T0235964

Lecture Notes in Computer Science   9967

Commenced Publication in 1973
Founding and Former Series Editors:
Gerhard Goos, Juris Hartmanis, and Jan van Leeuwen

Editorial Board

David Hutchison
  Lancaster University, Lancaster, UK
Takeo Kanade
  Carnegie Mellon University, Pittsburgh, PA, USA
Josef Kittler
  University of Surrey, Guildford, UK
Jon M. Kleinberg
  Cornell University, Ithaca, NY, USA
Friedemann Mattern
  ETH Zurich, Zurich, Switzerland
John C. Mitchell
  Stanford University, Stanford, CA, USA
Moni Naor
  Weizmann Institute of Science, Rehovot, Israel
C. Pandu Rangan
  Indian Institute of Technology, Madras, India
Bernhard Steffen
  TU Dortmund University, Dortmund, Germany
Demetri Terzopoulos
  University of California, Los Angeles, CA, USA
Doug Tygar
  University of California, Berkeley, CA, USA
Gerhard Weikum
  Max Planck Institute for Informatics, Saarbrücken, Germany

More information about this series at http://www.springer.com/series/7412

Zhisheng You · Jie Zhou
Yunhong Wang · Zhenan Sun
Shiguang Shan · Weishi Zheng
Jianjiang Feng · Qijun Zhao (Eds.)

Biometric Recognition

11th Chinese Conference, CCBR 2016
Chengdu, China, October 14–16, 2016
Proceedings

 Springer

Editors

Zhisheng You
Sichuan University
Chengdu
China

Jie Zhou
Tsinghua University
Beijing
China

Yunhong Wang
Beihang University
Beijing
China

Zhenan Sun
Chinese Academy of Sciences
Beijing
China

Shiguang Shan
Chinese Academy of Sciences
Beijing
China

Weishi Zheng
Sun Yat-sen University
Guangzhou
China

Jianjiang Feng
Tsinghua University
Beijing
China

Qijun Zhao
Sichuan University
Chengdu
China

ISSN 0302-9743   ISSN 1611-3349 (electronic)
Lecture Notes in Computer Science
ISBN 978-3-319-46653-8   ISBN 978-3-319-46654-5 (eBook)
DOI 10.1007/978-3-319-46654-5

Library of Congress Control Number: 2016951979

LNCS Sublibrary: SL6 – Image Processing, Computer Vision, Pattern Recognition, and Graphics

© Springer International Publishing AG 2016
This work is subject to copyright. All rights are reserved by the Publisher, whether the whole or part of the material is concerned, specifically the rights of translation, reprinting, reuse of illustrations, recitation, broadcasting, reproduction on microfilms or in any other physical way, and transmission or information storage and retrieval, electronic adaptation, computer software, or by similar or dissimilar methodology now known or hereafter developed.
The use of general descriptive names, registered names, trademarks, service marks, etc. in this publication does not imply, even in the absence of a specific statement, that such names are exempt from the relevant protective laws and regulations and therefore free for general use.
The publisher, the authors and the editors are safe to assume that the advice and information in this book are believed to be true and accurate at the date of publication. Neither the publisher nor the authors or the editors give a warranty, express or implied, with respect to the material contained herein or for any errors or omissions that may have been made.

Printed on acid-free paper

This Springer imprint is published by Springer Nature
The registered company is Springer International Publishing AG
The registered company address is: Gewerbestrasse 11, 6330 Cham, Switzerland

Preface

Security and privacy issues are topics of growing concern in the Internet era and as a result of the growing demand for anti-terrorism activity. This raises great interest in biometric technology, which provides substantial advantages over traditional password- or token-based solutions. Biometric recognition systems have been extensively deployed worldwide in law-enforcement, government, and consumer applications. In China, thanks to the huge population using the Internet and smart phones and to the great investment of the government in security and privacy protection, the biometric market is rapidly growing and biometric research keeps attracting the attention of numerous scholars and practitioners. These researchers have been addressing various biometric problems, promoting diverse biometric techniques, and making significant contributions to the biometrics field. The Chinese Conference on Biometric Recognition (CCBR), an annual conference held in China, provides an excellent platform for biometric researchers to share their progress and advances in the development and applications of biometric theory, technology, and systems.

CCBR 2016 was held in Chengdu during October 14–16, 2016, and was the 11th in the series that has been successfully held in Beijing, Hangzhou, Xi'an, Guangzhou, Jinan, Shenyang, and Tianjin since 2000. CCBR 2016 received 138 submissions, each of which was reviewed in a double-blind manner by at least three experts from the Program Committee. Based on the rigorous review comments, 18 papers (13%) were selected for oral presentation and 66 papers (48%) for poster presentation. These papers comprise this volume of the CCBR 2016 conference proceedings covering a wide range of topics: face recognition and analysis; fingerprint, palm-print, and vascular biometrics; iris and ocular biometrics; behavioral biometrics; affective computing; feature extraction, and classification theory; anti-spoofing and privacy; surveillance; and DNA and emerging biometrics.

We would like to thank all the authors, reviewers, invited speakers, volunteers, and Organizing Committee members, without whom CCBR 2016 would not have been successful. We also wish to acknowledge the support of the Chinese Association for Artificial Intelligence, Institute of Automation of Chinese Academy of Sciences, Springer, Sichuan University, and Wisesoft Co., Ltd. for sponsoring this conference. Special thanks are due to Yang Wang, Xiaofeng Li, Zhihong Wu, Ying Chang, Ling Mao, Hu Chen, Yanli Liu, Yanci Zhang, Wei Jia, and Fuxuan Chen for their hard work in organizing the conference.

October 2016

Zhisheng You
Jie Zhou
Yunhong Wang
Zhenan Sun
Shiguang Shan
Weishi Zheng
Jianjiang Feng
Qijun Zhao

Organization

Advisors

Anil K. Jain	Michigan State University, USA
Tieniu Tan	Institute of Automation, Chinese Academy of Sciences, China
David Zhang	The Hong Kong Polytechnic University, Hong Kong SAR, China
Jingyu Yang	Nanjing University of Science and Technology, China
Xilin Chen	Institute of Computing Technology, Chinese Academy of Sciences, China
Jianhuang Lai	Sun Yat-sen University, China

General Chairs

Zhisheng You	Sichuan University, China
Jie Zhou	Tsinghua University, China
Yunhong Wang	Beihang University, China
Zhenan Sun	Institute of Automation, Chinese Academy of Sciences, China

Program Chairs

Shiguang Shan	Institute of Computing Technology, Chinese Academy of Sciences, China
Weishi Zheng	Sun Yat-sen University, China
Jianjiang Feng	Tsinghua University, China
Qijun Zhao	Sichuan University, China

Program Committee

Caikou Chen	Yangzhou University, China
Cunjian Chen	Canon Information Technology (Beijing), China
Fanglin Chen	National University of Defense Technology, China
Weihong Deng	Beijing University of Posts and Telecommunications, China
Yuchun Fang	Shanghai University, China
Quanxue Gao	Xidian University, China
Shenghua Gao	ShanghaiTech University, China
Yongxin Ge	Chongqing University, China
Xun Gong	Southwest Jiaotong University, China

Zhe Guo	Northwestern Polytechnical University, China
Zhenhua Guo	Graduate School at Shenzhen, Tsinghua University, China
Hu Han	Institute of Computing Technology, Chinese Academy of Sciences, China
Ran He	Institute of Automation, Chinese Academy of Sciences, China
Zhenyu He	Harbin Institute of Technology Shenzhen Graduate School, China
Qingyang Hong	Xiamen University, China
Dewen Hu	National University of Defense Technology, China
Di Huang	Beihang University, China
Wei Jia	Hefei University of Technology, China
Xiaoyuan Jing	Wuhan University, China
Wenxiong Kang	South China University of Technology, China
Zhihui Lai	Shenzhen University, China
Huibin Li	Xi'an Jiaotong University, China
Qin Li	Shenzhen Institute of Information Technology, China
Weijun Li	Institute of Semiconductors, Chinese Academy of Sciences, China
Wenxin Li	Peking University, China
Zhifeng Li	Shenzhen Institutes of Advanced Technology, Chinese Academy of Sciences, China
Shengcai Liao	Institute of Automation, Chinese Academy of Sciences, China
Eryun Liu	Zhejiang University, China
Feng Liu	Shenzhen University, China
Heng Liu	Anhui University of Technology, China
Kai Liu	Sichuan University, China
Manhua Liu	Shanghai Jiao Tong University, China
Yiguang Liu	Sichuan University, China
Zhi Liu	Shandong University, China
Guangming Lu	Harbin Institute of Technology Shenzhen Graduate School, China
Jiwen Lu	Tsinghua University, China
Xiao Luan	Chongqing University of Posts and Telecommunications, China
Haifeng Sang	Shenyang University of Technology, China
Fumin Shen	University of Electronic Science and Technology of China, China
Linlin Shen	Shenzhen University, China
Kurban Ubul	Xinjiang University, China
Kejun Wang	Harbin Engineering University, China
Yi Wang	Hong Kong Baptist University, Hong Kong SAR, China
Yiding Wang	North China University of Technology, China
Xiangqian Wu	Harbin Institute of Technology, China
Lifang Wu	Beijing University of Technology, China

Xiaohua Xie	Sun Yat-sen University, China
Yong Xu	Harbin Institute of Technology Shenzhen Graduate School, China
Yuli Xue	Beihang University, China
Haibin Yan	Beijing University of Posts and Telecommunications, China
Gongping Yang	Shandong University, China
Jinfeng Yang	Civil Aviation University of China, China
Jucheng Yang	Tianjin University of Science and Technology, China
Wankou Yang	Southeast university, China
Yingchun Yang	Zhejiang University, China
Yilong Yin	Shandong University, China
Shiqi Yu	Shenzhen University, China
Weiqi Yuan	Shenyang University of Technology, China
Baochang Zhang	Beihang University, China
Lei Zhang	The Hong Kong Polytechnic University, Hong Kong SAR, China
Lin Zhang	Tongji University, China
Man Zhang	Institute of Automation, Chinese Academy of Sciences, China
Yongliang Zhang	Zhejiang University of Technology, China
Zhaoxiang Zhang	Institute of Automation, Chinese Academy of Sciences, China
Cairong Zhao	Tongji University, China
Xiuzhuang Zhou	Capital Normal University, China
En Zhu	National University of Defense Technology, China
Wangmeng Zuo	Harbin Institute of Technology, China

Publication Chairs

| Arun Ross | Michigan State University, USA |
| Di Huang | Beihang University, China |

Doctoral Consortium Chairs

| Jiwen Lu | Tsinghua University, China |
| Min Zhu | Sichuan University, China |

Organizing Committee Chairs

Yang Wang	Sichuan University, China
Zhihong Wu	Sichuan University, China
Xiaofeng Li	Wisesoft Co., Ltd., China
Ying Chang	Wisesoft Co., Ltd., China

Organizing Committee

Hu Chen	Sichuan University, China
Jing Li	Sichuan University, China
Menglong Yang	Sichuan University, China
Yanli Liu	Sichuan University, China
Yanci Zhang	Sichuan University, China
Ziliang Feng	Sichuan University, China
Ling Mao	Wisesoft Co., Ltd., China
Lun Xu	Wisesoft Co., Ltd., China
Sha Ma	Wisesoft Co., Ltd., China

Contents

Fingerprint, Palm-print and Vascular Biometrics

Iris and Ocular Biometrics

Behavioral Biometrics

Affective Computing

Feature Extraction and Classification Theory

Anti-Spoofing and Privacy

Surveillance

DNA and Emerging Biometrics

Face Recognition and Analysis

Occlusion-Robust Face Detection Using Shallow and Deep Proposal Based Faster R-CNN

Jingbo Guo[1], Jie Xu[2], Songtao Liu[1], Di Huang[1(✉)], and Yunhong Wang[1]

[1] Laboratory of Intelligent Recognition and Image Processing, School of Computer Science and Engineering, Beihang University, Beijing 100191, China
{buaa11061069,dhuang,yhwang}@buaa.edu.cn
[2] National Computer Network and Information Security Administrative Center, Beijing 100031, China

Abstract. As the first essential step of automatic face analysis, face detection always receives high attention. The performance of current state-of-the-art face detectors cannot fulfill the requirements in real-world scenarios especially in the presence of severe occlusions. This paper proposes a novel and effective approach to occlusion-robust face detection. It combines two major phases, *i.e.* proposal generation and classification. In the former, we combine both the proposals given by a coarse-to-fine shallow pipeline and a Region Proposal Network (RPN) based deep one respectively, to generate a more comprehensive set of candidate regions. In the latter, we further decide whether the regions are faces using a well-trained Faster R-CNN. Experiments are conducted on the WIDER FACE benchmark, and the results clearly prove the competency of the proposed method at detecting occluded faces.

Keywords: Face detection · Occlusion · Shallow and deep proposal · Faster R-CNN

1 Introduction

Face detection is to locate any face within a given image, and it is a fundamental step of machine based face analysis, involving face landmarking, face recognition, face parsing *etc.*, which plays an important role in a variety of related applications. Despite the great progress achieved by recent advanced techniques, the gap still remains between the state of the art face detectors and the real world requirements, since some factors, such as illumination and pose variations, occlusions, and low resolutions, form the bottleneck which largely degrades the face detection performance. Among these factors, occlusion is a very challenging problem [2] due to a diversity of styles. For example, in common cases, ordinary people wear hat, glasses, and scarfs at times; women of some nationality wear veils; hockey players wear protecting helmets; and doctors and nurses wear medical masks; while in unusual ones, criminals related to severe security issues like robbers and thieves always wear atypical covers (see Fig. 1 for illustration of some occluded face samples).

© Springer International Publishing AG 2016
Z. You et al. (Eds.): CCBR 2016, LNCS 9967, pp. 3–12, 2016.
DOI: 10.1007/978-3-319-46654-5_1

Fig. 1. Illustration of face samples with different types of occlusions.

In the past several decades, many studies have appeared to address such an issue. Earlier methods mainly make use of dimensionality reduction techniques. In [6], Moghaddam and Pentland proposed an eigenface based face detector; Yang *et al.* [14] developed a face detector based on Fisher Linear Discriminant (FLD); Sung and Poggio [11] introduced a neural network to detect faces; Osuna *et al.* [7] employed SVM to decide whether a given patch contains a face and this idea was further enhanced by Romdhani *et al.* [9] using the reduced set vectors. These approaches report good results on some small databases, but seem out of date for the following more complex benchmarks. In the beginning of 2000s, Viola and Jones [12] brought us the Haar-like feature, the integral image, and the Boosting algorithm, which were combined to construct a powerful face detector. Since then, face detection has entered VJ' times and this method as well as its variants [1] have achieved state-of-the-art performance in many more difficult datasets, making Adaboost a milestone. Recently, Yang *et al.* [13] replaced Haar with Aggregated Channel Features (ACF) to better describe faces, and promoted the accuracy of the Adaboost framework. Regarding the solution to face detection in the presence of occlusion, Deformable Part Models (DPM) show some promising results [5], where are represented in pictorial structures by a collection of parts arranged in a deformable configuration and significant variations in their appearances can be captured, and have become another landmark. The methods mentioned above are all based on shallow features, which are designed according to the knowledge of human beings in specific areas. Although they prove effective in many face detection evaluations, they are still far from competent in real-world applications, because of insufficient face representation incurred by our incomplete cognition.

Considering the fact that deep learning models, especially the Convolutional Neural Networks (CNNs), have been successfully applied to a number of image classification and retrieval tasks, such techniques are also investigated to facilitate the face detection accuracy in more practical scenarios. Li *et al.* [3] presented a cascade CNN face detector, which operates at multiple resolutions, quickly rejecting the background regions in the fast low resolution stages and carefully evaluating a small number of challenging candidates in the last high resolution stage. It achieves state-of-the-art performance on the major benchmark, *i.e.* FDDB. In [15], Yang *et al.* proposed a Deep Convolutional Network (DCN) based method for face detection, namely Faceness, in particular handling the problem of severe external occlusions and unconstrained pose variations. It locates faces through scoring facial parts responses by their spatial structure and arrangement, and reports competitive results on FDDB, Pascal Face, and AFW.

More recently, a more challenging database, namely WIDER FACE [16], has been built to trigger progress and inspire novel ideas of face detection in real-world conditions, as the performance of existing ones continuously increases to a very high level in more restricted cases. Specifically, current public benchmarks, *e.g.*, FDDB, AFW, Pascal Face, generally contain a few thousand faces, with limited variations in pose, scale, expression, occlusion, and background clutter [16], making them not so practical. Such limitations have partially induced the failure of some reputable algorithms in coping with atypical changes, evidenced by the evaluation on WIDER FACE that the result of the occlusion subset of Faceness, the most advanced occlusion robust face detector, is very disappointing. A possible reason lies in that region proposals generated are not accurate enough, for the presence of scale, illumination, pose, and make up changes, which confuse the deep models.

This paper proposes a novel and effective approach to occlusion-robust face detection. It first combines both the shallow and deep proposals to produce a more comprehensive set of candidate regions and then decides whether they are faces through a well-trained deep model. Region Proposal Network (RPN) [8] is adopted to generate deep proposals, which proves efficient in most cases but tends to fail in some extreme conditions caused by low resolution, severe pose, and large occlusion. To solve this problem, we embed extra knowledge using shallow proposals, provided by a human upper body detector consisting of a coarse Harr-like feature based cascade classier and a fine SVM classifier. The state of the art object detection deep network, Faster R-CNN [8], is further employed for final decision making. Experiments are carried out on the WIDER FACE benchmark, and the result on the occlusion subset clearly demonstrates the competency of the proposed method to detect occluded faces.

The remainder of this paper is organized as follows. In Sect. 2, we describe the proposed method in detail, including the framework overview, shallow and deep proposal generation, and faster R-CNN based decision. Experimental results are presented and analyzed in Sect. 3. Finally, we conclude this paper in Sect. 4.

2 Occlusion-Robust Face Detector

In this section, we describe the proposed approach in detail. First, we give an overview of the occlusion-robust face detection system in Sect. 2.1. The shallow proposal generator as well as the deep one are then presented in Sect. 2.2 and Sect. 2.3, respectively. Finally, we introduce Faster R-CNN based face detection in Sect. 2.4.

2.1 Approach Overview

The whole process of the proposed approach is shown in Fig. 2. A given input image goes to two pipelines, *i.e.* shallow proposal generator and deep proposal generator, in a parallel way. In the deep pipeline, the image is first sent to CNN to compute the convolutional feature map. RPN then makes use of a sliding window to traverse this map and generate deep region proposals. In the shallow pipeline, we first extract fast Haar-like features from the input image, and a boosted cascade classifier is adopted to locate the region of the human upper-body. We then give a coarse estimation of the face region according to the prior of human body configuration. A pre-trained linear SVM classifier is further exploited to finely filtrate the shallow proposals. Finally, both the shallow and deep proposals are integrated and dropped in Faster R-CNN to decide whether the proposals are faces and return the positions of faces in this image.

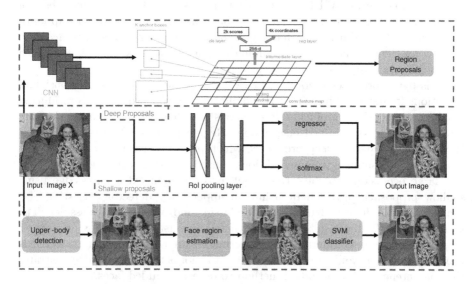

Fig. 2. Flowchart of the proposed face detector.

2.2 Shallow Proposal Generator

Upper-body detection. The mechanism of this generator is a cascaded Haar-like feature based classifier [4] used to detect the human upper-body. Different from the traditional methodology directly determining if the given image patch is a face with certain types of occlusions, which tends to incur unexpected errors, the proposed solution makes use of prior knowledge of upper-body as the constraint to enhance the performance. It coarsely estimates the possible face area based on the location of the upper body taking the common configuration of human bodies into account. Haar-like features which can be regarded as some rectangles containing black and white parts are very efficient to calculate and widely adopted in detection tasks. Three types of Haar-like features are used in this paper including edge features, center-surround features, and line features. The AdaBoost algorithm is employed to build the cascaded Haar-like feature based classifier.

SVM based proposal filter. When the coarse candidates of the face are given, we further finely analyze if they are faces in the presence of occlusions. On each proposal, we extract the Histogram of Oriented Gradient (HOG) feature and employ the well-known Support Vector Machines (SVM) in this binary classification problem, distinguishing occluded faces from background, for its robust performance on linear and non-linear data as well as good generalization ability (see the bottom part of Fig. 2 for the illustration of shallow proposal generation).

2.3 Deep Proposal Generator

Region Proposal Network (RPN) uses a fully convolutional network to propose face regions with confidence scores. RPN is a sliding window based method, and a small network is used to slide over the whole convolutional feature map which is extracted by CNN. The sliding window is then projected to a lower-dimensional feature. The box-classification layer (cls) and box-regression layer (reg) are constructed on the feature. The architecture is implemented with the reg and cls 1×1 convolutional layer extracted from the $n \times n$ fully-connected layer. Each sliding window can generate k proposals. The reg layer outputs $4k$ coordinates of the k regions, while the cls layer outputs $2k$ confidence scores. An anchor is centered at the sliding window indicating the proposals parameterized to the reference boxes. There are WHk anchors used for a convolutional feature map of the size $W \times H$ (see the upper part of Fig. 2 for the illustration of deep proposal generation). Additionally, multi-scale anchors are used in our RPN training.

2.4 Face Detection by Faster R-CNN

When the proposals are generated in the shallow and deep pipeline respectively, the two types of regions are combined to form a more comprehensive candidate set, from which we analyze if they are faces. For this objective, the advanced object detection framework, *i.e.* Fast R-CNN, is adopted to find occluded faces. Faster R-CNN and RPN share the same convolutional network feature. We iteratively train the model: the first step is RPN training, where the proposals of RPN are treated as the input of Fast R-CNN training; the second step is to reverse the process, where we use the output of Fast R-CNN training, a tuned network, to launch RPN, thus building an end-to-end detection system. In our face detection approach, we initialize RPN with pre-trained ImageNet models, and fine-tune them using the training samples.

3 Experimental Results

We validate the proposed face detection approach on the WIDER FACE benchmark, and the database, setting and protocol, and results are presented in the subsequent.

3.1 Database

WIDER FACE is a benchmark for face detection with images selected from the public WIDER dataset. It consists of 32,203 images and 393,703 faces are annotated. Faces have high degree of variabilities in scale, pose, and occlusion, as shown in Fig. 3. WIDER FACE is categorized based on 60 event classes, and for each of them, 40 %, 10 %, and 50 % data are randomly selected for training, validation, and testing respectively. Each face is assigned one of the three categories: no occlusion, partial occlusion, and heavy occlusion, according to the portion of the occluded region measured by annotator. A face is labeled as partially occluded if 1 %–30 % of the entire face area is occluded, while is labeled as heavily occluded if the face area is with over 30 % occlusion. We focus on the subset of heavy occlusion to evaluate the robustness of our method to occlusions.

Fig. 3. Illustration of samples in the WIDER FACE dataset (best scene in color).

3.2 Setting and Protocol

The performance of face detection is measured in terms of Recall and Average Precision (AP) as in other databases. Meanwhile, we compare two network models, *i.e.* the Zeiler and Fergus model (ZF) [17] and the Simonyan and Zisserman model (VGG-16) [10], which are integrated in the proposed method to compute the convolutional layer and initialize the training process of RPN and Faster R-CNN. A single NVIDIA GTX TITAN GPU is equipped on a PC with mainstream hardware configuration for computation.

3.3   Results

The precision curves with respect to recall of the ZF and VGG-16 model on the validation images in the subset of heavy occlusion of the WIDER FACE dataset are shown in Fig. 4. From this figure, we can see that VGG-16 performs better than ZF. The detailed AP value per event class in WIDER FACE is displayed in Table 1. We only show abbreviations of the category names, and refer to [16] for complete information. Table 2 gives the comparison between the proposed method and the state of the art ones. From that table, we can see that the AP based on the ZF model is 13.8 %, 3 point better than that of ACF (10.3 %) but slightly inferior to that of Faceness (14.4 %), while the AP based on the VGG-16 model is 15.7, outperforming all the counterparts. In addition, we can see that by embedding

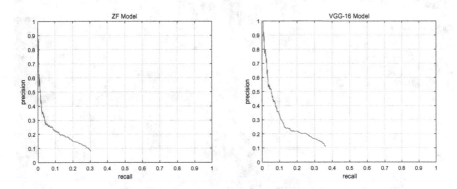

Fig. 4. Precision curves with respect to recall using the ZF (left) and VGG-16 (right) models on the subset of heavy occlusion WIDER FACE validation benchmark.

Table 1. Comparison of AP of each event class on the WIDER FACE dataset with heavy occlusion tags using both the ZF and VGG-16 models.

	March.	Grou.	Inte.	Stoc.	Coup.	Demo.	Picn.	Firi.	Patr.	Danc.	Spor.	Stud.
ZF	9.2	10.5	13.2	33.6	14.5	20.6	6.2	7.1	10.9	22.8	15.5	12.1
VGG	10.6	13.8	12.0	68.2	37.5	11.7	11.1	13.8	24.7	26.1	11.4	14.0

	Shop.	Dril.	Base.	Bask.	Riot.	Surg.	Gymn.	Work.	Runn.	Socc.	Tenn.	Skat.
ZF	7.2	7.6	5.3	1.4	16.7	11.8	20.5	23.1	9.2	10.6	18.7	9.5
VGG	7.9	8.8	9.1	2.7	15.5	15.3	24.6	25.6	17.9	15.0	23.9	15.7

	Para.	Gree.	Cele.	Dres.	Phot.	Raid.	Resc.	Parach.	Acci.	Stre.	Elec.	Pres.
ZF	25.6	20.2	12.9	32.8	46.3	23.2	18.5	7.2	4.9	3.4	6.9	10.1
VGG	23.1	27.2	17.7	37.6	54.2	27.8	20.2	9.0	7.4	5.2	8.1	12.5

	Swim.	Raci.	Aero.	Ball.	Foot.	Boat.	Jock.	Mata.	Hock.	Driv.	Fune.	Chee.
ZF	16.7	10.1	9.9	26.1	3.6	4.5	5.9	1.6	13.2	18.8	12.7	5.1
VGG	22.3	13.2	13.3	44.5	4.5	6.1	9.7	1.8	16.3	18.2	12.0	12.5

	Wait.	Coac.	Vote.	Angl.	Hand.	Meet.	Traf.	Awar.	Cere.	Conc.	Fami.	Fest.
ZF	17.8	16.2	9.4	10.1	1.6	3.7	4.1	6.1	3.3	4.2	6.6	7.3
VGG	24.6	18.7	12.1	10.5	2.3	5.5	5.8	8.8	4.7	7.1	7.5	9.1

Fig. 5. Face detection results of some selected samples on the WIDER FACE validation dataset (VGG-16; 198 ms per image).

shallow proposals in Faster R-CNN, the performance is ameliorated (compared with the original version), indicating the necessity of the clues conveyed in the shallow model. The face detection results of some selected samples on the WIDER FACE validation dataset are demonstrated in Fig. 5, where the labeled images are composed of various extreme facial occlusions in the real-world scenario including hats, glasses, hands, profiles, medicine masks *etc.* All the results clearly prove the effectiveness of the proposed approach and the robustness to occlusions.

Table 2. Comparison with the state of the art methods on the subset of heavy occlusion of WIDER FACE in terms of AP (results of ACF and Faceness are directly cited from [16]).

	AP (%)
ACF [16]	10.3
Faceness [16]	14.4
ZF (Original Faster R-CNN)	12.0
VGG (Original Faster R-CNN)	14.1
ZF (proposed approach)	13.8
VGG (proposed approach)	15.7

4   Conclusion

In this paper, we propose an approach to facilitate the performance of face detection under severe occlusions. With the purpose of improving the quality of proposals, we make use of the prior of human body configuration and thus combine the candidates provided by the shallow and deep pipeline. The well-trained Faster R-CNN is further adopted to decide whether the proposals are faces. We conduct experiments on the WIDER FACE benchmark, and the results achieved are competitive, which highlight the advantage of the proposed method for face detection in the presence of occlusions.

Acknowledgments. This work was supported in part by the national key research and development plan under Grant 2016YFC0801002, the Hong Kong, Macao, and Taiwan Science and Technology Cooperation Program of China under Grant L2015TGA9004, and the National Natural Science Foundation of China under Grant 61540048 and 61673033.

References

1. Chen, D., Ren, S., Wei, Y., Cao, X., Sun, J.: Joint cascade face detection and alignment. In: Fleet, D., Pajdla, T., Schiele, B., Tuytelaars, T. (eds.) ECCV 2014, Part VI. LNCS, vol. 8694, pp. 109–122. Springer, Heidelberg (2014). doi:10.1007/978-3-319-10599-4_8
2. Ekenel, H.K., Stiefelhagen, R.: Why is facial occlusion a challenging problem? In: Tistarelli, M., Nixon, M.S. (eds.) ICB 2009. LNCS, vol. 5558, pp. 299–308. Springer, Heidelberg (2009). doi:10.1007/978-3-642-01793-3_31
3. Li, H., Lin, Z., Shen, X., Brandt, J., Hua, G.: A convolutional neural network cascade for face detection. In: Proceedings of the IEEE Conference on Computer Vision and Pattern Recognition, pp. 5325–5334 (2015)
4. Lienhart, R., Maydt, J.: An extended set of haar-like features for rapid object detection. In: Proceedings of the 2002 International Conference on Image Processing, vol. 1, pp. I-900–I-903. IEEE (2002)

5. Mathias, M., Benenson, R., Pedersoli, M., Van Gool, L.: Face detection without bells and whistles. In: Fleet, D., Pajdla, T., Schiele, B., Tuytelaars, T. (eds.) ECCV 2014, Part IV. LNCS, vol. 8692, pp. 720–735. Springer, Heidelberg (2014). doi:10. 1007/978-3-319-10593-2_47
6. Moghaddam, B., Pentland, A.: Probabilistic visual learning for object representation. IEEE Trans. Pattern Anal. Mach. Intell. **19**(7), 696–710 (1997)
7. Osuna, E., Freund, R., Girosi, F.: Training support vector machines: an application to face detection. In: Proceedings of the 1997 IEEE Computer Society Conference on Computer Vision and Pattern Recognition, pp. 130–136. IEEE (1997)
8. Ren, S., He, K., Girshick, R., Sun, J.: Faster r-cnn: towards real-time object detection with region proposal networks. In: Advances in Neural Information Processing Systems, pp. 91–99 (2015)
9. Romdhani, S., Torr, P., Schölkopf, B., Blake, A.: Computationally efficient face detection. In: Proceedings of the Eighth IEEE International Conference on Computer Vision, ICCV 2001, vol. 2, pp. 695–700. IEEE (2001)
10. Simonyan, K., Zisserman, A.: Very deep convolutional networks for large-scale image recognition (2014). arXiv preprint: arXiv:1409.1556
11. Sung, K.K., Poggio, T.: Example-based learning for view-based human face detection. IEEE Trans. Pattern Anal. Mach. Intell. **20**(1), 39–51 (1998)
12. Viola, P., Jones, M.J.: Robust real-time face detection. Int. J. Comput. Vis. **57**(2), 137–154 (2004)
13. Yang, B., Yan, J., Lei, Z., Li, S.Z.: Aggregate channel features for multi-view face detection. In: 2014 IEEE International Joint Conference on Biometrics (IJCB), pp. 1–8. IEEE (2014)
14. Yang, M.H., Abuja, N., Kriegman, D.: Face detection using mixtures of linear subspaces. In: Proceedings of the Fourth IEEE International Conference on Automatic Face and Gesture Recognition, pp. 70–76. IEEE (2000)
15. Yang, S., Luo, P., Loy, C.C., Tang, X.: From facial parts responses to face detection: a deep learning approach. In: Proceedings of the IEEE International Conference on Computer Vision, pp. 3676–3684 (2015)
16. Yang, S., Luo, P., Loy, C.C., Tang, X.: Wider face: a face detection benchmark (2016)
17. Zeiler, M.D., Fergus, R.: Visualizing and understanding convolutional networks. In: Fleet, D., Pajdla, T., Schiele, B., Tuytelaars, T. (eds.) ECCV 2014, Part I. LNCS, vol. 8689, pp. 818–833. Springer, Heidelberg (2014). doi:10.1007/ 978-3-319-10590-1_53

Locally Rejected Metric Learning Based False Positives Filtering for Face Detection

Nanhai Zhang$^{(\boxtimes)}$, Jiajie Han, Jiani Hu, and Weihong Deng

Beijing University of Posts and Telecommunications, Beijing, China
{nhzhang,dxs,jnhu,whdeng}@bupt.edu.cn
http://www.bupt.edu.cn/

Abstract. Face detection in the wild needs to deal with various challenging conditions, which often leads to the situation where intraclass difference of faces exceeds interclass difference between faces and non-faces. Based on this observation, in this paper we propose a locally rejected metric learning (LRML) based false positives filtering method. We firstly learn some prototype faces with affinity propagation clustering algorithm, and then apply locally rejected metric learning to seek a linear transformation to reduce the differences between each face and prototype faces while enlarging the differences between non-faces and prototype faces and preserving the distribution of learned prototype faces with locally rejected term. With the learned transformation, data are mapped into a new domain where face can be exactly detected. Results on FDDB and a self-collected dataset indicate our method is better than Viola-Jones face detectors. And the combination of the two methods shows an improvement in face detection.

Keywords: Locally rejected · Face detection · Prototype faces

1 Introduction

Great success of face detection in constrained environments have been made over past years. However it is still a challenge to detect face in wild environments, due to various variations like lighting, illumination, expression and occlusion.

From the view of metric learning, failure of face detection results from that intraclass distance (between faces) may be larger than interclass distance (between faces and complex background). Figure 1 shows this situation. To deal with various challenging variations, researchers have proposed diverse approaches. For the feature-based methods, researchers try to extract robust feature, e.g. SURF [1], or feature learned by CNN [2]. For the model-based methods, researchers try to model large variations with deformable part-based model [3]. Nevertheless, most of these approaches are time consuming or have expensive computation.

To deal with various challenging variations, borrowing the idea of metric learning, we can map the feature from the origin domain into a new domain where differences of interclass are larger than the differences of intra-class. Therefore,

© Springer International Publishing AG 2016
Z. You et al. (Eds.): CCBR 2016, LNCS 9967, pp. 13–21, 2016.
DOI: 10.1007/978-3-319-46654-5_2

Face   Average Face   Non-Face

Fig. 1. Example illustrates the situation where intraclass distance exceeds interclass distance. *Left* is a face image, *middle* is a average face[1] and *right* is a non-face image. The cosine similarity between the face image and the average face is 0.37 which is lower than 0.62 that is the cosine similarity between the non-face image and the average face.

we propose a new false positives filtering approach for face detection based on locally rejected metric learning and affinity propagation clustering algorithm, which can efficiently improve the results of classical Viola-Jones detector [4]. Since the training process can be done off-line and the predication procedure is simple, the whole procedure of face detection can be done fast and efficiently.

In summary, the contributions of this paper are threefold:

(1) We propose to use affinity propagation clustering algorithm to learn some prototype faces being more representative than average faces.
(2) We propose a robust framework of false positives filtering for face detection based on locally rejected metric learning by reducing the intraclass differences while enlarging the interclass differences and preserving the distribution of prototype faces with the locally rejected term.
(3) We evaluate our approach on self-collected dataset and FDDB [5], both of which are collected from unconstrained conditions. Results on the two datasets show an efficient improvement of Viola-Jones detector.

2   Related Work

Clustering: The goal of clustering analysis is to mine the underlying structure of an unlabeled dataset. Most of clustering algorithms can be broadly categorized into three groups: partitioning based clustering, such as K-means [6], graph based clustering, such as spectral clustering [7] and density based clustering, such as mean-shift [8]. K-means proposed in 1955 is still a popular algorithm. Frey [9] proposed a powerful cluster algorithm with the ability of discovering representative faces from a gallery of face images dataset in 2007. With this method, we can learn some prototype faces from real world face datasets.

Face Detection: The seminal work of face detection was done by Viola and Jones [4], which has become a standard paradigm for face detection. Recently, Chen [10] proposes a new framework for cascade face detection with the help of aligned shape indexed feature. Li [2] proposes a CNN cascade based face detection. As far as we know, few papers discuss the post process for face detection

---

[1] http://faceresearch.org/.

except Chen's work [10]. It introduces a simple SVM classifier for post process to prove facial point based features can improve face detector performance. Different from it, our false positives filtering approach is more universal and faster.

Metric Learning: Since the pioneering work of Xing [11], researchers have proposed many metric learning algorithms. Most metric learning algorithms can be roughly categorized into linear metrics and non-linear metrics. For linear metrics, the mahalanobis distance takes the dominant place. Most classic metric learning methods adopt the mahalanobis distance form including LMNN [12], ITML [13], OASIS [14]. For non-linear metrics, besides the kernel tricks, neural network is also used to map data into a non-linear space [15]. Our approach benefits from these works, especially Hu's work DDML [15]. Differently, our approach is more suitable this point-to-set metric learning problem while most conventional methods focus on point-to-point metric learning problem.

3 Proposed Approach

3.1 Learning Prototype Faces

To reduce the intraclass difference, a straightforward idea is to minimize the differences between real world faces and average faces. However average faces are usually influenced by age, gender and race. To avoid this problem, we propose to learn some prototype faces from real world face dataset.

For the powerful ability of affinity propagation clustering algorithm [9], we adopt it to discover underlying prototype faces from face datasets. Affinity propagation clustering algorithm has a good performance in clustering face. The key idea of affinity propagation clustering is to take similarity as input and exchange "responsibility" and "availability" messages between data points. In this way, a high-quality set of exemplars and corresponding clusters will gradually emerge. The procedure of messages exchange is as following:

$$r(i,k) \leftarrow s(i,k) - \max_{k' \neq k}\{a(i,k') + s(i,k')\} \tag{1}$$

$$a(i,k) \leftarrow \begin{cases} min\{0, r(k,k) + \sum_{i' \notin \{i,k\}} max\{0, r(i',k)\}\} & i \neq k \\ \sum_{i' \notin \{i,k\}} max\{0, r(i',k)\} & i = k \end{cases} \tag{2}$$

where $s(i,k)$ indicates similarity between i and k, $r(i,k)$ denotes responsibility from i to k and $a(i,k)$ indicates availability sent from k to i. $r(i,k)$ reflects the accumulated probability for how well-suited K is to serve as the exemplar for point i. $a(i,k)$ reflects the accumulated probability for how well-suited for i choosing k as its exemplar. After some iterations, points with high responsibility and availability will be chosen as prototype faces. Details can refer to [9].

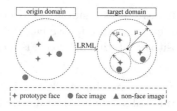

Fig. 2. Schematic illustration of our method. *Left* shows the data distribution in the origin domain, there are some easily misclassified samples. *right* shows the new data distribution in target domain after LRML. Samples can be easily classified in the new domain.

3.2 Locally Rejected Metric Learning

Basic Idea: The goal of metric learning is to seek a transformation that reduces the distance between face images and prototype faces while enlarges distance between non-face images and prototype faces. Figure 2 intuitively illustrates the proposed method. In the origin domain, distance between face image and prototype face is larger than distance between non-face image and prototype face. With the transformation function, data points can be mapped into a new domain where distance between face and prototype face has been reduced to less than threshold μ_1 while distance between non-face and prototype face has been increased to over threshold μ_2.

Besides, considering that different prototype faces learned by affinity propagation clustering stand for different kinds of faces. To preserve the structure, we believe there should be a gap between inter-prototype-faces, which means a face image is not necessary to keep a small distance to all prototype faces. Therefore, it motivates us to propose a new locally rejected metric learning method that a face image is pushed closer to the nearest prototype face, while keeping a gap with other prototype faces.

LRML: Let $X = \{x_i | i = 1, 2, \cdots, N\}$ be the set of N training samples, where $x_i \in \mathbb{R}^d$ denotes the ith training sample, and $Y = \{y_i | i = 1, 2, \cdots, K\}$ be the set of K prototype faces, where $y_i \in \mathbb{R}^d$ denotes the ith prototype face. Our approach adopts the Mahalanobis distance form and the distance between a sample from X and a sample from Y can be computed as: $d_M(x_i, y_j) = \|Wx_i - Wy_j\|_2$. Data points parameterized by W are mapped into a new space where the distance between two data points can be computed with squared L2 distances.

As discussed in **Basic Idea**, our approach can be formulated as:

$$\min_W J(W) = J_1(W) + J_2(W) + J_3(W) + J_4(W)$$

$$= \frac{1}{NK} \sum_i^N \sum_j^K h_\beta((1 - l_{ij})(\mu_2 - d_M^2(x_i, y_j))) + \frac{1}{N} \sum_i^N h_\beta(l_{iit}(d_M^2(x_i, y_{it}) - \mu_1)) \quad (3)$$

$$+ \frac{1}{N(K-1)} \sum_i^N \sum_{j \neq t}^K h_\beta(l_{ij}(\mu_1 - d_M^2(x_i, y_j))) + \gamma \|W\|_F^2$$

where l_{ij} is the label of image pair (x_i, y_j), $l_{ij} = 1$ for (x_i, y_j) being intraclass pair (face and prototype face) and $l_{ij} = 0$ for (x_i, y_j) being interclass pair(non-face and prototype face). μ_1 and μ_2 are respectively the threshold for similar pair and dissimilar pair. $h_\beta(z)$ is a generalized logistic loss function to smoothly approximate the hinge loss [16], where $h_\beta(z) = \frac{1}{\beta} log(1 + exp(\beta z))$ and β is a sharpness parameter. $h_\beta(z)$ converges to hinge loss as β increases. y_{it} denotes the nearest prototype face to sample face x_i, where $t \in [1, K]$ and l_{iit} is label for (x_i, y_{it}). γ is a parameter to trade off the regularization term and the hinge loss.

The cost function defined in Eq. (3) consists of four parts. $J_1(W)$ in Eq. (3) is to ensure distance is larger than threshold u_2 if it is a dissimilar pair. $J_2(W)$ in Eq. (3) is to ensure distance is smaller than threshold u_1 if x_1 is a face sample and y_1 is the nearest prototype face to x_i. $J_3(W)$ in Eq. (3) is to preserve the structure of prototype face by keeping a gap between face sample x_i and nonnearest prototype face to x_i. $J_4(W)$ in Eq. (3) is a regularization term.

To solve the objective function defined in Eq. (3), we utilize a batch-stochastic gradient descent scheme. With this scheme, we can obtain a robust solution quickly. Besides, considering that l_{ij} is either 0 or 1, the gradient of cost function can be computed with a classified discussion idea:

$$J(W) = \begin{cases} J_1(W) + J_4(W) & l_{ij} = 0 \quad (4a) \\ J_2(W) + J_3(W) + J_4(W) & l_{ij} = 1 \quad (4b) \end{cases}$$

Therefore the batch-stochastic gradient of $J(W)$ can be computed as:

For $l_{ij} = 0$,

$$\frac{\partial J}{\partial W} = \frac{2}{K} \sum_j^K (h'_\beta(\mu_2 - d_M^2(x_i, y_j))(Wx_i - Wy_j)x_i^T + h'_\beta(\mu_2 - d_M^2(x_i, y_j))(Wy_j - Wx_i)y_j^T) + 2\gamma W \quad (5)$$

For $l_{ij} = 1$,

$$\frac{\partial J}{\partial W} = 2(h'_\beta(d_M^2(x_i, y_{it}) - \mu_1)W(x_i - y_{it})x_i^T + h'_\beta(d_M^2(x_i, y_{it}) - \mu_1)W(y_{it} - x_i)y_{it}^T +$$
$$\frac{2}{K-1} \sum_{j \neq t}^K (h'_\beta(\mu_1 - d_M^2(x_i, y_j))W(x_i - y_j)x_i^T + h'_\beta(\mu_1 - d_M^2(x_i, y_j))W(y_j - x_i)y_j^T) + 2\gamma W \quad (6)$$

For the batch-stochastic gradient descent scheme, batch means a batch of K or $K - 1$ prototype faces while stochastic means randomly selecting a sample from dataset X. Then parameter W can be updated by multiplying the batch-stochastic gradient by a learning rate. The main procedure of our method is shown as Algorithm 1.

Score of our method can be computed as:

$$score = \exp(- \min_{j \in [1, K]} (d_M^2(t_m, y_j))). \quad (7)$$

where t_m denotes the m-th test sample.

Combine: Besides, to achieve advanced performance of false positives filtering, we combine the results of our method with Viola-Jones detector. Since the Viola-Jones detector adopts the number of neighbors for filtering false face, we propose following formulation for combining:

$$Score\_combine = num\_neighbors \times \exp(-\theta \min_{j \in [1, K]} (d_M^2(t_m, y_j))) \quad (8)$$

Algorithm 1. LRML

Input: Training set X and Y, threshold μ_1, μ_2, regularization parameter γ, learning rate ν, convergence error ε
Output: parameter W
  (training the parameter W):
  Initialization W with diagonal position set 1, otherwise 0
  for $iter = 1, 2, 3, \ldots$ **do**
    Randomly select a sample x_i from X, y_i from Y
    if $l_{ij} = 0$ **then**
      Compute gradient according to Eq. (5)
    else
      Compute gradient according to Eq. (6)
    end if
    Update W with $W = W - \nu \dfrac{\partial J}{\partial W}$
    if $|J(W)_{iter} - J(W)_{iter-1}| < \varepsilon$ **then**
      break
    end if
  end for

---

where θ is a parameter to balance the weight of our method and Viola-Jones detector. *num_neighbors* is the confidence score of Viola-Jones detector.

4   Experiments

To evaluate the proposed approach, we test it on the challenging FDDB dataset and our self-collected face dataset. Following describes it in detail.

4.1   Implementation Details

The training set for clustering and metric learning is collected as following: we firstly collect a large set of images containing faces from Flickr. Then we use Viola-Jones detector [4] to detect faces in these images. Due to the limited performance, the results of Viola-Jones detector may contain many non-face images. Lastly, we annotate these detected results and obtain the training set consisting of about 20000 face images and 10000 non-face images. This training set is just used to train a transformation function W.

We extract two kinds of features: histogram of oriented gradients (HOG) and local binary patterns (LBP). Before that we align all images with face alignment algorithm Supervised Descent Method (SDM) [17]. For LBP, we divide each image into 10×10 non-overlapping blocks with size 10×10. For each block we extract a 59-dimensional LBP feature. Lastly we apply LDA to project the 5900-dimensional feature into a 100-dimensional feature. For HOG, we also divide each image into 10×10 non-overlapping blocks with size 10×10. For each block, we choose 5×5 cell size and 18 directions. LDA is applied to project get a 100-dimensional feature too. Finally we concatenate the two kinds of feature and get a 200-dimensional feature for each face. Before training, we apply WPCA to the feature. For the parameters of metric learning, we set threshold $\mu_1 = 1, \mu_2 = 10$, regularization parameter $\gamma = 0.01$ and learning rate $\nu = 0.0005$.

4.2   Learned Prototype Faces

We select the true face images from the training set and get a small image dataset only containing faces. Then we apply affinity propagation clustering

Fig. 3. Illustration of 3 kinds of faces learned by affinity propagation clustering algorithm. The learned prototype faces are roughly categorized into: (a) woman face, (b) man face, and (c) children face

algorithm to this dataset to obtain some learned prototype faces. For the affinity propagation clustering algorithm, we set 3 clusters. The clustering algorithm discovers three kinds of face and we roughly category them into woman face, man face and children face, as Fig. 3 shows. Every category contains expression and pose variations, as the left image of each pair in Fig. 3 shows. The reason for pose variation not taking the dominant position is that we have aligned images before extracting feature.

4.3 Experiments on Our Self-collected Dataset

We collect an unconstrained face detection dataset in the wild to evaluate our approach. This dataset is from personal photo album. Different from FDDB, our face dataset contains various poses pictures, scenery and multi-person pictures. It altogether contains 225 images with totally 630 faces. Following the discrete evaluation protocols as FDDB, we count the correct detections according to intersection ratio. We compare our method with original Viola-Jones detector

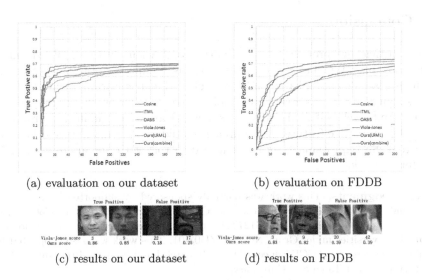

(a) evaluation on our dataset   (b) evaluation on FDDB

(c) results on our dataset   (d) results on FDDB

Fig. 4. (a) Evaluation on our dataset (Discontinuous score), (b) Evaluation on FDDB (Discontinuous score), (c)(d) some results of two detectors on two datasets, numbers are the score of two models, the greater score means the greater probability of face.

[4], the cosine similarity and two other classic metric learning based false positives filtering. From Fig. 4(a), we can see that our approach is sightly better than ITML [13] and OASIS [14] while outperforms the cosine similarity significantly. Besides, all of the three metric learning based methods show an efficient improvement to original Viola-Jones detector (implemented by OpenCv). The reason for four post-processing methods achieve good performance to improve Viola-Jones detector may be that most images in dataset are high resolution and have no complex background. Figure 4(b) shows some examples of easily misclassified images. From the result we can see that our approach outperforms the Viola-Jones detector in detecting these hard examples.

4.4 Experiments on FDDB

The Face Detection Data Set and Benchmark (FDDB) is a challenging dataset for evaluating the performance of face detector [5]. The FDDB contains 2845 images with a total of 5171 faces. For the evaluation protocols, we also use the discrete setting. From Fig. 4(b), we can see that our result outperforms cosine similarity significantly while achieves competitive result comparing with ITML [13] and OASIS [14]. Comparing with Viola-Jones detector, our single model of metric learning sightly outperforms it while the combining method is superior to both two single models and achieve the best result. Figure 4(d) shows some examples of easily misclassified images. From the result, we can see that two examples misclassified by Viola-Jones detector is well classified by our approach, which shows the better performance of our approach.

5   Conclusion

In this article, we propose to use affinity propagation clustering algorithm to learn some prototype faces and propose a robust framework of false positives filtering for face detection based on locally rejected metric learning. Our approach shows significant improvements for Viola Jones detector on challenging FDDB dataset and a self-collected dataset. As metric learning is a unified approach to learn discriminative feature, our approach should be able to improve other face detectors. So improvements of other face detectors with our approach will be our future work.

Acknowledgments. This work was partially sponsored by supported by the NSFC (National Natural Science Foundation of China) under Grant No. 61375031, No. 61573068, No. 61471048, and No. 61273217, the Fundamental Research Funds for the Central Universities under Grant No. 2014ZD03-01, This work was also supported by Beijing Nova Program, CCF-Tencent Open Research Fund, and the Program for New Century Excellent Talents in University.

References

1. Li, J., Wang, T., Zhang, Y.: Face detection using surf cascade. In: 2011 IEEE International Conference on Computer Vision Workshops (ICCV Workshops), pp. 2183–2190. IEEE (2011)
2. Li, H., Lin, Z., Shen, X., Brandt, J., Hua, G.: A convolutional neural network cascade for face detection. In: Proceedings of the IEEE Conference on Computer Vision and Pattern Recognition, pp. 5325–5334 (2015)
3. Felzenszwalb, P.F., Girshick, R.B., McAllester, D., Ramanan, D.: Object detection with discriminatively trained part-based models. IEEE Trans. Pattern Anal. Mach. Intell. **32**(9), 1627–1645 (2010)
4. Viola, P., Jones, M.: Rapid object detection using a boosted cascade of simple features. In: Proceedings of the 2001 IEEE Computer Society Conference on Computer Vision and Pattern Recognition, CVPR 2001, vol. 1, p. I-511. IEEE (2001)
5. Jain, V., Learned-Miller, E.G.: FDDB: A benchmark for face detection in unconstrained settings. UMass Amherst Technical Report (2010)
6. Steinhaus, H.: Sur la division des corp materiels en parties. Bull. Acad. Polon. Sci **1**, 801–804 (1956)
7. Ng, A.Y., Jordan, M.I., Weiss, Y., et al.: On spectral clustering: analysis and an algorithm. Adv. Neural Inf. Process. Syst. **2**, 849–856 (2002)
8. Comaniciu, D., Meer, P.: Mean shift: a robust approach toward feature space analysis. IEEE Trans. Pattern Anal. Mach. Intell. **24**(5), 603–619 (2002)
9. Frey, B.J., Dueck, D.: Clustering by passing messages between data points. Science **315**(5814), 972–976 (2007)
10. Chen, D., Ren, S., Wei, Y., Cao, X., Sun, J.: Joint cascade face detection and alignment. In: Fleet, D., Pajdla, T., Schiele, B., Tuytelaars, T. (eds.) ECCV 2014. LNCS, vol. 8694, pp. 109–122. Springer, Heidelberg (2014). doi:10.1007/978-3-319-10599-4_8
11. Xing, E.P., Jordan, M.I., Russell, S., Ng, A.Y.: Distance metric learning with application to clustering with side-information. In: Advances in Neural Information Processing Systems, pp. 505–512 (2002)
12. Weinberger, K.Q., Blitzer, J., Saul, L.K.: Distance metric learning for large margin nearest neighbor classification. In: Advances in Neural Information Processing Systems, pp. 1473–1480 (2005)
13. Davis, J.V., Kulis, B., Jain, P., Sra, S., Dhillon, I.S.: Information-theoretic metric learning. In: Proceedings of the 24th International Conference on Machine Learning, pp. 209–216. ACM (2007)
14. Chechik, G., Sharma, V., Shalit, U., Bengio, S.: Large scale online learning of image similarity through ranking. J. Mach. Learn. Res. **11**, 1109–1135 (2010)
15. Hu, J., Lu, J., Tan, Y.P.: Discriminative deep metric learning for face verification in the wild. In: 2014 IEEE Conference on Computer Vision and Pattern Recognition (CVPR), pp. 1875–1882. IEEE (2014)
16. Mignon, A., Jurie, F.: PCCA: a new approach for distance learning from sparse pairwise constraints. In: 2012 IEEE Conference on Computer Vision and Pattern Recognition (CVPR), pp. 2666–2672. IEEE (2012)
17. Xiong, X., De la Torre, F.: Supervised descent method and its applications to face alignment. In: 2013 IEEE Conference on Computer Vision and Pattern Recognition (CVPR), pp. 532–539. IEEE (2013)

Face Classification:
A Specialized Benchmark Study

Jiali Duan[1]([✉]), Shengcai Liao[2], Shuai Zhou[3], and Stan Z. Li[2]

[1] School Of Electronic, Electrical and Communication Engineering,
University of Chinese Academy of Sciences, Beijing, China
jli.duan@gmail.com
[2] Center for Biometrics and Security Research & National Laboratory
of Pattern Recognition, Institute of Automation, University of Chinese
Academy of Sciences, Beijing, China
{scliao,szli}@nlpr.ia.ac.cn
[3] Macau University of Science and Technology, Taipa, Macau
shuaizhou.palm@gmail.com

Abstract. Face detection evaluation generally involves three steps: block generation, face classification, and post-processing. However, firstly, face detection performance is largely influenced by block generation and post-processing, concealing the performance of face classification core module. Secondly, implementing and optimizing all the three steps results in a very heavy work, which is a big barrier for researchers who only cares about classification. Motivated by this, we conduct a specialized benchmark study in this paper, which focuses purely on face classification. We start with face proposals, and build a benchmark dataset with about 3.5 million patches for two-class face/non-face classification. Results with several baseline algorithms show that, without the help of post-processing, the performance of face classification itself is still not very satisfactory, even with a powerful CNN method. We'll release this benchmark to help assess performance of face classification only, and ease the participation of other related researchers.

Keywords: Face detection · Face classification · Benchmark evaluation

1 Introduction

Face detection is a key and fundamental problem in facial analysis as it is usually the first step to other high-level tasks such as face alignment, face recognition, face attribute analysis, etc. Therefore, a well-designed benchmark is essential to analyze the performance of face detection algorithms and advance the face detection research.

In the literature, face detection is evaluated by scanning a set of images containing faces in background, and counting true positives and false positives by matching the detected bounding boxes with the ground truth. This evaluation procedure generally involves three steps: block generation (multi-scale sliding subwindows or objectness proposals), face classification, and post-processing

© Springer International Publishing AG 2016
Z. You et al. (Eds.): CCBR 2016, LNCS 9967, pp. 22–29, 2016.
DOI: 10.1007/978-3-319-46654-5_3

(non-maximum suppression, bounding box regression, etc.). Today, popular face detection benchmarks such as AFW [4], FDDB [2], and WIDER FACE [3] still continue to use such evaluation procedure.

However, on one hand, the performance of face detection methods is largely influenced by specific settings of block generation and post-processing, therefore, it is not easy to know the specific performance of the core module, namely the face classification part in existing methods. On the other hand, implementing all the three steps and achieving a good overall face detection performance results in a very heavy work, sometimes preventing researchers of related fields (e.g. feature and classification researchers) in introducing their ideas for face detection. For example, the AFW [4], FDDB [2], and WIDER FACE [3] benchmarks all require that researchers start from scratch, from generating blocks, classifying faces, to post-processing.

Motivated by this, we conduct a specialized large-scale benchmark study in this paper, which focuses purely on face classification. We start with face proposals, by which about 3.5 millions of face and non-face sample patches are collected. Then, we build a large-scale benchmark dataset for two-class face classification evaluation. Accordingly, we evaluate several feature extraction methods and classification algorithms and compare their performance. Our results show that, without the help of post-processing, the performance of face classification itself is still not very satisfactory, even with a powerful CNN method.

The data and evaluation code of this study will be released to the public[1] to help assess performance of face classification, and ease the participation of related researchers who want to try their algorithms for face detection. With this benchmark, researchers only need to do feature extraction and face classification per image patch, regardless the troubling block generation and post-processing tasks. Even more easily, we provide some baseline features, so that general classification researchers are able to evaluate their classification algorithms.

2   Face Classification Benchmark

2.1   Face Proposals

RPN network is employed to extract proposals inspired by the work of Faster R-CNN [9] and its recent application in face detection [10]. Note that generic object proposal-generating methods such as [17–19] are not very suitable for our classification benchmark because the amount of positive face patches generated is too scarce and those patches are not as discriminative as a specially trained RPN face proposal network.

We trained a 4-anchor RPN network with some slight modifications on the fc6 and fc7 InnerProduct layer of Zeiler and Fergus model [12]. The default anchor ratio was set to 1:1 and we compute anchors at 4 different scales (2,8,16,32). During training, the number of categories are modified to 2 (face and background) with 2 * 4 bounding box coordinates to be predicted. Softmax and smoothL1 loss are deployed for training classification and bounding box prediction respectively.

---

[1] https://davidsonic.github.io/index/ccbr_2016

(a) Face patches extracted from RPN.

(b) Non-face patches extracted from RPN.

Fig. 1. Sample proposals generated by RPN. When the IOU between a face proposal generated by RPN and a ground-truth label is greater than 0.5, we treat it as a face patch. Otherwise, when the IOU is below 0.3, we treat it as a non-face patch

All the proposals are generated from the training set of WIDER FACE [3] containing 12,880 high-resolution images through this RPN convolutional neural network. There are about 300 proposals extracted from each image. WIDER FACE contains 393,703 labelled faces collected from 32,203 images with a wide variety in scales, poses, occlusions and expressions. What's worth noticing about WIDER FACE is that the images collected are taken in crowded scenes and proves to be an effective training set and challenging evaluation set.

In our benchmark dataset, when the Intersection over Union (IOU) between a face proposal generated by RPN and a ground-truth label is greater than 0.5, we treat it as a face patch. Otherwise, when the IOU is below 0.3, we treat it as a non-face patch. As a result, we collected a face classification benchmark (FCB) database, which contains 3,558,142 proposals in total, of which 198,616 being face patches. All images are resized to 24 × 24 for face classification benchmark. Note that by doing so there may be some changes to the original aspect ratio. Sample face patches and non-face patches extracted from the RPN network are displayed in Fig. 1.

2.2 Benchmark Protocol

As shown in Table 1, proposals are extracted from the first 6,440 images in WIDER_FACE are used as the training set, while the remaining proposals from the next 6,440 images are used as testing set. In the testing set the size of Non-face patches are about 20 times the size of face proposals. So if an algorithm

Table 1. Details of FCB Benchmark

Dataset	#Img	#Face patches	#Non-face patches
Training	6,440	112,124	1,666,947
Testing	6,440	86,492	1,692,579
Total	12,880	198,616	3,359,526

classifies all the positive samples as negative ones, it would still get 95 % two-class classification accuracy. Under such circumstances, it would be biased in the choice of our face detection algorithms if we solely take the two-class classification accuracy as our evaluation index.

To reveal the 'true' performance of a face classifier, we put stress on performance at low False Accept Rate (FAR). Following the method in [5], the performance of the proposed algorithms are displayed via ROC curve by varying the confident score threshold, with FAR in log space being the x axis and True Positive Rate (TPR) being the y axis. Specifically, we measure the true positive rate at FAR=10^{-3} to compare the performance of different algorithms. Since there are altogether 1,779,071 proposals extracted from 6,440 images in the test set, it means we only allow for False Positive Per Image (FPPI) of 0.28 in an image, which is both challenging and persuasive in terms of real world applications.

3 Evaluation and Results

3.1 Feature Extraction and Classification Methods

Traditional Methods: Illumination changes, occlusions and pose variations are three fundamental problems for face detection under unconstrained settings. Illumination-invariance is obtained in LOMO [8] by applying the Retinex transform and the Scale Invariant Local Ternary Pattern (SILTP) for feature representation. NPD [7] gives the nice properties of scale-invariance, boundedness and its feature involves only two pixel values, hence robust to occlusion and blur or low image resolution. We use the open source code of these two feature representation methods in our experiments. Besides, LBP [14] together with its variant MB-LBP [15] are also re-implemented for evaluation. We adopt DQT+boosting [7] as our baseline classifier. We also tried SVM, but it appears to be not effective to handle this challenging problem, and it is also not efficient for our large-scale data. Therefore, we leaved SVM out finally.

CNN Methods: Convolutional Neural Network based methods have received more and more attention due to its effectiveness in computer vision tasks. In our experiments, a CIFAR-10 Net [6] based binary classification CNN and a Cascade-CNN following the paradigm of [11] have been implemented.

Several CNN structures have been explored and we picked one with the best performance based on CIFAR-10 and its detailed information is listed in Table 2.

Table 2. Model structure of CIFAR10-based CNN

Layer name	Filter number	Filter size	Stride	Padding	AF
conv1	32	3×3	1	2	-
max_pool1	-	2×2	2	-	RELU
conv2	32	3×3	1	2	RELU
ave_pool2	-	2×2	2	-	-
conv3	64	3×3	1	2	RELU
ave_pool3	-	2×2	2	-	-
ip1	64	-	-	-	-
ip2	2	-	-	-	-

As for the structure of Cascade-CNN, please refer to [11]. Note that for training Cascade-CNN, hard negative samples mined by the former net are used as non-face samples to be used for the following net training and in training each net, hard positive samples mined are aggregated to face proposals for further fine-tuning.

3.2   Results and Discussion

The evaluation results on the whole test set are shown in Fig. 2. From the results, we can see that the CIFAR-10 based CNN beats other methods due to its powerful representation ability. Besides, it also outperforms Cascade-CNN by a large margin. This is probably because in the process of cascade training, hard negative samples mined by the last net contain a proportion of non-face patches that actually contain faces but with a IOU less than 0.3, thus 'too hard' to identify for a shallow net structure (see Fig. 3). Another possible reason is that Cascade-CNN in [11] followed a pipeline of alternation between classification net and calibration net; the Non Maximum Suppresion (NMS) is also deployed during the Cascade-CNN training process, in contrast to the FCB evaluation, which only requires classification net.

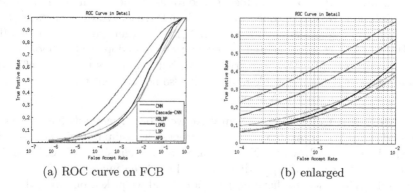

(a) ROC curve on FCB   (b) enlarged

Fig. 2. Evaluation results on FCB test set, best viewed in color

However, even with the best performer CIFAR-10, the performance on FCB is still far from satisfactory as observed from Fig. 2, revealing that FCB is a large-scale and challenging benchmark on face classification. Note that we only used two CNN based methods while a more sophisticated network structure should be able to achieve better performance.

(a) Hard positive samples mined by 24-net.

(b) Hard negative samples mined by 24-net.

Fig. 3. Some hard positive samples and some hard negative samples mined by the 24-net in the Cascade-CNN method [11]

As for hand-crafted features, MB-LBP obtains about 20 % detection rate compared to LBP (about 16 %) detection rate at FAR of 10^{-3}, which is reasonable considering that MB-LBP encodes not only microstructures but also macrostructures of image patterns, thus more comprehensive and robust than LBP.

Table 3. Detection rate (%) of each algorithm at FAR $= 10^{-3}$

LOMO	LBP	MB-LBP	NPD	CNN	Cascade CNN
17.42	15.98	19.42	15.47	**43.10**	32.66

At FAR of 10^{-3}, LOMO performs slightly better than LBP, but its true positive rate increases rapidly as we move along the righthand direction of x axis. It is not until FAR of 0.3 % that LOMO outperforms MB-LBP. NPD achieves comparable performance compared to LBP. As its values are computed involving only two pixels of an image, NPD is more sensitive than other algorithms considering that face patches on FCB are not aligned. At FAR of 10^{-2}, the overall rank is almost the same except that LOMO performs better than MB-LBP. Please refer to Table 3 for more details.

Table 4 is a further illustration about the dimension of the original features and selected features by the DQT based AdaBoost, as well as the training time, testing time and platform of each algorithm employed in our evaluation. Note that LOMO requires RGB images while other methods use gray images as input. The first 4 algorithms are all combination of feature extraction and boosting with Deep Quadratic Trees (DQT) while the last two are end to end CNN

Table 4. Model details and speed of each algorithm

Algorithm	#Features	#Selected features	Training time (h)	Testing time (h)	Platform
LOMO	7,252	283,323	5.35	1.52	X5650CPU
LBP	768	20,269	1.80	0.44	X5650CPU
NPD	165,600	6,877,535	6.42	1.10	X5650CPU
MB-LBP	5,120	228,606	3.91	0.34	X5650CPU
CIFAR-10 CNN	64	64	2.20	0.50	K40-GPU
Cascade-CNN	560	560	5.85	0.60	Titan-GPU

methods, therefore the dimension of original features and selected features are the same. Besides, CNN is generally faster to train since it takes the advantage of GPU parallelization, but it's also due to this fact that CNN runs less efficiently compared to traditional methods on CPU or hand-held devices.

4   Conclusion

Face detection generally involves three steps with face classification being its core module. However, it is not easy to determine the actual performance of the face classification part due to the large influence of block generation and post-processing in traditional benchmarks. Motivated by this, we conduct a specialized benchmark study in this paper, which focuses purely on face classification. We start with face proposals by collecting about 3.5 millions of face and non-face sample patches, and build a benchmark dataset (FCB) for two-class face classification evaluation. Our results show that, without the help of post-processing, the performance of face classification itself is still not very satisfactory, even with a powerful CNN method. The data and evaluation code of this study will be released to the public to help assess performance of face classification, and ease the participation of other related researchers who want to try their algorithms for face detection.

Acknowledgements. This work was supported by the National Key Research and Development Plan (Grant No.2016YFC0801002), the Chinese National Natural Science Foundation Projects #61473291, #61572501, #61502491, #61572536, NVIDIA GPU donation program and AuthenMetric R&D Funds.

References

1. Kostinger, M., Wohlhart, P., Roth, P.M., et al.: Annotated facial landmarks in the wild: a large-scale, real-world database for facial landmark localization. In: 2011 IEEE International Conference on Computer Vision Workshops (ICCV Workshops), pp. 2144–2151. IEEE (2011)
2. Jain, V., Erik Learned-Miller, F.: A benchmark for face detection in unconstrained settings. Technical Report: UM-CS-2010-009 (2010)
3. Yang, S., Luo, P., Loy, C.C., Tang, X., WIDER FACE: a face detection benchmark. In: IEEE Conference on Computer Vision and Pattern Recognition (CVPR) (2016)

4. Zhu, X., Ramanan, D.: Face detection, pose estimation, landmark localization in the wild. In: Computer Vision and Pattern Recognition (CVPR) (2012)
5. Dollar, P., Wojek, C., Schiele, B., et al.: Pedestrian detection: an evaluation of the state of the art. IEEE Trans. Pattern Anal. Mach. Intell. **34**(4), 743–761 (2012)
6. The CIFAR-10 dataset. https://www.cs.toronto.edu/~kriz/cifar.html
7. Liao, S., Jain, A.K., Li, S.Z.: A fast and accurate unconstrained face detector. IEEE Trans. Pattern Anal. Mach. Intell. **38**(2), 211–223 (2016)
8. Liao, S., Hu, Y., Zhu, X., et al.: Person re-identification by local maximal occurrence representation, metric learning. In: Proceedings of the IEEE Conference on Computer Vision and Pattern Recognition, pp. 2197–2206 (2015)
9. Ren, S., He, K., Girshick, R., et al.: Faster R-CNN: towards real-time object detection with region proposal networks. In: Advances in Neural Information Processing Systems, pp. 91–99 (2015)
10. Jiang, H., Learned-Miller, E.: Face detection with the faster R-CNN. arXiv preprint (2016). arXiv:1606.03473
11. Li, H., Lin, Z., Shen, X., et al.: A convolutional neural network cascade for face detection. In: Proceedings of the IEEE Conference on Computer Vision and Pattern Recognition, pp. 5325–5334 (2015)
12. Zeiler, M.D., Fergus, R.: Visualizing and understanding convolutional networks. In: Fleet, D., Pajdla, T., Schiele, B., Tuytelaars, T. (eds.) ECCV 2014. LNCS, vol. 8689, pp. 818–833. Springer, Heidelberg (2014). doi:10.1007/978-3-319-10590-1_53
13. Mathias, M., Benenson, R., Pedersoli, M., Gool, L.: Face detection without bells and whistles. In: Fleet, D., Pajdla, T., Schiele, B., Tuytelaars, T. (eds.) ECCV 2014. LNCS, vol. 8692, pp. 720–735. Springer, Heidelberg (2014). doi:10.1007/978-3-319-10593-2_47
14. Ojala, T., Pietikainen, M., Maenpaa, T.: Multiresolution gray-scale and rotation invariant texture classification with local binary patterns. IEEE Trans. Pattern Anal. Mach. Intell. **24**(7), 971–987 (2002)
15. Liao, S., Zhu, X., Lei, Z., Zhang, L., Li, S.Z.: Learning multi-scale block local binary patterns for face recognition. In: Lee, S.-W., Li, S.Z. (eds.) ICB 2007. LNCS, vol. 4642, pp. 828–837. Springer, Heidelberg (2007). doi:10.1007/978-3-540-74549-5_87
16. Yan, J., Zhang, X., Lei, Z., et al.: Face detection by structural models. Image Vis. Comput. **32**(10), 790–799 (2014)
17. Van de Sande, K.E.A., Uijlings, J.R.R., Gevers, T., et al.: Segmentation as selective search for object recognition. In: International Conference on Computer Vision, pp. 1879–1886. IEEE (2011)
18. Zitnick, C.L., Dollár, P.: Edge boxes: locating object proposals from edges. In: Fleet, D., Pajdla, T., Schiele, B., Tuytelaars, T. (eds.) ECCV 2014. LNCS, vol. 8693, pp. 391–405. Springer, Heidelberg (2014). doi:10.1007/978-3-319-10602-1_26
19. Arbelez, P., Pont-Tuset, J., Barron, J.T., et al.: Multiscale combinatorial grouping. In: Proceedings of the IEEE Conference on Computer Vision and Pattern Recognition, pp. 328–335 (2014)

Binary Classifiers and Radial Symmetry Transform for Fast and Accurate Eye Localization

Pei Qin[✉], Junxiong Gao[✉], Shuangshuang Li, Chunyu Ma,
Kaijun Yi[✉], and Tomas Fernandes

Wuhan Hongshi Technologies Co., Ltd., Wuhan 430200, China
{qinpei,junxiong.gao,shuangshuang.li,chunyu.ma,
kaijun.yi,fernandes}@hongshi-tech.com

Abstract. In order to locate eyes for iris recognition, this paper presents a fast and accurate eye localization algorithm under active infrared (IR) illumination. The algorithm is based on binary classifiers and fast radial symmetry transform. First, eye candidates can be detected by the fast radial symmetry transform in infrared image. Then three-stage binary classifiers are used to eliminate most unreliable eye candidates. Finally, the mean eye template is employed to identify the real eyes from the reliable eye candidates. A large number of tests have been completed to verify the performance of the proposed algorithm. Experimental results demonstrate that the algorithm proposed in this article is robust and efficient.

Keywords: Binary classifiers · Fast radial symmetry transform · Mean eye template · Eye localization

1 Introduction

At present, iris recognition is regarded as one of the most reliable and accurate biometrics in all biological recognition technologies [1]. It will gain a wide range of application for personal identification in the public security system, military, counter-terrorism and bank payment system etc. The wide application of iris recognition could create a safer and more convenient living environment for society. In order to exploit the capability of iris recognition, it is extremely crucial to develop the eye localization technology with low complexity and high accuracy.

The existing technologies could be classified into three categories based on the information or patterns [2]. One of the three categories is based on measuring eye characteristics [3–6]. This type of method exploits the inherent features of eyes, such as their distinct shapes and strong intensity contrast [2]. This approach is relatively simple, however, its accuracy is highly affected by eyebrow, fringe, glass frame and illumination etc. Another type of method is based on learning statistic appearance model [2], which extracts useful visual features from a large set of training images [7, 8]. The performance of this method is limited by the training sample space and the high complexity is inevitable. The third type of method is based on structural information [9, 10]. This approach

© Springer International Publishing AG 2016
Z. You et al. (Eds.): CCBR 2016, LNCS 9967, pp. 30–39, 2016.
DOI: 10.1007/978-3-319-46654-5_4

exploits the spatial structure of interior components of eyes or the geometrical regularity between eyes and other facial features in the face context [2]. To overcome the complicated uncontrolled conditions, a statistical eye model is usually integrated into the third type of method.

For our proposed method in this paper, both eye characteristics and structural information are considered. In the next section, the theory of fast radial symmetry transform will be introduced. In Sect. 3, the proposed eye localization method will be described in detail. Assessment method of eye localization precision and experimental results are presented in Sect. 4. The last section concludes this work.

2 Fast Radial Symmetry Transform

Fast radial symmetry transform (FRST) [11] is regarded as the extension of general symmetry transform and a gradient-based interest descriptor in space domain. It can be used to detect high radial symmetry objects. Firstly, it is necessary to introduce two important concepts: orientation projection image O_n and magnitude projection image M_n. Orientation projection image O_n denotes the projection count accumulation of each pixel on its gradient orientation under radius n. Magnitude projection image M_n denotes the gradient magnitude accumulation of each pixel on its gradient orientation under radius n.

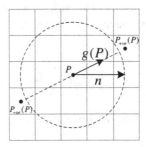

Fig. 1. The locations of positively-affected pixel $P_{+ve}(P)$ and negatively-affected pixel $P_{-ve}(P)$ affected by the gradient element g(P) for a range of $n = 2$.

As shown in Fig. 1, $P_{+ve}(P)$ represents the positively-affected pixel location on the positive gradient direction of pixel P. Similarly, $P_{-ve}(P)$ represents the negatively-affected pixel location on the negative gradient direction of pixel P. The coordinates of $P_{+ve}(P)$ and $P_{-ve}(P)$ are given by

$$P_{+ve}(P) = P + round\left(\frac{g(P)}{\|g(P)\|}n\right), \ P_{-ve}(P) = P - round\left(\frac{g(P)}{\|g(P)\|}n\right). \quad (1)$$

Where $round(\cdot)$ denotes the operation of getting the nearest integer of each vector element. g(P) is the gradient vector.

Orientation projection image O_n and magnitude projection image M_n should be initialized to zero [11]. For each pair of affected pixels, the values of orientation projection and magnitude projection corresponding points $P_{+ve}(P)$ and $P_{-ve}(P)$ are given by

$$O_n(P_{+ve}(P)) = O_n(P_{+ve}(P)) + 1, \ O_n(P_{-ve}(P)) = O_n(P_{-ve}(P)) - 1, \qquad (2)$$

$$M_n(P_{+ve}(P)) = M_n(P_{+ve}(P)) + \|g(P)\|, \ M_n(P_{-ve}(P)) = M_n(P_{-ve}(P)) - \|g(P)\|. \qquad (3)$$

For the radius n, fast radial symmetry contribution S_n is defined as the convolution

$$S_n = F_n(P) * A_n. \qquad (4)$$

Where

$$F_n(P) = \frac{M_n(P)}{k_n} \left(\frac{|\tilde{O}_n(P)|}{k_n} \right)^{\alpha},$$

$$\tilde{O}_n(P) = \begin{cases} O_n(P), & if \ O_n(P) < k_n \\ k_n, & otherwise \end{cases}. \qquad (5)$$

A_n is a 2-D Gaussian filter. α is the radial strictness parameter. k_n is a scaling factor. The final symmetry transform image S is determined by the average of all radial symmetry contribution S_n

$$S = \frac{1}{len(N)} \sum_{n \in N} S_n. \qquad (6)$$

Where N is a vector which is composed of radius n considered, $len(\cdot)$ calculates the length of the input vector.

3 Eye Localization Method

3.1 Eye Candidate Detection

Since the excellent performance of FRST on detecting radial symmetry structure, it is exploited to detect the eye candidates in the target image because of the highly symmetry irises and pupils.

The first step of detecting candidates is to search the regions of interest (ROI) in the target image and scale each ROI to 256×256 pixels. A ROI is a relatively small region where contains two eyes. While the visual angle of iris camera is usually very small in recognition products, so the whole target image can be an available ROI as shown in Fig. 2. If the background of the target image is extremely rich, it is necessary to employ face detection technology [15] to search ROIs in the target image.

Fig. 2. The target image from the iris camera with small visual angle which can be a ROI (Authorized by Institute of Automation of China Academia Sciences, CASIA).

Fig. 3. The output image of FRST.

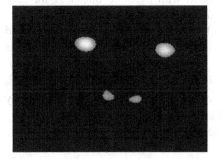

Fig. 4. The binarization result of FRST image S.

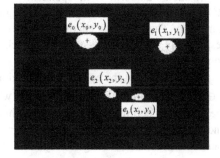

Fig. 5. The coordinates of eye candidates after region generation process and binarization.

Next, gradient vector $\left[g_x(P)g_y(P)\right]^T$ of each pixel in every ROI is computed by 3×3 Sobel operator. Then each ROI can be processed by the FRST according to Sect. 2 and the output image S is shown in Fig. 3. The considered radii values can be set according to the size of ROI. Here, we set the vector N of considered radius to be $\{7, 9, 11, 12\}$.

In the FRST output image S, it is obvious that there are some bright regions. These bright regions contain eyes, nostrils, node pads of glasses etc. In order to eliminate the background from the bright regions, we utilize the binarization method to process the image S and the processing result is shown in Fig. 4. Then region generation skill is employed to generate the coordinate of the middle pixel of each eye candidate region as shown in Fig. 5. The coordinate vector of eye candidates could be denoted as $\{e_0(x_0, y_0), \ldots, e_{M-1}(x_{M-1}, y_{M-1})\}$, where M is the number of eye candidates.

3.2 Binary Classifiers

Although it is efficient and reliable to detect eye candidates by FRST, binarization and region generation, it also remains a great challenge to identify the eye(s) accurately from the candidates. Because the candidates may also be nostrils, nevus, node pads of glasses etc.

Three-stage binary classifiers are designed to further exclude unreliable eye candidates. The binary classifiers are denoted as $C_k(w_k, h_k)$, $k \in \{0, 1, 2\}$ shown in Fig. 6, where w_k and h_k are respectively the width and height of classifier C_k. Classifier C_0 is only a $2n_{max} \times 2n_{max}$ square and classifier C_1 is composed of three $2n_{max} \times 2n_{max}$ squares, where black color represents "1" and white color represents "0", n_{max} is the maximum element of radius value vector N. Classifier C_2 is a little bit complex and this paper only describes the black region for simplicity. The black region is composed of a $2n_{max} \times 2n_{max}$ square, two $n_{max} \times 0.5n_{max}$ rectangles and two $0.25n_{max} \times 0.25n_{max}$ squares. Here n_{max} is equal to 12.

These binary classifiers are used to classify the binary eye candidates. Then, binarization transform is independently processed with dynamic threshold for each ROI, not for the whole target image. Figure 7 shows the result of ROI binarization transform. Then the eye candidates $\{e_0(x_0, y_0), \ldots, e_{M-1}(x_{M-1}, y_{M-1})\}$ are classified respectively by the three-stage binary classifiers. And the steps of classification is shown below.

Firstly, segment the eye candidate regions $B_{i,k}(s_{i,k}, t_{i,k}, w_{i,k}, h_{i,k})$, $i \in [0, M-1]$, $k \in \{0, 1, 2\}$ from the ROI binary image, where $(s_{i,k}, t_{i,k})$, $w_{i,k}$ and $h_{i,k}$ are respectively the left corner coordinate, width and height of the eye candidate regions. The width $w_{i,k}$ and height $h_{i,k}$ are the same as these of classifier C_k. The left corner coordinates of eye candidate regions $B_{i,k}$ are given by

$$
\begin{aligned}
S_{i,0} &= x_i - n_{max}, \quad t_{i,0} = y_i - n_{max}; \\
S_{i,1} &= x_i - n_{max}, \quad t_{i,1} = y_i - 5n_{max}; \\
S_{i,2} &= round(x_i - 1.625n_{max}), \quad t_{i,2} = y_i - n_{max}.
\end{aligned}
\tag{7}
$$

Where $1.625n_{max}$ is a half of the black region width in Classifier C_2 and the mean of $round(\cdot)$ is the same with Eq. (1). If $s_{i,k} < 0$ or $t_{i,k} < 0$, the eye candidate $e_i(x_i, y_i)$ should be rejected.

Secondly, calculate eigenvalue difference $\Delta v_{k,i}$, $i \in [0, M-1]$, $k \in \{0, 1, 2\}$. Eigenvalue difference $\Delta v_{k,i}$ is defined as

$$
\Delta v_{k,i} = v_{k,i} - \min\{v_{k,i}\}.
\tag{8}
$$

Where $v_{k,i}$ is given by

$$
v_{k,i} = C_k \times B_i.
\tag{9}
$$

Thirdly, compare the eigenvalue difference $\Delta v_{k,i}$ with the threshold λ_k. If $\Delta v_{k,i} < \lambda_k$, it represents the eye candidate $e_i(x_i, y_i)$ passes the classification of classifier C_k.

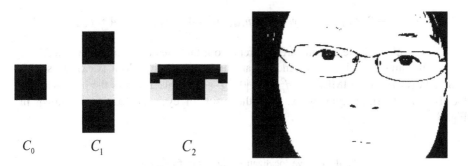

C_0 $\quad\quad$ C_1 $\quad\quad\quad$ C_2

Fig. 6. Three binary classifiers. $\quad\quad$ **Fig. 7.** Output of ROI binarization transform.

Suppose there are Q eye candidates passed the classification of the three-stage classifiers, which are denoted as $\left\{\tilde{e}_0(x_0, y_0), \ldots, \tilde{e}_{Q-1}(x_{Q-1}, y_{Q-1})\right\}$.

3.3 Eye Localization by IMED Matching

After three-stage classification, one or more non-eye candidates maybe also exist. To detect the real eyes from $\left\{\tilde{e}_0(x_0, y_0), \ldots, \tilde{e}_{Q-1}(x_{Q-1}, y_{Q-1})\right\}$, template matching is employed which is based on intensity appearance [12]. This approach is relatively reliable and does not require any training. The template is obtained by the average result of 200 eye samples with $4n_{\max} \times 4n_{\max}$ pixels cut from CASIA-Iirs-Distance database (CASIA-Iirs-Distance database is authorized by CASIA). Suppose S_n^e is the eye samples cut from ROIs of database images, the mean eye template T_e is given by

$$T_e = \frac{1}{200} \sum_{n=1}^{200} S_n^e. \tag{10}$$

Finally, the real eyes are identified through the similarity between eye candidates and eye template T_e. Image Euclidean Distance (IMED) [13] is proved to be an excellent assessment of image similarity. Because it can reduce mismatching caused by eye rotation or deformation. The IMED $d_r^2(G_e, G_T)$ between eye template and eye candidates is calculated by

$$d_r^2(G_e, G_T) = \frac{1}{2\pi} \sum_{i,j=1}^{WH} \exp\left\{-|P_i - P_j|^2/2\right\}(g_e^i - g_T^i)(g_e^j - g_T^j). \tag{11}$$

Where G_T and G_e are the vectors $\left\{g_T^1, g_T^2, \cdots, g_T^{WH}\right\}$ and $\left\{g_e^1, g_e^2, \cdots, g_e^{WH}\right\}$ which are respectively composed of all the pixels of eye template T_e and each eye candidate region $D_r(s, t, w, h)$, $r \in [0, Q-1]$. s, t, w and h are given by

$$s = x_i - 2 \times n_{\max}, \quad t = y_i - 2 \times n_{\max}, \quad w = 4 \times n_{\max}, \quad h = 4 \times n_{\max}. \quad (12)$$

These eye candidate regions are different from the ones used to be classified.

Smaller image Euclidean distance means higher similarity. So it is easy to search two real eyes from the IMED set d_r^2, $r \in [0,\ Q-1]$. Table 1 shows the proposed eye localization algorithm framework. And the result of eyes localization is shown in Fig. 8.

Table 1. Eye localization algorithm framework.

- Input a target image I;
- Initialize $N = \{7,9,11,12\}$, $[\lambda_0, \lambda_1, \lambda_2] = [35, 70, 85]$;
- Search ROIs in the target image $\{R_0, ..., R_{P-1}\}$ and scale each ROI to 256×256 pixels;
- for $r = 0, \cdots, P-1$:
  1. Detect the eye candidates $e_i(x_i, y_i), i \in [0, M-1]$ in the ROI R_r;
  2. for $i = 0,\ ,M-1$:
     - (1). Binarization transform for ROI R_r;
     - (2). Segment the eye candidate regions $B_{i,k}(s_{i,k},\ t_{i,k},\ w_{i,k},\ h_{i,k})$, then reject the eye candidate $e_i(x_i, y_i)$ and jump to next loop if $s_{i,k} < 0$ or $t_{i,k} < 0$;
     - (3). Calculate eigenvalue difference $\Delta v_{k,i}$;
     - (4). Compare the eigenvalue difference $\Delta v_{k,i}$ with λ_k, then put the eye candidate $e_i(x_i, y_i)$ into the eye candidate set of passed classification if $\Delta v_{k,i} < \lambda_k$.
  3. Template matching to locate the real eyes.

Fig. 8. The result of eyes localization.

4 Experimental Results

4.1 Assessment Method of Eye Localization Precision

In order to assess the precision of the proposed method, the most commonly used measurement proposed in [14] is used in this article, which is given by

$$d_{eye} = \frac{\max(d_l,\, d_r)}{\|C_l - C_r\|}. \tag{13}$$

Where C_l and C_r are the true eye center. d_l and d_r are the Euclidean distances between the detected eye center and the true eye center.

4.2 Results and Analysis

The proposed method is tested on the JAFFE and CASIA-Iirs-Distance databases for its performance. The database of CASIA-Iirs-Distance is from the Center for Biometrics and Security Research of CASIA. There are 2576 images in the database which are taken under active infrared (IR) illumination. People on the images have different postures and some wear glasses.

Table 2. The experimental results on JAFFE database.

Method	Accuracy	
	$d_{eye} < 0.1$	$d_{eye} < 0.25$
Multi-view eyes localization [16]	60.9 %	98.6 %
AdaBoost + SVM [17]	99.5 %	100 %
Proposed method	96.82 %	98.90 %

Table 3. The experimental results on CASIA-Iirs-Distance database.

Method	Accuracy
AdaBoost [15]	89.74 % (with glasses + without glasses)
SVM [3]	95.50 % (with glasses + without glasses)
Appearance model + GST [18]	99.4 % (without glasses)
	88.3 % (with glasses)
Proposed method	96.26 % (with glasses + without glasses)

The experimental results on JAFFE database are shown in the Table 2. The proposed method performance is superior to multi-view eyes localization method [16], and worse than Tang's [17]. Tang's method employs the Adaboost and SVM skills to obtain excellent performance, but it introduces a large amount of computation and complex training. So it is extremely difficult to achieve real-time eye localization.

The methods proposed by Zhu [3] and Zhao [18] can be compared with the method proposed in this article since they also exploit the active infrared illumination. Table 3 shows the eye localization performance of proposed method when comparing with other representative ones. From Table 3, the proposed method is superior to other representative methods except the one proposed by Zhao. But Zhao's method is sensitive to the interference of glasses.

5 Conclusions

A novel method based on binary classifiers and fast radial symmetry transform is proposed to improve the accuracy rate of eye localization under active infrared (IR) illumination. It is able to efficiently overcome the detrimental interference from eyebrow, fringe, glass frame and the reflected light from glasses etc. Because besides the geometric structure and intensity information, binary information is also considered in this research. From the experimental results, the proposed method is proved to be superior to most of other states-of-art methods. It is worth mentioning that the complexity degree of our method is highly reduced because the training step is eliminated. Therefore the proposed method could achieve a better tradeoff between eye localization performance and complexity.

References

1. Sachin, G., Chander, K.: Iris recognition: the safest biometrics. Int. J. Eng. Sci. **4**, 265–273 (2011)
2. Song, F., Tan, X., Chen, S., Zhou, Z.H.: A literature survey on robust and efficient eye localization in real-life scenarios. J. Pattern Recogn. **46**(12), 3157–3173 (2013)
3. Zhu, Z., Fujimura, K., Ji, Q.: Real-time eye detection and tracking under various light conditions. In: Proceedings of the 2002 Symposium on Eye Tracking Research and Applications, vol. 25, pp. 139–144 (2002)
4. Yuille, A.L., Cohen, D.S., Hallinan, P.W.: Feature extraction from faces using deformable templates. In: Proceedings of IEEE Conference on Computer Vision and Pattern Recognition, pp. 104–109 (1989)
5. Feng, G.C., Yuen, P.C.: Variance projection function and its application to eye detection for human face recognition. Pattern Recogn. Lett. **19**(9), 899–906 (1998)
6. Kothari, R., Mitchell, J.L.: Detection of eye locations in unconstrained visual images. In: Proceedings of International Conference on Image Processing, vol. 3, pp. 519–522 (1996)
7. Everingham, M.R., Zisserman, A.: Regression and classification approaches to eye localization in face images. In: Proceedings of IEEE Conference on Automatic Face and Gesture Recognition, pp. 441–448 (2006)
8. Wang, P., Green, M., Ji, Q., Wayman, J.: Automatic eye detection and its validation. In: Proceedings of IEEE Conference on Computer Vision and Pattern Recognition, vol. 3, pp. 164–172 (2005)
9. Cootes, T.F., Taylor, C.J., Cooper, D.H., Graham, J.: Active shape models-their training and application. Comput. Vis. Image Underst. **61**(1), 38–59 (1995)

10. Tan, X., Song, F., Zhou, Z.H., Chen, S.: Enhanced pictorial structures for precise eye localization under uncontrolled conditions. In: Proceedings of IEEE Conference on Computer Vision and Pattern Recognition, pp. 1621–1628, 20–25 June 2009

11. Loy, G., Zelinsky, A.: Fast radial symmetry for detecting points of interest. IEEE Trans. PAMI **25**(8), 959–973 (2003). IEEE Press

12. Li, W., Wang, Y., Wang, Y.: Eye location via a novel integral projection function and radial symmetry transform. Int. J. Digital Content Technol. Appl. **5**(8), 70–80 (2011)

13. Wang, L., Zhang, Y., Feng, J.: On the euclidean distance of images. IEEE Trans. PAMI **27**(8), 1334–1339 (2005). IEEE Press

14. Jesorsky, O., Kirchberg, K., Frischholz, R.: Robust face detection using the hausdorff distance. In: Proceedings of International Conference on Audio and Video-Based Biometric Person Authentication, pp. 90–95 (2001)

15. Viola, P., Jones, M.: Robust real-time face detection. Int. J. Comput. Vis. **57**(2), 137–154 (2004)

16. Fu, Y., Yan, H., Li, J., Xiang, R.: Robust facial features localization on rotation arbitrary multi-view face in complex background. J. Comput. **6**(2), 337–342 (2011)

17. Tang, X., Ou, Z., Su, T., Sun, H., Zhao, P.: Robust precise eye location by AdaBoost and SVM techniques. In: Proceedings of International Conference on Advances in Neural Networks, pp. 93–98 (2005)

18. Zhao, S., Grigat, R.: Robust Eye Detection under active infrared illumination. In: Proceedings of International Conference on Pattern Recognition, vol. 4, pp. 481–484 (2006)

Robust Multi-view Face Alignment Based on Cascaded 2D/3D Face Shape Regression

Fuxuan Chen, Feng Liu, and Qijun Zhao[✉]

National Key Laboratory of Fundamental Science on Synthetic Vision,
College of Computer Science, Sichuan University, Chengdu, China
qjzhao@scu.edu.cn
http://vs.scu.edu.cn/

Abstract. In this paper, we present a cascaded regression algorithm for multi-view face alignment. Our method employs a two-stage cascaded regression framework and estimates 2D and 3D facial feature points simultaneously. In stage one, 2D and 3D facial feature points are roughly detected on the input face image, and head pose analysis is applied based on the 3D facial feature points to estimate its head pose. The face is then classified into one of three categories, namely left profile faces, frontal faces and right profile faces, according to its pose. In stage two, accurate facial feature points are detected by using an appropriate regression model corresponding to the pose category of the input face. Compared with existing face alignment methods, our proposed method can better deal with arbitrary view facial images whose yaw angles range from -90 to $90°$. Moreover, in order to enhance its robustness to facial bounding box variations, we randomly generate multiple bounding boxes according to the statistical distributions of bounding boxes and use them for initialization during training. Extensive experiments on public databases prove the superiority of our proposed method over state-of-the-art methods, especially in aligning large off-angle faces.

Keywords: Face alignment · Multi-view · Cascaded regression · Pose analysis

1 Introduction

Face alignment is a process to detect facial feature points in a facial image. Facial feature points, also known as facial fiducial points or facial landmarks, are located at semantic positions, such as eyebrows, eye-corners, and lips. Many related research topics and real-world applications, e.g., face recognition and expression analysis, could benefit from the accurately detected facial feature points. Face alignment is an interesting but challenging problem that has attracted substantial attention over the recent years [2,14–16].

With the fast development of face alignment algorithms in the last several years, especially the introduction of cascaded regression [1], state-of-the-art face

© Springer International Publishing AG 2016
Z. You et al. (Eds.): CCBR 2016, LNCS 9967, pp. 40–49, 2016.
DOI: 10.1007/978-3-319-46654-5_5

alignment methods almost can process frontal face and near-frontal face well. Yet, large pose face alignment is still a hard problem that has not been solved satisfactorily. Another factor that may affect face alignment accuracy is the variation of facial bounding boxes. As a necessary input of face alignment, it greatly affects the results of face alignment. Existing face alignment algorithms either use manually marked ground truth bounding boxes, or employ some automated face detection algorithms. However, they mostly do not consider the variation in detected facial bounding boxes.

Cascaded regression based alignment, which is composed of a set of cascaded regressors, has been used extensively because of its high performance and low computational complexity. Three dimensional (3D) face model has recently been utilized to assist the alignment of large off-angle two dimensional (2D) facial images. In this paper, we propose a novel multi-view face alignment algorithm based on cascaded 2D/3D face shape regression. It consists of two stages. In stage one, it applies coarse face shape regressors to analyze the head pose of the input face; and then in stage two, appropriate fine face shape regressors are chosen according to the head pose to locate the landmarks in the input face. When training these regressors, distributions of automatically detected facial bounding boxes are analyzed for different pose angles, respectively, and used to enhance the robustness of face alignment to bounding box variations.

2   Related Work

Multi-view Face Alignment. Few prior approaches have proposed to handle faces with a wide range of poses. Zhu and Ramanan [15] proposed a method called TSPM to fulfill multi-view face alignment and pose estimation. It achieves multi-view face alignment by employing multi-view trees. However, it cannot deal with in-the-wild faces well and has high computational complexity. Cascaded Deformable Shape Model (CDM) [14], which proposed for the first time pose-free face alignment, is a regression-based method. It can handle both laboratory environmental and in-the-wild face images, but it has been applied only to faces within ±45°. Facial Landmark Detection by Deep Multi-task Learning (TCDCN) [16] is a deep learning based method and effectively achieves good performance, but it only detects five landmarks and mainly handles faces within ±60°. More recently, Pose-Invariant 3D Face Alignment (PIFA) [2] was proposed to estimate both 2D and 3D landmarks and their visibilities. Using 3D landmarks and their visibility information enables this method to handle faces with arbitrary poses. Although these methods aim to accomplish pose-invariant face alignment, none of them have attempted to align profile faces with yaw angle near ±90°. In comparison, our proposed method can consistently well cope with faces with yaw angles from −90 to 90° via two-stage cascaded regression in 2D/3D face shape space.

Robustness to Bounding Box Variations. One characteristic of regression-based face alignment is that it heavily relies on initialization, which is usually decided by the facial bounding box. Most face alignment algorithms [2,4] assume that a face detection algorithm is available that can provide fairly good facial bounding boxes, and they initialize their algorithms with bounding boxes directly calculated from ground truth landmarks. Consequently, these algorithms usually cannot fit into real-world applications due to the variation of detected facial bounding boxes. Very few algorithms consider about this problem, and adapt the alignment procedure according to the results of automated face detection [14,15]. However, these algorithms not only are limited by the poor performance of face detection algorithms, but can only adapt to their own face detection algorithms. Some other algorithms [5] train their alignment models with multiple initializations, i.e., multiple facial bounding boxes, which are obtained by disturbing the ground truth bounding boxes according to the rule of automatically detected ones. This way, the resulting alignment models can better handle bounding box variations. They consider the faces of all different views together with one single distribution of facial bounding boxes. However, faces of different views may not share the same distribution. We thus propose to establish different distributions for different views, respectively, so that faces with varying pose angles all can have good initialization and be better aligned.

3   Proposed Method

Detecting facial feature points of frontal faces has reached very high accuracy nowadays, while the performance of face alignment of large pose facial images still cannot be satisfied. One reason is the serious self-occlusion in large pose facial images. When extracting features from the surrounding of an obstructed point, wrong information may be provided, which will consequently mislead the process of face alignment. Another reason may be that frontal face and profile face should be seen as different objects, while past methods use a common model to deal with multi-view faces. Towards the first reason, we propose to estimate visibility of each fiducial point by utilizing 3D face alignment, and thus we can get rid of the misleading information from invisible fiducial points. As for the second problem, we use a two-stage regression framework. The stage-one regression estimates pose of each image via rough shape estimation, then the stage-two regression estimates facial feature points accurately according to the estimated pose angles. Besides, we propose a novel method to initialize the training samples with proper bounding boxes. In the following sections, we introduce in detail our method from four aspects: (1) The framework of our method; (2) The structure of cascaded regression; (3) The method of head pose analysis; 4) The initialization of facial bounding boxes.

3.1   The Framework of the Proposed Method

In this work, we employ a two-stage regression framework. In stage one, we use a common cascaded regression model for all different views, to locate facial feature points. A rough result of face alignment can be obtained via this model. However, because of the large difference between frontal and profile faces,

Fig. 1. The flowchart of our method

this result may be not very accurate. So in stage two, we achieve face align-ment via multiple models. Fortunately, based on the roughly detected 2D and 3D landmarks on the input face, its head pose can be estimated. According to the head pose angle, the face can be categorized into one of three classes, namely faces within $-90° \sim -45°$ yaw, faces within $-45° \sim 45°$ yaw, faces within $45° \sim 90°$ yaw. Among pitch, yaw, and roll rotation of a head, it is yaw rotation that most likely causes self-occlusion and changes image appearance. This is the reason why the classification is based on yaw angle; but the proposed method can be easily extended to other rotation dimensions. Then, in stage two, another appropriate cascaded regression model is chosen according to the category of the input face and used to achieve fine alignment of the input face. Figure 1 shows the flowchart of the proposed method. In this work, each regression model is a set of cascaded coupled-regressors.

3.2   The Structure of Cascaded Regression

Cascaded regression contains a set of regressors, each of which is a mapping from feature to target. Our regression structure is similar to [3] and we will introduce some definitions at first. Let us use the vector concatenated by the coordinates of all facial landmarks to define the face shape of each image. Assume each shape is composed of u facial fiducial points. $S = (x_1, y_1, z_1, x_2, y_2, z_2, \cdots, x_u, y_u, z_u) \in R^{3u \times 1}$ denotes a 3D shape and $P = (x_1', y_1', x_2', y_2', \cdots, x_u', y_u') \in R^{2u \times 1}$ denotes a 2D shape where x, y, z is the 3D-coordinates of a point and x', y' is the cor-responding 2D-coordinates. $\hat{S}^k$ represents the current 3D-estimation of a face and $\hat{P}^k$ corresponding to the current 2D-estimation of the face at k^{th} iteration.

R_s^k and R_p^k are the associated 3D-regressor and 2D-regressor. Here, we employ a simple linear regression. In each iteration of regression, $\hat{S}^k$ and $\hat{P}^k$ are respectively updated according to Eqs. (1) and (2).

$$\hat{S}^{k+1} = \hat{S}^k + R_s^k(f(P^k)), \tag{1}$$

$$\hat{P}^{k+1} = \hat{P}^k + R_p^k(f(P^k)), \tag{2}$$

where f denotes appearance (feature) of the face image based on the current shape estimation. The R_s^k and R_p^k are the mappings from image appearance to their target shapes. They are the least-squares solutions of Eqs. (3) and (4).

$$R_s^k = \underset{R_s^k}{argmin} \sum_{i=1}^{N} \left\| \triangle S_i^k - R_s^k(f_i(P_i^k)) \right\|, \tag{3}$$

$$R_p^k = \underset{R_p^k}{argmin} \sum_{i=1}^{N} \left\| \triangle P_i^k - R_p^k(f_i(P_i^k)) \right\|, \tag{4}$$

where $\triangle S_i^k$ is the 3D shape residual between ground truth S_i^* and currently estimated 3D shape S_i^k of the ith face image, and $\triangle P_i^k$ is the corresponding 2D shape residual:

$$\triangle S_i^k = S_i^* - \hat{S}_i^k, \tag{5}$$

$$\triangle P_i^k = P_i^* - \hat{P}_i^k, \tag{6}$$

In each iteration, after the above update of $\hat{S}^k$ and $\hat{P}^k$, we further refine $\hat{P}^k$, particularly the invisible landmarks, according to the projection of $\hat{S}^k$. Let M denote the perspective projection matrix, which can be estimated by fitting $\hat{S}^k$ to $\hat{P}^k$. $\hat{P}^k$ is then revised by Eq. (7). This refinement guarantees the 2D shape staying in the limitation of a real face:

$$P = M \times S \tag{7}$$

The training procedure of the regression is summarized in Algorithm 1:

Visibility. A face may have some invisible landmarks due to self-conclusion, especially when the face has a large pose angle. The features based on these invisible landmarks may mislead regression direction. Thus we estimate visibility of each facial landmark to avoid this problem. If a landmark is invisible, we set its feature value to zeros. As mentioned before, projection matrix M_i can be computed between the 3D shape and 2D shape. The computation of visibility is similar to [2]:

$$v = sgn(\overrightarrow{N_j} \cdot (\frac{m1}{\|m1\|} \times \frac{m2}{\|m2\|})), \tag{8}$$

where $m1$ is the first row vector of M_i, $m2$ is the second row vector of M_i, $\overrightarrow{N_j}$ is the normal vector of landmark j in 3D space, and sgn denotes the sign function. If v is positive, this landmark is visible; otherwise invisible.

Algorithm 1. The learning of the cascaded coupled-regressor

Input: Training data$\{(I_i, S_i^*, P_i^*)|i = 1, 2, \cdots, N\}$, and initial shape pair (S_i^0, P_i^0)

Output: Two level cascaded coupled-regressors $\{R_s^k, R_p^k\}_{k=1}^K$

1 **for** $k = 1, \cdots, K$ **do**
2   Estimate R_s^k via Eq. (3) ;
3   Update S_i^k via Eq. (1) for all images;
4   Estimate R_p^k via Eq. (4);
5   Update P_i^k via Eq. (2) for all images;
6   Compute the 3D-to-2D mapping matrix M_i^k and revise P_i^k via Eq. (7) ;

3.3 Head Pose Analysis

Benefiting from 3D estimation, we can easily analyze head pose [6]. Let $\vec{n_1}$ denote the vector pointing from left eye to right eye, q_j denote the 3D coordinate of landmark j, and $\bar{q}$ denote mean 3D coordinate of all landmarks. Let $C_t \in R^{3\times3}$ be defined as:

$$C_t = \frac{1}{u}\sum_{j=1}^{u}(q_j - \bar{q})(q_j - \bar{q})^T. \qquad (9)$$

Suppose $\vec{n_3}$ is the eigenvector of C_t, corresponding to the minimal eigenvalue. Mathematically, it represents the face normal. $\vec{n_2}$ is computed by the cross product of $\vec{n_1}$ and $\vec{n_3}$. Now the three vectors, which respectively correspond to a coordinate axis, form the camera coordinate system of this face. We compute the rotation angle between the x-axis of this coordinate system and the x-axis of the normal coordinate system of a frontal face, and then project it into x-y plane and x-z plane. These two projected angles respectively represent yaw angle and roll angle of this face. Similarly, pitch angle can be computed by comparing the y-axes of these two coordinate systems.

3.4 Bounding Boxes

In this section, we study the statistical distribution of detected facial bounding boxes. Two face detection methods [12,17] are used to detect the faces in all images of enlarged LFW [8], which includes 3D ground truth landmarks and a great number of additional face images with large pose angles synthesized from the original face images in LFW. We compare all detected bounding boxes with corresponding ground truth bounding boxes, and find that both face detection methods have similar results. The deviation of the detected bounding boxes from the ground truth ones is closely related to head poses of the detected faces. Figure 2 shows the histograms of the bounding box deviations of [12] along x and y directions.

Bearing the above observations in mind, we divide face images into three classes according to their yaw angles, namely left-profile face images, near-frontal

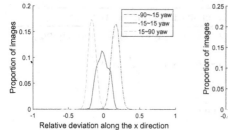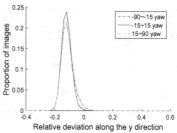

Fig. 2. Distribution of the deviation of detected bounding boxes

face images, and right-profile face images, and compute the statistical distributions of facial bounding box deviations for these three classes respectively. In training phase, we analyze the head pose of a face, classify it into one of the three classes, and then give it one or more random initial bounding boxes according to the bounding box deviation distribution of its corresponding class. Additionally, we set the initial shape to the mean of all training shapes transformed with regard to random bounding box. As a result, our method fits better with automated face detection.

4   Experiments

Data Preparation. The particular characteristics of our learning structure require data containing 2D and 3D ground truth landmarks. LFW [8] contains 13,233 face images of 5,749 different individuals. The work of [18] provides each face of LFW with 68 landmarks, based on which the 3D models of the faces in

Table 1. The MAPE of four methods on AFW

CDM	PIFA	Proposed-Single	Proposed-Multi
9.13	8.61	8.21	6.76

Table 2. The NME of four methods on Multi-PIE

Yaw angle	N_t	CDM	PIFA	Proposed-Single	Proposed-Multi
±90°	8	–	0.0958	0.0632	0.0584
±75°	8	–	0.1151	0.0536	0.0541
±60°	8	–	0.0948	0.0586	0.0544
±45°	15	0.0724	0.0615	0.0466	0.0434
±30°	15	0.0546	0.0520	0.0510	0.0393
±15°	15	0.0365	0.0610	0.0317	0.0295
0°	15	0.0358	0.0527	0.0300	0.0299

LFW are obtained via 3DMM [9]. It is worth mentioning that we augment this database because the pose variation of the original LFW is limited. We rotate each 3D face until the yaw angle is close to 90 degrees to generate corresponding 2D images. After this process, LFW database is enlarged with a great number of multi-view images. We use this enlarged LFW database for training.

Baseline Methods. We compare our proposed method with other state-of-the-art methods. The codes of PIFA and CDM are publicly available and both of them aim to solve large pose face alignment. In order to prove the robustness of our initialization method to bounding box variations, we also implement our method in another way by using a single deviation distribution for all poses instead of multiple pose-specific deviation distributions to disturb initial bounding boxes. We denote this implementation of our method as Proposed-Single, while the one with multiple distributions as Proposed-Multi. Normalized Mean

Fig. 3. Some results of the proposed method on Multi-PIE and AFW. The yellow boxes show the detected bounding boxes. And the green/red dots show the visible/invisible landmarks. First row to Forth row: estimated 68 landmarks with yaw angle ranging from $-90°$ to $90°$ for Multi-PIE. Fifth row: estimated 68 landmarks for AFW (Color figure online)

Error (NME) [7] and Mean Average Pixel Error (MAPE) [14] are used to measure the landmarks estimation error.

Comparison on AFW. The Annotated Faces in-the-wild (AFW) database [10] contains faces with complex background. 68 landmark points are provided for 337 faces in the database by [11]. We use initial bounding boxes detected by [12], and give a manual bounding box if a face is not detected. Table 1 shows our results, and results of PIFA and CDM which are directly cited from their papers. It can be clearly seen from these results that the proposed method significantly improves the alignment accuracy.

Comparison on Multi-PIE. The CMU Multi-Pose Illumination, and Expression (Multi-PIE) Database [13] contains around 750,000 images for 15 different poses in lab environment. We select 13 poses with yaw angles ranging from $-90°$ to $90°$ in our experiments. PIFA uses ground truth bounding box, and CDM uses the bounding boxes obtained by its own detection algorithm. Because the face detection algorithm of CDM almost cannot detect faces with yaw angles beyond $45°$, we only show its results on faces with yaw angles varying between $-45°$ and $45°$. Furthermore, the number of facial feature points detected by PIFA is 21, which is different from ours (68) and CDM's (66), so only the same semantic points are selected to make comparison. Results in Table 2 show that our proposed method has obvious advantages when dealing with large pose faces. Note that the training of CDM is based on Multi-PIE, while ours is not. Figure 3 shows some example alignment results by our proposed method.

5   Conclusions

In this paper, we have proposed a multi-view face alignment algorithm to locate 2D and 3D facial feature points simultaneously. Our motivation mainly comes from two aspects. One is frontal faces and profile faces should be seen as different objects, and the other is each face is a 3D object in real-world. Thus, we use a two-stage cascaded regression framework which utilizes different models to deal with faces of different poses, and explicitly handles invisible feature points with assistance of 3D face shapes. In addition, we investigate the statistical distributions of facial bounding boxes obtained by automated face detection algorithms, and utilize these distributions to enhance the robustness of our method to facial bounding box variations. We have compared our proposed method with state-of-the-art methods on public databases, and the results prove the effectiveness of our method.

Acknowledgments. This work is supported by the National Natural Science Foundation of China (No. 61202161) and the National Key Scientific Instrument and Equipment Development Projects of China (No. 2013YQ49087904).

References

1. Zhou, S., Comaniciu, D.: Shape regression machine. In: Information Proceeding in Medical, Imaging, pp. 13–25 (2007)
2. Jourabloo, A., Liu, X.: Pose-invariant 3D face alignment. In: ICCV, pp. 3694–3702 (2015)
3. Liu, F., Zeng, D., Zhao, Q., Liu, X.: Joint face alignment and 3D face reconstruction. In: ECCV (2016, in press)
4. Dollar, P., Welinder, P., Perona, P.: Cascaded pose regression. In: CVPR, pp. 1078–1085 (2010)
5. Xiong, X., De la Torre, F.: Supervised descent method and its applications to face alignment. In: CVPR, pp. 532–539 (2013)
6. Tulyakov, S., Sebe, N.: Regressing a 3D face shape from a single image. In: ICCV, pp. 1109–1119 (2015)
7. Yu, X., Huang, J., Zhang, S., Yan, W., Metaxas, D.N.: Pose-free facial landmark fitting via optimized part mixtures and cascaded deformable shape model. In: ICCV, pp. 1994–1951 (2013)
8. Huang, G.B., Ramesh, M., Berg, T., Learned-Miller, E.: Labeled faces in the wild: a database for studying face recognition in unconstrained environments. University of Massachusetts, Amherst, Technical Report 07–49 (2007)
9. Blanz, V., Vetter, T.: A morphable model for the sunthesis of 3D faces. In: SIG-GRAPH 1999, pp. 187–194 (1999)
10. Zhu, X., Ramanan, D.: Face detection, pose estimation, and landmark localization in the wild. In: CVPR, pp. 2879–2886 (2012)
11. Sagonas, C., Tzimiropoulos, G., Zafeiriou, S., Pantic, M.: 300 Faces in-the-wild challenge: the first facial landmark localization challenge. In: ICCV-W, pp. 397–403 (2013)
12. Sun, Y., Wang, X., Tang, X.: Deep convolutional network cascade for facial point detection. In: CVPR, pp. 3476–3483 (2013)
13. Gross, R., Matthews, I., Cohn, J., Kanade, T., Baker, S.: Multi-pie. In: Proceedings of IEEE International Conference on Automatic Face Gesture Recognition, In Image and Vision Computing, pp. 807–813 (2010)
14. Yu, X., Huang, J., Zhang, S., Yan, W., Metaxas, D.N.: Pose-free facial landmark fitting via optimized part mixtures and cascaded deformable shape model. In: ICCV, pp. 1944–1951 (2013)
15. Zhu, X., Ramanan, D.: Face detection, pose estimation, and landmark localization in the wild. In: CVPR, pp. 2879–2886 (2012)
16. Zhang, Z., Luo, P., Loy, C.C., Tang, X.: Facial landmark detection by deep multi-task learning. In: Fleet, D., Pajdla, T., Schiele, B., Tuytelaars, T. (eds.) ECCV 2014. LNCS, vol. 8694, pp. 94–108. Springer, Heidelberg (2014). doi:10.1007/978-3-319-10599-4_7
17. Yu, S.: Shenzhen University face detector (2014). https://github.com/ShiqiYu/libfacedetection
18. Zhu, X., Lei, Z., Liu, X., Shi, H., Li, S.Z.: Face alignment across large poses: a 3D solution (2015). arXiv:1511.07212

Extended Robust Cascaded Pose Regression for Face Alignment

Yongxin Ge[1(✉)], Xinyu Ren[1], Cheng Peng[1], and Xuchu Wang[2]

[1] School of Software Engineering, Chongqing 400044, China
{yongxinge,20121850,20152413008}@cqu.edu.cn
[2] College of Optoelectronic Engineering, Chongqing 400044, China
xcwang@cqu.edu.cn

Abstract. We present a highly accurate and very efficient approach for face alignment, called Extended Robust Cascaded Pose Regression (ERCPR), which is robust to large variations due to differences in expressions and pose. Unlike previous shape regression-based approaches, we propose to reference features weighted by three different face landmarks, which are much more robust to shape variations. Then, a correlation-based feature selection method and a two-level boosted regression are applied to establish accurate relation between features and shapes. Experiments on two challenging face datasets (LFPW, COFW) show that our proposed approach significantly outperforms the state-of-art in terms of both efficiency and accuracy.

Keywords: Face alignment · Cascade Pose Regression · Face landmark

1 Introduction

Face alignment (a.k.a., face landmark localization) is a foundational task in many computer vision applications such as face recognition [1], facial expression recognition [2], and age estimation [3]. Therefore, it has been a popular topic in recent years. However, it is still challenging due to the complex variations in face appearance caused by illumination, expressions, pose and partial occlusions under uncontrolled conditions.

Various methods for face alignment have been proposed recently [4–8]. As a typical model, active appearance model (AAM) is a flexible linear model that models the shape and appearance variations of non-rigid objects [9]. However, AAM uses holistic feature of face, which make it difficult to handle large variations and partial occlusion problems. Moreover, AAM usually fails in case of complex variations of facial appearance, mainly because a single linear model can hardly deal with all the nonlinear variations in facial appearance.

To address the first problem, local feature based methods like ASM [10] and CLM [11–13] have been proposed, which build appearance models with local image patches instead of the entire face. These local image patches are generally sampled around the current facial landmarks. However, these local features are still not robust enough against large shape deformation, illumination changes and pose variations. If the number

© Springer International Publishing AG 2016
Z. You et al. (Eds.): CCBR 2016, LNCS 9967, pp. 50–58, 2016.
DOI: 10.1007/978-3-319-46654-5_6

of face landmarks is low in some regions, it is likely that many of the local patches far from any landmark, becoming increasingly subject to small variations.

In the state-of-the-art work [14], s supervised descent method (SDM) is proposed to solve nonlinear least squares optimization problem by using the supervised descent strategy. Despite of the promising performance of SDM in face alignment, it requires manually defined energy functions that measure goodness of fit. Some simple weak regressors such as decision stump [15] and a fern [16] are used in a similar boosted regression manner for face alignment. However, such regressors are too weak and result in every slow convergence in training and poor performance in the testing.

In this paper, to better extract robust shape-index features and model efficient relationship between the shape-index features and their corresponding face shape, we propose an Extended Robust Cascaded Pose Regression (ERCPR) approach for face alignment. Figure 1 illustrates the basic idea for shape-index features extraction. Every reference feature is weighted by three original shape features. Both the three original shape features and weights are generated randomly. So these reference features are distributed more reasonably in the face region and also are more robust. Subsequently, a correlation-based feature selection method and a two-level boosted regression are used to establish the relationship between features and their corresponding shapes.

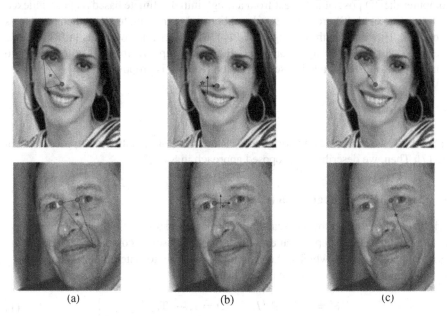

(a)   (b)   (c)

Fig. 1. Referencing shape-indexed features from face landmarks by using different approaches. (a) Features from our method. (b) Features from [8]. (c) Features from [17] (Color figure online)

2   Related Work

Shape-Index Features: Faces in the wild usually present large variations due to difference in pose, expressions and illumination. So extracting shape-index features invariant to these conditions is a key step to shape estimation. Dollar et al. [16] propose shape-index features, which are relative to the currently estimated shapes. To achieve feature invariance against face rotations and scales, Cao et al. [8] propose to compute a similarity transform to normalize the current shape to a mean shape by least squares fitting of all facial landmarks. Specially, they suggest to index a pixel by its local coordinates with respect to its nearest face landmark, which is illustrated in Fig. 1(b). Both of the above mentioned methods for feature extraction are based on the currently estimated face landmarks. However, if the number of face landmarks is low in some regions, it is likely that many of the local patches far from any landmark, becoming increasingly subject to small variations. To overcome this issue, interpolated shape-indexed features are proposed by linear interpolation between two landmarks. As show in Fig. 1(c), these new feature could cover more face region and are much more robust to shape variations. However, all the reference features are limited in the lines determined by any two face landmarks.

Regression: Most of the proposed face alignment methods in recent years exploit the idea of regression on shape-indexed features by using a feature to shape mapping function [8, 16–23]. Dollar et al. [16] present the cascaded Pose Regression (CPR) to computer the 2D pose of an object from a rough initial estimate based on pose-indexed features. Cao et al. [8] propose a two-level boosted regression to strengthen regressors over CPR. However, both the original CPR [16] and its improvements in [8] struggle against occlusions and large shape variations. To improve robustness to these two conditions, Robust Cascaded Pose Regression (RCPR) is proposed in [15].

3   Method

In Sect. 3.1, we first review the original CPR method [14] and its two improvements in [8, 17]. Then, we describe our proposed approach in Sect. 3.2.

3.1   Cascaded Pose Regression (CPR)

Original CPR is formed by a cascade of T weak regressors $R^{1 \cdots T}$. Given a face image I and a raw initial face shape S^0, at each iteration, regressor R^t computes a shape update δS from image features, which is then combined with previous iteration's estimation S^{t-1} in an additive manner to form the updated shape:

$$S^t = S^{t-1} + R^t(I, S^{t-1}), t = 1, \cdots, T, \tag{1}$$

During learning, given N training examples $\left\{ (I_i, \hat{S}_i) \right\}_{i=1}^N$, each regressor R^t is trained by minimizing the error between the true shape and the shape estimation of the previous stage. The key to CPR lies on extracting robust shape-indexed features and learning regressors, which are able to progressively reduce the estimation error at each iteration.

Cao et al. [8] propose three main improvements over CPR: (1) To effectively exploit shape constraints, Cao et al. perform regression on all shape parameters at once instead of one parameter at a time; (2) Two-level boosted regression are proposed to strengthen regressor in [8]; (3) Cao et al. propose to extract features referenced locally with respect to their closest landmark, which could improve feature to shape variations.

Although the extracted features in [8] is more robust than referencing features directly with respect to the global shape proposed in original CPR, these features are still not robust enough against to large variations of shape and pose. Specifically, the referencing features are not distributed properly in the face region, so the number of landmarks is low in some regions, which will result in many useful features could not be extracted. To address this issue, Burgos-Artizzu et al. [17] propose to reference features by linear interpolation between two face landmarks selected randomly.

3.2   Extended Robust Cascaded Pose Regression (ERCPR)

Their experiments in [17] demonstrate that the proposed features are much more robust and computation efficient. However, all these shape-indexed features are limited to the lines between any two face landmarks.

To overcome this issue, we propose to reference features by weighting any three face landmarks selected by randomly. These new features are able to cover the entire face region and much more robust to shape variations as show in Fig. 1(a).

The main processes of our approach for referencing shape-indexed features are three steps. First, we randomly select three different face landmarks, as three red face landmarks show in Fig. 1(a). And we mark the coordinates of these three landmarks as P_1, P_2 and P_3 respectively. Then, the corresponding weights for each landmark are generated randomly, labeled as w_1, w_2 and w_3 respectively. Finally, the coordinate of a new point termed as P_{new} (as the green star in Fig. 1(a)) is generated according to Eq. (2), which is considered as our referencing feature point.

$$P_{new} = P_1 w_1 + P_2 w_2 + P_3 w_3 \qquad (2)$$

Comparing to the approach in [17], referencing feature could be selected in the plane composed of three face landmarks instead of a line between two face landmarks. So more features in the face are the candidates for our referencing features, reflecting more real variations of the face. Moreover, for each feature, there is no longer need to fitting a line between the two face landmarks, so computation is much faster.

4   Datasets and Implementation Details

We first introduce two popular and challenging dataset: Labeled Face Parts in the Wild (**LFPW**) [6] and Caltech Occluded Faces in the Wild (**COFW**) [17]. Then, in Sect. 4.2, we describe implementation details in all experiments.

4.1   Datasets

LFPW was created in [6], and is one of the most used datasets to benchmark face alignment in unconstrained conditions, including 1300 face images. This dataset shares only web image URLs, so all the images are downloaded from internet which contain large variations in expressions, illumination, pose and occlusions. But now some URLs are no longer valid. We only downloaded 811 of the 1000 training images and 224 of the test images with 68 annotated landmarks from IBUG website [24].

COFW was produced in [17], and is designed to present faces in real world conditions, it is much more challenging since it contains faces showing large variations in pose, expressions and occlusions. Specifically, with the clear goal of collecting challenging dataset, four people with different level of computer vision knowledge are asked to each collect 250 typical real-world face images. Totally, 1007 face images are obtained from a variety of sources, and each is hand annotated using the same 29 landmark as in LFPW.

4.2   Implementation Details

Code for [17] is publicly available, and we implemented our method starting from it. To achieve better generalization, we augment the training data by the factor of 20, which is found to be very robust against large pose variations and rough initial shapes during testing. To compare with the methods fairly, all the parameters are set the same as these in [17]: number of boosted regressors and iterations respectively $T = 100$ and $K = 50$, number of features $F = 400$. We also use depth 5 random fern regressors and 5 restarts during testing.

5   Experiments

In this section, we compare the proposed ERCPR approach with the two state-of-art methods in [8, 17] on LFPW and COFW datasets. Each case is evaluated on the average error and percentage of failure cases.

The code of the method in [17] is publicly available, and we use it directly, but the released code estimates only 29 landmarks located in the inner regions of the face.

In this paper, errors are measured as the average landmark distance to ground-truth, which are normalized as percentages with respect to interocular distance. Average, any error above 10 % is considered as failure.

5.1   Comparison on LFPW Dataset

We evaluate our proposed ERCP and the two methods in [8, 17] on LFPW dataset [6], and the cumulative error distribution curves of the three methods mentioned above are shown in Fig. 2. As seen, both our method performs and RCPR perform much better than the method in [8] on this dataset, and achieves better localization accuracy with an improvement up to about 15 % when error is below 0.10. Our method performs the best all the time, which attributes to more robust selected features.

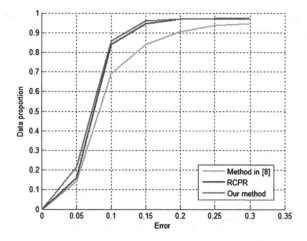

Fig. 2. The cumulative error distribution curves of all the method on LFPW.

Figure 3 shows the localization results of our ERCPR on some extremely challenging example faces from LFPW. It can be observed that our approach is robust to the variations from illumination, expressions, pose and partial occlusions.

Fig. 3. Example results from LFPW dataset, containing diverse in illumination, expression, pose and partial occlusion.

5.2 Comparison on COFW Dataset

Similar to Fig. 2, the comparison results on COFW dataset are show in Fig. 4. To increase the number of training images, the training images of both LFPW and COFW are used for training. Particularly, The original non-augmented 845 LFPW face images and 500

COFW face images are collected for training (1345 total), and the remaining 507 face images for testing, which are provided in [17].

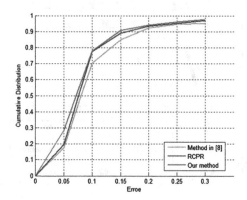

Fig. 4. The cumulative error distribution curves of all the method on COFW.

As seen in Fig. 4, our ERCPR still performs the best, which illustrates the superiority to the other two methods again.

Both RCPR and method in [8] discussed the tradeoff between two-level cascade regression, and they proposed different optimal tradeoffs for their own methods respectively (T = 100, K = 50 for RCPR and T = 10, K = 500 for RCPR). To compare with RCPR fairly, we keep K the same number as that of RCPR (K = 50), and show the relation between failure and T in Fig. 5. From Fig. 5, we can conclude that our method can achieve the smallest failure rate with much more less iterations compare to that of RCPR).

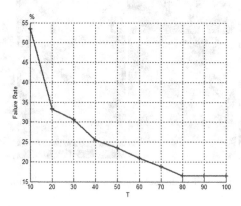

Fig. 5. The relation between failure rate and T. In our method, the iteration T is set as 100.

6   Conclusion

Aiming at dealing with challenging face landmark estimation due to complex variations in face appearance cause by illumination, expressions, pose and partial occlusions, we propose a novel method, called Extended Robust Cascade Pose Regression (ERCPR). We first generated the new feature reference points in the planes formed by three different face landmarks, which are selected randomly. Then, based on these points, a correlation-based feature selection method is used to get the features. Finally, a two-level boosted regression approach is adopted to establish accurate relation between features and shapes. Experimental results demonstrate that our proposed method clearly improves both accuracy and robustness of previous state-of-art methods on two challenging datasets.

References

1. Wiskott, L., Fellous, J.-M., Krüger, N., Von der Malsburg, C.: Face recognition by elastic bunch graph matching. IEEE Trans. Pattern Anal. Mach. Intell. **19**(7), 775–779 (1997)
2. Lucey, S., Matthews, I., Hu, C., Ambadar, Z., De la Torre, F., Cohn, J.: AAM derived face representations for robust facial action recognition. In: FG (2006)
3. Fu, Y., Guo, G., Huang, T.S.: Age synthesis and estimation via faces: a survey. IEEE Trans. Pattern Anal. Mach. Intell. **32**(11), 1955–1976 (2010)
4. Ge, Y., Yang, D., Jiwen, L., Li, B., Zhang, X.: Active appearance models using statistical characteristics of gabor based texture representation. J. Vis. Commun. Image Representation **24**(5), 627–634 (2013)
5. Burgos-Artizzu, X., Perona, P., Dollar, P.: Robust face landmark estimation under occlusion. In: IEEE International Conference on Computer Vision (ICCV), Sydney, Australia, 1−8 December 2013, pp. 1513–1520 (2013)
6. Belhumeur, P.N., Jacobs, D.W., Kriegman, D.J., Kumar, N.: Localizing parts of faces using a consensus of exemplars. IEEE Trans. Pattern Anal. Mach. Intell. **35**(12), 2930–2940 (2013)
7. Zhou, F., Linm, J.: Exemplar-based graph matching for robust facial landmark localization. IEEE International Conference on Computer Vision (ICCV), Sydney, Australia, 1−8 December 2013, pp. 1025–1032 (2013)
8. Cao, X., Wei, Y., Wen, F., Sun, J.: Face alignment by explicit shape regression. In: IEEE Conference on Computer Vision and Pattern Recognition (CVPR), Providence, RI, USA, 16 − 21 June 2012, pp. 2887–2894 (2012)
9. Cootes, T., Edwards, G., Taylor, C.: Active appearance models. IEEE Trans. Pattern Anal. Mach. Intell. **23**(6), 681–685 (2001)
10. Cootes, T.F., Taylor, C.J., Cooper, D.H., Graham, J.: Active shape modelstheir training and application. Comput. Vis. Image Underst. (CVIU) **61**(1), 38–59 (1995)
11. Cristinacce, D., Cootes, T.F.: Feature detection and tracking with constrained local models. Br. Mach. Vis. Conf. (BMVC) **17**, 929–938 (2006)
12. Lucey, S., Wang, Y., Saragih, J.M., Cohn, J.F.: Non-rigid face tracking with enforced convexity and local appearance consistency constraint. Image Vis. Comput. **28**(5), 781–789 (2010)
13. Saragih, J.M., Lucey, S., Cohn, J.F.: Deformable model fitting by regularized landmark mean-shift. Int. J. Comput. Vis. **91**(2), 200–215 (2011)

14. Xiong, X., De la Torre, F.: Supervised descent method and its applications to face alignment. In: IEEE Conference on Computer Vision and Pattern Recognition, CVPR (2013)
15. Cristinacce, D., Cootes, T.: Boosted regression active shape models. In: BMVC (2007)
16. Dollar, P., Welinder, P., Perona, P.: Cascaded pose regression. In CVPR (2010)
17. Burgos-Artizzu, X.P., Perona, P., Doll'ar, P.: Robust face landmark estimation under occlusion. In: ICCV, pp. 1513–1520 (2013)
18. Zhang, J., Shan, S., Kan, M., Chen, X.: Coarse-to-fine auto-encoder networks (CFAN) for real-time face alignment. In: Fleet, D., Pajdla, T., Schiele, B., Tuytelaars, T. (eds.) ECCV 2014, Part II. LNCS, vol. 8690, pp. 1–16. Springer, Heidelberg (2014)
19. Valstar, M., Martinez, B., Binefa, X., Pantic, M.: Facial point detection using boosted regression and graph models. In: IEEE Conference on Computer Vision and Pattern Recognition (CVPR), San Francisco, CA, USA, 13–18 June 2010, pp. 2729-2736 (2010)
20. Dantone, M., Gall, J., Fanelli, G., VanGool, L.: Real-time facial feature detection using conditional regression forests. In: IEEE Conference on Computer Vision and Pattern Recognition (CVPR), Providence, RI, USA, 16–21 June 2012, pp. 2578–2585 (2012)
21. Chen, D., Ren, S., Wei, Y., Cao, X., Sun, J.: Joint cascade face detection and alignment. In: Fleet, D., Pajdla, T., Schiele, B., Tuytelaars, T. (eds.) ECCV 2014, Part VI. LNCS, vol. 8694, pp. 109–122. Springer, Heidelberg (2014)
22. Cao, C., Weng, Y., Lin, S., Zhou, K.: 3D shape regression for real-time facial animation. ACM Trans. Graph. (SIGGRAPH) **32**(4), 41:1–41:10 (2013)
23. Yu, X., Lin, Z., Brandt, J., Metaxas, D.N.: Consensus of regression for occlusion-robust facial feature localization. In: Fleet, D., Pajdla, T., Schiele, B., Tuytelaars, T. (eds.) ECCV 2014, Part IV. LNCS, vol. 8692, pp. 105–118. Springer, Heidelberg (2014)
24. 300 faces in-the-wild challenge. http://ibug.doc.ic.ac.uk/resources/300-W/

Pose Aided Deep Convolutional Neural Networks for Face Alignment

Shuying Liu, Jiani Hu, and Weihong Deng[✉]

School of Information and Communication Engineering,
Beijing University of Posts and Telecommunications, Beijing, China
{liushuying668,jnhu,whdeng}@bupt.edu.com

Abstract. Recently, deep convolutional neural networks have been widely used and achieved state-of-the-art performance in face recognition tasks such as face verification, face detection and face alignment. However, face alignment remains a challenging problem due to large pose variation and the lack of data. Although researchers have designed various network architecture to handle this problem, pose information was rarely used explicitly. In this paper, we propose Pose Aided Convolutional Neural Networks (PACN) which uses different networks for faces with different poses. We first train a CNN to do pose classification and a base CNN, then different networks are finetuned from the base CNN for faces of different pose. Since there wouldn't be many images for each pose, we propose a data augmentation strategy which augment the data without affecting the pose. Experiment results show that the proposed PACN achieves better or comparable results than the state-of-the-art methods.

Keywords: Deep Convolutional Neural Network · Pose aided · Data augmentation

1 Introduction

Pose matters. Face alignment is a vital procedure in many face recognition tasks. It serves as the preprocessing stage of face verification, face animation, emotion recognition, etc.

In the research of face alignment, significant progress has been made in the past few years [2,11,12,17,19]. But face alignment still remains a challenge problem due to various head poses and the lack of data. Researches [1,3] show that the features extracted by deep convolutional neural networks (DCNN) can be robust to variants of illumination, occlution and poses. So we choose DCNN as our basic model. But simply training DCNN does not utilize the pose information explicitly. However, we use pose information explicitly in the proposed method. We first use a DCNN to classify the face images into different poses, then we use different DCNNs to train faces in different poses. This bring us the problem that there wouldn't be much data for each pose class, which is not enough to train a

© Springer International Publishing AG 2016
Z. You et al. (Eds.): CCBR 2016, LNCS 9967, pp. 59–67, 2016.
DOI: 10.1007/978-3-319-46654-5_7

network. So data augmentation is needed with the requirement of not affecting the original pose of the image. We propose to enlarge the dataset using gaussian noise, gaussian blur, motion blur and jpeg compression.

This paper might have following contributions: We utilize the pose information explicitly by first classify the face images into different poses and train different regression networks for different poses. We propose a data augmentation method which keeps the poses of images unchanged. Experiment results shows that our method achieved better or comparable performance than the state-of-the-arts.

The remainder of the paper is organized as follows. Section 2 will introduce some related works of face alignment. In Sect. 3, we will discuss the proposed Pose Aided Convolutional Neural Networks (PACN). Then the experiments and the results will be discussed in Sect. 4. And finally, we made a conclusion in Sect. 5.

2   Related Works

Face alignment has developed rapidly in the past few years. Here we divide the face alignment methods into conventional methods and deep learning methods.

Regression-based methods can be a typical kind of conventional methods which directly learn the regression function from images to the locations of the landmarks. Some typical regression-based methods are SDM, Xiong et al. [8], ESR, Cao et al. [9], LBF, Ren et al. [10]. Those algorithms start from a initial shape estimation(always mean shape) and predict shape increment iteratively, which means their performance still depends on a good initial shape.

Recently, deep learning has made breakthroughs in face alignment. Sun et al. [2] trained 23 deep convotional neural networks cascaded to do five-point face landmark detection and achieved state-of-the-art performance on LFPW dataset. Zhang et al. [11] trained a Coarse to Fine Autoencoder Networks to do real time face alignment. Zhang [12] trained a multi-task DCNN which gains state-of-the-art performance on the challenging 300 W dataset [13]. Very recently, some researchers began to use Fully Convolutional Networks(FCN) to do landmark detection in a segmentation way [14,15]. However, the proposed method needs neither cascaded networks training nor multi-task learning which requires very carefully tuning. So our methods achieves good performance with relatively low model complexity.

3   Pose Aided Convolutional Neural Networks

The Pose Aided Convolutional Neural Networks consist of three stages. In the first stage, we train a DCNN to do pose classification and face images are classified into different poses. A base DCNN for five-point detection is trained in the second stage. Finally, different DCNNs for dense-landmark detection are fine-tuning from the base DCNN using different pose images. The overall framework of PACN is shown in Fig. 1, and the network architecture of each stage is shown in Table 1.

Table 1. The model architecture used in three stages. As for CONV, a x a, b means convolution kernel size and output size, respectively. We use 2×2 pooling to down sample the feature map for all the experiments. For all stages, we use 80×80 gray images. Bounding boxes provided by 300 W dataset are used to crop faces

Model / Layer type	Stage 1	Stage 2	Stage 3
CONV-POOL	5x5, 16	5x5, 16	5x5, 16
CONV-POOL	5x5, 48	5x5, 48	5x5, 48
CONV-POOL	5x5, 48	5x5, 48	5x5, 48
CONV-POOL	4x4, 64	4x4, 64	4x4, 64
CONV	3x3, 64	3x3, 64	3x3, 64
FC	100	100	256
FC	5	10	136

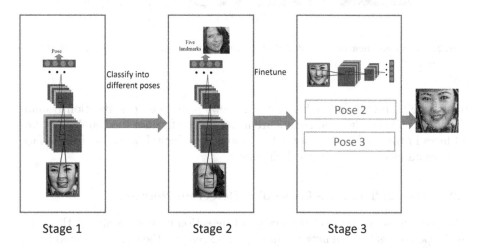

Fig. 1. The overall framework of the proposed method

3.1   Stage 1. Pose Classification Network

The pose classification network consists of four convolution layers and two fully connected layers. We use dropout after the first fully connected layer at a rate of 0.8.

The TCDCN paper [12] provides a five-point detection dataset called MTFL dataset which consists of 10,000 training images and 2,995 images for validation. All the images are not only labeled with landmarks but also poses. The dataset divides poses into five categories, namely, $-60°, -30°, 0°, 30°, 60°$. We use MTFL dataset to train the pose classification network and obtain a model of 80 % validation accuracy. Then the model is used to do classification on the 300 W dataset. So we combine the images in the $-60°$, $-30°$ classes, and the images in the $30°$, $60°$ classes because the number of face images classified into the large pose class, i.e. $-60°$ and $60°$, is very small. Now we get three pose classes,

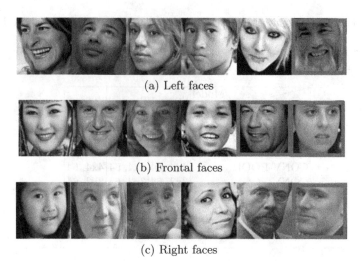

(a) Left faces

(b) Frontal faces

(c) Right faces

Fig. 2. Pose classification results. Red bounding boxes indicate the failures (Color figure online)

namely, left, frontal and right. Figure 2 shows some pose classification results. Note that the classification results are mostly correct. Since the 300 W faces are all faces in the wild, there may not be many pure frontal faces, the frontal face class contains some faces with slight poses.

3.2 Stage 2. The Base Five-Point Detection Network

The network architecture of the five-point detection network is almost the same as the pose classification network in stage 1, except for the fully connected layer.

The network is trained for a regression task which learns a regression function to map input images directly to landmark locations. Unlike classification network, the performance of the regression network is very sensitive to the parameter initialization and hyper-parameter tuning. To get rid of this problem, we use Batch Normalization (BN) [16]. Batch Normalization normalize the input of every layer which makes the input become more gaussian so that the network can converge much faster and can find better local minimal.

We train the base five-point network using the MTFL dataset [12]. Batch Normalization is very effective, Fig. 3 compare the loss/iteration curve with or without using BN.

We can see that both training loss and testing loss get lower with BN. Some landmark detection results of the base model are shown in Fig. 4.

Stage 3. Different Networks for Different Poses: The network architecture is identical to the base network except for the fully connected layer.

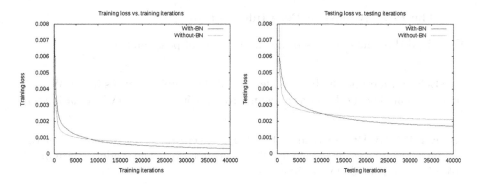

Fig. 3. Training and testing loss vs iterations with or without using BN

Finetune: We have to do finetune because face images in each pose are not enough to train a network from scratch.

Augmentation: Obviously, data augmentation should be done. But normal augmentation strategies like mirroring and rotating would change the pose of the original image. So we propose some new strategies which consists of four operations: Gaussian Noise, Gaussian Blur, Motion Blur and JPEG compression. Those operation wouldn't change the original pose and can make the model more robust.

Fig. 4. Localization results of the base model

4   Experiments

We first introduce the datasets used in our experiments, then we discuss and compare the effectiveness of using pose information explicitly, finally we compare our methods with some state-of-the-arts methods.

4.1   Datasets

300W consists of 3,837 face images, 3,148 for training and 689 for validation. The training set includes 811 images from LFPW [17], 2000 images from Helen [18] and 337 images from AFW [19]. The validation set includes 330 images from Helen, 224 images from LFPW and 135 images from IBUG [13]. We use training images in different poses to finetune the base model and evaluate the final models on the validation set.

4.2   The Effectiveness of Pose Information

We trained three models to see the effectiveness of pose information.

BASE-FT: Finetune the base model use all the training images in 300 W with augmentation. The model gains a mean error of 6.50 on the 300 W validation set.

BASE-FT-DROP: Identical to BASE-FT except for using dropout after the last convolution layer and the first fully connected layer. The model gains a mean error of 5.83 on the 300 W validation set.

PACN: Use images in different poses to train different model with both data augmentation and dropout. The model gains a mean error of 5.75 on the 300 W validation set. The mean errors of three left, frontal, right poses are 6.51, 5.268, 6.597, respectively.

We can see that the model which use pose information explicitly achieves best performance. But the performance of **PACN** does not improve so much compared to **BASE-FT-DROP**. This must be caused by the lack of data, we believe that better performance can be achieved using pose information along with more data.

The detailed results of the models can be found in Table 2.

Table 2. Some results of the comparative experiments. In *italic* are methods achieved by others

Method	Common subset	Challenging subset	Fullset
RCPR	6.18	17.26	8.35
SDM	5.57	15.40	7.50
CFAN	5.50	16.78	7.69
CFSS	4.73	9.98	5.76
CFSS-PRACTICAL	4.79	10.92	5.99
TCDCN	4.80	8.60	**5.54**
BASE-FT	5.41	11.05	6.50
BASE-FT-DROP	**4.69**	10.59	5.85
PACN	**4.69**	10.12	**5.75**

4.3   Comparison with State-of-the-Art Methods

We compare our methods with some state-of-the-art methods using mean error as the evaluation metric which is calculated by the distance between the estimate shape and ground truth, normalize using inter-ocular distance. The results

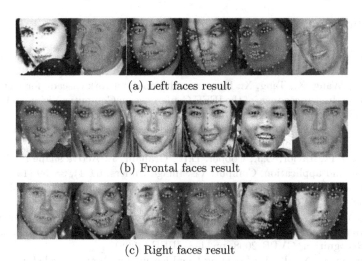

(a) Left faces result

(b) Frontal faces result

(c) Right faces result

Fig. 5. 300W localization result samples

is shown in Table 2. Results show that **PACN** achieves better or comparable performance than the state-of-the-arts, which proved the effectiveness of using pose information explicitly. Figure 5 shows some landmark localization results on the 300 W validation set.

5 Conclusion

We proposed a novel face alignment methods, i.e. Pose Aided Convolutional Neural Networks, which use pose information explicitly. The Pose Aided Convolutional Neural Networks consist of three stages. We first train a DCNN to do pose classification and face images are classified into different poses. A base DCNN for five-point detection is trained in the second stage. Finally, different DCNNs for dense-landmark detection are finetuning from the base DCNN using different pose images. Experiments results show that our method achieves better or comparable results than the state-of-the-art methods. We believe the proposed methods can achieve better results when we have more data.

Acknowledgments. This work was partially sponsored by supported by the NSFC (National Natural Science Foundation of China) under Grant No. 61375031, No. 61573068, No. 61471048, and No. 61273217, the Fundamental Research Funds for the Central Universities under Grant No. 2014ZD03-01, This work was also supported by Beijing Nova Program, CCF-Tencent Open Research Fund, and the Program for New Century Excellent Talents in University.

References

1. Krizhevsky, A., Sutskever, I., Hinton, G.E.: Imagenet classification with deep convolutional neural networks. Adv. Neural Inf. Process. Syst. **25**(2), 2012 (2012)
2. Sun, Y., Wang, X., Tang, X.: Deep convolutional network cascade for facial point detection. In: Proceedings of the IEEE Conference on Computer Vision and Pattern Recognition, pp. 3476–3483 (2013)
3. Sun, Y., Wang, X., Tang, X.: Deeply learned face representations are sparse, selective, and robust. Computer Science, pp. 2892–2900 (2014)
4. Cootes, T.F., Taylor, C.J., Cooper, D.H., Graham, J.: Active shape models-their training and application. Comput. Vis. Image Unders. **61**(1), 38–59 (1995)
5. Cristinacce, D., Cootes, T.F.: Feature detection and tracking with constrained local models. In: BMVC, vol. 2, p. 6. Citeseer (2006)
6. Wang, Y., Lucey, S., Cohn, J.F.: Enforcing convexity for improved alignment with constrained local models. In: 2008 IEEE Conference on Computer Vision and Pattern Recognition, CVPR 2008, pp. 1–8. IEEE (2008)
7. Milborrow, S., Nicolls, F.: Locating facial features with an extended active shape model. In: Forsyth, D., Torr, P., Zisserman, A. (eds.) ECCV 2008. LNCS, vol. 5305, pp. 504–513. Springer, Heidelberg (2008). doi:10.1007/978-3-540-88693-8_37
8. Xiong, X., Torre, F.: Supervised descent method and its applications to face alignment. In: Proceedings of the IEEE Conference on Computer Vision and Pattern Recognition, pp. 532–539 (2013)
9. Cao, X., Wei, Y., Wen, F., Sun, J.: Face alignment by explicit shape regression. Int. J. Comput. Vision **107**(2), 177–190 (2014)
10. Ren, S., Cao, X., Wei, Y., Sun, J.: Face alignment at 3000 FPS via regressing local binary features. In: Proceedings of the IEEE Conference on Computer Vision and Pattern Recognition, pp. 1685–1692 (2014)
11. Zhang, J., Shan, S., Kan, M., Chen, X.: Coarse-to-fine auto-encoder networks (CFAN) for real-time face alignment. In: Fleet, D., Pajdla, T., Schiele, B., Tuytelaars, T. (eds.) ECCV 2014. LNCS, vol. 8690, pp. 1–16. Springer, Heidelberg (2014). doi:10.1007/978-3-319-10605-2_1
12. Zhang, Z., Luo, P., Loy, C.C., Tang, X.: Facial landmark detection by deep multitask learning. In: Fleet, D., Pajdla, T., Schiele, B., Tuytelaars, T. (eds.) ECCV 2014. LNCS, vol. 8694, pp. 94–108. Springer, Heidelberg (2014). doi:10.1007/978-3-319-10599-4_7
13. Sagonas, C., Tzimiropoulos, G., Zafeiriou, S., Pantic, M.: 300 faces in-the-wild challenge: the first facial landmark localization challenge. In: Proceedings of the IEEE International Conference on Computer Vision Workshops, pp. 397–403 (2013)
14. Liang, Z., Ding, S., Lin, L.: Unconstrained facial landmark localization with backbone-branches fully-convolutional networks. arXiv preprint arXiv:1507.03409 (2015)
15. Lai, H., Xiao, S., Cui, Z., Pan, Y., Xu, C., Yan, S.: Deep cascaded regression for face alignment. arXiv preprint arXiv:1510.09083 (2015)
16. Ioffe, S., Szegedy, C.: Batch normalization: accelerating deep network training by reducing internal covariate shift. arXiv preprint arXiv:1502.03167 (2015)
17. Belhumeur, P.N., Jacobs, D.W., Kriegman, D.J., Kumar, N.: Localizing parts of faces using a consensus of exemplars. IEEE Trans. Pattern Anal. Mach. Intell. **35**(12), 2930–2940 (2013)

18. Le, V., Brandt, J., Lin, Z., Bourdev, L., Huang, T.S.: Interactive facial feature localization. In: Fitzgibbon, A., Lazebnik, S., Perona, P., Sato, Y., Schmid, C. (eds.) ECCV 2012. LNCS, vol. 7574, pp. 679–692. Springer, Heidelberg (2012). doi:10.1007/978-3-642-33712-3_49
19. Zhu, X., Ramanan, D.: Face detection, pose estimation, and landmark localization in the wild. In: 2012 IEEE Conference on Computer Vision and Pattern Recognition (CVPR), pp. 2879–2886. IEEE (2012)

Face Landmark Localization Using a Single Deep Network

Zongping Deng, Ke Li, Qijun Zhao, and Hu Chen[✉]

College of Computer Science, Sichuan University, No. 24 South Section 1, Yihuan Road,
Chengdu, 610065, Sichuan, China
huchen@scu.edu.cn

Abstract. Existing Deep Convolutional Neural Network (DCNN) methods for Face Landmark Localization are based on Cascaded Networks or Tasks-Constrained Deep Convolutional Network (TCDCN), which are complicated and difficult to train. To solve this problem, this paper proposes a new Single Deep CNN (SDN). Unlike cascaded CNNs, SDN stacks three layer groups: each group consists of two convolutional layers and a max-pooling layer. This network structure can extract more global high-level features, which express the face landmarks more precisely. Extensive experiments show that SDN outperforms existing DCNN methods and is robust to large pose variation, lighting and even severe occlusion. While the network complexity is also reduced obviously compared to other methods.

Keywords: DCNN · Face landmark localization · SDN

1 Introduction

Face landmark localization plays a very important role in the tasks for face alignment, face pose estimation and face recognition. Recent years have witnessed significant improvements in face landmark localization [1–7]. Generally, there are two categories of approaches for face landmark localization: conventional approaches and DCNN-based approaches. Typical conventional approaches include regression-based or template-fitting-based methods. They use classifying search windows for scanning features or shape parameters for predicting key point positions directly. DCNN-based approaches benefit from the development of Deep Learning (DL). These approaches provide state-of-the-art performance.

Face landmark localization methods are usually restrained by pose, lighting, expression and severe occlusion. Conventional methods cannot find a universal model that can be applied in all these situations, and thus often perform badly when facing these challenges. However, DCNN can learn efficient features from the complicated input data and these features can be robust to the above challenges. Sun et al. [1] show that their proposed DCNN-based approach can improve the landmark localization accuracy significantly compared to state-of-art methods and latest commercial software. The main reason is that convolutional networks take the full face as input to make the best use of texture context information, and extract global high-level features at higher layers of the deep structures, which can effectively predict keypoints. Zhang et al. [2, 3] used deep

© Springer International Publishing AG 2016
Z. You et al. (Eds.): CCBR 2016, LNCS 9967, pp. 68–76, 2016.
DOI: 10.1007/978-3-319-46654-5_8

Multi-task Learning for face points detection, and showed possibility of improving detection robustness through Multi-task Learning with DCNN.

However, these approaches are complicated and difficult to train. Sun et al. cascaded three levels of 13 convolutional networks. Zhang et al. trained the convolutional network with five tasks (i.e., landmarks, wearing glasses, smiling, gender and pose). Obviously, their structures and training process are both very complicated, and consequently, their detection speed is also slow. To solve these problems, we propose a new simple network, i.e., a single deep network (SDN), for face landmark localization. Compared to the cascaded Networks and Multi-task Learning network, SDN can reduce the complexity of face landmark localization significantly and meanwhile improve the accuracy and reliability of facial points. Figure 1 shows some example face landmark localization results by cascaded CNN and our proposed SDN.

Fig. 1. Examples of face landmark localization by the Cascaded CNN [1] (upper row) and our SDN (lower row).

2 Related Work

Many convolutional networks and other deep learning approaches have been applied in computer vision field or other related work. However, the applications in face landmark localization are rare. There are mainly two works.

Sun et al. [1] adopt a new way for Facial Point Detection by using cascaded networks. This approach partitions the faces into different segments and each of them is trained by deep CNN respectively. It is a coarse-to-fine process. Finally, it achieves a high accuracy for the detection of 5 landmarks. However, due to the complexity of Cascaded Networks, the detection is slow.

Zhang et al. [2, 3] use the same deep CNN to Sun et al.. The difference is that they train the network with Multi-task Learning (Auxiliary Attributes). Each task corresponds to one attribute of face image such as pose, smiling, gender etc., which makes the landmark localization robust. The results show that the accuracy of landmark position is higher. However, Multi-task learning makes higher demand of datasets and it is difficult to repeat the complicated training.

What's more, Zhou et al. [21] present a new approach to localize extensive facial landmarks with a coarse-to-fine convolutional network cascaded by using four DCNN levels. While Hou et al. [22] present a novel cascade multi-channel convolutional neural networks (CMC-CNN) approach for face alignment with jointing several CNNs for the final output. Both the two methods are also cascaded-based networks that are complexity and hard to realize.

In this paper, we propose a new network named SDN, whose network and training process are both simple. Comparing to the methods above, it makes the landmark localization faster and more accurate.

3   Proposed Single Deep Network

In this section, we focus on the SDN design. Similar to other DCNN methods, five landmarks will be detected [1], the center of left eye (LE), the right eye center (RE), the nose tip (NS), the left mouth corner (LM) and the right mouth corner (RM). The five facial points are predicted simultaneously. Figure 2 is the overview of our DCNN. Since a stack of two convolutional layers n × n (without spatial max-pooling in between) has an effective receptive field of $(2n - 1) \times (2n - 1)$ and two non-linear rectification layers makes the feature exacted more discriminative than a single one [8, 9], the layer group which consists of two convolutional layers and followed by one max-pooling layer is designed instead of the structure of one convolutional layer followed by one max-pooling layer.

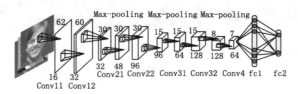

Fig. 2. The structure of our proposed SDN

The network contains a stack of 3 layer groups to extract the features hierarchically, followed by two fully-connected layers and the output indicating the position of the five facial landmarks. The dimension of input layer is 64 × 64 × 1 for gray image. The first layer group includes first two convolutional layers (Conv11, Conv12) whose filter size is 5 × 5 and the corresponding stride is 1. The filter size of convolutional layers in group 2 and group 3 is 3 × 3 and the corresponding stride is 1. Every group has a max-pooling layer whose filter size is 2 and stride is 1. The first fully connected layer (fc1) connects the neurons of Conv4 and its output number is 100, and the second one (fc2) connect 5 facial points whose output number is 10 (the coordinates of 5 face landmarks).

4   Training SDN

4.1   Training Data

The training face images are mainly collected from existing public datasets and the internet, such as MORPH [10], Color FERET [11] and other databases, and the total number of training images is about 30 k. The input images of our network must be face detected and be cropped by the face bounding box. Here, we choose face detector from the DLIB C++ Library [12] for detecting face, which can detect multi-view face exactly. The cropped face for input are labeled with five points (LE, RE, NS, LM, RM) for training. Since deep convolution network needs huge data and our data is not enough, we enhance the training data manually. Firstly, we rotate the images in plane and the rotation degrees are $-25, -15, 0, 15$ and 25. Secondly, we augment the face bound box with a certain ratio. Thirdly, we apply different lighting on these images. By the operations above, we generate about 0.2 million images for training and make the data robust to light variation, face rotation and other adverse cases for face landmark localization.

4.2 Training Methodology

Deep learning tool CAFFE [13] is used to train the network. The learn rate is set to a small value 1e-2 at first and reduce to 1e-5 gradually. To choose the best trained model, we store the model per 50,000 iterations when training. Moreover, fine-turning process is also adopted in our training, once we found the training process can't converge easily, we interrupt the training using fine-turning process or early termination.

5 Experiments

By investigating different designs of deep convolutional networks, we design our new SDN and get its optimal model from training phase. We compare our SDN with the similar approach of DCNNs, conventional methods [12, 14], and other commercial method on Bioid [15], LFPW [6], COFW [16] database and our collected MFID. Our training sets have no overlap with these test sets.

5.1 Performance Measurement

Accuracy and Reliability: Performance is measured with the average detection error and failure rate of each face landmark. We adopt mean error of each point as is defined follows, which is the same to Sun et al.

$$err_i = \sqrt{(x_i - x_i')^2 + (y_i - y_i')^2}/l \tag{1}$$

Where i is the index of five points (LE, RE, NS, LM, RM) respectively, (x_i, y_i) is the ground truth, and (x_i', y_i') is the predict result, l is the width of the bounding box returned by face detector. If the mean error of all five points is larger than 5 %, it is counted as failure. The failure rate f is defined as follows:

$$f = \frac{n_f}{N_f} \times 100\% \tag{2}$$

Where n_f is the failure images number and N_f is the number of face detected images.

Complexity: Real-time performance is measured by the average time-consuming of detections which also shows the complexity of methods. The average time-consuming on the test sets is defined as:

$$t = t_{i-in} - t_{i-out} \tag{3}$$

Where t_{i-in} and t_{i-out} is the beginning time point and end time point of the detection respectively. The time of data pre-processing is not included in t.

5.2   Results

Bioid [15] has 1,521 images of 23 subjects, all the faces are frontal. The face detector detects faces of 1,477 images in Bioid. We compare with Component based discriminative search [14], commercial software of Luxand [17], DLIB approach from DLIB project [12, 18], the cascaded CNNs [1] and the TCDCN [3]. Since [3, 12] do not detect eye centers, we only compare nose tip and mouth corners with it. Compared to conventional approaches, our method reduces the detection errors and failure rates significantly. Figure 3a and b show the results.

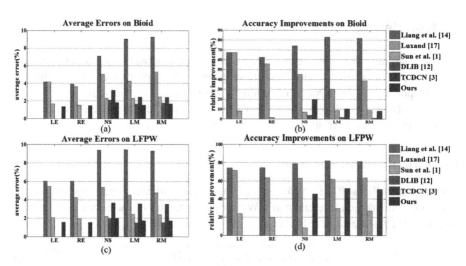

Fig. 3. Comparison on Bioid and LFPW (Our test results of TCDCN may different from [3], the main reason may be that the test images are simple, or only 3 of its 68 points are measured, or the definitions of landmarks may be different.)

LFPW [6] contains 1,432 face images from internet. Since some URLs of images are no longer valid, we adopt about 949 valid images for testing. All the testing images are out of our training sets. Our approach again performs better than most methods. Although the accuracy of our approach is little lower than that DLIB, they are very close (the difference of average error is about 0.1 pixels). Figure 3c and d show the result details on LFPW.

COFW (Caltech Occluded Faces in the Wild) database has 1,007 images of faces obtained from a variety of sources. All images were hand annotated by [16] with 29 landmarks. It is designed to present faces in severe occlusions due to pose, sunglasses, and interaction with objects (e.g., food, hands, hat). Here, the performance of five facial points is measured. Our method shows superior performance, whose average error and the failure rate are both the lowest among all tested methods. Figure 4a, b show the results.

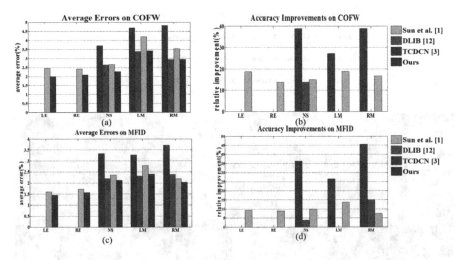

Fig. 4. Comparison on COFW and MFID (The missing bars value are zeros)

MFID[1] (Multiple Face Images Database)**:** To evaluate the model of our method better, we construct a new database by annotating 5 facial points (LE, RE, NS, LM, RM), it has 827 images collected from FDDB [19] (232 images), LFW [20] (400 images) and the internet (195 images), all the face images are different in pose, expression, illumination and full backgrounds. We compare with the best methods of relevant work: DLIB approach from DLIB project [12], the cascaded CNNs [1] and the TCDCN [3]. Our method once again shows superior performance on face landmark localization, and our failure rate is lowest of all methods. Figure 4c, d show the results.

5.3 Complexity

Furthermore, we compare our approach with DLIB [12], the cascaded CNNs [1] and the TCDCN [3] in the datasets above (Bioid, LFPW, COFW, MFID) under the same conditions with different optimization tool in time-consuming. Our method without optimization is much faster than cascaded CNNs and in the same level with TCDCN. It is slower than DLIB. However, our approach is much faster than all approaches after optimization. It indicates that the complexity of our approach is reduced obviously and

---

[1] The database will be released soon.

satisfies the practical real-time application. Table 1 shows the results of our experiments (Fig. 5).

Table 1. Comparison (*The data of Sun et al. gets from his paper [1].)

Method Database	Ours		DLIB	TCDCN	Sun et al.*
Optimization Tool	NO	GPU	Intel	NO	NO
Bioid	12.08ms	0.175ms	3.41ms	12.12ms	120ms*
LFPW	13.01ms	0.181ms	3.54ms	12.68ms	120ms*
COFW	12.98ms	0.172ms	3.56ms	12.80ms	120ms*
MFID	12.50ms	0.180ms	3.88ms	12.56ms	120ms*

Fig. 5. The results of our experiments

6 Summary

We proposed an effective convolutional network for face landmark localization, which uses a single deep convolutional network with single task of training and extracts global high-level features exactly. The experimental results have demonstrated that the proposed method achieves very high accuracy and performs much better than other competing methods. Moreover, the proposed method is real-time and robust to pose, expression, lighting, severe occlusion which are commonly seen in uncontrolled scenarios.

Acknowledgment. This work is supported by the National Natural Science Foundation of China (No.61202160) and the National Key Scientific Instrument and Equipment Development Projects of China (No. 2013YQ49087904).

References

1. Yi, S., Wang, X., Tang, X.: Deep convolutional network cascade for facial point detection. In: 2013 IEEE Conference on IEEE Computer Vision and Pattern Recognition (CVPR), pp. 3476–3483 (2013)
2. Zhang, Z., Luo, P., Loy, C.C., Tang, X.: Facial landmark detection by deep multi-task learning. In: Fleet, D., Pajdla, T., Schiele, B., Tuytelaars, T. (eds.) ECCV 2014, Part VI. LNCS, vol. 8694, pp. 94–108. Springer, Heidelberg (2014)
3. Zhang, Z., et al.: Learning deep representation for face alignment with auxiliary attributes. IEEE Trans. Pattern Anal. Mach. Intell. **1** (2014)
4. Amberg, B., Vetter, T.: Optimal landmark detection using shape models and branch and bound. In: 2011 IEEE International Conference on IEEE Computer Vision (ICCV), pp. 455–462 (2011)
5. Cao, X., et al.: Face alignment by Explicit Shape Regression. Int. J. Comput. Vis. **107**(2), 2887–2894 (2012)
6. Belhumeur, P.N., et al.: Localizing parts of faces using a consensus of exemplars. IEEE Trans. Pattern Anal. Mach. Intell. **35**(12), 545–552 (2013)
7. Tzimiropoulos, G.: Project-Out Cascaded Regression with an application to face alignment. In: 2015 IEEE Conference on IEEE Computer Vision and Pattern Recognition (CVPR) (2015)
8. Wu, X., He, R., Sun, Z.: A lightened CNN for deep face representation. In: 2015 IEEE Conference on IEEE Computer Vision and Pattern Recognition (CVPR) (2015)
9. Simonyan, K., Zisserman, A.: Very deep convolutional networks for large-scale image recognition. Eprint Arxiv (2014)
10. Ricanek Jr, K., Tesafaye, T.: MORPH: A longitudinal image database of normal adult age-progression. In: IEEE 7th International Conference on Automatic Face and Gesture Recognition, Southampton, UK, pp. 341–345, April 2006
11. Phillips, P.J., Moon, H., Rizvi, S.A., Rauss, P.J.: The FERET evaluation methodology for face recognition algorithms. IEEE Trans. Pattern Anal. Mach. Intell. 22, 1090–1104 (2000)
12. http://dlib.net/
13. Turchenko, V., Luczak, A.: Caffe: convolutional architecture for fast feature embedding. Eprint Arxiv, pp. 675–678 (2014)
14. Liang, L., Xiao, R., Wen, F., Sun, J.: Face alignment via component-based discriminative search. In: Forsyth, D., Torr, P., Zisserman, A. (eds.) ECCV 2008, Part II. LNCS, vol. 5303, pp. 72–85. Springer, Heidelberg (2008)
15. Jesorsky, O., Kirchberg, K.J., Frischholz, R.W.: Robust face detection using the Hausdorff distance. In: Bigun, J., Smeraldi, F. (eds.) AVBPA 2001. LNCS, vol. 2091, pp. 90–95. Springer, Heidelberg (2001)
16. Burgos-Artizzu, X.P., Perona, P., Dollár, P.: Robust Face Landmark Estimation under Occlusion. 2013 IEEE International Conference on Computer Vision (ICCV), pp. 1513–1520. IEEE Computer Society (2013)
17. http://www.luxand.com/facesdk/. 6
18. Kazemi, V., Sullivan, J.: One millisecond face alignment with an ensemble of regression trees. In: IEEE Conference on Computer Vision & Pattern Recognition IEEE Computer Society, pp. 1867–1874 (2014)

19. Jain, V., Erik, G.: Learned-Miller. FDDB: a benchmark for face detection in unconstrained settings. UMass Amherst Technical Report (2010)
20. Huang, G.B., et al.: Labeled faces in the wild: a database for studying face recognition in unconstrained environments, vol. 1, No. 2. Technical Report 07-49, University of Massachusetts, Amherst (2007)
21. Zhou, E., et al.: Extensive facial landmark localization with coarse-to-fine convolutional network cascade. In: IEEE International Conference on Computer Vision Workshops, pp. 386–391 (2013)
22. Hou, Q., et al.: Facial landmark detection via cascade multi-channel convolutional neural network. In: IEEE International Conference on Image Processing IEEE (2015)

Cascaded Regression for 3D Face Alignment

Jinwen Xu and Qijun Zhao[⊠]

National Key Laboratory of Fundamental Science on Synthetic Vision,
School of Computer Science, Sichuan University, Chengdu, China
qjzhao@scu.edu.cn
http://vs.scu.edu.cn/

Abstract. Although 2D facial landmark detection methods built on the cascaded regression framework have been widely researched, their performance was still limited by face shape deformations and poor light conditions. With the assist of extra shape information provided by 3D facial model, these difficulties can be eased to some degree. In this paper, we propose 3D Cascaded Regression for detecting facial landmarks on 3D faces. Our algorithm makes full use of both texture and depth information to overcome the difficulties caused by expression variations, and generates shape increments based on a weighted mixture of two separated shape updates regressed from texture and depth, respectively. Finally, the shape estimation is mapped into the original 3D facial data to obtain three-dimensional landmark coordinates. Experimental results on the BU-4DFE database demonstrate that our proposed approach achieves satisfactory performance in terms of detection accuracy and robustness, significantly superior to state-of-the-art method.

Keywords: 3D facial landmarking · Cascaded Regression · Weighted mixture

1 Introduction

Face image analysis is a key and significant research issue in the field of computer vision. Face alignment or detection of facial landmarks such as eye corners, nose tip and mouth corners is an indispensable step for many facial analysis tasks, *e.g.* face recognition [1], face animation [3], and facial expression recognition [2].

In the wake of the explosive increase of personal and Internet images, two-dimensional face alignment methods have been successfully developed, such as the seminal work Active Shape Model (ASM) [8], Active Appearance Model (AAM) [9] and Constrained Local Model (CLM) [10]. Among all different methods, a new family of face alignment algorithms has emerged as one of the most popular and state-of-the-art methods which are based on the cascaded regression (CR) framework [4–7]. These CR-based approaches directly learn a regression function from image appearance to the target shape update. The recent developments in CR feature learning and optimization strategy have achieved better accuracy than before. However, they still suffer from the difficulties caused by

© Springer International Publishing AG 2016
Z. You et al. (Eds.): CCBR 2016, LNCS 9967, pp. 77–84, 2016.
DOI: 10.1007/978-3-319-46654-5_9

large expression variations and varing lighting conditions. Recently, benefited from the advance of 3D face acquisition technology, these difficulties in face alignment are lightened somewhat owing to additional shape information from 3D facial data.

With the wide use of 3D faces, there is a strong need for robust and accurate algorithms to detect facial landmarks on 3D data. Therefore, various 3D facial landmark detection algorithms have been presented over these years. A.A. Salah et al. [20] exploited three-dimensional information to reduce the effect of illumination conditions on 2D face image and to acquire robust depth or curvature feature. Zhao et al. [12] used a statistical facial feature model to detect 3D landmarks. Canavan et al. [13] involved fitting the trained SI-SSM model to the input range data. Nair et al. [15] fitted a learned point distribution model (PDM) to the input face using a transformation between the predefined landmarks of model and localized candidate points on 3D mesh. However, problems occur while existing variations in expressions and lack of coverage around the nose. de Jong et al. [14] presented a new automatic algorithm to locate certain landmarks of interest from 3D face using 2D Gabor wavelets transform. Baltrusaitis et al. [11] had success with rigid and non-rigid facial tracking using a 3D Constrained Local Model (a.k.a CLM-Z). Due to many of the remaining challenges, the performance in terms of accuracy and stability still needs to be improved.

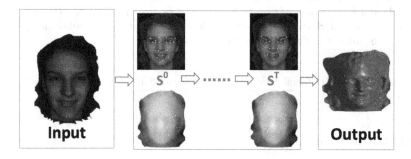

Fig. 1. Algorithm framework of 3D Cascaded Regression for facial landmark detection

In this paper, we propose a 3D Cascaded Regression-based method to address the problem of facial landmark detection on 3D faces. As shown in Fig. 1, it makes full use of both texture and depth information to detect facial points in image pair, which is a pair of texture image and depth image, computed from original 3D facial model and then map the detected points into the corresponding 3D face model. We adopt histogram of gradient (HOG) descriptors [18] to represent the neighbor information of a landmark. Extracting HOG features at relatively large window not only performs best in CR framework, but can be capable of dealing with large shape variations resulting from differences in expressions by the first few regressors [19]. The CR-based algorithm updates the face shape in a cascaded manner.

The key contributions of this work are as follows:

- A novel 3D Cascaded Regression method for 3D facial landmark localization. This method has for the first time extended 2D CR-based framework to accurately detect facial landmarks on 3D facial models.
- We evaluate our method on the Binghamton University 3D dynamic facial expression database (BU-4DFE) [16]. The experimental results show the superiority of our presented method in accurately dealing with various facial expressions, and better performance in accuracy and stability than CLM-Z [11].

The remainder of this paper is organized as follows. First, we detail our proposed approach in Sect. 2. Then we describe our algorithm implementation and report the evaluation results in Sect. 3. Finally, we give a conclusion of our approach in Sect. 4.

2   Proposed Method

Here the face shape $S = [x_1, ..., x_P, y_1, ..., y_P]'$ is represented by a series of pre-defined facial landmarks, where P is the number of landmarks, $[x_p, y_p]'$ is the location of the pth landmark in texture image I and the corresponding depth image D, and $'$ denotes the transpose operation. Given N training image pairs $\{I_i, D_i\}_{i=1}^N$ with the initial shape guesses $\{S_i^0\}_{i=1}^N$, the main idea is then to train a mapping function R by minimizing the difference between the final shape estimation and the true shape:

$$\sum_{i=1}^N \left\| R\left(I_i, D_i, S_i^0\right) - \hat{S}_i \right\|_2^2 . \tag{1}$$

where i is the ith pair of training examples and $\hat{S}$ denotes the true shape. In general, we can use any regression method (*e.g.* random forest, linear regression and random fern regressor) to learn the mapping function in Eq. (1). While only one regressor is unable to understand the highly non-linear problem, we use a CR-based framework, proving its effectiveness and robustness [4,5].

In CR framework, the following mapping function R is a composition of a cascade of weak regressors:

$$R = R^1 \circ R^2 \circ \cdots \circ R^{T-1} \circ R^T . \tag{2}$$

where T is the number of cascaded weak regressors. Each regressor R^t $(t = 1, ..., T)$ is defined as:

$$\begin{aligned} R^t\left(I_i, D_i, S_i^{t-1}\right) &= S_i^{t-1} + \Delta S_i^t \\ &= S_i^{t-1} + (1 - w(t))\,\Delta S_{I_i}^t \\ &\quad + w(t)\,\Delta S_{D_i}^t . \end{aligned} \tag{3}$$

$\Delta S_{I_i}^t$ is the shape increment computed from the texture image I_i:

$$\Delta S_{I_i}^t = W_I^t \Phi^t \left(I_i, S_i^{t-1} \right) . \tag{4}$$

and $\Delta S_{D_i}^t$ is the shape increment computed from the depth image D_i:

$$\Delta S_{D_i}^t = W_D^t \Phi^t \left(D_i, S_i^{t-1} \right) . \tag{5}$$

where W_I^t and W_D^t are linear regression matrices learned from texture images and depth images, respectively. Φ^t is the classical HOG feature mapping proposed by N. Dalal and B. Triggs et al. [18] which provided superior performance in face alignment task, proved in [19]. The texture images cooperate with the corresponding depth images via the weighting parameter $w(t)$. In our 3D Cascaded Regression, the first few stages compute coarse shape increments to adapt expression variations, while the following stages compute finer shape increments.

Next, we need to sequentially learn the mapping function in Eq. (2) until convergence. Each regressor R^t is trained by incorporating Eq. (3) into Eq. (1). In order to avoid over-fitting, we append a regularization term to the following objective function:

$$\min_{W_I^t, W_D^t} \sum_{i=1}^{N} \left\| \Delta \hat{S}_i^t - \Delta S_i^t \right\|_2^2 + \lambda \left\| W_I^t \right\|_2^2 + \gamma \left\| W_D^t \right\|_2^2 . \tag{6}$$

where $\Delta \hat{S}_i^t$ is the regression target for training R^t, which is the ground truth shape increment with reference to the current shape. $\Delta S_i^t = (1 - w(t)) \Delta S_{I_i}^t + w(t) \Delta S_{D_i}^t$ is the output shape update at stage t. λ and γ are regularization parameters that control the regularization strength.

After pre-training the mapping function, given a pair of texture and depth images (I, D) and a raw initial shape S^0, the first regressor R^1 predicts a shape update ΔS^1 based on the previous shape S^0 and its feature calculation, which is applied to update S^0 to the new shape estimate S^1. And then feed S^1 to the following regressors until the final shape S^T is obtained. More specifically, this is an iterative method where the tth shape is obtained by:

$$\begin{aligned} S^t = {} & S^{t-1} + (1 - w(t)) W_I^t \Phi^t \left(I, S^{t-1} \right) \\ & + w(t) W_D^t \Phi^t \left(D, S^{t-1} \right) . \end{aligned} \tag{7}$$

Notice that the available shape-related feature depends on the current shape estimate S^{t-1}, thus it is also updated at every iteration of our proposed method.

3   Experiments

3.1   Database

Our experiments are conducted on the BU-4DFE database, which contains 101 participants with various ethnic/racial ancestries. Each participant has six video sequences showing one of six different facial expressions (including anger, disgust, fear, happiness, sadness and surprise) with labelled landmarks. To implement our proposed approach, we divide available 3D facial data into two parts: training set and testing set. Training set includes 23 male participants and 33 female participants, while testing set includes 20 male participants and 25 female participants. Finally, 33,208 3D facial models are used in training phase and 25,788 models used for testing. We select 18 landmarks to represent each 3D face as shown in Fig. 3. Due to the input requirement of our designed framework, we need to preprocess 3D models of faces in BU-4DFE database to generate corresponding image pairs.

3.2 Implementation Details

In our MATLAB implementation, the number of cascaded weak regressors T is set to 15, and the regularization parameters (λ, γ) are both set to 1000. The initial shape estimate is set as the mean shape of the normalized training shapes transformed with respect to the face bounding box which is obtained by using the software in [17]. We set the neighboring window size around a landmark, a.k.a block size, to 30×30 pixels while extracting HOG features [18] on texture and depth images, split each neighborhood into 3×3 cells, compute HOG features using 9 orientation bins on each cell and finally concatenate all HOG features from all its cells into a whole feature vector. In fact, there are neighbourhoods around some landmarks close to image border, which need to be resized to 30×30 before splitting. The weighting parameter is set as a function of t, namely dynamic weighting:

$$w(t) = \frac{1}{1 + e^{K(t-1)}}, \tag{8}$$

where $K = 2$ denotes a shrinking rate that controls the contribution of $\Delta S_{I_i}^t$ and $\Delta S_{D_i}^t$.

3.3 Evaluation Results

We use the following two measurement metrics to evaluate the landmark localization accuracy of our proposed method.

Absolute Euclid-distance error: The Euclidean distance in millimeters between the ground truth and estimated position of the landmark on a 3D model.

Detection success rate: The proportion of successful detection cases of a landmark on a testing set, where successful detection case is defined as the absolute Euclid-distance error of the landmark below a certain threshold (*e.g.* 5 mm).

To better illustrate the impact of expression variations on detection accuracy, we manually pick out 3D facial models displaying neutral expression from all

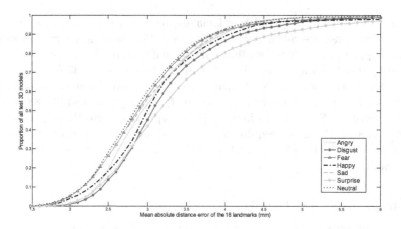

Fig. 2. Depiction of AED curves on facial landmarking for different expressions. The x-axis is the overall mean absolute distance error of the 18 landmarks and the y-axis is the proportion of all 3D facial models in testing set

testing models in purpose of conducting the evaluation experiments, and the AED curves for each expression are plotted in Fig. 2. Our implemented algorithm provides a consistently reliable and stable way to overcome the difficulty due to different expressions, while the accuracy of handling the surprise expression is slightly lower than the other five expressions. We also compare our presented method against CLM-Z [11], a state-of-the-art method for 3D face landmark localization. As depicted in Fig. 3, we use 18 landmarks to represent face shape while CLM-Z used 66 landmarks, so we select the landmarks common to the two methods to compare their performance.

Table 1 reports the mean and standard deviation of absolute Euclid-distance error of each landmark and detection success rate of the two methods. As can be seen from Table 1, our method can achieve an average distance error of 3.10 mm which is significantly superior to 4.31 mm of CLM-Z, and also has a lower standard deviation. Moreover, the detection success rate of our proposed method is much higher than CLM-Z over the entire testing set. Some example results of our proposed method are shown in Fig. 3.

Table 1. Detection accuracy of CLM-Z and our proposed method on BU-4DFE

Index		1	2	3	4	5	6	7	8	9	10	11	12	13	14	15	16	17	18	Avg
Ours	mean (mm)	2.02	2.34	2.68	2.09	2.08	2.35	2.88	2.08	3.53	5.23	3.22	5.31	3.81	3.90	3.32	2.49	2.93	3.52	3.10
	std. (mm)	1.11	1.69	2.63	1.26	1.26	1.58	1.91	1.27	2.12	4.10	2.16	3.65	2.22	2.64	2.02	1.82	2.11	2.67	2.12
	<5 mm (%)	99.3	93.2	90.1	98.2	98.3	93.4	86.5	97.5	79.5	59.2	84.8	55.0	73.5	73.1	83.4	93.4	89.0	81.2	84.9
CLM-Z	<5 mm (%)	3.87	x	5.26	x	2.44	x	8.82	x	3.38	x	4.28	x	x	x	3.82	2.40	3.40	5.42	4.31
	std. (mm)	1.68	x	2.62	x	1.33	x	2.99	x	2.17	x	2.46	x	x	x	2.31	2.01	2.60	5.17	2.53
	<5 mm (%)	74.7	x	53.2	x	96.4	x	8.0	x	82.5	x	67.4	x	x	x	76.3	92.6	80.9	57.7	69.0

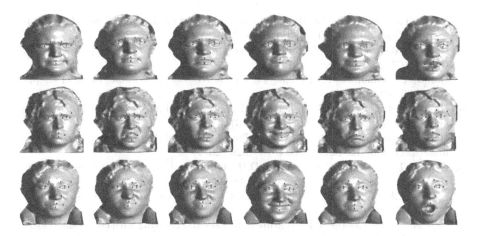

Fig. 3. Example 3D face landmark localization results of our proposed method on the BU-4DFE

4 Conclusion

In this paper, we have presented a novel 3D Cascaded Regression approach that fully exploits texture and depth information to automatically detect facial landmarks on 3D facial data. The presented method is the first attempt to extend 2D CR-based framework to solve the issue of 3D facial landmark localization. Our algorithm starts from a raw initial shape estimation, and progressively refine the final shape estimation by combining each shape update stage by stage. Each update is base on two sub-increments with a weighting scheme, one computed from texture image and the other one computed from the corresponding depth image. Finally, we map the shape increments into the corresponding 3D face to obtain the three-dimensional positions of 18 facial landmarks. We have extensively evaluated our method on the BU-4DFE database. The test results demonstrate that our proposed approach achieves high landmark detection accuracy which is robust to large shape variations resulting from different expressions, performing significantly better than previous published method [11].

Acknowledgments. This work is supported by the National Natural Science Foundation of China (No. 61202161) and the National Key Scientific Instrument and Equipment Development Projects of China (No. 2013YQ49087904).

References

1. Lee, H.-S., Kim, D.: Tensor-based AAM with continuous variation estimation: application to variation-robust face recognition. TPAMI **31**(6), 1102–1116 (2009)
2. Chew, S.W., Lucey, P., Lucey, S., Saragih, J.M., Cohn, J.F., Sridharan, S.: Person-independent facial expression detection using costrained local models. In: FGR, pp. 915–920 (2011)

3. Weise, T., Bouaziz, S., Li, H., Pauly, M.: Realtime performance-based facial animation. TOG **30**(4), 77:1–77:10 (2011)
4. Cao, X., Wei, Y., Wen, F., Sun, J.: Face alignment by explicit shape regression. CVPR **107**(2), 2887–2894 (2012)
5. Dollar, P., Welinder, P., Perona, P.: Cascaded pose regression. In: CVPR, pp. 1078–1085 (2010)
6. Xiong, X., De la Torre, F.: Supervised descent method and its applications to face alignment. In: CVPR, pp. 532–539 (2013)
7. Burgos-Artizzu, X.P., Perona, P., Dollar, P.: Robust face landmark estimation under occlusion. In: ICCV, pp. 1513–1520 (2013)
8. Cootes, T.F., Taylor, C.J., Cooper, D.H., Graham, J.: Active shape models-their training and application. CVIU **61**(1), 18–23 (1995)
9. Cootes, T.F., Walker, K., Taylor, C.J.: View-based active appearance models. IVC **20**(9), 657–664 (2002)
10. Cristinacce, D., Cootes, T.F.: Feature detection and tracking with constrained local models. BMVC **1**(2), 3 (2006)
11. Baltrusaitis, T., Robinson, P., Morency, L.: 3D constrained local model for rigid and non-rigid facial tracking. In: CVPR, pp. 2610–2617 (2012)
12. Zhao, X., Dellandrea, E., Chen, L., Kakadiaris, I.A.: Accurate landmarking of three-dimensional facial data in the presence of facial expressions and occlusions using a three-dimensional statistical facial feature model. SMC **41**(5), 1417–1428 (2011)
13. Canavan, S., Liu, P., Zhang, X., Yin, L.: Landmark localization on 3D/4D range data using a shape index-based statistical shape model with global and local constraints. CVIU **139**, 136–148 (2015)
14. de Jong, M.A., et al.: An automatic 3D facial landmarking algorithm using 2D Gabor wavelets. TIP **25**(2), 580–588 (2015)
15. Nair, P., Cavallaro, A.: 3-D Face detection, landmark localization, and registration using a point ditribution model. IEEE Trans. Multimedia **11**(4), 611–623 (2009)
16. Yin, L., Chen, X., Sun, Y., Worm, T., Reale, M.: A high-resolution 3D dynamic facial expression database. In: FG, pp. 1–6 (2008)
17. Yu, S.: https://github.com/ShiqiYu/libfacedetection
18. Dalal, N., Triggs, B.: Histograms of oriented gradients for human detection. In: CVPR, vol. 1, pp. 886–893 (2005)
19. Yan, J., Lei, Z., Yi, D., Li, S.Z.: Learn to combine multiple hypotheses for accurate face alignment. In: ICCVW, pp. 392–396 (2013)
20. Salah, A.A., Akarun, L.: 3D facial feature localization for registration. In: Gunsel, B., Jain, A.K., Tekalp, A.M., Sankur, B. (eds.) MRCS 2006. LNCS, vol. 4105, pp. 338–345. Springer, Heidelberg (2006). doi:10.1007/11848035_45

Deep CNNs for Face Verification

Xiaojun Lu[1(✉)], Yang Wang[1], Weilin Zhang[2], Song Ding[3], and Wuming Jiang[3]

[1] College of Sciences, Northeastern University, Shenyang 110819, China
{luxiaojun0625,wangy_neu}@163.com
[2] New York University Shanghai,
1555 Century Ave, Pudong, Shanghai 200122, China
wz723@nyu.edu
[3] Beijing Smartshino Technology Co., Ltd., Beijing, China
{15941424333,jwmneu}@163.com

Abstract. This paper proposes a method based on two deep convolutional neural networks for face verification. In the process of face normalization, we propose to use different landmarks of faces to solve the problems caused by poses. In order to increase the ability of verification, semi-verification signal is used for training one network. The final face representation is formed by catenating features of two deep CNNs after PCA reduction. What's more, each feature is a combination of multi-scale representations through making use of auxiliary classifiers. For the final verification, we only adopt the face representation from one region and one resolution of a face jointing Joint Bayesian classifier. Experiments show that our method can extract effective face representation and our algorithm achieves 99.71 % verification accuracy on LFW dataset.

Keywords: CNN · Joint Bayesian · Face verification

1 Introduction

In recent years, face verification based on deep convolutional neural networks (CNNs) has achieved high performance [1–4]. Some researchers combine deep face representation and verification into one system, that is learning to map faces into similarity space directly [4]. However, it is much harder to learn the mapping in terms of a lack of training data. In this paper, we use the deep CNN as feature extractor and adopting extra classifier to make face representation more discriminative as in [1–3].

For face pre-processing, it is hard to do great normalization for faces with variation caused by poses. In [5], the authors proposed to use the distance of landmarks instead of eye centers for face normalization, which is said to be relatively invariant to pose variations in yaw poses. In our system, we combine this method with the most used eye centers method to do face normalization.

Most face verification methods catenate face representations of multi-resolutions and multi-regions based on deep CNNs to construct a high dimension feature [2,3]. This conducts high computation cost and a large burden of storage

© Springer International Publishing AG 2016
Z. You et al. (Eds.): CCBR 2016, LNCS 9967, pp. 85–92, 2016.
DOI: 10.1007/978-3-319-46654-5_10

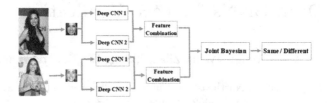

Fig. 1. The overall framework of face verification.

cost. In our work, we draw a compact face representation from only one region and one resolution by two CNNs. Inspired by DeepID2 [2] and Facenet [4], we design two networks in terms of face representation from which can have strong abilities of identification and verification. In order to achieve such purposes, one network is designed for setting different identity apart and the other one is to make the distance of the same person small enough. The overall framework of our face verification method is illustrated in Fig. 1. And we achieve high performance (99.71 %) on LFW database with small training dataset.

The rest of this paper is organised as follows: In Sect. 2, we introduce two deep CNNs. Face verification based on the proposed framework will be presented in Sect. 3. In Sect. 4, we present the performance of our algorithm comparing with other methods based on deep CNN. Discussion and conclusion will be drawn in Sect. 5.

2   The CNN Architectures and Signals Used for Training

Our face representation is a combination of features from two deep CNNs. The first neural network (NN1) is supervised by identification signal only and the second one (NN2) is supervised by jointing identification and semi-verification signals.

2.1   Deep CNN Architectures

NN1 is constructed by ordinary convolution in shallow layers and Inception Architectures [6] in deep layers. Inception can not only increase the depth and width of CNN at a certain computation cost, but also can extract multi-scale features for face representation. The framework of Inception used in NN1 is shown in Fig. 2.

As shown in Fig. 2, we catenate different sizes of convolution (1×1, 3×3, 5×5) and Max-Pooling in one layer. Smaller size convolution layer focus more on local information, and the lager one focus more on global information. In order to reduce high computation cost, 1×1 convolution is used before 3×3 and 5×5 convolution layers, and we also adopt Batch Normalization (BN) [7] after each convolution. BN can help our algorithm coverage at a high speed and solve the problem of overfitting. For the activation function, we explore to use Rectified Linear Units

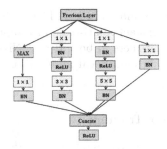

Fig. 2. Inception used in NN1

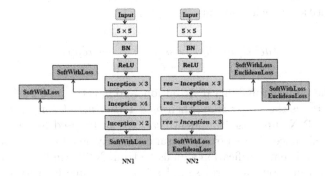

Fig. 3. The overall frameworks of NNs.

(ReLU) [8] after BN for each convolution in Inception. But for the output of Inception, which catenates the results of multi-scale convolution, we adopt ReLU after catenating layer. The overall framework of NN1 is shown in Fig. 3.

One difference between two NNs is that we explore to use extra residual networks in NN2. Residual network [9] is not only used for ordinary convolution but also for Inception, which is called res-Inception. The framework of res-Inception is shown in Fig. 4. Residual networks can make information propagation much smoother from former to later. And it also solves the problems of overfitting and

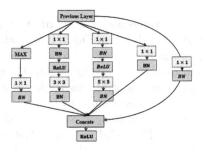

Fig. 4. Res-Inception used in NN2.

low speed of coverage in the training process. The overall framework of NN2 is shown in Fig. 3. In order to extract multi-scale face representation features, we investigate three auxiliary classifiers in both deep CNNs. By this way, features from the former layers contain more local information and the latter ones are much more global.

2.2 The Signals Used for Training

The training of NN1 and NN2 are based on gradient descent algorithm with different supervisory signals. NN1 is supervised by identification signal. Identification signal can make the face representation has a strong ability of distinguishing different identities, which is formulated in Eq. (1)

$$Identification\ Loss = -\sum_{i=1}^{n} -p_i logp_i \tag{1}$$

where p_i is the target probability distribution, and p_i is the predicted probability distribution. If t is the target class, then $p_t = 1$, and $p_j = 0$ for $j \neq t$.

Although CNN supervised by identification can be used for verification, it cannot make distance of faces from the same identity small enough. So we joint identification and semi-verification signals to train NN2. Similar to verification signal, semi-verification only uses samples from the same identity to compute loss. It can either decrease the distance of the intra-identity.

The loss of two signals can be formulated as follows:

$$Loss = -\sum_{i=1}^{n} -p_i logp_i + \frac{\lambda}{2\,|\,S\,|} \sum_{(i,j)\in S}^{|S|} \|\,f_i - f_j\,\|_2^2 \tag{2}$$

where $-\sum_{i=1}^{n} -p_i logp_i$ represent identification part, and $\|\,f_i - f_j\,\|_2^2$ denotes semi-verification signal. S is a index set of face pairs belong to the same identity, and λ is a hyper-parameter used to balance the contributions of two signals.

3   Face Verification with Classifier

Verifying faces with different poses is one of the hardest tasks in face verification, especially ones in yaw angles. As shown in Fig. 5, if normalized with eye centers, faces with large yaw angles will be normalized to a part of faces. It has negative effects for face verification. However, normalization by the distance between two landmarks of noses is relative invariant to yaw angles. But accurate landmarks of nose is much harder to be detected than eyes.

In order to solve two problems mentioned above, we adopt different methods to deal with face normalization. First of all, an image is detected by a face detector based on CNN [10]. Then, we estimate the pose and detect face landmarks of the detected face through 3D poses algorithm [11]. For those faces, whose yaw

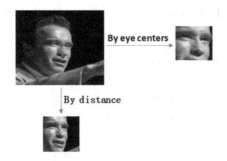

Fig. 5. Face normalization by eye centers and distance.

angles belong to $[-15, 15]$, we adopt landmarks of eye centers for normalization. For others, we use the distance of landmarks from noses for alignment. By this method, it can not only ensure the accuracy of face normalization for faces with no or small pose variance, but also ensure that results of faces with poses in yaw angles are the whole face regions.

After face pre-processing, we can obtain images only contain face regions. The normalized face image is as the input of two networks, and outputs are catenated to form the final face representation after PCA reduction.

In order to increase the ability of discriminant of face representation, we explore Cosine Distance and Joint Bayesian [12] respective. This two classifiers both compute the similarity of a pair of features.

4 Experiments

Our experiments are based on Caffe, with NVIDIA GT980X GPU with 4 GB of onboard memory, using single GPU. We train our model on TesoFaces Database, which contains 100,000 face images of 15340 celebrities from Internet. We evaluate our method on LFW [13].

4.1 Learning Effective Face Representation

In order to learn the most effective face representation, we evaluate various combinations of features from auxiliary classifiers by Cosine Distance for face verification. As shown in Table 1, ensembling different results from more auxiliary classifiers can improve the performance.

As a result, feature of the deeper layer has the much stronger ability of classification. And the face verification accuracy is much higher with the increasement of the number of features. The performance shows that the more auxiliary classifiers are used, the higher accuracy can be achieved. Combining three auxiliary classifiers can achieve the highest accuracy for each NN.

Furthermore, we compare face verification rate of each NN and that of the combination of two NNs. The result is shown in Table 2 which shows that the

Table 1. Accuracy in differently combined manners.

NN1		NN2	
Combination manner	Accuracy	Combination manner	Accuracy
cls 1	95.73 %	cls 1	95.92 %
cls 2	96.60 %	cls 2	96.42 %
cls 3	97.85 %	cls 3	98.07 %
cls 1 & cls 2	96.78 %	cls 1 & cls 2	96.68 %
cls 1 & cls 3	98.10 %	cls 1 & cls 3	97.93 %
cls 2 & cls 3	98.22 %	cls 2 & cls 3	98.12 %
cls 1 & cls 2 & cls 3	**98.25 %**	**cls 1 & cls 2 & cls 3**	**98.18 %**

Table 2. Accuracy of different face representation.

Classifier	NN1	NN2	NN1 & NN2
Cosine Distance	98.25 %	97.77 %	98.50 %
Joint Bayesian	98.45 %	97.94 %	99.71 %

combination of two features has the best performance. So our final effective face representation is formed by catenating two features from NN1 and NN2, with each feature is a combination of three outputs of auxiliary classifiers.

4.2   Evaluation on Classifiers

Learning more compact and discriminative features is the key for face verification task. For final face verification, we explore Cosine Distance and Joint Bayesian to improve discrimination of features. The verification rate of two methods is shown in Table 2. As the result, Joint Bayesian is more appropriate for our face representation and it has a much better performance on face verification task.

4.3   Comparision with Other Methods

To show the performance of our algorithm, we compare pair-wise accuracy on LFW dataset with the state-of-art deep methods. In Table 3, we show the results of comparison and the scales of databases used for training in different methods. Our method achieves 99.71 % test accuracy.

As the result, our method outperforms mostly deep face verification algorithm. The method in [1] is only 0.06 % higher than us, but the number of faces they used for training is 12 times the amount of data we have. So our face verification method is a high product with a small cost.

Figure 6 compares ROC curves of diffenent methods, and the curve of our algorithm is much more smooth than others. In the experiment, there are 17 wrong pairs in which 3 of them are wrongly labeled. So our the final pair-wise accuracy is 99.75 %.

Table 3. Accuracy of different methods.

Method	Accuracy	Identities	Faces
Baidu [1]	99.77 %	18K	1.2M
Ours	**99.71 %**	**15K**	**0.1M**
FaceNet [4]	99.63 %	NA	260M
DeepID3 [14]	99.53 %	16K	NA
Face++ [15]	99.50 %	16K	NA
DeepID2+ [16]	99.47 %	NA	NA
DeepID2 [3]	99.15 %	10K	NA
DeepID [2]	97.45 %	10K	NA
DeepFace [17]	97.35 %	NA	NA

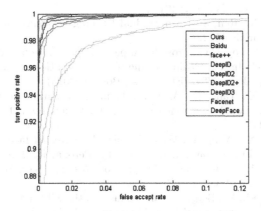

Fig. 6. ROC curves of different methods.

5   Conclusion and Discussion

In this paper, we propose a face verification method based on two deep convolutional neural networks with Joint Bayesian classifier. And our algorithm has achieved high performance (99.71 %) on LFW dataset. What's more, we only use one region and one resolution in our face representation process. In the real-life case which requires less computational storage, our method is more practical than the others.

References

1. Liu, J., Deng, Y., Huang, C.: Targeting ultimate accuracy: face recognition via deep embedding (2015). arXiv preprint: arXiv:1506.07310
2. Sun, Y., Wang, X., Tang, X.: Deep learning face representation from predicting 10,000 classes. In: Proceedings of the 2014 IEEE Conference on Computer Vision and Pattern Recognition, pp. 1891–1898. IEEE Press, Washington (2014)

3. Sun, Y., Chen, Y., Wang, X.: Deep learning face representation by joint identification-verification. In: Advances in Neural Information Processing Systems, pp. 1988–1996. MIT Press, Canada (2014)

4. Schroff, F., Kalenichenko, D., Philbin, J.: Facenet: A unified embedding for face recognition and clustering. In: Proceedings of the IEEE Conference on Computer Vision and Pattern Recognition, pp. 815–823. IEEE Press, Boston (2015)

5. Yi, D., Lei, Z., Liao, S.: Learning face representation from scratch (2014). arXiv preprint: arXiv:1411.7923

6. Szegedy, C., Liu, W., Jia, Y.: Going deeper with convolutions. In: Proceedings of the IEEE Conference on Computer Vision and Pattern Recognition, pp. 1–9. IEEE Press, Boston (2015)

7. Ioffe, S., Szegedy, C.: Batch normalization: accelerating deep network training by reducing internal covariate shift (2015). arXiv preprint: arXiv:1502.03167

8. Nair, V., Hinton, E.: Rectified linear units improve restricted boltzmann machines. In: Proceedings of the 27th International Conference on Machine Learning, pp. 807–814. ACM Press, Israel (2010)

9. He, K., Zhang, X., Ren, S.: Deep residual learning for image recognition (2015). arXiv preprint: arXiv:1512.03385

10. Yang, S., Luo, P., Loy, C.C.: From facial parts responses to face detection: a deep learning approach. In: Proceedings of the IEEE International Conference on Computer Vision, pp. 3676–3684. IEEE Press, Boston (2015)

11. Ye, M., Wang, X., Yang, R.: Accurate 3d pose estimation from a single depth image. In: International Conference on Computer Vision, pp. 731–738. IEEE Press, Barcelona (2011)

12. Chen, D., Cao, X., Wang, L., Wen, F., Sun, J.: Bayesian face revisited: a joint formulation. In: Fitzgibbon, A., Lazebnik, S., Perona, P., Sato, Y., Schmid, C. (eds.) ECCV 2012. LNCS, vol. 7574, pp. 566–579. Springer, Heidelberg (2012). doi:10.1007/978-3-642-33712-3_41

13. Huang, B., Ramesh, M., Berg, T.: Labeled faces in the wild: a database for studying face recognition in unconstrained environments. Technical report, University of Massachusetts (2007)

14. Sun, Y., Liang, D., Wang, X.: Deepid3: Face recognition with very deep neural networks (2015). arXiv preprint: arXiv:1502.00873

15. Zhou, E., Cao, Z., Yin, Q.: Naive-deep face recognition: touching the limit of LFW benchmark or not? (2015). arXiv preprint: arXiv:1501.04690

16. Sun, Y., Wang, X., Tang, X.: Deeply learned face representations are sparse, selective, and robust. In: Proceedings of the IEEE Conference on Computer Vision and Pattern Recognition, pp. 2892–2900. IEEE Press, Boston (2015)

17. Taigman, Y., Yang, M., Ranzato, M.A.: Deepface: closing the gap to human-level performance in face verification. In: Proceedings of the IEEE Conference on Computer Vision and Pattern Recognition, pp. 1701–1708. IEEE Press, Columbus (2014)

Robust Face Recognition Under Varying Illumination and Occlusion via Single Layer Networks

Shu Feng[(✉)]

College of Mathematics and Statistics, Chongqing University,
Chongqing, People's Republic of China
fengshu@cqu.edu.cn

Abstract. Feature extraction plays a significant role in face recognition, it is desired to extract robust feature to eliminate the effect of variations caused by illumination and occlusion. Motivated by convolutional architecture of deep learning and the advantages of KMeans algorithm in filters learning. In this paper, a simple yet effective face recognition approach is proposed, which consists of three components: convolutional filters learning, nonlinear transformation and feature pooling. Concretely, firstly, KMeans is employed to construct the convolutional filters quickly on preprocessed image patches. Secondly, hyperbolic tangent is applied for nonlinear transformation on the convoluted images. Thirdly, multi levels of spatial pyramid pooling is utilized to incorporate spatial geometry information of learned features. Recognition phase only requires an efficient linear regression classifier. Experimental results on two representative databases AR and ExtendedYaleB demonstrate strong robustness of our method against real disguise, illumination, block occlusion, as well as pixel corruption.

Keywords: Face recognition · Convolutional architecture · KMeans · Spatial Pyramid Pooling · Linear Regression

1 Introduction

In the past two decades, face recognition (FR) has been extensively studied due to its vast range of applications in virtual reality, social security and human computer interaction, etc. A large number of works have been developed on FR. Among these works, Eigenface and Fisherface are two classical holistic feature methods, LBP and Gabor are two representative local feature methods. Even though current FR methods have made great progress, the performance of FR under unconstrained environment remains to be improved. Therefore, how to design robust feature to eliminate the effect of variations of illumination, pose, age, and occlusion, still is a great challenge.

Recently, the pioneer work Sparse Representation Classification (SRC) [1] has achieved great success in FR, which shows impressive performance with

© Springer International Publishing AG 2016
Z. You et al. (Eds.): CCBR 2016, LNCS 9967, pp. 93–101, 2016.
DOI: 10.1007/978-3-319-46654-5_11

occlusion variations. Then considerable extensions, such as CRC, GSRC, RSC, RCR, JRPL [2–6], have been proposed to enhance the discriminative power and robustness. Wright et al. [1] claimed that SRC is insensitive to image feature as long as feature dimension is large enough, however, researchers have pointed out that SRC suffers from two drawbacks. Firstly, the computational cost of SRC via L1 norm constraints is too high. Secondly, the performance of SRC drops heavily when the training sample per subject is insufficient, which makes it inefficient in practical usage.

Since 2006, deep learning has attracted much attention in computer vision, then feature learning becomes a hot and new topic, the aim of which is to discover semantic information automatically from low level to high level layer by layer. The critical factor to the success of deep learning is the stacked convolutional architectures. Each convolutional architecture consists of three parts: convolutional filters learning, nonlinear transformation and feature pooling. For filters learning part, popular techniques, such as Sparse Auto Encoder and Restricted Boltzmann Machine, are time consuming and require rich experience for vast parameters tuning. However, classical clustering algorithm KMeans has fast convergence speed and stable performance in filters (centroids) learning. For feature pooling part, the overlapping blockwise strategy only focus on local information, so its descriptive power is limited. Spatial Pyramid Pooling (SPP) [7], an efficient extension of Bag of Feature model, has made remarkable success in image classification by partitioning image into increasingly fine subregions and computing features in each subregion. Obviously, SPP can capture spatial geometry information and extract both local and holistic information, which is more useful for FR.

Based on above analysis and motivation from convolutional architecture, we construct a novel single (not deep) layer networks for FR, three components are included: convolution filters learning by KMeans, hyperbolic tangent (tanh) for nonlinear transformation, SPP for feature pooling. The pipeline of our method is illustrated in Fig. 1, some good properties are summarized as follows:

(1) The usage of KMeans avoids expensive computation and enormous parameters tuning which always needs prior knowledge and rich experience.
(2) SPP could joint the local information and holistic information and preserve spatial layout of image feature, which is beneficial to robust FR.
(3) It is robust to illumination and block occlusion, getting 100 % rate in sungalsses disguise and 99.3 % accuracy when block occlusion level is 60 %.

2 The Proposed Approach

2.1 Local Patches and Filters Learning

Without loss of generality, raw image patches of size $w \times w$ are extracted then each patch is arranged into a column vector $p \in R^{w^2}$. Two preprocessing operations are conducted, contrast normalization and ZCA whitening, to remove the overall brightness and make the patch less redundant for generating sharply localized filters.

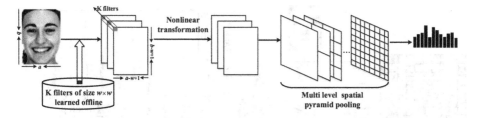

Fig. 1. The pipeline of the proposed method for face representation.

Due to popular filters learning methods suffers from time-consuming, we exploit KMeans to learn convolutional filters because of its fast convergence speed and stable performance. Let $P = \{p_1, \ldots, p_N\} \in R^{w^2}$ be a set of patches from training set, given K randomly initialized centroids $\mu = \{\mu_1, \ldots, \mu_K\} \in R^{w^2}$. KMeans algorithms optimizes the centroids by two steps alternate iterations, namely, searching nearest centroid of each patch and updating centroids, until $\sum_{i=1}^{N} ||p_i - \mu_{c_i}|| < \epsilon$, here ϵ is the tolerance coefficient.

LeCun et al. [8] firstly proposed image convolution operation, it can learn significant local structure information from image. Hence, each converged centroid $\mu_j \in R^{w^2}$ is converted to a matrix $W_j \in R^{w \times w}$, which is regarded as convolution filter. Some learned filters are visualized in Fig. 2(Left), clearly, these filters contains information of different directions and edges. In particular, face image has stationary property, i.e., statistics of one part of image are similar to any other parts. Moreover, images belonging to same class share some common low level features, therefore, the learned filters can be convolved over the whole image to extract discriminative and sufficient low level features, see Fig. 2(Middle) for illustration, it is clear that different filters indeed extract features of different directions, edges and scales.

2.2   Nonlinear Transformation

Since convolution operation is incapable of capturing nonlinear information from the source images, we employ nonlinear transformation to obtain more semantic and discriminative nonlinear features on the convoluted images, which is analogous to the activation function in neural networks:

$$H = T\left(W_j \otimes X\right), j = 1, 2, \cdots, K \tag{1}$$

where $\otimes$ is a convolution operator, X is a facial image, $T(\cdot)$ is a nonlinear function which applies element wisely. In this paper, tanh is used for nonlinear transformation because of its better performance than other two nonlinear functions (sigmoid and relu), which will be corroborated in Sect. 3.

2.3   Multi Levels of Spatial Pyramid Pooling

In general, in the literature of image classification, 3 levels of SPP is adopted due to the fact that no more significant improvement can be observed when SPP

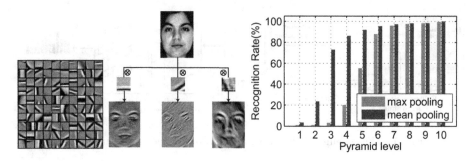

Fig. 2. (Left) Some learned filters. (Middle) Convolutional feature extraction. (Right) Recognition rates of two pooling methods under varying SPP levels. K is set to 10.

level is greater than 3. However, in this paper, we find that multi levels (more than 3) of SPP will enhance the performance of FR remarkably. Firstly, suppose L levels of SPP: $\{s_1, \ldots, s_L\}$ are used and H is divided into $s_1 \times s_1$, $s_2 \times s_2$, and $s_L \times s_L$ subregions, in total $C = \sum_{l=1}^{L} s_l^2$. Then pooling is performed to extract robust and discriminative feature vector in each subregion. Finally all feature vectors are concatenated to form the face representation for image X:

$$f(X) = [\phi(X, 1)^T, \ldots, \phi(X, C)^T]^T \in R^{CK \times 1} \tag{2}$$

where $\phi(\cdot, \cdot)$ pooling function, common and widely used pooling function contains mean pooling and max pooling.

In classification phase, Linear Regression (LR) is adopted. The reasons for selecting LR are mainly of two folds. On one hand, compared with Nearest Neighborhood (NN) and Support Vector Machine (SVM), LR has lower computational complexity and closed form solution. On the other hand, it achieves better and stable performance than NN and SVM on the extracted features of our proposed method, which will be explained in Sect. 3.

3   Parameters Selection

In this section, we thoroughly evaluate the impact of two key parameters in the proposed approach: (1) the levels of SPP, (2) the number of filters, i.e., K. All experiments are conducted on AR database with eight non-occluded images per subject for training and two sunglasses disguised images per subject for testing, see Sect. 4.1 for datasets description.

The levels of SPP: Firstly, the impact of SPP levels on recognition performance under the two pooling methods, i.e., max and mean is evaluated. Different SPP levels ranging from 1 level $\{1\}$ to 10 levels $\{1, 2, 4, 6, 8, 10, 12, 14, 16, 32\}$ are tested. The recognition rates are plotted in Fig. 2(Right). Obviously, multi levels SPP boosts the recognition rate for both pooling methods. Moreover, mean pooling outperforms max pooling under all pooling levels, especially when pooling level less than 7, the advantage is clearer. The reason may be that max pooling with small level discards structure information in the pooling region while mean pooling retains the information in average manner. Hence, mean pooling and 10 levels of SPP are chosen in our final experiments in Sect. 4.

The Number of filters: The impact of filters number, ranging from 5 to 70, on the recognition rates is studied. By varying SPP levels, the average rates are reported in Table 1. From each column, the performance reveals an upward tendency with the number of filters increases, it may attribute to larger K makes more similar patches differentiated. Also, more SPP levels yield higher performance in all types of K. When $K \geq 30$, the recognition rate comes to a steady state and achieves 100 % accuracy under 10 levels SPP. So, K is set to 30 in the following sections if no special statement.

Table 1. Recognition rates (%) with varying number of filters and SPP levels.

K	SPP levels									
	1	2	3	4	5	6	7	8	9	10
5	2.4	8.4	53.5	79	89.6	91.6	95.9	96.2	96.9	98.5
10	4.2	23.4	74.9	86.2	91.6	95.1	97.5	97.9	98.1	99.9
30	20.5	44.2	82.8	92.9	97	97.7	99	99.5	99.5	**100**
50	26.2	46	82.2	95.2	97.9	98.5	99.1	99.5	99.5	**100**
70	27.7	42.4	80.1	96	98	99	99.2	99.5	99.5	**100**

Comparison of different classifiers and nonlinear functions: We further compare the performance of three classifiers, i.e., NN, SVM and LR, with different nonlinear functions, as shown in Table 2. Here, 10 levels SPP is adopted, two types of K are tested. Clearly, tanh performs much better than relu and slightly better than sigmoid under all situations. From each row of Table 2, one can observe that LR gets better performance than NN and SVM under tanh and sigmoid, achieving 100 % accuracy when tanh is used and K is 30. Consequently, the combination of tanh with LR is adopted in this paper.

Table 2. Recognition rates (%) with varing classifiers and nonlinear functions.

Classifier	$K = 30$			$K = 5$		
	tanh	sigmoid	relu	tanh	sigmoid	relu
NN	99.9	99.6	56.8	97.5	97.1	49.2
LR	**100**	**100**	47.7	98.5	97.5	40.1
SVM	99.5	99.5	54.8	98.4	96.2	41.9

4   Experimental Results

In this section, two widely used databases, i.e., ExtendedYaleB and AR, are utilized to evaluate our method. Several representative algorithms are compared, including sparse representation based SRC, CRC, GSRC, RSC, RCR, JPRL, RRC, SSRC [1–6,9,14], filters based method Volterra [10], and subspace based method RPCAweight and RPCAratio [11]. The reported results from the corresponding published articles are quoted directly. For fair comparisons, all competing algorithms share the same experiment settings: same training samples and same testing samples.

4.1   Databases

ExtendedYaleB [12]. There are 2414 images of 38 subjects with various illumination conditions, about 64 samples for each subject. It is divided into five subsets according to azimuth and elevation, the image number per subject of each subset is 7, 12, 12, 14, and 19. Subsets 2 and 3 characterize slight to moderate light changes, while subset 4 and 5 suffer from extreme illumination variations.

AR [13]. Over 4000 frontal images from 126 individuals are contained, each individual has 26 images captured in two separate sessions under different variations of expression changes, illumination changes and occlusion by sunglasses and scarves. Following [1,3], a subset contains 100 individuals is selected.

4.2   Face Recognition with Illumination

We first validate the robustness of our approach against illumination on ExtendedYaleB database. Subset 1 is regarded as training, while other four subsets are used for testing. The comparison results are plotted in Fig. 3(Left). It is clear that, on subset 2 and subset 3, the accuracy of our method is 100 %. Moreover, our method gets the best performance of 98.4 % accuracy on subset 4, outperforming SRC by a margin of 30.5 %. Additionally, except for our method and Gradientface, the performance of other methods decreases dramatically from subset4 to subset 5. It implies that our method is more robust to illumination variations.

Table 3. Recognition rates (%) on AR database with sunglasses and scarves disguise.

Method	SRC [1]	CRC [3]	GSRC [2]	RSC [4]	RCR [5]
Sunglasses	97.5	91.5	93	99	98.5
Scarves	93.5	95	79	97	96.5
Method	Volterra [10]	SSRC [14]	RRC-L1 [9]	JRPL-L1 [6]	Our method
Sunglasses	96.1	90.9	**100**	**100**	**100**
Scarves	92.1	90.9	97.5	**99**	**99**

4.3   Face Recognition with Occlusion

In this subsection, we validate the robustness of our method to different kinds of occlusions, namely, real disguise, random block occlusion and random pixel corruption, on AR and ExtendedYaleB.

Recognition with real disguise: AR is used in this experiment, as in [1,5], 800 frontal view images with expression changes are for training, 200 images with sunglasses or scarves disguises are for testing separately. The recognition rates of competing methods are listed in Table 3. Our method gets perfect recognition rate of 100 % for sunglasses disguise and comparable rate of 99 % for scarves disguise. Although JRPL-L1 offers the same results, but our method is less time-consuming. Note that our method significantly outperforms filter based method Volterra [10] by 3.9 % and 6.9 %, respectively.

Recognition with block occlusion and pixel corruption: According to [1], subset 1 and 2 of ExtendedYaleB are used as training samples and subset 3 as testing samples. For block occlusion, seven levels of block occlusion, from 0 % to 60 %, are simulated by replacing a randomly located square block of each testing image with a baboon image. Comparison results are plotted in Fig. 3(Middle). Obviously, our method achieves best results than all other algorithms in all levels of block occlusion. Moreover, our method get almost perfect recognition rate of 99.3 % when 60 % occlusion, which outperforms SRC, GSRC, RRC-L1, JRPL-L1 by large margin of 71.5 %, 35.3 %, 38.5 %, 13.6 %, respectively. For pixel corruption, a certain percentage of pixels in each testing image are replaced by uniformly distributed random values from 0 to 255. The comparison results are shown in Fig. 3(Right). It can noted that our method obtains acceptable and comparable performance and offers similar results with RRC-L1 [9].

In summary, our method has shown strong robust with respect to block occlusion and real disguise and promising robustness to pixel corruption.

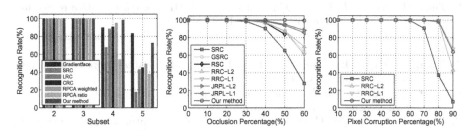

Fig. 3. Recognition rates (%) on ExtendedYaleB database with different levels of (Left) illumination (Middle) block occlusion (Right) pixel corruption.

4.4   Experiments on FERET and LFW

Two experiments on challenging databases, i.e., FERET and LFW, were conducted to further testify the ability of our method. For FERET database, we follows [15] to select a subset that contains 436 images of 72 persons, which includes variations of expression, illumination, poses and ages. Our method obtained comparable performance of 98.15 % accuracy, which again deduces the effectiveness of our method. For the more challenging database, LFW, it contains 13,233 images with great variations of pose, age, misalignment and viewpoint, following [5], two subsets are chosed in our experiment, subset1(subset2) consists of 311(143) subjects with no less than 6(11) samples per subject. However, the performance of our method is not promising, achieving accuracy of 46.8 % on subset1 and 68.9 % on subset2. The reason may be that the specific and informative filters corresponding to variations of misalignment and viewpoint can not be learned effectively.

5   Conclusions

In this paper, a novel yet effective face representation method for recognition is presented inspired by convolutional architecture and the convergence speed and stable performance of KMeans, which mainly consists of three components: convolutional filters learning by KMeans, tanh for nonlinear transformation and 10-levels SPP for feature pooling. The results of experiments on representative databases demonstrate the effectiveness and strong robustness of our method to illumination changes, real disguise, block occlusion, and pixel corruption.

References

1. Wright, J., Yang, A.J., Ganesh, A., et al.: Robust face recognition via sparse representation. TPAMI **31**(2), 210–227 (2009)
2. Yang, M., Zhang, L.: Gabor feature based sparse representation for face recognition with gabor occlusion dictionary. In: Daniilidis, K., Maragos, P., Paragios, N. (eds.) ECCV 2010, Part VI. LNCS, vol. 6316, pp. 448–461. Springer, Heidelberg (2010). doi:10.1007/978-3-642-15567-3_33
3. Zhang, L., Yang, M., Feng, X.C.: Sparse representation or collaborative representation: which helps face recognition? In: ICCV (2011)
4. Yang, M., Zhang, L., Yang, J., et al.: Robust sparse coding for face recognition. In: CVPR (2011)
5. Yang, M., Zhang, L., Zhang, D., et al.: Relaxed collaborative representation for pattern classification. In: CVPR (2012)
6. Yang, M., Zhu, P., Liu, F., et al.: Joint representation and pattern learning for robust face recognition. Neurocomputing **168**, 70–80 (2015)
7. Lazebnik, S., Schmid, C., Ponce, J.: Beyond bags of features: spatial pyramid matching for recognizing natural scene categories. In: CVPR (2006)
8. LeCun, Y., Boser, B., Denker, J.S., et al.: Backpropagation applied to handwritten zip code recognition. Neural Comput. **1**(4), 541–551 (1989)
9. Yang, M., Zhang, L., Yang, J., et al.: Regularized robust coding for face recognition. TIP **22**(5), 1753–1766 (2013)
10. Kumar, R., Banerjee, A., Vemuri, B.C., et al.: Trainable convolution filters and their application to face recognition. TPAMI **34**(7), 1423–1436 (2012)
11. Luan, X., Fang, B., Liu, L., et al.: Extracting sparse error of robust PCA for face recognition in the presence of varying illumination and occlusion. Pattern Recogn. **47**(2), 495–508 (2014)

12. Georighiades, A.S., Belhumeur, P.N., Kriegman, D.J.: From few to many: illumination cone models for face recognition under variable lighting and pose. TPAMI **23**(6), 643–660 (2001)
13. Martinez, A., Benavente, R.: The AR face database. Technical report 24, CVC (1998)
14. Deng, W., Hu, J., Guo, J.: In defense of sparsity based face recognition. In: CVPR (2013)
15. Pan, B., Lai, J., Chen, W.: Nonlinear nonnegative matrix factorization based on Mercer kernel construction. Pattern Recogn. **44**(10), 2800–2810 (2011)

Sample Diversity, Discriminative and Comprehensive Dictionary Learning for Face Recognition

Guojun Lin[1,2], Meng Yang[1,3(✉)], Linlin Shen[1], Weicheng Xie[1], and Zhonglong Zheng[3]

[1] College of Computer Science and Software Engineering,
Shenzhen University, Shenzhen, China
[2] College of Automation and Electric Information,
Sichuan University of Science and Engineering, Zigong, China
[3] College of Mathematics, Physics and Information Engineering,
Zhejiang Normal University, Jinhua, China
yangmengpolyu@gmail.com, tiemujian123400@163.com

Abstract. For face recognition, conventional dictionary learning (DL) methods have disadvantages. In the paper, we propose a novel robust, discriminative and comprehensive DL (RDCDL) model. The proposed model uses sample diversities of the same face image to make the dictionary robust. The model includes class-specific dictionary atoms and disturbance dictionary atoms, which can well represent the data from different classes. Both the dictionary and the representation coefficients of data on the dictionary introduce discriminative information, which improves effectively the discrimination capability of the dictionary. The proposed RDCDL is extensively evaluated on benchmark face image databases, and it shows superior performance to many state-of-the-art sparse representation and dictionary learning methods for face recognition.

Keywords: Dictionary learning · Face recognition · Sparse representation

1 Introduction

Recently sparse representation technology has been successfully used in image restoration [1] and image classification [2, 17]. For the success of sparse representation, the dictionary is very important. Dictionary learning (DL) aims to learn the desired dictionary from the training samples. The desired dictionary can well represent or code the given signal. Many latest DL methods learn properly the desired dictionary from the original training data have led to state-of-the-art results in many practical applications, such as face recognition [3, 4, 8, 16, 18].

Though dictionary learning has achieved promising performance in face recognition, previous DL methods suffer from the severe problem for face recognition. First, because face images of the same person vary with facial expressions, illuminations and disguises, conventional DL for face recognition is hard to obtain a very robust dictionary. For face recognition tasks, only if the dictionary is not very sensitive to variations of expressions, illuminations and disguises, it is able to get relatively stable descriptions of the face

© Springer International Publishing AG 2016
Z. You et al. (Eds.): CCBR 2016, LNCS 9967, pp. 102–111, 2016.
DOI: 10.1007/978-3-319-46654-5_12

image and obtain a high accuracy. Second, conventional DL methods don't cover important components (e.g., particularity and disturbance) completely, which limit their performance. In order to address the above two problems, in the paper, we propose a novel robust, discriminative and comprehensive DL (RDCDL) model.

The proposed RDCDL uses the training sample diversities of the same face image to get a robust dictionary. For face recognition tasks, RDCDL achieves the robustness by generating virtual face images that convey new possible expressions, illuminations and disguises of the face. The virtual training samples are the alternative training samples, which are obtained by corrupting the original training samples. RDCDL is applied to the original and virtual training samples. The dictionary of RDCDL includes the class-specific dictionary atoms and the disturbance dictionary atoms, which can completely represent the practical data (e.g., the data of the different classes has class-specific component and disturbance component such as noise, outlier and occlusion). Both the comprehensive dictionary and the representation coefficients of data on the dictionary exploit the discriminative information, which improves effectively the discriminative capability of the dictionary.

The rest of this paper is organized as follows. Section 2 briefly introduces related work. Section 3 presents the proposed RDCDL model. Section 4 describes the optimization procedure of RDCDL. Section 5 presents the RDCDL based classification. Section 6 conducts experiments, and Sect. 7 concludes the paper.

2 Related Work

According to the relationship between dictionary atoms and class labels, current supervised dictionary learning can be categorized into three main types: class-shared dictionary learning, class-specific dictionary learning and hybrid dictionary learning.

In the first category, a dictionary whose atoms are shared by all classes of data is learned while the discrimination of coding coefficients is exploited. Based on KSVD [6], Zhang and Li [3] proposed a dictionary learning method called discriminative KSVD (DKSVD). Based on DKSVD [3], Jiang et al. [4] added a label consistent term and proposed so-called Label-Consistent KSVD (LCKSVD). Because each class-shared dictionary atom can represent all classes of data, the class-shared dictionary loses the correspondence between the dictionary atoms and the class labels, weakening the classification capability of the class-shared dictionary. Classifiers based on the class-shared dictionary cannot perform classification based on the class-specific representation residuals.

In the second category, class-specific dictionary learning requires that each dictionary atom should be corresponded to a single class label. Inspired by SRC [2], the class-specific dictionary is widely applied to the design of classifiers. Based on the KSVD [6] model, Mairal et al. [9] introduced a discriminative reconstruction penalty term. Ramirez et al. [7] proposed DLSI which minimized the coherence term of the dictionary to improve the discriminative capability of the dictionary. Yang et al. [8, 16] proposed Fisher discrimination dictionary learning (FDDL), where both the representation residual and the representation coefficients achieved the discriminative information. Although class-specific dictionary learning can achieve better performance, the coherence among the different class-specific dictionaries is inevitable. The number of the dictionary is usually large.

In the third category, hybrid dictionary is the dictionary which combines the class-specific dictionary atoms with the class-shared dictionary atoms. Recently, some hybrid DL methods are proposed. Deng *et al.* [10] proposed extended sparse representation based classification (ESRC) which constructed an intra-class variation dictionary as a shared dictionary. Kong *et al.* [5] proposed dictionary learning with commonality and particularity (COPAR) which learned a hybrid dictionary by introducing an incoherence penalty term to the class-specific sub-dictionaries. However, these hybrid DL methods cannot well describe the disturbance such as noise, outlier and occlusion. In addition, these methods don't introduce the discriminative information to both the dictionary and the representation coefficients.

3 Robust, Discriminative and Comprehensive Dictionary Learning

In order to improve the performance of previous DL methods, we propose a new robust, discriminative and comprehensive dictionary learning (RDCDL) model. Suppose that we have N classes of subjects, the comprehensive dictionary D includes a class-specific dictionaries $D_i(i = 1, 2, \cdots, N)$ and a disturbance dictionary D_b. The class-specific dictionaries represent the particularity of different class data, and the high-performance class-specific representation residual can be used. While the disturbance dictionary can represent other components not related to the identity of data (e.g., noise, outlier and occlusion).

Denote by $Y = [Y_1, Y_2, \cdots, Y_N]$ a set of training samples, where Y_i is the training samples of class i. Denote by $Z = [Z_1, Z_2, \cdots, Z_N]$ a set of alternative training samples. Z_i has the same size and structure as the original training samples Y_i $(i = 1, 2, \cdots, N)$. Let $X = [X_1, X_2, \cdots, X_N]$, $B = [B_1, B_2, \cdots, B_N]$, where X_i is the coding coefficient matrix of Y_i over the dictionary $[D_1, D_2, \cdots, D_N]$. B_i is the coding coefficient matrix of $Z_i - D_i X_i^i$ over the dictionary D_b. In order to make the learned dictionary robust to variations of facial expressions, illuminations and disguises of the same person, we can obtain alternative training samples using a special scheme. For the comprehensive dictionary $D = [D_1, D_2, \cdots, D_N, D_b]$, we propose the followed RDCDL model:

$$J_{(D,X,B)} = \arg \min_{D,X,B} \sum_{i=1}^{N} \left[\begin{array}{c} \left\| Y_i - D_i X_i^i - \sum_{j \neq i} D_j X_i^j \right\|_F^2 + \lambda_1 \left\| Z_i - D_i X_i^i - D_b B_i \right\|_F^2 \\ + \lambda_2 (\|X_i\|_1 + \|B_i\|_1) + \lambda_3 \phi(X_i) + \lambda_4 \varphi(D) \end{array} \right] \quad (1)$$

where λ_1, λ_2, λ_3 and λ_4 are scalar parameters, X_i^i is the coding coefficient matrix of Y_i over the dictionary D_i, X_i^j is the coding coefficient matrix of Y_i over the dictionary D_j. $\phi(X_i)$ is the representation coefficient discrimination constraint term and $\varphi(D)$ is the dictionary discrimination constraint term.

The proposed model obtains alternative training samples using a special scheme. In this paper, we use two methods to generate the alternative training samples, the procedures to generate alternative training samples are presented as follows:

(1) We use the corrupted images of original training samples as alternative training samples. Figure 1 shows alternative training samples by corrupting the original face images by using the Salt & Pepper noise.

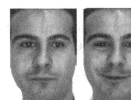 

Fig. 1. The left two images are original training samples, the right two images are alternative training samples by corrupting the left two images.

(2) We use the original training samples with random block occlusion as alternative training samples. Figure 2 shows the original training samples and the alternative training samples.

Fig. 2. The left two images are original training samples, the right two images are alternative training samples by occluding the left two images by the random block.

$X_i = \left[X_i^1, X_i^2, \cdots, X_i^N \right]$ is the coding coefficients of Y_i over the dictionary $[D_1, D_2, \cdots, D_N]$. In order to improve classification capability of the spare, we require that Y_i should be only represented on D_i and not be represented on the other class-special dictionaries, i.e., $X_i^j = 0$. At the same time, we also require that the within-class scatter of the representation coefficient X_i^i of Y_i over D_i is small, i.e., the representation coefficients of the same class data over the class-special dictionary are similar. Thus, the discrimination constraint of X_i is defined as:

$$\phi(X_i) = \left\| X_i^i - M_i \right\|_F^2 \tag{2}$$

where M_i is the coefficient mean value matrix, each column of M_i is the mean vector of X_i^i. Because the sparse constraint on X_i^j results in $X_i^j = 0$, here, we do not show $X_i^j = 0$.

In order to improve the discrimination capability of the dictionary, the correlation among the different dictionaries should be very small, i.e., $\left\|D_i^T D_j\right\|_F^2$ is small for $i \neq j$, and $\left\|D_b^T D_i\right\|_F^2$ is small. Therefore, the dictionary discrimination constraint term is designed as:

$$\varphi(D) = \sum_{j \neq i} \left\|D_j^T D_i\right\|_F^2 + \sum_i \left\|D_b^T D_i\right\|_F^2 \tag{3}$$

By incorporating Eqs. (2) and (3) into Eq. (1) and the discrimination representation coefficient constraint $X_i^j = 0, \forall j \neq i$, we have the following RDCDL model:

$$J_{(D,X,B)} = \operatorname*{arg\,min}_{D,X,B} \sum_{i=1}^{N} \left[\begin{array}{l} \left\|Y_i - D_i X_i^i\right\|_F^2 + \lambda_1 \left\|Z_i - D_i X_i^i - D_b B_i\right\|_F^2 + \lambda_2 \left(\left\|X_i^i\right\|_1 + \left\|B_i\right\|_1 \right) \\ + \lambda_3 \left\|X_i^i - M_i\right\|_F^2 + \lambda_4 \left(\sum_{j \neq i} \left\|D_j^T D_i\right\|_F^2 + \sum_i \left\|D_b^T D_i\right\|_F^2 \right) \end{array} \right] \tag{4}$$

We require that l_2-norm of the atoms of the dictionary D should be less than or equal to 1 (i.e., $\|d\|_2^2 \leq 1$) to avoid the trivial solution. Although the objective function J in Eq. (4) is not jointly convex to (D, X, B), it is convex with respect to each of D and (X, B) when the other is fixed. Equation (4) can be solved by alternatively optimizing D and (X, B). Optimization procedures are presented in Sect. 4.

4 Optimization of RDCDL

We can solve Eq. (4) by alternatively optimizing D and (X, B): Updating (X, B) by fixing D; Updating D by fixing (X, B).

When D, B and all X_j^i $(j = 1, \cdots, N, j \neq i)$ are fixed, we can compute X_i^i one by one; When D, X and all B_j $(j = 1, \cdots, N, j \neq i)$ are fixed, we can compute B_i one by one. Thus the objective function J in Eq. (4) is respectively reduced to:

$$J_{(X_i^i)} = \operatorname*{arg\,min}_{(X_i^i)} \left\{ Q_1\left(X_i^i\right) + 2\tau \left\|X_i^i\right\|_1 \right\} \tag{5}$$

$$J_{(B_i)} = \operatorname*{arg\,min}_{(B_i)} \left\{ Q_2(B_i) + 2\tau \left\|B_i\right\|_1 \right\} \tag{6}$$

where $Q_1\left(X_i^i\right) = \left\|Y_i - D_i X_i^i\right\|_F^2 + \lambda_1 \left\|Z_i - D_i X_i^i - D_b B_i\right\|_F^2 + \lambda_2 \left\|X_i^i - M_i\right\|_F^2$, $\tau = \frac{\lambda_1}{2}$, $Q_2(B_i) = \lambda_1 \left\|Z_i - D_i X_i^i - D_b B_i\right\|_F^2$. The iterative projection method (IPM) [11] can be used to solve Eqs. (5) and (6).

When X, B, D_b and all D_j $(j = 1, \cdots, N, j \neq i)$ are fixed, we can update D_i atom by atom. When X, B and $[D_1, D_2, \cdots, D_N]$ are fixed, we can update D_b atom by atom. Thus the objective function J in Eq. (4) is respectively reduced to:

$$D_i = \arg\min_{D_i}\left[\left\|Y_i - D_iX_i^i\right\|_F^2 + \lambda_1\left\|Z_i - D_iX_i^i - D_bB_i\right\|_F^2\right] + \lambda_4\left[\sum_{j\neq i}\left\|D_j^TD_i\right\|_F^2 + \left\|D_b^TD_i\right\|_F^2\right] \quad (7)$$

$$D_b = \arg\min_{D_b}\sum_{i=1}^N \lambda_1\left\|Z_i - D_iX_i^i - D_bB_i\right\|_F^2 + \lambda_4\sum_i\left\|D_b^TD_i\right\|_F^2 \quad (8)$$

The COPAR [5] can be used to solve Eqs. (7) and (8). The algorithm of DCDL is summarized in Table 1.

Table 1. Algorithm of robust, discriminative and comprehensive dictionary learning

Robust, Discriminative and Comprehensive Dictionary Learning
1. **Initialization** $D = [D_c, D_1, D_2, \cdots, D_N, D_b]$.
We use PCA to initialize the atoms of D_i by Y_i ($i = 1, 2, \cdots, N$) and the atoms of D_b by $Z_i - Y_i$.
2. **Update the representation coefficient X and B.**
Fix D and B and update X_i^i ($i = 1, 2, \cdots, N$) one by one.
Fix D and X and update B_i ($i = 1, 2, \cdots, N$) one by one.
3. **Update the dictionary D.**
Fix X, B and D_b and update D_i ($i = 1, 2, \cdots, N$) one by one.
Fix X, B and $[D_1, D_2, \cdots, D_N]$ and update D_b one by one.
4. **Output.**
Return to step 2 until the values of $J_{(D,X,B)}$ in adjacent iterations are closed enough, or the maximum of iterations is reached. Output D, X and B.

5   The Classification Scheme

After the comprehensive dictionary $D = [D_1, D_2, \cdots, D_N, D_b]$ is got, we can code a testing sample y over the dictionary D. In this case, the coding coefficient can be got by solving:

$$\hat{\alpha} = \arg\min_{\alpha}\left\{\left\|y - [D_1, \cdots, D_N, D_b][\alpha_1; \cdots; \alpha_N; \alpha_b]\right\|_2^2 + \lambda\left\|[\alpha_1; \cdots; \alpha_N; \alpha_b]\right\|_1\right\} \quad (9)$$

where λ is a constant. Denoted by $\hat{\alpha} = [\hat{\alpha}_1; \cdots; \hat{\alpha}_N; \hat{\alpha}_b]$. The reconstruction error of each class is represented as:

$$e_i = \left\|y - D_i\hat{\alpha}_i - D_b\hat{\alpha}_b\right\|_2 \quad (10)$$

where $\hat{\alpha}_i$ is the coefficient vector associated with class i. The classification is defined as:

$$\text{identity}(y) = \arg\min_i\{e_i\} \quad (11)$$

6   Experimental Results and Analysis

In order to well show the advantage of RDCDL, we compare it with NN, SVM, LCKSVD [4], DLSI [7], FDDL [8], SRC [2], and COPAR [5] algorithms by experiments on the Extended Yale B [12,13], AR [14] and Multi-PIE [15].

6.1   Experimental Setting

In this section, we give the experimental details. For Extended Yale B database, the alternative training images are produced by occluding the original images by the random block, whose level is 0.3, $\lambda_1 = 0.001$, $\lambda_2 = 0.01$, $\lambda_3 = 0.01$, $\lambda_4 = 0.001$ and $\lambda = 0.001$. For AR database, the alternative training images are produced by occluding the original images by the random block, whose level is 0.2, $\lambda_1 = 0.001$, $\lambda_2 = 0.01$, $\lambda_3 = 0.001$, $\lambda_4 = 0.0001$ and $\lambda = 0.001$. For Multi-PIE database, the alternative training images are produced by corrupting the original images by the salt & pepper noise, whose density is 0.5, $\lambda_1 = 0.001$, $\lambda_2 = 0.0005$, $\lambda_3 = 0.1$, $\lambda_4 = 0.0005$ and $\lambda = 0.001$.

6.2   Experimental Results on the Extended Yale B Database

The Extended Yale B database consists of 2414 frontal face images from 38 individuals (about 64 images per subject) captured under various laboratory controlled lighting conditions. In the experiment, the size of the original face images is 96×84, we select the former 2 images per subject from subset 1 for training and the subjects from subset 3 for testing. Then we use PCA to reduce the image dimension to 70. The results of RDCDL, SRC, NN, SVM, LCKSVD, DLSI, FDDL and COPAR are listed in Table 2. It can be seen that RDCDL achieves higher recognition rates than the other compared methods.

Table 2. The recognition rates (%) of competing methods on the Extended Yale B database

Methods	Accuracy (%)	Methods	Accuracy (%)
SRC	83.5	COPAR	77.8
NN	55.4	FDDL	84.2
SVM	47.7	DLSI	83.9
LCKSVD	78.9	**RDCDL**	**91.0**

6.3   Experimental Results on the AR Database

The AR database consists of over 4,000 frontal images from 126 individuals. For each individual, 26 pictures were taken in two separated sessions. As in [2], we chose a subset consisting of 50 male subjects and 50 female subjects in the experiment. The size of the original face images is 165×120. For each subject, the 7 images with illumination and expression changes from session 1 are used for training, and the 13 images (with illumination, expression changes, sunglasses and scarf) from session 2 are used for testing. Then we use PCA to reduce the image dimension to 300. The results of competing methods are shown in Table 3. It can be seen that RDCDL achieves the best recognition rates.

Table 3. The recognition rates (%) of competing methods on the AR database

Methods	Accuracy (%)	Methods	Accuracy (%)
SRC	69.2	COPAR	65.6
NN	48.2	FDDL	69.5
SVM	58.6	DLSI	68.4
LCKSVD	65.5	**RDCDL**	**75.3**

6.4 Experimental Results on the CMU Multi-PIE Database

The CMU Multi-PIE face database is a large scale database of 337 subjects including four sessions with simultaneous variations of pose, expression and illumination. Among the 337 subjects, we chose the former 60 subjects from session 1 as the training set, and the same subjects from session 3 as the testing set. For each subject, we chose the 3 frontal images with illumination {0, 1, 3} and smile expression from session 1 for training, and the 10 frontal images with illumination {0, 2, 4, 6, 8, 10, 12, 14, 16, 18} and smile expression from session 3 for testing. Then we use PCA to reduce the image dimension to 170. Table 4 shows the results of competing methods. It can be seen that RDCDL improves at least 3 % over the other compared methods.

Table 4. The recognition rates (%) of competing methods on the Multi-PIE database

Methods	Accuracy (%)	Methods	Accuracy (%)
SRC	85.3	COPAR	83.5
NN	69.3	FDDL	87.7
SVM	72.2	DLSI	86.5
LCKSVD	82.3	**RDCDL**	**90.8**

6.5 Experimental Analysis

The above experiments show that the proposed RDCDL achieves higher recognition rates than SRC, NN and SVM, which directly use original training samples to perform face recognition. It demonstrates that the obtained dictionaries have more discriminative ability than the original training samples. The experiments also show that the recognition rates of the proposed RDCDL are higher than those of LCKSVD, COPAR, FDDL and DLSI, which are DL methods. It demonstrates that the proposed RDCDL has more power discriminative ability than them.

7 Conclusion

In the paper, we propose a new robust, discriminative and comprehensive DL (RDCDL) model. The proposed model uses sample diversities of the same face image to make the dictionary robust. The model includes class-specific dictionary atoms and disturbance dictionary atoms, which can well represent the data from different classes. Both the dictionary and the representation coefficients of data on the dictionary introduce discriminative information, which improves effectively the discrimination capability of the dictionary. The experiments on face recognition demonstrated the effectiveness of RDCDL to those state-of-the-art methods. Face recognition with a single sample per person is very important in the practical application. In the future, we will apply RDCDL to face recognition with a single sample per person.

Acknowledgment. This work is supported by the Projects under Grant no. 2015RC16 and 2015RZY01. This work is partially supported by the National Natural Science Foundation for Young Scientists of China (Grant no. 61402289) and National Science Foundation of Guangdong Province (Grant no. 2014A030313558).

References

1. Yang, J.C., Wright, J., Ma, Y., Huang, T.: Image super-resolution as sparse representation of raw image patches. In: CVPR (2008)
2. Wright, J., Yang, A.Y., Ganesh, A., Sastry, S.S., Ma, Y.: Robust face recognition via sparse representation. IEEE Trans. Pattern Anal. Mach. Intell. **31**(2), 210–227 (2009)
3. Zhang, Q., Li, B.X.: Discriminative K-SVD for Dictionary Learning in Face Recognition. In: CVPR (2010)
4. Jiang, Z.L., Lin, Z., Davis, L.S.: Label consistent K-SVD: learning a discriminative dictionary for recognition. IEEE Trans. Pattern Anal. Mach. Intell. **35**(11), 2651–2664 (2009)
5. Kong, S., Wang, D.: A dictionary learning approach for classification: separating the particularity and the commonality. In: Fitzgibbon, A., Lazebnik, S., Perona, P., Sato, Y., Schmid, C. (eds.) ECCV 2012, Part I. LNCS, vol. 7572, pp. 186–199. Springer, Heidelberg (2012)
6. Aharon, M., Elad, M., Bruckstein, A.: K-SVD: an algorithm for designing over complete dictionaries for sparse representation. IEEE Trans. Sig. Process. **54**(11), 4311–4322 (2006)
7. Ramirez, I., Sprechmann, P., Sapiro, G.: Classification and clustering via dictionary learning with structured incoherence and shared features. In: CVPR (2010)
8. Yang, M., Zhang, L., Feng, X.C., Zhang, D.: Fisher discrimination dictionary learning for sparse representation. In: ICCV (2011)
9. Mairal, J., Bach, F., Ponce, J., Sapiro, G., Zissserman, A.: Learning discriminative dictionaries for local image analysis. In: CVPR (2008)
10. Deng, W.H., Hu, J.N., Guo, J.: Extended SRC: undersampled face recognition via intraclass variation dictionary. IEEE Trans. Pattern Anal. Mach. Intell. **34**(9), 1864–1870 (2012)
11. Rosasco, L., Verri, A., Santoro, M., Mosci, S., Villa, S.: Iterative Projection Methods for Structured Sparsity Regularization. MIT Technical reports, MIT-CSAIL-TR-2009-050, CBCL-282 (2009)
12. Lee, K., Ho, J., Kriegman, D.: Acquiring linear subspaces for face recognition under variable lighting. IEEE Trans. on Pattern Anal. Mach. Intell. **27**(5), 684–698 (2005)
13. Georghiades, A., Belhumeur, P., Kriegman, D.: From few to many: illumination cone models for face recognition under variable lighting and pose. IEEE Trans. Pattern Anal. Mach. Intell. **23**(6), 643–660 (2001)
14. Martinez, A., Benavente, R.: The AR Face Database. CVC Technical report No. 24 (1998)
15. Gross, R., Matthews, I., Cohn, J., Kanade, T., Baker, S.: Multi-PIE. Image Vis. Comput. **28**, 807–813 (2010)

16. Yang, M., Zhang, L., Feng, X.C., Zhang, D.: Sparse representation based Fisher discrimination dictionary learning for image classification. Int. J. Comput. Vis. **109**, 209–232 (2014)
17. Zhang, B.C., Perina, A., Murino, V., Bue, A.D.: Sparse representation classification with manifold constraints transfer. In: CVPR (2015)
18. Jing, X.Y., Wu, F., Zhu, X.K., Dong, X.W., Ma, F., Li, Z.Q.: Multi-spectral low-rank structured dictionary learning for face recognition. Pattern Recogn. (2016). doi:10.1016/j. patcog.2016.01.023

Compact Face Representation via Forward Model Selection

Weiyuan Shao, Hong Wang, Yingbin Zheng, and Hao Ye[✉]

Shanghai Advanced Research Institute,
Chinese Academy of Sciences, Shanghai, China
yeh@sari.ac.cn

Abstract. This paper proposes a compact face representation for face recognition. The face with landmark points in the image is detected and then used to generate transformed face regions. Different types of regions form the transformed face region datasets, and face networks are trained. A novel forward model selection algorithm is designed to simultaneously select the complementary face models and generate the compact representation. Employing a public dataset as training set and fusing by only six selected face networks, the recognition system with this compact face representation achieves 99.05 % accuracy on LFW benchmark.

Keywords: Face recognition · Model selection · Deep learning

1 Introduction

Face recognition in unconstrained environment is a challenge problem in computer vision research. Various hand-crafted representations such as LBP [1], Gabor [2], fisher faces [3] and eigenfaces [4] were designed to train the face recognition models. However, there still exists a gap between the recognition results and human visual system. Recently, Krizhevsky et al. [5] proposed to train the deep convolutional neural network (CNN) for image classification. A significant amount of progress has gone into recognizing faces via the deep networks and achieved human-level performance [6–14].

Previous deep learning based face recognition systems usually use two directions when generating the representations. One approach is to train a very deep network, e.g., the GoogLeNet style Inception with more than 20 layers [10], and obtain a well-defined representation of human faces. Another is to train several medium scale networks and then combine their output features to form a compound feature, e.g., [6–8]. In this paper, we present a compact face representation based on the forward model selection of deep networks for recognition task. The networks are trained from face dataset with machine labeled landmark points; each of them are corresponding to a specific face region and scale. We develop the forward model selection algorithm to select the complementary network set and dimensional reduction is finally applied on the concatenation of selected features to generate a compact representation.

© Springer International Publishing AG 2016
Z. You et al. (Eds.): CCBR 2016, LNCS 9967, pp. 112–120, 2016.
DOI: 10.1007/978-3-319-46654-5_13

The highlights of this work are: (i) compared with previous approaches such as [9], smaller number of networks are needed for the final representation; (ii) we present the analysis on different face regions and investigate the contribution of the regions on the model combination; (iii) as trained using a published available dataset, our compact face representation outperforms previous approaches based on the same dataset, and achieve comparable result with recognition systems from private datasets.

The rest of this paper is organized as follows. Section 2 discusses related works on face recognition. Our approach is described in Sect. 3 and evaluated on LFW dataset in Sect. 4. Finally, Sect. 5 concludes this paper.

2   Related Works

There have been a number of works focusing on recognizing faces in images. A few papers investigated the problem by using one deep network. For example, [10] presented the FaceNet system by employing more than 200 million face images for training and achieved state-of-the-art. However, this large-scale dataset is not publicly available. Based on the relatively small datasets, a popular strategy is to embed multiple networks. In [6], the DeepFace system was proposed with four stages, i.e., detection, alignment, representing and classification. It employed explicit 3D face modeling to apply a piecewise affine transformation on the original face images and generated new aligned face images. Three 8-layer networks are trained on the images using different alignments and color channels, and then combined by various protocols. The DeepFace was extended by the DeepID system [8], which trained 25 small deep convolutional networks from fixed regions and formed the representation by using the last hidden layer of each network. The successive research along this direction focused on improving the network structure [9]. Contrast to the previous approaches, our method chooses regions around the landmark points of human face as input, and performs forward model selection and dimensional reduction on networks to get compact representation. Figure 1 shows our face recognition pipeline.

3   Compact Face Representation

3.1   Pre-processing

The first step of our pipeline is to detect the faces. The face detector from the open source software dlib [15] is used. We choose this off-the-shelf solution as the focus of this work is on the recognition task. However, we believe that our method is complementary to state-of-the-art face detection methods such as cascaded CNN [16] since they perform on different steps of the whole framework.

Through a network with the structure of [5], the corresponding facial landmark points in each face are obtained. Consider the time complexity, we select in-plane 2D alignment method which only use 5 landmark points (i.e., nose, left eye, right eye, left mouth, and right mouth) to align the face image. Then we

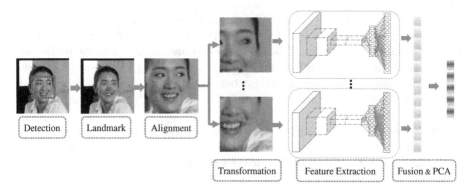

Fig. 1. Face recognition pipeline. We first detect the face region in the given image. The facial landmark points are calculated and used to align the face. Then we apply several transformation strategies, each of which is applied on the aligned face to generate the corresponding transformed face. The transformed face datasets are formed by grouping different kind of transformed faces and we use each of the datasets to train individual networks. The features are extracted from the fully connected layers in each network. Finally, forward model selection and dimensional reduction are applied on the features and the generated representation is used for face recognition task (Color figure online)

can align and transform the faces based on the landmark points to weaken the influence from the pose variation and augment the versatility of faces. The transform matrix is shown in Eq. (1), where s controls the distance between two eyes, θ makes two eyes horizontal, and (dx, dy) makes the transformed face centered by a certain landmark point.

$$T = \begin{bmatrix} 1 & 0 & \frac{w}{2} \\ 0 & 1 & \frac{h}{2} \\ 0 & 0 & 1 \end{bmatrix} \begin{bmatrix} s & 0 & 0 \\ 0 & s & 0 \\ 0 & 0 & 1 \end{bmatrix} \begin{bmatrix} \cos(\theta) & -\sin(\theta) & 0 \\ \sin(\theta) & \cos(\theta) & 0 \\ 0 & 0 & 1 \end{bmatrix} \begin{bmatrix} 1 & 0 & dx \\ 0 & 1 & dy \\ 0 & 0 & 1 \end{bmatrix} \tag{1}$$

3.2 Face Networks

We use a few deep networks to classify unique individuals. The input of the network is $X = \{(x_1, y_1), (x_2, y_2), ..., (x_n, y_n)\}$, where x_i is the face image after transformation and y_i is the corresponding identity. We follow the network architecture of lighted CNN [12], which consists of 9 convolutional layers (conv) and 2 fully connected layers (fc). Different from traditional CNN, here the active function is Maxout [17], which outperforms the ReLU function in both our evaluation and previous face recognition work [12]. The detail network configuration is listed in Table 1.

As mentioned in previous works (e.g., [8]), if the network can discriminate large number of individuals, the feature from the fully connected layer is a good representation in face recognition task, and the recognition problem can be transformed to classification problem. We choose cross entropy loss

Table 1. Face network configuration

Layer name	conv1	conv2_x	conv3_x	conv4_x	conv5_x	fc1	fc2	prob
Output size	128×128	64×64	32×32	16×16	8×8	512	10,575	10,575
Patch size, #channel	5×5, 96	1×1, 96	1×1, 192	1×1, 384	1×1, 256	-	-	-
		3×3, 192	3×3, 384	3×3, 256	3×3, 256			

Algorithm 1. Forward Model Selection

1: **procedure** FORWARDMODELSELECTION($CandidateSet$)
2:     $SelectedSet \leftarrow \emptyset$
3:     $PreviousAccuracy \leftarrow 0.0$
4:     **for all** $Feature \in CandidateSet$ **do**
5:         $WorkSet \leftarrow SelectedSet \bigcup \{Feature\}$
6:         $WorkRepresentation \leftarrow PCA(Concat(WorkSet))$
7:         $CurrentAccuracy \leftarrow Accuracy(Representation)$
8:         **if** $CurrentAccuracy > PreviousAccuracy$ **then**
9:             $PreviousAccuracy \leftarrow CurrentAccuracy$
10:             $SelectedSet \leftarrow WorkSet$
11:             $SelectedRepresentation \leftarrow WorkRepresentation$
12:         **end if**
13:     **end for**
14:     return $(SelectedSet, SelectedRepresentation)$
15: **end procedure**

$entropyLoss = -\sum_{i=1}^{n} y_i \log \hat{p}_i$ as the supervisory signal, where $\hat{p}_i$ is the predicted probability of the ith identity. Since multiple face region datasets based on different affine transformation are generated in previous sub-section, we denote the features set as $F = \{f_1, f_2, ..., f_k\}$, where k is the amount of datasets.

3.3 Forward Model Selection

Traditionally, face features are obtained by concatenate feature vectors in set F [8]. In this subsection, we will introduce a forward model selection algorithm on k kinds of feature vectors. Each feature vector is corresponding to a specific transformed face region and with different representing ability. For example, we found that regions centered by the nose are more discriminant than that centered by mouth corners in our experiments. However, simply selecting the best models and concatenating them directly may not get a good performance, since some models are not complementary with others. On the other hand, traversing all the subset of F to find the optimal solution is not practical, since the search space will grow exponentially when the size of F increases. Therefore, we propose a greedy forward model selection algorithm to find the near optimal solution; the pseudocode is detailed in Algorithm 1.

Initially, we set the Candidate Set $C = F$. In each iteration, one model will be extracted from C and added to S. The selected one can mostly improve the previous performance from S. Principal Component Analysis (PCA) is applied

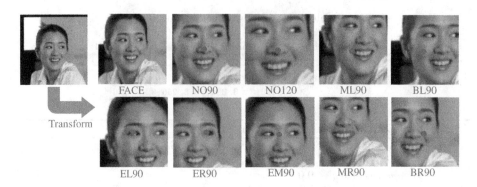

Fig. 2. Example of transformed face and partial regions

on the concatenation of selected features. This step not only plays a dimensionality reduction role, but also drops the noise that may influent the recognition performance. We observe that most elements of the selected set are the models trained from the regions near eyes and nose, and the final performance is influenced by the traverse order. Different traverse order strategies will be discussed in next section. Finally, we use cosine distance as the similarity metric on the compact face representation for face recognition.

4   Experiments

4.1   Setup

Dataset. We evaluate our method in the Labeled Faces in the Wild (LFW) benchmark [18], which is the most popular benchmark for face recognition task. The dataset contains 13,233 face images with 5,749 individuals, and our experiments follow the unrestricted settings protocol which allows using external data in the training period. The benchmark randomly generates 6,000 face pairs and uses 10-fold cross-validation to avoid unfairly overfitting. Our models are trained using CASIA-WebFace dataset [7]. It contains 49,414 images with 10,575 individuals, and is a large public available face recognition dataset.

Pre-processing. In our experiments, several anchor points are defined based on facial landmark points, i.e., left eye (EL), right eye (ER), middle of two eyes (EM), below left eye (BL), below right eye (BR), nose (NO), left mouth corner (ML) and right mouth corner (MR). The face images are scaled according to the distance between two eyes with 90 or 120 pixels. Then different images centered by each landmark point are cropped with the size of 144 × 144 pixels, and form the transformed face datasets for the further training of different face recognition network. To discriminate each dataset and the corresponding model, we use FACE as the model trained based on the whole detected faces, and {AnchorPoint + DistanceBetweenTwoEyes} to nominate the network from the

Table 2. Comparison of networks from different transformed face datasets

Model	FACE	ER90	EL90	NO90	MR90	ML90
Accuracy	98.26 %	98.09 %	98.04 %	97.92 %	97.18 %	96.75 %

partial region. For example, the network trained by the transformed face centered by nose and scaled the distance between two eyes to 90 pixels is nominated as NO90. An example of the regions are illustrated in Fig. 2.

Network training. In order to overcome the overfitting, the dropout is used after fully connected layer with ratio 0.75. Our mini-batch is 40 and the momentum is set to 0.9. The weight decay is set to be 0.0005 and 0.005 in convolutional layer and fully connected layer, respectively. The weights in each layer are initialized by xavier strategy. The learning rate is set to 0.001 and each network is trained on an Nvidia Titan X GPU for about 3 days.

4.2   Comparisons

Transformed face regions. We start by evaluating models from different transformed face datasets. Regions near the 5 facial landmark points are selected to find their importance and the result is illustrated in Table 2. FACE model obtains the highest performance, as they contain all of the face information. The ER and EL models get 98 % accuracy, while ML and MR have around 97 % accuracy. It denotes that the transformed faces fetched from the upper part of face may be more discriminant than these from lower part in face recognition task. The reason may be that the variation in the lower part of face is larger than the upper part in the unconstraint environment, which will confuse the network.

Model traverse orders. The forward model selection solution is highly dependent on the traverse order. As shown in Table 3, we find that if we traverse under

Table 3. Comparison with different model traverse orders

Model traverse order	Selected models	Accuracy
FACE, ER90, EL90, NO90, MR90, ML90	FACE, ER90, EL90	98.66 %
NO90, FACE, ER90, EL90, ML90, MR90	NO90, FACE, ER90, EL90, MR90	98.61 %
ML90, MR90, EL90, ER90, NO90, FACE	ML90, MR90, EL90, ER90, NO90, FACE	98.54 %

Table 4. Performance of forward model selection for different PCA compression rates

Dimensions	w/o PCA	256	128	64	32	16
Accuracy	98.71 %	99.00 %	**99.05 %**	98.97 %	98.26 %	96.81 %

the decreasing order based on the performance[1] of different models (row 1 in Table 3), the performance after fusing will be higher than random order (row 2 in Table 3) and increasing order (row 3 in Table 3). Another observation is that fusing more number of models may not improve the results.

Forward model selection. We construct a larger candidate set including the FACE model and all combinations of the 8 anchor points (see Fig. 2) and 2 scales (90 and 120 pixels). After running the forward model selection algorithm, a selected set is generated with 6 networks, i.e., {EM90, FACE, ER90, EL90, NO90, NO120}. We evaluate the performance of different versions of forward model selection without PCA or after PCA compression to a different number of dimensions (Table 4). PCA works surprisingly well; the forward model selection can be compressed to 128 or even to 64 dimensions almost without any quality loss. Overall, the forward model selection boosts the performance from 98.26 % (FACE model only) to 99.05 % (128 dimension), and meanwhile keeps the face representation compact.

Comparison with state-of-the-art. Tables 5 and 6 compare our method with the state-of-the-art methods in LFW. Our result is better than the methods trained based on CASIA-WebFace. And the performance reaches the same magnitude of methods trained using other public or private datasets.

Table 5. Comparison with previous works using CASIA-WebFace for training

Approach	#Nets	Accuracy
WebFace [7]	1	97.73 %
Lightened CNN [12]	1	98.13 %
Face Search [13]	7	98.23 %
MM-DFR-JB [14]	8	99.02 %
Ours	6	99.05 %

Table 6. Comparison with state-of-the-art approaches with different training datasets

Approach	Dataset	Available	People	Images	Accuracy
DeepFace [6]	SFC	private	4,030	4.4M	97.35 %
VGG Net [11]	VGG Face	public	2,622	2.6M	98.95 %
DeepID2+ [9]	CelebFaces+	private	10,177	202K	99.47 %
FaceNet [10]	Google	private	8M	200M	99.63 %
Ours	CASIA-WebFace	public	10,575	500K	99.05 %

---

[1] The performance is the cross-validation result on CASIA-WebFace, which has a same order with the result of LFW.

5 Conclusion

In this paper, we have introduced a compact face representation based on the forward model selection of deep networks for face recognition. After setting up the pre-processing methods, given an image, the face with landmark points is detected and then used to generate transformed face regions. Several face networks are trained using the transformed face region datasets. The forward model selection algorithm is designed to simultaneously select the complementary face models and generate the compact representation. Experiments on the LFW benchmark demonstrate the effectiveness of our compact face representation.

Acknowledgements. We would like to thank the anonymous reviewers for their helpful comments. This work was supported by the STCSM's Program (No. 16511104802).

References

1. Ahonen, T., Hadid, A., Pietikainen, M.: Face description with local binary patterns: application to face recognition. IEEE Trans. Pattern Anal. Mach. Intell. **28**(12), 2037–2041 (2006)
2. Liu, C., Wechsler, H.: Gabor feature based classification using the enhanced fisher linear discriminant model for face recognition. IEEE Trans. Image Process. **11**(4), 467–476 (2002)
3. Guillaumin, M., Verbeek, J., Schmid, C.: Is that you? Metric learning approaches for face identification. In: ICCV, pp. 498–505 (2009)
4. Turk, M.A., Pentland, A.P.: Face recognition using eigenfaces. In: CVPR (1991)
5. Krizhevsky, A., Sutskever, I., Hinton, G.E.: ImageNet classification with deep convolutional neural networks. In: NIPS, pp. 1097–1105 (2012)
6. Taigman, Y., Yang, M., Ranzato, M., Wolf, L.: DeepFace: closing the gap to human-level performance in face verification. In: CVPR, pp. 1701–1708 (2014)
7. Yi, D., Lei, Z., Liao, S., Li, S.Z.: Learning face representation from scratch. arXiv preprint arXiv:1411.7923 (2014)
8. Sun, Y., Wang, X., Tang, X.: Deep learning face representation from predicting 10,000 classes. In: CVPR, pp. 1891–1898 (2014)
9. Sun, Y., Wang, X., Tang, X.: Deeply learned face representations are sparse, selective, and robust. In: CVPR, pp. 2892–2900 (2015)
10. Schroff, F., Kalenichenko, D., Philbin, J.: FaceNet: a unified embedding for face recognition and clustering. In: CVPR, pp. 815–823 (2015)
11. Parkhi, O.M., Vedaldi, A., Zisserman, A.: Deep face recognition. In: BMVC (2015)
12. Wu, X., He, R., Sun, Z.: A lightened CNN for deep face representation. arXiv preprint arXiv:1511.02683 (2015)
13. Wang, D., Otto, C., Jain, A.K.: Face search at scale: 80 million gallery. arXiv preprint arXiv:1507.07242 (2015)
14. Ding, C., Tao, D.: Robust face recognition via multimodal deep face representation. IEEE Trans. Multimedia **17**(11), 2049–2058 (2015)
15. King, D.E.: Dlib-ml: a machine learning toolkit. J. Mach. Learn. Res. **10**, 1755–1758 (2009)
16. Li, H., Lin, Z., Shen, X., Brandt, J., Hua, G.: A convolutional neural network cascade for face detection. In: CVPR, pp. 5325–5334 (2015)

17. Goodfellow, I.J., Warde-Farley, D., Mirza, M., Courville, A., Bengio, Y.: Maxout networks. arXiv preprint arXiv:1302.4389 (2013)
18. Huang, G.B., Ramesh, M., Berg, T., Learned-Miller, E.: Labeled faces in the wild: a database for studying face recognition in unconstrained environments. Technical report, Technical Report 07–49, University of Massachusetts, Amherst (2007)

A Semi-supervised Learning Algorithm Based on Low Rank and Weighted Sparse Graph for Face Recognition

Tao Zhang$^{(\boxtimes)}$, Zhenmin Tang, and Bin Qian

School of Computer Science and Engineering, Nanjing University of Science and Technology, Nanjing 210094, China
`njustztwork@126.com`, {`Tzm.cs,311062198`}`@njust.edu.cn`

Abstract. Traditional graph-based semi-supervised learning can not capture both the global and local structures of the data exactly. In this paper, we propose a novel low rank and weighted sparse graph. First, we utilize exact low rank representation by the nuclear norm and Forbenius norm to capture the global subspace structure. Meanwhile, we build the weighted sparse regularization term with shape interaction information to capture the local linear structure. Then, we employ the linearized alternating direction method with adaptive penalty to solve the objective function. Finally, the graph is constructed by an effective post-processing method. We evaluate the proposed method by performing semi-supervised classification experiments on ORL, Extended Yale B and AR face database. The experimental results show that our approach improves the accuracy of semi-supervised learning and achieves the state-of-the-art performance.

Keywords: Semi-supervised learning · Graph construction · Low rank · Sparse

1 Introduction

For many machine learning and pattern recognition applications, it is difficult to get enough labeled samples, while a large number of unlabeled samples are widely available over the Internet. Semi-supervised learning (SSL) can utilize both limited labeled samples and abundant unlabeled samples, which has become a research focus in learning tasks. In the current method, graph-based SSL has attracted much attention because it can effectively capture the structure information hidden in the data and obtain a better performance in the practical application [1].

Graph-based SSL employs a graph to represent data structures, where the set of vertices corresponds to the samples, and the set of edges is associated with an adjacency matrix which measures the pairwise weights between vertices. Label information of the labeled samples can be propagated to the unlabeled samples over the graph by label propagation algorithm, such as local and global consistency (LGC) [2] and Gaussian random field and harmonic function (GHFH) [3]. How to construct a good graph is the difficulty of the algorithms, and it is still an open problem. Liu et al. [4] propose low rank representation (LRR), which constructs a low rank graph by solving the nuclear norm minimization problem. LRR can capture the global structure of the

© Springer International Publishing AG 2016
Z. You et al. (Eds.): CCBR 2016, LNCS 9967, pp. 121–129, 2016.
DOI: 10.1007/978-3-319-46654-5_14

data and performs well on the subspace clustering problem. Zhuang et al. [5] extend
LRR and propose non-negative low rank and sparse graph (NNLRS). Compared with
LRR, NNLRS adds a sparse constraint in the objective function, and it can capture the
global and local structure of the data. In [6, 7], based on NNLRS, the authors propose
weighted sparse constraint, where the sparse regularization term is weighted by different weight matrix and it can effectively protect the local structure of the data.

We observe that the above algorithms use the nuclear norm to estimate the rank of
the matrix. Nevertheless, the nuclear norm is a convex relaxation of the rank function,
and it can not estimate the rank accurately. Choosing a suitable function to estimate the
rank can improve the performance of algorithms. Kang et al. [8] propose a rank
approximation based on Logarithm-Determinant and it improves the accuracy of
subspace clustering. Inspired by elastic net [9] in learning theory, we use both the
nuclear norm and Forbenius norm as a replacement function. The rank can be estimated
effectively and we can get a more exact LRR. On the other hand, in order to improve
the ability to capture the local structure of the data, we also add a weighted sparse
regularization term into the objective function. Different from [6, 7], we utilize the
shape interaction information to construct weight matrix, which makes the graph
contain more information.

The remainder of this paper is organized as follows. We give an overview of the
LRR algorithm in Sect. 2. In Sect. 3, we present the proposed low rank and weighted
sparse graph (LRWSG) and its optimization by linearized alternating direction method
with adaptive penalty (LADMAP) [10]. The experimental results on three widely used
face database are presented in Sect. 4. Finally, we conclude this paper in Sect. 5.

2 Related Work

This section briefly introduces LRR. Let $X = [x_1, x_2, \ldots, x_n] \in \mathbb{R}^{d \times n}$ be a matrix whose
columns are n data samples in the d dimensional space. LRR seeks the coefficient
matrix $Z = [z_1, z_2, \ldots, z_n] \in \mathbb{R}^{n \times n}$ which is the lowest rank representation that can
represent X as a linear combination of itself. The LRR problem is defined as follows:

$$\min_{Z} ||Z||_* + \lambda ||E||_{2,1}, s.t. X = XZ + E. \qquad (1)$$

where $|| \cdot ||_*$ is the nuclear norm of a matrix (the sum of the singular values of a matrix).
$||E||_{2,1} = \sum_{j=1}^{n} (\sum_{i=1}^{d} E_{ij}^2)^{1/2}$ is 2,1-norm and it is used to represent noise. The
parameter λ is used to balance the effect of noise. The inexact augmented Lagrange
multiplier (IALM) [11] method is employed to solve the problem (1), and we can get
the optimal solution (Z^*, E^*). The adjacency matrix of the low rank graph can be
calculated as follows:

$$G = (|Z^*| + |Z^*|^T)/2 \qquad (2)$$

After we get the adjacency matrix, LGC or GHFH algorithm is used to propagate
label information and obtain the results of semi-supervised classification.

3   The Proposed Method

3.1   Problem Formulation

Elastic net which utilizes both the 1-norm and 2-norm as penalty function is an effective model in statistical learning [9]. The 1-norm guarantees the sparsity of the solution, while the 2-norm guarantees the stability of the solution. And the model performs well on the low rank matrix completion problem [12].

We observe that $||Z||_*$ in Eq. (1) can be represented as $\sum_{i=1}^{r} |\sigma_i|$, where σ_i is the ith singular value of Z, r is the rank of Z. Obviously, $\sum_{i=1}^{r} |\sigma_i|$ is the 1-norm penalty of the singular value of Z. To improve the stability of the algorithm, we introduce $\sum_{i=1}^{r} |\sigma_i|^2$ as a 2-norm penalty of the singular value of Z. Actually, $||Z||_F^2 = Tr(V\Lambda U^T U\Lambda V^T) = Tr(\Lambda^2) = \sum_{i=1}^{r} |\sigma_i|^2$, where $Z = U\Lambda V^T$ is SVD of Z. By combining the 1-norm penalty and 2-norm penalty, we can rewrite Eq. (1) as follows:

$$\min_{Z} ||Z||_* + \alpha||Z||_F^2 + \lambda||E||_{2,1}, s.t. X = XZ + E. \tag{3}$$

where the parameter α is used to trade off the effect of 1-norm penalty and 2-norm penalty. Compared with Eqs. (1), (3) is a stable model which can estimate the rank of Z and capture the global subspace structure more exactly.

In order to capture the local linear structure, $||Z||_1$ is added into Eq. (1) [5]. Later on, [6, 7] propose weighted sparse constraint $||W \odot Z||_1$, where $\odot$ denotes the Hadamard product, if $M = A \odot B$, then $M_{ij} = A_{ij} \times B_{ij}$. Constructing a weight matrix W with more information can protect the local structure of the data. Inspired by [13], we utilize shape interaction information to construct W. Let $X = U_r \Lambda_r V_r^T$ be the skinny SVD of X, where r is the rank of X. The shape interaction representation of each data sample x_i is $R_i = \Lambda_r^{-1} U_r^T x_i$. Normalize all column vectors of R_i by $R_i^* = R_i / ||R_i||_2$, and the shape interaction weight matrix W can be defined as follows:

$$W_{ij} = || R_i^* - R_j^* ||_2 \tag{4}$$

In summary, we formulate the objective function of LRWSG as follows:

$$\min_{Z} || Z ||_* + \alpha || Z ||_F^2 + \beta || W \odot Z ||_1 + \lambda || E ||_{2,1}, \quad s.t. \ X = XZ + E, Z \geq 0. \tag{5}$$

3.2   Optimization

Similar to [5], we utilize LADMAP to solve problem (5). We first introduce an auxiliary variable J to separate the variable in the objective function. Thus Eq. (5) can be rewritten as follows:

$$\min_{Z} \| Z \|_* + \alpha \| Z \|_F^2 + \beta \| W \odot J \|_1 + \lambda \| E \|_{2,1}, \quad s.t. \ X = XZ + E, Z = J, J \geq 0. \quad (6)$$

The augmented Lagrange function of Eq. (6) is

$$L = \| Z \|_* + \alpha \| Z \|_F^2 + \beta \| W \odot J \|_1 + \lambda \| E \|_{2,1} + Tr\left[Y_1^T \left(X - XZ - E \right) \right]$$
$$+ Tr\left[Y_2^T \left(Z - J \right) \right] + \frac{\mu}{2} [\| X - XZ - E \|_F^2 + \| Z - J \|_F^2] \quad (7)$$

where Y_1 and Y_2 are Lagrange multipliers, $\mu > 0$ is a penalty parameter.
Update Z_{k+1} with Z_k, J_k, E_k fixed.

$$Z_{k+1} = \arg\min_{Z} \frac{1}{\eta\mu_k} \| Z \|_* + \frac{1}{2} \| Z - (Z_k + (X^T(X - XZ_k - E + Y_{1,k}/\mu_k)$$
$$- (Z_k - J_k + Y_{2,k}/\mu_k) - (2\alpha/\mu)Z_k)/\eta) \|_F^2 \quad (8)$$

where $\eta = \|X\|_2^2$, Eq. (8) can be solved by singular value thresholding operator [14].
We set $A = (Z_k + (X^T(X - XZ_k - E + Y_{1,k}/\mu_k) - (Z_k - J_k + Y_{2,k}/\mu_k) - (2\alpha/\mu)Z_k)/\eta$,
$A = U\Lambda V^T$ is the SVD of A, the solution of Eq. (8) is $Z_{k+1} = US_{1/\beta}(\Lambda)V^T$, where S is
soft thresholding operator [11], defined as $S_\varepsilon[x] = \max(x - \varepsilon, 0) + \min(x + \varepsilon, 0)$.
Update J_{k+1} with Z_{k+1}, J_k, E_k fixed.

$$J_{k+1} = \arg\min_{J \geq 0} \frac{\beta}{\mu_k} \| W \odot J \|_1 + \frac{1}{2} \| J - (Z_{k+1} + Y_{2,k}/\mu_k) \|_F^2 \quad (9)$$

Equation (9) can be solved by soft thresholding operator and the solution is

$$(J_{k+1})_{ij} = \max(S_{\varepsilon_{ij}}[(Z_{k+1})_{ij} + (Y_{2,k})_{ij}/\mu_k], 0) \quad (10)$$

where $\varepsilon_{ij} = (\beta/\mu_k)W_{ij}$.

Update E_{k+1} with Z_{k+1}, J_{k+1}, E_k fixed.

$$E_{k+1} = \arg\min_{E} \frac{\lambda}{\mu_k} \|E\|_{2,1} + \frac{1}{2} \|E - (X - XZ_{k+1} + Y_{1,k}/\mu_k)\|_F^2 \quad (11)$$

The solution of Eq. (11) is

$$E_{k+1} = \Omega_{\lambda/\mu_k}(X - XZ_{k+1} + Y_{1,k}/\mu_k) \quad (12)$$

where Ω is 2,1-norm minimization operator [4]. If $Y = \Omega_\varepsilon(X)$, then the ith column of Y
is

$$Y(:,i) = \begin{cases} \frac{\|X(:,i)\|_2 - \varepsilon}{\|X(:,i)\|_2} X(:,i), & \varepsilon < \|X(:,i)\|_2 \\ 0, & \varepsilon \geq \|X(:,i)\|_2 \end{cases} \tag{13}$$

The complete optimization to LRWSG is summarized in Algorithm 1.

3.3 Graph Construction

Once problem (5) is solved, we can obtain an optimal Z^*. Different from the traditional graph-based SSL construct the adjacency matrix by Eq. (2), we utilize the method which is used on the subspace clustering problem [4]. Let $Z^* = U^* \Lambda^* (V^*)^T$ be the skinny SVD of Z^*, we define $P = U^* (\Lambda^*)^{1/2}$, the adjacency matrix of LRWSG is calculated as follows:

Algorithm 1: LRWSG

Input: data matrix X, parameters α, β and λ, weight matrix W;

Initialization: $Z_0 = J_0 = E_0 = Y_{1,0} = Y_{2,0} = 0$, $\mu_0 = 0.1$, $\mu_{max} = 10^{10}$, $\rho_0 = 1.1$,
$\quad \varepsilon_1 = 10^{-4}$, $\varepsilon_2 = 10^{-2}$, $\eta = \|X\|_2^2$, $k = 0$;

Definition: $\varepsilon = \mu_k \max(\sqrt{\eta} \| Z_{k+1} - Z_k \|_F, \| J_{k+1} - J_k \|_F, \| E_{k+1} - E_k \|_F)/\| X \|_F$;

while $\| X - XZ_{k+1} - E_{k+1} \|_F / \| X \|_F \geq \varepsilon_1$ or $\varepsilon \geq \varepsilon_2$ **do**

(1) Update the variables (Z, J, E) as Eq. (8), Eq. (9) and Eq. (11);

(2) Update Lagrangian multipliers as
$\quad Y_{1,k+1} = Y_{1,k} + \mu_k (X - XZ_{k+1} - E_{k+1})$, $Y_{2,k+1} = Y_{2,k} + \mu_k (Z_{k+1} - J_{k+1})$;

(3) Update μ as $\mu_{k+1} = \min(\mu_{max}, \rho \mu_k)$, where
$$\rho = \begin{cases} \rho_0, & \varepsilon < \varepsilon_2, \\ 1, & \varepsilon \geq \varepsilon_2, \end{cases};$$

(4) Update k as $k = k + 1$;

end while

Output: optimal solution (Z^*, E^*).

$$(G)_{ij} = (PP^T)_{ij}^2 \tag{14}$$

After we obtain the adjacency matrix G, LGC algorithm is employed to solve the semi-supervised classification problem.

4 Experiment

In this section, we evaluate the effectiveness of LRWSG on semi-supervised classification experiments. LRWSG is compared with several LRR related graphs including LRR [4], NNLRS [5], LRRLC [6], SCLRR [7] and CLAR [8]. The classification accuracy is used to evaluate the semi-supervised classification performance, which is defined to be the percentage of correctly classified samples versus the test samples. The parameters of the compared algorithms are tuned to achieve the best performance. In LRWSG, the parameter α balances the effect of nuclear norm and Forbenius norm. According to a large number of experiments, the classification accuracy is better when we set $\alpha = 1$. The parameter λ is used to describe the noise of data, we set $\lambda = 10$ for our experiments. The parameter β controls the effect of sparse regularization term, we set $\beta = 0.3$ on ORL database and EYaleB database and we set $\beta = 0.1$ on AR database. The experiments are implemented on Intel Core i7 4710MQ CPU with 8 G memory.

4.1   Databases

We select three face databases for our experiments: ORL, Extended Yale B (EYaleB) and AR. The ORL database contains 40 distinct subjects, and each subject has 10 different images. The images were taken at different times, varying the lighting, facial expressions and facial details. There are 64 face images under different illuminations of each of 38 individuals in the EYaleB database. In our experiments, we use the first 20 subjects and each subject chooses the first 50 images. The AR database contains 3120 images of 120 subjects with different facial expressions, lighting conditions and occlusions. The first 50 subjects are chosen for our experiments, and each subject chooses the first 20 images. All the images are resized to 32×32. Several sample images of the three face databases are shown in Fig. 1.

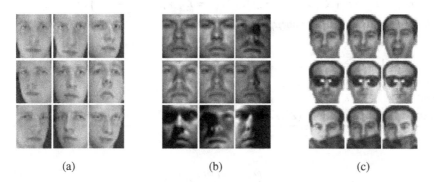

(a)   (b)   (c)

Fig. 1. Some sample images from three databases: (a) ORL, (b) EYaleB, (c) AR

4.2   Experimental Results and Analysis

For each database, we randomly choose 10 % to 60 % samples from each class as labeled samples, and the rest samples are used for testing. For each percentage of labeled samples, we repeat the experiment 20 trials for each algorithm. Tables 1, 2 and 3 report the classification accuracies and standard deviations of each algorithm on ORL, EYaleB and AR.

Table 1. The classification accuracies and standard deviations (%) on ORL

Label	LRR	CLAR	NNLRS	LRRLC	SCLRR	LRWSG
10 %	63.83 ± 2.21	68.53 ± 1.88	72.76 ± 2.03	69.78 ± 1.86	75.93 ± 2.22	**82.10 ± 2.32**
20 %	73.19 ± 2.54	80.45 ± 2.48	82.78 ± 2.69	80.98 ± 2.25	84.31 ± 2.77	**87.63 ± 2.22**
30 %	78.00 ± 2.19	86.23 ± 2.71	87.96 ± 1.94	86.41 ± 2.55	88.89 ± 2.00	**91.04 ± 2.10**
40 %	80.56 ± 2.42	89.96 ± 1.69	91.04 ± 1.87	89.98 ± 1.77	92.35 ± 1.64	**93.17 ± 1.98**
50 %	82.03 ± 2.06	91.18 ± 1.47	92.55 ± 1.42	91.53 ± 1.49	93.50 ± 1.47	**94.20 ± 1.66**
60 %	83.75 ± 2.94	93.06 ± 1.89	93.78 ± 1.65	93.28 ± 1.69	94.22 ± 1.61	**94.75 ± 2.08**

Table 2. The classification accuracies and standard deviations (%) on EYaleB

Label	LRR	CLAR	NNLRS	LRRLC	SCLRR	LRWSG
10 %	86.43 ± 1.56	87.57 ± 1.47	92.64 ± 1.02	87.17 ± 1.41	88.90 ± 1.21	**92.99 ± 1.02**
20 %	91.76 ± 1.37	93.01 ± 1.39	95.00 ± 0.79	92.65 ± 1.31	93.21 ± 1.31	**95.36 ± 0.73**
30 %	93.13 ± 0.98	94.69 ± 0.79	96.02 ± 0.61	94.53 ± 0.72	94.98 ± 0.72	**96.45 ± 0.60**
40 %	94.56 ± 0.88	96.25 ± 0.92	96.99 ± 0.61	96.13 ± 0.78	96.43 ± 0.67	**97.32 ± 0.60**
50 %	95.14 ± 1.17	96.85 ± 0.79	97.28 ± 0.59	97.09 ± 0.57	97.41 ± 0.62	**97.69 ± 0.56**
60 %	95.39 ± 0.83	97.50 ± 0.59	97.61 ± 0.70	97.60 ± 0.67	97.60 ± 0.67	**97.96 ± 0.63**

Table 3. The classification accuracies and standard deviations (%) on AR

Label	LRR	CLAR	NNLRS	LRRLC	SCLRR	LRWSG
10 %	85.70 ± 1.78	84.06 ± 2.09	83.68 ± 1.81	85.83 ± 1.88	85.07 ± 1.88	**93.53 ± 1.40**
20 %	92.34 ± 0.89	93.17 ± 1.02	91.63 ± 1.11	93.26 ± 1.01	93.24 ± 1.06	**95.96 ± 0.91**
30 %	94.82 ± 1.04	96.01 ± 0.98	94.96 ± 1.14	95.84 ± 0.97	95.96 ± 0.90	**97.19 ± 0.99**
40 %	95.88 ± 0.72	97.41 ± 0.63	96.99 ± 0.75	97.07 ± 0.58	97.48 ± 0.68	**98.23 ± 0.58**
50 %	96.12 ± 0.88	97.63 ± 0.67	97.37 ± 0.80	97.18 ± 0.83	97.68 ± 0.77	**98.35 ± 0.64**
60 %	96.81 ± 0.64	98.11 ± 0.71	98.24 ± 0.83	97.84 ± 0.80	98.31 ± 0.77	**98.70 ± 0.70**

From the results, we can observe that:

(1) LRWSG achieves the highest accuracies on both databases. LRWSG utilizes the nuclear norm and Forbenius norm to estimate the rank function. Meanwhile, the weighted sparse regularization term with shape interaction information is joined into the objective function. Therefore, LRWSG can capture both the global subspace structure and local linear structure exactly. And the standard deviations of LRWSG are often small, which shows the stability of LRWSG.

(2) CLAR uses the logarithm determinant function to estimate the rank function, which improves the performance of LRR. But compared with the algorithms which consider both low rank and sparse property, CLAR performs worse. Depend on LRR, NNLRS, LRRLC and SCLRR propose different sparsity constraint. Although the weight matrices of sparse regularization term are different, the performance of these

three algorithms are similar. With exact rank estimation and informational weighted sparse matrix, LRWSG performs better than these three algorithms.

(3) With the increase of the number of labeled samples, the classification accuracies of each algorithm are also increased. When given more labeled samples, the label information is more abundant, and each algorithm performs well. When given less labeled samples, the classification becomes more difficult, but LRWSG can still get a higher classification accuracies. For example, with 10 % labeled samples, the accuracy of LRWSG is 82.10 % on ORL database, which is 6.17 % higher than the best result obtained from other algorithms

5 Conclusion

This paper proposes a novel semi-supervised learning algorithm based on low rank and weighted sparse graph (LRWSG), and applies it to face recognition. In order to capture the data structure exactly, LRWSG makes use of the nuclear norm and Forbenius norm to estimate the rank function, and adds a weighted sparse constraint with shape interaction information into the object function. LADMAP is employed to solve the optimization problem. And with an effective post-processing method, the graph is constructed and used for semi-supervised classification. Experimental results on ORL, EYaleB and AR databases show that the proposed approach achieves better classification performance.

References

1. Zhu, X.: Semi-supervised Learning Literature Survey. Technical report, University of Wisconsin, Madison (2006)
2. Zhou, D., Bousquet, O., Lal, T.N., Weston, J., Schölkopf, B.: Learning with local and global consistency. In: Advances in Neural Information Processing Systems, pp. 321–328. MIT Press, Cambridge (2004)
3. Zhu, X., Ghahramani, Z., Lafferty, J.: Semi-supervised learning using gaussian fields and harmonic functions. In: Proceedings of the 20th International Conference on Machine Learning, pp. 912–919. AAAI Press, Washington, DC (2003)
4. Liu, G., Lin, Z., Yan, S., Sun, J., Yu, Y., Ma, Y.: Robust recovery of subspace structures by low-rank representation. IEEE Trans. Pattern Anal. Mach. Intell. **35**(1), 171–184 (2013)
5. Zhuang, L., Gao, H., Lin, Z., Ma, Y., Zhang, X., Yu, N.: Non-negative low rank and sparse graph for semi-supervised learning. In: Proceedings of the IEEE Conference on Computer Vision and Pattern Recognition, pp. 2328–2335. IEEE Press, Providence (2012)
6. Zheng, Y., Zhang, X., Yang, S., Jiao, L.: Low-rank representation with local constraint for graph construction. Neurocomputing **122**, 398–405 (2013)
7. Tang, K., Liu, R., Su, Z., Zhang, J.: Structure-constrained low-rank representation. IEEE Trans. Neural Netw. Learn. Systems **25**(12), 2167–2179 (2014)
8. Kang, Z., Peng, C., Cheng, Q.: Robust subspace clustering via smoothed rank approximation. IEEE Signal Process. Lett. **22**(11), 2088–2092 (2015)
9. De Mol, C., De Vito, E., Rosasco, L.: Elastic-net regularization in learning theory. J. Complex. **25**(2), 201–230 (2009)

10. Lin, Z., Liu, R., Su, Z.: Linearized alternating direction method with adaptive penalty for low-rank representation. In: Advances in Neural Information Processing Systems, pp. 612–620. Springer Press, Granada (2011)
11. Lin, Z., Chen, M., Ma, Y.: The augmented lagrange multiplier method for exact recovery of corrupted low-rank matrices. Technical report, UILU-ENG-09-2215 (2009)
12. Li, H., Chen, N., Li, L.: Error analysis for matrix elastic-net regularization algorithms. IEEE Trans. Neural Netw. Learn. Syst. **23**(5), 737–748 (2012)
13. Liu, B., Jing, L., Yu, J., Li, J.: Robust graph learning via constrained elastic-net regularization. Neurocomputing **171**, 299–312 (2016)
14. Cai, J.F., Candès, E.J., Shen, Z.: A singular value thresholding algorithm for matrix completion. SIAM J. Optim. **20**(4), 1956–1982 (2010)

Multilinear Local Fisher Discriminant Analysis for Face Recognition

Yucong Peng[1,2], Peng Zhou[1,2], Hao Zheng[3], Baochang Zhang[4], and Wankou Yang[1,2(✉)]

[1] School of Automation, Southeast University, Nanjing 210096, China
pyc3611@163.com, wankou.yang@yahoo.com
[2] Key Lab of Measurement and Control of Complex Systems of Engineering, Ministry of Education, Nanjing 210096, China
[3] Key Laboratory of Trusted Cloud Computing and Big Data Analysis, Nanjing Xiaozhuang University, Nanjing 211171, People's Republic of China
[4] School of Automation Science and Electrical Engineering, Beihang University, Beijing 100191, China

Abstract. In this paper, a multilinear local fisher discriminant analysis (MLFDA) framework is introduced for tensor object dimensionality reduction and recognition. MLFDA achieves feature extraction by finding a multilinear projection to map the original tensor space into a tensor subspace that maximize the local between-class scatter as well as minimize the local within-class scatter. The experimental result shows that MLFDA has an outperformance.

Keywords: Local Fisher Discriminant Analysis (LFDA) · Dimensionality reduction · Tensor · Face recognition

1 Introduction

The traditional algorithms of subspace learning, such as Principal Component Analysis (PCA) [1], Linear Discriminant Analysis (LDA) [2] and Locality Preserving Projections (LPP) [3] have been used in many areas. Traditional Linear discriminant analysis tends to give undesired results if samples in some class form several separate clusters, i.e., multimodal. To solve this problem, a new dimensionality reduction method called Local Fisher Discriminant Analysis (LFDA) [4] is proposed, which is a localized variant of Fisher Discriminant Analysis. LFDA takes local structure of the data into account so that the multimodal data can be embedded appropriately.

All these methods process an image object as a high-dimensional vector (1D vector) by concatenating the rows or columns of the images [5]. Because of this, they will lose some useful structural information embedded in the original images and can cause a lot of calculations. To solve this problem, the Two Dimensional PCA (2DPCA) [6] had been proposed based on the classical PCA. With the similar idea of 2DPCA, researchers proposed 2DLDA [7] and 2DLPP [8].

© Springer International Publishing AG 2016
Z. You et al. (Eds.): CCBR 2016, LNCS 9967, pp. 130–138, 2016.
DOI: 10.1007/978-3-319-46654-5_15

D Zhang and ZH Zhou improved the 2DPCA and proposed a new algorithm called Two-directional two-dimensional PCA ($(2D)^2PCA$) [13] which achieves the same or even higher recognition accuracy than 2DPCA in face recognition.

Although two dimensional algorithms have good effect on image dimension reduction, they still cannot function well on multidimensional objects. For example, the gait silhouette sequences are the input to most of gait recognition algorithms [9]. In this case, tensor is used here to denote a multi-dimensional object [10]. Tensors are considered to be the extensions of vectors and matrices, the elements of which are to be addressed by more than two indices [11], where the number of indices used in the description defines the order of the tensor object and each index defines one mode [10]. By this definition, we can use tensor to represent different kind of data in high-dimensional space. For example, a video sequence or a gait silhouette sequence is a 3rd-order tensor. Therefore, researchers focused on multilinear dimensionality reduction algorithms using tensor as the input data because it applies to all kinds of high-dimensional data rather than one or two specific kinds. Researchers combined tensor with traditional algorithms and developed the Multilinear Principal Component Analysis (MPCA) [10] and the Multilinear Discriminant Analysis (MLDA) [12].

In this paper, a new multilinear approach Multilinear Local Fisher Discriminant Analysis (MLFDA) algorithm is proposed. Compared with LFDA, MLFDA gives natural representations of samples using tensor framework, and has better performance in face recognition. The rest of the paper is organized as follows: Sect. 2 reviews the LFDA algorithm. And in Sect. 3, we introduce the basic multilinear algebra notations and the notion of multilinear projection for dimensionality reduction and propose the problem of MLFDA and its iterative solution. Section 4 do experiments on face recognition and compares the result to other algorithm. Finally, the conclusions are given in Sect. 5.

2   Local Fisher Discriminant Analysis

LFDA is a localized variant of Fisher discriminant analysis [4]. Here we briefly review the definition of Local Fisher Discriminant Analysis (LFDA): let $X = (x_1, x_2, \ldots, x_M), x_i \in \mathbb{R}^n$ be n-dimensional samples and $c_i \in \{1, 2, \ldots, N_c\}$ be the class labels of each samples, where M is the number of the samples and N_c is the number of classes. Let m_c be the number of samples in the class c, then: $\sum_{c=1}^{N_c} m_c = M$.

LFDA finds a $n \times d$ projection matrix T to project sample x_i into low-dimensional subspace $\mathbb{R}^d$, where $y_i = T^T x_i \in \mathbb{R}^d$ and $d \ll n$. Based on the above declaration, the local within-class scatter matrix S_W and the local between-class scatter matrix S_B as follows.

$$S_B = \frac{1}{2} \sum_{i,j=1}^{M} (X_i - X_j)(X_i - X_j)^T A_{ij}^B \tag{1}$$

$$S_W = \frac{1}{2} \sum_{i,j=1}^{M} (X_i - X_j)(X_i - X_j)^T A_{ij}^W \tag{2}$$

where

$$A_{ij}^B = \begin{cases} w_{ij}(\frac{1}{M} - \frac{1}{m_c}) & if \ c_i = c_j \\ \frac{1}{M} & if \ c_i \neq c_j \end{cases} \qquad A_{ij}^W = \begin{cases} \frac{w_{ij}}{m_c} & if \ c_i = c_j \\ 0 & if \ c_i \neq c_j \end{cases} \tag{3}$$

In above formula, the values of A_{ij}^W and A_{ij}^B are weighted by the affinity of samples x_i and x_j. The W is a sparse symmetric $M \times M$ matrix with w_{ij} having the weight of the edge joining vertices x_i and x_j. There are two common ways of defining W:

$$Heat\_kernel: \quad W_{ij} = \begin{cases} e^{-\frac{||x_i - x_j||^2}{t}} & if \ i \ and \ j \ are \ connected \\ 0 & else \end{cases}$$

$$Simple\_minded: \quad W_{ij} = \begin{cases} 1 & if \ i \ and \ j \ are \ connected \\ 0 & else \end{cases}$$

The objective function of LFDA can be defined as

$$T_{LFDA} = arg \max_{T \in \mathbb{R}^{n \times d}} \frac{tr(T^T S_B T)}{tr(T^T S_W T)} \tag{4}$$

By matrix transformation, the objective function of T_{LFDA} can be given by $T_{LFDA} = (\varphi_1 | \varphi_2 | \dots | \varphi_d)$ where φ_i is the generalized eigenvectors associated to the generalized eigenvalues $\lambda_1 \geq \lambda_2 \geq \cdots \geq \lambda_d$ of the following generalized eigenvalue problem: $S_B T = \lambda S_W T$

3   Multilinear Local Fisher Discriminant Analysis

In this section, a multilinear local fisher discriminant analysis (MLFDA) solution to the problem of dimensionality reduction for tensor objects is introduced. Before formally stating the objective, we need to review some basic multilinear concepts used in the MLFDA framework and introduce the multilinear projection of tensor objects for the purpose of dimensionality reduction.

3.1   Preparations

In this paper, if there are no special instructions, the fundamental symbols of different variables will be defined as follows. Tensors are denoted by calligraphic uppercase letters, e.g. $\mathcal{A}, \mathcal{B}$; matrices by uppercase boldface, e.g. $\mathbf{X}, \mathbf{Y}$; and vectors by lowercase boldface letters, e.g. $\mathbf{x}, \mathbf{y}$.

Assume that an Nth-order tensor is denoted as: $\mathcal{A} \in \mathbb{R}^{I_1 \times I_2 \times \cdots \times I_N}$. It is addressed by N indices $i_n, n = 1, 2, \dots, N$ and each i_n addresses the n-mode of $\mathcal{A}$ e.g. $\mathcal{A}_{i_1,i_2,\ldots,i_N}$. The Frobenius norm of tensor $\mathcal{A}$ is defined as $||\mathcal{A}||_F^2 = \sqrt{\sum_{i_1=1}^{I_1} \sum_{i_2=1}^{I_2} \cdots \sum_{i_N=1}^{I_N} \mathcal{A}^2_{i_1,i_2,\ldots,i_N}}$, where $||\mathcal{A}||_F^2 = \langle \mathcal{A}, \mathcal{A} \rangle$. In the same way, we can also define the norm of two different tensor $\mathcal{A}, \mathcal{B} \in \mathbb{R}^{I_1 \times I_2 \times \cdots \times I_N}$ as $||\mathcal{A}, \mathcal{B}||_F^2 = \sqrt{\sum_{i_1=1}^{I_1} \sum_{i_2=1}^{I_2} \cdots \sum_{i_N=1}^{I_N} \mathcal{A}_{i_1,i_2,\ldots,i_N} \mathcal{B}_{i_1,i_2,\ldots,i_N}}$.

The unfolding of tensor is the process by which the elements in the tensor are rearranged into a matrix. The n-mode vectors of $\mathcal{A}$ are defined as the i_n-dimensional vectors obtained from $\mathcal{A}$ by varying the index in while keeping all the other indices fixed. The n-mode unfolding of a tensor is expressed as $\mathbf{A}_{(n)} \in \mathbb{R}^{I_n \times (I_1 \times \cdots \times I_{n-1} \times I_{n+1} \times \cdots \times I_N)}$, and defined as making all the vectors into the columns of the matrix. Assume we project the element of the tensor $\mathcal{A}_{i_1,i_2,\ldots,i_N}$ into the matrix $\mathbf{A}_{(n)i_n,j}$, where $j = 1 + \sum_{k=1;k\neq n}^{N} (i_k - 1)j_k$.

The n-mode product of a tensor is defined as $\mathcal{A} \times_n \mathbf{U}$ where $\mathbf{U} \in \mathbb{R}^{J_n \times I_n}$ is a matrix. The result of n-mode product is a new tensor belonging to the subspace $\mathbb{R}^{I_n \times (I_1 \times \cdots \times I_{n-1} \times J_n \times I_{n+1} \times \cdots \times I_N)}$, it can be proposed as:

$$(\mathcal{A} \times_n \mathbf{U})_{i_1 i_2 \ldots i_{n-1} j_n i_{n+1} \ldots i_N} = \sum_{i_n=1}^{I_n} \mathcal{A}_{i_1 i_2 \ldots i_{n-1} i_n i_{n+1} \ldots i_N} \mathbf{U}_{j_n i_n} \tag{5}$$

the n-mode product of a tensor can also be n-mode unfolded:

$$\mathcal{B} = \mathcal{A} \times_n \mathbf{U} \Leftrightarrow \mathbf{B}_{(n)} = \mathbf{U} \mathbf{A}_{(n)} \tag{6}$$

For an Nth-order tensor: $\mathcal{X} \in \mathbb{R}^{I_1 \times I_2 \times \cdots \times I_N}$, if we want to map the tensor into low-dimensional subspace $\mathbb{R}^{P_1 \times P_2 \times \cdots \times P_N}$, we must define a group of projection matrix $\mathbf{U}^{(n)} \in \mathbb{R}^{P_n \times I_n}, n \in \{1, 2, \ldots, N\}$.

The projection and its n-mode unfolding are defined as:

$$\mathcal{Y} = \mathcal{X} \times_1 \mathbf{U}^{(1)} \times_2 \mathbf{U}^{(2)} \cdots \times_N \mathbf{U}^{(N)} \Leftrightarrow$$
$$\mathbf{Y}_{(n)} = \mathbf{U}_n \mathbf{X}_{(n)} (\mathbf{U}^{(N)} \otimes \cdots \otimes \mathbf{U}^{(n-1)} \otimes \mathbf{U}^{(n+1)} \otimes \cdots \otimes \mathbf{U}^{(1)}) \tag{7}$$

where $\otimes$ denotes the Kronecker product.

3.2 The Objective Function of MLFDA

Let $\{\mathcal{X}_m, m = 1, 2, \ldots, M\}$ be a set of tensor samples in $\mathbb{R}^{I_1 \times I_2 \times \cdots \times I_N}$, where I_n represent the n-mode dimension of the tensor, M is the number of tensor samples. The labels of each tensor samples are $c_i \in \{1, 2, \ldots, N_c\}$. The MLFDA objective is to seek a multilinear transformation $\{\mathbf{U}^{(n)} \in \mathbb{R}^{P_n \times I_n}, n = 1, 2, \ldots, N\}$ to maps the original tensor space $\mathbb{R}^{I_1 \times I_2 \times \cdots \times I_N}$ into a tensor subspace $\mathbb{R}^{P_1 \times P_2 \times \cdots \times P_N}$ with $P_n < I_n, n = 1, 2, \ldots, N$. The transformation can be in the form like

$$\mathcal{Y} = \mathcal{X} \times_1 \mathbf{U}^{(1)} \times_2 \mathbf{U}^{(2)} \cdots \times_N \mathbf{U}^{(N)} \tag{8}$$

The MLFDA objective is the determination of the N projection matrices $\mathbf{U}^{(n)} \in \mathbb{R}^{P_n \times I_n}$ that maximize the local between-class scatter and at the same time minimize the local within-class scatter:

$$\{\mathbf{U}^{(n)} \in \mathbb{R}^{P_n \times I_n}\} = \max_{\mathcal{Y} = \mathcal{X} \times_1 \mathbf{U}^{(1)} \cdots \times_N \mathbf{U}^{(N)}} \frac{\sum_{i,j}^M ||\mathcal{Y}_i - \mathcal{Y}_j||_F^2 A_{ij}^B}{\sum_{i,j}^M ||\mathcal{Y}_i - \mathcal{Y}_j||_F^2 A_{ij}^W} \tag{9}$$

3.3   n-Mode Optimization

We now discuss how to optimize the objective function from only one direction of the tensor. Under this circumstances, the tensor samples $\mathcal{X}_m$ only need to project to n^{th}-mode subspace, e.g. $\mathcal{Y}_i = \mathcal{X}_i \times_n \mathbf{U}^{(n)}$. And the objective function is changed into:

$$\mathbf{U}^{(n)} = \arg\max_{\mathbf{U}^{(n)}} \frac{\sum_{i,j}^M ||\mathcal{X}_i \times_n \mathbf{U}^{(n)} - \mathcal{X}_j \times_n \mathbf{U}^{(n)}||_F^2 A_{ij}^B}{\sum_{i,j}^M ||\mathcal{X}_i \times_n \mathbf{U}^{(n)} - \mathcal{X}_j \times_n \mathbf{U}^{(n)}||_F^2 A_{ij}^W} \tag{10}$$

where A_{ij}^B and A_{ij}^W are the same definition in Sect. 2. N-mode unfolding the molecular part and the denominator part in the objective function, we will get:

$$\sum_{i,j}^M ||(\mathcal{X}_i - \mathcal{X}_j) \times_n \mathbf{U}^{(n)}||_F^2 A_{ij}^B \Leftrightarrow \sum_{i,j}^M ||\mathbf{U}^{(n)}(\mathbf{X}_{i(n)} - \mathbf{X}_{j(n)})||_F^2 A_{ij}^B$$

$$= \sum_{i,j}^M Tr\big(\mathbf{U}^{(n)}(\mathbf{X}_{i(n)} - \mathbf{X}_{i(n)})(\mathbf{X}_{i(n)} - \mathbf{X}_{i(n)})^T \mathbf{U}^{(n)^T} A_{ij}^B\big) \tag{11}$$

$$= Tr\Big(\mathbf{U}^{(n)}\big(\sum_{i,j}^M (\mathbf{X}_{i(n)} - \mathbf{X}_{i(n)})(\mathbf{X}_{i(n)} - \mathbf{X}_{i(n)})^T A_{ij}^B\big)\mathbf{U}^{(n)^T}\Big)$$

According to the same matrix transformation, the denominator of the Eq. (10) can be the same form of above formula. In summary, the n- mode optimization problem can be transformed into the following form:

$$\mathbf{U}^{(n)} = \arg\max_{\mathbf{U}^{(n)}} \frac{Tr(\mathbf{U}^{(n)} S_B \mathbf{U}^{(n)^T})}{Tr(\mathbf{U}^{(n)} S_W \mathbf{U}^{(n)^T})} \tag{12}$$

where

$$S_B = \frac{1}{2} \sum_{i,j=1}^M (\mathbf{X}_{i(n)} - \mathbf{X}_{j(n)})(\mathbf{X}_{i(n)} - \mathbf{X}_{j(n)})^T A_{ij}^B$$

$$S_W = \frac{1}{2} \sum_{i,j=1}^M (\mathbf{X}_{i(n)} - \mathbf{X}_{j(n)})(\mathbf{X}_{i(n)} - \mathbf{X}_{j(n)})^T A_{ij}^W \tag{13}$$

According to the transformation, the problem can be solved in the same way as the traditional LDA algorithm.

3.4   Multilinear Dimensionality Reduction

As described above, the objective of MFLDA is to find the N projection matrices to make the following objective function optimal:

$$\mathbf{U}^{(n)} = \arg \max_{\{\mathbf{U}^{(n)}\}} \frac{\sum_{i,j}^{M} ||(\mathcal{X}_i - \mathcal{X}_j) \times_1 \mathbf{U}^{(1)} \cdots \times_N \mathbf{U}^{(N)}||_F^2 A_{ij}^B}{\sum_{i,j}^{M} ||(\mathcal{X}_i \times_1 - \mathcal{X}_j) \times_1 \mathbf{U}^{(1)} \cdots \times_N \mathbf{U}^{(N)}||_F^2 A_{ij}^W} \tag{14}$$

The molecular part of the objective function can be n- mode unfolded to:

$$\sum_{i,j} ||(\mathcal{X}_i - \mathcal{X}_j) \times_1 \mathbf{U}^{(1)} \cdots \times_N \mathbf{U}^{(N)}||_F^2 A_{ij}^B \Leftrightarrow \sum_{i,j} ||\mathbf{U}^{(n)}(\mathcal{X}_i - \mathcal{X}_j)\mathbf{U}_{\phi(n)}||_F^2 A_{ij}^B \tag{15}$$

where $\mathbf{U}_{\phi(n)} = (\mathbf{U}^{(N)} \otimes \cdots \otimes \mathbf{U}^{(n+1)} \otimes \mathbf{U}^{(n-1)} \otimes \cdots \otimes \mathbf{U}^{(1)})$. The above formula can be further simplified to:

$$\sum_{i,j} ||\mathbf{U}^{(n)}(\mathcal{X}_i - \mathcal{X}_j)\mathbf{U}_{\phi(n)}||_F^2 A_{ij}^B$$

$$= \sum_{i,j}^{M} Tr\left(\mathbf{U}^{(n)}(\mathbf{X}_{i(n)} - \mathbf{X}_{i(n)})\mathbf{U}_{\phi(n)}\mathbf{U}_{\phi(n)}^T(\mathbf{X}_{i(n)} - \mathbf{X}_{i(n)})^T \mathbf{U}^{(n)T} A_{ij}^B\right) \tag{16}$$

$$= Tr\left(\mathbf{U}^{(n)}\left(\sum_{i,j}^{M} (\mathbf{X}_{i(n)} - \mathbf{X}_{i(n)})\mathbf{U}_{\phi(n)}\mathbf{U}_{\phi(n)}^T(\mathbf{X}_{i(n)} - \mathbf{X}_{i(n)})^T A_{ij}^B\right)\mathbf{U}^{(n)T}\right)$$

Since the product $\mathbf{U}_{\phi(n)}\mathbf{U}_{\phi(n)}^T$ depends on the Kronecker product $\mathbf{U}^{(N)} \otimes \cdots \otimes \mathbf{U}^{(n+1)} \otimes \mathbf{U}^{(n-1)} \otimes \cdots \otimes \mathbf{U}^{(1)}$, the optimization of $\mathbf{U}^{(n)}$ has no closed solution. In this case, an iterative procedure can be utilized to solve the objective function optimization problem. In each iteration, the projection matrices $\mathbf{U}^{(N)}, \ldots, \mathbf{U}^{(n+1)}, \mathbf{U}^{(n-1)}, \ldots, \mathbf{U}^{(1)}$ are assumed known, then the objective function is changed to

$$\mathbf{U}^{(n)} = \arg \max_{\mathbf{U}^{(n)}} \frac{\sum_{i,j}^{M} ||\hat{\mathcal{Y}}_i \times_n \mathbf{U}^{(n)} - \hat{\mathcal{y}}_j \times_n \mathbf{U}^{(n)}||_F^2 A_{ij}^B}{\sum_{i,j}^{M} ||\hat{\mathcal{Y}}_i \times_n \mathbf{U}^{(n)} - \hat{\mathcal{y}}_j \times_n \mathbf{U}^{(n)}||_F^2 A_{ij}^W} \tag{17}$$

where $\hat{\mathcal{y}}_i = \mathcal{X}_i \times_1 \mathbf{U}^{(1)} \cdots \times_{n-1} \mathbf{U}^{(n-1)} \times_{n+1} \mathbf{U}^{(n+1)} \cdots \times_N \mathbf{U}^{(N)}$. The formula has the same formulation as the objective function in Sect. 3.3 by replacing $\mathcal{X}_i$ with $\hat{\mathcal{y}}_i$. In that case, objective function in each iteration can be solved using the above described n-mode optimization approach.

4   Experiments

In this section, experiments are performed on the ORL and FERET face database to compare our algorithm with the PCA, LPP, LFDA and MPCA, some popular linear methods for face recognition.

4.1   Face Database

ORL face database contains 400 images of 40 individuals. Those images have different variations in facial expressions such as open or closed eyes, smiling or unsmiling, and glasses or no glasses. Every image is in grayscaling and normalized to the resolution of 112×92 pixels.

The FERET face database is often used as a standard database for evaluating face recognition algorithms. The proposed method was tested on a subset of the FERET database. This subset includes 1400 images of 200 individuals. Each individual involves variations in facial expression, illumination, and pose. The images are cropped and resized to 40×40 pixels.

4.2   Experimental Settings and Result

Two sets of experiments were conducted to compare the performance of MLFDA with Eigenface(PCA), LPP, LFDA and MPCA. Each face database has one experiment. In each experiment, the image set was partitioned into the gallery and probe set with different numbers. Every set randomly chose the images for training and testing 20 times and calculate the average recognition results.

For ease of representation, the experiments are named as Train/Test. The Train means the number of images per person selected for training and the Test represent the quantity of testing samples. Furthermore, the basic parameters of the MLFDA algorithm are: the maximum number of iterations is 3, the affinity matrix W is determined by k nearest neighbors with $k = 5$ and the heat kernel function with $t = 1$. The results of the four experiments are shown in the following tables.

Table 1. The average recognition on ORL random face database

Train/Test	3/7	4/6	5/5	6/4
PCA	85.57 %	89.06 %	91.55 %	94.22 %
LPP	81.92 %	86.29 %	88.68 %	92.44 %
LFDA	48.52 %	67.85 %	77.88 %	82.78 %
MPCA	88.80 %	93.31 %	94.77 %	96.06 %
MLFDA	91.34 %	92.90 %	95.72 %	96.25 %

Table 1 shows the face recognition accuracies of all the algorithms in experiments of ORL database. The comparative results show that MLFDA have better performance than PCA, LPP, LFDA and MPCA on all four sets of experiments, especially in the cases with a small number of training samples. Table 2 shows the face recognition accuracies of all the algorithms in experiments of FERET database. In this experiment, it is obvious to see that MLFDA performs much better than the other methods.

Table 2. The average recognition on FERET random face database

Train/Test	2/5	3/4	4/3	5/2
PCA	32.15 %	40.29 %	43.18 %	46.04 %
LPP	37.44 %	42.34 %	51.28 %	55.66 %
LFDA	10.54 %	15.91 %	33.42 %	43.52 %
MPCA	26.84 %	33.44 %	40.02 %	41.46 %
MLFDA	42.17 %	52.76 %	62.28 %	67.22 %

5 Conclusions

In this paper, a novel algorithm, MLFDA, has been proposed for supervised dimensionality reduction. The algorithm works on tensor objects and determines a multilinear transformation to map the original tensor object into a low-dimension tensor subspace that maximize the local between-class scatter and at the same time minimize the local within-class scatter. Based on the MLFDA framework, an iterative algorithm used on computer programming was given to solve the problem of face recognition. Compared with the popular algorithms like PCA, LFDA and MPCA, the novel algorithm has a better performance on FERET and ORL face database. We think MLFDA is a useful algorithm and we are going to explore this application in our future researches.

Acknowledgments. This project is partly supported by NSF of China (61375001, 31200747), the Natural Science Foundation of Jiangsu Province (No. BK20140638, BK2012437), the Fundamental Research Funds for the Central Universities.

References

1. Yang, M.H., Ahuja, N., Kriegman, D.: Face recognition using kernel eigenfaces. In: International Conference on Image Processing, pp. 37–40. IEEE (2000)
2. Belhumeur, P.N., Hespanha, J.P., Kriengman, D.J.: Eigenfaces vs. Fisherfaces: recognition using class specific linear projection. IEEE Trans. Pattern Anal. Mach. Intell. **19**(7), 711–720 (1997)
3. He, X.: Locality preserving projections. Adv. Neural Inf. Process. Syst. **45**(1), 186–197 (2010)
4. Sugiyama, M.: Dimensionality reduction of multimodal labeled data by local fisher discriminant analysis. J. Mach. Learn. Res. **8**(1), 1027–1061 (2007)
5. Zhihui, L., Yong, X., Jian, Y., et al.: Sparse tensor discriminant analysis. IEEE Trans. Image Process. **22**(10), 3904–3915 (2013). A Publication of the IEEE Signal Processing Society
6. Yang, J., Zhang, D., Frangi, A.F., Yang, J.Y.: Two-dimensional PCA: a new approach to appearance-based face representation and recognition. IEEE Trans. Pattern Anal. Mach. Intell. **26**(1), 131–137 (2004)
7. Li, M., Yuan, B.: 2D-LDA: a statistical linear discriminant analysis for image matrix. Pattern Recogn. Lett. **26**(5), 527–532 (2005)

8. Chen, S., Zhao, H., Kong, M., et al.: 2D-LPP: a two-dimensional extension of locality preserving projections. Neurocomputing **70**(4), 912–921 (2007)
9. Boulgouris, N.V., Hatzinakos, D., Plataniotis, K.N.: Gait recognition: a challenging signal processing technology for biometric identification. IEEE Signal Process. Mag. **22**(6), 78–90 (2005)
10. Lu, H., Plataniotis, K.N., Venetsanopoulos, A.N.: MPCA: multilinear principal component analysis of tensor objects. IEEE Trans. Neural Netw. **19**(1), 18–39 (2010)
11. Lathauwer, L.D., Moor, B.D., Vandewalle, J.: On the best RANK-1 and RANK-(R 1, R 2, R N) approximation of higher-order tensors. SIAM J. Matrix Anal. Appl. **21**(4), 1324–1342 (2000)
12. Shuicheng, Y., Dong, X., Qiang, Y., et al.: Multilinear discriminant analysis for face recognition. IEEE Trans. Image Process. **16**(1), 212–220 (2007). A Publication of the IEEE Signal Processing Society
13. Zhang, D., Zhou, Z.H.: (2D)2PCA: two-directional two-dimensional PCA for efficient face representation and recognition. Neurocomputing **69**(1–3), 224–231 (2005)

Combining Multiple Features for Cross-Domain Face Sketch Recognition

Yang Liu[1], Jing Li[1(✉)], ZhaoYang Lu[1], Tao Yang[2], and ZiJian Liu[1]

[1] Insititute of Telecommunication, Xidian University, Xi'an, China
jinglixd@mail.xidian.edu.cn
[2] School of Computer Science, Northwestern Polytechnical University, Xi'an, China

Abstract. Cross-domain face sketch recognition plays an important role in biometrics research and industry. In this paper, we propose a novel algorithm combing an intra-modality method called the Eigentransformation and two inter-modality methods based on modality invariant features, namely the Multiscale Local Binary Pattern (MLBP) and the Histogram of Averaged Orientation Gradients (HAOG). Meanwhile, a sum-score fusion of min-max normalized scores is applied to fuse these recognition outputs. Experimental results on the CUFS (Chinese University of Hong Kong (CUHK) Face Sketch Database) and the CUFSF (CUHK Face Sketch FERET Database) datasets reveal that the intra-modality method and inter-modality methods provide complementary information and fusing of them yields better performance.

Keywords: Face sketch recognition · Intra-modality · Modality invariant features

1 Introduction

Face sketch recognition has attracted great attention due to its vital role in video surveillance, banking, security system access attention and law enforcement. For example, automatic retrieval of photos of suspects from mug-shot databases using a face sketch is potentially useful. It will not only help the police to narrow down potential suspects quickly, but also help the eyewitness and the artist to modify the face sketch drawing of the suspect based on similar images retrieved [1].

To date, various algorithms have been proposed in the literature to address the problem of face sketch recognition, which can be categorized into two general approaches: intra-modality and inter-modality approaches [1]. Intra-modality methods attempt to reduce the modality gap by transforming a photo (sketch) to a sketch (photo). Then, any kind of face recognition methods can be applied to match the synthesized pseudo-sketches (photos) with original sketches (photos). However, the performance of face sketch recognition is highly relied on the accuracy of photo (sketch) synthesis, which is more complicated than face recognition task itself. On the other hand, inter-modality methods perform face sketch recognition by extracting discriminative local features to compare sketches

© Springer International Publishing AG 2016
Z. You et al. (Eds.): CCBR 2016, LNCS 9967, pp. 139–146, 2016.
DOI: 10.1007/978-3-319-46654-5_16

with photos directly. However, most of these algorithms focus on either intra-modality methods or inter-modality methods. A limited number of algorithms consider fusing both intra-modality and inter-modality methods. A method in [2] combing Eigentransformation with Eigenpatches fused with an inter-modality algorithms called HAOG was proposed. It utilized only one modality invariant feature and the hair region of face images was excluded.

Inspired by [2], we propose a novel face sketch recognition algorithm combining an intra-modality method, namely Eigentransformation [3] with two inter-modality methods based on modality invariant features, namely Multiscale Local Binary Pattern (MLBP) [4] and Histogram of Averaged Orientation Gradients (HAOG) [1]. The main difference between ours and [2] is that we adopts two modality invariant features and PCA and LDA is used to achieve more discriminative feature vectors. In addition, we take hair region into consideration and evaluate our algorithm in two different databases.

The main contributions of this paper are summarized as follows:

(1) We employ two inter-modality discriminative descriptors which are invariant to the modality gap and fuse their outputs in an efficient way;
(2) PCA and LDA are adopted to achieve discriminative facial descriptors;
(3) We take hair region of face images into consideration, which is closer to practical face sketch recognition task.

The organization of the rest of this paper is as follows. Section 2 gives an overview of our proposed face sketch recognition system. Section 3 presents the intra-modality approach, namely the Eigentransformation. Section 4 presents two inter-modality descriptors and the fusion method. Section 5 shows the experimental results and analysis and the conclusion is in Sect. 6.

2   Proposed Method

The proposed approach combines the recognition scores output by three methods, namely the Eigentransformation [3], Multiscale Local Binary Pattern

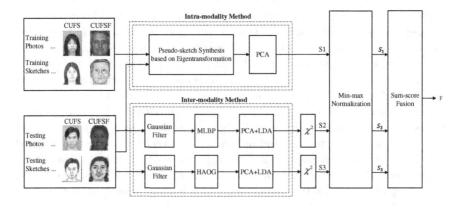

Fig. 1. Overview of the proposed face sketch recognition approach

(MLBP) [4] and Histogram of Averaged Orientation Gradients (HAOG) [1]. The overview of our proposed method is shown in Fig. 1.

Eigentransformation utilize a set of photo/sketch pairs from training set to synthesize a pseudo-sketch, while the MLBP method and HAOG method directly extracts the inter-modality features for each image in the testing set. The synthesized pseudo-sketches are matched to probe sketches using the PCA face recognition method while the Chi-Square (χ^2) histogram matching method is used to evaluate the distance between the MLBP or HAOG descriptors of probe sketches and those of the gallery photos. Finally, sum-score fusion of the min-max normalized scores is applied to obtain the resulting scores.

3 Intra-modality Method

In this section, we detail the intra-modality method based on Eigentransformation. The start point of Eigentransformation is to transform a face photo to a face sketch, so that recognition can be performed in the same modality.

3.1 Photo-to-Sketch Transformation

For the classic Eigentransformation method [3,5,6], a face photo can be reconstructed by a weighted summation of a set of eigenvectors U_p, as follows:

$$\boldsymbol{P_r} = U_p \boldsymbol{b_p} \tag{1}$$

where $\boldsymbol{P_r}$ is a column vector representing a sample face image and $\boldsymbol{b_p}$ is an Eigentransformation weight vector. As demonstrated in [3], (1) can be rewritten in summation form as follows:

$$\boldsymbol{P_r} = \bar{P} + \sum_{i=1}^{M} c_p^i (P^i - \bar{P}) \tag{2}$$

where $\bar{P}$ is the mean face computed over M face photos in the training set, the coefficient c_p^i describe the contribution weight of ith training face photo P^i in the reconstruction of a test face photo. Given the assumption that the structure between photos and sketches should be similar, we can modify (2) by replacing training face photos P^i with their corresponding training sketches S^i as follows:

$$\boldsymbol{S_r} = \bar{S} + \sum_{i=1}^{M} c_p^i (S^i - \bar{S}) \tag{3}$$

where $\boldsymbol{S_r}$ is the reconstructed pseudo-sketch, $\bar{S}$ is the mean sketch in the training set. Through such mapping, we can transform a face photo image into a pseudo-sketch.

3.2   Sketch Recognition

After photo-to-sketch transformation, sketch recognition becomes straightforward. We use PCA face recognizer [3] as its widespread use in intra-modality methods. Hence, the generated pseudo-sketches and the probe sketches are projected onto the eigensketch vectors, then the projection coefficients are then utilized as feature vectors for final classification [3]. Finally, the sketch is matched to the face photo with minimum value of distance.

4   Inter-modality Methods

An obvious limitation of intra-modality face recognition is that the performance is highly dependent on the results of photo-sketch synthesis [1]. Inspired by [1,4,7,8], we adopt two modality-invariant face descriptors, namely Multiscale Local Binary Pattern (MLBP) [4,7] and Histogram of Averaged Orientation Gradients (HAOG) [1]. The choice of the MLBP and HAOG feature descriptors was based on the reported success in face sketch recognition and through a quantitative evaluation of their ability to discriminate between subjects in photos and sketches [4].

4.1   Multiscale Local Binary Pattern (MLBP)

In previous works [7,9], LBP was introduced as face representation for face recognition. LBP has gained reputation as a powerful face texture descriptor showing excellent results in terms of accuracy and computational complexity in many empirical studies [9] but inefficient in case of heterogeneous faces. Therefore, MLBP is used in place of LBP in [4,7,10] by extending the LBP to describe the face image at multiple scales and combining the LBP descriptors computed with radius $r \in \{1, 3, 5, 7\}$ in one histogram. MLBP encodes not only microstructure but also macrostructure of face image patterns. Hence provides more complete image representation than LBP.

4.2   Histogram of Averaged Orientation Gradients (HAOG)

The HAOG [1] is proposed as a novel modality-invariant descriptor for face sketch recognition. HAOG is inspired by the fact that orientations of stronger gradients are more modality invariant than weaker gradients. The modality difference between face photos and face sketches can be reduced by emphasizing features extracted from stronger gradients. More details on the HAOG descriptors is provided in [1].

4.3   Score Level Fusion

Sum-score fusion of the min-max normalized scores method is adopted. The matching scores of Eigentransformation and two inter-modality methods are fused at the matching score level. The normalization of these scores is achieved by using min-max normalization [11]:

$$\hat{S} = \frac{S - S_{min}}{S_{max} - S_{min}} \tag{4}$$

where S is a vector of dimension M containing the scores output by a face sketch recognition algorithm, $\hat{S}$ contains the corresponding normalized scores, and S_{min} and S_{max} represent the minimum and maximum values of s.

The sum-score method is then utilized to fuse the normalized scores together:

$$F = \sum_{k=1}^{N} \hat{s_k} \tag{5}$$

where $\hat{s_k}$ is the score of kth face sketch recognition method, N represents the number of intra- and inter- modality methods considered, and F is the final similarity score [11].

5   Experiments

In this section, we evaluate the performance of our proposed method on two representative databases.

The CUHK Face Sketch Database (CUFS) [12]: We use 88 photo-sketch pairs as training set and the other 100 photo-sketch pairs for testing. For the inter-modality methods, only testing set is used and the images are divided into over-lapped patches of 32 × 32 with 16 pixels of horizontal and vertical intersection.

The CUHK Face Sketch FERET Database (CUFSF) [13]: We use 500 photo-sketch pairs as training set and the other 694 photo-sketch pairs for testing. For the inter-modality methods, only testing set is used and the images are divided into overlapped patches of 16 × 16 with 8 pixels of horizontal and vertical intersection.

For our proposed method, the most time-consuming part lies in the χ^2 distance calculation phase and the feature extraction phase. As the photo size in two datasets is different, the time consumption also varies. It takes about 171 s for distance calculation and 2.225 s for feature extraction in CUFS dataset, while in CUFSF dataset, it takes about 0.176 s and 643.468 s respectively.

In the first experiment, we evaluate the performance of various descriptors in face sketch recognition: SIFT and MLBP used in [14]; HAOG proposed in [1]; LRBP proposed in [10]; LBP used in [7,9]. In Fig. 2, the results of comparing all the descriptors in the CUFSF database are shown. As we can see, HAOG out-performs other descriptors while LBP has the worst performance. To be noticed, MLBP yields noticeable improvements by extending the LBP to multiple scales and performs better than SIFT, LRBP and LBP. Even in cases the performance of MLBP is less than HAOG, the difference is only marginal, which indicates that MLBP is also a good modality invariant feature in heterogeneous face sketch recognition like HAOG. In the second experiment, we evaluate the performance

Table 1. Cumulative match scores for the methods evaluated on the CUFS dataset. E = Eigentransformation, M = MLBP, H = HAOG

Rank	1	2	3	4	5	6	7	8	9	10
E	0.70	0.78	0.82	0.87	0.87	0.89	0.89	0.91	0.92	0.94
M	0.84	0.90	0.92	0.93	0.95	0.97	0.97	0.97	0.97	0.97
H	0.97	0.99	1	1	1	1	1	1	1	1
E+M	0.99	0.99	0.99	0.99	0.99	0.99	0.99	0.99	0.99	1
E+H	0.99	0.99	0.99	0.99	0.99	0.99	1	1	1	1
M+H	0.98	1	1	1	1	1	1	1	1	1
Proposed	1	1	1	1	1	1	1	1	1	1

Table 2. Cumulative match scores for the methods evaluated on the CUFSF dataset. E = Eigentransformation, M = MLBP, H = HAOG

Rank	1	5	10	20	30	40	50	100	150	200
E	0.08	0.21	0.29	0.37	0.43	0.49	0.55	0.71	0.79	0.86
M	0.14	0.29	0.38	0.47	0.53	0.57	0.61	0.73	0.80	0.85
H	0.15	0.32	0.41	0.50	0.55	0.59	0.63	0.76	0.82	0.88
E+M	0.17	0.34	0.44	0.55	0.63	0.69	0.73	0.84	0.89	0.93
E+H	0.20	0.40	0.50	0.61	0.67	0.73	0.76	0.86	0.90	0.93
M+H	0.20	0.37	0.45	0.54	0.58	0.62	0.65	0.79	0.84	0.89
Proposed	**0.21**	**0.42**	**0.51**	**0.61**	**0.68**	**0.74**	**0.77**	**0.86**	**0.91**	**0.94**

of the intra-modality method, inter-modality methods, their arbitrary combinations and our proposed method. In Tables 1 and 2, we show the cumulative match scores of the methods discussed above in the CUFS and CUFSF databases. Both the MLBP and HAOG outperform the Eigentransformation method across all ranks, which indicates that these two cross-modality invariant descriptors are more effective in addressing the problem of modality gap than the Eigentransformation approach. The combination of any two algorithms performs better than these algorithms independently, which shows the effectiveness in improving the matching performance by the fusion of these methods.

From Table 1, it is noticed that our proposed method yields the best performance and achieve retrieval rates of 100 % at Rank 1. In Table 2, our proposed method also performs the best on CUFSF database although it merely achieves marginal performance improvement compared with E+H, which not only demonstrates that Eigentransformation, MLBP and HAOG contain complementary information to improve face-sketch matching accuracies, but also the combination of intra- and inter-modality algorithms may be an ideal approach for face sketch recognition rather than using either intra- or inter-modality approaches.

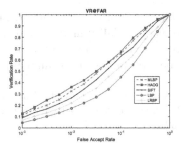

Fig. 2. Comparison between the descriptors using Chi-Square distance on CUFSF database. The figure displays the ROC curve (horizontal axis is in log scale). VR@FAR: Verification Rate versus False Accept Rate

From Fig. 3, we show the comparison of these methods in a more intuitive way. As the CUFS dataset is relatively easy for state-of-the-art methods including MLBP and HAOG to achieve high accuracies, our proposed method cannot have evident performance improvement. Nevertheless, our proposed method can achieve matching rates of 100 % at Rank 1 which verifies our methods effectiveness to some extent. As the photos and sketches in CUFSF involve lighting variations and shape exaggerations, the performance of face recognition degrades. In CUFSF, our proposed method yields noticeable improvements at most ranks compared with these methods independently, which verifies that our proposed method is effective in improving the face sketch recognition performance by combining intra- and inter-modality methods at matching score level.

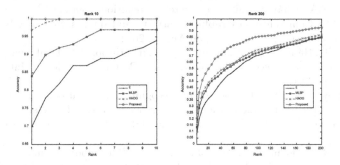

Fig. 3. Comparison of results on CUFS (left) and CUFSF (right) database. E= Eigentransformation

6   Conclusion

We proposed a new approach for face sketch recognition based on the combination of Eigentransformation, MLBP and HAOG algorithms. Experiments on the CUFS and CUFSF databases show that our proposed method yields the best performance among all the algorithms evaluated in this paper. This indicates that not only do the intra-modality method and the inter-modality methods considered in this paper provide complementary information, but also their combination provides the best performance for matching sketches with photos.

Acknowledgments. This work is supported by the National Natural Science Foundation of China (No.61502364 No.61272288), ShenZhen Science and Technology Foundation (JCYJ20160229172932237).

References

1. Galoogahi, H.K., Sim, T.: Inter-modality face sketch recognition. In: Proceedings of the 2012 IEEE International Conference on Multimedia and Expo, ICME 2012, Melbourne, Australia, pp. 224–229, 9–13 July 2012
2. Galea, C., Farrugia, R.A.: Fusion of intra- and inter-modality algorithms for face-sketch recognition. In: Azzopardi, G., Petkov, N. (eds.) CAIP 2015. LNCS, vol. 9257, pp. 700–711. Springer, Heidelberg (2015). doi:10.1007/978-3-319-23117-4_60
3. Tang, X., Wang, X.: Face sketch recognition. IEEE Trans. Circ. Syst. Video Technol. **14**(1), 50–57 (2004)
4. Klare, B., Li, Z., Jain, A.K.: Matching forensic sketches to mug shot photos. IEEE Trans. Pattern Anal. Mach. Intell. **33**(3), 639–646 (2011)
5. Tang, X., Wang, X.: Face sketch synthesis and recognition. In: 9th IEEE International Conference on Computer Vision (ICCV 2003), Nice, France, pp. 687–694, 14–17 October 2003
6. Tang, X., Wang, X.: Face photo recognition using sketch. ICIP **1**, 257–260 (2002)
7. Chan, C.-H., Kittler, J., Messer, K.: Multi-scale local binary pattern histograms for face recognition. In: Lee, S.-W., Li, S.Z. (eds.) ICB 2007. LNCS, vol. 4642, pp. 809–818. Springer, Heidelberg (2007). doi:10.1007/978-3-540-74549-5_85
8. Silva, M.A.A., Chávez, G.C.: Face sketch recognition from local features. In: 27th SIBGRAPI Conference on Graphics, Patterns and Images, SIBGRAPI 2014, Rio de Janeiro, Brazil, pp. 57–64, 27–30 August 2014
9. Ahonen, T., Hadid, A., Pietikäinen, M.: Face description with local binary patterns: application to face recognition. IEEE Trans. Pattern Anal. Mach. Intell. **28**(12), 2037–2041 (2006)
10. Galoogahi, H.K., Sim, T.: Face sketch recognition by local radon binary pattern: LRBP. In: 19th IEEE International Conference on Image Processing, ICIP 2012, Lake Buena Vista, Orlando, FL, USA, pp. 1837–1840, September 30–October 3, 2012
11. Snelick, R., Indovina, M., Yen, J., Mink, A.: Multimodal biometrics: issues in design and testing. In: Proceedings of the 5th International Conference on Multimodal Interfaces, ICMI 2003, Vancouver, British Columbia, Canada, pp. 68–72, 5–7 November 2003
12. Wang, X., Tang, X.: Face photo-sketch synthesis and recognition. IEEE Trans. Pattern Anal. Mach. Intell. **31**(11), 1955–1967 (2009)
13. Zhang, W., Wang, X., Tang, X.: Coupled information-theoretic encoding for face photo-sketch recognition. In: The 24th IEEE Conference on Computer Vision and Pattern Recognition, CVPR 2011, Colorado Springs, CO, USA, pp. 513–520, 20–25 June 2011
14. Klare, B., Jain, A.K.: Heterogeneous face recognition using kernel prototype similarities. IEEE Trans. Pattern Anal. Mach. Intell. **35**(6), 1410–1422 (2013)

Recent Advances on Cross-Domain Face Recognition

Xiaoxiang Liu[1,2,3(✉)], Xiaobo Sun[1], Ran He[2,3,4], and Tieniu Tan[2,3,4]

[1] School of Automation, Harbin University of Science and Technology,
Harbin 150080, China
xiaoxiang.liu@cripac.ia.ac.cn
[2] Center for Research on Intelligent Perception and Computing,
Institute of Automation, Chinese Academy of Sciences, Beijing 100190, China
13845092768@163.com
[3] CAS Center for Excellent in Brain Science and Intelligence Technology,
Chinese Academy of Sciences, Beijing 100190, China
[4] University of Chinese Academy of Sciences, Beijing 100049, China
{rhe,tnt}@nlpr.ia.ac.cn

Abstract. Face recognition is a significant and pervasively applied computer vision task. With the specific application scenarios being explored gradually, general face recognition methods dealing with visible light images are unqualified. Cross-domain face recognition refers to a series of methods in response to face recognition problems whose inputs may come from multiple modalities, such as visible light images, sketch, near infrared images, 3D data, low-resolution images, thermal infrared images, or cross different ages, expressions, and ethnicities. Compared with general face recognition, cross-domain face recognition has not been widely explored and only few literatures systematically discuss this topic. Face recognition aiming at matching face images from photographs and other image modalities, which is usually called heterogeneous face recognition, has larger cross-domain gap and is a harder problem in this topic. This paper mainly investigates heterogeneous face databases, provides an up-to-date review of research efforts, and addresses common problems and related issues in cross-domain face recognition techniques.

Keywords: Cross-domain · Heterogeneous · Face recognition · Survey

1 Introduction

When appearing before a camera, the automated face recognition system can accurately tell who you are, which makes our society move further towards intellectualization. The rapid increase of requirements in different application scenarios, like public security, financial domain, personal safety, and etc., brings big challenges to face recognition. With the development of imaging techniques, the acquirement of image data becomes easier and face images can be collected from kinds of sources, resulting in the emergence of some researches on cross-domain

© Springer International Publishing AG 2016
Z. You et al. (Eds.): CCBR 2016, LNCS 9967, pp. 147–157, 2016.
DOI: 10.1007/978-3-319-46654-5_17

face recognition. We mainly discuss some of the heterogeneous face recognition tasks in this paper, since they are more difficult cross-domain problems: sketches is often used to match a suspect for forensic use; near infrared face images can help eliminate the impact of ambient light; 3D images can model real three dimensional face structures, and capture the surface shape; thermal infrared face images recognition is not very mature but of huge potential which can also be used in medical treatment; low resolution recognition is useful for identifying a person in surveillance video.

Different statistical distribution of face images in kinds of domains makes traditional methods simply computing the distance between the features of two face images invalid. The cross-domain gap from the intra-class distance is bigger than that from inter-class distance. If features of different modalities are pull closer to each other compulsively, the data space will become misshapen and thus cause the over-fitting problem. There are often three ideas to alleviate the cross-modality differences throughout the related literatures: exploring invariant face representation by designing universal face features; synchronizing other modalities based on a corresponding modality; projecting images in multiple domains to a common subspace based on some subspace learning methods. Due to the differences in imaging techniques, the recognition methods are specific in detail for different heterogeneous face recognition tasks. The following parts of this paper will introduce the existing heterogeneous face databases which contain both visible light images (VIS) and face images from other modalities in Sect. 2, list and summarize established heterogeneous face recognition methods in Sect. 3, compare and analyze the experimental results in Sect. 4, and discuss some challenging problems and future research direction in Sect. 5.

Fig. 1. Heterogeneous face image pairs. The images in the first row are sketch, near infrared image, thermal infrared image, 3D image and low resolution image respectively and the second row shows the corresponding visible light face images.

2   Database

Heterogeneous face image databases provide intuitional experience and first-hand information for heterogeneous face recognition system. These heterogeneous face databases are used for normal research and as standard test data sets. The general situation is that the images collected in these databases are small-scale, due to that special and professional imaging equipment or manual work are needed.

2.1 Sketch-VIS Face Database

Sketch database is originally used for the research of criminal investigations. However, real forensic sketch is hard to collect and the number of sketch is limited. To create more images for research, there are often four kinds of sketch databases: forensic sketch database, sketches are drawn by artists according to the description of eyewitnesses based on their recollection of the suspects; viewed sketch database, sketches are drawn by artists viewing the corresponding digital photos; semi-forensic sketch database, facial sketches are drawn based on the memory of sketch artists rather than the description of eyewitnesses; composite sketch database, the sketches are composited with candidate facial components using soft kits. The composite sketches are more affordable and easy-acquired than forensic sketches.

- CUHK Face Sketch Database (CUFS) [viewed]
  CUFS includes a total of 606 frontal view faces and the corresponding sketches drawn by artists. The face images are collected under normal lighting condition and with a neutral expression.
- CUHK Face Sketch FERET Database (CUFSF) [viewed]
  CUFSF includes 1,194 photo-sketch pairs in total, being the biggest available sketch database. The photos are from 1194 persons from the FERET database with lighting variations, and the sketches are drawn by artists when viewing the photos with shape exaggeration.
- IIIT-Delhi Semi-forensic Sketch Database [semi-forensic]
  Totally, 140 photos in III-D Viewed Sketch Database are used to compose the semi-forensic sketch database.
- Forensic Sketch Database [forensic]
  This database is collected by Image Analysis and Biometrics Lab. It contains 190 forensic sketch-digital image pairs.
- PRIP-VSGC Database [composite]
  The PRIP-VSGC Database is a software-generated sketch database. There are 123 subjects from the AR database, each with one digital image and 3 composite images using two different kits.

2.2 NIR-VIS Face Database

Owing to the intensity of the near infrared light (NIR) is stronger than visible light, the gray values of face images collected under near infrared lights are only relevant to the distances between objects and the near infrared light sources, which is an excellent characteristic for face recognition.

- CASIA HFB Database
  This database collects face images from 3 modalities: visual, near infrared and three-dimensional (3D) face images. 57 females, and 43 males are included and each has 4 VIS and 4 NIR face images.
- CASIA NIR-VIS 2.0 Database
  It is the existing biggest NIR-VIS database, which consists of NIR and VIS images from 725 subjects in total, each with 1–22 VIS and 5–50 NIR face images. Two views are developed to report unbiased performance. This database also has standard protocols for performance evaluation and reporting.

2.3   Thermal-VIS Face Database

Thermal infrared images are taken under thermal infrared imagery systems and are generated due to the specific heat pattern of each individual. The characteristic of not relying on ambient light helps lower the intra-class variability and contributes to improve the recognition rate. Thermal infrared images can be captured in night environments and are very useful for crime investigation.

- IRIS Thermal/Visible Face Database (OTCBVS Benchmark Dataset Collection)
  This database contains both thermal and visible face images and includes pose, expression and illumination variations. There are 30 identities in the database and 4228 pairs of thermal/visible face images are generated.
- Natural Visible and Infrared Facial Expression Database(NVIE Database)
  The NVIE database collectes images recorded simultaneously by a visible and thermal infrared camera from more than 100 subjects. Expression, illumination and wearing glasses variations are included.
- PUCV- Visible Thermal-Face (VTF) Database
  A total of 12160 images in both visible and thermal spectra from 76 individuals are collected in the PUCV-VTF database. Images from two modalities are acquired simultaneously. There are variations in wearing glasses and facial expressions such as frown, smile, and vowel.
- Other Thermal Face Recognition Database
  The database collected in [4] has 385 participants and different collecting sessions. Wilder et al. [5] acquire a 101 subjects thermal database. A co-registered visual and LWIR images of 3244 face images from 90 individuals are collected by the Equinox Company [6]. A database simultaneously acquired in visible, near-infrared and thermal spectrums is published in [7] which can undergo the research on multiple modalities and get more general perspective on face recognition.

2.4   3D-2D Face Database

Besides can be captured in different spectral bands, faces can also be recorded as measurements of 3D facial shape. The 3D face data has good performance when dealing with illumination and pose variations.

- UHDB11 Database
  The UHDB11 database is collected for 3D-2D face recognition and consists of samples from 23 individuals. This database is generated with different illumination conditions and head poses, and is very challenging companying with the 3D-2D variations.
- Texas 3D Face Recognition Database (Texas 3DFRD)
  This database is a collection of 1149 pairs of facial color and range images of 105 human subjects with high resolution. The images pairs are captured simultaneously. Besides, facial points are located in both 2D and 3D images manually which can help face recognition.
- FRGCv2.0 database
  The FRGCv2.0 database is the biggest 3D-2D face database to the best of my knowledge which consists of 4007 3D-2D face image pairs from 466 individuals and includes pose and expression variations.

3   Methods

3.1   Sketch-VIS Face Recognition

To address the sketch recognition problem, researchers propose photo/sketch synthesis method. It is the earliest proposed method, and once images from different modalities are synthesized into the same modality, traditional face recognition methods can be used. The whole trends for face synthesis methods are: the approximation relation of two modalities is from linear [8], locally linear [9], to nonlinear [1]; the concerned object is from basic pixels [10] to their statistical distribution with subspace method [11]. Linear approximate methods apply transformation globally and may not work well if the hair region is included. Thus patch-based methods are proposed to simulate the nonlinear projection but ignore the spatial relationship of patches. To reduce the blurring and aliasing effects, embedded hidden Markov model are applied into the theme which can approximate the nonlinear relationship well and achieve better performance. Since the synthesis task is more complicate than recognition, some researchers study another method for heterogeneous face recognition omitting the synthesis procedure. Such methods aim to project two image modalities on to an intermediate modality and conduct recognition in the common subspace [12]. Another breakthrough in heterogeneous face recognition methods is on the feature extraction stage, and the key point lies in finding the modality-invariable features [2]. The acquired near infrared face image and sketch share much similarities with normal visible face images intuitively though they are different at pixel-level, and the data is both two dimensional, so some methods are applicable for both sketch and near infrared face recognition and in fact some articles do experiments in these two modalities with their proposed methods.

3.2   NIR-VIS Face Recognition

Near infrared face images are mainly to deal with the illumination variations [38]. Due to the distinction of imagery technology, the data distribution of NIR and

VIS face images in high dimensional space are inconsistency. Thus general face recognition methods are not suitable. The three common methods for heterogeneous face recognition are applied in NIR and VIS domain as follows: in the work of [9,33], synthesis based methods are employed to transform one face modality to the other. Tang et al. [33] propose an Eigen-transformation method while Liu et al. [9] reconstruct image patches using LLE. A recent work done by Felix et al. [39] proposes a ℓ_0-Dictionary based approach to reconstruct the corresponding image modalities and acquires good performance; the common subspace methods are used respectively in [31,34] by employing LDA and TCA (transfer component analysis) respectively; modal-invariant features are often based on SIFT or LBP. The development of deep learning driving the heterogeneous face recognition algorithm further. Some unsupervised deep learning methods are used in this topic: J. Ngiam et al. [30] propose a Bimodal Deep AE method based on denoising auto encoder; To exert the potential effects of all layers, a multi-modal DBM approach is suggested by [32]; a RBM method combined with removed PCA features is proposed in the work of [35]. With these methods, the matching accuracies of heterogeneous face images are improved gradually, but still far below than the state-of-the-art VIS face recognition rates. Recently, a unified CNN framework is proposed in the study of [29], which integrates the deep representation transferring and the triplet loss to get consolidated feature representations for face images in two modalities. It alleviates the over-fitting problem for CNNs on small-scale datasets, and achieves great performance on the existing publicly available biggest CASIA 2.0 NIR-VIS Face Database.

3.3   Thermal-VIS Face Recognition

Different with visible imaging receiving the reflected lights, the thermal images are acquired by receiving the emitted radiation, thus causing a large cross-modal gap [16]. The emitted radiation is affected by many factors, and usually time-lapse, physical exercise and mental tasks are considered, which makes the recognition tasks even more challenging. There are already some studies on the within-domain thermal infrared face image recognition, but few addressed on the cross-modal thermal-visible face recognition. The first work on thermal to visible face recognition is done by [13], which resorts to a partial least squares-discriminant analysis (PLS-DA) method; A MWIR-to-visible face recognition system which consists of preprocessing, feature extraction (HOG, SIFT, LBP), and similarity matching is proposed by [14]; Klare and Jain [15] propose a nonlinear kernel prototype representation method for both thermal and visible light images and use LDA to improve the discriminative capabilities of the prototype representations; The authors of [13] improve their methods by incorporating multi-modal information into the PLS model building stage, and design different preprocessing and feature extraction stages to reduce the modality gap [16]; Recently, a graphical representation method which employs Markov networks and considers the spatial compatibility between neighboring image patches is proposed by [17], and the method achieves excellent performance on multiple heterogeneous face modalities including the thermal-visible scenario.

3.4   3D-2D Face Recognition

3D images are robust to illumination and pose variations compared to 2D images. The face recognition based on 3D dada is more accurate than visible light images and more practical than 3D-3D. Early work focus more on 3d-aided face recognition or 3D images reconstruction and little work explore the cross-modal 3D-2D face recognition. Partial Principle Component Analysis based method is used in [18] to extract features in two modalities and reduce the feature dimension. Kernel Canonical Correlation Analysis (CCA) is employed in [20] to maximize the feature correlation between patches in 2D texture images and 3D depth images. A fusion scheme based on Partial Least Square (PLS) and CCA is suggested in [21] to further improve the performance by learning the correlation mapping between 2D-3D. In the work of Riccio et al. [19], they propose to calculate the geometrical invariants based on several control points where locating the fiducial points accurately in both 2D and 3D modalities is also a challenging problem. Di Huang et al. [9] present a new biological vision-based facial description method, namely Oriented Gradient Maps (OGMs) which can simulate the response of complex neuron to gradient information in a pre-defined neighborhood and hence describe local texture changes of 2D faces and local shape variations of 3D face models. Recently, a 3D-2D face recognition framework is proposed in [23]. They use a bidirectional relighting method for non-linear, local illumination normalization and a global orientation-based correlation metric for pairwise similarity scoring, which can generalize well for diverse illumination conditions.

3.5   High-Low Resolution Face Recognition

The HR-LR face recognition is mainly used in video surveillance scenario where the face images acquired in surveillance pictures are usually of very low resolution. To match the detected faces with the enrolled face images of high resolution, a large cross-modal gap should be bridged. Existing related investigates try to improve the recognition rate of a LR image by reconstructing HR face, but the matching between faces in these two modalities are less studied. Since the reconstruction can help asymmetric face recognition, this paper will introduce some super resolution reconstruction (SR) algorithm. Usually two classes of methods are used in this topic [24]: multi-frames SR retrieving high-frequency details from a set of images, and single-frame SR inferring the HR counterpart of a single image based on extra information from the training samples. Specific to the topic of heterogeneous HR-LR face recognition, the subspace projection based method which is efficient to the similarity measure between different resolutions plays an important role, such as [25,26]. A recent study done by [27] proposes a local optimization based coupled mappings algorithm and constrains the LR/HR consistency, intraclass compactness and interclass separability. The newest work up to now is proposed in [28] which employs a coupled kernel-based enhanced discriminant analysis (CKEDA) method to maximize the discrimination property of the projected common space. This work is demonstrated effectiveness on a public face database and the LR face images are acquired by downsampling as other HR/LR face experiments set.

4 Results

To evaluate the recognition performance of heterogeneous face recognition, usually rank-1 recognition rate and verification rate at certain false accept rate are computed. As there are too many possible factors affecting the final results, different methods are not comparable if their experiments are employed on distinct datasets or with diverse experimental protocols. Sketch and near infrared face images are studied early and extensively, so there are some widely used datasets and standard protocols and related recognition results are listed in Tables 1 and 2. The recognition rate of sketch-VIS faces achieves a level of nearly 100 percent on CUFS database, but there are still promotion spaces for real world forensic sketch recognition. The highest rank-1 recognition rate and verification rate on the existing publicly available biggest NIR-VIS database, CASIA 2.0 NIR-VIS Face Database, are achieved by [29] as shown in Table 2. As for other above mentioned domains, transverse comparison is hard for the non-unified experimental settings. There is a trend that patch based methods are better than global based methods, non-linear based methods are better than linear based methods and usually the combination of related methods may generate higher accuracy.

Table 1. Rank1 recognition rates and VR@FAR=0.1 % of various methods on CUFS [19].

	Rank-1 Accuracy	VR@FAR=0.1 %
Gabor [35]	$99.50 \pm 0.39\%$	$94.70 \pm 1.2\%$
Gabor+Remove 20 PCs [35]	$100 \pm 0\%$	$100 \pm 0\%$
MRF+RS-LDA [1]	96.30 %	N/A
LFDA [37]	99.47 %	N/A
CITE [2]	99.87 %	N/A

Table 2. Rank1 recognition rates and VR@FAR=0.1 % of various methods on CASIA 2.0 NIR-VIS Face Databse [29].

	Rank-1 Accuracy	VR@FAR=0.1 %
PCA+Sym+HCA [3]	$23.70 \pm 1.89\%$	19.27 %
DSIFT+LDA [36]	$73.28 \pm 1.10\%$	N/A
Gabor + RBM + Remove 11 PCs [35]	$86.16 \pm 0.98\%$	$81.29 \pm 1.82\%$
NIR-VIS Reconstruction + UDP (DLBP) [39]	$78.46 \pm 1.67\%$	85.80 %
TRIVET [29]	$95.74 \pm 0.52\%$	$91.03 \pm 1.26\%$

5 Discussion

A good face recognition algorithm should have the power to deal with face images coming from different image sources or even different modalities, and is general adaptive for different scenes. Due to different characteristics for heterogeneous modalities or scenes, most existing algorithms have to deal with different data respectively though few methods try to deal with two or three modalities. However, humans can recognize an identity quickly no matter in sketch, near infrared image or long-distance monitoring scene. Neurologists and psychologists have been studying this phenomenon, and they want to find the recognition mechanism for face images having a low correlation with the phenomenological information. Specific to the problem of limited data, long life learning might be the future solution which can learn with one or two inputs even without labels and remember the knowledge learned before. The challenges in live detection would find their solutions if two or more modalities can be combined and well fused for recognition, which is deserved to study further.

Acknowledgments. This work is supported by the Youth Innovation Promotion Association of the Chinese Academy of Sciences (CAS) (Grant No. 2015190), the National Natural Science Foundation of China (Grant No. 61473289) and the Strategic Priority Research Program of the Chinese Academy of Sciences (Grant No. XDB02070000).

References

1. Wang, X., Tang, X.: Face photo-sketch synthesis and recognition. IEEE Trans. Pattern Anal. Mach. Intell. **31**(11), 1955–1967 (2009)
2. Zhang, W., Wang, X., Tang, X.: Coupled information-theoretic encoding for face photo-sketch recognition. In: IEEE Conference on Computer Vision and Pattern Recognition, pp. 513–520 (2011)
3. Li, S., Yi, D., Lei, Z., et al.: The casia nir-vis 2.0 face database. In: IEEE Conference on Computer Vision and Pattern Recognition Workshops (2013)
4. Socolinsky, D.A., Selinger, A.: Thermal face recognition in an operational scenario. In: IEEE Computer Society Conference on Computer Vision and Pattern Recognition, vol. 2, pp. II-1012–II-1019 (2004)
5. Kevin, X., Bowyer, W.: Visible-light, infrared face recognition. In: Workshop on Multimodal User Authentication, p. 48 (2003)
6. Socolinsky, D.A., Selinger, A.: A comparative analysis of face recognition performance with visible and thermal infrared imagery. Equinox Corp., Baltimore (2002)
7. Espinosa-Dur, V., Faundez-Zanuy, M., Mekyska, J.: A new face database simultaneously acquired in visible, near-infrared and thermal spectrums. Cogn. Comput. **5**(1), 119–135 (2013)
8. Tang, X., Wang, X.: Face photo recognition using sketch. In: IEEE International Conference on Image Processing, pp. I-257–I-260 (2002)
9. Liu, Q., Tang, X., Jin, H., et al.: A nonlinear approach for face sketch synthesis and recognition. In: IEEE Computer Society Conference on Computer Vision and Pattern Recognition, vol. 1, pp. 1005–1010 (2005)

10. Uhl Jr., R.G., Lobo, N.D.V., Kwon, Y.H.: Recognizing a facial image from a police sketch. In: IEEE Conference on Applications of Computer Vision Workshop, pp. 129–137 (1994)
11. Li, Y., Savvides, M., Bhagavatula, V.: Illumination tolerant face recognition using a novel facefrom sketch synthesis approach and advanced correlation filters. In: IEEE Conference on Acoustics, Speech, and Signal Processing, pp. 357–360 (2006)
12. Lei, Z., Liao, S., Jain, A.K., et al.: Coupled discriminant analysis for heterogeneous face recognition. IEEE Trans. Inf. Forensics Secur. **7**(6), 1707–1716 (2012)
13. Choi, J., Hu, S., Young, S.S., et al.: Thermal to visible face recognition. In: SPIE Defense, Security, Sensing. International Society for Optics, Photonics, pp. 83711L–83711L-10 (2012)
14. Bourlai, T., Ross, A., Chen, C., et al.: A study on using mid-wave infrared images for face recognition. In: SPIE Defense, Security, and Sensing. International Society for Optics and Photonics, pp. 83711K–83711K-13 (2012)
15. Klare, B.F., Jain, A.K.: Heterogeneous face recognition using kernel prototype similarities. IEEE Trans. Pattern Anal. Mach. Intell. **35**(6), 1410–1422 (2013)
16. Hu, S., Choi, J., Chan, A.L., et al.: Thermal-to-visible face recognition using partial least squares. JOSA A **32**(3), 431–442 (2015)
17. Peng, C., Gao, X., Wang, N., et al.: Graphical Representation for Heterogeneous Face Recognition. arXiv preprint arXiv:1503.00488 (2015)
18. Rama, A., Tarres, F., Onofrio, D., et al.: Mixed 2D-3D Information for pose estimation and facerecognition. In: IEEE Conference on Acoustics, Speech and Signal Processing, vol. 2, pp. II-211–II-217 (2006)
19. Riccio, D., Dugelay, J.L.: Geometric invariants for 2D/3D face recognition. Pattern Recogn. Lett. **28**(14), 1907–1914 (2007)
20. Yang, W., Yi, D., Lei, Z., et al.: 2D3D face matching using CCA. In: IEEE Conference on Automatic Face & Gesture Recognition, pp. 1–6 (2008)
21. Wang, X., Ly, V., Guo, G., et al.: A new approach for 2d-3d heterogeneous face recognition. In: IEEE International Symposium on Multimedia, pp. 301–304 (2013)
22. Huang, D., Ardabilian, M., Wang, Y., et al.: Oriented gradient maps based automatic asymmetric 3D-2D face recognition. In: International Conference on Biometrics, pp. 125–131 (2012)
23. Kakadiaris, I.A., Toderici, G., Evangelopoulos, G., et al.: 3D-2D face recognition with pose and illumination normalization. Comput. Vis. Image Underst. (2016)
24. Zhang, Q., Zhou, F., Yang, F., et al.: Face super-resolution via semi-kernel partial least squares and dictionaries coding. In: IEEE Conference on Digital Signal Processing, pp. 590–594 (2015)
25. Li, B., Chang, H., Shan, S., et al.: Low-resolution face recognition via coupled locality preserving mappings. IEEE Sig. Process. Lett. **17**(1), 20–23 (2010)
26. Biswas, S., Bowyer, K.W., Flynn, P.J.: Multidimensional scaling for matching low-resolution face images. IEEE Trans. Pattern Anal. Mach. Intell. **34**(10), 2019–2030 (2012)
27. Shi, J., Qi, C.: From local geometry to global structure: learning latent subspace for low-resolution face image recognition. IEEE Sig. Process. Lett. **22**(5), 554–558 (2015)
28. Wang, X., Hu, H., Gu, J.: Pose robust low-resolution face recognition via coupled kernel-based enhanced discriminant analysis. IEEE/CAA J. Autom. Sin. **3**(2), 203–212 (2016)
29. Liu, X., Song, L., Wu, X., Tan, T.: Transferring deep representation for NIR-VIS heterogeneous face recognition. In: International Conference on Biometrics (2016)

30. Ngiam, J., Khosla, A., Kim, M., et al.: Multimodal deep learning. In: International Conference on Machine Learning, pp. 689–696 (2011)
31. Pan, S.J., Tsang, I.W., Kwok, J.T., et al.: Domain adaptation via transfer component analysis. IEEE Trans. Neural Netw. **22**(2), 199–210 (2011)
32. Srivastava, N., Salakhutdinov, R.R.: Multimodal learning with deep boltzmann machines. In: Advances in Neural Information Processing Systems, pp. 2222–2230 (2012)
33. Tang, X., Wang, X.: Face sketch synthesis and recognition. In: IEEE Conference on Computer Vision, pp. 687–694 (2003)
34. Wang, R., Yang, J., Yi, D., Li, S.Z.: An analysis-by-synthesis method for heterogeneous face biometrics. In: Tistarelli, M., Nixon, M.S. (eds.) ICB 2009. LNCS, vol. 5558, pp. 319–326. Springer, Heidelberg (2009). doi:10.1007/978-3-642-01793-3_33
35. Yi, D., Lei, Z., Li, S.Z.: Shared representation learning for heterogeneous face recognition. In: IEEE Conference and Workshops on Automatic Face and Gesture Recognition, vol. 1, pp. 1–7 (2015)
36. Dhamecha, T.I., Sharma, P., Singh, R., et al.: On effectiveness of histogram of oriented gradient features for visible to near infrared face matching. In: International Conference on Pattern Recognition, pp. 1788–1793 (2014)
37. Klare, B.F., Li, Z., Jain, A.K.: Matching forensic sketches to mug shot photos. IEEE Trans. Pattern Anal. Mach. Intell. **33**(3), 639–646 (2011)
38. Li, S.Z., Zhang, L., Liao, S.C., et al.: A near-infrared image based face recognition system. In: FG, pp. 455–460 (2006)
39. Juefei-Xu, F., Pal, D., Savvides, M.: NIR-VIS heterogeneous face recognition via cross-spectral joint dictionary learning and reconstruction. In: IEEE Conference on Computer Vision and Pattern Recognition Workshops, pp. 141–150 (2015)

Exploring Deep Features with Different Distance Measures for Still to Video Face Matching

Yu Zhu and Guodong Guo[✉]

Lane Department of Computer Science and Electrical Engineering,
West Virginia University, Morgantown, WV 26506, USA
yzhu4@mix.wvu.edu, guodong.guo@mail.wvu.edu

Abstract. Still to video (S2V) face recognition attracts many interests for researchers in computer vision and biometrics. In S2V scenarios, the still images are often captured with high quality and cooperative user condition. On the contrary, video clips usually show more variations and of low quality. In this paper, we primarily focus on the S2V face recognition where face gallery is formed by a few still face images, and the query is the video clip. We utilized the deep convolutional neural network to deal with the S2V face recognition. We also studied the choice of different similarity measures for the face matching, and suggest the more appropriate measure for the deep representations. Our results for both S2V face identification and verification yield a significant improvement over the previous results on two databases, i.e., COX-S2V and PaSC.

1 Introduction

Face recognition has been attracting researchers' attentions for several decades in computer vision and biometrics. With the fast development of video surveillance systems and low cost video cameras, video based face recognition becomes an important topic in face recognition [2,3,5,11,12,16]. In practice, face recognition systems usually have still face images in gallery and the probe faces come from videos. In such scenario, it is necessary to study the problem of automatically matching video faces and still faces, a.k.a., Still-to-Video (S2V) face recognition. In this work, we focus on the S2V face recognition where each subject is enrolled with only few still images, while the query is coming from video clips which consist of uncontrolled image frames. One of the major challenges for S2V face recognition lies in the disparity between still images and video clips. Faces captured by video cameras usually show more variations in illumination, head pose, expression, or motion blur, while the still images could be with a high quality.

Recently, several approaches are proposed for S2V face recognition [1–4,9,10,15,20]. One way is to apply still face recognition methods to the S2V scenario [1,9,15]. Another popular methodology for S2V face recognition is by using metric learning, e.g., Neighborhood Components Analysis (NCA) [7], Information Theoretic Metric Learning (ITML) [6], Local Fisher Discriminant Analysis (LFDA) [13] and Large Margin Nearest Neighbor (LMNN) [17]. More recently, point to set metric learning methods, such as Point-to-Set Distance

© Springer International Publishing AG 2016
Z. You et al. (Eds.): CCBR 2016, LNCS 9967, pp. 158–166, 2016.
DOI: 10.1007/978-3-319-46654-5_18

Metric Learning (PSDML) [19] and Learning Euclidean-to-Riemannian Metric (LERM) [10], have been proposed. Moreover, in [20], the authors considered the S2V face recognition as a heterogeneous problem.

However, the above mentioned previous works utilized either gray level features or low level features in their approaches, which to some extent impact the overall face recognition performance. Especially for the still to video face recognition where great variations occurs in video faces, low level features are not sufficient. Therefore, we study the performance of still to video face recognition using deep representations, which has been established as a powerful model for many recognition problems. Our proposed method is the first time that applying deep representations to the Still to Video (S2V) face recognition problem, to the best of our knowledge.

Moreover, classification of faces often involves identifying samples that are close or similar to each other. Distances or similarities are mathematical representations of what are defined by close or similar. Since the choice of distance measures is a critical for S2V face recognition, we also study the choice of distances or similarities when deep features is used.

The rest of this paper is organized as following: The proposed method and distance measures are described in Sect. 2. Experimental results on two databases with comparisons are shown in Sect. 3. Finally, we draw some conclusions in Sect. 4.

2 Approach

2.1 Deep Neural Network

Recently, deep learning methods especially the deep convolutional neural networks (DCNN) have been applied to many computer vision tasks with promising performance, such as object recognition [14], still image based face recognition [18], etc. However, it has not been well studied yet on using deep learning techniques for still to video face matching. In this study, we explore the performance of deeply learned face representations (features) for still to video face recognition. Then, we further studied different distance measures for deep features on S2V face matching.

In exploring the deep features for still to video face matching, we hope that the trained deep network is capable of capturing the face structures with discriminative power, at the same time being robust to the variations, such as head poses, illuminations and blurs. Accordingly, it usually requires a large number of training data for the deep network. However, the size of public S2V databases is usually small, e.g., in PaSC database, there are only 2802 videos collected from 293 subjects. Therefore, we propose to utilize a large number of still face images to train a deep network, e.g., from the WebFace database [18]. Besides, we utilized a much deeper network architecture so that the deep features are expected to be more robust and representative. We applied the GoogLeNet [14], which contains 22-layers with an "inception" structure, to train our deep face model. The main idea of "inception" structure that was included in the GoogLeNet is a combination of network-in-network filters, along with different convolutional filters in each layer. Within the inception module, a 3×3 filter, a 5×5 filter and a max pooling are performed and then combined together. In this way, there are multiple filter sizes per layer so each layer can have the ability to character different "feature resolutions" that may have in its input. Another property of the GoogLeNet is that auxiliary classifiers are added to connect to intermediate layers. The total loss of the network during training is a weighted sum of the auxiliary classifiers.

2.2   Distance Measures for Face Matching

In our approach, matching of still images and video clips is done by fusing the deep feature distances between still images and video frames in each video clip. Note that, the training data provided with the database are not used in our study. Deep features extracted from the deep model are used directly for face matching without any fine-tuning. There are different measures for the distance between two deep features, however, there is no systematic study or evaluation of different measures. In the following, we study six different distance measures for measuring the similarity between deep features.

Euclidean Distance. Among various distance metrics, the Euclidean distance is one of the most commonly used metric due to its simplicity. The Euclidean distance between 1-D arrays u and v, is defined as:

$$d(u, v) = ||u - v||_2, \tag{1}$$

where $||u - v||_2 = \sqrt{(u - v) \cdot (u - v)}$.

Manhattan Distance. The Manhattan distance is the L1-norm of the difference, which is also a special case of the Minkowski distance (with p=1). The Manhattan distance (a.k.a., City Block distance) between 1-D arrays u and v, is defined as:

$$d(u, v) = \Sigma_i |u_i - v_i|. \tag{2}$$

In other words, the Manhattan distance computes the sum of absolute differences between two vectors.

Canberra Distance. The Canberra distance between 1-D arrays u and v, is defined as:

$$d(u, v) = \Sigma_i \frac{|u_i - v_i|}{|u_i| + |v_i|}. \tag{3}$$

When u_i and v_i are 0 for given i, then the fraction is set to 0. The Canberra is similar to the Manhattan distance, with the distinction that prior to summation, the absolute difference between the variables of the two vectors is divided by the sum of the absolute variable values. It is thus more sensitive to proportional than to absolute differences.

Correlation Distance. Correlation distance is another widely used measures for data analysis, which defined by subtracting the correlation coefficient from 1. Specifically, the Correlation distance between 1-D arrays u and v, is defined as:

$$d\left(u,v\right) = 1 - \frac{(u - \bar{u}) \cdot (v - \bar{v})}{||\left(u - \bar{u}\right)||_2 ||\left(v - \bar{v}\right)||_2}, \tag{4}$$

where $\bar{u}$ is the mean of the elements of u, and $\cdot$ is the dot product operation.

BrayCurtis Distance. The computation of BrayCurtis distance involves summation of the absolute differences between the variables and dividing this by the sum of the variables in the two vectors. Mathematically, the BrayCurtis distance between 1-D arrays u and v, is defined as:

$$d\left(u,v\right) = \frac{\Sigma |u_i - v_i|}{\Sigma |u_i + v_i|}. \tag{5}$$

Bray-Curtis distance can be considered as a modified version of Manhattan distance, where the summed differences between the vectors are weighed by the sum of corresponding vector components.

Cosine Distance. The cosine distance is a measure that calculates the cosine of the angle between two vectors. The cosine distance between 1-D arrays u and v, is defined as:

$$d\left(u,v\right) = 1 - \frac{u \cdot v}{||u||_2 ||v||_2}, \tag{6}$$

where $u \cdot v$ is the dot product of u and v. Cosine distance between two vectors can be seen as a comparison on a normalized space, since the magnitude is not considered but the angle is used to measure how related between the two vectors.

3 Experimental Results

3.1 Databases

COX-S2V Database. COX-S2V database [9] was collected with both still images and video clips. The faces in this database contain large variations, such as illumination, head pose, and motion blurs. Totally there are 1,000 subjects in this database. For each subject, there is one still image with high resolution, and three video clips corresponding to three different camera locations, denoted as Cam1, Cam2 and Cam3, respectively.

Point and Shoot Face Recognition Challenge (PaSC) Database. The PaSC database [1] was collected for the point and shoot face recognition challenge. For both still images and video clips in this database, the faces show different variations such as head pose, background locations, motion blur and poor focus. There are 9,376 still images and 2,802 video clips that have been collected from 293 subjects in this database.

3.2   Experimental Settings

On the COX-S2V database, we follow the same experimental protocol in [9], where face identification is performed between still images and three camera settings, respectively. On the PaSC database, we followed the same protocol in [1], for the face verification task. We use CASIA-WebFace [18] to train the deep network for our S2V face matching. CASIA-WebFace is a large database including about 10,595 subjects and 494,414 images.

On the COX-S2V database, 700 subjects with their still images and video clips formed the test set. The remaining 300 subjects' data are used for training. The experiments ran 10 times with randomly selected gallery/probe combinations. The averaging recognition rates are used as the performance measurement on this database.

On the PaSC database, there are 2872 still images and 280 video clips for training. The 4688 still images formed the target set, while 1401 handheld video clips is the query set in testing. Therefore, the verification is conducted based on the similarity matrix of size 4688×1401. The ROC curve and verification rate (when FAR equals to 0.01) are used as the performance measurements.

Experimental Settings for Deep Network. Firstly, face detection and landmark localization are applied on both COX-S2V and PaSC database. The detected faces are then cropped and aligned to the size of 256×256.

The training of GoogLeNet is implemented using the Caffe toolbox [14] with the WebFace database. We used the mini-batch SDG (Stochasitc gradient descent) with momentum settings (set to 0.9) and the batch size is set to 32. The learning rate is set to 0.01 with decrease in polynomial decay (power of 0.5). The training procedure stops after 2,400,000 iterations.

During the test, the aligned face images from both gallery and probe sets are fed into deep network, we used the layer ($pool5/7x7\_s1$) to get the face deep features. Each face image is then represented as the deep feature vector of size 1024. Matching is conducted according to the protocols described above. All experiments are tested on the 64 bit Ubuntu 14.04 platform with 6-Core i7 CPU, 32 G RAM and Titan X GPU.

3.3   Experimental Results on the COX-S2V Database

The experimental results on COX-S2V are shown in Table 1. From the table one can see that, the Euclidean distance gets the worst performance in all three experiments (i.e., Cam 1, 2 and 3), the recognition rates are 30.97 %, 34.53 % and 54.50 %, respectively. One of the reasons might lie in the fact that it suffers from a high sensitivity even to small deformation. For the high dimension (i.e., 1024) deep features, a small deformation may result in a large Euclidean distance change. The Manhanttan and Canberra distances show better performance then the Euclidean distance, but still quite lower than the other three distances. The performance obtained by Cosine distance is slightly higher than the results using correlation distance, but is lower than the BrayCurtis distance. The best

Table 1. The experimental results for S2V face identification on COX-S2V database, and face verification on PaSC database.

Method	COX-S2V			PaSC	
	Still-Video1	Still-Video2	Still-Video3	VR(FAR = 0.01)	VR (FAR = 0.01)
Euclidean	30.97 ± 0.75	34.53 ± 0.86	54.50 ± 1.36	0.04	0.52
Manhattan	36.43 ± 2.38	44.57 ± 4.02	68.93 ± 2.11	0.02	0.48
Canberra	55.31 ± 1.03	65.50 ± 1.38	77.29 ± 0.84	0.08	0.67
Correlation	74.37 ± 1.17	79.61 ± 1.05	94.90 ± 0.64	0.58	**0.82**
Cosine	74.81 ± 1.22	79.76 ± 0.91	95.04 ± 0.59	0.60	0.80
Braycurtis	**77.29±0.84**	**83.10±1.09**	**96.17±0.74**	**0.61**	0.79

Table 2. Comparison with other approaches for S2V face identification on COX-S2V database.

Method	COX-S2V		
	Still-Video1	Still-Video2	Still-Video3
NNC [8]	9.96 ± 0.61	7.14 ± 0.68	17.37 ± 6.16
NCA [7]	39.14 ± 1.33	31.57 ± 1.56	57.57 ± 2.03
LMNN [17]	34.44 ± 1.02	30.03 ± 1.36	58.06 ± 1.35
LERM [10]	45.71 ± 2.05	42.80 ± 1.86	58.37 ± 3.31
GFK [20]	49.86 ± 1.22	42.99 ± 2.17	69.81 ± 1.72
Ours	**77.29±0.84**	**83.10±1.09**	**96.17±0.74**

performance is achieved by the BrayCurtis distance, which gives the recognition rates 77.29 %, 83.10 % and 96.17 % for Cam1, 2 and 3, respectively. These results show that, when the deep feature is used, the choice of distance measures impacts the S2V face recognition performance significantly.

Next we compare the results to other state-of-the-art methods on the COX-S2V database. The results are shown in Table 2. The gray level features were utilized to those methods according to the original papers. From the table one can see that, our proposed approach achieved better results than the other listed methods, where the recognition rates are 77.29 %, 83.10 % and 96.17 %, respectively. The comparisons suggest that deep features are more appropriate for still-to-video face matching.

3.4   Experimental Results on PaSC Database

On the PaSC database, we firstly show the verification results using different distance measures in Table 1. We listed the verification rate (VR) then FAR equals to 0.01 and 0.1, in column 5 and 6, respectively. From the table, one can see that Correlation, Cosine and BrayCurtis distances shows much better performances than the other three distances: Euclidean, Manhattan, and Canberra. The best

Table 3. The experimental results (verification rate) for S2V face verification on PaSC dataset, when FAR equals to 0.01.

Method	Verification rate	Method	Verification rate
NNC [8]	0.05	PLDA-WPCA-LLR [1]	0.26
NCA [7]	0.16	Eigen-PEP [1]	0.24
LMNN [17]	0.17	LPB-SIFT-WPCA-SILD [1]	0.23
LERM [10]	0.17	ISV-GMM [1]	0.11
GFK [20]	0.22	LRPCA [1]	0.10
Ours	**0.61**		

VR (FAR = 0.01) achieves the value 0.61 by BrayCurtis distance. These observations illustrates that, when deep features are utilized as the face representation, different distance measures perform quite differently. The selection of distance measures effects the matching results significantly.

Next we compared our results to the other state-of-the-art approaches on the PaSC dataset in Table 3. The results are shown the verification rate when FAR equals to 0.01, which is the same for the PaSC challenge [1]. In Table 3, it shows that deep feature obtains the best verification rate of 0.61, using the BrayCurtis distance. One can also see that our result is significantly better than the other approaches in the PaSC challenge from [1]. Similar observations can be found in the ROC curves shown in Fig. 1 This further demonstrates the robustness and effectiveness of our method for still to video face recognition.

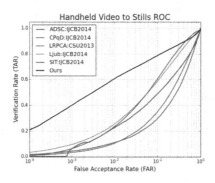

Fig. 1. ROC of the PaSC dataset for S2V face verification.

4   Conclusions

We proposed to utilize the face representations from deep convolutional neural networks dealing with the still to video (S2V) face recognition. We found deeply learned features provides more robustness and discriminative power for face matching, which is a more appropriate way for the S2V face recognition. We further studied the choice of different similarity measure and show the impact to the final recognition performance. Experimental results on two still to video face databases illustrate that, the deep features achieved significantly better performance in both verification and identification, than the other state-of-the-art approaches. Besides, the recognition performance using deep features varies according to different choices of the similarity measures. Among the six different similarity measures, the BrayCurtis measure is considered more appropriate for the S2V.

References

1. Beveridge, J.R., Phillips, P.J., Bolme, D.S., Draper, B.A., Givens, G.H., Lui, Y.M., Teli, M.N., Zhang, H., Scruggs, W.T., Bowyer, K.W., et al.: The challenge of face recognition from digital point-and-shoot cameras. In: IEEE Biometrics: Theory, Applications and Systems (BTAS), pp. 1–8 (2013)
2. Beveridge, J.R., Zhang, H., Draper, B.A., Flynn, P.J., Feng, Z., Huber, P., Kittler, J., Huang, Z., Li, S., Li, Y., et al.: Report on the fg 2015 video person recognition evaluation. In: 2015 11th IEEE International Conference and Workshops on Automatic Face and Gesture Recognition (FG), vol. 1, pp. 1–8. IEEE (2015)
3. Chen, X., Wang, C., Xiao, B., Cai, X.: Scenario oriented discriminant analysis for still-to-video face recognition. In: IEEE International Conference on Image Processing (ICIP), pp. 738–742 (2014)
4. Chen, X., Wang, C., Xiao, B., Zhang, C.: Still-to-video face recognition via weighted scenario oriented discriminant analysis. In: IEEE International Joint Conference on Biometrics (IJCB), pp. 1–6 (2014)
5. Cui, Z., Chang, H., Shan, S., Ma, B., Chen, X.: Joint sparse representation for video-based face recognition. Neurocomputing **135**, 306–312 (2014)
6. Davis, J.V., Kulis, B., Jain, P., Sra, S., Dhillon, I.S.: Information-theoretic metric learning. In: Proceedings of the 24th International Conference on Machine Learning, pp. 209–216. ACM (2007)
7. Goldberger, J., Hinton, G.E., Roweis, S.T., Salakhutdinov, R.R.: Neighbourhood components analysis. In: Advances in Neural Information Processing Systems, pp. 513–520 (2005)
8. Gong, B., Shi, Y., Sha, F., Grauman, K.: Geodesic flow kernel for unsupervised domain adaptation. In: IEEE Conference on Computer Vision and Pattern Recognition (CVPR), pp. 2066–2073 (2012)
9. Huang, Z., Shan, S., Zhang, H., Lao, S., Kuerban, A., Chen, X.: Benchmarking still-to-video face recognition via partial and local linear discriminant analysis on COX-S2V dataset. In: Lee, K.M., Matsushita, Y., Rehg, J.M., Hu, Z. (eds.) ACCV 2012. LNCS, vol. 7725, pp. 589–600. Springer, Heidelberg (2013). doi:10.1007/978-3-642-37444-9_46
10. Huang, Z., Wang, R., Shan, S., Chen, X.: Learning euclidean-to-riemannian metric for point-to-set classification. In: IEEE Conference on Computer Vision and Pattern Recognition (CVPR), pp. 1677–1684 (2014)
11. Kim, T.-K., Kittler, J., Cipolla, R.: Discriminative learning and recognition of image set classes using canonical correlations. IEEE Trans. Pattern Anal. Mach. Intell. **29**(6), 1005–1018 (2007)

12. Liu, X., Chen, T.: Video-based face recognition using adaptive hidden markov models. In: IEEE Computer Vision and Pattern Recognition, vol. 1, p. I-340 (2003)
13. Sugiyama, M.: Dimensionality reduction of multimodal labeled data by local fisher discriminant analysis. J. Mach. Learn. Res. **8**, 1027–1061 (2007)
14. Szegedy, C., Liu, W., Jia, Y., Sermanet, P., Reed, S., Anguelov, D., Erhan, D., Vanhoucke, V., Rabinovich, A.: Going deeper with convolutions. In: Proceedings of the IEEE Conference on Computer Vision and Pattern Recognition, pp. 1–9 (2015)
15. Wang, H., Liu, C., Ding, X.: Still-to-video face recognition in unconstrained environments. In: IS&T/SPIE Electronic Imaging, p. 94050O. International Society for Optics and Photonics (2015)
16. Wang, R., Guo, H., Davis, L.S., Dai, Q., Covariance discriminative learning: a natural and efficient approach to image set classification. In: IEEE Conference on Computer Vision and Pattern Recognition (CVPR), pp. 2496–2503 (2012)
17. Weinberger, K.Q., Blitzer, J., Saul, L.K.: Distance metric learning for large margin nearest neighbor classification. In: Advances in Neural Information Processing Systems, pp. 1473–1480 (2005)
18. Yi, D., Lei, Z., Liao, S., Li, S.Z.: Learning face representation from scratch. arXiv preprint arXiv:1411.7923 (2014)
19. Zhu, P., Zhang, L., Zuo, W., Zhang, D.: From point to set: extend the learning of distance metrics. In: IEEE International Conference on Computer Vision, pp. 2664–2671 (2013)
20. Zhu, Y., Zheng, Z., Li, Y., Mu, G., Shan, S., Guo, G.: Still to video face recognition using a heterogeneous matching approach. In: IEEE Biometrics: Theory, Applications and Systems (BTAS) (2015)

Face Hallucination Using Convolutional Neural Network with Iterative Back Projection

Dongdong Huang and Heng Liu[✉]

School of Computer Science and Technology, Anhui University of Technology,
Maxiang Road, Ma'anshan 243032, China
ddl2huang@163.com, hengliusky@aliyun.com

Abstract. Face hallucination aims to generate a high-resolution (HR) face image from an input low-resolution (LR) face image, which is a specific application field of image super resolution for face image. Due to the complex and sensitive structures of face image, obtaining a super-resolved face image is more difficult than generic image super resolution. Recently, deep learning based methods have been introduced in face hallucination. In this work, we develop a novel network architecture which integrates image super-resolution convolutional neural network with network style iterative back projection (IBP) method. Extensive experiments demonstrate that the proposed improved model can obtain better performance.

Keywords: Face hallucination · Super resolution · Convolutional network · Iterative back projection

1 Introduction

The research of face image processing is one of classical problems in many related fields such as face recognition and video surveillance. However, in many scenarios, these related tasks are particularly challenging due to the little information provided by very low resolution input face image. Face hallucination, which aims at recovering a high-resolution face image from a low-resolution input face image, is a specific field of super resolution for human face. Unlike generic image super resolution, face hallucination is more difficult because of the complex and sensitive structures in human face, which comes up in practice in many applications.

Generally, a low-resolution image can be obtained from high-resolution image through a degradation model [1], which can be formulated as follows.

$$y = DH_x \tag{1}$$

where y is the observed low-resolution image, x is the high-resolution image. D and H act as down sampling operator and low pass filters separately. Therefore face hallucination is an inverse problem of face image degradation process, that is, given an input low-resolution face image y, face hallucination aims at estimating the original high-resolution face image x. It is an ill-posed problem because of the non-unique solution.

© Springer International Publishing AG 2016
Z. You et al. (Eds.): CCBR 2016, LNCS 9967, pp. 167–175, 2016.
DOI: 10.1007/978-3-319-46654-5_19

Face hallucination can be summarized into different categories according to different factors [12]. Some of the classical works have been listed in the following. The basic methods for upscaling a face image are interpolation based methods, including nearest neighbour interpolation, bilinear interpolation and bicubic interpolation. These methods are widely used owing to their simplicity and low complexity. However, they are limited as a result of the over-smoothed regions and artifacts in the reconstructed face image.

Learning based face hallucination generates a target image from a corresponding input source image by using training image pairs (LR and HR image pairs) based on various machine learning algorithms. These methods mainly learn an underlying mapping between LR images and the corresponding HR images, and then reconstruct an HR face image using the learned mapping. Recently, sparse representation has achieved great progress in computer vision and data analysis. In particular, these methods have been applied into face image super resolution and better results have been obtained. Yang et al. [2] introduced the idea of sparse representation with dictionary learning for face hallucination. The solution is approached in two steps: first use reconstruction constraint to recover a medium high-resolution face images, then use the local sparse model to recover the image details. Liu et al. [3] also proposed a two-step method for face upscaling according to global and local constraint. First, a global face is estimated using an Eigen face model. Then an enhanced face image was obtained by introducing local constraint. Yang et al. [17] partitioned a face image into three groups of facial components, contours and smooth regions based on a facial landmark detection. They used the nearest neighbour search for each of the facial components with the training images, while for contours and smooth regions edge-based statistics and nearest neighbour patch search were used. The final result was generated by integrating gradient maps from the three groups and imposing them on the high-resolution image.

In the past several years, deep learning based methods update state-of-the-art constantly of computer vision field from image classification [4], face recognition [5] to semantic segmentation [6]. Recently, these methods have also been applied into low-level vision tasks, such as image denoising [7], image enhancement [8], and image super resolution included [9–11]. The seminal work of image super-resolution convolutional neural network (SRCNN) was done by Dong et al. [10]. They first introduced convolutional neural network into image super resolution. The proposed model mainly consists of three convolutional layers, which approximately simulated a sparse representation based scheme to generate an HR image. The three layers implement the following tasks separately: patch extraction and representation, non-linear mapping and reconstruction. However, it is not effective to solve face hallucination due to the only goal of minimizing the loss function without exploiting any face image priors, such as face specific structures, which is an important component for face image recovery tasks to regularize the problem to an extent.

In this work, inspired by SRCNN model, we also inherit such three layers convolutional neural network for face image super resolution, that is, face hallucination. Moreover, we introduce some face image priors through iterative back projection way [13] to form a novel convolutional neural network face image super-resolution framework. In summary, our contributions can be summarized as follows:

- We integrates image super-resolution convolutional neural network with iterative back projection (IBP) to form a new network model for face hallucination.
- The merit of the proposed model is the prior introduction of ground truth image in face hallucination procedure. This prior guidance updating way will be helpful to the improving of performance. In addition, it provides a way of introducing image priors.

The remainder of this work is organized as follows. The proposed SRCNN-IBP framework is discussed in detail in Sect. 2. In Sect. 3, many experimental results and comparisons are presented and discussed. Finally, we conclude this work in Sect. 4.

2 SRCNN-IBP Model

2.1 Motivation of SRCNN-IBP Model

To our knowledge, back projection algorithm is usually utilized as a post processing step, which is a common approach used in many super resolution methods [2, 15]. Iterative back projection was proposed by Irani et al. [13]. First, an initial estimate of HR image is regarded as an intermediate result. And then the result can be mapped onto LR observation image by the degradation model to acquire LR simulation image. Then the difference between LR simulation image and actual observed LR image is calculated, which can be called simulation error. And the estimated HR image can be updated based on the simulation error. The processing procedure is looped to get the final result. The process can be formulated as following equations:

$$y^0 = W_k x^0 + n_k \tag{2}$$

$$x^1 = x^0 + H^{BP}(y - y^0) \tag{3}$$

where x^0 and x^1 denote the HR images of initial estimation and first improved respectively, y^0 represents LR simulation image calculated by degradation model, y is the LR observation image, n_k denotes the additional noise and H^{BP} represents back projection operator.

Although the reconstruction quality for IBP is not impressive, it can be still combined with other super resolution approaches to improve performance. Many super resolution methods exploit it as a post processing step. For example, work [2] utilizes the corresponding result as the HR image of initial estimation, i.e. x^0 in Eq. (2). Then gain the final result by multiple iterations. In this work, we integrate IBP algorithm into SRCNN framework avoiding extra post-processing. The flow chart of our modified model can be viewed in Fig. 1.

Despite the better results have been achieved in [10], there is still further space for face hallucination. Therefore, one motivation of this work is to impose more image prior or constraint in reconstruction process. In our thinking, iterative back projection approach can introduce ground truth image prior continually by producing LR simulation image and calculating the simulation error, which can improve reconstruction effect by updating estimated HR image iteratively. We implement each step of IBP with

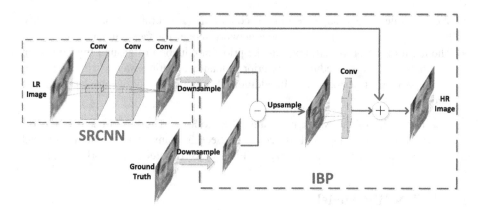

Fig. 1. The compositional model of SRCNN with IBP algorithm.

a neural network operation, and make it integrated into convolutional neural network. That is, we combine SRCNN model with iterative back projection algorithm based on deep convolutional network to form a new model, termed SRCNN-IBP model. The following Fig. 1 gives the sketch map of such compositional model.

2.2 Architecture of SRCNN-IBP

As is illustrated above, the whole proposed SRCNN-IBP model consists of seven layers which includes four convolution layers, two sub-sampling layers (one for down sampling and another for up sampling), and one for difference layer. The specific functions of each layer are described in detail as following:

(1) First three layers. The first three layers of our model are the same as those in SRCNN model. These layers are all taking the form of convolution, and they achieve the following functions separately: patch extraction and expression, non-linear mapping, and reconstruction.

(2) Downsampling layer. This operation downsamples the image derived from the third layer. As a result, a LR version of reconstruction image is obtained.

(3) Difference layer. This operation calculates the difference between downsampling version of the original HR image and the corresponding counterpart we acquired above. The difference is treated as reconstruction simulation error, and it also can be considered as a prior guidance that has been introduced.

(4) Upsampling layer. This operation upsamples the simulation error to generate the simulation error of HR version.

(5) Update layer. This operation performs a convolution with the above simulation error, and then the final HR image is updated based on the synthesis of the third layer's result with the convolution version of simulation error.

Extensive experimental results demonstrate that our SRCNN-IBP model surpass the performance of SRCNN because of the function of introducing the ground truth HR image prior, which also declares the significance of image prior.

2.3 Model Training

For image SR task, we expect to obtain a set of parameters to represent the mapping between the HR output and the LR input optimally. Giving a training dataset $\{x^i, y^i\}_{i=1}^N$, our goal can be depicted by the following equation.

$$y = F(x, \emptyset) \tag{4}$$

where x, y denote the LR image and the estimated HR image separately, $\emptyset$ represents the learned parameter. Given a LR image x and the corresponding HR image x^H, we expect to minimize the difference between y and x^H using mean square error. Formally, this operation can be expressed as follow.

$$\min_{\emptyset} \frac{1}{N} \sum_{i=1}^N \left\| F(x_i, \emptyset) - x_i^H \right\|^2 \tag{5}$$

where N denotes the number of sample images in dataset. Then we train the network using the *Caffe* package [14] of deep learning. During training, we use stochastic gradient descend (SGD) to update the parameter, which is described in Sect. 3.1.

3 Experiments

In this section, we first provide implementation details of our experiments. Then, we compared our proposed method with some other face hallucination algorithms.

3.1 Implementation Details

In our experiments, we use the Labeled Faced in the Wild dataset (LFW) [16] for training. This dataset contains 13233 face images from 1680 people, where we used 12000 for training and 1233 for testing. In our work, the network is only training on the single channel. For colour images, we first convert the original images into YCbCr colour space and then extract features from the luminance component Y. The image was cropped into small patches with size 40×40 (larger than 33×33 in SRCNN [10]). The cropped ground truth patches were regarded as the HR patches, namely the label in experiments, the corresponding LR pairs can be obtained by bicubic interpolation. There is a little difference between the last convolutional layer with former convolutional layers. In [10], all the three convolutional layers have no padding, however, we impose a zero-padding for the last convolutional layer so that the network produces a same size output as SRCNN model. Similar as other super resolution methods, our proposed network can be applied on images of arbitrary sizes during testing, though the fixed image size is used in training.

The specific configurations of our model can be referred in Table 1. All the convolutional layers' parameters are initialized using a Gaussian distribution with zero mean and standard deviation 0.001, and the biases are set as 0. In addition, we set the learning rate of 0.0001 and training uses a batch size of 128 in our experiment. Momentum and weight decay parameters are set to 0.9 and 0.0001, respectively.

Table 1. Configurations of our modified network. "conv9-64" stands for a convolutional layer, where the kernels size is 9 × 9 and has 64 feature maps. The others are similar. "eltwise (sum)" acts as a summation of two corresponding layers' feature maps, corresponding to an eltwise layer in *Caffe*. And unpooling executes an upsampling operation.

SRCNN-IBP Model		
data		
conv1-1	conv9-64	
	conv1-32	
	conv5-1	
	pooling	
eltwise(sum)		
unpooling		
conv3-1		
eltwise(sum)		

3.2 Quality Evaluation

We evaluate and compare the performance of our proposed models in terms of peak signal to noise ratio (PSNR) and structure similarity (SSIM). The model is tested on 1233 images of LFW dataset. Here are the visual qualities of the face hallucination results generated by our method and other competing ones in Fig. 2.

Table 2 shows the comparison results in terms of PSNR and SSIM between the proposed improved method and some competing methods. The best results are highlighted in bold. As one can see, our proposed method improves the results both in terms of PSNR and SSIM. And they all have an upscaling factor of 4 in our experiments. We can make some observations from the results. Obviously, the proposed modified network has already achieved better results than the competing methods, which validates that introducing image prior for face hallucination works well.

For LFW dataset, Table 3 shows another comparison results in terms of more evaluation index such as information fidelity criterion (IFC) [18], and noise quality measure (NQM) [19]. The proposed method is compared with more competing methods, for example, Liu et al.'s algorithm (LSF) [20] and Yang et al.'s (YLY) [21].

| NN | Bicubic | SRCNN | SRCNN-IBP | GT |

Fig. 2. Qualitative comparisons of 4x upsampling results for different algorithms. NN refers to nearest neighbour interpolation. GT denotes the ground truth image.

Table 2. The result of PSNR (dB) and SSIM on test images using different methods.

Images	NN		Bicubic		ScSR [2]		SRCNN [10]		SRCNN-IBP	
	PSNR	SSIM	PSNR	SSIM	PSNR	SSIM	PSNR	SSIM	PSNR	SSIM
1	26.17	0.679	28.58	0.789	29.27	0.809	29.51	0.819	**29.56**	**0.823**
2	27.73	0.737	29.94	0.825	30.69	0.841	30.89	0.847	**30.91**	**0.849**
3	26.32	0.733	30.61	0.844	29.99	0.871	31.90	0.874	**31.98**	**0.877**
4	24.35	0.689	31.31	0.853	28.59	0.849	32.28	0.875	**32.32**	**0.877**
5	26.39	0.710	29.12	0.850	28.84	0.831	30.38	0.875	**30.41**	**0.878**
6	28.77	0.754	28.23	0.815	28.94	0.828	29.03	0.839	**29.11**	**0.842**
7	26.16	0.737	27.73	0.778	28.46	0.801	28.76	0.809	**28.80**	**0.811**
8	28.90	0.796	32.48	0.897	33.45	0.905	34.00	0.914	**34.07**	**0.916**
Average	26.84	0.729	29.75	0.831	29.77	0.841	30.84	0.856	**30.90**	**0.859**

Table 3. More quality evaluation index comparisons by using different methods.

Methods	PSNR	SSIM	IFC	NQM
NN	24.16	0.687	1.23	7.97
Bicubic	26.62	0.796	1.84	10.72
LSF	22.97	0.600	0.79	7.01
YLY	25.16	0.738	1.47	9.11
SRCNN	27.55	0.827	2.03	11.05
SRCNN-IBP	**27.60**	**0.830**	**2.05**	**11.08**

4   Conclusion

In this work, we propose to develop and integrate iterative back projection network with image super-resolution convolutional neural network to form an improved model for face hallucination. Based on the introduced image prior, the SRCNN-IBP model achieves competitive performance compared with competing methods. In this way, we avoid additional post-processing existing in some other face hallucination methods. Furthermore, it can be applied to generic image super resolution. In future work, more image priors maybe considered into our model to enrich the details of super-resolved image.

References

1. Kamal, N., Thomas, B.: Super-resolution: a comprehensive survey. Mach. Vis. Appl. **556**, 1423–1468 (2014)
2. Yang, J.C., Wright, J., Huang, T., Ma, Y.: Image super-resolution via sparse representation. IEEE Trans. Image Process. **19**, 2861–2873 (2010)
3. Liu, C., Shum, H., Freeman, W.: Face hallucination: theory and practice. Int. J. Comput. Vis. **75**, 115–134 (2007)

4. Krizhevsky, A., Sutskever, I., Hinton, G.: Imagenet classification with deep convolutional neural networks. In: Advances in Neural Information Processing Systems, pp. 1097–1105 (2012)
5. Taigman, Y., Yang, M., Ranzato, M., Wolf, L.: Deepface: closing the gap to human-level performance in face verification. In: Proceedings of the IEEE Conference on Computer Vision and Pattern Recognition (CVPR), pp. 1701–1708 (2014)
6. Noh, H., Hong, S., Han, B.: Learning deconvolution network for semantic segmentation. In: Proceedings of IEEE International Conference of Computer Vision, pp. 1520–1528 (2015)
7. Mao, X.J., Shen, C.H., Yang, Y.: Image Denoising Using Very Deep Fully Convolutional Encoder-Decoder Networks with Symmetric Skip Connections (2016). arXiv preprint: arXiv:1603.09056
8. Xie, J., Xu, L., Chen, E.: Image denoising and inpainting with deep neural networks. In: Advances in Neural Information Processing Systems, pp. 341–349 (2012)
9. Dong, C., Loy, C.C., He, K., Tang, X.: Learning a deep convolutional network for image super-resolution. In: Fleet, D., Pajdla, T., Schiele, B., Tuytelaars, T. (eds.) ECCV 2014, Part IV. LNCS, vol. 8692, pp. 184–199. Springer, Heidelberg (2014)
10. Dong, C., Loy, C., He, K., Tang, X.: Image super-resolution using deep convolutional networks. IEEE Trans. Pattern Anal. Mach. Intell. (TPAMI) 38(2), 295–307 (2016)
11. Wang Z., Liu D., Yang J., Huang, T.: Deep networks for image super-resolution with sparse prior. In: Conference on Computer Vision and Pattern Recognition (CVPR), pp. 370–378 (2015)
12. Wang, N., Tao, D., Gao, X.: A comprehensive survey to face hallucination. Int. J. Comput. Vis. 106, 9–30 (2014)
13. Irani, M., Peleg, S.: Improving resolution by image registration. Graph. Models Image Process. 53, 231–239 (1991)
14. Jia, Y., Shelhamer, E., Donahue, J., Karayev, S., Long, J., Girshick, R., Guadarrama, S., Darrel, T.: Caffe: convolutional architecture for fast feature embedding (2014). arXiv preprint: arXiv:1408.5093
15. Gu, S., Zuo, W., Xie, Q., Meng, D., Feng, X., Zhang, L.: Convolutional sparse coding for image super-resolution. In: Proceedings of the IEEE International Conference on Computer Vision (ICCV), pp. 1823–1831 (2015)
16. Huang, G., Ramesh, M., Berg, T., Learned-Miller, E.: Labeled faces in the wild: a database for studying face recognition in unconstrained environments. Technical report, University of Massachusetts, Amherst, 1, 3 (2007)
17. Yang, C., Liu, S., Yang, M.: Structured face hallucination. In: Proceedings of the IEEE Conference on Computer Vision and Pattern Recognition (CVPR), pp. 1099–1106 (2013)
18. Sheikh, H.R., Bovik, A.C., De Veciana, G.: An information fidelity criterion for image quality assessment using natural scene statistics. IEEE Trans. Image Proc. 14(12), 2117–2128 (2005)
19. Damera-Venkata, N., Kite, T.D., Geisler, W.S., Evans, B.L., Bovik, A.C.: Image quality assessment based on a degradation model. IEEE Trans. Image Proc. 9(4), 636–650 (2000)
20. Liu, C., Shum, H.Y., Freeman, W.T.: Face hallucination: theory and practice. Int. J. Comput. Vis. 75(1), 115–134 (2007)
21. Yang, C.Y., Liu, S., Yang, M.H.: Structured face hallucination. In: Proceedings of the IEEE Conference on Computer Vision and Pattern Recognition (CVPR), pp. 1099–1106 (2013)

Facial Ethnicity Classification with Deep Convolutional Neural Networks

Wei Wang, Feixiang He, and Qijun Zhao[(⊠)]

National Key Laboratory of Fundamental Science on Synthetic Vision,
School of Computer Science, Sichuan University, Chengdu, China
qjzhao@scu.edu.cn

Abstract. As an important attribute of human beings, ethnicity plays a very basic and crucial role in biometric recognition. In this paper, we propose a novel approach to solve the problem of ethnicity classification. Existing methods of ethnicity classification normally consist of two stages: extracting features on face images and training a classifier based on the extracted features. Instead, we tackle the problem via using Deep Convolution Neural Networks to extract features and classify them simultaneously. The proposed method is evaluated in three scenarios: (i) the classification of black and white people, (ii) the classification of Chinese and Non-Chinese people, and (iii) the classification of Han, Uyghurs and Non-Chinese. Experimental results on both public and self-collected databases demonstrate the effectiveness of the proposed method.

1 Introduction

Human faces carry a large amount of information of soft biometric attributes, such as ethnicity, age and gender. These attributes can be very useful for face recognition, person re-identification, and video surveillance etc. [15, 16]. Increasing attention has thus been paid to the recognition of such soft biometric attributes. In this paper, we focus on the problem of facial ethnicity classification from 2D images.

Facial ethnicity classification is a typical pattern recognition task, which can be usually accomplished in two main steps: feature extraction and classification. Many methods have been proposed in the past decades with different features and classifiers [1–6, 13, 14]. These methods mostly extract hand-crafted features, e.g., local binary patterns (LBP) and Gabor filter responses, and apply some feature selection/transformation methods to improve the separability between faces of different ethnicities. They finally use certain classifiers, e.g., k-nearest neighbor classifiers (kNN) and support vector machines (SVM), to categorize the input face into one ethnicity. These methods have achieved impressive accuracy when trained and tested on same database. Yet, it is still unknown how they will work for multi large scale databases or when training and test data are from different sources.

Deep learning techniques have recently lead to breakthrough progress in many computer vision tasks, including image classification [17, 18], object detection [19–21], and face recognition [22, 23]. This motivates us to adopt deep learning techniques, particularly deep convolutional neural networks (DCNN), to solve the problem of large-scale facial ethnicity classification. Compared with previous approaches, our

© Springer International Publishing AG 2016
Z. You et al. (Eds.): CCBR 2016, LNCS 9967, pp. 176–185, 2016.
DOI: 10.1007/978-3-319-46654-5_20

proposed DCNN-based method can automatically learn appropriate feature representations for facial ethnicity classification, and well adapt to face databases from different sources. Extensive evaluation experiments on both public and private databases demonstrate the effectiveness and efficiency of the proposed DCNN-based facial ethnicity classification method.

2 Related Work

In the past decade, the field of ethnicity classification has drawn considerable attention and developed significantly. Enormous methods have been applied in ethnicity classification, which can achieve a high accuracy and perform effectively. All these approaches are made up with two components: feature extraction, and training classifiers. Guo et al. [5] use the biologically-inspired features (BIF) with (or without) manifold learning to study the ethnicity classification with variations of gender and age. Their experiments are conducted on the whole MORPH-II database with about 55,000 face images, in which White faces make up 19 %, Black faces provide 77 %, and the remaining faces (4 %) belong to Asian, Indian, Hispanic and other. When classifying two races, White and Black, within the same gender, their method can achieve an accuracy of 99 %, while the accuracy would reduce by 6 % to 8 % if female faces are used for training and males for testing. It is well accepted that good results can be gained when the training and test images have the same gender; but in most cases, the gender of the test images is not known in prior. For the experiment in five races classification within the cases of unknown genders and age, they can predict ethnicity on Black and White races with the success rates of 98.3 % and 97.1 % respectively. However, for the other three races, Named Hispanic, Asian and Indian, the success rates are relatively low, 74.2 %, 59.5 %, and 6.9 % respectively. Xie et al. [14] proposed an approach using Kernel Class-dependent Feature Analysis (KCFA) and facial color based features to tackle the ethnicity classification on large face databases. It works on the periorbital regions instead of the entire face region. Their highest accuracy for Caucasian, Asian and African American is, respectively, 98 %, 95 %, and 96 % on a Mugshot database (50,000 Caucasian, 50,000 African, 4,000 Asian) collected by their lab, and 97 %, 97 %, and 95 % on the MBGC database (20,000 Caucasian, 10,000 African, 10,000 Asian).

In addition to the two state of art methods described above, there are still enormous researches in ethnicity classification in 2-D images [1–3, 13] and 3-D images [4, 6], showed in Table 1.

To summarize, although these methods have gained a high ethnicity recognition rate, there are still some problems. None of them evaluated their performance with images from different databases that were not included in the training data. In this paper, we will do evaluation experiments not only on the same database, but also for the cross-database situation.

Table 1. Previous work on ethnicity classification.

Authors and Year	Approaches	Databases	Ethnicity	Accuracy
Hosoi et al. [1], 2004	Gabor wavelets and SVM	1,991 face photos	Asian, European and African	96.3 %, 93.1 %, 94.3 %
Lu et al. [2], 2004	Linear Discriminant Analysis (LDA)	A union database (2,630 samples of 263 subjects)	Asian vs. non-Asian	96.3 % (average)
Yang et al. [3], 2007	Real AdaBoost (Haar) Real AdaBoost (LBPH)	FERET and PIE (11,680 Asian characters and 1,016 non-Asian)	Asian vs. non-Asian	92.1 %, 93.2 %
Toderici et al. [4], 2010	KNN K-KNN MDS Wavelets	Face Recognition Grand Challenge v2 dataset. (4,007 facial meshes)	White vs. Asian	99.1 %, 98.4 % 99.1 %, 98.4 % 99.6 %, 99.5 % 98.2 %, 97.1 %
Lyle et al. [13], 2010	Periocular regions, LBP and SVM	FRGC (4,232 faces, 404 subjects)	Asian v.s. Non-Asian	91 % (average)
Guo et al. [5], 2010	Biologically-Inspired Features (BIF)	MORPH-II (10,530 Black and 10,530 White)	Black and White	99 % (average)
Xie et al. [14], 2012	Kernel Class-dependent Feature Analysis (KCFA)	MBGC database (20,000 Caucasian, 10,000 African, 10,000 Asian)	Caucasian, African American and Asian	97 %, 97 %, 95 %
Huang et al. [6], 2014	Boosted local texture and shape features, local circular patterns (LCP)	FRGC v2.0 and BU-3DFE databases (3,676 textured 3D face models of 418 subjects)	White v.s Asian	97 % (average)

3   Proposed Method

In this section we will introduce our proposed method in detail, include image pre-processing and our network. Convolutional neural network plays an important role in our racial classification experiments. We designed the network on the basis of CIFAR-10 network [7]. And it has achieved very good effects on our ethnicity classification experiments.

3.1   Facial Image Preprocessing

Figure 1 shows the facial image pre-processing step in the proposed method. Face detection and face landmarking [12] are first applied to the face images. The face images are then aligned based on the five landmarks, i.e., two eye centers, nose tip, two corners of mouth. These face images are finally normalized to the size of 100×100 and cropped to the size of 64×64, in which most background is excluded. Note that gray-scale images are used in this paper. If color facial images are provided, they will be converted into gray-scale images.

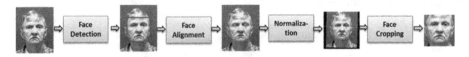

Fig. 1. Block diagram of image preprocessing method

3.2 Network Structure

Figure 2 shows the architecture of the network in detail which takes a 64 × 64 image as input and predicts its ethnicity class. The network architecture contains five learnable layers—three convolutional and two fully-connected layers.

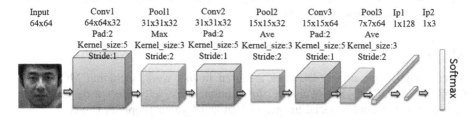

Fig. 2. The architecture of the proposed Convolutional Neural Network for ethnicity classification.

The output of the network is an *n-way* softmax layer, which outputs a probability distribution over the *n* classes:

$$y_p = \frac{\exp(y_p')}{\sum_{k=1}^{n} \exp(y_k')}$$

Where $y_k' = \sum_{k=1}^{128} x_p \cdot w_{k,p} + b_k$ combine the 128 dimensional features as the input of neuron k, and its output is y_k. We train the network to minimize the cross-entropy loss, expressed as:

$$L = -\sum_{y-1}^{n} -y_p \log \widehat{y_p} = -\log \widehat{y_t}$$

Where y_p is the target probability distribution, and $\widehat{y_p}$ is the predicted probability distribution. The stochastic gradient descent (SGD) is used in the phase of back propagation, the network minimize the loss over the parameters by computing the gradient of L. And in the implementation of the program, we use the minibatch stochastic gradient descent (MSGD), which calculates the gradient and update parameters after each traversal of a batch of samples, and a batch of samples generally have dozens to hundreds of individual samples.

4 Experiments and Results

In this section, we first introduce the databases used in the experiments, then the detail of the experiment setup, and finally report the results for three scenarios: (i) classification of White and Black people, (ii) classification of Chinese and Non-Chinese people, and (iii) classification of Han, Uyghur, and Non-Chinese people (Fig. 3).

Fig. 3. Some example facial images of different ethnicities: Black (MORPH-II), White (MORPH-II), and Chinese (CAS-PEAL).

4.1 Databases

Several public face image databases are used in this work, including MORPH-II, CASIA-PEAL and CASIA-WebFace. In addition, some self-collected databases are also used, which contain facial images of Han and Uyghur people in China.

MORPH-II [8] contains more than 55,000 face images, in which about 77 % face images are Black, 19 % are White, and the remaining 4 % are Asian, Hispanic, Indian, and Other. In Sects. 4.3 and 4.4, we chose 43,130 faces images of White and Black from MORPH-II. These face images are divided into 10 parts, in which 9/10 of them are used in training data, and the remaining are used in test.

The CASIA-WebFace database [9] is a large scale dataset of face images collected from Internet, containing 10,575 subjects and 494,414 images. We randomly select 91,594 face images about black and white races of them as part of the training data, and 10,177 face images for test.

The CAS-PEAL database [10] is a large-scale Chinese face image database containing 99,594 images of 1,040 individuals (595 males and 445 females). We choose 5,429 images of 1,040 individuals, with 9/10 for training and 1/10 for test.

The FERET database [11] contains 14,126 images of 1,199 individuals. We choose 3,407 images of black or white as our test data.

The CMU Multi-PIE [24] database contains more than 750,000 images of 337 people recorded in up to four sessions over the span of five months. Subjects were imaged under 15 view points and 19 illumination conditions while displaying a range of facial expressions.

In addition to the above public databases, we also collected by ourselves a large number of face images of Chinese people, including both Han and Ugyhur ethnicities. This private dataset consists of two parts: (i) High resolution identity photos of 198,775 Han Chinese people and 137,395 Ugyhur Chinese people, each having one frontal face images, and (ii) 71,319 face images of 4,335 people captured by surveillance cameras at railway stations and shopping malls. We denote these two subsets as IDPhotos and SurvImages, respectively.

4.2 Classification of Black and White

For a fair comparison with [5], 10,530 white and 10,530 black face images are randomly chosen from MORPH-II. Ten-fold cross validation is done for the proposed method. The average accuracy achieved by the proposed method is 100 % and 99.4 % for Black and White people, respectively. This is obviously better than that obtained by

[5]. It is worth mentioning that the method in [5] assumes that the gender of test images is known in advance in order to achieve the best accuracy. In contrast, our proposed method does not rely on such assumption.

4.3 Classification of Chinese and Non-Chinese

Training data in this experiment consist of 110,000 face images of Chinese people and 130,000 face images of Non-Chinese people from the IDPhotos, SurvImages, CAS-PEAL, CASIA-WebFace and MORPh-II databases (see Table 2). The remaining images of Chinese people in the IDPhotos and CAS-PEAL databases and those of Non-Chinese people in the CASIA-WebFace and MORPH-II databases are used as test data. Table 3 shows the confusion matrix of the proposed method. As can be seen, the accuracy on the four databases is, respectively, 99.84 %, 99.81 %, 99.65 % and 99.93 %. The above test and train sets are in the same database, now we test the different databases whose images are not used in training data. As showed in Table 3, our approach achieves the accuracy rate of 99.62 % and 99.38 % for Chinese and Non-Chinese.

In order to further evaluate the generalization capability of the trained facial ethnicity classification model, we also test it on another database (Multi-PIE) that is not used during training. As shown in Table 3, the accuracy is degraded to 91.6 % and 93.5 % for test images of Chinese and Non-Chinese people, respectively. This demonstrates the difficulty in cross-database (or more generally, cross-domain) facial ethnicity classification caused by varying subjects and imaging conditions.

Table 2. Databases used for training in the experiment of Chinese and Non-Chinese Classification.

Database	# Images	Ethnicity
IDPhotos	40,000	Chinese
SurvImages	71,319	Chinese
CAS-PEAL	4,886	Chinese
CASIA-WebFace	91,594	Non-Chinese
MORPH-II	38,817	Non-Chinese

Table 3. Confusion matrix of the proposed method in classifying Chinese and Non-Chinese on different test databases.

	Chinese	Non-Chinese
10,000 Chinese (IDPhotos)	99.84 %	0.16 %
542 Chinese (CAS-PEAL)	99.81 %	0.19 %
10,000 Non-Chinese (CASIA-WebFace)	0.35 %	99.65 %
4,313 Non-Chinese (MORPH-II)	0.07 %	99.93 %
1,578 Chinese (SHJT)	99.62 %	0.38 %
3,407 Non-Chinese (FERET)	0.62 %	99.38 %
1,824 Chinese (Multi-PIE)	91.6 %	8.4 %
2,819 Non-Chinese (Multi-PIE)	6.5 %	93.5 %

4.4   Classification of Han, Uyghur and Non-Chinese

To train the classification model for Han, Uyghur and Non-Chinese, 100,000 images of Han, 100,000 images of Uyghur, and 130,411 images of Non-Chinese are used (see Table 4). The results are reported in Table 5: The accuracy for Han and Ugyhur on the IDPhotos database, and for Non-Chinese on the CASIA-WebFace and MORPH-II databases is 99.40 %, 99.51 %, 99.87 % and 99.93 %, respectively.

Table 6 summarizes the accuracy achieved by the proposed method and some existing methods. From this comparison, we can clearly see that the proposed method achieves state-of-the-art performance for facial ethnicity classification.

Table 4. Databases used for training in the experiment of classifying Han, Uyghur and Non-Chinese people.

Database	# Images	Ethnicity
IDPhotos (Han)	100,000	Han
IDPhotos (Uyghur)	100,000	Uyghur
CASIA-WebFace	91,594	Non-Chinese
MORPH-II	38,817	Non-Chinese

Table 5. Confusion matrix of the proposed method for classifying Han, Uyghur and Non-Chinese on different test databases.

	Han	Uyghur	Non-Chinese
10,000 Han (IDPhotos)	99.40 %	0.48 %	0.12 %
10,000 Uyghur (IDPhotos)	0.44 %	99.51 %	0.05 %
10,000 Non-Chinese (CASIA-WebFace)	0.11 %	0.02 %	99.87 %
4,313 Non-Chinese (MORPH-II)	0.07 %	0	99.93 %
1,578 Han (SHJT)	98.04 %	1.08 %	0.88 %
3,406 Non-Chinese (FERET)	0.62 %	0.03 %	99.35 %

4.5   Computational Efficiency

According to our experiments on a PC with i7 CPU, NVIDIA GeForce GTX 980Ti graphics and 32 GB memory, the C++ implementation of the proposed method takes around 3.58 ms to process one face image. This indicates that the proposed method can do facial ethnicity classification in real time.

5   Conclusions

In this paper, we have proposed a deep convolutional neural network based method for facial ethnicity classification. Unlike traditional methods, it automatically learns effective feature representations and meanwhile does ethnicity classification for facial images.

Evaluation experiments have been done with large-scale datasets, and the results demonstrate the superiority of the proposed approach over existing methods. However, the generalization capability of the trained facial ethnicity classification model is still limited, especially when the test images have different acquisition conditions such as illumination and head pose. Our future work is to further improve the robustness of the proposed method to such varying factors.

Table 6. Comparison between the proposed approach and some existing methods.

Authors	Approaches	The Highest accuracy (%)	Databases	Ethnicities
Lyle et al. [13]	Grayscale and LBP	94 %	FRGC (4,232 faces, 404 subjects)	Asian v.s. Non-Asian
Guo et al. [5]	BIF (Biologically Inspired Features)	99 %	MORPH-II (21,060 faces)	White v.s. Black (only on the same gender)
Xie et al. [14]	KCFA and color features (on periorbital region)	97 % (Caucasian) 97 % (African) 95 % (Asian)	MBGC DB (20,000 Caucasian, 10,000 African, 10,000 Asian)	Caucasian, African American and Asian
Proposed Approach	CNN	100 % (Black) 99.4 % (White)	MORPH-II (21,060 faces)	White v.s. Black
	CNN	99.8 % (Chinese) 99.9 % (Non-Chinese)	Multiple large databases given above (240,000 faces)	Chinese v.s. Non-Chinese
	CNN	99.4 % (Han) 99.5 % (Uyghur) 99.9 % (Non-Chinese)	Multiple large databases given above (330,411 faces)	Han, Uyghur and Non-Chinese

Acknowledgments. This work is supported by the National Natural Science Foundation of China (No. 61202161) and the National Key Scientific Instrument and Equipment Development Projects of China (No. 2013YQ49087904).

References

1. Hosoi, S., Takikawa, E, Kawade, M.: Ethnicity estimation with facial images. In: IEEE International Conference on Automatic Face and Gesture Recognition, pp. 195–200. IEEE Computer Society (2004)
2. Lu, X., Jain, A.K.: Ethnicity identification from face images. In: Proceedings of SPIE - The International Society for Optical Engineering, vol. 5404, pp. 114–123 (2004)
3. Yang, Z., Ai, H.: Demographic classification with local binary patterns. In: Lee, S.-W., Li, S. Z. (eds.) ICB 2007. LNCS, vol. 4642, pp. 464–473. Springer, Heidelberg (2007)
4. Toderici, G., O'Malley, S.M., Passalis, G., Theoharis, T., Kakadiaris, I.A.: Ethnicity- and gender-based subject retrieval using 3-D face-recognition techniques. Int. J. Comput. Vis. **89**(2–3), 382–391 (2010)
5. Guo, G., Mu, G.: A study of large-scale ethnicity estimation with gender and age variations. In: Computer Vision and Pattern Recognition Workshops (CVPRW), pp. 79–86 (2010)
6. Huang, D., Ding, H., Wang, C., Wang, Y., Zhang, G., Chen, L.: Local circular patterns for multi-modal facial gender and ethnicity classification. Image Vis. Comput. **32**(12), 1181–1193 (2014)
7. Krizhevsky, A.: Convolutional Deep Belief Networks on CIFAR-10 (2012)
8. Ricanek, K., Tesafaye, T.: MORPH: a longitudinal image database of normal adult age-progression. In: IEEE Conference on AFGR, pp. 341–345 (2006)
9. Yi, D., Lei, Z., Liao, S., Li, S.Z.: Learning face representation from scratch. arXiv preprint arXiv, pp. 341–345 (2014)
10. Gao, W., Cao, B., Shan, S., Chen, X., Zhou, D., Zhang, X., Zhao, D.: The CAS-PEAL large-scale chinese face database and baseline evaluations. IEEE Trans. Syst. Man Cybern. Part A Syst. Hum. **38**(1), 149–161 (2008)
11. Phillips, P.J., Moon, H., Rizvi, S., Rauss, P.J.: The FERET evaluation methodology for face-recognition algorithms. IEEE Trans. Pattern Anal. Mach. Intell. **22**(10), 1090–1104 (2000)
12. Wang, Z., Miao, Z., Wu, Q.M.J., Wan, Y., Tang, Z.: Low-resolution face recognition: a review. Vis. Comput. **30**(4), 359–386 (2014)
13. Lyle, J.R.: Soft biometric classification using periocular region features. In: Fourth IEEE International Conference on Biometrics: Theory Applications and Systems, IEEE (2010)
14. Xie, Y., Luu, K., Savvides, M.: A robust approach to facial ethnicity classification on large scale face databases. In: IEEE Fifth International Conference on Biometrics: Theory, Applications and Systems, pp. 143–149 (2012)
15. Liu, Z., Luo, P., Wang, X., Tang, X.: Deep learning face attributes in the wild. In: Computer Science, pp. 3730–3738 (2014)
16. Zhong, Y., Sullivan, J., Li, H.: Face attribute prediction with classification CNN. In: Computer Science (2016)
17. KYan, Z., Jagadeesh, V., Decoste, D., Di, W., Piramuthu, R.: HD-CNN: Hierarchical Deep convolutional neural network for image classification. Eprint Arxiv (2014)
18. Krizhevsky, A., Sutskever, I., Hinton, G.E.: ImageNet Classification with Deep Convolutional Neural Networks. In: Advances in Neural Information Processing Systems, vol. 25(2) (2012)
19. Tomè, D., Monti, F., Baroffio, L., Bondi, L., Tagliasacchi, M., Tubaro, S.: Deep convolutional neural networks for pedestrian detection. In: Computer Science (2015)
20. Li, H., Lin, Z., Shen, X., Brandt, J., Hua, G.: A convolutional neural network cascade for face detection. In: IEEE Conference on Computer Vision and Pattern Recognition, pp. 5325–5334 (2015)

21. Ranjan, R., Patel, V.M., Chellappa, R.: Hyperface: a deep multi-task learning framework for face detection, landmark localization, pose estimation, and gender recognition. In: Computer Vision and Pattern Recognition (2016)
22. Sun, Y., Wang, X., Tang, X.: Sparsifying neural network connections for face recognition. In: Computer Science (2015)
23. Masi, L., Rawls, S., Medioni, G., Natarajan, P.: Pose-aware face recognition in the wild. In: Computer Vision and Pattern Recognition (2016)
24. Gross, R., Matthews, I., Cohn, J., Kanade, T., Baker, S.: Multi-PIE. In: IEEE International Conference on Automatic Face and Gesture Recognition, pp. 1–8 (2008)

Age Estimation Based on Multi-Region Convolutional Neural Network

Ting Liu[1,2], Jun Wan[1,2], Tingzhao Yu[1,2], Zhen Lei[1,2], and Stan Z. Li[1,2(✉)]

[1] Institute of Automation, Chinese Academy of Sciences, Beijing, China
{ting.liu,jun.wan,zlei,szli}@nlpr.ia.ac.cn, yutingzhao2013@ia.ac.cn
[2] University of Chinese Academy of Sciences, Beijing, China

Abstract. As one of the most important biologic features, age has tremendous application potential in various areas such as surveillance, human-computer interface and video detection. In this paper, a new convolutional neural network, namely MRCNN (Multi-Region Convolutional Neural Network), is proposed based on multiple face subregions. It joins multiple face subregions together to estimation age. Each targeted region is analyzed to explore the contribution degree to age estimation. According to the face geometrical property, we select 8 subregions, and construct 8 sub-network structures respectively, and then fuse at feature-level. The proposed MRCNN has two principle advantages: 8 sub-networks are able to learn the unique age characteristics of the corresponding subregion and the eight networks are packaged together to complement age-related information. Further, we analyze the estimation accuracy on all age groups. Experiments on MORPH illustrate the superior performance of the proposed MRCNN.

Keywords: Facial age estimation · MRCNN · Convolutional Neural Network · Age group analyzing

1 Introduction

Age estimation based upon facial images, as an emerging soft biometrics identification technology, has become a hot topic among computer vision areas. The task of age estimation is to compute the appearance age of a given facial image.

Most of the traditional age estimation methods published are reviewed in [1,2]. Texture features such as Gabor, LBP, PCA, Haar, and BIF have been widely used to represent both the holistic and local face regions. Then, classification, regression methods or the combination of the two are adopted to predict the age of face image, such as SVM, SVR, PLS, CCA. Among existing traditional methods, BIF+KCCA [14] is almost the best method in terms of accuracy. However, traditional ways of age estimation are often broken down into several incoherent steps, including data preprocessing, hand-crafted feature extraction, feature selection or down-sampling, classification or regression, etc. As a consequence, it exists some gaps between above-mentioned steps. Recently,

© Springer International Publishing AG 2016
Z. You et al. (Eds.): CCBR 2016, LNCS 9967, pp. 186–194, 2016.
DOI: 10.1007/978-3-319-46654-5_21

deep learning has achieved state-of-the-art results in the field of computer vision. Convolutional Neural Network (CNN) has also been introduced into age estimation. Wang et al. [3] applies CNN for age estimation for the first time. Instead of using the feature obtained at the top layer, they use feature maps obtained in different layers, and adopt manifold learning to learn aging patterns. Levi et al. [4] improves AlexNet for sex and age prediction. They regard the age estimation problem as a 8-classification problems, because ages are divided into eight groups. Yi et al. [5] introduces multi-scale analysis strategy, which improves the age estimation performance significantly. To make further improvement on the performance of age estimation based on CNN, similar to [5], we utilize individual facial landmarks to locate several face subregions which have abundant texture information, e.g., wrinkle and facial marks. Early researches have demonstrated that pose, illumination and expression (PIE) variation have less effects on local areas than the entire face image. Face representation based on local regions are more robust and hold greater potential. In this paper, we propose a novel framework, Multi-Region Convolutional Neural Network (MRCNN). The highlights and main contributions of the paper are summarized as follow.

1. A novel Convolutional Neural Network framework MRCNN for face age prediction is proposed. MRCNN makes full use of multiple subregions which contain rich age information.
2. MRCNN achieves state-of-the-art performance on MORPH database, validating its effectiveness and superiority.
3. Each facial component is analyzed to examine its contribution to age estimation. And we also reveal some prediction facts in and across all age groups.

2 Multi-Region Convolutional Neural Network

2.1 Facial Component Location

Intuitively, the locations where have the richest age information are eyes, nose, mouse, etc. Based on above cognition, given a face image, we first localize 21 facial landmarks with reasonable accuracy using ASM [6]. And then, we align the face images based on the two pupils and the middle of the mouth. The remaining landmarks follows the transformation. All images are resized and cropped into 300×300 (as shown in Fig. 1(a). The effect of age irrelevant features (e.g. posture) can be eliminated via face alignment, which is indeed helpful for age estimation. Beside, we convert color images into gray images, for that color information has poor stability and little effect on age estimation.

In this paper, we empirically select 12 local areas for face representation. The 12 local areas include the *head, face, eyes, nose, mouth, eyecorners, eyebags* and *nosewings*. In Fig. 1(a), they are described by face rectangles with different colors. And details can be found in Table 1.

Considering the facial symmetry, we group the 12 local areas into 8 groups as follow, the head and its mirror, the face and its mirror, the left-eye and the right-eye' mirror, the nose and its mirror, the mouth and its mirror, the outer corners

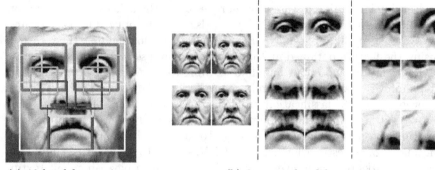

(a) 12 local face regions.   (b) 8 groups local face regions.

Fig. 1. Facial component location.

Table 1. The detailed description of facial component location.

Regions	Rectangle color	Size	Characteristics
head	-	300×300	-
face	white	240×240	no unrelated background
eyes	purple	100×100	vital component
nose	yellow	100×100	vital component
mouth	red	100×100	vital component
eyecorners	cyan	60×60	crows feet, wrinkle
eyebags	green	60×60	skin sag, dark circles and pigmentation
nosewings	blue	60×60	edict wrinkle

of left-eye and right-eye' mirror, the eyebags left-eye and right-eye' mirror, the left wing and the mirror of the right wing of nose. And the 8 groups pathes are normalized as 60×60, as shown in Fig. 1(b).

2.2   The Architecture of MRCNN

In this paper, a new convolutional neural network, namely MRCNN (Multi-Region Convolutional Neural Network), is proposed based on multiple face subregions. The whole architecture of our MRCNN model is described in Fig. 2, which is designed to predict the age of the given face image. The input is the 8 groups preprocessed local face regions, with 60×60 size, and the output is a age label. For the eight local face areas, we construct eight sub-networks respectively. The details of each sub-network is illustrated as Fig. 3. The sub-network of each group is composed of three convolution layers and two max-pooling layers. The input of sub-network is a certain group of local face areas. The output C3 layer is feature maps, and its dimension is $16 \times 15 \times 15 = 3600$. All feature maps of eight groups are concatenated in channel dimension. As a consequence, the input

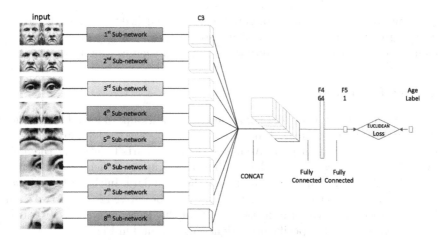

Fig. 2. The entire architecture of MRCNN.

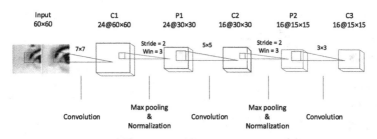

Fig. 3. The detailed architecture of the sub-network.

of F4 layer is $8 \times 3600 = 28800$ dimensions. Then, we fuse these responses in the two following full connected layers. $L2$ loss is chosen to be the loss function which can be regarded as a linear regression layer. Stochastic Gradient Descent (SGD) is adopted to optimize the network. The detailed parameter settings are clearly laid out in Fig. 3.

Multiple face subregions join together to estimation age. MRCNN has several principle advantages: 8 sub-networks are able to learn the unique age characteristics of the corresponding sub-region and the final fully connected layer packages the eight together to complement age-related information. Compare with global-face representation, local-face representation is robust against rotation etc. image transformation. Unlike existing traditional methods, MRCNN automatically learns global optimal parameters instead of manual designed features and classifiers. Followed experiments can prove the effectiveness of MRCNN.

3   Experiments

We evaluate our proposed method on the MORPH database [7], which is the biggest available database for facial age estimation. We follow the standard evaluation protocol as [8]. Each targeted region is analyzed to explore the contribution degree to age estimation, and it also illustrates the superiority of multi-region method. Further, we analyze the estimation accuracy on all age groups.

3.1   Age Estimation

As referred in Sect. 2.1, each face image derives eight groups of local face patches. In the training phases, we regard the non-mirror patches as the left part, while the mirror patches as the right part. We merge these two parts together as the input of MRCNN. As a consequence, the number of the input of each sub-network is $10634 \times 2 = 21268$, which is equal to double the train data. In the testing phases, for a new given face image, two predicted results can be derived from the two training parts respectively. We fuse the two results at the decision level by calculating their average value. The specific operations can be found in Fig. 4.

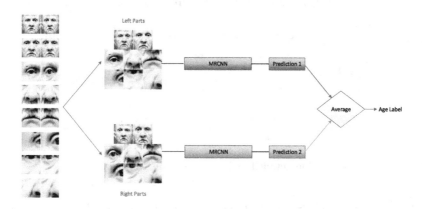

Fig. 4. The test phase of MRCNN.

3.2   Comparison of Age Estimation by Single and Multiple Regions

The MAE (Mean Absolute Error) and CS (Cumulate Score) [8] of our proposed method based on single region and multiple regions are shown in Table 2 and Fig. 5. The MAE is the smaller the better, while the CS is the bigger the better. The facts are indicated with the red arrows in following Tables. MAE_{left} is the error with left parts, while MAE_{right} is the error with right parts. MAE_{avg} is the error with average values. It is obviously that the performance of MRCNN is much superior to those methods based only upon global area and single region.

From the point of view of the horizontal comparison, we can separate the eight groups into four scales, namely, $head > face > eyes\&nose\&mouth > eyecorners\&eyebags\&nosewings$, thus MRCNN can be robust to distortion. Theoretically, the larger the scale is, the more information of age it will preserve. The MAE of head is much lower than nosewings'. Through the vertical

Table 2. The contribution degree of single and multiple regions.

Architecture		MAE↓			CS(5-year)↑
		MAE_{left}	MAE_{right}	**MAE_{avg}**	
MultiRegion		3.60	3.63	3.48	0.76
SingleRegion	Head	4.08	4.15	3.97	0.70
	Face	4.06	4.05	3.92	0.70
	LeftEye	4.85	5.02	4.55	0.62
	Mouse	5.60	5.62	5.44	0.55
	Nose	5.31	5.39	5.21	0.56
	LeftEyeCorner	5.62	5.61	5.17	0.56
	LeftLowEye	5.35	5.43	4.99	0.58
	LeftNose	6.25	6.52	6.02	0.47

comparison, it is obviously that *eyes* contains the most richest age information, and the MAE of *eyes* is lower than MAEs of *nose* and *mouth*, which are at the same scale with *eyes*. Even the methods based on the much smaller scale *eyecorners* and *eyebags* achieve better performances than *mouth* and *nose*. This emphasizes the importance of *eyes*. What's more, the contribution of *nose* is greater than *mouth*.

Though the different scales achieve different performances, they can complement each other via learning from all regions simultaneously. And the MAE of MRCNN is reduced to 3.48 years, which is superior to state-of-the-art algorithms.

3.3   Comparison of Age Estimation in Different Age Groups

In order to demonstrate the effectiveness of our method on each age group, we implement our method on different age groups. The distribution of all age

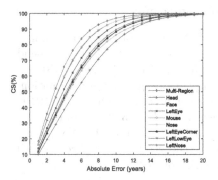

Fig. 5. The CS curves based on single and multiple regions.

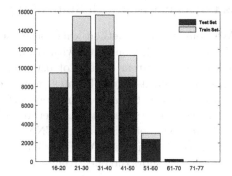

Fig. 6. The train and test set distribution of MORPH.

Table 3. Age estimation in different age groups.

Indicators	Architecture		16–20	21–30	31–40	41–50	51–60	61–70	71–77
$MAE\downarrow$	MultiRegion		3.49	2.88	3.32	3.93	5.32	9.58	16.50
	SingleRegion	Head	4.27	3.31	3.64	4.46	5.89	9.57	17.14
		Face	4.02	3.25	3.68	4.44	5.95	10.00	15.04
		LeftEye	5.86	3.78	3.77	4.69	7.23	12.00	22.32
		Mouse	6.37	4.13	4.41	6.55	9.70	14.95	29.21
		Nose	6.60	4.16	4.25	5.92	8.03	12.44	22.05
		LeftEyeCorner	6.39	3.81	4.10	6.07	9.65	15.99	26.92
		LeftLowEye	6.33	3.91	4.23	5.55	7.64	12.45	21.87
		LeftNose	9.01	5.17	4.09	6.13	9.43	15.44	22.02
$CS(5-year)\uparrow$	MultiRegion		0.78	0.84	0.77	0.70	0.54	0.22	0
	SingleRegion	Head	0.67	0.78	0.73	0.63	0.50	0.25	0
		Face	0.70	0.79	0.72	0.63	0.49	0.18	0
		LeftEye	0.45	0.72	0.71	0.60	0.37	0.07	0
		Mouse	0.42	0.69	0.63	0.42	0.26	0.09	0
		Nose	0.37	0.67	0.65	0.49	0.33	0.10	0
		LeftEyeCorner	0.38	0.72	0.67	0.46	0.22	0.03	0
		LeftLowEye	0.41	0.71	0.65	0.51	0.36	0.13	0
		LeftNose	0.15	0.55	0.67	0.45	0.23	0.03	0

groups is shown in Fig. 6. The performances in different age groups are listed in Table 3. Except the age groups of 61–70 and 71–77 whose numbers are too small, MRCNN get the best results in all age groups.

It is generally known that one's apparent age and biological age may be inconsistent. Apparent is affected by various intrinsic and extrinsic factors. With time going on, their gaps are increasing. Our experiments results reflected that well. Another finding is that MAE of mouse is lower than nose' in the youth, while contrary in the older. We consider the emerging edict wrinkle around nose can account for it.

3.4   Comparison with State-of-the-Art Algorithms

We compare our method with other state-of-the-art algorithms, as summarized in Table 4. Compared with traditional methods, MRCNN is a end-to-end self-learning system instead of using hand-crafted features. Besides, MRCNN introduces multi-regions fusion strategy to complement age-related information, which improves the age estimation performance significantly. On the MORPH database, the best traditional method achieves a MAE of 3.98 (BIF+KCCA), and the best method based on CNN achieves a MAE of 3.63 (MSCNN), while our method achieves a MAE of 3.63, reducing the error by 4.1 percents. All experiments show the effectiveness and superiority of MRCNN.

Table 4. Comparison with state-of-the-art algorithms.

Methods	MAE↓	CS(5-year)↑
BIF+CCA [9]	5.37	-
BIF+KCCA [9]	3.98	-
BIF+KPLS [10]	4.04	-
DFDnet [11]	4.65	0.60
LDL [12]	4.87	-
MSCNN [5]	3.63	-
DLA [3]	4.77	0.63
MRCNN(Ours)	**3.48**	**0.76**

4 Conclusion

In this paper, we propose a novel method for age estimation, named MRCNN. We select eight face subregions, and construct eight sub-network structures respectively, and then fuse at feature-level. Eight sub-networks are able to learn the unique age characteristics of the corresponding subregion and the eight sub-networks are packaged together to complement age-related information. Each facial component is analyzed to examine its contribution to age estimation. We also analyze the estimation accuracy on all age groups. Experiments on MORPH illustrate the superior performance of the proposed MRCNN.

Acknowledgement. This work was supported by the National Key Research and Development Plan (Grant No.2016YFC0801002), the Chinese National Natural Science Foundation Projects ♯61473291, ♯61572501, ♯61502491, ♯61572536, NVIDIA GPU donation program and AuthenMetric R&D Funds.

References

1. Fu, Y., Guo, G., Huang, T.S.: Age synthesis and estimation via faces: a survey. IEEE Trans. Pattern Anal. Mach. Intell. **32**(11), 1955–1976 (2010)
2. Han, H., Otto, C., Liu, X., Jain, A.K.: Demographic estimation from face images: human vs. machine performance. IEEE Trans. Pattern Anal. Mach. Intell. **37**(6), 1148–1161 (2015)
3. Wang, X., Guo, R., Kambhamettu, C.: Deeply-learned feature for age estimation. In: IEEE Winter Conference on Applications of Computer Vision, WACV 2015, pp. 534–541. IEEE (2015)
4. Levi, G., Hassner, T.: Age and gender classification using convolutional neural networks. In: IEEE Conference on Computer Vision and Pattern Recognition Workshops, CVPRW 2015, pp. 34–42. IEEE (2015)
5. Yi, D., Lei, Z., Li, S.Z.: Age estimation by multi-scale convolutional network. In: Cremers, D., Reid, I., Saito, H., Yang, M.-H. (eds.) ACCV 2014. LNCS, vol. 9005, pp. 144–158. Springer, Heidelberg (2015). doi:10.1007/978-3-319-16811-1_10

6. Cootes, T.F., Taylor, C.J., Cooper, D.H., Graham, J.: Active shape models-their training and application. Comput. Vis. Image Underst. **61**(1), 38–59 (1995)
7. Ricanek, K., Tesafaye, T.: Morph: A longitudinal image database of normal adult age-progression. In: International Conference on Automatic Face and Gesture Recognition, FGR 2006, pp. 341–345. IEEE (2006)
8. Guo, G., Mu, G., Fu, Y., Huang, T.S.: Human age estimation using bio-inspired features. In: IEEE Conference on Computer Vision and Pattern Recognition, CVPR 2009, pp. 112–119 (IEEE)
9. Guo, G., Mu, G.: Joint estimation of age, gender and ethnicity: CCA vs. PLS. In: Automatic Face and Gesture Recognition, FG 2013, pp. 1–6. IEEE (2013)
10. Guo, G., Mu, G.: Simultaneous dimensionality reduction and human age estimation via kernel partial least squares regression. In: IEEE Conference on Computer Vision and Pattern Recognition, CVPR 2011, pp. 657–664. IEEE (2011)
11. Liu, T., Lei, Z., Wan, J., Li, S.Z.: DFDnet: discriminant face descriptor network for facial age estimation. In:Yang, J., Yang, J., Sun, Z., Shan, S., Zheng, W., Feng, J. (eds.) CCBR 2015. LNCS, vol. 9428, pp. 649–658. Springer, Heidelberg (2015). doi:10.1007/978-3-319-25417-3_76
12. Geng, X., Yin, C., Zhou, Z.: Facial age estimation by learning from label distributions. IEEE Trans. Pattern Anal. Mach. Intell. **35**(10), 2401–2412 (2013)

Interval Type-2 Fuzzy Linear Discriminant Analysis for Gender Recognition

Yijun Du[1,2], Xiaobo Lu[1,2(✉)], Weili Zeng[3], and Changhui Hu[1,2]

[1] School of Automation, Southeast University, Nanjing 210096, China
xblu2013@126.com
[2] Key Laboratory of Measurement and Control of Complex Systems
of Engineering, Ministry of Education, Nanjing 210096, China
[3] College of Civil Aviation, Nanjing University of Aeronautics and Astronautics,
Nanjing 210096, China

Abstract. In this paper, we propose the interval type-2 fuzzy linear discriminant analysis (IT2FLDA) algorithm for gender recognition. In this algorithm, we first proposed the supervised interval type-2 fuzzy C-Mean (IT2FCM), which introduces the classified information to the IT2FCM, and then the supervised IT2FCM is incorporated into traditional linear discriminant analysis (LDA). By this way, means of each class that are estimated by the supervised IT2FCM can converge to a more desirable location than means of each class obtained by class sample average and the type-1 fuzzy k-nearest neighbor (FKNN) method in the presence of noise. Furthermore, the IT2FLDA is able to minimize the effects of uncertainties, find the optimal projective directions and make the feature subspace discriminating and robust, which inherits the benefits of the supervised IT2FCM and traditional LDA. The experimental results show that the IT2FLDA improved the gender recognition rate when compared to the results from the previous techniques.

Keywords: Type-2 fuzzy set · Linear discriminant analysis · Type-2 fuzzy C-Means algorithm · Fuzzy membership degree

1 Introduction

Attention has been widely paid to the gender recognition which is an important part of face recognition. Currently, a number of techniques have been introduced in the literature for gender recognition. Generally two types of feature are present. These are geometric-based features [1, 2] and appearance-based features [3, 4]. Among the appearance based techniques, LDA is the famous algorithms for supervised dimensionality reduction. LDA seeks the projection matrix by maximizing the ratio of between-scatter matrix to within-scatter matrix [5]. However, we note that the relationship of each face to a class is assumed to be crisp. As the faces are significantly affected by numerous environmental conditions, it is advantageous to investigate these factors and quantify their impact on their "internal" class assignment. Hence, Kwak and Pedrycz [6] introduced the membership degree of each face pattern to a class in LDA based upon the fuzzy k-nearest neighbor (KNN) algorithm [7]. Yang et al. [8] extended

© Springer International Publishing AG 2016
Z. You et al. (Eds.): CCBR 2016, LNCS 9967, pp. 195–202, 2016.
DOI: 10.1007/978-3-319-46654-5_22

the idea of incorporating the membership degree of each face pattern into the definition of the between-class and within-class scatter matrices in LDA. Khoukhi et al. [9] further modified by optimizing the parameters of the membership functions of the training images and the number of nearest neighbors used to calculate the membership degrees through genetic algorithm. In references [6–9], the membership degree is calculated by weighting the contribution of the k-nearest neighbor vectors, the dominant membership is assigned an offset of 0.51 and only to ensure that the dominant membership remains intact. However, there is no reason reported for assigning this particular value of offset. Therefore, it appears that the value of the offset in assigning the membership grades will have some influence of artificial factors on the recognition rate. A genetic algorithm is employed to optimize these parameters of the membership functions in Refs. [9]. However, it is well-known that the genetic algorithm consumes more time to perform the search and is easy to fall into local optimum.

Based on above analysis, the management of uncertainty using type-2 fuzzy sets may be applied to various fields where we cannot obtain satisfactory performance with type-1 fuzzy sets [10–12]. From this point of view, we propose the IT2FLDA algorithm. The IT2FLDA utilizes the supervised IT2FCM algorithm to weight each face pattern to a class with membership degree and calculate means of each class. They are then applied to the definition of within-class scatter matrix and between-class scatter matrix, respectively. The proposed IT2FLDA is able to minimize the effects of uncertainties, find the optimal projective directions and make the feature subspace discriminating and robust, which inherits the benefits of type-2 fuzzy set theory.

This paper is organized as follows. In Sect. 2, the proposed IT2FLDA algorithm is addressed in detail. Section 3 presents implementation details and compares the performance of the proposed method with other previous feature extraction techniques in gender recognition. The conclusions are drawn in Sect. 4.

2   The Proposed IT2FLDA Algorithm

In IT2FLDA algorithm, the fuzzy membership degree and the mean vector of each class can be gained by our proposed supervised IT2FCM algorithm. The supervised IT2FCM algorithm is an extension of the IT2FCM algorithm [13, 14], which introduces the classified information to the IT2FCM algorithm. Therefore, the supervised IT2FCM is able to use the classified information and handle uncertainty found in a given set of feature vectors during the process of feature clustering, thereby makes feature clustering less susceptible to noise to achieve the goal that feature vectors can be clustered more appropriately and more accurately, especially when pattern distributions contain partitions of different size volumes.

Given a set of feature vectors $X = \{x_1, x_2, \cdots, x_N\}$ transformed by the PCA. The number of feature vectors is equal to N and they belong to $c = 2$ classes. Due to considering the classified information, initialize the fuzzy cluster centers $V = \{v_1, v_2\}$ using the following equation.

$$v_i = \frac{1}{N_i} \sum_{x_j \in X_i} x_j \quad j = 1, 2, \cdots, N_i, \quad i = 1, 2 \tag{1}$$

where N_i is the number of samples in class X_i. In doing so, it can be easy to get the optimal fuzzy cluster centers and reduce iterations.

The fuzzification weighting exponent $\tilde{p}(\tilde{p} = [p_1, p_2])$ in the supervised IT2FCM algorithm is represented by an interval rather than a precise numerical value, where p_1 and $p_2(1 < p_1 < p_2 < \infty)$ represent the lower and upper limits of the fuzzification weighting exponent respectively, which reflect the fuzziness of the input data.

Because the $\tilde{p}$ value is represented by an interval, the fuzzy partition matrix $U(U = [\mu_{ij}] \in R^{c \times N})$ must be calculated to the interval $[p_1, p_2]$, for this reason μ_{ij} would be given by the belonging interval $\left[\underline{\mu}_{ij}, \bar{\mu}_{ij}\right]$, where $\underline{\mu}_{ij}$ and $\bar{\mu}_{ij}$ stand for the lower and upper fuzzy membership degrees of j th vector in the i th class. Update the lower and upper limits of the range of the fuzzy partition matrix $\underline{U} = [\underline{\mu}_{ij}] \in R^{c \times N}$, $\bar{U} = [\bar{\mu}_{ij}] \in R^{c \times N}$ can be expressed as:

$$\underline{\mu}_{ij} = \min\left\{\left[\sum_{k=1}^{c}\left(\frac{d_{ij}}{d_{kj}}\right)^{\frac{2}{(p_1-1)}}\right]^{-1}, \left[\sum_{k=1}^{c}\left(\frac{d_{ij}}{d_{kj}}\right)^{\frac{2}{(p_2-1)}}\right]^{-1}\right\} \tag{2}$$

$$\bar{\mu}_{ij} = \max\left\{\left[\sum_{k=1}^{c}\left(\frac{d_{ij}}{d_{kj}}\right)^{\frac{2}{(p_1-1)}}\right]^{-1}, \left[\sum_{k=1}^{c}\left(\frac{d_{ij}}{d_{kj}}\right)^{\frac{2}{(p_2-1)}}\right]^{-1}\right\} \tag{3}$$

where $c = 2$, $i = 1, 2$ and $j = 1, 2, \cdots, N$, d_{ij} is the Euclidean distance between feature vector x_j and cluster center v_i. The distance matrix is defined as $D = [d_{ij}] \in R^{c \times N}$.

In order to ensure that the sample has the maximum degree of membership in its own class, the lower and upper membership degree $\underline{\mu}_{ij}$ and $\bar{\mu}_{ij}$ are adjusted according to the category information. If $\underline{\mu}_{ij}$ is the maximum degree of membership, when i is the same as the label of the j th vector, the value of $\underline{\mu}_{ij}$ is retained; If $\underline{\mu}_{ij}$ is not the maximum degree of membership, when i is the same as the label of the j th vector, we must find the maximum degree of membership $\underline{\mu}_{kj}(k \neq i)$ and exchange value of them. The procedure for adjustment $\bar{\mu}_{ij}$ is the same as $\underline{\mu}_{ij}$.

The procedure for updating the type-2 fuzzy cluster center matrix $\tilde{V}(\tilde{V} = [V_L, V_R])$ in the supervised IT2FCM algorithm should take into account the type-2 fuzzy partition matrix $\tilde{U} = [\underline{U}, \bar{U}]$. The interval of fuzzy cluster centers $V_L = \{v_{1L}, v_{2L}\}$ and $V_R = \{v_{1R}, v_{2R}\}$ will be given by the following equations:

$$v_{iL} = \frac{\sum_{j=1}^{L_i} \bar{\mu}_{ij}^p x_j + \sum_{j=L_i+1}^{N} \underline{\mu}_{ij}^p x_j}{\sum_{j=1}^{L_i} \bar{\mu}_{ij}^p + \sum_{j=L_i+1}^{N} \underline{\mu}_{ij}^p} \tag{4}$$

$$v_{iR} = \frac{\sum_{j=1}^{R_i} \underline{\mu}_{ij}^p x_j + \sum_{j=R_i+1}^{N} \bar{\mu}_{ij}^p x_j}{\sum_{j=1}^{R_i} \underline{\mu}_{ij}^p + \sum_{j=R_i+1}^{N} \bar{\mu}_{ij}^p} \tag{5}$$

where N is the number of feature vectors, and $p = (p_1 + p_2)/2$. The detailed enhanced Karnik-Mendel (EKM) algorithm for computing v_{iL} and v_{iR} can be found in [15] and is omitted here.

The interval of the coordinates for cluster centers is obtained. They are defuzzified by using the average of v_{iL} and v_{iR}. Hence, the crisp cluster centers and the fuzzy membership degrees are obtained by the defuzzification as shown in the following equations:

$$v_i = \frac{v_{iL} + v_{iR}}{2} \tag{6}$$

$$\mu_{ij} = \frac{\underline{\mu}_{ij} + \bar{\mu}_{ij}}{2} \tag{7}$$

Based on all this, the supervised IT2FCM algorithm consists of the following steps:

Step1:   Initialize the fuzzy cluster centers $V^{(l)}$ using Eq. (1); Set iteration counter $l = 0$; Assign the fuzzification weighting exponent p_1 and p_2

Step 2:   Calculate the lower and upper fuzzy partition matrix $\underline{U}^{(l)}$ and $\bar{U}^{(l)}$ using Eqs. (2) and (3). It consists of computing the Euclidean distance d_{ij}, and adjusting the lower and upper membership degree $\bar{\mu}_{ij}$ and $\underline{\mu}_{ij}$

Step 3:   Update the fuzzy cluster centers $V^{(l+1)}$ using Eqs. (4)–(6)

Step 4:   Compare $V^{(l+1)}$ and $V^{(l)}$ until $\|V^{(l+1)} - V^{(l)}\| < \varepsilon$; otherwise, Let $l = l+1$, back to step 2;

Therefore, the fuzzy mean vector of each class $\tilde{m}_i$ and the fuzzy membership matrix U can be achieved with the result of the supervised IT2FCM.

$$U = [\mu_{ij}] \quad i = 1, 2 \quad j = 1, \cdots, N \tag{8}$$

$$\tilde{m}_i = v_i \quad i = 1, 2 \tag{9}$$

The membership degree of each vector (contribution to each class) is considered and the corresponding fuzzy within-class scatter matrix and fuzzy between-class scatter matrix are redefined as follows:

$$\tilde{S}_{FB} = \sum_{i=1}^{c} \sum_{j=1}^{N} \mu_{ij}^p (\tilde{m}_i - \bar{m})(\tilde{m}_i - \bar{m})^T \tag{10}$$

$$\tilde{S}_{FW} = \sum_{i=1}^{c} \sum_{x_k \in X_i} \mu_{ij}^p (x_i - \tilde{m}_i)(x_i - \tilde{m}_i)^T \tag{11}$$

where $\bar{m}$ is a mean vector of training set X, $c = 2$, p is a constant which controls the influence of the fuzzy membership degree.

The optimal interval type-2 fuzzy projection $W_{IT2FLDA}$ is given by the following expression:

$$W_{IT2FLDA} = \arg\max_{W} \frac{\left|W^T \tilde{S}_{FB} W\right|}{\left|W^T \tilde{S}_{FW} W\right|} \tag{12}$$

The feature vectors $Y = \{y_1, y_2, \cdots, y_N\}$ transformed by IT2FLDA algorithm can be calculated as follows:

$$y_j = W_{IT2FLDA}^T x_j = W_{IT2FLDA}^T W_{PCA}^T (z_j - \bar{z}) \tag{13}$$

where $\bar{z}$ describes a mean facial image in the training set Z.

3   Experimental Results

In this section, we verify the performance of the IT2FLDA algorithm from gender recognition accuracy and the robustness. In all scenarios we use the nearest neighbor classification. Experiments are performed on a personal computer with Intel Core i3 CPU at 3.10 GHz and 2.00 GB RAM. All the algorithms have been implemented using MATLAB programming language.

3.1   Gender Classification Using Proposed Method

In the experiments, we first reduce the dimension of the training set using PCA and determine 100 eigenvectors; then, we extract discriminant vectors using IT2FLDA. The parameters of the supervised IT2FCM are chosen with $p_1 = 1.5$, $p_2 = 2.5$ and $p = 2$.

The proposed algorithm for gender recognition is tested on the Internet facial database. The Internet facial database consists of 1130 frontal images from 1130 individuals (with only one image per person), 501 of which belong to class male and 629 to class female. These images mostly come from digital pictures and posters, which has the characteristics of pose complexities, rich facial expressions and so on. In this database, we randomly select 566 images (251 males and 315 females) for training, and 564 images (250 males and 314 females) for testing. Original images were normalized (in scale and orientation) such that the two eyes were aligned at the same position. The size of each cropped image is 96×112. Some of face images in the Internet facial database are shown in Fig. 1. This procedure was repeated 20 times by randomly choosing different training and testing sets.

The gender recognition rates for various feature extraction methods are shown in Fig. 2. Table 1 contains a comparative analysis of the mean and standard deviation for the obtained gender recognition rates. The proposed IT2FLDA algorithm outperformed LDA and FLDA. IT2FLDA achieves the average gender recognition rates of 90.77 % and gets the best result. FLDA and LDA achieve the average gender recognition rates

Fig. 1. The Internet facial database

of 89.35 % and 88.53 %, respectively. Compare with FLDA and LDA, IT2FLDA has minimum standard deviation. Hence, the proposed IT2FLDA algorithm outperformed LDA and FLDA.

Table 1. Comparison of the mean and standard deviation for the gender recognition rates

Method	Total	Male	Female
Proposed method	90.77 ± 1.07	89.24 ± 2.13	91.99 ± 1.49
FLDA [6]	89.35 ± 1.13	86.54 ± 2.21	91.59 ± 1.86
LDA [5]	88.53 ± 1.25	85.98 ± 2.34	90.56 ± 1.79

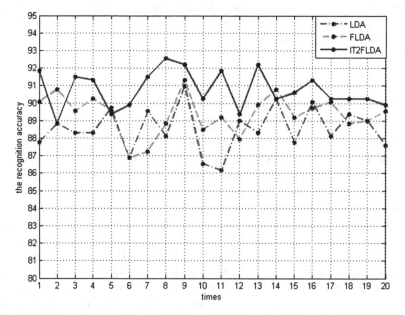

Fig. 2. The gender recognition rates of various methods

3.2 The Robustness of the Algorithm Under Noise Environment

In order to verify the robustness of the proposed method, experiments are conducted under "salt and pepper" noise environments on Internet facial database. All images incorporate "salt and pepper" noise, whose density is 0.1.

The gender recognition rates for various feature extraction method with "salt and pepper" noise are shown in Fig. 3. Compare Tables 1 and 2, we can see that the mean and the standard deviation of gender recognition rates have a great change, which are caused by noise. The standard deviation of the IT2FLDA is smaller than other two methods. In LDA method, the sample must be fully belongs to one class. It means that the sample fully contribute to computing the class mean, even through the sample stay away from other samples of this class. That caused the class mean is not exact. In the IT2FLDA and FLDA methods, the sample belongs to one class according its fuzzy membership degree. Hence, if the sample is isolated, it has less contribution to computing the class mean. It can reduce the influence and make the class mean to be more reasonable.

Table 2. The mean and standard deviation for gender recognition with "salt & pepper" noise

Method	Total	Male	Female
Proposed method	88.10 ± 1.16	85.66 ± 2.78	90.04 ± 1.84
FLDA [6]	85.48 ± 1.23	82.66 ± 2.05	87.72 ± 2.25
LDA [5]	84.90 ± 1.65	81.14 ± 3.01	87.89 ± 2.16

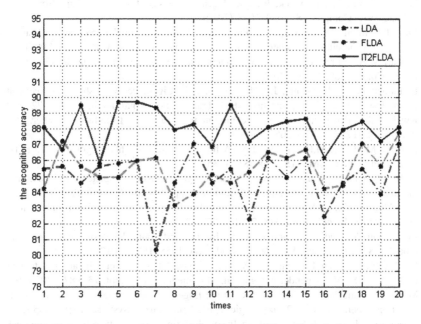

Fig. 3. The gender recognition rates of various methods with "salt & pepper" noise

4 Conclusions

In this paper, we proposed the IT2FLDA algorithm for gender recognition. We first proposed the supervised IT2FCM. Then the supervised IT2FCM is incorporated into traditional LDA to reduce these outer effects to obtain the correct local distribution information to ensure good performance. Experimental results show a better recognition rate in comparison to LDA and FLDA. It is worth stressing that the algorithm developed in the setting of type-2 fuzzy sets revealed more robust characteristics as far as the uncertainty occur due to large variation.

Acknowledgments. This work was supported by the National Key Science & Technology Pillar Program of China (No.2014BAG01B03), the National Natural Science Foundation of China (No. 61374194 & No. 61403081), the Natural Science Foundation of Jiangsu Province (No. BK20140638), Scientific Research Foundation of Graduate School of Southeast University (YBJJ1519) and a Project Funded by the Priority Academic Program Development of Jiangsu Higher Education Institutions.

References

1. Mozaffari, S., Behravan, H., Akbari, R.: Gender classification using single frontal image per person: combination of appearance and geometric based features. In: 20th IEEE International Conference on Pattern Recognition, pp. 1192–1195. IEEE Press, Istanbul (2010)
2. Wu, J., Smith, W., Hancock, E.: Facial gender classification using shape-from-shading. J. Image Vis. Comput. **28**, 1039–1048 (2010)
3. Lu, H., Huang, Y., Chen, Y., Yang, D.: Automatic gender recognition based on pixel-pattern-based texture feature. J. Real-Time Image Process. **3**, 109–116 (2008)
4. Berbar, M.A.: Three robust features extraction approaches for facial gender classification. J. Vis. Comput. **30**, 19–31 (2014)
5. Belhumeur, P.N., Hespanha, J.P., Kriegman, D.J.: Eigenfaces vs. fisherfaces: recognition using class specific linear projection. IEEE Trans. Pattern Anal. Intell. **19**, 711–720 (1997)
6. Kwak, K.C., Pedrycz, W.: Face recognition using a fuzzy fisherface classifier. Pattern Recogn. **38**, 1717–1732 (2005)
7. Keller, J.M., Gray, M.R., Givens, J.A.: A fuzzy k-nearest neighbor algorithm. IEEE Trans. Syst. Man Cybern. **SMC-15**, 580–585 (1985)
8. Yang, W., Yan, H., Wang, J., Yang, J.: Face recognition using complete fuzzy LDA. In: 19th International Conference on Pattern Recognition, pp. 1–4. IEEE Press, Tampa (2008)
9. Khoukhi, A., Ahmed, S.F.: A genetically modified fuzzy linear discriminant analysis for face recognition. J. Franklin Inst. **348**, 2701–2717 (2011)
10. Li, Y., Du, Y.: Indirect adaptive fuzzy observer and controller design based on interval type-2 T-S fuzzy model. Appl. Math. Model. **36**, 1558–1569 (2012)
11. Du, Y., Lu, X., Chen, L., Zeng, W.: An interval type-2 T-S fuzzy classification system based on PSO and SVM for gender recognition. Multimedia Tools Appl. **75**, 987–1007 (2016)
12. Melin, P., Gonzalez, C.I., Castro, J.R., et al.: Edge-detection method for image processing based on generalized type-2 fuzzy logic. IEEE Trans. Fuzzy Syst. **22**, 1515–1525 (2014)
13. Hwang, C., Rhee, F.C.H.: Uncertain fuzzy clustering: interval type-2 fuzzy approach to C-means. IEEE Trans. Fuzzy Syst. **15**, 107–120 (2007)
14. Linda, O., Manic, M.: General type-2 fuzzy c-means algorithm for uncertain fuzzy clustering. IEEE Trans. Fuzzy Syst. **20**, 883–897 (2012)
15. Wu, D., Mendel, J.M.: Enhanced Karnik-Mendel algorithms. IEEE Trans. Fuzzy Syst. **17**, 923–934 (2009)

Fingerprint, Palm-print and Vascular Biometrics

Latent Fingerprint Enhancement Based on Orientation Guided Sparse Representation

Kaifeng Wei and Manhua Liu(✉)

Department of Instrument Science and Engineering, SEIEE, Shanghai Jiao Tong University, Shanghai, China
wkf8092@163.com, mhliu@sjtu.edu.cn

Abstract. Latent fingerprints are the finger skin impressions left at the crime scene by accident. They are usually of poor quality with unclear ridge structure and various overlapping patterns. This paper proposes a latent fingerprint enhancement algorithm which combines the TV image decomposition model and image reconstruction by orientation guided sparse representation. Firstly, the TV model is applied to decompose a latent fingerprint image into the texture and cartoon components. Secondly, we calculate the orientation field and the reliability of the texture image. Finally, for the low reliability region, sparse representation based on the redundant dictionary, which is constructed with Gabor functions and the specific local ridge orientation, is iteratively used to reconstruct the image. Experimental results based on NIST SD27 latent fingerprint database indicate that the proposed algorithm can not only remove various noises, but also restore the corrupted ridge structure well.

Keywords: Latent fingerprint enhancement · Sparse representation · Orientation field · Gabor dictionary · TV model

1 Introduction

Latent fingerprints are the finger skin impressions unintentionally left by a person at crime scenes, which have been considered as an important evidence for identifying and convicting criminals in law enforcement agencies [1]. Compared with rolled and plain fingerprints (see Fig. 1), latent fingerprints are usually of low quality overlapped with various non-fingerprint patterns such as writing letters, lines or even other latent fingerprints. Due to the poor quality, the fingerprint features may be falsely extracted or missed so that the accuracy of latent fingerprint identification is lower than that of rolled and plain fingerprints [1]. Thus, latent fingerprint enhancement is a necessary pre-processing step for fingerprint identification (or matching). Although great progress has been made in rolled and plain fingerprints enhancement, most of these methods cannot perform well for latent fingerprints due to the low image quality [2].

Generally, there are two main difficulties for latent fingerprint enhancement. First, since most of latent fingerprints are overlapped by various non-fingerprint patterns such as writing letters and lines, how to remove these structured noises is still an important

© Springer International Publishing AG 2016
Z. You et al. (Eds.): CCBR 2016, LNCS 9967, pp. 205–213, 2016.
DOI: 10.1007/978-3-319-46654-5_23

Fig. 1. Three types of latent fingerprints: (a) rolled (b) plain and (c) latent.

task for enhancement. Second, it is still a challenging task to restore the noise corrupted fingerprint ridge structure without introducing false features.

There are many methods proposed to enhance the latent fingerprint. Yoon et al. [3] proposed an algorithm for latent fingerprint enhancement based on Gabor filters. In this algorithm, a robust algorithm was conducted for orientation field estimation and Gabor filtering was performed for enhancement [3]. Feng et al. [4] proposed an orientation field estimation algorithm by utilizing the prior knowledge of the fingerprint ridge structure for latent fingerprint enhancement. With robust orientation field estimation, a Gabor filter was applied to enhance latent fingerprints. Cao et al. [1] proposed a latent fingerprint enhancement algorithm which applied the coarse to fine ridge structure dictionaries to estimate the orientation and frequency fields for Gabor filtering. Liu et al. [5] proposed an enhancement algorithm via multi-scale patch based sparse representation, which applied the Gabor dictionary and sparse representation to reconstruct the corrupted fingerprint image.

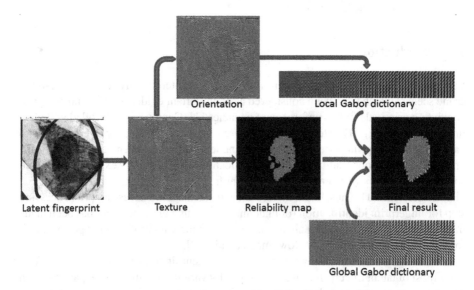

Fig. 2. The flowchart of the proposed latent fingerprint enhancement algorithm

In this paper, we propose a latent fingerprint enhancement method based on orientation guided sparse representation. The flowchart of the proposed algorithm is shown in Fig. 2. First, each latent fingerprint image is decomposed into texture and cartoon components with the total-variation (TV) image model. The local ridge orientation field and the reliability were then computed with the texture component. For each image patch, in addition to the global Gabor dictionary, a local Gabor dictionary is constructed with the specific local ridge orientation. Finally, orientation guided sparse representation was iteratively applied to reconstruct the low reliability regions of the texture component. This paper is organized as follows. In Sect. 2, the proposed enhancement algorithm is described in detail. Section 3 presents the experimental results on NIST SD27 latent fingerprint database and comparisons with other related algorithms. Finally, we conclude the paper in Sect. 4.

2   The Proposed Algorithm

This will present the proposed latent fingerprint enhancement algorithm in detail, which includes three main steps: latent fingerprint decomposition by TV model, orientation field computation and fingerprint restoration via sparse representation.

2.1   Latent Fingerprint Decomposition by Total-Variation Model

The total-variation model (TV) has been proved to be an efficient model for regularizing images without smoothing the boundaries of targets [6]. Given an image y, it can be decomposed into texture v and cartoon u through TV model, i.e., $y = u+v$. Texture v includes the oscillatory and noise component, while cartoon u consists of the piecewise smooth component [5]. Mathematically, the decomposition can be obtained by minimizing the total variation [7]:

$$\min_{(u,v)\in L^2(\Omega)} \{TV(u) + \lambda\|u - y\|_2^2\} \tag{1}$$

where $TV(u)$ denotes the total variation of u and the parameter λ is used to balance the tradeoff between the fidelity of u and the minimization of TV. The range of λ is set from 0 to 1 and larger λ will produce stronger texture and vice versa. Figure 3 shows the decomposition of a sample latent fingerprint image by TV model with λ set to 0.7.

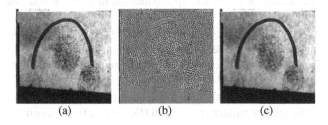

(a)   (b)   (c)

Fig. 3. Latent fingerprint decomposition: (a) latent fingerprint, (b) texture and (c) cartoon.

2.2   Orientation Field Computation

Orientation field is an important feature to describe the fingerprint ridge flow structure, which plays an important role for fingerprint processing and recognition [3]. It is usually computed by uniformly dividing the fingerprint into blocks and estimating the orientation for each block. There are many methods proposed for computation of orientation field such as gradient based methods, Fourier series model and low-pass filtering based method [3, 4]. In this paper, we compute the orientation field using the method proposed by Feng et al. [4]. The orientation field estimation algorithm includes two stages: off-line dictionary construction and on-line orientation field estimation [4]. In the offline stage, a dictionary of orientation patches is constructed from the orientation fields, which are manually selected from a set of good quality fingerprints [4]. The on-line orientation field estimation consisted of three steps: initial estimation, dictionary lookup and context-based correction [4].

2.3   Fingerprint Reconstruction via Orientation Guided Sparse Representation

Sparse representation has been widely used in many fields such as image processing, pattern recognition and signal processing [8]. Generally, a signal can be decomposed into a combination of elementary atoms as follows [9]:

$$y = X\alpha \tag{2}$$

where $y \in R^d$ is the input sample by a column vector. $X = [x_1, x_2, ..., x_n]$ is composed of the elementary atoms for representation [8]. $\alpha = [\alpha_1, \alpha_2, ..., \alpha_n]^T$ is the coefficient vector of X. If there is no limiting condition or prior knowledge for the representation coefficient α, it is impossible to get a unique solution for this equation.

Sparse representation considers that the coefficients α should be sparse, which means that most of coefficients in α should be zero or very close to zero [8]. Although the l_0-norm minimization of α can acquire the sparse representation but it is difficult to approximate [10]. To solve this problem, l_0-norm is replaced with the l_1-norm regularized minimization to get the solution as those in the literature [11–13]:

$$\hat{\alpha} = \arg\min \|\alpha\|_1 \text{ s.t. } \|y - X\alpha\|_2^2 \le \varepsilon \tag{3}$$

where $\|\alpha\|_1$ i.e., the l_1-norm of α, is the penalty quantifying sparsity, ε is a tuning parameter to control the fidelity of the model approximation to y, and X is the dictionary for sparse representation.

In this work, we model the fingerprint enhancement as a sparse representation and reconstruction problem. To achieve good approximation, dictionary should characterize all kinds of ridge structures and details. The local fingerprint patch usually forms a 2D sinusoidal-shaped wave with well-defined orientation and frequency. Gabor functions have both good frequency- and orientation-selective properties which can capture the characteristics of fingerprint pattern [14]. The 2D Gabor functions have the general form:

$$h(x,y,\theta,f) = \exp\left\{-\frac{1}{2}\left[\frac{x_\theta^2}{\delta_x^2} + \frac{y_\theta^2}{\delta_y^2}\right]\right\}\cos(2\pi f x_\theta + \varphi_0) \tag{4}$$

$$x_\theta = x\cos\theta + y\sin\theta \tag{5}$$

$$y_\theta = -x\sin\theta + y\cos\theta \tag{6}$$

where δ_x and δ_y are the space constants of Gaussian envelope along x and y axes, respectively; θ and f represent the orientation and frequency of the Gabor functions, respectively; φ_0 is the initial phase of Gabor functions [14]. The dictionary can be constructed by varying the parameters of Gabor functions.

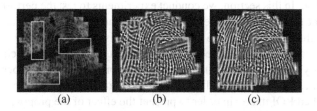

(a)   (b)   (c)

Fig. 4. One sample of sparse representation: (a) latent fingerprint, (b) sparse representation on global Gabor dictionary and (c) sparse representation on local Gabor dictionary.

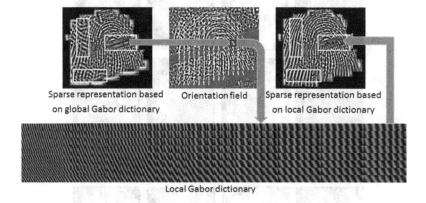

Sparse representation based   Orientation field   Sparse representation based
on global Gabor dictionary   on local Gabor dictionary

Local Gabor dictionary

Fig. 5. The procedure of fingerprint reconstruction via sparse representation on local Gabor dictionary guided by the local ridge orientation.

First, similar to the method [5], a global dictionary is constructed with the Gabor function specified as 16 orientations, 9 frequencies and 6 initial phases varying in their whole ranges. Fingerprint reconstruction via the global dictionary performs well to reconstruct the corrupted ridge by the small noise. But it cannot perform well to restore the corrupted image by the structured noises as shown in Fig. 4. To address this problem, we proposed to construct a local dictionary with the orientation specified as the local ridge orientation and the other two parameters same as those of global dictionary.

Figure 5 shows the procedure of image reconstruction by sparse representation based on local dictionary. For a noise corrupted patch (see the blue rectangle in Fig. 5), its orientation is obtained from the orientation field and is used to guide the construction of a local dictionary. Finally, the sparse representation on the local dictionary is applied to reconstruct the image region where the global dictionary cannot achieve good results as shown in Fig. 5.

3   Experimental Results

The main purpose of latent fingerprint enhancement is to remove the complex structure noises while restore the corrupted ridge details for reliable feature extraction and fingerprint recognition. In this section, we conduct experiments to test the performance of the proposed latent fingerprint enhancement algorithm and compare the results with those of other algorithms [4, 5]. The NIST SD27 database is used in the experiments, which consists of 258 latent and their mated rolled fingerprints. This database includes "good", "bad" and "ugly" three different quality latent fingerprints and the number of them are 88, 85 and 85, respectively. In addition, all of the comparisons are based on the same manually marked ROI masks in order to present the effect of the proposed algorithm.

(a)   (b)   (c)   (d)

Fig. 6.   (a) Latent fingerprint, (b) Feng method [4], (c) Liu method [5] and (d) proposed method.

Figure 6 shows the comparison of enhancement results for three sampled latent fingerprints of NIST SD27 with "bad", "good" and "ugly" qualities. From these results, we can see that Feng method [4] by Gabor filtering can remove the noise well but it cannot restore the corrupted ridge patterns. Liu method [5] can reconstruct well the ridge patterns when the noise is small, but it may result in false ridge structure when the ridge is corrupted by heavy noises because the reconstruction is not guided by global pattern. The proposed method can perform better to restore the ridge pattern corrupted by heavy structure noises. It should be noted that reconstruction is performed only on the regions of low reliability in proposed method. The unclear ridge patterns Fig. 6(d) are due to the display of weak texture image, but these regions have high reliability of ridge structure and thus no reconstruction is performed to reduce the computation.

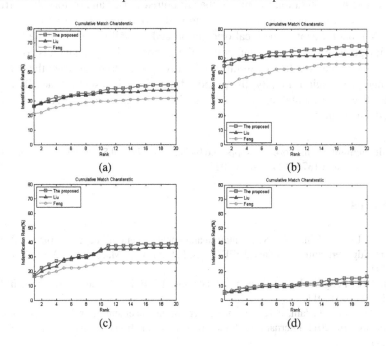

Fig. 7. Comparison of CMC curves on NIST SD27: (a) all, (b) good, (c) bad and (d) ugly fingerprints.

As the final objective of enhancement is to improve the performance of latent fingerprint identification, we conduct the latent fingerprint identification experiment and compute the identification accuracy to evaluate the performance of the proposed algorithm. In this paper, the fingerprint identification is conducted in the template database which includes 27000 fingerprint images of NIST SD14 and 258 mated rolled fingerprint images. In addition, the commercial software Neurotechnology VeriFinger SDK 6.5 is used for the following feature extraction and fingerprint matching. For matching the enhanced latent fingerprint with all templates, 27258 matching scores are generated and sorted in descending order. Finally, a Cumulative Match Characteristic (CMC) curve plots the identification rate with rank k varying from 1 to 20. The identification rate indicates the proportion of times that the genuine rolled fingerprint appears in the top k matches [5]. Figure 7 shows the comparison of the CMC curves of the proposed method and other methods [4, 5]. Figure 7(a), (b), (c) and (d) show the CMC curves on the all, good, bad and ugly latent fingerprints, respectively. The results demonstrate that the proposed method performs better than other method, especially for good quality fingerprints.

4   Conclusion

In this paper, we propose a latent fingerprint enhancement algorithm based on orientation guided sparse representation to remove the structured noises and restore the corrupted ridge structures. First, latent image is decomposed into texture and cartoon components by the TV model. Second, the local orientation and reliability are calculated with the texture image. The sparse representation on the Gabor dictionary, which is constructed with the local ridge orientation guiding, is iteratively used to reconstruct the low reliability fingerprint region. Finally, the proposed algorithm is tested on the NIST SD27 database. The experimental results and comparison demonstrate the effectiveness of the proposed algorithm.

Acknowledgement. This work was supported by National Natural Science Foundation of China under the grants No. 61375112 and 61005024.

References

1. Cao, K., Liu, E., Jain, A.K.: Segmentation and enhancement of latent fingerprints: A coarse to fine ridge structure dictionary. IEEE Trans. Pattern Anal. Mach. Intell. **36**(9), 1847–1859 (2014)
2. Jain, A.K., Feng, J.: Latent fingerprint matching. IEEE Trans. Pattern Anal. Mach. Intell. **33**(1), 88–100 (2011)
3. Yoon, S., Feng, J., Jain, A.K.: Latent fingerprint enhancement via robust orientation field estimation. In: 2011 International Joint Conference on Biometrics (IJCB), pp. 1–8. IEEE (2011)
4. Feng, J., Zhou, J., Jain, A.K.: Orientation field estimation for latent fingerprint enhancement. IEEE Trans. Pattern Anal. Mach. Intell. **35**(4), 925–940 (2013)
5. Liu, M., Chen, X., Wang, X.: Latent fingerprint enhancement via multi-scale patch based sparse representation. IEEE Trans. Inf. Forensics Secur. **10**(1), 6–15 (2015)
6. Chambolle, A.: An algorithm for total variation minimization and applications. J. Math. Imag. Vis. **20**(1–2), 89–97 (2004)
7. Buades, A., Le, T.M., Morel, J.M.: Fast cartoon+texture image filters. IEEE Trans. Image Process. **19**(8), 1978–1986 (2010)
8. Zhang. Z., Xu, Y., Yang, J.: A survey of sparse representation: algorithms and applications. IEEE Access **3**, 490–530 (2015)
9. Rubinstein, R., Bruckstein, A.M., Elad, M.: Dictionaries for sparse representation modeling. Proc. IEEE **98**(6), 1045–1057 (2010)
10. Amaldi, E., Kann, V.: On the approximability of minimizing nonzero variables or unsatisfied relations in linear systems. Theoret. Comput. Sci. **209**(1), 237–260 (1998)

11. Wright, J., Yang, A.Y., Ganesh, A.: Robust face recognition via sparse representation. IEEE Trans. Pattern Anal. Mach. Intell. **31**(2), 210–227 (2009)
12. Donoho, D.L.: For most large underdetermined systems of linear equations the minimal l1-norm solution is also the sparsest solution. Commun. Pure Appl. Math. **59**(6), 797–829 (2006)
13. Candes, E.J., Tao, T.: Near-optimal signal recovery from random projections: Universal encoding strategies? IEEE Trans. Inf. Theory **52**(12), 5406–5425 (2006)
14. Hong, L., Wan, Y., Jain, A.: Fingerprint image enhancement: algorithm and performance evaluation. IEEE Trans. Pattern Anal. Mach. Intell. **20**(8), 777–789 (1998)

A Hybrid Quality Estimation Algorithm for Fingerprint Images

Xin Li[1], Ruxin Wang[1], Mingqiang Li[1], Chaochao Bai[1], and Tong Zhao[1,2($\boxtimes$)]

[1] University of Chinese Academy of Sciences, Beijing, China
{lixin14,wangruxin12,limingqiang14,baichaochao12}@mails.ucas.ac.cn,
zhaotong@ucas.ac.cn
[2] Key Laboratory of Big Data Mining and Knowledge Management,
CAS, Beijing, China

Abstract. Estimating the quality of a fingerprint image is very important in an automatic fingerprint identification system. It helps to reject poor-quality samples during enrollment and adjust the enhancement, feature extraction and matching strategies according to the quality of fingerprints, thus upgrading the performance of the overall system. In this paper, we propose a locality sensitive algorithm for fingerprint image quality assessment. For low curvature parts, we estimate their quality based on the sparse coefficients computed against a redundant Gabor dictionary. For high curvature parts, the quality is measured with their responses of a set of symmetric descriptors. Besides, the ridge and valley clarity is evaluated for the whole foreground. By integrating these information, the quality assessment of a fingerprint image is obtained. We test the proposed method on the FVC2002 Db1 and FVC2004 Db1 databases. Experimental results demonstrate that the proposed method is an effective predictor of biometrics performance.

Keywords: Fingerprint image quality assessment · Sparse representation · Symmetric descriptors · Ridge and Valley Clarity

1 Introduction

Over the last years, biometric recognition has been receiving considerable attention due to increasing concerns about security and identity authentication. Biometrics refers to automatic individual recognition based on anatomical (e.g., fingerprint, face, iris) and behavioral (e.g., speech) characteristics, which represent the individuals bodily identity and cannot be shared or misplaced [1]. Among these biometric traits, fingerprint is the most widespread in personal identification systems due to its permanence and uniqueness [2]. Automatic fingerprint identification systems, like other applications of pattern recognition and machine learning, are affected a lot by the quality of input data. Fingerprint quality is usually defined as a measure of the clarity of the ridge and valley structures, as well as the extractability of features used for recognition such as minutiae and singular points [3]. A good estimate of fingerprint quality should be predictive of the utility

© Springer International Publishing AG 2016
Z. You et al. (Eds.): CCBR 2016, LNCS 9967, pp. 214–223, 2016.
DOI: 10.1007/978-3-319-46654-5_24

of features and matching performance of fingerprint images [1]. If we can estimate the quality of a fingerprint image firstly, we are able to reject the very poor-quality samples, and then new samples can be collected. We can also improve the performance of identification process by combining quality information into the procedure of enhancement, feature extraction and matching [4].

Until now, a number of methods have been proposed to estimate fingerprint quality, which can be divided into: (1) those that use local features of the image, such as local orientation reliability [5], symmetric features [6]; (2) those that use global features of images, such as Fourier spectrum [3]; (3) those that address the problem as a classification problem, such as NFIQ [8]. A comprehensive review of them has been given in [2]. However, these approaches usually process on the full regions of a fingerprint, and most of them cannot work well on some parts. For example, whenever the ridge to valley structure on the neighborhood around singular points is distinct or not, orientation coherence usually tends to give a bad quality evaluation there, which is not that expected.

In this paper, we propose a locality sensitive method to assess the fingerprint quality, which can overcome this shortcoming. For low curvature parts of a fingerprint, we construct a dictionary based on a set of Gabor elementary functions and calculate the sparse representation of blocks against the Gabor dictionary. Since a good-quality fingerprint block in low curvature parts usually has a specific ridge frequency and orientation, so it can be well characterized by one or some given Gabor filters and the coefficients should be sparse. As for poor-quality blocks, the coefficients will be more evenly distributed. Therefore, for blocks in low curvature parts, it is reasonable to use sparsity as a quality measurement. However, for high curvature parts, considering that singular points may be in the neighborhood, sparse representation cannot work well, so we decompose the orientation tensor of these parts into symmetric representation [6] and measure how well these parts comprise the expected symmetry. If there exists an apparent singular point, it will give a good quality assessment. Besides, through analysing gray level distributions of ridge and valley, the clarity is evaluated for the full foreground. By integrating the information of frequency, orientation, symmetry and clarity, we get the final quality evaluation of a fingerprint image. Some intermediate results are shown in Fig. 1.

This paper is organized as follows. Section 2 details the proposed method. Section 3 presents and analyses experimental data and results. Finally, Sect. 4 concludes the paper.

2 Methodology

In this work, we detail how we employ the sparse representation based on a Gabor dictionary, the symmetry representation and the clarity of ridge and valley.

2.1 Sparse Representation

Signals can be usually described as linear combinations of elementary signals or dictionary atoms [9]. Research on image statistics suggests that image patches

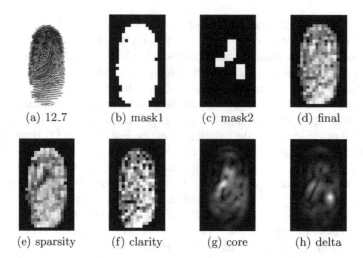

(a) 12_7   (b) mask1   (c) mask2   (d) final

(e) sparsity   (f) clarity   (g) core   (h) delta

Fig. 1. Illustration of intermediate results. The image id is 12_7 of FVC2004 Db1. (a) Gray scale fingerprint image, (b) foreground mask, (c) high curvature mask, (d) final quality map, (e) sparsity quality map, (f) clarity quality map, (g) symmetry quality map for core points detection, (h) symmetry quality map for delta points detection. We obtain the high curvature mask by analyzing the distribution of orientations in each block. Note that, symmetry quality maps are only calculated in high curvature parts in experiments.

can be well represented as a sparse linear combination of elements from a proper over-complete dictionary [10]. This dictionary-based approach has been successfully used in fingerprint orientation field estimation [11], segmentation [12] and enhancement [12].

Mathematically speaking, a real valued signal $y \in R^N$ can be represented by a linear combination of a set of N-dimensional basis atoms:

$$y = \sum_i \alpha_i \phi_i + e = \Phi\alpha + e, \tag{1}$$

where $\Phi = [\phi_1, \phi_2, ..., \phi_M] \in R^{N \times M}$ is a dictionary consisting of a set of basis atoms; $\alpha = [\alpha_1, \alpha_2, ..., \alpha_M] \in R^M$ denotes the basis coefficient vector; e represents the additive noise imposed on the signal. As a local fingerprint block usually has a specific frequency and orientation, the representation coefficients are expected to be sparse which means that only a few values are nonzero. Measuring the sparsity as $l_0 - norm$ of α is a nonconvex problem and cannot be efficiently solved. Therefore, a convex relaxation is adopted to use a $l_1 - norm$ regularization:

$$\min \|\alpha\|_1 \quad s.t. \quad \|y - \Phi\alpha\|_2^2 < \epsilon, \tag{2}$$

where $\|\alpha\|_1$ is the $l_1 - norm$ of α and $\epsilon > 0$ is a tuning parameter to control the fidelity of the model approximately to y.

To compute the sparse representation of a local fingerprint block, a redundant dictionary needs to be constructed firstly. The local fingerprint block in low Curvature regions usually forms a sinusoidal plane wave with well-defined frequency and orientation. Gabor functions have both frequency and orientation selective properties and have optimal joint resolution in both spatial and frequency domains [13]. To obtain good representation, we construct the dictionary with a set of Gabor elementary functions with different parameters [14].

The 2D Gabor functions have the general form:

$$h(x, y, \theta, f) = \exp\{-\frac{1}{2}[\frac{x_\theta^2}{\delta_x^2} + \frac{y_\theta^2}{\delta_y^2}]\} \cos(2\pi f x_0 + \phi_0), \tag{3}$$

$$x_\theta = x \cos\theta + y \sin\theta, \tag{4}$$

$$y_\theta = -x \sin\theta + y \cos\theta, \tag{5}$$

where δ_x and δ_y are the space constants of the Gaussian envelope along x and y axes and we set $\delta_x = \delta_y$ equal to the patch size; f is the frequency of a sinusoidal plan wave and it ranges from 5 to 21 at a step of 2; θ is the orientation of Gabor function and it varies from 0 to $15\pi/16$ at a step of $\pi/16$; ϕ_0 is the phase offset of Gabor function and it ranges from 0 to $5\pi/6$ at a step of $\pi/6$. Figure 2 presents the dictionary consisting of 864 Gabor atoms.

After dictionary construction, the sparse representation of patches against the Gabor dictionary is computed. Since a good-quality local fingerprint path in low curvature regions always has a specific frequency and orientation, the representation coefficient is usually sparse. As for other patches of bad quality or in the non-fingerprint or high curvature regions, the coefficients are more evenly distributed. Therefore, we use the sparsity as a quality evaluation of a local fingerprint block:

$$q_1 = \frac{\max |\alpha_i|}{\sum_{i=1}^N |\alpha_i|}. \tag{6}$$

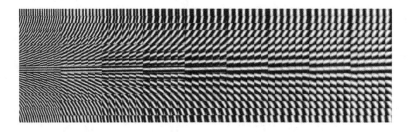

Fig. 2. The dictionary used for sparse representation in low curvature parts, consisting of the Gabor basis atoms at 16 different orientations, 9 different frequencies and 6 different phases.

2.2 Symmetry Representation

From biometrics performance viewpoint, the quality of a fingerprint is concerned with the extraction of certain points(singular points, minutiae). In this work, we decompose the orientation tensor of high curvature parts into symmetry representations with symmetric descriptors designed based on a prior knowledge about fingerprint [6], and the resulting quality is evaluated by how well it comprises the expected symmetry.

The orientation tensor is given by the equation:

$$z = (D_x f + i D_y f)^2, \tag{7}$$

where $D_x f$ and $D_y f$ denote the partial derivatives of the image along $x-$ and $y-axes$. To compute the derivatives, separable Gaussians with a small standard deviation δ_1 are used. Filters modeling the symmetry description are calculated by

$$h_n = \begin{cases} (x + iy)^n \cdot g & for\ n \geq 0 \\ (x - iy)^{|n|} \cdot g & for\ n < 0, \end{cases} \tag{8}$$

where g is a $2D$ Gaussian with standard deviation δ_2 in x and y direction.

Normalized filter response are obtained by

$$s_n = \frac{\langle z, h_n \rangle}{\langle |z|, h_0 \rangle}. \tag{9}$$

The corresponding patterns to detect are shown in Fig. 3, e.g. straight lines for n = 0, parabolic curves and line endings for $n = \pm 1$. Refer to [6,15] for a more detailed review of symmetry filters.

The quality of a specific block is represented as the maximum average response of all pixels in the block. Mathematically,

$$q_2 = \max_{s_n} \frac{1}{M} \sum_i^M s_n^{(i)}, \ for\ n = \pm 1, \tag{10}$$

where M is the number of pixels in a specific block.

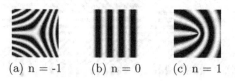

(a) n = -1   (b) n = 0   (c) n = 1

Fig. 3. Symmetric patterns (global orientation is zero) to detect: Straight lines for $n = 0$ (linear symmetry); parabolic curves and line endings for $n = \pm 1$ (parabolic/triangular symmetry). Note that, in high curvature parts of fingerprints, only $n = \pm 1$ are used.

2.3   Ridge and Valley Clarity

Ridge and valley clarity was firstly proposed in [7] to evaluate how distinguishing the ridge and valley structure is along the direction. The traditional ridge and valley clarity analysis calculates the average gray values of 32×13 pixels of each block along the perpendicular direction to the ridge, which extremely depends on the block's orientation coherence. In this paper, we introduce a modified ridge and valley clarity analysis method. To perform local clarity analysis, the binarized fingerprint image is obtained by a simple method firstly (here, we use the approach based on [16]) and further, we get the gray level distributions of the segmented ridge and valley just as Fig. 4 shows. The overlapping area is an ambiguous region, which cannot be determined as ridge or valley accurately. Therefore, this overlapping area can be an estimation of the clarity of ridge and valley. Mathematically, the clarity score is calculated by

$$\alpha = v_b/v_t, \tag{11}$$

$$\beta = r_b/r_t, \tag{12}$$

$$LRVC = (\alpha + \beta)/2, \tag{13}$$

where v_b is the number of bad pixels in the valley that the intensity is lower than ridge; v_t is the total number of pixels in the valley region; r_b is the number of bad pixels in the ridge that the intensity is higher than valley; α and β are the portion of bad pixels; the Local Ridge and Valley Clarity (LRVC) is the average value of α and β.

To normalize LRVC, a low threshold t_0 and a high threshold t_1 is needed. Specifically,

$$q_3 = 1 - LRVC_{norm} = \begin{cases} 1 & LRVC \leq t_0 \\ 0 & LRVC \geq t_1 \\ 1 - \frac{LRVC - t_0}{t_1 - t_0} & otherwise. \end{cases} \tag{14}$$

In experiments, we set $t_0 = 0.08$ and $t_1 = 0.35$ experientially.

2.4   Final Image Quality

Combining the above quality indices, the quality value of each block can be calculated by

$$Q_i = \begin{cases} (q_1^{(i)} + q_3^{(i)})/2 & for \ B_i \in R_L \\ (q_2^{(i)} + q_3^{(i)})/2 & for \ B_i \in R_H, \end{cases} \tag{15}$$

where B_i represents the i–th block; R_L and R_H represents low curvature and high curvature parts of a fingerprint; q_1, q_2 and q_3 are normalized sparsity quality, symmetry quality and clarity quality respectively.

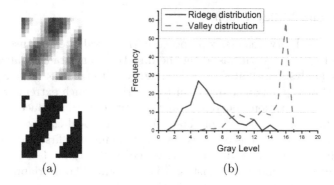

(a)   (b)

Fig. 4. Computation of the local ridge and valley clarity. (a) A fingerprint block and its ridge and valley mask, (b) the renormalized gray-level distributions of the ridges (solid line) and valleys (dashed line).

The global fingerprint image quality can be obtained by the weighted mean quality of all foreground blocks. Mathematically,

$$Q = \begin{cases} 0 & N < N_{min} \\ \sum_i^N w_i Q_i & otherwise, \end{cases} \tag{16}$$

where N is the number of foreground blocks; N_{min} represents the expected minimum number of foreground blocks; w_i is weight of each block, which can be set as $\frac{1}{N}$ simply or Gaussian weight based on the distance between the center block and the current block.

3   Experiments and Results

In this section, we describe experiments carried out to evaluate the proposed method. For the utility study, we compare the proposed method with existing methods in the performance of a widely available fingerprint matcher that matches fingerprints based on minutiae.

3.1   Datasets and Setup

The experimental evaluation of the proposed method and its comparison with existing methods are performed on two public databases:

FVC2002 Db1 contains 800 fingerprints, 8 impressions of 100 different fingers, with the size of 388 × 344.

FVC2004 Db1 contains 800 fingerprints, 8 impressions of 100 different fingers, with the size of 640 × 480.

As a fingerprint matcher for experiments, we use the minutia-based matcher included in the freely available NIST Fingerprint Image Software (NBIS) [17], MINDTCT for feature extraction and BOZORTH3 for matching.

3.2   Evaluation Indicators

To evaluate the ability of predicting matching performance, the False Non-Match Rate (FNMR) versus reject curve is adopted to demonstrate how efficiently the rejection of low-quality samples results in improving biometrics performance. FNMR is calculated by

$$FNMR = P(D_0|H_1),   \tag{17}$$

where H_1 represents verification feature set from the same finger as the template; D_0 represents the non-match decision [1].

If the quality value can perfectly mirror the genuine comparison score, it should result in FNMR of zero by setting threshold τ to get an overall FNMR of p and then rejecting p percent fingerprints with the lowest quality. As rejecting the fingerprints with the lowest quality, the FNMR versus reject curve should show a descending tendency. An almost flat curve suggests that the quality assessment algorithm is not effective in predicting biometrics performance.

Additionally, we also generate heat maps of three variables Q_{tmp} (quality of template fingerprints), Q_{probe} (quality of probe fingerprints) and *score* (comparison scores), to examine the relationship between quality scores obtained by the proposed method and genuine comparison scores. If the quality can be a predictor for biometrics performance, the matcher should give high comparison scores (shown in light gray in the heat map) for high-quality images of the same finger.

3.3   Results and Discussions

In the experiments, We set the value of τ of 45 for FVC2002 Db1 and 30 for FVC2004 Db1 to give a clear illustration. The block size is set as 16×16. To give a point of reference for benchmarking our method and existing methods, Figs. 5 and 6 includes two existing known quality assessment method Orientation Certainty Level (OCL) [5] and Local Clarity Score (LCS) [7] - the traditional ridge and valley clarity method.

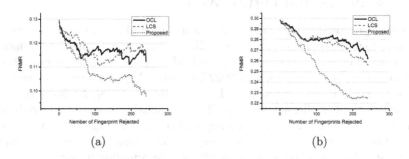

	(a)			(b)

Fig. 5. FNMR vs reject curves on (a) FVC2002 Db1 and (b) FVC2004 Db1.

The FNMR versus reject curves on FVC2002 Db1 and FVC2004 Db1 are illustrated in Fig. 5. As the figure shows, the OCL curve and LCS curve are similar and show a weak descending tendency but have a strong oscillation. However, the curve of our proposed method shows a much stronger descending tendency and weaker oscillation.

Figure 6 shows the heat maps of Q_{tmp}, Q_{prob} and *score* obtained by our method and NFIQ [8] on FVC2004 Db1. We quantize quality values into 5 levels, where 1 represents the best quality and 5 represents the worst quality, just like NFIQ. As the figure shows, our method and NFIQ have similar tendency, where gray values in the lower left corner are much lighter than those in the upper right corner, which means that good-quality images (1 and 2) result in the highest comparison scores and poor-quality images (4 and 5) result in the lowest comparison scores. The heat map of NFIQ has a little higher contrast than our method, probably because it considers more minutiae information, which is not that necessary in rejecting poor-quality samples in enrollment process, but our method can give an similar estimation before minutiae extraction.

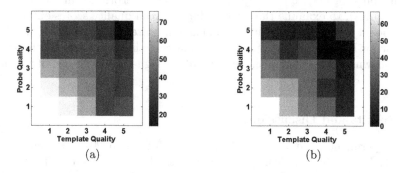

Fig. 6. Heat maps of q_{tmp}, q_{prob} and *score* by the proposed method (a) and NFIQ (b) on FVC2004 Db1.

4   Conclusions and Future Work

This paper proposes a new image quality assessment algorithm based on a combination of sparse coefficients of Gabor dictionary, the responses of symmetric descriptors and clarity measure of ridge and valley. To test our proposed method, experiments are conducted on FVC2002 Db1 and FVC2004 Db1 databases and results are compared with OCL [5], LCS [7] and NFIQ [8]. It shows that the proposed method is efficient in discarding poor-quality images and predicting biometrics performance. In order to improve the method further, we will consider the information of minutiae and may introduce machine learning method, such as neural network, to incorporate all these information in our future work.

Acknowledgement. This work was supported by Technology Research Project of Ministry of Public Security (2016JSYJA01).

References

1. Maltoni, D., Maio, D., Jain, A., Prabhakar, S.: Handbook of Fingerprint Recognition. Springer Science & Business Media, London (2009)
2. Alonso-Fernandez, F., Fierrez, J., Ortega-Garcia, J., Gonzalez-Rodriguez, J., Fronthaler, H., Kollreider, K., Bigun, J.: A comparative study of fingerprint image-quality estimation methods. IEEE Trans. Inf. Forensics Secur. **2**(4), 734–743 (2007)
3. Chen, Y., Dass, S.C., Jain, A.K.: Fingerprint quality indices for predicting authentication performance. In: Kanade, T., Jain, A., Ratha, N.K. (eds.) AVBPA 2005. LNCS, vol. 3546, pp. 160–170. Springer, Heidelberg (2005). doi:10.1007/11527923_17
4. Shen, L.L., Kot, A., Koo, W.M.: Quality measures of fingerprint images. In: Bigun, J., Smeraldi, F. (eds.) AVBPA 2001. LNCS, vol. 2091, pp. 266–271. Springer, Heidelberg (2001). doi:10.1007/3-540-45344-X_39
5. Lim, E., Jiang, X., Yau, W.: Fingerprint Quality and Validity Analysis. In: International Conference on Image Processing, vol. 1, pp. I–469. IEEE Press (2002)
6. Fronthaler, H., Kollreider, K., Bigun, J., et al.: Fingerprint image-quality estimation and its application to multialgorithm verification. IEEE Trans. Inf. Forensics Secur. **3**(2), 331–338 (2008)
7. Chen, T.P., Jiang, X., Yau, W.Y.: Fingerprint image quality analysis. In: International Conference on Image Processing, vol. 2, pp. 1253–1256. IEEE Press (2004)
8. Tabassi, E., Wilson, C., Watson, C.: NIST Fingerprint Image Quality. NIST Res. Rep. NISTIR7151, pp. 34–36 (2004)
9. Rubinstein, R., Bruckstein, A.M., Elad, M.: Dictionaries for sparse representation modeling. Proc. IEEE **98**(6), 1045–1057 (2010)
10. Yang, J., Wright, J., Huang, T.S., Ma, Y.: Image super-resolution via sparse representation. IEEE Trans. Image Process. **19**(11), 2861–2873 (2010)
11. Feng, J., Zhou, J., Jain, A.K.: Orientation field estimation for latent fingerprint enhancement. IEEE Trans. Pattern Anal. Mach. Intell. **35**(4), 925–940 (2013)
12. Cao, K., Liu, E., Jain, A.K.: Segmentation and enhancement of latent fingerprints: a coarse to fine ridge structure dictionary. IEEE Trans. Pattern Anal. Mach. Intell. **36**(9), 1847–1859 (2014)
13. Jain, A.K., Feng, J.: Latent fingerprint matching. IEEE Trans. Pattern Anal. Mach. Intell. **33**(1), 88–100 (2011)
14. Liu, M., Chen, X., Wang, X.: Latent fingerprint enhancement via multi-scale patch based sparse representation. IEEE Trans. Inf. Forensics Secur. **10**(1), 6–15 (2015)
15. Bigun, J., Bigun, T., Nilsson, K.: Recognition by symmetry derivatives and the generalized structure tensor. IEEE Trans. Pattern Anal. Mach. Intell. **26**(12), 1590–1605 (2004)
16. Hong, L., Wan, Y., Jain, A.: Fingerprint image enhancement: algorithm and performance evaluation. IEEE Trans. Pattern Anal. Mach. Intell. **20**(8), 777–789 (1998)
17. NIST Biometric Image Software. http://www.nist.gov/itl/iad/ig/nbis.cfm

A Preprocessing Algorithm for Touchless Fingerprint Images

Kejun Wang[1], Huitao Cui[1], Yi Cao[1], Xianglei Xing[1(✉)],
and Rongyi Zhang[2]

[1] College of Automation, Harbin Engineering University, Harbin 150001, China
xingxl@hrbeu.edu.cn
[2] College of Mechanical and Electrical Engineering,
Heilongjiang Institute of Technology, Harbin 150050, China

Abstract. Touchless fingerprint recognition with high acceptance, high security, hygiene advantages, is currently a hot research field of biometrics. The background areas of touchless fingerprints are more complex than those of the contact: the touchless fingerprint image will appear rotation and translation phenomenon, what's more, the contrast of the ridge and valley lines is much lower. These factors seriously affected the performance of the touchless fingerprint recognition. So the general methods for contact fingerprint images are difficult to achieve a good effect. A novel method is proposed to preprocess the images reasonably aiming at these features of touchless fingerprint images. Firstly, the Otsu based on the Cb component of the YCbCr model is adopted to extract the finger area. Secondly, we combined the high-frequency enhancement filter with the iterative adaptive histogram equalization technique to enhance fingerprint images. Thirdly, we proposed a new method to extract the ROI fingerprint area. Lastly, the AR–LBP algorithm is adopted for feature extraction and the nearest neighbor classifier is used for feature matching. Experimental results show that the proposed method can achieve excellent image identify results.

Keywords: Touchless fingerprint · High frequency emphasis filtering · Otsu · Adaptive histogram equalization · ROI area · AR-LBP algorithm

1 Introduction

With its high practicability and feasibility, fingerprint identification technology has become the most common and legally binding biometric technology. Even so, since the fingerprint image is collected by a touchable sensor, there are still many problems in the conventional fingerprint identification like fingerprint deformation, fingerprint residue, sensitive to skin conditions and the spread of germs at the time of collection, etc. In contrast, touchless fingerprint can not only eliminate these negative factors, but also has high recognition performance and anti-counterfeiting performance.

The background areas of touchless fingerprints are more complex than those of the contact. Fingerprint image will appear rotation and translation phenomenon. What's more, the contrast of the ridge and valley lines is much lower. Many scholars have studied touchless fingerprint recognition. The shape-from-silhouette method can get a

© Springer International Publishing AG 2016
Z. You et al. (Eds.): CCBR 2016, LNCS 9967, pp. 224–234, 2016.
DOI: 10.1007/978-3-319-46654-5_25

three-dimensional fingerprint image with five cameras from multiple perspectives, and then expand it into an equivalent two-dimensional fingerprint image [1]. Choi H. and Kim J. [2] proposed a new touchless fingerprint sensing device capturing three different views at one time and a method for mosaicking these view-different images. They can get a high-quality fingerprint template to solve problems caused by a touch-based sensing device such as a view difference problem and a limited usable area due to perspective distortion and rotation. The device is large and expensive, so its application scope is limited.

Scholars conducted a study of touchless fingerprint identification technology based on simple acquisition devices in order to overcome these difficulties. Literature [3] obtained the fingerprint image with mobile cameras and delved into a low contrast between ridges and valleys. Ajay Kumar and Cyril Kwong [4] developed a 3-D fingerprint identification system that employs only single camera and a new representation of 3D finger surface features using Finger Surface Codes which is very effective in matching three dimensional fingerprints. This kind of method, using the cheap fingerprint acquisition device and simple fingerprint acquisition method, has broad prospects. However, its fingerprint image quality is relatively poor. The recognition algorithm's effect of touchless fingerprint recognition is so poor now.

Fingerprint image preprocessing directly affects the performance of the fingerprint identification. Using the color information of fingerprint images, literature [5] proposed a fingerprint segmentation method based on skin color and the adaptive threshold point. Preprocess the image by using the Lucy-Richardson algorithm, wiener filter and the inverse convolution [6]. Literature [7] adopted the method of homomorphic filtering and coherent filtering for image preprocessing. However, the characteristics of touchless fingerprint image cannot be fully considered by these methods without targeted treatment measures. So the touchless fingerprint recognition algorithm still needs further study.

The study found that fingerprint images show more detail changes under blue light [8]. Therefore, a fingerprint sampling device, which is made up of common CMOS cameras under blue light, is adopted in this paper. The Otsu based on the Cb component of the YCbCr model is adopted to extract the finger area. When the fingerprint images are enhanced, combining the high frequency emphasis filtering and iterative adaptive histogram equalization technique is adopted firstly and then the simplified Gabor function template is used to enhance them again. Due to the phenomena such as fingerprint rotation, translation and edge blurring caused by factors like the touchless acquisition method and low camera depth of field, this paper proposed a new method of extracting the ROI fingerprint area. The AR–LBP algorithm [9] is adopted for feature extraction and the nearest neighbor classifier based on the chi-square distance is used for feature matching.

2 Extraction of Full Finger Area

The size of fingerprint image collected by the finger fingerprint acquisition system in our lab is 1280 × 720 pixels. As is shown in Fig. 1, background region takes so much space of the image that processing the whole image will not only increase computational cost, but also takes up more storage space. To reduce the background region interference, we need to extract the finger area.

By observing the fingerprint image, we can see that finger area is mainly the blue part while the background is not. According to this feature, the paper converts the RGB images collected into YCbCr format images which can detach the color component from the luminance component, and then the Otsu [10] based on the Cb component of the YCbCr model is adopted to extract the finger area.

2.1   Color Model Based on YCbCr Space

The YCbCr color model uses CaR601 as the encoding. Y/Cb/Cr refers to the luminance/blue color/red color component, YCbCr space has the characteristic to detach the color component from the luminance component. The YCbCr format can be linear changed from the RGB formatas is shown in the Eq. (1):

$$\begin{bmatrix} Y \\ Cb \\ Cr \\ 1 \end{bmatrix} = \begin{bmatrix} 0.2990 & 0.5870 & 0.1140 & 0 \\ -0.1687 & -0.3313 & 0.5000 & 0.5 \\ 0.5000 & -0.4187 & -0.0813 & 0.5 \\ 0 & 0 & 0 & 1 \end{bmatrix} \begin{bmatrix} R \\ G \\ B \\ 1 \end{bmatrix} \qquad (1)$$

So that we can get the component diagram (Fig. 1(b), (c)) of the Cb component and Cr component in Fig. 1(a):

  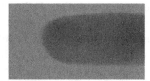

(a)Fingerprint image collected   (b) The component diagram of Cb.   (c) The component diagram of Cr

Fig. 1. The component diagrams

As is shown in Fig. 1(b) and (c), the pixel difference of the target and background in Cb component diagram is more apparently than that in Cr component diagram.

2.2   Otsu

Otsu [10] is a kind of adaptive threshold selection method which analyzes the class attribute. The optimum threshold is obtained, when the variance between the target one and the fingerprint image background is maximal. In Otsu, we first obtain the probability of each gray value from a m gray-level image. Secondly, we divide them into two parts with variable T and then calculate the probability of each part and the inter-class variance $\delta^2(T)$:

$$\delta^2(T) = \omega_0(\mu_0 - \mu)^2 + \omega_1(\mu_1 - \mu)^2 \tag{2}$$

Where μ_0, μ_1 is the average gray-value of each part, ω_0, ω_1 are their probability, μ is the average gray-value of the whole image. The variable T, changing from 0 to m − 1, is the threshold when δ^2 is the biggest.

Otsu, utilizing the statistical property of the gray value, is strict with the size of the target picture, which means the finger area should be neither too big nor too small. As is shown in the experiment, Otsu is robust, and we can get a better image segmentation effect even when the background is complex. The decomposition diagram of fingerprint image is shown in Fig. 2. The grayscale map of the extracting finger area is shown in Fig. 3. The extracted finger area in complex background is shown in Fig. 4.

Fig. 2. The decomposition diagram

Fig. 3. The grayscale map of finger area

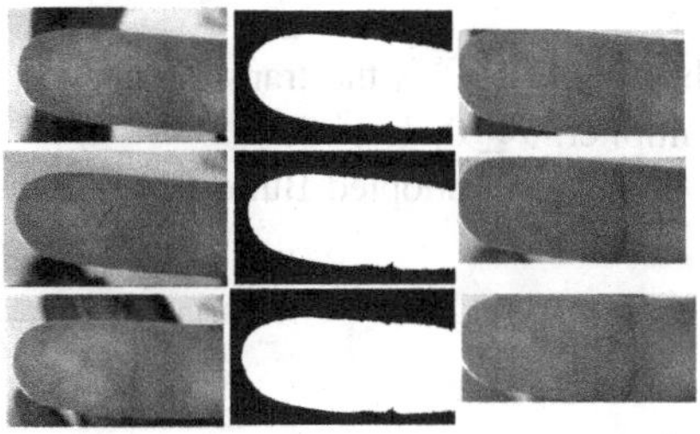

Fig. 4. Extract finger area in complex backgrounds

3 Fingerprint Image Enhancement

Because of the low-contrast of touchless fingerprint images and abrupt ridge-valley change, fingerprint information is distributed mainly over the high frequency region which is too dark to see straight. When the fingerprint images are enhanced, combining the high frequency emphasis filtering and iterative adaptive histogram equalization technique is adopted firstly and then the simplified Gabor function template is used to enhance them again.

3.1 High Frequency Emphasize Filter

Filters can realize the enhancement in the frequency domain. A high-pass filter attenuates low frequency and enhances high frequency which shows image details in time domain. A high-pass filter is used to enhance image details. The transfer function of Ideal High-pass Filter (IHPF) should meet the condition as follows:

$$H(\mu, v) = \begin{cases} 0 & D(\mu, v) \le D_0 \\ 1 & D(\mu, v) > D_0 \end{cases} \tag{3}$$

where D_0 is the designated nonnegative number, and $D(\mu, \gamma)$ is the distance between (μ, γ) and the center of filter. The track of points satisfying $D(\mu, \gamma) = D_0$. is a circle. As is shown in the formula (3), in high-pass filter, the output of low frequency and DC component, which corresponds to most part of the backgroundis zero.

A compensation method to overcome the problem of blocking direct-current in high-pass filter is to multiply the high-pass filter with a constant bigger than 1 and then plus an offset to the result, which is called high frequency emphasis filtering. The transfer function of high frequency emphasize filter is:

$$H_{hfe}(\mu, v) = \alpha + b H_{hp}(\mu, v) \tag{4}$$

where, $H_{hp}(\mu, \gamma)$ is the transfer function of a high-pass filter. α is the offset, b is the multiplier. $\alpha \ge 0$, $b > \alpha$.

This paper adopted Butterworth high pass filter, whose transfer function is:

$$H(\mu, v) = \frac{1}{1 + [D_0/D(\mu, v)]^{2n}} \tag{5}$$

By using this filter, the detail definition can be effectively increased.

3.2   Contrast Limited Adaptive Histogram Equalization (CLAHE)

There are mainly two kinds of conventional methods of histogram equalization based on probability: local area histogram equalization and full frame histogram equalization. Histogram equalization increases the dynamic range of pixel gray value by the gray mapping and redistributing the gray levels. The discrete function of grey statistics histogram:

$$p(r_k) = \frac{n_k}{n}, k = 0, 1, 2, \cdots, l - 1 \tag{6}$$

where n is the total image pixels, n_k is the number of pixels in the gray value k, and r_k is the k-level grayscale of image $f(x, y)$. L is the gray levels of the image.

CLAHE [11] is the improvement of these two histogram equalizations above. The substance of CLAHE is to consider the influence of nearby region and local area. The processed image has the effect of both full frame histogram equalization and local area histogram equalization. $H_b(s)$ shows histogram equalization out of the window and $H_\omega(s)$ shows histogram equalization inside the window. CLAHE can be expressed as a formula (7):

$$h(s) = \beta H_w(s) + (1 - \beta) H_b(s) \tag{7}$$

where $0 \leq \beta \leq 1$. We can adjust the influence of the external environment to the transformation within the window by adjusting β. We can take pixels near the window as external pixels considering the low-correlation between pixels in the window and far-away from the window region.

3.3   Fingerprint Image Enhancement Algorithm Realization

The steps are as follows:

Step 1: Determine the related area of any point in the image according to the size of rectangular-window.
Step 2: Calculate the histogram of rectangular window using the formula (7).
Step 3: Process the center pixel by equalizing the histogram in rectangular window.
Step 4: Move the rectangle window to the next adjacent pixel, then repeat these steps above until the whole image is finished.
Step 5: Repeat Step1 to Step4 several times.
Step 6: Process the adaptive histogram equalization to strengthen the details.
Step 7: The simplified Gabor function template [7] is used to enhance them.

Figure 5 is the visual effect of Fig. 3 processed by the algorithm proposed in the paper. Obviously, experiments showed that the enhancement algorithm, which not only highlights the image edges and details but also improved the contrast and brightness of the image, obviously improved the image.

Fig. 5. Visual effect of the proposed algorithm

4   The Extraction of ROI

4.1   Rotation Compensation of Fingerprint Image

It is important to extract the region of interest in the image-defocus blurred and uneven illumination caused by collection devices. Different fingerprint samples from the same people are not always alike because of the difference in horizontal offset and rotation angle caused by the lack of retaining latches when collecting touchless fingerprint images. Therefore, we should extract the ROI after rotating the image with the rotation compensation method proposed in literature [12] to guarantee the accuracy of fingerprint identification. Figure 6(a), (b) and (c), (d) show the effect picture before and after correction.

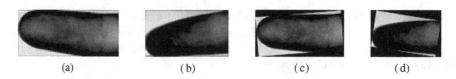

Fig. 6. The gray-scale map before (a), (b), and after correction (c), (d).

4.2   Fingertip Estimation and ROI Location

There are usually one or two knuckles in the full fingerprint image, and according to the images collected, the fingerprint is clearer between the fingertip and the center of the first knuckle. So we choose this region for feature extraction.

This paper proposed a method to determine the ROI according to the arc center and radius of a fingertip. Different people have different fingertip-arcs, and the center of it is nearly located in the center place in front of the first joint. So it is a feasible idea to use the center of fingertip-arc as ROI anchor point.

In the area of fingerprint after rotation correction, assume that the left side of the fingerprint midline is starting point, and the distance between the starting point to the center of the circle is the radius. The center point moves from the starting point to the right along the midline, and get the maximum likelihood estimator when the radius is longer than half the width of the finger. Then the exact value of fingertip-arc is determined by calculating the circle fitting based on points of fingertip-arc estimation. Figure 7 shows how to confirm fingertip radius.

   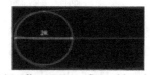

(a) Fingertip radius by rough estimate   (b) Arc diameter confirmed by circle fitting

Fig. 7. Confirming fingertip radius

The least-square correction algorithm is adopted to fit the fingertip arc. Assume that the point (X, Y) on the circle satisfies the Eq. (8):

$$R^2 = (X - A)^2 + (Y - B)^2 \qquad (8)$$

Where A, B is the ordinate and abscissa of the center point, R is the radius of the circle, the formulas are as follows:

$$A = -\frac{a}{2} \quad B = -\frac{b}{2} \quad R = \frac{1}{2}\sqrt{a^2 + b^2 - 4c} \qquad (9)$$

$$a = \frac{HD - EG}{CG - D^2} \quad b = \frac{HC - ED}{D^2 - GC} \quad c = -\frac{\sum \left(X_i^2 + Y_i^2\right) + a\sum X_i + b\sum Y_i}{N} \qquad (10)$$

$$C = \left(N \sum X_i^2 - \sum X_i \sum X_i\right)$$
$$D = \left(N \sum X_i \sum Y_i - \sum X_i \sum Y_i\right)$$
$$E = N \sum X_i^3 + N \sum X_i \sum Y_i^2 - \sum (X_i^2 + Y_i^2) \sum X_i \qquad (11)$$
$$G = \left(N \sum Y_i^2 - \sum Y_i \sum Y_i\right)$$
$$H = N \sum Y_i^3 + N \sum Y_i \sum X_i^2 - \sum (X_i^2 + Y_i^2) \sum Y_i$$

where $(X_i, Y_i)\ i \in (1, 2 ..., N)$ are contour points on the fingertip.

Get the radius and center of fingertip by fitting the fingertip-arc. The center of the fingertip is the anchor point of the rotation corrected fingerprint image. The vertical segment line on the left of ROI is $L_1 : x = A - R/2$; the vertical segment line on the right is $L_2 : x = A + R \times 2$; the upside horizontal segment line of the ROI is $L_3 : y = B - 4 \times R/5$; the downside horizontal segment line of the ROI is $L_4 : y = B + 4 \times R/5$. The ROI is surrounded by these four lines as shown in Fig. 8. Figure 9 is the ROI of the fingerprint image in Fig. 1.

Fig. 8. Confirming the size of ROI   **Fig. 9.** ROI of a fingerprint image

5 Experimental Results

Experiments in the paper are trained and tested on fingerprint databases built in our lab. The collection device is made up of a web camera and a series of blue LED, and is connected with the computer by USB. The database consists of 105 fingers, 5 images of each finger including thumbs, index fingers and middle fingers.

5.1 Experiment Description

The framework of contactless fingerprint identification system is illustrated in Fig. 10. Experimental procedures are as follows:

Step 1: Preprocess the fingerprint image with the method proposed in this paper, and then normalize the images to 300 × 500 pixels as shown in Fig. 11.
Step 2: There are m × n blocks in a preprocessed fingerprint image. Apply AR-LBP algorithm to extract texture features of each block and cascade the histograms of all the blocks. The cascaded histograms represent for the feature of fingerprint image.

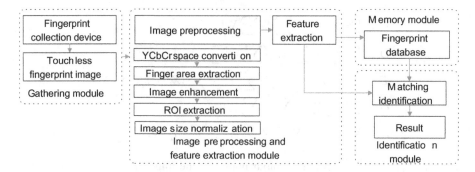

Fig. 10. The framework of contactless fingerprint identification system

Fig. 11. Example of fingerprint image preprocessing

Step 3: Calculate the histogram feature of Chi-square distance between registry and test samples. And finally, the nearest neighbor classifier is adopted for fingerprint classification.

5.2   Analysis of Experimental Results

To illustrate the effectiveness of the proposed algorithm, the paper conducted two experiments: In the first group, we choose 3 in the fingerprint images for training and 2 for testing randomly. Repeat the experiments 10 times and choose their average amount as the final experimental result. In the second experiment, we choose 4 images randomly for training and one for testing. Take the average result of the 10 experiments as the final result.

5.2.1   Analysis of Image Enhancement

The paper takes contrastive analysis to find the difference between enhanced and unenhanced fingerprint ROI images in order to verify the validity of the enhancement algorithm. Using the matching method based on the AR-LBP algorithm (the neighborhood size of AR-LBP is 5 × 5, dividing the fingerprint image into 25 blockettes), we obtained experimental results tabulated in Table 1.

According to Table 1, although the computing time increased to some extant after enhancement, its recognition rate achieved great increase. The rise of recognition rate deserves the expenditure of computing time. Thus, the fingerprint image enhancement method proposed in the paper can achieve good results according to this experiment.

Table 1. Performance comparison of two image databases

Data	Computation time (s)	Recognition rate (%)	
		First	Second
Original ROI image	2.12	73.81	75.25
Enhanced ROI image	2.52	93.81	96.67

5.2.2 Analysis of ROI Extraction Method

This paper takes contrastive analysis to find the difference between the full fingerprint images and enhanced ROI images in order to verify the validity of ROI extraction method. Using the matching method based on the AR-LBP algorithm (the neighborhood size of AR-LBP is 5×5, dividing the fingerprint image into 5×5 blockettes), we got experimental results tabulated in Table 2.

Table 2. Performance comparison of two image databases

Data	Computing time (s)	Recognition rate (%)	
		First	Second
Enhanced full fingerprint	3.47	80.48	82.86
Enhanced ROI image	2.52	93.81	96.67

According to Table 2, the recognition rate of the extracted ROI image is much higher than full fingerprint image. What's more, the computing time decreases after extracting the region of interest. The ROI extraction method can achieve good results according to this experiment.

Analyzing the experimental results, fingerprint identification based on the AR-LBP algorithm can realize the majority of the images. However, its recognition effect is not ideal for some poor quality images because of the influence of rotation, translation and blur, which affect the feature extraction a lot and then have a negative effect on matching identification. The preprocessing method proposed in this paper improved the recognition rate of a fingerprint recognition system. Although fingerprint image preprocessing need more time, we spend less computing time on the ROI image, which is smaller than the original image. So, altogether, it costs less time on identifying a preprocessed image. The improvement of recognition rate and computational complexity proved the effectiveness of the preprocessing algorithm proposed in the paper.

6 Conclusion

Taking example by the traditional touch-based fingerprint image preprocessing algorithm and the existing touchless fingerprint image preprocessing algorithm, the paper proposed a touchless fingerprint preprocessing algorithm with high practicability according to features of touchless fingerprint image collected in our lab. Through experimental analysis, the algorithm proposed in this paper has more advantages on both time complexity and recognition effect.

Acknowledgments. This work was supported by the Fundamental Research Funds for the Central Universities of China, Natural Science Fund of Heilongjiang Province of China, and Natural Science Foundation of China, under Grand No HEUCF160415, F2015033, and 61573114.

References

1. Parziale, G., Diaz-Santana, E., Hauke, R.: The surround imager^{TM}: a multi-camera touchless device to acquire 3D rolled-equivalent fingerprints. In: Zhang, D., Jain, A.K. (eds.) ICB 2005. LNCS, vol. 3832, pp. 244–250. Springer, Heidelberg (2005)
2. Choi, H., Choi, K., Kim, J.: Mosaicing touchless and mirror-reflected fingerprint images. IEEE Trans. Inf. Forensics Secur. 5(1), 52–61 (2010)
3. Derawi, M.O., Yang, B., Busch, C.: Fingerprint recognition with embedded cameras on mobile phones. In: Prasad, R., Farkas, K., Schmidt, A.U., Lioy, A., Russello, G., Luccio, F. L. (eds.) MobiSec 2011. LNICST, vol. 94, pp. 136–147. Springer, Heidelberg (2012)
4. Kumar, A., Kwong, C.: Towards contactless, low-cost and accurate 3D fingerprint identification. IEEE Trans. Pattern Anal. Mach. Intell. 37(3), 681–696 (2015)
5. Kaur, P., Jain, A., Mittal, S.: Touch-less fingerprint analysis—a review and comparison. Int. J. Intell. Syst. Appl. (IJISA) 4(6), 46 (2012)
6. Labati, R.D., Genovese, A., Piuri, V., et al.: Contactless fingerprint recognition: a neural approach for perspective and rotation effects reduction. In: 2013 IEEE Workshop on Computational Intelligence in Biometrics and Identity Management (CIBIM), pp. 22–30. IEEE (2013)
7. Qin, F., Liao, B.: Contactless fingerprint image segmentation and enhancement method research. J. Sens. World 8, 16–19 (2014)
8. Angelopoulou, E.: Understanding the color of human skin. In: Photonics West 2001-Electronic Imaging. International Society for Optics and Photonics, pp. 243–251 (2001)
9. Naika, C.L.S., Das, P.K., Nair, S.B.: Asymmetric region local binary pattern operator for person-dependent facial expression recognition. In: 2012 International Conference on Computing, Communication and Applications (ICCCA), pp. 1–5. IEEE (2012)
10. Xie, F., Zhao, D.-P., et al.: Visual C++ Digital Image Processing, pp. 285–288. Electronic Industry Press, Beijing (2008)
11. Zhou, W.-X., Liao, H.: Based on the high frequency emphasis filtering and CLAHE image contrast enhancement method. J. TV Technol. 7, 38–40 (2010)
12. Ma, H., Wang, K.: A region of interest extraction method using rotation rectified finger vein images. J. Intell. Syst. 7(3), 230–234 (2012)

Palmprint Recognition via Sparse Coding Spatial Pyramid Matching Representation of SIFT Feature

Ligang Liu, Jianxin Zhang[(✉)], and Aoqi Yang

Key Lab of Advanced Design and Intelligent Computing,
Ministry of Education, Dalian University,
Dalian, People's Republic of China
zjx99326@163.com

Abstract. Spatial pyramid matching using sparse coding (ScSPM) algorithm can construct the palmprint image descriptors which may effectively express local features and global features of palmprint image. In the paper, we adopt sparse coding and max pooling instead of vector quantization coding and sum pooling to extract descriptors, and it improves the nonlinear coding to linear coding. Then, the linear SVM classifier is applied to replace the nonlinear classifier in pyramid matching. We apply this algorithm to the recognition of palmprint images and exactly analyze the effects of parameters on the recognition, including the size of a complete dictionary and sparse coding parameter. The experimental results illuminate the excellent effectiveness of the ScSPM algorithm for palmprint recognition.

Keywords: Sparse coding · Spatial pyramid matching · Palmprint recognition

1 Introduction

Bag-of-Words model has been widely applied in the field of image classification [1] and video semantic retrieval [2, 3] in recent years. The model is also called Bag of Features (BoF), which comes from text categorization. Csurka et al. [4] introduced it into computer vision in 2014, and its core idea is that the image is regarded as a kind of document object and different local area in the image or its characteristics are regarded as the vocabulary of the image, and a similar area or feature can be regarded as a word. Thus, each image can be described as an unordered collection of local Patches/key point features.

However, BoF method ignores the spatial information of the image features, and is often powerless to capture the image shape or position, which severely limits the descriptive power of the image representation. In order to overcome this problem, researchers have made a lot of improvements, and the more successful extension was SPM (spatial pyramid matching) by Schmid et al. [5]. SPM takes into account the spatial information, and its main idea consists of the following parts. Firstly, the image is divided according to different resolutions in two-dimensional space, and each local feature is quantified as a visual vocabulary of the visual dictionary; Secondly, it counts

© Springer International Publishing AG 2016
Z. You et al. (Eds.): CCBR 2016, LNCS 9967, pp. 235–243, 2016.
DOI: 10.1007/978-3-319-46654-5_26

the same number of visual words in the same sub region and obtains the statistical histogram based on the visual word in each resolution; Finally, the weighted sums of the histograms is calculated to obtain the finally representation. The SPM algorithm is an efficient expansion of BoF model, which shows a very good performance in large-scale image classification task.

But SPM algorithm also has some limitations [6, 7] such as: (1) the spatial partitioning method did not take into account the integrity of the image; (2) in order to achieve good classification result, it combined with nonlinear classifier for classification, but the computational complexity of nonlinear classifier was high and its scalability was poor for real applications.

To improve the scalability, obtaining nonlinear feature representations and linear classifiers becomes the focus of the research [8–12]. Yang et al. [13] proposed an extension of the SPM approach, which computed spatial pyramid image representation based on sparse coding (SC) of SIFT features, replacing the Hard vector quantization coding (Hard-VQ) to obtain nonlinear codes, and it was called spatial pyramid matching using sparse coding (ScSPM). In this paper, we introduce ScSPM algorithm into palmprint recognition, and give an exactly recognition performance test on the PolyU and CASIA palmprint databases.

2 Review of SPM

SPM is an algorithm for image matching, recognition and classification in spatial pyramid. The image of each layer is divided into 4 bins, and we count histogram features on each bins, and finally the histogram features of all the layers are connected together to form a vector as the image feature.

Suppose X and Y are two sets of features in a D dimensional space and the feature space is divided into different scales $(0, \ldots, L)$. The matching extent of two images is defined as [5]:

$$
\begin{aligned}
k^L(X, Y) &= I^L + \sum_{l=0}^{L-1} \frac{1}{2^{L-l}}(I^l - I^{l+1}) \\
&= \frac{1}{2^L}I^0 + \sum_{l=1}^{L} \frac{1}{2^{L-l+1}}I^l
\end{aligned}
$$

(1)

$I^l - I^{l+1}(l = 0, \ldots, L - 1)$ represents the increment between the two levels. Combined with BoF algorithm, SPM added spatial information, and counted the number of times each visual word in each level, and calculated the matching degree of each visual word. Here, we can give the similarity of the two images:

$$
k^L(X, Y) = \sum_{m=1}^{K} k^l(X_m, Y_m)
$$

(2)

where K is the size of codebook. In the process of matching, we calculate the similarity by Eq. (2), which measures the matching degree between the features of two groups. The classification and matching are closely related, so, SVM (support vector machine) final decision function can be written [5, 6, 14]:

$$f(x) = \left(\sum_{i=1}^{n} a_i y_i x_i \right)^T x + b$$
$$= w^T x + b$$

(3)

where x_i is training samples, x is testing samples.

3 Linear SPM Using SIFT Sparse Codes

We introduce ScSPM algorithm into palmprint image recognition, which greatly reduce the time and space complexity of recognition. In order to more clearly express the application of the ScSPM algorithm in palmprint recognition, we draw the workflow, as shown in Fig. 1.

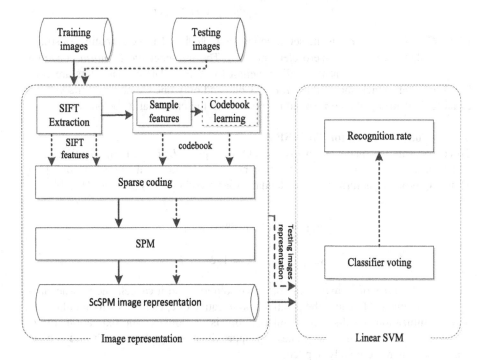

Fig. 1. The workflow of ScSPM method for palmprint recognition. Training process is along the solid arrow while testing process is along the dotted arrow.

3.1   Encoding SIFT

Making X be a set of SIFT descriptors in a D dimensional feature space, i.e. $X = [x_1, \ldots x_N] \in R^{D \times N}$. Given a codebook with K entries, $V = [v_1, v_2, \ldots, v_K] \in R^{D \times K}$, is a set of over complete base($K > D$). Different coding algorithms (here VQ, SC) will eventually transform each descriptor into M dimensional vector, to generate the final image representation.

3.1.1   Coding Descriptors in VQ

The vector quantization (VQ) method applies the *K-means* clustering algorithm to solve the following problem [11, 13]:

$$\min_{V} \sum_{i=1}^{N} \min_{k=1\ldots K} \|x_i - V_k\|_2^2 \tag{4}$$

where K is the number of cluster centers, $\|\cdot\|_2$ denotes the L_2 *norm* of vector. The Eq. (4) problems can also be written as following form:

$$\min_{C,V} \sum_{i=1}^{N} \|x_i - c_i V\|_2^2 \tag{5}$$
$$s.t. \quad \|c_i\|_0 = 1, \|c_i\|_1 = 1, c_i \geq 0, \forall i$$

where $C = [c_1, c_2, \ldots, c_N]$ is the set of codes for X. $\|c_i\|_0 = 1$ is a cardinality constraint, meaning that only one non-zero element of c_i. The non-negative L_1 *norm* constraint $\|c_i\|_1 = 1, c_i \geq 0$ means that the coding weight for X is 1. These constraints are combined together, which shows that $\forall i$, c_i has one and only one element and the value is equal to 1. It means the corresponding position is the class that X_i belongs to.

3.1.2   Coding Descriptors in ScSPM

To compensate the quantization loss of VQ, they put a L_1 *norm* regularization on c_i, which makes c_i to have small number of nonzero elements but more than one [12]. Thus VQ problem is turned into a standard sparse coding (SC) problem [12, 14]:

$$\min_{C,V} \sum_{i=1}^{N} \|x_i - c_i V\|_2^2 + \lambda \|c_i\|_1 \tag{6}$$
$$s.t. \|v_k\| \leq 1, \forall k = 1, 2, \ldots, K$$

where the L_2 *norm* of v_k avoids the ordinary solution, and it cancels the non-negative limit of c_i elements. Because the positive and negative of c_i elements will not affect the final optimization results. L_1 regularization is a convex approximation of L_0 non-convex function, and the process of approximation can be smooth and achieve sparse, so it is more widely applied.

In the training phase of sparse coding, to solve this optimization problem of the Eq. (6), the traditional method is iteratively by alternatingly optimizing over C or V

while fixing the other. Fixing the codebook V, the optimization is a standard LASSO problem by optimizing over each coefficient c_i individually [13, 15, 16]:

$$\min_{c_i} \sum_{i=1}^{N} \|x_i - c_i V\|_2^2 + \lambda \|c_i\|_1 \tag{7}$$

The Eq. (7) has many solving methods, such as feature-sign search algorithm [18]. Fixing C, It translates into a least square problem:

$$\min_{V} \|x_m - CV\|_2^2$$
$$s.t. \|v_k\| \leq 1, \forall k = 1, 2, \ldots, K \tag{8}$$

The Eq. (8) can be done by the Lagrange algorithm. In our experiments, we use 40,000 SIFT descriptors extracted from random patches to train the codebook. After getting the codebook V, we can obtain sparse coding coefficient c_i by Eq. (7) on each descriptors of an image.

3.2 Linear SVM

In this paper, multi-class linear support vector machine (SVM) is used for classification. Given the training data $(x_i, y_i), i = 1, 2, \ldots, n$, x_i denotes the histograms representation for image I_i, $y_i \in \{-1, +1\}$ indicates labels. Such that, for a test data x, its class label is predicted by [15–17]:

$$y = w^T x + b \tag{9}$$

taking a one-against-all strategy, the unconstrained optimization objective function corresponding to the linear SVM model is [15]:

$$\min_{w,c} \left\{ \|w_c\|_2^2 + C \sum_{i=1}^{n} l(w_c; y_i^c, x_i) \right\} \tag{10}$$

where $l(w_c; y_i^c, x_i)$ is a hinge loss function. But the standard hinge loss function is not differentiable everywhere, so, using gradient-based optimization methods to solve it. Such that, a differentiable quadratic hinge loss is obtained [16, 18]:

$$l(w_c; y_i^c, x_i) = [\max(0, w_c^T x \cdot y_i^c - 1)]^2 \tag{11}$$

The loss function of various algorithm usually has fisher consistency, and the classifier obtained by optimizing these loss functions can be regarded as the "agent" of the posterior probability.

4 Experiment and Analysis

In this section, the PolyU and the CASIA palmprint image databases are used to test the performance of the ScSPM. Finally, the effect of parameters on the recognition result is analysed, respectively, the size of complete dictionary and sparse coding parameter. We use the SIFT descriptors that are extracted from 16×16 pixel patches from each image on a grid space with 8 pixels. The dimension of each SIFT descriptors is 128. In the stage of pooling, we adopt max pooling combined with l_2 normalization [12]. All of our experiments are carried out on a PC machine with 3.30 GHz CPU, 4G memory and Matlab R2013a.

4.1 Results on the PolyU Database

The PolyU palmprint database is the largest and most authoritative public palmprint database. It collects the original palmprint image size of 384×284 pixels. Our experiment is tested on a subset of this database. The subset consists of 1000 images from 100 palms, and for each palm there are 10 images. We segment the region of interest (ROI) [19] and its size is 128×128 the pixels. Each person was taken 3, 5 training images, and the rest as a test. In the experiment, the size of codebook is 128×1024. Table 1 shows the different training sample and SIFT the extracted features under different block size corresponding to the recognition rate, and we compare to various palmprint authentication methods on PolyU database.

Table 1. Comparison of various palmprint authentication methods on PolyU database, '–'indicates non-reported value

Algorithms	Patch size	3 training	5 training
ScSPM	16×16	100 %	100 %
	25×25	100 %	100 %
	31×31	99.9 %	100 %
LLDP [10]		99.28 %	
Contourlet transform [20]	–	88.91 %	–
BDCT [21]	–	98.93 %	–
OWE [22]	–	–	98.9 %
2D-DOST [23]	–	–	100 %

4.2 Results on the CASIA Database

CASIA palmprint database samples are 256 gray level images, which contains 5502 palmprint images captured from 312 subjects and the original size is 480×640 pixels. This experiment uses 2432 right hand effective image of the database, and for each palm there are 8 images. We segment the region of interest (ROI) [19] and its size is 200×200 pixels. Each person was taken 2, 4 training images, and the rest as a test.

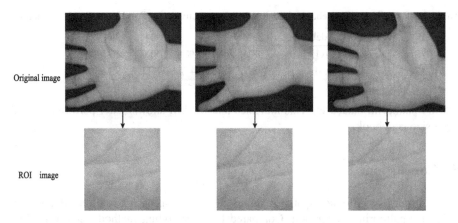

Fig. 2. Sample images in CASIA database with corresponding ROI images

Table 2. Comparison of various palmprint recognition methods on CASIA database, '–' indicates non-reported value

Algorithms	Patch size	2 training	4 training
ScSPM	16 × 16	99.2 %	99.68 %
	25 × 25	99.0 %	99.46 %
	31 × 31	98.89 %	99.57 %
BDPCA [24]	–	95 %	–
2D-DOST [23]	–	97.29 %	98.44 %

In this experiment, the size of codebook is 128 × 1024. Figure 2 shows sample images of a person right palm in the CASIA database and corresponding ROI image (Table 2).

4.3   Parameter Analysis

4.3.1   Sparse Coding Parameter

During sparse coding phase, λ is a parameter that controls the sparsity of sparse coding coefficients in Eq. (7). In practical experience, the sparsity of the coefficient is relatively good at about 10 %. In our experiments, by testing $\lambda = 0.1/0.15/0.2/0.25/0.3/0.4$, we can obtain average sparsity of coefficients at about 10 % when λ is 0.1 to 0.2. Therefore, our experiment takes $\lambda = 0.15$ for sparse coding.

4.3.2   Codebook Size

We know that codebook size has little effect on the result of SPM algorithm, therefore, we test the impact of codebook size on ScSPM method. Generally, if the codebook size is smaller, the histogram feature will lose the ability to discriminate; if the codebook size is too large, the histogram from the same class of image will never match. In our experiments, we try four sizes: 256, 512, 1024 and 2048. As shown in Table 3, the recognition rate continues to increase as the codebook size grows further on PolyU and

Table 3. The effects of codebook size on ScSPM respectively on PolyU and CASIA databases

	Codebook size	256	512	1024	2048
3 training	PolyU	98.6 %	100 %	100 %	100 %
	CASIA	98.79 %	99.24 %	99.22 %	99.56 %

CASIA palmprint databases. This indicates that ScSPM shows better performance for large size codebook.

5 Conclusion

In this paper, we introduce spatial pyramid matching approach based on SIFT sparse codes for palmprint recognition. Compared to other coding methods, sparse coding method has the advantages in palmprint recognition: (1) the constraint conditions are more relaxed and it performs much better on reconstruction effect; (2) it describes the statistical properties and the essential of image; (3) there are obvious block sparse characteristics in the palmprint image, which is beneficial to linear separability. The experimental results show the validity for palmprint recognition.

Acknowledgements. This work is supported by the National Natural Science Foundation of China (No. 61202251), the China Postdoctoral Science Foundation (No. 2014M551086), the Liaoning Provincial Natural Science Foundation (No. 201602035), and by the Program for Liaoning Excellent Talents in University (No. LJQ2013133).

References

1. Lu, Z., Wang, L., Wen, J.: Image classification by visual bag-of-words refinement and reduction. Neurocomputing **173**, 373–384 (2016)
2. Wang, F., Zhao, W., Ngo, C.W., et al.: A hamming embedding kernel with informative bag-of-visual words for video semantic indexing. ACM Trans. Multimedia Comput. Commun. Appl. 3(10) (2014)
3. Jia, W., Hu, R.X., Lei, Y.K., et al.: Histogram of oriented lines for palmprint recognition. IEEE Trans. Syst. Man Cybern. Syst. **44**, 385–395 (2014)
4. Csurka, G., Dance, C.R., Fan, L., et al.: Visual categorization with bags of keypoints. In: ECCV (2004)
5. Schmid, C., Lazebnik, S., Ponce, J.: Beyond bags of features: spatial pyramid matching for recognizing natural scene categories. In: Proceedings of CVPR 2006, vol. 2, pp. 2169–2178 (2006)
6. Peng, X., Yan, R., Zhao, B.: Fast low rank representation based spatial pyramid matching for image classification. Knowl. Based Syst. **10**(16), 817–828 (2015)
7. Mei, X., Ma, Y., Li, C.: A real-time infrared ultra-spectral signature classification method via spatial pyramid matching. Sensors **29**, 79–88 (2015)
8. Lu, P., Xu, Z., Yu, H., Chang, Y., et al.: Object class recognition based on compressive sensing with sparse features inspired by hierarchical model in visual cortex. In: Proceedings of the SPIE. Optoelectronic Imaging and Multimedia Technology II, vol. 8558, p. 85581X, 30 November 2012

9. Yu, K., Zhang, T., Gong, Y.H.: Nonlinear learning using local coordinate coding. In: Proceedings of the 2009 Advances in Neural Information Processing Systems, pp. 2223–2231. NIPS, Vancouver (2009)
10. Luo, Y.T., Zhao, L.Y., Zhang, B., et al.: Local line directional pattern for palmprint recognition. Pattern Recogn. **50**, 26–44 (2016)
11. Wu, X., Zhao, Q.: Deformed palmprint matching based on stable regions. IEEE Trans. Image Process. **24**, 4978–4989 (2015)
12. Zhang, L., Shen, Y., Li, H., et al.: 3D palmprint identification using block-wise features and collaborative representation. IEEE Trans. Pattern Anal. Mach. Intell. **37**(8), 1730–1736 (2015)
13. Yang, J., Yu, K., Gong, Y., Huang, T.: Linear spatial pyramid matching using sparse coding for image classification. In: CVPR (2009)
14. Xu, Y., Fei, L., Zhang, D.: Combining left and right palmprint images for more accurate personal identification. IEEE Trans. Image Process. **24**, 549–559 (2015)
15. Zhao, Z., Ji, H., Gao, J., et al.: Sparse coding based multi-scale spatial latent semantic analysis for image classification. Chin. J. Comput. **37**(6), 1251–1260 (2014)
16. Wang, J., Yang, J., Yu, K., et al.: Locality-constrained linear coding for image classification. In: CVPR (2010)
17. Liu, P., Liu, G., Guo, M., et al.: Image classification based on non-negative locality-constrained linear coding. Acta Automatica Sin. **41**(7), 1235–1243 (2015)
18. Lee, H., Battle, A., Raina, R., et al.: Efficient sparse coding algorithms. In: Neural Information Processing Systems (2007)
19. Shang, L., Su, P., Huai, W.: New location method of palmprint ROI images. Laser Infrared **7**(42), 815–820 (2012)
20. Butt, M.A.A., Masood, H., Mumtaz, M., et al.: Palmprint identification using contourlet transform. In: Proceedings of IEEE Conference on Biometrics, Theory, Applications and Systems, pp. 1–5 (2008)
21. Badrinath, G.S., Gupta, P.: Stockwell transform based palm-print recognition. Appl. Soft Comput. **11**(7), 4267–4281 (2011)
22. Meraoumia, A., Chitroub, S., Bouridane, A.: Gaussian modeling and discrete cosine transform for efficient and automatic palmprint identification. In: International Conference on Machine and Web Intelligence (ICMWI), pp. 121–125 (2010)
23. Saedi, S., Charkari, N.M.: Palmprint authentication based on discrete orthonormal S-Transform. Appl. Soft Comput. **21**, 341–351 (2014)
24. Xue, Y., Liu, Y., Liu, C., et al.: Improved BDPCA method for palmprint recognition. Comput. Eng. Appl. **50**(15), 150–152 (2014)

A Finger Vein Identification System Based on Image Quality Assessment

Zhixing Huang[1], Wenxiong Kang[1(✉)], Qiuxia Wu[2], Junhong Zhao[1], and Wei Jia[3]

[1] School of Automation Science and Engineering, South China University of Technology,
Guangzhou, China
auwxkang@scut.edu.cn

[2] School of Software Engineering, South China University of Technology, Guangzhou, China

[3] School of Computer and Information, Hefei University of Technology, Hefei, China

Abstract. Generally, the quality of the acquired finger vein images makes a significant impact on the performance of finger vein identification system. Therefore, aimed at the characteristics of the vein images, we propose a novel finger vein identification system taking the image quality assessment into account. The embedded image quality assessment method is able to improve the performance of finger vein identification system by filtering the low quality images. In order to make better representation of the finger vein images, a score-level fusion strategy is proposed for the combination of the texture information and the structural information, wherein the texture information and the structural information are obtained from the Local Binary Pattern (LBP) and the histogram of oriented gradients (HOG), respectively. The comprehensive experiments on two finger vein image datasets have demonstrated that our proposed image quality assessment method and the score-level fusion method can achieve outperformed performance for the finger vein identification system.

Keywords: Finger vein identification · Image quality assessment · Score fusion

1 Introduction

The biometric technology is a way of identifying a person by means of his biological information such as fingerprints, palm prints, palm vein, finger vein, face and iris. Compared with the traditional authentication techniques based on passwords, the emerging biometric techniques are more convenient and secure [1]. Among the above-mentioned biometrics, finger vein recognition has attracted more and more attention because of its advantages of small size, easy to carry as well as anti-counterfeit.

Since the finger vein images include rich texture information, the effective vein texture representation has still been the most common way for the feature extraction. Based on local binary pattern (LBP) [2], Ojala et al. [3] proposed a new texture descriptor called local line binary pattern (LLBP), which achieved better performance than the LBP and local derivative pattern (LDP). And in [4], a method was proposed to describe the texture of local gradient patterns (LGP), which had obtained ideal performance in face detection. Meng et al. [5] represented finger vein by a novel local descriptor called

© Springer International Publishing AG 2016
Z. You et al. (Eds.): CCBR 2016, LNCS 9967, pp. 244–254, 2016.
DOI: 10.1007/978-3-319-46654-5_27

Local Directional Code (LDC), which outperformed the LLBP. Another alternative way for finger vein feature extraction is to obtain structural features from binary images. As in [6], a finger-vein recognition method with modified binary tree (MBT) model was proposed which is robust to translation, slight rotation, local difference and segmentation error. Based on a personalized best patches map (PBPM), a robust finger vein verification method was proposed in [7], which achieved strong robustness to rotation and translation. To resolve the influence of the poor-quality images, a new strategy based on both the Gaussian low-pass filter and the direction detection was presented for finger vein image recognition [8]. Nevertheless, there are also some research works to identify the finger vein image based on neural network by self-learned features. In [18], a method was proposed to learn a set of representative features based on auto-encoders, which achieved outperformed recognition accuracy without preprocessing on the finger vein images.

So far, there has been a predominant issue for the finger vein identification system that the quality of images is poor. In order to evaluate the quality of the images, an image quality evaluation index was presented to simulate the characteristics of human visual system [13]. To improve the performance of the finger vein recognition system, they presented a novel image quality assessment based on Radon transform [10], and the quality score was estimated from the curvature of corresponding Radon space. In [11], a novel quality metrics from the hierarchical structure of finger vein was proposed which was demonstrated with better performance but the outperformed segmentation results should be obtained in advance. A novel image quality assessment method was proposed according to detecting the vein points by the depth thresholds from the gray finger vein images in order to improve the performance of finger vein recognition system [12]. Yang *et al.* proposed an image quality assessment method using support vector machines (SVMs) based on the gradient, image contrast, and information capacity from the image [9]. And in [14], a new method based on the Support Vector Regression (SVR) also was proposed for finger vein image quality evaluation, but the scores of the images in the training set needed to be annotated manually in advance. A novel approach to predicting the quality of finger vein images based on deep Neural Network (DNN) was proposed, but it is relatively complicated in application and more training data are necessary [15].

In fact, it doesn't only depend on the contrast, mean and energy of finger vein image for image quality assessment in the practical finger vein identification system. If the blurred images are successfully enhanced and the useful invariant features are extracted, it won't make any impact on achieving good performance for the finger vein identification system. Therefore, the image quality evaluation also needs to take both the feature extraction method and recognition strategy into account. If the stable and distinguished features can be extracted from finger vein images, the quality of finger vein image is supposed to be good. Otherwise, it is supposed to be poor.

To improve the accuracy of the finger vein identification system, we present a recognition algorithm based on the information fusion of texture and structure first. In combination of the recognition algorithm, we also propose a novel finger vein image quality assessment method to filter the poor-quality images. The method has been demonstrated to be effective and objective even without manually annotation on the training set. Nevertheless, our finger vein recognition system based on the image quality assessment method also has the ability of refusing to the poor-quality images in order to improve the recognition performance. As the algorithm has less computational complexity, so the system is able to run faster, without other additional processing except for vein points detection and statistical operation, which reveals its stability, real-time, and reliability for the practical system.

2   The Proposed Finger Vein Recognition System

The overview of our proposed recognition system is illustrated in Fig. 1, which combined the image quality assessment method with the fusion recognition method in the system. First, the finger vein image has been captured. Then the preprocessing is conducted, including the region of interests (ROI) extraction [17]. Subsequently we evaluate the quality of captured images based on our proposed image quality assessment method. If the quality of an image is poor, wherein the score is below the set threshold, the image would be refused to register and identify. Otherwise, we perform texture matching on the gray image and Matching score 1 is obtained. In addition, the structure feature is calculated from the binary image, and the feature matching is performed to obtain Matching score 2. The final recognition results are achieved by the score-level fusion strategy on the formerly obtained matching scores.

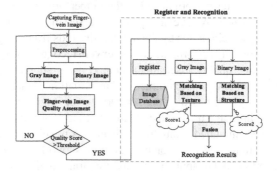

Fig. 1. The block diagram of proposed system

The quality of images mainly determined from whether the stable and discriminative feature could be extracted. Hence, the image quality assessment method also has the relation to the subsequent feature extraction and matching methods. As our recognition method is based on the information fusion of texture and structure, so we take the following two aspects into account for the image quality assessment, including the number of the vein point, and the variance of the image.

2.1   The Vein Point Detection

First, the Gaussian filter is used for denoising the obtained ROI images, and then the normalization is conducted on the gray-scale. Subsequently, the vein texture is segmented from the gray image by detecting the vein valley direction [8]. Next, we search the possible vein points based on binary images. As shown in Fig. 2(a), the distribution of finger vein is mainly along the horizontal direction, so we can search in the vertical direction when looking for vein points. The search is conducted from top to bottom, from left to right. During searching the binary image from top to bottom, a point can be viewed as the upper bound point if its last point is black and the following point is white. Then continuing searching, a point can be viewed as the lower bound point if the next point is black. And the vein point is located at the right middle between the upper and the lower bound point. To speed up the searching and prune the redundant vein points, we implement an equidistant pixels search method when searching vein points from left to right. In this paper, a vein point's upper bound point, lower bound point, as well as the vein point itself are taken as a vein point pair.

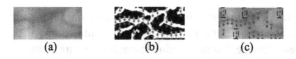

(a)   (b)   (c)

Fig. 2. Finger vein image (a) the gray ROI image; (b) the binary image, the red points are the candidate vein points, the green points are the upper bound points, the blue points are the lower bound points; (c) the illustration of the detected vein point pairs on a gray image. (Color figure online)

More pseudo vein point pairs might be detected from the binary images probably, if the quality of the finger vein image is poor. In order to prune the pseudo vein points, we verify the candidate vein points one by one. The candidate vein point pairs are illustrated in the gray image, as shown in Fig. 2(c). The yellow boxes denote the pseudo vein point pairs. It is obvious that the gray difference is relatively small between the pseudo vein point and its upper bound point or its lower bound point.

2.2   Calculating the Finger Vein Quality Score Based on the Vein Points

For each vein point pair, the value of vein point's gray difference is obtained from the average of the gray difference between the upper point and the vein point, and the gray difference between the lower point and the vein point. More accurately, we move the upper bound point four pixels up and the lower bound point four pixels down. To reduce the impact of the noise, we calculate a point gray difference by the average of its surrounding point pairs. We suppose that $f(x_0, y_0)$ denotes the gray value of a vein point, $f(x_{up}, y_{up})$ is the gray value of its upper bound point and $f(x_{down}, y_{down})$ is the gray value of its lower bound point, and then the gray difference of a vein point is as follows:

$$GrayDiff = \frac{1}{5} \sum_{i=-2}^{2} f(x_{up} + i, y_{up}) + f(x_{down} + i, y_{down}) - 2 * f(x_0 + i, y_0) \qquad (1)$$

The range of a real vein point' gray difference is set as [a, b]. Theoretically, the larger the value of the vein point's gray difference is, the clearer the vein image is. As a result, the larger value of the vein point's gray difference contributes much to the quality score of finger vein image. The image quality score is calculated as,

$$score = \sum_{i=a}^{b} FVPGFN_i \tag{2}$$

where $FVPGFN_i$ denotes the number of the vein points which the gray difference is larger than i. Then, the score is normalized to the range of [0, 1] by the Min-Max method, where 1 indicates the best quality of the images and 0 indicates the worst.

2.3 The Recognition Methods and Score Level Fusion

In this paper, both the texture information and the structure information are extracted from the images. The texture information obtained from the gray image retains many details of the original image, but the obtained minutiae feature is quite not stable due to illumination fluctuations, finger deformation and noise interference. Thus, only based on the texture information won't achieve high robustness for the finger vein image recognition system. However, it is well known that the structure feature is not sensitive to the illumination changes and translation. But the vein image contains relatively less vein structural information, which will decrease the recognition accuracy in large-scale database. In light of the complementary of both types of features, we fuse them to improve the performance of the recognition system. To prove the universality of the strategy, we choose Local Binary Patterns (LBP) to extract the texture feature and the Histogram of Oriented Gradient (HOG) is used to extract the structure feature. In [19], the LBP operator was first introduced for analyzing the image texture feature, which reveals its strong discrimination in texture classification. We use an improved operator, Uniform LBP, which performs better and has stronger ability for representing most of texture patterns. Similar to [16], we adopt the HOG feature to recognize the finger veins, and also achieve outperformed results. For our proposed finger vein identification system, the final matching score is obtained by fusing the scores of LBP feature matching and HOG feature matching. The block diagram of recognition is shown in Fig. 3.

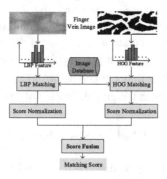

Fig. 3. Block diagram of recognition

As the LBP histogram is a statistical feature, so it is better to adopt the strategy of matching the intersection of LBP histogram. The larger the intersection is, the more similar the two samples, otherwise smaller. The matching score is defined as follows,

$$score_{LBP} = \left\{ \sum_{i=1}^{m} \min\left(F_1^{(i)}, F_2^{(i)}\right) \right\} / (|F_{LBP}|) \times 100 \tag{3}$$

wherein, F_1 and F_2 are the LBP feature vectors, and m is the length of the vector. It is noticed that the cosine similarity has the ability to measure the difference in the direction of the two vectors. So, we measure the similarity of HOG features based on cosine similarity. Finally, we normalize the cosine similarity score into [0, 100].

$$score_{HOG} = (F_{HOG1} \bullet F_{HOG2}) / (|F_{HOG1}| * |F_{HOG2}|) \times 100 \tag{4}$$

Here, F_{HOG1} and F_{HOG2} are the HOG feature vectors, $score_{HOG}$ denotes the HOG feature matching score. The final score is calculated as follows,

$$score = w * score_{LBP} + (1 - w) * score_{HOG} \tag{5}$$

wherein, w is the weight of the LBP score, w ranges from 0 to 1. The distribution of matching scores obtained by LBP and HOG in the Universiti Sains Malaysia finger-vein database is shown in Fig. 4. The black points denote match scores from genuine finger vein image, and the yellow points are the impostor match scores. As seen the two methods are complementary, so it is advisable to use the weight fusion method.

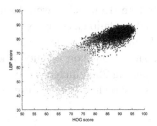

Fig. 4. The distribution of matching scores obtained by LBP and HOG in the Universiti Sains Malaysia finger-vein database

3   Experiment

To validate the effectiveness of our proposed finger vein identification system, we designed a set of comparative experiments on the purpose of: (1) Evaluating the performance of our proposed image quality assessment method by using several recognition methods; (2) Comparing the performance of the fusion recognition method with the single recognition method.

A. Database

The experiments are conducted on two different finger-vein databases. The first database is the Universiti Sains Malaysia finger-vein database [20], denoted as "Database 1" and collected from two different sessions. There are a total of 2952 finger vein images from 123 volunteers in each session. And each volunteer provided 24 images from left index, left middle, right index and right middle (6 images from each finger) in each session. And the size and depth of the captured images are 640 × 480 and 256 gray levels, respectively.

The second database is denoted as "Database 2", which is established by us. The database is collected from 300 volunteers, and each volunteer provided 20 images from left index, left middle, right index and right middle (5 images from each finger). And the size and depth of the images are 752 × 480 and 256 gray levels, respectively. So, there are a total of 6000 images in our own established database. There are many reasons accounted for the decreasing performance of the system. Therefore, it is better for the volunteer to keep the same finger attitude during the acquisition process.

B. Experimental results and analysis

(1) Experiment 1 on the Database 1

We compared the performance of different finger vein recognition methods on original database and the selected database where the quality score of images was greater than the threshold, and show how much it can be improved by adopting our quality assessment scheme and the fusion method. In our experiments, we adopted the following matching strategies. Intragroup match: pair-wise matching was performed among six images of each finger in the group. Therefore, 15 matches were identified for each finger. Inter-group matching: to reduce the computational complexity of the matching process, pair-wise matching was conducted among each image and other 100 images of other finger. A total of 122 images in session 2 are poor-quality when the image quality score threshold is 0.12. And the remaining 2806 image can be accepted by the system. The comparison on the EER curves is shown as follows (Fig. 5).

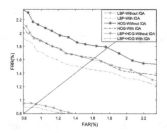

Fig. 5. The EER curve comparisons

Experimental results show that a total of 2952 images only 122 were refused when the quality score was not greater than 0.12. The EER without our proposed image quality assessment method is 1.6 % with the LBP-based method, but after we conduct the image quality assessment method the EER decreases to 1.483 % using the same LBP-based method. And for the HOG-based recognition, the EER was 1.798 % without the image quality assessment method, but it was also higher than the EER of 1.627 % with our proposed image quality assessment method. After fusion on the LBP-based recognition and the HOG-based recognition, the EER was 0.939 % without the proposed image quality assessment method, and the EER was the lowest (0.887 %) with the image quality assessment method (Tables 1 and 2).

Table 1. The performance of different methods

	Without image quality assessment	With image quality assessment
LBP(uniform)	1.6 %	1.483 %
HOG	1.798 %	1.627 %
LBP + HOG	0.939 %	0.887 %

Table 2. The comparison on the amount of images with different quality score thresholds

Quality value	Original	>0.13	>0.18	>0.21	>0.25	>0.29	>0.33
Amount of images	2952	2806	2673	2476	2173	1838	1518

As shown in Fig. 6, with the increasing of the image quality score threshold, the EER decreased at first, increased then and decreased again. We should both consider the EER and the number of the poor-quality images when setting the threshold. If the threshold was set too high, there would result in more poor-quality images and also degrade the user experience. But using the proposed image quality assessment would hardly affect the performance of the identification system when the threshold was set too low. Therefore, it is necessary to select a proper threshold. In above-mentioned experiments, the EER appeared to a decreasing tendency when the quality score threshold was 0.12 and the rate of the poor images was 122/2952 = 4.13 %.

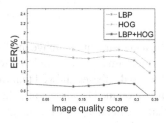

Fig. 6. The EER when changing in the quality score

(2) Experiment 2 on the Database 2

The matching strategies on the "Database 2" were the same as that on the "Database 1". On the database, a total of 6000 images only 860 were refused when the quality score was not greater than 0.31. And the EER curve is shown in Fig. 7 (Table 3).

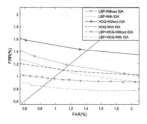

Fig. 7. The EER curve comparisons

Table 3. The performance of different methods

	Without image quality assessment	With image quality assessment
LBP(uniform)	1.18 %	1.095 %
HOG	1.417 %	1.106 %
LBP + HOG	0.964 %	0.836 %

On the "Database 2", when the image quality score threshold was 0.31, the EER dropped from 1.18 % to 1.095 % with the same LBP-based recognition method. Using the HOG-based recognition method, the EER also dropped from 1.417 % to 1.106 %. And the EER dropped from 0.964 % to 0.836 % when fusing both of them. This also indicated that the performance of the finger vein recognition was improved by means of the fusion method and our proposed image quality assessment method (Table 4).

Table 4. The comparison on the amount of image with different quality score thresholds

Quality value	Original	>0.25	>0.31	>0.38	>0.44
Amount of image	6000	5548	5130	4565	3707

As shown in Fig. 8, with the increasing of the image quality score threshold, the EER decreased. However, there are more images that would be refused by the system.

Experimental results on the two databases showed that the distribution of the image quality scores was a little different on the Database 1 and the Database 2. But it is same that the EER would decrease after using the proposed image quality assessment method on both databases, regardless of whichever the matching method is. And the performance of the finger vein recognition system based on the fusion recognition method was better than that before the methods fusing.

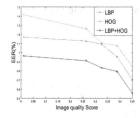

Fig. 8. The EER when changing in the quality score

(3) Experiment 3

In the experiment, we measured the average processing time of our proposed finger-vein verification system, and the computation time was shown in details as Table 5. The experiment was implemented in Visual Studio 2013, and conducted on a PC with a 3.3 GHz CPU. From the Table 5 we can see the total running time of the system is less than 11.9 ms because the features of the registered images had been extracted before recognition. So, our proposed system can be taken as a real-time system.

Table 5. The average processing time.

Method	Preprocessing	Quality Assessing	LBP matching	HOG matching
Time (ms)	9	0.5	1	1.4

4   Conclusion

In this paper, we propose a finger vein identification system based on the fusion of texture matching and structure matching. Combined with the recognition algorithm, we also develop a novel image quality assessment method. Experimental results show that the fusion method could improve the accuracy of the system. And using our proposed image quality assessment method, the recognition system could refuse to register and identify the poor-quality images, which is able to improve the recognition accuracy. However, the further research on more effective identification system based on our proposed image quality assessment is still needed in the future.

Acknowledgments. This work was supported by the National Natural Science Foundation of China (Nos. 61573151, 61105019, 61503141, 61175022), the Guangdong Natural Science Foundation (No. 2016A030313468), the Fundamental Research Funds for the Central Universities, SCUT (No. 2015ZM080).

References

1. Jain, A.K., Ross, A., Pankanti, S.: Biometrics: a tool for information security. IEEE Trans. Inf. Forensics Secur. **1**(2), 125–143 (2006)

2. Ojala, T., Pietikäinen, M., Mäenpää, T.: Multiresolution gray-scale and rotation invariant texture classification with local binary patterns. IEEE Trans. Pattern Anal. Mach. Intell. **24**(7), 971–987 (2002)
3. Rosdi, B.A., Shing, C.W., Suandi, S.A.: Finger vein recognition using local line binary pattern. Sensors **11**(12), 11357–11371 (2011)
4. Jun, B., Kim, D.: Robust face detection using local gradient patterns and evidence accumulation. Pattern Recogn. **45**(9), 3304–3316 (2012)
5. Meng, X., Yang, G., Yin, Y., et al.: Finger vein recognition based on local directional code. Sensors **12**(11), 14937–14952 (2012)
6. Liu, T., Xie, J., Yan, W., et al.: Finger-vein recognition with modified binary tree model. Neural Comput. Appl. **26**(4), 969–977 (2015)
7. Dong, L., et al.: Finger vein verification based on a personalized best patches map. In: 2014 IEEE International Joint Conference on Biometrics (IJCB), pp. 1–8. IEEE (2014)
8. You, L., Li, X., Sun, L., et al.: Finger vein recognition method based on Gaussian low-pass filter and direction detection. In: 2014 International Conference on Information and Communications Technologies (ICT 2014), pp. 1–8. IET (2014)
9. Yang, L., Yang, G., Yin, Y., Xiao, R.: Finger vein image quality evaluation using support vector matchines. Opt. Eng. **52**(2), 1–10 (2013)
10. Qin H, Li S, Kot A C, et al.: Quality assessment of finger-vein image. In: 2012 Asia-Pacific Signal & Information Processing Association Annual Summit and Conference (APSIPA ASC), pp. 1–4. IEEE (2012)
11. Xie, S.J., Zhou, B., Yang, J., Lu, Y., Pan, Y.: Novel hierarchical structure based finger vein image quality assessment. In: Sun, Z., Shan, S., Yang, G., Zhou, J., Wang, Y., Yin, Y.L. (eds.) CCBR 2013. LNCS, vol. 8232, pp. 266–273. Springer, Heidelberg (2013)
12. Nguyen, D.T., Park, Y.H., Shin, K.Y., et al.: New finger-vein recognition method based on image quality assessment. KSII Trans. Internet Inf. Syst. (TIIS) **7**(2), 347–365 (2013)
13. Ma, H., Wang, K., Fan, L., Cui, F.: A finger vein image quality assessment method using object and human visual system index. In: Yang, J., Fang, F., Sun, C. (eds.) IScIDE 2012. LNCS, vol. 7751, pp. 498–506. Springer, Heidelberg (2013)
14. Zhou, L., Yang, G., Yang, L., et al.: Finger Vein Image Quality Evaluation based on Support Vector Regression. Int. J. Sig. Process. Image Process. Pattern Recogn. **8**(8), 211–222 (2015)
15. Qin, H., El-Yacoubi, M.A.: Finger-vein quality assessment by representation learning from binary images. In: Arik, S., Huang, T., Lai, W.K., Liu, Q. (eds.) ICONIP 2015. LNCS, vol. 9489, pp. 421–431. Springer International Publishing, Heidelberg (2015)
16. Dalal, N., Triggs, B.: Histograms of oriented gradients for human detection. In: 2005 IEEE Computer Society Conference on Computer Vision and Pattern Recognition, CVPR 2005, vol. 1, pp. 886–893. IEEE (2005)
17. Yang, L., Yang, G., Yin, Y., et al.: Sliding window-based region of interest extraction for finger vein images. Sensors **13**(3), 3799–3815 (2013)
18. Fayyaz, M., PourReza, M., Saffar, M.H., et al.: A novel approach for finger vein verification based on self-taught learning. arXiv preprint arXiv:1508.03710 (2015)
19. Ojala, T., Pietikäinen, M., Harwood, D.: A comparative study of texture measures with classification based on featured distributions. Pattern Recogn. **29**(1), 51–59 (1996)
20. http://blog.eng.usm.my/fendi/

An Edge Detection Algorithm for Nonuniformly Illuminated Images in Finger-vein Authentication

Hongyu Ren, Da Xu, and Wenxin Li[(✉)]

School of Electronics Engineering and Computer Science, Peking University,
Beijing 100871, People's Republic of China
{rhy,xuda1996,lwx}@pku.edu.cn

Abstract. Recently, finger-vein authentication has been a rising bio-detection technique for its outstanding security, biologic maintenance, accuracy and speed. To deal with the rotation in finger-vein image, the edge of finger in the image is detected and the inclination angle is calculated. However, considering the device universally used in finger-vein authentication, in order to detect finger-veins more clearly and get more features, illumination is not evenly distributed, so the conventional edge detection methods are affected by different illuminative backgrounds of the finger. Therefore, a new simple but effective edge detection algorithm specially designed for finger-vein authentication is proposed and evaluated in this paper. Experiments based on 5,000 finger-vein images show that the proposed algorithm provides higher accuracy than conventional methods.

Keywords: Biometrics · Finger-vein recognition · Edge detection

1 Introduction

As a practical and proved biometric technique, finger-vein authentication has been widely researched in recent years because of its superiority in accuracy, speed and security. However, there are also some problems in finger-vein authentication, such as image quality loss due to environment and image distortion due to various finger position. The impact caused by the first problem can be effectively reduced by the device we use to capture finger-vein images because it can automatically examine under which circumstances the image quality (particular the finger-vein clarity) can be the best. As for the second one, normalization is required. It is necessary to calculate the inclination angle, which can be deduced by two edge lines. However, conventional methods do not perform well enough since they neglect the characteristics of finger-vein images. We propose an algorithm to figure out finger edge accurately based on the ubiquitous and notable characteristics. Furthermore, we normalize every finger-vein image in order to test the improvement.

We run our algorithm on a database of 5,000 finger-vein images, and test 6 criterions, Equal Error Rate included, as an evaluation of the performance. We also compare our algorithm with algorithm without rotation and Canny algorithm with rotation [1].

© Springer International Publishing AG 2016
Z. You et al. (Eds.): CCBR 2016, LNCS 9967, pp. 255–262, 2016.
DOI: 10.1007/978-3-319-46654-5_28

2   Brief Introduction of the Device

The device is manufactured by Beijing Yannan Tech Co., Ltd., which contains four parts, a camera to capture the image, a computer to process the image, an infrared LED array and its control circuit, a microcomputer unit to receive the control signal from the computer and to control the LED array [2]. The device works as follows. The camera may capture an image and send it to the computer. After the computer calculates the standard deviation of the grey level, total length of the vein and number of bifurcations, the MCU will change the intensity of the LED array based on the three criterions and the camera takes an image repeatedly until the image is considered eligible [2]. The device is extensively used in various scenarios, such as Chinese College Entrance Examination in Neimeng and Guangdong Province, China Minsheng Bank ATM etc. (Fig. 1).

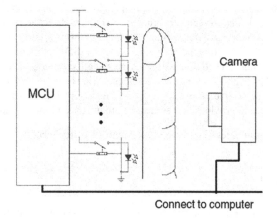

Fig. 1.   Sketch map of the device

3   Characteristics of Finger-vein Images

As is shown in Fig. 2, there are many characteristics affecting the detection of edge. Due to nonuniformly distributed illumination, first and foremost, the central part of background of the upper edge line is generally lighter than other parts of background, so it is harder to detect it, though it is quite clear for human eyes. Conventional edge detection method will print an arc instead of a line when detecting the central part of edge. Furthermore, the light on the left part and right part of the image can be confusing for algorithm to find out the exact edge line.

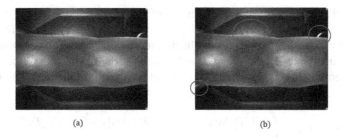

Fig. 2. (a) A typical finger-vein image. (b) Characteristics of finger-vein image.

4 Procedure of Finger-vein Authentication

To solve the problem mentioned in Sect. 3, an edge detection algorithm is proposed. The overall process is listed below.

Step 1. Image normalization
       Step 1-1. Finding potential edge pixels
       Step 1-2. Determining a standard pixel for both upper edge and lower edge
       Step 1-3. Two-way extension of the edge lines
       Step 1-4. Fetching the middle line and rotating
Step 2. Binarization
Step 3. Matching and cutting

The details of these steps are as follows:
Step 1. Image normalization
As we can see in Fig. 3, these two finger-vein images belong to one person. However, the finger in Fig. 3a tilts upward slightly while that in Fig. 3b is not. Therefore, rotation is necessary when normalizing the images. We need to decide the inclination angle based on the edges of finger in each image.

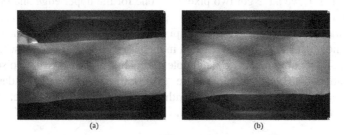

Fig. 3. Same finger with different positions. (a) Upward tilting. (b) Level.

Step 1-1. Finding potential edge pixels

$$P\_New[x][y] = \left(\sum_{i=x-1}^{i=x+1} \sum_{j=y-1}^{j=y+1} Pixel[i][j] \right)/9 \qquad (1)$$

First of all, the image is reduced to one third of its original size in both dimensions by taking the averages of all non-overlapping 3 × 3 squares, which is illustrated in Eq. 1. We use a parameter to represent the difference between the chosen pixel and the pixel for comparison. If the difference is higher than the parameter, we consider this pixel as potential edge pixel. Then two pixel sets, up node set and down node set, are obtained by separation of y coordinate value (Fig. 4).

$$Potential[x][y] = \begin{cases} 1 \ if \ |P\_New[x][y] - P\_New[x][y - 3]| > P\_Diff \\ 0 \ else \end{cases} \tag{2}$$

Step 1-2. Determining a standard pixel for both upper edge and lower edge

$$Stan\_Up\_Y = \underset{1 \leq i \leq Up\_Node\_Sum}{most} (Up\_Node[i].y) \tag{3}$$

$$Stan\_Down\_Y = \underset{1 \leq i \leq Down\_Node\_Sum}{most} (Down\_Node[i].y) \tag{4}$$

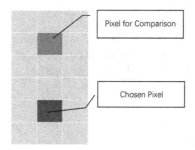

Fig. 4. Illustration of chosen pixel and pixel for comparison.

After Step 1-1, we have got two pixel sets, one for the upper edge and one for the lower edge. Take upper edge as an example, pixels in upper set are only potential edge pixels. In order to find a standard pixel (a pixel which is most likely on the edge), we notice that the most y coordinate appeared in the point set would be the most possible standard pixel's y coordinate. Although potential pixels are sensitive to noise, yet the method mentioned above can sort out those "fake" edge pixels. As for standard pixel's x coordinate, we use limited random algorithm to pick a pixel from the set which has the same y coordinate as the most appeared y coordinate.

$$Stan\_Up\_Node = Up\_Node[i] \ if \ Up\_Node[i].y = Stan\_Up\_Y$$
$$\&\& \ Col/3 \leq Up\_Node[i].x \leq 2 * Col/3 \tag{5}$$

$$Stan\_Down\_Node = Down\_Node[i] \ if \ Down\_Node[i].y = Stan\_Down\_Y$$
$$\&\& \ Col/3 \leq Down\_Node[i].x \tag{6}$$
$$\leq 2 * Col/3$$

Step 1-3. Two-way extension of the edge lines

We extend the edge line based on the standard pixel. Sort needs to be done first. There are 2 situations.

S1: From the standard pixel, if the horizontal distance between the nearest pixel in pixel set and the standard pixel more than 2 units, then we find the pixel which is only 1 unit away from the standard pixel horizontally and is also the most different than the pixel just above it.

S2: Otherwise, if the vertical distance between the nearest pixel and the standard pixel is less than 2, we can affirm that it is on the edge because two pixels make an edge line when and only when the distance between them is 1 at most both horizontally and vertically.

As shown in Fig. 5a, assume the red pixel is the standard pixel and if we extend rightwards, then the blue pixel is the nearest pixel in set. Since they are 3 units away from each other, we should find 3 pixels within the yellow rectangle area. As for the situation in Fig. 5b, although the nearest pixel is only 1 unit away from the standard horizontally, it is 5 units away from the standard vertically, which is unacceptable and needs to be corrected. We should abandon the point, and find another one in the red rectangle area.

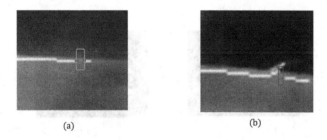

(a)   (b)

Fig. 5. (a) Situation 1 happens. (b) Situation 2 happens. (Color figure online)

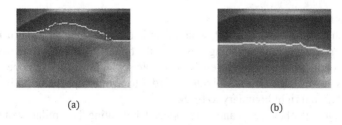

(a)   (b)

Fig. 6. (a) Edge found by snake algorithm. (b) Edge found by proposed algorithm.

Also, considering the fact that the light intensity is not evenly distributed, the rectangle area should shift downwards if the algorithm is currently detecting the central part of finger edge, which ensures that the edge the algorithm finds tends to be a straight line instead of an arc. As is shown in Fig. 6, we compare our algorithm with snake contour algorithm [3], the snake algorithm gets an arc while our algorithm figures out the exact edge line in the central part.

Step 1-4. Fetching the middle line and rotating

We then get each point of the middle line by simply averaging the y coordinate of the upper edge and lower edge. With the middle line, it is easy for us to calculate the angle thanks to linear fitting of the middle points and rotate the picture in order to level the finger.

Step 2. Binarization

We apply the wide line detector for feature extraction [4] to binarize the finger-vein image. The value of pixels in vein region and is set to 255 and other pixels set to 0. We also notice that there are little dots in binarized image which obviously are noise and they cannot be eliminated effectively simply by filtering. So we use floodfill algorithm to detect little dots and erase them (Fig. 7).

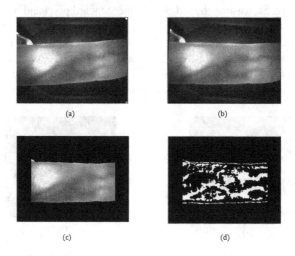

Fig. 7. (a) Original finger-vein image. (b) Normalized. (c) Denoised. (d) Binarized.

Step 3. Matching and cutting

We use the matching method in [5], which is able to correct the shifting of fingers in four directions. Before each matching, since it is the finger-veins that we are to compare, other background factors should be eliminated. We set all pixels above upper edge and pixels below lower edge as black pixels. In order to avoid impact caused by rotation, we also set left and right boundary to black.

Finally, a number between 0 and 1 is produced, indicating the similarity of two input images.

5   Experiments

5.1   Data Set

We use the test database named DS1 in [6]. It consists of 5000 images from 1000 fingers (5 images per finger), collected in indoor environment, under slight guidance and strict supervision. Data for each finger were captured in one day or two. All images are in 8-bit BMP format, 256 grayscale and 512 × 384 pixel resolution.

5.2 Experimental Process

To examine the performance of proposed algorithm, we conduct three experiments — no rotation, rotation using canny algorithm and rotation using proposed algorithm. The evaluation is run on RATE, which is short for Recognition Algorithm Test Engine (http://rate.pku.edu.cn), an automatic evaluation system. Key parameters such as FAR, FMR, EER and response time are calculated.

5.3 Evaluation Criterions

There are 6 criterions we use for evaluation. EER, the main evaluation criterion, is computed as the point where FNMR curve intersects FMR curve. FMR 100 and FMR 1000 are the values of FNMR for FMR = 1/100 and 1/1000. ZeroFMR means the lowest FNMR at which no False Matches occur. FTE and FTM represent failure to enroll and failure to match, respectively [7].

Table 1. Experimental results

	EER	FMR100	FMR100	zeroFMR	FTE	FTM
No rotation	4.792	8.42	15.71	40.24	0	0
Canny with rotation	3.205	4.87	10.44	37.45	2	0
Proposed with rotation	1.925	2.47	4.98	12.71	0	0

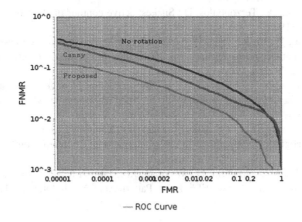

Fig. 8. ROC curve of the 3 algorithms.

5.4 Results

The ROC curves and criterions of three experiments are shown in Fig. 8 and Table 1. Firstly, both algorithms with rotation perform better than the version without rotation. Secondly, the proposed method whose EER is 1.925 %, shows its advantage over Canny algorithm, producing the best result in every criterion.

6 Conclusion and Outlook

In this paper, we design an edge detection algorithm special for nonuniformly illuminated finger-vein images. It can detect the finger position in a finger-vein image and rotate the image to normalize it accurately. Experiments show that our proposed algorithm performs better than conventional edge detection methods.

Furthermore, we do believe that there is potential in processing the finger-vein. Although the illumination is in good condition, there are still images in which finger-veins are so blurred that few algorithms can tell the difference between finger-vein and background within finger. So we speculate that some blurred finger-vein can be detected and forecast by machine learning, which may also improve performance and accuracy.

References

1. Canny, J.: A computational approach to edge detection. IEEE Trans. Pattern Anal. Mach. Intell. **6**, 679–698 (1986)
2. Dai, Y., Huang, B., Li, W., Xu, Z.: A method for capturing the finger-vein image using nonuniform intensity infrared light. In: Congress on Image and Signal Processing, CISP 2008, vol. 4, pp. 501–505. IEEE (2008)
3. Kass, M., Witkin, A., Terzopoulos, D.: Snakes: active contour models. Int. J. Comput. Vis. **1**(4), 321–331 (1988)
4. Huang, B., Dai, Y., Li, R., Tang, D., Li, W.: Finger-vein authentication based on wide line detector and pattern normalization. In: 2010 20th International Conference on Pattern Recognition (ICPR), pp. 1269–1272. IEEE (2010)
5. Miura, N., Nagasaka, A., Miyatake, T.: Feature extraction of finger-vein patterns based on repeated line tracking and its application to personal identification. Mach. Vis. Appl. **15**(4), 194–203 (2004)
6. Ye, Y., Ni, L., Zheng, H., Liu, S., Zhu, Y., Zhang, D., Xiang, W., Li, W.: FVRC 2016: the 2nd finger vein recognition competition. In: 2016 International Conference on Biometrics (ICB). IEEE (2016)
7. Cappelli, R., Maio, D., Maltoni, D., Wayman, J.L., Jain, A.K.: Performance evaluation of fingerprint verification systems. IEEE Trans. Pattern Anal. Mach. Intell. **28**(1), 3–18 (2006)

Finger-Vein Recognition Based on an Enhanced HMAX Model

Wenhui Sun, Jucheng Yang$^{(\boxtimes)}$, Ying Xie, Shanshan Fang, and Na Liu

College of Computer Science and Information Engineering,
Tianjin University of Science and Technology, Tianjin, China
jcyang@tust.edu.cn

Abstract. To overcome the shortcomings of the traditional methods, in this paper, we investigate the role of a biologically-inspired network for finger-vein recognition. Firstly, robust feature representation of finger-vein images are obtained from an enhanced Hierarchical and X (HMAX) model, and successively class by the extreme learning machine (ELM). The enhanced HMAX model could calculate complex feature representations by the way of simulating the hierarchical processing mechanism in primate visual cortex. ELM performs well in classification while keeping a faster learning speed. Our proposed method is tested on the MMCBNU-6000 dataset, and achieved good performances compared with state-of-the-art methods. The results further the case for biologically-motivated approaches for finger-vein recognition.

Keywords: Finger vein recognition · Biometrics · HMAX model · Feature representation · ELM

1 Introduction

Finger-vein recognition, as a highly secure and efficient technique for biometric identification [1], has been attract much attention. Compared with traditional biometric characteristics (e.g. fingerprints, iris, and face), finger–vein hold some excellent advantages such as security, stability, universality and so on.

There are many research works done for finger-vein recognition. Kono et al. [2] proposed the finger-vein pattern matching as a new method for identification of individuals. In 1996, Ojala et al. [3] proposed a LBP algorithm which focus on the local information of feature extraction for facial recognition. Unfortunately, it has not enough ability to extract large texture features. Successively, extended LBP algorithms such as LLBP (Rosdi et al. [4]) was presented. However, LLBP only extracts horizontal and vertical line patterns. In 2004, Miura et al. [5] proposed a method which extracts the finger-vein pattern from the unclear image by using line tracking that starts from various positions. Xie et al. [6] applied a Guided Gabor filter to improve the extraction of finger vein features while it holds a very expensive amount of computations.

G.B. Huang [7] proposed a novel learning algorithm for single hidden layer feedforward networks (SLFNs), namely, extreme learning machine (ELM), and also proved

© Springer International Publishing AG 2016
Z. You et al. (Eds.): CCBR 2016, LNCS 9967, pp. 263–270, 2016.
DOI: 10.1007/978-3-319-46654-5_29

that it can be applied to regression and classification problems while keeping a faster learning speed [8].

In this paper, we introduce a novel biologically inspired network for image recognition. In the network, previous four layers obtained from enhanced HMAX model [9] are used for feature representation of finger-vein image and ELM is introduced for feature classification in ultimate layer. Four groups of experiments will be performed on the database, to demonstrate the novelty and superiority of our proposed network. Our proposed method combines the two biologically inspired mechanisms together. And our motivation of this paper is to provide a new idea for finger-vein recognition.

The rest of the paper is organized as follows. Section 2 states the finger-vein recognition system simply. In Sect. 3, related works about HMAX model and ELM is briefly presented. Section 4 details our proposed network. In Sect. 5, experiments are performed on the database. Finally, the paper is concluded in Sect. 6.

2   Finger-Vein Recognition System

The typical finger-vein recognition system is shown in Fig. 1. Firstly, the finger-vein images are acquired through the devices. Then, acquired finger-vein images will be preprocessed by gray scaling, cropping and resizing to build the datasets [10]. Next, images are to generate the feature representation vector. The classifier is to generate output labels used for biometric identification.

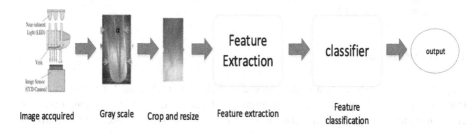

Fig. 1. A general finger-vein recognition system

3   Related Theory

3.1   Brief of the HMAX Model

Now, we will introduce the HMAX model briefly. It is described in Fig. 2.

The whole network starts with an image layer of grayscale pixels and successively compute higher layers, alternating "S" and "C" layers:

- Simple ("S") layers use convolution with local filters to compute higher-order features by combining different types of units in the previous layer.
- Complex ("C") layers increase invariance by pooling units of the same type in the previous layer over limited ranges.

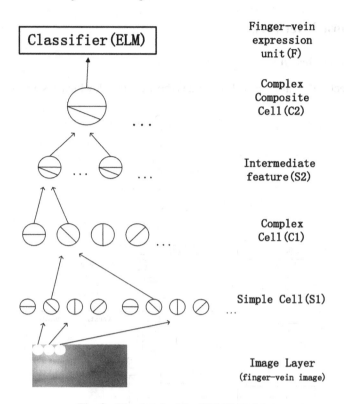

Fig. 2. The sketch of the HAMX model

A standard HMAX model [11] has four layers of hierarchy (S1-C1-S2-C2). It's lower two layers (S1 and C1) contain neurons selective in various orientations, while the upper two layers (S2 and C2) contain model neurons. Template-learning simply involves storing "snapshots" of C1 activity produced in response to some set of training images. Subsequently, these snapshots become templates that new images are matched. This template-matching produces the S2 layer, and pooling of the S2 model neurons over all image positions and scales produces the C2 layer. At the final stage, the C2 output feature vectors are used to train classifiers, such as ELM, SVM and so on.

3.2 Brief of the Extreme Learning Machine (ELM)

Extreme learning machine (ELM) [7] is a type of "generalized" SLFNs whose hidden layer need not be tuned. Moreover, ELM keeps both very fast learning speed and higher accuracy. A SLFNs with L hidden nodes is described as follows:

$$fL(x) = \sum_{i=1}^{L} \beta ihi(\mathbf{x}) = \sum_{i=1}^{L} \beta iG(\mathbf{ai}, bi, \mathbf{x}) = \mathbf{h(x)\beta} \tag{1}$$

Where $G(\mathbf{ai}, bi, \mathbf{x})$ is the activation function hold parameters of $\mathbf{ai}$ and bi.

4 Proposed Network

4.1 Network Design

The architecture of our proposed network is shown in Fig. 3, which has 5-layer structure.

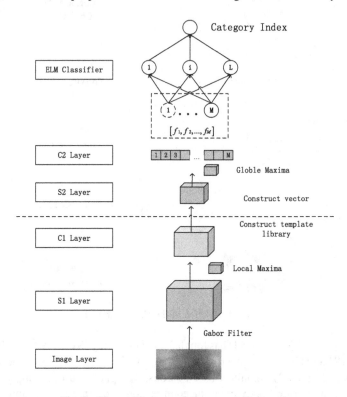

Fig. 3. The architecture of our proposed network

Image layer. We convert the image to grayscale and scaled the shorter edge to fix the aspect ratio.

Gabor filter (S1) layer. We applied 2D Gabor filters to the image layer from 4 orientations at each position and scale. The Gabor filters are described as:

$$G(x, y) = \exp\left(-\frac{(X^2 + \gamma^2 Y^2)}{2\sigma^2}\right)\cos\left(\frac{2\pi}{\lambda}X\right) \tag{2}$$

Local invariance (C1) layer. We pool nearby S1 units (of the same orientation) to create position/ scale invariance. A C1 unit's value is calculated by maximize S1 unit that falls within the max filter.

Intermediate feature (S2) layer. At each position and scale in the C1 layer, we perform template matches between the patch of C1 units and each of d prototype patches which are randomly sampled from the C1 layers.

The response of a patch of C1 units X to a particular S2 feature/prototype P, of size n × n, is given by a Gaussian radial basis function:

$$R(X, P) = \exp(-\frac{\|X - P\|^2}{2\sigma^2\alpha})$$ (3)

Global invariance (C2) layer. Finally we generate a d-dimensional vector, each element of which is the maximum response (anywhere in the image) to one of the model's d prototype patches.

ELM classifier (F) layer. ELM is employed to map the generated feature vector to the category index for predicting unknown images.

4.2 Enhanced HMAX

In this paper, we involve two main contributions to enhance the HMAX model for finger-vein recognition task, they are described as following:

(1) **Select template that are highly correlation to classified features.** After the stage of learning S2 Dictionary, we get d prototypes which testing images are matched subsequently. We calculate the absolute value of correlation coefficient between each template and every testing images. While smaller value of correlation coefficient indicate less similar. We discard the template which hold bigger correlation coefficient and remain the rest for further matched.

(2) **Select more than one scale of C2 vector.** In the final stage, we calculate C2 vector at two different scales to represent more abundant information for finger-vein images. In our experiment, we calculate 8192 (d*2) features (d is 4096 and represent C2 features in the standard HMAX model).

4.3 Algorithm Description

Our proposed image recognition network is shown in Fig. 4, and the complete algorithm as follows:

(1) Select N samples from training images, leave rest images to the test set;
(2) Generate S2 Dictionary by learning from the training images at random positions and scales;
(3) Generate C2 vectors for the training set;
(4) Train the ELM using training images and corresponding labels;
(5) Generate C2 vectors for the test set and then classify the test images.

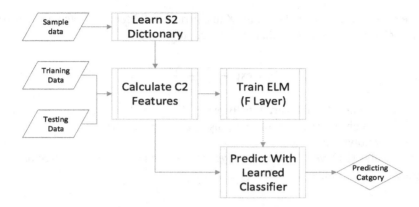

Fig. 4. The schematic diagram of finger-vein recognition network

5   Experiment and Analysis

5.1   Database of Experiment

We utilize a high-quality finger vein database established and named MMCBNU 6000 [12]. Among which, each person contains finger-vein images for the index, middle, ring finger of both hands. Since each finger produces 10 images, it means $6 \times 10 = 60$ images for one person. The size of each image is 128×60 as shown in Fig. 5.

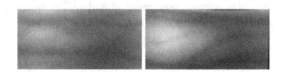

Fig. 5. Finger-vein images on the database

All the experiments are performed with MATLAB R2014a for PC which contains windows 10 OS and 2.8 GHz CPU and 4.0 GB memory.

5.2   Experimental Results

5.2.1   Determine the Best Number of Hidden Neurons

Firstly, experiment is performed to search the proper number of hidden neurons for ELM, we used 6 training images and 4 testing with each finger. According to the result, we choose 2000 as the number of hidden neurons for ELM in the later experiments.

5.2.2   Comparison of Performance with Different C2 Vector Features

In the experiment, we perform with different C2 feature templates. From Table 1, we conclude that more feature template bring higher recognition rate for the recognition system. When the feature is 8192, we get a higher recognition rate at 98.88%.

Table 1. Recognition rate with different number of feature

The number of features	512	1024	2048	4096	8192
Recognition rate (%)	84.84	89.04	89.33	91.14	98.88

5.2.3   Comparison of Performance Using Different Algorithms

We conduct an experiment to compare the performance with different algorithms [13], the result is shown in Table 2 and Fig. 6.

Table 2. Recognition rate with different algorithms

Samples	LBP	LGS	LDC	LGP	Proposed method
N=3	0.3890	0.5798	0.4539	0.4379	0.8972
N=4	0.5706	0.7272	0.7021	0.6520	0.9744
N=5	0.7727	0.8343	0.7430	0.7438	0.9830
N=6	0.8300	0.8760	0.8554	0.8630	0.9867
N=7	0.8733	0.9211	0.9432	0.9472	0.9917

To analyze the following Table 2: the proposed method has higher recognition rate compared with LBP, LGS, LDC and LGP; and the recognition rate for all methods grows along with the addition of the samples numbers. Hence our proposed method perform best on the same database.

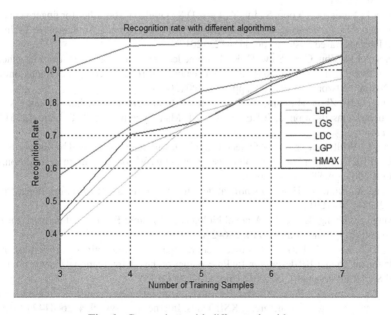

Fig. 6. Comparison with different algorithms

6 Conclusion

In this paper, we propose a biologically inspired network for finger-vein recognition. We combine the two biologically inspired mechanisms (HMAX and ELM) and construct a five-layer network (S1–C1–S2–C2–F) to complete the whole finger-vein recognition task. Experimental results show that the proposed method achieve a better performance for finger-vein recognition task.

Acknowledgments. This work was supported by the National Natural Science Foundation of China under Grant No. 61502338 and No. 61502339, the 2015 key projects of Tianjin science and technology support program No. 15ZCZDGX00200, and the Open Fund of Guangdong Provincial Key Laboratory of Petrochemical Equipment Fault Diagnosis No. GDUPTKLAB201504.

References

1. Jain, A.K., Flynn, P., Ross, A.A.: Handbook of Biometrics, 1st edn. Springer, Berlin (2008)
2. Kono, M., Ueki, H. and Umemura, S.: A new method for the identification of individuals by using of vein pattern matching of a finger. In: Proceedings of Fifth Symposium on Pattern Measurement, pp. 9–12 (2000)
3. Ojala, T., Pietikainen, M., Harwood, D.: A comparative study of texture measures with classification based on feature distributions. J. Pattern Recogn. **29**, 51–59 (1996)
4. Rosdi, B.A., Shing, C.W., Suandi, S.A.: Finger vein recognition using local line binary pattern. J. Sens. **11**, 11357–11371 (2011)
5. Miura, N., Nagasaka, A., Miyatake, T.: Feature extraction of finger-vein patterns based on repeated line tracking and its application to personal identification. Mach. Vis. Appl. **15**, 194–203 (2004)
6. Xie, S.J., Yang, J.C., Yoon, S., Lu, Y., Park, D.S.: Guided Gabor filter for finger vein pattern extraction. In: Proceedings of the 8th International Conference on Signal Image Technology and Internet Based Systems, pp. 118–123 (2012)
7. Huang, G.B., Zhu, Q.Y., Siew, C.-K.: Extreme learning machine: a new learning scheme of feedforward neural networks. In: 2004 Proceedings of IEEE International Joint Conference on Neural Networks, IEEE 2004, pp. 985–990 (2004)
8. Huang, G.B., Zhou, H., Ding, X., Zhang, R.: Extreme learning machine for regression and multiclass classification. J. IEEE Trans. Syst. Man Cybern. Part B: Cybern. **42**, 513–529 (2012)
9. Serre, T., Wolf, L., Poggio, T.: Object recognition with features inspired by visual cortex. In: 2005 IEEE Computer Society Conference on Computer Vision and Pattern Recognition, IEEE CVPR 2005, pp. 994–1000 (2005)
10. Kumar, A., Zhou, Y.: Human identification using finger images. IEEE Trans. Image Process. **21**, 2228–2244 (2012)
11. Zhang, Y., Zhang, L., Li, P.: A novel biologically inspired ELM-based network for image recognition. J. Neurocomput. **174**, 286–298 (2016)
12. Liu, B.C., Xie, S.J., Park, D.S.: Finger vein recognition using optimal partitioning uniform rotation invariant LBP descriptor. In: Proceedings of the 6th International Congress on Image and Signal Processing (CISP 2015), pp. 410–415 (2015)
13. Dong, S., Yang, J.C., Park, D.S.: Finger vein recognition based on multi-orientation weighted symmetric local graph structure. J. KSII Trans. Internet Inf. Syst. **9**, 4126–4142 (2015)

Finger Vein Recognition via Local Multilayer Ternary Pattern

Hu Zhang[✉], Xianliang Wang, and Zhixiang He

Beijing Hisign Corp. Ltd., Hanwei International Square,
Area4, No. 186, West Road, 4th South Ring Road,
Fengtai District, Beijing 100160, China
{zhanghu,wangxianliang,hezhixiang}@hisign.com.cn

Abstract. We propose a novel method for finger vein recognition in this paper. We use even symmetrical Gabor filters to smooth images and remove noise, then Contrast Limited Adaptive Histogram Equalization (CLAHE) is utilized for image enhancement. Finger Vein is extracted via Maximum Curvature (MC), and after thinning by morphological filter, we use Local multilayer Ternary Pattern (LmTP) descriptor proposed in this paper to extract finger vein features. We also propose an algorithm to calculating the similarity of LmTP features. Experiment results show the performance of the proposed method is better than other well-known metrics and LmTP is more robust than other local feature descriptors like LBP, LTP and LmBP.

Keywords: Finger vein recognition · Local multilayer ternary pattern · Affine transform · Biometric identification

1 Introduction

Finger veins have many properties, like it can only authenticate the finger of a living person, it is clean because finger does not need to touch the equipment and its security level is high. There are mainly two categories for finger vein recognition: one is based on local shape information and another is based on global texture information.

In the first category, the structure of finger vein network is extracted. The most famous ones are repeated Line Tracking (LT) and Maximum Curvature (MC), both proposed by Miura [1, 2], but they are susceptible to image rotation. One common rotation invariant feature descriptor is Local Binary Patterns (LBP). LBP and Local Derivative Patterns (LDP) were combined together by Lee [3] to extract binary code of finger vein with the same weighting. In fact, only parts of binary code can reflect the difference of different finger veins. Meanwhile LBP is sensitive to noise in near-uniform image regions because the threshold value is exactly the center pixel. There are many other local feature model based on LBP, like Local Ternary Pattern (LTP) [4] and Elongated Quinary pattern(EQP) [5]. LTP extends two value codes of LBP into three value codes, while EQP extends to five value codes. SIFT [6] is another well-known local feature descriptor for finger vein recognition [7–9].

In the second category, image is first preprocessed by filter and transform. Mean filter is used in [8] to reduce the influence of noise. Yang et al. [10, 11] used different

© Springer International Publishing AG 2016
Z. You et al. (Eds.): CCBR 2016, LNCS 9967, pp. 271–278, 2016.
DOI: 10.1007/978-3-319-46654-5_30

kinds of filters to enhance the structure of finger vein. Gabor was also utilized in [12]. FFT [13], DFT [14], wavelet [15] and Contourlet [16] are major transformation methods for recognition. Local information and global information were fused for recognition in [17, 18]. This can improve the accuracy of matching, but it also increases recognition time.

The main contributions of this paper include: 1 We propose LmTP descriptor and experiment results demonstrate the proposed LmTP is better than LBP, LTP and LmBP descriptor. 2 We propose global and local similarity metric for LmTP feature. We utilize local similarity in affine transform to obtain the matched pairs, and global similarity is utilized to calculate the final similarity of two images.

The remainder of this paper is organized as follows. Section 2 propose Local multilayer Ternary Pattern (LmTP) descriptor and the whole scheme for finger vein recognition. Experiment results and analysis are given in Sect. 3. Section 4 concludes the paper.

2   Proposed Method

2.1   LmTP Descriptor and Its Similarity

Ojala et al. [19] proposed the Local Binary Pattern (LBP) descriptor in 1996 to extract local gray-level feature and then it is widely used in face recognition systems. Given a 3×3 window patch, the gray value of the center pixel is compared with its 8-neighboring pixels, so as to get the LBP code of the center pixel.

The disadvantage of LBP is obvious, LBP is quite sensitive to noise especially in near-uniform image regions because the threshold value is just the value of the center pixel [4]. So Tan et al. [4] extended LBP into 3-valued codes, called Local Ternary Patterns (LTP). Compared with LBP, LTP is more discriminant and less sensitive to noise in uniform regions. Another disadvantage of LBP is it cannot capture features in a large scale, LTP suffers this problem too. Liu et al. [20] proposed Local extensive Binary Pattern (LeBP) by combining Local multilayer Binary Pattern (LmBP) and Local directional binary pattern (LdBP) together. Experiment results shows that the performance of LmBP is quite similar to LeBP, so we just recommended LmBP here. The gray value of the center pixel is compared with its 8-neighboring pixels (1st layer), 16-neighboring pixels (2nd layer) and 24-neighboring pixels (3rd layer), the pixel in the 1st and the 2nd layers are compared with the outer layers, and these features are jointed together to get the LmBP feature, its length is 64.

Although LmBP can capture features in a large scale, it still could not avoid the disadvantage of LBP, which is quite sensitive to noise. In the meantime, because the finger vein images are captured with near-infrared light sources, there are a lot of noises in the image. So we adopt the advantage of LTP and LmBP, and proposed the Local multilayer Ternary Pattern (LmTP). Calculation of LmTP is similar with LmBP, shown in Fig. 1. LmTP can be calculated as follows.

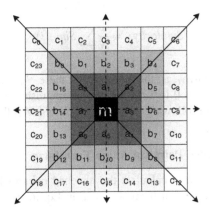

Fig. 1. Calculation of LmBP discriptor

$$LmTP(t) = \left[v(t)_8^1 \, v(t)_{16}^2 \, v(t)_{24}^3 \, v(t)_8^4 \, v(t)_8^5 \right] \tag{1}$$

where

$$
\begin{aligned}
v(t)_8^1 &= [a_0 a_1 a_2 a_3 a_4 a_5 a_6 a_7]_{\wp_t} m \\
v(t)_{16}^2 &= [b_0 b_1 b_2 \cdots b_{13} b_{14} b_{15}]_{\wp_t} m \\
v(t)_{24}^3 &= [c_0 c_1 c_2 \cdots c_{21} c_{22} c_{23}]_{\wp_t} m \\
v(t)_8^4 &= [b_0 \wp_t a_0 \cdots b_{2i} \wp_t a_i \cdots b_{14} \wp_t a_7] \\
v(t)_8^5 &= [c_0 \wp_t b_0 \cdots c_{3i} \wp_t b_{2i} \cdots c_{21} \wp_t b_{14}]
\end{aligned}
\tag{2}
$$

t is the threshold like LTP and fixed at 5 in the proposed method, and the symbol $\wp_t$ in the above equations means

$$
x \, \wp_t \, y = \begin{cases} 1 & x \geq y + t \\ 0 & |x - y| < t \\ -1 & x \leq y - t \end{cases} \tag{3}
$$

We cannot calculate the similarity of two LmTP descriptors by XOR, because LmTP is not binary. In this paper, we calculate the similarity of two LmTP descriptors, saying, L_{i1} and L_{i2}, as follows

$$Sim_G(i) = \frac{1}{2Len} \sum_{j=1}^{Len} |L_{i1}(j) - L_{i2}(j)| \tag{4}$$

where $Len = 64$ is the length of each LmTP feature. The similarity of N pairs of LmTP descriptors can be calculated as

$$Similarity_G = \frac{1}{N} \sum_{i=1}^{N} Sim_G(i) \qquad (5)$$

The smaller the $Similarity_G$ is, the more similar these N pairs will be. The range of both Sim_G and $Similarity_G$ is 0 to 1. In order to distinguish $Similarity_G$ from the local similarity proposed in the following part, we call $Similarity_G$ the global similarity.

2.2   Calculating Matched Pairs via Affine Transform

We utilized affine transform to calculate the matched pairs of LmTP descriptor. The homogeneous form of affine transform is shown in Eq. (6) with rotation, scaling and shift.

$$\begin{bmatrix} p_1 & p_2 & p_3 \\ p_4 & p_5 & p_6 \\ 0 & 0 & 1 \end{bmatrix} \begin{bmatrix} f_x \\ f_y \\ 1 \end{bmatrix} = \begin{bmatrix} g_x \\ g_y \\ 1 \end{bmatrix} \qquad (6)$$

where $\mathbf{P} = [p_1, p_2, p_3, p_4, p_5, p_6]$ is affine transformation parameter. We can calculate $\mathbf{P}$ by three feature points in input image and three feature points in template image. After obtained $\mathbf{P}$, locations of input image are transformed into (f_{xi}^t, f_{yi}^t), $i = 1,\ldots,n_1$. Given template image G and locations of feature point (g_{xj}, g_{yj}), $j = 1,\ldots,n_2$, the Euclidean distance between (f_{xi}^t, f_{yi}^t) and (g_{xj}, g_{yj}) is calculated by Eq. (7) and the distance matrix $\mathbf{D}$ is obtained by Eq. (8), where $D_{ij} = \exp(-d_{ij})$. If D_{ij} is the biggest in both i-th row and j-th column, the i-th feature point in input image and the j-th feature point in template image is marked as matched pair with current affine parameter $\mathbf{P}$.

$$d_{ij} = ((f_{xi}^t - g_{xj})^2 + (f_{yi}^t - g_{yj})^2)^{0.5} \qquad (7)$$

$$\mathbf{D} = \begin{bmatrix} D_{11} & \cdots & D_{1n_2} \\ \vdots & \ddots & \vdots \\ D_{n_1 1} & \cdots & D_{n_1 n_2} \end{bmatrix} \qquad (8)$$

The similarity of these pairs may be small when there are a few matched pairs via global similarity. To address this, we future propose local similarity. The local similarity of L_{i1} and L_{i2} can be calculated by Eq. (9)

$$Sim_L(i) = \frac{1}{Len} \sum_{j=1}^{Len} (1 - \left| \frac{L_{i1}(j) - L_{i2}(j)}{2} \right|) \qquad (9)$$

The local similarity of N matched pairs with $\mathbf{P}$ can be obtained by

$$Similarity_L = \sum_{i=1}^{N} Sim_L(i) \qquad (10)$$

The range of local similarity is 0 to N. The larger the local similarity is, the more similarity these two images will be. The global similarity will not be too large with a few matched pairs, thus mismatch is avoided. After selected 200 groups of feature points in input image and template image, the largest local similarity corresponded to the best affine transformation parameter $\mathbf{P}_b$.

2.3 Proposed Method

In registration stage, even Gabor filters is utilized to smooth the image and remove noise, and the image is future enhanced by Contrast Limited Adaptive Histogram Equalization (CLAHE). Finger region is detected by the gray values of the image and finger vein network is obtained via MC. After thinning, we followed the steps in [20] to get the locations of bifurcation point (BP) and ending point (EP). The LmTP features are calculated in the original image with the locations of these feature point.

In recognition stage, best affine transform parameter $\mathbf{P}_b$ and matched BP pairs are obtained by the locations of BP point because it is more stable than EP point. After that, the locations of EP point are transformed by the affine transform parameter $\mathbf{P}_b$ and compared with the EP locations of the template image to get the matched pairs of EP point. Then the global similarity of all matched pairs is calculated by Eq. (5) and compared with the threshold to decide whether it is the same person.

3   Results and Analysis

We tested the performance of the proposed method on PolyU database [21], constructed by Hong Kong Polytechnic University. There are 3132 finger vein images acquired from 156 volunteers over a period of 11 months. The finger vein images were acquired in two separate sessions (Session 1 and Session, marked as S1 and S2) and a total of 105 subjects turned up during the second session. Each of the subjects provided six image samples from the index finger to the middle finger. Different fingers form the same subjects were treated as belonging to different classes. So there are 1872 finger vein images with 312 classes in S1, and 1260 finger vein images with 210 classes in S2.

We compare the performance of the proposed method with other finger vein recognition methods, including Local Line Binary Pattern(LLBP) [22], Local Directional Code(LDC) [23], Scale Invariant feature Transform(SIFT) [9], Singular Value Decomposition based Minutiae Matching(SVDMM) [20], method proposed in [24] and Superpixel-based Features(SPF) [25]. Note that all these compared methods were tested on S1. We list the results of our proposed method on both S1 and the whole database (marked as ALL). Table 1 lists equal error rate (EER) of all these methods and the receiver operating characteristic (ROC) curve of parts of the methods are illustrated in Fig. 2. We can see that the performance of the proposed method is the better than all other methods except SPF, and the performance difference between the proposed method and SPF is small.

Table 1. Performance of different methods

Method	EER
LLBP [22]	4.27 %
LDC [23]	3.59 %
SIFT [9]	4.72 %
SVDMM [20]	2.45 %
paper [24]	4.47 %
SPF [25]	1.47 %
proposed (S1)	1.67 %
proposed (ALL)	3.87 %

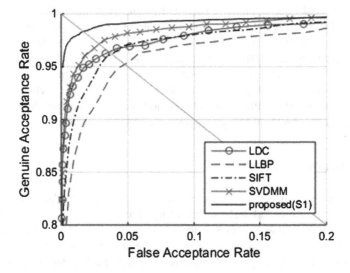

Fig. 2. ROCs of different methods

Table 2 lists the EER of LBP, LTP, LmBP, LmTP on PolyU database [21]. The ROC of the proposed method via these descriptors are shown in Fig. 3. LBP got the worst performance, LTP was better than LBP, LmBP was future better, and LmTP got the best performance. The reason is that LBP is sensitive to noise while finger vein image is full of noise. Due to the threshold method, LTP is tolerant of a certain degree of noise. LmBP is better because it can capture features in a large scale. Finally, the performance method via LmTP is the best because it adopts the advantages of both LTP and LmBP, it can capture features in a large scale and it is tolerant to noise.

We randomly selected 10 images from PolyU database, calculated the mean time of obtaining template and calculating similarity, with an intel core i5 4590 @3.3 GHz and 8 GB RAM. The mean time of obtaining template is about 600 ms and the mean time of calculating similarity is about 4.3 ms using single thread with C++. We can see that the proposed method has practical value.

Table 2. EER of LBP, LTP, LmBP and LmTP on PolyU database

	S1	S2
LBP	4.64 %	4.14 %
LTP	3.09 %	2.65 %
LmBP	2.18 %	1.6 %
LmTP	1.67 %	1.21 %

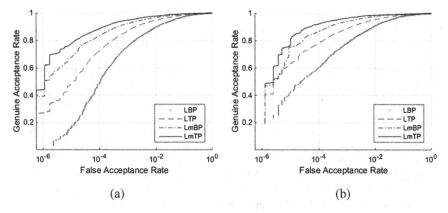

(a)   (b)

Fig. 3. ROCs of different methods on S1(a) and S2(b) of PolyU Database

4   Conclusion

This paper proposes a novel method for finger vein recognition. We proposed Local multilayer Ternary Pattern (LmTP) descriptor by combining LTP and LmBP together. LmTP is unsusceptible to noise and can capture features in a large scale. We future proposed global and local similarity metric for LmTP. Experiment results show the performance of proposed method is better than other well-known methods, and the proposed LmTP descriptor outperforms LBP, LTP and LmBP descriptors.

References

1. Miura, N., Nagasaka, A., Miyatake, T.: Feature extraction of finger-vein patterns based on repeated line tracking and its application to personal identification. Mach. Vis. Appl. **15**, 194–203 (2004)
2. Miura, N., Nagasaka, A., Miyatake, T.: Extraction of finger-vein patterns using maximum curvature points in image profiles. IEICE Trans. Inf. Syst. **90**, 1185–1194 (2007)
3. Lee, E.C., Jung, H., Kim, D.: New finger biometric method using near infrared imaging. Sensors **11**, 2319–2333 (2011)
4. Tan, X., Triggs, B.: Enhanced local texture feature sets for face recognition under difficult lighting conditions. IEEE Trans. Image Process. **19**, 1635–1650 (2010)
5. Nanni, L., Lumini, A., Brahnam, S.: Local binary patterns variants as texture descriptors for medical image analysis. Artif. Intell. Med. **49**, 117–125 (2010)

6. Lowe, D.G.: Distinctive image features from scale-invariant keypoints. Int. J. Comput. Vis. **60**, 91–110 (2004)

7. Peng, J., Wang, N., El-Latif, A.A.A., Li, Q., Niu, X.: Finger-vein verification using Gabor filter and sift feature matching. In: 2012 Eighth International Conference on Intelligent Information Hiding and Multimedia Signal Processing (IIH-MSP), pp. 45–48. IEEE (2012)

8. Kim, H.-G., Lee, E.J., Yoon, G.-J., Yang, S.-D., Lee, E.C., Yoon, S.M.: Illumination normalization for SIFT based finger vein authentication. In: Bebis, G., Boyle, R., Parvin, B., Koracin, D., Fowlkes, C., Wang, S., Choi, M.-H., Mantler, S., Schulze, J., Acevedo, D., Mueller, K., Papka, M. (eds.) ISVC 2012, Part II. LNCS, vol. 7432, pp. 21–30. Springer, Heidelberg (2012)

9. Pang, S., Yin, Y., Yang, G., Li, Y.: Rotation invariant finger vein recognition. In: Zheng, W.-S., Sun, Z., Wang, Y., Chen, X., Yuen, P.C., Lai, J. (eds.) CCBR 2012. LNCS, vol. 7701, pp. 151–156. Springer, Heidelberg (2012)

10. Yang, J., Shi, Y.: Finger–vein ROI localization and vein ridge enhancement. Pattern Recogn. Lett. **33**, 1569–1579 (2012)

11. Yang, J., Yang, J.: Multi-channel Gabor filter design for finger-vein image enhancement. In: Fifth International Conference on Image and Graphics, ICIG 2009, pp. 87–91. IEEE (2009)

12. Yang, J., Yang, J., Shi, Y.: Finger-vein segmentation based on multi-channel even-symmetric Gabor filters. In: IEEE International Conference on Intelligent Computing and Intelligent Systems, ICIS 2009, pp. 500–503. IEEE (2009)

13. Mahri, N., Suandi, S.A.S., Rosdi, B.A.: Finger vein recognition algorithm using phase only correlation. In: 2010 International Workshop on Emerging Techniques and Challenges for Hand-Based Biometrics (ETCHB), pp. 1–6. IEEE (2010)

14. Nakajima, H., Kobayashi, K., Higuchi, T.: A fingerprint matching algorithm using phase-only correlation. IEICE Trans. Fundam. Electron. Commun. Comput. Sci. **87**, 682–691 (2004)

15. Wang, K., Yuan, Z.: Finger vein recognition based on wavelet moment fused with PCA transform. Pattern Recogn. Artif. Intell. **20**, 692–697 (2008)

16. Xu, J., Dingyu, X., Jianjiang, C.: Vein recognition based on fusing multi HMMs with contourlet subband energy observations. J. Electron. Inf. Technol. **33**, 1877–1882 (2011)

17. Yang, Y., Yin, Y., Yang, G., Xi, X.: Finger vein recognition by combining local and global feature. Comput. Eng. Appl. **48**, 158–162 (2012)

18. Yang, J., Zhang, X.: Feature-level fusion of global and local features for finger-vein recognition. In: 2010 IEEE 10th International Conference on Signal Processing (ICSP), pp. 1702–1705. IEEE (2010)

19. Ojala, T., Pietikäinen, M., Harwood, D.: A comparative study of texture measures with classification based on featured distributions. Pattern Recogn. **29**, 51–59 (1996)

20. Liu, F., Yang, G., Yin, Y., Wang, S.: Singular value decomposition based minutiae matching method for finger vein recognition. Neurocomputing **145**, 75–89 (2014)

21. Kumar, A., Zhou, Y.: Human identification using finger images. IEEE Trans. Image Process. **21**, 2228–2244 (2012)

22. Rosdi, B.A., Shing, C.W., Suandi, S.A.: Finger vein recognition using local line binary pattern. Sensors **11**, 11357–11371 (2011)

23. Meng, X., Yang, G., Yin, Y., Xiao, R.: Finger vein recognition based on local directional code. Sensors **12**, 14937–14952 (2012)

24. Gupta, P., Gupta, P.: An accurate finger vein based verification system. Digit. Sig. Process. **38**, 43–52 (2014)

25. Liu, F., Yin, Y., Yang, G., Dong, L., Xi, X.: Finger vein recognition with superpixel-based features. In: IEEE International Joint Conference on Biometrics, pp. 1–8 (2014)

A Performance Evaluation of Local Descriptors, Direction Coding and Correlation Filters for Palm Vein Recognition

Jingting Lu[1,2], Hui Ye[1,2], Wei Jia[2,4(✉)], Yang Zhao[2], Hai Min[2],
Wenxiong Kang[3], and Bob Zhang[4]

[1] Institution of Industry and Equipment Technology,
Hefei University of Technology, Hefei, China
[2] School of Computer and Information, Hefei University of Technology, Hefei, China
[3] School of Automation Science and Engineering, South China University of Technology,
Guangzhou, China
[4] Faculty of Science and Technology, University of Macau, Macau, China
china.jiawei@139.com

Abstract. As one of new-emerging biometrics techniques, palm vein recognition has received wide attentions recently. In recent years, local descriptor, direction coding and correlation filters-based methods are popular for palmprint, palm vein, and finger vein recognition. In this paper, we make a performance evaluation for palm vein recognition using these methods. The experimental results show that the methods based on direction information can achieve better recognition performance.

Keywords: Biometrics · Palm vein · Direction feature · Performance evaluation

1 Introduction

Among all kinds of biometrics technologies, palm vein recognition have received wide attentions recently. In recent years, local descriptor, direction coding and correlation filters-based methods are popular for palmprint, palm vein, and finger vein recognition [1–3]. The objective of this work is to make a performance evaluation for palm vein recognition using these methods.

2 Related Work

So far, many approaches have been proposed for palm vein recognition. Generally existing methods can be roughly divided into several different categories such as subspace learning-based methods, texture-based methods, structure-based methods, direction coding-based methods and local descriptor-based methods. In the past two decades, the study on subspace learning techniques has made a great progress. Many different representative subspace learning methods have been applied to palm vein recognition. As two simple and representative subspace learning methods, principal component analysis (PCA) and linear discriminant analysis (LDA) require that the 2-D

© Springer International Publishing AG 2016
Z. You et al. (Eds.): CCBR 2016, LNCS 9967, pp. 279–287, 2016.
DOI: 10.1007/978-3-319-46654-5_31

image data must be reshaped into 1-D vector, which can be referred to as the strategy of "image-as-vector". In recent years, kernel method, manifold learning method [4], matrix and tensor embedding method [5] were also applied for palm vein recognition. For texture based methods, Gabor wavelet [6], discrete orthonormal S-transform [7] and other statistical methods have been used for palm vein texture feature extraction. Structure based methods are also very important in palm vein recognition field. Zhang et al. [8] proposed a palm vein line detection method using the matched filters. Kang et al. [9] proposed a palm vein line detector using normalized gradient-based maximal principal curvature algorithm. In [10], Wirayuda et al. proposed a palm vein recognition method using minutiae feature. So far, coding methods have achieved very promising recognition performance in terms of accuracy and matching speed. Ordinal code [11], robust line orientation code (RLOC) [11], competitive code [12], and their variations [13, 14] have been successfully used for palm vein recognition. In computer vision, local image descriptor plays an important role for image recognition. Up to now, a lot of local image descriptors have been proposed for palm vein recognition. Kang et al. [9] proposed a method named mutual foreground-based LBP (MFLBP) for palm vein recognition. Mirmohamadsadeghi et al. exploited Local derivative patterns (LDP) for palm vein recognition. In [15], Kang et al. investigated SIFT-based method for palm vein recognition. For palm vein recognition, subspace learning methods are known to be sensitive to the illumination, translation and rotation variations. Structure-based methods have not achieved desirable performance since the problem of exact palm vein line extraction and precise matching remain unsolved. Texture-based methods have not achieved state-of-the-art performance due to the lack of powerful texture features. In this paper, we will exploit three kinds of methods for performance evaluation including local descriptors, direction coding and correlation filters since they are very promising for palm vein recognition.

3   Evaluation Methods

3.1   Local Descriptors

For different local descriptors, we divide palm vein image into 8×8 splits to generate coding image.

Method 1: LBP. The basic idea for developing the LBP operator was that two-dimensional surface textures can be described by two complementary measures: local spatial patterns and gray scale contrast [16, 17]. The original LBP operator forms labels for the image pixels by thresholding the 3×3 neighborhood of each pixel with the center value and considering the result as a binary number. The histogram of different labels can then be used as a texture descriptor. This operator used jointly with a simple local contrast measure provided very good performance in unsupervised texture segmentation.

Method 2: Local Ternary Patterns (LTP). LBP is sensitive to noise since only using the value of center pixel as a threshold cannot robustly reflect the texture changes in near-uniform image regions. Tan et al. [18] extended LBP to 3-valued codes to form a new descriptor, i.e., LTP. In LTP, conventional 2-valued (0, 1) LBP code is extended to 3-valued $(-1, 0, 1)$ ternary code by using threshold t. Then the upper pattern and lower pattern are coded, respectively. LTP codes are more robust to noise, but no longer strictly invariant to monotonic gray scale transformation.

Method 3: Local Directional Pattern (LDP). The LDP of each pixel is an eight-bit binary code calculated by comparing the edge response values of different directions in local 3×3 neighborhood [19]. Given a central pixel in the image, the eight-directional edge response values are computed by Kirsch masks in eight different orientations centered on the pixel's position. Then the top k response values are selected and the corresponding directional bits are set to 1. The remaining $(8-k)$ bits are set to 0. Finally, LDP code is derived by the LBP coding rule.

Method 4: Enhanced LDP (ELDP). LDP is encoded using the absolute values of the convolving results. However, LDP ignores the sign of the original convolving values, which may contain useful information. In order to improve the performance of the original LDP, ELDP utilizes the directions of maximum edge response value and the second most prominent one [20]. Similar to LDP, ELDP also uses Kirsch masks to calculate edge responses at different directions. But, ELDP exploits the direction index number to calculate the code instead of bit string. Thus, eight gradient directions can be represented by eight octal codes, respectively. Another main difference between LDP and ELDP is that ELDP assigns a fixed position for the maximum edge's direction index number, as the three most significant bits in the code, and the three least significant bits are the second prominent edge's direction index number.

Method 5: Local Directional Number Pattern (LDN). LDN and ELDP are similar to some extent. ELDP pays attention to the maximum direction index number and the second most prominent one. LDN considers the maximum direction index number and the minimum direction index number [21]. Like EDLP, LDN also assigns fixed positions for the top direction index number and the minimum direction index number.

Method 6: HOL. Histogram of oriented gradients (HOG) descriptor has been successfully applied to recognition tasks. However, gradient exploited in HOG is not a good tool to detect the line responses and orientation of pixels since different palm vein lines have different widths and there are complicated intersections between lines. Jia et al. [22] proposed the HOL descriptor, a variant of HOG, for palmprint recognition, which exploits line-shape filters or tools such as the real part of Gabor filter and modified finite radon transform (MFRAT) to extract line responses and orientation of pixels. HOL has two obvious advantages. First, using oriented lines and histogram normalization, HOL has better invariance to changes of illumination. Second, HOL has the robustness against transformations because slight translations and rotations make small histogram value changes.

Method 7: LLDP. In [23], Luo et al. proposed a LLDP descriptor. In LLDP, MFRAT and the real part of Gabor filters were exploited to extract robust directional palmprint features. Similar to LDN, LLDP also exploits directional index number to generate

LLDP code. In addition, LLDP considers the maximum direction index number and the minimum direction index number for coding. That is, in LLDP, two directions in DR image are jointly encoded, and then a histogram is constructed as the final feature.

3.2 Orientation Coding Methods

Method 8: CompC. The method of CompC is firstly proposed for palmprint recognition. In the first step of CompC [24], six real parts of 2D ellipsoidal Gabor filters with different directions are used to convolute an image to obtain six Gabor response. Then, CompC selects the index number of the minimum line response to construct an orientation representation image. In CompC, the size of palmprint ROI image is 128×128, which is too large for matching. Therefore, a small feature map with the size of 32×32 is created by down-sampling. Since there are totally 6 different orientations, we encode them by 3 bits. The difference between two direction maps can be measured by the Hamming distance.

Method 9: Sparse Multiscale Competitive Code (SMCC). In [25], Zuo et al. propose a novel multiscale palmprint verification method, called the sparse multiscale competitive code (SMCC). The SMCC method first defines a filter bank of second derivatives of Gaussians with different orientations and scales, and then uses the l_1-norm sparse coding to obtain a robust estimation of the multiscale/multiorientation filter responses. Finally, the competitive code is extended to encode the dominant orientation of the filter responses.

Method 10: Robust Line Orientation Code (RLOC). In [26], Jia et al. proposed RLOC for palmprint verification. Firstly, the MFRAT is proposed, which can extract the orientation feature of palmprint more accurately and solve the problem of sub-sampling better. Secondly, a matching algorithm based on pixel-to-area comparison has been designed, which has better fault tolerant ability.

Method 11: OrdinalC. In [27], Sun et al. proposed the method of OrdinalC, in which employed three groups of orthogonal Gaussian filters to extract three binary codes, i.e. the Ordinal Code, in terms of the sign of the filtered results. Then, the difference between two direction maps can be measured by the Hamming distance.

3.3 Correlation Filter

Method 12: BLPOC. Phase correlation is an approach to estimate the relative translative offset between two similar images. It is commonly used in image registration and relies on a frequency-domain representation of the data, usually calculated by fast Fourier transforms. The term is applied particularly to a subset of cross-correlation techniques that isolate the phase information from the Fourier-space representation of the cross-correlogram. In the original Phase-Only Correlation (POC) method, POC exploits all components of the image's 2D DFT to generate the output plane. It was found that BLPOC can be improved by removing the high frequency components and using only the inherent frequency band for matching. In this paper, the method of BLPOC means that we apply BLPOC on original palm vein images for matching.

Method 13: BLPOC_DR. In [28], Zhu et al. proposed a method combining Band-Limited Phase-Only Correlation (BLPOC) and DR for palmprint recognition. In this methods, we firstly using MFRAT to extract DR images from original palm vein images, and then apply BLPOC on DR images for matching.

4 Evaluation Protocol and Experimental Results

4.1 Database

The proposed method is tested on the near-infrared band of PolyU multispectral palmprint databases (PolyU M_NIR) [12]. PolyU M_NIR database contains 6000 grayscale palm vein images from 500 palms corresponding to 250 individuals. In this database, about 12 samples from each of these palms were collected in two sessions, where 6 samples were captured in the first session and the remaining 6 samples were captured in the second session. Figure 1(a) shows the palm vein collection scenes and device for PolyU M_NIR database. It could be seen that this database was captured by contact manner with pegs. For preprocessing, each palm vein image is rotated for alignment and an ROI of size 128 × 128 is cropped. Figure 1(b) shows six ROI samples.

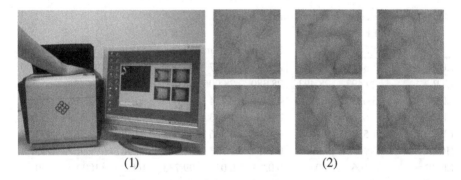

                    (1)   (2)

Fig. 1. (1) The palm vein image collection scenes and devices for PolyU M_NIR database, (2) Six palm vein images captured from six different palms in PolyU M_NIR database

4.2 Evaluation Protocol

In this paper, both verification and identification experiments are conducted. Verification is a one-to-one comparison, which answers the question of "whether the person is whom he claims to be". In the verification experiments, the statistical value of Equal Error Rate (EER) is adopted to evaluate the performance of different methods. Identification is a one-to-many comparison, which answers the question of "who the person is?". In this paper, the close-set identification is conducted. That is we know all enrollments exist in the training set. In order to obtain identification accuracy, the statistical value of Accurate Recognition Rate (ARR) is used, which is the rank 1 identification rate. In this paper, the nearest neighbor classifier is used for classification. In this database, the palm veins from the first session are used for training and the palm veins from the second session are adopted for test. In order to study the performances using different numbers of training images, we use the first 1 (1Train), 2 (2Train), 3 (3Train), and 4 (4Train) images from the first session for training, respectively.

4.3 Evaluation Results

Table 1 lists the evaluation results on PolyU M_NIR palm vein database. For local descriptors, we find that LLDP achieves the best results among several local descriptors. For orientation coding-based methods, RLOC has better recognition performance than other coding-based methods. For correlation filters-based methods, the performance of BLPOC_DR is obviously better than original BLPOC methods. Among all methods, RLOC achieves the best recognition performance. In order to better illustrate the verification performances, the Receiver Operating Characteristic (ROC) curves of several methods are given in Fig. 2, which plots the False Accept Rate (FAR) against the Genuine Accept Rate (GAR).

Table 1. Evaluation results on PolyU M_NIR palm vein database

Method	Recognition performance							
	EER (%)				ARR (%)			
	1Train	2Train	3Train	4Train	1Train	2Train	3Train	4Train
LBP	3.341	2.184	1.954	1.757	93.900	96.733	97.533	98.300
LTP	29.492	28.493	28.380	28.006	53.400	60.167	64.233	66.566
LDP	5.633	4.489	4.049	3.714	83.800	90.200	92.100	93.167
ELDP	3.670	2.353	2.083	1.833	87.000	92.767	94.633	95.800
LDN	1.533	0.766	0.660	0.566	97.967	99.400	99.767	99.833
HOL	0.969	0.300	0.275	0.233	99.300	99.967	99.967	100
LLDP	0.166	0.067	0.0291	0.031	99.733	100	100	100
RLOC	0.130	0.026	0.0005	0.0001	99.933	100	100	100
OrdinalC	0.135	0.100	0.006	0.003	100	100	100	100
CompC	0.368	0.166	0.133	0.109	99.600	99.900	99.967	100
SMCC	0.101	0.028	0.005	0.003	100	100	100	100
BLPOC	0.499	0.204	0.193	0.132	98.733	99.567	99.733	99.967
BLPOC_DR	0.332	0.095	0.033	0.033	99.53	99.93	100	100

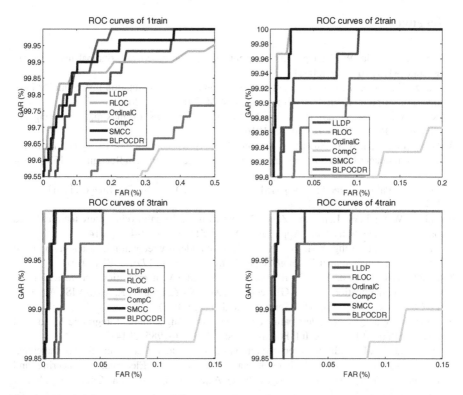

Fig. 2. The ROC curves under different numbers of training images on the PolyU M_NIR database.

5   Conclusions

In this paper, we made a performance evaluation for palm vein recognition using different methods. Three kinds of methods were investigated including local descriptor, direction coding and correlation filters. Among all methods, HOL, LLDP, and BLPOC_DR can be viewed as DR-based methods since they exploit direction information for feature designing or matching. It should be noted that it is the first time that DR-bases methods in frequency and histogram domains are investigated for palm vein recognition. The experimental results have shown that the methods based on direction information can achieve better recognition performance.

Acknowledgement. This work is partly supported by the grants of the National Science Foundation of China, Nos. 61175022, 61573151, 61305006, 61305093, 61402018, 61370167, 61472115, and science and technology project of Anhui Province under Grant No.1401b042009.

References

1. Huang, D.S., Jia, W., Zhang, D.: Palmprint verification based on principal lines. Pattern Recogn. **41**, 1316–1328 (2008)
2. Kang, W., Chen, X.: Fast representation based on a double orientation histogram for local image descriptors. IEEE Trans. Image Process. **24**, 2915–2927 (2015)
3. Kang, W.: Vein pattern extraction based on vectorgrams of maximal intra-neighbor difference. Pattern Recogn. Lett. **33**, 1916–1923 (2012)
4. Wang, J.G., Yau, W.Y., Suwandy, A., Sung, E.: Person recognition by fusing palmprint and palm vein images based on "Laplacianpalm" representation. Pattern Recogn. **41**, 1531–1544 (2008)
5. Lee, Y.P.: Palm vein recognition based on a modified (2D)2 LDA. Sig. Image Video Process. **9**, 229–242 (2015)
6. Shi, Y., Wang, L.W., Lan, H.Y., Zeng, G.: Extraction of the palm vein texture features based on gabor wavelet transforms. Appl. Mech. Mater. **511–512**, 429–432 (2014)
7. Lin, S., Xu, T.Y., Tang, Y.H., Hui, X.W.: Palm vein identity recognition based on improved S-transform. Guangdianzi Jiguang/J. Optoelectron. Laser **26**, 1776–1782 (2015)
8. Zhang, Y.-B., Li, Q., You, J., Bhattacharya, P.: Palm vein extraction and matching for personal authentication. In: Qiu, G., Leung, C., Xue, X.-Y., Laurini, R. (eds.) VISUAL 2007. LNCS, vol. 4781, pp. 154–164. Springer, Heidelberg (2007)
9. Kang, W., Wu, Q.: Contactless palm vein recognition using a mutual foreground-based local binary pattern. IEEE Trans. Inf. Forensics Secur. **9**, 1974–1985 (2014)
10. Wirayuda, T.A.B.: Palm vein recognition based-on minutiae feature and feature matching. In: Proceedings of the 5th International Conference on Electrical Engineering and Informatics: Bridging the Knowledge between Academic, Industry, and Community, ICEEI 2015, pp. 350–355 (2015)
11. Zhou, Y., Kumar, A.: Human identification using palm-vein images. IEEE Trans. Inf. Forensics Secur. **6**, 1259–1274 (2011)
12. Zhang, D., Guo, Z., Lu, G., Zhang, L., Zuo, W.: An online system of multispectral palmprint verification. IEEE Trans. Instrum. Meas. **59**, 480–490 (2010)
13. Lee, J.C.: A novel biometric system based on palm vein image. Pattern Recogn. Lett. **33**, 1520–1528 (2012)
14. Zhou, Y., Liu, Y., Feng, Q., Yang, F., Huang, J., Nie, Y.: Palm-vein classification based on principal orientation features. PLoS ONE **9**, e112429 (2014)
15. Kang, W., Liu, Y., Wu, Q., Yue, X.: Contact-free palm-vein recognition based on local invariant features. PLoS ONE **9**, e97548 (2014)
16. Ojala, T., Pietikäinen, M., Mäenpää, T.: Multiresolution gray-scale and rotation invariant texture classification with local binary patterns. IEEE Trans. Pattern Anal. Mach. Intell. **24**, 971–987 (2002)
17. Zhao, Y., Huang, D.S., Jia, W.: Completed local binary count for rotation invariant texture classification. IEEE Trans. Image Process. **21**, 4492–4497 (2012)
18. Tan, X., Triggs, B.: Enhanced local texture feature sets for face recognition under difficult lighting conditions. IEEE Trans. Image Process. **19**, 1635–1650 (2010)
19. Jabid, T., Kabir, M.H., Chae, O.: Robust facial expression recognition based on local directional pattern. ETRI J. **32**, 784–794 (2010)
20. Zhong, F., Zhang, J.: Face recognition with enhanced local directional patterns. Neurocomputing **119**, 375–384 (2013)

21. Rivera, A.R., Castillo, J.R., Chae, O.: Local directional number pattern for face analysis: face and expression recognition. IEEE Trans. Image Process. Publ. IEEE Sig. Process. Soc. **22**, 1740–1752 (2013)
22. Jia, W., Hu, R.X., Lei, Y.K., Zhao, Y., Gui, J.: Histogram of Oriented Lines for Palmprint Recognition. IEEE Trans. Syst. Man Cybern. Syst. **44**, 385–395 (2014)
23. Luo, Y.-T., Zhao, L.-Y., Zhang, B., Jia, W., Xue, F., Lu, J.-T., Zhu, Y.-H., Xu, B.-Q.: Local line directional pattern for palmprint recognition. Pattern Recogn. **50**, 26–44 (2016)
24. Kong, A.W.K., Zhang, D.: Competitive coding scheme for palmprint verification. In: Proceedings of the International Conference on Pattern Recognition, pp. 520–523
25. Zuo, W., Lin, Z., Guo, Z., Zhang, D.: The multiscale competitive code via sparse representation for palmprint verification. In: Proceedings of the IEEE Computer Society Conference on Computer Vision and Pattern Recognition, pp. 2265–2272
26. Jia, W., Huang, D.S., Zhang, D.: Palmprint verification based on robust line orientation code. Pattern Recogn. **41**, 1521–1530 (2008)
27. Sun, Z., Tan, T., Wang, Y., Li, S.Z.: Ordinal palmprint representation for personal identification. In: Proceedings of the IEEE Computer Society Conference on Computer Vision and Pattern Recognition, pp. 279–284
28. Zhu, Y.-H., Jia, W., Liu, L.-F.: Palmprint recognition using band-limited phase-only correlation and different representations. In: Huang, D.-S., Jo, K.-H., Lee, H.-H., Kang, H.-J., Bevilacqua, V. (eds.) ICIC 2009. LNCS, vol. 5754, pp. 270–277. Springer, Heidelberg (2009)

Enlargement of the Hand-Dorsa Vein Database Based on PCA Reconstruction

Kefeng Li[1(✉)], Guangyuan Zhang[1], Yiding Wang[2], Peng Wang[1], and Cui Ni[1]

[1] School of Information Science and Electric Engineering, Shandong Jiaotong University, Jinan, China
seafrog1984@hotmail.com, xdzhanggy@163.com,
{121602121,81001630}@qq.com
[2] College of Information Engineering, North China University of Technology, Beijing, China
wangyd@ncut.edu.cn

Abstract. This paper introduces a novel method to enlarge the hand-dorsa vein database using principal component analysis (PCA), which will be applied to increase the samples of each class. The ten samples of each hand is divided into two sets, feature set B and projection set M. Set B is used to provide the feature space using PCA methods. Set M is used to obtain projection coefficients for new image. A new sample can be constructed with the feature space and projection coefficient using PCA reconstruction method. In this work, the database is enlarged from 2040 images to 10200 images, with the samples of each hand increasing from 10 to 50. The experimental results show that the enlarged database has a satisfied recognition rate of 98.66 % using Partition Local Binary Patterns (PLBP), which indicates the proposed method performs well and would be applicable in the simulation test.

Keywords: Biometrics · Hand-dorsa vein images · PCA reconstruction

1 Introduction

Hand vein patterns have attracted significant attention in the research community recently, as a new means of biometric based recognition. Compared to more established biometric patterns, such as fingerprints, facial characteristics and iris patterns, hand vein patterns have higher user convenience as the manner of image acquisition is perceived to be less intrusive and more user friendly; and higher security as it does not rely on surface or appearance based features [1–3].

Recently, deep learning performs well in face recognition and some other biometrics [4, 5]. But the performance is not ideal in applying this method in hand-dorsa vein recognition for its small database, especially not enough samples of one class. To solve this problem, an enlargement method of hand-dorsa vein database is proposed in this paper.

© Springer International Publishing AG 2016
Z. You et al. (Eds.): CCBR 2016, LNCS 9967, pp. 288–295, 2016.
DOI: 10.1007/978-3-319-46654-5_32

2   Vein Image Acquisition

The acquisition of hand vein images using near IR (NIR) imaging has been studied in [6–8] and [9]. In this work, a low-cost reflection-mode NIR imaging device developed by the authors was employed for hand-dorsa vein image acquisition. Figure 1 shows the photo and schematic of the vein image acquisition device, where the back of the hand is seen to be illuminated from two sides by two LED arrays acting as the infrared sources and the light reflected from the hand is captured by the camera placed directly above the hand. Attached to front of the camera is an infrared filter to prevent unwanted visible light from entering the camera.

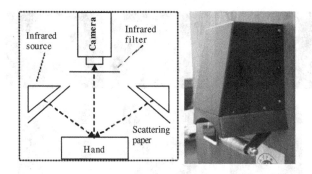

Fig. 1. Schematic and picture of vein image acquisition device

A database of hand-dorsa vein images has been built using the vein image acquisition device developed. It contains 2,040 images from 102 individuals in which 52 are female and 50 are male. Ten images of each hand were captured for every individual with each individual placing alternately the left hand and right hand under the image acquisition device. Some image samples in the database are illustrated in Fig. 2.

Fig. 2. Sample images acquired

3   Vein Image Preprocessing

3.1   Region of Interest (ROI)

With the image coverage area larger than the back of the hand as shown in Fig. 2, the region of interest (ROI) containing the vein pattern needs to be extracted. Extraction of

ROI has been discussed in. In this work, the image centroid was employed as the center to extract the ROI. Let (x0, y0) be the centroid of vein image f(x, y) calculated using

$$x_0 = \frac{\sum\limits_{i,j} i \times f(i,j)}{\sum\limits_{i,j} f(i,j)}; \quad y_0 = \frac{\sum\limits_{i,j} j \times f(i,j)}{\sum\limits_{i,j} f(i,j)} \tag{1}$$

With the image centroid defining the center of ROI, image cropping is subsequently performed to yield a sub-image of 380 × 380 pixels. For the vein images shown in Fig. 4, the corresponding ROIs extracted are illustrated in Fig. 3.

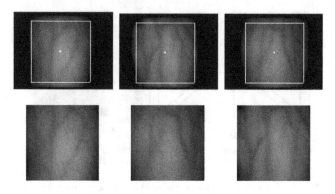

Fig. 3. ROI of the vein images

Since the centroid is invariant to translation, it enables correct ROI to be extracted without being affected by the shift of hand-dorsa vein region in the image (caused by a difference in hand positioning in each image acquisition).

3.2 Gray Level Normalization

Since the light intensity may vary at different times, the gray levels of vein images are distributed over different ranges. To reduce the difference and thereby providing a more uniform vein pattern representation among different vein images, gray level normalization based on the following equation is carried out

$$y = ((x - \min) \times 255)/(\max - \min). \tag{2}$$

where x and y denote the gray level values of the original and normalized images, respectively; min and max denote the minimum and maximum gray level values of the original image, respectively.

4   Enlargement of Hand-Dorsa Vein Database

The basic structure of the method is shown in the Fig. 4.

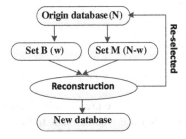

Fig. 4. Basic structure of the method

The first step is to divide the origin database into two sets. w samples are selected from the database to compose the feature set B. The left N-w samples compose the projection set M. Then the reconstruction is carried out by merging the information from both sets to get new images. Then w samples are re-selected different from last time to update set B and M. The reconstruction with these two new sets is carried out again. At last, a new database combined with the origin database and the reconstructed database is established.

Set B is to provide feature space which could reflect the common characteristics of the hand-dorsa vein image. The other set M is projected into feature space to achieve the construction of the new image. The purpose of the reconstruction method is to merge the common information from set B and personal information from set M to produce a new image using PCA method.

In order to achieve the reconstruction of the hand-dorsa vein image, original ROI images are needed to be represented. An image (I) which has $m \times n$ pixels could be represented by an $m \times n$-dimensional vector v_{ij} (the jth image from the ith hand) as in Eq. (3).

$$I = \begin{bmatrix} i_{11} & \cdots & i_{1n} \\ \vdots & \ddots & \vdots \\ i_{m1} & \cdots & i_{mn} \end{bmatrix} \Rightarrow v_{ij} = \begin{bmatrix} i_{11} \\ \vdots \\ i_{1n} \\ \vdots \\ i_{m1} \\ \vdots \\ i_{mn} \end{bmatrix} \tag{3}$$

With these vectors, a matrix can be built:

$$v_i = \begin{bmatrix} v_{i1} & \cdots & v_{iN} \end{bmatrix} \tag{4}$$

Where, N means that each individual has N images. The ith hand in the origin ROI database can be represented by this matrix.

Then the database is constituted by the matrices which are on behalf of the individuals in the origin ROI database. Set B which provides feature space is composed of the matrices from w selected samples of one hand,

$$B = \begin{bmatrix} v_1 & \cdots & v_w \end{bmatrix} \tag{5}$$

The left matrices constitute set M.

$$M = \begin{bmatrix} v_1 & \cdots & v_{N-w} \end{bmatrix} \tag{6}$$

After obtaining set B and set M in the preparation, feature space is extracted from set B. The covariance matrix of set B is calculated as follow:

$$mean_B = \left(\sum_{i=1}^{w} B \right) / w \tag{7}$$

$$m_B = B - mean_B \tag{8}$$

$$C = m_B \times m_B^T \tag{9}$$

Here, C is the covariance matrix of the set B. Feature vectors u_i corresponding to the nonzero eigenvalues of the matrix C ($\lambda = \begin{bmatrix} \lambda_1, \lambda_2, \ldots, \lambda_r \end{bmatrix}$, in descending order) are adopted to form the feature space U:

$$U = \begin{bmatrix} u_1, u_2, \ldots, u_r \end{bmatrix} \in R^{(m \times n) \times r} \tag{10}$$

Due to the compression of dimension, the feature space does not contain all the characteristics of the base set and just remains common characteristics of set B.

The projection coefficients can be obtained from set M as following:

$$mean_M = \left(\sum_{i=1}^{(N-w)} M \right) / (N - w) \tag{11}$$

$$m_M = M - mean_M \tag{12}$$

$$Y_{ij} = m_{ij} \times m_B^T \tag{13}$$

Where, $mean_M$ is the average vector of the set M. m_{ij} is the vector which contains the information of the jth image from the ith individual in m_M. Y_{ij} is the projection coefficients of m_{ij} in the feature space, which contains the information of the images in set M.

By merging the common features of set B with the personality characteristics from set M, a new image can be reconstructed by the projection coefficient and the eigenvector as following:

$$y' = mean_M + Y_{ij} \times U^T \times \lambda^{1/2} \tag{14}$$

where, Y_{ij} is the projection coefficients of M_{ij}. U is composed by the feature vectors. λ is the nonzero eigenvalues vector of the covariance matrix of the set B. y' is the new vector which represents a new image belonging to the ith class.

This new hand-dorsa vein image vector inherits the characteristics of the projection vector from set M and the features from set B. A new image can be created by reshaping the vector y' into image matrix as follow:

$$y' = \begin{bmatrix} i'_{11} \\ \vdots \\ i'_{1n} \\ \vdots \\ i'_{m1} \\ \vdots \\ i'_{mn} \end{bmatrix} \Rightarrow I_y = \begin{bmatrix} i'_{11} & \cdots & i'_{1n} \\ \vdots & \ddots & \vdots \\ i'_{m1} & \cdots & i'_{mn} \end{bmatrix} \tag{15}$$

Some new images are shown with the original ones in Fig. 5.

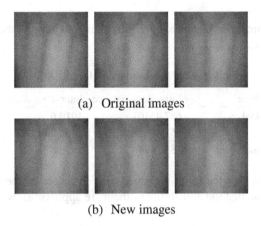

(a) Original images

(b) New images

Fig. 5. Original and new images of one hand

As the selection of set B is different, massive new images can be generated. Theoretically, given a database containing N images of each class, the number of new images of each class could be calculated as follow:

$$Num = C_N^i \times (N - i) \tag{16}$$

In this paper, there are 10 samples of each hand in the origin database, and selecting 5 as set B with the left 5 as set M. Theoretically, the number of new reconstructed samples of one hand can reach 1260.

5   Experiments and Results

In this work, 40 new samples of one hand are reconstructed to form a new database. The original and new databases are investigated separately and also be tested together.

5.1 Intra- and Inter-class Distances

For each hand, there are N images. The feature vector of the nth image of the mth hand is represented as $V_{mn}(m = 1, 2, \cdots, 204; n = 1, 2, \cdots, 50)$. The intra-class distance $IntraD$ and inter-class distance $InterD$ are defined as:

$$IntraD_{mn} = \|V_{mn} - C_m\| \tag{17}$$

$$InterD_{mn}(k) = \|V_{mn} - C_k\| \quad (k \neq m) \tag{18}$$

where, C_m denotes the average feature vector of the mth hand class:

$$C_m = \frac{1}{N} \sum_{n=1}^{N} V_{mn} \tag{19}$$

The intra- and inter-class distances of original, new and joint databases are calculated and listed in Table 1.

Table 1. The intra- and inter-class distances

Database	Intra-class distance	Inter-class distance
Original	687.4510	1919.6
New	551.4063	1982.2
Original+New	588.5494	1979.8

The results show that the intra- and inter-class distances of these three databases differ slight, meaning that the divisibility of them are approximately the same.

5.2 Recognition Rate

To evaluate the new database, recognition experiments using integral histogram and PLPB [10] features with nearest neighbourhood (NN) classifier are carried out on the new database, original database and a joint database. In the experiments, the database is divided into set A containing five images of each hand as register set, and set B containing the left images as test set. The recognition results are shown in Table 2.

Table 2. Recognition results

Database	PLBP (%)	Integral histogram (%)
Original	98.43	88.63
New	99.73	91.35
Original+New	98.66	90.01

The results show that the performance of the new database is similar to the original one. The new database can be used to test algorithms as a supplement of the original one.

6 Conclusions

In this work, PCA method is adopted to enlarge the database from 2040 images to 10200 images, with the samples of each hand increasing from 10 to 50. The experimental results show that the enlarged database has a satisfied recognition rate of 98.66 % using PLBP and NN classifier, which indicates the proposed method performs well and new database is available for simulation test.

Acknowledgments. This work is supported by National Natural Science Foundation of Shandong Province (ZR2015FL018).

References

1. Ding, Y., Zhuang, D., Wang, K.: A study of hand vein recognition method. In: Gu, J., Liu, P.X. (eds.): 2005 IEEE International Conference on Mechatronics and Automations, vols. 1–4, Conference Proceedings, pp. 2106–2110 (2005)
2. Delac, K., Grgic, M.: A survey of biometric recognition methods. In: 46th International Symposium Electronics in Marine, pp. 184–193 (2004)
3. Wang, R., et al.: A palm vein identification system based on Gabor wavelet features. Neural Comput. Appl. **24**(1), 161–168 (2014)
4. LeCun, Y., Bengio, Y., Hinton, G.: Deep learning. Nature **521**, 436–444 (2015)
5. Liu, Z., et al.: Deep learning face attributes in the wild. In: The IEEE International Conference on Computer Vision, pp. 3730–3738 (2015)
6. Wang, Y., Li, K., Cui, J.: Hand-dorsa vein recognition based on partition local binary pattern. In: Yuan, B.Z., Ruan, Q.Q., Tang, X.F. (eds.) 2010 IEEE 10th International Conference on Signal Processing Proceedings, pp. 1671–1674 (2010)
7. Zhao, S., Wang, Y., Wang, Y.: Biometric verification by extracting hand vein patterns from low-quality images. In: Proceedings of the Fourth International Conference on Image and Graphics (2007)
8. Cross, J.M., Smith, C.L.: Thermo graphic imaging of the subcutaneous vascular network of the back of the hand for biometric identification. In: Proceedings of IEEE 29th Annual International Carnahan Conference on Security Technology (1995)
9. Wang, L., Leedham, G.: Near- and far-infrared imaging for vein pattern biometrics. In: Proceedings of IEEE International Conference on Video Signal Based Surveillance, Sydney, pp. 52–57, Nov. 2006
10. Li, K., et al.: Hand-dorsa vein recognition based on improved partition local binary patterns. In: The 11th Chinese Conference on Biometric Recognition, pp. 312–320 (2015)

Comparative Study of Deep Learning Methods on Dorsal Hand Vein Recognition

Xiaoxia Li[1,3], Di Huang[1,3(✉)], and Yunhong Wang[2,3]

[1] State Key Laboratory of Software Development Environment,
Beihang University, Beijing 100191, China
[2] IRIP Lab, Beihang University, Beijing 100191, China
[3] School of Computer Science and Engineering,
Beihang University, Beijing 100191, China
pheobego@163.com,{dhuang,yhwang}@buaa.edu.cn

Abstract. In recent years, deep learning techniques have facilitated the results of many image classification and retrieval tasks. This paper investigates deep learning based methods on dorsal hand vein recognition and makes a comparative study of popular Convolutional Neural Network (CNN) architectures (*i.e.*, AlexNet, VGG Net and GoogLeNet) for such an issue. To the best of our knowledge, it is the first attempt that applies deep models to dorsal hand vein recognition. The evaluation is conducted on the NCUT database, and state-of-the-art accuracies are reached. Meanwhile, the experimental results also demonstrate the advantage of deep features to the shallow ones to discriminate dorsal hand venous network and confirm the necessity of the fine-tuning phase.

Keywords: Dorsal hand vein recognition · Deep learning · Fine-tuning

1 Introduction

In recent years, hand vein pattern based biometric recognition has drawn considerable attention both in the academia as well as industry. Similar to other biometric traits, such as iris, face, and fingerprint, hand vascular networks are individually different even between identical twins [1]. In contrast to the majority of the other biometrics, vessels are under skin, and they are thus difficult to forge. Furthermore, hand vein recognition offers an easy way for liveness detection due to the nature of Near Infrared (NIR) or Far Infrared (FIR) imaging which captures the temperature difference between blood flow in the vein and its surrounding skin of the living body. Additionally, the acquisition of dorsal hand vein images is user friendly, non-invasive, and contactless.

In literature, dorsal hand vein recognition methods generally follow the similar procedure including pre-processing, feature extraction and similarity measurement. According to the feature adopted to represent vascular patterns, these methods can be roughly split into two groups, shape-based and texture-based. The former focuses on the shape characteristics acquired from the skeleton map

© Springer International Publishing AG 2016
Z. You et al. (Eds.): CCBR 2016, LNCS 9967, pp. 296–306, 2016.
DOI: 10.1007/978-3-319-46654-5_33

of the hand vein network for people identification. In some early attempts, the positions and angles of short straight vectors [2] and minutiae points [3–5] including endpoints and crossing points are exploited to describe the distinctiveness between the vein shapes. Recently, Zhu and Huang [6] propose a Graph-based vein shape representation for recognition which simultaneously encodes both the similarities of minutiae and line segments by a single model. For the latter, texton variations are extracted within the Region of Interest (ROI) of the hand vein image as the feature to distinguish different individuals. For example, textures can be encoded both in the Principal Component Analysis (PCA) [7] or Linear Discriminant Analysis (LDA) [8] subspace on the entire image, and in Local Binary Patterns (LBP) [9,10] or Scale-Invariant Feature Transform (SIFT) [11–14] within specific areas. From the perspective of the manner of feature extraction, those approaches mentioned above can be classified into holistic based and local based as well. The holistic ones employ the texture or shape information of dorsal hand vein region as a whole for similarity measurement, and the PCA [7], LDA [8] and Graph [6,15] based methods belong to this stream. However, they tend to be sensitive to illumination, distortion and occlusion variations, leading to degraded performance. While the local ones such as LBP and SIFT, which extract the texture or shape attributes in a specific region, show better robustness to these factors and become dominant for such an issue.

In spite of the continuously boosted accuracy, current dorsal hand vein recognition methods still mainly depend on hand-crafted features, which are designed based on the knowledge of human beings in the specific domain. As the cognition of human beings is still far from sufficient, such features probably incur incomplete representation of the vein network either in terms of shape or texture, leaving space for further improvement. More recently, deep learning techniques, in particular Convolutional Neural Networks (CNNs), have demonstrated their competency at many image recognition applications, including the ones of face recognition and speech recognition in the field of biometrics. Deep learning is able to automatically discover the intrinsic structures of high-dimensional training data. The characterization of the input data is actualized by learning a deep neural network formed with a number of layers of simple but non-linear modules. More concretely, multiple levels (usually more than three layers except the input and output layer) of representation are generated from the raw input data through a series of nonlinear transformation from the low to higher layer with slightly more abstracted level. In general, higher layers which represent simplified aspects of the input data possess better discrimination power and robustness to irrelevant variations. Furthermore, these layers of features are entirely learned from data in a general-purpose learning procedure, which alleviates human intervention required in traditional recognition framework.

The objective of this paper is to investigate deep learning methods on dorsal hand vein recognition. We evaluate four popular CNN models, namely Caffe Alex Net, Caffe Reference Net [16], VGG-16 Net [17] and GoogLeNet [18], constructed from external generic large-scale datasets such as ImageNet [19], in representing and recognizing dorsal hand vein patterns. The experiments are conducted on

NCUT, one of the most comprehensive databases, and the state of the art results are achieved, which demonstrate the advantage of the deep features to the shallow ones on dorsal hand vein recognition. Additionally, the comparison of performance with and without fine-tuning confirms the necessity of this step.

The remainder of this paper is organized as follows. Section 2 introduces the deep learning architectures and compares the configurations of four typical pre-trained deep neural models. Experimental results achieved on the NCUT dorsal hand vein dataset are presented and analyzed in Sect. 3. Section 4 is the conclusion of this paper.

2   Deep Learning Architectures

CNN is a typical deep neural network designed to process the data which comes in the form of multiple arrays such as the gray image (one 2D array) and the color image (three 2D arrays). The input image passes through a stack of multiple processing layers which are connected using spatially organized patterns. This conforms to the way that the human visual cortex processes image data [20]. A typical architecture of convolutional network (ConvNet) is structured as a series of stages. The first few stages consist of two types of layers namely convolutional layers and pooling layers. A convolutional layer takes the form of the feature maps, in which each unit connects to local patches in the feature maps of previous layer through a set of weights. The result of this local weighted sum is then passed through a non-linear activation function, such as Rectified Linear Unit (ReLU), to accelerate the training phase. A pooling layer consists of a grid of pooling units, each of which computes the maximum or the average of a local patch of units in one or a few feature maps. Neighboring pooling can not only reduce the dimension of the representation, but also create an invariance to small shifts and distortions. After a few stages of convolution and pooling are following fully-connected (FC) layers, which have full connections to all activations in the previous layer.

Currently, there are some typical ConvNets that prove efficient for image classification in literature, e.g., AlexNet proposed by Krizhevsky et al. [16], VGG Net proposed by Simonyan and Zisserman [17], and GoogLeNet proposed by Szegedy et al. [18]. Their architectures are greatly different from each other. In this paper, we adopt 4 pre-trained CNN models for texture based vein feature extraction, including two implementations of AlexNet namely Caffe Reference Net model (Caffe-Ref) and Caffe AlexNet model (Caffe-Alex), an implementation of VGG Net namely VGG-16 and an implementation of GoogLeNet. They all have been well trained on the ImageNet dataset [19], which consists of about 1.5 million labeled photographs divided into 1000 categories, based on the Caffe library [21]. Table 1 summarizes the configurations of the ConvNets mentioned. Remarkably, they share the same input data size of $224 \times 224 \times 3$ (the RGB image).

Table 1. Configurations of different ConvNets (The ReLU activation function is not shown for brevity).

Caffe-Alex/Ref		VGG-16		GoogLeNet	
Input (224×224 RGB image)					
Filter	Channel	Filter	Channel	Type	Output size
11×11	96	3×3	64	convolution (7×7)	112×112×64
		3×3	64		
Max pooling					
5×5	256	3×3	128	convolution (3×3)	56×56×192
		3×3	128		
				Max pooling	
		3×3	256	inception (3a)	28×28×256
		3×3	256	inception (3b)	28×28×480
		3×3	256		
Max pooling					
3×3	384	3×3	512	inception (4a)	14×14×512
		3×3	512	inception (4b)	14×14×512
		3×3	512	inception (4c)	14×14×512
3×3	384			inception (4d)	14×14×528
				inception (4e)	14×14×832
				Max pooling	
3×3	256	3×3	512	inception (5a)	7×7×832
		3×3	512	inception (5b)	7×7×1024
		3×3	512		
Max pooling				Avg pooling	1×1×1024
FC-4096				Dropout(40%)	1×1×1024
FC-4096				Linear	1×1×1000
FC-1000					
Softmax					

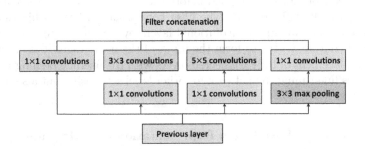

Fig. 1. Inception module with dimension reductions in GoogLeNet.

2.1 AlexNet

AlexNet contains eight learned layers, five convolutional and three fully connected ones. A 1000-way softmax connected with the last fully-connected layer produces the classification results. The neurons in the fully-connected layers are connected to all the neurons in the previous layer. Max-pooling layers follow both response-normalization layers as well as the fifth convolutional layer. The ReLU non-linearity is applied to the output of every convolutional and fully-connected layer. The difference between Caffe-Ref and Caffe-Alex lies in the order of the pooling and normalization layer.

2.2 VGG Net

The input layer and fully-connected layers in the VGG-16 Net are the same as the ones in the AlexNet. The difference only exists in the hidden layers. There are a total of 5 pooling layers and 13 convolutional layers where all the filters used are with a very small size: 3×3. All the hidden layers are equipped with ReLU non-linearity. The configurations of the AlexNet and VGG Net are shown in Table 1. We can see that compared with AlexNet, VGG-16 ConvNet is deeper and smaller in filter size.

2.3 GoogLeNet

GoogLeNet has a typical very deep network containing 22 layers with parameters and 5 pooling layers in all. Nevertheless, compared with the deep network VGG-16, GoogLeNet performs better in computational efficiency and practicality thanks to the inception module, which aims to utilize a readily available dense component to approximate and cover an optimal local sparse structure in a convolutional network. The inception module is considered as a whole in the architecture of GoogLeNet as shown in Fig. 1. There exist a set of filters with fixed sizes of 1×1, 3×3, and 5×5 in the module to avoid patch-alignment issues. Additionally, a pooling operation is essential in each of such stages. To reduce the expensive computational consumption caused by the convolutional operations, 1×1 convolutions are applied before the ones of 3×3 and 5×5 and after pooling separately. Subsequently, the filter concatenation layer achieves a combination of the pooling and convolutional layers by concatenating their outputs into a single output vector to form the input of the next stage. It is noteworthy that the replacement of fully connected layers with the average pooling layer not only enables fine-tuning the network for other label sets easily, but also improves the accuracy.

2.4 Deep Model Based Vein Representation and Matching

In the deep neural network, high-level features are abstracted from low-level ones, possessing stronger discriminative power and better robustness to small rotations and distortions. Accordingly, we extract high-level features from the input ROI image of the dorsal hand vein image using the pre-trained deep models. For the AlexNet and VGG ConvNets, three fully-connected layers are feasible for feature extraction, while for the GoogLeNet we have to extract features from the average pool layer which is the substitute for the fully-connected layer. These deep features are used to represent vascular patterns for recognition. Then a simple KNN classifier is exploited to measure the similarity for the sake of highlighting the discriminative power of deep model based vein representation.

3 Experimental Results

To validate the effectiveness of the deep learning based methods for hand dorsal vein recognition, we carry out a series of experiments on the North China University of Technology (NCUT) dorsal hand vein dataset [22], which is publicly available within the community. Subsequently, the database, protocol and results are presented.

3.1 Database

NCUT is one of the largest public dorsal hand vein databases, composed of two parts, *i.e.*, NCUT Part A and NCUT Part B. There are 2040 Near-Infrared (NIR) images of dorsal hand veins in NCUT Part A, collected from the left and right hands of 102 individuals (10 samples for each hand) including 52 females and 50 males. Similar to NCUT Part A, NCUT Part B contains 10 right and 10 left dorsal hand images from 101 individuals, which has the total number of 2020 samples. Both the two parts of the dataset have the same image resolution of 640×480. In contrast to the samples in NCUT Part B, the ones in Part A have better a quality with less noise and higher contrast due to the more expensive acquisition device used.

3.2 Protocol

The left hand and right hand can be regarded as different subjects due to the discrepancy between the two hands of the same person, which makes the number of subjects double. NCUT Part A has 204 classes and Part B has 202 classes. Since most state-of-the-art results are reported on NCUT Part A, we use it for validation in our experiments, where a number of samples from each subject are stochastically chosen to compose the gallery set and the others are regarded as the probe samples. The size of the gallery sample set varies from 1 to 5 for the comparison with the studies that make use of different protocols. When fine-tuning the deep model, entire NCUT Part B are exploited. The gallery set of NCUT Part A is also added for fine-tuning if there are more than one sample of each class in it.

We conduct three experiments in the scenario of identification: the first is to analyze the difference of deep features in various FC layers; the second is to validate the fine-tuning step with different gallery sizes; and the third is to compare the results with the state-of-the-art ones under different protocols in literature.

3.3   Results

Difference in FC Layers. There are three fully-connected (FC) layers in Caffe-Alex, Caffe-Ref and VGG-16. To analyze the difference amongst them, we extract features from three FC layers respectively, and thus report 9 results with the same gallery size set to 5 as shown in Table 2. We can see that the ones from the first FC layers achieve the best performance for all the ConvNets, which is evident that the first FC layer contains more discriminative information than the other two. Therefore, in the subsequent experiments, the deep feature is extracted from the first FC layer for Caffe-Alex, Caffe-Ref and VGG-16.

Necessity of Fine-Tuning. Figure 2 shows the recognition rates of the 4 deep feature based methods as well as their models after fine-tuning. It can be seen from Fig. 2(a) that for various gallery sizes, Caffe-Alex and Caffe-Ref always achieve the best performance among the three kinds of ConvNets. On the other hand, after fine-tuning, all their accuracies are ameliorated as shown in Fig. 2(b). Although GoogLeNet obviously performs worse than other approaches before fine-tuning, its performance is largely improved by about 9 % to 15 %, which are comparable to the ones of the counterparts with more data in this step, *i.e.* the gallery size is 3 to 5. The increases in results of the other three models are with the range of 5 % to 15 % for VGG-16 and 0.5 % to 4 % for Caffe-Alex and

Table 2. Recognition rates based on features extracted from the three FC layers of Caffe-Alex, Caffe-Ref and VGG-16 respectively, on NCUT Part A (the ratio of gallery size to probe size is 5:5).

FC Layer	Caffe-Alex	Caffe-Ref	VGG-16
First Fully-Connected layer (FC-4096)	**97.35 %**	**97.84 %**	**94.41 %**
Second Fully-Connected layer (FC-4096)	95.88 %	96.76 %	91.76 %
Last Fully-Connected layer (FC-1000)	91.67 %	93.43 %	85.69 %

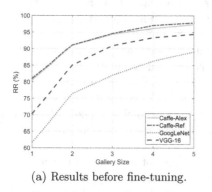 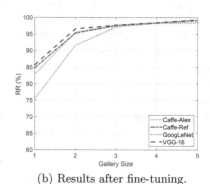

(a) Results before fine-tuning.   (b) Results after fine-tuning.

Fig. 2. Recognition rates (RR) of the 4 pre-trained deep models: (a) before fine-tuning and (b) after fine-tuning, with the gallery size varying from 1 to 5.

Caffe-Ref. These CNN based deep features reach good recognition rates, and to some extent, it is evident that the deep learning models pre-trained on very large datasets with plenty of categories, possess certain universality for domain independent feature representation. The promotions in performance demonstrate that the deep model fine-tuned with a small amount of domain-dependent data gives much better discriminative power in the specific area. Such a fact clearly illustrates the necessity of the fine-tuning phase.

Table 3. Comparison with the state of the arts in rank-one recognition rate on NCUT Part A.

Methods	Year	G:P	Recognition rate
CP-LBP [9]	2010	5:5	90.88 %
LBP+Graph [6]	2012	5:5	96.67 %
OMGs+SIFT [11]	2012	5:5	99.02 %
Multi-level Keypoint+SIFT [12]	2012	5:5	98.04 %
BC+Graph [23]	2013	5:5	97.82 %
MPLBP [10]	2015	5:5	98.83 %
Multi-source Keypoint+SIFT [13]	2015	5:5	99.61 %
GDRKG+SIFT+MtSRC [24]	2015	5:5	99.66± 0.07 %
WSM [25]	2016	5:5	99.31 %
This paper (VGG-16)	2016	5:5	**99.31 %**
Binary+SIFT [26]	2012	4:6	97.95 %
OMGs+SIFT [11]	2012	4:6	98.20 %
Multi-source Keypoint+SIFT [13]	2015	4:6	99.35 %
GDRKG+SIFT+MtSRC [24]	2015	4:6	99.74± 0.07 %
This paper (VGG-16)	2016	4:6	**98.45 %**
LBP [27]	2015	3:7	97.53 %
This paper (VGG-16)	2016	3:7	**97.69 %**
OMGs+SIFT [11]	2012	2:8	91.67 %
This paper (VGG-16)	2016	2:8	**96.57 %**
OGMs+SIFT [11]	2012	1:9	85.89 %
GDRKG+SIFT+MtSRC [24]	2015	1:9	96.46±0.05 %
This paper (VGG-16)	2016	1:9	**85.62 %**

Among all the models including the original ones and their fine-tuned versions, VGG-16 after fine-tuning reaches the best recognition rates when the gallery size is 1, 2, 4 and 5, and is only slightly inferior (0.07 %) to the one Caffe-Alex (97.76 %) with the gallery size at 3. Therefore, VGG-16 is used in the comparison with the state-of-the-art methods in the subsequence.

Additionally, the time consumed online per sample in the extraction deep learning based feature step through Caffe-Alex, Caffe-Ref, GoogLeNet and

VGG-16 are respectively 1.9 ms, 1.6 ms, 5.9 ms and 11.24 ms. It shows that these models are efficient in online processing, comparable to the level of hand-crafted feature based ones.

Comparison with the State-of-the-Art. We compare our best results, *i.e.*, fine-tuned VGG-16, with the top ones reported on the same benchmark using different experimental protocols. Our method achieves the state-of-the-art recognition rates when gallery size is 2 and 3. When G:P is 5:5, 4:6 and 1:9, our method outperforms most of the others and is only slightly inferior to the Multisource Keypoint+SIFT [13] and GDRKG+SIFT+MtSRC [24]. The main reason lies in that the specific data for fine-tuning are limited. In addition, compared with the handcrafted feature based methods, deep feature based ones need little pre-processing and are more convenient to be applied in the real world.

4   Conclusion

In this paper, we discuss deep learning based methods on dorsal hand vein recognition, and present a comparative study of four deep neural models pre-trained on ImageNet. Deep features are extracted as the representations of vascular patterns, and a simple KNN classifier is adopted for classification. After fine-tuning deep models on a number of dorsal hand vein data, the features abstracted exhibit better ability to distinguish different individuals. The recognition rates achieved on the NCUT database are state-of-the-art, clearly demonstrating the feasibility and efficiency of deep learning techniques for this issue.

Acknowledgments. This work was supported in part by the National Natural Science Foundation of China under Grant 61540048; the Beijing Municipal Natural Science Foundation under Grant 4142032; the Research Program of State Key Laboratory of Software Development Environment (SKLSDE-2015ZX-30); and the Fundamental Research Funds for the Central Universities.

References

1. Kumar, A., Hanmandlu, M., Gupta, H.: Online biometric authentication using hand vein patterns. In: IEEE Symposium on Computational Intelligence for Security and Defense Applications, pp. 1–7. IEEE (2009)
2. Cross, J., Smith, C.: Thermographic imaging of the subcutaneous vascular network of the back of the hand for biometric identification. In: IEEE International Carnahan Conference on Security Technology, pp. 20–35. IEEE (1995)
3. Wang, K., Zhang, Y., Yuan, Z., Zhuang, D.: Hand vein recognition based on multi supplemental features of multi-classifier fusion decision. In: International Conference on Mechatronics and Automation, pp. 1790–1795. IEEE (2006)
4. Lin, C.L., Fan, K.C.: Biometric verification using thermal images of palm-dorsa vein patterns. IEEE Trans. Circ. Syst. Video Technol. 14(2), 199–213 (2004)
5. Kumar, A., Prathyusha, K.V.: Personal authentication using hand vein triangulation and knuckle shape. IEEE Trans. Image Process. 18(9), 2127–2136 (2009)

6. Zhu, X., Huang, D.: Hand dorsal vein recognition based on hierarchically structured texture and geometry features. In: Zheng, W.-S., Sun, Z., Wang, Y., Chen, X., Yuen, P.C., Lai, J. (eds.) CCBR 2012. LNCS, vol. 7701, pp. 157–164. Springer, Heidelberg (2012). doi:10.1007/978-3-642-35136-5_20

7. Khan, M.H.M., Subramanian, R.K., Khan, N.A.M.: Representation of hand dorsal vein features using a low dimensional representation integrating cholesky decomposition. In: 2009 International Congress on Image and Signal Processing, CISP 2009, pp. 1–6. IEEE (2009)

8. Khan, M.H.M., Khan, N.A.M.: Investigating linear discriminant analysis (lda) on dorsal hand vein images. In: International Conference on Innovative Computing Technology (INTECH), pp. 54–59. IEEE (2013)

9. Wang, Y., Li, K., Cui, J., Shark, L.-K., Varley, M.: Study of hand-dorsa vein recognition. In: Huang, D.-S., Zhao, Z., Bevilacqua, V., Figueroa, J.C. (eds.) ICIC 2010. LNCS, vol. 6215, pp. 490–498. Springer, Heidelberg (2010). doi:10.1007/978-3-642-14922-1_61

10. Li, K., Zhang, G., Wang, Y., Wang, P., Ni, C.: Hand-dorsa vein recognition based on improved partition local binary patterns. In: Yang, J., Yang, J., Sun, Z., Shan, S., Zheng, W., Feng, J. (eds.) CCBR 2015. LNCS, vol. 9428, pp. 312–320. Springer, Heidelberg (2015). doi:10.1007/978-3-319-25417-3_37

11. Huang, D., Tang, Y., Wang, Y., Chen, L., Wang, Y.: Hand vein recognition based on oriented gradient maps and local feature matching. In: Lee, K.M., Matsushita, Y., Rehg, J.M., Hu, Z. (eds.) ACCV 2012. LNCS, vol. 7727, pp. 430–444. Springer, Heidelberg (2013). doi:10.1007/978-3-642-37447-0_33

12. Tang, Y., Huang, D., Wang, Y.: Hand-dorsa vein recognition based on multi-level keypoint detection and local feature matching. In: International Conference on Pattern Recognition (ICPR), pp. 2837–2840. IEEE (2012)

13. Huang, D., Tang, Y., Wang, Y., Chen, L., Wang, Y.: Hand-dorsa vein recognition by matching local features of multisource keypoints. IEEE Trans. Cybern. 45(9), 1823–1837 (2015)

14. Huang, D., Zhang, R., Yin, Y., Wang, Y., Wang, Y.: Local feature approach to dorsal hand vein recognition by centroid-based circular key-point grid and fine-grained matching. Image Vis. Comput. (2016). http://dx.doi.org/10.1016/j.imavis.2016.07.001

15. Huang, D., Zhu, X., Wang, Y., Zhang, D.: Dorsal hand vein recognition via hierarchical combination of texture and shape clues. Neurocomputing (2016). http://dx.doi.org/10.1016/j.neucom.2016.06.057

16. Krizhevsky, A., Sutskever, I., Hinton, G.E.: Imagenet classification with deep convolutional neural networks. In: Advances in Neural Information Processing Systems, pp. 1097–1105 (2012)

17. Simonyan, K., Zisserman, A.: Very deep convolutional networks for large-scale image recognition. arXiv preprint (2014). arXiv:1409.1556

18. Szegedy, C., Liu, W., Jia, Y., Sermanet, P., Reed, S., Anguelov, D., Erhan, D., Vanhoucke, V., Rabinovich, A.: Going deeper with convolutions. In: Proceedings of the IEEE Conference on Computer Vision and Pattern Recognition, pp. 1–9 (2015)

19. Russakovsky, O., Deng, J., Su, H., Krause, J., Satheesh, S., Ma, S., Huang, Z., Karpathy, A., Khosla, A., Bernstein, M., et al.: Imagenet large scale visual recognition challenge. Int. J. Comput. Vis. 115(3), 211–252 (2015)

20. Felleman, D.J., Van Essen, D.C.: Distributed hierarchical processing in the primate cerebral cortex. Cereb. Cortex 1(1), 1–47 (1991)

21. Jia, Y., Shelhamer, E., Donahue, J., Karayev, S., Long, J., Girshick, R., Guadarrama, S., Darrell, T.: Caffe: convolutional architecture for fast feature embedding. In: Proceedings of the ACM International Conference on Multimedia, pp. 675–678. ACM (2014)

22. Zhao, S., Wang, Y.D., Wang, Y.H.: Biometric identification based on low-quality hand vein pattern images. In: International Conference on Machine Learning and Cybernetics, vol. 2, pp. 1172–1177. IEEE (2008)

23. Zhu, X., Huang, D., Wang, Y.: Hand dorsal vein recognition based on shape representation of the venous network. In: Huet, B., Ngo, C.-W., Tang, J., Zhou, Z.-H., Hauptmann, A.G., Yan, S. (eds.) PCM 2013. LNCS, vol. 8294, pp. 158–169. Springer, Heidelberg (2013). doi:10.1007/978-3-319-03731-8_15

24. Zhang, R., Huang, D., Wang, Y., Wang, Y.: Improving feature based dorsal hand vein recognition through random keypoint generation and fine-grained matching. In: IAPR International Conference on Biometrics (ICB), pp. 326–333. IEEE (2015)

25. Li, X., Huang, D., Zhang, R., Wang, Y., Xie, X.: Hand dorsal vein recognition by matching width skeleton models. In: IEEE International Conference on Image Processing (ICIP) (2016)

26. Wang, Y., Fan, Y., Liao, W., Li, K., Shark, L.K., Varley, M.R.: Hand vein recognition based on multiple keypoints sets. In: IAPR International Conference on Biometrics (ICB), pp. 367–371. IEEE (2012)

27. Wang, Y., Xie, W., Yu, X., Shark, L.K.: An automatic physical access control system based on hand vein biometric identification. IEEE Trans. Consum. Electron. **61**(3), 320–327 (2015)

Dorsal Hand Vein Recognition Across Different Devices

YiDing Wang, Xuan Zheng[✉], and CongCong Wang

North China University of Technology, Beijing, China
xuan_zheng1993@163.com

Abstract. With the fast development of the information, the application of distributed recognition system becomes more widespread. But the difference of hardware condition of terminal acquisition and all kinds of environments in distributed recognition system made biometric feature images different, which were gathered by different hardware. Include contrast, lightness, shifting, angle of rotation, size and so on. These differences will inevitably reduce accuracy of recognition and will not satisfy the development needs of the times. This paper synthetically analyses the important factors of heterogeneous dorsal hand vein images which are resulted by different devices. After normalizing grayscale images, this paper uses a segmentation method based on gradient difference to segment the texture of veins and uses SIFT to extract and match features. Discrimination in this paper can improve to 90.17 %, which is higher than other algorithms. This method can effectively solve the problem about dorsal hand vein recognition across different devices.

Keywords: Across devices · Dorsal hand vein · Heterogenic · Normalization · Gradient segmentation · SIFT feature points

1 Introduction

In the time of intelligence, biologic feature recognition methods are more and more popular. They use connatural and unique biologic feature to recognize identity, such as face, fingerprint, iris, vein, palm print, voice, pace and so on. Be contrasted with the traditional methods, these biologic recognition methods are more reliable and safe.

Dorsal hand vein's physiological structure is unique and stable [1], and hand vein under the skin with the different infrared absorptivity about fat and blood. In addition, it's easily for hand vein to defend outside environments. These features are contributed to the living property and uneasy forgery of hand vein [2–4]. Because of these advantages, hand vein recognition is widely applied on many fields. For example, roll machines in many companies and enterprise factories, entrance guard system in airport, school, governmental agency and so on.

With the fast development of the information age, single hand vein adopting device hasn't been satisfied with the network development, but distributed hand vein recognition system can solve the problem very well. However, the difference of the hardware condition of terminal acquisition and all kinds of acquisition environments in distributed system will inevitably result in different quality of hand vein images. In addition, almost all of traditional hand vein recognition system works in controlled condition to

© Springer International Publishing AG 2016
Z. You et al. (Eds.): CCBR 2016, LNCS 9967, pp. 307–316, 2016.
DOI: 10.1007/978-3-319-46654-5_34

accurately recognize people who cooperate it very well. Including imaging equipment, acquisition environments and users' condition, many controlled conditions make current hand vein recognition system can't adapt to identity recognition without controlled condition. The unique advantage and potential about the feature of hand vein haven't been exploited to the full.

Because of the difference of imaging equipment, acquisition environments and users' condition, we called the acquisition images with different quality were heterogeneous hand vein images. But almost recent researches of this problem went ahead based on face, fingerprint and iris recognition. Just a few people do the research about heterogeneous hand vein recognition. Be contrasted with face, fingerprint and iris, dorsal hand vein has its own advantage and uniqueness. For the research of hand vein, it's significant to research heterogeneous hand vein recognition.

2   Collection of Images

This recognition system includes two aspects, register and recognition. There are 50 volunteers. Everyone should be collected dorsal hand vein images by 3 devices, and 10 images each left and right hand so that makes up the database of hand vein images across different devices. The main procedure of recognition is showed in Fig. 1.

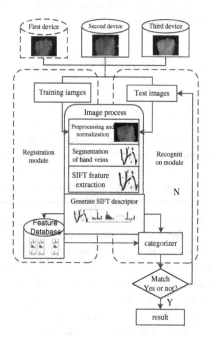

Fig. 1. Procedure of hand vein recognition

2.1   Collection Device

This experiment chooses the reflection infrared light source and CCD (Charged Couple Device) with IR filter to collect hand veins. Near-infrared light can automatically launch infrared ray whose wavelength is 850 nm. This wavelength can penetrate skin very well and makes vein blood absorb more infrared ray than surroundings [5]. The color will be much darker when hand veins go through. Thus, we can get the structure of veins. Be made up with three aspects: light source, camera, lens, collection device is showed in Fig. 2.

Fig. 2. Device (left), and device internal structure (right)

2.2   Create Database of Hand Vein Images Across Different Devices

There are 50 (25 males, 25 females) volunteers aged from 20 to 25. Everyone should be collected dorsal hand vein images by 3 devices, and 10 images each left and right hand. Some dorsal hand vein images are shown in Fig. 3.

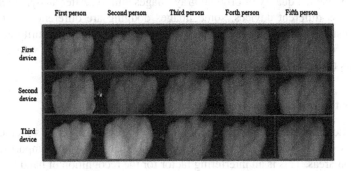

Fig. 3. Some images across different device

Because of the difference about collection environment and camera's parameter (lightness, contrast, focal distance, optical character), the collection quality of the same hand in different devices will be very different. In addition, volunteers need to replace left and right hand alternately, and the location or angle of hands is also different. In Fig. 3, longitudinal direction is the collection results in different device for the same hand. It can be found that the hand vein images, whose dorsal part's size, lightness, angle of rotation are different, collected by 3 devices. To show the influence of recognition results by hand vein images across different devices, this experiment compared average recognition rates about two algorithms, LBP and PCA, including different devices and single device.

Compared Tables 1 with 2, it shows that the influence of heterogeneous hand vein images to recognition rates is very serious. Even the better algorithm LBP, it's recognition rate is just not higher than 38.62 %. Next, in order to improve the recognition of hand vein images across different devices, this paper will choose SIFT algorithm because of its robustness to heterogeneous hand vein images.

Table 1. Average recognition rates in single device

Algorithms	1	2	3
LBP	93.5 %	90.1 %	86.7 %
PCA	90.4 %	86.5 %	81.6 %

Table 2. Average recognition rates in different devices

Across devices	1–2	1–3	2–3
PCA	20.03 %	15.50 %	16.05 %
LBP	38.62 %	36.50 %	37.90 %

3 Preprocessing of Images

In order to segment hand vein region from original gray images as effectively as possible, there must make the quality of original gray images unitary. After analyzing hand vein images across different devices, some images dodging are different because of the devices. Besides, hand shank area of the device and surrounding impurity is different, and non-uniform light of images won't benefit the segmentation about veins. Thus, this paper filters the hand shank area and normalize images' gray.

3.1 Filter the Hand Shank Areas

Although there is black shield outside the device to prevent light, it's ineluctable for some devices to be influenced by light so that hand shank areas and impurities appear in collection areas. This is an interfering factor for the recognition of hand vein images across different devices. After filtering hand shank area using morphologic opening, in order to protect pixels stable, this paper maps the result after opening into the original image so that we can get the result filtering hand shank area image shown in Fig. 4 (right).

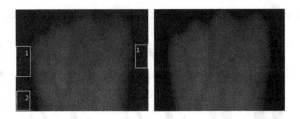

Fig. 4. Image with hand shank area (left), image after processing (right)

3.2 Normalization About Gray Scale

Because of the difference about lighting condition and about each thickness of hand, distribution of gray scale in images can't be equal. Thus, we need to normalize gray scale from 0 to 255 by:

$$N(x, y) = \frac{(R(x, y) - min) \times 255}{max - min} \tag{1}$$

where R(x, y) denotes grayscale after rotating, max and min denote respectively the highest and the lowest grayscale, N(x, y) denotes grayscale after normalized. The result after preprocessing of three devices is shown in Fig. 5.

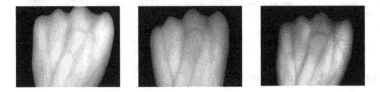

Fig. 5. Normalization about grayscale for three devices

3.3 Binary Segmentation

In the collection images, female's veins are too fine to be segmented unsuccessfully. Or be influenced by asymmetric light, background of dorsal hand will be error to be segmented. Experiment found that edge detected performance of segmentation based on gradient is better than other method [6] (Fig. 6). Segment threshold by:

$$T(x, y) = m(x, y) \times [1 - k(x, y) \times \frac{g(x, y)}{255}] \tag{2}$$

where m(x, y) denotes the average in N × N neighbourhood, g(x, y) denotes the gradient of N(x, y), k(x, y) is the adaptive coefficient decided by:

$$k(x, y) = \alpha + \beta \frac{G(x, y)}{255} \tag{3}$$

where G(x, y) denotes the max gradient, αandβ are set severally for 0.01 and 0.02.

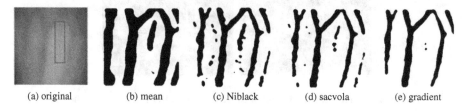

(a) original   (b) mean   (c) Niblack   (d) sacvola   (e) gradient

Fig. 6. Segmentation method for hand veins

4   Extraction and Choice for SIFT Feature Points

Feature extraction about hand vein images includes global and local features [7]. SIFT belongs to local features. SIFT algorithm has been globally applied to many biologic feature extraction including veins [8–12]. It not only has invariance of size and rotation, but also has resistance to lightness and geometric. This algorithm described feature points after extracting them and finally turned every picture into assemblage of feature vector. The flowsheet of SIFT is shown in Fig. 7.

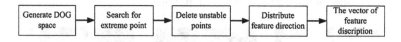

Fig. 7. Flowsheet of SIFT feature extraction

4.1   Search for Extreme Point

When detecting extreme points, there are 26 points shown in Fig. 8 to be contrasted with each other. The point which is the extreme in 26 points will be the local feature point.

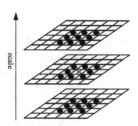

Fig. 8. Searching neighborhood of extreme point

4.2   Vector to Describe Feature

After confirming the main direction, we first turn the Axes to the main direction in order to assure rotation stable. Then we divides 16 × 16 neighborhood's pixels regarding feature point as the center into 16 areas the size is 4 × 4. Every small area need to be calculated gradient and counted gradient directions histogram about 8 directions. Thus, every small area becomes a seed pixel. Because there are 8 directions need to be calculated, the descriptor of SIFT feature points is 4 × 4 × 8 = 128 dimensions vector which is shown in Fig. 9. Normalizing SIFT feature vector can wipe off deformable light.

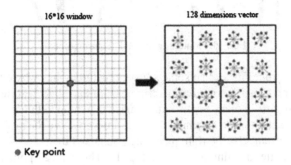

Fig. 9. SIFT describing vectors

4.3 Choice and Matching for SIFT Feature Points

Given the feature points, how to match points accurately is a problem. All the SIFT features are 128 dimensions vector extracted from test images and register images, so their similarity can be calculated by Euclidean distance, absolute difference, Cosine angle and the intersection of histograms. Taking time and accurate of calculation into consideration, this paper uses Cosine angle to match by:

$$\theta_{(p,q)} = \cos^{-1}\left(\frac{\mathrm{des}_p \cdot \mathrm{des}_{q(q,Q)}}{\left|\mathrm{des}_p\right| \cdot \left|\mathrm{des}_{q(q,Q)}\right|}\right) \tag{4}$$

where des_p denotes the feature vector of SIFT feature point p in test image P. $\mathrm{des}_{q(q,Q)}$ denotes the feature vector of SIFT feature point q in register image Q. We consider these two vectors matching successfully if they satisfy:

$$\frac{\theta(p,q)}{\theta(p,q')} \le R \ (q' \in Q, q' \ne q) \tag{5}$$

where q' denotes all the feature points except q in register image Q. R denotes an threshold. (5) shows that when we calculate the distance between all of the feature vectors in register image and in recognition image, if there are two vectors' distance is the min and is almost R times than other vectors' distance in recognition image, then we consider these two vectors are matched successfully. The result of matching is shown in Fig. 10. There 127 matching pairs in total.

Fig. 10. Matching of SIFT feature points

We can know from Fig. 10 that some adjacent feature points where the arrowheads point out have the same distribution of local feature and their feature vector is also approximate. It results in many points in test image matching with one point in register image. This is a many-to-one matching error. In order to solve the problem, this paper chooses the min distance as the right matching points and then deletes other matching points. The result after deleting is shown in Fig. 11. There are 27 points are deleted.

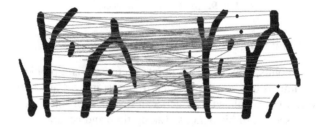

Fig. 11. Matching of SIFT feature points without repeat

Because the segmentation images of hand vein are binary texture and their structure is very simple, there should be enough feature points to match. However, when there are more and more feature points, errors will also increase. So, decreasing error is an important problem. After analyzing matching points, we can find that it is almost horizontal for right matching points, but some wrong matching points are declining. Now, we can set a slope threshold to choose right matching points which is shown in Fig. 12. It can be found that 76 remaining feature points have high matching rate. After selecting accurately feature points, it improves the robustness of the algorithm.

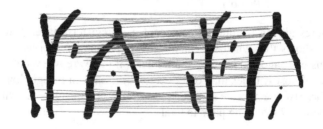

Fig. 12. SIFT feature points after selecting

5 Result and Analyzation of Experiment

In order to prove adequately the result of hand vein images recognition across different database after SIFT algorithm, this experiment adopts three devices with different parameters which are marked as first device, second device and third device to collect and classify 50 people's hand vein images. And their right and left hand are collected 10 images respectively.

This experiment uses one device to register and another to recognize. In order to guarantee the heterogenic of images, it adopts auto-collection and doesn't limit volunteers' posture. This experiment chooses the optimal parameters to compare the result of our algorithm with other previous algorithms for heterogeneous images (Table 3).

Table 3. Contrast with other algorithms

Algorithms	1–2	1–3	2–3	Average discrimination
SIFT	91.54 %	89.80 %	89.17 %	90.17 %
PCA	20.03 %	15.50 %	16.05 %	17.19 %
LBP	38.62 %	36.50 %	37.90 %	37.67 %
GDRKG	69.08 %	66.32 %	68.93 %	68.11 %
Deep learning	71.38 %	78.24 %	75.32 %	74.98 %

From this experiment, it can be found that PCA, LBP, GDRKG and Deep Learning didn't achieve a high discrimination. But, the SIFT algorithm in this paper normalized images first, and segment accurately hand veins from images with segmentation based on gradient. Then, we selected appropriate scale factor, threshold for matching, and this increased extractive as well as matching feature points. Finally, we selected accurately SIFT feature points, which made extractive hand vein feature more stable and improved accuracy of matching. So, discrimination can achieve 90.17 % for heterogeneous images with large difference. Compared with previous algorithms, this improved all kinds of results.

6 Conclusion

This paper proposed a normalized method of polygenetic heterogeneous hand vein images in the aspect of image preprocessing for heterogeneous problem of hand vein images across different devices. Using robustness SIFT itself has for rotation, zooming and panning, it selected accurately feature points through position, so that it decreased error matching rate and increased accuracy of classifying. In addition, compared with other recognized results of previous algorithms, it is obvious for this algorithm to increase discrimination. But with the increasing of dimensions and samples, the speed of recognition becomes slower and the complexity becomes higher. So effect of recognition will be researched mainly next.

References

1. Standring, S.: Gray's Anatomy, 39th edn. Elsevier Churchill Livingston, Edinburgh (2005)
2. Cross, J.M., Smith, C.L.: Thermographic imaging of the subcutaneous vascular network of the back of the hand for biometric identification. In: 29th International Carnahan Conference on Security Technology, pp. 20–35 (1995)
3. Wang, L., Leedham, G., Cho, S.Y.: Infrared imaging of hand vein patterns for biometric purposes. Comput. Vis. **1**(3–4), 113–122 (2007)
4. Kumar, A., Prathyusha, K.V.: Personal authentication using hand vein triangulation and knuckle shape. IEEE Trans. Image Process. **18**, 2127–2136 (2009)
5. Shahin, M., Badawi, A., Kamel, M.: Biometric authentication using fast correlation of near infrared hand vein patterns. Int. J. Biomed. Sci. **2**(3), 141–148 (2007)
6. Wang, Y., Wang, H.: Gradient based image segmentation for vein pattern. In: Fourth International Conference on Computer Sciences and Convergence Information Technology, pp. 1614–1618 (2009)
7. Lowe, D.G.: Distinctive image features from scale-invariant keypoints. Int. J. Comput. Vis. **60**(2), 91–110 (2004)
8. Bakshi, S., Mehrotra, H., Majhi, B.: Postmatch pruning of SIFT pairs for iris recognition. International Journal of Biometrics **5**(2), 160–180 (2013)
9. Morales, A., Ferrer, M.A., Kumar, A.: Towards contactless palmprint authentication. IET Comput. Vis. **5**(6), 407–416 (2011)
10. Meng, X., Yin, Y., Yang, G., et al.: Retinal identification based on an improved circular Gabor filter and scale invariant feature transform. Sensors **13**(7), 9248–9266 (2013)
11. Abaza, A., Bourlai, T.: On ear-based human identification in the mid-wave infrared spectrum. Image Vis. Comput. **31**(9), 640–648 (2013)
12. Tan, C., Wang, H., Pei, D.: SWF-SIFT approach for infrared face recognition. Tsinghua Sci. Technol. **15**(3), 357–362 (2010)

A New Finger Feature Fusion Method Based on Local Gabor Binary Pattern

Yihua Shi, Zheng Zhong, and Jinfeng Yang[(✉)]

Tianjin Key Lab for Advanced Signal Processing,
Civil Aviation University of China, Tianjin, China
jfyang@cauc.edu.cn

Abstract. This paper proposes a novel multimodal feature fusion method based on local Gabor binary pattern (LGBP). First, the feature maps of three modalities of finger, fingerprint (FP), finger vein (FV) and finger knuckle print (FKP), are respectively extracted using LGBP. The obtained LGBP-coded maps are further explored using local-invariant gray description to generate Local Gabor based Invariant Gray Features (LGIGFs). To reduce pose variations of fingers in imaging, LGIGFs are then weighed by a Gaussian modal. The experimental results show that the proposed method is capable of fusing multimodal feature effectively, and improve correct recognition rate greatly.

Keywords: Local Gabor Binary Pattern · Fingerprint · Finger Vein · Finger Knuckle Print · Rotation invariance

1 Introduction

Multimodal biometrics recognition has been an active research topic in biometric community. A multimodal biometric system usually fuses two or more biometric traits together for personal identification [1, 2]. In this paper, we combine fingerprint (FP) [3, 4], finger-vein (FV) [5–7], finger-knuckle-print (FKP) [8, 9] together for personal recognition. In order to fuse these three modalities reliably and effectively, a feature level fusion scheme is reported here.

In recent years, many feature analysis methods have been proposed for image content description. Daugman [10] proposed 2D Gabor filter which can exploit the image information in multi-orientation and multi-scale. Ojala [11] proposed a Local Binary Pattern (LBP) descriptor which combined local and global features. Zhang [12] proposed Local Gabor binary pattern (LGBP). LBP-based feature analysis is robust to illumination change, while it is sensitive to the pose variation. Therefore, Fan [13] proposed a multi-support region rotation and intensity monotonic invariant descriptor (MRRID) for reducing rotation variation. However, MRRID is a kind of interest-point-dependence method. This limits its performance on reliably representing multimodal finger features. First, extracting interest points enough for feature analysis is not practical for finger images, since FP, FV and FKP can not contribute a lot of candidate meaningful points. This inevitably impairs the accuracy of MRRID in recognition. Besides, MRRID is only local invariant in feature representation.

© Springer International Publishing AG 2016
Z. You et al. (Eds.): CCBR 2016, LNCS 9967, pp. 317–325, 2016.
DOI: 10.1007/978-3-319-46654-5_35

In order to effectively overcome the above limitations and solve finger-pose variation problem, we present a new descriptor in finger-feature description which named Weighted Local-Gabor-based Invariant Gray Features (WLGIGFs). First, a bank of even-symmetric Gabor filters is used to enhance FP, FV, FKP images, and then they are encoded using LGBP. Second, the LGBP feature maps are granulated and the intension of feature granules (FGs) are described using improved MRRID. Finally, the feature of each FG is weighted by Gaussian modal to further reduce the finger pose variations. The experimental results show that the proposed method has better effect on finger-pose variation suppression and yields higher identification accuracy in a large homemade database.

2   The Proposed Method

2.1   Multimodal Finger Image Acquisition

To obtain FP, FV and FKP images, we have designed a homemade imaging system [14], which can capture these three modalities images automatically and simultaneously when a finger is available in a collection groove, as shown in Fig. 1(a). Since the sizes of uni-modal region of interest (ROI) images are different, FV, FKP and FP images are resized in 91×203, 91×203, 154×154 and shown as Fig. 1(b).

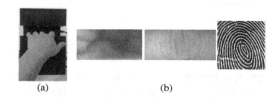

(a)   (b)

Fig. 1. A homemade imaging system. (a) An imaging device. (b) The extracted ROI images.

2.2   LGBP Feature Extraction

The LGBP is a descriptor on LBP coding derived from Gabor magnitude features of images, and it has robustness in illumination and translation variation. A bank of even-symmetric Gabor filter with eight orientations proposed in [15] is used here to obtain 8-orientations Gabor magnitude images (GMIs) of three modalities of finger images, as shown in Fig. 2. To obtain the illumination and translation invariant feature, the GMIs are respectively encoded with LBP descriptor [12], as shown in Fig. 3.

2.3   Feature Granule Intension Description

In order to overcome the MRRID limitation which only has rotation invariance in local feature analysis, the LGBP feature maps of three modal respectively are divided into rectangle granules with different scales, as shown in Fig. 4.

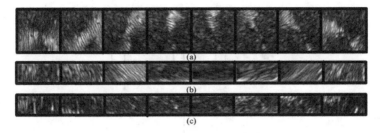

Fig. 2. The Gabor magnitude images of three modalities of figure. (a) FP, (b) FV, (c) FKP.

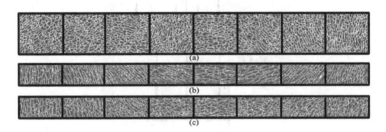

Fig. 3. The LGBP-coded images of finger. (a) FP, (b) FV, (c) FKP.

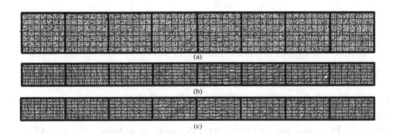

Fig. 4. The rectangle blocks of the finger-feature images. (a) FP, (b) FV, (c) FKP.

The local gray feature vectors are generated as the following procedure:

Step 1: gray-based grouping. The intensities of pixel points are sorted in non-descending order. According to the number of the pixels, this sequence is divided into k groups [13]. The parameter k is determined by the scale of each feature granule (FG).

Step 2: calculating the gray vector. We extract its eight nearest neighboring points regularly for each pixel. By comparing the gray of opposite adjacent points, we get a 4-bin binary vector: $(sign(I(X_i^{4+4}) - I(X_i^4)),\ sign(I(X_i^{3+4}) - I(X_i^3)),\ sign(I(X_i^{2+4}) - I(X_i^2)),\ sign(I(X_i^{1+4}) - I(X_i^1)))$. A local gray feature vector can be obtained by mapping the 4-bin binary vector into 16-bin binary vector:

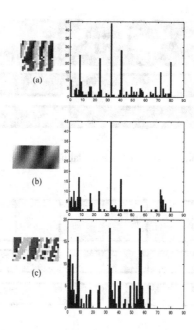

Fig. 5. The LGIGF histogram of each FG. (a) FP, (b) FV, (c) FKP.

$$f_j = \begin{cases} 1, & if \sum_{m=1}^{4} sign(I(X_i^{m+4}) - I(X_i^m)) \times 2^{m-1} = j - 1 \\ 0, & otherwise \end{cases}, \; j = 1, 2, \cdots, 2^4. \quad (1)$$

Here, f_j is 1, and the others are 0. Secondly, all the vectors of every gray-based group are accumulated. Then, the accumulated vectors are concatenated together to represent each FG, and the constructed intension descriptor of each FG is called Local-Gabor-based Invariant Gray Feature (LGIGF), as shown in Fig. 5.

2.4   Feature Granule Fusion

According to the inner regions of finger with less sensitivity to pose variation, we adopt a method which is used for weighing each FG of uni-modal finger-feature images based on 2D-Gaussian modal.

$$\alpha(i,j) = \frac{1}{2\pi\sigma^2} e^{\frac{-[(i-mid(i))^2 + (j-mid(j))^2]}{2\sigma^2}}, \; i = 1, 2, \cdots, M, \; j = 1, 2, \cdots, K. \quad (2)$$

Here, M is the number of granule in row, and K is the number of granule in column, $mid(i)$ and $mid(j)$ respectively denote the center granule of finger-feature image in ith row and jth column, as shown in Fig. 6. The robustness of uni-modal finger-feature images are determined by the size of σ. When the number of granule is same, the

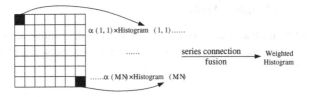

α (1, 1) ×Histogram (1, 1)......

......

series connection
fusion

Weighted
Histogram

......α (MN) ×Histogram (MN)

Fig. 6. The fusion processing of uni-modal finger-feature granules.

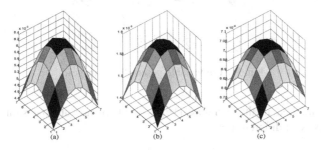

Fig. 7. 2D-Gaussian modal with different σ values. (a) $\sigma = 5$, (b) $\sigma = 10$, (c) $\sigma = 15$.

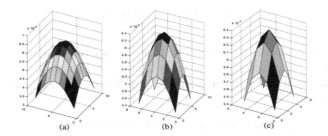

Fig. 8. 2D-Gaussian modal with different N value. (a) $N = 9 \times 9$, (b) $N = 7 \times 7$, (c) $N = 5 \times 5$.

smaller σ value is, the greater the weight of center granule is, as shown in Fig. 7. When the values of σ are same, the greater the number of granule (N) is, the fewer the weight of edge granule is, as shown in Fig. 8. Then, these three modal features are fused using a feature series connection strategy.

3 Experiments and Analysis

Here, a homemade database containing 1000 subsets of FP, FV, FKP images is used for performance evaluation. These multimodal images of a finger are collected simultaneously at different time.

3.1   LGIGF Poses Reliably Analysis

To testify the rotation invariance performance of LGIGF descriptor, we select four FV images from the homemade database which belong to one person and have variable poses (Fig. 9).

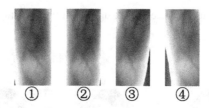

Fig. 9. The variable poses of FV images.

Here, the method in the literature [16] is used to measure the similarity of FV feature images with different poses.

$$sim(m_1, m_2) = \frac{\sum\limits_{l=1}^{L} \min[H_{m_1}(l), H_{m_2}(l)]}{\sum\limits_{l=1}^{L} H_{m_1}(l)} \tag{3}$$

Here, m_1, m_2 respectively denote two matching images, L is the dimension of histogram. From the presented data in Table 1, the conclusion shows that the LGIGF descriptor can effectively deal with the problem of finger-pose variation.

Table 1. The similarity coefficient of histogram.

Labeled matching image	LGIGF	LGBP	Improved MRRID
①—②	0.7063	0.6700	0.5499
①—③	0.6619	0.6064	0.4211
①—④	0.6661	0.6028	0.5136
②—③	0.6959	0.6709	0.6179
②—④	0.6737	0.6147	0.4420
③—④	0.6524	0.6004	0.3498

3.2   WLGIGF Parameter Selection

In the processing of LGIGF descriptor, the parameter of gray-based groups (k) and the granules of finger-feature images (N) would affect the recognition performance of finger feature, Fig. 10 shows the comparison of different values. From Fig. 10 we can clearly see that the finger-feature recognition performs better in $k = 5$, $N = 7 \times 7$.

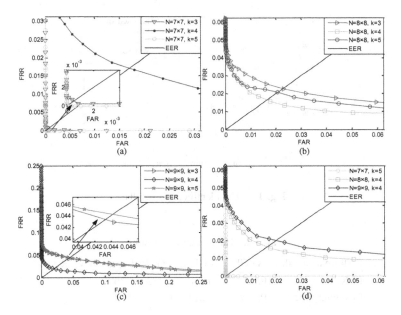

Fig. 10. The comparison of different parameter.

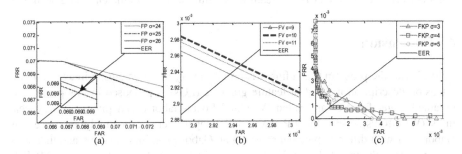

Fig. 11. The comparison of different σ. (a) FP, (b) FV, (c) FKP.

In the processing of the feature fusion, to achieve better recognition performance, the parameter σ of WLGIGF should be determined in the case of known N value. From the presented ROC in Fig. 11, we can see the WLGIGF descriptor of three modalities has the best recognition performance when $\sigma = 25, 10, 4$ respectively.

3.3 Recognition Results

The proposed algorithm is implemented using MATLAB R2010a on a standard desktop PC which is equipped with a Quad-Core, CPU 3.3 GHz and 4 GB RAM. The identification result is shown in Fig. 12. From this we can see that combining the WLGIGF descriptor has the best performance.

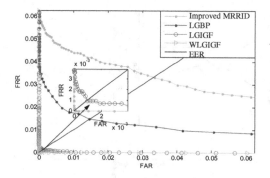

Fig. 12. The identification results.

Table 2. The recognition results.

Performance index	WLGIGF	LGIGF	LGBP	Improved MRRID
EER(%)	0.022	0.088	1.533	3.267
Matching time(s)	0.225	0.217	0.553	0.221

From the presented data in Table 2, the conclusions show that the descriptor has a good performance in finger-based feature recognition both in efficiency and accuracy.

4   Conclusion

To deal with the problem that a finger is prone to vary in poses during imaging, a new intension description method of feature granules (FGs) is proposed in this paper. The obtained finger features are called Weighted Local-Gabor-based Invariant Gray Features (WLGIGFs). First, the FP, FV, FKP images were respectively processed by Gabor filter with different parameters to obtain Gabor magnitude feature, and then they were respectively encoded by LBP. Second, to overcome the shortcoming of MRRID and reduce rotation variation, the three modal LGBP features were granulated and the intension of each FG was described by improved MRRID. It could improve intension description robustness of finger-based FG. Finally, considering the inner regions of finger with less sensitivity to pose variation, the LGIGF of each FG is weighted by a Gaussian modal. The experimental results showed that the proposed method had a superior performance in improving the finger-feature recognition accuracy as well as efficiency.

Acknowledgements. This work is jointly supported by National Natural Science Foundation of China (No. 61379102, No. U1343120, No. 61502498).

References

1. Jain, A., Ross, A., Prabhakar, S.: An introduction to biometric recognition. IEEE Trans. Circ. Syst. Video Technol. **14**(1), 4–20 (2004)
2. Ross, A., Jain, A.K., Qian, J.Z.: Information fusion in biometrics. Pattern Recogn. Lett. **24**(13), 2115–2125 (2003)
3. Upendra, K., Singh, S., Kumar, V., et al.: Online fingerprint verification. J. Med. Eng. Technol. **31**(1), 36–45 (2007)
4. Jain, A.K., Chen, Y., Demirkus, M.: Pores and ridges: high-resolution fingerprint matching using level 3 features. IEEE Trans. Pattern Anal. Mach. Intell. **29**(1), 15–27 (2007)
5. Lee, E.C., Lee, H.C., Park, K.R.: Finger vein recognition using minutia-based alignment and local binary pattern-based feature extraction. Int. J. Imaging Syst. Technol. **19**(19), 179–186 (2009)
6. Yang, J., Shi, Y., Yang, J.: Finger-vein recognition based on a bank of Gabor filters. In: Zha, H., Taniguchi, R-i, Maybank, S. (eds.) ACCV 2009, Part I. LNCS, vol. 5994, pp. 374–383. Springer, Heidelberg (2010)
7. Yang, J.F., Shi, Y.H., Yang, J.L.: Personal identification based on finger-vein features. Comput. Hum. Behav. **27**(5), 1565–1570 (2011)
8. Zhang, L., Zhang, L., Zhang, D., Zhu, H.: Ensemble of local and global information for Finger-Knuckle-Print recognition. Pattern Recogn. **44**(9), 1990–1998 (2011)
9. Zhang, L., Zhang, L.: Online finger-knuckle-print verification for personal authentication. Pattern Recogn. **43**(7), 2560–2571 (2010)
10. Yang, J.F., Yang, J.L., Shi, Y.H.: Finger-vein segmentation based on multi-channel even-symmetric Gabor filters. In: IEEE International Conference on Intelligent Computing and Intelligent Systems, vol. 4, pp. 500–503. IEEE Press, ShangHai (2009)
11. Ojala, T., Pietikainen, M., Maenpaa, T.T.: Multiresolution gray-scale and rotation invariant texture classification with local binary pattern. IEEE Trans. Pattern Anal. Mach. Intell. **24**(7), 971–987 (2002)
12. Zhang, W.C., Shan, S.G., Chen, X.L., et al.: Local Gabor binary patterns based on mutual information for face recognition. Int. J. Image Graph. **7**(4), 777–793 (2011)
13. Fan, B., Wu, F., Hu, Z.: Rotationally invariant descriptors using intensity order pooling. IEEE Trans. Pattern Anal. Mach. Intell. **34**(10), 2031–2045 (2012)
14. Yang, J.F., Meng, F.S., Shi, Y.K., Ma, Y.B.: Embedded imaging system for multimodal finger feature acquisition. J. Civ. Aviat. Univ. China (Chinese) **34**(1), 40–44 (2016)
15. Yang, J.F., Zhang, X.: Feature-level fusion of fingerprint and finger-vein for personal identification. Pattern Recogn. Lett. **33**(5), 623–628 (2012)
16. Xue, L.Y., Liu, Y.Y., Feng, H.F., et al.: The Color Histogram Image Retrieval Method Based on Granular Computing. Science Press (2013). (in Chinese)

Palmprint and Palm Vein Multimodal Fusion Biometrics Based on MMNBP

Sen Lin[1(✉)], Ying Wang[1], Tianyang Xu[1], and Yonghua Tang[2]

[1] School of Electronic and Information Engineering,
Liaoning Technical University, Huludao 125105, Liaoning, China
lin_sen6@126.com
[2] Computer Vision Group, Shenyang University of Technology,
Shenyang 110870, Liaoning, China

Abstract. This paper presents a multi-biometrics recognition method based on the fusion of palmprint and palm vein. Firstly, the traditional LBP method is improved, a novel algorithm called neighbor based binary pattern (NBP) is presented, which uses the relationship of gray value between adjacent pixels in the local area to encode the image. Secondly, the images of palm vein and palmprint are subdivided into several uniform size blocks, the gray mean value of each block is calculated. Furthermore, the multi-block mean image is encoded by the NBP method, which is called multi-block mean neighbor based binary pattern (MMNBP), and the feature fusion operation is implemented. Finally, the Hamming distance is used for matching. The comparison experiments are carried out with the current typical and popular approaches in the PolyU contact public database and self-built non-contact database. The experimental results indicate the superiority and effectiveness of the approach, which has good application prospect.

Keywords: Texture feature · Neighbor based binary pattern (NBP) · Palmprint and palm vein · Feature fusion

1 Introduction

With the rapid development of information technology, the requirements for identity recognition become higher, so biometric identification technology is becoming more and more popular for its safety and convenience [1]. However, there are some shortcomings in the typical biometrics methods, for example, the fingerprint is easy to be forged; the methods based on face recognition are easy to be interfered by gesture and decoration. In the last few years, the biometric identification technology based on the palmprint and palm vein have shown significant advantages [2]. Moreover, the identification of palmprint and palm vein can be designed in only one non-contact system, which is more friendly and widely accepted.

When reviewing the literature of current research, the recognition methods of palmprint and palm vein mainly include the following categories: the first is the method based on structural features [3], the second is based on subspace [4], and the third is based on invariant features [5]. The method based on texture is a very active research

© Springer International Publishing AG 2016
Z. You et al. (Eds.): CCBR 2016, LNCS 9967, pp. 326–336, 2016.
DOI: 10.1007/978-3-319-46654-5_36

direction, which is used to extract the global or local statistical information of the palmprint or palm vein image as features. For example, a new feature input space and a descriptor that operates in the local line-geometry space is proposed by Luo [6], and a new image descriptor called LLDP (local line directional patterns) is presented for palmprint recognition. The effects of two methods as LBP (local binary patterns) and LDP (local derivative patterns) were studied in detail for palm vein recognition [7]. The texture analysis methods have stronger versatility, and they are fit the own characteristics of the palmprint or palm vein images intuitively, so they have a broad prospect in application [8]. Obviously, identification by the fusion of palmprint and palm vein feature is very simple and practical [9], because it can be designed in the same acquisition device.

In this paper, the fusion identification method of the palmprint and palm vein based on the neighbor binary pattern (NBP) is proposed. To improve the traditional LBP coding method, the NBP encoding is informed according to the relations of gray values based on the local neighbor pixels of the images. The pictures of palmprint and palm vein are divided into several uniform region blocks, and the gray mean of each block is calculated namely multi-mean NBP (MMNBP) to enhance the robustness of the algorithm. After that, we connect the different features by using fusion method, and finally we do the matching by using Hamming distance.

2 Principle Method

2.1 LBP Algorithm and NBP Algorithm

The traditional LBP algorithm is mainly concerned with the relationship between the local neighbor pixels and the center pixel [10]. The formulas are described as follows:

$$LBP_{P,R}(x_c, y_c) = \sum_{i=0}^{p-1} 2^i \times s(p_i - p_c) \tag{1}$$

$$s(p_i - p_c) = \begin{cases} 1, p_i - p_c \geq 0 \\ 0, p_i - p_c < 0 \end{cases} \tag{2}$$

Where (x_c, y_c) is the coordinate of the center pixel and the gray value is p_c. p_i is the gray value of the neighborhood; i is the neighborhood position; R is the neighborhood radius; P is the number of pixels in the neighborhood. Figure 1(a) shows the LBP encoding process when $P = 8$, $R = 1$.

NBP is an improved texture description method, which mainly focus on the relationships of gray values among the neighbor pixels [11]. The method of the pixel arrangement in the 3×3 window is shown in Fig. 1(b).

There are three steps for NBP encoding:

Step 1, in 3×3 window, based on the center pixel, 8 points around the center pixel are extracted and arranged in a line by taking the pixel in the left corner as the starting point;

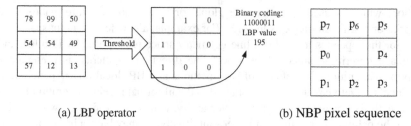

(a) LBP operator   (b) NBP pixel sequence

Fig. 1. LBP operator and NBP pixel sequence

Step 2, starting from the pixel on the most left side, each pixel can be operated as follows: the gray values are compared between the current pixel and the next neighbor pixel on the right by the formula as:

$$s_{i+1}(p_{i+1} - p_i) = \begin{cases} 1, p_{i+1} - p_i > 0 \\ 0, p_{i+1} - p_i \leq 0 \end{cases} \quad i = 0, 1, 2, \ldots, 6 \quad (3)$$

Specially,

$$s_0(p_0 - p_7) = \begin{cases} 1, p_0 - p_7 > 0 \\ 0, p_0 - p_7 \leq 0 \end{cases} \quad (4)$$

So a binary code of 8 bit can be formed.

Step 3, the binary encoding bit string is transformed into a decimal number, which is the NBP value of center pixel, the formula is:

$$D_{NBP} = \sum_{i=0}^{7} s_i \times 2^i \quad (5)$$

The schematic of NBP encoding principle and the examples are showed in Fig. 2.

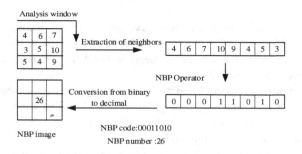

Fig. 2. NBP coding principle

2.2 NBP Feature Map

When an image of palmprint or palm vein is encoded by NBP, the decimal number can be regarded as the gray value, which can form NBP feature map, as shown in Fig. 3. Figure 3(a) is the ROI (region of interest) of palmprint and the corresponding NBP feature map, Fig. 3(b) is the ROI of palm vein and the corresponding NBP feature map. As shown in Fig. 3, we can see that after operating by NBP, the network structure of palmprint and palm vein will be clearer, the texture features are obviously prominent, which is beneficial for subsequent identification.

(a) Palmprint image and its NBP feature map (b) Palm vein image and its NBP feature map

Fig. 3. Palmprint and palm vein images and NBP feature maps

2.3 MMNBP and Feature Extraction of Palmprint and Palm Vein

The texture information is rich in palmprint and palm vein images, which is proper for the use of NBP feature extraction, but the dimension is high when NBP operation is implemented directly on the whole image. Meanwhile the comparisons of original NBP single pixel are more easily affected by noise. Therefore, this paper proposes a feature extraction method of palmprint and palm vein based on the multi-block mean neighbor binary pattern (MMNBP).

First of all, the image of palmprint and palm vein is processed by ROI extraction and gray enhancement, then a series of uniform block are formed, which is to transform an image matrix of v whose size is $M \times M$ into image blocks, as follow:

$$
V = \begin{bmatrix}
V_{11} & V_{12} & \cdots & V_{1k} \\
V_{21} & V_{22} & \cdots & V_{2k} \\
\cdots & \cdots & \cdots & \cdots \\
V_{k1} & V_{k2} & \cdots & V_{kk}
\end{bmatrix}
\tag{6}
$$

Here each block V_{ij} ($i, j = 1, 2, \ldots, k$) is a $m \times m$ matrix ($M = k \times m$).

Secondly, the gray value of each block can be calculated by the following formula:

$$
u_{ij} = \frac{1}{m^2} \sum_{x=1}^{m} \sum_{y=1}^{m} f_{ij}(x, y) \quad (i, j = 1, 2, \cdots, k)
\tag{7}
$$

Here $f_{ij}(x, y)$ shows the gray value of point (x, y) in the block. The image block average matrix of $k \times k$ size is formed by using the gray mean values of all blocks:

$$I = \begin{bmatrix} u_{11} & u_{12} & \cdots & u_{1k} \\ u_{21} & u_{22} & \cdots & u_{2k} \\ \cdots & \cdots & \cdots & \cdots \\ u_{k1} & u_{k2} & \cdots & u_{kk} \end{bmatrix} \qquad (8)$$

The multi-block mean calculation is shown in Fig. 4 (take palm vein image as an example). The advantages of the block mean calculation can be summarized as follows:

(1) The block mean calculation can further reduce the noise effect of the gray value comparison between single pixels.
(2) Reduce the possible impact of the image rotation caused by the acquisition, and enhance the robustness of the method.
(3) It can reduce the original data dimension and improve the operation efficiency, which is simple and easy to operate.

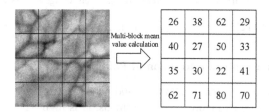

Fig. 4. Multi-block mean value calculation

Finally, NBP operation is implemented by using the matrix of the multi-block mean image, and the final MMNBP encoding result of the palmprint or the palm vein is obtained.

3   Palmprint and Palm Vein Feature Fusion and Matching

3.1   Feature Fusion

Image fusion is an effective method in multi-biometric recognition [12]. There are three main types of image fusion at present, and among them the application of feature level fusion is the most common [13]. The pictures of palmprint and palm vein all have rich texture information, from this perspective, they have a certain similarity, so they are suitable for the fusion operation. At the same time, the feature fusion of palmprint and palm vein can provide more abundant information for identity identification, and significantly increase the difficulty of forgery, which can effectively improve the security and reliability of the system.

If the MMNBP binary encoding of a sample palmprint image is $S_{\text{PP-MMNBP}}$, the MMNBP binary encoding of a sample palm vein image is $S_{\text{PV-MMNBP}}$, then the fusion feature $S_{\text{F-MMNBP}}$ is the connection of two codes, which can be defined as:

$$S_{\text{F-MMNBP}} = [S_{\text{PP-MMNBP}}\ S_{\text{PV-MMNBP}}] \tag{9}$$

Since the encoding of the binary is the type of bit in both $S_{\text{PP-MMNBP}}$ and $S_{\text{PV-MMNBP}}$, so there is no need to implement feature normalization operation, which is more convenient.

3.2   Feature Matching

During the match, the Hamming distance between MMNBP encoding after feature fusion are calculated. If there are two MMNBP codes called $S_{\text{F-MMNBP1}}$ and $S_{\text{F-MMNBP2}}$ respectively, the forms of bit string are:

$$s_{\text{F-MMNBP1}} = x_1 x_2 \cdots x_N \tag{10}$$

$$s_{\text{F-MMNBP2}} = y_1 y_2 \cdots y_N \tag{11}$$

Here x, y are 0 or 1.

The Hamming distance between them is defined as:

$$R_{\text{HD}}(S_{\text{F-MMNBP1}}, S_{\text{F-MMNBP2}}) = \frac{\sum\limits_{i=1}^{N} x_i \oplus y_i}{N} \tag{12}$$

Symbol $\oplus$ indicates the XOR operation, and N is the length of the bit string.

During the match, the similarity degree of two features is measured by using Hamming distance R_{HD}. The R_{HD} value ranges from 0 to 1, and a smaller value indicates a higher similarity. A threshold t is set in the specific identification. When R_{HD} satisfies follow:

$$R_{\text{HD}} < t \tag{13}$$

The two images are from the same person, and will be accepted, otherwise be refused.

4   Experimental Results

The whole identification system of dual modality fusion of palmprint and palm vein can be described as Fig. 5:

4.1   Evaluation Index Definition and Algorithm Test Environment

In this paper, the experimental evaluation algorithm of intra-class and inter-class matching has been used [8]. We can select the appropriate threshold value, and

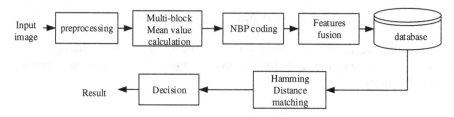

Fig. 5. Flow chart of the recognition system

complete the identification according to the matching principle above by drawing the distribution curve of intra-class and inter-class matching.

EER (error rate equal) is adopted as the evaluation index. Generally speaking, the value of EER is smaller, the effect of recognition is better [9]. The EER can be obtained as follow: take the FAR (false accept rate) as the horizontal coordinate and FRR (false rejection rate) as the vertical coordinate in the rectangular coordinate system of the same plane to draw ROC curve (receiver operating characteristics curve), the point at which the FRR equal to FAR is EER. The calculation formulas of FAR and FRR are as follow:

$$W_{FAR} = \frac{V_A}{V_J} \times 100\% \qquad (14)$$

$$W_{FRR} = \frac{V_E}{V_H} \times 100\% \qquad (15)$$

Among them, V_J is the login times of fake users; V_H is the registration number of legitimate users; V_A is the number of false acceptance, that is, the number of accepting the fake user into the system; V_E is the number of false rejection, which is the number of rejecting the legitimate users out of the system.

The test environment of the algorithm in this paper is the desktop computer which has been installed MATLAB software (version number: 2011b), and the CPU frequency is 3.0 GHz with 12 GB RAM.

4.2   Experimental Database and Results

To fully test the effectiveness of the algorithm, we use two image database described as follows:

(1) PolyU database. In this paper, the NIR (near infrared) of 850 nm band was adopted to collect palm vein images for 100 people, 5 ROI images per person were used as experimental samples. The white LED (light emitting diode) was selected to obtain palmprint images, the sample number was also 100 people, and 5 images per person [14].

(2) Self-built database. Dual optical CCD images sensor camera AD080GE was used as acquisition equipment. A non-contact database of palm vein was built. The NIR LED which wavelength is 850 nm has been selected as the light source indoor, and the images of 50 persons were obtained with 10 images of right hand palm

vein per person. Then we chose white LED as the light source for palmprint collection, the number of samples was also 50 people with 10 images per person.

The sample images of two databases are given in Fig. 6 and ROI size is 128 × 128. Different block division is selected, and the EER of every case for the fusion is calculated, as shown in Table 1. We can see that if the block is too large or too small, the EER will rise. This phenomenon can be interpreted as follow: the size of the block must be adapted to palmprint or palm vein texture, too large or too small blocks will affect the EER. And we can also find that the EER of self-built database is higher than the PolyU, this because the environmental reasons of image collection, or there may be some errors in the ROI extraction. Next step we will improve on these.

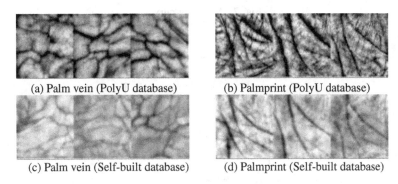

(a) Palm vein (PolyU database)   (b) Palmprint (PolyU database)

(c) Palm vein (Self-built database)   (d) Palmprint (Self-built database)

Fig. 6. Examples of two databases

Table 1. EER of the different blocks for fusion method (%)

Block size	PolyU database	Self-built database
2 × 2	0.1001	3.3838
4 × 4	0.0008	1.9745
8 × 8	0	1.4103
16 × 16	0.0097	1.7202
32 × 32	2.5288	5.1093
64 × 64	27.2662	22.4902

The matching curve of intra-class and inter-class in PolyU database is given in Fig. 7 (a), when the blocks are subdivided by 8 × 8 pixels, the times of intra-class and inter-class is 1000 and 123750 respectively. The threshold is set at the point of intersection of two curves, which is $t = 0.5598$. The result in self-built database is given in Fig. 7(b), the times of intra-class and inter-class is 2250 and 122500 respectively, and $t = 0.6132$. The curve of ROC is given on the corresponding database in Fig. 8.

To reflect the advantages of the proposed method, the MMNBP (before and after fusion) is compared with LBP and some typical and popular approaches currently [4, 8] on the palmprint and palm vein database, as shown in Table 2. We can see that our fusion method is the best.

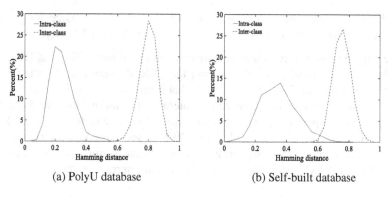

(a) PolyU database   (b) Self-built database

Fig. 7. Matching curve

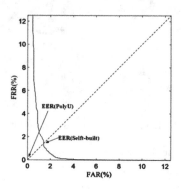

Fig. 8. ROC curve

Table 2. EER comparison of different methods (%)

Algorithm	PolyU database		Self-built database	
	Palmprint	Palm vein	Palmprint	Palm vein
2DGabor	0.3023	0.8068	24.0487	3.6111
2DPCA	0.4981	2.3006	10.6574	2.5912
WGS	0.7205	2.3889	11.5655	3.4744
SURF	3.3161	3.1397	7.4488	3.3312
LBP	1.8938	0.7106	13.2341	1.9873
MMNBP	0.4364	0.6983	13.0294	1.6036
MMNBP	0 (fusion)		1.4103 (fusion)	

The comparison of MMNBP execution time before and after the fusion is given in Table 3. We can see that the execution time of the method is satisfactory.

Table 3. Execution time of the algorithm

	PolyU database			Self-built database		
	Palmprint	Palm vein	Fusion	Palmprint	Palm vein	Fusion
Features extraction time (s)	0.094	0.095	0.165	0.092	0.097	0.164
Matching time (s)	0.015	0.015	0.016	0.016	0.017	0.018
Total time (s)	0.109	0.11	0.181	0.108	0.114	0.182

5 Conclusions and Discussion

From the perspective of texture image analysis, the operation of texture neighbor pattern is adopted in this paper, and the identification method of dual modality and multi-biometric feature fusion of palmprint and palm vein based on MMNBP is proposed. The core of this approach is NBP operation, by improving the encoding method of traditional LBP and combining the method of multi-block mean operation, the NBP is further enhanced. The experimental results in the two databases show that the MMNBP method of dual modality fusion could obtain the minimum EER of 0 and 1.4103 %, and the recognition time is only 0.181 s and 0.182 s. These show that the method is straightforward and feasible, which has a practical prospect.

Acknowledgement. This work is supported by (1) General Scientific Research Project of Liaoning Provincial Committee of Education (L2014132); (2) Natural Science Foundation of Liaoning Province of China (2015020100).

References

1. Unar, J.A., Seng, W.C., Abbasi, A.: A review of biometric technology along with trends and prospect. Pattern Recogn. **47**(8), 2673–2688 (2014)
2. Wu, W., Yuan, W.Q.: A survey of palm-vein image recognition. J. Image Graph. **18**(10), 1215–1224 (2013)
3. Jia, W., Hu, R.X., Lei, Y.K., et al.: Histogram of oriented lines for palmprint recognition. IEEE Trans. Syst. Man Cybern. Syst. **44**(3), 385–395 (2014)
4. Wu, W., Yuan, W.Q., Lin, S., et al.: Selection of topical wavelength for palm vein recognition. Acta Opt. Sin. **32**(12), 1211002 (2013)
5. Kang, W.X., Liu, Y., Wu, X.Q.: Contact-free palm-vein recognition based on local invariant features. PLoS ONE **9**(5), e97548 (2014)
6. Luo, Y.T., Zhao, L.Y., Zhang, B., et al.: Local line directional pattern for palmprint recognition. Pattern Recogn. **50**, 26–44 (2016)
7. Mirmohamadsadeghi, L., Drygajlo, A.: Palm vein recognition with local texture patterns. IET Biometrics **3**(4), 198–206 (2014)
8. Wu, W., Yuan, W.Q., Lin, S., et al.: Fast palm vein identification algorithm Based on grayscale surface matching. Acta Opt. Sin. **33**(10), 1015004 (2013)
9. Zhang, D., Guo, Z.H., Lu, G.M.: Online joint palmprint and palmvein verification. Expert Syst. Appl. **38**(3), 2621–2631 (2011)

10. Zhao, Y.: Theories and applications of LBP: a survey. In: 7th International Conference on Advanced Intelligent Computing Theories and Applications, pp. 112–120. IEEE Press, Zhengzhou (2011)
11. Hamouchene, I., Aouat, S.: A cognitive approach for texture analysis using neighbors-based binary patterns. In: 13th International Conference on Cognitive Informatics & Cognitive Computing, pp. 94–99. IEEE Press, London (2014)
12. Ahmad, M.I., Woo, W.L., Dlay, S.: Non-stationary feature fusion of face and palmprint multimodal biometrics. Neurocomputing **177**, 49–61 (2016)
13. Zhang, Y.Q., Sun, D.M., Qiu, Z.D.: Hand-based feature level fusion for single sample biometrics recognition. In: 1st International Workshop on Emerging Techniques and Challenges for Hand-Based Biometrics, pp. 1–4. IEEE Press, Istanbul (2010)
14. Guo, Z.H., Zhang, D., Zhang, L., et al.: Feature band selection for online multispectral palmprint recognition. IEEE Trans. Inf. Forensics Secur. **7**(3), 1136–1139 (2010)

Iris and Ocular Biometrics

Design of a Wide Working Range Lens for Iris Recognition

Wenzhe Liao[✉], Kaijun Yi[✉], Junxiong Gao[✉], Xiaoyu Lv, and Jinping Wang

Wuhan Hongshi Technologies Co., Ltd., C2-801, No. 999 Gaoxin Avenue, East Lake High-Tech Development Zon, Wuhan 430200, Hubei Province, China
{Wenzhe.Liao,Kaijun.Yi,Junxiong.Gao, Xiaoyu.Lv}@hongshi-tech.com

Abstract. This paper presents a methodology to solve the problem of narrow working range of lens for iris recognition. For iris recognition, working range of the lens is limited by the depth of field of the imaging lens. This paper proposes a design of a lens with liquid lens as a key component. The designed lens has a wide working range and can acquire high resolution images. The designed parameters include 19.2–20.3 mm focal lens, work distance from 250 mm to 450 mm, less than 0.5 % distortion, 2.8 working F number, 4 mm image diameter, 840 nm–870 nm wavelength of operating spectrum. At 166 lp/mm, the lens can acquire iris image over all field of view with MTF > 0.3. The lens is composed of fours spherical lenses and one liquid lens. Without moving parts inside, the structure of designed lens is simple and convenient to control.

Keywords: Iris recognition · Wide working range · Liquid lens

1 Introduction

Nowadays, iris recognition is becoming one of the most widely used technology at security industry. Compared to other biometric modalities, iris has characteristics of stability, uniqueness and contactless use. While the commonly deployed prime lens for iris recognition has narrow depth of field [1, 2]. Three solutions are proposed by researchers to solve this problem.

The first scheme is to reduce the resolution using modified blur algorithm with prime lens. This method is introduced in Chinese patent CN201110366654. The shortcoming of this scheme is obvious. While blurred iris images can make the depth of field broaden ostensibly, iris image quality decreases dramatically. While products from this approach are flexible and efficient of use, however their safety is seriously compromised.

The second scheme is using a combination of several prime lens. An iris lens with wide operating distance can compose of several prime lens with different work distance, as the patent CN200610113410 represents. Certainty, this kind of wide operating range device can obtain good iris images, but it has large volume and needs more response time to combine iris images together.

© Springer International Publishing AG 2016
Z. You et al. (Eds.): CCBR 2016, LNCS 9967, pp. 339–348, 2016.
DOI: 10.1007/978-3-319-46654-5_37

The third way to solve the problem is using zoom lens substituted for prime lens. It is convenient to use but difficult to acquire high definition iris image. Besides, zoom lens is hard for design and production. In order to zoom, image quality must be reduced at different focal length. And zoom lens needs a complicated mechanical structure to adjust lenses with motor or manual control.

A novel solution to extending the working range is presented in this paper. This paper presents an lens with liquid lens to gain wide working range for iris recognition which allows variable focus by changing the curvature of the single liquid lens surface.

2   The Optical Properties of Iris

2.1   Optical Principle of the Lens System

A ray model is built by geometrical optics which demonstrates the imaging procedure of lens from object plane to image plane [3]. The lens system is shown in Fig. 1 where y, $-x-f$, $f'+x'$, f' and $-y'$ is respectively the object height, object distance, image distance, focal length and image height. The relationship between them could be described by Newton formula [3]:

$$l = -x - f. \tag{1}$$

$$-f = f'. \tag{2}$$

$$y/y' = (l - f)/f. \tag{3}$$

$$f = l/[(y/y') + l]. \tag{4}$$

2.2   Depth of Field

From geometrical optics, depth of field (DoF) can be calculated by

$$DoF = 2f^2 F\delta l^2/(f^4 - F^2\delta^2 l^2). \tag{5}$$

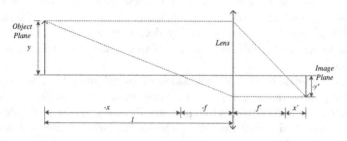

Fig. 1. Optical principle of the lens system.

Where l is object distance, F is lens F number, δ is the subjective quantity circle of confusion, f is the focal length. Generally, δ is equal to 2 pixels. As an example of normal prime lens, focal length f is 20 mm, F is 2.8, l length is 300 mm, and δ is 6 μm, then $DoF = 7.56$ mm. This value of Dof is too small comparing with the object distance 300 mm. So, a conclusion could be draw that the normal prime iris lens is not good enough.

3   Requirements of a Wide Working Range Iris Lens

3.1   The International Standard for Iris Image

According to international standard ISO/IEC29794-6 [4] and the government standard GB/T20979-2007, the requirements of iris recognition image quality standard is shown as Table 1.

Table 1. Iris image quality standard.

Image quality standard	Evaluation value	Pixels across iris diameter	Conclusion
Poor	0–25	50–100	Unacceptable
Low	26–50	100–149	Marginal
Medium	51–75	150–199	Acceptable
High	76–100	200 or more	Good

3.2   Illumination Requirements for Iris Recognition

Considering particularity of iris, the diffuse reflectivity of an iris connects with its albedo which is dependent on illumination wavelength. In NIR band of 700–850 nm illumination, the unique pattern of iris can be presented.

According to literature [2], the reflectivity and transmissivity of iris in different wavelength of illumination is shown in Table 2.

Table 2. The reflectivity and transmissivity of iris in different wavelength.

Wavelength (nm)	Reflectivity (%)	Transmissivity (%)	Absorptivity (%)	Absorption coefficient
440	8	4	88	2.75
488	17	20	63	1.25
632	19	24	57	1.07
749	28	40	31	0.45
850	34	48	16	0.22

According to the results given in Table 2, 850 nm wavelength has the highest reflectivity and the lowest absorption coefficient. So we choose a LED chip product with wavelength 850 nm span of 30 nm as the illumination to design iris system.

3.3   Appropriate CMOS Chip

In order to make iris recognition device small and compact, small size of CMOS is needed in iris recognition. So we select a 1/4 inch monochrome CMOS sensor with good quantum efficiency at 850 nm. Table 3 shows the key parameters [5].

Table 3. Key parameters of CMOS chip.

Parameters	Typical value
Optical format	1/4inch
Active pixels	1280 (H) × 800 (V)
Pixel size	3.0 μm × 3.0 μm

3.4   Parameters of Liquid Lens

Currently, wide working range of lens need the support of complicated mechanical structure. This paper describes a new method to gain wide working range of lens which uses a liquid lens. This liquid lens allows variable focus with absolutely no moving parts inside.

The operating principle is to change the curvature of single liquid lens surface with input voltage while the other surface of this liquid lens is not changed. As Fig. 2 shows, there are four surfaces in liquid lens. Surface1, Surface2 and Surface4 are fixed and the curvature of Surface3 can be changed by the value R with the switch of input voltage (V) and the distance between surface2 and surface3 (U) is changed at the same time.

The relationship between Voltage U and R is shown in Table 4.

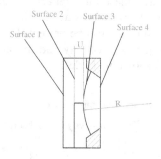

Fig. 2. The structure of the liquid lens.

3.5   Determination of Work Range Parameters

According to test, it is found that 250 mm–350 mm is the best operating range of object distance for single eye iris recognition. Too close work distance always gives the feeling of pressure and discomfort to user. Conversely, too far work distance is inconvenient to use. In our design, 250 mm–400 mm is the suitable work distance range.

Table 4. The relationship between Voltage, U, and R.

Voltage (V)	R (mm) example	Optical power (m^{-1})	U (mm)
29	−10.2	−10.7	1.43
30	−10.9	−10.0	1.42
31	−11.8	−9.3	1.41
32	−12.8	−8.5	1.39
33	−14.1	−7.8	1.38
34	−15.7	−7.0	1.37
35	−17.7	−6.2	1.35
36	−20.3	−5.4	1.34

4 Optical Lens Design

4.1 Design Requirements of Iris Lens

With above analysis, the design specification of wide working range iris lens can be obtained. According to literature [1], available high resolution iris cameras operate at approximately 30 cm and it could capture iris image at least 200 pixels across the iris diameter.

It is essential that at least 200 pixels are needed to cross an iris diameter at the farthest working distance 450 mm is to ensure the quality of iris image. The regular iris diameter is 12 mm. Suppose there are 200 pixels cross an iris diameter in object plane with working distance 450 mm, so y = 12/200 = 0.06 mm. The corresponding image plane y' equal to 0.003 mm (the pixels size). According to geometrical optics formulas (1)–(4), we can gain that the focal length of the appropriate is 21 mm. Then the design requirements of iris lens are shown in Table 5.

Table 5. Design requirements of iris lens.

Technical parameters	Target valve
Work distance	250 mm–400 mm
Focus length	20 mm ± 1 mm
Image diameter	4 mm
Wavelength	840 nm–870 nm
Distortion	<0.5 %
MTF/lp·mm^{-1}	166
F number	2.8

4.2 Structure Type of Iris Lens

According to literature [7], a three separation modified objective is selected as the initial structure. focal length of the objective is 100 mm and F number is 2.8. The structure of the initial structure is shown in Fig. 3.

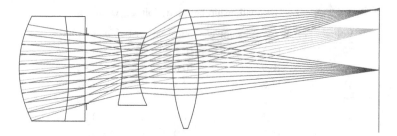

Fig. 3. The initial structure of three separation modified objective.

Next, scale the focal length to 20 mm and place the liquid lens behind the objective through optical design software. We should note that the structure of lens must be simple and each lens is suitable for production.

4.3   Optimization

Optical design software is used to optimize the initial structure of wide working distance iris lens which could adjust the distance between lens, specification of optical glass and radius of lens surface. Finally, a design with good image quality and wide working range of iris lens is given.

4.4   Optimized Results

In the final optimized design, iris lens with focus length of 19.26 mm–20.37 mm meets the wide working range requirement of 250 mm to 450 mm. Figure 4 shows a design of wide working distance of iris lens in preview. From Fig. 4, it is found that the lens has a wide object distance. And Fig. 5 shows the detail structure of the lens elements. From Fig. 5, we can see this iris lens is composed of four simple spherical lenses and one liquid lens.

Figures 6 and 7 show that this lens can acquire good image quality with all field of view at working distance of 250 mm and 450 mm. The spot diagram shows that RMS radius are less than the size of a CMOS pixel, so it perfectly matches the CMOS resolution. At 166lp/mm, over all field of view, the valve of MTF > 0.3. And the distortion is less than 0.5 %. All these parameters meet the design requirements.

4.5   Prototype Performance

With deliberate consideration in design, the iris lens prototype shows excellent performance. The prototype is shown in Fig. 8. The focal length of lens is 19.26 mm at 250 mm working distance and 20.37 mm at 450 mm working distance.

By inversely calculating the number of pixels across iris diameter with formula (1)–(4), the iris diameters are respectively 334 pixels at 250 mm working distance and 190

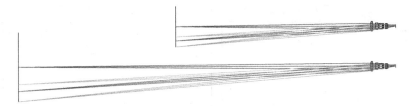

Fig. 4. The preview of nearest and farthest working distance.

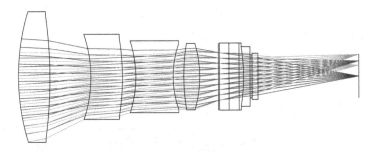

Fig. 5. The detail structure of designed iris lens.

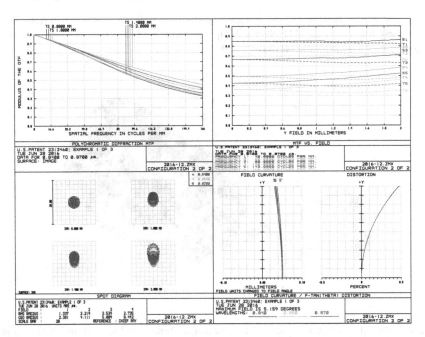

Fig. 6. The optical aberration chart at working distance of 250 mm. From left to right, up to bottom, these four charts are MTF chart at 166lp/mm, MTF chart with all field from 40lp/mm to 166lp/mm, spot diagram, field curvature and distortion.

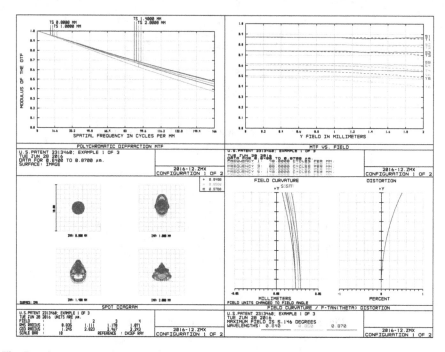

Fig. 7. The optical aberration chart at working distance of 450 mm. From left to right, up to bottom, these four charts are MTF chart at 166lp/mm, MTF chart with all field from 40lp/mm to 166lp/mm, spot diagram, field curvature and distortion.

Fig. 8. The iris lens prototype.

pixels at 450 mm. Then iris pictures in working distance of 250 mm and 450 mm are shown in Fig. 9.

From Fig. 10, there are 330 pixels across iris image at 250 mm working distance and 193 pixels at 450 mm by Windows Paint software testing. The results meet design requirements.

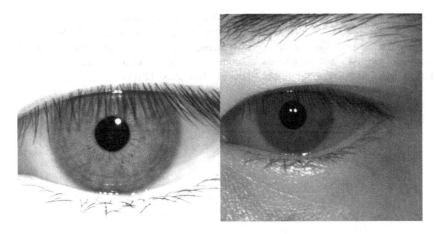

Fig. 9. The iris images are obtained with designed wide working range iris lens. The left one with working distance of 250 mm and the right one with working distance of 450 mm.

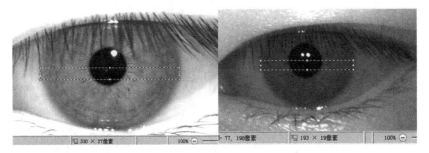

Fig. 10. The number of pixels across in iris. The left one is 330 pixels and the right one is 193 pixels.

5 Conclusion

This paper presents a lens with liquid lens for iris recognition. Without moving parts, this lens has a focal length of 19.26 mm–20.37 mm and a working range from 250 mm to 450 mm. The lens can match 1/4 inch CMOS image sensor perfectly and can produce pictures with high resolution. This lens has a very compact mechanical structure and easy to assemble. Besides iris recognition, this lens also has great market potential for machine vision.

References

1. Burge, M.J., Bowyer, K.W. (eds.): Handbook of Iris Recognition. Springer, London (2013)
2. Sachin, G., Chander, K.: Iris recognition: the safest biometrics. Int. J. Eng. Sci. **4**, 265–273 (2011)

3. Yu, D., Tan, H.: Engineering Optics. China Machine Press (2006)
4. Iris Image Quality Standard, SC 37 N 3331. ISO/IEC 29794-6 Annex A (2009)
5. 1/4-Inch Digital Image Sensor. http://www.onsemi.cn/pub_link/Collateral/AR0141CS-D.PDF
6. Varioptic-ARCTIC 39N. http://www.varioptic.com/products/variable-focus/arctic-39n/
7. Laikin, M.: Lens Design, Forth edn. China Machine Press (2011)

Iris Image Quality Assessment Based on Saliency Detection

Xiaonan Liu[1]([⊠]), Yuwen Luo[1], Silu Yin[1], and Shan Gao[2]

[1] Computer Vision Group, Shenyang University of Technology, No. 111,
Shenliao West Road, Economic and Technological Development Zone,
Shenyang 110870, People's Republic of China
april05_liu@126.com
[2] Yixun Technology Co. Ltd., No. 16, Zhuke Street, HunNan District, Shenyang
110168, People's Republic of China

Abstract. There are few restrictions in the image capture of mobile iris recognition, so the iris texture is easily interfered and the images may fail to meet the requirements of the identification. If the quality of captured iris images can be pre-evaluated, the unrecognizable iris images could be removed, which can reduce the operational burden and be more efficient. Therefore, an approach for iris image quality assessment based on saliency detection is proposed in this paper. First, Frequency-tuned (FT) method is used to detect image salient regions, then the binary image is obtained by segmenting saliency maps with threshold, and finally the image quality is evaluated according to the shape characteristics of the connected regions in binary images. As the results shown, the proposed method is capable of evaluating the image quality under the ideal and disturbing conditions, and removing the unrecognizable iris images because of the interference.

Keywords: Quality assessment · Frequency-tuned · Saliency detection · Mobile iris recognition

1 Introduction

Mobile iris recognition is an iris recognition technology applied in intelligent mobile devices. Image acquisition of mobile iris recognition is achieved by non-professionals using intelligent device with visible light camera. Therefore, the changes of illumination and other factors are not constant, which will result in a series of interference such as illumination variation, defocus, squint, eye close, occlusion, etc. These interference make pre-processing and iris texture feature extraction difficult and the accuracy of identification is influenced. It might even lead directly to the failure of the identification when the interference is serious.

At present, in the field of pre-processing of the iris image, scholars have carried out a lot of researches aimed at iris location under non-ideal conditions, including an analysis method based on color composition [1, 2], method based on SVM [3], gradually accurate localization [4], the normalization of edge [5], positioning method combining clustering algorithm and CHT [6] and so on. In recent years, a watershed-based

© Springer International Publishing AG 2016
Z. You et al. (Eds.): CCBR 2016, LNCS 9967, pp. 349–356, 2016.
DOI: 10.1007/978-3-319-46654-5_38

approach [7] and texture classification based on SVM [8] specifically for the acquisition conditions of mobile devices have been proposed. All the methods mentioned above are basically followed the traditional methods of iris recognition. It has never been discussed that whether the quality of the iris texture is able to meet the conditions of identification. If the quality of the iris texture can be assessed preliminarily, and the evaluation criteria measuring the quality of iris texture can be established. It can remove the images whose qualities of the texture are not qualified, and it can remind the collectors of recapture, which will improve the efficiency of the mobile iris recognition system.

Therefore, an approach for iris image quality assessment based on saliency detection is proposed in this paper. Frequency-tuned method is used for saliency detection towards the captured iris images. And the saliency map is segmented by threshold. Finally, it is determined whether the iris regions of the captured images have a good texture which can provide the information of the identity according to the shape feature of the salient region.

2 Visual Saliency and Quality of Iris Image

Visual saliency is the perceptual quality that makes an object, person, or pixel stand out relative to its neighbors and thus capture our attention [9]. The saliency calculation based on the mechanism of human visual perception models and quantizes the ability of the human visual attention. It forms a series of modeled analysis and calculation method which reveals the saliency of the image region [10]. The analysis of saliency has been widely applied to object detection and segmentation, image analysis and understanding, scene analysis and visual tracking. Since the detection of the image saliency is based on the focus-attention principle of human visual system, it can pick out the most concerned regions of the image.

Frequency-tuned salient region detection is a method based on the global contrast, which analyzes the image frequency [9]. It uses the low-frequency part of an image that includes the overall information of an image. FT method achieved good testing results in image retrieval [11], content-based target detection [12] and so on. Saliency map of original image can be obtained by using FT method to detect the salient regions of image. In the saliency map, the brightness of the pixels represents the value of its saliency, and the brighter it is, the more salient the pixel is. Consequently the concerned objects of the iris images can be highlighted by FT method.

For iris images captured by mobile intelligent devices, if the quality of the irises regions in this image are good, that means the most salient objects of the image must be the iris or pupil, as shown in Figs. 2(a) and 3(a). As the saliency maps show, the most attractive regions in the saliency map are the regions of the iris and eyebrow in Fig. 2(b), or the pupils and eyebrow in Fig. 3(b), while the visual attention of other regions are weak.

However, as for the iris images in some non-ideal conditions such as squint, occlusion, incorrect illumination, closed eyes, incorrect location of the camera in Fig. 4, the salient objects of these images are not irises or pupils. In Fig. 4(a), because of the squint, the salient object is the hair; In Fig. 4(b), the iris region is interfered by the specular reflection caused by eyeglasses, thus the iris is not the salient one. In Fig. 4 (c) and (d), due to the incorrect illumination, the face regions have the highest saliency. In Fig. 4(e), the salient region is the closed eye rather than the iris. In Fig. 4(f), the original image was taken in non-appropriate camera location, therefore salient region is the face.

To sum up, the content, illumination and texture of the image can be showed in the saliency map of iris image, so that the feature of iris region in that image can be obtained by analyzing the salient objects of the images. Based on the features, if the salient regions of the salient map are looked like the iris or pupil, this image may have an iris region in good quality. Otherwise, it may be disturbed by some kind of interference. Thus, the quality of the iris can be evaluated to determine whether it is a recognizable iris image.

3 The Proposed Method

Based on the relationship between the quality of iris images and the saliency of the objects, a method of iris image quality assessment based on FT salient region detection is proposed in this paper. Firstly, the salient region of iris image is detected by FT method. Secondly, the saliency map is binarized using automatic threshold. Then the shape of all the connected regions of the binary image is analyzed to determine whether there is a good iris region which satisfies the criteria of the iris recognition. Through the above steps, the quality of the captured iris image is evaluated to remove the iris image which can not satisfy the criteria of the iris texture feature extraction and identification due to the serious interference. Algorithm flow chart is shown in Fig. 1.

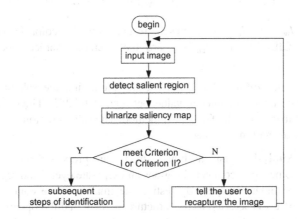

Fig. 1. Algorithm flow chart of the proposed method

Salient Region Detection. First, the Difference of Gaussian (DoG) filter is used to filter the value component of the input image. The DoG filter is defined as Eq. (1).

$$\text{DoG(x,y)} = \frac{1}{2\pi} \left[\frac{1}{\sigma_1^2} e^{-\frac{(x^2+y^2)}{2\sigma_1^2}} - \frac{1}{\sigma_2^2} e^{-\frac{(x^2+y^2)}{2\sigma_2^2}} \right] = G(x,y,\sigma_1) - G(x,y,\sigma_2) \quad (1)$$

A DoG filter is a simple band-pass Gaussian filter, and its pass-band width is controlled by the ratio σ_1/σ_2. Combine several narrow band-pass DoG filters as a DoG filter bank F_N.

$$F_N = \sum_{n=0}^{N-1} G(x,y,\rho^{n+1}\sigma) - G(x,y,\rho^n\sigma) = G(x,y,\rho^N\sigma) - G(x,y,\sigma) \quad (2)$$

In the Eq. (2), $\rho = \sigma_1/\sigma_2$, and when $\rho = 1.6$, a better result of the edge detection of the object can be achieved [13]. Gaussian filter is used with 3×3 window, its variance $\sigma = 0.5$. When $N = \infty$, $G(x,y,\rho^n\sigma)$ is actually the average vector of the entire image. So the saliency of the pixel p is:

$$S(p) = \left\| I_\mu - I_{w_{hc}}(p) \right\| \quad (3)$$

Where I_μ is the mean feature vector of the image, i.e. the color feature of CIELAB. $I_{w_{hc}}(p)$ is the color feature of CIELAB after the processing of the original image by Gaussian filter. $\|\cdot\|$ is L_2 norm, that is the Euclidean distance of all the components of I_μ and $I_{w_{hc}}(p)$ in the color space of CLELAB.

In order to calculate conveniently, $S(p)$ was calculated as followed Eq. (4).

$$S(p) = \left(I_{wl_{hc}}(p) - I_{\mu l} \right)^2 + \left(I_{wa_{hc}}(p) - I_{\mu a} \right)^2 + \left(I_{wb_{hc}}(p) - I_{\mu b} \right)^2 \quad (4)$$

Where $I_{wl_{hc}}(p)$, $I_{wa_{hc}}(p)$, $I_{wb_{hc}}(p)$ represent respectively the color feature of all the components of CIELAB; $I_{\mu l}$, $I_{\mu a}$, $I_{\mu b}$ are the average characteristics of all the components.

Saliency Map Binarization. To simplify calculation, first the salient value of the image are normalized to an integer value between 0 to 255. Then the normalized saliency map is binarized with OTSU [14] method. The salient regions of the image are the white region of the binary image.

Image Quality Analysis. First, the binary images are processed with opening operation to remove some small connected regions and separate eyelid and region of the iris and pupil in some binary images. By testing the images in the dataset, the circular structure with 6 pixels is selected as the structure element and the opening operation is executed for three times. Since all the iris regions of the image in the dataset are not in the boundary, the connected regions which in the boundary are removed.

And then, each connected regions are expressed by topology, and the area and circularity of the regions is selected as its shape descriptor. They are defined as Eqs. (5) and (6).

$$F = \|P_B\|^2 \Big/ 4\pi A_R \tag{5}$$

When the connected region is a circle, the value of F is 1, otherwise it is bigger than 1. The value of F will be the smallest when the region is a circle. In Eq. (5), A_R is the area of the connected region, P_B is the perimeter of the connected region, which are defined in Eqs. (6) and (7).

$$A_R = \sum_{(x,y)\in R} 1 \tag{6}$$

$$P_B = \sum_{i=1}^{N-1} Dis(p_i, p_{i+1}) \tag{7}$$

Where N is the number of pixel of the boundary; $\mathbf{p}_i = \{p_1, p_2, \cdots, p_N\}$ is the sequence of the pixel of the boundary; $Dis(\bullet)$ is the distance between two pixels.

By statistics of the images in the dataset, two criteria are defined to recognize the iris region based on the characteristics of iris. According to these two criteria, it could determine preliminarily whether there is an iris image region which can be used for the subsequent identification in the binary image.

Criterion I for a large number of iris images with good quality: The saliency of the iris and pupil is quite high in saliency maps of these images, and the binary images obtained by the opening operation present oval-like regions with great areas. Therefore, the criterion is $\{A_R > 12000, |F - 1| < 0.35\}$.

Criterion II for the iris images with highly salient pupil regions: The saliency of the pupil regions in these images is pretty high, and the binary images obtained by the opening operation present circle-like regions with smaller areas comparing with the areas of the iris. Therefore, the criterion is $\{4500 < A_R < 5500, |F - 1| < 0.18\}$.

4 Experiment and Analysis

In this paper, the algorithm has been tested by using some of the iris images in the mobile iris dataset MICHE, which were captured by iphone5.

There are 1262 iris color images captured by visual light in this dataset, including 16 or 20 left and right iris images respectively of 75 persons, which half of them were taken outside while the others were taken inside respectively. There are occlusion, specular reflection, uneven illumination, squint and other interference of iris images in the dataset, which include various disturbing conditions of image capture in the mobile iris recognition. In order to illustrate the applicability and effectiveness of the proposed method, the images with various types of interference are randomly selected to analyze the experiment results.

354 X. Liu et al.

4.1 Ideal Iris Image

The results under ideal conditions are showed in Figs. 2 and 3.

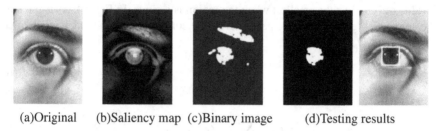

(a)Original   (b)Saliency map (c)Binary image   (d)Testing results

Fig. 2. The testing results based on the first criterion

The case showed in Fig. 2 meets the Criterion I. The most salient regions in this image are the regions of iris, pupil and eyebrow in Fig. 2(b). The testing results are obtained based on the Criterion I, which are showed in Fig. 2(d). (In order to highlight, the iris regions being recognized are marked by the enclosing rectangle, and the accurate iris can be located by more precise methods afterwards.)

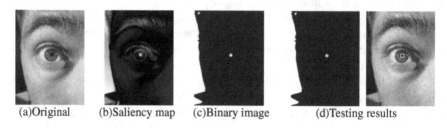

(a)Original   (b)Saliency map   (c)Binary image   (d)Testing results

Fig. 3. The testing results based on the second criterion

The case showed in Fig. 3 meets the Criterion II. As shown in the Fig. 3(b), the saliency of the pupil region is higher than the saliency of any other regions, and such region in the binary image is very close to a circle. The testing results are showed in Fig. 3(d).

Therefore, these two criteria are both able to get the ideal testing results based on the ideal images with good quality. As the results show, the proposed method is capable of evaluating the quality of the images under the ideal conditions.

4.2 Disturbing Iris Image

The results under non-ideal disturbing conditions are showed in Fig. 4.

Under these disturbing conditions, the iris texture failed to meet the criteria of identification due to the serious interference. The irises are not the salient objects in any the above saliency maps. The segmented salient regions in the binary images cannot match the proposed criteria, and the iris regions fail to be detected. Therefore, the proposed method is also capable of evaluating the quality of the image under the disturbing conditions.

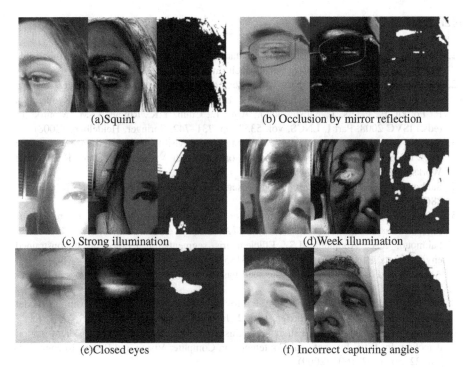

(a)Squint

(b) Occlusion by mirror reflection

(c) Strong illumination

(d)Week illumination

(e)Closed eyes

(f) Incorrect capturing angles

Fig. 4. Interfered images

5   Conclusions

An approach for iris image quality assessment applied to mobile iris recognition is proposed in this paper. It is capable of detecting the quality of the iris texture and picking out the iris images which can be used for subsequent identification. First, the saliency map of the iris image is calculated with FT method; then, the quality of the iris region us evaluated based on the saliency map of the iris image and the shape of the salient region. With the criteria proposed, the iris image is assessed to determine whether it could be used for identification. If the image cannot meet the criteria, it will be removed and the user will be reminded of recapture. The experimental results show that the salient region of the iris image can be correctly detected by FT and the criteria proposed are able to classify the ideal and disturbing iris images. With this method, the iris texture quality is assessed correctly and efficiently. By this kind of assessment, the efficiency of the whole system can be improved and the burden of the intelligent mobile devices can be reduced.

Acknowledgment.   All the images are from the dataset MICHE, all rights reserved.

References

1. Proenca, H.: Iris recognition: on the segmentation of degraded images acquired in the visible wavelength. IEEE Trans. Pattern Anal. Mach. Intell. **32**(8), 502–1516 (2010)
2. Proença, H.: Iris recognition: a method to segment visible wavelength iris images acquired on-the-move and at-a-distance. In: Bebis, G., Boyle, R., Parvin, B., Koracin, D., Remagnino, P., Porikli, F., Peters, J., Klosowski, J., Arns, L., Chun, Y.K., Rhyne, T.-M., Monroe, L. (eds.) ISVC 2008, Part I. LNCS, vol. 5358, pp. 731–742. Springer, Heidelberg (2008)
3. Tan, K.: Automated segmentation of iris images using visible wave-length face images. In: 2011 IEEE Computer Society Conference on Computer Vision and Pattern Recognition Workshops (CVPRW), pp. 9–14 (2011)
4. Sankowski, G.: Reliable algorithm for iris segmentation in eye image. Image Vis. Comput. **28**(2), 231–237 (2010)
5. Labati, R., Scotti, F.: Noisy iris segmentation with boundary regularization and reflections removal. Image Vis. Comput. **28**(2), 270–277 (2010)
6. Sahmoud, S.A., Abuhaiba, I.S.: Efficient iris segmentation method in unconstrained environments. Pattern Recogn. **46**, 3174–3185 (2013)
7. Abate, A.F., Frucci, M.: BIRD: watershed based iris detection for mobile devices. Pattern Recogn. Lett. **11**, 1–9 (2014)
8. Hu, Y., Sirlantzis, K., Howells, G.: Improving color iris segmentation using a model selection technique. Pattern Recogn. Lett. **2**, 1–9 (2015)
9. Achanta, R., Hemami, S., Estrada, F., Susstrunk, S.: Frequency-tuned salient region detection. In: IEEE International Conference on Computer Vision and Pattern Recognition, vol. 22, pp. 1597–1604 (2009)
10. Cheng, M.-M., Zhang, G.-X.: Global contrast based salient region detection. Comput. Vis. Pattern Recogn. **37**, 409–416 (2011)
11. Liu, Y., Li, X.Q., Wang, L., Niu, Y.Z.: Interpolation-tuned salient region detection. Sci. China Inf. Sci. **57**(1), 1–9 (2013)
12. Chen, Z., Xiong, S., Mao, Q., Fang, Z., Yu, X.: An improved saliency detection approach for Flying Apsaras in the Dunhuang Grotto Murals, China. Adv. Multimedia, 1–11 (2015)
13. Marr, D.: Vision: A Computational Investigation into the Human Representation and Processing of Visual Information. W. H. Freeman, San Francisco (1982)
14. Otsu, N.: A threshold selection method from gray-level histograms. IEEE Trans. Syst. Man Cybern. **9**(1), 62–66 (1979)

An Accurate Iris Segmentation Method Based on Union-Find-Set

Lijun Zhu[1,2(✉)] and Weiqi Yuan[1]

[1] School of Information Science and Engineering, Shenyang University of Technology, Shenyang, China
zhulijun@yeah.net
[2] School of Computer Science and Technology, Shenyang University of Chemical Technology, Shenyang, China

Abstract. Iris segmentation is one of the most important steps in iris recognition system, many existing localization methods model the iris outer boundary by a circle. However the iris outer boundary are not a circle in case of partially opened eye image. In this paper, we propose a method based on Union-Find-Set to extract the accurate iris boundary. The proposed method have been tested on the a visible light iris database captured by our own laboratory. The experimental results show that the proposed method outperforms the state-of-the-art method not only on localization accuracy rate but also on localization speed.

Keywords: Iris segmentation · Union-Find-Set · Level set · Inner boundary · Outer boundary

1 Introduction

In the last two decades, biometric techniques is becoming more and more popular. The practice have proved that many physical traits like face, fingerprint, iris, palm print, hand geometry and ear shape tend to change very little throughout the individual's life and can be applied to person identification and verification [1]. Among all of the mentioned biometric traits, iris is considered to be the most reliable, stable, and unique biometric trait [2].

Generally, the premise of ensuring the accuracy of iris recognition is ensuring the accuracy of iris location and segmentation. Iris segmentation deals with isolation of the iris from other parts of an eye like pupil, sclera, surrounding skin, eyelashes, and eyebrows [3]. Generally, the methods proposed for iris segmentation can be divided into two major categories. The first category is to model the iris by two circles, where iris and parts of eyelid are all extracted in case of partially opened eye. And the second category can isolate the iris without including any eyelids.

In this paper, a Union-Find-Set based iris segmentation method has been proposed. The proposed method starts by implementing Union-Find-Set to obtain a coarse segmentation result of iris and then eliminating the flaws that lies in the coarse segmentation result. At last, a final boundary of iris is obtained in the predefined region.

© Springer International Publishing AG 2016
Z. You et al. (Eds.): CCBR 2016, LNCS 9967, pp. 357–365, 2016.
DOI: 10.1007/978-3-319-46654-5_39

Rest of the paper is organized as follows. Section 2 introduces the background and the related work. Section 3 presents the process of accurate Iris segmentation based on Union-Find-Set. Section 4 exhibits the experimental results. Section 5 explains the limitations of the proposed method. Finally, conclusions are presented in the last section of this paper.

2   Background and Related Work

Generally, circle is used to model the iris by first finding the iris center and then fitting a circle to localize the iris. A circle-based method was proposed by Daugman [2, 4] to estimate the outer boundaries of the iris, where an Integro-differential operator was applied to estimate the three parameters (x,y,r), where (x,y) is the center of a circle, r is the radius of the circle. To high quality iris image, this method is effective, but its performance degrades in case of low contrast images and specular reflection.

Wildes [5] presents a two-stage iris localization method. In the first stage, the image was binarized to binary edge maps while in the second stage, votes were casted for the parameters of the circle. Ma et al. [6, 7] first localizes the center of the pupil by projecting the iris image in horizontal and vertical directions, then the canny edge detector was used in conjunction with the Hough transform to detect the inner and outer boundaries of the iris.

In [8], For determining the outer boundary of the iris, three points were detected, which represented the three vertices of a triangle inscribed in a circumference. [9] proposed a thresholding based method to locate the inner boundary of the iris, and Geodesic active contours were used to find the outer boundary of the iris. In [10], Hough transform along with active contours were used to locate the iris.

The methods above mentioned are effective in high quality iris image, but theirs performance degrades in case of partially opened eye image. In resent years, in order to extract outer boundary of the iris without involving eyelids, Level Set based methods [11–14] have been applied to localize the iris, where the method is demonstrated to be very effective not only to blurred image but also to the image with noise. However, it's performance degrades to the image having uneven grey level, and the result of localization can be affected by the setting of initial contour, furthermore this method is very time consuming.

In this paper, a new two stages segmentation method of outer boundary of iris has been proposed. In the first stage, the outer boundary of iris is modeled by a circle. In the second stage, a method based on Union-Find-Set is used to obtain the final outer boundary of iris.

3   Iris Segmentation Based on Union-Find-Set

3.1   Definition of the Union-Find-Set

In some practical application, if there exist some relations between different elements in a Set, then it is usually necessary to divide this Set into several disjoint subsets. One solution to this kind of problem is first to let each element form an independent set, if there is a direct or indirect connection between the elements in different sets, then these two sets will be merged. The process is repeated until there is not a relation between elements in a different Set. Because this kind of problem is mainly related to 'union' and 'find' two operations, accordingly, the name of it is call Union-Find-Set. Suppose $S = \{A,B,C,...\}$ represents a number of mutually disjoint dynamic sets, which support the following operations:

1. *Initial(A,x)*: construct a Set A, which only have one element x.
2. *Merge(A,B)*: merge Set A and B and select A or B as the label of the sub-set.
3. *Find(x)*: Find the Set to which the element x belong and return the label of the Set.

The Union-Find-Set is performed as follows:

(1) By *initial(A,x)*, construct a Set for every element.
(2) For each associated elements(x,y), By *Find(x)*, find the corresponding Sets S_1 and S_2 in which element x,y lie, separately.
(3) If S_1 is different with S_2, then the two Sets will be merged.
(4) Move to (2), until all the associated elements are dealt with.

In order to improve the executing efficiency of Union-Find-Set, tree is applied to carry out this algorithm. The tree root is considered as a label to represent a subset which is composed of all the elements in the tree. Any two elements in a tree have a direct or indirect relation, while any two elements in different trees don't have a direct or indirect relation. When merging two trees, we first find the root of each tree, then take one tree as a sub-tree of the other tree.

For example, suppose $Set = \{1,2,3,4,5,6,7,8,9,10\}$, the couple of associated elements include $\{5,1\}$, $\{7,4\}$, $\{10,4\}$, $\{4,2\}$, $\{6,3\}$, $\{8,3\}$, $\{9,3\}$. Figure 1 is the result of *Initial(A,x)*. The first row represents all the elements in the *Set*, while the second row represents the labels of the *Set* to which the element belong. In the beginning, the *Set* only have one element, so the label of the *Set* related is just the element itself. Figure 2 is the final result, it can be observed that the quantity that the element is the same with the label of corresponding *Set* is the final amount of sub-sets obtained by the proposed method. The sub-trees correspond to the subsets is shown in Fig. 3.

i	1	2	3	4	5	6	7	8	9	10
Set(i)	1	2	3	4	5	6	7	8	9	10

Fig. 1. Initial result of Union-Find-Set

i	1	2	3	4	5	6	7	8	9	10
Set(i)	1	2	3	2	1	3	4	3	3	4

Fig. 2. Processing results of Union-Find-Set

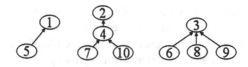

Fig. 3. Sub-trees corresponding to the subset

3.2   Determination of Iris Extracting Region

The iris images that we prepare to deal with are the kind of iris images in which the iris have been modeled by circles accurately, as shown in Fig. 4. On this basis, our task in this paper is to extract the accurate iris outer boundary Regardless of whether the iris boundary is covered by eyelids or not. In order to reduce the effect of other parts of an eye like pupil, sclera, surrounding skin, eyelashes and eyebrows, we take the circumscribed square of the outer circle as the iris extracting area (*IEA*) as shown in Fig. 5, and all the portion of the eye image beyond the square region will be neglected.

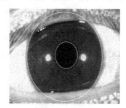

Fig. 4. The iris modeled by two circles

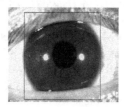

Fig. 5. The determination of iris extracting region

3.3   Iris Coarse Segmentation Based on Union-Find-Set

Generally, it can be observed that the grey level corresponding to the pupil region tend to be less than that of the iris, while the grey level of iris is less than that of the sclera and eyelids, as shown in Fig. 1. If the grey level difference between two adjacent pixels i and j in iris image is less than a threshold k, then there is a correlation between them, which is denoted by $\{i,j\}$. On this basis, we can obtain many correlations from an iris image, after that, Union-Find-Set can be applied to divide the iris into many independent areas where the grey level difference of two adjacent pixels is less than a threshold k. It is believed that the area of the iris is large than that of other region like pupil, eyelid and scelar, so, the iris region can be found based on the size of area of different region acquired. As the effect of the specular reflection in visible light iris image, the iris region acquired tend to be a region with some flaws, as shown in Fig. 6, which can be considered as a result of iris coarse segmentation.

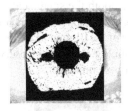

Fig. 6. The result of Union-Find-Set

3.4   Iris Fine Segmentation

By performing Union-Find-Set, we obtain a result of iris rough segmentation having some flaws which is made by specular reflections, pigments, freckles and crypts. In order to eliminate these flaws, we first use row-scanning and column-scanning method to fill these flaws, then a triangle is obtained to smooth the edge of the iris. The details are given below:

1. By scanning each horizontal line from up to down in IEA, we can obtain two white pixels that is the left most and the right most pixel on the iris in each row, and then draw a white line (the grey level is 255) to connect the two white pixels, by doing that, the black pixels (the grey level is 0) on the line will be replaced by white pixels. The above process is repeated row by row.
2. Each column is also dealt with in the same manner as step 1. Finally, all the black pixels within the iris will be filled by white pixels, as shown in Fig. 7.

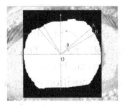

Fig. 7. The iris in which the flaw is eliminated

3. The value of θ is initialized to $5°$
4. The value of i is initialized to 1.
5. From the origin O(the center of the outer iris), we draw outwards two rays with the angle θ between them and two points of intersection of rays and the iris boundary can be obtained, denoted as A and B respectively, thus we get a triangle $\triangle OAB$, as shown in Fig. 7.
6. All grey levels of the pixels in $\triangle OAB$ are changed to 255.

7. By taking the point O as the origin, the $\triangle$OAB is rotated from 0° to i × θ anti-clockwise.
8. If i × θ is less than 360° then increase i by 1 and move to step 5.
9. If θ <=30° then increase θ by 5° and move to step 4.

The smaller angle is used to smooth the small scale variations, whereas the bigger angle is applied to obtain the practical shape of the iris. Figure 8 sows the final segmentation result. At last, the boundary of the iris can be extracted and mapped to the original iris image as shown in Fig. 8. From Fig. 9 it can be observed that the boundary obtained is mostly consistent with the real iris boundary.

Fig. 8. The iris dealt by smoothing

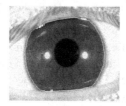

Fig. 9. The final iris boundary

4   Experimental Results

Experimental results are collected on a visible light iris database which contains 150 subjects with a resolution of 800 * 600 pixels. The database is captured by our own laboratory under the non-ideal imaging condition, so, the quality of the images acquired will be affected by specular reflection, position offset and low contrast. The computer configuration used by laboratory is as follows: the type of computer processor is Intel core i3, frequency is 2.53 GHz 2.53, memory is 2 G, operating system is Windows XP Professional 2002, development tool is Visual studio C++ 2010 and OpenCV 2.44. Empirically, the value of threshold k was set to 2.

In order to demonstrate the superiority of the proposed method, the iris segmentation method based on Level Set and our method have been tested on the whole database. We use the accuracy rate (*AR*) as a measure to evaluate the performance of the proposed method [3]. The *AR* is based on the accuracy error (*AE*), which is defined as

$$AE = \frac{|N_a - N_d|}{N_a} \times 100 \tag{1}$$

Where N_a and N_d are the number of actual and detected iris pixels lied in the iris region, respectively. If AE is less than 10 %, then the detected iris is considered as an iris that is segmented successfully. The AR is defined as follows:

$$AR = \frac{N_s}{N_t} \times 100 \tag{2}$$

where N_s is the total number of eye images in which the iris has been successfully segmented and N_t is the total number of images in the database.

The proposed method only take 2.65 s to implement an iris segmentation with an accuracy rate (AR) of 86 %, Table 1 show the comparison of the proposed method with the Level Set based method. Figure 10 shows some segmentation results: Fig. 10(a), (b), (c), (d) is the results by the Level Set based method, whereas Fig. 10(e), (f), (g), (h) is the results by our method. It can be observed that if the quality of iris image to be dealt with is ideal, then these two methods all can extract the accurate iris boundary. However, in case of non-ideal iris image, the phenomena of less and over segmentation will appear by the method based on the Level Set, as shown in Fig. 10(c), (d), while the proposed method still have a satisfactory segmentation results, as shown in Fig. 10(g), (h).

Table 1. Comparation with Level Set based methods

Location method	Accuracy rate (%)	Location time (s)
The method based on Level Set	76.0	16.14
The proposed method	86.0	2.65

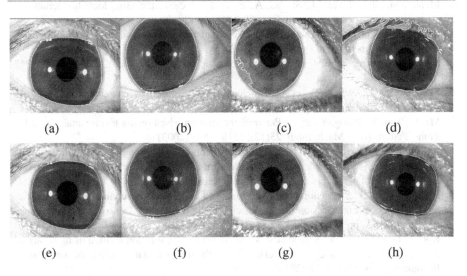

Fig. 10. Comparison of the proposed method with Level Set based. (a) ~ (d): iris segmentation by Level Set. (e) ~ (h):iris segmentation by the proposed method

5   Limitation of the Proposed Method

The proposed method fails to localize the outer boundary of the near infrared iris image, as the color of iris in such image is very similar with sclera, which will result in poor iris localization. Furthermore, the performance of this method degrades in case of the iris with dense eyelashes. To handle the above-mentioned limitation, the robustness of the method needs to be improved further.

6   Conclusion

In this paper, an iris outer boundary localization method has been proposed. In this method, the use of rectangular window helps to improve location accuracy of the iris outer boundary. Moreover, the use of Union-Find-Set helps in estimating the outer boundary of the iris in case of specular reflection and scattered eyelashes. Experimental results demonstrate the superiority of this method in this field of study.

Acknowledgements. The work was supported by the National Natural Science Foundation of China under Grant 61271365.

References

1. Jain, A., Ross, A., Prabhakar, S.: An introduction to biometric recognition. IEEE Trans. Circuits Syst. Video Technol. **14**(1), 4–20 (2004)
2. Daugman, J.: High confidence visual recognition of person by a test of statistical independence. IEEE Trans. Pattern Anal. Mach. Intell. **1115**, 1148–1161 (1993)
3. Muhammad, T.I., Tarid, M., Shahid, A., et al.: Iris localization using local histogram and other image statistics. Opt. Lasers Eng. **50**, 645–654 (2012)
4. Daugman, J.: The importance of being random: statistical principles of iris recognition. IEEE Trans. Pattern Recogn. **36**(2), 279–291 (2003)
5. Wildes, R.: Iris recognition: an emerging biometric technology. Proc. IEEE **85**, 1348–1363 (1997)
6. Ma, L., Tan, T., Wand, Y., et al.: Efficient iris recognition by characterizing key local variations. IEEE Trans. Image Process. **13**(6), 739–750 (2004)
7. Ma, L., Tan, T., Wang, Y., et al.: Personal recognition based on iris texture analysis. IEEE Trans. Pattern Anal. Mach. Intell. **25**(12), 1519–1533 (2003)
8. Rodríguez, J.L.G., Rubio, Y.D.: A new method for iris pupil contour delimitation and its application in iris texture parameter estimation. In: Sanfeliu, A., Cortés, M.L. (eds.) CIARP 2005. LNCS, vol. 3773, pp. 631–641. Springer, Heidelberg (2005)
9. Ross, A., Shah, S.: Segmenting non-ideal iris using geodesic active contours. In: Biometrics Symposium: Special Session on Research at the Biometric Consortium Conference, Baltimore, USA, pp. 1–6 (2006)
10. Koh, J., Govindaraju, V., Chaudhary, V.: A robust iris localization method using an active contour model and hough transform. In: 20th International Conference on Pattern Recognition, pp. 2852–2856 (2010)
11. Chen, R., Lin, X.R., Ding, T.H.: Iris segmentation for non-cooperative recognition system. IET Image Process. **5**(5), 448–456 (2011)

12. Ror, K., Bhattacharya, P., Suen, C.Y.: Iris segmentation using variational level set method. Opt. Laser Eng. **49**(4), 578–588 (2011)
13. Roy, K., Bhattacharya, P., Suen, C.Y.: Towards nonideal iris recognition based on level set method, genetic algorithms and adaptive asymmetrical SVMs. Eng. Appl. Artif. Intell. **24**(3), 458–475 (2011)
14. Connor, B.O., Roy, K.: Iris recognition using level set and local binary pattern. Int. J. Comput. Theor. Eng. **6**(5), 416–420 (2014)

Combining Multiple Color Components for Efficient Visible Spectral Iris Localization

Xue Wang, Yuqing He[(✉)], Kuo Pei, Mengmeng Liang, and Jingxi He

Key Laboratory of Photoelectronic Imaging Tehcnology and System,
Ministry of Education of China, School of Optoelectronics, Beijing Institute of Technology,
Beijing 100081, China
yuqinghe@bit.edu.cn

Abstract. Iris localization is the prerequisite for the precise iris recognition. Compared with near-infrared iris images, the visible spectral iris images may have more fuzzy boundaries, which impair the iris detection. We can use multiple color components of different color spaces to realize the visible spectral iris localization. Firstly, the sclera is segmented and eyelids are located on α component image through contrast adjustment and polynomial fitting. Secondly, morphological processing and CHT (Circular Hough Transform) is applied to localize the limbic boundary on R component image. Similarly, the pupillary boundary is localized on R component image and α component image. Experimental results on visible spectral iris image dataset indicate that the proposed method has good performance on iris localization.

Keywords: Color component · Visible spectral iris image localization · CHT

1 Introduction

The iris is one of the most reliable biometrics for individual recognition because of its rich textural details such as furrows, collarette, freckles, and crypts. A typical iris recognition system comprises preprocessing, iris localization, feature extraction and matching. The incorrect iris localization will affect the feature extraction and recognition accuracy.

The iris localization in visible spectrum has more difficulties due to some factors such as light reflection and fuzzy boundary. In order to solve this problem, many methods have been proposed for unconstrained visible spectral iris segmentation such as knowledge-based approach [1], grow cut based algorithm [2] and classifier based methods [3, 4]. Tan et al. [5] used clustering for iris localization followed with prediction and curvature models for eyelid and eyelash detection. Other methods [6, 7] based on clustering are also put forward successively. Wojciech Sankowski [8] and Yu Chen [9] determined the threshold in YIQ and HIS color space respectively, and localized iris boundaries through Daugman's operator. Abduljalil Radman et al. [10] utilized Circular Gabor Filters to get the pupil center roughly and localized the iris (pupil) boundary by optimization process. Michal Haindl et al. [11] put forward to apply Hough transform and Integro-diff operator to detect the pupil, and removed the eyelids and reflection by

© Springer International Publishing AG 2016
Z. You et al. (Eds.): CCBR 2016, LNCS 9967, pp. 366–373, 2016.
DOI: 10.1007/978-3-319-46654-5_40

adaptive thresholding in normalized iris. Yang Hu et al. [12] located the iris region by a coarse iris map based on the correlation histogram of super-pixels and combined three individual models with Daugman's integro-differential operator to localize iris boundary. It turned out that these algorithms all have wonderful performance on visible spectral iris localization. However the problem of incorrect iris segmentation still exist. Consqunetly, it is necessary to design a robust segmentation algorithm for iris images.

Here, we proposed an efficient visible spectral iris localization method through multiple color components of different color spaces. α component and R component iris images are used to localize the sclera region, limbic boundary and pupillary boundary.

The rest of paper is organized as follows. In Sect. 2, the features of different color components are analyzed for iris localization. In Sect. 3, we introduce the proposed method for iris localization. In Sect. 4, different localization methods are compared and the experimental results are described. Finally, some conclusions are drawn in Sect. 5.

2   Color Component Analysis for Iris Localization

Most of the digital images are stored in RGB color space, from which other models such as HSI and $l\alpha\beta$ can be converted. For HSI color space, H, S, I stands for hue, saturation and luminance respectively. H relates to the wavelength of light, S represents the color depth, and I represents luminance. For $l\alpha\beta$ color space, l stands for luminance, α represents yellow and blue components, and β represents red and green components.

The iris image in RGB and $l\alpha\beta$ color spaces have a certain difference which is shown in Fig. 1. The R component iris image has the minimum noise, the obvious limbic boundaries and the prominent reflected light. The α component iris image has clear sclera boundary. In addition, both of them have more clear pupillary boundaries. However, it's obvious that some iris images have different pupillary boundary definition in R component and α component. As is shown in Fig. 2, for color iris image Fig. 2(a), the pupillary boundary in R component is more obvious than α component. While for color iris image Fig. 2(d), the pupillary boundary in α component is more distinct. Accordingly, the limbic boundary can be localized on the R component iris image. And the R component combined with α component is used to localize pupillary boundary. In addition, the α component iris image can be utilized to segment sclera region.

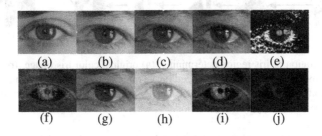

Fig. 1. Iris image in different color components. (a) Original image; (b) R component image; (c) G component image; (d) B component image; (e) H component image; (f) S component image; (g) I component image; (h) l component image; (i) α component image; (j) β component image.

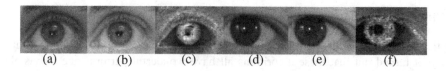

Fig. 2. Comparison of definition between R component iris image and α component iris image for different color iris image. (a) A color iris image; (b) the R component iris image of (a); (c) the α component iris image of (a); (d) another color iris image; (e) the R component iris image of (d); (f) the α component iris image of (d).

3   Multiple Color Component Based Iris Localization

The proposed iris segmentation scheme comprises three major steps: (1) determining iris region: sclera segmentation and eyelids localization based on polynomial fitting on the α component image; (2) limbic boundary localization: morphological processing and CHT are applied on R component iris image; (3) pupillary boundary localization: using morphological processing and CHT combining R component iris image with α component iris image.

3.1   Determining Iris Region

Unconstrained visible spectral iris images usually contain some noise generated by eyelids, eyebrows, skin, etc. Those noise is one of the most predominant sources of incorrect segmentation. As a result, excluding the non-iris regions before the iris segmentation step will be of great help to avoid such segmentation errors. The processing of determining the iris region is explained in Fig. 3.

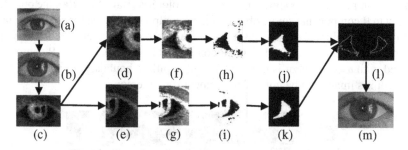

Fig. 3. An illustration of iris region determining. (a) original color iris image; (b) cropped iris image; (c) α component iris image; (d) cropped image on the left; (e) cropped image on the right; (f)(g) iris image after contrast adjustment; (h)(i) binary image; (j)(k) sclera region; (l) canny edge detection; (m) the result of eyelids localization.

First, we employ the eye detector based on Haar cascade object detectors to eliminate the influence of the eyebrows. Figure 3(a) illustrates the input image and Fig. 3(b) depicts the detected eye region using the Haar cascade eye detector.

According to the analysis in the Sect. 2, the sclera region has lower pixel values on α component iris image. Therefore, after locating the eye region, we segment the sclera region and locate the eyelids to determine the iris region. The specific process is described as follow:

1. Crop image. The sclera exist difference between left and right on the α component. Therefore, the α component iris image is cropped into two blocks in horizontal direction for precise segmentation via setting threshold.
2. Conduct contrast adjustment on each block image respectively. For α component, pixels whose intensity value lies between a low threshold T_1 and a high threshold T_2 are mapped to [0, 1], and the remaining pixels are clipped. Setting m_r as the mean intensity value of the normalized red channel. We set T_1 and T_2 as follow:

$$T_1 = \begin{cases} 0 & \text{if } m_r < \sigma \\ m_r - \sigma & \text{if } m_r \geq \sigma \end{cases} \tag{1}$$

$$T_2 = \begin{cases} 2 * m_r & \text{if } m_r < \sigma \\ m_r + \sigma & \text{if } m_r \geq \sigma \end{cases} \tag{2}$$

where σ is a parameter set as 0.2. We found that σ is almost unaffected by image quality, and 0.2 has the best performance for contrast enhancement of sclera experimentally. Figure 3(f) and (g) are contrast adjusted images.
3. Binarization. Binarizing iris images with m_r.
4. Sclera segmentation. Morphological processing is used to segment the sclera region shown as Fig. 3(j) and (k).
5. Edge detection. Figure 3(j) and (k) are stitched together and a canny edge detector is used to get the sclera edge shown as Fig. 3(l).
6. Determining iris region. Localize the upper and lower eyelids by polynomial fitting. The result is shown in Fig. 3(m). Finally, the iris region between upper and lower eyelids is determined.

3.2 Limbic Boundary Localization

According to Sect. 2, we localize the limbic boundary on R component iris image, which is more sensitive to light. As described in Fig. 4, in order to eliminate the impact of the uneven illumination, we firstly adopt median filter on iris image. After filtering, iris image reconstruction based on the open and close operation is implemented to enhance the limbic border contrast. Then, we binarize the iris image via OTSU threshold and remove the eyelids using the method in Sect. 3.1. Finally, the eyeball region mask is segmented by a series of morphological processing.

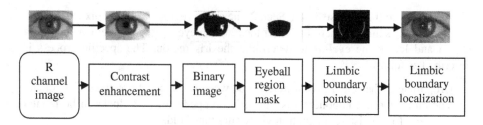

Fig. 4. The procedure of limbic boundary localization.

For the eyeball region mask, the rough iris center (x_{out}, y_{out}) can be determined. Then, canny edge detector is applied and the rough radius r_{out} is obtained by rough (x_{out}, y_{out}) and boundary points.

In the end, we apply CHT to get the precise limbic boundary parameters.

3.3 Pupillary Boundary Localization

Once the circular limbic region is extracted, the coarse pupillary region can be localized. Here, we combine the R component iris image with α component iris image to obtain the accurate pupillary boundary localization.

Depending on the exact positioning of the iris outer boundary, the R component iris image and the α component iris image are cropped. Next, we calculate S_R and S_α to represent the contrast between the pupil and the iris on the R component and α component iris images respectively. The higher contrast component is utilized to segment the pupil. According to the limbic position, we choose two blocks P and I with $M \times M$ pixels in pupil and iris region respectively. We assume that the radius of pupil is less than $\frac{1}{2}r_{out}$, and the center of pupil is same as the limbic center. Therefore, the block P is cropped below the limbic center, and the block I is cropped below the pupil, since those areas are experimentally determined to be the ones most unlikely to be affected by reflections or overlap with eyelids. The size of block has crucial impact on results. Overlarger block will contain reflections and boundary information, and undersized block cannot represent the average gray intensity sufficiently. Experimentally, M is set to $\frac{1}{10}r_{out}$. S_R and S_α are defined as follow:

$$S = \left| \left(\sum_{i=1}^{M^2} P_i - \sum_{j=1}^{M^2} I_j \right) \middle/ \left(\sum_{i=1}^{M^2} P_i + \sum_{j=1}^{M^2} I_j \right) \right| \tag{3}$$

where P_i is the i_{th} pixel in block P, I_j is the j_{th} pixel in block I.

Similarly to the procedure of limbic boundary localization, the pupillary boundary localization can be calculated through border contrast enhancement, edge detection and CHT. Figure 5 illustrates the procedure of the pupillary boundary localization.

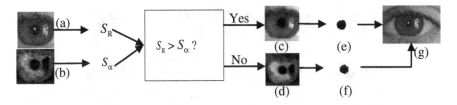

Fig. 5. Pupillary boundary location. (a) Cropped R component image; (b) cropped α component image; (c) R component image after open and close operation; (d) α component image after open and close operation; (e) segmented pupil on R component image; (f) segmented pupil on α channel component; (g) the result of pupillary boundary localization.

4 Experimental Results

4.1 Dataset

We test the proposed method on randomly selecting 200 images from UBIRIS.v1 (S1), UBIRIS.v1 (S2) and UBIRIS.v2 [13] respectively.

The iris images in UBIRIS.v2 dataset were actually captured on non-constrained conditions (at-a-distance, on-the-move and on the visible wavelength), with corresponding more realistic noise factors. The iris images are 300 × 400 pixels in size. The UBIRIS.v1 dataset contains eye images with 300 × 400 pixels in visible spectrum range captured in two distinct sessions.

In order to test the performance of the method, a mobile dataset includes 100 iris image from 10 persons captured by MEIZU4 pro mobile phone. These iris images are 780 × 1280 pixels in size.

4.2 Results and Comparison

We use MatlabR2013b as the simulation platforms to prove and analyze the method mentioned above. The hardware of experimental platform is configured with 2.1 GHz CPU frequency, 2 GB memory on PC. The Segmentation performance is evaluated by visual inspection of each image and its segmentation results are classified as either correct or incorrect. The accuracy of the proposed localization algorithm by ratio of correct number of iris localization to total images in database.

To make comparison with other color iris segmentation methods, we achieve the method in [7] (Sahmoud's method) and test it on UBIRIS.v2 dataset and the mobile dataset. This method apply K-means algorithm to determine the iris region, and localize limbic in Ycbcr color space by CHT. The pupillary boundary is localized by using contrast enhancement and CHT. Figure 6 shows the segmentation results by the proposed method and the Sahmoud's method. As a result, the illumination and defocus are of great significance in incorrect iris localization. And we also find that the proposed method has better performance, especially for pupillary boundary localization.

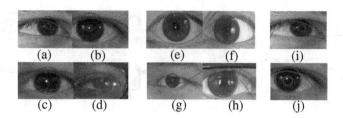

Fig. 6. The segmentation result. (a, b) Correct segmentation on UBIRIS.v2 dataset by the proposed method; (c, d) incorrect segmentation on UBIRIS.v2 dataset by the proposed method; (e, f) correct localization on mobile dataset by the proposed method; (g, h) incorrect localization on mobile by the proposed method; (i, j) the segmentation results by Sahmoud's method for the same original iris images as (a, b).

The segmentation accuracy for the proposed and existing methods are presented in Table 1. The segmentation accuracy results on UBIRIS.v1 (S1) for the four comparison methods in Table 1 are obtained from [7]. Obviously, the proposed method has higher accuracy for iris segmentation. And the Sahmoud's method has the shorter execution time due to scaling the image before CHT. In addition, we also test the execution time of the proposed method after scaling the image by factor of 0.5. While the precision remains, the execution time decrease from 3.276 s to 0.708 s which is shorter than Sahmoud's. The results show that the proposed method also has certain advantage in time.

Table 1. Comparison between the accuracy of the proposed method and some previous method on different datasets.

Method	Accuracy (%)				Average time(s)
	UBIRIS.v1 (S1)	UBIRIS.v1 (S2)	UBIRIS.v2	Mobile dataset	
Daugman	95.22	88.23	–	–	
Martin-Roche et al.	77.18	71.19	–	–	
Camus and Wildes	96.78	89.29	–	–	
Sahmoud	98.76	–	87.5	91	2.968
Proposed method	99	96.5	92.5	95	3.276

5 Conclusion

In this paper, a visible spectral iris localization algorithm based on multiple color channels is proposed. The method combines different color channels of iris image to achieve precise iris image localization. It is verified on UBIRIS dataset and a mobile dataset. Experiment results show that the method can achieve good performance on iris image localization. However, the unconstrained iris segmentation in visible spectral still remains uncertain and is likely to lead to error in localization, as shown in Fig. 6. Future work may utilize other algorithms taking place of the CHT and combine other color components for the higher accuracy visible spectral iris localization.

Acknowledgments. This work is supported by National Science Foundation of China (No. 60905012, 60572058) and International Fund of Beijing Institute of Technology.

References

1. Almeida, P.D.: A knowledge-based approach to the iris segmentation problem. J. Image Vis. Comput. **28**(2), 238–245 (2010)
2. Tan, C., Kumar, A.: Efficient iris segmentation using grow-cut algorithm for remotely acquired iris images. In: IEEE International Conference on Biometrics: Theory, Applications and Systems (BTAS), pp. 99–104 (2012)
3. Proenca, H.: Iris recognition: on the segmentation of degraded images acquired in the visible wavelength. J. IEEE Trans. Pattern Anal. Mach. Intell. **32**(8), 1502–1516 (2010)
4. Tan, C., Kumar, A.: Unified framework for automated iris segmentation using distantly acquired face images. J. IEEE Trans. Image Process. **21**(9), 4068–4079 (2012)
5. Tan, T., He, Z., Sun, Z.: Efficient and robust segmentation of noisy iris images for non-cooperative iris recognition. J. Image Vis. Comput. **28**(2), 223–230 (2010)
6. Li, P., Liu, X., Xiao, L., et al.: Robust and accurate iris segmentation in very noisy iris images. J. Image Vis. Comput. **28**(2), 246–253 (2010)
7. Sahmoud, S.A., Abuhaiba, I.S.: Efficient iris segmentation method in unconstrained environments. J. Pattern Recogn. **46**(46), 3174–3185 (2013)
8. Sankowski, W., Grabowski, K., Napieralska, M., et al.: Reliable algorithm for iris segmentation in eye image. J. Image Vis. Comput. **28**(28), 231–237 (2010)
9. Chen, Y., Adjouadi, M., Han, C., et al.: A highly accurate and computationally efficient approach for unconstrained iris segmentation. J. Image Vis. Comput. **28**(2), 261–269 (2010)
10. Radman, A., Jumari, K., Zainal, N.: Iris segmentation in visible wavelength images using circular gabor filters and optimization. J. Arabian J. Forence Eng. **39**(4), 1–11 (2014)
11. Haindl, M., Krupicka, M.: Unsupervised detection of non-iris occlusions. J. Pattern Recogn. Lett. **57**, 60–65 (2015)
12. Hu, Y., Sirlantzis, K., Howells, G.: Improving colour iris segmentation using a model selection technique. J. Pattern Recogn. Lett. **57**(1), 24–32 (2015)
13. Proença, H., Filipe, S., Santos, R., et al.: The UBIRIS.v2: a database of visible wavelength iris images captured on-the-move and at-a-distance. IEEE Trans. Pattern Anal. Mach. Intell. **32**(8), 1529–1535 (2010)

Extraction of the Iris Collarette Based on Constraint Interruption CV Model

Jing Huang[⊠] and Weiqi Yuan

School of Information Science and Engineering,
Shenyang University of Technology, Shenyang 110870, China
hj4393@sohu.com

Abstract. This paper proposes a method to extract collarette based on CV model with constraints. With different degrees of strength of multi-border iris image, this method realized the extraction of such complex collarette with weak border. The method analyzes the variation of the model parameters during optimization, controls model parameters by detecting errors under different applications, and establishes constraints of CV model to ensure that iteration interrupt at local optima, namely collarette boundary. In this experiment samples from our database, the experimental results show that the method is effective, and rapid to extract the iris collarette.

Keywords: Iris collarette · CV model · Constraints

1 Introduction

The traditional iris recognition system uses the global texture feature as the basis for recognition. In recent years, many researchers began to look at some of the iris texture feature and characteristic of local features as the basis of computer-aided identification [1–4], and achieved some results. Iris images have rich texture features with different shapes such as block, strip, collarette, etc. [5, 6]. The texture of the iris has a transitional boundary that are shown in the images of the iris along the radial direction. This boundary divides the whole iris image into internal and external two parts. The internal texture is radially, while outer texture is relatively flat, as shown in Fig. 1. This transitional boundary in medicine is called the collarette [7]. The distribution and texture of Iris images' collarette vary from different types of human. These differences dominated the whole iris images. If the collarette information extracted as a feature of iris recognition, will help to improve the recognition rate. Therefore, it is the key to study how to extract the feature efficiently.

The collarette locates on the iris have kinds of shapes, and most of collarette are relatively vague. The gray-scale of collarette image varies slowly within a certain range of pixels. The collarette of everyone change complex and different, which is weak boundary. In recent years, only few scholars do some research about extracting collarette. Xin guodong [8], who use gradient method of gray-scale on the normalized iris image to search for the largest gradient gray-scale to extract the boundary. The algorithm's detection results is unsatisfactory for the large number of boundary fuzzy image. The literature [9] effectively extracts the fuzzy collarette. However, these

© Springer International Publishing AG 2016
Z. You et al. (Eds.): CCBR 2016, LNCS 9967, pp. 374–382, 2016.
DOI: 10.1007/978-3-319-46654-5_41

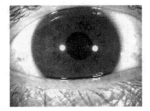

Fig. 1. The iris collarette

methods are needed for line-by-line image processing. As for this kind of complicated collarette contour, the results still need to be improved.

Active contour models (ACM) are often used for complex contour extraction. The basic idea of ACM is to evolve a curve to extract the desired object based on an energy-minimizing method. For instance, starting with a curve around the object to be detected, the curve moves toward its interior normal and has to stop on the boundary of the object. Without loss of generality, most of the ACMs studied under the level set framework can be categorized into two types: edge-based and region-based ones. One of the most popular edge-based models is the Snake [10]. The edge-based models utilize image gradient to construct force to direct the contours toward the boundaries of desired objects. Yu Li, who use the improved method of snake to extract collarette [11]. This method is not only very sensitive to the noise, but also difficult to detect the weak boundaries. The region-based models utilize the image statistical information to construct constraints, which have many advantages of region-based approaches when compared with edge-based methods. The Chan-Vese (CV) [12] model is a well-established region-based, that aims at minimizing the variance of two regions [13]. It extends the Mumford-Shah energy functional, by providing an implicit representation of the curve. So, we attempt to extract collarette by CV model. Meanwhile, in this paper, a novel scheme is proposed, called Constraint CV. This algorithm makes iterative disruption to local optimal solution, which can extract the weak boundary of the collarette.

2   Constraint Chan-Vese Model for Collarette Extraction

2.1   Chan-Vese Model for Collarette Extraction

The CV model is to look for a particular partition of a given image I(x) into two regions, one representing the objects to be detected and the other representing the back-ground. For a given image I(x) on the image domain O. In the CV model, they also have a regularizing term, such as the length of C and the area inside C to control the smoothness of the boundary. Therefore, the energy $E^{CV}(c_1, c_2, C)$ is defined by

$$E^{CV}(c_1, c_2, C) = \lambda_1 \int_{in(C)} (I(x) - c_1)^2 dx + \lambda_2 \int_{out(C)} (I(x) - c_2)^2 dx + \mu Length(C) + \upsilon Area(in(C)) \tag{1}$$

where C represents the curve, the constants c1 and c2 denote the average intensities inside and outside the curve, respectively, and the coefficients $\lambda 1$ and $\lambda 2$ are fixed parameters.

Using the level set to represent C, that is, C is the zero level set of a Lipschitz function $\phi(x)$, we can replace the unknown variable C by the unknown variable $\phi(x)$, and the energy function $E^{CV}(c_1, c_2, C)$ can be written as

$$E^{CV}(c_1, c_2, \phi) = \lambda_1 \int_{\Omega} (I(x) - c_1)^2 H(\phi(x)) dx + \lambda_2 \int_{\Omega} (I(x) - c_2)^2 (1 - H(\phi(x))) dx$$
$$+ \mu \int_{\Omega} \delta(\phi(x)) |\nabla \phi(x)| dx + \upsilon \int_{\Omega} H(\phi(x)) dx \tag{2}$$

where $H(\phi)$ and $\delta(\phi)$ are Heaviside function and Dirac function, respectively. Generally, the regularized versions are selected as

$$\begin{cases} H_\varepsilon(z) = \dfrac{1}{2}(1 + \dfrac{2}{\pi} \arctan(\dfrac{z}{\varepsilon})) \\ \delta_\varepsilon(z) = \dfrac{1}{\pi} \dfrac{\varepsilon}{\varepsilon^2 + z^2} \end{cases} \quad z \in R \tag{3}$$

Keeping $\phi(x)$ fixed and minimizing the energy $E^{CV}(c_1, c_2, C)$ with respect to the constants c1 and c2, we have

$$\begin{cases} c_1(\phi) = \dfrac{\int_{\Omega} I(x) H(\phi(x)) dx}{\int_{\Omega} H(\phi(x)) dx} \\ c_2(\phi) = \dfrac{\int_{\Omega} I(x)(1 - H(\phi(x))) dx}{\int_{\Omega} (1 - H(\phi(x))) dx} \end{cases} \tag{4}$$

At the same time, keeping c1 and c2 fixed, we minimize $E^{CV}(c_1, c_2, C)$ with respect to $\phi(x)$, and deduce the associated Euler–Lagrange equation for $\phi(x)$. We can obtain the corresponding variation level set formulation as follows:

$$\frac{\partial \phi(x, t)}{\partial t} = \delta(\phi)[-\lambda_1 (I(x) - c_1)^2 + \lambda_2 (I(x) - c_2)^2 + \mu div(\frac{\nabla \phi}{|\nabla \phi|}) - \upsilon]. \tag{5}$$

The CV method utilizes the local gradient information to control the curve deformation movement and the evolution of the contour curve.

From the iris image can be seen, pupil boundary and the outer boundary is more obvious gradient change than collarette, which are step boundary. By using the traditional CV model for several iterations, the result can extract collarette. However, the algorithm can't converge to the collarette boundary of the iris image. This work extracts a weak boundary between the two step boundaries, namely the collarette. If according to the characteristics of iris image in the iterative process to establish a constraint condition. The iterative is disrupted in the weak boundary, so can achieve the collarette contour extraction.

2.2 Constraint Chan-Vese Model for Collarette Extraction

Detection of the target is the collarette which is a weak boundary, is a local optimal solution of the optimization process. In order to find the local optimal solution, it is needed to establish the stopping criterion with some constraint conditions.

The main steps of establishing criterion is as follows:

Step1: Number of iterations n for selecting M images by traditional CV model, and saving results for each iteration;

Step2: Calculating the deviation between the results of each iteration and the calibration, figuring out the overall correct rate R_k(k = 1...n) of the detected position after each iteration is obtained, as following:

$$R_k = \frac{N1((w_i - w_{bi}) < \varepsilon)}{N} \tag{6}$$

where N is the total number of calibration points collarette position; N1 is the total number of conditions of the error after the test; w_i is the position coordinates detected; w_{bi} is calibrated position coordinates; ε is the pixel error value is set according to different application requirements.

Step3: The gradient value diff1, diff2 of the parameter C1, C2 obtained after the n iterations by the CV model is calculated;

Step4: Select the appropriate threshold from diff1, diff2 all samples, as far as possible to meet all the samples at the set of ε R_k is the best. The threshold is a stop condition.

3 Experiments Results and Discussion

3.1 Data Sets

Ours iris image capture device uses a handheld iris instrument. This equipment can collect 24-bit color image. Image size is 800 * 600. There are 688 taken from student volunteers at the Shenyang University of Technology. We named database 1. There are 1000 samples taken from the Central Hospital Affiliated to Shenyang Medical College. We named database 2.

In order to establish the model, this paper makes a manual calibration experiment for 1688 human eye images of the two image database. As shown in Fig. 2, in the iris coordinate calibration reference chart of all the radial direction, according to the observed collarette position calibration. Selecting the following three groups were calibrated. If calibration results deviation is within 10 pixels, average as the standard point. Calibration results deviation exceed the 10 pixels, so require further discussion finalized standard point.

Groups1: no prior knowledge of the 10 people (three undergraduates, three graduate students, three teachers, a family) on the image calibration

Groups2: 10 people in this group (6 graduate students, 4 doctoral students) on the image calibration

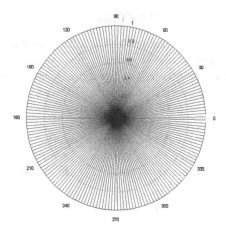

Fig. 2. Iris coordinate calibration reference

Groups3:   cooperate with the hospital's 8 doctors in the endoscope room of the hospital to calibrate the image

Based on the above three groups of calibration results obtained collarette the standard position of the iris image library.

3.2   Establishing Constraints

Randomly selected 200 images from the database, utilized the model CV 100 iterations, Calculated the deviation between the results of each iteration and the calibration results, the overall accuracy of the detection position of each iteration is R_k. As shown in Fig. 3 iteration results for an image. The horizontal coordinate is the CV model parameter C1. The vertical coordinate is the accuracy, where ε is 3, 5, 10.

Figure 3 show with the increase of the number of iterations, collarette the correct extraction rate increases. However, when it reaches the maximum value, and continue the iteration, the accuracy does not remain constant, but decreases. It presents that the traditional CV model can't converge to the boundary collarette. Therefore, the algorithm needs to set a constraint, when the accuracy reaches the maximum iteration stops. That is to say, the algorithm breaks into the boundary of the collarette.

All samples is iterated by using the traditional CV model, Fig. 4 shows the maximum accuracy of 200 samples extracted the collarette corresponding to the gradient diff1 of parameters C1. The horizontal coordinate is the number of samples. The principal of vertical coordinate is diff1, the secondary of vertical coordinate is the maximum accuracy of collarette extraction.

In this paper, we select the parameters that is 0.25 according to the correspondence between Fig. 4. For any image, when the diff1 is less than the threshold value, the iteration is interrupted. When the threshold is selected 0.25, there is undesirable problems including over detection and missed detection in a small number of samples.

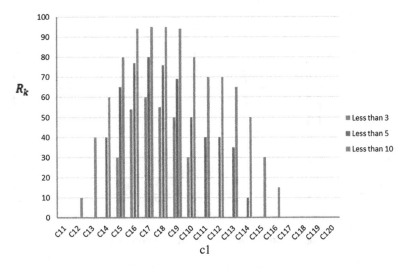

Fig. 3. Correspondence between the pattern parameters and the detection accuracy of the position

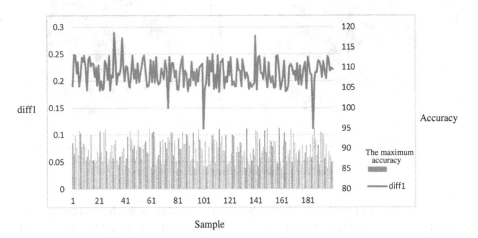

Fig. 4. Correspondence between the maximum accuracy

But most of the images can be interrupted to ensure maximum accuracy corresponding to the position, as shown in Fig. 5. The gradient diff2 of the parameter C2 is set to 1.5 according to the method mentioned above.

3.3   Experiments Results

From the above analysis it shows that the use of traditional CV model checking collarette, which detects the termination condition is pre-set number of iterations. When the number of iterations is set to 500, the result is shown in Fig. 6(a). According to the

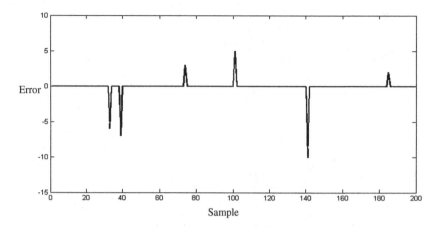

Fig. 5. Error diagram of maximum correct rate

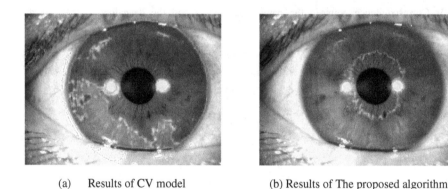

(a)   Results of CV model   (b) Results of The proposed algorithm

Fig. 6. Results of collarette extraction

traditional CV model can't follow the convergence conditions or the number of iterations to converge to collarette boundary. With the use of the proposed CV model with constraints of collarette detection, the results shown in Fig. 6(b).

3.4   The Comparison of Results of Extraction

In our sample databases, 1488 images were detected using our method. We fix the parameters as presented in above subsection. Besides, ε is 3, 5, 10. There are 2 levels of the detection accuracy Rk at each level ε. The result as shown in Table 1. At the same time, we compare the proposed method with the method of literature [9]. We can see from the results that with ε increases, the number of samples to meet the set the correct rates are gradually increased in these methods, our method slightly better than literature method. But in the detection time, our method has obvious advantages.

Table 1. Performance comparison for the different methods

ε	$R_{k\ (\%)}$	Samples of extraction accuracy		Extraction time(s)	
		Literature [9]	Proposed	Literature [9]	Proposed
3	50	1057	1096	25	5
	60	1007	1082		
5	65	1205	1213		
	75	1167	1184		
10	85	1390	1401		
	90	1214	1256		

4 Conclusion

Iris collarette is an important local feature. Collarette is extracted as a feature will improve the accuracy rate of iris recognition. However, there are three reasons to the detection difficult. Frist, collarette shape in the iris image is different. Second, boundary is fuzzy. The last one, location is not fixed. In this paper, CV model detecting method with constraints was presented, experimental results show that the method can effectively extract collarette. In addition, the test results can be seen, there is the impact of the light spot on the test results. The next step in image acquisition, pre-processing to remove spots, improve the detection efficiency.

References

1. Hosseini, M.S., Araabi, B.N., Soltanian-Zadeh, H.: Pigment melanin: pattern for iris recognition. IEEE Trans. Instrum. Meas. **59**(4), 792–804 (2010)
2. Shen, F., Flynn, P.J.: Iris matching by crypts and anti-crypts. In: 2012 IEEE Conference on Technologies for Homeland Security (HST), pp. 208–213 (2012)
3. Shen, F., Flynn, P.J.: Iris crypts: multi-scale detection and shape-based matching. In: 2014 IEEE Winter International Conference on Applications of Computer Vision, pp. 977–983 (2014)
4. Shen, F., Flynn, P.J.: Are iris crypts useful in identity recognition. In: IEEE International Conference on Biometrics: Theory, Applications and Systems, pp. 1–6 (2013)
5. Ling, Wang: Known Health by Iris Observation: Illustration of Holographic Iridology. Liaoning Science and Technology Publishing House, Shenyang (2010)
6. Jiangfan,J.: Interpretation of the Iris Visible Subhealth. China Citic Press, Beijing (2010)
7. Li, F.: System of Ophthalmology. People's Medical Publishing House, Beijing (1996)
8. Xin, G.,Wang, W.: Study on collarette extraction. Comput. Eng. Des. **29**(9), 2290–2292 (2008)
9. Jing, H., Weiqi, Y.: Collarette extraction based on primitive's pattern statistics. J. Comput. Aided Des. Comput. Graph. **26**(8), 1326–1332 (2014)
10. Kass, M., Witkin, A., Terzopoulos, D.: Snakes: active contour models. Int. J. Comput. Vis **1**, 321–331 (1988)

11. Li, Y., Kuanquan, W., Zhang, D.: Extracting the autonomic nerve wreath of iris based on an improved snake approach. Neuro computing **70**(4–6), 743–748 (2007)
12. Chan, Tony F., Vese, Luminita A.: Active contours without edges. Trans. Image Process. **2**(10), 266–277 (2001)
13. Yuzhu, C., Yong, C.: Corn seedling image segmentation using PCA and CV model. J. Comput. Inf. Syst. **11**(21), 7825–7832 (2015)

A Method of Vessel Segmentation Based on BP Neural Network for Color Fundus Images

Haiying Xia[✉] and Shuaifei Deng

Department of Electronic Engineering, Guangxi Normal University,
Guilin 541004, Guangxi, China
xhyhust@gmail.com

Abstract. The morphological and structural changes of retinal vessels are very important for the early diagnosis of many diseases. In view of the characteristics of retinal vessels, we present a new method for vessel segmentation based on BP neural network. This method consists of four steps: histogram equalization of green channel, morphological processing, Gaussian matched filter and Hessian matrix. The fundus vessels are segmented by BP neural network. We conduct the experiments on DRIVE and STARE database. The experiment results show that our method has good effect on the segmentation of fundus retinal vessels.x

Keywords: Color fundus image · Vessel segmentation · Gaussian matched filter · Hessian matrix · BP neural network

1 Introduction

Many cardiac and cerebral vascular diseases can cause human retinal changes. Color fundus image analysis plays an important role in the diagnosis of human eye diseases. Color fundus image analysis includes the extraction of retinal vessels, detection of bleeding points and leakage, etc. Among them, the segmentation of retinal vessels is an important foundation for the analysis of the color fundus image.

At present, there are many methods for retinal vessel segmentation. Chaudhuri et al. presents a matched filter method, which uses Gaussian functions to fit the gray distribution of the cross section of retinal vessels and generates 12 matching filters to detect the vessels [1]. Frangi et al. uses the Hessian matrix to extract the tubular vascular structure of the retinal image [2]. Zhao et al. proposes a method of retinal vessel segmentation based on level set and region growing [3]. First, the contrast of the fundus image is enhanced by a limited histogram equalization and Gabor wavelet. Then anisotropic diffusion filters are used to smooth the image and keep vessel edges clear. Finally, region active contour model and region growing are applied to extract the retinal vessel. Karthika et al. proposes a method to segment vessels using curvelet transform and multi structuring morphological elements [4]. This method uses a plurality of directions of curvelet transform to enhance the contrast of image, and uses morphological operations to remove the spinal cord not belonging the vessels. Finally, an

© Springer International Publishing AG 2016
Z. You et al. (Eds.): CCBR 2016, LNCS 9967, pp. 383–390, 2016.
DOI: 10.1007/978-3-319-46654-5_42

improved Otsu method combined with a strong connected component analysis is utilized to further confirmation. In 2014, Salazar-Gonzalez et al. proposes a graph cut method based on vector flow to segment vessels. This method first uses the adaptive histogram equalization and robust distance transform to pre-process the image, use the graph cut algorithm for vessel segmentation. All of the above methods belong to the unsupervised retinal vascular extraction method, and do not need to train the model in advance. The rule of thumb is to train the classifier using the hand labeled images to realize the vessel extraction [5]. Soares uses Gabor-Wavelet transform algorithm to extract image features to train the Gauss mixture model for vessel segmentation [6]. Staal et al. proposes a K- nearest neighbor method to locate the vessels [7], which makes use of the vessel diameter, the brightness and the edge intensity. Fraz et al. presents a similar segmentation method for fundus image of children, which uses a combination of second derivative of Gaussian, Gabor filtering, multi-scale line detection and morphological transformation [8]. Wang et al. proposes new method for vessel segmentation based on hierarchical structure [9].

Due to the linear distribution of retinal vessels and the Gaussian distribution of gray value of the cross section we propose a method of vascular segmentation of color fundus image based on BP neural network. In this method, the adaptive histogram equalization is firstly applied to the green channel; Morphological operation, Gaussian matched filter and Hessian matrix are used to enhance the vessel enhancement of the green channel; At last, the BP neural network is used to segment vessels.

2   Extracting Features of Color Fundus Image

2.1   Gray Features of Green Channel

The fundus images used in this paper are 565*584*24 and 605*700*24. From the comparisons among three channels, we can find that blue channel contains a lot of noise, the red channel is more sensitive to light, and the green channel contains more vascular texture information. In order to better highlight the vessels, the adaptive histogram equalization is applied to the green channel. Figure 1 shows the images of each channel and the image of green channel after histogram equalization.

2.2   Morphological Processing

If the shape of the object is known, morphological processing is a good way for image preprocessing. The curvature change and the width of the retinal vessels are smooth, the local linear structure can be seen as the width of the vessel. Therefore, it can be used to deal with the vascular segmentation. Specific operations are as follows:

(1) Invert the gray value of green channel image after histogram equalization;

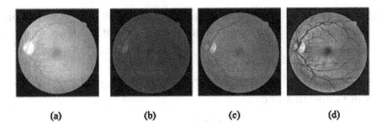

Fig. 1. Comparisons of each channel. (a) Red channel image. (b) Blue channel image. (c) Green channel image. (d) The image of green channel after histogram equalization.

(2) 12 linear structural elements with different orientations and lengths are constructed, which are used as open operators. The maximum response and the minimum response are taken as the output;

(3) The difference between the maximum response and the minimum response is taken as a morphological feature;

The linear structure elements in 12 directions are used as open operators, and the best response of the output can better retain the linear vessels, while the minimum response output canretain a large area of the background. then, the difference between the two can weaken the background and highlight the vessels. Morphological processing results are shown in Fig. 2:

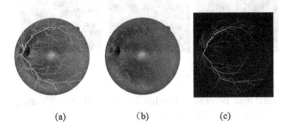

Fig. 2. Morphological processing. (a) Maximum output; (b) Minimum output; (c) The difference between the two.

2.3   Gaussian Matched Filtering

The gray distribution of retinal vessels is similar to that of Gaussian. Therefore, the Gaussian function is used to match the image, and the filter response is a kind of feature of vessel segmentation. The Gaussian function is:

$$G(x,y) = -exp(-\frac{x^2}{2\sigma x^2} - \frac{y^2}{2\sigma y^2}) \qquad (1)$$

The direction of vessels in the retina is different from each other. In order to get the Gaussian filters with different direction, it needs to rotate the Gaussian core.

Assuming that the rotation of the coordinates is *(u,v)*, The rotation angle of Gaussian nucleus is θ_i, If the origin is the center of rotation, then rotated coordinates is:

$$\begin{bmatrix} u \\ v \end{bmatrix} = \begin{bmatrix} \cos\theta_i & -\sin\theta_i \\ \sin\theta_i & \cos\theta_i \end{bmatrix} \begin{bmatrix} x \\ y \end{bmatrix} \tag{2}$$

The mean of Gaussian's nucleus is:

$$m_i = \sum G_i(u,v)/N \tag{3}$$

N is the number of the elements in the Gaussian core. Gaussian convolution kernel of the matched filter is:

$$G'_i(u,v) = G_i(u,v) - m_i \tag{4}$$

The size of the Gaussian core is 13*13, and the angle resolution is 15°. Taking into account the length of the vessel is greater than the width, the σ_x is 2 times as much as σ_y. The convolution of 12 different directions is used to filter the green channel, and the maximum value of the convolution result is used as the output features of Gaussian matched filters. The results of 45°, 135° and 12 directions are presented in Fig. 3.

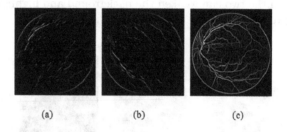

(a)   (b)   (c)

Fig. 3. Gaussian matched filters of fundus image. (a) 45° filtering result; (b) 135° filtering result; (c) 12 direction filtering result.

2.4   Hessian Matrix Features

Hessian matrix is a square matrix consisting of two order derivative. The gray curvature of the image can be expressed by the Hessian matrix. A Hessian matrix has two eigenvalues. Assuming that the eigenvalue λ_1 is the large one, the eigenvalue λ_2 is the small. The λ_1 represents the maximum curvature, and the eigenvector corresponding to the λ_1 represents the direction of the maximum curvature. The λ_2 represents the minimum curvature, and the eigenvector corresponding to the λ_2 represents the direction of the minimum curvature. Two eigenvector s are orthogonal to each other. In the fundus image, the gradient along the vessel direction changes slowly, and the gradient perpendicular to the vessel changes dramatically.

So it can achieve the purpose of enhancing the vessels by a similar function of the vascular structure. Here, we take the similarity function proposed by Frangi [7], which is described as follows:

$$v_0(\lambda) = \begin{cases} 0 & if \lambda_1 > 0 \\ exp(-\frac{R_B}{2\beta^2})(1 - exp(-\frac{S_B}{2C^2})) & otherwise \end{cases} \tag{5}$$

Where β is generally set to 0.5, and the C is half of the maximum norm of the matrix, R_B is λ_2/λ_1 and S_B is $\sqrt{\lambda_1^2 + \lambda_2^2}$.

According to the characteristic of the distribution of the vessels, we use the kernel of Gaussian function to construct the Hessian matrix. Because of the great change of vessel width, the single scale of Hessian matrix can't detect the vessels in a large range, so multiple scales are used. For each scale of the Hessian matrix, the vascular similarity function has an output response. When the size of the vessels is consistent with the maximum size of the vessel similar function, the maximum response of each pixel at different scales can be obtained by fusing the output response of all scales.

3 Vessel Segmentation Based on BP Neural Network

BP neural network can realize the complex mapping from input to output, and is especially suitable for solving the complex classification problem. We do not need to understand its internal process. As long as the node number, transfer function and the features of BP network are set, you can get the corresponding classification output. Here, the classical 3 layer BP neural network is taken, and its structure is shown in Fig. 4. BP neural network includes two aspects: data forward propagation and error back propagation. The network will forward the input data depending on the current threshold of the weight. The output of the sth node of the output layer is:

$$o_s = \psi[\sum_{i=1}^{q} w_{ij}\phi(\sum_{j=1}^{m} w_{ij}x_j + \theta_i) + a_s] \tag{6}$$

Where $_{ij}$ is the weight between the input layer and hidden layer; $_{si}$ is the weight between the hidden layer and input layer; θ_i and a_s represent the node thresholds in the hidden layer and output layer respectively; ϕ and ψ are the transfer functions in the hidden layer and output layer respectively.

The output error is calculated depending on the output, and is propagated reversely. Then, the weight and threshold of the network are adjusted by the gradient descent method, in order to make the output close to the ground truth. Error function is listed in the following.

$$E_p = \frac{1}{2}\sum_{k=1}^{} L(T_k - o_k)^2 \tag{7}$$

Where T_k is the output reference value of the kth node.

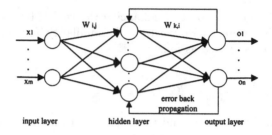

Fig. 4. The BP neural network with three layer structure.

In our method, we use four sets of image features to classify the images into two types: vessels and non-vessels. So the number of input layer node is set to 4, and the number of output layer node is set to 2. At present, there is no exact setting ways to set the number of hidden layer nodes. *logsig* function is used as the transfer function from the input layer to the hidden layer, and *purelin* function is taken as the transfer function from the hidden layer to the output layer. Moreover, the additional momentum is added to avoid the local minimum.

The process of vessel segmentation with BP neural network is described as follows:

(1) Norm the four types of training features extracted by the ways described above and design the corresponding feature vectors;
(2) Train the BP network based on the ground truth labeled by experts, and terminate the training when reach the defined iterations.
(3) Norm the test features, design the test feature vectors, input to the trained BP network and get the classified vessels.

4   Experimental Results and Analysis

We test the performance of our method on DRIVE and STARE [10] database. The DRIVE database contains 20 training images and 20 test images. The ground truth of test images are provided by the manual segmentation results of two experts, while the ground truth of training images are given by one expert. STARE database contains 20 images that are manually annotated by two independent human observers. Here, ten images represent patients with retinal abnormalities. The other ten images represent normal retina. The experiments are conducted on a platform of 2010a MATLAB with a Core i3-3240 Intel processor and a 4G memory bank. Figure 5 shows the results of our method and the ground truth. We can see from the Fig. 5 that our method get a lot of retinal capillary with the advantage of BP neural network. The segmentation performance of our method is also quantitatively analyzed. We employ three evaluating indicators to compare the performance of our method with others, which are the true positive rate (TPR), the false positive rate (FPR) and the detection accuracy (Acc) defined as follows:

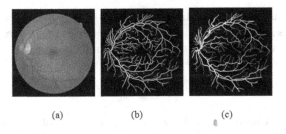

(a)   (b)   (c)

Fig. 5. Segmentation results. (a) The original image; (b) The result by our method; (c) The result by one expert.

Table 1. Comparison of the performance of our method with others

Test data	DRIVE			STARE		
Methods	TPR	FPR	Acc	TPR	FPR	Acc
Matched filter [2]	0.6167	0.0261	0.9283	0.6608	0.0301	0.9357
Soares [6]	0.7282	0.0213	0.9462	0.7211	0.0253	0.9479
Fathi [11]	0.7223	0.0399	0.9354	0.7396	0.0395	0.9435
Staal [7]	0.7192	0.0228	0.9439	0.6972	0.0193	0.9522
Our method	0.7436	0.0243	0.9425	0.7564	0.0202	0.9513

$$TPR = TP/(TP + FN)$$
$$FPR = FP/(FP + TN) \tag{8}$$
$$Acc = (TP + TN)/(TP + TN + FP + FN)$$

Where True positive (TP) represents the correct segmented vessel pixels; false positive (FP) represents the false segmented vessel pixels; True negative (TN) represents the correct segmented non-vessel pixels; False negative (FN) represents the false segmented non-vessel pixles.

As can be seen from Table 1, the performance of TPR of our method is the best among the five segmentation methods. It is because that our method can correctly segment the capillary. Also, our method achieves a good result in the segmentation accuracy. On the whole, our method can detect a large number of capillaries, and get a better segmentation result.

5   Conclusions

Retinal vessel segmentation plays an important role in the diagnosis and treatment of diabetes, hypertension and other diseases. In this paper, we propose a new method for vessel segmentation based on BP neural network. Our method uses the responses of histogram equalization of green channel, morphological processing, Gaussian matched filters, and the Hessian matrix enhancement as the feature vectors to train a BP neural network with three layers. Then the trained BP neural network is utilized to segment vessels in a color fundus image. The experiments show that our method can detect more capillaries and is feasible and effective for vessel segmentation of color fundus images.

References

1. Chaudhuri, S., Chatterjee, S., Katz, N., Nelson, M., Goldbaum, M.: Detection of blood vessels in retinal images using two-dimensional matched filters. IEEE Trans. Med. Imaging 8(3), 263–269 (1989)
2. Frangi, A.F., Niessen, W.J., Vincken, K.L., Viergever, M.A.: Multiscale vessel enhancement filtering. In: Wells, W.M., Colchester, A., Delp, S. (eds.) MICCAI 1998. LNCS, vol. 1496, pp. 130–137. Springer, Heidelberg (1998). doi:10.1007/BFb0056195
3. Zhao, Y.Q., Wang, X.H., Wang, X.F., Shih, F.Y.: Retinal vessels segmentation based on level set and region growing. Pattern Recogn. 47(7), 2437–2446 (2014)
4. Karthika, D., Marimuthu, A., Retinal image analysis using contourlet transform and multistructure elements morphology by reconstruction. In: 2014 World Congress on Computing and Communication Technologies (WCCCT), pp. 54–59. IEEE (2014)
5. Salazar-Gonzalez, A., Kaba, D., Li, Y., Liu, X.: Segmentation of the blood vessels and optic disk in retinal images. IEEE J. Biomed. Health Inf. 18(6), 1874–1886 (2014)
6. Soares, J.V., Leandro, J.J., Cesar Jr., R.M., Jelinek, H.F., Cree, M.J.: Retinal vessel segmentation using the 2-d gabor wavelet and supervised classification. IEEE Trans. Med. Imaging 25(9), 1214–1222 (2006)
7. Staal, J., Abràmoff, M.D., Niemeijer, M., Viergever, M.A., Van Ginneken, B.: Ridge-based vessel segmentation in color images of the retina. IEEE Trans. Med. Imaging 23(4), 501–509 (2004)
8. Fraz, M.M., Rudnicka, A.R., Owen, C.G., Barman, S.A.: Delineation of blood vessels in pediatric retinal images using decision trees-based ensemble classification. Int. J. Comput. Assist. Radiol. Surg. 9(5), 795–811 (2014)
9. Wang, S., Yin, Y., Cao, G., Wei, B., Zheng, Y., Yang, G.: Hierarchical retinal blood vessel segmentation based on feature and ensemble learning. Neurocomputing 149, 708–717 (2015)
10. Hoover, V.K.A., Goldbaum, M.: Locating blood vessels in retinal images by piecewise threhsold probing of a matched filter response. IEEE Trans. Med. Imaging 19(3), 203–210 (2000)
11. Fathi, A., Naghsh-Nilchi, A.R.: General rotation-invariant local binary patterns operator with application to blood vessel detection in retinal images. Pattern Anal. Appl. 17(1), 69–81 (2014)

Corneal Arcus Segmentation Method in Eyes Opened Naturally

Le Chang[1,2(✉)] and Weiqi Yuan[1]

[1] Computer Vision Group, Shenyang University of Technology, No.111,
ShenLiao West Road, Economic and Technological Development Zone,
Shenyang 110087, People's Republic of China
changle1105@163.com
[2] Guidaojiaotong Polytechnic Institute, No.13 Street,
Economic and Technological Development Zone, Shenyang 110023
People's Republic of China

Abstract. Detection of the corneal arcus by image analysis has important significance for the disintegration of the abnormal lipid metabolism. The traditional method is accompanied with the problem of robustness when the image is collected by non-invasive way. In this paper, an improved corneal arcus segmentation method is proposed. Firstly, locate the candidate area by detecting the eyelid and eyelash. Secondly, on the definition of similarity and the projection of color components, the Union-Find algorithm is used to accomplish the clustering of the target. Finally, the color metrics is defined to complete the segmentation of the corneal arcus. 1968 images from our database are analyzed segmentation accuracy reaches 95.4 % respectively.

Keywords: Medical image processing · Corneal arcus · Union-Find

1 Introduction

When an abnormality of human lipid metabolism, cholesterol, lecithin, glycerin three greases and other lipids in blood will deposit in the cornea and this kind of symptom is called corneal arcus [1, 2]. Corneal arcus has an important significance in screening and diagnosis of people's high cholesterol [3], atherosclerosis [4] and so on. Image-based detection of corneal arcus play an important role in discovers or confirms some diseases timely. R.A. Ramlee used iris recognition algorithm to detect the cholesterol presence. By extracting the 30 % of the normalized image and through the analysis of the histogram, then use the threshold of OTSU to detection Corneal arcus [5]. Yuan Weiqi presents Corneal Arcus Detection method based on HSI color space [6]. S.V. Mahesh Kumar detecting the corneal arcus by using the statistical feature extraction and support vector machine [7]. In training phase, this method achieved a classification accuracy of 1 and in testing phase, this method achieved a classification accuracy of 0.96.

All existing methods need to locate the fixed candidate area in image before detection,besides, the corneal arcus in image is not occluded by eyelid. The fixed candidate area not only includes the corneal arcus, but also contains some interfering organ such as iris, sclera eyelash and so on. These factors have influence on the

© Springer International Publishing AG 2016
Z. You et al. (Eds.): CCBR 2016, LNCS 9967, pp. 391–398, 2016.
DOI: 10.1007/978-3-319-46654-5_43

effectiveness of the existing algorithm. In addition, the corneal arcus is usually occluded by eyelid randomly when the image is collected in eyes opened naturally, the effectiveness of existing methods will be reduced significantly when the eyelid is appeared in candidate area. This article carries on the segmentation method of the corneal arcus based on image collected in eyes opened naturally.

2   Image Acquisition and Occlusion Detection

2.1   Image Acquisition

In order to collect enough images for testing algorithm, our research groups cooperate with Shenyang Medical College Fengtian Hospital assistance. All images are collected by noninvasive way and participant 'eyes are opened naturally. We collected more than 1968 iris images and include 984 individuals. The differences between individuals bring the randomness of occlusion, as shown in Fig. 1.

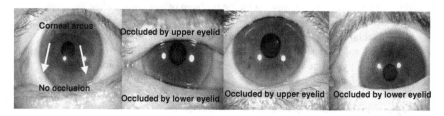

Fig. 1. Iris image with corneal arcus in database

2.2   Occlusion Detection

In this paper, the median filtering algorithm is used to detect the eyelash and eyelid [8]. Suppose the $MOD(x,y)$ is the candidate regions of corneal arcus by method [8]. When the pixel in location (x,y) is not in the candidate region, $MOD(x,y) = 0$, otherwise, $MOD(x,y) = 1$. Figure 2 shows the candidate region for the final determination of the various types of occlusions in Fig. 1.

Fig. 2. Candidate regions for the segmentation of the corneal arcus

3   The Corneal Arcus Segmentation Algorithm

3.1   Segmentation Procedure

The corneal arcus is adjacent to scleral, iris and eyelashes. The main purpose of the segmentation is to get the possible area of corneal arcus and remove the adjacent interference region from the color image. Color image segmentation is an important technique in image processing, pattern recognition and computer vision. Until now, thousands of various types of segmentation algorithm based on a variety of theories have been proposed. However, there is still no general segmentation algorithm suitable for all images [9]. Aiming at the target of this paper, there are lots of interference information on the color image which collected by eyes opened naturally, such as light, occlusion and so on. In order to locate the region of corneal arcus effectively the segmentation procedure is shown in Fig. 3.

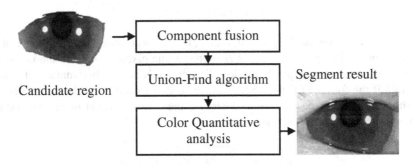

Fig. 3. The segmentation procedure of proposed method

The main purpose of occlusion detection is to determine the candidate regions for the segmentation of the corneal arcus by detecting the eyelashes and eyelids. We used the Union-Find clustering method to project the different components of the pixels in the candidate regions. After that, different scales of isolated regions are connected by the definition of similarity. Finally, the normal iris images are excluded by color quantitative analysis.

3.2   Segmentation of Corneal Arcus

For the color image $F(x,y)$ in HSI color space, any point in image can be described as a vector $\mu = (H(x,y),S(x,y),I(x,y))$. $H(x,y)$ represent the hue component of the image, $S(x,y)$ represent the saturation component of the image and $I(x,y)$ represent the luminance of the image.

Assuming that W is the width of image and H is the Height of image. Out_x is the outer boundary of iris and (c_x,c_y) is the center coordinates of the iris. (out_x,out_y) is one point of iris outer boundary. The segmentation mainly includes as follows:

1. Component fusion

In order to increase the difference between cornea arcus and surrounding tissues as much as possible, three components of the image are projected by formula (1).

$$Q(x,y) = H(x,y) \times \alpha + S(x,y) \times \beta + I(x,y) \times \delta \tag{1}$$

The vector μ can be located by calculating the max value of the $M(x,y)$ between the point (out_x, out_y) to point $(out\_x, out\_y - out\_r)$.

$$M(x,y) = (\frac{\partial(H(x,y) \times \alpha + S(x,y) \times \beta) + I(x,y) \times \delta}{\partial x})^2 \tag{2}$$

Assuming the projection vector is $\mu = (\mu_{x0}, \mu_{y0}, \mu_{z0})$, the similarity measured between the point (x_0, y_0) and the point (x_1, y_1) is defined as follows:

$$P = |Q(x_0, y_0) - Q(x_1, y_1)| \tag{3}$$

We define the vector $C(x), x = 0, 1, 2 \ldots, W \times H$ represents the initial label of the image F, and $C_1(x), x = 0, 1 \ldots, W \times H$ represent the pixels number of the labeled X. Calculating the P of each pixel with its adjacent pixels in both horizontal and vertical direction if the formula (4) and (5) are satisfied. If the similarity P is greater than the threshold θ_1 will not be processed, otherwise these two adjacent pixels will be performed by combination function.

$$\sqrt{(i - c\_x)^2 + (j - c\_y)^2} < out\_r \tag{4}$$

$$MOD(x,y) = 1 \tag{5}$$

2. Union-Find algorithm

Determine the average projection ψ of the outer boundary of corneal arcus in point (out_x, out_y). Calculate the $Q(x,y)$ in candidate regions and if the results are in $[\psi - 3\theta_1/2, \psi + 3\theta_1/2]$, then update the number of the corresponding set by formula (5).

$$\psi = \frac{\sum_{i=0}^{5} Q(c\_r, c\_y - out\_r - i)}{6} \tag{4}$$

$$C_1(find(x \times W + y)) = C_1(find(x \times W + y)) + 1 \tag{5}$$

$find(x)$ is the query function of the Union-Find. After the above processing, We get the label of each pixel $C(x), x = 0, 1, 2 \ldots, W \times H$ and the number of different sets $C_1(x), x = 0, 1 \ldots, W \times H$.

By analysis and comparison the image in our database, about 91.9 % of the image are affected by the upper eyelid occlusion, 77.4 % of the image are affected by both upper and lower eyelid occlusion. In our method, we divide the region of corneal arcus into different number of connected regions based on fact (as shown in Fig. 4). In order to remove the influence of the normal iris, we need to analyze the maximum two connected regions by calculating the $C_1(x), x = 0, 1 \ldots, W \times H$ and met the following conditions.

$$MOD(|c\_x - c\_r|, c\_y) = 1 \tag{6}$$

$$MOD(c\_x + c\_r, c\_y) = 1 \tag{7}$$

If the pixel number of second region is bigger than θ_2, then marked the two largest regions are corneal arcus. Otherwise, only the largest region is marked as corneal arcus. θ_2 is mainly used to remove the influence of the spot.

Two connected regions   One connected region

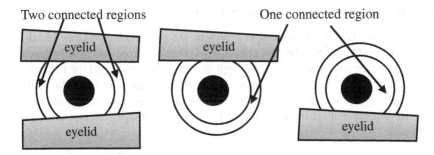

Fig. 4. The connected area of corneal arcus in segmentation result

3. Color quantitative analysis

Assume S' is the results of segmentation by our tracking method, n is the pixel number of S'. The color of corneal arcus is showed cloudy, some are light grey, some are dark grey. In other words three components of S' in RGB space is approximately the same or similar.

Calculate the mean of each RGB component $(\overline{M_r}, \overline{M_g} \overline{M_b})$. Subsequently, we define the color descriptor J, which can be obtained by the following expression:

$$J = \frac{2\sqrt{3}}{3} \times \sqrt{p \times (p - l) \times (p - l') \times (p - \sqrt{3})} \tag{8}$$

where $l = \sqrt{\overline{M_r}^2 + \overline{M_g}^2 + \overline{M_b}^2}, l' = \sqrt{(\overline{M_r} - 1)^2 + (\overline{M_g} - 1)^2 + (\overline{M_b} - 1)^2}, p = \frac{1}{2}(l + l' + \sqrt{3})$.

4 Experiment Results

4.1 Occlusion Detection Experiment

1968 images in our database are used for experiment, and 353 images with corneal arcus. Finally, 1854 images are segment correctly and 114 images are segmented wrong by our method. The main reason of error for our method is image blurs due to out of focus. Table 1 shows the segmentation results of effective region.

Table 1. Experimental analysis of effective region segmentation algorithm

Type	No occlusion	Eyelid occlusion	Accuracy
All images	159	1809	94.2 %
Normal images	111	1504	94.2 %
Corneal arcus	48	305	94.1 %

4.2 The Experiment of Parameters Selection

In the candidate region, θ_1 is used to represent the projection similarity of adjacent pixels, θ_2 is used to remove the spot effects. θ_2 is relatively fixed and usually depend on acquisition equipment. Combining with application of the device and the value of θ_2 is taken 323-388 can obtain the stable results of segmentation. In order to verify the performance of θ_1 selection, further experiments and tests have been executed. We select 10 images with corneal arcus and 10 normal images in our database for experiment.

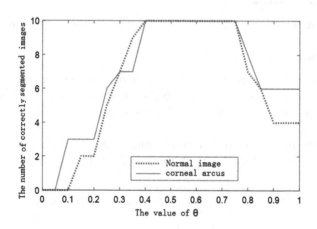

Fig. 5. The analysis of parameter θ_1 selection

From the experiment results shown as Fig. 5, with the parameters of different values, the segmentation accuracy is different about the normal image and the image with corneal arcus. Through experimental analysis, the image in our experiment can segment all correctly when the value of θ_1 is from 0.55 to 0.7.

The color quantization operator J is used to eliminate the influence of normal image. The J is relatively stable and will not be changed with the difference in the devices. The value of J is calculated by the following formula:

$$J_0 = \frac{1}{2} \times \frac{\sum_{i=1}^{10} J(i)}{10} + \frac{1}{2} \times \frac{\sum_{i=1}^{10} J'(i)}{10} \tag{9}$$

$J(i)$ is calculated according to the formula (8) and indicate the J of iris image which have corneal arcus and the index of image is i. $J'(i)$ is indicating the J of normal image and the index of image is i.

4.3 Validation Experiments

The previous segmentation algorithm has been tested in order to verify its accuracy and effectiveness. Let us consider for example the image in Fig. 1. The image has been segmented by our method, the results are shown in Fig. 6. Two different methods are used in same database to compare with our method. The experimental results are shown in Table 2.

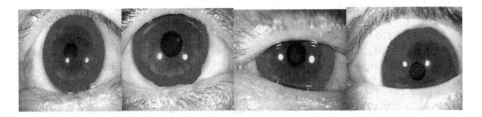

Fig. 6. The segmentation of corneal arcus

Table 2. The comparison of different algorithms

Algorithm	Normal image	Corneal arcus	Error accept	Error refuse	Accuracy rate
Our method	1523	331	2	84	95.4 %
K-means [10]	1523	331	208	96	83.6 %
Watershed [11]	1523	331	159	114	85.3 %

As shown in Table 2, the segmentation accuracy of our method has been significantly improved. The effect of seed selection of K-mean method is relatively large. The randomness of the spot position and iris texture is main reason for watershed method.

5 Conclusions

This article proposed a segmentation method for corneal arcus. Experimental results show the effectiveness of the method we proposed in this paper. As a noninvasive way, this method can be used as a preprocessing step in screening and diagnosis of people's health condition timely. All images are collected while the participant 'eyes is opened naturally, our segmentation method still not performance well if the image is because out of focus. These issues will be the main content of our future research.

Acknowledgments. This work is supported by the National Natural Science Foundation of China (No.61271365)

References

1. Raj, K.M., Subhash, P.A., Vikram, C.: Significance of corneal arcus. J. Pharm. Bioallied Sci. **7**, 14–15 (2015)
2. Macchiaiolo, M., Valente, P., et al.: Corneal arcus as first sign of familial hypercholesterolemia. J. Pediatr. **164**, 670 (2014)
3. Sarika, G., Songire, M., Joshi, S.: Automated detection of cholesterol presence using iris recognition algorithm. Int. J. Comput. Appl. **113**, 40–41 (2016)
4. Loren, A.Z., Jeffery, M.: Correlating corneal arcus with atherosclerosis in familial hypercholesterolemia. Lipids Health Dis. **22**, 132–135 (2013)
5. Ramlee, R., Aziz, K.A., Ranjit, S., Esro, M.: Automated detecting arcus senilis, symptom for cholesterol presence using iris recognition algorithm. J. Telecommun. Electron. Comput. Eng. **3**, 117–119 (2015)
6. Chang, L., Yuan, W.Q.: Research on corneal arcus detection method. Chin. J. Sci Instrum. **10**, 2312–2320 (2015)
7. Kumar, S.V.M., Gunasundari, R.: Diagnosis of corneal arcus using statistical feature extraction and support vector machine. In: Dash, S.S., Bhaskar, M.A., Panigrahi, B.K., Das, S. (eds.) Artificial Intelligence and Evolutionary Computations in Engineering Systems, vol. 394, pp. 481–492. Springer, India (2016)
8. Chang, L., Yuan, W.Q.: A new effective method of eyelash and eyelid detection. Micro Electron. Comput. **4**, 122–125 (2011)
9. Guo, X.: Color image segmentation method of statistical region merging. J. XiAn Univ. Sci. Technol. **3**, 393 (2015)
10. Li, D.D., Shi, X.Z.: A kind of color image segmentation algorithm based on HSI space and k-means method. Micro Electron. Comput. **7**, 121–124 (2010)
11. Li, J.Q., Yang, C.H., Cao, B.F.: Improved watershed segmentation method for flotation froth image based on parameter measurement. Chin. J. Sci. Instrum. **6**, 1233–1235 (2013)

Image Super-Resolution for Mobile Iris Recognition

Qi Zhang[1,2], Haiqing Li[1(✉)], Zhaofeng He[1], and Zhenan Sun[1]

[1] Center for Research on Intelligent Perception and Computing,
Institute of Automation, Chinese Academy of Sciences, Beijing, China
{qi.zhang,hqli,znsun}@nlpr.ia.ac.cn, hezhf@irisking.com
[2] School of Engineering Science,
University of Chinese Academy of Sciences, Beijing, China

Abstract. Iris recognition is a reliable method to protect the security of mobile devices. Low resolution (LR) iris images are inevitably acquired by mobile devices, which makes mobile iris recognition very challenging. This paper adopts two pixel level super-resolution (SR) methods: Super-Resolution Convolutional Neural Networks (SRCNN) and Super-Resolution Forests (SRF). The SR methods are conducted on the normalized iris images to recover more iris texture. Ordinal measures (OMs) are applied to extract robust iris features and the Hamming distance is used to calculate the matching score. Experiments are performed on two mobile iris databases. Results show that the pixel level SR technology has limited effectiveness in improving the iris recognition accuracy. The SRCNN and SRF methods get comparable recognition results. The SRF method is much faster at both the training and testing stage.

Keywords: Super-resolution · Iris recognition · Mobile devices

1 Introduction

With the growing demand for high security of smartphones, iris recognition is an emerging method for mobile authentication. Iris has merits of high uniqueness and distinctiveness. Compared with traditional knowledge-based mobile authentication systems, iris recognition is more reliable and user-friendly. Mobile iris recognition is generally used in more flexible conditions. It extends the applicability of a traditional iris recognition system but also brings about new challenges. Due to limitations of mobile imaging sensors, many low resolution (LR) iris images are acquired. Figure 1 shows the comparison of iris images obtained by a mobile device and a specific equipment from IrisGuard. We can see the resolution of mobile iris images is lower and some iris texture details are inevitably lost. This will degrade mobile iris authentication accuracy. A straightforward idea is to increase the resolution of iris images.

Super-resolution (SR) is widely used to enhance image resolution. It usually takes one or more low resolution images as input and maps them to a high

© Springer International Publishing AG 2016
Z. You et al. (Eds.): CCBR 2016, LNCS 9967, pp. 399–406, 2016.
DOI: 10.1007/978-3-319-46654-5_44

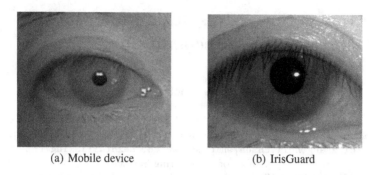

(a) Mobile device   (b) IrisGuard

Fig. 1. Comparison of iris images obtained by a mobile device and IrisGuard. The resolution of mobile iris images is lower and some iris texture details are inevitably lost.

resolution (HR) output image [1]. Single image super resolution (SISR) receives much attention nowadays. Most of SR methods only focus on visual effect, while SR in biometrics mainly aims at improving the recognition rate. Super-resolution technology used for iris recognition can be conducted at pixel level [2], feature level [3] and code level [4]. Among them, pixel level SR occupies the majority because it is simpler and more direct. After SR, higher resolution iris images or enhanced feature codes are fed into the traditional recognition procedure [5]. In this way, the recognition accuracy can be improved.

In this paper, to solve the problem of low resolution iris images acquired by mobile devices, two SISR methods are adopted: (1) the first one is the Super-Resolution Convolutional Neural Networks (SRCNN) [6], which is based on deep learning that can directly learns an end-to-end mapping between LR and HR images; (2) the second one uses Super-Resolution Forests (SRF) [7], which is fast in both training and evaluation. Both of the above SR methods are conducted at the pixel level on the normalized iris images. Afterwards, iris features of higher resolution images are represented by ordinal measures (OMs) [8]. The Hamming distance is used to calculate the matching score of two iris codes. The schematic diagram is shown in Fig. 2. Experiments are performed on two mobile iris databases to verify the effectiveness of SR technology in improving the recognition rate. The remainder of this paper is organized as follows: Sect. 2 describes technical details. The experimental results are presented in Sect. 3 and finally Sect. 4 concludes the paper and outlines future works.

2   Technical Details

2.1   Image Preprocessing

Images acquired by mobile devices contain two eyes. Image preprocessing includes three steps. Firstly, coarse eye regions are detected by Adaboost eye detectors [9]. Then iris boundaries and eye centers are localized using the method proposed by He et al. [10]. Thirdly, the annular iris image is unfolded to a 70×540

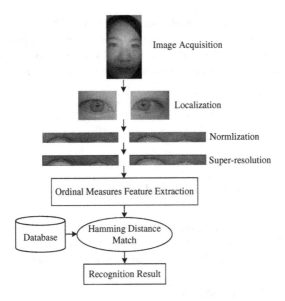

Fig. 2. The schematic diagram.

rectangle image using the rubber sheet model [11]. Subsequently, pixel level super-resolution is performed on the normalized iris images.

2.2 Image Super-Resolution

Super-Resolution Convolutional Neural Networks (SRCNN). The convolutional neural networks (CNNs) are adopted to learn the non-linear mapping function between LR images to HR images [6]. The used CNNs have a lightweight structure that only has three convolutional layers: the first layer extracts n_1-dimensional feature maps of LR image patches; the second layer maps these n_1-dimensional feature vectors into n_2-dimensional feature maps of corresponding HR image patches; the last layer aggregates above HR patches to generate the final HR image. The loss function is mean squared error between the reconstructed images and the corresponding ground-truth HR images.

Super-Resolution Forests (SRF). Random forests are used to directly map from LR to HR patches [7]. Random forests have merits of highly non-linear that are usually extremely fast during both training and evaluation. SRF build on linear prediction models in leaf nodes. During tree growing, a novel regularized objective function is adopted that operates on both output and input domains. In this way, higher quality results for SISR can be achieved.

2.3 Iris Feature Extraction and Matching

The robust local feature descriptor ordinal measures (OMs) are used to extract iris features [12]. We use both the di-lobe and tri-lobe ordinal filters, as shown in

Fig. 3. At first, a large feature pool is generated. We divide the normalized iris image into multiple regions and various ordinal filters are applied on different regions. Afterwards, the AdaBoost algorithm [13] is used for feature dimensionality reduction that only the most distinctive features are selected.

Fig. 3. The di-lobe and tri-lobe ordinal filters.

We calculate the Hamming distance (HD) [11] of two iris feature templates to get the matching score. To overcome iris rotation variations, we rotate iris feature templates several angles to get the best matching score.

3 Experimental Results

3.1 Training

The training set includes 91 images that is widely used in SR technology [1]. The LR images are synthesized from the ground truth HR images through down-sampling and Gaussian blur. SRF can be trained within minutes on a single CPU core, which is very efficient. However, it takes three days to train the SRCNN on a GTX 770 GPU.

We also use HR iris images obtained by IrisGuard and corresponding LR iris images by down-sampling to train the models. But similar recognition results with using the models trained in [6,7] are acquired. Hence, in our subsequent experiments, we use the models in [6,7]. One normalized mobile iris image is input into the trained SR model and the corresponding HR image is output.

3.2 Test Databases

CASIA-Iris-Mobile-V1.0. This is the first public near-infrared (NIR) mobile iris database [14]. It includes 1400 face images and 2800 iris images from 70 Asians. A small NIR imaging module that connected to smartphones by USB is used. Images are captured at about 25 cm standoff distance. The resolution of the whole image is 1080 × 1920 while the diameter of an iris is about 110 pixels. Example images are shown in Fig. 4.

CASIA-Iris-Mobile-V2.0. This is the largest NIR mobile iris database that contains 6000 images from 200 Asians [15]. It uses a new NIR imaging module that connected to smartphones by USB. Images are acquired at varying standoff distances: 20, 25, 30 cm and the corresponding iris diameter is about 132, 153, 195 pixels, respectively. The resolution of the whole image is 1968 × 1024. Example images are shown in Fig. 5.

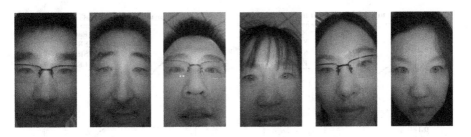

Fig. 4. Example images in the CASIA-Iris-Mobile-V1.0 database.

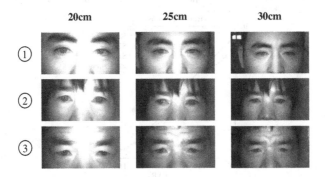

Fig. 5. Example images in the CASIA-Iris-Mobile-V2.0 database.

Table 1. EER results, where 'Iris LR Fusion' represents the score level fusion of left and right iris by the sum rule.

	Right iris	Left iris	Iris LR Fusion
Raw image	7.57 %	5.36 %	3.89 %
SRCNN	6.94 %	4.95 %	3.65 %
SRF	6.98 %	5.01 %	3.61 %

3.3   Results on CASIA-Iris-Mobile-V1.0 Database

We use the same testing images as used in [14] that contains 1800 iris images from 45 subjects. Both the SRCNN and SRF super-resolution methods are used to enhance the resolution of iris images. We implement both methods by MATLAB and run in a PC with 2.67 GHz CPUs. Experiments are conducted on left and right iris images separately and then score level fusion of left and right iris by the sum rule is performed to boost the recognition accuracy. The equal error rate (EER) results are listed in Table 1. The receiver operating characteristic (ROC) curves are shown in Fig. 6.

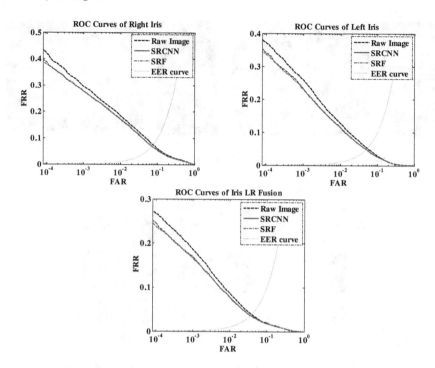

Fig. 6. ROC curves of SRCNN and SRF on CASIA-Iris-Mobile-V1.0 database.

Table 2. EER results at various distances.

	20–20 cm	20–25 cm	20–30 cm
Raw image	0.64 %	1.69 %	1.83 %
SRCNN	0.54 %	1.49 %	1.82 %
SRF	0.55 %	1.51 %	1.83 %

3.4   Results on CASIA-Iris-Mobile-V2.0 Database

We use the same testing images as used in [15] that contains 6000 iris images
from 100 subjects. Both the SRCNN and SRF super-resolution methods are used
to enhance the resolution of iris images. Experiments are performed at various
distances (20–20 cm, 20–25 cm, 20–30 cm) using a single eye. The EER results
are listed in Table 2. The ROC curves are shown in Fig. 7.

Experiments on the two databases get similar conclusions: (1) the SRCNN
and SRF methods get comparable recognition results. SRCNN method takes
about 3 s on one normalized image with size of 70 × 540 while the SRF method
takes only about 0.3 s on the same image. The SRF method is much faster;
(2) the SR technology has limited effectiveness in improving the recognition
accuracy. The limitations are as follows: pixel level SR is not directly related to

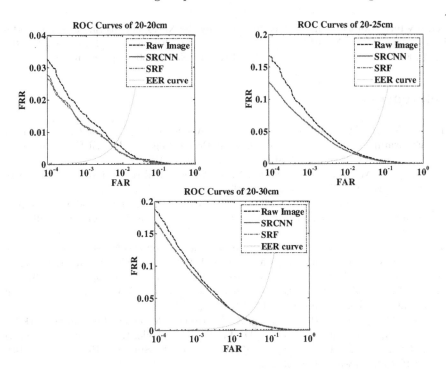

Fig. 7. ROC curves of SRCNN and SRF on CASIA-Iris-Mobile-V2.0 database.

recognition and may introduce spurious information; the SR model is trained with synthesizing LR images that are very different with real-world LR images.

4   Conclusions

In this paper, to solve the problem of low resolution iris images acquired by mobile devices, we have adopted two super-resolution methods: SRCNN and SRF at the pixel level. Acquired images are first preprocessed and the SR methods are performed on the normalized iris images. Afterwards, ordinal measures are used to extract robust iris features and the Hamming distance is used to calculate the matching score. The methods are evaluated on two mobile iris databases. We have found the SRCNN and SRF methods get comparable recognition results. The SRF method is much faster at both the training and testing stage. Experimental results show that the pixel level SR technology has limited effectiveness in improving the recognition accuracy because it is not directly related to recognition and may introduce spurious information. We should pay more attention to access more information, such as multi-frame SR that can use complementary information of various images. Our future work will also focus on adding recognition supervision to SR and performing SR at the feature and code level to directly boost the recognition accuracy.

Acknowledgments. This work is supported by the National Natural Science Foundation of China (Grant No. 61403389), the Beijing Nova Programme (Grant No. Z141101-001814090), and the Beijing Talents Fund (Grant No. 2015000021223ZK30).

References

1. Timofte, R., De Smet, V., Van Gool, L.: Anchored neighborhood regression for fast example-based super-resolution. In: Proceedings of the IEEE International Conference on Computer Vision, pp. 1920–1927 (2013)
2. Huang, J., Ma, L., Tan, T., Wang, Y.: Learning based resolution enhancement of iris images. In: BMVC, pp. 1–10 (2003)
3. Nguyen, K., Fookes, C., Sridharan, S., Denman, S.: Feature-domain super-resolution for iris recognition. Comput. Vis. Image Underst. **117**(10), 1526–1535 (2013)
4. Liu, J., Sun, Z., Tan, T.: Code-level information fusion of low-resolution iris image sequences for personal identification at a distance. In: IEEE Sixth International Conference on Biometrics: Theory, Applications and Systems, pp. 1–6 (2013)
5. Liu, J., Sun, Z., Tan, T.: Distance metric learning for recognizing low-resolution iris images. Neurocomputing **144**, 484–492 (2014)
6. Dong, C., Loy, C.C., He, K., Tang, X.: Learning a deep convolutional network for image super-resolution. In: Fleet, D., Pajdla, T., Schiele, B., Tuytelaars, T. (eds.) ECCV 2014, Part IV. LNCS, vol. 8692, pp. 184–199. Springer, Heidelberg (2014). doi:10.1007/978-3-319-10593-2_13
7. Schulter, S., Leistner, C., Bischof, H.: Fast and accurate image upscaling with super-resolution forests. In: Proceedings of the IEEE Conference on Computer Vision and Pattern Recognition, pp. 3791–3799 (2015)
8. Sun, Z., Tan, T.: Ordinal measures for iris recognition. IEEE Trans. Pattern Anal. Mach. Intell. **31**(12), 2211–2226 (2009)
9. Viola, P., Jones, M.J.: Robust real-time face detection. Int. J. Comput. Vis. **57**(2), 137–154 (2004)
10. He, Z., Tan, T., Sun, Z., Qiu, X.: Toward accurate and fast iris segmentation for iris biometrics. IEEE Trans. Pattern Anal. Mach. Intell. **31**(9), 1670–1684 (2009)
11. Daugman, J.G.: How iris recognition works. IEEE Trans. Circuits Syst. Video Technol. **14**(1), 21–30 (2004)
12. Wang, L., Sun, Z., Tan, T.: Robust regularized feature selection for iris recognition via linear programming. In: International Conference on Pattern Recognition, pp. 3358–3361 (2012)
13. He, Z., Sun, Z., Tan, T., Qiu, X., Zhong, C., Dong, W.: Boosting ordinal features for accurate and fast iris recognition. In: IEEE Conference on Computer Vision and Pattern Recognition, pp. 1–8 (2008)
14. Zhang, Q., Li, H., Zhang, M., He, Z., Sun, Z., Tan, T.: Fusion of face and iris biometrics on mobile devices using near-infrared images. In: Yang, J., et al. (eds.) CCBR 2015. LNCS, vol. 9428, pp. 569–578. Springer, Switzerland (2015). doi:10.1007/978-3-319-25417-3_67
15. Zhang, Q., Li, H., Sun, Z., He, Z., Tan, T.: Exploring complementary features for iris recognition on mobile devices. In: International Conference on Biometrics (2016, to appear)

Behavioral Biometrics

Online Finger-Writing Signature Verification on Mobile Device for Local Authentication

Lei Tang[1], Yuxun Fang[1], Qiuxia Wu[2(✉)], Wenxiong Kang[1(✉)], and Junhong Zhao[1]

[1] School of Automation Science and Engineering, South China University of Technology, Guangzhou, China
auwxkang@scut.edu.cn
[2] School of Software Engineering, South China University of Technology, Guangzhou, China
qxwu@scut.edu.cn

Abstract. Most of the existing works for the online signature verification system have focused on the algorithm improvement of each stage, such as feature extraction, matching and classifier design. However, there are less of them related to the design of a real system and its issue in practical application. In this paper, we have designed a novel system for online finger-writing signature verification on mobile device. By means of our proposed protocol for data collection, a small Chinese signature database has been established. Finally, we also have developed a signature verification App embed with simpler and more efficient algorithms for evaluating the performance and time-consuming of real system.

Keywords: Finger-writing signature · Online signature verification · Smart phone · DTW-based system · Local authentication

1 Introduction

With the popularity of mobile devices like smartphones as well as their updated functions, people have been paying their increased attention on them, such as storing more and more sensitive and private information, using them for frequent shopping, paying and trading online [1]. Thus, the more secure and reliable user authentication on smartphones has been emerging as an important issue. As a promising and effective solution, online signature verification on mobile device has caught more and more attention from researchers recently.

According to the instruments employed for signing, *online signature verification on mobile device (M-OSV)* can be classified into two categories, *finger-based signature* and *stylus-based signature*. Compared with the stylus-based signature, the finger-based signature always signs with index finger instead of stylus and most of smartphones are without stylus. Therefore, it can be denoted as *online finger-writing signature verification on mobile device (M-OFSV)* and becomes more popular and convenient in real application. Nevertheless, M-OSV can be classified into *local authentication* and *cloud authentication* according to its real applications. For the local authentication, the whole system runs locally on a designated device, and can be employed for Mcode, App Lock, and File Lock. For the cloud authentication, when enrollment and verification are

© Springer International Publishing AG 2016
Z. You et al. (Eds.): CCBR 2016, LNCS 9967, pp. 409–416, 2016.
DOI: 10.1007/978-3-319-46654-5_45

conducted on different devices, the templates will be stored in cloud, which can be used for online paying, online trading and loading. As shown in Table 1, Owing to large differences between local authentication and cloud authentication, the system's test protocol and actual demand will be easily distinguished to some extent.

Table 1. The comparison between local authentication and cloud authentication

	Local authentication	Cloud authentication
Templates and reference samples	Stored in a designated device	Stored in cloud or servers
	Small amount	Small or lager amount
Enrollment	On a designated device	On a device
	Small amount	Small amount
Verification	Sample on the designated device	Sample on different devices
	Run on the designated device	Run on servers
Classifier and training	Easy and fewer calculation	Maybe complex and higher calculation
	One classifier, DTW, template matching, HMM, SVM, etc.	One classifier, template matching, SVM, HMM, DTW, deep leaning, etc.
Application	Mcode, App Lock, and File Lock	User loading, online playing, and online transfer
	Used more frequently	———

Due to the huge potential market, many online verification systems have been proposed on smartphone, such as DTW-based system [2], histogram-based system [3], feature-based system fusion with HMM-based system [4]. However, most of works still paid their attention on stylus-based signature verification, and less of them discussed or tested the proposed system in real finger-based signature verification. Nevertheless, there is no literature made any different treatment for local authentication and cloud authentication, even without any research work for employing them in Chinese database. As a result, in this paper, we designed a DTW-based system and employed it into M-OFSV for local authentication, then discussed and tested it in practical. The reasons why we chose DTW-based system rather than HMM-based system or feature-based system are as follow: (1) compared with GMM-HMM, DTW is simpler and easier to be implemented in real system; (2) it is demonstrated that the DTW-based system [5] can get the highest accuracy in SVC2004 [6]; (3) DTW-based system has the ability to make use of multicore, which will be described in session III.

The main contributions of our work are as follows: (1) given a detailed analysis and comparison between local authentication and cloud authentication according to the practical situation; (2) proposed a protocol for M-OFSV of local authentication (3); built a finger-writing Chinese signature database on mobile device; (4) discussed and tested the performance of a designed system according to practical situation for the first time.

The remainder of the paper is organized as follows. Section 2 presents a detailed description of the proposed DTW-based system. Section 3 introduces the software which is used to test the actual time-consuming of the designed system, and some experiments and discussions on practical application are presented in Sect. 4. Finally Sect. 5 concludes the paper.

2 The Proposed DTW-Based System

The framework of this proposed DTW-based system can be classified into enrollment and verification phase. Both of them include pre-processing and feature extraction. During the enrollment phase, the user enrolls a set of samples as reference samples which will be used in training and testing phase. When there is an input of a test signature, DTW algorithms will be adopted to calculate the distances between the test sample and the reference samples, then the template matching method [7] will be used to judge whether this test sample is genuine or not. The details are outlined below.

2.1 Pre-processing

Taking the consideration of real-time performance emphasized in the real system, we only translate the signature position to let the mass of the signature be 0.

2.2 Feature Extraction

The feature set of sample points is $o = [x, y, dx, dy, \theta, \rho]$, where x and y are the horizontal and vertical position of this point, dx and dy are the derivative of x and y, where the derivatives of discrete-time signals are calculated by using a second-order regression for removing small noisy variations, as described in Eq. 1, θ is the Path-tangent angle, and ρ is the Log curvature radius. In addition, since the range of this 4 discrete-time signals are different, we take advantage of signal normalization, where they are normalized to zero mean and unit standard deviation [8].

$$\dot{f}_i = \frac{\sum_{\tau=1}^{2} \tau(f_{i+\tau} - f_{i-\tau})}{2 \cdot \sum_{\tau=1}^{2} \tau^2} \tag{1}$$

2.3 DTW Algorithm

In both training and verification stages, we need to calculate the distances between sample and reference samples. In order to compare the signatures with different lengths, we employ the dynamic time warping (DTW) algorithm [9]. The details of employed DTW algorithm is as follows.

For two different length discrete sequences $X = (x_1, x_2,..., x_n)$ and $Y = (y_1, y_2, ..., y_m)$, the distance of x_i and y_j are calculated firstly as Eq. 4, where x_i and y_j are the ith ($i = 1, 2,..., n$) element of X and j^{th} ($j = 1, 2,..., m$) element of Y,

$$d(i,j) = \sum_{z=1}^{k} (x_{i,z} - y_{j,z})^2 \tag{2}$$

k is the length of x_i and y_j; $x_{i,z}$ and $y_{i,z}$ are the zth element of x_i and y_j, respectively, $d(i, j)$ is the distance of x_i and y_j. The overall distance between two discrete sequences X and Y is calculated as follows,

$$D(i,j) = \min\begin{cases} D(i,j-1) + d(i,j) \\ D(i-1,j-1) + d(i,j) \\ D(i-1,j) + d(i,j) \end{cases} \tag{3}$$

Finally, the distance between X and Y is denoted as $D(n, m)/l$, l is the length of the response reference sample.

2.4 Template Matching

In test phase, the mean of distances between the test samples with all reference samples ($mean(d_{rt})$) will be employed to obtain a final similarity measurement. To improve the accuracy, an effective strategy named target dependent (TC-1) score normalization [10] is employed to decrease the adverse impact on target specificities. Thus, the distinction between the test sample with its claims client calculated by follow equation:

$$s = mean(d_{rt}) - mean(d_{ref}) \tag{4}$$

Where $mean(d_{ref})$ is the mean of distances between reference samples.

2.5 Complexity Analysis

For a real smartphone verification system, the analysis on the time complexity is essential. Given n as the length of online signature, the process of pre-processing and feature extraction can be computed in time $O(n)$, and the process of DTW matching will be computed in time $O(n^2)$, while the template matching almost have no time consuming. That's to say, most of the time has been spent in the comparison between samples, and the dim of feature vector and the number of reference sample play an important part for the real-time authentication. Thus, we only employ a 6-dim feature descriptor for sample points.

3   Verification Software

In this paper, an online signature software was developed by using android studio [11]. The software consists of 4 phases, *enrollment*, *verification*, *reproduce* and *logout*. The framework of the verification software is shown in Fig. 1.

- *Enrollment*: collecting some genuine samples to build reference sample set.
- *Verification*: judging the sample is genuine or not and recording the time-consuming.
- *Reproduce*: providing the dynamic trajectory of reference samples to forger.
- *Logout*: deleting the user's samples and their associated documentation.

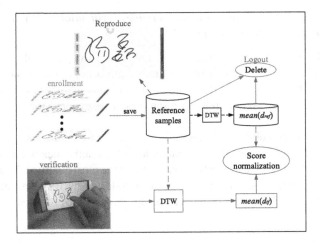

Fig. 1. The framework of the verification software

The locally stored signature is the original signatures which are captured by smartphone instead of extracted features from them, the reasons are as follows: (1) Most of the time spent in the comparison of samples rather than the pre-processing and feature extraction as described in session II; (2) Considering the convenience for system upgrade, the real system prefers to store the encryption original information of samples.

In order to improve the efficiency of the system, the mean of distances between reference samples will be calculated and stored in advance, which can be used directly during verification phase. Additionally, multithreading technology is also used in the comparison of the sample and reference samples in our real system.

However, this software is only a simple simulation of the practical application. As for an App of online finger-writing signature verification, the developer should take more aspects into consideration, such as signature storage form, record location, and templates protection and file encryption.

4   Protocol and Experiments

In light of the characteristics of local authentication as described in Table 1, the online finger-writing signature on mobile device should satisfy the, following requirements for database constructing and experiments designing.

(1) Sign with a finger. As the analysis in Sect. 1, finger-writing style is the latest tendency of signature verification on mobile device.
(2) The interval of samples should not last too long, since the Apps like Mcode are generally used frequently.
(3) Multi-session sampling and multi-device collection. A better signature verification system should have the ability to cope with template aging problem, and also robust to the various devices.

(4) Taking account of both *few reference samples verification* (<=5) and *acceptable reference samples verification* (<=10).

It should be pointed out that in actual use only fewer samples could be captured as reference samples in enrollment phase. The limited number of reference sample is owing to the following two aspects, (1) the memory of chip, (2) time-consuming limitation in real system, which means more reference samples are accounted for larger amount of calculation.

So far, there are no public databases satisfied all above requirements, since they make no different treatment for local authentication and cloud authentication and are lack of analysis on M-OSV for local authentication. Even for the most qualified database [3] still isn't able to obtain multi-device collection (only collected by IOS device) and the 4th requirement. Thus, we build our own database and evaluate the proposed system on it.

4.1   Database

All samples in the database are collected by 6 different smart phones, each device captures 3~5 targets, and there are 25 targets in total. Each target includes 28 genuine samples and 20 skilled forger samples, and the dynamic trajectories of genuine samples are provided for forgers to imitate. All genuine samples are collected from 5 sessions. The first session includes 8 samples, while other sessions include 5 samples, and the time-span between two successive sessions is 24 h, 48 h, 72 h, and 96 h, respectively. The samples from session 1 are taken as reference samples both in few reference samples verification (first 4 samples) and in acceptable reference samples verification (all 8 samples), while the samples from other sessions and all skilled forger samples are used for testing. Additionally, since the screen size of smartphone is limited, it is difficult for all participators to sign whole name on it. As a result, partial signing is allowed.

Depending on the hardware used, the following features are commonly measured at each sample point on signature trajectory: (1) x and y coordinates of the fingertip, (2) time stamp, (3) finger up or down with respect to the signing surface. It is observed from the database that the sampling frequency of most sample points in all devices is 58.8 Hz. The other impacts caused by different configurations among devices, such as screen size and sensitivity of touch screen, are beyond the scope of this article.

4.2   Experiments

In our experiments, the Equal Error Rate (EER), that is the rate at false acceptance rate (FAR) for skilled forgeries and false rejection rate (FRR) are equal, are applied to evaluated the systems' performance. To get the running time in practical system, 10 smart phones with different specifications are used to test the software, and each device includes 2–3 users, 26 participators in total, and each participator tests 3 times. The EER and running time are shown in Table 2. The mean and maximum of running time are 413 ms and 1249 ms, respectively, when using 8 reference samples, which demonstrates that the designed system is able to attain the requirements of real-time verification. The mean running time of using 8 reference samples is only 1.54 times of using 4 reference samples rather than nearly 2 times, indicating the effectiveness by taking full advantage of multicore in smartphone.

Table 2. The EER and time-consuming of the proposed system

	EER	Running time		
		mean	std	maximum
4 reference sample	7.3%	268 ms	105 ms	607 ms
8 reference sample	6.7%	413 ms	221 ms	1249 ms

The greater the number of reference samples, the higher the precision of system. In our system, the distinction between the test sample and its claimed client is measured by $mean(d_{rt})$ and $mean(d_{ref})$ described in Eq. 4. When the number of reference samples increases, the value of $mean(d_{rt})$ and $mean(d_{ref})$ will become close to reality, and the EER will decrease at the same time. In the actual practice, to ensure real-time authentication, the number of reference samples which used to compare with the test sample should be limited, but the number of reference samples which used to calculate $mean(d_{ref})$ can be greater. That's to say, the strategy of employing greater number of reference samples to calculate $mean(d_{ref})$ can be adopted in practice, which might able to improve the performance without substantially changed running time. To test the effectiveness of this strategy, SUSIG [12] and MCYT-100 [13] also have been evaluated in our experiment and the results showed in Table 3.

Table 3. The EER of the system with different number of reference samples which used to calculate $mean(d_{ref})$

	SUSIG	MCYT-100	Our database
Test 4_8	5.56%	4.0%	7.6%
Test 4_4	5.75%	4.67%	7.3 %

Test a_b: a and b are the reference samples used for $mean(d_{rt})$ and $mean(d_{ref})$ respectively, the sample which is not reference samples is used for testing.

The results on SUSIG and MCYT-100 show that the EER will decrease 3.3 % and 14.3 % respectively when more reference samples are used to calculate $mean(d_{ref})$. This indicates that increase the number of reference samples to calculate $mean(d_{ref})$ may able to increase the system performance. However, the EER on our database does not decrease, one of the reasons might be that our database is relatively small. In the future, we will enlarge our database by collecting more samples, in order that more convincing results could be obtained.

5   Conclusion

In this paper, an online finger-writing signature verification system has been presented on mobile device, including designed protocol for data collection, enrollment and verification, and established Chinese signature database. After the validation experiments on actual system, the detailed analysis on technical feasibility of our proposed system has be delivered. In addition, we also have pointed out that local authentication and cloud authentication should be treated different when constructing a real system, such as the strategy of database collection and the complexity of the system. Unlike other existing work, the running time of our proposed system has been obtained by our developed App. Finally, an acceptable strategy is adopted which may increase the performance without sacrificing time consumption, and its validity has been convincingly demonstrated on two public access databases.

Acknowledgments. This work was supported by the National Natural Science Foundation of China (Nos. 61573151, 61105019, 61503141), the Guangdong Natural Science Foundation (No. 2016A030313468) and the Science and Technology Program of Guangzhou (201510010088), the Fundamental Research Funds for the Central Universities, SCUT (No. 2015ZM080).

References

1. Meng, W., et al.: Surveying the development of biometric user authentication on mobile phones. IEEE Commun. Surv. Tutorials **17**(3), 1268–1293 (2015)
2. Blanco-Gonzalo, R., et al.: Handwritten signature recognition in mobile scenarios: performance evaluation. In: 2012 IEEE International Carnahan Conference on Security Technology (ICCST). IEEE (2012)
3. Sae-Bae, N., Memon, N.: Online signature verification on mobile devices. IEEE Trans. Inf. Forensics Secur. **9**(6), 933–947 (2014)
4. Martinez-Diaz, M., et al.: Towards mobile authentication using dynamic signature verification: useful features and performance evaluation. In: 2008 19th International Conference on Pattern Recognition, 2008, ICPR 2008. IEEE (2008)
5. Kholmatov, A., Yanikoglu, B.: Identity authentication using improved online signature verification method. Pattern Recogn. Lett. **26**(15), 2400–2408 (2005)
6. Yeung, D.-Y., Chang, H., Xiong, Y., George, S.E., Kashi, R.S., Matsumoto, T., Rigoll, G.: SVC2004: first international signature verification competition. In: Zhang, D., Jain, A.K. (eds.) ICBA 2004. LNCS, vol. 3072, pp. 16–22. Springer, Heidelberg (2004)
7. Vivaracho-Pascual, C., Faundez-Zanuy, M., Pascual, J.M.: An efficient low cost approach for on-line signature recognition based on length normalization and fractional distances. Pattern Recogn. **42**(1), 183–193 (2009)
8. Fierrez, J., et al.: HMM-based on-line signature verification: Feature extraction and signature modeling. Pattern Recogn. Lett. **28**(16), 2325–2334 (2007)
9. Sakoe, H., Chiba, S.: Dynamic programming algorithm optimization for spoken word recognition. IEEE Trans. Acoust. Speech Signal Process. **26**(1), 43–49 (1978)
10. Fierrez-Aguilar, J., Ortega-Garcia, J., Gonzalez-Rodriguez, J.: Target dependent score normalization techniques and their application to signature verification. IEEE Trans. Syst. Man Cybern. Part C Appl. Rev. **35**(3), 418–425 (2005)
11. Android studio. http://www.android-studio.org/
12. Kholmatov, A., Yanikoglu, B.: SUSIG: an on-line signature database, associated protocols and benchmark results. Pattern Anal. Appl. **12**(3), 227–236 (2009)
13. Ortega-Garcia, J., et al.: MCYT baseline corpus: a bimodal biometric database. IEE Proc. Vis. Image Signal Process. **150**(6), 395–401 (2003)

Uyghur Off-line Signature Recognition Based on Modified Corner Curve Features

Kurban Ubul[1], Ruxianguli Abudurexiti[2], Hornisa Mamat[1], Nurbiya Yadikar[1], and Tuergen Yibulayin[1(✉)]

[1] School of Information Science and Engineering, Xinjiang University, Urumqi 830046, China
{kurbanu,Tuergen}@xju.edu.cn
[2] Xinjiang Police Institute, Urumqi 830013, Xinjiang, China

Abstract. In this paper, modified corner curve features based off-line signature recognition method proposed for Uyghur handwritten signature. The signature images were preprocessed according to the nature of Uyghur signature. Then corner curve features (CCF) and modified corner curve features (MCCF) with different 3 dimensional vectors were extracted respectively. Experiments were performed using Euclidean distance classifier, and non-linear SVM classifier for Uyghur signature samples from 50 different people with 1000 signatures, two kinds of experiments were performed for and variations in the number of training and testing datasets, and a high recognition rate of 98.9 % was achieved with MCCF-16. The experimental results indicated that modified corner curve features can efficiently capture the writing style of Uyghur signature.

Keywords: Uyghur · Handwritten signature · MCCF · Recognition

1 Introduction

Handwritten signatures are the most widely accepted biometric to human identity recognition and verification both socially and legally [1]. The aim of the recognition process is to identify the writer of a given sample [2]. There are two kinds of signature recognition approach: on-line and off-line signature recognition. On-line systems use a digitizer (or an instrumented pen) to generate signals; while off-line systems produce an image of a signature with the help of a scanner (or camera) [3].

The handwritten signature recognition and verification Techniques were studied extensively for more than 30 years. Ismayil et al. [2] proposed an off-line Arabic signature recognition and verification system that its recognition phase was used the multistage classifier and a combination of global and local based features whereas the verification was done using fuzzy concepts. Neural network based approaches for signature recognition and verification indicated in [4, 5]. Lv et al. [6] used static and dynamic features and verify the Chinese signatures with Support Vector Machine (SVM) classifier. Kisku et al. proposed Euclidean distance classifier based signature verification in [7]. Off-line Persian signature identification and verification based on image registration, discrete wavelet transform and image fusion was proposed in report [8]. Shanker et al. [9] proposed signature verification system based on Dynamic Time Warping (DTW)

© Springer International Publishing AG 2016
Z. You et al. (Eds.): CCBR 2016, LNCS 9967, pp. 417–423, 2016.
DOI: 10.1007/978-3-319-46654-5_46

that the system works by extracting the vertical projection features from the signature images, and then comparing it to a reference. An off-line signature recognition system based on local radon features is presented in work [10]. These reports about signature recognitions were mostly based on Latin handwriting, Chinese handwriting, Arabic handwriting, and so on. However, there are a few reports that were our previous research for off-line Uyghur signature recognition. Modified grid information features was proposed for Uyghur signature recognition in [11], and thinning effects on the accuracy of Uyghur signature recognition are studied in [12], and a report about Uyghur hand-written signature verification [13]. So there is a great need and much research room for Uyghur handwritten signatures by implementing existing algorithms creatively or developing new algorithms.

In this paper, modified corner curve features based off-line signature recognition method was proposed for Uyghur signature. The signature images were preprocessed according to the nature of Uyghur signature. Then 3 kinds of corner curve features and modified corner curve features were extracted respectively. Experiments were performed using Euclidean distance classifier, and non-linear SVM classifier.

2   Data Acquisition and Pre-processing

It is including common steps for signature recognition that data acquisition, pre-processing, feature extraction and classification. Native Uyghur persons are selected to give their natural signatures on paper for data acquisition. The signature image must be pre-processed to useful for feature extraction.

2.1   Data Acquisition

The handwritten signatures used in here were selected from Uyghur signatures datasets collected in [11], which 7980 samples were written by 380 Uyghur persons (21 samples/person). Each person asked to sign 21 times on a white A4 sheet of a paper with 21 same sized boxes. The area of each box is big enough to give enough space to use his/her natural signature, and to allow size deviation of signature. The signatures are scanned using Canon MP810 scanner, and stored with .bmp format in 256 grey levels and 300 dpi of resolution.

2.2   Pre-processing

The pre-processing steps for Uyghur signature recognition here include noise reduction, binarization, and size normalization. Since pre-processing is not key point in this paper and it is adapted to the nature of Uyghur signature in our previous work [12, 13]. So it is taken same pre-processing methods for Uyghur signature in this paper explained in [12, 13], and it is omitted to describe here.

3   Feature Extraction

The corner curve features described in [2] and modified corner curve features were extracted in this paper. They were introduced as below.

3.1   Corner Curve Features

The corner curve features composed of coordinates of points which curves crossed with black pixels of signatures. The corner curves and points were indicated as the following Fig. 1:

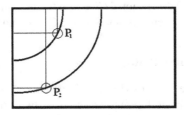

Fig. 1. Corner curves

In the above Fig. 1, the origin point of corner curves is upper left corner. Assume that, there are two corner curves and two points $P_1(x_1, y_1)$, and $P_2(x_2, y_2)$, corner curve features F composed of m points $P_1(x_1, y_1)$, $P_2(x_2, y_2)$,..., $P_m(x_m, y_m)$:

$$F = [P_1, P_2, \ldots, P_m] = [x_1, y_1, x_2, y_2, \ldots, x_m, y_m] \tag{1}$$

Since the size of Uyghur signature image is normalized to 384×96 based on the nature of Uyghur signature, the distances between the two curves was to be selected as 32 pixels, 16 pixels and 8 pixels separately in this paper. They are abbreviated as CCF-32, CCF-16 and CCF-8 respectively. Because the variety of Uyghur handwritten signature, there are several crossed points in some curves and there is no crossed point in some curves, such as illustrated as the following Fig. 2:

Fig. 2. Crossed points in a Uyghur handwritten signature

It is clear from the above Fig. 2 that the numbers of crossed points are different in the different corner curves. It is pointed out that, only one word is illustrated in Fig. 2, and common Uyghur signature is composed of two words, first name and surname, and first name comes first. It is complicated if the crossed points are concerned in the two words in a Uyghur signature. This phenomenon was became much more complex if different kinds of Uyghur signatures are concerned when feature extraction.

For the quantifying the feature extraction and feature matching, only one (first) point in one curve is selected, and coordinates is set zero if there is no crossed point in a curve. If there is no crossed points in ith $(2 < i < m)$ curves, this kind of point is called blank point, and the coordinate of related point is taken $P_i(0,0)$. For CCF-32 here, the distances between the two curves is 32 pixels, and 16 crossed points were selected from 16 curves in Uyghur signature, thus 32 dimensional CCF is extracted. Similarity, it is extracted 64 and 96 dimensional features were extracted with CCF-16 and CCF-8 respectively.

3.2   Modified Corner Curve Features

The modified corner curve features (MCCF) is composed of coordinates of crossed points which are selected from different curves from two original points at the same time. The modified corner curves and points were indicated as the following Fig. 3:

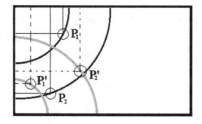

Fig. 3. Modified corner curves and points (Color figure online)

In the Fig. 3, the origin point of corner curves is upper and lower left corner at the same time. Based on the corner curves and point on the Fig. 1, there are other two corner curves (in red) and two points $P'_1(x'_1, y'_1)$ and $P'_2(x'_2, y'_2)$ originated from lower left corner. MCCF include crossed m points $P_1(x_1, y_1)$, $P_2(x_2, y_2)$,..., $P_m(x_m, y_m)$ from upper left corner, and crossed n points $P'_1(x'_1, y'_1), P'_2(x'_2, y'_2), ..., P'_n(x'_n, y'_n)$ from lower left corner:

$$F = [p_1, p_{2,...,}p_m; p'_1, p'_2, ..., p'_n] \tag{2}$$

Where m, n is the number of point selected from curves originated from upper left corners and lower left corners. All the feature extraction rules of MCCF are same as the CCF except the number originated corner points. Thus, the numbers of features are doubled MCCF than CCF. So, it is extracted 64, 128 and 192 dimensional features were extracted with MCCF-32, MCCF-16 and MCCF-8 separately.

4   Classification

Euclidean distance classifier and non-linear SVM classifier were used in recognition step. If the weight vector can be expressed as a linear combination of the training examples, i.e. $w = \sum_{i=1}^{n} a_i x_i$, then:

$$f(x) = \sum_{i=1}^{n} a_i x_i^T x + b \tag{3}$$

In the feature space F, this expression takes the form:

$$f(x) = \sum_{i=1}^{n} a_i \phi(x_i)^T \phi(x) + b \tag{4}$$

where α_i is known as the dual representation of the decision boundary. The feature space F may be high dimensional as indicated Eq. (4), making this trick impractical unless the kernel function $k(x, x')$ can be computed efficiently denoted as:

$$k(x, x') = \phi(x)^T \phi(x') \tag{5}$$

In terms of the kernel function the discriminate function is:

$$f(x) = \sum_{i=1}^{n} a_i k(x, x_i) + b \tag{6}$$

5   Experimental Results

For the demonstrating the efficiency of the proposed method, two types of classifiers, Euclidean distance classifier, and non-linear SVM classifier were used in our experiment. To the experiment, 1000 samples collected from 50 Uyghur people (20 samples per person) were selected from our database. Three types CCF and MCCF features were extracted respectively after preprocessing. Two kinds of experiments were performed based on the training data set with 800 and 500 images from the database separately. The rest of the signature images of the data set were separately used as the testing data set. For the distribution of the training and test set, take 800 samples for training as an example, 16 samples of each classes are used for the training, and rest of them are used for the testing. The accuracy of signature recognition using Euclidean classifier based trial of training 800 and 500 signature image dataset indicated as in Table 1.

It can be seen from the Table 1 that the 87.1 % of highest recognition rate was achieved when MCCF-16 were extracted during Euclidean classifier based trial of training 800 dataset. While the other features were indicated lower recognition rate than MCCF-16. The accuracy of signature recognition using non-liner SVM classifier based trial of training 800 and 500 signature image dataset indicated as in the following Table 2.

Table 1. Identification rates using Euclidean distance

Trial Features	training 800 samples	training 500 samples
CCF-32	79.4%	73.9%
CCF-16	82.6%	76.5%
CCF-8	85.7%	81.8%
MCCF-32	84.3%	80.4%
MCCF-16	87.1%	83.2%
MCCF-8	88.3%	82.5%

Table 2. Identification rates using non-liner SVM classifier

Trial Features	training 800 samples	training 500 samples
CCF-32	93.6%	89.5%
CCF-16	94.1%	90.3%
CCF-8	96.2%	91.8%
MCCF-32	95.4%	90.9%
MCCF-16	98.9%	94.3%
MCCF-8	96.8%	93.7%

It was clear from the Table 2 that the 98.9 % of highest recognition rate in this paper was obtained when MCCF-16 was extracted using non-linear SVM classifier based trial of training 800 dataset. While the other features were indicated lower recognition rate than MCCF-16 in this kind of experiment.

It can be seen from the two tables (Tables 1 and 2) that non-linear SVM classifier indicates higher accuracy than Euclidean distance classifier with CCF and MCCF, that is, its identification rates is at least 11.5 % higher than Euclidean distances' both the two kinds of experiments. CCF-8 was indicates higher identification rates than CCF-16, and CCF-32 during the same kind of experiment; similarly, MCCF-16 presents higher accuracy than MCCF-32 and MCCF-8. The average accuracy of MCCF-16 is about 2.5 % higher than accuracy of CCF-8. Also, it is higher than our earlier results using modified grid information features about 4.2 % presented in [11]. And it is also higher than our earlier results using directional features about 2.9 % described in [12].

6   Conclusions and Future Work

In this paper, modified corner curve features based off-line signature recognition method was proposed for Uyghur handwritten signature. The signature images were preprocessed according to the nature of Uyghur signature. Then 3 types of corner curve features (CCF-32, CCF-16, and CCF-8) and modified corner curve features (MCCF-32, MCCF-16, and MCCF-8) were extracted separately. Experiments were performed using Euclidean distance classifier, and non-linear SVM classifier for Uyghur signature samples from 50 different people with 1000 signatures, two kinds of experiments were performed for and variations in the number of training and testing datasets, and a high recognition rate of 98.9 % was achieved with MCCF-16. The experimental results indicated that MCCF in this paper can efficiently capture the writing style of Uyghur signature. So it is worth to considering that it is a kind of method to improving accuracy of signature recognition when the structural features are extracted in different scripts signature, especially in Arabic, Persian, and Urdu etc. In future work, this methods described in this paper will upgraded by including more signatures in the database, exploring more efficient features, and performing more experiments with other efficient methods.

Acknowledgments. This work is supported by the National Natural Science Foundation of China (No. 61163028, 61563052), College Scientific Research Plan Project of Xinjiang Uyghur Autonomous Region (No. XJEDU2013I11), and Special Training Plan Project of Xinjiang Uyghur Autonomous Region's Minority Science and Technological Talents (No. 201323121).

References

1. Plamondon, R., Srihari, S.N.: On-line and off-line handwriting recognition: a comprehensive survey. IEEE Trans. Pattern Anal. Mach. Intell. **22**(1), 63–84 (2000)
2. Ismail, M.A., Gad, S.: Off-line Arabic signature recognition and verification. Pattern Recogn. **33**(10), 1727–1740 (2000)
3. Plamondon, R., Lorette, G.: Automatic signature verification and writer identification – the state of the art. Pattern Recogn. **22**(2), 107–131 (1989)
4. Baltzakisa, H., Papamarkos, N.: A new signature verification technique based on a two-stage neural network classifier. Eng. Appl. Artif. Intell. **14**(1), 95–103 (2001)
5. Karounia, A., Dayab, B., Bahlak, S.: Offline signature recognition using neural networks approach. Procedia Comput. Sci. **3**, 155–161 (2011)
6. Lv, H., Wang, W., Wang, C., Zhuo, Q.: Off-line Chinese signature verification based on support vector machines. Pattern Recogn. Lett. **26**(15), 2390–2399 (2005)
7. Kisku, D.R., Gupta, P., Sing, J.K.: Off-line signature identification by fusion of multiple classifiers using statistical learning theory. Int. J. Secur. Appl. **4**(3), 35–45 (2010)
8. Ghandali, S., Moghaddam, M.E.: Off-line Persian signature identification and verification based on image registration and fusion. J. Multimedia **4**, 137–144 (2009)
9. Shanker, A., Rajagopalan, A.: Off-line signature verification using DTW. Pattern Recogn. Lett. **28**(12), 1407–1414 (2007)
10. Angadi, S.A., Gour, S., Bajantri, G.: Offline signature recognition system using radon transform. In: 2014 Fifth International Conference on Signals and Image Processing, pp. 56–61 (2014)
11. Ubul, K., Adler, A., Abliz, G., Yasheng, M., Hamdulla, A.: Off-line Uyghur signature recognition based on modified grid information features. In: 11th International Conference on Information Sciences, Signal Processing and Their Applications, pp. 1083–1088. IEEE Press, New York (2012)
12. Ubul, K., Adler, A., Yadikar, N.: Effects on accuracy of Uyghur handwritten signature recognition. In: Liu, C.-L., Zhang, C., Wang, L. (eds.) CCPR 2012. CCIS, vol. 321, pp. 548–555. Springer, Heidelberg (2012)
13. Ubul, K., Yibulayin, T., Aysa, A.: Off-line Uyghur handwritten signature verification based on combined features. In: Li, S., Liu, C., Wang, Y. (eds.) CCPR 2014, Part II. CCIS, vol. 484, pp. 491–498. Springer, Heidelberg (2014)

Improved i-vector Speaker Verification Based on WCCN and ZT-norm

Yujuan Xing$^{(\boxtimes)}$, Ping Tan, and Chengwen Zhang

School of Digital Media, Lanzhou University of Arts and Science,
Lanzhou 730000, China
Xyj19811010@126.com

Abstract. For the purpose of improving system performance in high channel variability, an improved i-vector speaker verification algorithm is proposed in this paper. Firstly, i-vectors are obtained from GMM-UBM of registered speakers. And then, the weighted linear discriminant analysis is utilized to play the role of channel compensation and dimensionality reduction in i-vectors. By doing this, more discriminant vectors could be extracted. Immediately following, WCCN and ZT-norm are combined to normalize the scores from cosine distance score classifier for the sake of removing channel disturbance. Finally, cosine distance score classifier of high robustness is generated to find target speaker. Experiment results demonstrate that our proposed i-vector system has better performance.

Keywords: Speaker verification · i-vector · Weighting linear fisher discriminant · Within-class covariance normalization · ZT-norm

1 Introduction

Speaker verification is an important branch of speaker recognition. Gaussian mixture model (GMM) has achieved widespread application in this research field with its excellent classification performance. Campbell, W [1] proposed the conception of GMM super-vector based on speaker Gaussian mixture model universal background models(GMM-UBM) and applied it in SVM speaker verification. Good experimental results had been achieved. Most researchers utilized GMM super-vector to generate SVM sequence kernel [2–4]. However, the dimension of GMM super-vector is high and it contains more channel information [5]. These problems result in a mass of matrix manipulation which exist in the process of dimension reduction and channel compensation in GMM super-vector. So the computational complexity of GMM super-vector is higher. How to extract lower dimensional and more discriminant feature vectors becomes the research hotspot recently. N. Dehak [6] pointed that the feature extraction should comprehensively consider the speech space and channel space. And N. Dehak proposed lower dimensional i-vector based on total variability space, linear discriminant analysis (LDA) was used for channel compensation. References [8] established a simple classifier called cosine distance score classifier (CDSC) based on i-vector to replace support vector machine (SVM). Experiments were carried out on NIST SRE2010 to verify the algorithm's effectiveness and feasibility. However, in the

© Springer International Publishing AG 2016
Z. You et al. (Eds.): CCBR 2016, LNCS 9967, pp. 424–431, 2016.
DOI: 10.1007/978-3-319-46654-5_47

cased of similar channel and closer speech, LDA is not a ideal compensation method since that it could not sufficiently utilize the discrimination between classes. Meanwhile, independent threshold should be set for each target speaker since that the target sample size is far less than imposter sample size in CDSC. This problem will reduce the system robustness.

For the sake of solving the problem of poor robustness in CDSC, References [9] utilized ZT-norm technology to normalize the classifier score. Based on the inspiration of above research, we proposed a improved i-vector extraction method to apply in speaker verification. We utilized weight linear discriminant analysis (WLDA) for channel compensation to extract more discriminant and lower dimensional i-vector. And then, we combined within class covariance normalization (WCCN) with ZT-norm to normalized score and restrain channel interference.

The reminder of this paper is organized as follows. Section 2 gives a detailed description of our speaker verification based on improved i-vector. Experimental evaluation and results discussion are presented in Sect. 3. Finally, conclusions are drawn in Sect. 4.

2 Speaker Verification Based on Improved i-vector

The system framework of speaker verification based on our proposed i-vector is showed as Fig. 1. From Fig. 1, we could see that the system constitute of three processing blocks, which are the generation of i-vector, channel compensation and CDSC decision.

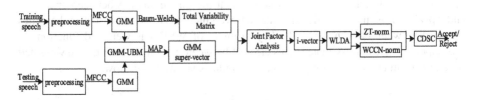

Fig. 1. The system diagram of improved i-vector speaker verification

2.1 The Generation of i-vector

The basic idea of i-vector is that more discriminant vectors are extracted based on GMM super-vector, in which the speech space and channel space are not distinguished strictly. So GMM super-vector can be represented as follows.

$$\mu = \bar{\mu} + Tw \tag{1}$$

where μ is speaker's GMM super-vector, and it is related to speaker voice and channel. $\bar{\mu}$ is the mean super-vector of GMM Universal Background Model (GMM-UBM) that is channel-independent. T is a low rank matrix representing the primary directions across all development data. w is total-variability factors, which has a standard normal distribution $N(0,1)$ and is referred to as i-vector.

We assumed that GMM-UBM of our speaker verification system as follows.

$$p(x)^{(u)} = \sum_{i=1}^{M} \omega_i N(x; m_i, \sum_i)$$ (2)

where $N(x; m_i, \sum_i)$ indicates the Gaussian density function of vector x. ω_i, μ_i and $\sum_i$ are the mixture weights, mean and covariance of ith Gaussian density component respectively. A Maximum-Likelihood estimate of matrix T is usually obtained by minor modifications of the Joint Factor Analysis approach [10].

2.2   Channel Compensation Based on WLDA

Linear discriminant analysis is a common channel compensation technology. However, LDA don't consider separability of similar classes sufficiently. So some useful discriminant information in speech will lost. In this paper, we utilized WLDA [11] to replace LDA for i-vector channel compensation. The main difference between WLDA and LDA is that between-class matrix is redefined by weighted function of similar classes. The weighted between-class matrix can be calculated as follows.

$$S_b^W = \frac{1}{N} \sum_{s=1}^{S-1} \sum_{t=s+1}^{S} \omega(d_{st}) n_s n_t (\bar{w}_s - \bar{w}_t)(\bar{w}_s - \bar{w}_t)^T$$ (3)

In Eq. (3), the weighted function $\omega(d_{st})$ is used to weight similar classes for better discrimination. When $\omega(d_{st}) = 1$, it shows that the discrimination between speaker s and speaker t is not considered, and the weighted between-class matrix becomes standard between-class matrix. The key problem of WLDA is weighted function. In this paper, we use approximate Bayes error of between-class mean to estimate weighted function parameters. The computational formula is showed as follows.

$$\omega(d_{st})_{Bayes} = \frac{1}{2(\sigma_{st})^2} Erf(\frac{\sigma_{st}}{2\sqrt{2}})$$ (4)

where $\sigma_{st} = \sqrt{(\bar{w}_s - \bar{w}_t)^T (S_w)^{-1}(\bar{w}_s - \bar{w}_t)}$ is Mahalanobis distance of i-vector mean between speaker s and speaker t. $Erf(\frac{\sigma_{st}}{2\sqrt{2}}) = \frac{2}{\pi} \int_0^{\frac{\sigma_{st}}{2\sqrt{2}}} e^{-t^2} dx$ is error function. We compute optimal projection direction H using $S_b v = \lambda S_w v$. And then, compensated i-vector is extracted by $\hat{w}_{LDA} = H^T w$.

2.3   Robust Cosine Distance Score Classifier

Suppose that the compensated i-vector is w', the traditional cosine distance score classifier (CDSC) is showed as follows.

$$s(w'_{t\,arg\,et}, w'_{test}) = \frac{(w'_{t\,arg\,et})^t w'_{test}}{\left\| w'_{t\,arg\,et} \right\| \left\| w'_{test} \right\|} \begin{array}{c} > \\ < \end{array} \theta \tag{5}$$

where $s(w'_{t\,arg\,et}, w'_{test})$ represents the matching score between testing speech and target speech. $w'_{t\,arg\,et}$ and w'_{test} is the compensated i-vector of testing speech and target speech respectively. θ is the decision threshold. The robustness of θ is poor because of channel interference and sample size gap between target samples and imposter samples. Score normalization could restrain the channel affection that is calculated by follows.

$$\tilde{s}(w'_{t\,arg\,et}, w'_{test}) = \frac{s(w'_{t\,arg\,et}, w'_{test}) - \mu}{\sigma} \tag{6}$$

where $\tilde{s}(w'_{t\,arg\,et}, w'_{test})$ is the score after normalization, μ and σ is mean and variance of imposter i-vector respectively. In this paper, we combined zero normalization (Z-norm) and test normalization (T-norm) to normalize the CDSC score.

We firstly use Z-norm for Eq. (4) as follows.

$$\tilde{s}_{z-norm}(w'_{t\,arg\,et}, w'_{test}) = \frac{s(w'_{t\,arg\,et}, w'_{test}) - m_{z-norm}}{\sigma_{z-norm}} \tag{7}$$

where $m_{z-norm} = \frac{1}{N}(w'_{t\,arg\,et})^t \sum\limits_{i=1}^{N} w'_{z-imp_i}$, N is the imposter sample number. w'_{z-imp_i} is i-vector of ith imposter.

$$\begin{aligned} \sigma^2_{z-norm} &= Ei[((w'_{t\,arg\,et})^t(w'_{z-imp_i}) - m_{z-norm}) * ((w'_{t\,arg\,et})^t(w'_{z-imp_i}) - m_{z-norm})^t] \\ &= Ei[((w'_{t\,arg\,et})^t(w'_{z-imp_i}) - (\frac{1}{N}(w'_{t\,arg\,et})^t \sum\limits_{i=1}^{N} w'_{z-imp_i})) * ((w'_{t\,arg\,et})^t(w'_{z-imp_i}) \\ &\quad - (\frac{1}{N}(w'_{t\,arg\,et})^t \sum\limits_{i=1}^{N} w'_{z-imp_i}))] \\ &= (w'_{t\,arg\,et})^t \Sigma_{z-imp}(w'_{t\,arg\,et}) \end{aligned} \tag{8}$$

where $\Sigma_{z-imp} = Ei[((w'_{z-imp_i}) - \frac{1}{N}\sum\limits_{i=1}^{N} w'_{z-imp_i}) * ((w'_{z-imp_i}) - \frac{1}{N}\sum\limits_{i=1}^{N} w'_{z-imp_i})^t]$. So the computational formula of Z-norm is showed as follows.

$$\begin{aligned} \tilde{s}_{z-norm}(w'_{t\,arg\,et}, w'_{test}) &= \frac{s(w'_{t\,arg\,et}, w'_{test}) - \frac{1}{N}(w'_{t\,arg\,et})^t \sum\limits_{i=1}^{N} w'_{z-imp_i}}{\sqrt{(w'_{t\,arg\,et})^t \Sigma_{z-imp}(w'_{t\,arg\,et})}} \\ &= \frac{(w'_{t\,arg\,et})^t(w'_{test} - \frac{1}{N}\sum\limits_{i=1}^{N} w'_{z-imp_i})}{\sqrt{(w'_{t\,arg\,et})^t \Sigma_{z-imp}(w'_{t\,arg\,et})}} \end{aligned} \tag{9}$$

Suppose that Σ_{z-imp} is diagonal matrix, we could simply above equation as follows.

$$\tilde{s}_{z-norm}(w'_{t\,arg\,et}, w'_{test}) = \frac{(w'_{t\,arg\,et})^t (w'_{test} - \frac{1}{N}\sum_{i=1}^{N} w'_{z-imp_i})}{\left\| C_{z-imp} w'_{t\,arg\,et} \right\|} \tag{10}$$

where C_{z-imp} is the square root of imposter i-vector covariance matrix. Also it is a diagonal matrix. Similar to Z-norm, the computational formula of T-norm is showed as follows.

$$\tilde{s}_{t-norm}(w'_{t\,arg\,et}, w'_{test}) = \frac{(w'_{t\,arg\,et} - \frac{1}{N}\sum_{i=1}^{N} w'_{t-imp_i})^t (w'_{test})}{\left\| C_{t-imp} w'_{test} \right\|} \tag{11}$$

We combined Z-norm and T-norm to normalize CDSC as follows.

$$\tilde{s}(w'_{t\,arg\,et}, w'_{test}) = \frac{(w'_{t\,arg\,et} - \bar{w}'_{imp})^T (w'_{t\,arg\,et} - \bar{w}'_{imp})^T}{\left\| C_{imp}.w'_{t\,arg\,et} \right\| \left\| C_{imp}.w'_{test} \right\|} \tag{12}$$

where $\bar{w}_{imp}$ is mean of imposter i-vector, C_{imp} is the square root of imposter i-vector covariance matrix.

After score normalization based on ZT-norm, we utilized WCCN [12] to further normalize score immediate following. By doing so, the channel affection in score could be reduced. The WCCN transformation matrix U could be calculated as follows.

$$UU^T = W^{-1} \tag{13}$$

$$W = \frac{1}{S}\sum_{s=1}^{S}\sum_{i=1}^{n_s} \left(H^T \left(w'^s_i - \bar{w}'_s\right)\right) \left(H^T \left(w'^s_i - \bar{w}'_s\right)\right)^T \tag{14}$$

$$w' = \frac{U^t H^t w}{\left\| U^t H^t w \right\|} \tag{15}$$

Where H is projection matrix of WLDA. We not only normalized the score but also identify the target speaker by substituting Eq. (15) into Eq. (12).

3   Experiments

3.1   Speech Corpus

Our experiments are primarily to test the performance of speaker verification system based on improved i-vector. Therefore, how to build better speech corpus is the key problem. In our corpus, we record speech data of 58 speakers, which contains 27 males and 31 females. In order to embody the channel variation in speech, the speech is collected at twice. The first speech record is carried out in quiet environment using microphone. We record 15 utterances for each speaker. In these utterances, 6 utterances is ordinary speed, 5 utterances vary in high, medium and low tone, the rest 4 utterances' speed is slow. The second speech record is carried out using telephone. The utterance allocation is the same as first speech allocation. In our corpus, we totally record 30 utterances for each speaker by twice speech collection. We randomly select 15 utterances for training and the rest is used for testing. The first-order digital filter was $H(z) = 1 - 0.95z^{-1}$. We extract 13 dimensional Mel-Frequency Cepstral Coefficients (MFCCs) and their first and second derivatives and combine them into a 39 dimensional vector as input features of all our experiments. Therefore, the number of training vectors was $5 \times 1999 = 9995$. The original MFCC coefficients extracted from the feature vectors have wide variations. These variations not only come from speaking at different times, but also come from different channels. We adopted cepstral mean variance normalization (CMVN) to compensate for these changes. The calculation was showed as $x_i' = \frac{x_i - \mu}{\sigma}$, where x_i is original coefficient and x_i' indicated normalized speech coefficient of the ith frame. μ is mean vector and σ is standard deviation: $\mu = \frac{1}{N} \sum_{i=1}^{N} x_i$,

$\sigma = \sqrt{\frac{\sum_{i=1}^{N} (x_i - \mu)^2}{N-1}}$, where N is the frame number of a single speech utterance. The dimension of i-vector is set 550. Equal Error Rate (EER) and Minimum Decision Cost Function (minDCF) are adopt as performance measurement index.

3.2 Experiments and Analysis

Experiment 1: The comparison of LDA and WLDA

In order to test the channel interference suppression and dimension reduction, we applied LDA and WLDA to i-vector in this experiment. The experimental results were showed as Table 1.

Table 1. Performance analysis between LDA and WLDA

i-vector dimension	LDA		WLDA	
	EER(%)	MinDCF	EER(%)	MinDCF
550	13.64	0.07229	11.93	0.0701
400	10.13	0.06326	9.06	0.0628
350	8.47	0.05823	7.22	0.0533
300	7.32	0.05101	6.46	0.0455
200	6.11	0.04379	**4.93**	**0.0373**
100	6.78	0.04925	6.01	0.0416
50	7.92	0.05778	7.83	0.0539
20	9.03	0.07002	8.94	0.0643

The experiment results of Table 1 showed that the performance of LDA and WLDA was worst when the dimension of i-vector was 550. However, with the decrease of i-vector dimension, WLDA could take full advantage that was to maximize phonetic differences and minimize the channel different. When i-vector dimension was 200, the best system performance was achieved. But i-vector dimension should not decrease sharply. When i-vector dimension was less than 200, the discriminant information would be lost. In the case of i-vector dimension was 200, the WLDA EER fell by 1.18 % compared with LDA and WLDA minDCF also fell by 0.0065. Therefore, WLDA was superior to LDA.

Experiment 2:The performance comparison of i-vector speaker verification based on different classifier

In this experiment, we applied SVM, original CDSC, CDSC based on ZT-norm and CDSC based on WCCN and ZT-norm to i-vector speaker verification. WLDA was used for channel compensation and i-vector dimension was 200. The experimental results were showed as Table 2.

Table 2. Performance comparison analysis in different classification algorithm

Classifier	EER(%)	MinDCF
SVM	15.21	0.0981
Original CDSC	13.49	0.0790
ZT-norm CDSC	5.31	0.0316
WCCN + ZT-norm CDSC	4.28	0.0202

From Table 2, we could see that our proposed method is optimal. Compared to SVM, the EER of our proposed method reduced almost 11 % and minDCF reduced 0.0779. Compared to original CDSC, the EER of our proposed method reduced 9.29 % and minDCF fell by 0.0588. Compared to CDSC based on ZT-norm, The EER of our proposed method reduced 1.03 % and minDCF reduced 0.0114. Therefore, the experiment result fully verified that the combination of WCCN and ZT-norm could improve the robustness of CDSC effectively.

4   Conclusion

A novel improve i-vector speaker verification algorithm was proposed based on in-depth study of i-vector and channel compensation. WLDA not merely was used to channel compensation and dimension reduction but also set different weight for similar speech. It could overcome the LDA defects that discrimination was weak in the case of similar channel and similar speech. With the aid of combination of WCCN and ZT-norm, we normalized the score of CDSC and restrained the channel interference. Experiment results showed that our proposed method had better performance. However, the computation of total variability space is higher. So, how to explore effective training algorithm is our research emphasis in future.

Acknowledgments. This paper is supported by youth science and technology foundation of Gansu (1506RJYA111), china.

References

1. Campbell, W., Sturim, D., Reynolds, D.: Support vector machines using GMM supervectors for speaker verification. IEEE Sig. Process. Lett. **13**(5), 308–311 (2006)
2. Sarkar, A.K., Bonastre, J.F., Matrouf, D.: A study on the roles of total variability space and session variability modeling in speaker recognition. Int. J. Speech Technol. **19**(1), 111–120 (2016)
3. Ma, X., Tan D.T., Jin, Y.K., et al.: Speaker verification using a modified adaptive GMM approach based on low rank matrix recovery. Mobile and Wireless Technologies (2016)
4. Xing, Y.J., Tan, P.: A novel SVM Kernel with GMM super-vector based on Bhattacharyya distance clustering plus within class covariance normalization. In: International Conference on Natural Computation. IEEE, pp. 47–51 (2015)
5. Solomonoff, A., Campbell, W.M., Boardman, I.: Advances in channel compensation for svm speaker recognition. In: International Conference on Acoustics, Speech, and Signal Processing. IEEE, Pennsylvania, pp. I-629−I-632 (2005)
6. Dehak, N.: Front-end factor analysis for speaker verification. Audio Speech Lang. Process. **19**(4), 788–798 (2011)
7. Gang, L.V., Heming, Z.H.A.O.: Joint factor analysis of channel mismatch in whispering speaker verification. Arch. Acoust. **37**(4), 555–559 (2012)
8. McLaren, M., van Leeuwen, D.: Improved speaker recognition when using i-vectors from multiple speech sources. In: IEEE International Conference on Acoustics, Speech and Signal Processing. IEEE, Prague, pp. 5460−5463 (2011)
9. Kenny, P., Boulianne, G., Ouellet, P., et al.: Joint factor analysis versus eigenchannels in speaker recognition. IEEE Trans. Audio Speech Lang. Process. **15**(4), 1435–1447 (2007)
10. Cumani, S., Plchot, O., Laface, P.: On the use of i−vector posterior distributions in probabilistic linear discriminant analysis. IEEE/ACM Trans. Audio Speech Lang. Process. **22**(4), 846–857 (2014)
11. Aronowitz, H.: Inter dataset variability compensation for speaker recognition. In: IEEE International Conference on Acoustics, Speech and Signal Processing, pp. 4002–4006. IEEE (2014)
12. Gao, X.J., Bi-Cheng, L.I.: Method for speaker recognition based on with-in class covariance normalization and SVM. Comput. Eng. Appl. **45**(10), 168–171 (2009)

Gesture Recognition Benchmark Based on Mobile Phone

Chunyu Xie[1], Shangzhen Luan[1], Hainan Wang[1,2], and Baochang Zhang[1(✉)]

[1] School of Automation Science and Electrical Engineering, Beihang University, Beijing, China
bczhang@buaa.edu.cn
[2] School of Mechanical Engineering, Guizhou University, Guiyang, China

Abstract. Mobile phone plays an important role in our daily life. This paper develops a gesture recognition benchmark based on sensors of mobile phone. The built-in micro gyroscope and accelerometer of mobile phone can efficiently measure the accelerations and angular velocities along x-, y- and z-axis, which are used as the input data. We calculate the energy of the input data to reduce the effect of the phone's posture variations. A large database is collected, which contains more than 1,000 samples of 8 gestures. The Hidden Markov Model (HMM), K-Nearest Neighbor (KNN) and Support Vector Machine (SVM) are tested on the benchmark. The experimental results indicated that the employed methods can effectively recognize the gestures. To promote research on this topic, the source code and database are made available to the public. (mpl.buaa.edu.cn or correspondence author)

Keywords: SVM · HMM · KNN · Gesture recognition · Mobile phone

1 Introduction

With the advance of electronic technology, daily activities are closely related to computer and network technology. Human-computer interaction (HCI) becomes an important part of our daily life. The emergence of smart phones allows HCI to be performed effectively through touch screen. However, the touch screen, affected by environmental constraints, is prone to many uncontrollable problems. Therefore, other types of interaction, such as gesture input [1], attract the attention of researchers.

For HCI using gesture input, the key component is the recognition of gestures. As an efficient way of communication, human gesture is easy to implement and understand [2]. Currently, there are two kinds of gesture recognition methods, including vision-based recognition and inertial sensor-based recognition [14–17]. However, because of

B. Zhang—This work was supported in part by the Natural Science Foundation of China under Contract 61272052 and Contract 61473086, in part by PAPD, in part by CICAEET, and in part by the National Basic Research Program of China under Grant 2015CB352501. The work of B. Zhang was supported by the Program for New Century Excellent Talents University within the Ministry of Education, China, and Beijing Municipal Science & Technology Commission Z161100001616005. Baochang Zhang is the corresponding author.

© Springer International Publishing AG 2016
Z. You et al. (Eds.): CCBR 2016, LNCS 9967, pp. 432–440, 2016.
DOI: 10.1007/978-3-319-46654-5_48

the diverse gestures and demanding environment, the first method is relatively time consuming. For the second method, it is in constant development in recent years [3–5].

In the last two decades, researchers have carried out experiments by using inertial sensors to identify simple operations and achieved some good results. Due to the huge volume and expense of related equipment, the device cannot be used in individual level. Therefore this technology has been difficult to make progress. At the beginning of this century, the rapid development of mobile phones provided hardware platforms, which made gesture recognition by acceleration usher in the dawn. In 2000, Rekimoto tried to use a specific type of wearable device to detect the motion of the arm, but the size of the equipment is too large, and the precision obtained is very low, making this method not suitable in practice [6]. In 2004, the theory of static acceleration and dynamic acceleration was published by Jang and Park, and at the same time they put forward their own views about recognition issues [7]. Fresca and Resmritas categorized gestures through a law developed, including two categories of basic gestures and combined gestures. They established a database of gestures, and classified gestures based on the database [8]. Juha put forward the concept of base interfaces, and obtain different features of different gestures [9]. F. G. Hofmann proposed a recognition scheme based on the acceleration vectors from different gestures [10]. Baek, who further refined gestures and obtained better results [11].

Most studies of gesture recognition are based on an accelerometer, which pose restriction on the type of gestures and the recognition accuracy. With MEMS sensors are first built in iphone4, including linear accelerometers and micro-gyroscopes, various Android phones also include these basic functions, which provide more excellent hardware conditions of mobile phone gesture recognition. Based on inertial sensors such as accelerometers and gyroscopes, mobile phones can measure gesture information directly. At present, the main ways of gesture recognition are: decision trees, dynamic time warping technique, support vector machines, hidden Markov models, etc.

Similar to other areas of recognition, public databases are very important to researchers in the field of gesture recognition. However, as far as we know, there is no such database related to gesture recognition based on inertial sensors of mobile phones, while the benchmark databases in other biometric problems are normally ample. For example, the FERET and FRGC databases are commonly used in face recognition [12, 13].

Our database was created to enable more researchers and practitioners to evaluate and compare their algorithms by using the same data. We record the inertial sensor data of each gesture in a text file. It is worth noting that most of the previous experiments were conducted in a laboratory environment, using their own data. Therefore creating an open and comprehensive database for gesture recognition is of benefit to the research community.

In this paper, we focus more on data preprocessing, feature extraction, and recognition algorithms of HMM, KNN and SVM. The rest of the paper is organized as follows. In Sect. 2, we introduce the gesture recognition system, describing the basic theory and processes. The specific methods of preprocessing and feature extraction are presented in Sects. 3 and 4. Section 5 displays our experiment results of HMM, KNN and SVM. Section 6 concludes this paper and makes some discussions on future work.

2   Gesture Recognition Based on Mobile

By using mobile phone, we obtain the original data from the phone's built-in accelerometer and gyroscope. We carry out data preprocessing and feature extraction. The
gestures include English alphabet and Arabic numerals, which are very common characters and have a standard way of writing. This paper selects four representative capital
letters of A, B, C, D and four Arabic numerals of 1, 2, 3, 4 to carry out gesture recognition
research.

The flowchart of the gesture recognition approach is shown in Fig. 1. When the phone
records gestures, we transfer data into digital signal of three-dimensional acceleration
and angular velocity by A/D conversion. Then we train an HMM or SVM for each type
of gesture through the preprocessing and feature extraction, and finally make a classification decision.

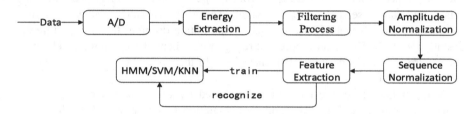

Fig. 1. Flowchart of the gesture recognition system

3   Data Preprocessing

3.1   Energy Calculation

In the experiments, we collect gestures of the capital letters C in different ways.
Figure 2 shows angular velocity and acceleration. The angular velocity and acceleration
have three directions, X, Y and Z. Z-axis direction is perpendicular to the screen of the
phone. The X-axis direction represents right direction of the phone, and Y-axis means
upward direction. The data curves are quite different when the phone does not have the
same attitude, even if it has the same action, which makes it difficult for accurate recognition.

If we denote the XYZ-axis acceleration data as accx, accy and accz, the XYZ-axis
angular velocity data as gyrox, gyroy and gyroz, and the energy signal of the acceleration
data and angular velocity data as accs and gyros, acceleration data, angular velocity data
and energy signal will have the following relationships:

$$accs = accx^2 + accy^2 + accz^2. \tag{1}$$

$$gyros = gyrox^2 + gyroy^2 + gyroz^2. \tag{2}$$

Using Eqs. (1) and (2), the data in Fig. 2 is converted to the data shown in Fig. 3. As
it is apparent from Fig. 3, different postures we draw C, using a mobile phone, have

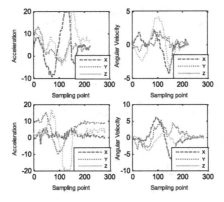

Fig. 2. Different postures for Gesture C in each row.

almost the same energy signal of the acceleration and angular velocity. The energy signal of angular velocity and acceleration have a clear advantage on gesture clustering and recognition, which can greatly increases the recognition rate.

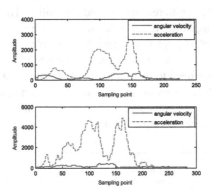

Fig. 3. Energy signals for Fig. 2

3.2 Wave Filtering

Affected by laboratory equipment and the environment, the data from the sensor inevitably contain noise. Therefore, we further carry out a filtering process to reduce noise. For time-domain signal, we can use Average Filter or Median Filter to remove high-frequency interference of background signal in the data. Since the gesture signals have relatively low frequency in the frequency domain, so we should use a low-pass filter.

Figure 4 shows the original data and the processed data by the Average Filter, Median Filter and Butterworth Filter. We can obviously find the Average Filter and Butterworth Filter are better. However, it should be noted that Butterworth Filter has the process of DFT or FFT, which cannot meet the requirement of less calculation cost. Thus, we choose the Average Filter which is relatively simple and efficient.

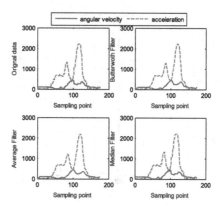

Fig. 4. From top (left) to bottom (right): the original data, and the processed data by Average Filter, Median Filter, Butterworth Filter

3.3 Amplitude Normalization and Sequence Normalization

Different gestures may have different speeds and intensities. The difference of intensity has an impact on the amplitude of data. Meanwhile, when the speeds of action are different, gestures completed relatively fast have fewer sampling points since the sampling frequency (200 Hz) of acceleration and the angular velocity signals is fixed for a mobile phone. So we need to carry out amplitude normalization to mitigate interference caused by the differences in action's intensity. In addition, we normalize the data obtained at different speeds to have the same length, which eliminates the impact of action's speed by sequence normalization.

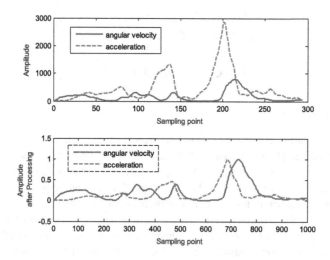

Fig. 5. The original data (top) and the preprocessed data (bottom).

This paper uses cubic spline interpolation to set the sampling point of data to the same number. Figure 5 shows the waveform of data after the process of amplitude normalization and sequence normalization, which has effectively eliminated the influence of intensity and speed variations.

4   Feature Extraction

After preprocessing, the length of each sample is of 1000 sampling points. For a gesture, if we simply use these data, the difference between the samples corresponding to the same gesture is large, thus we cannot achieve a good recognition performance. We have to extract compact and discriminative features, not only effective for gesture recognition, but also for compression.

We utilize the method of computing the mean of the energy signal. The segment length is set to be 30 sampling points, and the segment shift has 20 sampling points, which can guarantee the continuity of data. We calculate the mean of every segment's acceleration energy and angular velocity energy to obtain their characteristic sequences. Figure 6 shows characteristic curves of the capital letters of A in different poses, intensities and speeds.

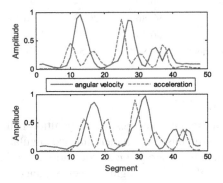

Fig. 6. The curve of different As

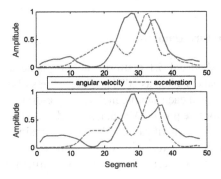

Fig. 7. The curve of different Cs

5 Baseline Algorithms and Results

There are several methods widely used in statistical classifications. In this paper, we use 3 state-of-the-art algorithms: SVM, KNN and HMM based methods. The SVM solution uses maximum-margin hyperplanes to classify, while the KNN solution selects the nearest Euclidean distance and the HMM uses the maximum of likelihood as a decision rule. The details of the parameters of the baseline algorithms can be found in the source codes that will be publically available. In the following, we use a 14-fold cross validation, where each category training set has 130 samples and test set has 10 samples. Based on these algorithms, the paper obtains the overall recognition accuracy rate (see Table 1).

Table 1. Recognition results comparison on the BUAA mobile gesture dataset

Algorithm	SVM	KNN	HMM
A	97.14	92.14	95.00
B	88.57	82.14	95.71
C	89.29	89.29	84.29
D	93.57	89.29	80.00
1	97.86	95.00	97.14
2	90.00	92.14	93.57
3	97.86	96.43	96.43
4	86.43	90.71	94.29
Average	93.84	90.54	91.79

6 Conclusion

This paper introduces a mobile based gesture recognition benchmark by building a gesture database of three-dimensional acceleration and angular velocity. Data preprocessing is performed including energy signal calculation, filtering, normalization and feature extraction. To evaluate the recognition performance, we use the algorithms of HMM, SVM and KNN. Our future work will focus on boosting the classifiers and finding more powerful features to improve the performance. Related work can also refer to [18–21].

The BUAA Mobile Gesture Database

This paper uses an Android 5.1 platform mobile phone to collect data, and the sampling frequency of data is taken as 200 Hz. For gestures of A, B, C, D, 1, 2, 3, 4 we collected 1,120 samples, and each sample includes three-dimensional acceleration and angular velocity of the mobile phone. All data is saved in text file, which are originally collected without any manual modification. The data is classified and stored in different folders, named by the type of gesture. To download the database for research purpose, one can send an email to the corresponding author or visiting mpl.buaa.edu.cn.

References

1. Lane, N.D., Miluzzo, E., Lu, H., et al.: A survey of mobile phone sensing. J. IEEE Commun. Mag. **48**(9), 140–150 (2010)
2. Choi, E.S., Bang, W.C., Cho, S.J., et al.: Beatbox music phone: gesture-based interactive mobile phone using a tri-axis accelerometer. In: 2005 IEEE International Conference on Industrial Technology, pp. 97–102. IEEE Press, Hong Kong (2005)
3. Mantyla, V.M, Mantyjarvi, J., Seppanen, T., et al.: Hand gesture recognition of a mobile device user. In: 2000 IEEE International Conference on Multimedia and Expo, pp. 281–284. IEEE Press, New York (2000)
4. Liu, J., Zhong, L., Wickramasuriya, J., et al.: uWave: accelerometer-based personalized gesture recognition and its applications. Pervasive Mob. Comput. **5**, 657–675 (2009)
5. Yazdi, N., Ayazi, F., Najafi, K.: Micromachined inertial sensors. Proc. IEEE **86**, 1640–1659 (1998)
6. Rekimoto, J.: Gesturewrist and Gesturepad: unobtrusive wearable interaction devices. In: Fifth International Symposium on Wearable Computers, pp. 21–27. IEEE Press, Zurich (2001)
7. Jang, I.J., Park, W.B.: Signal processing of the accelerometer for gesture awareness on handheld devices. In: The 12th IEEE International Workshop on Robot and Human Interactive Communication, pp. 139–144. IEEE Press, Roman (2003)
8. Ferscha, A., Resmerita, S.: Gestural interaction in the pervasive computing landscape. e & i Elektrotechnik und Informationstechnik. **124**, 17–25 (2007)
9. Kallio, S., Kela, J., Mantyjarvi, J.: Online gesture recognition system for mobile interaction. In: IEEE International Conference on Man and Cybernetics, pp. 2070–2076. IEEE Press, Washington, D.C (2003)
10. Hofmann, F.G., Heyer, P., Hommel, G.: Velocity profile based recognition of dynamic gestures with discrete hidden markov models. In: Wachsmuth, I., Fröhlich, M. (eds.) GW 1997. LNCS (LNAI), vol. 1371, pp. 81–95. Springer, Heidelberg (1998)
11. Baek, J., Jang, I.-J., Park, K., Kang, H.-S., Yun, B.-J.: Human computer interaction for the accelerometer-based mobile game. In: Sha, E., Han, S.-K., Xu, C.-Z., Kim, M.-H., Yang, L.T., Xiao, B. (eds.) EUC 2006. LNCS, vol. 4096, pp. 509–518. Springer, Heidelberg (2006)
12. Phillips, P.J, Flynn, P.J, Scruggs, T., et al.: Overview of the face recognition grand challenge. In: 2005 IEEE Computer Society Conference on Computer Vision and Pattern Recognition (CVPR 2005), pp. 947–954. IEEE Press, San Diego (2005)
13. Phillips, P.J., Moon, H., Rizvi, S.A., et al.: The FERET evaluation methodology for face-recognition algorithms. IEEE Trans. Pattern Anal. Mach. Intell. **22**, 1090–1104 (2000)
14. Chen, C., Jafari, R., Kehtarnavaz, N.: Improving human action recognition using fusion of depth camera and inertial sensors. IEEE Trans. Hum.-Mach. Syst. **45**, 51–61 (2015)
15. Chen, C., Jafari, R., Kehtarnavaz, N.: A real-time human action recognition system using depth and inertial sensor fusion. IEEE Sens. J. **16**, 773–781 (2016)
16. Liu, K., Chen, C., Jafari, R., et al.: Fusion of inertial and depth sensor data for robust hand gesture recognition. IEEE Sens. J. **14**, 1898–1903 (2014)
17. Chen, C., Jafari, R., Kehtarnavaz, N.: A survey of depth and inertial sensor fusion for human action recognition. Multimedia Tools Appl. 1–21 (2015)
18. Chen, C., Liu, M., Zhang, B., Han, J., Jiang, J., Liu, H.: 3D action recognition using multi-temporal depth motion maps and fisher vector. In: International Joint Conference on Artificial Intelligence, pp. 3331–3337 (2016)
19. Zhang, B., Perina, A., Li, Z., Murino, V., Liu, J., Ji, R.: Bounding multiple gaussians uncertainty with application to object tracking. Int. J. Comput. Vis. **118**, 364–379 (2016)

20. Zhang, B., Li, Z., Perina, A., Del Bue, A., Murino, V.: Adaptive local movement modeling (ALMM) for object tracking, IEEE TCSVT (2016). doi:10.1109/TCSVT.2016.2540978
21. Zhang, B., Perina, A., Murino, V., Bue, A.D.: Sparse representation classification with manifold constraints transfer. In: Computer Vision and Pattern Recognition, pp. 4557–4565. IEEE press, Boston (2015)

Improved GLOH Approach for One-Shot Learning Human Gesture Recognition

Nabin Kumar Karn[(⊠)] and Feng Jiang

School of Computer Science and Technology, Harbin Institute of Technology, Harbin, China
{karnnabin,fjiang}@hit.edu.cn

Abstract. A method is presented for One-Shot Learning Human Gesture Recognition. Shi-Tomasi corner detector and sparse optical flow are used to quickly detect and track robust key-points around motion patterns in scale space. Then Improved Gradient Location and Orientation Histogram feature descriptor is applied to capture the description of robust key interest point. All the extracted features from the training samples are clustered with the k-means algorithm to learn a visual codebook. Subsequently, simulation orthogonal matching pursuit is applied to achieve descriptor coding which map each feature into a certain visual codeword. K-NN classifier is used to recognizing the gesture. The proposed approach has been evaluated on ChaLearn gesture database.

Keywords: Gesture · Bag of Features (BoF) model · Feature extraction · K-means algorithms · Improved Gradient Location and Orientation Histogram (IGLOH)

1 Introduction

Human Gesture Recognition transcribes the actions or activity into speech which play significant roles in our normal daily life among humans and computers. They are frequently considered as natural and inborn way of communication between humans and machines [1]. Due to the vibrant research areas and rapid development of computer vision and machine learning, it has gained increasing popularity and attracted great interests from computer vision scholar, whose extensive applications such as human computer interaction (HCI) [8], robot control [3] and sign language recognition [21]. These days gesture recognition is extensively practiced in the field of cinema, sports, medicine, bio-mechanics etc. for advance analysis. Record RGB videos by the sensing devices are capable to capture only color information and still limited in complex scenes such as occlusions, clutter and illumination changes. Recently, the Kinect[TM] camera introduced by Microsoft has revolutionized both industry and research communities [6] of the computer vision field capturing both RGB and depth images of gesture at available of low cost. Kinect[TM] has been extensively used in numerous vision-base tasks due to its attractive performance at reasonable cost, such as hand tracking [7], human action recognition [8], gesture recognition [9] and face tracking [10]. RGB-D video came up with two significant aspects to explore more informative. First adopted method is to select 3D points of joints from skeleton detector [11].

© Springer International Publishing AG 2016
Z. You et al. (Eds.): CCBR 2016, LNCS 9967, pp. 441–452, 2016.
DOI: 10.1007/978-3-319-46654-5_49

However, if the complicated occlusions occur, the skeleton model fails to maintain enough stable to capture 3D position of tracked joints, which will escort to increased intra-class variations in actions.

Another adopted approach is conventional color-base (gray-scale-based), related to extracting the spatiotemporal interest feature points (STIP), which are becoming promising for action representation [12] for only depth or RGB-D data sequences. Harries3D detector used [13] to detects the keypoints on RGB and depth succession. A method 3D MoSIFT proposed by [14], compute SIFT-descriptor by merging RGB data and depth information. Although this 3DMoSIFT method is robust to detect keypoints around the body motion, it still cannot accurately detect interest points if some slight movements occur in the background. Later, an extension of work carried out by [15] and proposed a new method named 3D EMoSIFT. This method is more robust to detect keypoints and gains better results. However, both the methods 3DMoSIFT and 3DEMoSIFT are time consuming to detect keypoints, due to making Gaussian pyramid and dense optical flow pyramid. Again 3D Sparse MoSIFT, proposed by [16], which obtained the high performance even it takes time. Getting motivation from the previous works [14–16], we developed a new feature for Gesture Recognition from single example in this paper. The new method gains some more impressive characteristics that others haven't. The main contribution of this paper is proposing a new gesture feature descriptor: "Improved Gradient Location and Orientation Histogram (IGLOH)" based on "Gradient Location and Orientation Histogram (GLOH)" which are computed from the tracked features. We model the feature descriptor 17 log-polar sub region having 8 quantized bins resulting 136 bins histogram which gives almost same strength, but computation time reduced by half that maintain invariance for scale changing, rotation and illumination variations and proposing an effective and efficient learning classification framework for gesture recognition based on the proposed gesture descriptor.

The remainder of the paper is organized as follows. Section 2 reviews the background of both local spatiotemporal features and one-shot learning gesture recognition. Then we describe new proposed method in Sect. 3. Extensive experiment results are reported in Sect. 4. Section 5 concludes the paper.

2 Related Works

Earlier, the color information is extensively used to locate human hands and recognize the hand's gestures. The users are mandatory to wear different colored gloves for the simplicity of the color based segmentation [18]. The shape [19] and motion [20] are also method used to locate and recognize the human hand gestures. While to exploit the color information is difficult to segment the hands from an image [21], motion features extracted from two successive frames is used for human gesture recognition. Shao [22] calculates the optical flow from individual frame and then compute a motion histogram by using different combinations of the magnitude and direction of optical flow. The above introduced features are usually extracted from RGB image captured by a traditional optical camera and such type of extracted features from RGB images are not robust due to clutter backgrounds, sensitive to lighting conditions and the nature of

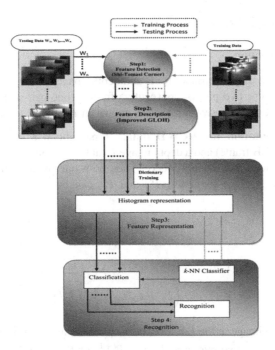

Fig. 1. Proposed method of gesture recognition

optical sensing. Recently, Microsoft Kinect[TM] has been used in Human gesture recognition which is more effective and robust to noises and illumination changes than traditional optical camera. Ren [23] proposed the parts based finger shape features using Kinect[TM] which extract more robust features from depth image for gesture recognition and no need to depend on proper segmentation of the hands. Wan [14, 15] proposed methods to extract features from RGB and depth information extending the SIFT, which has more compact and richer visual representations and are invariant to scale and rotation. Gesture recognition method performance is not only depends on used features but also depends up on classifier used. Traditional classifier for general recognition problem like Dynamic Time Wrapping (DTW) [24] and Liner SVMs [25] can be used. However, Hidden Markov Model is possibly the most well known classifier due to the ability of modeling, temporal signals for gesture recognition.

Most of the methods need dozens or hundreds of training samples to achieve gesture recognition. In the case of insufficient availability of training samples, most of classification methods are unlikely to fit, however, the collection of large dataset of gestures is also difficult. Several methods has been developed in past which require small training data set. Euclidean distance based classifiers to classify gestures has been employed by [20]. Authors [14–16] proposed bag of feature model using sparse coding method for codewords and Euclidean distance based classifiers to classify gestures.

3   The Proposed Approach

3.1   Feature Detection

First, the scale space of every frame (RGB and depth image) is constructed by pyramid representation and use two pair of consecutive frames (one pair of RGB frames, one pair of depth frames). Proposed approach is shown in Fig. 1.

Pyramid Representation for RGB-D data. First, obtain a gray-scale image G_t (converted from RGB frame) and a depth image D_t at time t from a given sample of two videos (an RGB video and a depth video). Then built one pyramid from G_t or D_t via down- sampled way. Two pyramids, P_G^t and P_D^t can be constructed at time t via Eq. (1).

$$
\begin{aligned}
G_t^l(x,y) &= G_t\left(2^{(l-1)}x, 2^{(l-1)}y\right) \ 1 \le l \le \mathrm{L} \\
D_t^l(x,y) &= D_t\left(2^{(l-1)}x, 2^{(l-1)}y\right) \ 1 \le l \le \mathrm{L}
\end{aligned}
\tag{1}
$$

where $G_t^l(D_t^l)$ is the image at the l'th level in the pyramid and (x,y) is the coordinate of $G_t^l(D_t^l)$. Figure 2 shows two pyramids P_G^t and P_G^{t+1} (or P_D^t and P_D^{t+1}) compromise the frames size 320×240 is built from two consecutive gray-scale (or depth) frames at times t and $t + 1$.

Keypoint Detection. Shi-Tomasi corner detector [26] is adopted for spatiotemporal interest point detection is a 2×2 Hessian matrix H_p can be computed for every point p in an image I (G_t or D_t). H_p is a square matrix of second-order partial derivatives of I.

$$
H_p = \begin{bmatrix} \frac{\partial^2 I}{\partial^2 x} & \frac{\partial^2 I}{\partial x \partial y} \\ \frac{\partial^2 I}{\partial x \partial y} & \frac{\partial^2 I}{\partial^2 y} \end{bmatrix}_p = \begin{bmatrix} a & b \\ b & c \end{bmatrix}_p
\tag{2}
$$

Keypoint detection via tracking and filtering. Pyramidal tracking algorithm proposed by Bouguet [27] to track the same interest point at the time $t + 1$. So, suppose at time t an interest point $p = [p_x \ p_y]^T$ on and image I^t then the location of $q = p+v$ at time $t + 1$ on image I^{t+1} is $[p_x + v_x \ p_y + v_y]^T$. The vector $v = [v_x \ v_y]^T$ is the velocity of p, which is known as optical flow of p and the absolute velocity can be defined as $|v| = \sqrt{v_x^2 + v_y^2}$. The velocity v is to minimize the residual function ε and ε is defined as

$$
\begin{aligned}
\varepsilon(v) &= \varepsilon(v_x, v_y) \\
&= \sum_{x=p_x-N}^{p_x+N} \sum_{y=p_y-N}^{p_y+N} [I^t(x,y) - I^{t+1}(x+v_x, y+v_y)]^2
\end{aligned}
\tag{3}
$$

where ε is measured on image neighborhood of size $(2N+1) \times (2N+1)$. To optimize the Eq. (3), the first derivative of ε with respect to v is zero:

$$\frac{\partial \varepsilon(v)}{\partial v} = [0 \quad 0]^T \qquad (4)$$

Then, the optimized optical flow vector is calculated. Since this optical flow is sparse, so it tracks a few points in two consecutive frames and calculated the velocity for each interest point at time t, and $t+1$.

3.2 Feature Description

During the last three decades, several local descriptors have been proposed to represent local image structures and usually combined with one or several feature detectors.

Improved Gradient Location and Orientation Histogram. Gradient Location and Orientation Histogram (GLOH) proposed by Mikolajczyk [28] is an extension of the SIFT descriptor designed to enhance its robustness and distinctiveness. For proposed method, 25×25 local patch size is used. Further the grid patch size 25×25 is converted into three bins in radial direction having the radius 4, 7 and 11, which is modified and 17 log-polar bins having quantized 8-bins. In the proposed method the quantized bins is also reduced from 16 to 8, so that to avoid the use of other method to reduce the dimensions of descriptor vectors.

Feature Descriptor Calculation. A keypoint is detected at the l'th level in the pyramid at time t. Then local patches are extracted around the keypoint from four pyramids: P_G^t, P_G^{t+1}, P_D^t and P_D^{t+1} (Fig. 3).

The Fig. 2 shows that a keypoint which is marked as red and encircled with blue rectangles is detected at the second level in the pyramid in any instance at time t, and then four local patches are extracted from blue rectangles. The extracted local patches are denoted by Γ_G^t from G_t^2, Γ_D^t from D_t^2, Γ_G^{t+1} from G_{t+1}^2 and Γ_D^{t+1} from D_{t+1}^2. The four local patches are used to calculate gradient images and motion fields. Firstly, the

Fig. 2. Building four pyramids from two pairs of consecutive frames. (a) P_G^t at time t. (b) P_D^t at time t. (c) P_G^{t+1} at time t + 1. (d) P_D^{t+1} at time t + 1. (Color figure online)

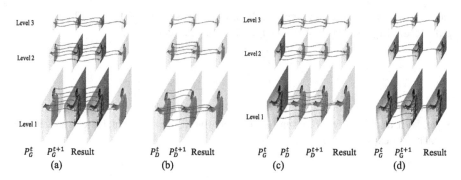

$$P_G^t \quad P_G^{t+1} \quad \text{Result} \qquad P_D^t \quad P_D^{t+1} \quad \text{Result} \qquad P_G^t \quad P_D^t \quad P_D^{t+1} \quad \text{Result} \qquad P_G^t \quad P_G^{t+1} \quad \text{Result}$$
$$\text{(a)} \qquad\qquad\qquad \text{(b)} \qquad\qquad\qquad\qquad \text{(c)} \qquad\qquad\qquad\qquad \text{(d)}$$

Fig. 3. The flow graph of keypoint detection from RGB-D data in the scale space.

Gaussian filter is used to smooth the extracted patches (Γ_G^t, Γ_D^t, Γ_G^{t+1}, Γ_D^{t+1}) to reduce the effects of noise and the corresponding results are Γ_G'', Γ_D'', $\Gamma_G^{t+1\prime}$, $\Gamma_D^{t+1\prime}$; as shown in Fig. 4. Secondly, dense optical flow [29] is calculated using the two pairs of image [(Γ_G'', $\Gamma_G^{t+1\prime}$) and (Γ_D'', $\Gamma_D^{t+1\prime}$)]. To calculate the dense optical flow, calcOpticalFlowFarne- back () function [5] is used from opencv library. After that, the vertical and horizontal velocities (V_x, V_y, V_z^x, V_z^y) is obtained as shown in Fig. 4, where V_x and V_y are calculated from Γ_G'' and $\Gamma_G^{t+1\prime}$, and V_z^x, and V_z^y are calculated from Γ_D'', $\Gamma_D^{t+1\prime}$. The gradients can simply be calculated at time t using Γ_G'' and Γ_D''.

Feature Descriptor in 3D gradient space. 3D gradient space of a point P_t having the coordinate (i, j) is constructed by $I_x(i, j), I_y(i, j), D_z^x(i,j)$ and $D_z^y(i,j)$ as shown in Fig. 5 (a). First the xy plane is used to calculate the feature descriptor in the 3D gradient space. For each point p_t with its coordinate(i, j) the gradient magnitude is calculated, $\text{mag}(i, j) = \sqrt{I_x(i,j)^2 + I_y(i,j)^2}$, orientation, $ori(i,j) = tan^{-1}(I_y(i,j)/I_x(i,j))$ in the xy plane. Then in xy plane the local patch of size 25×25 around keypoints are converted into 17 log-polar location grids with 8 orientation bins and calculate Improved GLOH descriptor (17×8) with 136 dimensions. Similarly, Improved GLOH descriptors in xz

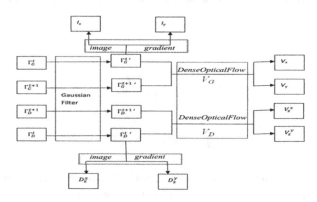

Fig. 4. Preprocessing portion of the descriptor calculation from the extracted local patches.

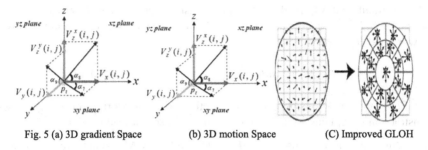

Fig. 5 (a) 3D gradient Space   (b) 3D motion Space   (C) Improved GLOH

Fig. 5. (a) 3D gradient space (b) 3D motion space (C) Improved GLOH

and yz planes is also calculating. Therefore, the descriptor vector has 408 (136 × 3) dimensions in 3D gradient space.

Feature Descriptor in 3D Modified Motion Space. In 3D modified motion space, the depth horizontal and vertical velocities $(V_z^x; V_z^y)$ is calculated by using dense optical flow (see Fig. 4). Here yz plane is used to calculate the feature descriptor in 3D modified motion space. For each point p_t coordinate (i, j), computed the gradient magnitude, $\mathrm{mag}(i,j) = \sqrt{V_y(i,j)^2 + V_z^y(i,j)^2}$, orientation, $ori(i,j) = tan^{-1}[V_z^y(i,j)/V_y(i,j)]$ in the yz plane. Then, in yz plane, the local patch is dividing of the size 25 × 25 around the keypoints as shown in Fig. 5(c) to calculate Improved GLOH descriptor, the patch is converted into 17 log-polar location grids with 8 orientations bins. Similarly it is computed the magnitude and orientation for the local patch around the detected points in other two planes. Therefore, the descriptors with 408 dimensions in the 3D motion space are obtained. Finally, integrating these two descriptor vectors gives a long descriptor vector with 816 dimensions.

3.3   Feature Representation

Codebook learning. Each training video is annotated with one gesture label (*e.g.* waving). Let η denote the number of gesture classes which means there are η training samples for one-shot learning, $\Omega = [X^1, X^2, ..., X^\eta]$, $\Omega \in \Re^{d \times L_{tr}}$ is the set of all the descriptor vectors extracted from all the training samples, $X^i \in \Re^{d \times N_i}$ with N_i descriptor vectors is the set extracted from the ith class, and $L_{tr} = \sum_{i=1}^{\eta} N_i$ is the number of features extracted from all the training samples. Then k-means algorithm Wang [17] is applied to learn the codebook $B \in \Re^{d \times M} (M < \sum_{i=1}^{\eta} N_i)$ to all over the descriptors Ω with M entries.

In proposed framework a new parameter $\gamma \in (0,1)$ is used to calculate the codebook size M rather than traditional BoF method of calculating codebook size. γ is expressed as a fraction of L_{tr}. So, the codebook size M is calculated as $M = L_{tr} \times \gamma$.

In the traditional VQ method, Euclidean distance is calculated between a given descriptor $x \in \mathfrak{R}^d$ and every codeword $b_i \in \mathfrak{R}^d$ of the codebook B and find the closest codeword and formulated as:

$$\min_C \|X - BC\|_F^2, \ subject \ to \| c_i\|_0 = 1, \|c_i\|_1 = 1, c_i \geq 0, \forall i \tag{5}$$

In Eq. 5, the conditions may be too restrictive, which gives rise to usually a coarse reconstruction of X, hence a sparse coding method used instead of VQ.

Descriptor Coding by Sparse Coding Method. SOMP stands for simulation orthogonal matching pursuit is a greedy pursuit algorithm that based on simultaneous sparse approximation techniques, based on the idea of selecting an element of the codebook and building all signal approximations as the projection of the signal matrix X on the span of these selected codewords. The problem can be stated as the following optimization problem:

$$\min_C \|X - BC\|_F^2, \ subject \ to \ \|c_i\|_0 \leq k \ \forall i \tag{6}$$

3.4   Coefficient Histogram Calculation and Classification

Coefficient histogram is used to denote the representation of each individual sample by equation $h = \frac{1}{N} \sum_{i=1}^N c_i$ where $c_i \in \mathfrak{R}^M$ is the ith descriptor of $c_i \in \mathfrak{R}^{M \times N}$, and the total number of descriptors extracted from a sample is N and $h \in \mathfrak{R}^M$.

Since for training only one sample is available, multi-class SVMs are not trivially applicable because in principle they require a large number of training examples. So Learn-and-predict NN classifier is selected for proposed framework of gesture recognition.

4   Performance and Evaluation

4.1   Parameter and Data Setting and Metric of Evaluation

Building the pyramid the number of levels L is used to maintain the new feature invariant to scale space. $L = 3$ is set for one image of size 320×240. The other parameters selected for codebook learning are sparsity $(k) = 10$ and γ with different values (ranging from 0.1 to 0.5). It is found that $\gamma = 0.5$ gives higher performance. Here the simple strategy is used to decide value of k and γ, since the field of sparse coding theory and the codebook learning are in a developing stage and selecting optimal parameters (γ and k) are still open topic [4]. To evaluate the performance, ChaLearn Gesture Dataset (CGD 2011) is selected which is rich but extremely complicated dataset made available to researchers under Microsoft ChaLearn Gesture Challenge Guyon [2].

Table 1. Comparison of proposed method with other methods

Methods \ γ	0.1	0.2	0.3	0.4	0.5
Cuboid(R)	0.36717	0.36495	0.34332	0.33111	0.31392
Cuboid(R+D)	0.33666	0.31559	0.30948	0.30782	0.28064
Harris3D hog(R)	0.30061	0.26012	0.25014	0.23516	0.23461
Harris3D hog(R+D)	0.24903	0.22795	0.22407	0.22795	0.22684
Harris3Dhof(R)	0.34831	0.32668	0.31281	0.29895	0.29063
Harris3D hof(R+D)	0.32169	0.29174	0.28508	0.27898	0.27121
Harris3D hoghof(R)	0.24237	0.21963	0.20022	0.19468	0.18857
Harris3D hoghof(R+D)	0.20965	0.18802	0.18303	0.18747	0.18192
MoSIFT(R)	0.41653	0.39601	0.35885	0.36606	0.33500
MoSIFT(R+D)	0.44426	0.44260	0.43594	0.42318	0.40488
3D MoSIFT(R+D)	0.19135	0.16694	0.16195	0.14476	0.14642
3D EMoSIFT(R+D)	0.16528	0.15419	0.14753	0.13977	0.13311
3D SMoSIFT(R+D)	0.135	0.1245	0.1185	0.1175	0.1105
Proposed Method	0.129	0.121	0.1165	**0.109**	**0.108**

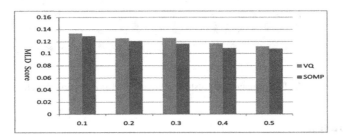

Fig. 6. Performance evaluations between VQ and SOMP in graph.

Levenshtein Distance (LD) measure is employed to calculate the score between the predicted labels and the truth labels to evaluate the gesture recognition performance. In our framework, the string contains the gesture labels detected in each sample. In order to facilitate a fair comparison with the existing methods, In our case, the strings contain the gesture labels detected in each sample. For all comparisons, mean Levenshtein distance (MLD) is computed over all video clips and batches. Then percentage LD is employed as the evaluation criteria.

4.2   Comparisons

First we evaluate the proposed method in terms of recognition rate and then compare it with other State-of-the-art methods that have been applied on the CGD. We also calculated the performance of VQ and SOMP. The standard BoF model is used to compare different spatio-temporal features with our proposed model. Some standard BoF modes used VQ for coding descriptor where as some used SOMP. The results are shown in Table 1. We can observe that results of our proposed method constantly surpass than other method. Evaluating SOMP and VQ coding method on final data set is shown in Fig. 6. Now Comparing with GLOH, the Gesture recognition rate of GLOH and Improved GLOH on final data set (final 20 ∼ final 40). The result is shown in Table 2. Batch wise on Fig. 7.

Table 2. Performance evaluation between GLOH and improve GLOH

Methods γ	0.5
GLOH	0.1075
Improved GLOH	0.108

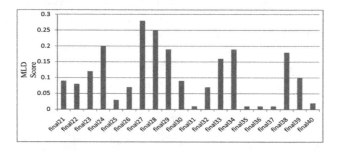

Fig. 7. Performance of Gesture recognition for each final batch.

5   Conclusion

A new unified framework for one-shot Learning Human Gesture Recognition is proposed which gets a fast way to detect keypoint via tracking and filtering and construct
3D gradient and motion space to calculate Improved GLOH descriptor which describes
the 3D patches from RGB-D sequence. SOMP is used replacing VQ in the descriptor
coding stage to represent each feature by some linear combination of a small number of
visual codewords. SOMP leads to a much lower reconstruction error and achieves
better performance. Compared to other exiting methods, it gets viable performance.
Although the proposed method has achieved promising results, several avenues are
which can to be explored. The first the existing spatio-temporal features are extracted
from a static or simple dynamic background.

References

1. Mitra, S., Acharya, T.: Gesture recognition: a survey. EEE Trans. Syst. Man Cybern. Part C
   Appl. Rev. **37**(3), 311–324 (2007)
2. Guyon, I., Athitsos, V., Jangyodsuk, P.: ChaLearn gesture challenge: design and first results.
   In: IEEE Conference on CVPR Workshops, pp. 1–6 (2012)
3. Malima, A., Ozgur, E., Çetin, M.: A fast algorithm for vision-based hand gesture recognition
   for robot control. In: IEEE Signal Processing and Communications Applications, pp. 1–4
   (2006)

4. Guha, T., Ward, R.K.: Learning sparse representations for human action recognition. IEEE Trans. Pattern Anal. Mach. Intell. **34**(8), 1576–1588 (2012)
5. Farneback (2003). http://docs.opencv.org/2.4/modules/video/doc/motion_analysis_and_object_tracking.html?highlight=meanshift#farneback2003
6. Han, J., Shao, L., Xu, D., Shotton, J.: Enhanced computer vision with Microsoft Kinect sensor: a review. IEEE Trans. Cybern. **43**(5), 1318–1334 (2013)
7. Oikonomidis, I., Kyriazis, N., Antonis, A.: Efficient model-based 3D tracking of hand articulations using Kinect. In: Proceedings of the BMVC, pp. 1–11 (2011)
8. Wang, J., Liu, Z., Wu, Y., Yuan, J.: Mining: actionlet ensemble for action recognition with depth cameras. In: Proceedings of the IEEE Conference on CVPR, pp. 1290–1297 (2012)
9. Ren, Z., Yuan, J., Meng, J., Zhang, Z.: Robust part-based hand gesture recognition using Kinect sensor. IEEE Trans. Multimedia **15**(5), 1110–1120 (2013)
10. Cai, Q., Gallup, D., Zhang, C., Zhang, Z.: 3D deformable face tracking with a commodity depth camera. In: Proceedings of the 11th European Conference on Computer Vision, pp. 229–242 (2010)
11. Shotton, J., Fitzgibbon, A.W., Cook, M., Sharp, T., Finocchio, M., Moore, R., Kipman, A., Blake, A.: Real-time human pose recognition in parts from single depth images. In: Proceedings of the IEEE Conference on CVPR, pp. 1297–1304 (2011)
12. Laptev, I.: On space-time interest points. Int. J. Comput. Vision **64**(2–3), 107–123 (2005)
13. Hernández-Vela, A.: BoVDW: bag-of-visual-and-depth-words for gestur recognition. In: 21st International Conference on Pattern Recognition, pp. 449–452 (2012)
14. Ming, Y., Ruan, Q., Hauptmann, A.: Activity recognition from RGB-D camera with 3D local spatio-temporal features. In: IEEE Conference on Multimedia and Expo, pp. 344–349 (2012)
15. Wan, J., Ruan, Q., Li, W.: One-shot learning gesture recognition from RGB-D data using bag of features. J. Mach. Learn. Res. **14**(9), 2549–2582 (2013)
16. Wan, J., Ruan, Q., Li, W., An, G., Zhao, R.: 3D SMoSIFT three-dimensional sparse motion scale invariant feature transform for activity recognition from RGB-D videos. J. Electron. Imaging **23**(2), 023017 (2014)
17. Wang, J., Yang, J., Yu, K., Lv, F., Huang, T., Gong, Y.: Locality-constrained linear coding for image classification. In: Proceedings of IEEE Conference on Computer Vision and Pattern Recognition, pp. 3360–3367 (2010)
18. Liang, G., Chen, Y., Fang, G., Chen, X., Gao, W.: A vision-based sign language recognition system using tied-mixture density HMM. In: Proceedings of the 6th International Conference on Multimodal Interfaces, pp. 198–204 (2004)
19. Ramamoorthy, A., Vaswani, N., Chaudhury, S., Banerjee, S.: Recognition of dynamic hand gestures. Pattern Recogn. **36**(9), 2069–2081 (2003)
20. Mahbub, U., Roy, T., Rahman, Md.S., Imtiaz, H.: One-shot-learning gesture recognition using motion history based gesture silhouettes. In: Proceedings of the International Conference on Industrial Application Engineering, pp. 186–193 (2013)
21. Wan, J., Ruan, Q., An, G., Li, W.: Hand tracking and segmentation via graph cuts and dynamic model in sign language videos. In: Proceedings of IEEE 11th International Conference on Signal Processing, vol. 2, pp. 1135–1138 (2012)
22. Shao, L., Ji, L.: Motion histogram analysis based key frame extraction for human action/activity representation. In: Proceedings of Canadian Conference on Computer and Robot Vision, pp. 88–92 (2009)
23. Zhou, R., Junsong, Y., Jingjing, M., Zhengyou, Z.: Robust part-based hand gesture recognition using Kinect sensor. IEEE Trans. Multimedia **15**(5), 1110–1120 (2013)

24. Reyes, M., Dominguez, G., Escalera, S.: Feature weighting in dynamic time warping for gesture recognition in depth data. In: Proceedings of the IEEE International Conference on Computer Vision Workshops, pp. 1182–1188 (2011)

25. Fanello, S.R., Gori, I., Metta, G., Odone, F.: One-shot learning for real-time action recognition. In: Sanches, J.M., Micó, L., Cardoso, J.S. (eds.) IbPRIA 2013. LNCS, vol. 7887, pp. 31–40. Springer, Heidelberg (2013)

26. Shi, J., Tomasi, C.: Good features to track. In: IEEE Conference on Computer Vision and Pattern Recognition, pp. 593–600 (1994)

27. Bouguet, J.Y.: Pyramidal implementation of the affine Lucas Kanade feature tracker description of the algorithm (2014). http://robots.stanford.edu/cs223b04/algotracking.pdf

28. Mikolajczyk, K., Schmid, C.: A performance evaluation of local descriptors. IEEE Trans. on Pattern Anal. Mach. Intell. (S0162-8828), 1615–1630 (2005)

29. Farnebäck, G.: Two-Frame motion estimation based on polynomial expansion. In: Bigun, J., Gustavsson, T. (eds.) SCIA 2003. LNCS, vol. 2749, pp. 363–370. Springer, Heidelberg (2003)

A Sign Language Recognition System in Complex Background

Haifeng Sang and Hongjiao Wu[✉]

School of Information Science and Engineering, Shenyang University of Technology,
Shenyang 110870, China
1196721257@qq.com

Abstract. In view of the complicity of background, similarity of hand shape and the limitations of the algorithm, we propose a new system for sign language recognition. To separate gesture from complex backgrounds we use initial division based on improved color clustering and the re-segmentation by graph cut method. After that, the outline of hand shape is detected by CV model, the convex defects are found, the Hu moments and the geometric features are calculated. Finally, utilizing the SVM to classification that consists of the first classification on the number of defects and the second classification through multi-feature fusion, the average recognition rate of 26 kinds of sign language is 91.18 % in our collection of images which shows the effectiveness of the proposed algorithms.

Keywords: Color clustering · Graph cut · CV model · Multi-feature · SVM

1 Introduction

The target extraction is one of the key steps in sign language recognition. [1] Proposed a detection method based on ellipse skin color model. This method has improved the check ability of skin color in the case of ellipse center determined. But it is only suitable for light moderate image. [2] Mentioned sign language finger spelling recognition by user-independent system based on the skin color-texture attributes and MLP neural network in complex background. Although the target and the background can be separated very well by this way, but the running time is too long. [3] Proposed the use of interactive Graph Cuts image segmentation. The algorithm has achieved good results in division. Due to the need of selection seed points for each image, it is not applicable. To overcome above shortages, we employ the improved skin color clustering. The algorithm is just to set the Cb and Cr range according to the value of Y. Then the better gestures will be obtained. Moreover, under the strong light, this way can achieve superior effect. With respect to the skin-like in the post clustered gesture, we take automatic segmentation algorithm based on energy optimization [4] to handle. This method can remove the non-target fine and has great applicability. In addition, for the similarity of the hand shapes, it is hard to identify by single feature while the fusion of multiple features [5] will improve the recognition rate. So in this paper, we use the CV model [6] to extract the contour of sign language. Then calculate the Hu moments [7] and geometric

© Springer International Publishing AG 2016
Z. You et al. (Eds.): CCBR 2016, LNCS 9967, pp. 453–461, 2016.
DOI: 10.1007/978-3-319-46654-5_50

features of the contour [8]. Finally, multiple features are fused [9] which apply to SVM for classification and recognition.

2   Sign Language Recognition System

Based on the computer camera to collect sign language images which need to segment, extract feature, build database and implement classification and recognition (see Fig. 1).

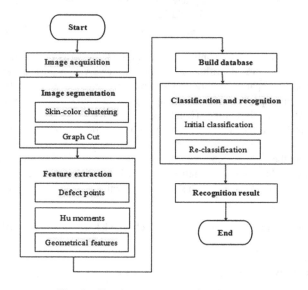

Fig. 1. Sign language recognition system

2.1   Sign Language Image Acquisition

In natural light conditions, using a computer camera to capture sign language images which including different people, different directions and different gestures. We need to set the collection area before the acquisition, if the gesture is contained in the range to start collect. And the distance between hands to the camera to control the 0.8 m ~ 1.2 m to ensure gesture clear.

2.2   Sign Language Image Segmentation

2.2.1   Improved Skin Color Clustering

Cr and Cb with the change of Y will present a certain rule in YCbCr space. When Y is modest, changes of Cr and Cb value are very small, the aggregation is better. Otherwise the value of Cr is decreased gradually and ultimately tends to 0, and Cb increased little by little until reaching 0, the effect of clustering is not obvious. Thus for the picture with strong illumination, the skin color detection is bad. So it is necessary to regulate Cr, Cb values non-linearly as follows:

When $60 \le Y_{min} \cup Y_{max} \le 235$

$if\left(Cr \in \left(103\ 163\right) \cup Cb \in \left(77\ 129\right)\right)$

Extracting original image pixels;

else Setting the pixel value to 0;

When $Y_{min} \le 60 \cup Y_{max} \le 235$

$if\left(Cr \in \left(134\ 173\right) \cup Cb \in \left(97\ 124\right)\right)$

Extracting original image pixels;

else Setting the pixel value to 0;

Improved skin color clustering results (see Fig. 2(B)).

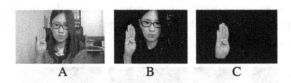

A   B   C

Fig. 2. (A) Original image (B) color clustering graph (C) Image segmentation by Graph cut. (Color figure online)

2.2.2 Graph Cut Segmentation

Modified skin color clustering algorithm can get better gestures, but due to the presence of skin-like affects the feature extraction, so it is imperative to be proposed that combining K-means algorithm with GMM model to represent the color distribution of the foreground and background. According to the similarity between pixels, establish energy function then find the minimum cut by max-flow. The specific steps are follows:

(1) Pixel labeling
(2) GMM model of target and background establishing
(3) Iterative minimization

The result is shown in Fig. 2(C).

2.3 Feature Extraction of Sign Language Image

Feature extraction is significant in sign language recognition technology. In this paper, we put the Hu moments and a set of geometrical characteristics of hand contour as the feature vectors.

2.3.1 Contour of Hand Shape Extract

The traditional edge detection usually applies the operator to extract the contour of the objective. It mainly depends on the threshold while the CV model can solve the problem of discontinuous border which is produced by traditional calculation. As for an image I which was divided into Ω_o and Ω_b by closed boundary C we can build energy function (1), let C_O and C_b as average gray value of Ω_o and Ω_b respectively.

$$E\left(C, C_o, C_b\right) = \lambda_1 \int \int_{\Omega_o} \left(I - C_o\right)^2 dxdy + \lambda_2 \int \int_{\Omega_b} \left(I - C_b\right)^2 dxdy + L(C) \qquad (1)$$

Where λ_1, λ_2 is weight coefficients and $L(C)$ is the perimeter of closed contour C.

Though variation method to obtain *Euler − Lagrange* equation and then acquire partial differential equations by gradient descent method as:

$$\frac{\partial \varphi}{\partial t} = \frac{\varphi_{i,j}^{n+1} - \varphi_{i,j}^{n}}{\Delta t} = \delta_\varepsilon(\varphi)\left\{ \nabla \cdot \frac{\nabla \varphi}{|\nabla \varphi|} - \lambda_1\left[\left(I - C_o\right)^2 - \left(I - C_b\right)^2\right]\right\} \tag{2}$$

Segmentation result is calculated via φ after converged.

CV model also can get rid of shadow that received due to the effects of light in image (see Fig. 3(A) and (B) and reduce the contour points by fitting algorithm to make preparation for convex defects (see Fig. 3(C)).

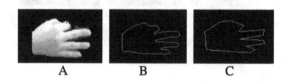

| A | B | C |

Fig. 3. (A) Extract contour by CV model (B) The filtered contour (C) Interpolated contour.

2.3.2 Hu Moments

The Hu moments are invariant to translation, scale change and rotation, so we use it to distinguish between the signs meaning different and have similar hand shapes. Since the Hu information is mainly concentrated in the first four, so in here only extract first four as Hu features, the specific formula are as follows:

$$\phi_1 = \mu_{20} + \mu_{02} \tag{3}$$

$$\phi_2 = (\mu_{20} - \mu_{02})^2 + 4\mu_{11} \tag{4}$$

$$\phi_3 = (\mu_{30} - 3\mu_{12})^2 + (3\mu_{12} - \mu_{03})^2 \tag{5}$$

$$\phi_4 = (\mu_{30} + \mu_{12})^2 + (\mu_{20} + \mu_{03})^2 \tag{6}$$

2.3.3 Geometric Features

Geometric features reflect configuration and orientation of hand shape such as minimum enclosing rectangle, minimum circum-circle, convex hull and some key points as shown in Fig. 4 and calculate four characteristic values as show Table 1.

Fig. 4. Geometric features of hand shape.

Table 1. Relative moment, circular ratio, filling ratio and perimeter ratio of hand shape

Geometric features	Formula	Performance
Relative moment	$lb = d/a$	The larger the lb, the more close to the ellipse;
Filling ratio	$tc = S/A$	The larger the tc, the more close to the circle;
Circular ratio	$c = (l * l)/4\pi S$	The larger the c, the more close to the rectangle;
Perimeter ratio	$f = l/2\pi R$	The greater the f, the more divergent hand shape;

where d is the maximum distance of convex points to the center of gravity; a is the major axis of minimum enclosing rectangle; S is area of contour; l is perimeter of contour; A is area of minimum circumscribed circle; R is the radius of minimum circumscribed circle.

2.4 Sign Language Recognition

For the diversity and similarity of hand shapes, the recognition rate by SVM is low and the classification speed is slow in 26 species of gestures classify, so we utilize SVM based on Gauss kernel function for two sessions. First, the 26 kinds of gestures are divided into four categories based on the number of convex defects as shown in Table 2. Second, use the same SVM to identify each class of sign language.

Table 2. Classification of sign language according to the number of defect points

The number of defects	Sign language
0	B, D, M, N, O, Q
1	A, C, G, H, I, J, P, S, T, U, X, Z
2	F, J, K, L, R, V, W
3	E, W, Y

As a result of the different directions the same gesture will have different number of points, so it will appear in various classes.

3   Experiment and Analysis

To assess the efficiency and capabilities of the proposed algorithms and features, we conducted experiments on ours databases.

3.1   Image Database

Sign language images which including train sample and test sample were collected by both myself and laboratory members. 20 individuals were collected and 10 were acquired per class by camera based on the computer HD720P and picture size is1280 × 720 (see Fig. 5).

Fig. 5. Twenty-six kinds of sign language images with complex backgrounds

3.2   Experimental Identification and Analysis

3.2.1   Comparison of Skin Color Clustering Algorithm

According to the empirical value the suitable center point of ellipse model is generally (119,152) in traditional method. To get a better color clustering, we need to change the center appropriately as show in Fig. 6(B)–(D) represent the color cluster map which center are (113,156), (119,152) and (125,152) respectively. For the light intensity image improved cluster algorithm will get better results than traditional (see Fig. 6G–H).

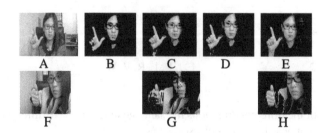

Fig. 6. Skin color cluster images. (Color figure online)

3.2.2   Comparison of Edge Detection Algorithm

As show in Fig. 7(A) and (B) utilizing operator to detect edge by threshold for (5 120) and (65 120) respectively which case border discontinuity, while using the CV model to extract the contour of the image can be a good way to solve the problem of edge discontinuities (see Fig. 7(C) and (D)).

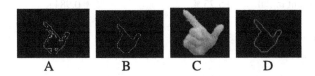

A   B   C   D

Fig. 7. A-B Traditional edge detection; C-D edge detection by CV model.

3.2.3   Comparison Between Single and Multiple Features

The comparison of the recognition results as shown in Fig. 8. Where H and G represent the Hu moments and geometric features respectively; H-G represent first classification by Hu moments and then according to the geometric features of fine classification while G-H represents in contrast. H, G represents according to the Hu moments and geometric features in parallel to classify.

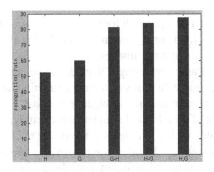

Fig. 8. Comparison of single feature and multi-feature recognition

Figure 8 shows the sign language recognition rate of multiple features fusion is higher than that of single from the whole point of view, which indicating multi-feature extraction is distinctive and can commendably reflect the characteristics of each hand shape. From the local point of view, the parallel fusion of multi-feature recognition rate is higher than the sequential fusion of multiple features recognition rate. It can be concluded that the parallel fusion can display the multiple features of the gesture at the same time, and it is comprehensive.

3.2.4   Classification and Recognition

Three images are randomly selected in each kind of gesture from per person as train sample, and the remaining seven as the test sample. Table 3 gives a comparison of the recognition results of classifications whether through the initial classification of 26 species sign languages.

Table 3. Comparison of the recognition results of classifications

Recognition method	Average recognition rate	Average time for each picture
Recognition without initial classification	85.73 %	0.984 s
Recognition by initial classification	91.18 %	1.031 s

Table 3 shows that the recognition rate of sign language is higher by the initial classification of the defect points. Although the average time for each picture is relatively long, but little impact. We can draw that the initial classification can eliminate the similarity of sign language gestures. However, the recognition rate is improved, but it is not very high. Because similar gestures in the same class, such as H and X, are difficult to distinguish by the features extracted in this article, therefore it is needed to consider the inner-contour of the hand shape, or other features to obtain a high recognition rate.

4   Conclusion

In this paper, we propose a new approach for hand segmentation based on the improved skin color clustering and graph cut algorithm, this method is able to accurately characterize skin region and segment hand images under different lighting conditions from complex backgrounds. In addition, using CV model to detect the edge can avoid the discontinuity of image contour. In terms of feature extraction, taking defect points, Hu moment and a set of geometric features as eigenvectors has a comprehensive and can reflect the characteristics of each kind of sign language primly. Finally, the initial classification according to the number of defects not only can reduce the error rate but also enhance the recognition stability. Besides, the recognition of gestures by SVM makes the calculation simple and the global optimum. For all sign language images, the average recognition rate is 91.18 % and average time of per gesture is 1.03 s.

Further work is to consider the inner contour of gestures as feature to distinguish between the signs meaning different letters but have similar hand shapes.

References

1. Jie, L., Xiaoli, H.: Face Detection Using Ellipse Skin Model. Comput. Measur. Control **14**, 170–172 (2006)
2. Dahmani, Djamila, Larabi, Slimane: User-independent System for Sign language finger spelling recognition. J. Vis. Commun. Image Represent. **25**, 1240–1250 (2014)
3. Wenbing, T., Feng, C., Liman, L., Hai, J., Tianjiang, W.: Interactively multiphase image segmentation based on variational formulation and graph cuts. Pattern Recogn. **43**, 3208–3218 (2010)

4. Yong, Y., Ling, G., Tianjiang, W.: Multi-scale structure based unsupervised color-texture image segmentation approach in multiclass. J. Comput. Aided Des. Comput. Graph. **26**, 812–825 (2014)
5. Haifeng, S., Yu, Z., Weiqi, Y.: Multi-biological feature recognition base on natural open of hand. Chin. J. Sci. Instrum. **32**, 15–22 (2011)
6. Fangmei, W., Hong, F., Fengni, W.: Survey on application of level set in image segmentation. Appl. Res. Comput. **29**, 1207–1210 (2012)
7. Padam Priyal, S., Bora, P.K.: A study on static hand gesture recognition using moments. In: IEEE International Conference on Signal Processing and Communications (SPCOM), pp. 1–5 (2010)
8. Wenxiong, K., Qixia, W.: Pose-invariant hand shape recognition based on finger geometry. IEEE Trans. Syst. Man Cybern. Syst. **44**, 1510–1521 (2014)
9. Haifeng, S., Hongjiao, W., Dakuo, H.: Hand shape, palm-print and palm vein multimodal fusion recognition. Chin. J. Sci. Instrum. **36**, 1356–1362 (2015)

Enhanced Active Color Image for Gait Recognition

Yufei Shang, Yonghong Song$^{(\boxtimes)}$, and Yuanlin Zhang

Xi'an Jiaotong University, Xi'an 710049, Shaanxi, People's Republic of China
syf2616209@stu.xjtu.edu.cn, {songyh,ylzhangxian}@mail.xjtu.edu.cn

Abstract. Active Energy Image (AEI) is an efficient template for gait recognition. However, the AEI is short of the temporal information. In this paper, we present a novel gait template, named Enhanced Active Color Image (EACI). The EACI is extract the difference of two interval in each gait frame, followed by calculating the width of that difference image and then mapping into RGB space with the ratio, describing the relative position, and composition them to a single EACI. To prove the validity of the EACI, we employ experiments on the USF HUMANID database. Experiment result shows that our EACI describes the dynamic, static and temporal information better. Compared with other published gait recognition approaches, we achieve competitive performance in gait recognition.

Keywords: Gait recognition · Biometric authentication · Enhanced active color image

1 Introduction

Biometrics has been widely used in our daily life, such as fingerprint payment or face recognition. However, fingerprint face or iris biometric generally require a cooperative subject and physical contact [1]. In real world, these methods cannot recognize individuals at automated visual surveillance. Gait, as one of behavioral biologic traits, has been shown that human are capable to recognize individuals by their gait signature. Compared with other biometric traits like fingerprint or iris, the most significant advantage of gait is that it can be used for remote human identification without subject cooperation. Therefore, gait is useful and irreplaceable in the long distance visual surveillance [2].

In the past few year, a volume of research has been published regarding gait recognition. There research can mainly be divided into model-based and model-free approaches, depending on the a structural model or a motion model. For crating a model, model-based approaches [3,4] use a series of static and dynamic argument to fit into several body structure like as limbs, legs arms and thighs. Model-free methods [1,5,6] draw more attention on the shape of the silhouette or extract the pattern of whole motion. However, model-based approaches are required high quality gait images and high computational cost for extracting the model from the body part [7].

© Springer International Publishing AG 2016
Z. You et al. (Eds.): CCBR 2016, LNCS 9967, pp. 462–470, 2016.
DOI: 10.1007/978-3-319-46654-5_51

In this paper, we use the model-free technique to avoid the limitation of model-based. We propose a new model-free approach named enhanced active color image (EACI), having less computational cost and easier condition unlike the model-based method.

2   Related Work

Compared with model-based methods, model-free methods achieve better performance and lower complexity. Gait energy Image (GEI) [1], which is one of the most model-free approach, represents gait as a single grey image by averaging the silhouettes in a whole gait cycle. Chen [8] proposed the frame difference energy image (FDEI) based on gait energy image. Zhang firstly extracted the active regions named active energy image (AEI) by calculating the difference of two adjacent silhouette images [9]. Bashir designed gait entropy image (GEnI) based on computing entropy [5]. Wang [6] present Chrono Gait Image (CGI), with temporal information of the gait sequence encoded. Yang introduced flow histogram energy image (FHEI) over extracting the Histograms of Optical Flow descriptors of each silhouette [10].

Fig. 1. The Gait Energy Image

For an individual gait, there are two types of useful information for gait recognition, which are dynamic and static [11]. Additionally, we think there is other important information that is temporal. It is known that the gait consists of a sequence, having a temporal information. The GEIs show in Fag.1. The static part likes head or body are bright, which has high intensity values in a Gait Energy Image, while the dynamic part are dim, which has low intensity values correspond to lower parts of legs and arms that move constantly. The bright area mainly contains information about body shape and stance, whilst the dim area tells us about how people move during walking [12]. However, the GEI may contain the static information, that are easily affected by clothing variety and carrying briefcase. Besides, the GEI is average the frame of the whole sequence, losing the temporal information. Like the GEI, the AEI could catch some dynamic information, and get the static information by averaging the frames. The AEI also lose the temporal information. For the CGI, it use the multichannel technique to express the temporal information, but it lose the dynamic information. Consequently, we propose the enhanced active color image to organization the dynamic, static and temporal information.

Although the existing methods have been able to achieve good performance, we focus on two key problems. The first is how to describe a gait with the dynamic part and static part better. The second is how to better characterize the time sequence information of each frame image in the whole gait sequence. Thus, we attempt to present a new gait representation, which we call Enhanced Active Color Image (EACI). The main idea of EACI has two steps. Firstly, the step is to extract enhanced active image(EAI), the dynamic and static part of a gait sequence by calculating the difference between two silhouette images, which have two intervals. Then, the sequence of EAI is encoded into a multichannel image with computing the width of EAI. In order to enhance the ability of EACIs, we also generate real and synthetic EACI templates. Experimental results on the USF HumanID Gait Database [13], which is one of the most widely used gait database, demonstrate the effectiveness of the proposed method.

3   Enhanced Active Image

To solve first problem, we propose the enhanced active image (EAI) in the following.

Assuming that silhouettes have been extracted from original human walking, the preprocessing [13] procedure is then applied on the silhouette sequences. Given the preprocessed binary gait silhouette images $B_t(x, y)$ at time t in a sequence, we first compute the difference image between two silhouettes which has an interval as follows:

$$D_t(x, y) = \|B_{t+2} - B_t\| \quad t \geq 0 \tag{1}$$

From Eq. (1), D_t is the difference between B_{t+2} and B_t. The D_t contains more dynamic information by extracting the moving part.

And then formally defined EAI as

$$EAI(x, y) = \frac{1}{N} \sum_{t=1}^{N-2} D_t(x, y), \tag{2}$$

where N is the number of frames in the complete cycles of a silhouette sequence, t is the frame number in the sequence, and x and y are values in the 2D image coordinate.

However, our EACI is similar to the AEI method, we have more dynamic information and less noisy. As the AEI method generated by the difference of the adjacent frames, those are easy to be disturbed by noisy and are less dynamic region. Moreover, the AEI using the first frame to contain the static region, which affect the performance by the quality of the first silhouette. Therefore, the ECAI is more robust with the difference of two intervals of frames.

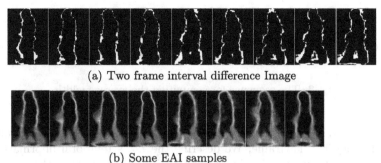

(a) Two frame interval difference Image

(b) Some EAI samples

Fig. 2. The Two frame interval difference Image are shown in (a), Some EAI samples (b) are generated by average the (a) image.

4   Temporal Representation

In spite of the EAI compromises useful information, that loses the important temporal information. The EAI just averages each difference, it can't tell us every D_t those position in a gait period sequence. So, we propose a new temporal representation.

First of all, we calculate the Individual's average width. Inspired by Wang's [6] and Yang's [10] period estimation, a walking person can be divided into two parts, those are moving part and motionless part. The moving part includes the leg and the arm, while the motionless part includes the head and torso. The average width is caught by moving part in a gait cycle. Thus, the average width is composed by the moving leg and the swing arm. It is unquestionable that human's arms always swing out of phase with human's legs, the right arm swinging forward with the left leg and vice versa [14]. In particular, the Wang and Yang's methods use the silhouette image from preprocessed gait sequence, but some silhouette quality are noisy and the width is easily suffered by the rightmost or leftmost noisy pixels. So, we consider using the moving leg and the swing arm compute the average width with the D_t, which has higher image quality and clearer edge. The sequence of D_t are show on Fig. 3. That defines as follows:

$$AdvWith = \alpha * W_{leg} + \beta * W_{arm}, \tag{3}$$

where W is defined as:

$$W = \frac{1}{\gamma h - \delta h + 1} \sum_{i=\gamma h}^{\delta h} (DR_i - DL_i). \tag{4}$$

As we know, h is the height of an individual, α and β are the parameters of describing the importance in $AdvWidth$. The parameter γ and δ constrain the leg region or arm region. DR_i and DL_i are the rightmost and leftmost foreground pixels in the ith line of D_t image. Then, we define a keyframe is the individual stands with two legs overlapping or takes a step with two leg apart from each

Fig. 3. The sequence for computing the average width.

other extremely. In other words, the *AvgWidth* reaches the local peak value or the local valley is a keyframe. We describe the D_t 's temporal information by reckoning the relative position in 1/4 gait period, where is from the local peak value to local valley. For 1/4 period, we define $ratio_t$ as follow:

$$z_t = \frac{(AvgWidth_t - \hat{\mu})}{\hat{\sigma}} \tag{5}$$

$$ratio_t = 1 - \left(\frac{1}{\sigma\sqrt{2\pi}} \int_{-\infty}^{1} e^{\frac{-(z_t-\mu)^2}{2\sigma^2}} dt\right), \tag{6}$$

where $AvgWidth_t$ is the average width of the leg and arm region of the tth difference gait image. The $\hat{\mu}$ and $\hat{\sigma}$ are the means and standard deviation of the average width from the peak (or valley) keyframe to valley (or peak) keyframe. z_t is the value normalized to the mean 0 and standard deviation of 1. And after, we map the difference gait image to RGB space by different $ratio_t$. The RGB gait enhanced active image R_t of the tth as:

$$R_t(x,y) = \begin{pmatrix} D_t(x,y) * R(ratio_t) \\ D_t(x,y) * G(ratio_t) \\ D_t(x,y) * B(ratio_t) \end{pmatrix} \tag{7}$$

where the

$$R(ratio_t) \begin{cases} 0, 0 \le ratio_t \le 1/2 \\ (2ratio_t - 1), 1/2 < ratio_t \le 1 \end{cases} \tag{8}$$

$$G(ratio_t) \begin{cases} 2ratio_t, 0 \le ratio_t \le 1/2 \\ (2 - 2ratio_t), 1/2 < ratio_t \le 1 \end{cases} \tag{9}$$

$$B(ratio_t) \begin{cases} (2 - 2ratio_t), 0 \le ratio_t \le 1/2 \\ 0, 1/2 < ratio_t \le 1 \end{cases} \tag{10}$$

Compared with CGI, experiments show that using the $B(ratio_t)$ reaches better performance. At last, we present the enhanced active color as:

$$EACI(x,y) = \frac{1}{N} \sum_{i=1}^{N-2} R_t(x,y). \tag{11}$$

The Fig. 4 is the EACI of three sequences. What's more, we propose that a new gait period for gait statistics, and using the Z-score standardization describes the relative position of gait. Besides, mapping every D_t into RGB space with the relative position information. It is not difficult to see that we obtain a more informative gait template, which will be demonstrate in experiments.

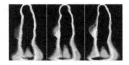

Fig. 4. The EACI Images of three individuals

5   Reduced Dimension and Classification

To avoid the curse of dimensionality of EACI, Principal Component Analysis (PCA) and Linear Discriminant Analysis (LDA) are employed to reduce the dimensionality before classification. Detailed explanation in [1]. Meanwhile, in order to solve the small sample problem we also generate the real and synthetic gait templates [1,6].

Given n d-dimensional real training EACI templates $\{x_1, x_2, ..., x_n\}$ and synthetic templates $\{x_1', x_2', ..., x_n'\}$, its feature vector is computed as $r_k = Tx_k$ and $s_k' = Tx_k'$, where T is the projection matrix calculated by PCA+LDA. The nearest neighbor (NN) is used by matching the similarity between gallery and probe templates. For the real templates and synthetic templates, we define the $d(\hat{R}_p, R_i)$ and $d(\hat{S}_p, S_i)$. More about $d(\hat{R}_p, R_i)$ and $d(\hat{S}_p, S_i)$ can be found in [1]. Furthermore, we improve the fusion strategy to enhance the recognition performance using the following:

$$d(\{\hat{R}_p, \hat{S}_p\}, \{R_k, S_k\}) = \frac{\zeta * d(\hat{R}_p, R_i)}{min_j d(\hat{R}_p, R_j)} + \frac{\eta * d(\hat{S}_p, S_i)}{min_j d(\hat{S}_p, S_j)}, \tag{12}$$

where $i, j = 1, ..., C$, C is the number of classes, ζ and η is the parameter of measuring the important of the real and synthetic gait templates. We assign the probe template to the kth class is

$$k = \min_{i=1}^{c} d(\{\hat{R}_p, \hat{S}_p\}, \{R_k, S_k\}). \tag{13}$$

6   Experiments

In this section, we performed experiments on the USF HumanID gait database to verify the validity of the EACI. The USF HumanID Gait Database includes 122 individuals walking in elliptical paths on concrete and grass surfaces, with or without a briefcase, wearing different shoes, and with different time. Sarkar et al. [13] developed 12 experiments, each of which is under a specific condition. The more about 12 experiments on Table 1. We evaluate the "Rank1" and "Rank5" performances with other state-of-the-art algorithms including baseline algorithm [13], gait energy image (GEI) [1], HMM [15], discriminant analysis with tensor representation (DATER) [16], GEnI [5], CGI [6], Multiple HOG [17], FHEI [10]. The Rank1 defined the percentage of the correct subjects ranked first, while Rank5 denotes the percentage of the correct subjects appeared in any of

Table 1. The details of the gallery and probe set

Data Label	A	B	C	D	E	F	G	H	I	J	K	L
Data Set Size	122	54	54	121	60	121	60	120	60	120	33	33
Variances	V	H	V,H	S	SH	SV	SHV	B	BS	BV	THC	TS

V-View,H-Shoe,S-Surface,B-Briefcase,T-Time and C-Clothing

Table 2. Rank1 rate comparison on the USF HUMANID gait dataBase.

Rank1	A	B	C	D	E	F	G	H	I	J	K	L	Avg
Baseline [13]	73	78	48	32	22	17	17	61	57	36	3	3	40.96
GEI [1]	90	91	81	56	64	25	36	64	60	60	6	15	57.72
HMM [15]	89	88	68	35	28	15	21	85	80	58	17	15	53.54
DATER [16]	87	93	78	42	42	23	28	80	79	59	18	21	56.99
GEnI [5]	89	89	80	30	38	20	22	82	63	66	6	9	53.5
CGI [6]	91	93	78	51	53	35	38	84	78	64	3	9	61.69
M-HOG [17]	96	91	83	33	33	18	25	91	82	82	9	6	59.39
FHEI [10]	92	91	83	49	40	36	19	89	91	75	9	6	62.74
Our Method	92	93	78	50	50	31	30	92	77	81	18	18	64.33

Table 3. Rank5 rate comparison on the USF HUMANID gait dataBase.

Rank5	A	B	C	D	E	F	G	H	I	J	K	L	Avg
Baseline [13]	88	93	78	66	55	42	38	85	78	62	12	15	40.96
GEI [1]	94	94	93	78	81	56	53	90	83	82	27	21	57.72
HMM [15]	-	-	-	-	-	-	-	-	-	-	-	-	-
DATER [16]	96	96	93	69	69	51	52	92	90	83	40	36	75.69
GEnI [5]	-	-	-	-	-	-	-	-	-	-	-	-	-
CGI [6]	97	96	94	77	77	56	58	98	97	86	27	24	79.12
M-HOG [17]	98	94	93	66	52	44	47	96	93	93	30	21	74.32
FHEI [10]	98	96	94	73	66	54	47	97	98	93	42	33	78.98
Our Method	97	94	93	77	75	55	62	95	93	92	36	30	79.66

the first five places. The Rank1 and Rank5 performances are listed as Tables 2 and 3. From the Table 2, the Rank1 performance of the EACI is better than that of the baseline algorithm, GEI, HMM, DATER, Multiple, CGI and FHEI. These results suggest that the EACI is able to capture more distinctive gait information and describe the temporal information better. In particular, our method achieves the best results in experiments B H K and the second result in experiment J. This indicates that the EACI are insensitive to the distortions caused by shoe and briefcase.

Table 4. The result of Rank1 and Rank5 with different intervals

Number	0	1(Our)	2
Rank1 Avg	62.61	64.33	62.42
Rank5 Avg	78.98	79.66	78.69

In contrast with other algorithm, the average of the Rank5 of the EACI is also better, from the Table 3. Specially, our method gets the best results in experiment G, and second result in experiment A B C D. Besides, for experiments A B C H I J, our result is over 90. This phenomenon shows that the proposed method is more robust to the changes of views, shoes and carrying condition.

To prove the validity of our method, we select three numbers of the interval. In our method, the interval number is the one. The result shows in Table 4. The Table 4 tells us that the Rank1 and Rank5 are best, when the number of interval is 1. And when choosing 0 or 2, the Rank1 and Rank5 decrease. It's evident that our method is robust, containing the static, dynamic and temporal effectively.

7 Conclusion

In this paper, we propose enhanced active color image to characterize the static, dynamic and temporal information of the gait sequence. On the USF HUMANID Gait Database, our method achieve the better performance than other published algorithm. And proving our method is robust. In the future, we will study how to solve the time changing and other gait challenge problems.

References

1. Han, J., Bhanu, B.: Individual recognition using gait energy image. IEEE Trans. Pattern Anal. Mach. Intell. **28**(2), 316–322 (2006)
2. Guan, Y., Li, C.-T., Roli, F.: On reducing the effect of covariate factors in gait recognition: a classifier ensemble method. IEEE Trans. Pattern Anal. Mach. Intell. **37**(7), 1521–1528 (2015)
3. Lee, L., Grimson, W.E.L.: Gait analysis for recognition and classification. In: 2002 Proceedings of Fifth IEEE International Conference on Automatic Face and Gesture Recognition, pp. 148–155 (2002)
4. Yam, C.Y., Nixon, M.S., Carter, J.N.: Automated person recognition by walking and running via model-based approaches. Pattern Recogn. **37**(5), 1057–1072 (2004)
5. Bashir, K., Xiang, T., Gong, S.: Gait recognition using gait entropy image. In: 3rd International Conference on Crime Detection and Prevention (ICDP 2009), pp. 1–6. IET (2009)
6. Wang, C., Zhang, J., Pu, J., Yuan, X., Wang, L.: Chrono-gait image: a novel temporal template for gait recognition. In: Daniilidis, K., Maragos, P., Paragios, N. (eds.) ECCV 2010. LNCS, vol. 6311, pp. 257–270. Springer, Heidelberg (2010). doi:10.1007/978-3-642-15549-9_19

7. Wang, J., She, M., Nahavandi, S., Kouzani, A.: A review of vision-based gait recognition methods for human identification. In: International Conference on Digital Image Computing: Techniques and Applications, Dicta 2010, Sydney, Australia, pp. 320–327, 1–3 December 2010
8. Chen, C., Liang, J., Zhao, H., Hu, H., Tian, J.: Frame difference energy image for gait recognition with incomplete silhouettes. Pattern Recogn. Lett. **30**(11), 977–984 (2009)
9. Zhang, E., Zhao, Y., Xiong, W.: Active energy image plus 2DLPP for gait recognition. Sig. Process. **90**(7), 2295–2302 (2010)
10. Yang, Y., Tu, D., Li, G.: Gait recognition using flow histogram energy image. In: International Conference on Pattern Recognition, pp. 444–449 (2014)
11. Yang, X., Zhou, Y., Zhang, T., Shu, G., Yang, J.: Gait recognition based on dynamic region analysis. Sig. Process. **88**(9), 2350–2356 (2008)
12. Bashir, K., Xiang, T., Gong, S.: Gait recognition without subject cooperation. Pattern Recogn. Lett. **31**(13), 2052–2060 (2010)
13. Sarkar, S., Phillips, P.J., Liu, Z., Vega, I.R., Grother, P., Bowyer, K.W.: The humanID gait challenge problem: data sets, performance, and analysis. IEEE Trans. Pattern Anal. Mach. Intell. **27**(2), 162–177 (2005)
14. Pontzer, H., Raichlen, D.A., Lieberman, D.E.: Control and function of arm swing in human walking and running. J. Exp. Biol. **212**(4), 523–534 (2009)
15. Kale, A., Sundaresan, A., Rajagopalan, A.N., Cuntoor, N.P.: Identification of humans using gait. IEEE Trans. Image Process. Publ. IEEE Sig. Process. Soc. **13**(9), 1163–1173 (2004)
16. Xu, D., Yan, S., Tao, D., Zhang, L., Li, X., Zhang, H.J.: Human gait recognition with matrix representation. IEEE Trans. Circ. Syst. Video Technol. **16**(7), 896–903 (2006)
17. Liu, Y., Zhang, J., Wang, C., Wang, L.: Multiple HOG templates for gait recognition. pp. 2930–2933 (2012)

Gait Recognition with Adaptively Fused GEI Parts

Bei Sun[✉], Wusheng Luo, Qin Lu, Liebo Du, and Xing Zeng

College of Mechatronics Engineering and Automation,
National University of Defense Technology, Changsha, China
beys1990@163.com

Abstract. Though the general gait energy image (GEI) preserves static and dynamic information, most GEI-based gait recognition approaches do not fully exploit it, which leads to inferior performance under the conditions of appearance change, dynamic variation and viewpoint variation. Therefore, this paper proposes a novel Silhouette-based method called GEI parts (GEIs) to identify individuals. The GEIs divides GEI, as the gray-value of GEI indicates different motion of body part. Furthermore, this paper uses k-nearest neighbor as classifier and develops a feature fusion method by adding scores to the recognition results of each GEI part. The proposed method is tested on publicly available CASIA-B dataset under different conditions, by using: (1) different GEI parts individually; (2) adaptively fused GEI parts. The experimental results show that with our proposed adaptive GEIs fusion on the dynamic-static information of walking, the fused GEIs outperforms the state-of-the-art GEI.

Keywords: Geis · Gait recognition · Feature fusion · KNN

1 Introduction

Gait, as a new biometric can be captured at a distance and still be valid in low resolution, has shown widely prospects in applications such as public security, surveillance and smart home [1].

Recently, numerous gait recognition approaches have been proposed [2], and they can be generally divided into two types: model-based approaches and silhouette-based approaches. Model-based approaches mainly use a mathematic model to describe the movement of body such as torso and legs. Aqmar [4] employed the phase fluctuations and trajectory fluctuations of walking to conduct recognition from temporal and spatial information. Lin [5] presented a method using three-dimensional parameters for lower limb joints. In contrast, silhouette-based approaches characterize the gait patterns with the statistics of silhouette variation. Due to its simplicity and low computational cost, the silhouette-based approach is a more popular gait recognition method.

The most common silhouette-based approach is gait energy image (GEI) [8]. Recently, Lee [6] adopted the Fourier coefficients of human silhouette to measure the similarity, Liu [7] introduced a Fourier transform on gait energy image, some other improved methods based on GEI such as Accumulated Frame Difference Energy

© Springer International Publishing AG 2016
Z. You et al. (Eds.): CCBR 2016, LNCS 9967, pp. 471–479, 2016.
DOI: 10.1007/978-3-319-46654-5_52

Image [9] (AFDEI) also lead a good performance. However, as silhouette is easily affected by appearance and viewpoint variation, the GEI has difficulties in providing effective solution under such conditions.

Numerous researches have proved that conducting gait recognition with static and dynamic feature is a novel and effective method in dealing with external disturbs [10, 11]. Wang [12] proposed a feature model fusing static and dynamic biometrics in gait recognition, Jing et al. [9] introduced an approach fusing GEI and AFDEI which included the static and dynamic feature of walking to conduct recognition. Actually, the GEI preserves the static and dynamic information of walking [13, 14], e.g., the torso usually has a large gray value and the small gray-level parts generally denote the limbs. However, most GEI-based approaches mainly focus on recognition using the overall gait energy image, while few fully uses these dynamic and static information.

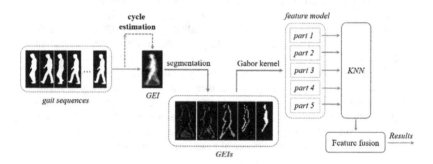

Fig. 1. Diagram of recognition based on GEIs.

In this paper, we propose an improved method called GEIs, where we first calculate and divide the GEI into several parts according to its gray-level, and then employ a feature fusion strategy on the segmented parts. As each GEI part preserves different static and dynamic information, this paper provides a new class of feature model based on the improved GEI. Figure 1 shows the diagram of the proposed algorithm. The gait cycle is first estimated based on the motion of lower limbs, then the GEI in a cycle is calculated and divided into different parts according to its gray value which generates GEIs. In order to simplify the calculation, we further use Gabor [15, 16] kernel as the feature representation and employ a fusion strategy to generate the fused GEIs. Finally, the experimental analysis is conducted based on the publicly available CASIA-B dataset in which the k-nearest neighbor [17] (KNN) is selected as the classifier.

Based on the feature fusion of GEI parts, the experimental analysis is mainly conducted from: (1) verifying which kind of feature, static or dynamic, can contribute a more robust recognition under external noise; (2) verifying variations, appearance or dynamics, can easily affect recognition; (3) evaluating the overall performance of GEIs, compared to other state-of-the-art algorithms (e.g. GEI).

2 Feature Model and Recognition

2.1 Gait Cycle Estimation

Most approaches [18–20] are based on gait cycle to extract feature and conduct recognition. Actually, the change of side silhouette implies the cycle information. And most recent approaches use parameters such as silhouette width, height or silhouette relevance in gait cycle estimation. However, the silhouette can be easily affected by external disturbance, which makes the silhouette-based cycle estimation methods limited.

To alleviate this problem, this paper conducts cycle estimation based on the legs swing. In fact, the regular limbs motion is a prominent characteristic in walking, furthermore, as a local feature, it can provide a more robust estimation than the overall silhouette-based methods. Figure 2 shows the diagram of the designed cycle estimation method. We first resize the images 90 * 150 with the silhouette centered and then calculate the silhouette width of lower limbs line by line. To facilitate the computation, this paper defines the lower one third of silhouette as the legs part. Moreover, in order to make a robust estimation, the average of ten max widths of each legs part is selected as its silhouette width count and a median filter is employed to remove some singularities. Finally, after all frames processed, the frequency of the width counts is computed and regarded as the gait cycle.

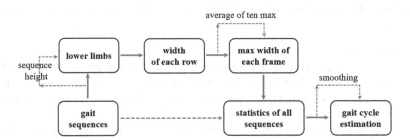

Fig. 2. Diagram of the cycle estimation based on lower limbs motion

2.2 GEIs Representation

(1) GEIs

GEI is a most common feature used in silhouette-based approaches. It usually utilizes a gait cycle to represent the gait energy [21]. Assuming $I(x, y, t)$ denotes a gait image, we can calculate the gait energy image by the following formula:

$$G(x, y) = \frac{1}{N} \sum_{t=1}^{N} I(x, y, t)$$

where N is the frame number of a cycle, and t denotes each frame of the sequence. As shown in Fig. 1, the gray value of GEI implies different spatial change of the body parts, e.g., the white points represent the parts with small changes, e.g. torso or head, while the gray points denote the parts with significantly movements, e.g. legs or arms. To fully exploit the static and dynamic information of GEI, this paper divides it into several parts based on its gray value and generates the fused GEI parts. Supposing $G_i(x, y)$ denotes the GEIs, then we have the following formula:

$$G_i(x, y) = \begin{cases} G(x, y), & 1 \leq i \leq k \, and \, 255 * \frac{i-1}{k} < G(x, y) \leq 255 * \frac{i}{k} \\ 0, & else \end{cases}$$

where k is the parts number of GEIs. The gray value of GEIs is equal to GEI if the pixel belongs to one part. Figure 1 shows the generation of GEIs, where k is set as 5.

As this paper mainly focuses on the experimental analysis of fused GEI parts, we select the popular Gabor kernel as feature representation, which has been widely used in image denoising, face detection and object tracking. Convolution with the Gabor kernel, the final gait feature is defined as:

$$I_{u,v}(z) = G_i(z) * \Psi_{u,v}(z)$$

where $*$ denotes the convolution operation, $\Psi_{u,v}(z)$ is the Gabor kernel and $\|I_{u,v}(z)\|$ denotes the amplitude spectrum of GEIs used as a feature representation. To reduce the computational cost, we also employ a PCA [3, 22] method to make a dimensionality reduction.

(2) Feature Fusion

Recently, two main approaches are widely used in feature fusion: one firstly generates a new feature model and then conduct recognition, while the other firstly implements recognition using each kind of features and then make a general evaluation based on the results.

This paper adopts the second fusion approach to recombine the GEI parts. Algorithm 1 shows the diagram of our designed feature fusion method (a little similar to the main idea of k-nearest neighbors). As the GEIs divides the GEI into five parts, we first conduct recognition using each GEI part as a feature model (we select k-nearest neighbors as classifier), and each GEI part will output a ranks based on the distance (which represents the similarity of two samples). Actually, the higher rank denotes the more likelihood the recognition result is, so we extract four top-rank results from the recognition results of each GEI part and add a score to them (e.g. 0.4, 0.3, 0.2 and 0.1) based on the ranks. Finally, after the 5 GEI parts processed, the class with highest score is selected as the recognition result.

Algorithm 1 The proposed late feature fusion algorithm for GEIs.

1: Initialization
  GEIs{5}   //5 divided parts of GEI;
  Scores(4)={0.4,0.3,0.2,0.1}   //fusion weights;
  Res(5, 4)   //the initial classify based on KNN;
  Score_of_Class(N)   //the final score of each class
2: *KNN* on Each GEI Part
  for i=1 to 5 **do**
     gei = *GEIs*{i};   *//conduct recognition using each GEI part*
     rank = *KNN_Classifier*{gei};
     Res(i, :) = *The_Four_Best_Rank*{rank};
                 //extract 4 top ranking results from each GEI part
  end
3: Late Fusion Approach
  for i=1 to 5 **do**
    for j=1 to 4 **do**
    class = Res(i, j);
    Score_of_Class (class) =+ *Scores*(j); *//add weight score according ranks*
    end
  end
4: Output Final Result
  Final_Class = *Class_With_Max_Score*{*Score_of_Class*}; *//final results*

Compared with GEI, our GEIs method provides a more flexible analysis: (1) we can make a detail evaluation of which kind of characteristics, static or dynamic, provides a robust recognition under external disturbance; (2) we can employ a feature fusion method on the 5 different GEI parts for recognition applications. Generally speaking, by exploiting static and dynamic information of different GEI parts, this paper provides a depth experimental analysis on gait identification.

2.3   Recognition Based on KNN

Actually, the process of recognition is an evaluation of the similarity of two samples. In recent years, researchers have proposed numerous machine learning algorithms such as k-means, SVM, HMM, random forest and ad-boost. While some algorithms conduct recognition according to a trained model and some others based on distance to make a measurement.

This paper adopts the k- nearest neighbors classifier (KNN) [17] for the identification task, where the distance of two samples is first measured. We use Euclidian distance to measure the distance:

$$L(\phi_1, \phi_2) = \sum_{i=1}^{n} \sqrt{(\phi_1(i) - \phi_2(i))^2}$$

where ϕ_1 and ϕ_2 denote two samples, and n is the dimension. Then the k nearest distances are calculated as the k-th likelihood classification of the unknown samples, and finally the smallest distance one is assessed as the class of the samples.

3 Experiments and Analysis

3.1 Dataset

The publicly available CASIA-B dataset is used in our experimental analysis. The dataset contains 124 people - each one includes 10 different conditions (6 normal situations and 4 variations: 2 carrying and 2 clothing) and each condition consist of 11 views ($0°$, $18°$, $36°$,..., $180°$). This paper mainly focus on the side silhouette, so only the sequences of $90°$ view are tested. Figure 3 shows some samples of side silhouettes in 3 different situations. In order to facilitate the calculation, all the sequences are first resized to 90 * 150 and centralize the silhouette.

Fig. 3. Samples of CASIA-B dataset (top row: sequences with variations of carrying bags; middle row: sequences with variations of clothing; bottom row: normal sequences.)

3.2 Results and Analysis

To make a depth analysis, we group the CASIA-B dataset into different sub-datasets and employ 3 different training strategies: (1) both trained and tested on normal situations, namely Test-1 (trained with nm-01, nm-03 and nm-05 and tested on nm-02, nm-04 and nm-06); (2) trained with normal samples and tested on situations with disturbance, namely Test-2 (the experiments trained with nm-01, nm-03 and nm-05 and tested on bg-01 and cl-01); (3) both trained and tested on all situations. In other words, Test-3 denotes the experiments trained with bg-01, cl-01, nm-01, nm-03, nm-05, and tested on bg-02, cl-02, nm-02, nm-04 and nm-06.

(1) Comparison of Different GEI Parts

Table 1 shows the results based on different GEI parts. G_i denotes different parts, where $i = \{1, 2, ..., 5\}$ represents different static and dynamic information.

In Table 1, each G_i obtains a higher accuracy in Test-1 and Test-3 but performs a little worse in Test-2. Note that though both Test-2 and Test-3 consist external disturbance in the test, but Test-2 is the experiments trained with normal sequences but

Table 1. Results based on different GEI parts (percentage)

Dataset	GEIs				
	G_1	G_2	G_3	G_4	G_5
Test-1	93.80	96.17	99.00	**99.50**	97.50
Test-2	69.25	**76.25**	74.75	71.75	56.00
Test-3	94.70	96.90	**97.80**	97.30	95.80

tested on variations, while in Test-3, both normal and noisy conditions are trained. From Table 1, we can see that each GEI part gains a higher accuracy in normal situations (more than 90 %), but has difficulties in dealing with the external noise (less than 75 %). On the other hand, G_4 performs best in Test-1, G_2 achieves the highest accuracy in Test-2, and G_3 gains the best performance in Test-3. This indicates the fact that, each GEI part contributes to the recognition, that is to say, dynamic and static information may play a different role in gait recognition under different variations. Note that as the static characters can be easily influenced under variations, and walking motions such as stride and arm-swing also easily changes in a real world. So this paper employs a fused GEI parts to expect a higher recognition accuracy.

(2) Comparison of GEI and Fusion based on GEIs

Table 2 provides the comparison of GEI and the fused GEI parts. From the results, both GEIs and GEI can achieve a high accuracy in Test-1 and Test-3, while in Test-2, GEIs leads a better performance due to the silhouette-based GEI is easier affected under external noise. The results show that, though GEI preserves the dynamic and static information, the proposed GEI-based approaches based on overall energy image do not performs well in dealing with external disturbance. However, when dividing the dynamic-static information of GEI into different parts, the method may perform more efficient and robust under those conditions.

Table 2. Results based on GEI and fusion of GEIs (percentage)

Dataset	GEIs	GEI
Test-1	**99.67**	99.33
Test-2	**82.75**	76.75
Test-3	**99.50**	99.10

However, note that Test-2 denotes the experiments trained with normal situations and tested on noisy sequences, the results of Test-2 indicate the general over-fitting problems existed in both GEIs and GEI methods. Actually, as can be easily affected by external disturbance, gait recognition approaches simply based on silhouette are not suitable in dealing with external variations.

(3) Discussion of Performance on Variations

This paper also provides a detailed analysis of the GEI and the fused GEI parts methods perform under single kind of variation, e.g. variation of clothing or variation of carrying items, in order to make clear which kind of the two disturbances significantly affects the recognition. As shown in Table 3, both GEIs and GEI gain a higher accuracy in variation of carrying than clothing. This may be related to the facts that carrying items only influences local silhouettes of torso or back while clothing influences the overall features of torso and limbs which make silhouette badly affected. Furthermore, our GEIs approach gains a higher accuracy than GEI, especially in Test-2. The experimental results show that, by individually represent the dynamic and static information of walking, our designed fused GEI parts model improves the performance of GEI-based approaches.

Table 3. Detail performance on variation of clothing and carrying (percentage)

Dataset		GEIs	GEI
Test-2	cl	73	65
	bg	**92.5**	**86.5**
Test-3	cl	97.5	97.5
	bg	**100**	**100**

4 Conclusion

The gait energy image (GEI) has difficulties handling variations such as carrying items, clothing and viewpoint changes. Therefore, this paper augmented a new original energy image named GEIs to exploit static-dynamic gait information implies in GEI, where we first divide the GEI into different parts based on the gray value and then fuse the GEI parts to generate a new robust feature model. The experimental results show that, the proposed GEIs using general dynamic and static feature can lead a higher accuracy. The other contributions of this paper include: (1) proposed a gait cycle estimation method based on lower limbs motion; (2) introduced a novel feature fusion method to fuse different GEI parts which leads a better recognition performance; (3) made a depth analysis of which kind of external noise (e.g. clothing or carrying items) is easier to affect the performance of silhouette-based approaches. Certainly, gait recognition is a difficult task due to the complexity walking style of each individual. Our ongoing works focus on the in-depth research of more robust gait feature models.

Acknowledgments. This work is supported by the National Natural Science Foundation of China (61171136).

References

1. Jain, A.K., Ross, A., Prabhakar, S.: An introduction to biometric recognition. IEEE Trans. Circ. Syst. Video Technol. **14**(1), 4–20 (2004)
2. Yu, S.Q., Tan, T.N., Huang, K.Q., et al.: A study on gait-based gender Classification. IEEE Trans. Image Process. **18**(8), 1905–1910 (2009)
3. Benbakreti, S., Benyettou, M.: Gait recognition based on leg motion and contour of silhouette. In: IEEE International Conference on Information Technology and e-Services (2012)

4. Aqmar, M.R., Fujihara, Y., Makihara, Y., Yagi, Y.: Gait recognition by fluctuation. Comput. Vis. Image Underst. **126**, 38–52 (2014)
5. Lin, Y.C., Yang, B.S., Lin, Y.T., Yang, Y.T.: Human recognition based on kinematics and kinetics of gait. J. Med. Biol. Eng. **31**(4), 255–263 (2010)
6. Lee, C.P., Tan, A.W.C., Tana, S.C.: Gait recognition via optimally interpolated deformable contours. Pattern Recogn. Lett. J. **34**(6), 663–669 (2013)
7. Liu, Y.Q., Wang, X.: Human gait recognition for multiple views. Proc. Eng. **15**, 1832–1836 (2011)
8. Han, J., Bhanu, B.: Individual recognition using gait energy image. IEEE Trans. Pattern Anal. Mach. Intell. **28**(2), 316–322 (2006)
9. Luo, J., Zhang, J.L., Zi, C.Y., et al.: Gait recognition using GEI and AFDEI. Int. J. Opt. **2015**, 1–5 (2015)
10. Lombardi, S., Nishino, K., et al.: Two-point gait: decoupling gait from body shape. In: ICCV (2013)
11. Yang, X., Zhou, Y., Zhang, T., et al.: Gait recognition based on dynamic region analysis. Sig. Process. **88**(9), 2350–2356 (2008)
12. Wang, L., Ning, H.Z., Tan, T., Hu, W.M.: Fusion of static and dynamic body biometrics for gait recognition. IEEE Trans. Circ. Syst. Video Technol. **14**, 149–158 (2004)
13. Lopez-Fernandez, D., Madrid-Cuevas, F.J., Carmona-Poyato, A., Munoz-Salinas, R., Medina-Carnicer, R.: Entropy volumes for viewpoint-independent gait recognition. Mach. Vis. Appl. **26**(7–8), 1079–1094 (2015)
14. Shroti, N., Khandekar, A.: A Survey paper on human gait recognition using PCA & Neural Network. Int. J. Eng. Sci. Res. Technol. (2015)
15. Tao, D., Li, X., Wu, X., Maybank, S.J.: General tensor discriminant analysis and gabor features for gait recognition. IEEE Trans. Pattern Anal. Mach. Intell. **29**(10), 1700–1715 (2007)
16. Hu, M., et al.: Combining spatial and temporal information for gait based gender classification. In: 20th IEEE International Conference on Pattern Recognition (2010)
17. Hastie, T., Tibshirani, R.: Discriminant Adaptive Nearest Neighbor Classification. IEEE Trans. Pattern Anal. Mach. Intell. **18**(6), 607–616 (1996)
18. Sarkar, S., Phillips, P., Liu, Z., Vega, I., Grother, P., Bowyer, K.: The human ID gait challenge problem: Data sets, performance, and analysis. IEEE Trans. PAMI **27**(2), 162–177 (2005)
19. Bashir, K., Xiang, T., Gong, S.G.: Gait recognition without subject cooperation. Pattern Recogn. Lett. **31**, 2052–2060 (2010)
20. Chattopadhyaya, P., Surala, S., Mukherjeeb, J.: Frontal gait recognition from occluded scenes. Pattern Recogn. Lett. **63**, 9–15 (2015)
21. Wang, C., Zhang, J., Wang, L., Pu, J., Yuan, X.: Human identification using temporal information preserving gait template. IEEE TPAMI **34**(11), 2164–2176 (2012)
22 Ekinci, M., Aykut, M.: Human gait recognition based on kernel PCA using projections. J. Comput. Sci. Technol. **22**, 867–876 (2007)

Affective Computing

A Computational Other-Race-Effect Analysis for 3D Facial Expression Recognition

Mingliang Xue[1], Xiaodong Duan[1]([✉]), Juxiang Zhou[2], Cunrui Wang[1], Yuangang Wang[1], Zedong Li[1], and Wanquan Liu[3]

[1] Dalian Key Lab of Digital Technology for National Culture,
College of Computer Science and Engineering, Dalian Minzu University,
Dalian 116600, Liaoning, China
duanxd_dlnu@126.com
[2] Key Laboratory of Education Informatization for Nationalities,
Ministry of Education, Yunnan Normal University,
Kunming 650500, Yunnan, China
[3] Department of Computing, Curtin University, Kent Street,
Perth, WA 6102, Australia

Abstract. This paper investigates the other-race-effects in automatic 3D facial expression recognition, giving the computational analysis of the recognition performance obtained from two races, namely white and east Asian. The 3D face information is represented by local depth feature, and then a feature learning process is used to obtain race-sensitive features to simulate the other-race-effect. The learned features from own race and other race are then used to do facial expression recognition. The proposed analysis is conducted on BU-3DFE database, and the results show that the learned features from one race achieve better recognition performance on the own-race faces. It reveals that the other-race-effect are significant in facial expression recognition problem, which confirms the results of psychological experiment results.

Keywords: Other-race-effect · 3D facial expression · Feature learning

1 Introduction

Human face carries various kinds of information, which related to a person's identity, race, gender and age etc. These information usually mix together with each other. This is the reason why discriminant feature extraction and selection process are quite a different task when doing face-based pattern recognition problems, such as face recognition [1], facial expression recognition [2–4], gender classification [5] and age estimation [6]. As one of demographic categories, race information has been noticed in behavioural research and the computer vision research. Psychological studies have long shown the existence of other-race-effect (ORE) [7], which means that human brain is superior in memorizing and recognizing the faces of our own race than for faces of other races. Moreover, the other-race-effect for face recognition algorithms is also demonstrated in [8].

© Springer International Publishing AG 2016
Z. You et al. (Eds.): CCBR 2016, LNCS 9967, pp. 483–493, 2016.
DOI: 10.1007/978-3-319-46654-5_53

This leads to the question of whether other-race-effect exists in facial expression recognition problem.

Facial expressions provide a non-verbal way for humans to convey their emotions and intentions, which makes expressions rather crucial to human social communications. Enabling machines to recognize human expressions has become increasingly popular, due to its wide application potentials, such as human computer interaction (HCI), affective computing, and psychological treatments. Many models and algorithms [9] have been proposed to represent and classify facial expressions, in which the factors that affect facial expression recognition are studied intensively. Some of the psychological works have shown that race information have influenced facial expression recognition. In [10], the authors investigate the evidence of cultural differences in facial expression and attempt to seek a computational explanation. The results reveal the existence of culture-specific facial expression dialect, which causes the own-group recognition advantage. This work inspires us to study on how race differences affect the performance of facial expression recognition computationally.

The investigation is based on 3D facial expression images, since 3D face images are more expressive and accurate in facial expression description [4,11–13]. The experiment employs the facial expression samples of two races in BU-3DFE database [14], i.e. White and East-Asian, to simulate the other-race-effect in expression recognition. A feature learning algorithm is proposed to obtain the race-sensitive features for expression representation. The learned features from own race and other race are then used for classification, which will give a computational explanation of other-race-effect in facial expression recognition.

The remainder of this paper is organized as follows. Section 2 reviews the related works about other-race-effect from psychological and computational perspectives. Section 3 gives the details of the feature extraction in facial expression recognition, and the race-sensitive feature learning is described in Sect. 4. We present the experimental results and analysis in Sect. 5, and finally conclude in Sect. 6.

2   Related Works

The other-race-effect was first observed and investigated in psychological researches. The behavioural experiments [15] have suggested that human show much better ability in memory and recognition of the own-race's human faces. The psychological researches tried to find out the factors that may cause these differences for decades. The progress in the domains of social and visual perception has inspired computer vision researchers to develop computational models for other-race-effect analysis. As reviewed in [16], these models could be grouped into two categories. One is based on the local Gabor wavelets connected with dynamic link structures. This type of models have the ability to analog visual cortex [17], but work independent of prior knowledge of faces, which makes this type of model unsuitable to encode the other-race-effect. The other type of model is based on holistic face analysis using principal components analysis (PCA) [18,19]. The face-space based on PCA provides a natural way to understand how we read and remember faces of own or other-race.

Based on the existing works [18,20], it can be seen that incorporating different kinds of experience into the model is essential in other-race effect simulation. Thus, this paper proposes a model based on local depth features of 3D faces, which focus on learning the race-sensitive features and then could be use to simulate other-race-effect in expression recognition.

3   Feature Extraction

The raw 3D faces in BU-3DFE are represented by point cloud, which is invariant to the changes caused by head position and illumination, and thus to be an adequate representation of facial expressions for recognition task. This section gives a method to generate 30 heuristic landmarks on 3D faces, and then local depth features are extracted around the detected landmarks to represent expressions.

3.1   Uniform Local Depth Feature

Presently, real time landmark detection on 3D faces is still an open problem due to the significant topology changes, such as opening mouth in surprise. Though some works such as [21] have been done on this topic, the time cost is still unbearable for real time application, especially when the probe 3D images are the expressive scans with high intensity. However, it is worth noting that facial geometric features change relatively little around some points when expression changes, such as the four eye corners and nose tip. Hence, these points are more likely to be detected with a decent accuracy. In the proposed methods, these five points are detected on a 3D facial surface, and their relative distances are used to generate another 25 heuristic points on the face. For more detail, please see paper [22].

As shown in Fig. 1(a), once a landmark point has been located on 3D face surface, a cluster of points around the landmark are cropped out to extract local information. This could be done by collecting the points within a sphere of radius r centered at this point. A cubic patch is then fitted to the cropped points by grid fitting [23], which describes the local facial surface. In order to obtain features of same pattern, the depth information of the fitted patch is then sampled uniformly by a $n \times n$ grid. The resulting local depth features of each patch could be recorded in a $n \times n$ depth matrix. Until now, all sampled patches end up with equal resolution, which enables the following feature learning and classification.

3.2   Patch Parameter Selection

There are two parameters, i.e. the radius r and the resolution $n \times n$, which control the patch shape and fitting resolution. When extracting local features from fitted

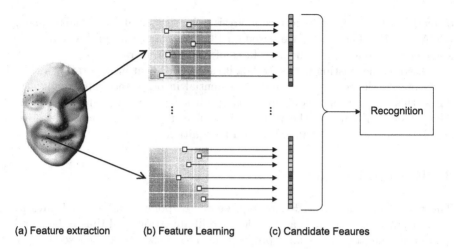

(a) Feature extraction   (b) Feature Learning   (c) Candidate Feaures

Fig. 1. The scheme of the feature extraction, learning and classification.

patches, the selection of the these two parameters will affect the quality of the resulting depth features. A relatively small radius will decrease the effectiveness of feature extraction, because an undersized patch would not be able to reflect the facial surface deformation caused by different expressions. However, if the radius are too large, the selected points will contain too much information that in-relevant to the expressions. Thus, an adequate radius r need to be selected before grid patch fitting.

Even a suitable radius of local patch has been fixed, the sampling resolution is another parameter to determine. As same as all the sampling process, the sampled data will lose the fidelity to the original data if the sampling resolution is too low. Obviously, this will affect the performance of following facial expression recognition. On the contrary, the computational cost will increase significantly if the resolution is too high. This means a right size patch with suitable resolution is required by feasible approach.

In order to determine these two parameters, we conduct facial expression recognition on BU-3DFE data following commonly used 54-vs-6 setup [4]. The depth features are extracted from patches with radius of $r = 20, 25, 30, 35, 40$ using sampling grid size of 20×20, 32×32, and 64×64. The average recognition rates of 10-fold cross-validation are recorded in Table 1. It can be seen that depth features extracted from patches with radius of $r = 30$ using sampling grid size of 64×64 achieve the best average recognition rate. It is worth noting that the sampling resolution is approximately than 1 mm when sampling a patch of $r = 30$ mm with 64×64 grid. In fact, the resolution of 3dMD scanner, which used to capture faces for BU-3DFE database, is 1 mm. That means it doesn't help to further increase the size of sampling grid, besides the rising computational cost. Hence, the parameters radius $r = 30$ and grid size 64×64 are used in all the following experiments.

Table 1. Facial expression recognition rates based on the features extracted from patches of different parameters (radius r and grid size $n \times n$). The results are obtained on BU-3DFE database.

Rates (%)	20×20	32×32	64×64
$r = 20\,\mathrm{mm}$	73.3	73.4	73.9
$r = 25\,\mathrm{mm}$	74.3	74.4	75.0
$r = 30\,\mathrm{mm}$	74.0	74.7	**75.4**
$r = 35\,\mathrm{mm}$	75.0	74.7	74.4
$r = 40\,\mathrm{mm}$	75.0	74.9	74.3

4 Race-Sensitive Expression Feature Learning and ORE Verification

To verify the other-race-effect in facial expression recognition, the race-sensitive features should be indentified first. After feature extraction, each face is now represented by 30 depth matrices, with each matrix corresponding to one local patch. It can be seen from Fig. 1(a) that the distances between neighbouring landmarks are far less than 30 mm, which means the patches around neighbouring landmarks will overlap with each other. Thus, the extracted local depth features have considerable redundancy, which will increase the computational cost if the local depth features are used directly. In fact, the depth feature are extracted around automatic landmarks may cause classification error since the heuristic points are usually not perfectly aligned. Hence, learning the compact race-sensitive features of the observed data is essential to other-race-effect simulation.

The purpose of feature learning is to obtain a optimal race-sensitive feature set, which can best represent the expressions of a target race for recognition. It could be done by a forward learning process, during which the relevance and redundancy between the features are considered. Given the training samples of the target race represented by features $F = \{x_1, x_2, \cdots, x_i, \cdots, x_N\}$ and the expression label e, the mutual information between feature x_i and the expression e could be calculated to measure the relevance by

$$I(x_i, e) = \int \int p(x_i, e) log \frac{p(x_i, e)}{p(x_i)P(e)} dx_i de. \tag{1}$$

where $p(x_i)$ and $p(e)$ is the probability distribution of feature x_i and expression class e, and $p(x_i, e)$ is the joint probability distribution of feature x_i and expression e. However, the combination of m most relevant features does not necessarily lead to the optimal feature set, due to the redundancy existing among the features. Thus, the mutual information between feature x_i and x_j is calculated by

$$I(x_i, x_j) = \int \int p(x_i, x_j) log \frac{p(x_i, x_j)}{p(x_i)p(x_j)} dx_i dx_j \tag{2}$$

Algorithm 1. Incremental Race-sensitive Feature Learning Algorithm

---

Require: Facial features $F = \{f_i | 1 \leq i \leq n\}$, Candidate feature set C
Ensure: Optimal Feature set: S_{opt}
   Initialize: Classification error: $E = 1$, count $= 1$;
                        Candidate feature set: $C_0 = F$
                        Optimal feature set: $S_0 = \Phi$ (empty set)
  while $count \leq n$ **do**
    for $k = 1 : sizeof(C_{count-1})$ **do**
      1. $Temp = \{S_{count-1}, f_k\}$
      2. Update classification error $e(k)$ based on $Temp$
      3. $i = argmin\ e(k)$
    end for
    if $min\ e(k) \leq E$ **then**
      1. $E = min\ e(k)$
      2. $S_{count} = \{S_{count-1}, f_i\}$
      3. $C_{count} = \{C_{count-1} - f_i\}$
    else
      Break
    end if
    $S_{opt} = S_{count}$;
    $count = count + 1$;
  end while

---

to measure the redundancy. The feature learning criterion is then formed based on mutual information as follows:

$$max \frac{\frac{1}{|F|} \sum_{f_i \in F} I(f_i; e)}{\frac{1}{|F|^2} \sum_{f_i, f_j \in F} I(f_i; f_j)} \tag{3}$$

where $|F|$ is the size of the depth feature set F. The most relevant features to target expression, which also have the least mutual redundancy, could be achieved simultaneously by max this feature learning criterion.

More specifically, the optimal race-sensitive features can be determined one by one by a incremental algorithm under the criterion in Eq. (3). After the samples are represented by candidate features, a wrapper which works with a nearest-neighbour classifier, are used to finish expression classification after Linear Discriminant Analysis (LDA) projection [24]. As shown in Fig. 1(b), the incremental learning process are conducted on each patch of a 3D face, and the learned optimal features are combined together to represent the whole face. It can been seen in Algorithm 1 that the classification error is initialized as 1. In the learning process, the feature which can reduce the classification error most are chosen in each round. This feature will be added into optimal feature set and deleted from candidate feature set. This operation is repeated until the classification error stop decreasing or all the candidate features have been used up. The learning process are performed on the samples of one race, where n-fold cross-validation is conducted. The intersection of the learned feature sets (n-fold) are taken for the race-sensitive expression representation.

5   Experimental Results

5.1   Experiment Setup

The paper analyzes the other-race-effect computationally based on the BU-3DFE database [14], which is originally created for the purpose of 3D facial expression recognition. This database contains 3D faces of 100 subjects. Each subject shows the 6 prototypic expressions with 4 different intensity. As shown in Table 2, the subjects of BU-3DFE database belong to 6 different races. Because of the imbalance of race distributions, our experiment employs 48 Whites and all the 24 East-Asians from BU-3DFE to analyze the other-race-effect in facial expression recognition. Normally, facial expression recognition are performed in person-independent way [22], in which the training samples and testing samples are from different individuals. However, in order to analyze other-race-effect, facial expression recognition needs to be done in cross and own-race ways. Thus, the 48 Whites are divided randomly into two parts (White-A and White-B), with each part containing 24 subjects. Until now, there are 3 parts of data, i.e. White-A, White-B and East-Asian, based on which the proposed experiment could be conducted. To ensure an unbiased results, the splitting of 48 Whites are repeated 10 times. In every split, White-A and White-B have no intersection and the union of them are the 48 Whites. The experiments are then accordingly performed, and the average results are reported.

Table 2. The Race distribution of BU-3DFE database.

Race	Number of subjects	Number of expressive faces
White	51	1224
East-Asian	24	576
Black	9	216
Hispanic-Latino	8	192
Indian	6	144
Middle-East Asian	2	48

5.2   ORE in Facial Expression Recognition

As shown in Table 3, four experiments are conducted to compare the recognition performance based on cross-race data and own-race data. Base on the setup in Table 3, the facial expression recognition is also person-independent. In cross-race setup (Experiment number 2 and 4), the East-Asian faces are used for training and White faces are used in testing. In training stage, the feature learning algorithm are performed based on East-Asian faces. The learned 'East-Asian' features are then used to represent White Faces for recognition. Similarly, in own-race setup (Experiment number 1 and 3), the classifier is trained on the

Table 3. The data configuration of facial expression recognition on BU-3DFE database.

Experiment ID	Training group	Testing group
1	White-A	White-B
2	East-Asian	White-B
3	White-B	White-A
4	East-Asian	White-A

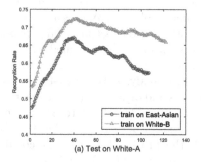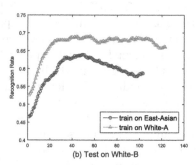

Fig. 2. The facial expression recognition performance comparison of Other-Race-Effect. The X-axis represents the size of candidate feature set in feature learning, while Y-axis records the corresponding expression recognition rate.

White-A faces and tested on the White-B faces, or vice versa. During the training process, the feature learning approach is used to obtain the best features for White race description. The testing samples are then represented by the learning 'White' features for classification.

The average recognition rates of six prototypic expressions in the four experiments are illustrated in Fig. 2. It can be seen that no matter how many the learned features are used, the own-race (White-A and White-B) trained method outperforms the cross-race (East-Asian and White) trained one significantly and consistently. Based on the average recognition rate of 6 prototypic expressions, the other-race-effect are very significant in 3D facial expression recognition.

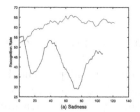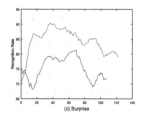

Fig. 3. The recognition performance comparison of sadness, happiness and surprise. The X-axis means the size of the candidate feature set in feature learning, and the Y-axis represents the corresponding facial expression recognition rate.

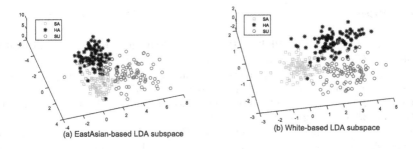

Fig. 4. The testing White samples distribution in subspace.

In order to find out the influence of the ORE to the specific expression, the recognition rates of expression sadness, happiness and surprise of own-race and cross-race are compared in Fig. 3. As same as the average recognition rate, the recognition rates of these 3 expressions based on own-race are far better than that of cross-race. This may caused by the features learned under own-race setup mainly reflect the own-race facial expression characteristics, which thereby could not represent the other-race's expression sufficiently and accurately.

Figure 4 illustrates the learned LDA subspace from East-Asian faces and White faces. The testing white facial expression samples are represented by features learned based on East-Asian faces and White faces. It shows clearly that the White-based features can separate White expressions better (Fig. 4(b)). The testing samples mix with each other when represented by the cross-race learned features. The geometric and appearance of faces from one race will bias the feature learning process to choose the features which can well describe the own-race faces, which is a computational explanation of other-race-effect. The separability of the test samples in Fig. 4 is the illustration of this biased effect.

6   Conclusion

This paper studied the other-race-effect in 3D facial expression recognition. First, local depth features are extracted from 3D faces to represent facial expressions. Based on the training samples of one specified race, the race-sensitive features are then obtained by an incremental feature learning process. The expression recognition is finally performed based on the features learned from own-race and other-race. The recognition rates drop significant when the features learned from other-race are used for representation, which reveals that the other-race-effect exists in 3D facial expression recognition computationally. However, what kind of differences in 3D faces caused other-race-effect is still not very clear, which is also the direction of our future investigation.

Acknowledgments. This work is supported by National Natural Science Foundation of China (Grant No. 61370146), Liaoning Science & Technology of Liaoning Province of China (Grant No. 2013405003), Natural Science Foundation of China (Grant No. 61262071) and Application Infrastructure Projects in Yunnan Province (Grant No. 2014FD016).

References

1. Zhao, W., Chellappa, R., Phillips, P.J., Rosenfeld, A.: Face recognition: a literature survey. ACM Comput. Surveys (CSUR) **35**(4), 399–458 (2003)
2. Samal, A., Iyengar, P.A.: Automatic recognition and analysis of human faces and facial expressions: a survey. Pattern Recogn. **25**(1), 65–77 (1992)
3. Fasel, B., Luettin, J.: Automatic facial expression analysis: a survey. Pattern Recogn. **36**(1), 259–275 (2003)
4. Sandbach, G., Zafeiriou, S., Pantic, M., Yin, L.: Static and dynamic 3d facial expression recognition: a comprehensive survey. Image Vis. Comput. **30**(10), 683–697 (2012)
5. Ng, C.B., Tay, Y.H., Goi, B.M.: Vision-based human gender recognition: a survey. arXiv preprint (2012). arXiv:1204.1611
6. Fu, Y., Guo, G., Huang, T.S.: Age synthesis and estimation via faces: a survey. IEEE Trans. Pattern Anal. Mach. Intell. **32**(11), 1955–1976 (2010)
7. Fu, S., He, H., Hou, Z.G.: Learning race from face: a survey. IEEE Trans. Pattern Anal. Mach. Intell. **36**(12), 2483–2509 (2014)
8. Phillips, P.J., Jiang, F., Narvekar, A., Ayyad, J., O'Toole, A.J.: An other-race effect for face recognition algorithms. ACM Trans. Appl. Percep. (TAP) **8**(2), 14 (2011)
9. Bettadapura, V.: Face expression recognition and analysis: the state of the art. arXiv preprint (2012). arXiv:1203.6722
10. Dailey, M.N., Joyce, C., Lyons, M.J., Kamachi, M., Ishi, H., Gyoba, J., Cottrell, G.W.: Evidence and a computational explanation of cultural differences in facial expression recognition. Emotion **10**(6), 874 (2010)
11. Huang, D., Ouji, K., Ardabilian, M., Wang, Y., Chen, L.: 3d face recognition based on local shape patterns and sparse representation classifier. In: Lee, K.-T., Tsai, W.-H., Mark Liao, H.-Y., Chen, T., Hsieh, J.-W., Tseng, C.-C. (eds.) MMM 2011, Part. LNCS, vol. 6523, pp. 206–216. Springer, Heidelberg (2011)
12. Zhen, Q., Huang, D., Wang, Y., Chen, L.: Muscular movement model based automatic 3d facial expression recognition. In: He, X., Luo, S., Tao, D., Xu, C., Yang, J., Hasan, M.A. (eds.) MMM 2015, Part I. LNCS, vol. 8935, pp. 522–533. Springer, Heidelberg (2015). doi:10.1007/978-3-319-14445-0_45
13. Yang, X., Huang, D., Wang, Y., Chen, L.: Automatic 3d facial expression recognition using geometric scattering representation. In: 2015 11th IEEE International Conference and Workshops on Automatic Face and Gesture Recognition (FG), vol. 1, pp. 1–6. IEEE (2015)
14. Yin, L., Wei, X., Sun, Y., Wang, J., Rosato, M.J.: A 3d facial expression database for facial behavior research. In: 7th International Conference on Automatic Face and Gesture Recognition (FGR06), pp. 211–216. IEEE (2006)
15. Malpass, R.S., Kravitz, J.: Recognition for faces of own and other race. J. Personal. Soc. Psychol. **13**(4), 330 (1969)
16. Jain, A.K., Li, S.Z.: Handbook of Face Recognition. Springer, London (2011)
17. Shen, L., Bai, L.: A review on gabor wavelets for face recognition. Pattern Anal. Appl. **9**(2–3), 273–292 (2006)
18. O'Toole, A.J., Deffenbacher, K., Abdi, H., Bartlett, J.C.: Simulating the other-race effect as a problem in perceptual learning. Connect. Sci. **3**(2), 163–178 (1991)
19. OToole, A.J., Deffenbacher, K., Valentin, D., Abdi, H.: Low-dimensional representation of faces in higher dimensions of the face space. JOSA A **10**(3), 405–411 (1993)

20. O'Toole, A.J., An, X., Dunlop, J., Natu, V., Phillips, P.J.: Comparing face recognition algorithms to humans on challenging tasks. ACM Trans. Appl. Percep. (TAP) **9**(4), 16 (2012)
21. Zulqarnain Gilani, S., Shafait, F., Mian, A.: Shape-based automatic detection of a large number of 3d facial landmarks. In: Proceedings of the IEEE Conference on Computer Vision and Pattern Recognition, pp. 4639–4648 (2015)
22. Xue, M., Mian, A., Liu, W., Li, L.: Fully automatic 3d facial expression recognition using local depth features. In: IEEE Winter Conference on Applications of Computer Vision, pp. 1096–1103. IEEE (2014)
23. D'Errico, J.R.: Understanding gridfit. Information (2006). http://www.mathworks.com/matlabcentral/fileexchange/loadFile.do
24. Belhumeur, P.N., Hespanha, J.P., Kriegman, D.J.: Eigenfaces vs. fisherfaces: recognition using class specific linear projection. IEEE Trans. Pattern Anal. Mach. Intell. **19**(7), 711–720 (1997)

Discriminative Low-Rank Linear Regression (DLLR) for Facial Expression Recognition

Jie Zhu[1,2(✉)], Hao Zheng[2,3], Hong Zhao[2], and Wenming Zheng[1]

[1] School of Biological Sciences and Medical Engineering, Southeast University, Nanjing 210096, People's Republic of China
Zhuj139130@163.com
[2] Key Laboratory of Trusted Cloud Computing and Big Data Analysis, Nanjing XiaoZhuang University, Nanjing 211171, People's Republic of China
[3] Key Laboratory of Computer Network and Information Integration, Ministry of Education, Southeast University, Nanjing 210096, People's Republic of China

Abstract. In this paper we focus on the need for seeking a robust low-rank linear regression algorithm for facial expression recognition. Motivated by low-rank matrix recovery, we assumed that the matrix whose data are from the same pattern as columns vectors is approximately low-rank. The proposed algorithm firstly decomposes the training images per class into the sum of the sparse error matrix, the low-rank matrix of the original images and the class discrimination criterion. Then accelerated proximal gradient algorithm was used to minimize the sum of ℓ1-norm and the nuclear matrix norm to get the set of tight linear regression base as the dictionary. Finally, we reconstruct the samples by tight dictionary and classified the face image by linear regression method according to the residual. The experimental results on facial expression databases show that the proposed method works well.

Keywords: Linear regression · Low rank · Facial expression recognition

1 Introduction

The last decade made substantial progress in facial expression recognition systems [1], and a handful of researchers focused on this field [2–5]. Kaltwang [4] et al. used Relevance Vector Regression to obtain a probabilistic prediction from facial expressions. Rudovic [5] et al. presented a regression-based scheme for multi-view facial expression recognition. However, the above methods didn't consider the images with noises.

One of the methods for face recognition is linear regression classification (LRC) [6, 7]. LRC is based on the assumption that the observations from each individual subject can be represented linearly by the same kind of samples, because the samples from the same class had great similarity. The experimental results showed that LRC can obtain better results under the constrained conditions, and the recognition speed was fast, but the LRC method will be affected by face transformation, rotation and scale change. Ideally, the matrix A whose columns come from the same pattern is

© Springer International Publishing AG 2016
Z. You et al. (Eds.): CCBR 2016, LNCS 9967, pp. 494–502, 2016.
DOI: 10.1007/978-3-319-46654-5_54

often low-rank or approximately low-rank, but under the influence of factors such as illumination changes and some of the shelter, the training images' structure is often destroyed by sparse matrix E. Based on low-rank matrix recovery and completion [1], robust principal component analysis [8, 9] (Robust PCA) was proposed to recover the underlying low-rank structure in the data. Benjamin [10] proposed that the minimum-rank solution can be recovered by solving a convex optimization problem if a certain restricted isometry property holds for the linear transformation definition. Peng and Ma [11] put forward the robust alignment by sparse low-rank decomposition method for linearly correlated images, which reduced the optimization problem to a sequence of convex programs that minimize the sum of L1-norm and nuclear norm of the component matrices. Inspired by above work, we can consider the images as the sum of low rank matrix and error matrix to decrease the noise effect.

All above methods have achieved promising results in many fields, but for image classification tasks they did not provide much attention to the class discrimination information which can result in better performance. Learning discriminative dictionary has been proved to improve the performance of face recognition dramatically [12]. LRC algorithm uses the training samples of the same class as the dictionary to represent the query face image, and classified it by evaluating which class leads to the minimal reconstruction error of it, but we need to consider the noise information in the raw training images, in addition the discriminative information should also be exploited. LDA [13, 14] is to extract the most discriminative features that can maximize the class separability, defined as the ratio of the between-class scatter matrix to the within-class scatter matrix. Parkhi [15] et al. propose a novel face track descriptor based on the Fisher Vector representation which aggregate local descriptors into an overall face descriptor. Ma [16] et al. propose a discriminative low-rank dictionary learning algorithm for sparse representation. Compared to Robust PCA, they optimized the dictionary under the framework of sparse representation. Yang et al. [17] presented a novel dictionary learning method based on the Fisher discrimination criterion which is called FDDL model to learn class-specific dictionary for each subject. Eleftheriadis [18] et al. proposed the discriminative automated systems that can accurately perform multi-pose and pose-invariant facial expression recognition. Both of them considered the discriminative information based on the sparse representation, but they deteriorate when there are noises in the training data. In this paper, both the discriminative information and the noises are considered, and we present a discriminative low-rank method based on the linear regression method to learn a robust dictionary.

The rest of the paper is organized as follows. In Sect. 2, we briefly review some related methods. Section 3 presents the proposed discriminative low-rank linear regression model. Section 4 provides experimental results on face databases to illustrate the superiority of DLLR. Some conclusions are drawn in Sect. 5.

2 Linear Regression Classification

In this section, we shall first briefly introduce linear regression algorithm, which is easy to use and powerful for face recognition. Suppose there are m individuals for recognition as the set of m samples $\{x_1, \ldots, x_m\}$, and n_i training images from the ith subject, i=1,2,...,c. Each sample belongs to one of the c classes $\{Z_1, \ldots, Z_c\}$. Using the concept that patterns from the same class lie on a linear subspace [17], we develop a class-specific model X_i,

$$X_i = [x_i^1 x_i^2 \ldots x_i^{n_i}], i = 1, 2, \ldots, C \tag{1}$$

Each vector x_i^j, j=1,2,..., n_i, is called the column space of X_i. Therefore, at the training level, each class i is represented by a vector subspace X_i, which is also called the regressor or predictor for class i. Let y be an unlabeled test image and our problem is to classify y as one of the classes i=1, 2,...,C. If y belongs to the ith class, it should be represented as a linear combination of the training images from the same class, i.e.

$$y = X_i \beta_i, i = 1, 2, \ldots, C, \tag{2}$$

where β_i is the vector of parameters corresponding to X_i. The system of equations in (2) is well conditioned and β_i along with the predictors X_i are used to predict the response vector for each class i:

$$\hat{y}_i = X_i \hat{\beta}_i, i = 1, 2, \ldots, C \tag{3}$$

$$\hat{\beta}_i = (X_i^T X_i)^{-1} X_i^T y, \hat{y}_i = X_i (X_i^T X_i)^{-1} X_i^T y \tag{4}$$

where the predicted vector $\hat{y}_i \in R^{q \times 1}$ is the projection of y onto the ith subspace. In other words, $\hat{y}_i$ is the closest vector in the ith subspace, to the observation vector y in the Euclidean senses. Here we calculate the distance measure between the predicted response vector $\hat{y}_i$, i=1,2,...,C, and the original response vector y. $di(y) = \|y - \hat{y}_i\|_2$, $i = 1, 2, \ldots, C$

Therefore, the rule of LRC in favor of the class with minimum distance, i.e. $\min_i di(y), i = 1, 2, \ldots, C$.

For LRC, the original training images are used to represent the query image. So when the original face images contain noise, that can be negative to recognition.

3   Discriminative Low-Rank Linear Regression Algorithm

3.1   Idea and Preparation for DLLR

In this section, we consider the frontal views. The samples from the same class are generally located on the same low-rank subspace. In practice, however, the low-rank structure can be easily violated due to partial shade or pollution, for example, shadow, sunglasses, hats, scarves and neckties. Therefore, the performance of LRC will deteriorate in this situation. Here, not directly observed linear correlation images $I_1^0, \cdots, I_n^0$, a matrix E should be added to approximate the error, therefore, we observed $I_1 = I_1^0 + e_1, \cdots, I_n = I_n^0 + e_n$ more practical. The sparse error matrix e_i represents the gross corruption of the training images. We set vec is $R^{m \times n} \rightarrow R^w$, so the whole model can be written as

$$D = [vec(I_1)|\cdots|vec(I_n)] = A + E \tag{5}$$

which $A = [vec(I_1^0)|\cdots|vec(I_n^0)] \in R^{mxn}$ is a low rank matrix that models the common linear structure in images, $E = [vec(e_1)|\cdots|vec(e_n)] \in R^{mxn}$ is a large - but - sparse error matrix modeling pollution, shade, occlusion, etc.

Based on Linear Discriminant Analysis (LDA), the within-class scatter and the between-class scatter of images are defined as

$$S_W(A) = \frac{1}{N}\sum_{i=1}\sum_{a_k \in A}(a_k - m_i)(a_k - m_i)^T \tag{6}$$

$$S_B(X) = \frac{1}{N}\sum_{i=1}^c n_i(m_i - m)(m_i - m)^T \tag{7}$$

where m_i and m are the mean vectors of A_i and A respectively, and n_i is the number of samples in class A_i. They decompose the original images into the class-specific feature and within-class variant feature. In this paper, the minimization problem satisfies a given equality constraints:

$$\min_{A,E}\|A\|_* + \lambda\|E\|_1 + \beta(tr(S_W(A) - S_B(A)) + \eta\|A\|_F^2), \text{ subject to } D = A + E. \tag{8}$$

where $\|\cdot\|_*$ denotes the nuclear norm of matrix, $\|\cdot\|_1$ denotes the sum of the absolute values of matrix entries.

3.2 Optimization to the Target Function of DLLR

The optimization problem of equality constraint relaxation to the target function, get the Lagrange function as follows: $L(A, E, \mu) = \mu\left(\|A\|_* + \lambda\|E\|_{1,1}\right) + \|D - A$ $-E\|_F^2/2 + \beta(\|A_i - M_i\|_F^2 - \sum_{k=1}^c \|A - M\|_F^2 + \eta\|A_i\|_F^2)$ $\quad g(A, E, \mu) = \mu(\|A\|_* + \lambda\|E\|_{1,1}), f(A, E) = \|D - A - E\|_F^2/2 + \beta(\|A_i - M_i\|_F^2 - \sum_{k=1}^c \|A - M\|_F^2 + \eta\|A_i\|_F^2)$ So $L(A, E, \mu) = g(A, E, \mu) + f(A, E)$. The function $g(A, E, \mu)$ is nondifferentiable, but $f(A, E)$ is smooth and has Lipschitz continuous gradient, it means $L_f > 0$, to make

$$\|\nabla f(A, E) - \nabla f(A', E')\|_F \leq L_f\|(A - A', E - E')\|_F \tag{9}$$

Among them: function f (A, E) represents Fréchet gradient of matrix variable A and E. Here take $L_f = 2$. We set $f'(A) = \beta(\|A_i - M_i\|_F^2 - \sum_{k=1}^c \|A - M\|_F^2 + \eta\|A_i\|_F^2)$. It can be proved that if $\eta > 1 - n_i/n$, $f'(A)$ is strictly convex to A [14]. When $E = E_k, Y_A = Y_A^k, Y_E = Y_E^k, \mu = \mu_k,$

$$A_{k+1} = \arg\min_A Q\left(A, E_k, \mu_k, Y_A^k, Y_E^k\right)$$

$$= \arg\min_A \mu_k\|A\|_* + <Y_A^k - (D - Y_E^k), A> + L_f\|A - Y_A^k\|_F^2/2 + \beta\|A_i\|_F^2$$

$$= \arg\min_A \mu_k\|A\|_* + L_f\|A - (Y_A^k + (D - (1-\beta)Y_A^k - Y_E^k)/L_f)\|_F^2/2$$

$$(10)$$

Similarly, when $A = A_{k+1}, Y_A = Y_A^k, Y_E = Y_E^k, \mu = \mu_k$,

$$E_{k+1} = \arg\min_E Q\left(A_{k+1}, E, \mu_k, Y_A^k, Y_E^k\right) \qquad (11)$$

In order to update the step length of Y_A and Y_E, we need make sure: $t_{k+1} = \left(1 + \sqrt{1 + 4t_k^2}\right)/2.$

So the iteration update formula is: $Y_A^{k+1} = A_k + (t_k - 1)(A_k - A_{k+1})/t_{k+1}$, $Y_E^{k+1} = E_k + (t_k - 1)(E_k - E_{k+1})/t_{k+1}$. The parameter μ's iteration update formula is: $\mu_{k+1} = \max(\eta\mu_k, \mu')$

Among them: μ' for a given positive number in advance and $0 < \eta < 1$. The max iteration number is 1000.

3.3   The Algorithm Steps of DLLR

INPUT: The ith training samples $x_i \in R^{m \times n_i}$, n_i is the number of the ith samples, one test sample $y \in R^{m \times 1}$. $\mu^0 > 0$, $(a^0, e^0) \in R^{m \times n_i} \times R^{m \times n_i}$. Set $t^1 = t^0 = 1$, $(a^1, e^1) = (a^0, e^0)$, k = 1.

while not converged do

Step 1. compute proximal points: $y_a^k = a^k + \frac{t^{k-1}-1}{t^k}(a^k - a^{k-1})$, $y_e^k = e^k + \frac{t^{k-1}-1}{t^k}(e^k - e^{k-1})$

Step 2. gradient step: $G^k = y_e^k + (1 + \beta)y_a^k - x_i$, $G_a^k = y_a^k - \rho^{-1}G^k$, $G_e^k = y_e^k - \rho^{-1}G^k$, $\beta > 0$ and $\rho > 0$ are the parameters to be specified.

Step 3. soft-thresholding: compute the reduced SVD (U,S,V) of G_a^k $a^{k+1} = UT_{\mu^k/\rho}(S)V^T$, $e^{k+1} = T_{\lambda\mu^k/\rho}(G_e^k)$

Step 4. update: $t^{k+1} = \frac{1}{2} + \frac{1}{2}\sqrt{1 + 4(t^k)^2}$, $\mu^{k+1} = \max\{0.9\mu^k, \mu'\}$

$$S_a^k = \rho(G_a^k - y_a^k) + (G_a^k + G_e^k - y_a^k - y_e^k), S_e^k = \rho(G_e^k - y_e^k) + (G_a^k + G_e^k - y_a^k - y_e^k)$$

According to [23], the stopping criterion is

$$S^k = \rho((y_a^{k-1}, y_e^{k-1}) - (a^k, e^k)) + \nabla f(a^k, e^k) - \nabla f(y_a^{k-1}, y_e^{k-1})$$

$$\frac{\|S^k\|_F}{\rho \max\{1, (\|a^k\|_F^2 + \|e^k\|_F^2)^{1/2}\}} \leq \varepsilon$$

where $\varepsilon = 10^{-6}$. End while

Step 5. d as the dictionary to compute the LRC.

$$\hat{y}_i = a_i \hat{d}_i, i = 1, 2, \ldots, C, \hat{d}_i = (a_i^T a_i)^{-1} a_i^T y, \hat{y}_i = a_i (a_i^T a_i)^{-1} a_i^T y$$

Step 6. computer the residual error: $Kdi(y)$(i=1,2,...,C).

OUTPUT: $identity(y) = \arg\min_i (Kdi(y))$.

4   Experiments

In this section, we will apply the proposed DLLR algorithm for facial expression recognition, at the same time we compare the results with SRC [23], LRC, LLRC. The parameter λ trades off the rank versus the sparsity of the error. Usually, we set $\lambda = 1/\sqrt{\max(m, n)}$ in the DLLR algorithm.

4.1   Experiment for Expression Recognition

JAFFE database is made up of ten Japanese female that have 7 kinds of positive expression(angry, disgust, fear, happy, sad, surprise and neutral) of 213 gray images, the image is the size of 256×256 8-bit grayscale, formatted as .tiff, the average person there were 2 to 4 each expression. We extracted the eye features and the mouth features as 50×130 images.

Usually the part of eye and mouth can extract the prominent characteristics of facial expressions and form the feature vector. First, the face area was histogram equalized to cope with noise and lighting variations. After that, the region of eyes and mouth are roughly segmented. Through the experiment, in SRC we choose the feature of eye, mouth and the whole face for the expression: angry, neuter, sad and surprise, and we choose the feature of eye for the expression: disgust, fear and happy. In other three methods, we choose the feature of eye, mouth and the whole face for the expression: angry, fear, neuter, sad, and we choose the feature of eye for the expression: disgust, happy and surprise. For classification, we have 20 different facial expressions as training sets, the rest as the testing sets. We choose some images from JAFFE database as Figs. 1, 2 and 3 are shown. The recognition rates under the images from JAFFE database are given in Table 1.

Fig. 1. Some of the whole face images from JAFFE database

Fig. 2. Some of the eye images from JAFFE database

Fig. 3. Some of the mouth images from JAFFE database

When the "salt&pepper" noise is 10 %, 20 %, 30 %, the recognition is shown as the Tables 2, 3 and 4.

Table 1. The recognition rates with different facial expressions

Expression	Angry	Disgust	Fear	Happy	Neuter	Sad	Surprise	Ave
DLLRC	50	80	70	70	100	80	80	75.7
LLRC	50	80	70	70	100	80	70	74.3
LRC	50	80	70	70	100	80	70	74.3
SRC	60	60	70	50	90	70	70	67.1

Table 2. The recognition rates with 10 % noises

Expression	Angry	Disgust	Fear	Happy	Neuter	Sad	Surprise	Ave
DLLRC	60	100	50	90	90	90	80	80
LLRC	60	90	40	80	100	70	80	74.3
LRC	60	90	50	70	90	70	70	71.4
SRC	60	80	60	30	40	70	80	60

Table 3. The recognition rates with 20 % noises

Expression	Angry	Disgust	Fear	Happy	Neuter	Sad	Surprise	Ave
DLLRC	40	100	40	60	90	60	80	67.1
LLRC	50	100	40	50	80	60	80	65.7
LRC	50	100	40	40	90	60	80	65.7
SRC	70	90	10	30	10	40	80	47.1

4.2 Experimental Comparison and Analysis

For facial expression recognition, there are some limitations. First, "pure" emotional expressions are seldom elicited. Most of the time, people show blends of emotional expressions. Therefore, classification of expression into a single emotion category isn't realistic. Second, even for people, it is not easy for them to classify the expression

Table 4. The recognition rates with 30 % noises

Expression	Angry	Disgust	Fear	Happy	Neuter	Sad	Surprise	Ave
DLLRC	40	100	40	50	60	40	80	58.6
LLRC	40	100	40	50	50	40	80	57.1
LRC	40	100	40	50	40	30	60	51.4
SRC	100	90	20	20	10	10	80	47.1

exactly. In this experiment, we use the eyes, mouth and the whole face as features. Especially, we found that the feature of eyes can distinct the expression of disgust more correctly, even with noises it can get the correct result. We find that when people feel disgust, they may narrow their eyes, and there may be horizontal stripes in the root of their nose. These features can make the expression disgust more easily be found by the image of eyes. Secondly, the expression of neuter and sad are effected most obviously when there are noises. The two expressions are similar as each other, when there are noises they cannot be distinguished clearly. Finally the expressions of happy and surprise also decreased obviously especially when added more noises.

5 Discussion and Future Work

In this paper, we proposed a discriminative low-rank linear regression method to get the compact base for recognition, which considered the effect of the noise, and it is robust to the noise. Then we add some noises personally to experiment and further verify its effectiveness. In the future we will consider how to make it more effective. Also for facial expression classification, we hope that it should not only the seven basic emotion category, we can find more suitable emotion categories. Recently large scale public datasets are used in face recognition methods [19], we should also consider larger face dataset.

References

1. Yang, P., Liua, Q., Metaxasa, D.N.: Boosting encoded dynamic feature for facial expression recognition. Pattern Recogn. Lett. **30**(2), 132–139 (2009)
2. Lin, K., Cheng, W., Li, J.: Facial Expression Recognition Based on Geometric Features and Geodesic Distance. Int. J. Sig. Process. Image Process. Pattern Recogn. **7**(1), 323–330 (2014)
3. Pantic, M., Rothkrantz, L.J.M.: Automatic analysis of facial expressions: The state of the art. IEEE Trans. Pattern Anal. Mach. Intell. **22**(12), 1424–1445 (2000)
4. Kaltwang, S., Rudovic, O., Pantic, M.: Continuous pain intensity estimation from facial expressions. In: Proceedings of the International Symposium on Visual Computing, pp. 368–377 (2012)
5. Rudovic, O., Patras, I., Pantic, M.: Regression-based multiview facial expression recognition. In: Proceedings of the 20th International Conference on Pattern Recognition (ICPR), pp. 4121–4124 (2010)

6. Chai, X., Shan, S., Chen, X., Gao, W.: Locally linear regression for pose-invariant face recognition. IEEE Trans. Image Process. **7**(16) (2007)
7. Naseem, I., Togneri, R., Bennamoun, M.: Linear regression for face recognition. IEEE Trans. Pattern Anal. Mach. Intell. **32**(11), 2106–2112 (2010)
8. Wright, J., Ganesh, A., Rao, S., Peng, Y., Ma, Y.: Robust principal component analysis: exact recovery of corrupted low-rank matrices via convex optimization. In: Proceedings of Advances in Neural Information Processing Systems (NIPS), vol. 12 (2009)
9. Candès, E.J., Li, X., Ma, Y., et al.: Robust principal component analysis? J. ACM (JACM) **58**(3), 11 (2011)
10. Recht, B., Fazel, M., Parrio, P.A.: Guaranteed minimum-rank solutions of linear matrix equations via nuclear norm minimization. Soc. Ind. Appl. Math. **52**(3), 471–501 (2010)
11. Peng, Y., Ganesh, A., Wright, J., Wenli, X., Ma, Y.: RASL: robust alignment by sparse and low-rank decomposition for linearly correlated images. IEEE Trans. Pattern Anal. Mach. Intell. **11**(34), 2233–2246 (2012)
12. Zhang, Q., Li, B.: Discriminative K-SVD for dictionary learning in face recognition. In: Proceedings of IEEE Conference on Computer Vision and Pattern Recognition, pp. 2691–2698 (2010)
13. Swets, D., Weng, J.: Using discriminant eigen features for image retrieval. IEEE Trans. Pattern Anal. Mach. Intell. **18**(8), 831–836 (1996)
14. Liu, C., Wechsler, H.: Enhanced fisher linear discriminant models for face recognition. In: Proceedings of Fourteenth International Conference on Pattern Recognition, vol. 2, 1368–1372 (1998)
15. Parkhi, O., Simonyan, K., Vedaldi, A., et al.: A compact and discriminative face track descriptor. In: Proceedings of the IEEE Conference on Computer Vision and Pattern Recognition, pp. 1693–1700 (2014)
16. Ma, L., Wang, C., Xiao, B., et al.: Sparse representation for face recognition based on discriminative low-rank dictionary learning. In: Computer Vision and Pattern Recognition (CVPR), pp. 2586–2593 (2012)
17. Yang, M., Zhang, L., Feng, X., Zhang, D.: Fisher discrimination dictionary learning for sparse representation. In: 2011 IEEE International Conference on Computer Vision (ICCV), pp. 543–550 (2011)
18. Eleftheriadis, S., Rudovic, O., Pantic, M.: Discriminative shared gaussian processes for multiview and view-invariant facial expression recognition. IEEE Trans. Image Process. **24**(1), 189–204 (2015)
19. Schroff, F., Kalenichenko, D., Philbin, J.: Facenet: a unified embedding for face recognition and clustering. In: Proceedings of the IEEE Conference on Computer Vision and Pattern Recognition, pp. 815–823 (2015)
20. Yang, M., Zhu, P., Van Gool, L., et al.: Face recognition based on regularized nearest points between image sets. In: 2013 10th IEEE International Conference and Workshops on Automatic Face and Gesture Recognition (FG), pp. 1–7 (2013)
21. Wright, J., Yang, A.Y., Ganesh, A., Sastry, S.S., Ma, Y.: Robust face recognition via sparse representation. IEEE Trans. Pattern Anal. Mach. Intell. **31**(2), 210–227 (2009)
22. Basri, R., Jacobs, D.W.: Lambertian reflectance and linear subspaces. IEEE Trans. Pattern Anal. Mach. Intell. **25**(2), 218–233 (2003)
23. Toh, K.C., Yun, S.: An accelerated proximal gradient algorithm for nuclear norm regularized linear least squares problems. Pac. J. Optim. (2010)
24. Bao, C., Wu, Y., Ling, H., Ji, H.: Real time robust l1 tracker using accelerated proximal gradient approach. Comput. Vis. Pattern Recogn. (2012)
25. Lin, Z., Liu, R., Su, Z.: Linearized alternating direction method with adaptive penalty for low-rank representation. Adv. Neural Inf. Process. Syst. **9** (2011)

Facial Expression Recognition Based on Multi-scale CNNs

Shuai Zhou[1,2,3], Yanyan Liang[1], Jun Wan[2,3(✉)], and Stan Z. Li[2,3]

[1] Faculty of Information Technology,
Macau University of Science and Technology, Macau, China
shuaizhou.palm@gmail.com, yyliang@must.edu.mo
[2] Institute of Automation, Chinese Academy of Sciences, Beijing, China
{jun.wan,szli}@nlpr.ia.ac.cn
[3] University of Chinese Academy of Sciences, Beijing, China

Abstract. This paper proposes a new method for facial expression recognition, called multi-scale CNNs. It consists several sub-CNNs with different scales of input images. The sub-CNNs of multi-scale CNNs are benefited from various scaled input images to learn the optimalized parameters. After trained all these sub-CNNs separately, we can predict the facial expression of an image by extracting its features from the last fully connected layer of sub-CNNs in different scales and mapping the averaged features to the final classification probability. Multi-scale CNNs can classify facial expression more accurately than any single scale sub-CNN. On Facial Expression Recognition 2013 database, multi-scale CNNs achieved an accuracy of 71.80 % on the testing set, which is comparative to other state-of-the-art methods.

Keywords: Facial expression recognition · Multi-scale CNNs · CNN · Deep learning · Patten recognition

1 Introduction

Human facial expression, as an external representation of psychological states, plays an important role in social communication and observation. We can learn one's emotion and mental activity better by seeing his or her facial expression than just listening to words. Researches on facial expression started from nineteen century, Darwin claimed the universality of emotions [2], later on in 1971, Paul Ekman classified six facial expressions as basic: anger, disgust, fear, happiness, sadness, and surprise [3].

In the future, facial expression recognition will be a vital part of artificial intelligence. It can be applied into different crucial fields, such as human computer interaction, criminal investigation and commercial analysis. It will be of great significance to national security and economic development.

Though facial expression recognition has been researched for years, there still are several obstacles to overcome. This is a cross-discipline research, it needs the

© Springer International Publishing AG 2016
Z. You et al. (Eds.): CCBR 2016, LNCS 9967, pp. 503–510, 2016.
DOI: 10.1007/978-3-319-46654-5_55

cooperation between computer science, social psychology and medical science. The difficulties that face detection research was facing remain in facial expression recognition. Large visual variations from human faces in the cluttered backgrounds and variational head poses and different lighting environments make this issue more and more complicated.

In recent years, convolutional neural network has been widely applied in image and video recognition [8,10], recommender systems and natural language processing, and have made great success in these fields. In image pattern recognition, most of the state of the art model were developed or constructed from convolutional neural network. In 2014, DeepID [10] convolutional neural network architecture were proposed by Tang et al. for face verification. In 2015, Kaiming He proposed deep residual networks [4] and won the 1st places in: ImageNet classification, ImageNet detection and ImageNet localisation. For face detection, a convolutional neural network cascade [8] were proposed by Li et al.

To solve facial expression and emotion recognition problem, some methods were reported in [7,9,11]. In particular, Tang [11] reported a deep CNN jointly learned with a linear support vector machine (SVM) output. This method achieved the first place on both validation and testing subset on the FER 2013 Challenge [1]. Liu et al. [9] proposed a facial expression recognition framework with 3D CNN and deformable action parts constraints in order to jointly localizing facial action parts and learning part-based representations for expression recognition. Yu and Zhang [12] proposed a method contains a face detection module based on the ensemble of three state-of-the-art face detectors, followed by a classification module with the ensemble of multiple deep convolutional neural networks (CNN). They used two schemes to learn the ensemble weights of the network responses: by minimizing the log likelihood loss, and by minimizing the hinge loss.

Considering the high quality features extracted from convolutional neutral network, we choose CNN to solve the facial expression recognition problem too. During this research, unlike using simple single CNN or even deep complex CNN, we proposed multi-scale CNNs, a method combined multiple simple CNNs with different input image size, and predicting classes together. Multi-scale CNNs can classify facial expression more accurately than any single scale sub-CNN of it. At last, the multi-scale CNNs got an accuracy of 71.80 % on FER database testing set, surpassed the result of the winner of FER Challenge 2013.

2   Multi-scale CNNs

Multi-scale CNNs are two or more CNN models which have different scales of input images. It predicts the result by fusing the features extracted from each sub-CNN, then makes the final prediction based on all the features extracted.

2.1   Training Multi-scale CNNs

To solve facial expression recognition problem, we use three sub-CNNs of different input scale rates of 1.0x, 2.0x, 2.14x. As showed in Fig. 1, we adopt similar network architecture of winner of FER Challenge 2013. There are three convolutional layers, three pooling layers and two fully connected layers in each net. The number of output neurons in last fully connected layer is 7, because the samples of facial expression images were labeled to seven categories: angry, disgust, fear, happy, sad, surprise and neutral.

The difference between sub-CNNs is that the input image size for 1.0x sub-CNN is 42×42 pixels, 84×84 for 2.0x sub-CNN and 90×90 for 2.14x sub-CNN, because the training images, training set from Facial Expression Recognition Challenge 2013, are in shape of 48 by 48 pixels grayscale. 1.0x sub-CNN uses randomly cropped images from the raw images, and 2.0x and 2.14x sub-CNNs use resized 96 by 96 pixels images with random cropping size of 84 by 84 and 90 by 90 pixels. Also the kernel sizes of convolutional layers are different. Since the input image size is larger for 2.0x and 2.14x sub-CNNs, the first convolutional layer's kernel size is enlarged to 7×7 and kernel size of second convolutional layer is 5×5 instead of 4×4 for 1.0x sub-CNN. We apply PReLU nonlinearity function [5], after each pooling layer and second last fully-connected layer.

In the training phase, training samples were first resized to three different sizes and each sub-CNNs were trained separately with corresponding scaled

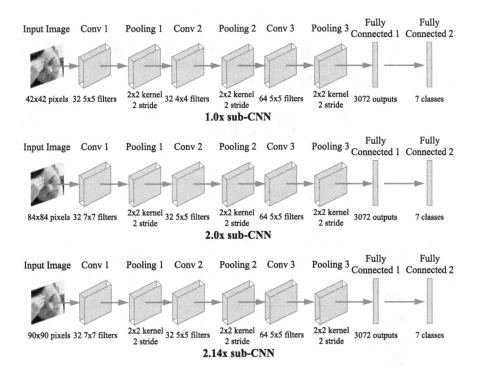

Fig. 1. Architecture of each sub-CNNs. Input image size and kernel size of partial convolutional layers are different. Please note that all these three sub-CNNs were trained separately.

training samples. In order to increase the classification accuracy, we compared the performances between softmax with loss and hinge loss as the loss function to train each sub-CNNs, and experiment of comparison between each loss function will be detailed later in Sect. 3.1. As proposed by [11], using hinge loss do enhanced the model a little.

2.2 Classification Using Multi-scale CNNs

As for predicting a test image, the image need to be resized to corresponding size and then feed into one of the different scale CNNs according to its size. After all the forward calculations of each network were done, extract features from the last fully connected layer, which should get three 7-dimensional vectors from three sub-CNNs, and we denote those feature matrixes as F_1, F_2 and F_3 for 1.0x scale, 2.0x scale and 2.14 scale CNNs. As shown in Eq. (1), we calculate the arithmetic mean on the same dimension, denoted by j, of extracted F_1, F_2 and F_3 as the averaged feature, then we got $\overline{F} : \{\overline{f_j}, j = 1, ..., 7\}$, since we have 7 categories of facial expressions. N is 3, because there are three sub-CNNs.

$$\overline{f_j} = \frac{1}{N} \sum_{i=1}^{N} f_{ij}, \ j = 1, ..., 7 . \tag{1}$$

At last, for seven classes, $K = 7$, we use softmax function Eq. (2) to map the averaged feature to categorical probability distribution. So that each $\sigma(f)_j$ represents the probability of that class.

$$\sigma(f)_j = \frac{\exp(\overline{f_j})}{\sum_{k=1}^{K} \exp(\overline{f_k})}, \ j = 1, ..., K . \tag{2}$$

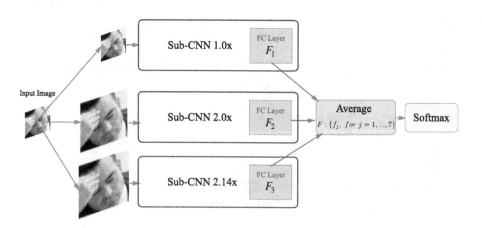

Fig. 2. Illustration of Multi-scale CNNs. Test images were first resized to different sizes then feed into corresponding sub-CNN, and features of last FC layer were extracted and combined, then using softmax to map the averaged features to classification probability.

3   Experiments on FER 2013 Database

The FER 2013 database was published for the challenge in facial expression recognition at [1]. There are 35,887 facial expression images in this database and they are in form of grayscale 48 × 48 pixels. The publisher claimed that all the faces have been automatically registered and the face is more or less centered at the picture. Image samples as shown in Fig. 3. The training set consists of 28,709 images, and both validation and testing sets have 3,589 images. All the images in this database were labeled to one of the seven categories: angry, disgust, fear, happy, sad, surprise and neutral. Table 1 showed the number distribution of each categories.

Angry   Disgust   Fear   Happy   Sad   Surprise   Neutral

Fig. 3. Example images of seven classes from FER 2013 database.

Table 1. Image number distribution of each categories of FER 2013 database

	Angry	Disgust	Fear	Happy	Sad	Surprise	Neutral	Total
Training Set	3995	436	4097	7215	4830	3171	4965	28709
Validation Set	467	56	496	895	653	415	607	3589
Testing Set	491	55	528	879	594	416	626	3589
Total	4953	547	5121	8989	6077	4002	6198	35887

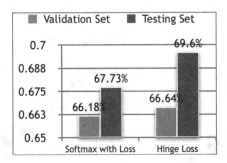

Fig. 4. Accuracy of 1.0x sub-CNN with softmax loss and hinge loss on FER 2013 database.

3.1 Comparison Between Softmax Loss and Hinge Loss

In Sect. 2.1, we tested softmax with loss and hinge loss functions to find the best loss function for solving this facial expression recognition problem. The experiment was conducted on FER 2013 using 1.0x scale CNN and only the last loss function is different. As shown in Fig. 4, by using hinge loss, the accuracy of the model do increase around one percent than softmax loss. So we choose to use the model with hinge loss in later experiments.

3.2 Performance of Sub-CNNs and Multi-scale CNNs

Figure 5 shows the accuracy of different scale sub-CNNs and the multi-scale CNNs. We can see that the accuracy of multi-scale CNNs overcomes all other single scale sub-CNNs. Various scaled input images benefit the models to learn the optimalized parameters, and multi-scale CNNs combined all of these representative features and fused them to make the final prediction together. Multiscale CNNs do need a little bit more time compared to single sub-CNN, and with the TITAN X GPU, it costs 43 ms to predict one image while 2.0x sub-CNN only takes 18 ms. Figure 6 shows the confusion matrix of multi-scale CNNs.

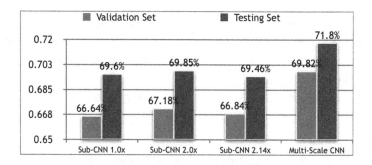

Fig. 5. Accuracy of single sub-CNNs with different scales and the multi-scale CNNs

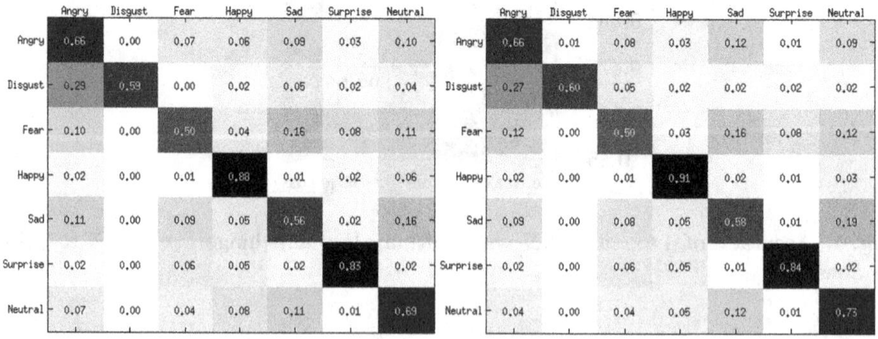

Fig. 6. Confusion matrix of multi-scale CNNs on FER 2013. (Left, validation set. Right, testing set)

3.3 Comparison with State-of-the-Art Methods

We compare our multi-scale CNNs with other state-of-the-art method, and Fig. 7 showed the performance of these methods on FER 2013 database. Our method surpassed the winner of FER 2013 Challenge on both validation and testing set of FER 2013 database. But Multiple Deep Network Learning [12] do perform a little better than us, and this may because that it used more complex data preprocessing like data perturbation and voting.

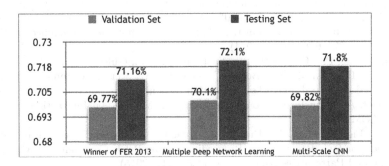

Fig. 7. The recognition accuracy of the proposed method is comparative to other methods.

4 Conclusion

In this work, we propose a new method for facial expression recognition, called multi-scale CNNs. Multi-scale CNNs consists of three sub-CNNs with different image input size and each sub-CNN is designed best to fit with the input size. After trained these sub-CNNs separately, the prediction extracted the output features of last fully connected layer and combined them by calculating the arithmetic mean on same dimension, then used softmax to map the averaged features to categorical probability of facial expression. At last, experiments on FER 2013 database showed that multi-scale CNNs is comparative to other state-of-the-art methods.

Acknowledgement. This work was supported by the National Key Research and Development Plan (Grant No.2016YFC0801002), the Chinese National Natural Science Foundation Projects ♮61473291, ♮61572501, ♮61502491, ♮61572536, Science and Technology Development Fund of Macau (No. 019/2014/A1), NVIDIA GPU donation program and AuthenMetric R&D Funds.

References

1. Challenges in representation learning: facial expression recognition challenge. https://www.kaggle.com/c/challenges-in-representation-learning-facial-expression-recognition-challenge. Accessed 30 June 2016

2. Darwin, C., Ekman, P., Prodger, P.: The Expression of the Emotions in Man and Animals. Oxford University Press, USA (1998)
3. Ekman, P., Friesen, W.V.: Constants across cultures in the face and emotion. J. Pers. Soc. Psychol. **17**(2), 124 (1971)
4. He, K., Zhang, X., Ren, S., Sun, J.: Deep residual learning for image recognition. ArXiv e-prints, 12 (2015)
5. He, K., Zhang, X., Ren, S., Sun, J. Delving deep into rectifiers: surpassing human-level performance on imagenet classification. In: Proceedings of the IEEE International Conference on Computer Vision, pp. 1026–1034 (2015)
6. Jia, Y., Shelhamer, E., Donahue, J., Karayev, S., Long, J., Girshick, R., Guadarrama, S., Darrell, T. Caffe: convolutional architecture for fast feature embedding. In: Proceedings of the 22nd ACM International Conference on Multimedia, pp. 675–678. ACM (2014)
7. Kahou, S.E., Pal, C., Bouthillier, X., Froumenty, P., Gülçehre, Ç., Memisevic, R., Vincent, P., Courville, A., Bengio, Y., Ferrari, R.C., et al.: Combining modality specific deep neural networks for emotion recognition in video. In: Proceedings of the 15th ACM on International Conference on Multimodal Interaction, pp. 543–550. ACM (2013)
8. Li, H., Lin, Z., Shen, X., Brandt, J., Hua, G.: A convolutional neural network cascade for face detection. In: Proceedings of the IEEE Conference on Computer Vision and Pattern Recognition, pp. 5325–5334 (2015)
9. Liu, P., Han, S., Meng, Z., Tong, Y.: Facial expression recognition via a boosted deep belief network. In: Proceedings of the IEEE Conference on Computer Vision and Pattern Recognition, pp. 1805–1812 (2014)
10. Sun, Y., Wang, X., Tang, X.: Deep learning face representation from predicting 10,000 classes. In: Proceedings of the IEEE Conference on Computer Vision and Pattern Recognition, pp. 1891–1898 (2014)
11. Tang, Y.: Deep learning using linear support vector machines (2013). arXiv preprint: arXiv:1306.0239
12. Yu, Z., Zhang, C.: Image based static facial expression recognition with multiple deep network learning. In: Proceedings of the ACM on International Conference on Multimodal Interaction, pp. 435–442. ACM (2015)

Facial Expression Recognition Based on Ensemble of Mulitple CNNs

Ruoxuan Cui, Minyi Liu, and Manhua Liu[✉]

Department of Instrument Science and Engineering, SEIEE, Shanghai Jiao Tong University,
Shanghai 200240, China
mhliu@sjtu.edu.cn

Abstract. Automatic recognition of facial expression is an important task in many applications such as face recognition and animation, human-computer interface and online/remote education. It is still challenging due to variations of expression, background and position. In this paper, we propose a method for facial expression recognition based on ensemble of multiple Convolutional Neural Networks (CNNs). First, the face region is extracted by a face detector from the pre-processed image. Second, five key points are detected for each image and the face images are aligned by two eye center points. Third, the face image is cropped into local eye and mouth regions, and three CNNs are trained for the whole face, eye and mouth regions, individually. Finally, the classification is made by ensemble of the outputs of three CNNs. Experiments were carried for recognition of six facial expressions on the Extended Cohn-Kanade database (CK+). The results and comparison show the proposed algorithm yields performance improvements for facial expression recognition.

Keywords: Facial expression · Convolutional networks · Machine learning · Machine vision

1 Introduction

In recent years, how to recognize human emotion in artificial intelligence systems has attracted great research interests. Facial expression is one of the most important cues for recognition of human emotion and behavior [1]. It is defined as the facial changes in response to person's internal emotional state, intentions, or social communications. Facial expression recognition has a wide variety of applications, such as face recognition and animation, human-computer interface, interactive games, online/remote education and intelligent transportation systems. However, different persons may have different ways to show their expressions. Even the facial images of the same person in one expression may be captured under different conditions such as brightness, position and background. Therefore, automatic recognition of facial expression is still a challenging problem to achieve the high accuracy and robustness, and it still has been an active research topic in computer vision [2–4].

Generally, facial expression recognition can be modeled as an image classification problem which consists of three main steps: image preprocessing, feature

© Springer International Publishing AG 2016
Z. You et al. (Eds.): CCBR 2016, LNCS 9967, pp. 511–518, 2016.
DOI: 10.1007/978-3-319-46654-5_56

extraction and classification. There have been a lot of approaches proposed for facial expression recognition in the past decade, which made great progresses in this research area. A detailed review of the facial expression recognition methods was presented in the literature [2, 3]. According to different input resources, facial expression recognition systems can be categorized into two main types which are input with static images [4, 5] and dynamic image sequences [6], respectively. The methods with the static images extract the representation features only from the current input image, while the methods with the image sequences can extract the temporal information of image sequences along with the features of each static image. Thus, more information can be used with the dynamic image sequences to recognize the facial expression. Based on the extracted feature vector, an output decision is made by training a classifier as one of the assigned expressions, e.g., the six basic expressions: angry, sad, surprise, happy, disgust and fear. In this work, we will focus on the methods based on the static images and consider the six basic expressions only.

After preprocessing the captured images by image normalization and alignment, and detection of the face region, a representation feature should be extracted from the facial image to characterize the facial appearance/geometry changes caused by variant expressions. Most of existing methods utilize the hand crafted features such as local binary patterns (LBP), Haar features, Histograms of Oriented Gradients (HOG) to characterize the facial expressions, followed by construction of classifiers such as support vector machine, linear discriminant analysis and linear programming to recognize the facial expression [7–9]. Recently, to become more adaptable to the real world, deep learning networks have been used for the applications of facial expression recognition [4, 5, 10, 11]. Instead of extracting the hand crafted features, these methods are able to learn the set of features that best model the facial expression recognition. A boosted deep belief network (BDBN) is proposed to learn and select a set of effective features to characterize expression-related facial appearance/shape changes for facial expression recognition [4]. This approach performs iteratively the training process of three stages: feature learning, feature selection and classifier construction in a unique framework for facial expression recognition, which is different from the traditional methods that perform sequentially these three training stages.

Recently, convolutional neural network (CNN) has been successfully used in a wide variety of image classification tasks and achieved good performance [5, 6, 10–12]. In general, the CNN based hierarchical network has alternating types of layers: convolutional and sub-sampling layers. CNN architectures vary in how convolutional and subsampling layers are applied and how the networks are trained. Convolutional layers are mainly parameterized by the number of kernels and generate maps. An efficient method was proposed to combine the CNN model with the specific image preprocessing steps for facial expression recognition [5]. One of the main advantages of CNN is that the models' input is a raw image rather than hand-coded features and the representative features can be automatically learned to model the specified classification [5]. A CNN architecture was proposed for image based static facial expression recognition based on ensemble of multiple CNNs with each CNN is randomly initialized and trained on the perturbated data set [10]. The careful design of local to global feature learning with convolution, pooling and layered architecture renders very strong visual representation ability, making it a powerful tool for facial expression recognition [10].

In the existing CNNs based method, the whole face region is employed as input and every part of the face is treated and fine-tuned equally no matter if it is relevant to the target facial expression. However, as suggested by the psychological studies, the information extracted around nose, eyes, and mouth is more critical for facial expression analysis [13]. Thus, construction of CNN model with the whole face region is not only computation expensive but also degrades the recognition accuracy. In this work, we proposed a facial expression recognition algorithm based on ensemble of multiple Convolutional Neural Networks (CNNs) with each CNN performed on a local face region. First, the face image is pre-processed by image normalization and the face region is extracted by a face detector. Second, five key points are detected and the face images are aligned with the detected eye points. Third, the face image is cropped into two smaller regions which are eye region and mouth region, and three CNNs are trained for the whole face region, eye region and mouth region, individually. Finally, the classification is made by ensemble of the outputs of three CNNs. The proposed method has been tested on the Extended Cohn-Kanade (CK+) database and achieves good performance.

The remainder of this paper is organized as follows. Section 2 presents the proposed facial expression recognition algorithm in detail. In Sect. 3, the experimental results are presented and compared with the other methods. Finally, a conclusion is presented in Sect. 4.

2   The Proposed Algorithm

In this section, we will present the proposed facial expression recognition algorithm based on ensemble of multiple CNNs, which includes three main processing steps, i.e., image preprocessing, facial region segmentation, classification by ensemble of CNNs. In the first step, the image preprocessing includes face detection, the intensity and spatial normalization, and facial point detection for an input raw image. In the facial region segmentation, the local regions around the eye and mouth are extracted from the detected facial region. In the final step, we construct the CNN model for the whole facial region, the eye image region, and the mouth image region, separately, and the final classification is performed by ensemble of the outputs of three CNNs. Figure 1 shows the overview of the proposed algorithm. In the implementation, the whole facial expression recognition algorithm consists of offline training and online testing. The image data set is divided into training image set and testing image set. For the whole image data set, each image is processed to extract the local regions round the eye and mouth. The training image set is used to training the CNN model for classification, while the testing image set is used for testing. The output of each trained CNN is the probabilities that the test image belongs to each of the expression classes, and the final classification output is a class label that indicates one of the six basic expressions.

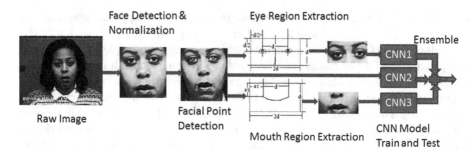

Fig. 1. The overview of the proposed facial expression recognition algorithm

2.1 Image Preprocessing

The captured raw image may vary in brightness, spatial transformation, size and background for the same face expression. Face expression recognition algorithm should be robust to these variations which will negatively affecting the accuracy rate of the expression recognition. To achieve the invariance of backgrounds, a face detector same as that in [12] is applied to detect the face region from the input raw image and then the various backgrounds are removed for more accurate recognition. In addition, the intensity normalization is performed to reduce the effect of varying brightness. Furthermore, the proposed method [12] is applied to detect the five facial points, which are left eye center, right eye center, nose tip, left mouth corner, and right mouth corner. A line segment is formed from one eye center to the other eye center. To correct the rotation of face region, the spatial normalization is performed by aligning the line segment with the horizontal axis of the image. Finally, the facial image region is cropped and the facial image is normalized into the same size of 64 × 64 pixels. Thus, the non-face components such as backgrounds and hairs, which are not related to facial expression, are removed to reduce their negative effects and the face components (eyes, mouth, eyebrow, etc) are captured in the image.

2.2 Facial Region Segmentation

In most existing CNNs based methods [5], the whole face region is employed as input and every part of the face is treated and fine-tuned equally. However, according to the psychological studies, the local face regions around eyes, nose, and mouth may have different effects on the recognition of facial expressions [16]. Construction of CNN model with the whole face region is not only computation expensive but also sacrifices the recognition accuracy. It is well known the eye and mouth components are mostly related to the recognition of facial expressions. Different from the existing methods that input the whole face region into the CNN, we partition the face region into two smaller local regions according to the eye and mouth positions as shown in Fig. 1.

Let $d1$ denote the length of the line segment between the left and right eye centers. The local region of $d1 \times 2d1$ around two eye centers is cropped from the detected face image to extract the eye region. Similarly, let $d2$ denote the length of the line segment between the left and right mouth corners. The local region of $d2 \times 2d2$ around the mouth is cropped from the detected face image to extract the mouth region (See Fig. 1). Finally, the cropped images of these local regions are resized into the same size of 32×64 pixels to facilitate further processing.

2.3 CNN Based Classification

In addition to construct one CNN for the whole face region, we also construct two CNNs for the eye and mouth regions separately. The CNN for the whole face region receives the grayscale image of size 64×64 pixels as input, while the CNNs for the other two local regions receives the grayscale image of size 64×32 pixels as the input. The outputs of all CNNs are the confidence of each expression. The class with the maximum value can be used as the expression of the face image. The architecture of our convolution networks comprise six layers: 2 convolutional layers, 2 subsampling layers, 1 full connection layers and 1 output layer. The first layer of each CNN is a convolution layer, which performs the convolution by the kernel of 5×5 to the input image and outputs a response image. In our implements, 5 different kernels are learned and 5 feature maps are output in the first layer. This layer is followed by a subsampling layer that uses max-pooling with a kernel size of 2×2 to reduce the image size to half. The maximum function is applied on the input over a local neighborhood to achieve some invariance in the max-pooling layer. Subsequently, a new convolution is applied to each feature map by 5 different kernels of size 5×5 and is followed by another max-pooling of size 2×2. These outputs are further given to a fully connected layer that is known as multi-layer perceptron connecting all neurons of the previous layer to every neuron of its own layer. Finally, the output layer has six output nodes with each node for each expression to output their confidence levels. These output nodes are fully connected to the previous layer. To combine multiple CNNs, the final classification is made by the average ensemble of the confidence outputs of multiple CNNs.

3 Experimental Results

The experiments were performed for recognition of six facial expressions on the Extended Cohn-Kanade (CK+) database [14]. This image dataset consists of 593 image sequences from 123 subjects aged from 18 to 50 years and varied with different back-grounds: 69 % female, 81 % Euro-American, 13 % Afro-American, and 6 % other groups. The image sequences were captured with two hardware synchronized Panasonic AG-7500 cameras directly located in front of subject according to instructions. Each image sequence begins and ends with the neutral expression. All images in the dataset are of size 640×480 pixels as well as 640×490 pixels with 8-bit gray-scale or 24-bit color values. Similar to the existing methods [5], the neutral and contempt expression images were not used in the experiments. Figure 2 shows some sample test images of the CK+ database with six facial expressions: Happy, Surprise, Disgust, Fear, Sad, and Angry. In our experiments, 2200 annotated images were selected from the last 4 frames of each expression sequence and have been used to do a 10-fold cross-validation for training and testing. The average classification accuracy is used to evaluate the perform-ance.

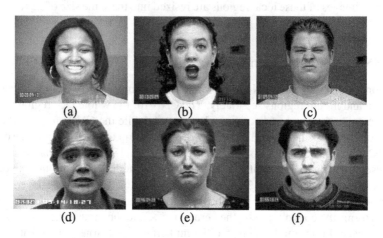

Fig. 2. The sample images of the CK+ database with six facial expressions: (a) Happy, (b) Surprise, (c) Disgust, (d) Fear, (e) Sad and (f) Angry.

The proposed facial expression recognition algorithm was implemented with the Matlab software and the deep learning toolbox downloaded from [15] was used to implement the CNN. All the experiments were carried out using a PC of Intel Core i5-2320 CPU @3.00 GHz and 8 G RAM. The image preprocessing and classification steps of our algorithm took about 0.1 and 0.2 s on average, respectively.

Table 1. The comparison of recognition accuracy of six facial expressions with different individual CNN and the ensemble of multiple CNNs w.r.t different numbers of iterations.

Iteration#	Whole face	Eye region	Mouth region	Eye+Mouth	Face+Eye+Mouth
20	88.1 %	91.7 %	92.2 %	94.3 %	95.9 %
40	88.4 %	94.6 %	95.3 %	96.8 %	97.4 %
60	90.3 %	95.4 %	95.5 %	97.2 %	97.9 %
80	93.6 %	96.0 %	95.9 %	97.7 %	98.0 %
100	96.0 %	95.6 %	95.6 %	97.7 %	97.9 %
120	**96.7 %**	**96.2 %**	**96.1 %**	**97.8 %**	**98.1 %**
140	96.7 %	95.9 %	96.0 %	97.8 %	98.0 %
160	96.7 %	89.8 %	96.1 %	97.7 %	97.9 %
180	96.7 %	90.5 %	96.2 %	97.7 %	98.0 %
200	96.8 %	94.1 %	96.2 %	97.6 %	98.1 %

First, we compare the recognition results of six facial expressions by the ensemble of multiple CNNs with the results by one CNN. The recognition accuracy is evaluated by considering one classifier for all expressions. Table 1 shows the comparisons of recognition accuracies with respect to different number of iterations. We can see that ensemble of multiple CNNs ("Eye+Mouth", "Face+Eye+Mouth") performs better than the individual CNN ("Whole face", "Eye region", "Mouth region"). With increasing the iteration number from 10 to 120, the recognition accuracy is gradually improved to 98.1 % and further increasing the iteration cannot improve the results.

In addition, recognition accuracy by ensemble of multiple CNNs is evaluated by one-versus-all classification strategy which considers one binary classifier for each expression. Table 2 shows the confusion matrix of the recognition accuracy for six facial expressions. We can see that the recognition accuracy of happy, sad, disgust and surprise expressions achieves no less than 98 %, while recognition accuracy of the angry and fear expressions was a little lower about 96.7 % and 94.7 %, respectively.

Table 2. The confusion matrix of the recognition accuracy of six facial expressions.

	Angry	Disgust	Fear	Happy	Sad	Surprise
Angry	96.7 %	0.3 %	0.7 %	2.0 %	0.3 %	0.0 %
Disgust	0.6 %	98.1 %	0.0 %	1.1 %	0.0 %	0.3 %
Fear	0.7 %	0.7 %	94.7 %	3.3 %	0.0 %	0.7 %
Happy	0.0 %	0.0 %	0.2 %	99.8 %	0.0 %	0.0 %
Sad	0.7 %	1.3 %	0.0 %	0.0 %	98.0 %	0.0 %
Surprise	0.2 %	0.0 %	0.2 %	0.9 %	0.6 %	98.1 %

Finally, we compare the recognition performance of our proposed algorithm to other methods [4–7] in terms of the average classification accuracy. The results presented in the published papers on the CK+ database are directly used for comparison as shown in Table 3. Compared with the method based on the handcrafted features [7], the proposed method achieved performance improvement from 95.1 % to 98.1 %. In addition, our proposed method performs better than other methods based on deep learning such as deep belief network and CNN [4–6].

Table 3. Performance comparison with other methods.

Methods	Recognition accuracy
BDBN [4]	96.70 %
LBPSVM [7]	95.10 %
3D CNN [6]	95.00 %
1-CNN [5]	97.81 %
The proposed method	98.10 %

4   Conclusions

This paper proposed a facial expression recognition algorithm by ensemble of multiple CNNs which is constructed on the local face regions. To enhance the local image features and reduce the variances of face components, the whole face region is partitioned into two smaller local regions and each local region is constructed with a CNN for classification. The final classification is made by ensemble of the multiple CNNs constructed on the whole face region and the local regions. Experimental results on the Extended Cohn-Kanade (CK+) database and comparison with other methods demonstrate the effectiveness of the proposed algorithm.

Acknowledgement. This work was supported by National Natural Science Foundation of China under the grants No. 61375112 and 61005024.

References

1. Wu, Y., Liu, H., Zha, H.: Modeling facial expression space for recognition. In: IEEE/RSJ International Conference on Intelligent Robots and Systems, pp. 1968–1973 (2005)
2. Caleanu, C.-D.: Face expression recognition: a brief overview of the last decade. In: 8th IEEE International Symposium on Applied Computational Intelligence and Informatics, pp. 157–161 (2013)
3. Bettadapura, V.: Face expression recognition and analysis: the state of the art. arXiv preprint arXiv:1203.6722 (2012)
4. Liu, P., Han, S., Meng, Z., Tong, Y.: Facial expression recognition via a boosted deep belief network. In: IEEE Conference on Computer Vision and Pattern Recognition, pp. 1805–1812 (2014)
5. Andre, T.L., Edilson, A., Thiago, O.-S.: A facial expression recognition system using convolutional networks. In: 28th SIBGRAPI Conference on Graphics, Patterns and Images, pp. 273–280 (2015)
6. Byeon, Y.-H., Kwak, K.-C.: Facial expression recognition using 3d convolutional neural network. Int. J. Adv. Comput. Sci. Appl. **5**(12) (2014)
7. Shan, C., Gong, S., McOwan, P.W.: Facial expression recognition based on local binary patterns: a comprehensive study. Image Vis. Comput. **27**(6), 803–816 (2009)
8. Jain, S., Hu, C., Aggarwal, J.K.: Facial expression recognition with temporal modeling of shapes. In: ICCV Workshops, pp. 1642–1649 (2011)
9. Whitehill, J., Bartlett, M.S., Littlewort, G., Fasel, I., Movellan, J.R.: Towards practical smile detection. IEEE T-PAMI **31**(11), 2106–2111 (2009)
10. Foster, I., Kesselman, C., Nick, J., Tuecke, S.: Image based static facial expression recognition with multiple deep network learning. In: Proceedings of the ACM on International Conference on Multimodal Interaction, Seattle, WA, USA, 09–13 November 2015
11. Burkert P., Trier, F., Afzal, M.Z., Dengel, A., Liwicki, M.: DeXpression deep convolutional neural network for expression recognition. arXiv:1509.05371 [cs.CV]
12. Sun, Y., Wang, X., Tang, X.: Deep convolutional network cascade for facial point detection. In: Proceedings of IEEE Conference on Computer Vision and Pattern Recognition (2013)
13. Cohn, J.F., Zlochower, A.: A Computerized Analysis of Facial Expression: Feasibility of Automated Discrimination. American Psychological Society, New York (1995)
14. Lucey, P., Cohn, J.F., Kanade, T., Saragih, J., Ambadar, Z., Matthews, I.: The extended cohn-kanade dataset (CK+): a complete dataset for action unit and emotion-specified expression. In: IEEE Conference on Computer Vision and Pattern Recognition Workshops, pp. 94–101 (2010)
15. Palm, R.B.: Prediction as a candidate for learning deep hierarchical models of data (2012). http://www2.imm.dtu.dk/pubdb/views/publication_details.php?id=6284
16. Zhen, Q., Huang, D., Wang, Y., Chen, L.: Muscular movement model based automatic 3d facial expression recognition. In: He, X., Luo, S., Tao, D., Xu, C., Yang, J., Hasan, M.A. (eds.) MMM 2015, Part I. LNCS, vol. 8935, pp. 522–533. Springer, Heidelberg (2015)

Real-World Facial Expression Recognition Using Metric Learning Method

Zhiwen Liu$^{(\boxtimes)}$, Shan Li, and Weihong Deng

School of Information and Communication Engineering,
Beijing University of Posts and Telecommunications, Bejing, China
timon@bupt.edu.cn

Abstract. Real-world human facial expressions recognition has great value in Human-Computer Interaction. Currently facial expression recognition methods perform quite poor in real-world compared with in traditional laboratory conditions. A key factor is the lack of reliable large real-world facial expression database. In this paper, a large and reliable real-world facial expression database and a Modified Metric Learning Method based on NCM classifier (PR-NCMML) to regress the probability distribution of emotional labels will be introduced. According to experiments, the six-dimension emotion probability vector derived by PR-NCMML is closer to human perception, which leads to better accuracy than the state-of-the-art methods, such as the SVM based algorithms, both dominant emotion prediction and multi-label emotion recognition.

Keywords: Real-world facial expressions · Metric Learning · Probability regression

1 Introduction

Facial expression recognition is currently a hot topic in the field of pattern recognition. Recently, many studies on expression recognition have achieved nearly perfect accuracy. However, these results are based on databases which are collected under strictly controlled laboratory conditions (e.g. Cohn-Kanade [1], CMU-PIE [2]). These databases all share common limitations of not representing the diverse set of illumination conditions, camera models and personal difference. Although, some recent database(e.g. AFEW/SFEW [3]) contains expressions in real-world. The labels in these databases are not always reliable. These limitations are the direct factors of poor performance when applied those nearly perfect classifiers to recognize the real world facial expressions. In this paper, a large Real-world database called *RAF-DB* will be introduced, which contains nearly 30,000 images all collected straightly from 'Flickr.com', and labeled by about 300 volunteers to ensure the reliability. The *RAF-DB* database will be described in Sect. 2.

Ekman [4] has defined that human emotions can be classified into seven-basic categories (Surprise, Fearful, Disgusted, Happy, Sad, Angry and Neutral). Former researchers always considered facial expression recognition as a multi-class

© Springer International Publishing AG 2016
Z. You et al. (Eds.): CCBR 2016, LNCS 9967, pp. 519–527, 2016.
DOI: 10.1007/978-3-319-46654-5_57

problem [5] to recognize the dominant emotion of the image. Commonly used classifiers including multi-class SVM [5,6], NCM [7], LDA [8], Decision Trees [9] etc. have achieved nearly perfect performance on 'posed expressions'. However, real-world expressions are much more complex than the dominant basic-emotion. Many of our expressions are mixed by different basic-emotions with different intensities (see Fig. 1). RAF-DB provides 7-dimensional probability distribution of the 7-basic-emotion for each image labeled by human. Each dimension of that indicates the intensity of this emotion in the image, which give us a chance to predicted multi-emotion as well as the intensity of the emotions in the images.

Therefore, we consider modifying a metric learning method based on NCM [10] classifier to regress the probability distribution of emotions. By doing this, the modified NCMML (called PR-NCMML) can re-weight the distance between sample and its class mean by the probability. Also, it can provide the probability for each sample, which not only can be used for dominant emotion recognition but also can provide multi-label result to solve the multi-emotion problem. And the performance of PR-NCMML in both dominant emotion and multi-emotion recognition are better than state-of-the-art methods(including SVM). The experiments will be described in Sect. 4.

2   Real-world Affect Face Database

Real-world Affect Face Database (RAF-DB) was collected straightly from the Internet. All images in RAF-DB are uploaded by thousands of users from world wide. In Fig. 2, it is obvious that images in RAF-DB have much more complexed background, illumination, characters, pose, angle etc. than most existing facial databases.

Labeling emotional expression in images in real-world always has much difficulties because different people may have different understanding. Therefore, images in RAF-DB were labeled by 300 volunteers to ensure that each image was voted by more than 40 volunteers. The final result of each image was calculated by the results of the 40 volunteers. In this way, the annotation of each expression image is much more reliable than most existing databases.

Calculating the annotation results, RAF-DB provided the probability distribution of the seven-basic emotions (including Neutral) for each facial image. In Fig. 1, we can obverse that in real-world some facial expression with significant one single dominant emotion label while other images with more than one labels (see Fig. 1). However, in most former researches, expression recognition algorithms only trained and tested with single label of images, which didn't have good performance in real-world emotion recognition.

2.1   Multi-emotion Recognition Problem

The emotion label with the largest probability called Dominant Emotion, and most former researches can be seen as dominant emotion recognition. In Fig. 1, it is obvious that only recognizing the dominant emotion in this image is far

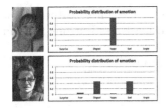

Fig. 1. Examples images with single or multiple emotions in *RAF-DB*

Fig. 2. Example image in *RAF-DB* and classical database

from enough. These images should be recognized as multi-emotion problem. Traditional researches always use multi-label classifiers to solve this problem. Since *RAF-DB* can provide the reliable 7-dimension of probability distribution of emotion labels, a considerable way is to use the probability based methods to recognize multi-emotion images in the real-world.

3 Metric Learning Method for NCM Based on Probability Distribution

There are two classic distance based method classifier—Nearest Class Mean (NCM) Classifier and K-Nearest Neighborhood (KNN) Classifier. NCM is more efficient and the outperformance of NCM is more flexible than KNN. The main idea of this NCM classifier is to classify samples by the distance between the sample and then center of each class.

$$c^* = \underset{c \in \{1,\dots,C\}}{\arg\min}\, d(x, \mu_c) \tag{1}$$

$$\mu_c = \frac{1}{N_c} \sum_{i:y^{(i)}=c} x^{(i)} \tag{2}$$

where $d(x, \mu_c)$ means the Euclidean distance between a sample x and the class mean μ_c. $y^{(i)}$ is the ground truth label of sample x. N_c is the number of samples in class c Thomas Mensink et al. [10] have proposed a metric learning method by replacing the Euclidean distance in NCM classifier with the Mahalanobis distance:$d_M(x, x') = (x - x')^T M (x - x')$, M is a positive defined matrix which can be seen as a weight matrix for each dimension. Consider that When the dimension of sample x is high, the matrix M will be extremely large ($D \times D$ dimension), M can be replaced with $M = W^T W, W \in \Re^{d \times D}, d << D$, and $d_W(x, \mu_j) = (x - \mu_j)^T W^T W (x - \mu_j)$. Defined the probability for sample $x^{(i)}$ belonging to class j as:

$$p(x^{(i)} \in C_j | x^{(i)}) = \frac{\exp d_W(x^{(i)}, \mu_j)}{\sum_{k=1}^{K} \exp d_W(x^{(i)}, \mu_k)} \tag{3}$$

$$\mu_j = \frac{1}{N_j} \sum_{i:y^{(i)}=j} x^{(i)} \tag{4}$$

To use the probability distribution of emotions to recognize real-world facial expressions, we define the object function Eq. 5 using Cross Entropy method:

$$J(W) = -\frac{1}{Q}[\sum_{i=1}^{Q}\sum_{j=1}^{C} t_j^{(i)} ln \frac{\exp[-\frac{1}{2}d_W(x^{(i)}, \mu_j)]}{\sum_{k=1}^{C} \exp[-\frac{1}{2}d_W(x^{(i)], \mu_k)}}] \tag{5}$$

where $t_j^{(i)}$ indicates the true probability of sample i belonging to class j. And Q is the number of samples in total, C is the number of categories. By minimizing Eq. 5, the predicted probability and ground truth will be converged. To optimize the object function (5), we consider using gradient descent method:

$$\nabla_W J = \frac{1}{Q} \sum_{i=1}^{Q}\sum_{j=1}^{C} \alpha_{ij} W (x^{(i)} - \mu_j)(x^{(i)} - \mu_j)^T \tag{6}$$

where $\alpha_{ij} = p(x^{(i)} \in C_j | x^{(i)}) - t_j^{(i)}$. Matrix W can mapping x from original feature space to a new subspace where the distance between samples and class centers and the probabilities are positive correlation.

4   Experiments

4.1   Exp 1: Results on the CK [1] database

Setup: In the first experiment, we use the famous CK [1] database. Because CK [1] is a sequence database and our classifiers are all based static images, we manually captured several frames from each image-sequence and manually labeled these static images with six-basic emotions. Totally, we got 486 static images in our CK-dataset.

Alignment: For each image in the CK-dataset, we manually mark face and then cut and resized the facial rectangle to 100×100 pixels. Using the landmark marked by ourselves for each images in the dataset, we applied affine transform for the cut facial images to make sure eyes and mouth in each aligned image are at the same location.

Features: Two kinds of features are extracted for each aligned image. Local binary patterns (LBP) [11] was proved to be a powerful texture description with illumination invariance. Here, we set 7×7 blocks for each image, and (8,1) uniform pattern. We got a 2891-dimensional feature vector each image. Histogram of Oriented Gradients(HOG) [12] feature is extracted by dividing each image into 15×15 patches and 20 different angles. The HOG feature we got for each image is a 4500-dimensional vector.

Results: In both HOG and LBP features, the NCMML method performed better than traditional SVM method (Show in Table 1). And it is observed that there is a gap between our experiment accuracy and existing researches' best accuracy on CK database. The key factor is that we just use static images cut from CK's sequences which will ignore the dynamics of expressions.

Table 1. Dominant Emotion recognition on CK-dataset

	Rate (%)	Surp.	Fear	Disg.	Happ.	Sad	Angr.	Mean
HOG	NCMML	**90.2**	**93.8**	**81.3**	**100**	**88**	**81**	**89.1**
	SVM	94.9	80.6	81.8	91.1	94.1	91.3	89.0
LBP	NCMML	**96.9**	**91.5**	**84.4**	**94.7**	**86.2**	**86.7**	**90.1**
	SVM	97.6	85	79.3	95.6	91.7	78.6	87.9

Table 2. Recall and precision rates of dominant emotion recognition

Rate (%)	HOG		LBP		Pixel	
	Rec.	Prec.	Rec.	Prec.	Rec.	Prec.
PR-NCMML	**57.7**	**53.7**	**55.6**	**51.1**	**50.1**	**47.0**
LDA [8]	47.0	42.9	43.2	40.4	28.3	28.8
SVM [6]	56.2	50.8	53.6	48.5	35.2	35.2
TREE [9]	33.7	31.0	25.9	25.1	27.9	26.5
NCM [7]	49.5	44.1	36.9	35.9	27.9	28.0
KNN	49.9	46.1	38.7	36.0	31.9	32.0
QDA	42.2	38.0	42.1	39.0	28.1	26.2

Table 3. Confusion matrix of dominant emotion recognition using HOG and PR-NCMML classifier

(%)	Surp.	Fear	Disg.	Happ.	Sad	Angr.
Surp.	**69.1**	17.2	6.6	6.6	6.4	8.5
Fear	8.7	**41.4**	1.5	1.9	4.0	4.2
Disg.	5.7	6.1	**48.2**	7.9	17.3	16.0
Happ.	5.7	9.1	4.7	**70.6**	9.8	2.9
Sad	5.1	11.1	24.8	7.8	**57.9**	9.6
Angr.	5.7	15.2	14.3	5.2	4.6	**58.8**

(Row, ground truth. Colunm, predicted label)

4.2 Exp 2: Real-world Dominant Expression Recognition

Dataset: In this paper, we only focus on frontal face images, so we select images whose face deflection angle are less than 20°. Because in *RAF-DB*, neutral images are far more than other emotion images, the definition whether an image considered as neutral or expressive is Eq. 7, where $\sum_{j \in E} 1\{p_j^{(i)} > \frac{1}{7}\} > 1$ indicates that image i contains at least one non-neutral expressions which can be recognized by human. We finally got nearly 17,000 images with frontal face and non-neutral expression.

$$img^{(i)} = \begin{cases} non-neutral & if \sum_{j \in E} 1\{p_j^{(i)} > \frac{1}{7}\} \geq 1 \\ neutral & otherwise \end{cases} \tag{7}$$

Up/Down-sampling: In the dataset with frontal and non-neutral facial images, we found that there is a serious imbalance problem: some categories (e.g. Happy and Surprised) have several times number of images than some negative emotion categories (e.g. Fear, disgusted). Considering many multi-class Classifiers may be influenced by the imbalanced problem, in this paper, by expanding 'small' categories in trainingset by copying themselves and randomly removing some images in 'large' categories, we make the scale of each category close.

Image processing: *RAF-DB* offers the coordinate of facial rectangle and 5-point landmark information. For each images, we cut the facial rectangle and resized it into 100×100 pixels. Then use 5-point landmark to aligned each image through affine transform. We extracted three kinds of feature for each image:

HOG [12], LBP [11] and original Pixel feature. The set of HOG and LBP features are the same as Exp.1 with 4500-dimension and 2891-dimension. To extract the original Pixel feature, we resized the rectangle facial image into 53×53 pixels and then transform it to a 2809-dimensonal vector.

Classifiers: Dominant emotion recognition can be seen as a multi-class problem. In Exp.2, we used several state-of-the-art multi-class classifiers for comparison. For multi-class SVM, we use Libsvm v3.20 [13] toolbox. For KNN and original NCM classifiers, we use PRTools v4.0 [14] toolbox. And LDA [15], QDA, Decision Tree are all used Matlab build-in function.

Results and Analysis: To evaluate the performance of the dominant expression recognition, we use 'Recall' and 'Precision' rates, which are defined as Eqs. (8) and (9) below:

$$RECALL = \frac{1}{C} \sum_{c=1}^{C} \frac{TP_c}{TP_c + FN_c} \tag{8}$$

$$PRECISION = \frac{1}{C} \sum_{c=1}^{C} \frac{TP_c}{TP_c + FP_c} \tag{9}$$

where C is the total number of emotion categories, TP_c, FN_c, FP_c indicate the 'True Positive', 'False Negative' and 'False Positive' of class c. Results are shown in Table 2. The PR-NCMML classifier achieved the highest performance in all three features. And compared with the performance in CK-dataset, the accuracy of recognition real-world facial expression is very low, which indicates the difficulty and complexity of real-world human expressions. Compared the accuracy of different features, feature type had less influence on PR-NCMML classifier than other classifier. From the confusion matrix shown in Table 3, that some categories (e.g. Fear, Disgust) have lower accuracy than other categories. The factor is that these two categories had less number of samples in the original training set, and the 'simply copy' up-sampling method did not expand the diversity of them.

4.3 Exp 3: Multi-label Emotions Recognition in the Real World

Multiple Emotion recognition can be considered as a multi-label problem. And the typical approaches include Binary Relevance(BR) [16], Multi-Label KNN (ML-KNN) [17], etc. Also the original NCM classifier can use the distance to each class mean to predict the probability of each class. So it can also provide multi-emotion outputs. Similarly, multi-class SVM can also output probability results, which means it can provide multi-label results. The dataset for this experiment was the same as Exp.2 and just two features — HOG and LBP features are extracted in Exp.3.

To evaluate this multi-label problem, we considered 'Hamming Loss' and 'Multi-Label Accuracy' rates, which are defined as below: As shown in Fig. 3, PR-NCMML has the lowest Hamming Loss and the highest Multi-Label Accuracy

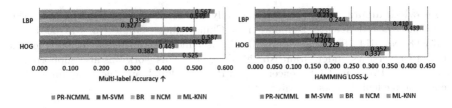

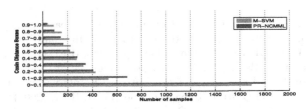

Fig. 3. Hamming Loss and Multi-Emotion Accuracy for HOG and LBP features

Fig. 4. Histogram Results of Cosine Distance (Color figure online)

among these five multi-label methods in both HOG and LBP feature, which indicates that PR-NCMML has the best performance for multi-emotion recognition among these classifiers. To evaluate the similarity between the predicted probability and the annotated one, we calculated the 'Cosine Distance' for each test sample, and histogram them in Fig. 4. We got the number of samples that 'Cosine Distance' values are less than 0.1, accounted 44 % output by PR-NCMML (see red bars in Fig. 4), nearly 4 % higher than M-SVM classifier. This means the probability distribution output by PR-NCMML is more consistent with the real intensity distribution voted by human.

5 Conclusion

In this paper, a comprehensive work for recognizing facial expressions in the real world is presented. Several state-of-the-art emotion classifiers and the PR-NCMML classifier are examined on the large real-world expression database *RAF-DB*. The key issue of this work can be summarized as follow: First, introducing a large and reliable real-world facial expression database called *RAF-DB*, in which nearly 30,000 images are all download straightly from social websites with true emotion and each image was labeled by 40 different volunteers to avoid the influence of personal factors. Second, a modified Metric Learning method (PR-NCMML) regressing the probability performed well on *RAF-DB*. PR-NCMML not only perform better than some state-of-the-art methods on dominant emotion recognition, but also do well on multi-label emotion recognition. What's more, the output probability by PR-NCMML is more consistent with human cognitions.

Acknowledgments. This work was partially sponsored by supported by the NSFC (National Natural Science Foundation of China) under Grant No. 61375031, No. 61573068, No. 61471048, and No.61273217, the Fundamental Research Funds for the Central Universities under Grant No. 2014ZD03-01, This work was also supported by Beijing Nova Program, CCF-Tencent Open Research Fund, and the Program for New Century Excellent Talents in University.

References

1. Kanade, T., Cohn, J.F., Tian, Y.: Comprehensive database for facial expression analysis. In: 2000 Proceedings of the Fourth IEEE International Conference on Automatic Face and Gesture Recognition, pp. 46–53. IEEE (2000)
2. Sim, T., Baker, S., Bsat, M.: The CMU pose, illumination, and expression (PIE) database. In: 2002 Proceedings of the Fifth IEEE International Conference on Automatic Face and Gesture Recognition, pp. 46–51. IEEE (2002)
3. Dhall, A., Goecke, R., Lucey, S., Gedeon, T.: Acted facial expressions in the wild database. Australian National University, Canberra, Australia, Technical report TR-CS-11-02 (2011)
4. Ekman, P., Scherer, K.: Expression and the nature of emotion. Approaches to emotion **3**, 19–344 (1984)
5. Kotsia, I., Pitas, I.: Facial expression recognition in image sequences using geometric deformation features and support vector machines. IEEE Trans. Image Process. **16**(1), 172–187 (2007)
6. Anderson, K., McOwan, P.W.: A real-time automated system for the recognition of human facial expressions. IEEE Trans. Syst. Man Cybern. Part B Cybern. **36**(1), 96–105 (2006)
7. Buciu, I., Pitas, I.: Application of non-negative and local non negative matrix factorization to facial expression recognition. In: Proceedings of the 17th International Conference on Pattern Recognition, ICPR2004, vol. 1, pp. 288–291. IEEE (2004)
8. Wang, J., Yin, L.: Static topographic modeling for facial expression recognition and analysis. Comput. Vis. Image Underst. **108**(1), 19–34 (2007)
9. Sebe, N., Lew, M.S., Sun, Y., Cohen, I., Gevers, T., Huang, T.S.: Authentic facial expression analysis. Image Vis. Comput. **25**(12), 1856–1863 (2007)
10. Mensink, T., Verbeek, J., Perronnin, F., Csurka, G.: Distance-based image classification: generalizing to new classes at near-zero cost. IEEE Trans. Pattern Anal. Mach. Intell. **35**(11), 2624–2637 (2013)
11. Moore, S., Bowden, R.: Local binary patterns for multi-view facial expression recognition. Comput. Vis. Image Underst. **115**(4), 541–558 (2011)
12. Dahmane, M., Meunier, J.: Emotion recognition using dynamic grid-based hog features. In: 2011 IEEE International Conference on Automatic Face & Gesture Recognition and Workshops (FG 2011), pp. 884–888. IEEE (2011)
13. Chang, C.C., Lin, C.J.: LIBSVM: a library for support vector machines. ACM Trans. Intell. Syst. Technol. **2**, 27:1–27:27 (2011). Software available at http://www.csie.ntu.edu.tw/cjlin/libsvm
14. Duin, R.: PRtools version 3.0: a matlab toolbox for pattern recognition. In: Proceedings of SPIE, Citeseer (2000)
15. Deng, H.B., Jin, L.W., Zhen, L.X., Huang, J.C.: A new facial expression recognition method based on local Gabor filter bank and PCA plus LDA. Int. J. Inf. Technol. **11**(11), 86–96 (2005)

16. Boutell, M.R., Luo, J., Shen, X., Brown, C.M.: Learning multi-label scene classification. Pattern Recogn. **37**(9), 1757–1771 (2004)
17. Zhang, M-L., Zhou, Z-H.: Multi-instance multi-label learning with application to scene classification

Recognizing Compound Emotional Expression in Real-World Using Metric Learning Method

Zhiwen Liu$^{(\boxtimes)}$, Shan Li, and Weihong Deng

School of Information and Communication Engineering,
Beijing University of Posts and Telecommunications, Beijing, China
timon@bupt.edu.cn

Abstract. Understanding human facial expressions plays an important role in Human-Computer-Interaction (HCI). Recent achievements on automatically recognizing facial expressions are mostly based on lab-controlled databases, in which facial images are a far cry from those in the real world. The main contribution of this paper is listed in the following three points. First, a large real-world facial expression database (*RAF-DB*), with nearly 30,000 images collected from Flickr and labeled by 300 volunteers will be introduced. Second, for the reason that human emotions are much more complexed than the six-basic-emotion defined by Ekman et al., we re-categories real-world facial expressions as compound emotional expressions, which can explain human emotions better. Finally, a metric learning method as well as several state-of-the-art facial expression classifying methods including SVM, are used to recognize our compound expression dataset. And we found that metric learning method performed better than other classifications.

Keywords: Compound facial expressions · Large Real-world Database · Metric learning

1 Introduction

Automatic Facial Expression Analysis has numerous potential applications in Human-Computer Interaction (HCI) and social media analysis. Recent years, recognizing facial expressions on posed and lab-controlled images (e.g. images in CK [1], JAFFE [2] etc. databases) have achieved nearly perfect accuracy. However, when detecting human facial expressions in the real world, accuracy tends to become very poor. One important factor is that there is almost no large real-world facial expressions database with reliable expression-labels. Therefore, in this paper, we will introduce a large real-world expression database called *RAF-DB*, in which nearly 30 thousand facial expression images collected from Flickr and labeled by 300 volunteers. Each image has a 7-dimension emotion probabilities (six-basic-emotion plus neutral) vector labeled by 40 volunteers.

For decades, researchers always consider that human have six basic expressions proposed by Ekman [3]. And almost all of facial expression recognition

© Springer International Publishing AG 2016
Z. You et al. (Eds.): CCBR 2016, LNCS 9967, pp. 528–536, 2016.
DOI: 10.1007/978-3-319-46654-5_58

researches are based on the six-basic-emotion as ground truth categories. However, according to real-world images, It can be easily observed that human expressions are much more complex than those six basic emotional expressions. For example, in Fig. 1, the face on the left is different from either single disgust or angry expression. Du et al. [4] proposed a new concept called compound emotional expressions based on posed images in lab-controlled conditions. Inspired by [4], we found that in real-world (show in Fig. 3) there are a large number of expressions similar to [4]'s definition. These expressions not only verified [4]'s theory but also were highly consistent with human sense (see Fig. 3).

In this work, we focus on compound expression recognition in the real-world. Classifiers including SVM [5,6], LDA [7], KNN [8], etc. are commonly used for expression recognition tasks. According to our experiments in Sect. 4, applying these state-of-the-art methods directly for real-world facial expression recognition problem didn't receive satisfying performance. However, a distance-based method called Nearest Class Mean (NCM) classifier can reach SVM base-line. Inspired by T. Mensink et al. [9], we considered using metric learning method for NCM classifier by displace the Euclidean distance in origin NCM with Mahalanobis distance. Compared with one-vs-one multi-class svm, the NCM classifier can use full information of training samples. Also it is more robust than multi-class SVM and KNN methods if the training dataset was suffering a serious imbalance problem. Adapting the metric learning method to NCM classifier can enhance the ability of classification, while maintaining robust and efficiency of original NCM classifier. According to Sect. 4, the metric learning NCM classifier performed better than many state-of-the-art facial expression classifiers in real-world compound expression recognition.

Fig. 1. Example image of compound emotional expressions

2 Database and Compound Facial Expressions

2.1 Large Real-World Database

The *RAF-DB* is a large facial expression image database collected straightly from the Internet (mostly downloaded from Flickr.com). The database contains 29,672 static images with at least one effective face, which is much larger than most existing facial expression database. Example images of *RAF-DB* are illustrated in Fig. 2. It is obvious that images in *RAF-DB* have more complex background, illumination, posture and a larger number of characters. Which means, images in *RAF-DB* are closer to the real-world, and the emotions are more realistic than those posed expressions under lab-conditions (see Fig. 2).

In most existing databases, expressions are labeled by a few people, which may cause personal factor greatly influence labels and labels can be unreliable. Therefore, *RAF-DB* was annotated by 300 volunteers with each image labeled by nearly 40 volunteers. The expression label in *RAF-DB* is much more reliable than most existing databases. A 7-dimensional distribution vector of probability per image was calculated by the annotation results of 40 volunteers. This probability vector is highly consistent with the true probability distributions of the 7 basic emotions, which are much more reliable than most existing databases. Also *RAF-DB* provides coordinate of face rectangle and five points landmarks (left and right eye centers, nose, right and left mouth coners) for each image.

Fig. 2. Images comparison of *RAF-DB* and Classical databases

2.2 Compound Facial Expressions in the Real-World

According to images in *RAF-DB*, it's obvious that human facial expressions are much more complex than the seven basic expressions. Roughly, in *RAF-DB*, there are more than 50 % of images with at least two possible expressions, which means a considerable number of facial images can not be simply recognized as single emotion label (shows in Fig. 1). Traditional methods always treat this like a multi-label problem. However, learning a multi-label classifier for expressions is not only inefficient but also ineffective, because a compound expression can not be seen as a simple sum of two basic expressions.

Inspired by Du et al. [4], It's considerable to use compound emotional expressions to expand traditional expressions categories. Du et al. [4] has proposed 15 compound emotional expressions including 12 typical expressions (See Fig. 3(a)) and 3 additional emotion categories (Appalled, Hatred, Awed) defined by different intensities of the two 'mixed' emotions. Faces in [4]'s work were all posed by professional volunteers photoed under controlled lab-condition and selected by strict protocols. In this work, we use the 7-dimensional probability distributions provided by *RAF-DB* to extract compound expressions in real-world facial images. If image i satisfies both $P_{max1}^{(i)} - P_{max2}^{(i)} \leq 0.4$ and $P_{max1}^{(i)} + P_{max2}^{(i)} \geq 0.8$ at the same time, image i is regarded as compound expressions, Where $P_{max1}^{(i)}$

(a) Compound emotional expressions

(b) Basic emotional expressions

Fig. 3. Examples images of basic and compound emotional expressions in *RAF-DB*

and $P_{max2}^{(i)}$ are the first and second largest probabilities of image i. These first equation ensures that the first and second possbile expressions in image i can be seen as the two predominant emotions and the second equation guarantees the difference between them is not too large.

In this paper, "basic" refers to those expressions which are more significant than compound expressions. In other words, images belonging to "basic" categories have only one predominant label. After extracting compound expression, we consider image satisfied $P_{max1}^{(i)} \geq threshold$ belongs to basic emotional expressions subset.

3   Metric Learning for Nearest Class Mean Classifier

The main idea of the Nearest Class Mean Classifier is to classify samples by distance between sample points and class mean points, see Eqs. (1), (2), where $d(x, \mu_c)$ is the Euclidean distance between image i and the mean of class c, and $y^{(i)}$ is the ground truth of image i.

$$c^* = \underset{c \in \{1,...,C\}}{\arg\min} \, d(x^{(i)}, \mu_c) \tag{1}$$

$$\mu_c = \frac{1}{N_c} \sum_{i:y^{(i)}=c} x^{(i)} \tag{2}$$

Mensink et al. [9] proposed that using Mahalanobis distance to replace the Euclidean distance when calculating $d(x, \mu_c)$.

$$d_M = (x - \mu_c)^T M (x - \mu_c) \tag{3}$$

where x is a D-dimensional feature vector for one image, μ_c is the mean vector of image in c class and M is a positive definite matrix. Matrix M can be seen as a weight matrix for each dimension to make sure image i close enough to the class mean if i belongs to the class. If applying $M = W^T W$, where $W \in \Re^{d \times D}, d < D$, the mahalanobis diatance is equivalent to the squared l_2 distance, which can greatly improve the efficiency for computing and storage:

$$d_W(x, \mu_c) = (x - \mu_c)^T W^T W (x - \mu_c) \tag{4}$$

Based on logistic regression, the probability for class c given a feature vector $x^{(i)}$ can be defined as below:

$$p(c|x^{(i)}) = \frac{\exp(-\frac{1}{2}d_W(x^{(i)}, \mu_c))}{\sum_{c'}^C \exp(-\frac{1}{2}d_W(x^{(i)}, \mu_{c'}))} \tag{5}$$

To learn the projection matrix W, we can use the method of softmax to minimize the cost function J in Eq. (6) and solve it through the SGD method:

$$J = -\frac{1}{N} \sum_{i=1}^N 1[y^{(i)} = c] \ln p(y^{(i)}|x^{(i)}) \tag{6}$$

$$\nabla_W J = \frac{1}{N} \sum_{i=1}^N \sum_{c=1}^C \alpha_{ic} W (x^{(i)} - \mu_c)(x^{(i)} - \mu_c)^T \tag{7}$$

Where $\alpha_{ic} = p(c|x^{(i)}) - [y^{(i)} = c]$, and $[y^{(i)} = c]$ means if $y^{(i)}$ equal c then the result is one otherwise zero. When W has been learned, the Mahalabia distance can be calculated in NCM to classify images.

4   Compound Emotion Experiments

4.1   Experiment Set

Dataset. Due to the imbalance problem in *RAF-DB*, some compound expression categories contain images far more than other. Therefore, we manually remove some images in those 'huge categories' to narrow the gap between 'small categories', and remove three categories (Sadly surprised, Fearfully disgusted and

Table 1. Confusion Matrix for NCMML method using HOG in compound expression sub-database

	1	2	3	4	5	6	7	8	9	10	11	12	13	14	15	16
1	**0.53**	0.05	0.08	0.00	0.02	0.07	0.12	0.13	0.02	0.07	0.08	0.01	0.08	0.03	0.03	0.03
2	0.02	**0.13**	0.04	0.00	0.01	0.00	0.00	0.03	0.04	0.00	0.02	0.02	0.06	0.01	0.03	0.02
3	0.02	0.00	**0.21**	0.03	0.02	0.04	0.03	0.00	0.00	0.01	0.02	0.00	0.01	0.02	0.00	0.01
4	0.01	0.00	0.04	**0.13**	0.00	0.00	0.01	0.03	0.04	0.00	0.00	0.02	0.00	0.01	0.02	0.04
5	0.01	0.10	0.08	0.16	**0.28**	0.07	0.05	0.03	0.13	0.02	0.03	0.10	0.00	0.12	0.01	0.12
6	0.01	0.00	0.04	0.03	0.00	**0.32**	0.00	0.00	0.00	0.00	0.08	0.00	0.00	0.00	0.02	0.00
7	0.09	0.10	0.04	0.00	0.03	0.11	**0.28**	0.07	0.02	0.05	0.18	0.06	0.02	0.05	0.01	0.02
8	0.04	0.03	0.00	0.00	0.02	0.04	0.00	**0.27**	0.02	0.03	0.00	0.04	0.00	0.00	0.08	0.02
9	0.03	0.18	0.04	0.25	0.17	0.04	0.07	0.07	**0.43**	0.01	0.03	0.17	0.01	0.03	0.17	0.12
10	0.10	0.05	0.04	0.00	0.01	0.00	0.10	0.13	0.02	**0.73**	0.05	0.04	0.01	0.01	0.00	0.05
11	0.03	0.00	0.13	0.06	0.02	0.21	0.15	0.07	0.00	0.01	**0.28**	0.01	0.01	0.01	0.05	0.00
12	0.01	0.05	0.00	0.06	0.13	0.00	0.02	0.00	0.08	0.00	0.02	**0.21**	0.01	0.06	0.05	0.04
13	0.08	0.13	0.00	0.00	0.04	0.00	0.02	0.00	0.02	0.01	0.05	0.04	**0.67**	0.09	0.02	0.03
14	0.01	0.05	0.17	0.09	0.11	0.00	0.04	0.07	0.03	0.00	0.07	0.09	0.05	**0.43**	0.02	0.08
15	0.01	0.13	0.04	0.16	0.03	0.11	0.07	0.10	0.10	0.00	0.03	0.04	0.01	0.03	**0.49**	0.01
16	0.00	0.03	0.04	0.03	0.12	0.00	0.05	0.00	0.06	0.07	0.07	0.18	0.06	0.11	0.03	**0.41**

Rows, ground truth. Columns, predicted label.
Emotional expression labels in this table are: 1. happily surprised, 2. happily disgusted, 3. sadly fearful, 4. sadly angry, 5. sadly disgusted, 6. fearfully angry, 7. fearfully surprised, 8. angrily surprised, 9. angrily disgusted, 10. surprised, 11. fearful, 12. disgust, 13. happy, 14. sad, 15. angry, 16. neutral

Table 2. Recall, Precision and Accuracy of methods using HOG and LBP features

	HOG			LBP		
	Recall	Precision	Accuracy	Recall	Precision	Accuracy
SVM (Linear) [10]	35.0 %	35.5 %	**45.9 %**	27.0 %	28.2 %	34.9 %
KNN-40 [8]	25.9 %	23.1 %	37.8 %	19.0 %	16.9 %	22.0 %
KNN-15 [8]	26.7 %	24.3 %	36.6 %	16.2 %	21.2 %	23.7 %
NCM [11]	32.4 %	32.5 %	38.6 %	23.7 %	22.1 %	28.0 %
LDA [7]	31.2 %	31.6 %	37.8 %	28.3 %	27.1 %	33.5 %
QDA	30.7 %	30.8 %	39.6 %	20.0 %	21.6 %	27.7 %
PCA+TREE [12]	15.6 %	15.6 %	19.1 %	12.1 %	14.1 %	17.2 %
NCMML	**36.9 %**	**37.0 %**	44.1 %	**30.1 %**	**29.2 %**	**36.7 %**

Disgustedly surprised) which contain less than 30 images. Finally, for compound expression dataset, 1460 images are selected from *RAF-DB* with 9 compound categories (shows in Fig. 3(a)). Similar to the steps above, we then extracted a basic expression subset with 1711 images through the balance processing. Finally, combined these two subsets into a sub-database with 16 categories (9 compound categories and 7 basic categories) of emotional expressions and divided it randomly in half on category level, one for training, the other for testing.

Alignment. *RAF-DB* offers coordinates of face and five-points-landmark marked manually for each images. After cutting face into a 100×100 pixel images, 3-point (left-eye-center, right-eye-center, mouth-center) are used for alignment. Make sure eyes and mouth in aligned images are almost at the same location.

Features. HOG [13] and LBP [6] features are extracted in both aligned trainset and testset. For HOG [13] feature, setting a 5×5 pixels cell and 2×2 cell in one block, 4000-dimensional feature vector for each image. For LBP [6] feature, setting 7×7 blocks for each image and histogram in (8,1) neighborhood, 2891-dimensional vector.

Classifiers. For comparison, several classic classifiers are tested, including SVM which can be seen as the state-of-art method in facial expression recognition. In this paper, Libsvm v3.1.9 [10] used for svm classifier and considering the high dimension of features, we select 'linear' as kernel. For KNN classifier [8], a function provided by PRTools v4.0 [14] is used, and set k=40, k=15 for the reason that compound emotion dataset still has imbalance problem. LDA [7] and QDA methods are built-in function in Matlab, and 'PCA+TREE' indicates using PCA for dimensionality reduction and use Decision Tree to classify emotional expressions.

4.2   Results and Analysis

For each classifier, 10 times test is done by randomly half-half dividing the compound sub-database into trainset and testset, and take the average of Accuracy, Recall and Precision rate as results of the performance of the classifier.

$$Recall = \frac{1}{C} \sum_{c=1}^{C} \frac{TP_c}{TP_c + FN_c} \tag{8}$$

$$Precision = \frac{1}{C} \sum_{c=1}^{C} \frac{TP_c}{TP_c + FP_c} \tag{9}$$

Show in Table 2. NUMML method get the highest recall rate (36.9%) and the highest precision rate (37.0%) for HOG [13] feature with NCMML method. Also, for LBP [6] feature, NCMML method achieves the best performance. Due to the space limitations, we can't show all classifiers' confusion matrix. Table 1 shows the confusion matrix of NCMML using HOG [13] feature. We can observe that in some categories (i.e. 2-happily disgusted and 4-sadly angry), the accuracy rates are very low (less than 20%), and images in these categories are more easily to be classified into some categories (i.e. 9-angily disgusted and 5-sadly disgusted). The reason is closely related to imbalance problem in the compound emotion sub-database. And the imbalance problem dose exist in the real-world environment since in social network, people prefer positive emotion rather than negative emotion.

5   Conclusions

In this paper, a large and reliable real-world facial expression static image database is introduced, which greatly improve the situation of the insufficiency of real-world facial expression database. It's obvious that human expressions in the real world are much more complex than the 7-basic-emotion. To this end, a concept called Compound Emotional Expression is proposed to re-categorize facial expressions in the real world. And we extracted a sub-database of compound emotional expressions with totally 19 categories. Then NCMML method and several other classifiers are tested to recognize the compound facial expressions in the sub-database, and the NCMML method performed best in both HOG [13] and LBP [6] features among the classifiers used.

Acknowledgments. This work was partially sponsored by supported by the NSFC (National Natural Science Foundation of China) under Grant No. 61375031, No. 61573068, No. 61471048, and No. 61273217, the Fundamental Research Funds for the Central Universities under Grant No. 2014ZD03-01, This work was also supported by Beijing Nova Program, CCF-Tencent Open Research Fund, and the Program for New Century Excellent Talents in University.

References

1. Kanade, T., Cohn, J.F., Tian, Y.: Comprehensive database for facial expression analysis. In: Proceedings of the Fourth IEEE International Conference on Automatic Face and Gesture Recognition, pp. 46–53. IEEE (2000)
2. Lyons, M., Akamatsu, S., Kamachi, M., Gyoba, J.: Coding facial expressions with gabor wavelets. In: Proceedings of the Third IEEE International Conference on Automatic Face and Gesture Recognition, pp. 200–205. IEEE (1998)
3. Ekman, P.: An argument for basic emotions. Cogn. Emot. **6**(3–4), 169–200 (1992)
4. Du, S., Tao, Y., Martinez, A.M.: Compound facial expressions of emotion. Proc. Nat. Acad. Sci. **111**(15), E1454–E1462 (2014)
5. Kotsia, I., Pitas, I.: Facial expression recognition in image sequences using geometric deformation features and support vector machines. IEEE Trans. Image Process. **16**(1), 172–187 (2007)
6. Luo, Y., Wu, C.M., Zhang, Y.: Facial expression recognition based on fusion feature of PCA and LBP with SVM. Optik - Int. J. Light Electron Opt. **124**(17), 2767–2770 (2013)
7. Deng, H.B., Jin, L.W., Zhen, L.X., Huang, J.C.: A new facial expression recognition method based on local gabor filter bank and PCA plus LDA. Int. J. Inf. Technol. **11**(11), 86–96 (2005)
8. George, T., Potty, S.P., Jose, S.: Smile detection from still images using KNN algorithm. In: International Conference on Control, Instrumentation, Communication and Computational Technologies, pp. 461–465 (2014)
9. Mensink, T., Verbeek, J., Perronnin, F., Csurka, G.: Distance-based image classification: generalizing to new classes at near-zero cost. IEEE Trans. Pattern Anal. Mach. Intell. **35**(11), 2624–2637 (2013)
10. Chang, C.C., Lin, C.J.: LIBSVM: A library for support vector machines. ACM Trans. Intell. Syst. Technol. **2**, 27:1–27:27 (2011). Software available at http://www.csie.ntu.edu.tw/~cjlin/libsvm
11. Buciu, I., Pitas, I.: Application of non-negative and local non negative matrixfactorization to facial expression recognition. In: Proceedings of the 17th International Conference on Pattern Recognition, ICPR 2004, vol. 1, pp. 288–291. IEEE (2004)

12. Sebe, N., Lew, M.S., Sun, Y., Cohen, I., Gevers, T., Huang, T.S.: Authentic facial expression analysis. Image Vis. Comput. **25**(12), 1856–1863 (2007)
13. Yun, W.H., Kim, D.H., Park, C., Kim, J.: Hybrid facial representations for emotion recognition. ETRI J. **35**(6), 1021–1028 (2013)
14. Duin, R.: Prtools version 3.0: a matlab toolbox for pattern recognition. In: Proceedings of SPIE. Citeseer (2000)

Feature Extraction and Classification Theory

Category Guided Sparse Preserving Projection for Biometric Data Dimensionality Reduction

Qianying Huang[1]([✉]), Yunsong Wu[2], Chenqiu Zhao[1], Xiaohong Zhang[1], and Dan Yang[1]

[1] School of Software Engineering, Chongqing University, Chongqing, China
{qianying.huang,zhaochenqiu,xhongz,dyang}@cqu.edu.cn
[2] College of Computer Science, Chongqing University, Chongqing, China
wuyunsong@cqu.edu.cn

Abstract. In biometric recognition tasks, dimensionality reduction is an important pre-process which might influence the effectiveness and efficiency of subsequent procedure. Many manifold learning algorithms arise to preserve the optimal data structure by learning a projective maps and achieve great success in biometric tasks like face recognition. In this paper, we proposed a new supervised manifold learning dimensionality reduction algorithm named Category Guided Sparse Preserving Projection (CG-SPP) which combines the global category information with the merits of sparse representation and Locality Preserving Projection (LPP). Besides the sparse graph Laplacian which preserves the intrinsic data structure of samples, a category guided graph is introduced to assist in better preserving the intrinsic data structure of subjects. We apply it to face recognition and gait recognition tasks in several datasets, namely Yale, FERET, ORL, AR and OA-ISIR-A. The experimental results show its power in dimensionality reduction in comparison with the state-of-the-art algorithms.

Keywords: Dimensionality reduction · Sparse representation · Manifold learning · Graph Laplacian

1 Introduction

A common challenge encountered by most appearance-based biometric tasks is raw data of entries are always represented in high-dimensional space. Therefore, dimensionality reduction is a fundamental procedure in many biometric systems. Although there are many efforts and achievements in this field, it is still a vivid topic nowadays. Up till now, many impressive dimensionality reduction algorithms have been proposed [1–5], including Principal Component Analysis (PCA) [6], Linear Discriminant Analysis (LDA) [7], Local Preserving Projection (LPP) [8], Neighborhood Preserving Embedding (NPE) [9] and Sparse Preserving Projection (SPP) [10]. Different from PCA and LDA assuming the Gaussian distribution in data space, the others are manifold learning based algorithms. The opinion behind is that intrinsic information of high-dimensional

© Springer International Publishing AG 2016
Z. You et al. (Eds.): CCBR 2016, LNCS 9967, pp. 539–546, 2016.
DOI: 10.1007/978-3-319-46654-5_59

data often reside on the nonlinear manifold subspace, therefore a mapping from high-dimensional data space to low-dimensional optimal space can be found to reduce dimensions in representing data samples. LPP is one of the representative manifold-based dimensionality reduction algorithms. It learns a projection from an adjacency matrix which weighting the distance between each pair of samples to a new space which the relationships of sample pairs, or local manifold structure of data will be preserved. The notion of the Laplacian of graph is used in LPP, and also in SPP while it leverages sparse regression to construct a different efficient and robust graph to preserve the locality information.

As far as we know, previous algorithms like LPP and SPP consider only preserving the structure of locality for each pair of samples, however, there are natural correlation between subjects which are not being considered. The similarity between subjects indicates that there might be some correlation between them, or they are belonging to the same category to some extent. In some scenario, these correlations can be essential to represent the characteristic of data samples. For example in face recognition tasks, the faces of the people from the same race often share more similarities which may further benefit the recognition.

In this paper, we propose a new dimensionality reduction algorithm named Category Guided Sparse Preserving Projection (CG-SPP) to answer these needs. As the name implies, the adjacency weight matrix in our algorithm is generated by sparse representation. There are several desired characteristics of sparse representation for constructing weighted graph or affinity matrix. First of all, it does not encounter the trouble of selecting appropriate neighborhood size like LPP which makes it very simple to use in practice. In addition, the sparsity property of affinity matrix is beneficial to computation. The graph Laplacian in our model consists of two parts, one for the manifold of samples and another of the manifold of subjects. These two parts are joint learned and can be easily solved as generalized eigenvalue problem. We apply this new method to biometric tasks in four face datasets and one gait dataset. The results show that it achieves a great improvement than SPP and other state-of-the-art algorithms.

2   Related Works

The general notation of dimensionality reduction problem is the following. Given a sample set $X = x_1, x_2, ..., x_m$ in R^n, the mission of dimensionality reduction is to find a transformation matrix A that maps these m samples to a different set of points $Y = y_1, y_2, ..., y_m$ in $R^l (l \ll n)$, and then x_i can be represented as y_i where $y_i = A^T x_i$.

2.1   Locality Preserving Projections

In LPP, such optimal map A is solved by minimizing the summation of the weighted distance between each pair of samples as

$$\sum_{i,j} (y_i - y_j)^2 S_{ij} \tag{1}$$

where the weight $S_{i}j$ is the i, jth entry of the adjacency weight matrix S, which depicts the similarity of two samples x_i and x_j in the original high-dimensional sample space. This constraint ensures that if samples x_i and x_j are close in original space then they remain close in the learned subspace. This linear transformation can be viewed as a linear discrete approximation to a continuous map Laplacian Eigenmaps [11]. There are several variations for weighting edges in adjacency matrix S, two common schemes are Heat Kernel and Simple-minded [8].

The objective function of LPP can be formulated as

$$\sum_{i,j} (y_i - y_j)^2 S_{ij}$$
$$= 2 \left(\sum_{i,j} a^T x_i D_{ii} x_i^T a - \sum_{i,j} a^T x_i D_{ij} x_j^T a \right) \quad (2)$$
$$= 2 \left(a^T X (D - S) X^T a \right)$$
$$= 2 \left(a^T X L X^T a \right)$$

where D is a diagonal matrix and $D_{ii} = \sum_j S_{ij}$. $L = D - S$ is the Laplacian matrix. This problem can be solved by eigenvalue decomposition

$$X L X^T a = \lambda X D X^T a \quad (3)$$

The best LPP map $A = [a_0, a_1, ..., a_{l-1}]$ is spanned by the solution of Eq. 3 ordered according to their eigenvalues.

2.2 Sparse Graph Laplacian

Sparsity is a common characteristic of most locality-based dimensionality reduction algorithms such as LPP and NPE. Motivated by this, researchers proposed a new approach to design the adjacency weight matrix based on sparse representation theory [10,12]. The goal of sparse representation is to construct a overcomplete dictionary X and represent x using as few entries of X as possible. Although l_0 minimization is more sparse but it is NP-hard problem. Therefore, for each x_i, we seek a sparse representation coefficients vector c_i through l_1 minimization problem. It is a common and might be a reasonable substitute since l_1 pays more attentions to the value of coefficients which indicts the degrees of similarity between sample pairs. Therefore, the equation for l_1-norm constraint is

$$\min_{c_i} \|c_i\|_1, \text{s.t.} \|x_i - X c_i\| < \varepsilon, 1 = 1^T c_i \quad (4)$$

where ε is the noise error tolerance. We adopt an efficient projection method for sparse learning in our experiments which is for the best trade-off between performance and running time [13]. Then the affinity weight matrix A is constructed as

$$s_{ij} = s_{ji} = \frac{|c_i(j) + c_j(i)|}{2} \quad (5)$$

In addition, the self-similarity of entry is $\sum_{i \neq j} s_{ij}$. The sparse graph Laplacian is derived following the Laplacian Eigenmapping [1] as in LPP. In this paper, the normalized graph Laplacian is defined as

$$L = D^{-1/2}\left(D - S\right)D^{-1/2} = I - D^{-1/2}SD^{-1/2} \tag{6}$$

where $D_{ii} = \sum_j S_{ij}$ and I is an identical matrix. In our method, the graph Laplacian in LPP is replaced by this sparse graph Laplacian, which is nearly the same as SPP [10] but there is a slightly difference between them since in SPP, the affinity matrix does not need to be symmetric and we make it symmetric here.

3   Category Guided Sparse Preserving Projection

The motivation of our method is that correlations naturally exist among objects, we often know something by putting it into a category or relating it to other subjects we already know.

Let vector $C = [1, 2, ..., p]$ be the subject labels for dataset and matrix X_c, $c \in C$ represents all the samples of subject c. Matrix $M = m_1, m_2, ..., m_p$ in R^l denotes the projected mean class space via projecting the original mean class space $U = u_1, u_2, ..., u_p$ in R^d into the optimal space.

First, we construct a class affinity graph from sparse affinity weight graph. In this graph, every entries depict the similarity between subjects (classes) instead of samples, that is

$$B_{kl} = \frac{1}{N} \sum_{k=1}^{N} s_k \tag{7}$$

where s_k is the coefficient between class i and class j and N is the total number of pairs between them. It depicts the relationship of classes which contains more information from original space.

Therefore, the objective function of our model consist of two parts

$$\varPsi = \min \mu \sum_{ij} \left(y_i - y_j\right)^2 S_{ij} + \sum_{k,l \in C} \left(\bar{m}_k - \bar{m}_l\right)^2 B_{kl} \tag{8}$$

where μ is a positive value to control the trade-off between samples sparse structure and category guided structure.

Eventually, the equation is deduced as

$$\begin{aligned}
&\mu \sum_{ij} \left(y_i - y_j\right)^2 S_{ij} + \sum_{k,l \in C} \left(\bar{m}_k - \bar{m}_l\right)^2 B_{kl} \\
&= \mu \sum_{ij} \left(w^T x_i - w^T x_j\right)^2 S_{ij} + \sum_{k,l \in C} \left(w^T u_k - w^T u_l\right)^2 B_{kl} \\
&= 2\mu \left(w^T X D X^T w - w^T X S X^T w\right) + 2 \left(w^T U G U^T w - w^T U B U^T w\right) \\
&= 2w^T \left(\mu X L X^T + U K U^T\right) w \\
&= w^T A w
\end{aligned} \tag{9}$$

where G is the column sum of B and $K = G - B$ is the graph Laplacian of class affinity graph B. Obviously, L and K are positive semi-definite matrices, hence A is also positive semi-define matrix. Therefore, this problem equals to

$$\hat{w} = \arg\min_{w} \left(w^T A w\right) \tag{10}$$

The solution of this equation can be given by solving generalized eigenvalue problem. The projection $W = [w_1, w_2, ..., w_k]$ spanned by the first k eigenvector corresponding to k minimun nonzero eigenvalue of A is our learned optimal projective subspace.

4   Experiments

To demonstrate the effectiveness of CG-SPP in biometric data dimensionality reduction, we conduct experiments on face recognition and gait recognition.

4.1   Face Recognition

Yale[1], FERET [14], ORL (Olivetti Research Laboratory)[2] and AR [15] face datasets are adopted in face recognition experiments. Yale datasets contains the variations in lighting conditions, facial expression, and with/without glasses. The face images from Yale and ORL are resized to 32×32 pixels. Note that the dimension size of FERET face feature is over 10 thousands, which is quite tough for recognition tasks. The detail information is listed in Table 1.

Table 1. The detail information of face datasets.

Name	Subjects	#Sample	Feature	Dimension
Yale	15	165	GrayScale	1024
FERET	72	432	GrayScale	10304
ORL	40	400	GrayScale	1024
AR	120	1680	GrayScale	2000

PCA and LDA are widely used manifold learning algorithms in face recognition, the main supposition behinds them is Gaussian distribution. Other manifold learning algorithms such as LPP and NPE, are manifold learning based which usually assume certain manifold structure in data space. These four state-of-the-art algorithms are used to compare with our method in the experiments.

We apply two-fold cross-validation to evaluate the algorithms. The subspace projection is learned in training samples and the rest of dataset is considered as testing set. In these tasks, simple Nearest Neighbor (NN) classifier is used as classifier. Table 2 presents the recognition results in four face datasets. Obviously, CG-SPP outperforms all the compared dimensionality reduction algorithms. And it makes a great improvement than SPP, especially in Yale, ORL and AR with 3.67 %, 3.5 % and 5.36 % respectively.

---

[1] http://vision.ucsd.edu/content/yale-face-database.
[2] http://www.cl.cam.ac.uk/research/dtg/attarchive/facedatabase.html.

Table 2. Recognition performance on Yale, ORL, FERET and AR datasets.

Methods	Accuracy Rates (Mean ± Standard Deviation, %)			
	Yale	ORL	FERET	AR
PCA [6]	88.67 ± 2.8	85.25 ± 0.4	84.03 ± 1.0	66.73 ± 0.1
LDA [7]	95.33 ± 4.7	93.00 ± 0.7	90.74 ± 3.3	58.57 ± 1.5
LPP [8]	96.67 ± 4.1	90.75 ± 3.9	92.82 ± 2.3	61.19 ± 0.3
NPE [9]	96.00 ± 5.7	90.00 ± 4.5	93.51 ± 1.3	61.61 ± 0.2
SPP [10]	93.33 ± 3.8	93.00 ± 4.9	92.59 ± 2.6	61.96 ± 0.1
CG-SPP (ours)	**97.00 ± 0.5**	**96.75 ± 0.4**	**92.82 ± 3.6**	**67.32 ± 0.1**

The size of feature dimension is an important aspect of performance in biometric dimensionality reduction since it has a great impacts on the efficiency and storage. Hence, we conduct another face recognition experiment in LFW-A [16] dataset to demonstrate the relationship between dimensions and accuracies. LFW-A dataset contains 274 subjects whose sample numbers are over 10. Samples are represented by LBP feature. Training set consist of 10 samples from each subjects whose total size is 2740. Compared algorithms are the same as previous face recognition task. From Fig. 1, it can be seen that CG-SPP has the best performance especially in lower dimension size which shows that it is competent for dimensionality reduction tasks.

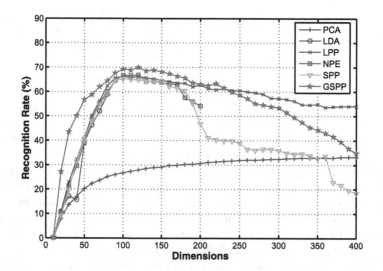

Fig. 1. Dimensions v.s. Accuracies in LFW-A dataset.

4.2 Gait Recognition

Experiments on dimensionality reduction for gait biometric task is done with OU-ISIR-A dataset [17]. This dataset consists of 3 subsets according to the walking speed. The speed range of subjects in subset1, subset2, and subset3 are 2–4 km/h, 5–7 km/h, and 8–10 km/h respectively. Results on Table 3 clearly shows that CG-SPP outperforms other compared algorithms, the improvement is remarkable in subset2 with 8.14 % higher than any other. SPP also shows its ability in gait recognition, especially in subset3. While CG-SPP exceeds it with 4.64 %, 8.14 % and 2.18 % in subset1, subset2, subset3 respectively, which is an evidence of the value of category guided information.

Table 3. Recognition performance (in percent) on OA-ISIR-A dataset.

Methods	1-Rank Recognition Rate (%)		
	subset1	subset2	subset3
PCA [6]	42.63	46.14	40.10
LDA [7]	64.53	73.59	53.79
LPP [8]	63.20	71.77	56.32
NPE [9]	65.10	72.12	55.62
SPP [10]	66.36	73.60	62.01
CG-SPP (ours)	**71.00**	**81.74**	**64.19**

5   Conclusion

In this paper, we proposed a new supervised manifold learning based dimensionality reduction algorithm named Category Guided Sparse Preserving Projection (CG-SPP). In this algorithm, we not only let it inherit the advantages of sparse representation to obtain the locality structure property of samples, but also introduced a category guided information for better representing the intrinsic relationship of classes. As a result, it went beyond SPP and had more discriminative information with category guided part.

We applied it to two different kinds of biometric recognition tasks, face recognition and gait recognition in Yale, FERET, ORL, AR and OA-ISIR-A. The results demonstrate its effectiveness and outperforms many other methods. The category guided part of our method can be easily plugged into other manifold learning algorithms as a supplement.

Acknowledgements. The work described in this paper was partially supported by the National Natural Science Foundation of China (Grant no. 61173131, 91118005, 11202249), Program for Changjiang Scholars and Innovative Research Team in University (Grant No. IRT1196) and the Fundamental Research Funds for the Central Universities (Grant No. CDJZR12098801, CDJRC091101 and CDJZR11095501).

References

1. Belkin, M., Niyogi, P.: Laplacian eigenmaps for dimensionality reduction and data representation. Neural Comput. **15**(6), 1373–1396 (2003)
2. Yan, S., Xu, D., Zhang, B., Zhang, H.J., Yang, Q., Lin, S.: Graph embedding and extensions: A general framework for dimensionality reduction. IEEE Trans. Pattern Anal. Mach. Intell. **29**(1), 40–51 (2007)
3. Huang, S., Cai, C., Zhang, Y.: Dimensionality reduction by using sparse reconstruction embedding. In: Qiu, G., Lam, K.M., Kiya, H., Xue, X.-Y., Kuo, C.-C.J., Lew, M.S. (eds.) PCM 2010, Part II. LNCS, vol. 6298, pp. 167–178. Springer, Heidelberg (2010)
4. Lan, C., Jing, X., Zhang, D., Gao, S., Yang, J.: Discriminant subclass-center manifold preserving projection for face feature extraction. In: 2011 18th IEEE International Conference on Image Processing, pp. 3013–3016. IEEE (2011)
5. Huang, S., Elgammal, A., Huangfu, L., Yang, D., Zhang, X.: Globality-locality preserving projections for biometric data dimensionality reduction. In: Proceedings of the IEEE Conference on Computer Vision and Pattern Recognition Workshops, vol. 53, pp. 15–20 (2014)
6. Turk, M., Pentland, A.: Eigenfaces for recognition. J. Cogn. Neurosci. **3**(1), 71–86 (1991)
7. Belhumeur, P.N., Hespanha, J.P., Kriegman, D.J.: Eigenfaces vs. fisherfaces: recognition using class specific linear projection. IEEE Trans. Pattern Anal. Mach. Intell. **19**(7), 711–720 (1997)
8. He, X., Niyogi, P.: Locality preserving projections. Neural Inf. Process. Syst. **16**, 153 (2004)
9. He, X., Cai, D., Yan, S., Zhang, H.-J.: Neighborhood preserving embedding. In: Tenth IEEE International Conference on Computer Vision Volume 1, vol. 2, 1208–1213 (2005)
10. Qiao, L., Chen, S., Tan, X.: Sparsity preserving projections with applications to face recognition. Pattern Recogn. **43**(1), 331–341 (2010)
11. Belkin, M., Niyogi, P.: Laplacian eigenmaps and spectral techniques for embedding and clustering. In: NIPS, vol. 14, pp. 585–591 (2001)
12. Timofte, R., Van Gool, L.: Sparse representation based projections. In: 22nd British Machine Vision Conference, pp. 61.1–61.12 (2011)
13. Liu, J., Ji, S., Ye, J., et al.: Slep: sparse learning with efficient projections. Ariz. State Univ. **6**, 491 (2009)
14. Phillips, P., Wechsler, H., Huang, J., Rauss, P.J.: The FERET database and evaluation procedure for face-recognition algorithms (1998)
15. Martinez, A.M.: The AR face database. CVC Tech. Rep. **24** (1998)
16. Wolf, L., Hassner, T., Taigman, Y.: Effective unconstrained face recognition by combining multiple descriptors and learned background statistics. IEEE Trans. Pattern Anal. Mach. Intell. **33**(10), 1978–1990 (2011)
17. Tsuji, A., Makihara, Y., Yagi, Y.: Silhouette transformation based on walking speed for gait identification. In: 2010 IEEE Conference on Computer Vision and Pattern Recognition (CVPR), pp. 717–722. IEEE (2010)

Sparse Nuclear Norm Two Dimensional Principal Component Analysis

Yudong Chen, Zhihui Lai$^{(\boxtimes)}$, and Ye Zhang

The College of Computer Science and Software Engineering,
Shenzhen University, Shenzhen 518060, China
lai_zhi_hui@163.com

Abstract. Feature extraction is an important way to improve the performance of image recognition. Compared to most of feature extraction methods, the 2-D principal component analysis (2-DPCA) better preserves the structural information of images since it is unnecessary to transform the small size image matrices into high dimensional vectors during the calculation process. In order to improve the robustness of 2-DPCA, nuclear norm-based 2-DPCA (N-2-DPCA) was proposed using nuclear norm as matrix distance measurement. However, 2-DPCA and N-2-DPCA lack the function of sparse feature extraction and selection. Thus, in this paper, we extend N-2-DPCA to sparse case, which is called SN-2-DPCA, for sparse subspace learning. To efficiently solve the model, an alternatively iterative algorithm will also be presented. The proposed SN-2-DPCA would be compared with some advanced 1-D and 2-D feature extraction methods using four well-known data sets. Experimental results indicate the competitive advantage of SN-2-DPCA.

Keywords: Sparse feature extraction · Nuclear norm · Image recognition

1 Introduction

There are many different types of feature extraction methods designed for image recognition [1], palmprint identification [2] and so on. The traditional methods include principal component analysis (PCA) [3, 4] and locally linear embedding (LLE) [5]. After extracting features from data points or image matrices by these methods, the efficiency and effectiveness of classification will be improved to a certain extent. However, the traditional methods get used to transform the 2-D image matrices into 1-D vectors which slow down the speed of computation. In addition, the structural information of image matrices is consequently destroyed.

To explore more structural information from image matrices, the feature extraction methods based on 2-D images were proposed such as 2-D linear discriminate analysis (2-DLDA) [6, 7], 2-D locality preserving projections (2-DLPP) [8], 2-D principal component analysis (2-DPCA) [9]. 2-DPCA is the two-dimensional extension of PCA. The traditional PCA method transforms image matrices to vectors in the first stage and then constructs a covariance matrix to compute the projection matrix. In contrast, 2-DPCA directly solves a covariance matrix based on image matrices and therefore speeds up the computation process. Experimental results demonstrate that 2-DPCA

© Springer International Publishing AG 2016
Z. You et al. (Eds.): CCBR 2016, LNCS 9967, pp. 547–555, 2016.
DOI: 10.1007/978-3-319-46654-5_60

performs better than PCA in feature extraction and face recognition [9]. Since the projections can be learned from both sides of the image matrix, the bilateral projection-based 2-DPCA (B2-DPCA) [10, 11] was further proposed for bilinear dimensionality reduction.

Nuclear norm computes the sum of the singular values of matrix and it was efficiently applied in pattern recognition such as robust PCA [12], low rank matrix recovery [13–15]. Since the optimal problems to constraint the rank of matrix is non-convex and difficult to solve, it can be approximated by an alternative nuclear norm [16]. To solve the optimal problems with nuclear norm, [17] has proposed an effective iterative algorithm. Moreover, experimental results show that the nuclear norm is more robust than L_1-norm and Frobenius norm as matrix distance measurement [18]. In order to improve the robustness of 2-DPCA, nuclear norm-based 2-DPCA (N-2-DPCA) [19] replaces Frobenius norm in 2-DPCA with nuclear norm.

Recently, sparse learning attracted great attention in machine learning. Sparse linear embedding (SLE) [20], sparse two-dimensional locality discriminant projections (S2DLDP) [21] and sparsity preserving projections (SPP) [22] were presented to obtain sparse projections for extracting features. The advantage of sparse learning is that most of elements of the optimal projections are zero and turn out to highlight the main features of images.

In this paper, in order to explore structural information of images, improve the robustness and obtain sparse projections simultaneously, we propose a sparse nuclear norm based 2-D method called SN-2-DPCA. The contributions of this paper include: (1) Inspired by the sparse principal component analysis (SPCA) [23] and N-2-DPCA, we proposed a novel regularized regression learning model for robust sparse regression learning, which generalizes the previous nuclear norm based regression model. And, an alternatively iterative algorithm is presented. (2) By adding L_1-norm and L_2-norm to the regression equation, the model can select more discriminative projection vectors for feature extraction, which is proved to be more robust than conventional PCA-based methods by a number of experiments.

2 Alternative Definition of Nuclear Norm

In this paper, given data matrix $X \in R^{m \times n \times s}$, m denotes the row number of data points and n denotes the columns number of data points. We use s to denote the number of data points. X_i denotes the i-th data point/matrix. The purpose of 2-D-based methods is to obtain the $n \times r$ projection matrix for dimensionality reduction.

Nuclear norm is defined as the sum of the singular values of matrix. In [17], nuclear norm is alternatively defined as

$$\|X_i\|_* = \|Z_i X_i\|_F^2 \tag{1}$$

where $Z_i = \left(X_i X_i^T\right)^{-1/4}$.

3 Sparse Model and Algorithm

3.1 Regression Representation of N-2-DPCA

In this section, we will improve N-2-DPCA to sparse case. We relax one of the projection matrix in the optimization model of N-2-DPCA, which will be derived a novel model as follow

$$\min_{A,B} \sum_{i=1}^{s} \left\| X_i - X_i A B^T \right\|_* \qquad \text{s.t.} \quad B^T B = I_r \qquad (2)$$

where $A, B \in R^{n \times r}$. In order to obtain sparse solution using the Elastic Net algorithm, a regularization term is added for obtaining discriminative projection matrix. Thus, we have the following regularized optimization problem:

$$\min_{A,B} \sum_{i=1}^{s} \left\| X_i - X_i A B^T \right\|_* + \alpha \|A\|_2 \qquad \text{s.t.} \quad B^T B = I_r \qquad (3)$$

where $\alpha > 0$. (3) converts the N-2-DPCA to a generalized regression model. However, (3) still cannot produce the sparse solution. Thus, the Elastic Net penalty is used to generate the sparse loadings, which will be introduced in Sect. 3.2.

3.2 Sparse Nuclear Norm-Based Model

In order to achieve the sparse projection matrix, we use the Elastic Net penalty on (3), which can shrink the coefficients of the model thus generate sparse solution. Hence, we have the following optimization problem:

$$\min_{A,B} \sum_{i=1}^{s} \left\| X_i - X_i A B^T \right\|_* + \alpha \|A\|_2 + \sum_{l=1}^{r} \gamma_l |a_l| \qquad \text{s.t.} \quad B^T B = I_r \qquad (4)$$

where $\gamma_l > 0$ and a_l denotes the l-th column vector of A.

Using above model, we are able to obtain the sparse projection matrix for extracting features from data matrices. In Sect. 3.3, we explain how to efficiently solve the model.

3.3 Iterative Algorithm

According to the alternative definition of nuclear norm, (4) is rewritten as

$$\min_{A,B} \sum_{i=1}^{s} \left\| W_i (X_i - X_i A B^T) \right\|_F^2 + \alpha \|A\|_2 + \sum_{l=1}^{r} \gamma_l |a_l| \qquad \text{s.t.} \quad B^T B = I_r \qquad (5)$$

where $W_i = \left((X_i - X_i A B^T)(X_i - X_i A B^T)^T \right)^{-1/4}$.

For fixed W_i, from (5), we can derive

$$\min_{A,B} \sum_{i=1}^{s} tr\left(W_i X_i X_i^T W_i^T - 2W_i X_i BA^T X_i^T W_i^T + W_i X_i AB^T BA^T X_i^T W_i^T\right)$$
$$+ \alpha tr(AA^T) + \sum_{l=1}^{r} \gamma_l |a_l| \tag{6}$$

Given B, from (6), we have the following problem

$$\min_{a} tr\left(A^T \left[\sum_{i=1}^{s} \left(X_i^T W_i^T W_i X_i\right)\right] A - 2A^T \sum_{i=1}^{s} \left(X_i^T W_i^T W_i X_i\right) B\right) + \alpha \|A\|_2 + \sum_{l=1}^{r} \gamma_l |a_l| \tag{7}$$

From Sect. 2.5 of [24], do SVD of $\sum_{i=1}^{s} \left(X_i^T W_i^T W_i X_i\right)$, we can obtain

$$\frac{\sum_{i=1}^{s} \left(X_i^T W_i^T W_i X_i\right) + \left(\sum_{i=1}^{s} \left(X_i^T W_i^T W_i X_i\right)\right)^T}{2} = UDU^T \tag{8}$$

So, (7) is similar to solve an Elastic Net problem:

$$\min_{a} \left\| \left(D^{\frac{1}{2}} U^T\right) B - \left(D^{\frac{1}{2}} U^T\right) A \right\|_2^2 + \alpha \|A\|_2^2 + \sum_{l=1}^{r} \gamma_l |a_l| \tag{9}$$

On the other hands, given A, $tr\left(W_i X_i X_i^T W_i^T\right)$ in (6) becomes a constant. In order to obtain B, we need to solve the maximization problem as follow:

$$\max_{B} tr\left(\sum_{i=1}^{s} B^T X_i^T W_i^T W_i X_i A\right) \quad \text{s.t.} \quad B^T B = I_r \tag{10}$$

From the Theorem 4 in [23], with SVD $\sum_{i=1}^{s} X_i^T W_i^T W_i X_i A = U_1 D_1 V_1^T$, then $B = U_1 V_1^T$. More details about the iterative algorithm are described in Sect. 3.4. According to the

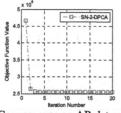

(a) Convergence on AR data set

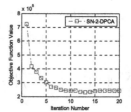

(b) Convergence on ORL data set

Fig. 1. Variations of objective function value by using iterative algorithm on two data sets.

proof of theorem 6 in [20], we know that the objective value in (4) will convergent by using the iterative algorithm. Figure 1 displays the descent speed of objective function value on AR and ORL data sets.

3.4   Program Code

An iterative algorithm designed to solve SN-2-DPCA is as follow.

```
Input: images X =[X₁,X₂,...Xₙ] , the number of iterations T ,
parameters α , r(r ≪ n) .
1: Initialize B=Iᵣ and W_{i=1:s} = I .
2: for j =1:T do
```

$$\text{Given } B, \text{ solve } \min_a \left\| \left(D^{\frac{1}{2}} U^T \right) B - \left(D^{\frac{1}{2}} U^T \right) A \right\|_2^2 + \alpha \|A\|_2^2 + \sum_{l=1}^r \gamma_l |a_l|$$

$$\text{Given } A, \text{ do SVD of } \sum_{i=1}^s X_i^T W_i^T W_i X_i A = U_1 D_1 V_1^T, \text{ then } B = U_1 V_1^T$$

$$\text{Update } W_i \text{ with } W_i = \left(\left(X_i - X_i A B^T \right) \left(X_i - X_i A B^T \right)^T \right)^{-\frac{1}{4}}$$

```
Output: compute Y_i = X_i A , Y =[Y₁,Y₂,...Yₙ] ∈ R^{m×r×s} .
```

The Matlab codes of this paper can be downloaded from http://www.scholat.com/laizhihui.

4   Experiment

In this section, we will compare the experimental results of six different feature extraction methods on AR data set, FERET data set, ORL data set and Yale data set for testing various situations. The feature extraction methods include PCA, sparse extension of PCA, i.e. SPCA, 2-D based method 2-DPCA, L_1-norm-based 2-DPCA (L_1-2-DPCA) [25] and nuclear norm-based method N-2-DPCA.

4.1   Data Sets Details

AR face data set [26] has 120 classes and each class includes 20 images used in the experiments. Every image has 50×40 pixels. For each classes of AR data set, we randomly chose T ($T = 6$) data points as training data and the remaining as testing data. **FERET** data set [27] has 200 individuals and each individual includes 7 images used in the experiments. Every image has 40×40 pixels. On FERET data set, we set $T = 4$. **ORL** data set is the same as in [21] which has 40 subjects and each subject includes 10 images used in the experiments. Every image has 46×46 pixels. On ORL data set, we set $T = 4$. **Yale** data set is the same as in [20] which has 15 individuals and each individual includes 11 images used in the experiments. Every image has 50×40 pixels. On Yale data set, we set $T = 6$. In order to test the robustness of the proposed method, we added 7×7 block or 10×10 block to the images. We report the average recognition rates under different cases.

4.2   Experimental Results Comparisons

On four data sets experiments, we used 1-NN classifier to perform classification. In order to present reliable results, in each experiment, the algorithms ran ten times to compute the average recognition rate. For SPCA and SN-2-DPCA, the parameter α utilized in Elastic Net varied from 10^{-8}, 10^{-7}, ..., 10^{8}.

Figure 2 displays the recognition rates of six algorithms on four data sets with 10×10 block. We can find that the proposed method obtains about 1%–17% improvements against other five methods on four data sets. From Table 1, we know that the proposed method did not perform the best when it was used for the original images. That is because we mainly focus on enhancing the robustness of the algorithm, so it is acceptable that the proposed method performed the same as other methods on the normal data sets. To prove this point, when we added 7×7 block or 10×10 block to the images, the proposed method showed the outstanding robustness and started to outperform other methods, which indicated that the proposed method was more robust

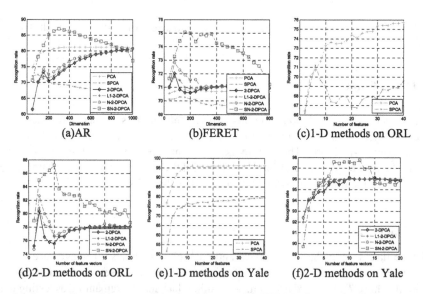

Fig. 2. Average recognition rate of six algorithms on AR, FERET, ORL and Yale data sets with 10×10 block (%). The independent variable on (a) and (b) is the desired dimension of images, on (c) and (e) is the desired number of features of image vectors and on (d) and (f) is the desired number of column of image matrices.

Table 1. Best average recognition rate on AR and FERET data sets with different block (%).

Method	AR data set			FERET data set		
	Original	7×7 block	10×10 block	Original	7×7 block	10×10 block
PCA	**90.72**	88.10	81.18	84.95	75.30	70.85
SPCA	82.52	76.57	72.51	74.52	70.63	70.32
2-DPCA	90.67	87.84	80.73	**86.32**	76.58	72.03
L_1-2-DPCA	90.64	87.84	80.75	86.23	76.75	71.78
N-2-DPCA	90.66	87.84	80.75	86.27	76.75	72.82
SN-2-DPCA	90.31	**88.42**	**87.07**	85.88	**76.85**	**75.10**

Table 2. Best average recognition rate on ORL and Yale data sets with different block (%).

Method	ORL data set			Yale data set		
	Original	7×7 block	10×10 block	Original	7×7 block	10×10 block
PCA	94.17	88.87	75.72	97.20	97.01	96.27
SPCA	84.54	75.88	71.21	87.07	79.87	79.20
2-DPCA	95.13	92.33	80.33	97.20	96.53	96.13
L_1-2-DPCA	95.12	92.46	80.88	97.47	96.53	96.00
N-2-DPCA	95.17	92.75	82.63	97.47	96.80	96.00
SN-2-DPCA	**95.33**	**92.79**	**87.21**	**98.27**	**98.00**	**97.73**

than the other methods. Furthermore, as shown in Table 2, the proposed method had better performance no matter in normal or noisy cases compared to the other methods. Based on all experimental results, we know that the SPCA obtains sparse solutions while reduces the efficiency. By extracting structural features from images and adding L_1-norm or nuclear norm to model, 2-DPCA, L_1-2-DPCA and N-2-DPCA increase the effectiveness against PCA. The proposed method appropriately preserves their advantages and therefore improves the robustness.

5 Conclusion

In this paper, a sparse and robust 2-D regularized model is presented by modifying the conventional 2-DPCA model and adding L_1-norm and L_2-norm for sparse subspace learning. The iterative algorithm is designed to solve the generalized regularized learning problem by integrating the Elastic Net and SVD. Experimental results indicate that the robustness of SN-2-DPCA is enhanced since we use the nuclear norm as the main metric and sparse regularized learning for feature extraction.

References

1. Hong, Z.Q.: Algebraic feature extraction of image for recognition. Pattern Recognit. **24**, 211–219 (1991)
2. You, J., Li, W., Zhang, D.: Hierarchical palmprint identification via multiple feature extraction. Pattern Recognit. **35**, 847–859 (2002)
3. Abdi, H., Williams, L.J.: Principal component analysis. Wiley Interdiscip. Rev. Comput. Stat. **2**, 433–459 (2010)
4. Jolliffe, I.T.: Principal Component Analysis, vol. 87, pp. 41–64. Springer, Berlin (2010)
5. Roweis, S.T., Saul, L.K.: Nonlinear dimensionality reduction by locally linear embedding. Science **290**, 2323–2326 (2009)
6. Noushath, S., Kumar, G.H., Shivakumara, P.: (2D) 2 LDA: an efficient approach for face recognition. Pattern Recognit. **39**, 1396–1400 (2006)
7. Zheng, W.S., Lai, J.H., Li, S.Z.: 1D-LDA vs. 2D-LDA: When is vector-based linear discriminant analysis better than matrix-based? Pattern Recognit. **41**, 2156–2172 (2008)
8. Chen, S., Zhao, H., Kong, M., Luo, B.: 2D-LPP: A two-dimensional extension of locality preserving projections. Neurocomputing **70**, 912–921 (2007)
9. Yang, J., Zhang, D., Frangi, A.F., Yang, J.Y.: Two-dimensional PCA: a new approach to appearance-based face representation and recognition. IEEE Trans. Pattern Anal. Mach. Intell. **26**, 131–137 (2004)
10. Yang, J., Liu, C.: Horizontal and Vertical 2DPCA-based discriminant analysis for face verification on a large-scale database. IEEE Trans. Inf. Forensics Secur. **2**, 781–792 (2008)
11. Kong, H., Li, X., Wang, L., Teoh, E.K., Wang, J.G., Venkateswarlu, R.: Generalized 2D principal component analysis. In: Proceedings of the IJCNN 2005 (2005)
12 Zhou, Z., Jin, Z.: Double nuclear norm-based robust principal component analysis for image disocclusion and object detection. Neurocomputing **205**, 481–489 (2016)
13. Candès, E.J., Recht, B.: Exact matrix completion via convex optimization. Found. Comput. Math. **9**, 717–772 (2008)
14. Zhang, F., Yang, J., Tai, Y., Tang, J.: Double nuclear norm-based matrix decomposition for occluded image recovery and background modeling. Image Process. IEEE Trans. **24**, 1956–1966 (2015)
15. He, R., Sun, Z., Tan, T., Zheng, W.S.: Recovery of corrupted low-rank matrices via half-quadratic based nonconvex minimization. In: 2011 IEEE Conference on Computer Vision and Pattern Recognition (CVPR). IEEE (2011)
16. Fazel, M., Hindi, H., Boyd, S.P.: A rank minimization heuristic with application to minimum order system approximation. In: Proceedings of the 2001 American Control Conference (2001)
17. Fornasier, M., Rauhut, H., Ward, R.: Low-rank matrix recovery via iteratively reweighted least squares minimization. SIAM J. Optim. **21**, 1614–1640 (2011)
18. Qian, J., Luo, L., Yang, J., Zhang, F., Lin, Z.: Robust nuclear norm regularized regression for face recognition with occlusion. Pattern Recognit. **48**, 3145–3159 (2015)
19. Zhang, F., Yang, J., Qian, J., Xu, Y.: Nuclear norm-based 2-DPCA for extracting features from images. IEEE Trans. Neural Networks Learn. Syst. **26**, 2247–2260 (2015)
20 Lai, Z., Wong, W.K., Xu, Y., Yang, J., Zhang, D.: Approximate orthogonal sparse embedding for dimensionality reduction. IEEE Trans. Neural Networks Learn. Syst. **27**, 1–13 (2015)
21. Lai, Z., Wan, M., Jin, Z., Yang, J.: Sparse two-dimensional local discriminant projections for feature extraction. Neurocomputing **74**, 629–637 (2011)

22. Yin, F., Jiao, L.C., Shang, F., Wang, S., Hou, B.: Fast fisher sparsity preserving projections. Neural Comput. Appl. **23**, 691–705 (2012)
23. Zou, H., Hastie, T., Tibshirani, R.: Sparse Principal Component Analysis. J. Comput. Graph. Stat. **15**, 265–286 (2014)
24. Zhou, T., Tao, D., Wu, X.: Manifold elastic net: a unified framework for sparse dimension reduction. Data Min. Knowl. Discov. **22**, 340–371 (2011)
25 Li, X., Pang, Y., Yuan, Y.: L1-norm-based 2DPCA. IEEE Trans. Syst. Man Cybern. Part B Cybern. A Publ. IEEE Syst. Man Cybern. Soc. **40**, 1170–1175 (2010)
26. Martinez, A.M.: The AR face database. CVC Technical report 24 (1998)
27. Jonathon Phillips, P., Moon, H., Rizvi, S.A., Rauss, P.J.: The FERET evaluation methodology for face-recognition algorithms. IEEE Trans. Pattern Anal. Mach. Intell. **22**, 1090–1104 (2000)

Unsupervised Subspace Learning via Analysis Dictionary Learning

Ke Gao, Pengfei Zhu$^{(\boxtimes)}$, Qinghua Hu, and Changqing Zhang

School of Computer Science and Technology, Tianjin University,
Tianjin 300072, China
{gaokeji,zhupengfei,huqinghua,zhangchangqing}@tju.edu.cn

Abstract. The ubiquitous digit devices, sensors and social networks bring tremendous high-dimensional data. The high-dimensionality leads to high time complexity, large storage burden, and degradation of the generalization ability. Subspace learning is one of the most effective ways to eliminate the curse of dimensionality by projecting the data to a low-dimensional feature subspace. In this paper, we proposed a novel unsupervised feature dimension reduction method via analysis dictionary learning. By learning an analysis dictionary, we project a sample to a low-dimensional space and the feature dimension is the number of atoms in the dictionary. The coding coefficient vector is used as the low-dimensional representation of data because it reflects the distribution on the synthesis dictionary atoms. Manifold regularization is imposed on the low-dimensional representation of data to keep the locality of the original feature space. Experiments on four datasets show that the proposed unsupervised dimension reduction model outperforms the state-of-the-art methods.

Keywords: Dimension reduction · Unsupervised learning · Dictionary learning

1 Introduction

In the field of computer vision and pattern recognition, the explosive growth of high-dimensional image and video data stimulates the demand for subspace learning. The high-dimensional data may increase the parameters of the learning machines, and therefore easily lead to over-fitting and degradation of the generalization ability. Additionally, the curse of dimensionality also increases the time complexity and storage burden.

Until now, researchers have developed a variety of subspace learning methods. Generally, according to the availability of the label information, subspace learning methods can be subclassified into three types, i.e., unsupervised [1], semi-supervised [2] and supervised [3] cases. Moreover, an instance usually has complex semantics and can be assigned to multiple labels. Hence, subspace learning algorithms are developed to reduce the feature dimension in multi-label circumstance [4]. One object can be represented by different features, described from

© Springer International Publishing AG 2016
Z. You et al. (Eds.): CCBR 2016, LNCS 9967, pp. 556–563, 2016.
DOI: 10.1007/978-3-319-46654-5_61

multi-views or collected from multi-sources. In this case, multi-view dimension reduction models are proposed to project samples to a low-dimensional feature subspace by using multi-view correlations [5]. All the linear or nonlinear subspace learning methods can be easily extended by the kernel tricks, e.g., kernel principle component analysis [6].

Among all the dimension reduction methods, unsupervised subspace learning is the most challenging due to the lack of label information. Principle component analysis (PCA) is a typical unsupervised dimension reduction method, which aims to find a group of orthogonal basis vectors by maximizing the covariance of the input data points [1]. Laplacian eigenmaps (LE) learns a projection that keeps the local neighborhood relations of a graph in high-dimension space [7]. Local preserving projections (LPP) is a linear variant of Laplacian eigenmaps [8]. Sparsity preserving projections (SPP) aims to preserve the sparse reconstruction relationship of the data [9]. In [10], a projection matrix is learned by minimizing the sparse representation residual in the projected low-dimensional feature subspace. When the training data is corrupted by sparse or gross noises, robust subspace learning methods are proposed, e.g., robust PCA [11], corruptions tolerant discriminant analysis [12]. Locality-preserving robust nonnegative patch alignment (LP-RNA) is a locally sparse graph to encode the local geometric structure of the manifold embedded in high-dimensional space [13]. When there are missing entries in the training data, subspace learning models are developed for data with partial information [14].

Subspace learning is a kind of feature extraction technique, which extracts low-dimensional salient features by maximizing covariance, preserving locality or reconstruction relationships, etc. Sparse representation has been widely used in signal reconstruction, face recognition and image classification. The coding coefficients reflect the distribution on the dictionary atoms and therefore become efficient features in image classification [15], texture classification [16], etc. Besides, coding coefficients alleviate the effect of noises and outliers, and therefore are more robust.

In this paper, motivated by the success of representation coefficients in classification task, we proposed a novel unsupervised subspace learning method by analysis-synthesis dictionary learning (ASDL). The analysis dictionary codes the query sample and the coefficients are used as the low-dimensional representation of data. By manifold regularization, the learned low-dimensional representation preserves the locality as well. Alternation minimization is used to solve the proposed analysis dictionary learning model with guaranteed convergence. Experiments on four benchmark face image databases show that ASDL outperforms the state-of-the-art unsupervised subspace learning algorithms.

2   Analysis Dictionary Learning

Subspace learning learns a low-dimensional representation of data, which keeps the intrinsic structure in the high-dimensional feature space. In this paper, we use coding coefficients as a low-dimensional representation of data because they reflect the data distribution on the dictionary atoms and are robust to noises. If we consider the dictionary atoms as the representative bases of different classes, the coding coefficients actually reflect the pseudo label distribution. Here, different from the existing subspace learning methods that extract salient features, we learn a new low-dimensional representation of data. Then the subspace learning problem is converted to find a matrix that can project one sample to the representation coefficients space. One effective way is to learn an analysis dictionary.

2.1   Problem Formulation

Let $\mathbf{X} \in \mathbb{R}^{\mathbf{d}} \times \mathbf{n} = \{\mathbf{x_1}, \mathbf{x_2}, ..., \mathbf{x_n}\}$ be the data matrix, and each column $\mathbf{x}_i \in \mathbb{R}^d$ be a sample. Given an analysis dictionary $\mathbf{V} \in \mathbb{R}^{\mathbf{k \times d}}$, where k is the number of dictionary atoms, $\mathbf{X}$ can be projected to the coefficient space $\mathbf{A} \in \mathbb{R}^{k \times n}$.

$$\mathbf{A} = \mathbf{VX} \tag{1}$$

The dictionary $\mathbf{V}$ can analytically code the signals and therefore is very efficient. We aim to seek a projection matrix $\mathbf{V} \in \mathbb{R}^{k \times d}$ such that the low-dimensional representation $\mathbf{A}$ can well characterize the discriminant structure embedded in high-dimensional data.

In signal reconstruction, $\mathbf{X}$ can be reconstructed by a synthesis dictionary $\mathbf{U} \in \mathbb{R}^{d \times k}$ as $\mathbf{X} = \mathbf{UA}$. The synthesis dictionary learning can be formulated as

$$\begin{aligned} \min \ & \| \mathbf{X} - \mathbf{UA} \|_F^2 \\ s.t. \ & \| \mathbf{u}_i \|_2^2 \leq 1, i = 1, 2, \ldots, k \end{aligned} \tag{2}$$

where $\mathbf{u}_i$ is the ith atom of the synthesis dictionary. The constraint on $\mathbf{U}$ is introduced to avoid the trivial solution. If we learn both an analysis dictionary and a synthesis dictionary, then a coupled dictionary learning model can be modeled as

$$\begin{aligned} \min \ & \|\mathbf{X} - \mathbf{UVX}\|_F^2 \\ s.t. \ & \|\mathbf{u}_i\|_2^2 \leq 1, i = 1, 2, ..., k \end{aligned} \tag{3}$$

By solving the optimization problem in Eq. (3), we can learn an analysis dictionary $\mathbf{V}$. Then, the low-dimensional representation can be obtained, i.e., $\mathbf{VX}$. The reduced feature dimension is k, which is the number of atoms in the dictionary. In [17], it is proved that $2k$ projection vectors are sufficient for the independence preservation of any k class data sampled from a union of independent subspaces. As the number of classes is unknown in unsupervised subspace learning, the option of feature dimension is still an unsolved problem.

The low-dimensional representation should preserve the locality as well, i.e., the spatial relationships of the data points in the raw feature space should be kept. Manifold regularization is imposed on the low-dimensional representation $\mathbf{VX}$. Then, we model manifold regularized analysis dictionary learning as

$$\begin{aligned} \min \ & \| \mathbf{X} - \mathbf{UVX} \|_F^2 + \lambda tr(\mathbf{VXLX}^T\mathbf{V}^T) \\ s.t. \ & \| \mathbf{u}_i \|_2^2 \leq 1, i = 1, 2, \ldots, k \end{aligned} \tag{4}$$

(a) The synthesis dictionary **U**   (b) The analysis dictionary **V**

Fig. 1. (a) the learned synthesis dictionary **U**; (b) the learned analysis dictionary **V**.

where $\mathbf{L} = \mathbf{D} - \mathbf{W}$ is a Laplacian matrix, and λ is a positive scalar constant. $\mathbf{W}$ is the affinity matrix that reflects the sample relationship. $\mathbf{D}$ is a diagonal matrix and the ith diagonal element of $\mathbf{D}$ is $\sum_{j=1}^{n} w_{ij}$.

We give a visual result of the analysis dictionary $\mathbf{V}$ and the synthesis dictionary $\mathbf{U}$ in Fig. 1.

2.2 Optimization and Algorithm

The model in Eq. (4) is generally non-convex. By introducing a variable matrix $\mathbf{A}$ to Eq. (4), we can get the following relaxed model

$$\min_{\mathbf{U},\mathbf{V},\mathbf{A}} \parallel \mathbf{X} - \mathbf{UA} \parallel_F^2 + \alpha \parallel \mathbf{A} - \mathbf{VX} \parallel_F^2 + \lambda tr(\mathbf{ALA}^T)$$
$$s.t. \parallel \mathbf{u}_i \parallel_2^2 \leq 1, i = 1, 2, \ldots, k \tag{5}$$

where α is a positive scalar constant. We use alteration minimization method to solve the optimization problem in Eq. (5). The analysis dictionary $\mathbf{V}$ and the synthesis dictionary $\mathbf{U}$ are initialized as random matrices with unit Frobenius norm. Then we iteratively update $\mathbf{A}$, $\mathbf{U}$ and $\mathbf{V}$, respectively. The detailed optimization procedures are summarized as follows:

Subproblem A. Fix $\mathbf{U}$ and $\mathbf{V}$, and update $\mathbf{A}$. We need to solve the following problem:

$$\widehat{\mathbf{A}} = \arg\min \parallel \mathbf{X} - \mathbf{UA} \parallel_F^2 + \alpha \parallel \mathbf{A} - \mathbf{VX} \parallel_F^2 + \lambda tr(\mathbf{ALA}^T) \tag{6}$$

By setting the derivative of Eq. (6) with respect to $\mathbf{A}$ to zero, we can get

$$(\mathbf{U}^T\mathbf{U} + \alpha\mathbf{I})\mathbf{A} + \lambda\mathbf{AL} = (\mathbf{U}^T + \alpha\mathbf{V})\mathbf{X} \tag{7}$$

The above equation is a standard Sylvester equation and it has a unique solution. After $\mathbf{A}$ is updated, we need to update $\mathbf{U}$ and $\mathbf{V}$. The optimization problem becomes:

$$\hat{\mathbf{U}} = \arg\min_{\mathbf{U}} \parallel \mathbf{X} - \mathbf{UA} \parallel_F^2 \quad s.t. \parallel \mathbf{u}_i \parallel_2^2 \leq 1, i = 1, 2, \ldots, k \tag{8}$$

$$\hat{\mathbf{V}} = \arg\min_{\mathbf{V}} \parallel \mathbf{A} - \mathbf{VX} \parallel_F^2 \tag{9}$$

Subproblem U. For the problem in Eq. (8), a variable matrix $\mathbf{H}$ can be introduced and the optimal solution of $\mathbf{U}$ can be got by Alternating Direction method of Multipliers (ADMM) [18].

$$\hat{\mathbf{U}} = \arg\min_{\mathbf{U}} \parallel \mathbf{X} - \mathbf{UA} \parallel_F^2$$
$$s.t. \mathbf{H} = \mathbf{U}, \parallel \mathbf{h}_i \parallel_2^2 \leq 1 \tag{10}$$

Then the $\hat{\mathbf{U}}$ is got by the following iteration steps:

$$\begin{cases} \mathbf{U}^{t+1} = \arg\min_{\mathbf{U}} \parallel \mathbf{X} - \mathbf{UA}^t \parallel_{\mathrm{F}}^2 + \beta \parallel \mathbf{U} - \mathbf{H}^t + \mathbf{S}^t \parallel_{F}^2 \\ \mathbf{H}^{t+1} = \arg\min_{\mathbf{H}} \beta \parallel \mathbf{U}^t - \mathbf{H} + \mathbf{S}^t \parallel_{\mathrm{F}}^2 \quad s.t. \parallel \mathbf{h}_i \parallel_2^2 \leq 1 \\ \mathbf{S}^{t+1} = \mathbf{S}^t + \mathbf{U}^{t+1} - \mathbf{H}^{t+1}, update \; \beta \; if \; appropriate. \end{cases} \quad (11)$$

Subproblem V. The analysis dictionary $\mathbf{V}$ is updated by solving the optimization problem in Eq. (9). The closed-form solution is

$$\hat{\mathbf{V}} = \mathbf{A}\mathbf{X}^T(\mathbf{X}\mathbf{X}^T + \varepsilon\mathbf{I})^{-1} \quad (12)$$

where ε is a positive scalar constant.

In each iteration, $\mathbf{A}$ has a unique solution and is updated by Eq. (7). $\mathbf{U}$ is updated by solving Eq. (11) and ADMM will rapidly converge. For updating $\mathbf{V}$, we also have a closed-form solution to solve the optimization problem.

2.3   Convergence Analysis

We use alternation minimization to solve the problem in Eq. (5). The optimization of $\mathbf{A}$ and $\mathbf{V}$ is convex, in the meantime both $\mathbf{A}$ and $\mathbf{V}$ have a unique solution. For synthesis dictionary, the ADMM algorithm can guarantee that the optimization of $\mathbf{U}$ converges to the optimum solution. According to the convergence of alternation optimization, as all the three subproblems are convex, the problem in Eq. (5) can converge.

2.4   Time Complexity Analysis

The time complexity of ASDL is composed of three parts, i.e., the updating of $\mathbf{A}$, $\mathbf{U}$ and $\mathbf{V}$ in each iteration. $\mathbf{A}$ has a unique solution and the time complexity of updating $\mathbf{A}$ is $O(n^3)$, where n is the number of samples. Let T_1 be the iteration number of the ADMM algorithm. The time complexity of updating $\mathbf{U}$ is $O(T_1(kdn + k^3 + k^2d + d^2k))$, where k is the number of atoms in the synthesis dictionary $\mathbf{U}$, and d is the dimension of samples. $\mathbf{V}$ also has a closed-form solution and the complexity of updating $\mathbf{V}$ is $O(knd + nd^2 + d^3)$.

3   Experimental Analysis

In this section, we evaluate the performance of the proposed analysis-synthesis dictionary learning (ASDL) on four benchmark datasets with comparison to five representative unsupervised dimension reduction methods, including principal component analysis (PCA), local preserving projections (LPP), Laplacian eigenmaps (LE), sparsity preserving projections (SPP), and the method put forward from ICPR 2010.

3.1   Parameter Setting

For PCA, the only model parameter is the subspace dimension. For LPP and LE, the neighborhood size in the experiment is set as 5 for all the four datasets. For SPP, we set the $\lambda = 0.1$. And for the method in ICPR2010, we set the $\lambda_1 = 0.0005$, $\lambda_2 = 2$. For the proposed method, only two parameters (α, λ) need to be set. We set $\alpha = 0.002$, $\lambda = 0.0001$ on dataset AR, Extended Yale B and Cmu Multi-PIE, while set $\alpha = 0.001$, $\lambda = 0.0001$ on LFW.

3.2   AR

AR face database [19] contains over 4000 face pictures of 154 people(82 males, 74 females). For each person there are two sections, and both sections include 13 images. These images include front view of faces with different expressions, illuminations and occlusions. In our work, we use a subset of the AR face database which include 1400 images of 100 people (50 males, 50 females) and each individual has 14 images. The original size of the images is 165×120 pixels.

Figure 2(a) shows that ASDL has the highest recognition accuracy among six approaches on the AR database when the feature dimension is more than 30. But ASDL is worse than PCA, LPP and ICPR 2010 when the feature dimension is less than 30.

3.3   Extended Yale B

The Extended Yale Face Database B [20] contains 2432 images of 38 people. For each person, there are 64 pictures taken under various laboratory-controlled lighting conditions. The original size of the images is 192×168 pixels. In this experiment, we have 1216 training images and 1216 testing images. The recognition rates are shown in Fig. 2(b).

The figure shows that ASDL still obtains the highest recognition accuracy among six approaches on the Extend Yale B database when the feature dimension is more than 30. ASDL is worse than SPP and ICPR 2010 when the feature dimension is less than 30.

3.4   CMU Multi-PIE

The CMU-PIE database [21] contains more than 40,000 facial images of 68 people. The images were acquired over different poses, under variable illumination conditions, and with different facial expressions. In this experiment, we use a subset include 1743 images of the database. The original size of the images is 100×82 pixels.

In this work, we have 747 training images and 996 testing images. And the recognition rates are shown in Fig. 2(c). From the result, we can learn that when feature dimension is more than 60, ASDL can achieve the best performance. Both ASDL and SPP perform better than other methods on CMU-PIE.

3.5   LFW

The LFW database [22] contains more than 13000 facial images of 1680 persons. In our work, we use a subset composed of 1580 images from 158 people and each individual has 10 images. The cropped image size is 121×121 pixels.

In this work, we have 1264 images for training and 316 for testing. The recognition rates are shown in Fig. 2(d). Figure 2(d) shows that ASDL outperforms others on CMU-PIE when the feature dimension is more than 20.

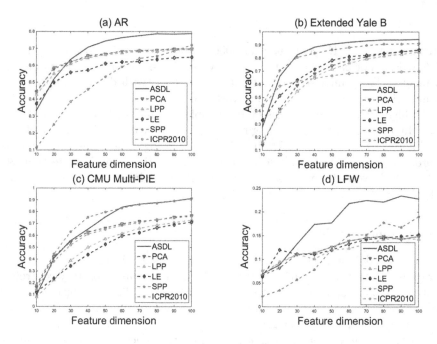

Fig. 2. The experiment results of all the four datasets.

4   Conclusion and Future Work

In this paper, we proposed a novel analysis-synthesis dictionary learning (ASDL) method for unsupervised dimension reduction. The synthesis dictionary is used to reconstruct the data while the analysis dictionary analytically codes the data. The coefficients coded by the analysis dictionary are used as the low-dimensional representation of data. To preserve the locality, we imposed manifold regularization on the low-dimensional representation, i.e., the coding coefficients. Experiment results show that ASDL is superior to the state-of-the-art unsupervised subspace learning algorithms. In the future, we will consider the multi-view case, and decrease the dimension of multi-view data.

References

1. Turk, M.A., Pentland, A.P.: Face recognition using eigenfaces. In: CVPR, pp. 586–591. IEEE (1991)
2. Huang, Y., Xu, D., Nie, F.: Semi-supervised dimension reduction using trace ratio criterion. IEEE Trans. Neural Netw. Learn. Syst. **23**(3), 519–526 (2010)
3. Ji, S., Ye, J.: Generalized linear discriminant analysis: a unified framework and efficient model selection. IEEE Trans. Neural Netw. **19**(10), 68–82 (2008)
4. Chen, Y.N., Lin, H.T.: Feature-aware label space dimension reduction for multi-label classification. NIPS **2**, 1529–1537 (2012)
5. Luo, Y., Tao, D., Ramamohanarao, K., Xu, C.: Tensor canonical correlation analysis for multi-view dimension reduction. IEEE Trans. Knowl. Data Eng. **27**(11), 3111–3124 (2015)
6. Mika, S., Schölkopf, B., Smola, A., Müller, K.R., Scholz, M., Rätsch, G.: Kernel PCA and de-noising in feature spaces. In: NIPS, pp. 536–542 (1999)
7. Belkin, M., Niyogi, P.: Laplacian eigenmaps for dimensionality reduction and data representation. Neural Comput. **15**(6), 1373–1396 (2003)
8. He, X.: Locality preserving projections. NIPS **45**(1), 186–197 (2005)
9. Qiao, L., Chen, S., Tan, X.: Sparsity preserving projections with applications to face recognition. Pattern Recogn. **43**(1), 331–341 (2010)
10. Zhang, L., Yang, M., Feng, Z., Zhang, D.: On the dimensionality reduction for sparse representation based face recognition. In: ICPR, pp. 1237–1240. IEEE (2010)
11. Candès, E.J., Li, X., Ma, Y., Wright, J.: Robust principal component analysis? J. ACM (JACM) **58**(3), 11 (2011)
12. Bao, B.K., Liu, G., Hong, R., Yan, S., Xu, C.: General subspace learning with corrupted training data via graph embedding. IEEE Trans. Image Process. **22**(11), 4380–4393 (2013)
13. You, X., Ou, W., Chen, C.L., Li, Q., Zhu, Z., Tang, Y.: Robust nonnegative patch alignment for dimensionality reduction. IEEE Trans. Neural Netw. Learn. Syst. **26**(11), 2760–2774 (2015)
14. Gonen, A., Rosenbaum, D., Eldar, Y.C., Shalev-Shwartz, S.: Subspace learning with partial information. J. Mach. Learn. Res. **17**(52), 1–21 (2016)
15. Yang, J., Yu, K., Gong, Y., Huang, T.: Linear spatial pyramid matching using sparse coding for image classification. In: CVPR, pp. 1794–1801. IEEE (2009)
16. Xie, J., Zhang, L., You, J., Shiu, S.: Effective texture classification by texton encoding induced statistical features. Pattern Recogn. **48**(2), 447–457 (2015)
17. Arpit, D., Nwogu, I., Govindaraju, V.: Dimensionality reduction with subspace structure preservation. NIPS **1**, 712–720 (2015)
18. Boyd, S., Parikh, N., Chu, E., Peleato, B., Eckstein, J.: Distributed optimization and statistical learning via the alternating direction method of multipliers. Found. Trends Mach. Learn. **3**(1), 1–122 (2011)
19. Martinez, A.M.: The AR face database. Cvc Technical report 24 (2010)
20. Comparison, D.L.: Extended yale face database b (b+)
21. Sim, T., Baker, S., Bsat, M.: The CMU pose, illumination, and expression (pie) database. In: FG, pp. 46–51 (2002)
22. Huang, G.B., Ramesh, M., Berg, T., Learned-Miller, E.: Labeled faces in the wild: a database for studying face recognition in unconstrained environments. Technical report 07–49, University of Massachusetts, Amherst, October 2007

Hybrid Manifold Regularized Non-negative Matrix Factorization for Data Representation

Peng Luo$^{(\boxtimes)}$, Jinye Peng, Ziyu Guan, and Jianping Fan

College of Information and Technology,
Northwest University of China, Xi'an 710127, China
luopengpeng@gmail.com, {pjy,ziyuguan,jfan}@nwu.edu.cn

Abstract. Non-negative Matrix Factorization (NMF) has received considerable attention due to its parts-based representation and interpretability of the issue correspondingly. On the other hand, data usually reside on a submanifold of the ambient space. One hopes to find a compact representation which captures the hidden semantic relationships between data items and reveals the intrinsic geometric structure simultaneously. However, it is difficult to estimate the intrinsic manifold of the data space in a principled way. In this paper, we propose a novel algorithm, called Hybrid Manifold Regularized Non-negative Matrix Factorization (HMNMF), for this purpose. In HMNMF, we develop a hybrid manifold regularization framework to approximate the intrinsic manifold by combining different initial guesses. Experiments on two real-world datasets validate the effectiveness of new method.

Keywords: Non-negative matrix factorization · Graph Laplacian · Manifold learning · Hessian

1 Introduction

Matrix factorization has become a widely used tool for data representation. The canonical methods include Principal Component Analysis (PCA), Linear Discriminant Analysis (LDA), Independent Component Analysis (ICA), Vector Quantization, LU-decomposition, QR-decomposition and Singular value Decomposition (SVD). The differences between them lie in the statistical properties attributable to the various constraints imposed on the component matrices and their hidden structures. However, these methods have the common property that there is no constraint in the sign of the elements in the factorized matrices. That is to say, the negative component is allowed in the representation.

By contrast, an emerging paradigm of matrix factorization is Non-negative Matrix Factorization (NMF) [15] which incorporates the nonnegative constraint in the factorized matrices. In NMF, each data item is reconstructed as an additive linear combination of nonnegative basis components. Therefore, NMF has the intuitive notion of combining parts to form a whole, which conforms to the cognitive process of human brains from psychological and physiological evidences.

© Springer International Publishing AG 2016
Z. You et al. (Eds.): CCBR 2016, LNCS 9967, pp. 564–574, 2016.
DOI: 10.1007/978-3-319-46654-5_62

Meanwhile, we have witnessed fast advance in manifold learning [3,19,22] in recent years. The data is more likely to reside on a low-dimensional sub-manifold which is embedded in a high dimensional ambient space [2]. In order to explore the underlying manifold structure, a lot of *manifold learning* algorithms have been proposed, such as Locally Linear Embedding (LLE) [16], ISOMAP [18], Laplacian Eigenmap [2], Locality Preserving Projection (LPP) [13] and Neighborhood Preserving Embedding (NPE) [12]. All these algorithms are motivated by the so-called locally invariant idea [10], i.e., the nearby samples usually have similar embeddings. Specifically, if two data points are close to each other in the intrinsic geometry of the submanifold, then their representation in semantic space are close to each other too [11].

In order to incorporate LPP technique [13] to NMF framework, Cai *et al.* proposed Graph Regularized NMF (GNMF) methods [6,7]. GNMF models the data space as a submanifold embedded in the ambient space and performs NMF on this manifold. Experimental results on several data sets show better performance than ordinary NMF approach. Despite GNMF's success, there are questions unanswered. GNMF used the common way to construct graph Laplacian, which could not estimate the intrinsic manifold of the data space. What's more, graph Laplacian has been identified to be biased towards a constant function due to its constant null space and the not well preserved local topology. Hence, a natural question is whether solving the two limitations of GNMF leads to a better method.

In this paper, we propose Hybrid Manifold Regularized Non-negative Matrix Factorization (HMNMF), which makes use of combining hybrid manifolds to approximate the true intrinsic manifold. To solve HMNMF, we develop an optimization method for HMNMF which optimizes the objective function with respect to the basic matrix and the encoding matrix alternately. Experimental results on two real-world data sets indicate that HMNMF is effective and outperforms baselines significantly.

2   Related Works

In this section, we primarily review some related works to our methods. We begin with a description of common notations in this paper.

2.1   Common Notations

In this paper, we use upper case letters in bold face and lower case letters in bold face to represent matrices and vectors, respectively. For matrix $\mathbf{M}$, we denote its (i,j)-th element by M_{ij}. The i-th element of a vector $\mathbf{a}$ is denoted by a_i. Given a set of N items, we use $\mathbf{X} \in \mathbb{R}_+^{M \times N}$ to denote the nonnegative data matrix where the i-th column vector is the feature vector for the i-th item. Throughout this paper, $\|\mathbf{M}\|_F$ denotes the Frobenius norm of matrix $\mathbf{M}$.

2.2   Non-negative Matrix Factorization

Non-negative Matrix Factorization (NMF) [15] is a matrix factorization algorithm that is designed for analyzing data matrices with nonnegative elements.

Given a non-negative data matrix $\mathbf{X}$ and a pre-specified positive integer $K < \min(M, N)$, the goal of NMF is to find two nonnegative matrices $\mathbf{U} \in \mathbb{R}_+^{M \times K}$ (basic matrix) and $\mathbf{V} \in \mathbb{R}_+^{K \times N}$ (encoding matrix) such that their product can well approximate the original data matrix:

$$\mathbf{X} \approx \mathbf{UV}.$$

When each column of $\mathbf{X}$ represents an item, NMF can be interpreted as approximating it by linear combinations of the column vectors in $\mathbf{U}$ using coefficients supplied by columns of $\mathbf{V}$. Therefore, the basis matrix $\mathbf{U}$ and the encoding matrix $\mathbf{V}$ together define a latent space representation for the data items. Due to the nonnegativity constraints, the NMF produces a so-called "additive parts-based" representation [15] of the data. Factors $\mathbf{U}$ and $\mathbf{V}$ are generally naturally sparse, thereby saving a great deal of storage when compared with the SVD's dense factors.

In order to quantify the difference between the original data $\mathbf{X}$ and the approximation $\mathbf{UV}$, Lee $et\ al.$ introduced two cost functions to measure the quality of the approximation: a least square cost and a divergence-style cost [15]. In this paper, we are focused on the least square cost which is defined as:

$$\mathcal{O} = \sum_{i=1}^{M} \sum_{j=1}^{N} \left(X_{ij} - \sum_{k=1}^{K} U_{ik} V_{kj} \right)^2 = \|\mathbf{X} - \mathbf{UV}\|_F^2. \tag{1}$$

The optimization problem in terms of $\mathcal{O}$ can be formulated as

$$\min_{\mathbf{U}, \mathbf{V}} \frac{1}{2} \|\mathbf{X} - \mathbf{UV}\|_F^2 \\ \text{s.t.} U_{ik} \geq 0, V_{kj} \geq 0, \quad \forall i, j, k. \tag{2}$$

The objective function $\mathcal{O}$ is not convex when both $\mathbf{U}$ and $\mathbf{V}$ are taken as variables. However, $\mathcal{O}$ is convex in $\mathbf{U}$ when $\mathbf{V}$ is fixed and vice versa. Lee and Seung [15] presented an iterative multiplicative update algorithm to find a local minimum of $\mathcal{O}$. In the t-th iteration, new values of $\mathbf{U}$ and $\mathbf{V}$ are calculated from their values in the last iteration:

$$U_{ik}^{t+1} = U_{ik}^t \frac{(\mathbf{X}(\mathbf{V}^t)^T)_{ik}}{(\mathbf{U}^t \mathbf{V}^t (\mathbf{V}^t)^T)_{ik}} \\ V_{kj}^{t+1} = V_{kj}^t \frac{((\mathbf{U}^{t+1})^T \mathbf{X})_{kj}}{((\mathbf{U}^{t+1})^T \mathbf{U}^{t+1} \mathbf{V}^t)_{kj}}. \tag{3}$$

By constructing auxiliary functions, it is proved that $\mathcal{O}$ is non-increasing under the above update rules.

2.3   Graph Regularized Non-negative Matrix Factorization

Cai *et al.* proposed a Graph Regularized Non-negative Matrix Factorization (GNMF) [6] method. Firstly, GNMF factorizes original data matrix $\mathbf{X}$ into a basic matrix $\mathbf{U}$ and an encoding matrix $\mathbf{V}$ with NMF. And then, GNMF constructs a nearest neighbor graph in a principled way to model the manifold structure. At last, combining the geometrically based regularizer with the original NMF objective function leads to the final Graph Regularized Non-negative Matrix Factorization (GNMF). The objective function of GNMF is formulated as follows:

$$\min_{\mathbf{U},\mathbf{V}} \|\mathbf{X} - \mathbf{U}\mathbf{V}^T\|_F^2 + \lambda Tr(\mathbf{V}^T\mathbf{L}\mathbf{V}),$$
$$\text{s.t.} U \geq 0, V \geq 0, \tag{4}$$

where the regularization parameter $\lambda \geq 0$ controls the smoothness of the new representation and $\mathbf{L} = \mathbf{D} - \mathbf{W}$ is graph Laplacian. $\mathbf{W}$ is the weight matrix and $\mathbf{D}$ is a diagonal matrix whose entries are column sums of $\mathbf{W}$, $\mathbf{D}_{ii} = \sum_j \mathbf{W}_{ij}$.

Because the objective function Eq. (4) is not convex in both $\mathbf{U}$ and $\mathbf{V}$ together, it is unrealistic to find the global minima for GNMF. [6] introduced the following updating rules to achieve local minima:

$$U_{ik}^{t+1} = U_{ik}^t \frac{(\mathbf{X}(\mathbf{V}^t)^T)_{ik}}{(\mathbf{U}^t\mathbf{V}^t(\mathbf{V}^t)^T)_{ik}}$$
$$V_{kj}^{t+1} = V_{kj}^t \frac{((\mathbf{U}^{t+1})^T\mathbf{X} + \lambda\mathbf{V}^t\mathbf{W})_{kj}}{((\mathbf{U}^{t+1})^T\mathbf{U}^{t+1}\mathbf{V}^t + \lambda\mathbf{V}^t\mathbf{D})_{kj}}. \tag{5}$$

The multiplicative updating rules (5) guarantee of the non-negativity of $\mathbf{U}$ and $\mathbf{V}$ and converge to a local optimum.

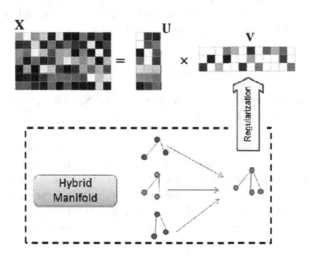

Fig. 1. An illustration of the work flow of the proposed approach.

3   Hybrid Manifold Regularized Non-negative Matrix Factorization

In this section, we introduce the Hybrid Manifold Regularized Non-negative Matrix Factorization (HMNMF) algorithm. Figure 1 illustrates the work flow of the proposed approach. We first obtain data matrix $\mathbf{X} \in \mathbb{R}_+^{M \times N}$. The data matrix is then factorized into basis matrix $\mathbf{U}$ and the encoding matrix $\mathbf{V}$. Because it is nontrivial to estimate the intrinsic manifold of the data space in a principle way, in the next, we approximate the intrinsic manifold with hybrid manifold. Details will be presented in the following section. At last, we constrain the encoding matrix $\mathbf{V}$ with hybrid manifold regulariztion and provide a good representation in the sense of semantic structure.

3.1   NMF with Hybrid Manifold Regularization

NMF tries to find a set of basis vectors for representing non-negative data. One might hope that the basic vectors can respect the intrinsic structure. The local invariance assumption [1] assumes that if two data points $\mathbf{x}_i$, $\mathbf{x}_j$ are close in the intrinsic geometrical of the data distribution, then $\mathbf{v}_i$ and $\mathbf{v}_j$, the representations of this two points with respect to the new basis, are also close to each other. This well known assumption plays an essential role in many algorithms including dimensionality reduction algorithms [1] and semi-supervised learning algorithms [4,23].

It is often the case that the local geometrical structure can be simple modeled through a nearest neighbor graph on a scatter of the data points. Given a graph with N data points, for each data point, we find its k nearest neighbors and then construct the weight matrix $\mathbf{W}^E$ on the graph. There are many choices to define matrix $\mathbf{W}^E$, here we use 0-1 weighting method, since it is simple and effective. Then we define the weight matrix $\mathbf{W}^E$ as follows:

$$W_{ij}^E = \begin{cases} 1, & \text{if } \mathbf{x}_i \in \mathcal{N}(\mathbf{x}_j) \ \text{or} \ \mathbf{x}_j \in \mathcal{N}(\mathbf{x}_i) \\ 0, & \text{otherwise} \end{cases} \tag{6}$$

where $\mathcal{N}(\mathbf{x}_i)$ indicates the k nearest neighbors of $\mathbf{x}_i$. The graph Laplacian of data graph is defined as $\mathbf{L}^E = \mathbf{D}^E - \mathbf{W^E}$, where $D_{ii}^E = \sum_j W_{ij}^E$ is the diagonal degree matrix.

On the other hand, *Self-expressiveness property* [8,9] of data shows that each data point in a union of subspace can be efficiently reconstructed by a combination of other points in the dataset. The key idea of Sparse subspace Clustering (SSC) [8,9] is that among the infinitely many possible representations of a data point in terms of other points, finds a sparse representation of each point in the dictionary of the other points. Specially, we can formulate data points as follow:

$$\mathbf{X} = \mathbf{XZ} \ s.t. \ diag(\mathbf{Z}) = 0 \tag{7}$$

where $\mathbf{Z}$ is the sparse representation of $\mathbf{X}$. Thus, we could find the optimal solution $\mathbf{Z}$ in Eq. (7) by minimizing a regression-like objective function with the sparse constraint [20]:

$$\min_{Z_{ij} \geq 0, Z_{ii} = 0} \gamma ||\mathbf{X} - \mathbf{XZ}||_F^2 + ||\mathbf{ZZ}^T||_1 \tag{8}$$

where $Z_{ij} \geq 0$ presents the nonnegative property of $\mathbf{Z}$, and $Z_{ii} = 0$ eliminates the trivial solution of writing a point as a linear combination of itself. Coefficient Z_{ij} represents the similarity between object $\mathbf{x}_i$ and $\mathbf{x}_j$. Furthermore, the regularization term $||\mathbf{ZZ}^T||_1$ can encourage more sparsity of the solution $\mathbf{Z}$ than ℓ_1 with less time consumption [20]. Equation (8) can be solved as a convex quadratic programming optimization problem. We choose to use Spectral Project Gradient (SPG) method [5] to solve it, for its simplicity and efficiency. For further details, please refer to [20]. Given the sparse representation $\mathbf{Z}$, the pair-wise affinity matrix is defined as [9]:

$$\mathbf{W}^S = \mathbf{Z} + \mathbf{Z}^T \tag{9}$$

According graph Laplacian $\mathbf{L}^S$ is:

$$\mathbf{L}^S = \mathbf{D}^S - \mathbf{W}^S \tag{10}$$

where $D_{ii}^S = \sum_j W_{ij}^S$ is the diagonal degree matrix. Thus, the heterogeneous manifold is built in the form of normalized graph Laplacian $\mathbf{L}$:

$$\mathbf{L} = \alpha \mathbf{L}^S + \mathbf{L}^E \tag{11}$$

The trade-off parameter α controls how two different types of relationships are combined. Then the graph Laplacian can be written in trace-form as

$$\mathbf{R}_1 = Tr(\mathbf{VLV}^T) \tag{12}$$

However, as denote in [14], the graph Laplacian based method suffers from the fact that the solution is biased towards a constant and extrapolating power is lost. The further proposed the second-order Hessian energy regularizer overcomes both these problems. Specially, the total estimated Hessian energy is shown by

$$\mathbf{R}_2 = Tr(\mathbf{V\Omega V}^T) \tag{13}$$

where $\mathbf{\Omega}$ is the Hessian energy matrix which is sparse since each data point has only contributions from its neighbors.

Therefore, for exploiting the advantage of both regularizers, the hybrid manifold model can be represented as:

$$\mathbf{R} = \lambda Tr(\mathbf{VLV}^T) + \mu Tr(\mathbf{V\Omega V}^T) \tag{14}$$

where $\lambda \geq 0$, $\mu \geq 0$ denote the contribution coefficients of Laplacian matrix $\mathbf{L}$ and Hessian energy matrix $\mathbf{\Omega}$ respectively.

3.2   Objective Function of HMNMF

By synthesizing the above objectives, the optimization problem of HMNMF is formulated as

$$
\min_{\mathbf{U},\mathbf{V}} \ \|\mathbf{X} - \mathbf{U}\mathbf{V}\|_F^2 + \lambda Tr(\mathbf{V}\mathbf{L}\mathbf{V}^T) + \mu Tr(\mathbf{V}\mathbf{\Omega}\mathbf{V}^T)
$$
$$
\text{s.t. } U \geq 0, V \geq 0, \mathbf{L} = \alpha \mathbf{L}^S + \mathbf{L}^E \tag{15}
$$

where the regularization parameter $\alpha \geq 0$ is used to govern the contribution of the composition manifold regularization to the objective, parameter $\lambda \geq 0$ denotes the contribution coefficient of Laplacian matrix and parameter $\mu \geq 0$ denotes the contribution coefficient of Hessian energy matrix.

4   Optimization

In this section, we introduce how to optimize Eq. (15). Since Eq. (15) are not convex in both $\mathbf{U}$ and $\mathbf{V}$ together. Therefore it is unrealistic to expect to find the global minima. In the following, we introduce iterative algorithm which can achieve local minima. The objective function in Eq. (15) can be rewritten as:

$$
\mathbf{J} = Tr(\mathbf{X}\mathbf{X}^T) - 2Tr(\mathbf{X}\mathbf{V}^T\mathbf{U}^T) + Tr(\mathbf{U}\mathbf{V}\mathbf{V}^T\mathbf{U}^T) + \lambda Tr(\mathbf{V}\mathbf{L}\mathbf{V}^T) + \mu Tr(\mathbf{V}\mathbf{\Omega}\mathbf{V}^T) \tag{16}
$$

Let Ψ_{ik} and Φ_{kj} be the Lagrange multiplier for constraint $U_{ik} \geq 0$ and $V_{kj} \geq 0$ respectively, then the Lagrange function $\mathscr{L}$ is

$$
\mathscr{L} = Tr(\mathbf{X}\mathbf{X}^T) - 2Tr(\mathbf{X}\mathbf{V}^T\mathbf{U}^T) + Tr(\mathbf{U}\mathbf{V}\mathbf{V}^T\mathbf{U}^T) + \lambda tr(\mathbf{V}\mathbf{L}\mathbf{V}^T) + \mu tr(\mathbf{V}\mathbf{\Omega}\mathbf{V}^T)
$$
$$
+ Tr(\Psi\mathbf{U}^T) + Tr(\Phi\mathbf{V}^T). \tag{17}
$$

4.1   Updating U

The partial derivation of $\mathscr{L}$ with respect to $\mathbf{U}$ is

$$
\frac{\partial \mathscr{L}}{\partial \mathbf{U}} = -2\mathbf{X}\mathbf{V}^T + 2\mathbf{U}\mathbf{V}\mathbf{V}^T + \Psi. \tag{18}
$$

Using the KKT condition $\psi_{ik}U_{ik} = 0$, we can get

$$
(-\mathbf{X}\mathbf{V}^T + \mathbf{U}\mathbf{V}\mathbf{V}^T)_{ik}U_{ik} = 0. \tag{19}
$$

Accoridng to Eq. (19), we present the following updating formula:

$$
U_{ik}^{t+1} = U_{ik}^t \frac{(\mathbf{X}(\mathbf{V}^t)^T)_{ik}}{(\mathbf{U}^t\mathbf{V}^t(\mathbf{V}^t)^T)_{ik}} \tag{20}
$$

4.2   Updating V

The partial derivation of $\mathscr{L}$ with respect to $\mathbf{V}$ is

$$\frac{\partial \mathscr{L}}{\partial \mathbf{U}} = -2\mathbf{U}^T\mathbf{X} + 2\mathbf{U}^T\mathbf{U}\mathbf{V} + 2\lambda\mathbf{V}\mathbf{L} + 2\mu\mathbf{V}\mathbf{\Omega} + \mathbf{\Phi}. \tag{21}$$

Using the KKT condition $\phi_{kj}V_{kj} = 0$, we can get

$$(-2\mathbf{U}^T\mathbf{X} + 2\mathbf{U}^T\mathbf{U}\mathbf{V} + 2\lambda\mathbf{V}\mathbf{L} + 2\mu\mathbf{V}\mathbf{\Omega})_{ik}U_{ik} = 0. \tag{22}$$

Since $\mathbf{L} = \mathbf{L}^+ - \mathbf{L}^-$, $\mathbf{\Omega} = \mathbf{\Omega}^+ - \mathbf{\Omega}^-$ and $\mathbf{L}^+ = (abs(\mathbf{V}) + \mathbf{V})/2$, $\mathbf{L}^- = (abs(\mathbf{V}) - \mathbf{V})/2$ (the same for $\mathbf{\Omega}$), then the above function can be rewritten as:

$$(-2\mathbf{U}^T\mathbf{X} + 2\mathbf{U}^T\mathbf{U}\mathbf{V} + 2\lambda\mathbf{V}(\mathbf{L}^+ - \mathbf{L}^-) + 2\mu\mathbf{V}(\mathbf{\Omega}^+ - \mathbf{\Omega}^-))_{ik}U_{ik} = 0. \tag{23}$$

Accoriding to Eq. (23), we present the following updating formula:

$$V_{ik}^{t+1} = V_{ik}^t \frac{(\mathbf{U}^{(t+1)^T}\mathbf{X} + \lambda\mathbf{V}^t\mathbf{L}^- + \mu\mathbf{V}^t\mathbf{\Omega}^-)_{ik}}{(\mathbf{U}^{(t+1)^T}\mathbf{U}^{(t+1)}\mathbf{V} + \lambda\mathbf{V}^t\mathbf{L}^+ + \mu\mathbf{V}^t\mathbf{\Omega}^+)_{ik}} \tag{24}$$

5   Experiments

Two image data sets are used in the experiment. The important statistics of these data sets are summarized in Table 1. The first data set is the COIL20 image library, which contains 32×32 gray scale images of 20 objects viewed from varying angles. The second data set is the CMU PIE face database, which contains 32×32 gray scale face images of 68 people. Each person has 42 facial images under different light and illumination conditions.

Table 1. Statistics of the datasets.

Dataset	Size	Dimensionality	# of classes
COIL20	1440	1024	20
PIE	2856	1024	68

In all experiments, we set the number of clusters equal to the true number of classes for all the clustering algorithms. And we use two popular evaluation metrics, the clustering accuracy (ACC) and the normalized mutual information (NMI), to measure the performance of all the clustering algorithms. For further details, please refer to [21].

5.1   Compared Algorithms

In order to show the effectiveness of HMNMF, we compared it with the following baseline methods:

- Canonical K-means clustering method (Kmeans for short).
- K-means clustering in the Principle Component subspace (PCA, in short).
- Normalized Cut [17], one of the typical spectral clustering algorithms (NCut in short).
- NMF-based clustering (NMF in short).
- Graph regularized Nonnegative Matrix Factorization (GNMF in short) [6].

Table 2. Clustering Accuracy on the 2 datasets.

Data Sets	KMeans	PCA	NCut	NMF	GNMF	HMNMF
COIL20	0.6049	0.6431	0.6963	0.6674	0.7222	**0.7556**
PIE	0.2454	0.2517	0.6597	0.3852	0.7556	**0.8085**

5.2   Clustering Results

Table 2 shows the clustering Accuracy on the two data sets. Table 3 shows the Normalized Mutual Information on the two data sets. These experiments reveal a number of interesting points:

- Both NMF and GNMF outperform the PCA method. It indicates the superiority of part-based representation idea in discovering the hidden factors.
- Methods consider the geometrical structure of the data, including NCut and GNMF, achieve better performance than Kmeans and NMF methods. This demonstrates the essential role of the geometrical structure in learning the hidden factors.
- GNMF achieve better performance than all the methods except HMNMF. It shows that both the parts-based representation and graph Laplacian regularization can lead to better performance.
- Regardless of the data sets, our HMNMF always results in the best performance. It suggestions that by leveraging the power of both the parts-based representation and hybrid manifold regularization, HMNMF can learn a better compact representation.

5.3   Parameters Selection

Our HMNMF model has three essential parameters: α, λ and μ. Experimental results demonstrate that when $\alpha = 2$, $\lambda = 700$ and $\mu = 0.016$, HMNMF achieves good performance.

Table 3. Normalized Mutual Information on the 2 datasets.

Data Sets	KMeans	PCA	NCut	NMF	GNMF	HMNMF
COIL20	0.7386	0.7437	0.7722	0.7536	0.8760	**0.8814**
PIE	0.5377	0.5473	0.8038	0.6982	0.8807	**0.9155**

6 Conclusion

We have presented a novel method for matrix factorization, called Hybrid Manifold Regularized Non-negative Matrix Factorization (HMNMF). The basic idea is to make use of hybrid manifold learning to approximate the intrinsic manifold and then integrate hybrid manifold regularization with NMF. To achieve this, we attempt to combine heterogeneous candidate manifolds so that it can maximally approximate the true intrinsic manifold. In order to optimize the objective function, we adopt the popular alternating optimization method to update the factorized matrices. The extensive experiments are conducted on real-world datasets to validate the effectiveness of our technique.

References

1. Belkin, M., Niyogi, P.: Laplacian eigenmaps and spectral techniques for embedding and clustering. NIPS **14**, 585–591 (2001)
2. Belkin, M., Niyogi, P.: Laplacian eigenmaps for dimensionality reduction and data representation. Neural Comput. **15**(6), 1373–1396 (2003)
3. Belkin, M., Niyogi, P.: Towards a theoretical foundation for Laplacian-based manifold methods. J. Comput. Syst. Sci. **74**(8), 1289–1308 (2008)
4. Belkin, M., Niyogi, P., Sindhwani, V.: Manifold regularization: a geometric framework for learning from labeled and unlabeled examples. J. Mach. Learn. Res. **7**, 2399–2434 (2006)
5. Birgin, E.G., Martínez, J.M., Raydan, M.: Nonmonotone spectral projected gradient methods on convex sets. SIAM J. Optim. **10**(4), 1196–1211 (2000)
6. Cai, D., He, X., Han, J., Huang, T.S.: Graph regularized nonnegative matrix factorization for data representation. IEEE Trans. PAMI **33**(8), 1548–1560 (2011)
7. Cai, D., He, X., Wu, X., Han, J.: Non-negative matrix factorization on manifold. In: Eighth IEEE ICDM, pp. 63–72. IEEE (2008)
8. Elhamifar, E., Vidal, R.: Sparse subspace clustering. In: IEEE Conference on CVPR, pp. 2790–2797. IEEE (2009)
9. Elhamifar, E., Vidal, R.: Sparse subspace clustering: algorithm, theory, and applications. IEEE Trans. PAMI **35**(11), 2765–2781 (2013)
10. Hadsell, R., Chopra, S., LeCun, Y.: Dimensionality reduction by learning an invariant mapping. In: IEEEComputer Society Conference on CVPR, vol. 2, pp. 1735–1742. IEEE (2006)
11. He, X., Cai, D., Shao, Y., Bao, H., Han, J.: Laplacian regularized gaussian mixture model for data clustering. IEEE TKDE **23**(9), 1406–1418 (2011)
12. He, X., Cai, D., Yan, S., Zhang, H.-J.: Neighborhood preserving embedding. In: Tenth IEEE International Conference on ICCV, vol. 2, pp. 1208–1213. IEEE (2005)

13. He, X., Yan, S., Hu, Y., Niyogi, P., Zhang, H.-J.: Face recognition using laplacian-faces. IEEE Trans. PAMI **27**(3), 328–340 (2005)

14. Kim, K.I., Steinke, F., Hein, M.: Semi-supervised regression using hessian energy with an application to semi-supervised dimensionality reduction. In: NIPS, pp. 979–987 (2009)

15. Lee, D.D., Seung, H.S.: Learning the parts of objects by non-negative matrix factorization. Nature **401**(6755), 788–791 (1999)

16. Roweis, S.T., Saul, L.K.: Nonlinear dimensionality reduction by locally linear embedding. Science **290**(5500), 2323–2326 (2000)

17. Shi, J., Malik, J.: Normalized cuts and image segmentation. IEEE Trans. PAMI **22**(8), 888–905 (2000)

18. Tenenbaum, J.B., De Silva, V., Langford, J.C.: A global geometric framework for nonlinear dimensionality reduction. Science **290**(5500), 2319–2323 (2000)

19. Turaga, P., Veeraraghavan, A., Chellappa, R.: Statistical analysis on stiefel and grassmann manifolds with applications in computer vision. In: IEEE Conference on CVPR, pp. 1–8. IEEE (2008)

20. Wang, S., Yuan, X., Yao, T., Yan, S., Shen, J.: Efficient subspace segmentation via quadratic programming. AAAI **1**, 519–524 (2011)

21. Xu, W., Liu, X., Gong, Y.: Document clustering based on non-negative matrix factorization. In: Proceedings of the 26th Annual International ACM SIGIR Conference on Research and Development in Informaion Retrieval, pp. 267–273. ACM (2003)

22. Zhang, Z., Zhao, K.: Low-rank matrix approximation with manifold regularization. IEEE Trans. PAMI **35**(7), 1717–1729 (2013)

23. Zhou, D., Bousquet, O., Lal, T.N., Weston, J., Schölkopf, B.: Learning with local and global consistency. NIPS **16**(16), 321–328 (2004)

A Novel Nonnegative Matrix Factorization Algorithm for Multi-manifold Learning

Qian Wang, Wen-Sheng Chen$^{(\boxtimes)}$, Binbin Pan, and Yugao Li

College of Mathematics and Statistics, Shenzhen University,
Shenzhen 518060, China
chenws@szu.edu.cn

Abstract. Nonnegative matrix factorization (NMF) is a promising approach to extract the sparse features of facial images. It is known that the facial images usually reside on multi-manifold due to the variations of illumination, pose and facial expression. However, NMF lacks the ability of modeling the structure of data manifold. To improve the performance of NMF for multi-manifold learning, we propose a novel Manifold based NMF (Mani-NMF) algorithm which incorporates the multi-manifold structure. The proposed algorithm simultaneously minimizes the local scatter in the same manifold and maximizes the non-local scatter between different manifolds. It theoretically proves the convergence of the algorithm. Finally, experiments on the face databases demonstrate the superiority of our method over some state of the art algorithms.

Keywords: Nonnegative Matrix Factorization · Face recognition · Multi-manifold learning

1 Introduction

Face recognition is a biometric technology which identifies the human with the face information. Feature extraction plays an important role in face recognition. The classical methods for linear feature extraction are Principal Component Analysis (PCA) [1], Linear Discriminant Analysis (LDA) [2] and Nonnegative Matrix Factorization (NMF) [3]. Different from PCA and LDA which extract the holistic features, NMF finds the sparse and localized features which are robust to the local deformations of facial images. Therefore, NMF is a promising method for face recognition. However, the facial images possibly lie on multiple manifolds. It is of interest to incorporate the multi-manifold structure into NMF for enhancing the performance.

Over the past few years, face recognition methods based on manifold learning have been proposed, such as Locality Preserving Projections (LPP) [4] and Unsupervised Discriminant Projection (UDP) [6]. LPP aims to find an optimal linear approximation to the eigenfunctions of the Laplace Beltrami operator on a smooth manifold. It forces the smoothness of the projected data points within their nearest neighbors. Nevertheless, LPP is limited in dealing with

© Springer International Publishing AG 2016
Z. You et al. (Eds.): CCBR 2016, LNCS 9967, pp. 575–582, 2016.
DOI: 10.1007/978-3-319-46654-5_63

multi-manifold structure. In contrast, UDP was posed as classification-oriented multi-manifold learning. UDP is able to discover the multi-manifold structure of the data effectively by maximizing the non-local scatter and minimizing the local scatter. But UDP cannot extract the sparse and localized features of the facial images.

Recently, a variant of NMF, named GLNMF [5], was presented to find the multi-manifold structure in the decomposed factors. In detail, GLNMF, which follows the idea of UDP method, decomposes a nonnegative matrix into two factors by minimizing the local scatter and maximizing the non-local scatter simultaneously. It designs iterative formulas to update the factors from the Karush-Kuhn-Tucker (KKT) conditions [8] of the optimization problem. However, it cannot ensure the convergence of the iterative formulas. Thus, it is less theoretically sound. Furthermore, the updated factors may exist negative elements since the Laplacian matrices appear in the iterative formulas. This indicates that GLNMF possibly results in unreasonable factorization. As illustrated in [7], the non-negativity of the factors is important for finding localized features.

To remedy the drawbacks of GLNMF, this paper proposes a new NMF algorithm for multi-manifold learning. We propose a new objective function for NMF by simultaneously minimizing the local scatter in the same manifold and maximizing the non-local scatter between different manifolds. The iterative formulae are obtained using the auxiliary functions. We theoretically show the convergence of the algorithm. Two face databases, namely ORL and FERET databases, are selected for evaluations. Compared with LPP, NMF and GLNMF algorithms, our algorithm achieves superior performance.

The rest of this paper is organized as follows. In Sect. 2, we propose our method and prove the convergence of the algorithm. Experimental results are reported in Sect. 3. Finally, Sect. 4 draws the conclusions.

2   Related Work

This section will briefly introduce some related work such as NMF and GLNMF. Details are as follows.

2.1   NMF

Let X be a non-negative data matrix and $X = [x_1, x_2, \cdots, x_n] \in R^{m \times n}$. NMF aims to approximately decompose X into two non-negative matrices $W \in R^{m \times d}$ and $H \in R^{d \times n}$, namely $X \approx WH$. Based on the error objective function with Frobenius norm, the following multiplicative update rules can be derived using gradient descent method [3]:

$$H = H \odot (W^T X) \oslash (W^T W H),$$
$$W = W \odot (X H^T) \oslash (W H H^T), \quad W = W \oslash S,$$

where $[S]_{jr} = \sum_{i=1}^{m} [W]_{ir}, j = 1, 2, ..., m$, notations $\odot$ and $\oslash$ stand for the element-wise multiplication and division respectively.

2.2 GLNMF

Following the idea of UDP method, GLNMF [5] is to find NMF which involves both the local and non-local scatter information. The local adjacency matrix $S = (S_{ij})_{n \times n}$ is defined by $S_{ij} = \begin{cases} 1, \text{ if } x_j \in N_i \text{ or } x_i \in N_j \\ 0, \text{ otherwise} \end{cases}$, where N_i and N_j denote the k-nearest neighbor set of x_i and x_j, respectively. The local Laplacian matrix L is $L = D - S$, where D is a diagonal matrix with diagonal entries $D_{ii} = \sum_j S_{ij}$. The non-local adjacency matrix S' is $S' = 1_{n \times n} - S$, where $1_{n \times n}$ denotes a n by n matrix with all entries equal to 1. The non-local Laplacian matrix L' is similarly defined by $L' = D' - S'$. The following update rules of GLNMF are obtained via the KKT conditions:

$$H = H \odot (W^T X + \mu H(L')^T) \oslash (W^T W H + \mu H L^T),$$
$$W = W \odot (XH^T) \oslash (WHH^T), \quad W = W \oslash S,$$

where $[S]_{jr} = \sum_{i=1}^{m}[W]_{ir}, j = 1, 2, ..., m$.

Obviously, the Laplacian matrices, contained in GLNMF update rules, are not non-negative. This means that H may not satisfy the non-negative condition. Also, since the update formulae are just derived from KKT conditions, it cannot guarantee the convergence of iterations. To overcome these problems, we will design a novel multi-manifold NMF algorithm in the following section.

3 The Proposed Method

This section proposes our multi-manifold NMF method, named Mani-NMF. The convergence of Mani-NMF will be proved as well.

3.1 Mani-NMF Update Rules

Our Mani-NMF aims to optimize the objective function by simultaneously minimizing the local scatter in the same manifold and maximizing the non-local scatter between different manifolds. The RBF kernel function is adopted in this paper to measure the closeness of x_i and x_j, namely $k(x_i, x_j) = \exp(\frac{-\|x_i - x_j\|^2}{t})$, where the parameter $t > 0$. The kernel matrix K is $K = (k(x_i, x_j))_{n \times n}$ and the local adjacency matrix S is

$$S_{ij} = \begin{cases} k(x_i, x_j), \text{ if } x_j \in N_i \text{ or } x_i \in N_j \\ 0, \qquad\quad \text{otherwise} \end{cases},$$

where N_i and N_j denote the k-nearest neighbor set of x_i and x_j, respectively.

The local scatter Q, which characterizes the mean of the weighted Euclidean distance between any pair of sample points that are within any local k-nearest neighbor, is defined as:

$$Q = \frac{1}{2} \sum_{i,j=1}^{n} \|h_i - h_j\|^2 S_{ij} = tr(HDH^T) - tr(HSH^T),$$

where $tr(\cdot)$ represents the trace of a matrix, D is a diagonal matrix with $D_{ii} = \sum_j S_{ij}$. While the non-local adjacency matrix $\widetilde{S}$ is given as $\widetilde{S} = K - S$ and the non-local scatter $\widetilde{Q}$ is defined below:

$$\widetilde{Q} = \frac{1}{2} \sum_{i,j=1}^{n} \|h_i - h_j\|^2 \widetilde{S}_{ij} = tr(H\widetilde{D}H^T) - tr(H\widetilde{S}H^T).$$

In order to make the data in the same manifold as close as possible and the data between different manifolds as far as possible, it should minimize the local scatter Q and maximize the non-local scatter $\widetilde{Q}$ simultaneously. To this end, this paper establishes the objective function as follows:

$$\begin{aligned} F(W,H) &= \frac{1}{2}\|X - WH\|_F^2 + \frac{\alpha}{2}Q - \frac{\beta}{2}\widetilde{Q} \\ &= \frac{1}{2}\|X - WH\|_F^2 + \frac{\alpha}{2}[tr(HDH^T) - tr(HSH^T)] \\ &\quad - \frac{\beta}{2}[tr(H\widetilde{D}H^T) - tr(H\widetilde{S}H^T)]. \end{aligned}$$

Mani-NMF needs to solve the following optimization problem:

$$\min_{W,H} F(W,H) \quad \text{s.t.} \quad W \geq 0, H \geq 0. \tag{1}$$

The problem (1) cannot be resolved directly. The general way is to convert the original problem into two convex subproblems by fixing W and H, respectively. Here, we mainly take into account the subproblem with respect to H as W is fixed. For simplification, it denotes that $f(H) = F(W,H)$, where W is fixed. By the gradient descent method, we have

$$H^{t+1} = H^t - \rho^t \odot \nabla_H f(H^t), \tag{2}$$

where $\nabla_H f(H)$ is the gradient of $f(H)$ with respect to H, and

$$\nabla_H f(H) = -W^T X + W^T WH + H(\alpha D + \beta \widetilde{S}) - H(\alpha S + \beta \widetilde{D}). \tag{3}$$

Substituting (3) into (2), it yields that

$$H^{t+1} = H^t - \rho^t \odot (W^T WH^t + \alpha H^t D + \beta H^t \widetilde{S}) + \rho^t \odot (W^T X + \alpha H^t S + \beta H^t \widetilde{D}). \tag{4}$$

To keep the nonnegativity of H^{t+1}, we set that $H^t - \rho^t \odot (W^T WH^t + \alpha H^t D + \beta H^t \widetilde{S}) = 0$, then ρ^t satisfies that

$$\rho^t = H^t \oslash (W^T WH^t + \alpha H^t D + \beta H^t \widetilde{S}). \tag{5}$$

We substitute (5) into (4) and obtain the iterative formula (6). The iterative formula (7) can be derived in a similar way.

Based on above analysis, the update rules of the proposed Mani-NMF are as follows:

$$H \leftarrow H \odot (W^T X + \alpha HS + \beta H\widetilde{D}) \oslash (W^T WH + \alpha HD + \beta H\widetilde{S}), \tag{6}$$

$$W \leftarrow W \odot (XH^T) \oslash (WHH^T), \quad W \leftarrow W \oslash Q, \tag{7}$$

where $[Q]_{jr} = \sum_{i=1}^{m} [W]_{ir}$, $j = 1, 2, ..., m$.

3.2 The Convergence of Mani-NMF

This subsection will show the convergence of Mani-NMF using the auxiliary function strategy.

Definition 1. [3] *For any column vectors* h, $h^{'} \in R^d$, $G(h, h^{'})$ *is called an auxiliary function for* $F(h)$ *if* $G(h, h^{'})$ *satisfies*

$$G(h, h^{'}) \geq F(h), \quad and \quad G(h, h) = F(h)$$

Lemma 1. *[3] If* $G(h, h^{'})$ *is an auxiliary function for* $F(h)$, *then* $F(h)$ *is a non-increasing function under the update rule*

$$h^{t+1} = \underset{h}{argmin}\, G(h, h^t) \tag{8}$$

To prove the convergence of Mani-NMF, we first establish the auxiliary function for objective function $f(H)$ with W fixed. Let h_q be the qth column of H and all the other columns of H are fixed, then we have $f(h_q)$ as

$$f(h_q) = \frac{1}{2}\|X - Wh_q\|_2^2 + \frac{\alpha}{2}[tr(HDH^T) - tr(HSH^T)]$$
$$-\frac{\beta}{2}[tr(H\widetilde{D}H^T) - tr(H\widetilde{S}H^T)]. \tag{9}$$

For the objective function (9), the following theorem holds.

Theorem 1. *We are given*

$$G(h_q, h_q^t) = f(h_q^t) + (h_q - h_q^t)^T \nabla f(h_q^t) + \frac{1}{2}(h_q - h_q^t)^T N(h_q^t)(h_q - h_q^t), \tag{10}$$

where $N(h_q^t)$ *is a diagonal matrix with the* ith *diagonal element*

$$[N(h_q^t)]_{ii} = [W^T W h_q^t \oslash h_q^t]_i + [H^t(\alpha D + \beta\widetilde{S})_q \oslash h_q^t]_i. \tag{11}$$

Then $G(h_q, h_q^t)$ *is an auxiliary function for* $f(h_q)$.

The proof of Theorem 1 is omitted here due to the limited room. The following Theorem 2 is concluded via combining Theorem 1 and Lemma 1.

Theorem 2. *For fixed* W, *the objective function* $f(h)$ *is non-increasing under the following update rule:*

$$h_q \leftarrow h_q \odot (W^T X_q + \alpha H S_q + \beta H\widetilde{D}_q) \oslash (WW^T h_q + \alpha H D_q + \beta H\widetilde{S}_q).$$

In addition, by reversing the role of W and H, Theorem 3 can be proven in a similar way.

Theorem 3. *For fixed* H, *the objective function* $F(W, H)$ *is non-increasing under the following update rules:*

$$W_q \leftarrow W_q \odot (XH_q^T) \oslash (WHH_q^T), \quad W_q \leftarrow W_q \oslash Q_q.$$

4   Algorithm Design

This section develops the following Mani-NNMF algorithm.

Step 1: Initialize kernel parameter t, regularization parameters α and β, factor matrices W and H.

Step 2: Calculate S, D, $\widetilde{S}$ and $\widetilde{D}$ using RBF kernel.

Step 3: Find the matrix W and H according to the update rules (6)–(7).

Step 4: Assume H contains features of c classes. Partition the columns of H into c blocks, namely $H = [H_1, H_2, \ldots, H_c]$, where the block H_i is the feature sub-matrix of the ith class. Compute the mean vector $\bar{h}_k$ of class k from H_k, where $k = 1, 2, \ldots, c$.

Step 5: For the testing sample y, compute the feature of y as $h = W^+ y$, where W^+ is the pseudo inverse of W.

Step 6: If $k = \text{argmin}_{1 \leq j \leq c} \|h - \bar{h}_j\|$, then the testing sample y is assigned to the kth class.

---

5   Experimental Results

This section evaluates the performance of Mani-NMF for face recognition on ORL and FERET databases. Some parameters are set as follows: $\alpha = \beta = 10^{-4}$, $r = 350$, and $Maxiter = 400$. The number of nearest neighbors $k = round(TN/2) + 1$, where TN means the number of training samples. The experiment is repeated ten times and the average results are recorded. LPP [4], NMF [3] and GLNMF [5] approaches are chosen for comparisons.

5.1   Facial Image Datasets

ORL face database is composed of a series of human face images, a total of 40 different ages, different genders and different ethnic groups. It includes 400 face images of 40 persons and each person has 10 images. The image size is 92×112. The human face has changed with different facial expressions, wearing or not wearing glasses and small variations in scales. The database is the most widely standard database currently, which contains a large number of comparative results.

For FERET database, we select 720 images from 120 persons, 6 images from each person. The image size is also 112×92. FERET database is more challenging than ORL database because the variations in FERET database include pose, illumination, facial expression and aging. These images are choosen from four sets, that is, Fa, Fb, Fc and duplicate. Fa and Fb were captured with the same camera on the same date and they had different facial expressions. Fc was taken from different camera. The duplicate was taken at different time.

5.2   Results on ORL Dataset

The setting of the experiments are as follows. The $n(n = 3, 4, \cdots, 9)$ face images are randomly taken from each individual for training, and the rest $(10-n)$ images of each people are for testing. The mean accuracies are described in Table 1.

In Table 1, we see that the recognition rate of Mani-NMF increases from 86.18 % with TN = 3 to 96.50 % with TN = 9. In contrast, the accuracies of LPP, NMF and GLNMF increase from 83.32 %, 84.14 % and 84.25 % with TN = 3 to 90.50 %, 93.25 % and 95.25 % with TN = 9, respectively. It shows that our method achieves the better performance.

Table 1. Mean accuracy(%) versus Training Number (TN) on ORL database.

TN	3	4	5	6	7	8	9
LPP	83.32	86.25	86.45	86.75	89.17	90.13	90.50
NMF	84.14	87.37	89.20	90.00	91.67	91.37	93.25
GLNMF	84.25	86.83	90.00	90.62	91.33	92.12	95.25
Mani-NMF	**86.18**	**88.79**	**91.90**	**92.75**	**93.92**	**93.50**	**96.50**

5.3   Results on FERET Dataset

The experimental setting of FERET is similar as that of ORL. We randomly take $n(n = 3, 4, 5)$ images from each individual for training, while the rest $(6-n)$ images of each people are taken for testing. The average accuracies are tabulated in Table 2. It can be seen that the recognition rate of Mani-NMF increases from 77.58 % with TN = 3 to 83.33 % with TN = 5. The accuracies of the LPP, NMF and GLNMF increase from 70.17 %, 74.11 % and 75.00 % with TN = 3 to 80.00 %, 82.66 % and 82.67 % with TN = 5 respectively. So, the proposed approach surpasses the other three methods as well.

Table 2. Mean accuracy (%) versus Training Number on FERET database.

TN	3	4	5
LPP	70.17	76.92	80.00
NMF	74.11	80.13	82.66
GLNMF	75.00	80.45	82.67
Mani-NMF	**77.58**	**81.13**	**83.33**

6   Conclusions

In this paper, we proposed a novel NMF for multi-manifold learning. The algorithm is theoretically proven to be convergence. The experiments on ORL and

FERET face databases demonstrate the effectiveness of our method. In the future, we will consider the problem of nonnegative nonlinear feature extraction by making use of kernel theory and multi-manifold learning.

Acknowledgements. This paper is partially supported by NSF of China under Grant (61272252, 11526145) and NSF of Guangdong Province under Grant 2015A030313544 and the postgraduate innovation development fund project of Shenzhen university (000360023409). We would like to thank Olivetti Research Laboratory and Amy Research Laboratory for providing the facial image databases.

References

1. Turk, M., Pentland, A.: Eigenfaces for recognition. J. Cogn. Neurosic. **3**(1), 71–86 (1991)
2. Belhumeur, P.N., Hespanha, J.P., Kriegman, D.J.: Eigenfaces vs. Fisherfaces: recognition using class specific linear projection. IEEE Trans. Pattern Anal. Mach. Intell. **19**(7), 711–720 (1997)
3. Lee, D.D., Seung, H.S.: Algorithms for non-negative matrix factorization. Adv. Neural Inf. Process. Syst. **13**, 556–562 (2001)
4. He, X.F., Niyogi, P.: Locality preserving projections. Adv. Neural Inf. Process. Syst. **15**, 186–197 (2003)
5. He, M., Wei, F., Jia, X.: Globally maximizing, locally minimizing, regularized nonnegative matrix factorization for hyperspectral dataset data feature extraction. In: The Workshop on Hyperspectral Image and Signal Processing: Evolution in Remote Sensing, pp. 1–4 (2012)
6. Yang, J., Zhang, D., Yang, J.Y., Niu, B.: Globally maximizing locally minimizing: unsupervised discriminant projection with applications to face and palm biometrics. IEEE Trans. Pattern Anal. Mach. Intell. **29**(4), 650–664 (2007)
7. Pan, B., Lai, J., Chen, W.S.: Nonlinear nonnegative matrix factorization based on Mercer kernel construction. Pattern Recogn. **44**(10–11), 2800–2810 (2011)
8. Boyd, S., Vandenberghe, L.: Convex Optimization. Cambridge University Press (2004)

Deep Convex NMF for Image Clustering

Bin Qian, Xiaobo Shen$^{(\boxtimes)}$, Zhenmin Tang, and Tao Zhang

School of Computer Science and Engineering,
Nanjing University of Science and Technology, Nanjing 210094, China
njustztwork@126.com, njust.shenxiaobo@gmail.com,
{311062198,Tzm.cs}@njust.edu.cn

Abstract. Conventional matrix factorization methods fail to exploit useful information from rather complex data due to their single-layer structure. In this paper, we propose a novel deep convex non-negative matrix factorization method (DCNMF) to improve the ability of feature representation. In addition, the manifold and sparsity regularizers are imposed on each layer to discover the inherent structure of the data. For the formulated multi-layer objective, we develop an efficient iterative optimization algorithm, which can enhance the stability via layer-by-layer factorization and fine-tuning. We evaluate the proposed method by performing clustering experiments on face and handwritten character benchmark datasets; the results show that the proposed method obviously outperforms the conventional single-layer methods, and achieves the state-of-the-art performance.

Keywords: Non-negative matrix factorization · Deep factorization · Image clustering · Manifold · Sparsity

1 Introduction

In many real world image applications, such as image clustering, image retrieval, and video tracking, the observed data often lie in a high-dimensional subspace, which leads to the increase of both storage and computational cost. Extracting their meaningful low-dimensional features not only avoids the curse of dimensionality problem, but also accomplish data analysis tasks at a low computational cost [1]. Therefore, feature extraction technique, as a tool for dimensionality reduction, has recently received a lot of attentions. Among them, non-negative matrix factorization (NMF) has been widely concerned [2].

NMF [3] aims to seek two non-negative matrices whose product provides a good approximation to the original matrix. It is optimal for learning the parts of objects because the non-negative constraints allow only additive combinations. NMF assumes that data points are sampled from a Euclidean space, thus it fails to exploit the geometric structure of the data. In order to consider the manifold information, graph regularized NMF (GNMF) [4] is proposed to preserve the local affinity structure of the data, by assuming that the close points in the original space should be also close in the low-dimensional subspace. Xu *et al.* [6]

© Springer International Publishing AG 2016
Z. You et al. (Eds.): CCBR 2016, LNCS 9967, pp. 583–590, 2016.
DOI: 10.1007/978-3-319-46654-5_64

extend NMF to the case with negative data and propose Concept Factorization (CF), which is also called convex non-negative matrix factorization. Compared with NMF, CF also has the "part representation" ability, and it is easier to be kernelized. Later on, Cai *et al.* [7] propose Locally Consistent Concept Factorization (LCCF) to further incorporate manifold information, and shows its brilliant performance on document clustering.

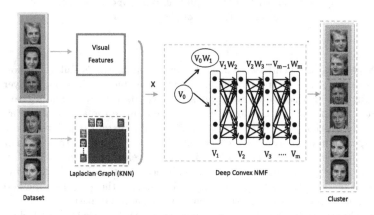

Fig. 1. The flowchart of the proposed DCNMF. First, visual feature is extracted from original images. Then the feature is further factorized by the proposed deep model, some additional information (*e.g.* manifold structure) is also incorporated. Finally, the coefficients from the last layer in the deep model represent the original data and can be used for the following clustering task.

To extract more abstract and effective features from complex data, some researchers have tried to apply multi-layer feature extraction methods to matrix factorization and achieved satisfying results in some fields [8–10]. Nevertheless, these methods are not designed for dimensionality reduction and they do not fully consider the dimensionality structure of multi-layer. If we reduce dimension directly using single-layer factorization model, then trouble may occur due to insufficient dimension provided for learning and the important discriminative information will be lost. An intuitive idea to solve this issue is to reduce the dimensionality of the original data in a descent order and perform matrix factorization multiple times. During each factorization process, most of the effect discriminative information is kept and meanwhile dimension reduction is achieved. Through these transitional dimensionalities and factorization processes, we can get better and more stable low-dimensional features.

Inspired with the success of multi-layer feature extraction, we propose a deep convex non-negative matrix factorization algorithm (DCNMF), which performs multiple factorization via a layer-by-layer strategy. The flowchart of DCNMF is outlined in Fig. 1. In DCNMF, the factorization result of each layer is treated as an initial value for proceeding fine-tuning, through which deeper structures can be effectively explored. In addition, manifold and sparsity regularized terms are further considered in each layer. Experimental results show that compared with single-layer matrix factorization methods, the proposed method is more effective for image clustering.

2 Related Works

This section briefly introduces Convex NMF, which is also named Concept Factorization. We are given nonnegative data matrix $X = [x_1, x_2, \cdots, x_n] \in \Re^{p \times n}$, where each vector x_i represents a sample and p denotes the dimension. In Convex NMF, the base vector u_j is obtained by a linear combination of the samples $u_j = \sum_i w_{ij} x_i$, where $w_{ij} \geq 0$. Let $W = [w_{ij}] \in \Re^{n \times r}$, the objective of Convex NMF can be expressed as:

$$\min_{W,V} F(W, V) = \|X - XWV\|_F^2 \quad s.t. W \geq 0, V \geq 0. \tag{1}$$

It is easy to check that Eq. (1) is not convex in both W and V together. The multiplicative updating rules of convex NMF can be introduced as follows:

$$W \leftarrow W. * \frac{KV^T}{KWVV^T}, \quad V \leftarrow V. * \frac{W^T K}{W^T KWV}, \tag{2}$$

where .* denotes element-wise multiplication and $K = X^T X$. These multiplicative updating rules in Eq. (2) only involve the inner product of X and thus Convex NMF can be easily kernelized. Details can be found in literature [6,11].

3 Approach

This section introduces the proposed deep convex nonnegative matrix factorization (DCNMF) model.

3.1 Formulation

Convex NMF inevitably loses important information of data as it is directly performed in a low-dimensional subspace. In order to alleviate this drawback, multi-factor factorization is developed by introducing the additional layers for transitional dimensionality reduction. Accordingly, deep convex NMF can be done as below:

$$V_0 = X_0,$$
$$V_0 \rightarrow V_0 W_1 V_1,$$
$$V_1 \rightarrow V_1 W_2 V_2,$$
$$\vdots$$
$$V_{m-1} \rightarrow V_{m-1} W_m V_m,$$

where $W_i \in \Re^{n \times r_i}$ and $V_i \in \Re^{r_i \times n}$ represent the basis matrix and coefficient matrix in the ith $(1 \leq i \leq m)$ layer, respectively. r_i is the dimensionality of the ith layer ($r_1 > r_2 > \cdots > r_m$). A layer-by-layer factorization strategy is developed. Specifically, V_i in the i-th layer can be used as the input of the $(i+1)$-th layer, and further be factorized into W_{i+1} and V_{i+1}. The procedure is repeated until the last layer, and generates the sequences of W_i and V_i. Besides, we also consider the manifold regularizer to capture the local structure of data. Thus, the objective of the i-th layer is defined as below:

$$\min_{W_i, V_i} F_i(W_i, V_i) = \|V_{i-1} - V_{i-1}W_iV_i\|_F^2 + \alpha Tr(V_iLV_i^T) \qquad s.t. W_i \geq 0, V_i \geq 0, \tag{3}$$

where $L = D - E$ denotes a Laplacian matrix, $E \in \Re^{n \times n}$ is a similarity matrix, and D represents a diagonal matrix, $D_{ii} = \sum_j E_{ij}$, α is the regularization parameter. Note that Eq. (3) cannot guarantee the uniqueness of the solution without the normalization step after factorization. To solve this issue, we therefore explicitly introduce the sparsity constraint to avoid such an ad-hoc step. The objective of the i-th layer can be reformulated as

$$\min_{W_i, V_i} F_i(W_i, V_i) = \|V_{i-1} - V_{i-1}W_iV_i\|_F^2 + \alpha Tr(V_iLV_i^T)$$
$$+ 2\beta\|W_i\|_{\frac{1}{2}} \quad s.t. W_i \geq 0, V_i \geq 0, \tag{4}$$

where β controls the weight of the sparse term, and $\|W\|_{\frac{1}{2}}$ is defined as:

$$\|W\|_{\frac{1}{2}} = \sum_{i=1}^{n}\sum_{j=1}^{r} W_{ij}^{\frac{1}{2}}. \tag{5}$$

$\|W\|_{\frac{1}{2}}$ explicitly ensures that V have certain local representation capability [12]. Compared with traditional sparse norm L_0 or L_1, $L_{1/2}$ here is beneficial for the deduction of multiplier updating rules [13]. To this end, the final objective of DCNMF is formulated as below:

$$\min_{W_i, V_i} F_{deep} = \|X - XW_1V_1W_2V_2\cdots W_mV_m\|_F^2 + \alpha \sum_{i=1}^{m} Tr(V_iLV_i^T)$$
$$+ 2\beta \sum_{i=1}^{m} \|W_i\|_{\frac{1}{2}} \quad s.t. \; \forall i \; W_i \geq 0, V_i \geq 0. \tag{6}$$

3.2   Optimization

In essence, the objective in Eq. (6) is a multivariable optimization problem. We develop an efficient alternate algorithm to update the variables layer-by-layer.

Let ϕ_i and ψ_i be the Lagrange multipliers for constraints $W_i \geq 0$, $V_i \geq 0$, respectively. For each layer, W_i and V_i are also iteratively updated. Taking the partial derivatives of Lagrange F_i with respect to W_i and V_i of Eq. (4), we have

$$\frac{\partial F_i}{\partial W_i} = -2V_{i-1}V_{i-1}^TV_i^T + 2V_{i-1}V_{i-1}^TW_iV_iV_i^T + \beta W_i^{-\frac{1}{2}} + \phi_i \tag{7}$$

Algorithm 1. DCNMF

Data: Image dataset X, parameters α, β, m, $r_i (1 \le i \le m)$.
1. Layer-by-Layer Factorization.
    $V_0 \leftarrow X$
    for $i = 1 : m$
       Update W_i, V_i by Eq. (9)
    endfor
2. Fine-tuning.
    for all layers do
       $\tilde{V}_m \leftarrow V_m$, $\tilde{V}_i \leftarrow \tilde{V}_i W_{i+1} \tilde{V}_{i+1}$, $(1 \le i < m)$
       $\varphi = W_1 V_1 W_2 V_2 \cdots W_{i-1} V_{i-1}$
       Update W_i, V_i by Eq. (10)
    endfor
Output: V_m

$$\frac{\partial F_i}{\partial V_i} = -2W_i^T V_{i-1} V_{i-1}^T + 2W_i^T V_{i-1} V_{i-1}^T W_i V_i + 2\alpha V_i D - 2\alpha V_i S + \psi_i \qquad (8)$$

Using KKT conditions $(\phi_i W_i)_{ak} = 0$, $(\psi_i V_i)_{kb} = 0$, we derive the following update rules:

$$W_i \leftarrow W_i .* \frac{2V_{i-1} V_{i-1}^T V_i^T}{2V_{i-1} V_{i-1}^T W_i V_i V_i^T + \beta W_i^{-\frac{1}{2}}}, \quad V_i \leftarrow V_i .* \frac{W_i^T V_{i-1} V_{i-1}^T + \alpha V_i S}{W_i^T V_{i-1} V_{i-1}^T W_i V_i + \alpha V_i D}.$$
$$(9)$$

Generally, the result of the former layer will accumulate to the latter layer. If the decomposition result of a certain layer is unsatisfactory, it will also affect the factorization in the following layers. To solve this problem, we adopt the fine-tuning [14] strategy to update all variables after layer-by-layer decomposition. Based on Eq. (9), we acquire the fine-tuning updating rules of W_i and V_i in any layer:

$$W_i \leftarrow W_i .* \frac{2\varphi^T K \tilde{V}_{i+1}^T}{2\varphi^T K \varphi W_i \tilde{V}_{i+1} \tilde{V}_{i+1}^T + \beta W_i^{-\frac{1}{2}}}, \quad V_i \leftarrow V_i .* \frac{W_i^T \varphi^T K + \alpha V_i S}{W_i^T \varphi^T K \varphi W_i V_i + \alpha V_i D},$$
$$(10)$$

where $\tilde{V}_{i+1}$ represents the reconstructed feature of the $(i+1)^{th}$ layer, $\varphi = W_1 V_1 W_2 V_2 \cdots W_{i-1} V_{i-1}$. The flowchart of the proposed method is shown in Algorithm 1.

4 Experiment

4.1 Experimental Settings

This section evaluates the proposed method by performing image clustering on two image databases: PIE face database and NUST603 Chinese handwritten character database [15]. Some sample images are shown in Fig. 2. Several related

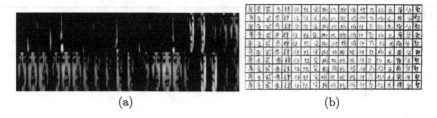

(a)   (b)

Fig. 2. Some sample images from two databases. (a) PIE face database. (b) NUST603 Chinese handwritten character database.

Table 1. Clustering performance on PIE database

c	PCA	NMF	CF	LCCF	DCNMF1	DCNMF2	DCNMF3
3	87.17	79.83	87.83	87.83	88.17	90.33	**90.50**
4	79.88	79.38	84.25	84.63	85.75	88.63	**90.47**
5	81.70	79.80	81.10	82.30	83.50	86.20	**87.80**
6	77.83	77.92	80.92	82.08	83.42	**84.08**	83.08
7	75.64	74.50	76.36	77.86	79.21	80.43	**81.50**
8	69.44	69.06	73.38	73.19	74.00	76.31	**77.63**
9	69.50	72.72	70.00	72.06	74.67	75.83	**76.06**
10	70.35	74.55	71.95	73.70	74.65	75.45	**76.05**
Avg	76.44	75.97	78.22	79.21	80.28	82.16	**82.89**

methods, *i.e.*, PCA, NMF, CF, and LCCF are adopted as the comparisons. In the experiment, we randomly select $c(= 3, 4, ..., 10)$ categories for clustering. The clustering results are evaluated by AC [5,7]. In order to verify the effectiveness of the proposed deep factorization, we report the results of the first three factorizations, and name them as DCNMF1, DCNMF2, and DCNMF3. For CF, LCCF, and DC-NMF, we kernelize them using the same gaussian kernel function. The kernel parameter σ on PIE and NUST603 databases are set as 0.15, and 0.3, respectively. In PIE, the original dimension of the samples is 1024, and we empirically set the reduced dimensions of the first three layers as $r_1 = 300, r_2 = 150, r_3 = c$. The original dimension of the samples in NUST603 is 256; here we set the reduced dimensions of the first three layers as $r_1 = 90, r_2 = 50, r_3 = c$.

4.2   Experimental Results and Analysis

Tables 1 and 2 report the clustering results on PIE and NUST603 databases, respectively. From the experimental results, we have the following conclusions:

(1) DCNMF3 achieves the highest average clustering accuracy on both databases. The results demonstrate that multi-layer factorization does help to improve the stability of dimensionality reduction.

Table 2. Clustering performance on NUST603 database

c	PCA	NMF	CF	LCCF	DCNMF1	DCNMF2	DCNMF3
3	94.10	91.27	95.33	96.93	**97.10**	96.77	97.07
4	91.55	83.50	94.45	95.15	95.15	**95.22**	95.17
5	82.84	79.08	90.98	90.76	91.84	**92.94**	90.88
6	82.25	77.17	85.42	89.48	88.45	**89.88**	89.46
7	79.84	77.46	79.57	84.61	85.57	86.71	**88.60**
8	79.24	77.84	79.04	83.04	83.02	84.97	**85.83**
9	73.99	73.78	74.48	76.52	77.13	78.42	**79.23**
10	70.35	74.55	71.95	73.70	74.65	75.45	**76.05**
Avg	82.07	79.10	83.79	87.00	87.26	87.88	**88.27**

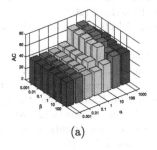
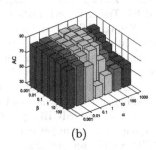

(a)   (b)

Fig. 3. Parameters analysis. (a) PIE face database. (b) NUST603 Chinese handwritten character database.

(2) The performance of the proposed DCNMF1 is also superior to CF. The main reason is that DCNMF1 further incorporates manifold and sparsity information, which helps to improve the ability of feature representation.

(3) DCNMF3 obviously outperforms DCNMF2 on PIE dataset, and achieves the similar performance on NUST603 dataset. This is because the difference between dimensions of the original and the extracted subspaces on PIE dataset is larger than NUST603, which makes it more likely to lead an unstable performance.

Figure 3 shows the performances of DCNMF3 with the varying parameters α and β. As we can see from Fig. 3, the performance of DCNMF3 is relatively stable when β varies from 0.001 to 0.1. On the other hand, α controls the weight of graph, playing a crucial role in the proposed algorithm. It needs to be chosen carefully.

5   Conclusions

In this paper, we propose a deep convex NMF method to enhance the stability of matrix factorization. It is achieved by making use of layer-by-layer factorization and fine-tuning. We also incorporate the graph information and sparse regularized term into the deep factorization model to promote the local ability of image expression. Experimental results on PIE and NUST603 databases demonstrate the superiority of our methods.

Acknowledgments. This paper is partially supported by Natural Science Foundation of Jiangsu Province of China (Grant No. BK20140794) and the Fundamental Research Funds for the Central Universities (No. 30916011326).

References

1. Li, Z.C., Liu, J., Tang, J.H.: Robust structured subspace learning for data representation. IEEE Trans. Pattern Anal. Mach. Intell. **37**, 2085–2098 (2015)
2. Wang, Y.X., Zhang, Y.J.: Nonnegative matrix factorization: a comprehensive review. IEEE Trans. Knowl. Data Eng. **25**, 1336–1353 (2013)
3. Lee, D.D., Seung, H.S.: Learning the parts of objects by non-negative matrix factorization. Nature **401**, 788–791 (1999)
4. Cai, D., He, X., Han, J.: Graph regularized nonnegative matrix factorization for data representation. IEEE Trans. Pattern Anal. Mach. Intell. **33**, 1548–1560 (2011)
5. Xu, W., Gong, Y.: Document clustering based on nonnegative matrix factorization. In: Proceedings of the International Conference on Research and Development in Information Retrieval (SIGIR), pp. 267–273, Toronto, Canada (2003)
6. Xu, W., Gong, Y.: Document clustering by concept factorization. In: Proceedings of the ACM SIGIR, pp. 202–209. ACM Press, Sheffield (2004)
7. Cai, D., He, X., Han, J.: Locally consistent concept factorization for document clustering. IEEE Trans. Knowl. Data Eng. **23**, 902–913 (2011)
8. Cichocki, A., Zdunek, R.: Multilayer nonnegative matrix factorization with projected gradient approaches. Int. J. Neural Syst. **17**, 431–446 (2007)
9. Lyu, S., Wang, X.: On algorithms for sparse multi-factor NMF. In: Advances in Neural Information Processing Systems, pp. 602–610. IEEE Press, Lake Tahoe (2013)
10. Song, H.A., Kim, B.K., Xuan, T.L., Lee, S.Y.: Hierarchical feature extraction by multi-layer non-negative matrix factorization network for classification task. Neurocomputing **165**, 63–74 (2015)
11. Ding, C., Li, T., Jordan, M.I.: Convex and semi-nonnegative matrix factorizations. IEEE Trans. Pattern Anal. Mach. Intell. **32**, 45–55 (2010)
12. Sun, F., Xu, M., Hu, X., Jiang, X.: Graph regularized and sparse nonnegative matrix factorization with hard constraints for data representation. Neurocomputing **173**, 233–244 (2016)
13. Qian, Y., Jia, S., Zhou, J., Robles-Kelly, A.: Hyperspectral unmixing via sparsity-constrained nonnegative matrix factorization. IEEE Trans. Geosci. Remote Sens. **49**, 4282–4297 (2011)
14. LeCun, Y., Bengio, Y., Hinton, G.: Deep learning. Nature **521**, 436–444 (2015)
15. Tao, Y.T., Yang, J., Chang, H.Y.: Enhanced iterative projection for subclass discriminant analysis under EM-alike framework. Pattern Recogn. **47**, 1113–1125 (2014)

Unsupervised Feature Selection with Graph Regularized Nonnegative Self-representation

Yugen Yi[1(✉)], Wei Zhou[2], Yuanlong Cao[1], Qinghua Liu[1],
and Jianzhong Wang[3(✉)]

[1] School of Software, Jiangxi Normal University, Nanchang, China
yiyg510@gmail.com
[2] College of Information Science and Engineering, Northeastern University,
Shenyang, China
[3] College of Computer Science and Information Technology,
Northeast Normal University, Changchun, China
wangjz019@nenu.edu.cn

Abstract. In this paper, we propose a novel algorithm called Graph Regularized Nonnegative Self Representation (GRNSR) for unsupervised feature selection. In our proposed GRNSR, each feature is first represented as a linear combination of its relevant features. Then, an affinity graph is constructed based on nonnegative least squares to capture the inherent local structure information of data. Finally, the $l_{2,1}$-norm and nonnegative constraint are imposed on the representation coefficient matrix to achieve feature selection in batch mode. Moreover, we develop a simple yet efficient iterative update algorithm to solve GRNSR. Extensive experiments are conducted on three publicly available databases (Extended YaleB, CMU PIE and AR) to demonstrate the efficiency of the proposed algorithm. Experimental results show that GRNSR obtains better recognition performance than some other state-of-the-art approaches.

Keywords: Unsupervised feature selection · Nonnegative self-representation · Local structure · Face recognition

1 Introduction

In recent years, feature selection has attracted much research attention along with the dramatically increasing data, particularly in bioinformatics and multimedia [1–3]. Many researchers have proposed various methods for feature selection [1]. These methods can be divided into three categories [1], i.e., supervised feature selection, semi-supervised feature selection and unsupervised feature selection. Supervised feature selection algorithms are able to select discriminative features by using the class information of training data [4, 5]. However, they cannot work under the circumstance in which the labels of training samples are absent [6, 7]. Since labeling all training samples often requires expensive human labor and takes much time, many semi-supervised feature selection approaches have been proposed to utilize the limited labeled data and abundant unlabeled data to improve the performance of feature selection [6, 7]. Compared with supervised and semi-supervised feature selection,

© Springer International Publishing AG 2016
Z. You et al. (Eds.): CCBR 2016, LNCS 9967, pp. 591–599, 2016.
DOI: 10.1007/978-3-319-46654-5_65

unsupervised feature selection is a more challenging task since the label information of the training data is unavailable [8]. Unsupervised feature selection is to select a feature subset that can effectively preserve or uncover the underlying structure of the high-dimensional data. The most representative and classical unsupervised feature selection algorithms are Laplacian Score (LS) [8], Spectral Feature Selection (SPEC) [9], Multi-Cluster Feature Selection (MCFS) [10], Unsupervised Discriminative Feature Selection (UDFS) [11] and Robust Unsupervised Feature Selection (RUFS) [12].

Recently, Zhu et al. [13] proposed a novel unsupervised feature selection algorithm called Regularized Self-Representation (RSR), in which each feature is represented as the linear combination of its relevant features. Although RSR can effectively select the most representative features and achieve state-of-the-art performance, the local structure information of the original data is ignored in it. In other words, RSR cannot guarantee that the nearby data samples in high-dimensional space are still close each other in low-dimensional space. In some recent studies [8, 9], it has been shown that persevering the local structure information is very important. Thus, the local structure information of features should be considered to improve the performance of RSR. Moreover, RSR did not consider the nonnegative property of learned feature weights, which may reduce its physical significance [14].

In this paper, we propose a novel unsupervised feature selection algorithm termed Graph Regularized Non-negative Self-Representation (GRNSR) to address the limitations of RSR. In GRNSR, we simultaneously explore the self-representation and local structure preserving abilities of features. Specifically, each feature is first represented by all other features in our GRNSR. Then, a similarity graph is constructed to uncover the local structure information of samples. Finally, an $l_{2,1}$-norm and a nonnegative constraint are introduced into our algorithm to achieve feature selection. More importantly, we design an efficient iterative algorithm to optimize our objective function. We apply our proposed algorithm to the face recognition task and conduct extensive experiments on three databases including Extended YaleB [15], CMU PIE [16] and AR [17]. The experimental results demonstrate that the proposed GRNSR algorithm outperforms some state-of-the-art unsupervised feature selection methods.

The rest of this paper is organized as follows. In Sect. 2, the proposed GRNSR algorithm is introduced. Section 3 shows the experimental results on three benchmark face image databases and the conclusions are given in Sect. 4.

2 The Proposed Method

In this section, the objective function of the proposed Graph Regularized Nonnegative Self Representation (GRNSR) algorithm is introduced. Then, an efficient iterative algorithm is also given to solve the objective function of GRNSR.

Let $X = [x_1; x_2;....,x_n] \in R^{n \times m}$ denotes a high-dimensional training data matrix, where $x_i \in R^{1 \times m}$ represents the i-th sample, m and n are the number of features and total number of samples. Let $f_1, f_2,...., f_m$ be the corresponding feature vectors that record the feature value in each sample. Thus, the data matrix X can also be represented as $X = [f_1, f_2,...., f_m]$. For any matrix $A \in R^{n \times m}$, we denote a^i and a_j as its i-th row and the j-th column, respectively. The Frobenius norm and $l_{2,1}$-norm of a matrix A are defined as $\|A\|_F = \sqrt{\sum_i^m \|a^i\|_2^2}$ and $\|A\|_{2,1} = \sum_i^m \|a^i\|_2$, respectively.

2.1 The Objective Function

Similar to RSR, the first object of GRNSR is also to exploit the self-representation capability of features. Therefore, we represent each feature as a non-negative linear combination of other features. Specifically, for each feature f_j from X, we have

$$f_j \approx \sum_{i=1}^m f_i w_{i,j} = X w_j \tag{1}$$

where $w_j = [w_{1,j}, \ldots, w_{2,j}, \ldots, w_{m,j}] \in R^{m \times 1}$ is a non-negative representation coefficient vector of feature f_j. Then, for all features, we have

$$X \approx XW \tag{2}$$

where $W = [w^1; \ldots, w^m] \in R^{m \times m}$ is a non-negative representation coefficient matrix, $w^i = [w_{i,1}, \ldots, w_{i,j}, \ldots, w_{i,m}] \in R^{1 \times m}$ is a i-th row vector of W.

In order to obtain matrix W, we can solve the following constrained least square regression problem

$$\min \|X - XW\|_F^2 \quad s.t. \quad W \geq 0 \tag{3}$$

However, Eq. (3) is sensitive to noise and outliers. Thus, the $l_{2,1}$-norm based loss function is introduced [13, 14]. As a result, we can get a robust regression model as

$$\min \|X - XW\|_{2,1} \quad s.t. \quad W \geq 0 \tag{4}$$

Inspired by the success of spectral analysis and manifold learning [8, 9], the second aim of our proposed GRNSR is to select the features which can well preserve the local geometrical structure of high-dimensional data. Therefore, we firstly construct a neighborhood weighted graph on given data by putting an edge between each sample and its k-nearest neighbors. Let $N_k(x_i)$ denotes the set of k-nearest neighbors of x_i, the weight matrix S can be obtained by minimizing the following objective function

$$\min \varepsilon(S) = \sum_{i=1}^n \|x_i - \sum_{j \in N_k(x_i)} S_{ij} x_j\|^2 \quad s.t. \quad S \geq 0 \tag{5}$$

Equation (5) is a typically Nonnegative Least Squares (NNLS) problem. In this paper, an active set method which is implemented as a function *lsqnonneg* in matlab is adopted to solve this problem. To ensure symmetry, S can be symmetrized as $S_{ij} = (S_{ij} + S_{ji})/2$.

Then, in order to ensure that the samples which are close to each other are also adjacent after feature selection, the proposed GRNSR needs to minimize the following problem

$$\min \sum_{i,j=1}^{n} ||W^T x_i^T - W^T x_j^T||_2^2 S_{ij} \qquad (6)$$

where $W^T x_i^T$ is an approximate representation of x_i in low-dimensional space.

By simple algebra formulation, Eq. (6) can be reformulated as

$$\min \sum_{i,j=1}^{n} ||W^T x_i^T - W^T x_j^T||_2^2 S_{ij} = tr(W^T X^T LXW) = tr(W^T MW) \qquad (7)$$

where $L = D-S$ is the Laplacian matrix, D is a diagonal matrix whose entries are column (or row, since S is symmetric) sums of S, that is $D_{ii} = \sum_{j=1}^{n} S_{ij}$, and $M = X^T LX$.

At last, in order to achieve feature selection, we impose an $l_{2,1}$-norm on matrix W to make sure that the matrix W is sparse in rows. Therefore, we can get the final objective function of our proposed GRNSR as

$$\min ||X - XW||_{2,1} + \alpha\, tr(W^T MW) + \beta\, ||W||_{2,1} \quad s.t.\ W \geq 0 \qquad (8)$$

where $\alpha \geq 0$ and $\beta \geq 0$ are two regularization parameters to control the tradeoff among the three terms.

Once W is learned, we can select the top p ranked features by sorting all m features according to $||w^i||_2$ $(i = 1,2,\ldots,m)$ in descending order.

2.2　Optimization Method

As can be seen in Eq. (8), the objective function involves the $l_{2,1}$-norm, which is non-smooth and cannot be solved by a closed form. Consequently, we design an iterative algorithm to optimize our GRNSR model.

For a matrix $A \in R^{n \times m}$, we have $||A||_{2,1} = tr(A^T GA)$, where G is a diagonal matrix with the i-th diagonal elements as $g_{ii} = 1/(2||a^i||_2)$ [18]. Thus, it can be easily verified that Eq. (8) is equivalent to the following function

$$\min tr((X - XW)^T R(X - XW)) + \alpha\, tr(W^T MW) + \beta\, tr(W^T QW) \quad s.t.\ W \geq 0 \qquad (9)$$

where R and Q are diagonal matrices with each diagonal elements $r_{ii} = 1/(2||x_i - x_i W||_2)$ and $q_{ii} = 1/(2||w^i||_2)$, respectively.

Let

$$\varphi(W) = tr((X - XW)^T R(X - XW)) + \alpha\, tr(W^T MW) + \lambda\, tr(W^T QW) \qquad (10)$$

Then we define $\psi = [\psi_{ij}]$ as the Lagrange multipliers for $W \geq 0$ and the Lagrangian function of Eq. (10) is

$$\rho(W) = \varphi(W) + tr(\psi\, W) \qquad (11)$$

The partial derivation of Eq. (11) with respect to W is

$$\partial \rho(W)/\partial W = X^T RXW + \alpha MW + \beta QW - X^T RX + \psi \qquad (12)$$

Using the KKT condition $\psi_{ij} W_{ij} = 0$ [19], we have

$$(PW + \alpha MW + \beta QW - P)_{ij} W_{ij} = 0 \qquad (13)$$

where $P = X^T RX$.

Similar to [19], we define $M = M^+ - M^-$, where

$$M_{ij}^+ = (|M_{ij}| + M_{ij})/2, \qquad M_{ij}^- = (|M_{ij}| - M_{ij})/2 \qquad (14)$$

We substitute the decomposed positive and negative parts into Eq. (14), which leads to the update rule of variable W as

$$W_{ij} \leftarrow W_{ij} \frac{(\alpha M^- W + P)_{ij}}{(PW + \beta QW + \alpha M^+ W)_{ij}} \qquad (15)$$

Therefore, we can solve Eq. (8) by updating W, R and Q alternately. At the t-th iteration, W_t is updated with R_{t-1} and Q_{t-1}, then R_t and Q_t is updated with W_t. This procedure is repeated until convergence.

3 Experiments Results and Analysis

In this section, the recognition performances of our GRNSR are evaluated and compared with Baseline, LS [8], SPEC [9], MCFS [10], UDFS [11], RUFS [12] and RSR [13] on three standard face databases (Extended YaleB [15], AR [16] and CMU PIE [17]). Here, baseline denotes that all features are adopted for face recognition. All images are manually aligned and cropped, and then resized to the resolution of 32×32 pixels. For each database, we randomly select l images from each person for training, and the remaining images are used for testing. The random training sample selection is repeated 10 times and the average recognition results are reported. The information of each database is given in Table 1.

In our GRNSR and other algorithms, there are some parameters which need to be set in advance. For LS, MCFS, SPEC UDFS, RUFS and NDFS, we fix the size of neighborhood k as 5 on all the databases. In order to fairly compare the performances of different unsupervised feature selection algorithms, we tune the parameters for all

Table 1. Summary of the three databases

Databases	Features	Classes	Number	Train	Test
Extended YaleB	1024	38	64	20	44
CMU PIE	1024	68	24	12	12
AR	1024	100	14	7	7

methods by a gird-search strategy from $\{10^{-3}, 10^{-2}, 10^{-1}, 1, 10^1, 10^2, 10^3\}$, and set the number of the selected features from 10 to 500 with the interval of 10. For all algorithms, we report the best recognition results from the optimal parameters. In our experiments, we employ the nearest neighbor classifier with Euclidean distance to classify the samples based on the selected features by different algorithms.

From the experimental results of different feature selection algorithms on three databases listed in Table 2, we have the following observations. (1) It can be seen that the performances of feature selection algorithms are generally better than using all features, which indicates that the feature selection procedure is beneficial to remove the noise and redundancy features to improve the classification performance. (2) The joint feature selection algorithms including MCFS, UDFS, RUFS and GRNSR are always superior to those methods which select the features in one by one manner, such as LS and SPEC. This is due to that MCFS, UDFS, RUFS and GRNSR select features in a batch model and the correlation among features is considered during feature selection. (3) RSR and GRNSR achieve better performance than other methods. This demonstrates that taking advantage of the self-representation ability of features is benefit to select the most representative features. In summary, GRNSR achieves the best performance on all databases due to GRNSR considers the self-representation and locality structure preserving abilities of features.

Then, the performances of different algorithms under various numbers of selected features are shown in Fig. 1. We can find that with the increase of the number of selected features at the beginning, the recognition rates of all algorithms are also improved. However, the trend is not maintained for all the numbers of selected features. When they achieve their best results, the recognition results of most algorithms begin to stay stable. For AR database, though the recognition results obtained by our algorithm are worse than some other methods (such as SPEC, UDFS and RUFS) when the number of selected features is relatively small. With the increase in number of selected features, the performance of our GRNSR becomes better and finally superior to all other unsupervised feature selection methods at higher dimension, which also demonstrates the advantage of our algorithm.

Table 2. The best average recognition rates (%) and standard deviations (%) of different feature selection algorithms on the three face databases

Methods	Extended YaleB	CMU PIE	AR
Baseline	61.93 ± 0.81(1024)	85.63 ± 0.72(1024)	62.06 ± 1.62(1024)
LS	48.50 ± 1.42(500)	81.96 ± 1.80(500)	58.51 ± 1.55(500)
SPEC	64.18 ± 0.96(500)	87.49 ± 0.82(470)	64.56 ± 1.54(500)
MCFS	65.89 ± 1.78(200)	87.91 ± 0.84(490)	65.21 ± 1.58(500)
UDFS	65.54 ± 2.33(500)	88.66 ± 0.93(410)	66.60 ± 1.50(500)
RUFS	66.97 ± 1.32(480)	88.99 ± 0.91(490)	66.61 ± 1.71(480)
RSR	68.83 ± 1.06(500)	89.37 ± 0.85(440)	66.71 ± 1.47(440)
GRNSR	70.86 ± 1.10(220)	90.99 ± 1.09(430)	68.62 ± 1.55(480)

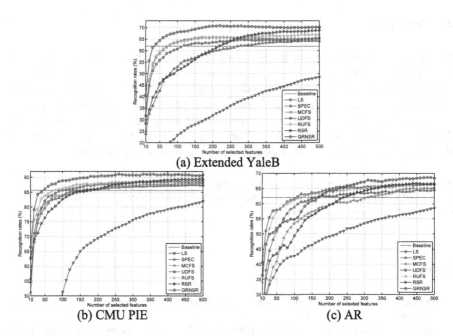

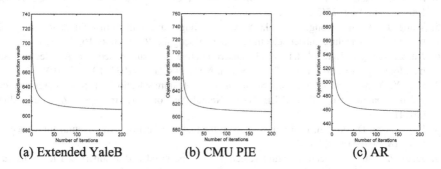

Fig. 1. Recognition rate versus the number of selected features of different feature selection algorithms on three databases.

Fig. 2. The convergence curves of GRNSR on three face databases.

Finally, the convergence curves of our GRNSR on three face databases are provided in Fig. 2. In this figure, the x-axis and y-axis represent the iteration number and value of objective function respectively. From this figure, we can clearly see that the proposed iterative updating scheme can be converged within 200 iterations.

4   Conclusions

In this paper, we propose a new unsupervised feature selection algorithm named Graph Regularized Non-negative Self-Representation (GRNSR), which considers self-representation and local structure information of features in high-dimensional data. Meanwhile, an efficient iterative algorithm is also provided to optimize the objective function of our algorithm. Through extensive face recognition experiments on three databases (Extended YaleB, CMU PIE and AR), it can be found that the proposed algorithm outperforms some state-of-the-art feature selection approaches.

Acknowledgment. This work is supported by National Natural Science Foundation of China (Nos. 61403078 and 61562044), Science and Technology Research Project of Liaoning Province Education Department (No. L2014450).

References

1. Alelyani, S., Tang, J., Liu, H.: Feature selection for clustering: a review. Data Clustering: Algorithms Appl. **29**, 59 (2013)
2. Zhang, B., Perina, A., Li, Z., et al.: Bounding multiple gaussians uncertainty with application to object tracking. Int. J. Comput. Vision **118**(3), 364–379 (2016). doi:10.1007/s11263-016-0880-y
3. Zhang, B., Perina, A., Murino, V., et al.: Sparse representation classification with manifold constraints transfer. IEEE Conf. on Comput. Vis. Pattern Recognit., 4557–4565 (2015)
4. Zhao, Z., Wang, L., Liu, H., et al.: On similarity preserving feature selection. IEEE Trans. Knowl. Data Eng. **25**(3), 619–632 (2013)
5. Wang, J., Wu, L., Kong, J., et al.: Maximum weight and minimum redundancy: a novel framework for feature subset selection. Pattern Recognit. **46**(6), 1616–1627 (2013)
6. Xu, Z., King, I., Lyu, M.R.T., et al.: Discriminative semi-supervised feature selection via manifold regularization. IEEE Trans. Neural Networks **21**(7), 1033–1047 (2010)
7. Han, Y., Yang, Y., Yan, Y., et al.: Semi-supervised feature selection via spline regression for video semantic recognition. IEEE Trans. Neural Networks. Learn. Syst. **26**(2), 252–264 (2014)
8. He, X., Cai, D., Niyogi, P.: Laplacian score for feature selection. Adv. Neural Inf. Process. Syst. **18**, 507–514 (2005)
9. Zhao, Z., Liu, H.: Spectral feature selection for supervised and unsupervised learning. In: Proceedings of the 24th International Conference on Machine Learning, pp. 1151–1157. ACM, New York (2007)
10. Cai, D., Zhang, C., He, X.: Unsupervised feature selection for multi-cluster data. In: Proceedings of the 16th ACM SIGKDD International Conference on Knowledge Discovery and Data Mining, pp. 333–342. ACM, New York (2010)
11. Yang, Y., Shen, H.T., Ma, Z., et al.: L2, 1-Norm regularized discriminative feature selection for unsupervised learning. In: Proceedings of International Joint Conference on Artificial Intelligence, vol. 22(1), p. 1589 (2011)
12. Qian, M., Zhai, C.: Robust unsupervised feature selection. In: Proceedings of the Twenty-Third International Joint Conference on Artificial Intelligence, pp. 1621–1627. AAAI Press, Menlo Park (2013)

13. Zhu, P., Zuo, W., Zhang, L., et al.: Unsupervised feature selection by regularized self-representation. Pattern Recognit. **48**(2), 438–446 (2015)
14. Yan, H., Yang, J., Yang, J.: Robust joint feature weights learning framework. IEEE Trans. Know. Data Eng. **28**(5), 1327–1339 (2016)
15. Lee, K., Ho, J., Kriegman, D.: Acquiring linear subspaces for face recognition under variable lighting. IEEE Trans. Pattern Anal. Mach. Intell. **27**(5), 684–698 (2005)
16. Terence, S., Simon, B., Maan, B.: The CMU pose, illumination, and expression (PIE) database. IEEE Trans. Pattern Anal. Mach. Intell. **25**(12), 1615–1618 (2003)
17. Martinez A M. The AR face database. CVC Technical report 24 (1998)
18. Nie, F., Huang, H., Cai, X., et al.: Efficient and robust feature selection via joint l2,1 norms minimization. Adv. Neural Inform. Process. Syst. **378**, 1813–1821 (2010)
19. Ding, C., Li, T.: Jordan MI convex and semi-nonnegative matrix factorizations. IEEE Trans. Pattern Anal. Mach. Intell. **32**(1), 45–55 (2010)

Local Dual-Cross Ternary Pattern for Feature Representation

Peng Zhou[1,2,3], Yucong Peng[1,2,3], Jifeng Shen[3], Baochang Zhang[4],
and Wankou Yang[1,2,3(✉)]

[1] School of Automation, Southeast University, Nanjing 210096, China
wankou.yang@yahoo.com
[2] Key Lab of Measurement and Control of Complex Systems of Engineering,
Ministry of Education, Nanjing 210096, China
[3] School of Electrical and Information Engineering, Jiangsu University, Zhenjiang 212013, China
[4] School of Automation Science and Electrical Engineering, Beihang University,
Beijing 100191, China

Abstract. Extracting effective features is a fundamental issue in image representation and recognition. In this paper, we present a new feature representation method for image recognition based on Local Ternary Pattern and Dual-Cross Pattern, named Local Dual-Cross Ternary Pattern (LDCTP). LDCTP is a feature representation inspired by the sole textural structure of human faces. It is efficient and only quadruples the cost of computing Local Binary Pattern. Experiments show that LDCTP outperforms other descriptors.

Keywords: LBP · LDCTP · Feature representation · Face recognition

1 Introduction

Face recognition is a longstanding computer vision problem and has been a hot research topic due to both the development of computer science and its potential application. However, only in controlled environments, satisfactory performance has been achieved. There has been increased demands for identification of unconstrained face images, such as face images captured by surveillance cameras or pictures selected from the internet. However, identification of unconstrained face images is a difficult issue due to the wide variations of illumination, pose, and expression.

A face recognition system usually consists of a face representation stage and a face matching stage [1]. In face representation, good representations discriminate interpersonal differences while being robust to intra-personal variations. For face matching, multi-class classifiers have been used for face identification, such as the nearest neighbor(NN) classifier and the sparse representation classifier (SRC) [2], and for two-class classifiers, such as support vector machine (SVM) [3] and Bayesian analysis [4] have been used for face recognition too. Consequently, extracting effective features (i.e. feature representation) is a fundamental step in face recognition.

In recent years, a number of face representation methods have been proposed, and they can be mainly classified into two categories: holistic features and local features.

© Springer International Publishing AG 2016
Z. You et al. (Eds.): CCBR 2016, LNCS 9967, pp. 600–608, 2016.
DOI: 10.1007/978-3-319-46654-5_66

Representative holistic features include principal component analysis (PCA) [5] and linear discriminant analysis (LDA) [6], and typical local features are local binary pattern (LBP) and Gabor wavelets [7]. Several variants of LBP have been proposed, e.g., Local Ternary Pattern (LTP) [8], three-patch LBP (TP-LBP) [9] and multi-block LBP (MB-LBP) [10]. While these descriptors have achieved encouraging recognition performance in controlled environments, their performance is still far from satisfactory in unconstrained environment.

Here we proposed a novel image descriptor, called Local Dual-Cross Ternary Pattern (LDCTP). Inspired by the unique textural structure of human faces, LDCTP extracts discriminative information for eight directions. By grouping the sampled pixels into two groups appropriately from the perspective of maximum joint Shannon entropy [11], we keep the feature size of LDCTP reasonable. LDCTP achieves superior performance and reasonable feature size.

2 Related Works

2.1 Local Binary Pattern

The local binary pattern (LBP) descriptor was proposed by Ojala et al. [12] as a gray-scale invariant texture pattern. LBP is a way to describe the characteristics of local texture. For a pixel A in an image, its LBP code is computed by thresholding its circularly symmetric n neighbors in a circle of radius r with the pixel value of the central point and arranging the results as a binary string. For clarity, we denote the LBP of pixel A by $LBP_{n,r}(A)$, which is defined as follows:

$$LBP_{n,r}(A) = \sum_{i=0}^{n-1} S(g_i - g_c)2^i \quad s(x) = \begin{cases} 1, & x \geq 0 \\ 0, & x < 0 \end{cases} \tag{1}$$

where A is a two-dimensional coordinates of a point in an image, g_c is the pixel value of point A, and g_i is the pixel value of point A's i^{th} neighbor. LBP is gray-scale invariant because the function (g_i-g_c) is invariant to monotonic change of illumination. The computation of LBP is illustrated in Fig. 1.

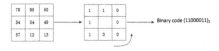

Fig. 1. Illustration of the basic local binary pattern

2.2 Local Ternary Pattern

Local ternary pattern (LTP) [13] is an extension of LBP. LTP extends LBP to 3-valued codes, in which gray-levels in a zone of width around are quantized to zero, ones above this are quantized to 1 and ones below it to −1, i.e., the indicator is replaced with a 3-valued function

$$s(x) = \begin{cases} 1 & g_i - g_c > t \\ 0 & |g_i - g_c| \le t \\ -1 & g_i - g_c < -t \end{cases} \qquad (2)$$

where $t > 0$ is the threshold. The computation of LTP is illustrated in Fig. 2.

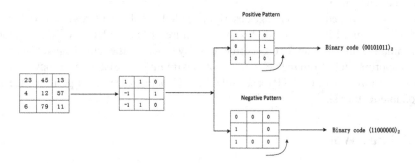

Fig. 2. Illustration of the computation of LTP

2.3   Dual-Cross Pattern

DCP (Dual-Cross Pattern) is proposed by C. Ding et al. [14]. The essence of DCP is to perform local sampling and pattern encoding in the most informative directions contained within face images.

Local sampling of DCP is conducted as shown in Fig. 3. Sixteen points are sampled around the central pixel O. The sampled points A_0 to A_7 are uniformly spaced on an inner circle of radius Rin, while B_0 to B_7 are evenly distributed on the exterior circle with radius Rex.

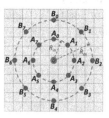

Fig. 3. Local sampling of DCP

We assign each of the eight directions a unique decimal number:

$$DCP_i = S(I_{A_i} - I_0) \times 2 + S(I_{B_i} - I_{A_i}), 0 \le i \le 7 \qquad s(x) = \begin{cases} 1, & x \ge 0 \\ 0, & x < 0 \end{cases} \qquad (3)$$

DCP_0~DCP_7 are grouped into two subsets from the perspective of maximum joint Shannon entropy. We define the subset $\{DCP_0, DCP_2, DCP_4, DCP_6\}$ as the first subset and $\{DCP_1, DCP_3, DCP_5, DCP_7\}$ as the second subset. We name the two cross encoders DCP-1 and DCP-2, respectively. The codes produced by the two encoders at each pixel are represented as

$$DCP\text{-}1 = \sum_{i=0}^{3} DCP_{2i} \times 4^i \tag{4}$$

$$DCP\text{-}2 = \sum_{i=0}^{3} DCP_{2i+1} \times 4^i \tag{5}$$

The DCP descriptor for a face image is the concatenation of the two codes produced by the two cross encoders:

$$DCP = \left\{ \sum_{i=0}^{3} DCP_{2i} \times 4^i, \ \sum_{i=0}^{3} DCP_{2i+1} \times 4^i \right\} \tag{6}$$

3 Local Dual-Cross Ternary Pattern

The design of a feature representation consists of three main parts: image filtering, local sampling, and pattern encoding. The implementation of image filtering is flexible: possible methods include Gabor wavelets [15], Difference of Gaussian (DoG) [16], or the recently proposed discriminative image filter [17]. In this paper, we focus on local sampling and pattern encoding, which are the core components of a image feature representation [18].

3.1 Local Sampling

Local sampling of LDCTP is the same as DCP descriptor, we sample in the local neighborhood along the 0, $\pi/4$, $\pi/2$, $3\pi/4$, π, $5\pi/4$, $3\pi/2$, and 7/4 directions, as illustrated in Fig. 3.

3.2 Pattern Encoding

Encoding of the sampled points is realized in two steps. First, textural information along each of the eight directions is independently encoded. Second, patterns in all eight directions are combined to form the final LTDCP codes. To quantize the textural information in each sampling direction, we assign each a number:

$$LDCTP_i = S\left(I_{A_i} - I_O\right) \times 2 + S\left(I_{B_i} - I_{A_i}\right), 0 \leq i \leq 7 \tag{7}$$

where $S(x)$ is the Eq. (3) in Sect. 2.2. I_O, I_{Ai}, and I_{Bi} are the gray value of points O, A_i, and B_i, respectively. Therefore, four patterns are defined in each direction and each of the four patterns denotes one type of textural structure.

The probable value of $LDCTP_i$ is $-3,-2,-1,0,1,2,3$. The results of the computation above can split in positive pattern and negative pattern. The example of the computation is show in Fig. 4.

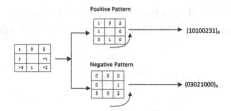

Fig. 4. The example of LDCTP computation

3.3 Image Feature Representation

By considering all eight directions, the total number of LDCTP is $4^8 = 65536$. We adopt grouping strategy to decrease the feature size of LDCTP like DCP. As a result, we define $\{\text{LDCTP}_0, \text{LDCTP}_2, \text{LDCTP}_4, \text{LDCTP}_6\}$ as the first subset and $\{\text{LDCTP}_1, \text{LDCTP}_3, \text{LDCTP}_5, \text{LDCTP}_7\}$ as the second subset.

We name the two cross encoders generated by positive pattern P1, P2, and the other two cross encoders generated by negative pattern N1, N2, respectively. The codes produced by the four encoders at each pixel O are represented as

$$P1 = \sum_{i=0}^{3} P_{2i} \times 4^i \tag{8}$$

$$P2 = \sum_{i=0}^{3} P_{2i} + 1 \times 4^i \tag{9}$$

$$N1 = \sum_{i=0}^{3} N_{2i} \times 4^i \tag{10}$$

$$N2 = \sum_{i=0}^{3} N_{2i+1} \times 4^i \tag{11}$$

The LDCTP descriptor for each pixel O in an image is the concatenation of the four codes generated by the four cross encoders:

$$LDCTP = \left\{ \sum_{i=0}^{3} P_{2i} \times 4^i, \ \sum_{i=0}^{3} N_{2i} \times 4^i, \ \sum_{i=0}^{3} P_{2i+1} \times 4^i, \ \sum_{i=0}^{3} N_{2i+1} \times 4^i \right\} \tag{12}$$

The example of the computation is shown in Fig. 5.

After encoding each pixel in the image using the local ternary dual-cross encoders, four code spectrums are produced and are respectively divided into a $M \times N$ grid of non-overlapping regions. Histograms of LDCTP codes are computed in each region and all histograms are concatenated to form the final feature. We can measure the similarity between a pair of images by measuring the final features via the chi-squared distance or histogram intersection.

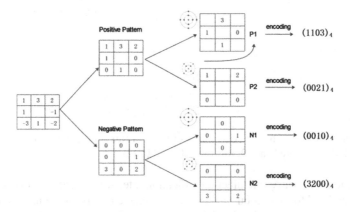

Fig. 5. An example of LDCTP computation

4 Experiments

In this section, the proposed LDCTP are evaluated in both controlled and uncontrolled face recognition. To perform fair comparison with existing methods, all experiments in this section are conducted on FERET database [19] and nearest neighbor classifier is used for all descriptors. We choose 1000 subjects from FERET database, every subject has 2 face images, which was captured with different facial expressions and under different illumination conditions. Every image is in grayscale and normalized to the resolution of 120×142. Example images of the database are shown in Fig. 6.

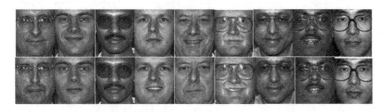

Fig. 6. Sample face images from FERET

There are four parameters for LDCTP, the threshold t and radius R_{in} and R_{ex} (different values of R_{in} and R_{ex} captures information on different scales) and the region number N. A larger value of N helps to preserve spatial information but makes the descriptor more sensitive to misalignment errors.

The mean identification rates against for different values of Radius R_{in} and R_{ex} are plotted in Fig. 7. Different values of R_{in} and R_{ex} capture information on different scales. This experiment shows that small value of R_{in} and large value of R_{ex} can achieve mean highest identification rate.

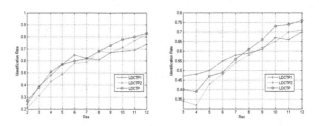

Fig. 7. Identification rate for different values of Rin and Rex. (left picture Rin = 1, Rex range from 2 to 12; right picture Rin = 2, Rex range from 3 to 12)

The region number N can affect identification rate. A larger value of N achieves to conserve spatial information but makes the face image descriptor be more sensitive to misalignment errors. We take the value of N range from 1 to 12. The results of the experiment are plotted in Fig. 8. Identification rate significantly increased as the value of region number N increases.

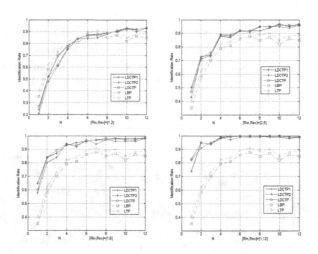

Fig. 8. Identification rate for different values of N.

In this section, the performance of LDCTP for face recognition tasks is evaluated and makes a contrast with other descriptor. Identification rates for different face image descriptors are listed in Table 1.

According to the results of experiments above, LDCTP outperforms LBP by 20 % and outperforms DCP by 10 %, respectively. LDCTP is shown to have strong discriminative power and consistently achieves excellent performance. Select the appropriate parameter is important to achieve high identification rate. The value of threshold range from 2 to 6 can achieve satisfied identification rate and we choose 5 as the value of threshold usually. The smaller value of R_{in} and the larger value of R_{ex} can achieve higher identification rate. Increase the value of region number N, the identification rate can be significantly increased.

Table 1. Identification rate for different face image descriptors

	Num = 100	Num = 200	Num = 500	Num = 1000
LBP	0.790	0.740	0.590	0.470
LTP	0.820	0.790	0.771	0.700
DCP1	0.870	0.890	0.826	0.811
DCP2	0.840	0.890	0.814	0.774
DCP	0.920	0.920	0.850	0.832
LTDCP1	*0.980*	0.965	0.882	0.864
LTDCP2	*0.990*	0.960	0.876	0.869
LTDCP	*0.990*	0.965	0.896	0.890

*Note that the region number N is 4 for all of the descriptors, for DCP, Rin = 2, Rex = 5, For LDCTP, Rin = 1, Rex = 12 and threshold=5; the number of images increase from 100 to 1000.

5   Conclusion

To extract efficient image feature and a comprehensive image representation scheme, we have presented a novel feature named LDCTP (Local Dual-Cross Ternary Pattern) using the textural characteristics of human faces, which consistently shows better performance and better discriminative power than other face descriptor. LTDCP is based on Local Ternary Pattern and Dual-Cross Pattern. Experiments demonstrated that LDCTP was efficient, effective and of a well-balanced tradeoff between the discriminative power and robustness. It is difficult to select a suitable threshold t like LTP. In the future, we will do more work to give automatic strategy to select the threshold.

Acknowledgments. This project is partly supported by NSF of China (61375001, 31200747), the Natural Science Foundation of Jiangsu Province (No. BK20140638, BK2012437, BK20140566, BK20150470), the Fundamental Research Funds for the Central Universities.

References

1. Turk, M., Pentland, A.P.: Face recognition system: U.S. Patent 5,164,992. 1992-11-17
2. Wright, J., Yang, A.Y., Ganesh, A., Sastry, S.S., Ma, Y.: Robust face recognition via sparse representation. IEEE Trans. Pattern Anal. Mach. Intell. **31**(2), 210–227 (2009)
3. Cortes, C., Vapnik, V.: Support vector machine. Mach. Learn. **20**(3), 273–297 (1995)
4. Berger, J.: The case for objective Bayesian analysis. Bayesian Anal. **1**(3), 385–402 (2006)
5. Turk, M., Pentland, A.: Eigenfaces for recognition. J. Cogn. Neurosci. **3**(1), 71–86 (1991)
6. Belhumeur, P.N., Hespanha, J.P., Kriegman, D.J.: Eigenfaces vs. fisherfaces: recognition using class specific linear projection. IEEE Trans. Pattern Anal. Mach. Intell. **19**(7), 711–720 (1997)
7. Liu, C., Wechsler, H.: Gabor feature based classification using the enhanced fisher linear discriminant model for face recognition. IEEE Trans. Image Process. **11**(4), 467–476 (2002)

8. Tan, X., Triggs, B.: Enhanced local texture feature sets for face recognition under difficult lighting conditions. IEEE Trans. Image Process. **19**(6), 1635–1650 (2010)

9. Wolf, L., Hassner, T., Taigman, Y.: Effective unconstrained face recognition by combining multiple descriptors and learned background statistics. IEEE Trans. Pattern Anal. Mach. Intell. **33**(10), 1978–1990 (2011)

10. Liao, S., Zhu, X., Lei, Z., Zhang, L., Li, S.Z.: Learning multi-scale block local binary patterns for face recognition. In: Lee, S.-W., Li, S.Z. (eds.) ICB 2007. LNCS, vol. 4642, pp. 828–837. Springer, Heidelberg (2007)

11. Lin, J.: Divergence measures based on the Shannon entropy. IEEE Trans. Inf. Theor. **37**(1), 145–151 (1991)

12. Ojala, T., Pietikäinen, M., Mäenpää, T.: Multiresolution gray-scale and rotation invariant texture classification with local binary patterns. IEEE Trans. Pattern Anal. Mach. Intell. **24**(7), 971–987 (2002)

13. Ren, J., Jiang, X., Yuan, J.: Relaxed local ternary pattern for face recognition. In: ICIP, pp. 3680–3684 (2013)

14. Ding, C., Choi, J., Tao, D., et al.: Multi-directional multi-level dual-cross patterns for robust face recognition. IEEE Trans. Pattern Anal. Mach. Intell. (1), 1

15. Xie, S., Shan, S., Chen, X., Chen, J.: Fusing local patterns of gabor magnitude and phase for face recognition. IEEE Trans. Image Process. **19**(5), 1349–1361 (2010)

16. Bay, H., Tuytelaars, T., Van Gool, L.: SURF: speeded up robust features. In: Leonardis, A., Bischof, H., Pinz, A. (eds.) ECCV 2006, Part I. LNCS, vol. 3951, pp. 404–417. Springer, Heidelberg (2006)

17. Lei, Z., Yi, D., Li, S.Z.: Discriminant image filter learning for face recognition with local binary pattern like representation. In: Proceedings of the IEEE Conference on Computer Vision and Pattern Recognition, pp. 2512–2517 (2012)

18. Zhang, B., Gao, Y., Zhao, S., et al.: Local derivative pattern versus local binary pattern: face recognition with high-order local pattern descriptor. IEEE Trans. Image Process. **19**(2), 533–544 (2010)

19. Phillips, P.J., Wechsler, H., Huang, J., et al.: The FERET database and evaluation procedure for face-recognition algorithms. Image Vis. Comput. **16**(5), 295–306 (1998)

Anti-Spoofing and Privacy

Cross-Database Face Antispoofing with Robust Feature Representation

Keyurkumar Patel[1], Hu Han[2(✉)], and Anil K. Jain[1]

[1] Department of Computer Science and Engineering, Michigan State University,
East Lansing, MI 48824, USA
{patelke6,jain}@msu.edu
[2] Key Lab of Intelligent Information Processing, Chinese Academy of Sciences
(CAS), Institute of Computing Technology, CAS, Beijing 100190, China
hanhu@ict.ac.cn

Abstract. With the wide applications of user authentication based on face recognition, face spoof attacks against face recognition systems are drawing increasing attentions. While emerging approaches of face anti-spoofing have been reported in recent years, most of them limit to the non-realistic intra-database testing scenarios instead of the cross-database testing scenarios. We propose a robust representation integrating deep texture features and face movement cue like eye-blink as countermeasures for presentation attacks like photos and replays. We learn deep texture features from both aligned facial images and whole frames, and use a frame difference based approach for eye-blink detection. A face video clip is classified as live if it is categorized as live using both cues. Cross-database testing on public-domain face databases shows that the proposed approach significantly outperforms the state-of-the-art.

Keywords: Face liveness detection · Cross-database generalizability · Deep texture feature · Eye-blinking detection

1 Introduction

A number of studies on spoof attacks against face recognition (FR) systems show that state-of-the-art (SOTA) FR systems are still vulnerable [1–4]. Additionally, most FR systems are designed to represent the individual face images of the same subject in a way that minimizes the intra-person variations like illumination, pose, and modality [5]. These properties of FR systems, to some degree, reduce their ability to distinguish between live and spoof face images. Such vulnerabilities can lead to financial loss and security breaches when FR alone is used for authentication. As more security systems leverage face for user authentication, an increasing focus is shifting towards developing face antispoofing algorithms to prevent malicious users from gaining access.

H. Han's research is partially supported by Natural Science Foundation of China (grant No. 61672496). H. Han would also like to thank NVIDIA for donating a GPU used in the research.

© Springer International Publishing AG 2016
Z. You et al. (Eds.): CCBR 2016, LNCS 9967, pp. 611–619, 2016.
DOI: 10.1007/978-3-319-46654-5_67

An authorized user's face images or videos can be easily obtained covertly by a smartphone camera or from social media, and used to spoof a FR system. Creating a realistic 3D face mask of an authorized user is also possible using multiple 2D face images. As spoof attacks are diverse in nature, a FR system may require a series of modules focusing on detecting each of the 2D and 3D attacks. In this paper, we focus on 2D attacks by photos and replays as they can be easily launched with low cost. However, even 2D face spoof detection alone is non-trivial. As shown in Fig. 1, even humans will find it difficult to distinguish between live and spoof face images.

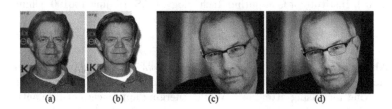

Fig. 1. Visual comparisons between spoof face images (a, c) captured from printed photos and real face images (b, d) indicate the challenges of face antispoofing.

A number of solutions to 2D face antispoofing have been proposed, but many of them do not generalize well to unconstrained scenarios. The generalization ability of face antispoofing approaches need to be significantly improved before they can be adopted by operational systems. Humans distinguish between a live face and a face photograph unconsciously by leveraging physical (*e.g.,* 3D shape, texture, and material) and behavioral (spontaneous facial motions like blink, sight, expression, etc.) cues that are generalizable. For example, human can easily distinguish between skin and other materials like paper and digital screen; facial motions are effective for identifying photographic attacks. These observations motivate us to use both physical and behavioral cues in designing our face antispoofing algorithms.

In the proposed approach, we integrate texture feature and eye-blink cue to achieve robust face antispoofing. We learn deep texture features from both aligned face images and whole video frames, because texture distortions in spoof face images exist in both face and non-face regions. We also design a frame difference based approach for efficient eye-blink detection. A face video clip is classified as live if it is categorized as live using both cues. The contributions of this paper include: (i) a novel texture representation using both aligned face images and whole video frames, highlighting general texture differences between live and spoof face images; (ii) a frame difference based approach for efficient eye-blink detection, complementing texture cue with low computational cost; and (iii) significantly improved cross-database testing performance than the SOTAs.

2   Related Work

Face antispoofing methods cover different categories from face motion analysis, texture analysis, image quality analysis to active methods [3,6]. In this paper, we briefly review related work on texture analysis and eye-blink detection.

2.1   Texture Analysis for Antispoofing

Face texture analysis based methods try to capture the texture differences between live and spoof face images from the perspective of surface reflection and material differences [7,8]. These methods can perform spoof detection using a single face image, and thus have relatively fast response. However, these methods may have poor generalizability, particularly under the relatively small training sets of public face spoof databases. Additionally, most of the face texture analysis based methods utilized hand-crafted features such as LBP. Antispoofing methods based on convolutional neural networks (CNNs) are rare, and limited to shallow CNNs [9]. Deep CNN models like CaffeNet [10] and GoogLeNet [11] were used for fingerprint antispoofing [12], but not for face antispoofing where the contactless image acquisition scenario of face is quite different. One important reason is that current face spoof datasets are small compared with the datasets of image classification and face recognition, which may easily lead to overfitting of CNN models.

2.2   Eye-Blink Detection for Antispoofing

Eye-blink is one of the spontaneous facial motions. On average, a human has one blink every 2-4 seconds [13]. Hence, eye-blink is a strong evidence to differentiate live faces from face photographs, particularly when the input is a video clip. Eye-blink detection is typically formulated as an eye state (open and close) change problem given a video sequence [13,14]. Approaches involved in the above publications include undirected conditional graphical model [13], and conditional random fields (CRF) model [14]. These approaches demonstrated their effectiveness in video based face antispoofing, but both approaches require training, and again their performance in cross-database testing scenarios were not known. In this work, we present a non-learning based method for efficient eye-blink detection. The proposed eye-blink detection and the deep texture features work together to handle input of both video clips and single images.

3   Proposed Approach

The proposed approach consists of three main modules: deep generalized texture feature learning, image difference based eye-blink detection, and fusion strategy.

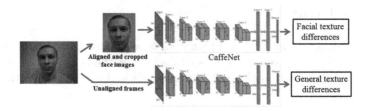

Fig. 2. Deep texture feature learning in the proposed antispoofing approach consists of learning features from both aligned faces and unaligned frames, which highlight facial and generalized image texture distortions in spoof face images, respectively.

3.1 Deep Generalized Texture Features

Considering the success of CNNs in feature learning for image classification tasks, we choose to use CNNs such as CaffeNet [10] and GoogLeNet [11]. Although CNNs were used in [9], it is shallow, and thus does not leverage the powerful non-linear learning ability of deep CNNs. Additionally, most of the published methods assume that the input to an antispoofing system is only the facial region. However, in real applications, no matter for a live or spoof face presentation, the input frames captured by the camera also contain non-face regions. Thus, texture distortions of spoof face image exist in the entire frame not only the facial region. Based on such an observation, we propose to learn texture features from both the aligned facial images and the whole frames under a deep CNN framework. This way, we believe the learned features will have better generalization ability. We formulated antispoofing as a live vs. spoof classification problem, and choose softmax loss

$$l(y, f) = -\log\left(\frac{e^{f_y}}{\sum_{j=1}^{m} e^{f_j}}\right),\tag{1}$$

where y is the sample's ground-truth label, and f denotes the output of the last fully-connected (fc) layer. We use the PittPatt SDK (acquired by Google in 2011) to detect the face and eye locations, and faces are aligned based on two-eye locations [15]. Both the aligned faces and whole frames are normalized into 256×256. During the task-specific fine-tuning, the last fc layer is set to have two nodes corresponding to two classes. Figure 2 gives an example using CaffeNet [10] model (with 5 conv layers and 3 fc layers) for feature learning.

Given the small sizes of existing face spoof databases, training such deep CNNs is prone to overfitting. Therefore, we design a generic-to-specific transfer learning scheme for network training. As shown in Fig. 3, the designed generic-to-specific learning first pre-train the network for classification in a related image classification domain. Such a pre-training assists in the network training by providing a reasonable initialization, which is usually better than random initialization. We then fine-tune the network w.r.t. face classification allowing the network to enhance face-specific feature learning, because we believe some face texture patterns could be shared between face classification and face antispoofing. Finally, task-specific fine-tuning with live and spoof face images is performed to build the capability of distinguishing between live and spoof face images. As we stated early, during the task-specific fine-tuning, we used both aligned face images and whole frames allowing feature learning of both face-specific texture features and generalized texture textures. Our experiments verified the effectiveness of such a deep texture feature learning.

General classification network
training on ImageNet   Face classification network
fine-tuned on WebFace   Task-specific network
fine-tuned on USSA

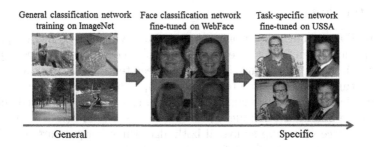

General   Specific

Fig. 3. The general-to-specific deep transfer learning strategy utilizes large databases of image and face classification (*e.g.*, ImageNet and WebFace) and a relatively small face spoof database (USSA).

3.2   Image Difference Based Eye-Blink Detection

An eye-blink activity is determined by the eye states ($\mathbb{S}$) in sequential frames ($\mathbb{F}$) of a video, where $\mathbb{F} = \{f_1, f_2, \cdots, f_n\}$, and $\mathbb{S} = \{s_1, s_2, \cdots, s_n\}$. For simplicity, we define two eye states, *i.e.*, $s_i \in \{o : open; c : close\}$. An eye-blink is reported if there is a state change in $\mathbb{S}$, either from open to close or from close to open. In our approach, we solve the eye-blink detection problem by detecting the state changes (*e.g.*, , $o \rightarrow c$ or $c \rightarrow o$) without explicitly predicting $\hat{\mathbb{S}}$. Formally, we look at the difference image ($\mathbb{D}$) between two image frames, and predict whether an eye state change ($\mathbb{G}$) occurs $\psi : \mathbb{D} \rightarrow \mathbb{G}$, where ψ is a mapping function from $\mathbb{D}$ to $\mathbb{G}$; $\mathbb{D} = \{d_j = (f_{j+1} - f_j)\}_{j=1}^{n-1}$; and $\mathbb{G} = \{g_j \in \{0 : no\ change; 1 : change\}\}_{j=1}^{n-1}$.

We crop the left and right eye regions separately into a 40×50 pixels. We dynamically threshold the periocular region and the pupil of the eyes to get binary eye images, and calculate the eye difference images d_j between successive frames. The following rule is used to determine the eye state changes

$$g_j = \psi(d_j) = \begin{cases} 1 & \text{if } \mathcal{V}(d_j) \geq T \\ 0 & \text{otherwise} \end{cases}, \tag{2}$$

where $\mathcal{V}(\cdot)$ calculates the percentage of pixels in a difference image d_j; as the difference images d_j is binary, the function $\mathcal{V}(\cdot)$ can simply count the percentage of white pixels; $\psi(\cdot)$ is the threshold mapping function, and the threshold $T = 0.1$ is choose based on our experimental verifications.

Such a simple eye-blink detection method may be affected by illumination, but it utilizes both the spatial information and the contextual information between sequential frames, making it fairly robust. The proposed method is also efficient in calculation (~100 fps on Windows 7 with Intel Core2 3.0 G CPU and 8 G RAM). Thus, it is possible to run the algorithm on commodity smartphones.

3.3   Voting Fusion

No matter if a spoof attack is from a photograph or video, the camera captures a video sequence. Therefore, it is reasonable to make a decision per video clip, *e.g.,* 1, 5, or 10 s in real applications. Thus, for the deep texture features (face-specific texture feature and generalized texture feature), a voting scheme can be used to generate a decision per video clip. This decision can be then combined with the output of eye-blink detection algorithm to generate a final decision. We choose to classify a face video clip as live, if both algorithms' outputs are live. Such a fusion scheme may cause a few false rejections of live faces, but our experiments show that the false reject rate is still in a reasonable level while the false accept rate is significantly reduced than the SOTA.

4   Experimental Results

We use three public-domain face spoof databases for evaluations: Idiap Replay-Attack [16], CASIA FASD [17], and MSU USSA [6], and follow their protocols of training, validation, and testing sets.

4.1   Comparisons with the STOA

Most of the earlier publications on face antispoofing did not report performance under cross-database testing. The baselines here are mainly the SOTAs in recent years. **CompRep** [6] analyzed the image distortions in spoof images, and provided a complementary representation of LBP and color moment. **JointCT** [18] extracted a joint color-texture feature from the luminance and the chrominance channels using LBP. **IDA** [3] proposed multiple image quality features for image distortion analysis of spoof face images. **VisCod** [2] performed face spoofing detection through visual codebooks of spectral temporal cubes. **SpoofNet** [9] is an early attempt of using a shallow CNN with three layers for antispoofing of face, fingerprint, and iris, but only *intra-database* performance is reported. So it is used as the baseline of intra-database testing.

USSA dataset is quite new, so most of the baselines did not report cross-database performance on USSA. So for the proposed approach, we follow the settings in [6], and use USSA as the training set for deep texture feature learning. Replay-Attack and FASD are used for testing. We set the base_lr as 0.01, use a polynomial learning rate policy with a power of 0.5. The momentum is set to 0.9, and the weight decay is set as 0.0002.

Table 1. Comparisons with the STOAs in cross-database testing (HTER in %).

Database	CompRep [6]	JointCT [18]	IDA [3]	VisCod [2]	Proposed
Replay-Attack	29.3	16.7	26.9	34.4	12.4
CASIA FASD	35.4	37.6	43.7	38.5	31.6

As shown in Table 1, the proposed approach achieves much lower HTERs than the best of the STOAs on both Replay-Attack and FASD databases. Figure 4 shows some live vs. spoof detection results by the proposed approach. Visualization of the images that have positive responses to the same nodes of the second-last fc layer shows that proposed approach learns generalized texture features such as photo-holding, non-natural illumination, and non-natural skin texture (see Fig. 5).

To compared with the intra-database testing performance of SpoofNet [9] on Replay-Attack, we further fine-tune the proposed approach using the training and development sets of Replay-Attack. The proposed approach achieves 0.5 % HTER, which is more than 30 % HTER reduction compared with SpoofNet [9].

4.2 Evaluations of Individual Modules

Face vs. non-face texture features. The face-specific texture feature alone achieves 17.5 % HTER on Replay-Attack, which outperforms most of the SOTA methods except for JointCT [18]. The generalized texture feature learning from the whole frames is new in face antispoofing studies. This feature alone achieves

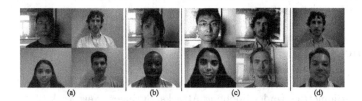

Fig. 4. Face spoof detection results on Replay-Attack: (a) true accept and (b) false reject of live face images, and (c) true reject and (d) false accept of spoof face images

Photo holding   Non-natural illumination   Non-natural skin texture

Fig. 5. Visualization of the images that have positive responses to the same nodes of the second-last fc layer indicates the generalized texture feature learning process

31.2 % HTER on Replay-Attack. Through the generalized texture features seem to be much less discriminative than the face-specific texture features, the integration of these two features shows impressive complementarity, leading to 13.8 % HTER. We also utilized different networks such as CaffeNet [10] and GoogLeNet [11], but we notice GoogLeNet outperforms CaffeNet.

Eye-blink detection. We evaluate the proposed eye-blink detection algorithm on the ZJU eye-blink dataset [13]. The proposed approach achieves 98.8 % accuracy, which outperforms the SOTA accuracy of 95.7 % [13] on ZJU dataset. Additionally, the proposed eye-blink detection is much faster than [13] (100 fps vs. 20 fps). After the eye-blink cue is fused with the deep texture features, HTER on Replay-Attack is further reduced from 13.8 % to 12.4 % (mainly reducing false acceptance of photograph attacks). These results show that the proposed eye-blink detection is helpful for assisting in photograph attack detection.

5   Summary and Conclusion

Cross-database face antispoofing replicates real application scenarios, and is a challenging problem for biometrics antispoofing. We propose a robust feature representation integrating deep texture features and eye-blink cue as countermeasures against presentation attacks of photographs and replays. Texture features are learned in a generic-to-specific way from both aligned face images and whole fames, which provide impressive complementarity. Eye-blink detection algorithm based on image difference is proposed to assist in texture cue with low computational cost. Cross-database testing on MSU USSA, Idiap Replay-Attack, and CASIA FASD databases shows that the proposed method outperforms the state-of-the-art. Our future work includes jointly learning spatial-temporal representation for antispoofing.

References

1. Marcel, S., Nixon, M.S., Li, S.Z. (eds.): Handbook of Biometric Anti-Spoofing: Trusted Biometrics Under Spoofing Attacks. Springer, New York (2014)
2. Pinto, A., Pedrini, H., Schwartz, W.R., Rocha, A.: Face spoofing detection through visual codebooks of spectral temporal cubes. IEEE Trans. Image Process. **24**(12), 4726–4740 (2015)
3. Wen, D., Han, H., Jain, A.K.: Face spoof detection with image distortion analysis. IEEE Trans. Inf. Forensics Secur. **10**(4), 746–761 (2015)
4. Smith, D.F., Wiliem, A., Lovell, B.C.: Face recognition on consumer devices: reflections on replay attacks. IEEE Trans. Inf. Forensics Secur. **10**(4), 736–745 (2015)
5. Han, H., Shan, S., Chen, X., Lao, S., Gao, W.: Separability oriented preprocessing for illumination-insensitive face recognition. In: Fitzgibbon, A., Lazebnik, S., Perona, P., Sato, Y., Schmid, C. (eds.) ECCV 2012. LNCS, vol. 7578, pp. 307–320. Springer, Heidelberg (2012). doi:10.1007/978-3-642-33786-4_23
6. Patel, K., Han, H., Jain, A.K.: Secure face unlock: spoof detection on smartphones. IEEE Trans. Inf. Forensics Secur. **11**(10), 2268–2283 (2016)

7. Li, J., Wang, Y., Tan, T., Jain, A.K.: Live face detection based on the analysis of fourier spectra. In: Proceedings of the SPIE, pp. 296–303 (2004)
8. Pereira, T.F., Anjos, A., De Martino, J.M., Marcel, S.: Can face anti-spoofing countermeasures work in a real world scenario? In: Proceedings of the ICB, pp. 1–8 (2013)
9. Menotti, D., Chiachia, G., Pinto, A., Robson Schwartz, W., Pedrini, H., Xavier Falcao, A., Rocha, A.: Deep representations for iris, face, and fingerprint spoofing detection. IEEE Trans. Inf. Forensics Secur. 10(4), 864–879 (2015)
10. Krizhevsky, A., Sutskever, I., Hinton, G.E.: Imagenet classification with deep convolutional neural networks. In Proceedings of the NIPS, pp. 1097–1105 (2012)
11. Szegedy, C., Liu, W., Jia, Y., Sermanet, P., Reed, S., Anguelov, D., Erhan, D., Vanhoucke, V., Rabinovich, A.: Going deeper with convolutions. In: Proceedings of the CVPR, pp. 1–9 (2015)
12. Wang, C., Li, K., Wu, Z., Zhao, Q.: A DCNN based fingerprint liveness detection algorithm with voting strategy. In: Yang, J., Yang, J., Sun, Z., Shan, S., Zheng, W., Feng, J. (eds.) CCBR 2015. LNCS, vol. 9428, pp. 241–249. Springer, Heidelberg (2015). doi:10.1007/978-3-319-25417-3_29
13. Pan, G., Sun, L., Wu, Z., Lao, S.: Eyeblink-based anti-spoofing in face recognition from a generic webcamera. In: Proceedings of the ICCV, pp. 1–8 (2007)
14. Szwoch, M., Pieniążek, P.: Eye blink based detection of liveness in biometric authentication systems using conditional random fields. In: Bolc, L., Tadeusiewicz, R., Chmielewski, L.J., Wojciechowski, K. (eds.) ICCVG 2012. LNCS, vol. 7594, pp. 669–676. Springer, Heidelberg (2012). doi:10.1007/978-3-642-33564-8_80
15. Han, H., Otto, C., Liu, X., Jain, A.K.: Demographic estimation from face images: Human vs. machine performance. IEEE Trans. Pattern Anal. Mach. Intell. 37(6), 1148–1161 (2015)
16. Chingovska, I., Anjos, A., Marcel, S.: On the effectiveness of local binary patterns in face anti-spoofing. In: Proceedings of the IEEE BIOSIG, pp. 1–7 (2012)
17. Zhuang, Z., Yan, J., Liu, S., Lei, Z., Yi, D., Li, S.Z.: A face antispoofing database with diverse attacks. In: Proceedings of the ICB, pp. 26–31 (2012)
18. Boulkenafet, Z., Komulainen, J., Hadid, A.: Face anti-spoofing based on color texture analysis. In: Proceedings of the ICIP, pp. 2636–2640 (2015)

Deep Representations Based on Sparse Auto-Encoder Networks for Face Spoofing Detection

Dakun Yang, Jianhuang Lai$^{(\boxtimes)}$, and Ling Mei

School of Data and Computer Science, Sun-Yat-Sen University,
Guangzhou 510006, China
ydk1026@163.com, stsljh@mail.sysu.edu.cn, meil3@mail2.sysu.edu.cn

Abstract. Automatic face recognition plays significant role in biometrics systems, and face spoofing has raised concerns at the same time, since a photo or video of an authorized uesr's face could be used for deceiving the system. In this paper, we propose a new hierarchical visual feature based on deep learning to discriminate spoof face. First, the LBP descriptor is used to extract low level face features of face images, and then these low level features are encoded to high level features via a deep learning architecture which is consists of sparse auto-encoder (SAE). Finally, SVM classifier is applied to detect face spoofing. We perform a experimental evaluation on two face liveness detection databases, CASIA database and NUAA database. The results indicate the robustness of the proposed approach for face spoofing detection.

Keywords: LBP · Deep learning · Sparse auto-encoder · SVM · Face spoofing

1 Introduction

Biometrics human features has become one of the most active research fields [1–4], the general public has enormous demands for people identification and authentication. Among the biometric human features, several biometric modalities such as face traits have been largely applied to authentication systems. Simultaneously, various spoofing attack techniques have been created to defeat these biometric systems, which has become a serious problem to the traditional biometric authentication techniques.

Among the different attack ways to spoof a biometric system, face spoofing attack is the most universal way. There are several ways to spoof face recognition systems such as facial pictures, videos and even portrait photographs. In order to guard against such spoofing, liveness detection is needed to distinguish "live" faces from "spoof" faces for a secure system. The main task of the liveness detection is to prevent imposters from accessing protected resources. However, in real life, imposters will try to introduce all kinds of face spoofing approaches to defeat the security systems, liveness detection is still a very challenging problem.

© Springer International Publishing AG 2016
Z. You et al. (Eds.): CCBR 2016, LNCS 9967, pp. 620–627, 2016.
DOI: 10.1007/978-3-319-46654-5_68

In recent years, many methods such as analysis based on motion, texture and life sign [5–7] are researched to address the liveness detection, but these methods can not handle the problem well. Therefore, we need a more effective and robust algorithm to solve the problem.

In recent years, a deep learning architecture named sparse auto coding (SAE) [8,9] has been more and more attention in automatic face recognition, which is a powerful technique in pattern recognition. It aims at selecting the least possible basis from the large basis pool to linearly recover the given signal under a small reconstruction error constraint. SAE learning algorithms [10] is an unsupervised approach to automatically learn features from unlabeled data. In this paper, we introduce SAE to encode low level descriptors so that the high level feature is captured by deep learning. The high level feature is more discrimination and robust than the low level feature, so the proposed method can address the face liveness detection better than the method based on low level descriptors.

The remainder of this work is organized into five sections, Sect. 2 presents the framework, principle and methodology of our proposed method, while Sect. 3 presents experiments, results and comparisons with the state-of-the-art methods. Finally, Sect. 4 draws conclusion of the paper and discusses some possible future directions.

2   The Proposed Countermeasures

The holistic contermeasures (See Fig. 1) consist of four primary steps which is like a bag of words framework (BOW). Different from the BOW, the SAE learning method is adopt to replace the encode way of BOW in the proposed countermeasures. The main purpose of the contermeasures is to encode robust low-level local descriptors of image patches for each image, such as LBP feature, and take advantage of a deep hierarchy of SAE (sparse-auto encoder) to obtain a high-level image presentation for face liveness detection. After that, we enhance the feature coding by combining the features of all image patches, which can derive the final results by a classifier such as SVM.

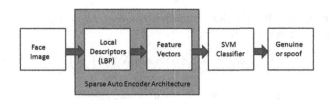

Fig. 1. The proposed framework.

2.1 Sparse Auto Encoder (SAE)

Auto-Encoder Networks. Recently, since deep multi-layer neural networks have many levels of non-linearities allowing them to compactly represent highly non-linear and highly-varying functions, deep learning has been shown great accomplishments in vision and learning since the first deep auto-encoder network was proposed by Hinton et al. in [11]. Auto-Encoder is an unsupervised feature learning algorithm [12] which aims to develop better feature representation of input high-dimensional data by finding the correlation among the data. Auto-Encoder is a three layers neural network with a single hidden layer including a encoder and a decoder. Below we briefly specify the traditional auto-encoder (AE) framework (See Fig. 2) and its encoder and decoder.

For a auto-encoder network, since the output vector is equal to the input vector, assuming that the numbers of neurons for the input, hidden and output layers are N, M, N, respectively. Let $\mathbf{W} = (\mathbf{w}_1^T, \mathbf{w}_2^T, \cdots, \mathbf{w}_M^T)^T \in \mathbb{R}^{M \times N}$ and $\mathbf{b} = (b_1, b_2, \cdots, b_M)^T \in \mathbb{R}^M$, where $\mathbf{w}_m = (w_{m1}, w_{m2}, \cdots, w_{mN})^T \in \mathbb{R}^N$, $m = 1, 2, \cdots, M$ be the weight matrix connecting the input and the hidden layers, and $b_m \in \mathbb{R}$, $m = 1, 2, \cdots, M$ be the threshold value of the neurons in the hidden layer. The weight vector connecting the hidden and the output layers is denoted by $\mathbf{W}' = (\mathbf{w}_1'^T, \mathbf{w}_2'^T, \cdots, \mathbf{w}_N'^T)^T \in \mathbb{R}^{N \times M}$, where $\mathbf{w}_n' = (w_{n1}', w_{n2}', \cdots, w_{nM}')^T \in \mathbb{R}^M$, $n = 1, 2, \cdots, N$. The threshold value of the neurons in the output layer is denoted by $\mathbf{b}' = (b_1', b_2', \cdots, b_N')^T \in \mathbb{R}^N$. In the auto-encoder network, a nonlinear activation function $f(x)$ is used in the hidden layer, and a nonlinear activation function $g(x)$ in the output layer.

Encoder: For an arbitrary input vector $\mathbf{x} = (x_1, x_2, \cdots, x_N)^T$, the output of the neurons in the hidden layer is given by

$$\mathbf{y} = (y_1, y_2, \cdots, y_M)^T = f(\mathbf{W}\mathbf{x} + \mathbf{b}),$$
$$y_m = f(\mathbf{w}_m^T \mathbf{x} + b_m) = f(\sum_{i=1}^{N} w_{mi} x_i + b_m), \tag{1}$$

where $m = 1, 2, \cdots, M$. Then the nonlinear activation function $f(x)$ that transforms an input vector $\mathbf{x}$ into hidden representation $\mathbf{y}$ is called the **encoder**.

Decoder: For the resulting hidden representation $\mathbf{y}$, the output of the neurons in the output layer is given by

$$\mathbf{z} = (z_1, z_2, \cdots, z_N)^T = g(\mathbf{W}'\mathbf{y} + \mathbf{b}'),$$
$$z_n = g(\mathbf{w}_n'^T \mathbf{y} + b_n') = g(\sum_{i=1}^{M} w_{ni}' y_i + b_n'), \tag{2}$$

where $n = 1, 2, \cdots, N$. Since the output vector $\mathbf{z}$ is used to reconstruct input vector $\mathbf{x}$ by hidden representation $\mathbf{y}$ for the auto-encoder network, the nonlinear activation function $g(x)$ is called the **decoder** [13].

According to the encoder and decoder above, we can know that training an autoencoder to minimize reconstruction error amounts to maximizing a lower bound on the mutual information between input and learnt representation. Intuitively, if a representation allows a good reconstruction of its input, it means that it has retained much of the information that was present in that input.

Sparse Representations in Auto-Encoders. Auto-Encoder (AE) is an unsupervised feature leaning methods which can avoid the labor-intensive and handcraft feature design. The goal of AE is to make the input to be equal to the output. When the number of hidden units in AE is less than that of the input units, a compression representation is learnt by AE. When the number of hidden units is larger, even more than that of the input units, a representation of input data is obtained by imposing a sparsity constraint on the hidden units. Therefore, In this way, in a sparse Auto-Encoder (SAE), there are only few hidden units being activated when given an input vector.

For a SAE network, let $\hat{\rho}_j$ be the mean activation probability in the jth hidden unit, namely $\hat{\rho}_j = (1/m)] \sum_{i=1}^{m} h_j$. Let ρ be the desired probability of being activated. Sparsity is imposed on the network, it is obvious that $\rho \ll 1$. Here KullbackCLeibler (KL) divergence is used to measure the similarity between the desired and actual distributions, as shown in the following equation

$$KL(\rho \parallel \hat{\rho}_j) = \rho \log \frac{\rho}{\hat{\rho}_j} + (1 - \rho) \log \frac{1 - \rho}{1 - \hat{\rho}_j}. \tag{3}$$

SAE model can be formulated as the following optimization problem

$$\min_{W,b} \left[\sum_{i=1}^{m} (h_{W,b}(x^{(i)}) - y^{(i)})^2 + \lambda(\|W\|_2^2) + \beta \sum_{j=1}^{k} KL(\rho \| \hat{\rho}_j) \right], \tag{4}$$

where the first term is the reconstruction cost, the second term is a regularization on weight to avoid over-fitting, and the last term enforces the mapping sparsity from the input layer to hidden layer. The parameters λ and β are regularization factors used to make a tradeoff between the reconstruction cost, weight decay and sparsity penalty term. Typically, back-propagation algorithm is used to solve Eq. (4).

Stacked Sparse Autoencoder (SSAE). The stacked autoencoder is a neural network consisting of multiple layers of basic SAE in which the outputs of each layer is wired to the inputs of the successive layer. In this paper, we construct two layers SSAE which consists of two basic SAE. The architecture of SSAE is shown in Fig. 3. For simplicity, we didnt show the decoder parts of each basic SAE in the figure.

3 Experiments

In our experiments, some outperforming features of spoof detection are evaluated for the CASIA face anti-spoofing database and NUAA database. For classification, we use LibSVM library to derive the authentication results.

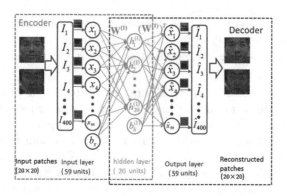

Fig. 2. The architecture of AE for face spoof detection.

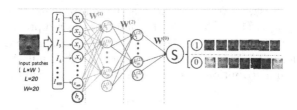

Fig. 3. The architecture of SSAE for face spoof detection.

3.1 Face Anti-spoofing Databases

CASIA database [14] is released in 2012, which consists of 50 subjects where 20 for training and 30 for testing. All subjects are captured in natural scenes with no artificial environmental unification. Specially, the database design three kinds of fake attacks: warped photo attack, cut photo attack and video attack. Additionally, three different cameras are used to record the data of different qualities: low quality, middle quality, high quality, so there are 600 video clips in CASIA database.

NUAA database [15] is released in 2010, which is one of the earliest public-domain spoof database. There are 12614 images of genuine and spoof attack attempts for 15 subjects. All the images are face gray images which normalized to 64*64 pixels size. Furthermore, NUAA database only included hand-held printed photo attack.

3.2 Results on CASIA Database

We evaluate 12 different types of spoof detection features on CASIA database: LBP features, LBP-TOP, WLD, WLD-TOP [16], CDD (weighted pooling) [17], CDD (no weighted pooling) [17], CDD (holistic coding) [17], MSLBP (H-face), MSLBP (Face), DOG (H-face) [17], DOG (Face) [17] and our proposed method. In this experiment, in the proposed method, the uniform LBP feature as input of SSAE is adopted for image patches of each face image, which is divided into 20*20 image patches. The ROC curves of overall test is shown in Fig. 4, as shown in above figure, the performance of our proposed method is better than the majority of state-of-art methods. Since we visualize the codewords trained on LBP descriptors extracted from the CASIA database, this leads to the potential that the shallow dictionaries learned are generic enough to discriminate the difference between genuine faces and spoof faces. On the other hand, the training and testing images are selected from continuous video frames, so we can obtain the important details whether the image is genuine face or not.

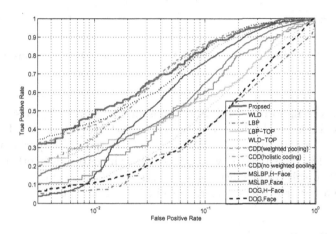

Fig. 4. The ROC graph of the proposed method and other methods for CASIA database

Figure 4 shows that the proposed hierarchical visual coding architecture outperform the other methods in CASIA database scenarios, which achieves TPR=83.04 % @ FPR=0.1 and TPR=50.67 % @ FPR=0.01. Since the authors divided a face image into 12 face patches where each patch took advantage of several LBP features, our method only use the one LBP feature for a face image, then our method can not outperform the CCD methods.

3.3 Results on NUAA Database

The images in NUAA database [15] are not continuous frame image, and the illumination changes quite much, which make the identification more difficult. In this experiment, in the proposed method, the uniform LBP feature as input of SSAE is also adopted for image patches of each face image, and two divided patterns is adopted for each face image. One is that each face image is divided into horizontal two blocks (denoted by "Proposed 2"), and the other is that each face image is divided into four equal blocks (denoted by "Proposed 4"). Figure 5 shows the ROC curves of some start-of-art methods, and the proposed method

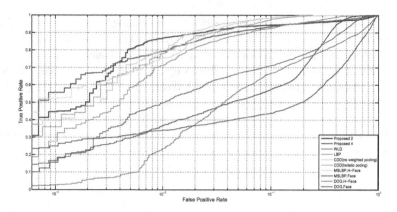

Fig. 5. The ROC graph of the proposed methods and other methods for NUAA database

outperforms the majority of other methods in the NUAA database scenarios. The Proposed 2 method achieves TPR=98.55 % @FAR=0.1 and the Proposed 4 method achieves TPR=93.43 % @FAR=0.1. The Proposed 4 reports an average TPR of 55.62 % @FAR=0.01, which is still much better than other methods except CDD (weighted pooling). These results show that the proposed approach can achieve a better liveness performance in NUAA database.

4   Conclusion

in this paper, we have presented a new approach based on SAE to address the problem of face spoof attack. LBP descriptor is used for extracting low-level feature code in the proposed architecture, deep learning based on SAE and image partition are exploited for encode more effective and robustness high-level feature code for classifying, while most published approaches use motion or texture based features. The encoded LBP features in different image patches are concatenated together, resulting in a high level feature vector. A classifier based on SVM trained for different spoof attacks is used for the classification of genuine and spoof faces. We have evaluated the proposed approach on two face liveness detection database, CASIA database and NUAA database, the results show that our method achieves great performance compared with the other methods.

Acknowledgment. This work was supported in part by the Guangzhou Program under Grant 201508010032, in part by the Guangdong Program under Grant 2015B010105005, and in part by the National Natural Science Foundation of China under Grant 61573387.

References

1. Menotti, D., Chiachia, G., Pinto, A.: Deep representations for iris, face, fingerprint spoofing detection. IEEE Trans. Inf. Forensics Secur. **10**(4), 864–879 (2015)
2. Gao, S., Tsang, I.W.-H., Chia, L.-T.: Kernel sparse representation for image classification and face recognition. In: Daniilidis, K., Maragos, P., Paragios, N. (eds.) ECCV 2010. LNCS, vol. 6314, pp. 1–14. Springer, Heidelberg (2010). doi:10.1007/978-3-642-15561-1_1
3. Lei, Z., Pietikainen, M., Li, S.: Learning discriminant face descriptor. IEEE Trans. Pattern Anal. Mach. Intell. **36**(2), 289–302 (2014)
4. Li, Z., Imai, J., Kaneko, M., Robust face recognition using block-based bag of words. In: Proceedings of 20th ICPR, pp. 1285–1288 (2010)
5. Maatta, J., Hadid, A., Pietikainen, M., Face spoofing detection from single image-susing micro-texture analysis. In: Proceedings of 2011 IJCB, pp. 1–7 (2011)
6. Jee, H., Jung, S., Yoo, J.: LIBSVM: liveness detection for embedded face recognition system. Int. J. Biol. Med. Sci. **1**(4), 235–238 (2006)
7. Chetty, G., Biometric liveness checking using multimodal fuzzy fusion. In: Proceedings of 2010 International Conference on Fuzzy Systems, pp. 1–8 (2010)
8. Goh, H., Thome, N., Cord, M., Lim, J.-H.: Unsupervised and supervised visual codes with restricted Boltzmann machines. In: Fitzgibbon, A., Lazebnik, S., Perona, P., Sato, Y., Schmid, C. (eds.) ECCV 2012. LNCS, vol. 7576, pp. 298–311. Springer, Heidelberg (2012). doi:10.1007/978-3-642-33715-4_22
9. Baccouche, M., Mamalet, F., Wolf, C.: Spatio-temporal convolutional sparse auto-encoder for sequence classification. In: BMVC 2012, pp. 1–12 (2012)
10. Ng, A.: Sparse Autoencoder, vol. 72. Stanford University Press, Stanford (2011)
11. Hinton, G.E., Salakhutdinov, R.R.: Reducing the dimensionality of data with neural networks. Science **313**(5786), 504–507 (2006)
12. Xu, J., Xiang, L., Hang, R., Stacked Sparse Autoencoder (SSAE) based framework for nuclei patch classification on breast cancer histopathology. In: Proceedings of 11th IEEE International Symposium on Biomedical Imaging, pp. 999–1002 (2014)
13. Su, S., Liu, Z., Xu, S.: Sparse auto-encoder based feature learning for human body detection in depth image. Sig. Process. **112**, 43–52 (2015)
14. Zhang, Z., Yan, J., Liu, S.: A face antispoofing database with diverse attacks. In: Proceedings of 5th IAPR, pp. 26–31 (2012)
15. Tan, X., Li, Y., Liu, J., Jiang, L.: Face liveness detection from a single image with sparse low rank bilinear discriminative model. In: Daniilidis, K., Maragos, P., Paragios, N. (eds.) ECCV 2010. LNCS, vol. 6316, pp. 504–517. Springer, Heidelberg (2010). doi:10.1007/978-3-642-15567-3_37
16. Mei, L., Yang, D., Feng, Z., Lai, J.: WLD-TOP based algorithm against face spoofing attacks. biometric recognition. In: Yang, J., Yang, J., Sun, Z., Shan, S., Zheng, W., Feng, J. (eds.) CCBR 2015. LNCS, vol. 9428, pp. 135–142. Springer, Heidelberg (2015). doi:10.1007/978-3-319-25417-3_17
17. Yang, J., Lei, Z., Liao, S., Li, S.Z., Face liveness detection with component dependent descriptor. In: International Conference on Biometrics, pp. 1–6 (2013)

A Face Liveness Detection
Scheme to Combining Static
and Dynamic Features

Lifang Wu$^{(\boxtimes)}$, Yaowen Xu, Xiao Xu, Wei Qi, and Meng Jian

School of Electronic Information and Control Engineering,
Beijing University of Technology, 100124 Beijing, China
lfwu@bjut.edu.cn, xuyao_wen@126.com,
{xuxiao2013,weiqi}@emails.bjut.edu.cn,
jianmeng648@163.com

Abstract. Face liveness detection is an interesting research topic in face-based online authentication. The current face liveness detection algorithms utilize either static or dynamic features, but not both. In fact, the dynamic and static features have different advantages in face liveness detection. In this paper, we discuss a scheme to combine dynamic and static features that combines the strength of each. First, the dynamic maps are obtained from the inter frame motion in the video. Then, using a Convolutional Neural Network (CNN), the dynamic and static features are extracted from the dynamic maps and the images, respectively. Next, the fully connected layers from the CNN that include the dynamic and static features are connected to form the fused features. Finally, the fused features are used to train a two-value Support Vector Machine (SVM) classifier, which classify the images into two groups, images with real faces and images with fake faces. We conduct experiments to assess our algorithm that includes classifying images from two public databases. Experimental results demonstrate that our algorithm outperforms current state-of-the-art face liveness detection algorithms.

Keywords: Face liveness detection · Deep learning · Convolutional Neural Network (CNN) · Static features · Dynamic features

1 Introduction

In recent years, there are increasingly more internet-based applications, such as e-commerce and social networks. These applications require reliable online identity authentication. In the traditional identity authentication systems, either a password or a key is used for authentication. However, the password or key could be separated from the true user. For example, if user B steals the password of user A, user B could then perform any action on the internet by using the identity of user A. In comparison, biometric-based online authentication could preserve the consistence of a user's physical identity and the digital identity which could be extracted from the true user. However, biometrics-based online authentication could be fooled by fake biometrics of the true user, so it is important that these systems can determine the real biometrics.

© Springer International Publishing AG 2016
Z. You et al. (Eds.): CCBR 2016, LNCS 9967, pp. 628–636, 2016.
DOI: 10.1007/978-3-319-46654-5_69

Consequently, it proposes a new research topic of liveness detection. In this paper we focus on face liveness detection.

The objective of face liveness detection is to determine that a face image is captured from the real face rather than from a fake face such as photographs, videos [1] or 3D-generated faces of the true user [2]. Related methods of face liveness could be classified into dynamic-based and static-based algorithms [3]. In dynamic-based algorithms, local or global motion, such as blinking [4, 5], facial expression change [6], head movements or motion style [7], is used for liveness detection. Conversely, the main idea of static-based algorithms is to extract the texture features for liveness detection. Generally used algorithms include Local Binary Patterns (LBP) [8, 9], Gabor wavelets [9], Histogram of Oriented Gradient (HOG) [9], Local Graph Structures (LGS) [10], focus variation [11], and features learnt using deep learning [13].

Static and dynamic features have different strengths for liveness detection. The static features are generally used to represent texture differences, while dynamic features are used for motion differences. Our algorithm combines these features to gain the strengths from both features. The static features are extracted from the image frame-by-frame by using a trained Convolutional Neural Network (CNN), which includes four convolutional layers, two pooling layers, and a fully connected layer. For the dynamic features, we first obtained the dynamic maps frame-by-frame by extracting the horizontal and vertical optical flow by using the Lucas Kanade (LK) Pyramid method [14]. Then, the dynamic features are extracted from the dynamic maps by using the CNN. Next, the fully connected layers of two networks are connected to form the fused features. Using the fused features, a Support Vector Machine (SVM) classifier is trained to determine the face image.

The contribution of this paper includes the following: (1) Both dynamic and static features are used for liveness detection and (2) Static and dynamic features are extracted using a CNN, which is more efficient than other feature extraction algorithms such as LBP, SIFT and so on.

The remainders of the paper are organized as follows: In Sect. 2, the proposed face liveness detection scheme is described in details. In Sect. 3, the compared experimental results on two public databases (Print-Attack, Replay-Attack) are presented, and the experimental results confirm the efficiency of the proposed scheme; finally, the paper is concluded in Sect. 4.

2 The Proposed Algorithm

2.1 Overview

The framework of the proposed scheme is shown in Fig. 1. Using input video, the static data is obtained from each video frame and the dynamic maps are obtained from the horizontal and vertical optic flows. The CNN is trained using the dynamic maps and the static data respectively, which is used to extract the dynamic and static features. These features are then connected to form the fused features. Finally, the face liveness detection is implemented using a SVM 2-value classifier.

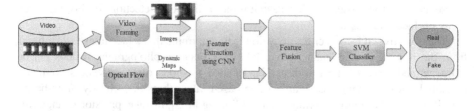

Fig. 1. The framework of the proposed scheme

2.2   Extracting the Dynamic Maps

We use the LK Pyramid optical flow method [14] to track the motion of objects in video. First, the current frame of the image is sampled, then the optical flow method is used to calculate the horizontal direction (F_x) and the vertical direction (F_y) of the current frame and the next frame image, and using the formula $D = \sqrt{F_x^2 + F_y^2}$ to calculate the displacement amplitude diagrams which form dynamic maps. Figure 2 shows dynamic maps from the real face and different fake faces. We can see that the motion style in the dynamic maps from real and fake faces is considerably different. In the dynamic map from the real face (Fig. 2a), there is distinct motion in the face region, and the motion in the region of the human eye is bigger than other regions. In the dynamic map from a photograph (Fig. 2b), there are very small motions in the region of face image. While in the dynamic map from video (Fig. 2c), there are uniform small motions in the face region.

(a) From real face   (b) From photograph   (c) From Video

Fig. 2. Dynamic maps from real face and fake faces

2.3   Training the CNN Network

The CNN extracts the static features from the original image and dynamic features from the dynamic maps. The architecture of the network is shown in Fig. 3. Four convolutional layers are stacked after the input layer. The first two convolutional layers share the same weight, and they are followed by two max-pooling layers. The last two convolutional layers are locally connected and have independent weights. In the last fully connected layer, each neuron is connected to all other neurons in the fourth convolutional layer. The soft-max output layer includes two values.

The first convolutional layer and the following max-pooling layer have 64 convolution kernels with the size of each kernel being 5 × 5 pixels. The second convolutional layer and the following max-pooling layer also have 64 convolution kernels, with the kernel size being 3 × 3 pixels. The last two convolutional layers are locally connected layers with unshared weights, and every layer has 32 convolution kernels with each kernel being 3 × 3 pixels. There are 160 neurons in the last fully connected layer, and the soft-max layer has two neurons.

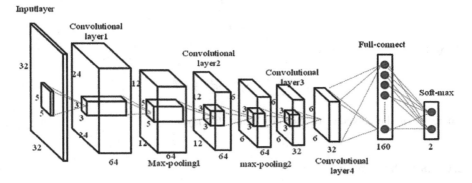

Fig. 3. The structure of CNN

The convolution function could be represented as follows:

$$y_j^{cov} = \max\{0, \sum_i W_{i,j} * x_i^{cov} + b_j\} \tag{1}$$

where x_i^{cov} is the ith input and y_j^{cov} is the jth output. W_{ij} is the convolution kernel between the ith input x_i^{cov} and the jth output y_j^{cov}. The symbol * denotes the operation of convolution. b_j is the bias of the jth output. The hidden neuron that we use is a rectified linear unit (ReLU) $f(x) = \max(0, x)$. It is proven to have better fitting abilities than the functions $f(x) = \tanh(x)$ and $f(x) = (1 + e^{-x})^{-1}$[15].

The max-pooling function is formulated as:

$$y_j^{pool} = \max_{k \in D}\{x_i^k\} \tag{2}$$

where D is the non-overlapping local region in the ith input map, y_j^{pool} is the max neuron in D.

The last fully connected layer is fully connected to the fourth convolutional layer, and the function can be formulated as:

$$y_j^{full} = \max\{0, \sum_i x_i^{full} \cdot W_{i,j}^{full} + b_j^{full}\} \tag{3}$$

where x_i^{full} is the ith input of the fully connected layer, which corresponds the ith output of the fourth convolutional layer. Moreover, y_j^{full} is the jth output of the fully connected layer.

The soft-max layer is an n-value output that predicts the probability distribution over n different classes. Our algorithm uses a two-value output, and the soft-max function can be formulated as:

$$y_j^{sm} = \frac{e^{y_j'}}{\sum_m e^{y_m'}}, \tag{4}$$

Where

$$y_j' = \sum_{i=1}^n y_i^{full} \cdot w_{i,j}^{sm} + b_j^{sm}, \tag{5}$$

where y_i^{full} is the ith vector of the fully connected layer.

2.4   Data Preparation

Prior to feature extraction, the original image and dynamic map are normalized to an image of size 32×32 pixels, and five overlapping patches of 24×24 pixels are cropped from the 32×32 input images. These patches correspond to the four corners and central region in the input image. Then, the five patches are flipped horizontally, resulting in a total of ten patches, as shown in Fig. 4.

For static feature extraction, the three components (R, G, B) of the original image are utilized as the input of CNN network, which consists of $32 \times 32 \times 3$ images. For dynamic feature extraction, the dynamic maps including horizontal and vertical motion components as the input of CNN network, which consist of $32 \times 32 \times 1$ images.

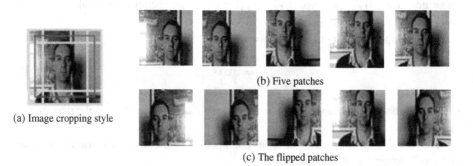

(a) Image cropping style

(b) Five patches

(c) The flipped patches

Fig. 4. Illustration of data preparation

2.5   Training the SVM Classifier

In the stage, the fully connected layers of two CNN networks of size 160 nodes are connected to form 320 dimensional fused features. The fused features are utilized to train the SVM classifier.

In the testing stage, only the central patch of size 24 × 24, marked in red color in Fig. 4(a), is cropped as the input of the CNN network for the static image and dynamic maps. The output of face liveness detection is obtained from the output of the SVM classifier.

3   Experimental Results

The algorithm is tested using two databases: Print-Attack [16] and Replay-Attack [17]. These databases are publicly available and there are numerous challenging benchmarks for them. Each database contains a training set, a testing set, and a development set. In our experiments, the training set is used to train the CNN network, the development set is used to train the SVM classifier, and the algorithm is tested using the testing set. The experimental results are evaluated using the Detection Rate and Half-Total Error Rate (HTER). Detection Rate is the ratio of the number of correctly classified videos to the total number of videos. HTER is defined as half of the sum of the False Rejection Rate (FRR) and the False Acceptance Rate (FAR).

3.1   Experiments on Idiap Print-Attack Database

The Print-Attack Database consists of 200 valid access videos and 200 print attack video attempts for 50 clients, which were captured in controlled and uncontrolled imagining conditions by using a webcam at 25 fps with a resolution of 320 × 240 pixels. The 400 video clips were divided into three groups: the training set (60 valid access videos and 60 print attack videos), the development set (60 valid access videos and 60 print attack videos), and the testing set (80 valid access and 80 print attack videos). This database includes two different scenarios: (i) controlled background (i.e., a uniform background), and (ii) adverse background (i.e., a non-uniform background). Example images from the database are shown in Fig. 5. In the experiments, we only use 200 frames of each video.

We compare our scheme with DMD + LBP + SVM^E [7], DMD + LBP + SVM^F [7], Partial Least Squares (PLS) [20], Non-rigid Motion Analysis [19], Face-Background Consistency Analysis [19], Image Banding Analysis [19], and Fusion of Multiple Clues [19]. The experimental results are shown in Table 1.

Fig. 5. Example images from Print-Attack Database

Table 1. Compared performance on Print-Attack Database

Method	Detection rate (%)	HTER (%)
DMD + LBP + SVM^E [7]	–	0
DMD + LBP + SVM^F [7]	–	0
PLS [20]	99.375	–
Non-rigid Motion Analysis [19]	90	–
Face-Background Consistency Analysis [19]	97.5	–
Image Banding Analysis [19]	97.5	–
Fusion of Multiple Clues [19]	100	–
The proposed scheme	100	0

From Table 1, we can see that our algorithm obtained the best performance. In [19], three clues are extracted for liveness detection, (1) Non-rigid Motion Analysis, (2) Face-Background Consistency, and (3) Image Banding Analysis. When these three clues are used independently, the detection rates are 90 %, 97.5 %, and 97.5 % respectively. The performances of these three algorithms are lower than our algorithm. When fused three clues, the detection rate can reached 100 %, however, it needs to make a choice according to the different backgrounds. In Ref [20], the features from HSC, CF, GLCM, and HOG are fused for face liveness detection and they could obtain the accuracy of 99.375 %.

3.2   Experiments on Idiap Replay-Attack Database

The Replay-Attack database consists of 1200 videos which include 200 valid access videos and 1000 attack videos. The attack videos were generated using three techniques: (1) print attack, (2) mobile attack, and (3) high-definition attack. The 1200 video clips were divided into three groups: the training set (60 valid access videos and 300 attack videos), the development set (60 valid access videos and 300 attack videos), and the testing set (80 valid access videos and 400 attack videos). The imaging conditions for the Replay-Attack database are similar to those for the Print-Attack database.

We compared our scheme with DMD + LBP + SVM^E (entire video as input) [7], DMD + LBP + SVM^F (face region as input) [7], AO + Random [13], Spoofnet + Random [13], LBP-TOP [21], LBP + LDA [22], HOOF + LDA (thresholding) [18], and HOOF + LDA (NN) [18], as shown in Table 2. LBP-TOP and HOOF + LDA are designed based on only the motion features and obtained the highest HTER 1.25 %. DMD + LBP + SVM, AO + Random and Spoofnet + Random used only the images as input. DMD + LBP + SVM obtained HTER 3.75 % with the entire video and HTER 0 % with the face region. AO + Random and Spoofnet + Random both are deep learning based algorithms. AO + Random algorithm is designed based on hyperopt-convnet. AO + Random is better and obtains a detection rate of 98.75 % and HTER of 0.75 %. Our algorithm obtains HTER 0 % and detection rate 100 %.

In our viewpoints, the proposed scheme performs better than other state-of-the-art algorithms because the following two reasons: First, we utilize both the static and

Table 2. Compared performance on Replay-Attack database.

Method	Detection rate (%)	HTER (%)
DMD + LBP + SVM^E [7]	–	0
DMD + LBP + SVM^F [7]	–	3.75
AO + Random [13]	98.75	0.75
Spoofnet + Random [13]	–	3.5
LBP-TOP [21]	–	8.51
LBP + LDA [22]	–	13.87
HOOF + LDA (thresholding) [18]	–	4.38
HOOF + LDA (NN) [18]	–	1.25
The proposed scheme	100	0

dynamic data. Second, the CNN framework could extract the dynamic and static features more efficiently.

4 Conclusion

In this paper, we discuss a face liveness detection algorithm that combines static and dynamic features. The static features are extracted directly from images by using the CNN network, and the dynamic features are extracted from dynamic maps by using the CNN network. The dynamic maps are obtained using LK optical flow. Finally, the static and dynamic features are connected to form fused features. The fused features are input to the two-value SVM classifier for liveness detection. The compared experimental results with the state-of-the-art algorithms show that the proposed algorithm achieved significantly better performance. From these experimental results, we could draw the following conclusions: (1) Both static and dynamic features are useful for face liveness detection; (2) Deep learning is an efficient method for feature extraction. But whether the fusion of static and dynamic features or the CNN framework is most important, this problem will be studied in our future research.

References

1. Pan, G., Sun, L., Wu, Z., Lao, S.: Eyeblink-based anti-spoofing in face recognition from a generic webcamera. In: Proceedings of the Computer Vision, IEEE ICCV, pp. 1–8 (2007)
2. Erdogmus, N., Marcel, S.: Spoofing face recognition with 3D masks. IEEE Trans. Inf. Forensics Secur. 9(7), 1084–1097 (2014)
3. Wu, L., Xu, X., Cao, Yu., Hou, Y., Qi, W.: Live face detection by combining the fourier statistics and LBP. In: Sun, Z., Shan, S., Sang, H., Zhou, J., Wang, Y., Yuan, W. (eds.) CCBR 2014. LNCS, vol. 8833, pp. 173–181. Springer, Heidelberg (2014)
4. Bharadwaj, S., Dhamecha, T.I., Vatsa, M., et al.: Computationally efficient face spoofing detection with motion magnification. In: 2013 IEEE Conference on Computer Vision and Pattern Recognition Workshops (CVPRW), pp. 105–110. IEEE (2013)

5. Jee, H.K., Jung, S.U., Yoo, J.H.: Liveness detection for embedded face recognition system. Enformatika, 235–238 (2011)
6. Komulainen, J., Hadid, A., Pietikäinen, M.: Face spoofing detection using dynamic texture. In: Park, J.-I., Kim, J. (eds.) ACCV Workshops 2012, Part I. LNCS, vol. 7728, pp. 146–157. Springer, Heidelberg (2013)
7. Tirunagari, S., Poh, N., Windridge, D., et al.: Detection of face spoofing using visual dynamics. IEEE Trans. Inf. Forensics Secur. **10**(4), 762–777 (2015)
8. Määttä, J., Hadid, A., Pietikainen, M.: Face spoofing detection from single images using micro-texture analysis. In: 2011 International Joint Conference on Biometrics (IJCB), pp. 1–7. IEEE (2011)
9. Määttä, J., Hadid, A., Pietikainen, M.: Face spoofing detection from single images using texture and local shape analysis. Biometrics, IET **1**(1), 3–10 (2012)
10. Housam, K.B., Lau, S.H., Pang, Y.H., et al.: Face spoofing detection based on improved local graph structure. In: 2014 International Conference on Information Science and Applications (ICISA), pp. 1–4. IEEE (2014)
11. Kim, S., Yu, S., Kim, K., et al.: Face liveness detection using variable focusing. In: 2013 International Conference on Biometrics (ICB), pp. 1–6. IEEE (2013)
12. Yang, J., Lei, Z., Liao, S., et al.: Face liveness detection with component dependent descriptor. In: 2013 International Conference on Biometrics (ICB), pp. 1–6. IEEE (2013)
13. Menotti, D., Chiachia, G., Pinto, A., et al.: Deep representations for iris, face, and fingerprint spoofing attack detection, EprintArxiv (2014)
14. Bouguet, J.Y.: Pyramidal implementation of the lucas kanade feature tracker description of the algorithm. Acta Pathologica Japonica **22**(2), 363–381 (2000)
15. Krizhevsky, A., Sutskever, I., Hinton, G.: Imagenet classification with deep convolutional neural networks. In: Proceedings of NIPS (2012)
16. Anjos, A., Chakka, M.M., Marcel, S.: Motion-based counter-measures to photo attacks in face recognition. IET Biometrics **3**(3), 147–158 (2014)
17. Chingovska, I., Anjos, A., Marcel, S.: On the effectiveness of local binary patterns in face anti-spoofing. In: Proceedings of International Conference on Biometrics Special Interest Group (BIOSIG), pp. 1–7, September 2012
18. Bharadwaj, S., Dhamecha, T.I., Vatsa, M., et al.: Computationally efficient face spoofing detection with motion magnification. In: 2013 IEEE Conference on Computer Vision and Pattern Recognition Workshops (CVPRW), pp. 105–110. IEEE Computer Society (2013)
19. Yan, J., Zhang, Z., Lei, Z., et al.: Face liveness detection by exploring multiple scenic clues. In: 2012 12th International Conference on Control Automation Robotics and Vision (ICARCV), pp. 188–193. IEEE (2012)
20. Schwartz, W., Rocha, A., Pedrini, H.: Face spoofing detection through partial least squares and low-level descriptors. In: IJCB. IEEE (2011)
21. de Freitas Pereira, T., Anjos, A., De Martino, J.M., Marcel, S.: Can face anti-spoofing countermeasures work in a real world scenario? In: Proceedings of International Conference on Biometrics (ICB), pp. 1–8, June 2013
22. Chingovska, I., Anjos, A., Marcel, S.: On the effectiveness of local binary patterns in face anti-spoofing. In: Proceedings of International Conference on Biometrics Special Interest Group (BIOSIG), pp. 1–7, September 2012

Liveness Detection Using Texture and 3D Structure Analysis

Qin Lin, Weijun Li, Xin Ning$^{(\boxtimes)}$, Xiaoli Dong, and Peng Chen

Institute of Semiconductors, Chinese Academy of Sciences, Beijing, China
{xinlideluoye,Wjli,ningxin,dongxiaoli,chenpeng}@semi.ac.cn

Abstract. We propose a novel face liveness detection method by analyzing the sparse structure information in 3D space based on binocular vision and texture information based on LBP (Local Binary Patterns). Structures of real faces have regular 3D structure information while structures of fake faces are usually presented in plane version or curve version different from real faces. Besides, fake faces containing quality defects caused by the printing technology can be detected by using the LBP texture feature. Three liveness detectors utilizing the 3D structure acquired from the binocular vision system, LBP and the combination of the aforementioned two methods are evaluated on a database. Experimental results show that the proposed methods can efficiently distinguish photo and real face.

Keywords: Binocular vision · 3D structure · LBP

1 Introduction

Recently, face recognition technique has developed rapidly. It has been widely used in our daily life, such as on cell phone or in verification system. The security of recognition systems has drawn more and more attention. Recognition systems are vulnerable to attacks forged by fake faces through using pictures, videos, or 3D models of human faces. Recently, due to the development of technology, it is easy to get photo or video of the target person from internet, cellphone or surveillance camera. Therefore, cost of forging fake faces has been further reduced and this may result in severe security problems. Face liveness detection is becoming an important technique for ensuring the security of face recognition systems.

According to the different features used, face spoofing detection methods can be divided into three categories [1]: methods based on additional hardware, methods based on biometric features, and methods based on additional data. The methods based on additional hardware use specific characteristics of liveness detection acquired by specialized sensors. This type of sensors generally includes thermal sensors, near infrared sensors, 3D scanners, and etc. [2–4]. The methods based on 3D scanner build face model and analyze the curvature of the face in order to distinguish the genuine and fake face images. However, it is not convenient to apply these methods in civil use since extra 3D scanner is necessary so that the application cost is increased thereby.

The methods based on biometric features analyze features of the picture to judge if the subject is human being. Several approaches focus on the dynamic changes of face,

© Springer International Publishing AG 2016
Z. You et al. (Eds.): CCBR 2016, LNCS 9967, pp. 637–645, 2016.
DOI: 10.1007/978-3-319-46654-5_70

including eye blinking, head rotation, and mouth movement [5, 6]. User has to respond to the special actions provided by computer accordingly in order that the computer can detect fake users. This may limit the application of such methods in practice. Some static methods detect spoofing attack using features of the picture. Z. Boulkenafet et al. [7] proposed a method to detect face spoofing using colour texture analysis. Kimet et al. [8] analyzed low frequency information as well as high frequency information of the image in combination with LBP to distinguish real face from two-dimension image. Diogo C. Garcia et al. [9] searched for Moiré patterns due to the overlap of digital grids, and detected peak in frequency domain for detection of face-spoofing. Maatta et al [10] analyzed facial micro-texture analysis to classify the real face and fake face. However, aforesaid methods are based on the hypothesis that the quality of the images of real face and fake face is different. Yet with the development of printing technology, these methods may be not applicable anymore.

The methods based on additional data use image capture device to get live additional information so as to detect liveness. Kim et al [11] proposed that two successive images at different focal lengths are different for real face and fake face. For real face, focus part is clear while other parts are fuzzy, while there is little change in fake face. However, it depends on the camera's depth of field for whether the result of this method is good or bad. Wang et al [12] proposed a face liveness detection approach to counter spoofing attacks by recovering sparse 3D facial structure from a single camera, but this method needs at least two images from different views and needs user to cooperate with the system.

In this article, we propose a novel face liveness detection method based on the sparse structure information in three dimensional spaces using binocular vision and LBP, respectively. 3D structures of real faces have regular 3D structure information, while structures of fake faces are usually presented in plane version. Even for warped pictures, the depth of the information is different from real faces (see Fig. 3). First, we get left and right face images at the same time and fit the Explicit Shape Regression (ESR) [13] model on both images to get the landmarks of the face. Then, according to the stereo matching method, we adjust the key points in right face image. Further, we use the matching key point based triangle's principle to compute the 3D structure of the face. Texture information based on LBP is used to classify fake and real faces by using enhanced feature histogram. Lastly, SVM classifier is trained based on the 3D facial structure, texture information and fusion-based two method from the real and fake faces.

The structure of the article is as follows: In Sect. 1, we introduce the basic idea of liveness detection. In Sects. 2 and 3, we describe sparse 3D facial structure recovery and LBP-based texture information respectively. In Sect. 4, we describe our proposed way of liveness detection. Experiments are presented in Sect. 5. Section 6 is the conclusion of this article.

2   Sparse 3D Face Structure Recovery

Binocular stereo camera system, which includes left camera and right camera, can capture a scene and get two images from two viewpoints. In order to estimate the disparity map, we adopt stereo matching method to get the corresponding points. Then we reconstruct the 3D information of the scene. Because of the low-textured region of the face, it is difficult to recover 3D face structure. It will be helpful to impose shape priors and adjust initial point by using local stereo matching algorithm.

For this purpose, we use an Explicit Shape Regression (ESR) model to obtain prior facial landmarks. In this way, we can limit the search area from the entire epipolar line to a small segment around the landmarks. This ensures topological information about the face and then we only need to adjust the landmarks of the right face which is not only under the epipolar constraints but also under the minimization of stereo matching cost constraints.

The coordinates of the landmarks of the left and right images are determined by applying the ESR algorithm on both images. After we apply two constraints to the right images, we will get more reliable coordinates of the corresponding points, which can be used to compute disparities. By combining with the similar triangle's principle, we can recover the sparse 3D facial structure.

2.1   Initial Facial Landmark Recovery

For the sake of establishing sparse matching, we apply the ESR model to the left and the right images to get the sparse facial landmarks. This model is obtained by the offline training process.

After fitting the ESR model, we get prior facial topological information including the shape SL of the left face and the shape SR of the right face. The 2D coordinates of the facial landmarks in the left are $L = \{(xL1, yL1), (xL2, yL2),........(xLn, yLn)\}$ and in the right are $R = \{(xR1, yR1), (xR2, yR2),........(xRn, yRn)\}$ (see Fig. 1).

Fig. 1. Optimization for the initial landmarks

Since we have rectified binocular stereo vision system, the corresponding points should be on the same scanlines. However, as we can see from Fig. 1, some of the corresponding points do not have equal row coordinates, that is, they are not on the same scanlines and they are not the best matching points. So we need to optimize the corresponding points.

2.2 Rectify Facial Landmarks of the Right Image

As we can see in Fig. 1, some of the landmarks on both images are actually not on the same scanlines. In fact, the landmarks on the left and the right images are not accurate corresponding points.

(1) Epipolar Geometry

A point in three dimensional space is imaged in both views, at p_l in the left view and p_r in the right view. p_l and p_r are under the constraint which is under the relative pose (R, t). The relation is showed in the formula (1):

$$p_r^T \varepsilon p_l = 0 \tag{1}$$

Essential matric ε has the form of $\varepsilon = [t_\times] R$. R is the relative rotation matrix and T is the relative translation matrix. $[t_\times]$ is the skew-symmetric cross-product matrix of $t = [t_x, t_y, t_z]$:

$$[t_\times] = \begin{bmatrix} 0 & -t_z & t_y \\ t_z & 0 & -t_x \\ -t_y & t_x & 0 \end{bmatrix} \tag{2}$$

we can get essential matrix by stereo calibration. Once the essential matrix is extracted, camera relative pose can be estimated. According points in the left image and the epipolar of the corresponding points in right images can be estimated. Because the binocular stereo vision system is rectified, the corresponding points are now on the same scanlines, which means they are on the same lines. By this means, we are able to limit the search area.

(2) Stereo Matching

Stereo matching is a method trying to find the corresponding points on the two views. There are two methods which include local algorithms and global algorithms. We assume that the matching search area is on the same scanlines so that we choose the local algorithms in combination with "winner takes all" principle to find the reliable corresponding points.

Stereo matching has four steps: cost computation, cost aggregation, disparity computation and disparity refinement. We concentrate on cost computation and disparity computation. Census measure [14] is used to compute matching cost. This measure encodes local image structures with relative orderings of the pixel intensity other than intensity values themselves. Therefore, it is more robust to noise. As shown in formulas (3) and (4):

$$\varepsilon(p, p') = \begin{cases} 1 & \text{if } I(p') < I(P) \\ 0 & \text{otherwise} \end{cases} \tag{3}$$

$$R_\tau(p) = \otimes \varepsilon(p, p'), \ p' \in N(p) \tag{4}$$

It is the comparative intensities of center pixel P versus the pixels.p'. in the neighborhood. Define $\varepsilon(p,p')$ to be 1 if $\left(p'\right) < I(P)$ and 0 otherwise. And the concatenation of $\varepsilon(p,p')$ in the neighborhood becomes the $R_\tau(p)$ map which is a bit string representing the set of neighboring pixel. The similarity of two pixels on the left and the right images is the harming distance of the census transform. To compute correspondence, we have minimized the Hamming distance after applying the census transform.

(3) Optimization

We take the initial facial alignment on both images as described in subsect. 2.1 as reference. It is a coarse alignment. The searching range of line in right image is the scanlines which is the same line with key points of the left image. And the searching range of columns in the right image is the neighborhood of columns of the key points in the right image. The two points which have the minimum Hamming distance are the corresponding points. The relation of these points is described in formula (5):

$$P_r = minR_\tau(p_l,p_r'), \text{ where } p_r' \in Ny\left(p_0\right) \tag{5}$$

p_l is the key point in the left face, p_0 is the initial key point in the right face. p_r' is the candidate point in the right image, which is the neighborhood of the point p_0.

Figure 1 is a comparison of the optimization for the initial landmarks. The red points in left image are the initial landmarks. The green points in the right face are the optimized points based on stereo matching and epipolar geometry. From the results we can see that it is more accurate matching cost as compared to the initial landmarks.

3   LBP-Based Method

This article utilizes the LBP [10] to analyze the micro-texture of the image. It is an effective method to describe the texture information of the image. As shown in formula (6), the value of pixel (x_c, y_c) is coded by considering the relative intensity of differences between the pixel and its neighbor.

$$LBP_{P,R} = \sum_{p=0}^{P-1} s(g_p - g_c)2^p, \quad s(x) = \begin{cases} 1, x \geq 0 \\ 0, x < 0 \end{cases} \tag{6}$$

where R is the radius from center to the neighboring pixels, P is the number of neighboring pixels. g_c corresponds to the gray value of the center pixel (x_c, y_c), g_p refers to the gray value of the P equally spaced pixels on the circle of radius of R,$s(x)$ is the threshold function of x. We use uniform patterns. The use of various values of P and R enables the analysis of multiresolution texture. The difference of P and R leads to different neighboring pixels (see Fig. 2).

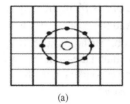 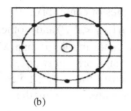 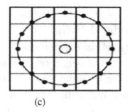

(a)   (b)   (c)

Fig. 2. LBP operator for different R and P (a) P = 8, R = 1 (b) P = 8, R = 2 (c) P = 16, R = 2

We firstly detect the face of the image and normalize it into 64 × 64 pixel image. We apply $LBP_{8,1}^{u2}$ operator on the normalized face image and divide the resulting LBP face image into 3 × 3 overlapping regions. And we also apply $LBP_{8,2}^{u2}$ and $LBP_{16,2}^{u2}$ operator on the face images. They all form the 833-bin histogram.

4 Liveness Detection

The depth differences of the landmarks are concatenated to form a feature vector. Then we use a nonlinear SVM classifier with radial basic function kernel, which is trained by the depth features, LBP features and fusion features, for deciding whether the input image is real face or not.

5 Experiments

In order to examine the proposed method of face liveness detection, we compare our method with other existing methods. There are some public databases designed for face liveness detection, such as NUAA database, Idiap database, and etc. However, these databases only obtain one image at a time, not two images from two views. So we have to establish a new database by ourselves in order to evaluate our proposed algorithm.

5.1 Experiment Data

We gathered 14 subjects and face images of people and their photographs are recorded using video cameras with 30 fps. The resolution of camera is 640 × 480. The photo used to forge fake face is captured from a camera with high resolution (ipad mini4 2448 × 3264). 200 pairs of images are collected for each subject with different motion style, including 50 pairs of real faces, and 150 pairs of fake faces. The database stores 700 pairs of real faces and 2100 pairs of fake faces. Specifically, the 2100 pairs of fake faces comprise 700 pairs of planar photos, 700 pairs of photos warped horizontally and 700 pairs of photos warped vertically. Table 1 presents the number of different kinds of images in the database.

Table 1. The number of images in the database

Real	Fake photos		
	Planar	Warp horizontally	Warp vertically
700	700	700	700

The images of the 14 subjects in the database are divided into two separate sets for training and testing purpose. The training set is constructed from 350 pairs of images of 7 real people and 1050 pairs of imposter images of the same 7 people. The test set contains 350 real people samples and 1035 imposter images.

5.2 Results

Figure 3 shows the recovery structure of the face of different type including the real face (see Fig. 3(a)), planar face (see Fig. 3(b)), photo warped horizontally (see Fig. 3(c)), photo warped vertically (see Fig. 3(d)). The real faces are the positive samples while the planar face, photo warped horizontally and photo warped vertically are the negative samples. Figure 3(e) to (f) are the 3D structure of the corresponding images. It shows that we can distinguish the real face from fake faces by using the difference of depth.

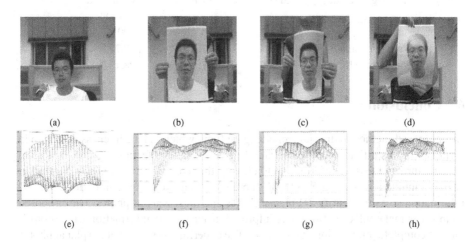

Fig. 3. 3D structure of the real face and fake face (a) real face (b) planar face (c) photo warped horizontally (d) photo warped vertically (e) 3D structure of genuine face (f) 3D structure of planar face (g) 3D structure of photo warped horizontally (h) 3D structure of photo warped vertically.

For the LBP and 3D structure methods, they both mistake some fake facial images for the real facial images. However, most of the samples mistaken by LBP-based methods are different with the samples mistaken by 3D structure-based method. And it inspired us that these two methods can be combined to improve the detection accuracy.

As shown in Table 2 and 3, the 3D structure-based method has higher true negative rate than the LBP-based method for the planar type photo, which is caused by the different features used in the two methods. Unlike real face, planar type photo has little variation in depth. But for the LBP-based method, image quality affects the results and consequently lowers the true negative rate. Otherwise, for the warped photo, 3D structure may fail when the photo is warped in large degree. Because the structure of this warped photo may be similar to the structure of the real face. However, variation in 3D structure has less influence on LBP feature, which leads to higher true negative rate for the horizontally warped photos. Furthermore, we combine these two methods to detect the warped photos. From Tables 2 and 3 it can be seen that the combined method increases the true negative rate of fake face detection, although it decreases the true positive rate of real faces. This implies that our proposed liveness detection algorithm is able to enhance the prevention rate of fake faces from passing the validation and thereby improve the system security.

Table 2. True acceptance rate of the test database

True positive rate	3D structure	LBP	Combined method
Real face	96.7 %	97.7 %	93.7 %

Table 3. True reject rate of the test database

True negative rate	3D structure	LBP	Combined method
Planar	100 %	98.72 %	100 %
Warp horizontally	96.5 %	97.14 %	98.73 %
Warp vertically	97.5 %	97.5 %	98.43 %

6   Conclusion

Our proposed method addresses a challenging topic which is face liveness detection in civil use. In this article, we propose an effective liveness detection method exploiting 3D structure and texture information to classify the live and facial images. We further utilize combined 3D structure and LBP approaches to make best use of both 2D and 3D information so as to identify 2D planar photos and most warped photos. Our proposed method can make full use of structure information and texture information which constitute the complete information of the image. The experiments show that 2D planar photos and most warped photos can be detected. The promising performance shows its capability to detect fake faces in real world. In the future, we will carry on our research on liveness detection dealing with attacks using video and we will increase the diversity of the fake facial image database.

References

1. Erdogmus, N., Marcel, S.: Introduction. In: Handbook of Biometric Anti-spoofing – Trusted Biometrics under Spoofing Attacks, pp. 1–11 (2014b)
2. Prokoski, J.: Disguise detection and identification using infrared imagery. **0339**, 27–31 (1983)

3. Wang, Y., Hao, X., Hou, Y., Guo, C.: A new multispectral method for face liveness detection. In: 2013 2nd IAPR Asian Conference on Pattern Recognition (ACPR), pp. 922–926, November 2013b

4. Lagorio, A., Tistarelli, M., Cadoni, M.: Liveness detection based on 3D face shape analysis. In: 2013 International Workshop on Biometrics and Forensics (IWBF), pp. 1–4 (2013)

5. Bao, W., Li, H., Li, N., Jiang, W.: A liveness detection method for face recognition based on optical flow field. In: 2009, International Conference on Image Analysis and Signal Processing, IASP 2009, pp. 233–236, April 2009

6. Pan, G., Sun, L., Wu, Z., Lao, S: Eyeblink-based anti-spoofing in face recognition from a generic webcamera. In: ICCV, pp. 1–8 (2007)

7. Boulkenafet, Z., Komulainen, J., Hadid, A.: Face spoofing detection using colour texture analysis. IEEE Trans. Inf. Forensics Secur. 11(8), 1818–1830 (2016)

8. Kim, G., Eum, S., Suhr, J.K., Kim, D.I., Park, K.R., Kim, J.: Face liveness detection based on texture and frequency analyses. In: 5th IAPR International Conference on Biometrics (ICB), New Delhi, India, pp. 67–72, March 2012

9. Garcia D.C., de Queiroz, R.L.: Evaluating the effects of image compression in Moiré-pattern-based face-spoofing detection. In: 2015 IEEE International Conference on Image Processing (ICIP), pp. 4843–4847. IEEE (2015)

10. Määttä, J., Hadid, A., Pietikäinen, M.: Face spoofing detection from single images using micro-texture analysis. In: 2011 International Joint Conference on Biometrics (IJCB), pp. 1–7. IEEE (2011)

11. Kim, S., Yu, S., Kim, K., Ban, Y., Lee, S.: Face liveness detection using variable focusing. In: 2013 International Conference on Biometrics (ICB), June 2013

12. Wang, T., Yang, J., Lei, Z., Liao, S., Li, S.Z.: Face liveness detection using 3D structure recovered from a single camera. In: 2013 International Conference on Biometrics (ICB) (2013a)

13. Cao, X., Wei, Y., Wen, F., et al.: Face alignment by explicit shape regression. Int. J. Comput. Vision 107(2), 177–190 (2014)

14. Zabih, R., Woodfill, J.: Non-parametric local transforms for computing visual correspondence. In: Eklundh, J.-O. (ed.) ECCV 1994. LNCS, vol. 801, pp. 151–158. Springer, Heidelberg (1994)

A Liveness Detection Method Based on Blood Volume Pulse Probing

Jianzheng Liu, Jucheng Yang[✉], Chao Wu, and Yarui Chen

College of Computer Science and Information Engineering,
Tianjin University of Science and Technology, No.1038, DaGu Road,
HeXi District, Tianjin 300222, China
{jz_leo,jcyang,superwoo,yrchen}@tust.edu.cn

Abstract. In this paper, we propose a novel method of detecting live body samples in biometrics, which is based on the detection of a blood volume pulse. We used an auto-encoder to extract a signal from the video captured from skin to determine whether the sample is alive or not. The experimental results confirmed that our method could accurately distinguish between live body samples and spoofed samples.

Keywords: Biometrics · Spoofing · Liveness detection

1 Introduction

Biometrics is defined as "automated methods for verifying or identifying the identity of a living individual based on physiological or behavioral characteristics" [1]. Recently, important research has been conducted that studies the vulnerabilities of biometric systems through direct attacks to the sensor by a constructed fake subject. These efforts were carried out using synthetic biometric traits such as gummy fingers, moldable plastic, clay, Play-Doh, wax, and silicon [2–5]. This illegitimate access to secured resources protected by a biometric recognition system through the use of faux biometric traits is called spoofing. Essentially, all kinds of biometric recognition systems will suffer if they cannot distinguish between a fake trait and that of a living human. Many efforts indicated that fingerprint authentication systems, facial recognition systems, iris recognition systems and even audio-video speaker authentication systems suffer from this weakness [2–8].

Here are a few studies that are most relevant to our research. Pan presented an approach that exploited the observation that humans blink once every 2 to 4 s. Experiments carried out with the ZJU Eye Blink Database (http://www.cs.zju.edu.cn/gpan/database/db_blink.html) showed an accuracy of 95.7 % [9]. However, the approach cannot protect a face recognition system from a Replay-Attack. Yan presented an approach based on Non-Rigid detection and Face-Background Consistency in [10]. But the method can be spoofed by Replay-Attack by using a large-screen display device. There are also some texture-based

© Springer International Publishing AG 2016
Z. You et al. (Eds.): CCBR 2016, LNCS 9967, pp. 646–654, 2016.
DOI: 10.1007/978-3-319-46654-5_71

methods such as [11,12]. But these methods require high user cooperation or costly equipments and are sensitive to the imaging quality and environments.

We presented a very simple but robust method to against a screen replay-attack [13]. So in this paper, we present a simple, cost-effective method for liveness detection based on blood volume pulse probing to against spoofing-attacks except replay-attack. There is a natural difference between forged and living biometric traits: a heartbeat. The blood flow under human skin can cause slight changes in skin color. These changes cannot be recognized visually, but signals can be extracted from videos or image sequences using conventional cameras, or even a webcam [14]. Because the finding proposed in this paper is not a texture-based method, it is unaffected by the imaging quality and environments. Unlike other methods, our approach can be used in almost biometric systems, including fingerprints, palm prints, face recognition, and iris recognition systems via capture videos from a region of subjects' skin.

2 Relevant Theories

2.1 SPA

SPA (smoothness prior approach) is a classical method proposed by Taravinen in [15] which was originally used to extract the HRV (heart rate variability) signals from ECG raw data. The raw signals we obtain from the video that have been captured by a biometric system consist of two components:

$$z = z_{stat} + z_{trend} \tag{1}$$

where z_{stat} is the signal we are interested in and z_{trend} is the low frequency aperiodic trend component caused by light and other factors that we want to remove. In [15], the signal we are interested in was modeled as :

$$\hat{z}_{stat} = z - H\hat{\theta}_\lambda = (I - (I + \lambda^2 D_2^T D_2)^{-1})z \tag{2}$$

where $D_2 \in \mathbb{R}^{(N-2)\times N}$ and is in the form:

$$D_2 = \begin{pmatrix} 1 & -2 & 1 & 0 & \dots & 0 \\ 0 & 1 & -2 & 1 & 0 & \vdots \\ \vdots & \ddots & \ddots & \ddots & \ddots & 0 \\ 0 & \dots & 0 & 1 & -2 & 1 \end{pmatrix}$$

According [15], SPA can be seen as a time-varying FIR high pass filter. If the smoothing parameter λ is set to 10, the cut-off frequency is 0.059 times the sampling frequency. If the λ is set to 20, the cut-off frequency is 0.041 times the sampling frequency.

2.2   RBM (Restricted Boltzmann Machine)

RBMs were invented by Paul Smolensky [16] and have gain popularity after Hinton published the paper [17] to propose a method of reducing the dimensionality of data. RBMs are probabilistic graphical models that can be interpreted as stochastic neural networks. They have attracted much attention as building blocks for the multi-layer learning systems called deep belief networks, and variants and extensions of RBMs have found applications in a wide range of pattern recognition tasks [18].

An RBM is an MRF associated with a bipartite undirected graph, and can be viewed as non-linear feature detectors [19]. We achieved an amenable result in extracting features by use a single layer RBM; the method and results are provided in Sects. 3 and 4.

3   Liveness Detection System

We present a method to detect living body in this paper. Figure 1 shows a block diagram of the proposed countermeasure.

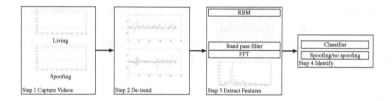

Fig. 1. General diagram of the liveness detection method presented in this paper (Color figure online)

3.1   Capture RGB Singals

In Fig. 1 Step 1, we captured a color video (24-bit RGB) from the sample using a camera. In our lab, we used a webcam and a built-in camera to capture videos at 15 fps or 30 fps. We captured videos with a pixel resolution of 640×480, which most face recognition systems can work on. Then, we selected the region that contained skin (face, palm or finger) in the video as ROI. Finally, we separated the ROI into RGB channels and recorded the average of all grayscale pixels. So we extracted three floating-point values from each frame in the video. In our lab, we defined 230 continuous frames as a sample. Experimental results showed that an increase of video length would not necessarily bring positive effects.

3.2   De-trended

In Step 2, the signals were de-trended using SPA with a smoothing parameter $\lambda = 20$ when the videos were captured at 30 fps (cut-off frequency of 1.23 Hz).

If the videos were captured at 15 fps, λ would have been better set to 10 (cut-off frequency of 0.89 Hz) [14]. The signals extracted from the R, G, B channels in Step 1 were de-trended. The size of D_2 was 228×230 in formula (2). According to the formula, the raw R, G, B channel signals were de-trended and the new signals are presented in Fig. 1 Step2. The top figure shows the de-trended R, G, B signals captured from a living body, whereas the bottom figure shows the signals captured from a photograph using the same method. The signals shown in the top figure have a significant cyclical characteristics, that corresponding the BVP (Blood Volume Pulse) signals. It is clearly that the SPA algorithm has the ability to extract BVP signals from a color video.

3.3 Extract Feature Signals Using RBM and Convert Signals to Frequency Domain

In this step, we put all the de-trended signals from each frame in a second together (i.e., 30 continuous frames if the video stream is captured at 30 fps or 15 continuous frames if the video stream is captured at 15 fps, R, G, B channels respectively) as an input of the RBM. We built an RBM with 90 (or 45 at 15 fps) units in the input layer and only one output unit in the hidden layer (which also can be seen as output layer). The continuous 230 frames of data were restructured using the following approach: we restructured the signals (R, G, B channels) between the 1st frame to the 30th frame to a 90-dimensional vector; the same approach was then used on the signals between the 2nd frame to the 31th frame, and so on. In this way, we built 200 vectors, and each vector was 90-dimensional. We fed the vectors into an RBM in order to extract the BVP signal. Experiments showed that an fps from 15 fps to 30 fps and a video contains 4~7 or more BVP cycles, which would be better for our method.

To train the RBM, we used two groups of vectors, one of which was extracted from a living body while the other was extracted from fake samples, such as photographs. The 400 vectors were mixed together in random order. We used the training approach presented in [17] to train the RBM, which was very effective. For our method we trained the RBM individually for each input signal. It means that the weight matrix of the RBM would be adjusted at each time to fit the input signal and extract output signal for each sample.

Next, the vectors were fed to the RBM again in the original order; The top fig in Fig. 1 shows the machine's output. The blue curve is the signal extracted from the living body and the red curve is the signal extracted from a photograph (spoof). In the top fig in Fig. 1, the blue curve shows an obvious characteristic at around 30 frames per cycle. That means the sample that had been tested was a living body and had an HR (heart rate) of approximately 1 Hz. We cannot find the same characteristic in the red curve, so it was a spoof. We are confident that the signal was caused by a BVP. In our view, the RBM can calculate the current frame's BVP state by extracting a feature using the data from the previous 30 frames.

The signals were filtered first with a band-pass filter and were then converted to frequency domain signals using the FFT (fast Fourier transform) theory. In fact, any available filter is OK if it can filter the DC part of the signal.

3.4   Classify and Identify

In the last Step, an AdaBoost classifier was trained using 2000 such vectors, including 1000 positive samples and 1000 negative samples. Each sample was a feature extracted from a living body (positive sample) or a spoofed trait (negative sample) using the approaches from Step 1 to Step 4. The frequency domain signals reflect the energy distribution of the time domain signals. However, there is a significant difference between living subjects and spoofed ones wherein the signal's energy is concentrated in a particular frequency if it had been extracted from a living body (in Fig. 1 Step 4, the blue curve is the signal extracted from living body and the red curve is the spoofed one). To clarify this feature further, the samples' values were normalized to 0~1 before they were used to train the AdaBoost classifier. After the training process, the classifier could then be used to discriminate spoofed traits from a living body.

4   Experiments

A webcam and a built-in camera were used to test our method. These two cameras achieved the same performance. All experiments reported in this section used a Microsoft LifeCam Studio 1080p HD Webcam.

4.1   Influence of Illumination

Almost all computer vision algorithms can be affected by illumination, and our method is no exception. There is no doubt that ambient sunlight is the best source of illumination. Here we present three results from our method using different types of illumination: ambient sunlight, an LED lamp with a 200 Hz strobe and an LED lamp with a 50 Hz strobe. We posted the BVP signal figures in Fig. 2. All of the signals were extracted from a living body's palm using our method.

In the curve "sunlight" we can see a perfect BVP signal, which was extracted using our method. In the curve there was a clear second peak in each cycle of the signal. The second peaks were caused by dicrotic waves. The curve "LED@200 Hz" reported a signal that was extracted in our lab used an LED lamp with a 200 Hz strobe. Compared with "sunlight", the signal can be seen to have some distortion without clear dicrotic wave curves in the signal. Because it was still a significant cyclical signal that conformed the BVP, so we can use the signal to identify a living body. But in the curve "LED@50 Hz", it is clear that the BVP signal could not be extracted; the only signal in the curve was the strobe signal. We used RBM to extract the signals; the machine can extract the strongest signal in the inputs. The 50 Hz strobe signal can be seen with a strong signal when we captured videos at 30 fps. In summary, our method can be used with ambient sunlight or high frequency LED lamps.

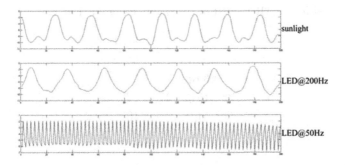

Fig. 2. Signals with sunlight, 200 Hz LED & 50 Hz LED

4.2   Results

Our living sample featured 10 participants of both genders (five of which were male and five female), from 25 to 60 years old. We captured video streams using a webcam on the subjects as positive samples (living body). We also created groups of subjects as spoofing sample sets containing 40 photographs and a hand model made of silica gel. The photographs captured from the persons who were in the living samples set. Video streams captured on the spoofing subjects can be seen as negative samples (spoofing attack). We used all of the videos as a training samples set.

In each experiment, the AdaBoost classifier mentioned in Sect. 3.4 was trained first. We trained the classifier using a training set extracted from the training samples set. The training set containing 2000 videos; 1000 were captured from the living samples, while others were captured from the spoofed samples. We extracted the 2000 samples using the approach covered in Steps 1 to 3 mentioned in Sect. 3 under the same conditions (illumination, capture rate, frame length, parameter λ). Then we used the classifier to test our method.

We tested our method on the continuous 100 and 200 frames mentioned previously. The 100 frames chosen fell between the 200 continuous frames, from the 51th frame to the 150th frame. In order to compare the results, we also extracted the odd frames from every 30 fps video stream to simulate video streams captured at 15 fps. Thus there were 4 tests and 4 identification results on test samples, consisting of 200 frames @ 30 fps, 100 frames @30 fps, 100 frames @15 fps and 50 frames @15 fps output by 4 classifiers. In the case of 30 fps, the parameter λ in formula (2) was set to 20, and set to 10 in the case of 15 fps. Tables 1, 2 and 3 summarize all the results.

Table 1 shows the results determined when we tested our method using ambient sunlight as the only source of illumination with a complex background. We selected 10 living subjects and 10 photographs captured from those living subjects as test samples. We tested our method 10 times for each sample. The results show that our method can achieve an FRR from 5 % to 10 % using the AdaBoost algorithm and an FAR from 1 % to 2 % with ambient sunlight. With the reduction of frames and capture rate, the FRR increased.

Table 1. FAR & FRR of the results using ambient sunlight

Samples	FAR	FRR
200@30 fps	1%	5%
100@30 fps	1%	5%
100@15 fps	2%	7%
50@15 fps	2%	10%

Table 2 shows the results found when we tested our method with an LED lamp (200 Hz) as the only source of illumination using a complex background. All experimental conditions were consistent with the previous experiment with the exception of illumination. By comparing the results, we observed that with a change of illumination, the FRR increased, but there was little change in the FAR.

Table 2. FAR & FRR of the results using an LED lamp at 200 Hz

Samples	FAR	FRR
200@30 fps	1%	6%
100@30 fps	1%	7%
100@15 fps	2%	10%
50@15 fps	3%	14%

Table 3 shows the results found when we tested our method with an LED lamp (200 Hz) as the only source of illumination. The experiment was implemented with a darkbox made in our lab to capture the video streams using a black background with front lighting. We tested our method using a hand model made of silica gel as the spoofing attack. The results were better than the previous two experiments as a result of better background conditions and stable subjects during video capture.

Table 3. FAR & FRR of the results using a white front light (LED lamp at 200 Hz) and a black background

Samples	FAR	FRR
200@30 fps	0%	3%
100@30 fps	0%	3%
100@15 fps	1%	3%
50@15 fps	1%	5%

5   Discussion

Based on the presented results, we demonstrated the feasibility of our method wherein liveness detection is possible using a webcam to measure the subject's BVP. In our view, the BVP can be seen as a key characteristic of a living body. There is a clear difference between the signals, which were extracted using a living body as well as spoofed subject (see Fig. 1 Step 3).

To summarize, the FAR in our method is relatively stable under different conditions. Degraded FRR occurred under less than ideal conditions, such as bad illumination, too few frames and a low video sampling rate. Illumination and video sampling rates have a direct impact on the signals generated using our method. However, reducing the signal quality or illumination condition does not make the signal extracted from a spoofed sample generate a cyclical feature.

Therefore, in our experiments, the results we obtained when we tested our method using an LED lamp as the sole source of illumination were a little better than those using ambient sunlight. We believed the reason was that when we used the LED source, the videos were captured from the subjects, which were fixed in the darkbox with a black background. These conditions were better than those when we used ambient sunlight (the subjects' faces had slight movements against a complex background).

Normally, a heart rate does not exceed 4 Hz. In our experiments, each test living subject was in a calm state. We had extracted BVP signals from several subjects who had a higher heart rate (from 100 to 150 per minute). The frequency domain signals were similar to the calm signals, and most energy from the BVP signals was concentrated at a certain frequency value (1.5 Hz or other value). Regardless of the heart rate, a BVP signal's energy should concentrated in a certain frequency, rather than spread over the frequency from 0~4 Hz. It is difficult to develop a database containing many high heart rate videos; consequently we tested our method with subjects who were in a calm state in our lab. However, our results suggest that this is sufficient to obtain accurate identifications of spoof attack. Our findings should motivate extensive validation and continued systematic exploration of the variables mentioned above.

Acknowledgment. This work was supported by the National Natural Science Foundation of China under Grant no. 61502338, the 2015 key projects of Tianjin Science and Technology Support Program no. 15ZCZDGX00200, and the Open Fund of Guangdong Provincial Key Laboratory of Petrochemical Equipment Fault Diagnosis no. GDUP-TKLAB201334.

References

1. Woodward, J.D., Orlans, N.M., Higgins, P.T.: Biometrics. McGraw-Hill/Osborne, New York (2003)
2. Matsumoto, T., Matsumoto, H., Yamada, K., Hoshino, S.: Impact of artificial gummy fingers on fingerprint systems. In: Electronic Imaging 2002, International Society for Optics and Photonics, pp. 275–289 (2002)

3. Schuckers, S.A.C.: Spoofing and anti-spoofing. Inf. Secur. Tech. Rep. **7**, 56–62 (2002)
4. Van der Putte, T., Keuning, J.: Biometrical fingerprint recognition: dont get your fingers burned. In: Smart Card Research and Advanced Applications, pp. 289–303. Springer, US (2000)
5. Derakhshani, R., Schuckers, S.A., Hornak, L.A., OGorman, L.: Determination of vitality from a non-invasive biomedical measurement for use in fingerprint scanners. Pattern Recogn. **36**, 383–396 (2003)
6. Johnson, P., Tan, B., Schuckers, S.: Multimodal fusion vulnerability to non-zero effort (spoof) imposters. In: 2010 IEEE International Workshop on Information Forensics and Security (WIFS), pp. 1–5. IEEE (2010)
7. Lee, E.C., Park, K.R., Ko, Y.J.: Fake iris detection method using purkinje images based on gaze position. Opt. Eng. **47**, 067204–067204 (2008)
8. Eveno, N., Besacier, L.: A speaker independent liveness test for audio-visual biometrics. In: INTERSPEECH, pp. 3081–3084 (2005)
9. Pan, G., Wu, Z., Sun, L.: Liveness detection for face recognition. In: Recent advances in face recognition, pp. 109–124 (2008)
10. Yan, J., Zhang, Z., Lei, Z., Yi, D., Li, S.Z.: Face liveness detection by exploring multiple scenic clues. In: 2012 12th International Conference on Control Automation Robotics & Vision (ICARCV), pp. 188–193. IEEE (2012)
11. Komulainen, J., Hadid, A., Pietikäinen, M.: Face spoofing detection using dynamic texture. In: Park, J.-I., Kim, J. (eds.) ACCV 2012. LNCS, vol. 7728, pp. 146–157. Springer, Heidelberg (2013). doi:10.1007/978-3-642-37410-4_13
12. Raghavendra, R., Raja, K.B., Busch, C.: Presentation attack detection for face recognition using light field camera. IEEE Trans. Image Process. **24**(3), 1060–1075 (2015)
13. Liu, J.Z., Yang, H.Y.: A Replay-attack detection method based on flashing illumination. Comput. Program. Skills Maintenance **349**(5–7), 11 (2016). (in Chinese)
14. Poh, M.Z., McDuff, D.J., Picard, R.W.: Advancements in noncontact, multiparameter physiological measurements using a webcam. IEEE Trans. Biomed. Eng. **58**, 7–11 (2011)
15. Tarvainen, M.P., Ranta-aho, P.O., Karjalainen, P.A.: An advanced detrending method with application to HRV analysis. IEEE Trans. Biomed. Eng. **49**, 172–175 (2002)
16. Smolensky, P.: Information Processing in Dynamical Systems: Foundations of Harmony Theory. MIT Press, Cambridge (1986)
17. Hinton, G.E., Salakhutdinov, R.R.: Reducing the dimensionality of data with neural networks. Science **313**, 504–507 (2006)
18. Fischer, A., Igel, C.: Training restricted Boltzmann machines: an introduction. Pattern Recogn. **47**, 25–39 (2014)
19. Hinton, G.E.: Boltzmann machine 2, 1668. Revision #91075 (2007)

2D Fake Fingerprint Detection Based on Improved CNN and Local Descriptors for Smart Phone

Yongliang Zhang[1(✉)], Bing Zhou[1], Hongtao Wu[2], and Conglin Wen[1]

[1] College of Computer Science and Technology, Zhejiang University of Technology,
Hangzhou 310023, China
titanzhang@zjut.edu.cn
[2] School of Computer Science and Engineering, Hebei University of Technology,
Tianjin 300130, China

Abstract. With the growing use of fingerprint authentication systems on smart phone, fake fingerprint detection has become increasingly important because fingerprints can be easily spoofed from a variety of readily available materials. The performance of the existing fake fingerprint detection methods is significantly influenced by the fabrication materials used to generate spoofs during the training stage. In order to enhance the robustness against spoof materials, this paper proposes a novel 2D fake fingerprint detection method mainly for smart phone by combining Convolutional Neural Networks (CNN) and two local descriptors (Local Binary Pattern and Local Phase Quantization). To optimize CNN, global average pooling and batch normalization are integrated. Besides, 2D printed fingerprint dataset created from capacitive fingerprint scanner is used for the first time to evaluate fake fingerprint detection algorithm. Experimental results show that the proposed algorithm has high accuracy and strong robustness, and can meet the requirements on smart phone.

Keywords: 2D fake fingerprint detection · Local binary pattern · Local phase quantization · Convolutional Neural Networks

1 Introduction

With the growing use of fingerprint authentication systems for smart phone in the recent years, Fake Fingerprint Detection (FFD) has become increasingly important because fingerprints can be easily spoofed from a variety of readily available materials, such as wood glue, electrosol or printed fingerprint [1, 2]. Different fabrication materials exhibit different intensity gradients and ridge shapes in fake fingerprints due to their different thickness. Therefore, the performance of the existing FFD methods is significantly influenced by the fabrication materials used to generate spoofs during the training stage [3–7]. The previous methods have shown that single feature-based approaches don't perform equally over different spoofing materials [3], and no feature has a good flexibility for all types of fake fingerprints [4].

A combination of different features becomes a practical way when there is no prior knowledge of the types of fabrication material. Dubey et al. [3] proposed to combine

© Springer International Publishing AG 2016
Z. You et al. (Eds.): CCBR 2016, LNCS 9967, pp. 655–662, 2016.
DOI: 10.1007/978-3-319-46654-5_72

gradient features from SURF, PHOG, and texture features from Gabor wavelet using dynamic score level integration. Their method performed well over a large open source dataset created using six different materials. Rattani and Ross [5] designed a scheme for automatic adaptation of a liveness detector to new spoof materials encountered during the operational phase by combining Grey Level Co-occurence Matrix (GLCM), Histogram of Oriented Gradients (HOG), Binary Statistical Image Features (BSIF), LPQ, Binary Gabor Patterns (BGP) and LBP using AdaBoost. In their further work, Rattani et al. [6] treated FFD as an open set recognition problem, and proposed a W-SVM-based fingerprint spoof detector for the automatic adaptation of new spoof materials based on LBP, LPQ and BSIF.

Recently, inspired by its strong learning ability from data and high efficient feature representation ability, deep learning has been applied to build image-based anti-spoofing systems [8–10], and achieved state-of-the-art performance. The experimental results in [8] strongly indicate that CNN based FFD was robust to attacks already known, and possibly adapted to image-based attacks that was yet to come. Experiments presented in [7] reveal good robustness with regards to unseen fabrication materials (−3.6 % to +4.6 % AUC deviation) on LivDet 2011 and 2013 databases.

Therefore, in order to further enhance the robustness against spoof materials, this paper proposes a novel 2D FFD method mainly for smart phone by combining improved CNN and local descriptors including LBP and LPQ. In the proposed method, Batch Normalization (BN) [11] and Global Average Pooling (GAP) [12] are integrated into CNN to further improve its efficiency and accuracy.

The duplication of a fingerprint can be a cooperative process, or a non-cooperative process [1, 2]. But, it is highly unlikely that a person will agree to produce a mold of his or her finger in a realistic scenario [1]. So the fake fingerprints used in this paper are created from fingerprints based on a non-cooperative process using photolithographic Printed Circuit Board (PCB) mold for smart phone. More importantly, a simpler yet effective method for spoofing the fingerprint scanner embedded in a smart phone was reported using a 2D fingerprint image printed on a special paper with special conductive ink in this year [13]. To the best of our knowledge, there are no FFD methods which discuss the detection performance under 2D printed fingerprint attack. The published LivDet2009, LivDet2011 and LivDet2013 are most of 3D fingerprints which are created from traditional optical fingerprint scanners and are general with enough ideal size. However, the current smart phone usually configures a capacitive fingerprint scanner and only can capture small fingerprint to some degree. Therefore, a dataset of 2D printed fingerprint and 2D PCB is created from capacitive fingerprint scanner of smart phone to evaluate the performance of our proposed FFD method.

The rest of the paper is organized as follows. In Sect. 2, the proposed method is described in detail. Experimental results are presented in Sect. 3. Finally, Sect. 4 concludes the paper.

2   Proposed Method

The procedure of the proposed FFD method is illustrated in Fig. 1. The proposed method consists of two classifiers. One is local descriptors based classifier in which LBP and LPQ are extracted and a SVM classifier is trained based on the fusion of LBP and LPQ. The other is CNN based classifier which is learned based on intercepting effective fingerprint region.

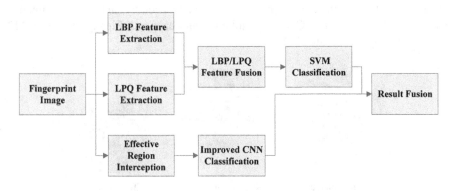

Fig. 1. The procedure of the proposed FFD

2.1   Local Descriptor Based Classification

The original LBP operator was first proposed by Ojala et al. [14]. LBP operator forms labels for the image pixels by thresholding each of the 8 neighbors of the 3 × 3-neighborhood of each pixel with the center value and considering the result as a binary number. LBP was first introduced in the fingerprint liveness detection literature in [15] where LBP descriptor was utilized to capture these structural, orientation, roughness, smoothness and regularity differences of diverse regions in a fingerprint image. LBP is considered as one of the best operators for FFD.

LPQ is a blur insensitive texture classification method proposed in [16]. LPQ encodes some phase information extracted through a short time Fourier transform of the local patch, rather than gradients. The first use of LPQ for fingerprint liveness detection is found in [17].

Because the image is usually captured from multiple subjects using different scanners, fingerprint images are typically found to be of different scales and rotations, or partially captured due to human errors [3]. Various features capturing properties of live fingerprint images are used to obtain features invariant to these problems [3]. Similarly, LBP and LPQ are chosen in this paper. After LBP feature vector *fea_LBP* and LPQ feature vector *fea_LPQ* are respectively extracted, they are combined into feature vector $Fusion_{LBP+LPQ}$ which serves as input to train a SVM-based spoof detector $P_{LBP+LPQ}$.

2.2   Convolutional Neural Networks Based Classification

In order to accelerate convergence and obtain ideal initial parameters, a pre-trained CNN named BVLC AlexNet Model [18] is used as the basic model to prevent falling into local optimum.

Additionally, in order to exclude the surrounding interference of the fingerprint region and make the results of CNN more accurate, effective region interception of the input fingerprint image is needed as shown in Fig. 2. Firstly, the weighted center coordinate C(x,y) of the original image pixels is calculated. Secondly, an 112×112 effective rectangle with the center of C(x,y) is calibrated and captured. Finally, the 112×112 effective region is input into CNN.

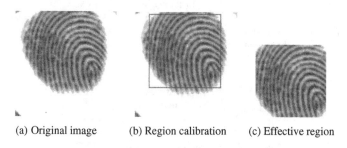

(a) Original image   (b) Region calibration   (c) Effective region

Fig. 2. An example of effective region interception

As the fully connected layers are prone to overfit, an alternative strategy called GAP is used to replace the traditional fully connected layers in CNN in this paper as shown in Fig. 3. The idea is to generate one feature map for each corresponding category of the classification task in the last convolutional layer. Instead of adding fully connected layers on top of the feature maps, the average of each feature map is taken and the resulting vector is fed directly into the softmax layer. The advantages of GAP over the fully connected layers are as follows:

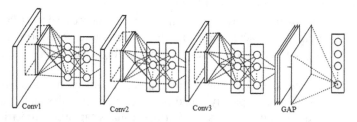

Fig. 3. An example of three convolutional layers and one global average pooling layer

(1) It is more native to the convolution structure by enforcing correspondences between feature maps and categories. Thus the feature maps can be easily interpreted as categories confidence maps.

(2) Overfitting can be avoided successfully at this layer because there is no parameter to be optimized in the GAP.

(3) Since GAP sums out the spatial information, it is more robust to spatial translations of the input.

GAP can be considered as a structural regularizer that explicitly enforces feature maps to be confidence maps of concepts (categories) [12]. This is made possible by the convolutional layers, as they make better approximation to the confidence maps than generalized linear modes [12].

In addition, the CNN is also improved by introducing BN which can accelerate deep network training by reducing internal covariate shift. Transforms are focused on that consist of an affine transformation followed by an element-wise nonlinearity:

$$z = g(W \cdot u + b) \tag{1}$$

where W and b are learned parameters of the model, and $g(\cdot)$ is the nonlinearity such as sigmoid or ReLU. This formulation covers both fully-connected and convolutional layers. We add the BN transform immediately before the nonlinearity, by normalizing $x = W \cdot u + b$. We don't choose to normalize the layer inputs u because u is likely to be the output of another nonlinearity, and the shape of its distribution is likely to be changed during training. Thus, constraining its first and second moments would not eliminate the covariate shift. In contrast, $W \cdot u + b$ is more likely to have a symmetric, non-sparse distribution, and normalizing it is likely to produce activations with a stable distribution.

When $W \cdot u + b$ is normalized, the bias b can be ignored since its effect will be canceled by the subsequent mean subtraction. Thus, Eq. 1 is replaced with

$$z = g(BN(W \cdot u)) \tag{2}$$

where the BN transform is applied independently to each dimension of $x = W \cdot u$, with a separate pair of learned parameters per dimension. Finally, The improved CNN can train a spoof detector P_{CNN}.

2.3 Classifier Fusion

From Sects. 2.1 and 2.2, two spoof detectors $P_{LBP+LPQ}$ and P_{CNN} are obtained, respectively. Then, $P_{LBP+LPQ}$ and P_{CNN} are combined into a detector P_{Fus} according to Eq. 3.

$$P_{Fus} = \omega \cdot P_{CNN} + (1 - \omega) \cdot P_{LBP+LPQ} \tag{3}$$

At last, the detection result η of the detector P_{Fus} can be calculated as follows:

$$\eta = \begin{cases} 1, & P_{Fus} > T_P \\ 0, & P_{Fus} \leq T_P \end{cases} \tag{4}$$

where ω is a weight and T_P is a threshold, and they are obtained by a 5-fold cross-validation. If $\eta = 1$, the input image is determined as a fake fingerprint; otherwise it is from a true fingerprint.

3   Experimental Results

3.1   Datasets

To the best of our knowledge, the published datasets are created from traditional optical fingerprint scanners and most of them only contain 3D fake fingerprints. There is no published dataset which is created from capacitive fingerprint scanner of smart phone and contians 2D fake fingerprints. However, it has been confirmed that some 2D fake fingerprints made of wood glue and electrosol from PCB, or printed by special conductive ink can cheat many current fingerprint verification systems on smart phone, lockfast or fingerprint lock [1, 2, 13]. Therefore, we create fake fingerprints with these materials and build a new dataset with FPC1021 capacitive fingerprint scanner for the first time. This dataset is divided into training dataset and testing dataset randomly which respectively include four different types of fingerprints such as real Fingerprint, 2D-Electrosol, 2D-Wood glue and 2D-Printed. Some examples are shown in Fig. 4. The detail information of our dataset is described in Table 1.

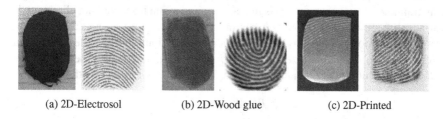

(a) 2D-Electrosol   (b) 2D-Wood glue   (c) 2D-Printed

Fig. 4.   Three kinds of 2D fake fingerprints and corresponding fingerprint images

Table 1.   The structure of dataset

Dataset	Real	2D-Electrosol	2D-Wood Glue	2D-Print	Total
Training dataset	67011	31524	17970	16087	132592
Testing dataset	8779	4464	5512	6007	24762

3.2   Results

In order to evaluate the performance of our proposed algorithm, Fake Fingerprint Accuracy (FFA), True Fingerprint Accuracy (TFA) and Weighted Accuracy (WA) are defined as follows:

$$FFA = \frac{N_1}{N_{Fake}} \times 100\,\% \tag{5}$$

$$TFA = \frac{N_2}{N_{True}} \times 100\,\% \tag{6}$$

$$WA = \frac{N_1 + N_2}{N_{Fake} + N_{True}} \times 100\% \tag{7}$$

Where N_{Fake} and N_{True} are the numbers of fake and true fingerprints in testing dataset, respectively, N_1 is the number of fake fingerprints which are verified fake successfully in N_{Fake}, and N_2 is the number of true fingerprints which are verified true successfully in N_{True}.

Due to there is no published dataset which is created from capacitive fingerprint scanner of smart phone and only contains 2D fingerprints, the proposed algorithm is compared with classical LBP+LPQ and CNN in our dataset. The testing platform is Inter®CPU i5-3450 and 8 G Memory. The experimental results are reported in Table 2. As shown in Table 2, the proposed algorithm has better accuracy, stronger robustness and good real-time performance on the testing dataset in generally, and can meet the requirements on smart phone.

Table 2. The performance of our proposed algorithm tested on dataset

Algorithm	LBP+LPQ	Improved CNN	Proposed algorithm
Real (TFA)	98.14 %	98.16 %	99.14 %
2D-Electrosol (FFA)	98.27 %	99.96 %	99.89 %
2D-Wood Glue (FFA)	98.73 %	95.53 %	98.53 %
2D-Print (FFA)	96.44 %	99.45 %	99.95 %
Weighted Accuracy (WA)	97.88 %	98.21 %	99.34 %
Average time	5.82 ms	54.90 ms	60.89 ms
Average memory	6.08 MB	37.55 MB	38.52 MB

4 Conclusion

A novel 2D fake fingerprint detection algorithm mainly for smart phone is proposed in this paper, which is based on improved CNN and local descriptors. In addition, a new dataset including 2D fingerprints of three fabrication materials is created from capacitive fingerprint scanner of smart phone for the first time. Experimental results show that the algorithm has high accuracy, strong robustness and good real-time performance, and can be applied on smart phone with a capacitive fingerprint sensor.

Currently, the fake fingerprints in testing dataset are captured only by a capacitive fingerprint scanner in smart phone. However, different sensors capture information differently. So, we will explore how to make our proposed method suit a new fake fingerprint dataset captured by different fingerprint sensors using fake fingerprints generated by different fabrication materials.

Acknowledgement. The project was supported by the Science and Technology Planning Project of Hebei Province, China (No. 15210124), and the Science and Technology Research Project of Higher School in Hebei Province, China (No. Z2015105).

References

1. Marasco, E., Ross, A.: A survey on antispoofing schemes for fingerprint recognition systems. ACM Comput. Surv. **47**(2), 28:1–28:36 (2014)
2. Sousedik, C., Busch, C.: Presentation attack detection methods for fingerprint recognition systems: a survey. IET Biometrics **3**(4), 219–233 (2014)
3. Dubey, R., Goh, J., Thing, V.L.L.: Fingerprint liveness detection from single image using low-level features and shape analysis. IEEE Trans. Inf. Forensics Secur. **11**(7), 1461–1475 (2016)
4. Huang, Q., Chang, S., Liu, C., et al.: An evaluation of fake fingerprint databases utilizing SVM Classification. Pattern Recogn. Lett. **60–61**, 1–7 (2015)
5. Rattani, A., Ross, A.: Automatic adaptation of fingerprint liveness detector to new spoof materials. In: 2014 IEEE International Joint Conference on Biometrics, pp. 1–8 (2014)
6. Rattani, A., Scheirer, W.J., Ross, A.: Open set fingerprint spoof detection across novel fabrication materials. IEEE Trans. Inf. Forensics Secur. **10**(11), 2447–2460 (2015)
7. Marasco, E., Wild, P., Cukic, B.: Robust and interoperable fingerprint spoof detection via convolutional neural networks. In: IEEE International Conference on Technologies for Homeland Security, pp. 1–6 (2016)
8. Menotti, D., Chiachia, G., Pinto, A.A., et al.: Deep representations for iris, face, and fingerprint spoofing detection. IEEE Trans. Inf. Forensics Secur. **10**(4), 864–879 (2015)
9. Wang, C., Li, K., Wu, Z., Zhao, Q.: A DCNN based fingerprint liveness detection algorithm with voting strategy. In: Yang, J., Yang, J., Sun, Z., Shan, S., Zheng, W., Feng, J. (eds.) CCBR 2015. LNCS, vol. 9428, pp. 241–249. Springer, Heidelberg (2015). doi: 10.1007/978-3-319-25417-3_29
10. Nogueira, R., Lotufo, R., Machado, R.: Fingerprint liveness detection using convolutional neural networks. IEEE Trans. Inf. Forensics Secur. **11**(6), 1206–1213 (2016)
11. Ioffe, S., Szegedy, C.: Batch normalization: accelerating deep network training by reducing internal covariate shift. In: Proceedings of the 32nd International Conference on Machine Learning, pp. 448–456 (2015)
12. Lin, M., Chen, Q., Yan, S.: Network in network. In: International Conference on Learning Representations (2014). http://arxiv.org/abs/1312.4400
13. Cao, K., Jain, A.K.: Hacking mobile phones using 2D Printed Fingerprints. MSU Technical report, MSU-CSE-16-2 (2016)
14. Ojala, T., Pietikinen, M., Menp, T.: Multiresolution Gray-scale and rotation invariant texture classification with local binary patterns. IEEE Trans. Pattern Anal. Mach. Intell. **24**(7), 971–987 (2002)
15. Nikam, S.B., Agarwal, S.: Texture and wavelet-based spoof fingerprint detection for fingerprint biometric systems. In: Proceedings of the 1st International Conference on Emerging Trends in Engineering and Technology, pp. 675–680, July 2008
16. Ojansivu, V., Rahtu, E., Heikkilä, J.: Rotation invariant local phase quantization for blur insensitive texture analysis. In: Proceedings of the 19th International Conference on Pattern Recognition, pp. 1–4, December 2008
17. Ghiani, L., Marcialis, G., Roli, F.: Fingerprint liveness detection by local phase quantization. In: Proceedings of International Conference on Pattern Recognition, pp. 537–540 (2012)
18. Caffe Github, https://github.com/BVLC/caffe/tree/master/models/bvlc_alexnet

Anonymized Distance Filter in Hamming Space

Yi Wang[1]([✉]), Jianwu Wan[2], Yiu-Ming Cheung[1], and Pong C. Yuen[1]

[1] Department of Computer Science, Hong Kong Baptist University, Kowloon Tong,
Hong Kong SAR, China
`alice.yi.wang@gmail.com`, {`ymc,pcyuen`}`@comp.hkbu.edu.hk`
[2] Department of Computer Science, Changzhou University, Changzhou, China
`jianwuwan@gmail.com`

Abstract. Search algorithms typically involve intensive distance computations and comparisons. In privacy-aware applications such as biometric identification, exposing the distance information may lead to compromise of sensitive data that have privacy and security implications. In this paper, we design an anonymized distance filter that can test and rank instances in a Hamming-ball search without knowing explicit distance values. We demonstrate the effectiveness of our method on both simulated and real data sets in the context of biometric identification.

Keywords: Filtering · Distance obfuscation · Hamming-ball search

1 Introduction

Due to query and storage benefits, there is a trend to learn binary projections for large-scale search of image or biometric features [1]. The binary embedding function is often designed to generate binary strings that can preserve some similarity metrics in Hamming space. Having done so, one can retrieve the most likely candidates (nearest neighbours) by exploring the Hamming-ball volume of a query.

In some applications such as biometric identification, privacy constraints need to be imposed on the storage and processing of the sensitive personal records. In general, a privacy-preserving nearest neighbour search may be classified into two categories [2]: (1) data transformation to conceal the data, and (2) secure multi-party computation to protect the search operations. The latter may be further decomposed into methods solving two distinct problems [3]: privacy-preserving distance computation followed by privacy-preserving minimum (distance) finding.

So, why is there a need to protect the distance information? Because the similarity measures exclusively reveal how the search records are inter related. Such information can be exploited by adversaries to infer some geometric and statistical properties of a data set and construct a number of privacy and security attacks. For example, knowing the empirical distribution of similarity match scores, it has been shown possible to recover the original biometric template

© Springer International Publishing AG 2016
Z. You et al. (Eds.): CCBR 2016, LNCS 9967, pp. 663–671, 2016.
DOI: 10.1007/978-3-319-46654-5_73

even from its non-invertible transforms [4] or perform a doppleganger attack [5]. The match scores can also be used to launch a hill-climbing attack in which modifications are made iteratively to an artificial input to spoof the biometric system [6].

Significant attention has been paid to biometric template protection for matching identities without disclosing the salient matching features [7]. Most of them were developed for one-to-one verification. For example, bio-cryptosystems are designed for secure matching of biometric features. They typically yield binary decisions (yes/no) for validity checks rather than producing numerical scores for similarity ranking. In other words, the systems output if a record matches a query but cannot distinguish which ones are *more* likely. Recently, secure computation methods are proposed to perform biometric matching in the encrypted domain [8]. However, the cryptography-based techniques generally incur excessive computational overhead and storage requirements. The efficiency and privacy requirements for near neighbour search motive us to study anonymized distance filters without evaluating explicit distance values. In this paper, we propose a randomized test based approach in Hamming space. The effectiveness of our approach is evaluated in the context of biometric identification.

The remainder of the paper is organized as follows. Section 2 provides problem formulation and proposes our approach. Section 3 presents simulation results and search experiments on binary face data. Finally, Sect. 4 concludes with future work.

2   Proposed Algorithms

For simplicity, we assume that the binary string representations are given, e.g., [9]. The problem under study is then formulated as follows. Consider a query string $\mathbf{q}$ and a data set $\Omega = \{\mathbf{p}_1, \mathbf{p}_2, ..., \mathbf{p}_N\}$ of D-bit length. For every $\mathbf{p} \in \Omega$, denote its Hamming distance to $\mathbf{q}$ by $H(\mathbf{p}, \mathbf{q})$ which is commonly defined as the number of bits that are different between two binary strings. Given a pre-fixed distance threshold r, we want to know if

$$H(\mathbf{p}, \mathbf{q}) \leq r \tag{1}$$

without evaluating the actual value of $H(\mathbf{p}, \mathbf{q})$. All $\mathbf{p} \in \Omega$ satisfying (1) constitutes a near neighbour subset of $\mathbf{q}$ with radius r, denoted by $\mathcal{B}_{\mathbf{q}}(\Omega, r)$. In the following section, we introduce a randomized protocol for testing (1) and ranking the detected near neighbours in $\mathcal{B}_{\mathbf{q}}(\Omega, r)$ without evaluating their Hamming distances to query.

2.1   A Randomized Protocol for Similarity Test

Let $x, y \in \mathcal{N}$ be the natural number representation for binary strings $\mathbf{p}$ and $\mathbf{q}$, respectively. To test $\mathbf{p} = \mathbf{q}$, it is equivalent to test the equality $x = y$.

Algorithm 1. Randomized Protocol for Equality Test

INITIAL STAGE

    Party I has $x \in \mathcal{N}$ for $p = p[1]p[2]...p[D] \in \{0, 1\}$,
    Party II has $y \in \mathcal{N}$ for $q = q[1]q[2]...q[D] \in \{0, 1\}$.

RANDOMIZED EQUALITY TEST

1   Party II selects a prime ϕ randomly with an equal probability in the range $[2, n]$
2   Party II computes $u = x \mod \phi$
3   Party II sends the u and ϕ to Party I
4   Party I computes $v = y \mod \phi$ and decides
5   **if** $u = v$
6   **then** $x = y$, approve the equality test
7   **else** $x \neq y$, fail the equality test

When D is large, it was shown that the equality test can be done more efficiently by randomly sampling primes from some given range $[2, n]$ and then comparing the corresponding remainders of x and y modulo the same prime [10]. Algorithm 1 outlines the randomized protocol for such an equality test.

It is worth noting that Algorithm 1 can only test whether two binary strings are identical or not, i.e., $H(\mathbf{p}, \mathbf{q}) = 0$, which is referred to as an *equality test* in our context. In a Hamming-ball search, however, we require a more general comparison between two binary strings to decide if $H(\mathbf{p}, \mathbf{q}) \leq r$ for an arbitrary integer value r, which we refer to as a *similarity test*. To resolve the problem, we thus modify Algorithm 1 based on the following proposition by applying the Drawer Principle.

Proposition 1. *Two binary strings* $\mathbf{p}$ *and* $\mathbf{q}$ *of D bits have* $H(\mathbf{p}, \mathbf{q}) \leq r$. *Divide* $\mathbf{p}$ *and* $\mathbf{q}$ *into $L > r$ non-overlapping substring segments in the same way. There must be $m \leq r$ unmatched substring pairs between* $\mathbf{p}$ *and* $\mathbf{q}$.

Proof. Divide the two binary strings into L segments: $\mathbf{p} = \mathbf{p}^{(1)} || \mathbf{p}^{(2)} || \ldots || \mathbf{p}^{(L)}$ and $\mathbf{q} = \mathbf{q}^{(1)} || \mathbf{q}^{(2)} || \ldots || \mathbf{q}^{(L)}$, where $||$ indicates concatenation. Suppose there are $m > r$ unmatched substring pairs between $\mathbf{p}$ and $\mathbf{q}$. Without loss of generality, assume the first m substring pairs are unmatched, i.e., $H(\mathbf{p}^{(i)}, \mathbf{q}^{(i)}) \geq 1$ for $i = 1, 2, \ldots, m$. We have $H(\mathbf{p}, \mathbf{q}) = \sum_{i=1}^{L} H(\mathbf{p}^{(i)}, \mathbf{q}^{(i)}) = \sum_{i=1}^{m} H(\mathbf{p}^{(i)}, \mathbf{q}^{(i)}) \geq m > r$, which gives a contradiction to $H(\mathbf{p}, \mathbf{q}) \leq r$.

Proposition 1 leads to a similarity test based on the number of *unmatched* substring pairs as follows. We use Algorithm 1 to test over all L substring pairs and find the value m. If $m > r$, we know immediately that p is not in the near neighbour subset $\mathcal{B}_{\mathbf{q}}(\Omega, r)$ because $H(\mathbf{p}, \mathbf{q}) \geq m$. In this case, $\mathbf{p}$ is filtered out.

If $m \leq r$, we may split each unmatched substring further into half and repeat the substring equality test. Suppose that m' out of these $2m$ new substring pairs fail the equality test. Update m with m'. If $m > r$, $\mathbf{p}$ is also filtered out.

The substring division may be iterated at finer scales. As the iteration going deeper, the tests yield more accurate results as m approximates to $H(\mathbf{p}, \mathbf{q})$ at $s = 1$. From a privacy perspective, however, s should not be too small as we want to protect the distance value $H(\mathbf{p}, \mathbf{q})$. The iterations also generate significant computation and communication costs.

To avoid iterative substring divisions, we propose a variable thresholding function to refine the similarity test over m. Let $d = H(\mathbf{p}, \mathbf{q})$. There must be $m \leq d \leq ms$. As the substring length s increases, the distance interval becomes larger. Intuitively, this introduces more uncertainty for deciding $\mathbf{p} \in \mathcal{B}_\mathbf{q}(\Omega, r)$ conditional on $m \leq r$. Assume that d is uniformly distributed within the distance interval. The conditional probability

$$\Pr(d \leq r | m \leq r) = \frac{r - m}{ms - m} = \frac{r/m - 1}{s - 1} \tag{2}$$

indicates how likely $m \leq r$ reflecting $d \leq r$. In this way, the number of unmatched substring m can be regarded as an obfuscated measure of the Hamming distance value.

We want to sort out instances that are more likely to be in the Hamming ball by the similarity test. Inspired by Eq. (2), we introduce a parameter $\epsilon \in [0, 1]$ corresponding to some latent variable m_ϵ such that those with

$$m < m_\epsilon = \frac{r}{1 + \epsilon(s - 1)} \tag{3}$$

have a higher probability than ϵ for $d \leq r$. Accordingly, we propose to rank all instances with $m \leq r$ by a serious of threshold values each updated with ϵ in the right-hand side of Eq. (3). Note that when $\epsilon = 0$, Eq. (3) is equivalent to test $m < r$. When $\epsilon = 1$, it is equivalent to test $m < r/s$. In the latter case, the test is associated with 100% certainty that $\mathbf{p} \in \mathcal{B}_\mathbf{q}(\Omega, r)$ because $d \leq ms < r$.

We generate T values of $\epsilon \in [0, 1]$ to test $\mathbf{p} \in \mathcal{B}_\mathbf{q}(\Omega, r)$ with Eq. (3). This results in T nested subsets $Set_{\epsilon_1} \subset Set_{\epsilon_2} ... \subset Set_{\epsilon_T}$ for $\epsilon_1 > \epsilon_2 > ... > \epsilon_T$. We group instances according to their nesting relationships. The top ranked groups are associated with larger ϵ values. Instances within the same group have no particular order and are regarded as of the same similarity level to query $\mathbf{q}$.

2.2   Estimation of Substring Test Error

In this section, we analyze the error probability of Algorithm 1 for substring equality test with $D = s$. It is worth noting that the randomized equality test is associated with some Type II error, i.e., false positive, which occurs when x and y are congruent modulo prime r, i.e., $u = v$ when $x \neq y$. Note that the probability of Type I error, i.e., false negative, is *zero* by the equality test. Because whenever $x = y$, their remainders are always the same modulo the same prime. In other words, it is possible that the proposed filtering test may underestimate a distance value and falsely augment $\mathcal{B}_\mathbf{q}(\Omega, r)$ with a misclassified $\mathbf{p}$ but it will never miss out a true Hamming-ball neighbour in the data set.

Since the prime number r is uniformly chosen at random in a given range, it can be expected that the larger the range is the lower the probability to have a Type II error. The number of available primes in $[2, n]$ is calculated by the prime counting function $\pi(n)$. By testing the equality of two s-bit substring binary codes independently for t times, the Type II error rate β is bounded by [10]

$$\beta \leq \left(\frac{s-1}{\pi(n)} \right)^t . \tag{4}$$

When s is fixed, to reduce the error rate β, we can either increase n for a bigger prime range or increase t to perform the randomized equality test independently for more times. The latter is equivalent to choose t primes independently at a time and pass the test only if all t pairs of remainders are equivalent.

The well-known prime number theorem says that $\pi(n)$ has an asymptotic form $\lim_{n->\infty} \pi(n) = \frac{n}{\ln n}$ and $\pi(n) > \frac{n}{\ln n}$ for $n \geq 17$ [11]. Let $n = s^3$ and $t = 3$. From (4), we have for $s > 2$

$$\beta < \left(\frac{s-1}{s^3/\ln s^3} \right)^t < \frac{27 \ln^3 s}{s^6} . \tag{5}$$

For example, the Type II error rate β is less than 0.000926 for $s = 8$ by Algorithm 1. From (5), it can be seen that the maximum error rate reduces drastically as the substring length s increases for a substring equality test.

2.3   Privacy Implications of m

Note that we are assuming a curious-but-honest computing environment. That is, everyone executes their part according to the protocol. As such, the system parameters are prefixed and cannot be changed during operation. The adversary can only observe the test result of *unmatched* substring pairs m in the proposed filtering scheme.

In this section, we discuss the privacy implication of m. The value of m is related to Hamming distance in the following way. If $H(\mathbf{p}, \mathbf{q})$ is large, m tends to be large for there can be more substring pairs that differ by more than 1 bit. It is worth noting that the m value also depends on the location of the error bit. Unless the substring length $s = 1$, one does not know the number of error bits in an unmatched substring from the randomized protocol.

The explicit value $d = H(\mathbf{p}, \mathbf{q})$ is projected into a variable interval $[m, ms]$ defined by both m and s. As long as $s > 1$, one cannot know the exact number of error bits in an unmatched substring. This is analogous to *anonymization* that attempts to classify data into fixed or variable intervals. In our context, an explicit distance value is replaced by a variable interval based on which a filtering decision for non-neighbours is made. Thus, we call our scheme *anonymized distance filter* (ADF). For convenience, we rewrite m with respect to d as follows:

$$\begin{cases} \dfrac{d}{s} \leq m \leq d, & \text{if } 0 \leq d \leq L \\ \dfrac{d}{s} \leq m \leq L, & \text{otherwise} \end{cases} \tag{6}$$

where L is the number of substring divisions. Accordingly, m approximates d when s is reduced to 1 or d is reduced to 0. Note that $s \gg 1$ in general. So, m reflects the distance value d more accurately as $\mathbf{p}$ is getting closer to query $\mathbf{q}$. The relation becomes more obscure with an enlarged interval as d increases. In fact, the value of m is capped at the number of substring division L for $d > L$. In this way, the number of unmatched substring pairs m can be viewed as an obfuscated measure of the Hamming distance value d. Note that the m value depends not only on d but also the distribution of error bits. The obfuscation introduces uncertainty and noise to the distance distribution that helps to foil adversaries from gleaning genuine geometric or statistical properties of the biometric dataset.

3   Experiment Results

We implemented the proposed algorithms in Matlab on a 3.40 GHz Intel(R) machine. In this section, we evaluate the proposed randomized similarity test on both simulation and biometric face data sets in Hamming space.

3.1   Hamming-Ball Simulation

We randomly generated *ten* binary strings as queries. For each query $\mathbf{q}$, we randomly generated 200 binary strings $\mathbf{p} \in \Omega$ such that ten of them are in the nearest neighbour subset $\mathcal{B}_{\mathbf{q}}(\Omega, r)$, i.e., $H(\mathbf{p}, \mathbf{q}) \leq r$ for $\mathbf{p} \in \mathcal{B}_{\mathbf{q}}(\Omega, r)$, and all the others are outside of the Hamming ball with radius $r = 75$. In this way, we know exactly the ground truth in the dataset Ω. All simulation data are of $1,600$-bit per code length, i.e., $D = 1,600$.

We divide each binary string into L non-overlapping substring segments. Given the full-string dimension D, the substring length $s = D/L$ if D is divisible by L. In cases where D is not divisible by L, we let the first $(D \mod L)$ substring codes have $s = \lceil D/L \rceil$ bits each and the remaining ones have $s = \lfloor D/L \rfloor$.

To evaluate the filtering performance, we define the filtering rate as the number of filtered outsiders divided by the total number of ground truth outsiders. It measures the effectiveness of identifying non-neighbours outside the Hamming ball radius r, i.e., $\mathbf{p} \notin \mathcal{B}_{\mathbf{q}}(\Omega, r)$, by the proposed test-based approach. In our simulation setting, the total number of ground truth outsiders is $190 \times 10 = 1,900$.

Figure 1 plots the filtering rates at different stages of the proposed similarity test for substring length $s = 4, 8, 10, 16, 20$, respectively. The dash line shows filtering rates at the initial condition $m > r$, which eliminates 90 % non-neighbours for $s = 4$ but not so much as s increases. The filtering performance can be largely compensated by refining the test with Eq. (3) as introduced in Sect. 2.1. In particular, we vary $\epsilon \in [0, 1]$ with step $\Delta\epsilon$ to generate a series of threshold values for testing the number of unmatched substring pairs m. In Fig. 1, the three solid lines show filtering rates at $\epsilon = 0, .01$, and $.05$, respectively. When $\epsilon = .01$, the filtering rate is improved by over 60 % for $s = 20$. ADF eliminates all non-neighbours at $\epsilon = 0.05$ for the simulation dataset.

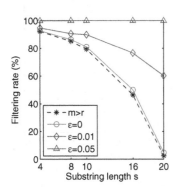

Fig. 1. ADF filtering rates at different testing stages for $s = 4, 8, 10, 16, 20$.

Table 1. Top ranked instances for a particular query.

Ground Truth	ADF Top Ranked ID (ϵ)		
NN ID (d)	$s = 20$	$s = 8$	$s = 8$
	$\Delta\epsilon = .1$	$\Delta\epsilon = .1$	$\Delta\epsilon = .05$
7 (1)	7 (1)	7 (1)	7 (1)
10 (2)	10 (1)	10 (1)	10 (1)
6 (15)	2 (0.2)	2 (0.6)	2 (0.6)
2 (16)	6 (0.2)	6 (0.5)	6 (0.55)
1 (19)	1 (0.1)	1 (0.4)	1 (0.45)
5 (20)	5 (0.1)	5 (0.3)	5 (0.35)
4 (34)	3 (0)	4 (0.1)	4 (0.15)
8 (41)	4 (0)	8 (0.1)	8 (0.1)
3 (50)	8 (0)	3 (0)	3 (0.05)
9 (71)	9 (0)	9 (0)	9 (0)

Table 1 shows an example of the top ranked instances for a particular query. The first column lists the ground truth ID's and in bracket their actual Hamming distance values to the query. The three columns on the right display the top ranked ID's returned by the proposed ADF scheme with different substring length s and ranking step $\Delta\epsilon$. For example, 7(1) denotes that the binary string with $ID = 7$ is placed at the top rank for $\epsilon = 1$. The one with $ID = 10$ is also in the top rank. The two are considered of the same proximity to query. The next non-empty rank for $s = 20, \Delta\epsilon = .1$ is at $\epsilon = .2$ which has two instances with $ID = 2$ and $ID = 6$. Table 1 shows that all instances in $\mathcal{B}_q(\Omega, r)$ are successfully returned after filtering the dataset. This is consistent with the zero Type I error rate in our previous error analysis in Sect. 2.2. The rank order is refiner with smaller substring length s and ranking step $\Delta\epsilon$ in the last column.

3.2 Face Search Experiments

We run the proposed anonymized distance filter on binary codes generated from the FERET dataset. The face data set contains 2,400 face images from 200 identities each with 12 images taken under a semi-controlled environment. We adopt the Linearly Separable Subcodes (LSSC) [12] to convert the real-valued face features into binary string representations. In particular, we used six face samples per identity for training and the remaining ones for test where each sample is represented by a 448-bit binary string.

We conducted six-fold experiments over the 6×200 test samples. That is, we iteratively enrolled each sample of the 200 identities while using the rest as query to search the gallery. The search performance is evaluated by the *hit rate* defined as the percentage of queries found with correct identities for the top k

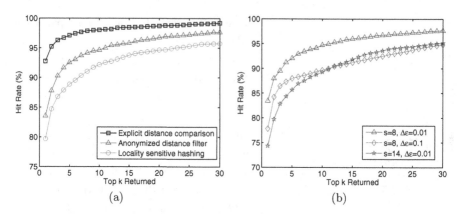

Fig. 2. Search results on FERET: (a) ADF comparing with others; (b) ADF varying s and $\Delta\epsilon$.

instances returned. The metric is commonly used in the biometric literature to indicate the search accuracy.

Figure 2(a) plots search results on FERET comparing ADF with that by explicit Hamming distance comparison and Locality Sensitive Hashing (LSH). In particular, the explicit approach based on pairwise distance comparison can be regarded as the upper-bound performance for search in Hamming space, while LSH is a popular approximate near neighbour method recently being extended to privacy-preserving applications [13]. We let LSH random sample s bits at a time for L hash tables. With the same s and L, ADF outperforms LSH. Figure 2(b) shows how the search accuracy can change with system parameters s and $\Delta\epsilon$. The result is consistent with that in Table 1 in which smaller s and $\Delta\epsilon$ improve the retrieval accuracy but at a cost of the distance anonymization level as the obfuscation interval shrinks.

4   Conclusions and Future Work

In this paper, we study anonymized distance filter in Hamming space. We show that it is possible to explore the Hamming ball volume of a query without evaluating explicit distance values. This can be done by randomized substring equality tests with designed threshold function values. The proposed method can be used for binary string-based comparison and decision making with privacy constraints on distance evaluation. Our future work includes more comprehensive theoretical analysis and performance evaluation for the distance anonymization schemes.

Acknowledgment. This work was supported by Hong Kong Research Grant Council (HKBU12202214) and National Natural Science Foundation of China (61403324 and 61502058).

References

1. Grauman, K., Fergus, R.: Learning binary hash codes for large-scale image search. In: Cipolla, R., Battiato, S., Farinella, G.M. (eds.) Machine Learning for Computer Vision, vol. 411, pp. 49–87 (2013)
2. Shaneck, M., Kim, Y., Kumar, V.: Privacy preserving nearest neighbor search. In: Machine Learning in Cyber Trust, pp. 247–276. Springer, Heidelberg (2009)
3. Rane, S., Boufounos, P.: Privacy-preserving nearest neighbor methods: comparing signals without revealing them. IEEE Signal Process. Mag. **30**(2), 18–28 (2013)
4. Gomez-Barrero, M., Galbally, J., Fierrez, J., Ortega-Garcia, J.: Face verification put to test: A hill-climbing attack based on the uphill-simplex algorithm. In: Proceedings of the International Conference on Biometrics, pp. 40–45, March 2012
5. Boult, T., Scheirer, W., Woodworth, R.: Revocable fingerprint biotokens: accuracy and security analysis. In: Proceedings of the IEEE Conference on Computer Vision and Pattern Recognition, pp. 1–8, June 2007
6. Galbally, J., McCool, C., Fierrez, J., Marcel, S., Ortega-Garcia, J.: On the vulnerability of face verification systems to hill-climbing attacks. Pattern Recogn. **43**(3), 1027–1038 (2010)
7. Nandakumar, K., Jain, A.K.: Biometric template protection: bridging the performance gap between theory and practice. IEEE Signal Process. Mag. **32**(5), 88–100 (2015)
8. Bringer, J., Chabanne, H., Patey, A.: Privacy-preserving biometric identification using secure multiparty computation: an overview and recent trends. IEEE Signal Process. Mag. **30**(2), 42–52 (2013)
9. Nagar, A., Nandakumar, K., Jain, A.: Multibiometric cryptosystems based on feature-level fusion. IEEE Trans. Inf. Forensics Secur. **7**(1), 255–268 (2012)
10. Hromkovic, J.: Design and Analysis of Randomized Algorithms: Introduction to Design Paradigms. Springer, Heidelberg (2005)
11. Rosser, J.B., Schoenfeld, L.: Approximate formulas for some functions of prime numbers. Ill. J. Math. **6**(1), 64–94 (1962)
12. Lim, M.H., Teoh, A.B.J.: A novel encoding scheme for effective biometric discretization: linearly separable subcode. IEEE Trans. Pattern Anal. Mach. Intell. **35**(2), 300–313 (2013)
13. Aghasaryan, A., Bouzid, M., Kostadinov, D., Kothari, M., et al.: On the use of lsh for privacy preserving personalization. In: IEEE International Conference on Trust, Security and Privacy in Computing and Communications (TrustCom), pp. 362–371 (2013)

Surveillance

Dictionary Co-Learning for Multiple-Shot Person Re-Identification

Yang Wu[1]([✉]), Dong Yang[2], Ru Zhou[2], and Dong Wang[2]

[1] Institute for Research Initiatives, Nara Institute of Science and Technology,
Ikoma, Japan
yangwu@rsc.naist.jp
[2] Athena Eyes Co. LTD., Beijing, China
{yangdong,zhouru,wangdong}@a-eye.cn

Abstract. Person re-identification concerns about identifying people across cameras using full-body appearance in a non-obtrusive way for video surveillance and other commercial applications, for which it is usually hard or even impossible to get other more reliable biometric data. In this paper, we present a novel approach for multiple-shot person re-identification when multiple images or video frames are available for each person, which is usually the case in real applications. Our approach collaboratively learns camera-specific dictionaries and utilizes the efficient l_2-norm based collaborative representation for coding, which has shown great superiority in terms of both effectiveness and efficiency to all related existing models.

1 Introduction

Identifying people in a non-obtrusive way is important for many applications such as video surveillance for security and customer recognition for personalized services. In such scenarios, it is usually hard or even impossible to get reliable biometric data such as faces, irises, and voice, no need to say any other data like fingerprints which require interactions. Currently, the most suitable way is to use cameras to get remotely sensed data, just like what we do with our eyes. And we may expect that the identification performance should be as robust as possible to the changes of camera views, human poses and environmental factors. Recently, a research topic named person re-identification has grown up and become popular. It targets at identifying a person again when he or she reappears in the view of a camera after disappearing from the view of the same or another camera in a camera network. This well fits the identification demands of video surveillance, and solutions for that can also be used for other applications.

Researches on person re-identification can be grouped into two categories based on which kind of data they are using: single-shot person re-identification and multiple-shot person re-identification. The former assumes that only one single image is available for each person in any camera view, while the later

Y. Wu—This work was supported by JSPS KAKENHI Grant Number 15K16024.

© Springer International Publishing AG 2016
Z. You et al. (Eds.): CCBR 2016, LNCS 9967, pp. 675–685, 2016.
DOI: 10.1007/978-3-319-46654-5_74

allows multiple shots (images or video frames) of the same person taken by each camera. Though single-shot re-identification is more suitable for testing the re-identification models' performance under extreme conditions, we believe that the multiple-shot cases are more common in real applications as usually videos rather than images are captured for re-identification purposes. Moreover, using as much information from the video frames as possible generally has higher potential to get better performances [1]. Therefore, in this paper, we focus on multiple-shot person re-identification.

When multiple-shot re-identification is concerned, it is closely related to a more general problem: set-based recognition, for which multiple instances of the same object/category are available and treated together as a whole set for recognition, as shown in Fig. 1. State-of-the-art approaches on set-based recognition can be grouped into two categories based on the availability of supervision information: unsupervised methods and supervised methods.

(a) Examples from iLIDS-MA dataset   (b) Set-based recognition problem setting

Fig. 1. Multiple-shot re-identification and set-based recognition.

Within unsupervised methods, there is a large group that compute independent set-to-set distances between each test-training pair of sets, and then classify the test set by ranking such distances. Representative methods include Minimum Point-wise Distance (MPD) [2] which finds the minimum distance between any pair (one from each set) of points (samples in the feature space), Affine/Convex Hull based Image Set Distance (AHISD/CHISD) [3] which computes the geometric distance between two affine/convex hulls generated from the two sets, Sparse Approximated Nearest Points (SANP) and its kernel version [4] which add sparsity constraints to the CHISD model, and Regularized Nearest points (RNP) [5] which adopts l_2-norm regularization terms to complement affine hulls and increase both effectiveness and efficiency. Besides that, recently collaborative models have show great advantages (especially in terms of efficiency). They treat all the training sets together as a large indiscriminate set and compute only one single geometric distance between it and the test set, which is also referred to as set-to-sets distance [1]. The collaboration of individual training sets in distance finding stimulates the competition among them which makes the linear combination coefficients discriminative.

Representative existing collaborative models are Collaborative Sparse Approximation (CSA) [6], Collaboratively Regularized Nearest Points (CRNP) [1] and its extended versions Locality-constrained Collaboratively Regularized Nearest Points (LCRNP) with sample/set pre-selection [7], and Collaborative Mean Attraction (CMA) [8].

Supervised methods for set-based recognition are relatively less studied, and there are two representatives: Set Based Discriminative Ranking (SBDR) [9] which iterates between CHISD or SANP and metric learning to find the geometric distance in a discriminative metric space, and Discriminative Collaborative Representation (DCR) [10] which combines collaborative representation and dictionary learning for the first time.

For person re-identification, usually a standard way is to model it with a pair of cameras, as that is a key building block for handling the more general setting of multiple cameras. Since the same person captured by different cameras may appear quite differently due to the variations of camera viewpoints and environmental factors, learning a common dictionary shared by them (like what DCR does) can be both hard and suboptimal.

In this paper we propose a supervised approach named Dictionary Collaborative Learning, or in a briefer form "Dictionary Co-learning" (DCL). It also combines collaborative representation and dictionary learning, but compared with DCR, it is much simpler, faster and also more effective. Unlike DCR, it learns camera-specific dictionaries and makes the learning collaborative, so that dictionary based representation is done within each camera and the identity correspondences can be properly modeled by the camera-specific dictionaries. Meanwhile, DCL inherits the efficiency from unsupervised collaborative methods, and goes further beyond it because of its compactness. We notice that recently there are some interesting models working on combining dictionary learning and multi-view learning for some other tasks such as image classification [11] and action recognition [12]. Due to the focus of this paper, we leave a more general comparison between our model and them in our future work. In the rest of the paper, we will detail DCL in Sect. 2 and provide extensive experiments in Sect. 3 to demonstrate its superiority to all the related methods.

2 Dictionary Co-Learning

2.1 Dictionary Learning

Given training input data in a d-dimensional space $\mathbf{X} \in \mathbb{R}^{d \times N}$ with N number of samples, generally speaking, dictionary learning tries to learn a representation (may also be called coding and usually it is preferred to be sparse) of the input data using a linear combination of basis elements/atoms. These elements/atoms compose a dictionary. It can be formulated as solving the following problem:

$$\langle \mathbf{D}^*, \boldsymbol{\alpha}^* \rangle = \arg\min_{\mathbf{D}, \boldsymbol{\alpha}} \left\{ \|\mathbf{X} - \mathbf{D}\alpha\|_2^2 + \lambda_1 \|\alpha\|_p + h(\mathbf{D}) \right\}, \tag{1}$$

where $D \in \mathbb{R}^{d \times k}$ with k items is the dictionary to be learned (usually $k \leq N$); α denotes the representation coefficients which is usually regularized by a p-norm (when sparsity is required, $p = 0$ or $p = 1$); $h(\mathbf{D})$ denotes the regularization part for the dictionary, and class label information may be used here (if it is available) for ensuring discriminative power of the learned dictionary.

2.2 Dictionary Collaborative Learning

Given training data in a d-dimensional space from two different camera views $\mathbf{X}_p \in \mathbb{R}^{d \times N_p}$ and $\mathbf{X}_g \in \mathbb{R}^{d \times N_g}$, which stand for probe camera data and gallery camera data with N_p and N_g number of samples, respectively, in general dictionary co-learning solves the following problem (for simplicity and also due to the space limitation, we ignore the probe and gallery denotations for $\mathbf{X}, \mathbf{D}, \alpha$, and β though in fact each of them should have the two different parts):

$$\langle \mathbf{D}^*, \alpha^*, \beta^* \rangle = \arg \min_{\mathbf{D}, \alpha, \beta} \left\{ r(\mathbf{X}, \mathbf{D}, \alpha, \beta) + h(\mathbf{D}, \alpha, \beta) + f(\beta) \right\}, \quad (2)$$

where "$\mathbf{D}_p \in \mathbb{R}^{d \times k}, \mathbf{D}_g \in \mathbb{R}^{d \times k}$" with k items each are the dictionaries to be learned (usually $k \leq \min(N_p, N_g)$); "α" and "β" denote the reconstruction coefficients for the training samples and dictionaries, respectively; $r(\mathbf{X}, \mathbf{D}, \alpha, \beta)$ is the reconstruction error; $h(\mathbf{D}, \alpha, \beta)$ denotes the regularization part for both the dictionaries and the reconstruction coefficients; $f(\beta)$ denotes the discrimination term ensuring discriminative power in the learned representation space.

Different from existing works, our proposed reconstruction model is:

$$r(\mathbf{X}, \mathbf{D}, \alpha, \beta) = \sum_{i=1}^{c} \left\{ \left\| \mathbf{X}_p^i \alpha_p^i - \mathbf{D}_p \beta_p^i \right\|_2^2 + \left\| \mathbf{X}_g^i \alpha_g^i - \mathbf{D}_g \beta_g^i \right\|_2^2 \right\}, \quad (3)$$

where $\mathbf{X}_p = \cup \mathbf{X}_p^i, i \in \{1, \ldots, c\}$, $\mathbf{X}_g = \cup \mathbf{X}_g^i, i \in \{1, \ldots, c\}$; c is the number of classes (identities); p and g stand for probe and gallery sides, respectively. The reconstruction model targets at learning a dictionary that can bridge the probe and gallery sets in terms of a good reconstruction of the closest points on the linear subspaces of both sets. Since $\mathbf{D}, \alpha$, and β need to be optimized iteratively which requires much computational cost, for simplicity, we choose a simplified version: $\alpha_p^i = \frac{\mathbf{1}_{N_p^i, 1}}{N_p^i}$ and $\alpha_g^i = \frac{\mathbf{1}_{N_g^i, 1}}{N_g^i}$, where $\mathbf{1}_{m,n}$ denotes the $m \times n$ dimensional matrix of ones. Let $\bar{\mathbf{x}}_p^i = \mathbf{X}_p^i \alpha_p^i$ and $\bar{\mathbf{x}}_g^i = \mathbf{X}_g^i \alpha_g^i$, then Eq. 3 can be rewritten as

$$r(\mathbf{X}, \mathbf{D}, \alpha, \beta) = \sum_{i=1}^{c} \left\{ \left\| \bar{\mathbf{x}}_p^i - \mathbf{D}_p \beta_p^i \right\|_2^2 + \left\| \bar{\mathbf{x}}_g^i - \mathbf{D}_g \beta_g^i \right\|_2^2 \right\}. \quad (4)$$

To regularize the linear subspaces and the dictionary, we choose the following model (since α is constant, it will be ignored here):

$$h(\mathbf{D}, \beta)$$
$$= \lambda_1 \left(\sum_{i=1}^{c} \left\| \beta_p^i \right\|_2^2 + \sum_{i=1}^{c} \left\| \beta_g^i \right\|_2^2 + \left\| \mathbf{D}_p \right\|_F^2 + \left\| \mathbf{D}_g \right\|_F^2 \right) + \lambda_2 \left(\left\| \mathbf{D}_p - \mathbf{D}_g \right\|_F^2 \right), \quad (5)$$

where the first part regularized the variables while the second part forces the learned dictionaries to be not too dissimilar to each other, and λ_1 and λ_2 are two trade-off parameters.

The discrimination power is generated by

$$f\left(\beta\right) = \sum_{i=1}^{c} \left\{ \gamma_1 \left\| \beta_p^i - \beta_g^i \right\|_2^2 + \gamma_2 \sum_{\substack{j=1, \\ j\neq i}}^{c} \left\| \beta_p^i - \beta_g^j \right\|_2^2 \right\}, \tag{6}$$

where γ_1 and γ_2 are two trade-off parameters. When γ_2 is set to be a small number, much smaller than γ_1, the distance between the reconstruction coefficients for the same class/identity $\left\| \beta_p^i - \beta_g^i \right\|_2$ is likely to be much smaller than that between the coefficients for different classes/identities $\left\| \beta_p^i - \beta_g^j \right\|_2, j \neq i$. In this way, it makes the dictionary discriminative, and the reconstruction coefficients can be used for classification.

2.3 Optimization for Dictionary Co-learning

Since both the dictionaries and the reconstruction coefficients are unknown, they can only be optimized alternatively.

Initializing D_p, D_g, β_p and β_g. We simply initialize D_p and D_g with randomly selected training samples from X_p and X_g, respectively. Then, we initialize $\beta_p^i, i \in \{1, \ldots, c\}$ by optimizing

$$\min_{\beta_p^i} \left\{ \left\| \bar{x}_p^i - D_p \beta_p^i \right\|_2^2 + \lambda_1 \left\| \beta_p^i \right\|_2^2 \right\}, \tag{7}$$

which has a closed-form solution

$$\beta_p^{i\,*} = \left(D_p^T D_p + \lambda_1 I_k \right)^{-1} D_p^T \bar{x}_p^i, \tag{8}$$

where I_k is a $k \times k$ identity matrix.

Similarly, we can get $\beta_g^{i\,*} = \left(D_g^T D_g + \lambda_1 I_k \right)^{-1} D_g^T \bar{x}_g^i$.

Optimizing D_p, D_g. Once β_p and β_g are given, optimizing D_p, D_g can be done sequentially. For optimizing D_p, the problem can be rewritten as

$$D_p^* = \arg\min_{D_p} \left\{ \left\| A_p - D_p B_p \right\|_F^2 + \lambda_1 \left\| D_p \right\|_F^2 \right\}, \tag{9}$$

where

$$A_p = \left[\bar{x}_p^1, \cdots, \bar{x}_p^c, \sqrt{\lambda_2} D_g \right], \quad B_p = \left[\beta_p^1, \cdots, \beta_p^c, \lambda_2 I_k \right]. \tag{10}$$

Equation 9 has a closed-form solution

$$D_p^* = A_p B_p^{\,T} \left(B_p B_p^{\,T} + \lambda_1 I_d \right)^{-1}. \tag{11}$$

Similarly, we have a closed-form solution for $\mathbf{D}_g$, which is

$$\mathbf{D}_g^* = \mathbf{A}_g\mathbf{B}_g{}^T\left(\mathbf{B}_g\mathbf{B}_g{}^T + \lambda_1\mathbf{I}_d\right)^{-1}, \tag{12}$$

with $\mathbf{A}_g = \left[\bar{\mathbf{x}}_g^1, \cdots, \bar{\mathbf{x}}_g^c, \sqrt{\lambda_2}\mathbf{D}_p\right]$ and $\mathbf{B}_g = \left[\boldsymbol{\beta}_g^1, \cdots, \boldsymbol{\beta}_g^c, \lambda_2\mathbf{I}_k\right]$.

Optimizing $\boldsymbol{\beta}_p^i$ and $\boldsymbol{\beta}_g^i$. Given $\mathbf{D}_p$ and $\mathbf{D}_g$, we can also optimize $\boldsymbol{\beta}_p^i$ and $\boldsymbol{\beta}_g^i$ sequentially (suppose the other one is fixed). Optimizing $\boldsymbol{\beta}_p^i$ equals solving the following problem

$$\boldsymbol{\beta}_g^{i\,*} = \arg\min_{\boldsymbol{\beta}_g^i}\left\{\left\|\mathbf{D}_p\boldsymbol{\beta}_g^i - \bar{\mathbf{x}}_p^i\right\|_2^2 + \lambda_1\left\|\boldsymbol{\beta}_g^i\right\|_2^2\right.$$
$$\left. + \gamma_2\sum_{j=1}^c\left\|\boldsymbol{\beta}_p^i - \boldsymbol{\beta}_g^j\right\|_2^2 + (\gamma_1 - \gamma_2)\left\|\boldsymbol{\beta}_p^i - \boldsymbol{\beta}_g^i\right\|_2^2\right\}, \tag{13}$$

which has a closed-form solution

$$\boldsymbol{\beta}_p^{i\,*} = \left(\mathbf{U}_p^{i\,T}\mathbf{U}_p^i\right)^{-1}\left(\mathbf{D}_p{}^T\bar{\mathbf{x}}_p^i + \lambda_1\sum_{j=1}^c\boldsymbol{\beta}_g^j + (\gamma_1 - \gamma_2)\boldsymbol{\beta}_g^i\right), \tag{14}$$

where

$$\mathbf{U}_p^i = \left[\mathbf{D}_p{}^T, \sqrt{\lambda_1}\mathbf{I}_k, \underbrace{\sqrt{\gamma_2}\mathbf{I}_k, \cdots, \sqrt{\gamma_2}\mathbf{I}_k}_{i-1}, \sqrt{\gamma_1}\mathbf{I}_k, \underbrace{\sqrt{\gamma_2}\mathbf{I}_k, \cdots, \sqrt{\gamma_2}\mathbf{I}_k}_{c-i}\right]. \tag{15}$$

Similarly, $\boldsymbol{\beta}_g^i$ has the following solution

$$\boldsymbol{\beta}_g^{i\,*} = \left(\mathbf{U}_g^{i\,T}\mathbf{U}_g^i\right)^{-1}\left(\mathbf{D}_g{}^T\bar{\mathbf{x}}_g^i + \lambda_1\sum_{j=1}^c\boldsymbol{\beta}_p^j + (\gamma_1 - \gamma_2)\boldsymbol{\beta}_p^i\right), \tag{16}$$

where

$$\mathbf{U}_g^i = \left[\mathbf{D}_g{}^T, \sqrt{\lambda_1}\mathbf{I}_k, \underbrace{\sqrt{\gamma_2}\mathbf{I}_k, \cdots, \sqrt{\gamma_2}\mathbf{I}_k}_{i-1}, \sqrt{\gamma_1}\mathbf{I}_k, \underbrace{\sqrt{\gamma_2}\mathbf{I}_k, \cdots, \sqrt{\gamma_2}\mathbf{I}_k}_{c-i}\right]. \tag{17}$$

The objective function in Eq. 2 has a lower bound of 0 and it is jointly convex w.r.t. $\mathbf{D}$ and $\boldsymbol{\beta}$. Since in the alternative optimization, each step on updating $\mathbf{D}$ and $\boldsymbol{\beta}$ decreases the objective, the iteration will converge to the global optimum. In our experiments to be presented, it always terminates in only a few steps.

2.4 Classification Model

Given the learned dictionaries $\mathbf{D}_p$ and $\mathbf{D}_g$, we use them to code each of the gallery and probe sets independently for the test data. Suppose $\hat{\mathbf{X}}_p$ is a test probe set and its mean (averaged sample) is $\hat{\mathbf{x}}_p$, then the coding is as simple as solving the following problem

$$\min_{\hat{\beta}_p}\left\{\left\|\hat{\mathbf{x}}_p - \mathbf{D}_p\hat{\beta}_p\right\|_2^2 + \lambda_1\left\|\hat{\beta}_p\right\|_2^2\right\}, \tag{18}$$

whose closed-form solution is

$$\hat{\beta}_p^* = \left(\mathbf{D}_p^T\mathbf{D}_p + \lambda_1\mathbf{I}_k\right)^{-1}\mathbf{D}_p^T\hat{\mathbf{x}}_p, \tag{19}$$

where $\mathbf{I}_k$ is a $k \times k$ identity matrix. For any test gallery set $\hat{\mathbf{X}}_g$, we can get the coding similarly:

$$\hat{\beta}_g^* = \left(\mathbf{D}_g^T\mathbf{D}_g + \lambda_1\mathbf{I}_k\right)^{-1}\mathbf{D}_g^T\hat{\mathbf{x}}_g. \tag{20}$$

Then the re-identification can be done by Euclidean distance based matching/ranking of the codes $\hat{\beta}_p$s and $\hat{\beta}_g$s.

3 Experiments and Results

In order to show the superiority of DCL, we compare it with all the related state-of-the-art methods when applicable (as detailed bellow), using exactly the same experimental settings (including the same training and test data).

3.1 Experimental Settings

Datasets and Experiments. We choose two representative and complementary datasets: iLIDS-MA [13] and CAVIAR4REID [14] for our experiments. Both of them were captured by two non-overlapping cameras with large viewpoint changes and have manually annotated bounding boxes. The first one was recorded at an airport, covering 40 persons. The second one consists of several sequences filmed in a shopping centre. Besides viewpoint changes, it has broader resolution changes and severer pose variations. We follow [14] on using the 50 people who have been covered by both cameras. We use the same 400-dimensional color and texture histograms based features as mentioned in [15] for both datasets. For a better understanding of how the probe/gallery set size s (number of images for each person) influences the performance, we choose different sizes for our experiments. In great details, $s = 10, 23, 46$ for iLIDS-MA, and $s = 5, 10, 10$ for CAVIAR4REID. Please notice that the second $s = 10$ for CAVIAR4REID is designed for a specially experiment on mixing the data from two cameras to check how much improvement each method can get if the camera difference is eliminated (the lower the better). We perform 10-time result averaging by randomly choosing images for each training/test set. In our experiments we split data into halves for training and testing and they cover different people.

Methods. We compare our proposal with as many related state-of-the-art methods as possible, including unsupervised ones such as MPD [2], SRC [16], CRC [17], CHISD [3], SANP [18], CSA [6], RNP [5], CRNP [1], CMA [8], and LCRNP [7], and supervised models such as SBDR [9] and DCR [10]. As mentioned in [1], here SRC and CRC stand for the version for set-based recognition extended from their original models. We get the results by running their codes either from their authors (such as SRC, CHISD, SANP, CSA, CRNP, LCRNP, SBDR, and DCR) or implemented by ourselves (such as MPD, CRC and RNP).

Parameters. We used the parameters recommended in their original papers for all the other methods, while for our proposed DCL model, we used the same parameters for all the experiments without fine tuning: $\lambda_1 = 2 \times 10^3$, $\lambda_2 = 1 \times 10^3$, $\gamma_1 = 100$, $\gamma_2 = 0.01$, and $k = 0.05 \times N_g$. Besides these key model parameters, we have two others controlling the convergence of iterative optimization: minimum change rate of the objective value set to be 1×10^{-10} (the iteration convergences very rapidly) and maximum number of iterations set to be 15.

3.2 Effectiveness

The results are shown in Table 1. Though person re-identification is widely treated as a ranking problem and evaluated by the Cumulative Matching Characteristic (CMC) curve [19], here we only report the rank-1 accuracy as it is most important for performance evaluation and generally also consistent with whole CMC curves. It is clear that our model (DCL) significantly outperforms all the other methods (the gain over the strongest competitors for each experiment is shown in the last row of Table 1). More interestingly, when we check the performance change of shifting from $s = 10$ without sample mixing to "$s = 10, mixed$" which mixes up the samples from two cameras, we can see that DCL has significantly lower change rate (especially when compared with other supervised learning models), showing that it has done a much better job in bridging the appearance gap between two cameras. This verifies the effectiveness of co-learning camera-specific dictionaries, which is the main reason for DCL's superiority.

3.3 Efficiency

We also provide efficiency comparison (Table 2) for the testing stage, which is most important for real applications. We exclude the time for feature extraction as it is constant for all methods. All the compared methods were implemented in Matlab and run on the same PC with a 3.60 GHz dual-core CPU and 16 GB memory. We choose CRNP and CMA as representatives of unsupervised methods as they have been proved to be more efficient than others (excluding CRC which doesn't perform well) [1,8]. The results indicate that DCL has great superiority especially when the number of classes is large, which is due to simple collaborative representation of only sample means of test sets. This is good for multiple-shot cases when a sequence of tracked frames are available for each person.

Table 1. Recognition accuracy (%) comparison. The first group are unsupervised methods, and the second group are supervised ones. The best ones are shown in bold, and the runner-ups are underlined. The relative performance improvement (named "Gain") over the runner-ups are listed in the last row.

Experiment	iLIDS-MA			CAVIAR4REID			
	$s = 10$	$s = 23$	$s = 46$	$s = 5$	$s = 10$	$s = 10$ mixed	Performance change
MPD[2]	52.0	56.5	55.0	25.2	28.0	48.8	74.3%
SRC[16]	<u>60.0</u>	58.5	<u>65.0</u>	28.0	28.0	48.0	71.4%
CRC[17]	25.5	30.5	25.0	16.8	8.0	42.8	435%
CHISD[3]	49.0	51.5	55.0	<u>31.6</u>	32.0	53.6	67.5%
SANP[4]	48.0	48.5	45.0	30.8	<u>36.0</u>	50.0	38.9%
CSA[6]	50.0	52.0	50.0	24.8	28.0	50.0	78.6%
RNP[5]	50.0	50.5	55.0	28.0	<u>36.0</u>	47.6	<u>32.2%</u>
CRNP[1]	59.5	57.0	55.0	29.6	28.0	48.8	74.3%
CMA[8]	55.5	52.0	50.0	31.2	32.0	<u>54.8</u>	71.3%
LCRNP[7]	54.0	55.5	60.0	30.0	32.0	48.0	50.0%
SBDR[9]	49.0	51.5	55.0	<u>31.6</u>	32.0	53.6	67.5%
DCR[10]	55.0	<u>60.0</u>	<u>65.0</u>	25.2	28.0	47.2	70.7%
DCL (ours)	**65.5**	**65.0**	**70.0**	**32.8**	**48.0**	**60.8**	**26.7%**
Gain	9.2%	8.3%	7.7%	3.8%	33.3%	11.0%	

Table 2. Runtime efficiency comparison on representative methods, averaged over 10 trials if applicable and measured in "milliseconds/person", with best results in bold.

Experiment	iLIDS-MA			CAVIAR4REID	
	$s = 10$	$s = 23$	$s = 46$	$s = 5$	$s = 10$
CRNP [1]	**1.44**	2.80	5.16	**1.12**	2.12
CMA [8]	**1.44**	3.72	7.56	1.30	2.18
SBDR [9]	76.3	116	328	95.4	85.6
DCR [10]	16.4	66.8	291	10.8	22.9
DCL (ours)	1.70	**2.37**	**2.68**	1.38	**1.98**

4   Conclusion and Future Work

This paper presents a novel multiple-shot person re-identification model named Dictionary Co-learning (DCL) which is significantly more effective and also faster than all the existing related methods. Experimental results on two benchmark datasets with various setting have demonstrated its superiority. A possible future work could be introducing affine/convex hull into the model for representing each person's probe images instead of the simplest averaging. It may increase the effectiveness but will likely sacrifice some efficiency. How to properly balance these two will be the key point for this direction. The co-learning is now only for a pair of camera views, how to extend it for directly handling multiple views will be an important future work. Moreover, it will be interesting to apply the model to other biometric recognition problems and see how it performs.

References

1. Wu, Y., Minoh, M., Mukunoki, M.: Collaboratively regularized nearest points for set based recognition. In: Proceedings of the British Machine Vision Conference, pp. 1–10. BMVA Press (2013)
2. Farenzena, M., Bazzani, L., Perina, A., Murino, V., Cristani, M.: Person re-identification by symmetry-driven accumulation of local features. In: CVPR (2010)
3. Cevikalp, H., Triggs, B.: Face recognition based on image sets. In: CVPR, pp. 2567–2573 (2010)
4. Hu, Y., Mian, A.S., Owens, R.: Face recognition using sparse approximated nearest points between image sets. IEEE Trans. Pattern Anal. Mach. Intell. 34(10), 1992–2004 (2012)
5. Yang, M., Zhu, P., Gool, L.V., Zhang, L.: Face recognition based on regularized nearest points between image sets. In: The 10th IEEE International Conference on Automatic Face and Gesture Recognition (FG) (2013)
6. Wu, Y., Minoh, M., Mukunoki, M., Li, W., Lao, S.: Collaborative sparse approximation for multiple-shot across-camera person re-identification. In: 2012 IEEE Ninth International Conference on Advanced Video and Signal-Based Surveillance (AVSS), pp. 209–214, September 2012
7. Wu, Y., Mukunoki, M., Minoh, M.: Locality-constrained collaboratively regularized nearest points for multiple-shot person re-identification. In: Proceedings of the 20th Korea-Japan Joint Workshop on Frontiers of Computer Vision (FCV) (2014)
8. Wu, Y., Mukunoki, M., Minoh, M.: Collaborative mean attraction for set based recognition. In: Proceedings of 17th Meeting on Image Recognition and Understanding (2014)
9. Wu, Y., Minoh, M., Mukunoki, M., Lao, S.: Set based discriminative ranking for recognition. In: Fitzgibbon, A., Lazebnik, S., Perona, P., Sato, Y., Schmid, C. (eds.) Computer Vision - ECCV 2012. LNCS, vol. 7574, pp. 497–510. Springer, Berlin Heidelberg (2012)
10. Wu, Y., Li, W., Mukunoki, M., Minoh, M., Lao, S.: Discriminative collaborative representation for classification. In: Cremers, D., Reid, I., Saito, H., Yang, M.-H. (eds.) ACCV 2014. LNCS, vol. 9006, pp. 205–221. Springer, Heidelberg (2015). doi:10.1007/978-3-319-16817-3_14
11. Wu, F., Jing, X.Y., You, X., Yue, D., Hu, R., Yang, J.Y.: Multi-view low-rank dictionary learning for image classification. Pattern Recogn. 50, 143–154 (2016)
12. Gao, Z., Zhang, H., Xu, G., Xue, Y., Hauptmann, A.: Multi-view discriminative and structured dictionary learning with group sparsity for human action recognition. Signal Process. 112, 83–97 (2015). Signal processing and learning methods for 3D semantic analysis
13. Bak, S., Corvee, E., Bremond, F., Thonnat, M.: Boosted human re-identification using riemannian manifolds. Image Vis. Comput. 30(6–7), 443–452 (2012)

14. Cheng, D.S., Cristani, M., Stoppa, M., Bazzani, L., Murino, V.: Custom pictorial structures for re-identification. In: British Machine Vision Conference (BMVC), pp. 68.1–68.11 (2011). http://dx.doi.org/10.5244/C.25.68
15. Wu, Y., Minoh, M., Mukunoki, M., Lao, S.: Robust object recognition via third-party collaborative representation. In: 21st International Conference on Pattern Recognition (ICPR), November 2012
16. Wright, J., Yang, A., Ganesh, A., Sastry, S., Ma, Y.: Robust face recognition via sparse representation. IEEE TPAMI **31**(2), 210–227 (2009)
17. Zhang, L., Yang, M., Feng, X.: Sparse representation or collaborative representation: which helps face recognition? In: ICCV (2011)
18. Yiqun, H., Mian, A.S., Owens, R.: Sparse approximated nearest points for image set classification. In: CVPR, pp. 121–128 (2011)
19. Wu, Y., Mukunoki, M., Funatomi, T., Minoh, M., Lao, S.: Optimizing mean reciprocal rank for person re-identification. In: 2011 8th IEEE International Conference on Advanced Video and Signal-Based Surveillance (AVSS), pp. 408–413, 30 August–2 September 2011

Weighted Local Metric Learning for Person Re-identification

Xinqian Gu[1] and Yongxin Ge[1,2(✉)]

[1] School of Software Engineering, Chongqing University,
Chongqing 400044, China
xinqiangu@gmail.com, yongxinge@cqu.edu.cn
[2] Key Laboratory of Dependable Service Computing
in Cyber Physical Society Ministry of Education, Chongqing 400044, China

Abstract. Person re-identification aims to match individual across non-overlapping camera networks. In this paper, we propose a weighted local metric learning (WLML) method for person re-identification. Motivated by the fact that local metric learning has been exploited to handle the data which varies locally, we break down the pedestrian images into several local sub-regions, among which different metric functions are learned. Then we use structured method to learn the weight for each metric function and the final distance is calculated from a weighted sum of these metric functions. Our approach can also combine the local metric functions with global metric functions to exploit their complementary strengths. Moreover it is possible to integrate multiple visual features to further promote the recognition rate. Experiments on two challenging datasets validate the effectiveness of our proposed method.

Keywords: Person re-identification · Local metric learning · Structured learning

1 Introduction

Person re-identification aims to recognize people who have been observed from different disjoint cameras, which play a crucial role in video surveillance and visual information retrieval. Due to the large changes in appearances caused by variations in viewing angle, illumination, background clutter and occlusions, person re-identification is still a very challenging problem.

Recently proposed approaches which improve the person re-identification performance [1–9] can be mainly divided into two categories: (1) extracting robust descriptors to deal with the changes in person appearances; (2) designing discriminative metric functions to measure the similarity of person images. For the first category, several effective descriptors have been proposed, such as covariance descriptor [7], and local maximal occurrence (LOMO) [2]. For the second category, a discriminative metric is learned, under which the distance between the same persons and the distance between different persons are increased and decreased, respectively. Among them, Liong et al. [6] model and regulate the eigen-spectrums of covariance matrices in a parametric manner. Pedagadi et al. [9] learned the distance function by maximizing the between-class scatter

© Springer International Publishing AG 2016
Z. You et al. (Eds.): CCBR 2016, LNCS 9967, pp. 686–694, 2016.
DOI: 10.1007/978-3-319-46654-5_75

matrix while minimizing the within-class scatter matrix using the Fisher discriminant objective. However, most metric learning methods only focus on the global measurement, neglecting the local discriminative power.

Chen et al. [1] proposed a similarity learning method with spatial constraints, which partitioned the person images into several sub-regions, and measured the similarity for each region, then, employed linear superposition to combine them together. He also collaborated the local measurements with global measurements and incorporated multiple visual cues to improve the performance. Experimental results show the effectiveness of this method. Considered different sub-regions and different features make different contribution to the final similarity, we proposed weighted local metric learning (WLML), which combines the similarity measurement of different sub-regions and different features by weighted summation. Then, we learn the weight by structured learning [3], instead of pre-defining. Experimental results on two widely used datasets demonstrate the efficacy of our proposed method.

2 Our Approach

In this section, we first propose weighted local metric learning and exploit structured method to learn the weight. Subsequently, we introduce metric method applied in our experiment.

2.1 Weighted Local Metric Learning

In this section, we introduce the overall similarity function first and then formulate the learning problem specifically.

Similarity Function. Given a pedestrian image, we divide it into R non-overlapping horizontal stripe regions and extract F types of color and texture features from each stripe region. After that, we can obtain the f-th descriptor $x^{r,f}$ for the r-th stripe region, where $r \in \{1, \ldots, R\}$ and $f \in \{1, \ldots, F\}$.

To measure the similarity between image descriptors $x_a, x_b \in \mathbb{R}^{d \times 1}$, where x_a and x_b are respectively from camera view A and camera view B, we employ the existing distance function $d(x_a, x_b)$ (will be introduced in Sect. 2.2) to calculate the distance between x_a and x_b. Correspondingly we define the similarity function for the f-th descriptor of the r-th stripe region as:

$$d^{r,f}(x_a, x_b) = d\left(x_a^{r,f}, x_b^{r,f}\right) \tag{1}$$

Considering one specific type of visual feature may not be powerful enough to discriminate individuals with similar visual appearance, we employ a weighted summation method to combine these features. The similarity function for r-th stripe region can be written as:

$$d^r(x_a, x_b) = \sum_{f=1}^{F} w_{r,f} d^{r,f}(x_a, x_b) \tag{2}$$

where $w_{r,f} \geq 0$ is the weight of $d^{r,f}(x_a, x_b)$. Since different regions make different contributions to the local similarity score. For all R regions, the local similarity function is represented as:

$$d^{local}(x_a, x_b) = \sum_{r=1}^{R} w_r d^r(x_a, x_b) \tag{3}$$

where $w_r \geq 0$ is the weight of $d^r(x_a, x_b)$. Since the horizontal stripe regions are non-overlapping, and the local descriptors can't describe the matching of large patterns across the stripes. We combine local similarity with global similarity, and the overall similarity function can be written as:

$$d(x_a, x_b) = d^{local}(x_a, x_b) + w_G d^{global}(x_a, x_b) \tag{4}$$

where $w_G \geq 0$ is the weight of $d^{global}(x_a, x_b)$, and the global similarity function $d^{global}(x_a, x_b)$ is defined as:

$$d^{global}(x_a, x_b) = \sum_{f=1}^{F} w_{G,f} d^{G,f}(x_a, x_b) \tag{5}$$

where $d^{G,f}(x_a, x_b) = d(x_a^{G,f}, x_b^{G,f})$ and $x_a^{G,f}$, $x_b^{G,f}$ are the f-th type global visual feature for image a and image b. Then, expansion formula of Eq. (4) can be written as:

$$d(x_a, x_b) = \sum_{r=1}^{R} \sum_{f=1}^{F} w_r w_{r,f} d^{r,f}(x_a, x_b) + \sum_{f=1}^{F} w_G w_{G,f} d^{G,f}(x_a, x_b) \tag{6}$$

Equation (6) can be simplified as follows by replacing $w_r w_{r,f}$ and $w_G w_{G,f}$ with $w'_{r,f}$ and $w'_{G,f}$:

$$d(x_a, x_b) = \sum_{r=1}^{R} \sum_{f=1}^{F} w'_{r,f} d^{r,f}(x_a, x_b) + \sum_{f=1}^{F} w'_{G,f} d^{G,f}(x_a, x_b) \tag{7}$$

$$= w^T \cdot d$$

where

$$w = [w'_{1,1}, \ldots w'_{R,F}, w'_{G,1}, \ldots w'_{G,F}]$$

and

$$d = [d^{1,1}(x_a, x_b), \ldots, d^{R,F}(x_a, x_b), d^{G,1}(x_a, x_b), \ldots, d^{G,F}(x_a, x_b)].$$

In next section, we will introduce the learning of the weighted similarity function Eq. (7) which makes $d(x_a, x_b)$ smaller when x_a and x_b are from the same individual.

Structured Learning of Similarity Model. In the training process, we randomly selected one image per individual form the gallery set and the remaining images are used to form the probe set. We denote the training set as $\chi = \{x_p^q\}_{p=a,b}^{q=1,...,N_p}$, where x_p^q denotes the q-th pedestrian form camera view p. We refer to probe set as camera view a, and gallery set as camera view b. We also denote the ground-truth ranking structure as $y^* = \{y_{ij}^*\}$, and $y_{ij}^* = 1$ if x_a^i and x_b^j are the same person; otherwise, $y_{ij}^* = 0$. Then training process can be formulated as the following structured learning problem:

$$\min_{w,\xi} \frac{1}{2}\|w\|_2^2 + C\xi$$

$$s.t. \ w^T(\psi(\chi, y^*) - \psi(\chi, y)) \geq \Delta(y^*, y) - \xi, \forall y \in \mathcal{Y}, \xi \geq 0$$

(8)

where w is the weight vector in Eq. (7), $y \in \mathcal{Y}$ denote any arbitrary predicted ranking structure, $\|\cdot\|_2$ denotes the l_2-norm of a vector, and $C > 0$ is the regularization parameter. We define the feature map $\psi(\chi, y)$ as:

$$\psi(\chi, y) = \frac{1}{N_a} \sum_{i=1}^{N_a} \sum_{k \in \chi_i^+} \sum_{j \in \chi_i^-} (1 - y_{ij}) \frac{d(x_a^i, x_b^j) - d(x_a^i, x_b^k)}{|\chi_i^+| \cdot |\chi_i^-|}$$

(9)

where χ_i^- denotes irrelevant individuals set of x_a^i, and χ_i^+ denotes the relevant individual set of x_a^i correspondingly. Since we use single-shot training, $|\chi_i^+| = 1$ and $|\chi_i^-| = (N_b - 1)$, Eq. (9) can be simplified as:

$$\psi(\chi, y) = \frac{1}{N_a(N_b - 1)} \sum_{i=1}^{N_a} \sum_{j \in \chi_i^-} (1 - y_{ij})(d(x_a^i, x_b^j) - d(x_a^i, x_b^k)), k \in \chi_i^+$$

(10)

The goal of constraints is to enforce the distance between irrelevant individuals and relevant individuals of the ground-truth ranking structure to be the largest among any arbitrary ranking structures. Following the large margin framework, we define the loss function as:

$$\Delta(y^*, y) = \frac{1}{N_a(N_b - 1)} \sum_{i=1}^{N_a} \sum_{j \in \chi_i^-} (y_{ij} - y_{ij}^*)$$

(11)

which denotes the mean loss incurred by predicting ranking structures instead of the ground-truth ranking structure. Note that other convex loss functions can also be applied.

Optimization. In principle we can solve the structured learning using cutting-plane algorithm [12]. The basic idea of cutting-plane algorithm is that it is sufficient to obtain a ε-approximate solution of optimization problem by using a small subset of all constraints. We list the algorithm steps in Algorithm 1. It begins with a null constraint set. At each iteration, we solve the optimization problem to find a suitable w over current constraint set. Based on the w, we can find the most violated ranking structure $\bar{y}$ and add it to constraint set. The cutting-plane algorithm repeats the above steps until it converges.

The calculation of the most violated constraint (Algorithm 1, step 2) can be written as:

$$\bar{y} = \arg\max_{y \in \mathcal{Y}} \Delta(y^*, y) - w^T(\psi(\chi, y^*) - \psi(\chi, y))$$

$$= \arg\max_{y \in \mathcal{Y}} \frac{1}{N_a(N_b - 1)} \sum_{i=1}^{N_a} \sum_{j \in \chi_i^-} y_{ij} - \frac{1}{N_a(N_b - 1)} \sum_{i=1}^{N_a} \sum_{j \in \chi_i^-} y_{ij} w^T(d(x_a^i, x_b^j) - d(x_a^i, x_b^k))$$

$$= \arg\max_{y \in \mathcal{Y}} \frac{1}{N_a(N_b - 1)} \sum_{i=1}^{N_a} \sum_{j \in \chi_i^-} (y_{ij}(1 - w^T d_{ij}))$$

$$(12)$$

where $d_{ij} = d(x_a^i, x_b^j) - d(x_a^i, x_b^k)$. Obviously, $\bar{y}$ can be written as:

$$\bar{y}_{ij} = \begin{cases} 1, & \text{if } w^T d_{ij} \leq 1 \\ 0, & \text{otherwise.} \end{cases} \qquad (13)$$

Algorithm 1 Cutting-plane algorithm for solving WLML

Input: training set χ, ground-truth ranking structure y^*, predefined regularization parameter $C \geq 0$, accuracy threshold $\varepsilon > 0$;
Output: weight vector w;
Initialize: The constraint set $\zeta \leftarrow \varnothing$;
repeat
    Step 1: Solve for the optimal metric and slack:

$$(w, \xi) \leftarrow \arg\min_{w, \xi} \frac{1}{2}\|w\|_2^2 + C\xi \qquad ;$$
$$s.t. \ \Delta(y^*, y) - w^T(\psi(\chi, y^*) - \psi(\chi, y)) \leq \xi, \forall y \in \zeta, \xi \geq 0$$

    Step 2: Calculate the most violated constraint:

$$\bar{y} \leftarrow \arg\max_{y \in \mathcal{Y}} \Delta(y^*, y) - w^T(\psi(\chi, y^*) - \psi(\chi, y)) \ ;$$

    Step 3: $\zeta \leftarrow \zeta \cup \bar{y}$;
until $\Delta(y^*, y) - w^T(\psi(\chi, y^*) - \psi(\chi, y)) \leq \xi + \varepsilon$.

2.2 Metric Method

Metric learning can be divided into linear [6, 9] and non-linear methods [2, 4]. As to linear method, a projection matrix M is sought, so that the distance between x_a and x_b can be denoted as $d(x_a, x_b) = (x_a - x_b)^T M(x_a - x_b)$, which will be small if x_a and x_b are from the same person and large otherwise. By kernelization, linear method can be extended to non-linear method easily. The distance of non-linear method can be written as $d(x_a, x_b) = (\phi(x_a) - \phi(x_b))^T M(\phi(x_a) - \phi(x_b))$, where $\phi(x)$ is mapping from feature to kernel space.

In our experiments, we used kernel Local Fisher Discriminant Analysis (kLFDA) [4], which is a non-linear extension to previously proposed LFDA [9]. Unlike LFDA, kLFDA learns projection matrix M in the kernel space $\phi(x)$. Note that there are more metric learning methods can be used in our framework and we just choose the kLFDA for our experiments.

3 Experiments

We evaluate the proposed WLML method on two widely used person re-identification datasets, namely the VIPeR [10] and i-LIDS [11] databases. The following describe the details of our experiments and results.

3.1 Feature Extraction

We divide a pedestrian image into 4 non-overlapping horizontal stripe regions. For each stripe region, we extract 4 types of basic features multi-HS, multi-RGB, SILTP [13] and dense SIFT [5], which describe different aspects of person images. Among them, multi-HS and multi-RGB are 8×8 and $8 \times 8 \times 8$ joint histograms respectively. SILTP and dense SIFT are texture descriptors extracted at RGB and LAB channel, respectively. Then each histogram feature is normalized with the l_2-norm. Finally, two visual cues F_1, F_2 are organized as multi-HS/SILTP and multi-RGB/SIFT. For global descriptor, we also extract HS and RGB concatenated histograms with each channel having 32 bins and concatenate them with HOG [14] histogram.

3.2 Settings

In our experiments, we used the single-shot training and testing where one image per person was randomly selected to form the gallery set and the remaining images were used to form the probe set. For our WLML method, we set the regularization parameter C as $10^{2.8}$ and accuracy threshold ε as 10^{-6} for all experiments. For the non-linear metric method kLFDA [4], we set the regularization parameter for class scatter matrix as 0.01 and apply the RBF-χ^2 kernel for all features. In this experiment, we set the value of σ^2 to be the same as the first quantile of all distances [4]. To evaluate our proposed method, the average cumulative matching curve (CMC) where a match is found at the top-n ranks by repeating the experiments 10 times.

3.3   Evaluation on the VIPeR Dataset

The VIPeR dataset [10] is one of the most popular datasets for person re-identification. It consists of 632 persons captured from two cameras with a viewpoint change of 90° and varying illumination conditions. We randomly select 316 persons to form the training set and the remaining 316 persons are used to form test set.

Table 1 show the matching results compared to 6 representative methods, which includes kLFDA [4], LOMO+XQDA [2], ME [3] and SCSP [1]. While kLFDA, LOMO+XQDA, ME and SCSP are state-of-the-art techniques that presented promising performance in person re-identification. We see that our proposed WLML method outperforms most existing methods. It achieved 50.9 % rank-1 accuracy in VIPeR dataset.

Table 1. Matching rates (%) of different metric learning methods on the VIPeR dataset

Rank	1	5	10	20
WLML	50.9	77.5	88.6	96.2
SCSP [1]	**53.5**	**82.6**	**91.5**	**96.6**
ME [3]	44.9	76.3	88.2	94.9
LOMO+XQDA [2]	40.0	68.0	80.5	91.1
kLFDA [4]	32.3	65.8	79.7	90.9

To validate the effectiveness of our proposed method, we compare our proposed method with other methods using multi-feature in Table 2. Since we haven't the source code of SCSP, we compare our proposed method with ME and the linear superposition of the local metric in our method (SLML). The difference between SCSP and SLML is that they used different local metric and kernel. To fairly compare these methods, all these approaches use the same features and testing/training set. We see that our proposed WLML method outperforms SLML and ME methods with as high as approximately 4 % and 3 % rank-1 accuracy, which validates the effectiveness of our proposed weighted method and local metric, respectively.

Table 3. Matching rates (%) of different metric learning methods on the i-LIDS dataset

Rank	1	5	10	20
WLML	**61.4**	**76.0**	**82.3**	**93.8**
ME [3]	50.3	–	–	–
kLFDA [4]	38.0	65.1	77.4	89.2
LFDA [9]	33.8	57.4	69.7	82.8

Table 2. Matching rates (%) of 3 methods using the same features and testing/training set

Rank	1	5	10	20
WLML	**50.9**	**77.5**	**88.6**	**96.2**
SLML	46.5	75.6	88.6	96.2
ME	47.5	76.9	87.0	94.9

3.4   Evaluation on the i-LIDS Dataset

The i-LIDS dataset consists of 476 images from 119 persons captured from eight disjoint cameras [11]. The number of images for each individual varies from 2 to 8. The dataset presents severe occlusions caused by busy crowd and luggage. We randomly select 59 persons to form the training set and the remaining 60 persons are used to form test set. Table 3 shows the matching rates compared to state-of-the-art method. We see that our proposed WLML method outperforms all other methods.

4   Conclusion

In this paper, we have proposed a weighted local metric learning (WLML) for person re-identification. The proposed method learns the weight of local metric and combines the similarity measurement of different sub-regions and different visual cues by weighted summation. Experimental results on two widely used re-identification datasets have shown the effectiveness of the proposed method.

References

1. Chen, D., Yuan, Z., Chen, B., Zheng, N.: Similarity learning with spatial constraints for person re-identification. In: CVPR, pp. 1268–1277 (2016)
2. Liao, S., Hu, Y., Zhu, X., Li, S.Z.: Person re-identification by local maximal occurrence representation and metric learning. In: CVPR, pp. 2197–2206 (2015)
3. Paisitkriangkrai, S., Shen, C., Hengel, A.V.D.: Learning to rank in person re-identification with metric ensembles. In: CVPR, pp. 1846–1855 (2015)
4. Xiong, F., Gou, M., Camps, O., Sznaier, M.: Person re-identification using kernel-based metric learning methods. In: Fleet, D., Pajdla, T., Schiele, B., Tuytelaars, T. (eds.) ECCV 2014, Part VII. LNCS, vol. 8695, pp. 1–16. Springer, Heidelberg (2014)
5. Zhao, R., Ouyang, W., Wang, X.: Unsupervised salience learning for person re-identification. In: CVPR, pp. 3586–3593 (2013)
6. Liong, V.E., Lu, J., Ge, Y.: Regularized Bayesian metric learning for person re-identification. In: Agapito, L., Bronstein, M.M., Rother, C. (eds.) ECCV 2014 Workshops. LNCS, vol. 8927, pp. 209–224. Springer, Heidelberg (2015)
7. Ma, B., Su, Y., Jurie, F.: Covariance descriptor based on bio-inspired features for person re-identification and face verification. Image Vis. Comput. **32**(6–7), 379–390 (2014)
8. Ma, B., Su, Y., Jurie, F.: Local descriptors encoded by fisher vectors for person re-identification. In: Fusiello, A., Murino, V., Cucchiara, R. (eds.) ECCV 2012 Ws/Demos, Part I. LNCS, vol. 7583, pp. 413–422. Springer, Heidelberg (2012)

9. Pedagadi, S., Orwell, J., Velastin, S., Boghossian, B.: Local fisher discriminant analysis for pedestrian re-identification. In: CVPR, pp. 3318–3325 (2013)
10. Gray, D., Brennan, S., Tao, H.: Evaluating appearance models for recognition, reacquisition, and tracking. In: PETS (2007)
11. Zheng, W.S., Gong, S., Xiang, T.: Associating groups of people. In: BMVC, pp. 1–11 (2009)
12. Joachims, T., Finley, T., Yu, C.-N.J.: Cutting-plane training of structural svms. Mach. Learn. **77**, 27–59 (2009)
13. Liao, S., Zhao, G., Kellokumpu, V., Pietikäinen, M., Li, S.Z.: Modeling pixel process with scale invariant local patterns for background subtraction in complex scenes. In: CVPR (2010)
14. Dalal, N., Triggs, B.: Histograms of oriented gradients for human detection. In: CVPR (2005)

Robust Color Invariant Model for Person Re-Identification

Yipeng Chen[1], Cairong Zhao[1(✉)], Xuekuan Wang[1], and Can Gao[2]

[1] Department of Computer Science and Technology,
Tongji University, Shanghai, China
zhaocairong@tongji.edu
[2] Institute of Textiles and Clothing,
The Hong Kong Polytechnic University, Hong Kong, China

Abstract. Person re-identification in a surveillance video is a challenging task because of wide variations in illumination, viewpoint, pose, and occlusion. In this paper, from feature representation and metric learning perspectives, we design a robust color invariant model for person re-identification. Firstly, we propose a novel feature representation called Color Invariant Feature (CIF), it is robust to illumination and viewpoint changes. Secondly, to learn a more discriminant metric for matching persons, XQDA metric learning algorithm is improved by adding a clustering step before computing metric, the new metric learning method is called Multiple Cross-view Quadratic Discriminant Analysis (MXQDA). Experiments on two challenging person re-identification datasets, VIPeR and CUHK1, show that our proposed approach outperforms the state of the art.

Keywords: Person re-identification · Color invariant · Feature representation · Metric learning

1 Introduction

Person re-identification plays an important role in a surveillance system. Given an image/video of a person taken from one camera, re-identification is the process of finding the same person from images/videos taken from a different camera [1]. It's a very challenging task because of wide variations in viewpoints, illumination, and pose. Meanwhile, low resolution and occlusion bring more difficulty to it.

Researchers have proposed many different methods to deal with this problem which can be summarized as two aspects: (1) feature representation [2–6], (2) metric learning [6–10].

For feature representation, it's necessary to extract features from images which are robust to viewpoint change and other variations. Usually, the features are based on visual information like color, texture, and shape. Among these visual information, color plays the most important role in person matching [4]. Several approaches have been proposed to capture color information in pedestrian images. In [12], a novel color descriptor (SCNCD) was proposed which utilized the probability of sixteen salient color names as feature representation. Ma et al. [13] turned local color descriptors into

© Springer International Publishing AG 2016
Z. You et al. (Eds.): CCBR 2016, LNCS 9967, pp. 695–702, 2016.
DOI: 10.1007/978-3-319-46654-5_76

the Fisher Vector to produce a global representation of an image. Liao et al. [6] proposed an effective feature representation called Local Maximal Occurrence (LOMO) which were composed of HSV histogram and SILTP. Among these methods, LOMO is the most effective feature which divided the HSV color space into $8 \times 8 \times 8$ bins and maximized the occurrence of local features to make a stable representation against viewpoint changes. However, when illumination change greatly, limited by the fixed bounds of bins in color space, the LOMO feature not work well. For example, Fig. 1 shows two images from VIPeR dataset [11] which belong to the same person. The first image looks brighter than second because of illumination change. There are two points locate at the knee respectively. The tuple $[X, Y]$ represents the location of pixel point within the image and the triple $[R, G, B]$ represents the value of pixel point in RGB space. As we can see, because of illumination change, the value of two points in RGB space differ greatly, so it's very difficult to extract a robust feature for matching person in this case.

Fig. 1. Two images from VIPeR dataset

To solve this problem, we propose a new feature representation called Color Invariant Feature(CIF) which is robust to viewpoint, pose and illumination changes. Because $[R, G, B]$ always increase or decrease proportional when illumination change, our goal is to design a variable of which the change is smaller than $[R, G, B]$'s change. We discover the value of $[\frac{Max-Mid}{Max}, \frac{Max-Min}{Max}]$ is meet our needs, where Max denotes the maximum value of R, G and B components, Mid denotes the mid-value and Min denotes the minimum.

Apart from designing a robust feature representation, metric learning is also an effective method for person re-identification. It focuses on learning a robust distance or similarity function to deal with the matching problem. Many discriminant metric learning algorithms have been widely applied for person re-identification. Martin et al. [10] proposed KISSME algorithm which considered a log likelihood ratio test of two Gaussian distributions and obtained a simplified and efficient solution to solve it. Li et al. [14] proposed to learn a decision function (LADF) for verification which can be viewed as a joint model of a distance metric and a locally adaptive thresholding rule. Liao et al. [6] proposed Cross-view Quadratic Discriminant Analysis (XQDA) which can be seen as an extension of Bayesian Face and KISSME, they considered learning a subspace W with cross-view data when most distance metric learning methods didn't consider it in the dimension reduction process. Among these methods, KISSME [10] is commonly used in metric learning, and XQDA [6] shows better result in pedestrian matching. In this paper, we have made an improvement for XQDA metric learning algorithm by adding a clustering process. The new metric learning method is called Multiple Cross-view Quadratic Discriminant Analysis (MXQDA).

The main contributions of our work are summarized as following two points:

(1) A novel Color Invariant Feature (CIF) is proposed for person re-identification. Experimental results demonstrate that the CIF feature obtains better performance than state of the art.
(2) A clustering process is applied to make an improvement for XQDA metric learning algorithm. Experimental results demonstrate that the new metric learning algorithm (MXQDA) is better than XQDA.

Experiments on two challenge public datasets, VIPeR and CHUK1, show that our proposed approach outperforms the state of the art when we combining CIF and MXQDA, and we also demonstrate how the proposed components lead to improvements.

2   Color Invariant Feature (CIF)

Many features consider color as the most important information for person re-identification. However, because of illumination changes, the color information in the images is not stable, especially at shadow and light spot. To focus on these 'incorrect regions', we design CIF descriptor.

In order to get CIF feature, we group the RGB space into six types ($R > G \geq B$, $R > B \geq G, G > R \geq B, G > B \geq R, B > R \geq G, B > G \geq R$), then group each type into one hundred smaller groups averagely according to the value of $[\frac{Max-Mid}{Max}, \frac{Max-Min}{Max}]$. If the value of $[\frac{Max-Mid}{Max}, \frac{Max-Min}{Max}]$ are smaller than a threshold θ, it means the color is similar to white, silver, gray or black, so we group them into four groups, in the experiments we set $\theta = 0.05$. Therefore, the RGB space is divided to $6 \times 100 + 4 = 604$ subspaces. Each subspace contains a set of colors which are similar and robust to illumination variations. This is the first step to getting CIF. Next step we will extract the feature from pedestrian images.

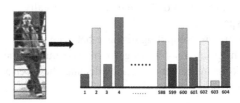

Fig. 2. Illustration of extracting a histogram from a stripe.

Images took from different cameras always have different viewpoints, resulting in the difficulty of matching pedestrians. For instance, a person with frontal view in a camera may appear in back view under other cameras. In order to address this problem, we divide a person image into twelve horizontal stripes equally. All pixels in each stripe will be computed to decide its index in subspaces respectively. This procedure is shown in Fig. 2. Finally, we can get twelve histograms $H_m = [n_1, n_2, \ldots, n_{603}, n_{604}]$, $(m = 1, 2, \ldots, 12)$, where m denotes the stripe's location in the image and n_i denotes the number of pixels in the i-th subspace. By concatenating all the histograms, the descriptors has $12 \times 604 = 7248$ dimensions. $[R, G, B]$ always increase or decrease proportionally when illumination change but the variation of $[\frac{Max-Mid}{Max}, \frac{Max-Min}{Max}]$ is much smaller, that is why CIF is robust to illumination change.

3   Multiple Cross-View Quadratic Discriminant Analysis (MXQDA)

Cross-view Quadratic Discriminant Analysis (XQDA) was proposed as a metric learning method which is very efficient for pedestrians matching. It not only learns a Mahalanobis metric M for computing Mahalanobis distances, but also learns a subspace W for reducing dimensions. However, in the training process, it doesn't consider 'hard examples' for matching. For example, the distance between two features of a pair of images may be very far which is called 'hard example'. Reducing the distances between 'hard examples' by computing Mahalanobis metric is not enough. To address this problem, we propose Multiple Cross-view Quadratic Discriminant Analysis (MXQDA) method for metric learning.

Suppose we have a training set $\{X, Z\}$, where $X = (x_1, x_2, \ldots, x_n) \in R^{d \times n}$ contains n samples in a d-dimensional space from one view and $Z = (z_1, z_2, \ldots, z_m) \in R^{d \times m}$ contains m samples from the other view. Before training, we use the k-means algorithm to divide them into three groups $G_k, (k = 1, 2, 3)$. If the images of a same person are divided into different groups, it means they have far distance in the feature space, so they are difficult to match and learn a Mahalanobis metric. In order to solve this, we use XQDA [6] metric learning method to compute M and W with different grouped training sets in Eq. (1)

$$[X_{mn}, W_{mn}] = XQDA(G_{mn}), (m, n = 1, 2, 3) \tag{1}$$

where G_{mn} denotes a combination of G_m and G_n. So we totally have nine Mahalanobis metrics and nine subspaces.

In the test process, before computing distance between two descriptors $\vec{x}_i$ and $\vec{x}_i$, we need to decide which group they belong to by computing the distances between descriptors and three k-means centers. Then the distance between $\vec{x}_i$ and $\vec{x}_i$ is computed by Eq. (2)

$$D_M(\vec{x}_i, \vec{x}_j) = (\vec{x}_i - \vec{x}_j)^T W_{ab} M_{ab} W_{ab}^T (\vec{x}_i - \vec{x}_j) \tag{2}$$

where a denotes $\vec{x}_i$'s group index and b denotes $\vec{x}_j$'s group index.

4 Experiments

4.1 Experiments on VIPeR

VIPeR [11] is a challenging person re-identification dataset which has been widely used for performance evaluation. It is composed of images of people from two different camera views but it only has one image of each person per camera. The dataset contains 632 pedestrian image pairs totally. All the images are cropped and scaled to be 128×48 pixels. Figure 3(a) shows some example images from this dataset. The VIPeR dataset is randomly divided into half for training and the other half for testing in this experiments, this procedure is repeated 50 times to get an average performance.

(a)   (b)

Fig. 3. (a) Example pairs of images from VIPeR dataset [11]. (b) Example images from CUHK1 dataset [18]. Images in the same column represent the same person.

Comparison of Features and Metric Learning Algorithms. To demonstrate our proposed CIF is effective for person re-identification, we applied both the XQDA algorithm to compare CIF with LOMO feature on VIPeR dataset. The experiment result is shown in Fig. 4(a). The rank-1 identification rate of LOMO feature is 38.27 % and the rank-1 identification rate of CIF can achieve 43.96 %. It shows that our proposed feature is more effective and robust for person re-identification and the improvement made by the CIF is mainly due to the specific consideration of handle illumination changes.

Next, we compare our proposed MXQDA algorithm with XQDA algorithm to prove that our metric learning method is better than XQDA. In this experiment, we both use LOMO feature for two metric learning methods, and the result is shown in Fig. 4(b). The rank-1 identification rate of MXQDA method is 40.0 %. The CMC curves show that our proposed MXQDA metric can achieve a better identification rate. The improvement mainly due to adding a clustering process before learning metric.

Comparison to the State of the Art. Finally, we compare the performance of the proposed approach (CIF+MXQDA) with the state-of-the-art methods on VIPeR dataset to demonstrate our proposed method is better for person re-identification. The experiment results are summarized in Fig. 5.

Among all the comparison methods, three methods, the MLAPG [15], LOMO +XQDA [6] and SCNCD [12] report the best performance on the VIPeR dataset. Experiment results show that our proposed method achieves the new state of the art, 45.49 % at rank 1, outperforming the second best one MLAPG by 6.03 %.

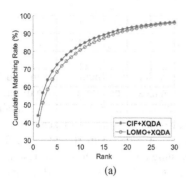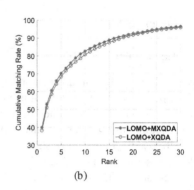

(a)   (b)

Fig. 4. CMC curves on the VIPeR dataset [11] (P=316). (a) Compare CIF with LOMO feature. (b) Compare MXQDA algorithm with XQDA algorithm.

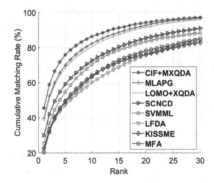

Fig. 5. CMC curves on the VIPeR dataset [11] (P=316) by comparing the proposed CIF +MXQDA method to other state-of-the-art methods.

4.2   Experiments on CUHK1

CUHK1 dataset [18] is another challenge person re-identification dataset which is captured with two camera views in a campus environment. It contains 971 pedestrians and each pedestrian has two images from two camera views. Camera A captures the frontal view or back view of people while camera B captures the side view. All the images are normalized to 160×60 for evaluations. Figure 3(b) shows some example images from the CHUK1 dataset. In this experiment, for each person re-identification method, all pedestrians are randomly divided to 485 for training and 486 for testing (multi-shot) and this procedure is repeated 20 times to average the performance.

We compare our proposed method with some state-of-the-art methods which are reported having good performances on CHUK1 dataset. The final results are shown in Table 1.

Using our proposed method, the rank-1 identification rate can achieve 67.32 % with an improvement of 9.37 %. It demonstrates that our proposed method also having great performance for the multi-shot case of person re-identification.

Table 1. Comparison of state of the art results on the CUHK1 dataset (P=486, M=2). The cumulative matching rates (%) at rank 1,5,10 and 20 are listed.

Method	r=1	r=5	r=10	r=20	Reference
CIF+MXQDA	**67.49**	**83.11**	**88.40**	**92.53**	Our method
LOMO+XQDA [6]	58.12	76.45	83.18	89.12	2015 CVPR
SVMML [16]	31.07	56.04	67.27	78.30	2013 CVPR
LFDA [17]	34.86	50.91	59.91	68.03	2013 CVPR
KISSME [10]	30.20	47.66	57.54	68.16	2012 CVPR

5 Conclusions and Future Works

In this paper, we have proposed an efficient feature and an effective metric learning method for person re-identification. The feature is called CIF and the metric learning method is called MXQDA. The CIF is shown to be robust against viewpoint and pose changes, especially for illumination changes. MXQDA is an improvement metric learning method for XQDA. We have tested our proposed method on two challenging person re-identification database, VIPeR, and CUHK1, show that our proposed method mostly achieves better identification rates than that of other methods. Especially on CUHK1 dataset, the proposed method improves the state-of-the-art rank-1 identification rate by 9.37 %. Because the metric learning of our method is easy to expand, it's interesting to see the application of our improved way to other metric learning algorithms.

Acknowledgements. The authors would like to thank the anonymous reviewers for their critical and constructive comments and suggestions. This work is partially supported by China National Natural Science Foundation under grant No. 61203247, 61573259 and 61573255. It is also supported by the Fundamental Research Funds for the Central Universities (Grant No. 2013KJ010). It is also partially supported by Changzhou Key Laboratory of Cloud Computing and Intelligent Information Processing grant No. CM20123004-KF01 and by the Open Project Program of Key Laboratory of Intelligent Perception and Systems for High-Dimensional Information of Ministry of Education under grant No. 30920130122005. It is also partially supported by the program of Further Accelerating the Development of Chinese Medicine Three Year Action of Shanghai grant No. ZY3-CCCX-3-6002.

References

1. Bedagkar-Gala, A., Shah, S.K.: A survey of approaches and trends in person re-identification. Image Vis. Comput. **32**(4), 270–286 (2014)
2. Farenzena M, Bazzani L, Perina A, et al.: Person re-identification by symmetry-driven accumulation of local features. In: 2010 IEEE Conference on Computer Vision and Pattern Recognition (CVPR), pp. 2360–2367. IEEE (2010)
3. Ma, B., Su, Y., Jurie, F.: Covariance descriptor based on bio-inspired features for person re-identification and face verification. Image Vis. Comput. **32**(6), 379–390 (2014)

4. Gray, D., Tao, H.: Viewpoint invariant pedestrian recognition with an ensemble of localized features. In: Forsyth, D., Torr, P., Zisserman, A. (eds.) ECCV 2008, Part I. LNCS, vol. 5302, pp. 262–275. Springer, Heidelberg (2008)

5. Zhao, R., Ouyang, W., Wang, X.: Person re-identification by salience matching. In: Proceedings of the IEEE International Conference on Computer Vision, pp. 2528–2535 (2013)

6. Liao, S., Hu, Y., Zhu, X., et al.: Person re-identification by local maximal occurrence representation and metric learning. In: Proceedings of the IEEE Conference on Computer Vision and Pattern Recognition, pp. 2197–2206 (2015)

7. Davis, J.V., Kulis, B., Jain, P., et al.: Information-theoretic metric learning. In: Proceedings of the 24th International Conference on Machine Learning, pp. 209–216. ACM (2007)

8. Weinberger, K.Q., Saul, L.K.: Distance metric learning for large margin nearest neighbor classification. J. Mach. Learn. Res. **10**, 207–244 (2009)

9. Mignon A, Jurie F. Pcca: A new approach for distance learning from sparse pairwise constraints. In: 2012 IEEE Conference on Computer Vision and Pattern Recognition (CVPR), pp. 2666–2672. IEEE (2012)

10. Koestinger, M., Hirzer, M., Wohlhart, P., et al.: Large scale metric learning from equivalence constraints. In: 2012 IEEE Conference on Computer Vision and Pattern Recognition (CVPR), pp. 2288–2295. IEEE (2012)

11. Gray, D., Brennan, S., Tao, H.: Evaluating appearance models for recognition, reacquisition, and tracking. In: Proceedings of the IEEE International Workshop on Performance Evaluation for Tracking and Surveillance (PETS), vol. 3(5) (2007)

12. Yang, Y., Yang, J., Yan, J., Liao, S., Yi, D., Li, S.Z.: Salient color names for person re-identification. In: Fleet, D., Pajdla, T., Schiele, B., Tuytelaars, T. (eds.) ECCV 2014, Part I. LNCS, vol. 8689, pp. 536–551. Springer, Heidelberg (2014)

13. Ma, B., Su, Yu., Jurie, F.: Local descriptors encoded by fisher vectors for person re-identification. In: Fusiello, A., Murino, V., Cucchiara, R. (eds.) ECCV 2012 Ws/Demos, Part I. LNCS, vol. 7583, pp. 413–422. Springer, Heidelberg (2012)

14. Li, Z., Chang, S., Liang, F., et al.: Learning locally-adaptive decision functions for person verification. In: Proceedings of the IEEE Conference on Computer Vision and Pattern Recognition, pp. 3610–3617 (2013)

15. Liao, S., Li, S.Z.: Efficient PSD constrained asymmetric metric learning for person re-identification. In: Proceedings of the IEEE International Conference on Computer Vision, pp. 3685–3693 (2015)

16. Li, Z., Chang, S., Liang, F., et al.: Learning locally-adaptive decision functions for person verification. In: Proceedings of the IEEE Conference on Computer Vision and Pattern Recognition, pp. 3610–3617 (2013)

17. Pedagadi, S., Orwell, J., Velastin, S., et al.: Local fisher discriminant analysis for pedestrian re-identification. In: Proceedings of the IEEE Conference on Computer Vision and Pattern Recognition, pp. 3318–3325 (2013)

18. Li, W., Zhao, R., Wang, X.: Human reidentification with transferred metric learning. In: Lee, K.M., Matsushita, Y., Rehg, J.M., Hu, Z. (eds.) ACCV 2012, Part I. LNCS, vol. 7724, pp. 31–44. Springer, Heidelberg (2013)

Fast Head Detection Algorithm
via Regions of Interest

Ling Li and Jiangtao Wang[✉]

Huaibei Normal University, Huaibei, China
1784656698@qq.com, jiangtaoking@126.com

Abstract. The traditional pedestrian detection systems usually scan the whole image through sliding window to find the pedestrian, this cause high computation cost. To solve this problem, this paper proposes a regions of interest based fast head detection algorithm. Motivated by the fact that the human head region usually has obvious gradient value and is not easy to be occluded, we set up the initial location model of the region of interest (ROI) by analyzing the distribution of the head gradient. After this, the K-means clustering algorithm is used to filter out the false ROIs and obtain refined candidates. Finally, the HOG-SVM framework is adopted to classify the ROIs after two times of choosing, so as to locate the human heads. Experimental results on real video sequences show that the proposed method can effectively improve the detection rate while ensuring the accuracy of detection.

Keywords: Regions of interest · K-means clustering · Head detection · HOG · SVM

1 Introduction

Recently, pedestrian detection has become one of the most important research topics in the field of computer vision [1–5]. Despite that many progress has been achieved in pedestrian detection, there still exist many challenges, such as dress, occlusion, posture, weather, light changing and other environmental factors, which make pedestrian detection system to be not enough robust. Currently, there exists a variety of pedestrian detection methods, and the most widely used one is the HOG-SVM framework proposed by Triggs and Dalal in 2005 [6]. In this framework, the HOG features of the candidate targets are first extracted, and then the SVM is employed to classify the candidate targets. Compared with other feature descriptors, HOG features are insensitive to light changing [7]. Based on the classic HOG-SVM framework, researchers have put forward many modified algorithms.

In summary, how to improve the real-time performance of pedestrian detection system is an urgent problem to be solved under the premise of ensuring the accuracy of detection. In order to address above mentioned problem, in this paper, we propose a fast head detection algorithm. In the presented algorithm, we first use the traditional background subtraction method to get the foreground region of the moving target, and then the region of interest is obtained by calculating the magnitude and direction of the foreground gradient. Furthermore, the K-means clustering algorithm is used to

© Springer International Publishing AG 2016
Z. You et al. (Eds.): CCBR 2016, LNCS 9967, pp. 703–710, 2016.
DOI: 10.1007/978-3-319-46654-5_77

eliminate the pseudo candidate regions. Finally, the HOG features of the area to be detected are extracted to be identified by a pre-trained SVM classifier.

2   Region of Interest Extraction

2.1   Gradient Direction Based ROI Generating

One of the main disadvantages of traditional sliding window is the heavy computation cost. To avoid this heavy cost, we consider that if the pedestrian position can be directly located in the background area, thus the detection speed can be accelerated. Through analyzing the characteristics of pedestrian heads, we find that the distribution of edge or gradient information can represent the outline and shape of the local object.

Because the camera used in video surveillance system is usually fixed. In this case, we can employ background difference method to find the approximate region of target motion by:

$$D(i,j) = \begin{cases} |I(i,j) - B(i,j)| & I(i,j) \neq B(i,j) \\ 0 & I(i,j) = B(i,j) \end{cases} \tag{1}$$

Where $I(i,j)$ is the image grabbed at current frame, $B(i,j)$ is the background image, and $D(i,j)$ is the detecting motion area.

If pedestrian density is high, the foreground region may still have a large ratio to the whole image. Notice that the human heads are usually showing a relatively fixed shape, therefore it is not easy to be occluded, and in addition the edges of these areas are more discriminative for the crowed dense scenes. In order to further reduce the possible existence of the target area, in this paper, a method based on gradient interest point is presented to obtain the gradient direction information effectively. In this method, we first calculate the gradient magnitude for each pixel by:

$$gx(i,j) = I(i,j-1) - I(i,j+1) \tag{2}$$

$$gy(i,j) = I(i-1,j) - I(i+1,j) \tag{3}$$

Where $gx(i,j)$ and $gy(i,j)$ represent the horizontal and vertical gradient of pixel $I(i,j)$, respectively. Usually, the contour of object can be depicted by its gradient magnitude $M(i,j)$ and gradient direction $O(i,j)$, so we can apply these two parameters to determine the extraction of interest points, and it can be computed by:

$$M(i,j) = \sqrt{gx(i,j)^2 + gy(i,j)^2} \tag{4}$$

$$O(i,j) = 1/\tan(gy(i,j)/gx(i,j)) \tag{5}$$

Given the gradient magnitude M and gradient direction O, a binary image of human head area can be yielded by:

$$B(i,j) = \begin{cases} 1 & \text{if } O(i,j) \subset [\pi_l, \pi_u] \quad M < th_m \\ 0 & \text{otherwise} \end{cases} \qquad (6)$$

where π_l and π_u indicate the upper and lower values of gradient direction of the head, respectively, th_m is a gradient threshold and B is generating binary image of the region of interest. Two samples of original head image and the corresponding generated ROIs are shown in Fig. 1.

Fig. 1. The human head and the generated ROIs

After getting the ROIs of the human head, the connected regions of ROIs are extracted. Each connected region is located with a bounding box. In order to separate the head region of interest from all of the connected regions, the width and height threshold of ROIs of the head is set, and the candidate region of head should meet with following rule:

$$th_l < width - height < th_h \qquad (7)$$

where th_h and th_l describe the upper and lower bounds of the difference between the width and the height of the ROIs.

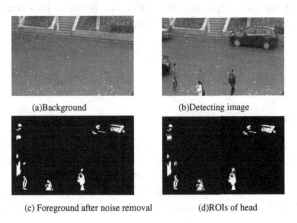

(a)Background   (b)Detecting image

(c) Foreground after noise removal   (d)ROIs of head

Fig. 2. Detection results of ROIs of head

To describe the ROIs extraction process more clearly, an example is shown in Fig. 2, where Fig. 2(a) is the original background, Fig. 2(b) is the detecting input image. Foreground image after denoising process is given in Fig. 2(c); Fig. 2(d) provide the detection results of the ROIs of human head, which is represented by the yellow bounding boxes.

2.2   K-Means Cluster Location Target Area

Based on the scheme described in Sect. 2.1, we can obtain the ROIs of human head, and the entire human head may exist in the region corresponding to the central coordinates of the bounding box of ROIs. However, there are still too many ROIs that do not belong to true human head. In order to eliminate the obvious non-head candidates, we further reduce the human head candidate region by means of using K-means clustering technique to detect the head hair region.

Foreground regions, especially the head hair part of human head usually have intensity which can obviously distinguish from the background. Motivated by this fact, we utilize the characteristics of the hair intensity clustering to refine the head candidate regions generated by Sect. 2.1. This is realized by the follow way.

First, we select k initial value of the k center u_k. This is usually done based on specific problems with some heuristic selection method, or most of the cases using random selection approach. For that K-means cannot always guarantee a global optimum and the initial value selection plays important role on whether it can converge to the global optimal solution. For this reason, sometimes we may select the initial value many times to get the best result. After the initial value is given, then each data point (pixel) is classified to the cluster it belongs to according to the distance between pixel intensity and the average intensity of every cluster. In the next step, the new average intensity each cluster is updated by:

$$u_k = \frac{1}{N_k} \sum_{j \in cluster} x_j \tag{8}$$

We repeat above two steps until the difference between two consecutive cluster center values is less than a given threshold value:

$$u_k^t - u_k^{t-1} < z \tag{9}$$

2.3   HOG Feature Extraction

Through the algorithm described in Sects. 2.1 and 2.2, we can obtain the refined pedestrian candidates. As reported in many literatures, the edge direction or the gradient direction distribution can be a good characterization of the contour and shape of the local object. Therefore, we employ HOG feature to depict the extracted candidate regions. The HOG feature can be constructed by the following means.

(1) Calculate the gradient of each pixel (including the size and direction), for pixel (x, y) the gradient can be computed by:

$$Gx(x, y) = H(x + 1, y) - H(x - 1, y) \tag{10}$$

$$Gy(x, y) = H(x, y + 1) - H(x, y - 1) \tag{11}$$

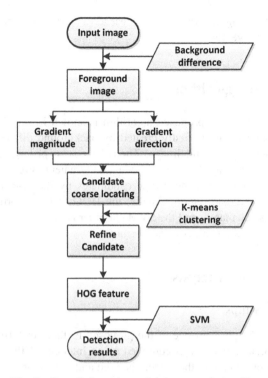

Fig. 3. Overall flow chart of the proposed algorithm

where $G_x(x,y)$, $G_y(x,y)$ and $H(x,y)$ represent the horizontal direction gradient, vertical gradient and pixel value of the pixel (x, y), respectively. The gradient and direction α of this pixel is given by:

$$G(x,y) = \sqrt{G_x(x,y)^2 + G_y(x,y)^2} \tag{12}$$

$$\alpha = 1/\tan(G_y(x,y)/G_x(x,y)) \tag{13}$$

(2) Divide the image into several small pieces of cell;
(3) Histogram of each cell is constructed according to α, and the bin number of each histogram is β;
(4) Let $n \times n$ cells incorporate into a block, that is to say, each block contains $\gamma = n \times n$ cells. Then the histograms of γ cells are concatenated to form the feature of this block. Finally, the HOG feature is obtained by concatenating δ block's feature and normalize it. In this work, the L2 norm is used to normalize the HOG:

$$v \leftarrow \sqrt{\|v\|^2 + \varepsilon^2} \tag{14}$$

$$\omega = \beta \times \gamma \times \delta \tag{15}$$

Where v is the original vector, ε represents a very small constant, ω is the dimension of the vector.

3   The Proposed Algorithm

The overall flow chart of the proposed algorithm is shown in Fig. 3. Given an input image, the foreground image is firstly created by background difference between the input image and the background image. Then the coarse pedestrian candidates are located according to the gradient magnitude and gradient direction. After that, a refining process is imposed on the coarse candidates by the K-means clustering to eliminate the false candidate region. Finally, the HOG features corresponding to the refined pedestrian is calculated, and the SVM classifier is introduced to decide whether the candidate region belong to pedestrian or not.

4   Experiment and Analysis

4.1   Experiment Setups

In order to validate the performance of the proposed method, experiments are carried out on MATLAB platform which is equipped on an Intel core CPU 3.40 GHZ, RAM 4.00G machine. In our database the camera is fixed and with a large perspective angle, so in the field of view of the camera the human heads have approximately equal scale. Here, the acquisition image size is 720×1280, and human head average scale is 46×46. When training the classifier, the training set contains 501 positive samples and 3269 negative samples. The test samples contain 200 positive samples and 800 negative samples. In the experiment, all the samples were normalized to 64×64 gray scale images. After extracting the HOG features, the features are fed into the classifier to get the identifying result. In this section, we select a SVM classifier with radial basis function (RBF) kernel function to realize the classification task.

4.2   Pedestrian Detection

For an inputting video sequence to be detected, the moving area of foreground object is obtained by background subtraction, and then the noise is removed by morphological processing to extract the region of interest. In our experiments, we experimentally found that when the value of gradient magnitude and direction, which is described in Sect. 2.1, were set as 15 and [0.45 PI, 0.75 PI], the system can get better results for the human head ROIs. In the k-mean clustering process, the center is initialized as central coordinate of each ROI. When the candidate area is finally determined, the HOG feature extracting step is executed. In this step, the cell size is set as 8×8, and the bin number of histogram corresponding to each cell is 9. The sliding step is set as 8, and each block corresponding to 4×4 cells as proposed, so each block feature is 36 dimensions vector. Based on Eq. (15), it can be acquired a 1764 dimensions HOG feature.

In order to verify the performance of the proposed algorithm; a comparison is conducted with the other two algorithms. The first method is to search the moving foreground region, which is called the sliding window method. The second method is only using the gradient feature to locate the ROIs, we name it as the gradient filter method. In this section, we analyze the performances of the three methods from two aspects of the detection time and the detection precision. The former is compared each detection algorithm with time required in different population density of the scene, and the latter is to compare the advantages and disadvantages of each algorithm's performance by the false detection rate, missing rate and precision. Tables 1 and 2 provide the experimental results for the three algorithms. Experimental results demonstrate that our proposed algorithm can ensure the detection accuracy while significantly improve the detection rate.

Table 1. Detection time for the three algorithms (s)

Detection method	1 person	3–5 persons	>5 persons
Sliding window +HOG	46.53	127.67	279.09
Gradient filter +HOG	3.07	6.32	14.11
Proposed method	2.43	3.09	5.97

Table 2. Comparison of detection performance of different methods

Detection method	Error rate (%)	Miss rate (%)	Precision (%)
Sliding window +HOG	56.6	4.4	95.6
Gradient filter +HOG	2.5	4.6	95.4
Proposed method	0	5.2	94.8

5 Conclusions

In this paper, a ROIs based fast head detection algorithm is proposed. Firstly, the background difference method is used to obtain the moving target area. Secondly, gradient direction information of the head is extracted and head point interest model is established, and then the initial candidate regions are furtherly refined by the k-means clustering technique. Finally, HOG features corresponding to each refined candidates are constructed and classified by SVM. The experimental results show that the proposed algorithm can improve the detection speed greatly while keep up with a high detection accuracy.

Acknowledgements. This work was partially supported by the Natural Science Foundation of China (61203272, 61572224), Natural Science Foundation of Anhui Province (1508085MF116, 1308085MF105), the seventh Batch of '115' Industrial Innovation Team of Anhui Province, Key Project of University Natural Science Research of Anhui Province (KJ2013A237) and the International Science & Technology Cooperation Plan of Anhui Province (10080703003). The Key Program in the Youth Elite Support Plan in Universities of Anhui Province (gxyqZD2016113).

References

1. Ouyang, W., Zeng, X., Wang, X.: Single-pedestrian detection aided by two- pedestrian detection. IEEE Trans. Pattern Anal. Mach. Intell. **37**(9), 1875–1889 (2015)
2. Yao, S., Pan, S., Wang, T., et al.: A new pedestrian detection method based on combined HOG and LSS features. Neurocomputing **151**, 1006–1014 (2015)
3. Wu, S., Laganière, R., Payeur, P.: Improving pedestrian detection with selective gradient self-similarity feature. Pattern Recogn. **48**(8), 2364–2376 (2015)
4. Yuan, Y., Lu, X., Chen, X.: Multi-spectral pedestrian detection. Sig. Process. **110**, 94–100 (2015)
5. Xiang, T., Li, T., Ye, M., et al.: Random forest with adaptive local template for pedestrian detection. Math. Prob. Eng. **2**, 1–11 (2015)
6. Dalal, N., Triggs, B.: Histograms of oriented gradients for human detection. In Proceeding of the IEEE Conference on Computer Vision and Pattern Recognition, pp. 886–893 (2005)
7. Ninomiya, H., Ohki, H., Gyohten, K.: An evaluation on robustness and brittleness of HOG feature of human detection. In: Proceeding of the 17th Korea-Japan Joint Workshop on Frontiers of Computer Vision, pp. 1–5. Ulsan IEEE (2011)

Glasses Detection Using Convolutional Neural Networks

Li Shao, Ronghang Zhu, and Qijun Zhao[✉]

National Key Laboratory of Fundamental Science on Synthetic Vision,
School of Computer Science, Sichuan University, Chengdu, China
qjzhao@scu.edu.cn
http://vs.scu.edu.cn/

Abstract. Glasses detection plays an important role in face recognition and soft biometrices for person identification. However, automatic glasses detection is still a challenging problem under real application scenarios, because face variations, light conditions, and self-occlusion, have significant influence on its performance. Inspired by the success of Deep Convolutional Neural Networks (DCNN) on face recognition, object detection and image classification, we propose a glasses detection method based on DCNN. Specifically, we devise a Glasses Network (GNet), and pre-train it as a face identification network with a large number of face images. The pre-trained GNet is finally fine-tuned as a glasses detection network by using another set of facial images wearing and not wearing glasses. Evaluation experiments have been done on two public databases, Multi-PIE and LFW. The results demonstrate the superior performance of the proposed method over competing methods.

Keywords: Glasses detection · Deep convolutional neural network · GNet · Deep learning

1 Introduction

Automatic face recognition is an active and important research topic due to its great potential in real world applications such as identity management, access control, attendance control, border control and surveillance [1]. Although a number of face recognition methods have been proposed, the performance of a face recognition system could still be affected by some negative factors, among which is the occlusion caused by glasses. A desirable solution is to let computers learn to deal with this situation. This requires that computers can do glasses detection, i.e., to tell if a face is wearing glasses or not. However, glasses detection is easily affected by many external factors, such as light changes, face rotation and expressions, which make glasses detection very challenging.

Many researchers have proposed different methods for detecting glasses in facial images [4,6–10,15,17]. As glasses detection is a typical two-class problem, these methods usually extract from the input face image hand-crafted features, e.g., wavelet features and local binary patterns (LBP) [8], and apply some

© Springer International Publishing AG 2016
Z. You et al. (Eds.): CCBR 2016, LNCS 9967, pp. 711–719, 2016.
DOI: 10.1007/978-3-319-46654-5_78

binary classifiers, e.g., nearest neighbor classifiers [2], support vector machines (SVM) [3] and Bayesian classifiers [5], to determine if the face has glasses or not. Although they achieve very high accuracy on face images captured in controlled conditions, their performance is obviously degraded when applied to in-the-wild face images [17]. One possible reason is due to the poor generalization capability of hand-crafted features under varying conditions (e.g., pose, illumination and expression, or PIE in short).

This paper aims to improve the robustness of glasses detection to PIE variations that are commonly observed in real-world applications. Motivated by the success of DCNN in various computer vision tasks, we propose a DCNN-based approach for glasses detection. To train the DCNN, we construct a large scale dataset of face images wearing and not wearing glasses from both public and private databases. These face images were acquired under different PIE conditions. To evaluate the robustness of the obtained DCNN model, we conduct experiments on the Labelled Faces in-the-Wild (LFW) database as well as a dataset collected by ourselves. The results demonstrate that our proposed method can achieve state-of-the-art performance on face images with obvious PIE variations.

2   Related Work

Table 1 lists major existing glasses detection methods published in the literature. In [4], glasses detection is achieved using edge information within a small area defined between the eyes. Although their accuracy is high, they test on their own images not public database. In [7], wavelet features are proposed and AdaBoost is utilized to detect the glasses. Impressive performance is obtained by this method on the public database FERET. However, all testing data in these methods are frontal facial images. A method that make use of 3D features obtained by a trinocular stereo vision system is proposed in [6] to detect glasses frames with 3D Hough transform. But this method requires more cameras and computational time than other 2D methods, like [4,7].

Recently, machine learning is used to improve performance of glasses detection. In [15], an eyeglasses detection algorithm is proposed for thermal face recognition, and a high detection accuracy is obtained. However, only 23 glasses-present images from ASUIR database are used to test the performance. Fernndez et al. [8] first normalized the facial images and then used Robust Local Binary Pattern and SVM for glasses detection. To detect glasses more robustly, Du et al. [9] proposed to use haar-like features and AdaBoost algorithm to detect glasses for in-plane rotated faces. To summarize, we can see that most existing glasses detection methods are using handcraft features.

More recently, deep learning has got a plenty of popularity. The main benefit of deep learning is that its algorithms can extract high-level, abstract information automatically as data representations through the complex learning process. Inspired by previous study [10], we propose in this paper a deep convolutional neural networks (DCNN) based method for glasses detection. Specifically, we devise a DCNN, namely GlassesNet or GNet, and pre-train it as

Table 1. Major existing glasses detection methods and the proposed method.

Approach	Test database	Accuracy	PIE variations
Deformable contours [4]	A set of 419 people, 151 wearing glasses under different imaging conditions	Glasses: 99.52%	Large
3D Hough Transform [6]	531 facial images of 19 people wearing 3 kinds of eyeglasses and 9 kinds of poses for training	Glasses:About 90%	Large
Real Adaboost [7]	3000 images obtained from FERET database and world wide web	Glasses: 98.1%; No Glasses: 99.7%	Slight
Block/Region Process [15]	23 images in ASUIR database	Glasses: 95.6%	Slight
AdaBoost [9]	1,309 glasses images and 1,293 no-glasses images from CAS-PEAL-R1	Glasses:95.11%	Median
LBP [8]	3000 facial images in FERET	Glasses: 98.65%	Large
LNet, ANet [10]	Some facial images form LFW	Glasses: 95%	Large
Proposed Method	2000 images from Multi-PIE	Glasses:99.35%	Large

a face identification network with a large number of face images of different people. We then fine-tune the GNet for the objective of discriminating face images wearing glasses from face images without glasses.

3   Proposed Method

In this section, we first describe the GNet structure and implementation of image pre-processing in detail. Then we introduce the pre-training and fine-tuning processes for GNet.

3.1   GlassesNet

The GlassesNet, as shown in Fig. 1, is composed by five convolutional layers and four pooling layers followed by two fully-connected layers. The Conv1 layer kernel size and stride are set as 5×5 and 1, and the rest of the four convolution layers kernel size and stride are set as 3×3 and 1. The five convolution layers output 96, 192, 192, 256 and 256 feature maps, respectively. The network structures (Conv1

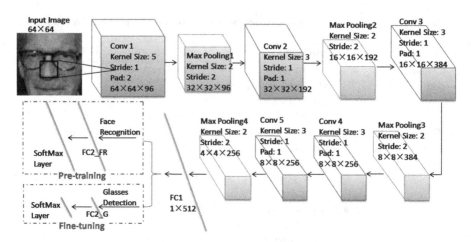

Fig. 1. The architecture of DCNN used in this paper for glasses detection.

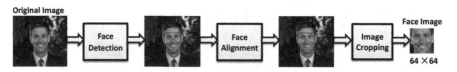

Fig. 2. The data pre-processing step.

to FC1) of pre-training and fine-tuning are the same. We only modify the second fully-connected layer (FC2_FR) of the pre-training network to compose the fine-tuning network.

In order to prepare training data, we pre-process images as follows. Firstly, we detect faces from all original images in the databases. Then we use recently proposed methods [11] to extract five facial landmarks: two eye centers, nose tip and two mouth corners. All the face images are aligned via similarity transformation such that the two eye centers of all faces stay at the same image location. Finally, based on the five landmarks we crop face images from original images. Figure 2 shows the data pre-processing in detail.

3.2   Training Process

We adopt 1.2 million face images of more than 80 thousand different people to pre-train the GNet. Each image has an annotation, referring to people identity information. All the labeled face images are fed into the network to pre-train GNet. As we can see from Fig. 1, we use two fully-connected layers at the end of the network. The first fully-connected layer has 512 dimensions, and the second one has 81,784 dimensions. For the pre-training network, softmax loss is employed as loss function.

All the filters of GNet are initialized after pre-training. GNet is fine-tuned by glasses images classification, where GNet employs face images and glasses labels as input. Prepared face images are used to fine-tune GNet, including about 30 thousand face images wearing glasses and 60 thousand face images not wearing glasses. As we mentioned above, fine-tuning network is the same as pre-training network, only the second fully-connected layer (FC2_G) dimensions of fine-tuning network are set to 2, indicating the probabilities of the presences of glasses images.

4   Experimental Results

4.1   Databases and Protocols

To evaluate the effectiveness of the proposed method, we use 8 databases, as summarized in Table 2, to conduct extensive experiments. Note that BRL is a large database which contains many face images obtained from railway stations, shopping malls and our biometrics research lab. All the facial images are resized to 64 × 64 pixels and 9 thousand of face images are used in the experiments, including 3.5 thousand glasses face images and 5.5 thousand no-glasses face images. Some training data samples are showed in Fig. 3.

Table 2. Databases used in our experiments.

Training databases	Description
BRL	84,354 face images under different conditions: 19,015 images with glasses; 65,339 images without glasses
CAS-PEAL [14]	99,594 images of 1,040 individuals: 620 images with glasses
LFW [17]	13,233 images of 5,749 individual collected from the web: 1,244 glasses-present images
CelebFaces [18]	10,000 subjects, 20 images per subject: 8,000 glasses-present images
CASIA-WebFace [19]	10,575 subjects and 494,414 images: 6,223 glasses-present images
FERET [20]	14,126 images of 1,199 individuals: 328 glasses-present images
FG-NET [21]	1,002 images of 82 individuals: 32 glasses-present images
Testing Databases	Description
Multi-PIE [16]	Including 337 subjects, imaged under 15 view points and 19 illumination conditions: 3,000 glasses-present images and 3,000 glasses-off images
LFW [17]	13,233 images of 5,749 individual collected from the web: 1,000 images with glasses and 1,000 images without glasses

Fig. 3. Example facial images from public databases.

We employ the open-source framework Caffe [12] to implement our proposed method. Caffe is a clear and efficient deep learning framework, which can be used to train, test, fine-tune and deploy deep learning models, particularly deep convolutional neural networks based models. The evaluation experiments are conducted on a PC with NVIDIA Geforce GTX 980 Ti.

We use the Overall Recognition Rate (ORR) to measure the accuracy of the proposed method, which is defined as:

$$OOR = \frac{(TPR + FPR)}{2}, \tag{1}$$

where TPR is True Positive Rate, which is the proportion of correctly detected glasses images among all the test glasses images, and FPR is False Positive Rate, which is the proportion of correctly detected no-glasses images among all the test no-glasses images.

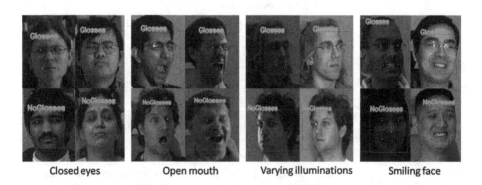

Fig. 4. Example results of the proposed method on Multi-PIE database.

4.2 Results

We randomly select 500 glasses images and 500 no-glasses images under four different conditions (closed eyes, open mouth, varying illuminations, and smiling face) from Multi-PIE [16]. Yaw angle of these test images is between $[-45°, 45°]$. Table 3 shows the glasses classification accuracy under these different conditions. It can be clearly seen by results that the proposed method is strongly robust to various challenging conditions. Some example results are shown in Fig. 4.

We also conduct two comparison evaluations: (i) comparing with Cifar-10 [13] to analysis the effect of neural network complexity to the final performance by randomly choosing 1000 glasses images and 1000 no-glasses images from Multi-PIE [16] as test data, and (ii) comparing with ANet [10] and Big Data [15] by randomly selecting 1000 glasses images and 1000 no-glasses images from LFW [17] as test data. There is no overlapping face images between the training data and the testing data. In the first comparison evaluation, the Cifar-10 network has 3 convolutional layers, 3 pooling layers and 1 innerproduct layer. Compared with Cifar-10, the proposed GNet is much more complex. The results are presented in Table 4, which clearly show that our proposed method outperforms Cifar-10. Table 5 shows the results of our proposed method and two state-of-the-art methods on the LFW database. Again, our proposed method achieves the best results.

Table 3. Recognition accuracy of the proposed method under different facial images conditions.

Test Data	TPR	FPR	OOR
Closed eyes	1	0.994	0.997
Open mouth	0.994	0.992	0.993
Varying illuminations	0.988	1	0.994
Smiling face	0.998	0.996	0.997

Table 4. Recognition accuracy of the proposed method and Cifar-10 on the Multi-PIE database.

Method	TPR	FPR	OOR
Cifar-10	0.997	0.944	0.9705
Proposed method	1	0.987	0.9935

Table 5. Recognition accuracy of the proposed method and two state-of-the-art methods on the LFW database.

Method	ANet [10]	Big Data [15]	Proposed method
OOR	0.95	0.9865	0.9922

5   Conclusion

In this paper, we have proposed a glasses detection method based on DCNN, called GlassesNet (GNet). We first pre-train the GNet for face identification and then the pre-trained GNet is fine-tuned as a glasses detection network. Experiments on the Multi-PIE database show that the proposed method is strongly robust to various challenging conditions. In addition, we have also compared the proposed GNet with the Cifar-10 network and two state-of-the-art methods. The results again prove the superiority of our proposed method. In the future, we will incorporate our method with other advanced attribute analysis methods to further improve its accuracy.

Acknowledgment. This work is supported by the National Natural Science Foundation of China (No. 61202161) and the National Key Scientific Instrument and Equipment Development Projects of China (No. 2013YQ49087904).

References

1. Shari, M., Mohsin, S., Javed, M.Y.: A survey: face recognition techniques. Res. J. Appl. Sci. Eng. Technol. **4**, 41–68 (2012)
2. Gumus, E., Kilik, N., Sertbas, A., Ucan, O.N.: Evaluation of face recognition techniques using PCA, wavelets and SVM. Expert Syst. Appl. **37**, 6404–6408 (2010)
3. Ahmed, A.M., Atul, S., Gulisong N.: Multi-label approach for human-face classification. In: International Congress on Image & Signal Processing, Australia, pp. 648–653 (2015)
4. Jing, Z., Mariani, R.: Glasses detection and extraction by deformable contour. In: International Conference on Pattern Recognition, pp. 933–936 (1998)
5. Jing, Z., Mariani, R., Wang, J.: Glasses detection for face recognition using Bayes rules. In: Tan, T., Shi, Y., Gao, W. (eds.) ICMI 2000. LNCS, vol. 1948, pp. 127–134. Springer, Heidelberg (2000). doi:10.1007/3-540-40063-X_17
6. Wu, H., Yoshikawa, G., Shioyama, T., Lao, S., Kawade, M.: Glasses frame detection with 3D Hough transform. In: International Conference on Pattern Recognition, pp. 346–349 (2002)
7. Wu, B., Ai, H., Liu, R.: Glasses detection by boosting simple wavelet features. In: International Conference on Pattern Recognition, pp. 292–295 (2004)
8. Fernández, A., Garcła, R., Usamentiaga, R., Casado, R.: Glasses detection on real images based on robust alignment. Mach. Vis. Appl. **26**, 519–531 (2015)
9. Du, S., Liu, J., Liu, Y., Zhang, X., Xue, J.: Precise glasses detection algorithm for face with in-plane rotation. Multimedia Syst., 1–10 (2015)
10. Wang, X., Liu, Z., Luo, P., Tang, X.: Deep learning face attributes in the wild. In: International Conference on Computer Vision (2015)
11. Sun, Y., Wang, X., Tang, X.: Deep convolutional network cascade for facial point detection. In: Computer Vision and Pattern Recognition, pp. 3474–3481 (2015)
12. Jia, Y., Shelhamer, E., Donahue, J., Karayev, S., Long, J., Girshick, R., et al.: Caffe: convolutional architecture for fast feature embedding. In: ACM International Conference on Multimedia, pp. 675–678 (2014)
13. Wan, L., Zeiler, M., Zhang, S., et al.: Regularization of neural networks using dropconnect. In: International Conference on Machine Learning, Atlanta, pp. 1058–1066 (2013)

14. Gao, W., Cao, B., Shan, S., et al.: The CAS-PEAL large-scale Chinese face database and baseline evaluations. IEEE Trans. Syst. Man Cybern. **38**, 149–161 (2008)
15. Fernández, A., et al.: A real-time big data architecture for glasses using computer vision techniques. In: International Conference on Future Internet of Things and Cloud, pp. 591–596 (2015)
16. Gross, R., Matthews, I., Baker, S.: Multi-pie. In: IEEE Conference on Automatic Face and Gesture Recognition (2008)
17. Huang, G.B., Ramesh, M., Berg, T., Learned-Miller, E.: Labeled faces in the wild: a database for studying face recognition in unconstrained environments. In: Technical Report 07–49, Amherst (2007)
18. Sun, Y., Wang, X., Tang, X.: Deep learning face representation by joint identification-verification. In: Advances in Neural Information Processing Systems (2014)
19. Yi, D., Lei, Z., Liao, S., Li, S.Z.: Learning face representation from scratch. In: Computer Science (2014)
20. Phillips, P.J., Moon, H., Rizvi, S., Rauss, P.J., et al.: The feret evaluation methodology for face-recognition algorithms. Pattern Anal. Mach. Intell. **22**, 1090–1104 (2000)
21. Han, H., Otto, C., Liu, X., Jain, A.K.: Demographic estimation from face images: human vs. machine performance. Pattern Anal. Mach. Intell. **37**(6), 1–14 (2014)

Face Occlusion Detection Using Cascaded Convolutional Neural Network

Yongliang Zhang[1(✉)], Yang Lu[1], Hongtao Wu[2], Conglin Wen[1], and Congcong Ge[1]

[1] College of Computer Science and Technology, Zhejiang University of Technology,
Hangzhou 310023, China
titanzhang@zjut.edu.cn
[2] School of Computer Science and Engineering, Hebei University of Technology,
Tianjin 300130, China

Abstract. With the rise of crimes associated with ATM, face occlusion detection has gained more and more attention because it facilitates the surveillance system of ATM to enhance the safety by pinpointing disguised among customers and giving alarms when suspicious customer is found. Inspired by strong learning ability of deep learning from data and high efficient feature representation ability, this paper proposes a cascaded Convolutional Neural Network (CNN) based face occlusion detection method. In the proposed method, three cascaded CNNs are used to detect head, eye occlusion and mouth occlusion. Experimental results show that the proposed method is very effective on two test datasets.

Keywords: Cascaded convolutional neural network · Face occlusion detection · ATM

1 Introduction

As Automatic Teller Machine (ATM) brings much convenience to everyone in life, it has attracted more and more attention from criminals especially when more services are provided from new ATMs. Criminals usually disguise themselves by wearing hats, masks, helmets, sunglasses and so on when they use ATM to withdraw illegal money. Two images of the suspects with heavy facial occlusions are shown in Fig. 1 captured by the actual ATMs. It is mostly difficult to recognize the suspects with occluded faces. So in order to prevent the crime and enhance the safety, it is the most straightforward technical solutions for the surveillance systems of ATM that using Face Occlusion Detection (FOD) pinpoints the disguised among customers and give real time automatic alarms when suspicious customer is found.

Face occlusion detection has been studied for several years in the field of security. The previous algorithms can be roughly divided into three categories: (i) specific attack detection, (ii) skin color-based occlusion detection, and (iii) frontal bare face detection [1]. Specific attack detection tries to detect specific occluding objects which are commonly used by the criminals, such as helmets [2, 3], masks [4], or scarves [5]. It is very feasible for those specific occluding objects which are included in training dataset. However, there are various occlusions that may occur in real ATM situations, but don't

© Springer International Publishing AG 2016
Z. You et al. (Eds.): CCBR 2016, LNCS 9967, pp. 720–727, 2016.
DOI: 10.1007/978-3-319-46654-5_79

Fig. 1. Suspects with face occlusion captured from ATM

appear in training dataset. Therefore, specific attack detection is inadequate. Skin color-based occlusion detection determines face occlusion based on skin color ratio [6–8]. The advantage of skin color-based methods is its robustness to various facial poses, and the disadvantage is its sensitivity to various lightings commonly occurred in the actual ATM environments. Frontal bare face detection-based approach recognizes face occlusion by detecting whether facial components present at appropriate locations [1, 9, 10]. Frontal bare face detection-based approach is able to handle users with various partial occlusions. But, it can hardly be used to deal with a low resolution face image [7]. In addition, using the local information of facial components is likely to result in: (i) rejecting a user with partial, yet acceptable, occlusion; (ii) falsely accepting a user by wrongly locating a local region closely similar to the regions in the actual facial components [1].

However, previous methods mostly relied on hand-crafted features which were carefully designed based on prior knowledge and task dependent. Recently, deep learning has drawn significant interest in computer vision community, and more and more promising results are published on a range of different vision tasks. Deep learning methods can learn hierarchical features directly from raw data for use in specific tasks. As one of deep learning models, Convolutional Neural Networks (CNN) integrates feature extraction and classification, and has achieved noteworthy success with its repeatedly confirmed superiorities in various computer vision tasks. So, it is straightforward to introduce CNN for face occlusion detection.

In this paper, we propose a new FOD method based on Cascaded CNN. In the proposed method, a cascaded CNN is firstly used to head detection. Then based on the fact that eye and mouth are often occlued, two cascaded CNNs are applied to detect eye and mouth occlusion, respectively.

The rest of the paper is organized as follows. In Sect. 2, the proposed method is described in detail. Experimental results are presented in Sect. 3. Finally, Sect. 4 concludes the paper.

2 Proposed Method

Eyes, nose and mouth are distinct facial features, and their shapes and sizes are different so that they make people's face different. These local features can be used as important features for face recognition. To avoid being captured their face information, suspects often occluded their eyes and mouths in the crimes related to ATM. Therefore, this paper mainly detects the occlusions of eyes and mouths.

Given a test image, the head position is firstly detected, and then the existence of eyes and mouth in the head position are detected. According to the existence of eyes and mouth to determine whether or not to be occluded. There are 7 CNNs in the cascade of face occlusion detector including 3 CNNs (head-16-net, head-32-net, and head-48-net) for head detection, 2 CNNs (eye-net) for eye detection and 2 CNNs (mouth-net) for mouth detection. The general procedure of our work is shown in Fig. 2. The unconstrained test image is transformed from color to gray. After histogram equalization is applied and sliding window approach is used to scan the entire image, the windows are classified by three cascaded head detection nets. We merge the region of interest (ROIs) and directly output the location of head position. Then the head area is cut out from the test image, and is operated by the Gamma transform. Finally the eye-net and mouth-net are used to detect the occlusions of the eyes and mouths.

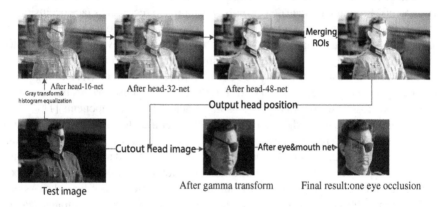

Fig. 2. The pipeline of our proposed method

2.1 Head Position Location

Head position location is implemented by cascading a head-16-net, a head-32-net, and a head-48-net. Given a test image, the head-16-net scans the whole image densely across different scales to quickly reject more than 90 % of the detection windows. The remaining detection windows are cropped out and resized into 32 × 32 as input images for head-32-net to further reject the remaining detection windows. The last 48-net accepts the passed detection windows as 48 × 48 images to evaluate the detection windows.

Head-16-net as shown in Fig. 3 refers to the first level CNN for head detection. This net is a very shallow CNN for binary classification which can scan the test image with 5-pixel spacing very quickly.

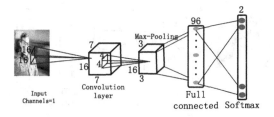

Fig. 3. The head-16-net architecture

The structure of head-32-net in Fig. 4 is as same as the structure of head-16-net except the fully connection layer connects to both Max-pooling layer 1 and convolutional layer 2. This idea refers to [11]. This connection can consider both local feature and global feature. The last hidden layer takes the function as Eq. 1

$$y_j = \max(0, x_i^1 \cdot w_{i,j}^1 + x_i^2 \cdot w_{i,j}^2 + b_j) \tag{1}$$

where $x_i^1, x_i^2, w_{i,j}^1, w_{i,j}^2$ denote neurons and weights in the first and second convolutional layers, respectively. It linearly combines features in the previous two convolutional layers, followed by ReLU non-linearity.

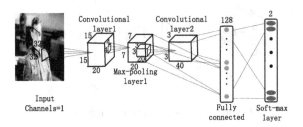

Fig. 4. The head-32-net architecture

The head-48-net decides all the remaining windows from head-32-net whether they are head or not. The structure is shown in Fig. 5. The candidate windows are deleted if they are not heads. Then we merge all remaining windows by the following way. For each input image, all the ROI candidates are sorted by the correlation coefficients in a descending order. Then the ROI candidate with the highest correlation coefficient is chosen as a positive region, and all other regions near this region are deleted. We repeat this operation until no region is left.

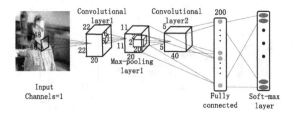

Fig. 5. The head-48-net architecture

2.2 Eye-Net and Mouse-Net

The eye-net structure is similar as head-net. The first level CNN quickly rejects most of detection windows. The second level CNN judges the remaining windows whether they are eye or not. The mouth-net has the same structure as eye-net except the input image size of its first level CNN is 32 * 16 and the input image size of its second level CNN is 64 * 32. The first level eye-net structure is shown in Fig. 6 and the second level eye-net structure is shown in Fig. 7.

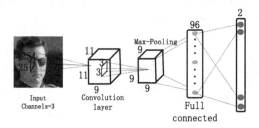

Fig. 6. The first level eye-net architecture

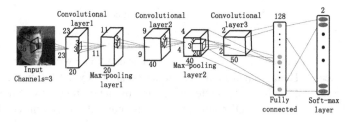

Fig. 7. The second level eye-net architecture

3   Experimental Results

In this paper, AR face dataset [12] and our self-building face occlusion dataset FO are used to evaluate our proposed method. The AR face dataset contains over 4,000 color images which cover frontal view faces with occlusions (sun glasses and scarf), different facial expressions and illumination conditions. FO dataset has 515 images, and includes

148 face images with no occlusion, 117 eye occlusion images, 139 mouth occlusion images and 111 both eye and mouth occlusion images. There is a variety of complex background and kinds of occlusions in FO dataset. Some examples of AR face dataset and our FO dataset are shown in Figs. 8 and 9, respectively. The difference of detection process between AR dataset and our FO dataset is that head detection is needed in our FO dataset.

Fig. 8. Samples of AR face dataset

Fig. 9. Samples of FO dataset

In order to train our proposed model, we collected both positive and negative samples between 150000 and 240000 for each net respectively from CACD2000 dataset [13] and CASIA-WebFace dataset [14]. The positive samples are cut out according to the given feature point, and the negative samples are mainly searched on the web like natural scenery, monuments, plants, pictures, as well as animals in the video, and the misjudging samples from upper level CNN test.

The testing results on AR dataset and our FO dataset are presented in Tables 1 and 2, respectively. It is noted that all the images in AR dataset are tested in [15] while 100 images are randomly selected from AR dataset and only the eye occlusions are detected in [16]. Experimental results show our method significantly improves the detection accuracy of human face occlusions. And also shows that the accuracy in FO dataset is very similar to AR dataset.

Table 1. Experimental results on AR face dataset

Algorithm	Eye detection accuracy	Mouth detection accuracy	Face occlusion detection accuracy
Proposed algorithm	98.5 %	94.2 %	92.7 %
MB-LBP [15]	83.5 %	85.6 %	–
Normalized gray level difference[16]	96 %	–	–

Table 2. Experimental results on FO dataset

Algorithm	Head detection accuracy	Eye detection accuracy	Mouth detection accuracy	Face occlusion detection accuracy
Proposed algorithm	96.1 %	97.2 %	95.2 %	93.1 %

4   Conclusion

Face occlusion detection is an effective way of security reinforcement by surveillance techniques for ATM applications. It can also be used in other places needing high security, such as Intelligent Visitors Management System and jewelry shop. In this paper, we propose a cascaded CNN based method for face occlusion detection. Three cascaded CNNs have been devised to locate head, and detect eye and mouth occlusion, respectively. The algorithm has strong robustness, could adapt to a variety of complex scenarios.

Acknowledgement. The project was supported by the Science and Technology Planning Project of Hebei Province, China (No. 15210124), and the Science and Technology Research Project of Higher School in Hebei Province, China (No. Z2015105).

References

1. Eum, S., Suhr, J.K., Kim, J.: Face recognition ability evaluation for ATM applications with exceptional occlusion handling. In: IEEE Computer Society Conference on Computer Vision and Pattern Recognition Workshops, pp. 82–89 (2011)
2. Wen, C.Y., Chiu, S.H., Liaw, J.J., Lu, C.P.: The safety helmet detection for ATM's surveillance system via the modified Hough transforms. In: Security Technology IEEE 37th Annual 2003 International Carnahan Conference, pp. 364–369 (2003)
3. Liu, C.-C., Liao, J.-S., Chen, W.-Y., Chen, J.-H.: The full motorcycle helmet detection scheme using canny detection. In: 18th IPPR Conference on Computer Vision, Graphics and Image Processing (CVGIP), pp. 1104–1110 (2005)
4. Wen, C., Chiu, S., Tseng, Y., Lu, C.: The mask detection technology for occluded face analysis in the surveillance system. J. Forensic Sci. **50**(3), 1–9 (2005)
5. Min, R., D'Angelo, A., Dugelay, J.-L.: Efficient scarf detection prior to face recognition. In: Proceedings of the 18th European Signal Processing Conference, August 2010, pp. 259–263 (2010)
6. Lin, D.-T., Liu, M.-J.: Face occlusion detection for automated teller machine surveillance. In: Chang, L.-W., Lie, W.-N. (eds.) PSIVT 2006. LNCS, vol. 4319, pp. 641–651. Springer, Heidelberg (2006)
7. Kim, G., Suhr, J.K., Jung, H.G., Kim, J.: Face occlusion detection by using B-spline active contour and skin color information. In: The 11th International Conference on Control Automation Robotics & Vision (ICARCV), pp. 627–632 (2010)
8. Zhang, X., Zhou, L., Zhang, T., Yang, J.: A novel efficient method for abnormal face detection in ATM. In: 2014 International Conference on Audio, Language and Image Processing (ICALIP), pp. 695–700 (2014)

9. Dong, W., Soh, Y.: Image-based fraud detection in automatic teller machine. Int. J. Comput. Sci. Netw. Secur. **6**, 13–18 (2006)
10. Choi, I., Kim, D.: Facial fraud discrimination using detection and classification. In: 6th International Symposium Advances in Visual Computing, pp. 199–208 (2010)
11. Sun, Y., Wang, X., Tang, X.: Deep learning face representation from predicting 10,000 classes. In: Computer Vision and Pattern Recognition, pp. 1891–1898. IEEE (2014)
12. Martinez, A.M., Benavente, R.: The AR face database. CVC Technical report #24 (1998)
13. Chen, B.-C., Chen, C.-S., Hsu, W.H.: Cross-age reference coding for age-invariant face recognition and retrieval. In: Fleet, D., Pajdla, T., Schiele, B., Tuytelaars, T. (eds.) ECCV 2014, Part VI. LNCS, vol. 8694, pp. 768–783. Springer, Heidelberg (2014)
14. Yi, D., Lei, Z., Liao, S., et al.: Learning face representation from scratch. Eprint Arxiv (2014)
15. Zhaohua, C.: Research of Occluded Face Detection and Recognition Based on Video. Soochow University, Suzhou (2012)
16. Gong, N.N,, Hai-Yan, W.U.: Projection curve gray level difference based face occlusion detection. Sci. Technol. Eng. (2013)

Multiple Pedestrian Tracking Based on Multi-layer Graph with Tracklet Segmentation and Merging

Wencheng Duan[1], Tao Yang[1(✉)], Jing Li[2], and Yanning Zhang[1]

[1] School of Computer Science, Northwestern Polytechnical University, Xian, China
tyang@nwpu.edu.cn
[2] School of Telecommunications Engineering, Xidian University, Xian, China

Abstract. Multiple pedestrian tracking is regarded as a challenging work due to difficulties of occlusion, abrupt motion and changes in appearance. In this paper, we propose a multi-layer graph based data association framework to address occlusion problem. Our framework is hierarchical with three association layers and each layer has its corresponding association method. We generate short tracklets and segment some of them into small pieces based on the segmentation condition in the first layer. The segmented tracklets are merged into long tracklets using spatial-temporal information in the second layer. In the last layer, tracklets in neighboring frame-window are merged to form object track mainly by searching the global maximum overlap ratio of the tracklets. Since appearance information is not available in various scenarios, we don't use any appearance features in our work. We evaluate our algorithm on extensive sequences including two categories and demonstrate superior experimental results.

Keywords: Multiple pedestrian tracking · Multi-layer graph based · Tracklet segmentation and merging

1 Introduction

As a fundamental problem in computer vision, multiple pedestrian tracking has been studied for years and numerous approaches [1–5] have been proposed. It is regarded as a challenging work due to difficulties of occlusion, abrupt motion and changes in appearance. Research about solving occlusion problem have made some achievement [6–11]. When dealing with occlusion problem, target missing and identity switches are likely to occur in many tracking algorithms. If two people are detected on partial occluded situations, identity switches may emerged especially when people are in close proximity for a long time. Besides, several clustered people are likely to be detected as one object in occluded scenes and this results in target missing. [7] formulates tracking problem as a hierarchical dense neighborhood searching problem. Some methods are limited in its application for emphasizing at particular occlusion occasion. In [8], the authors are

© Springer International Publishing AG 2016
Z. You et al. (Eds.): CCBR 2016, LNCS 9967, pp. 728–735, 2016.
DOI: 10.1007/978-3-319-46654-5_80

focused on handling partial occlusion using part-based multiple person tracking. [9] maintains the object track when objects occluded each other.

Various novel methods and frameworks [12–18] for multi-pedestrian tracking are published in recent years. [13] puts forward And-Or graph for simultaneously tracking and parses object using a spatial-temporal dynamic programming algorithm. In [15], the authors adopt psychology principles designing a flexible representation consisted of short-term and long-term memory. [17] states multi-target tracking as a minimum cost subgraph multicut problem.

In our work, we attend to figure out an effective multi-pedestrian tracking framework which is independent of the detection responses modalities of different detectors. Our algorithm is hierarchical with three association layers and each layer corresponding to a directed graph. According to the spatial-temporal information of moving objects, we calculate association cost between each pair of detection responses or tracklets as length of the corresponding side. Our algorithm is finding the specific group of paths in each layer which has the shortest length in total. Based on these viewpoints, we put forward an multi-layer graph based framework to solve multi-pedestrian tracking problem.

2 Proposed Framework

Our framework is illustrated in detail following three sections, tracklet generation and segmentation, intra frame-window tracklet merging and cross frame-window tracklet merging. A brief introduction of our work is shown in Fig. 1.

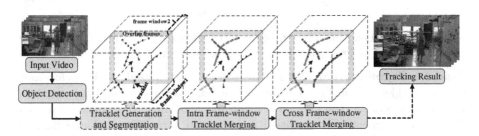

Fig. 1. Proposed framework: tracklets in each cubic are the association result of the corresponding step. Tracklets of different objects are labeled with different colors (Color figure online)

We assume that one detection response or tracklet can only belong to one tracklet or one object track. T_k^s denotes short tracklet in the association result of trackle generation and segmentation; $T^s = \{T_k^s\}$ is the short tracklet set; let T^l, T^t denote the association result set of long tracklets and object track. This basic unshared constraint formalized as:

$$T_m^\delta \cap T_n^\delta = \emptyset \qquad \delta \in \{s, l, t\} \tag{1}$$

The frame number of one frame window and the number of overlap frames between two neighbor windows are set as constants through our tracking algorithm. To each frame window, the three association steps are functioned hierarchically in our framework.

2.1   Trackle Generation and Segmentation

This step takes detection responses as input and generates reliable tracklets. Divided the tracklet into small pieces, we can find each shorter tracklet is associated appropriately in low density condition. Therefore, we segment the tracklet when more than one person are in close proximity in the image.

Short Tracklet Generation: Hungarian algorithm [19] which is simple and widely applied is employed in this layer to make sure an efficient association initialization. Supposing there are m and n detection responses in two consecutive frames, we calculate matrix C as the transition matrix. The association cost between two detection responses is measured by Euclidean distance. $d_{k1} = (x_{k1}, y_{k1}, w_{k1}, h_{k1})$ represents the detection response 1 in the frame f_k. The association cost value $c_d(d_{ki}, d_{lj})$ $(l = k+1)$ between d_{ki} and d_{lj} is formulated as:

$$c_d(d_{ki}, d_{lj}) = \sqrt{(x_{k1} - x_{l1})^2 + (y_{k1} - y_{l1})^2} \tag{2}$$

The distance an object can move in a constant time interval is limited, so this distance constraint is formulated as:

$$c_{i,j} = \begin{cases} c_d(d_{ki}, d_{lj}), & c_d(d_{ki}, d_{lj}) \leq d_t \\ \infty, & c_d(d_{ki}, d_{lj}) > d_t \end{cases} \tag{3}$$

where $c_{i,j}$ is the element in row i, column j of matrix C. The output association result is a global assignment scheme which has the minimum total cost.

Tracklet Segmentation: After generating the initialized tracklets for each object, tracklets should be extended till the end of the current frame-window. During this process, tracklets are segmented according to segmentation condition. The segmentation condition includes two parts. The first one handles spilt-merge condition. So we have this segmentation condition:

$$\exists d_{kx}, D_k^n \qquad loc(d_{kx}) \cap loc(D_k^n) \neq \emptyset \qquad n \geq 2 \tag{4}$$

where $loc(d_{kx})$ is the location of the detection response d_{kx}, D_k^n is the detection result set of frame f_k.

The other one is a correction measure to the possible deviation of data association when occlusion happens. If two detection responses d_{k1} and d_{k2} in frame f_k are associated with two detection responses d_{l1} and d_{l2} in frame f_k, and satisfied with Eq. 5, the associated result will be rejected.

$$dist(d_{k1}, d_{k2}) < dthresh \ \& \ dist(d_{l1}, d_{l2}) < dthresh \tag{5}$$

where dthresh is the distance threshold.

If d_{ki} is associated with d_{lj} and the new tracklet is satisfied with the segmentation condition, the trajectory of d_{ki} is terminated and d_{lj} is regarded as a new object with a new tracklet. Otherwise, the detection response d_{lj} is added to the tracklet of d_{ki}. Tracklet segmentation can correct the deviation engendered in data association and is the groundwork to guarantee the tracking accuracy of our proposed framework.

2.2 Intra Frame-Window Tracklet Merging

Some segmented tracklets are different temporal domain pieces belonging to the same object so these tracklets should be merged together. In this step, the tracklets which are concluded to be the same track are merged into long tracklet. The association elements in this step are short tracklets in the same frame-window. A cost matrix C is needed in this step as well but with the different defination. $c_r(t_i, t_j)$ represents the association cost of tracklet t_i and tracklet t_j. We have the new formulation of cost matrix as follows:

$$c_t(t_i, t_j) = w_1 * dt(t_i, t_j) + w_2 * fg(t_i, t_j) + w_3 * dd(t_i, t_j) + w_4 * vd(t_i, t_j) \quad (6)$$

where $dt(t_i, t_j)$, $fg(t_i, t_j)$, $dd(t_i, t_j)$, $vd(t_i, t_j)$ represent the spatial distance, frame gap, speed difference, direction difference respectively.

The distance an object can move in a frame-window interval doesn't distinct seriously. Besides, an object usually moves towards a destination so the direction of the object track is trending to a regular orientation rather than randomly. Considering from temporal domain, we take frame gap of two tracklets into account as well. When calculate $dt(t_i, t_j)$, we regard tracklet as line segment and calculate the minimum distance of two tracklets.

$$dt(t_i, t_j) = \mathbf{min}\{\left\|(x_{t_i}^s, y_{t_i}^s), (x_{t_j}^e, y_{t_j}^e))\right\|, \left\|(x_{t_i}^e, y_{t_i}^e), (x_{t_j}^s, y_{t_j}^s))\right\|\} \quad (7)$$

where $\|\cdot\|$ is the L2 norm and (x_{ti}^s, y_{ti}^s) is the start location of tracklet t_i, (x_{tj}^e, y_{tj}^e) is the end location of the tracklet t_j.

$$fg(t_i, t_j) = f_{t_j}^s - f_{t_i}^e \quad (8)$$

where $f_{t_j}^s$ is the start frame number of t_j and $f_{t_i}^e$ is the final frame number of t_i.

$$dd(t_i, t_j) = \cos(tanline(t_i))) - \cos(tanline(t_j)) \quad (9)$$

where $cos(tanline(t_i))$ is the cosine of the tangent line of t_i.

$$vd(t_i, t_j) = |vel(O_{ti}) - vel(O_{tj})| \quad (10)$$

where $vel(O_{ti})$ is the velocity of the object in t_i and $vel(O_{tj})$ is the velocity of the object in t_j.

The merging modalities can be sorted into two modes distinguished by the frame gap $fg(t_i, t_j)$ between two tracklets. If two tracklets are continuous in time domain, the long tracklet is formed by merging the two short tracklets following time order directly. If two tracklets are not successive in time domain, the object location in the frame gap need to be filled up at first. The location (x_m, y_m) of an object in a missed frame f_m is the arithmetic mean of the forward-backward prediction. This is formulated as:

$$x_m(t_i) = x_{t_i}^e + vel(O_{t_i}) * (f_m - f_{t_i}^e) \tag{11}$$

$$x_m(t_j) = x_{t_j}^s + vel(O_{t_j}) * (f_{t_j}^s - f_m) \tag{12}$$

where $x_m(t_i)$ and $x_m(t_i)$ represent the predicted location according to the information of t_i and t_j. After calculating the object location in each frame of the frame gap, the three parts are merged into a long tracklet following the temporal order. The long tracklet obtained by tracklet segmentation and merging is more accurate than the original data association result of detection responses.

2.3   Cross Frame-Window Tracklet Merging

The two consecutive frame-window have overlap frames to assure tracklets of the same object have common piece. We denote the overlap frames number of t_i and t_j in the consecutive frame-window by $f_o(t_i, t_j)$. The overlap of two tracks of the same object in consecutive frame-window constraints the candidate tracklet of an object. This constraint formulates as

$$iscandidate \begin{cases} = 0 & f_o(t_i, t_j) < f_{othre} \\ = 1 & f_o(t_i, t_j) \geq f_{othre} \end{cases} \tag{13}$$

where f_{othre} is overlap frame threshold.

If the value of *iscancidate* is 1, t_j is regarded as the candidate tracklet of t_i. t_j and t_i are merged into one complete track of the object. This association strategy works in most situations except when occlusion take place in the overlap frames of two consecutive frame-window. This causes the two tracklets belonging to the same object has no overlap tracklet piece. In order to handle this, we put the left tracklet into two tracklet sets, and calculate the association cost matrix following the equations in the second association step. Generally, association by overlap rate can match most pairs of the tracklets effectively. Tracklets in the second frame-window are associated with the tracklets in the first frame-window and form the object track of the first two frame-window. To the subsequent frame-window, tracklets need to be associated with the preservative track of the all the frame-window before it.

3   Experimental Results

We carry on two experiment sets with seven sequences of different pedestrian tracking scenarios. Experiment set1(S1) aims at pedestrians in surveillance environment including four sequences of DORM1(D1), DORM2(D2), PARK(P1) and RAIN(R1). For these medium or small objects, background modeling detection algorithms are usually adopted. We apply vibe [20] algorithm to obtain detection results in S1. Since the performance of many state-of-art face detectors is favorable, experiment set2(S2) is focused on detection responses obtained by face detector. The datasets we used in this set are sequences FACE1(F1), FACE2(F2) and FACE3(F3). Face detector designed by Shiqi Yu[1] is employed to get the detection results.

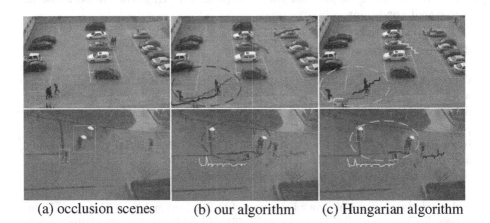

(a) occlusion scenes   (b) our algorithm   (c) Hungarian algorithm

Fig. 2. Tracking result of our algorithm and Hungarian algorithm handling spilt-merge conditions in sequences PARK and RAIN.

We use the same detection responses as input of Hungarian algorithm to carry on the comparative experiment. The experimental result is shown in Table 1. *OIC* is the objects number which is occluded in a sequence and *ROT* is the total number of tracks which are associated properly in the *OIC*. *AIO* means the tracking accuracy in handling occlusion, and $AIO = ROT/OIC$.

Table 1. Comparative results between our algorithm and Hungarian algorithm in seven sequences.

Dataset		OIC	Hungarian		Ours		Dataset		OIC	Hungarian		Ours	
			ROT	AIO	ROT	AIO				ROT	AIO	ROT	AIO
S1	D1	6.0	2.0	33.3 %	6.0	100.0 %	**S2**	F1	3.0	1.0	33.3 %	3.0	100.0 %
	D2	8.0	4.0	50.0 %	8.0	100.0 %		F2	3.0	0.0	0.0 %	3.0	100.0 %
	P1	10.0	1.0	10.0 %	9.0	90.0 %		F3	4.0	1.0	25.0 %	4.0	100.0 %
	R1	6.0	0.0	0.0 %	5.0	83.3 %	**S1+S2**		40.0	9.0	**22.5 %**	38.0	**95.0 %**

We can see in Table 1 that *AIO* of our algorithm is 95.0 % which is higher than 22.5 % of Hungarian Algorithm. The comparative tracking result is shown

---

[1] https://github.com/ShiqiYu/libfacedetection.

in Fig. 2. Besides, the missing detections don't influence the tracking result of our algorithm heavily because we associate tracklets intra frame-window. Since the appearance information is limited or even unavailable in some medium or small objects tracking scenes, we use no appearance information in our algorithm. Some experimental results can be more accurate if taking appearance information into account. In conclusion, these experiments prove that our algorithm are robust to occlusion and can maintain the pedestrian trajectory in occlusion or merge-spilt conditions.

4   Conclusions

Our work provides a multi-layer graph based multiple pedestrian tracking framework including three main steps, tracklet generation and segmentation, intra frame-window tracklet merging and cross frame-window tracklet merging. The proposed framework shows superior performance in different pedestrian tracking sequences including surveillance video and indoor video especially in merge-spilt and occlusion conditions. In future work, we plan to make our tracker reach real-time performance by more efficient implementation.

Acknowledgments. This work is supported by the National Natural Science Foundation of China (No. 61672429, No. 61502364, No. 61272288, No. 61231016), ShenZhen Science and Technology Foundation (JCYJ20160229172932237), Northwestern Polytechnical University (NPU) New AoXiang Star (No. G2015KY0301), Fundamental Research Funds for the Central Universities (No. 3102015AX007), NPU New People and Direction (No. 13GH014604).

References

1. Nagai, Y., Kamisaka, D., Makibuchi, N., Xu, J., Sakazawa, S.: 3D person tracking in world coordinates and attribute estimation with PDR. In: Proceedings of the 23rd ACM International Conference on Multimedia, MM 2015, pp. 1139–1142. ACM, New York (2015)
2. Tsokas, N.A., Kyriakopoulos, K.J.: Multi-robot multiple hypothesis tracking for pedestrian tracking. Auton. Robots 32(1), 63–79 (2012)
3. Kasuya, N., Kitahara, I., Kameda, Y., Ohta, Y.: Real-time soccer player tracking method by utilizing shadow regions. In: Proceedings of the 18th ACM International Conference on Multimedia, MM 2010, pp. 1319–1322. ACM, New York (2010)
4. Chu, C.-T., Hwang, J.-N., Pai, H.-I., Lan, K.-M.: Tracking human under occlusion based on adaptive multiple kernels with projected gradients. IEEE Trans. Multimedia 15(7), 1602–1615 (2013)
5. Wang, Z., Yoon, S., Park, D.S.: Online adaptive multiple pedestrian tracking in monocular surveillance video. Neural Comput. Appl. 1–15 (2016)
6. Kim, D., Kim, D.: Self-occlusion handling for human body motion tracking from 3D TOF image sequence. In: Proceedings of the 1st International Workshop on 3D Video Processing, 3DVP 2010, pp. 57–62. ACM, New York (2010)
7. Wen, L., Li, W., Yan, J., Lei, Z., Yi, D., Li, S.Z.: Multiple target tracking based on undirected hierarchical relation hypergraph. In: 2014 IEEE Conference on Computer Vision and Pattern Recognition (CVPR), pp. 1282–1289. IEEE (2014)

8. Shu, G., Dehghan, A., Oreifej, O., Hand, E., Shah, M.: Part-based multiple-person tracking with partial occlusion handling. In: 2012 IEEE Conference on Computer Vision and Pattern Recognition (CVPR), pp. 1815–1821. IEEE (2012)
9. Amitha Perera, A.G., Srinivas, C., Hoogs, A., Brooksby, G., Hu, W.: Multi-object tracking through simultaneous long occlusions and split-merge conditions. In: IEEE Computer Society Conference on Computer Vision and Pattern Recognition, vol. 1, pp. 666–673. IEEE (2006)
10. Tang, S., Andriluka, M., Schiele, B.: Detection and tracking of occluded people. Int. J. Comput. Vis. **110**(1), 58–69 (2014)
11. Possegger, H., Mauthner, T., Roth, P., Bischof, H.: Occlusion geodesics for online multi-object tracking. In: Proceedings of the IEEE Conference on Computer Vision and Pattern Recognition, pp. 1306–1313 (2014)
12. Lee, D.-Y., Sim, J.-Y., Kim, C.-S.: Multihypothesis trajectory analysis for robust visual tracking. In: The IEEE Conference on Computer Vision and Pattern Recognition (CVPR), June 2015
13. Lu, Y., Wu, T., Zhu, S.: Online object tracking, learning and parsing with and-or graphs. In: Proceedings of the IEEE Conference on Computer Vision and Pattern Recognition, pp. 3462–3469 (2014)
14. Li, Y., Zhu, J., Hoi, S.C.H.: Reliable patch trackers: robust visualtracking by exploiting reliable patches. In: The IEEE Conference on ComputerVision and Pattern Recognition (CVPR), June 2015
15. Hong, Z., Chen, Z., Wang, C., Mei, X., Prokhorov, D., Tao, D.: Multi-store tracker (muster): a cognitive psychology inspired approach toobject tracking. In: Proceedings of the IEEE Conference on Computer Vision and Pattern Recognition, pp. 749–758 (2015)
16. Vadivel, K.S., Ngo, T., Eckstein, M., Manjunath, B.S.: Eye tracking assisted extraction of attentionally important objects from videos. In: The IEEE Conference on Computer Vision and Pattern Recognition (CVPR), June 2015
17. Tang, S., Andres, B., Andriluka, M., Schiele, B.: Subgraph decomposition for multi-target tracking. In: Proceedings of the IEEE Conference on Computer Vision and Pattern Recognition, pp. 5033–5041 (2015)
18. Chari, V., Lacoste-Julien, S., Laptev, I., Sivic, J.: On pairwise costs for network flow multi-object tracking. In: The IEEE Conference on Computer Vision and Pattern Recognition (CVPR), June 2015
19. Kuhn, H.W.: The hungarian method for the assignment problem. Navalresearch Logistics Q. **2**(1–2), 83–97 (1955)
20. Hofmann, M., Tiefenbacher, P., Rigoll, G.: Background segmentation with feedback: the pixel-based adaptivesegmenter. In: 2012 IEEE Computer Society Conference on Computer Vision and Pattern Recognition Workshops (CVPRW), pp. 38–43. IEEE (2012)

DNA and Emerging Biometrics

An Adaptive Weighted Degree Kernel to Predict the Splice Site

Tianqi Wang$^{(\boxtimes)}$, Ke Yan, Yong Xu, and Jinxing Liu

Shenzhen Graduate School, Bio-Computing Research Center,
Harbin Institute of Technology, Shenzhen, China
hemaduhit@gmail.com

Abstract. The weighted degree kernel is a good means to predict the splice site. Its prediction performance is affected by positions in the DNA sequence of nucleotide bases. Based on this fact, we propose confusing positions in this article. Using the confusing positions and the key positions which we proposed in previous work, we construct a weight array to obtain adaptive weighted degree kernel, a kind of string kernel to predict the splice site. Then to prove the efficient and advance of the method, we use the public available dataset to train support vector machines to compare the performance of the adaptive weighted degree kernel and conventional weighted degree kernel. The results show that the adaptive weighted degree kernel has better performance than the weighted degree kernel.

Keywords: Splice site prediction · Adaptive weighted degree kernel · Confusing positions · Weight array · Support vector machine

1 Introduction

Owing to the development of the sequencing technology, the DNA sequences have an explosive growth. There is a pressing need for a set of tools to analyze these DNA sequences. An important problem is to locate genes in the DNA sequences, which is also called gene annotation. Most eukaryotic protein-coding genes are composed of exons and introns. The border between an exon and an intron is referred to as a splice site. The accurate prediction of splice sites plays a key role in the annotation of genes in eukaryotes [1]. Obviously, there exists two kinds of splice sites, the splice site at the beginning of an intron is termed as a donor site, and the splice site at the end of an intron is termed as an acceptor site. Fortunately, for both donor site and acceptor site, the dinucleotides in the intron are highly conserved. For a donor site, the dinucleotide in the intron contains G and T. For an acceptor site, the dinucleotide in the intron contains A and G. However, there are a large number of GT and AG dinucleotides in eukaryotic genes, but only 0.1 % of them are true splice sites [2]. So how to identify whether or not a GT/AG dinucleotide is a true splice site is always one of the most important and challenging tasks in bioinformatics [3].

Many methods have been proposed for splice site prediction. In recent years, support vector machines (SVMs) and related kernel methods are used widely due to their high accuracy and capability to deal with high-dimensional and large scale

© Springer International Publishing AG 2016
Z. You et al. (Eds.): CCBR 2016, LNCS 9967, pp. 739–746, 2016.
DOI: 10.1007/978-3-319-46654-5_81

datasets as well as flexibility of feature selection [4]. Among these methods, the string kernel is a simple but efficient means, which reflects the similarity of two sequences based on their content. For splice site prediction, the weighted degree (WD) kernel can get a more satisfactory performance than other string kernels [5]. Differing from other kernels, the WD kernel considers the positional information, in a way similar to the Position Weight Matrix (PWM). The PWM is popular in representing patterns in biological sequences. For splice site prediction, it can get a satisfactory performance. And this method shows that the bases near the splice site play key roles in splice site prediction.

Although the WD kernel considers the positional information, it only takes into account the base match in the two sequences in the same position. However, whether the position of the base match has effects on the performance of the WD kernel or not is still to be observed. In this article, we discuss the effect of the position on the performance of the WD kernel and construct an adaptive WD kernel to exploit the position information of the base match by assigning different multipliers to matches in different positions. The result shows that the new kernel can get a better performance in predicting the splice site.

In the next section, we will first introduce the PWM and WD kernel briefly. Then we will introduce a method to represent the probability of matching in each position. We will also show the concepts of the confusing positions. And we will introduce the adaptive WD kernel. Finally, we will have an experiment to compare the performance of the WD kernel and adaptive WD kernel.

2   Method

2.1   PWM and WD Kernel

The PWM is proposed to represent patterns in biological sequences. In PWM each row represents a symbol of the alphabet and each column represents a position. So the PWM proposed for nucleotides in DNA sequences has 4 rows, because there are 4 symbols, A, G, C and T. For splice site prediction, the PWM method has a satisfactory performance, which shows that the base near the splice site is important [6].

The WD kernel is a kind of string kernel and is defined as

$$k(x_1, x_2) = \sum_{\omega=1}^{d} w_\omega \sum_{i=1}^{N-d} I\big(u_{\omega,i}(x_1) = u_{\omega,i}(x_2)\big) \tag{1}$$

where $w_\omega = d - \omega + 1$, ω is so-called "degree", which represents the length of the match, $I(\cdot)$ is an indicator of the content in the brackets, x_1 and x_2 are two sequences, and $u_{\omega,i}(x) = x_i x_{i+1} \cdots x_{i+\omega-1}$ for all i and $1 \leq \omega \leq d$ [7].

The main idea of the WD kernel is to calculate the similarity of two sequences by counting the matches in the two sequences. The meaning of match is that two symbols or symbol strings which are in the same position of two sequences respectively are the same. The WD kernel considers that two sequences with more and longer matches have higher similarity, so such two sequences should get a higher score. Figure 1 shows an intuitive example. The figure tells us that there are four matches in the two sequences (shown as the highlighted regions). Since the lengths of these matches are different, the weight of each match in the WD kernel is also different. Note that due to the definition, the WD kernel needs to compare the two sequences again and again. At first, a comparison about a substring the length of which is 1 is performed at every position. If a match is found at this time, the weight of this match is w_1. Obviously, if the length of the two sequences is 20, there are totally 20 comparisons about a substring the length of which is 1. By that analogy, when the length of the match is over 1, we can get the meaning of w_2, w_3, and so on. So if there is a match 'AGA', the score of the WD kernel contains 3 w_1 for A, G, A respectively, 2 w_2 for AG, GA respectively and 1 w_3 for AGA [8].

Obviously, for two sequences, the result of the WD kernel depends on the number of the matches and the length of each match. Note that the WD kernel does not take the position of the match into account. So if the two sequences have one match the length of which is 3, the WD kernel will get the same value no matter where the match is. But according to the conclusion of the PWM, the base near the splice site is important to splice site prediction. So in the next section, we will explore whether the position of the match has the effect on the performance of the WD kernel.

2.2   Possibility of Matching

The WD kernel is based on the matches in the two sequences. In order to explore the relationship between the position of the match and the performance of the WD kernel, we should define a variable for each position to measure the possibility of matching in this position. We use the distribution of four nucleotide bases in one position to measure the possibility of matching. Specifically, we use the variance of the probability of the four nucleotide bases in one position to represent the distribution of four nucleotide bases. The formulation is as follows.

$$d_i = \sum_{b \in B} \left(p_{i,b} - \bar{p} \right)^2 \tag{2}$$

where $B = \{A, G, C, T\}$, $p_{i,b}$ is probability of each base b in position i and $\bar{p}$ is the average value of $p_{i,b}$.

Obviously, the higher the variance is, the higher the probability of there being a match is. Actually, if there is only one kind of nucleotide in a certain position, which means there must be a match in this position for any two sequences, the variance in this

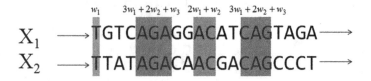

Fig. 1. The idea of the WD kernel

position will be the highest. So we think that the distribution of four nucleotide bases is a good choice to measure the possibility of matching. A position with a high variance is considered to be a conserved position.

2.3 Confusing Position

In our previous work, we have proved that some positions near the splice site have significant effect on the performance of the WD kernel. We call these positions "key positions". Besides these positions which contribute to splice site prediction significantly, some positions may limit the performance of the WD kernel. In this article, we intend to explore whether such positions exist. And these positions are called "confusing positions".

The main idea of selecting "confusing positions" is described in Fig. 2. The meaning of "confusing position" is that in such a position, the bases in the negatives are more conserved than those in the positives. Though it seems unreasonable, it really happens in the DNA sequences. When dealing with these positions, the WD kernel prefers to treat negatives as true splice site due to the higher possibility of matching.

In previous chapter, we have used the variance of the probability of the four nucleotide bases in one position to represent the possibility of matching. So we define a confusing factor f_i^c as follows.

$$f_i^c = d_i^+ - d_i^- \tag{3}$$

where d_i^+ is the variance of the four bases in position i in positives and d_i^- is the variance of the four bases in position i in negatives. In this article, we regard the position of which the confusing factor is below zero as a confusing position.

2.4 Weight Array and Adaptive WD Kernel

According to what we discussed above and the previous work, no matter for donor splice site or acceptor splice site, the effect of the positions near the splice site on the performance of the WD kernel is different. Some positions play a key role while some positions play a confusing role.

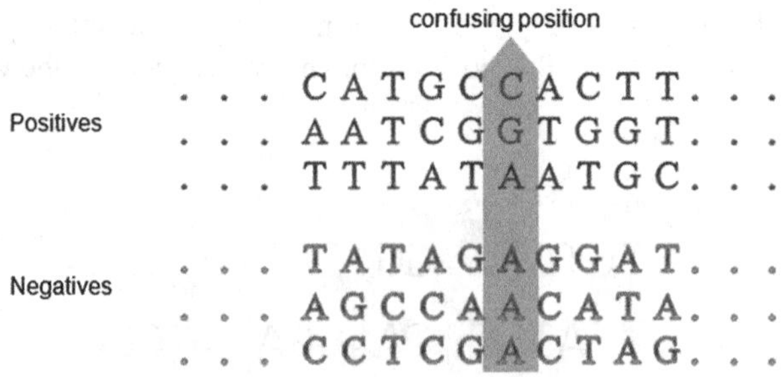

Fig. 2. The main idea of selecting confusing positions

Our previous work has shown that the effect of the positions on the performance of the WD kernel can be divided into 3 levels. Based on this fact and what we discussed above, in this article, we divide the positions near the target into four kinds include a special key position, some key positions, some common positions and some confusing positions. To distinguish these positions, we construct a weight array to assign different weight to each position. For key positions, we assign a high weight to strengthen their effect and for confusing positions we assign a low weight to weaken their effect. Based on this principle, the special key position is assigned the highest weight, and the second highest is the key positions. The confusing positions have the lowest weight.

Using this weight array, we adapt the WD kernel as follows.

$$k(x_1, x_2) = \sum_{\omega=1}^{d} w_\omega \sum_{i=1}^{N-d} \beta_{\omega,i} \cdot I\left(u_{\omega,i}(x_1) = u_{\omega,i}(x_2)\right) \tag{4}$$

where $\beta_{\omega,i}$ is the average weight ranging from the weight of the position i to the weight of the position $i + \omega$. In this article, this kernel is called "adaptive WD kernel".

3   Results and Discussions

3.1   Dataset

To construct a reliable experiment, we use the publicly available Homo sapiens splice site dataset (HS3D) [9] as the model dataset, which was derived from human genes. The dataset contains 2796 confirmed true donor splice sites, 271,937 pseudo-donor sites, 2880 confirmed true acceptor sites, and 329,374 pseudo-acceptor sites.

3.2   Selecting the Confusing Positions

In this step, we use the whole dataset to calculate the confusing factor for each position to select the confusing position. First we calculate each base's probability in each position in positives and negatives respectively, then we get two 140*4 position-base matrix, which is also called "PPM" [10]. Using PPM we can get the confusing factor for acceptor and donor easily. Due to our previous work, the key positions have been selected out. For selecting confusing positions, Figs. 3 and 4 are the graphs of the confusing factors for donor splice site and acceptor splice site respectively.

As we can see from the Figs. 3 and 4, if we set 0 as the threshold of the confusing position, there are 6 confusing positions near the donor splice site and 2 confusing positions near the acceptor splice site totally. In detail, we treat position 12, 66, 135, 136, 137 and 139 as the confusing positions for donor splice site and treat position 83 and 102 as the confusing positions for acceptor splice site.

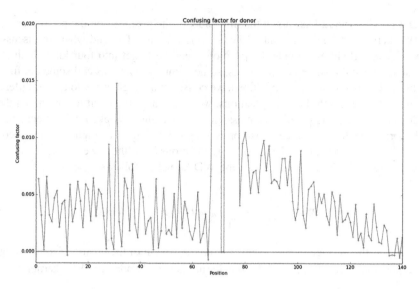

Fig. 3. The confusing factor for donor splice site

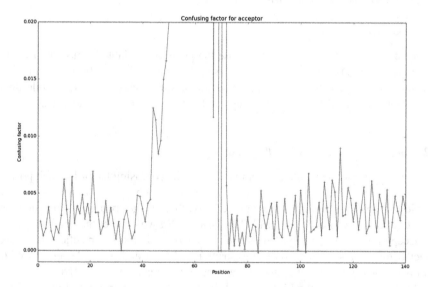

Fig. 4. The confusing factor for acceptor splice site

3.3   Performance of the Adaptive WD Kernel

In this step, in order to construct the weight array, we set the weight of common positions, key positions and special key positions as values 0.9, 1.0, and 1.1 respectively. Besides, we assign 0 to the weight of confusing positions. For the parameter of the WD kernel, we use the value ranging from 12 to 24.

Table 1. Performance of the WD and adaptive WD for donor (10-fold cross validation)

d	Recall		Precision		MCC	
	WD	Adaptive	WD	Adaptive	WD	Adaptive
12	0. 9673	0. 9670	0. 9308	0. 9317	0. 8962	0. 8969
13	0. 9663	0. 9666	0. 9307	0. 9316	0. 8951	0. 8966
14	0. 9655	0. 9663	0. 9306	0. 9319	0. 8944	0. 8965
15	0. 9655	0. 9659	0. 9313	0. 9313	0. 8951	0. 8955
16	0. 9659	0. 9662	0. 9310	0. 9313	0.8951	0. 8959
17	0. 9659	0. 9666	0. 9316	0. 9313	0. 8958	0. 8963
18	0. 9655	0. 9666	0. 9313	0. 9310	0. 8951	0. 8959
19	0. 9655	0. 9666	0. 9316	0. 9310	0. 8954	0. 8959
20	0. 9656	0. 9663	0. 9310	0. 9303	0. 8948	0. 8948
21	0. 9663	0. 9663	0. 9313	0. 9307	0. 8959	0. 8952
22	0. 9663	0. 9663	0. 9310	0. 9307	0. 8955	0. 8952
23	0. 9663	0. 9666	0. 9310	0. 9307	0. 8955	0. 8956
24	0. 9662	0. 9669	0. 9303	0. 9304	0. 8948	0. 8956

Table 2. Performance of the WD and adaptive WD for acceptor (10-fold cross validation)

d	Recall		Precision		MCC	
	WD	Adaptive	WD	Adaptive	WD	Adaptive
12	0. 9542	0. 9559	0. 9085	0. 9072	0. 8590	0. 8592
13	0. 9545	0. 9559	0. 9080	0. 9066	0. 8588	0. 8585
14	0. 9545	0. 9559	0. 9083	0. 9072	0. 8591	0. 8592
15	0. 9559	0. 9576	0. 9078	0. 9073	0. 8599	0. 8610
16	0. 9562	0. 9573	0. 9075	0. 9076	0. 8599	0. 8610
17	0. 9566	0. 9576	0. 9075	0. 9076	0. 8602	0. 8613
18	0. 9563	0. 9583	0. 9081	0. 9080	0. 8605	0. 8624
19	0. 9559	0. 9583	0. 9074	0. 9080	0. 8595	0. 8624
20	0. 9562	0. 9590	0. 9072	0. 9080	0. 8595	0. 8631
21	0. 9562	0. 9587	0. 9063	0. 9080	0. 8585	0. 8627
22	0. 9566	0. 9587	0. 9066	0. 9080	0. 8592	0. 8627
23	0. 9569	0. 9590	0. 9070	0. 9072	0. 8599	0. 8621
24	0. 9569	0. 9597	0. 9067	0. 9075	0. 8595	0. 8631

The SVMs are trained using the scikit-learn machine learning toolbox in Python [11] and the parameters of SVM were set to C = 1 and tol = 1e-3. Tables 1 and 2 show the performance of the adaptive WD kernel and the WD kernel.

As we can see from the table, for both donor splice site and acceptor splice site, the performance of the adaptive WD kernel is more satisfactory than the performance of the WD kernel.

4 Conclusion

Our previous work has shown that for splice site prediction, the positions have different effect on the performance of the WD kernel. In this article, we find that there are some confusing positions for donor splice site and acceptor splice site. Due to the different effect of each position, we construct a weight array to represent the effects. Then we propose an adaptive WD kernel using the weight array. And the results show that when the confusing position is taken into account, the adaptive WD kernel can get more satisfactory performance than the conventional WD kernel. So we can prove that the confusing position is useful and our method is feasible.

Acknowledgments. This research was partially supported by the Shenzhen Municipal Science and Technology Innovation Council (Nos. CXZZ20140904154910774).

References

1. Baten, A.K.M.A., Halgamuge, S.K., Chang, B., Wickramarachchi, N.: Biological sequence data preprocessing for classification: a case study in splice site identification. In: Liu, D., Fei, S., Hou, Z., Zhang, H., Sun, C. (eds.) ISNN 2007, Part II. LNCS, vol. 4492, pp. 1221–1230. Springer, Heidelberg (2007)
2. Sören, S., et al.: Accurate splice site prediction using support vector machines. BMC Bioinform. 8(Suppl. 10), S7 (2007)
3. Baten, K.M.A.A., Halgamuge, S.K., Chang, B.C.H.: Fast splice site detection using information content and feature reduction. BMC Bioinform. 9(Suppl. 12), S8 (2008)
4. Bari, A.T.M., Golam, M., Reaz, R., Jeong, B.-S.: Effective DNA encoding for splice site prediction using SVM. Match Commun. Math. Comput. Chem. 71(1), 241–258 (2014)
5. Benhur, A., et al.: Support vector machines and kernels for computational biology. PLoS Comput. Biol. 4(10), 1051–1056 (2008)
6. Staden, R.: Computer methods to locate signals in nucleic acid sequences. Nucleic Acids Res. 12(1 Pt 2), 505–519 (1984)
7. Gunnar, R., Sonnenburg, S.: Accurate splice site detection for Caenorhabditis elegans. In: Kernel Methods in Computational Biology, p. 277 (2004)
8. Sören, S., Rätsch, G., Rieck, K.: Large scale learning with string kernels. In: Large Scale Kernel Machines, pp. 73–103 (2007)
9. Pollastro, P., Rampone, S.: HS3D, a dataset of Homo Sapiens splice regions, and its extraction procedure from a major public database. Int. J. Mod. Phys. C 13(08), 1105–1117 (2002)
10. Roderic, G.: An Introduction to Position Specific Scoring Matrices. http://bioinformatica. upf.edu. Accessed 12 Nov 2013
11. Pedregosa, F., et al.: Scikit-learn: machine learning in Python. J. Mach. Learn. Res. 12, 2825–2830 (2011)

The Prediction of Human Genes in DNA Based on a Generalized Hidden Markov Model

Rui Guo[✉], Ke Yan, Wei He, and Jian Zhang

Bio-Computing Research Center, Shenzhen Graduate School, Harbin Institute of Technology, Shenzhen, China
570930945@qq.com

Abstract. The Generalized Hidden Markov Model (GHMM) has been proved to be an excellently general probabilistic model of the gene structure of human genomic sequences. It can simultaneously incorporate different signal descriptions like splicing sites and content descriptions, for instance, compositional features of exons and introns. Enjoying its flexibility and convincing probabilistic underpinnings, we integrate some other modification of submodels and then implement a prediction program of Human Genes in DNA. The program has the capacity to predict multiple genes in a sequence, to deal with partial as well as complete genes, and to predict consistent sets of genes occurring on either or both DNA strands. More importantly, it also can perform well for longer sequences with an unknown number of genes in them. In the experiments, the results show that the proposed method has better performance in prediction accuracy than some existing methods, and over 70 % of exons can be identified exactly.

Keywords: Gene prediction · WWAM · IMM · GHMM · The prefix sum arrays · The method based on similarity weighting of sequence patterns

1 Introduction

In recent years, with the development and gradual promotion of the third-generation gene sequencing technology [1], its sequencing cost becomes lower while each sequencing length becomes much longer and sequencing accuracy much higher, we have been accumulating the higher quality of genome sequences for all kinds of organisms at a faster rate. In order to tap the potential value of these data, a good many gene-finding programs, which identify gene in genomic DNA sequences by computational methods, are routinely used by gene annotation project members to help identify genes in that newly sequenced regions [2].

A complete gene structure in eukaryotes generally consists of some different functional elements which are divided into signal sensors and content sensors [3]. Signal sensors are regarded as the basic method of finding the presence of functional sites with fixed length, such as promoters, start and stop codons, splice sites, branch points, etc. As for content sensors, they are measures that try to classify a DNA region into coding and noncoding. The measures are mainly based on extrinsic similarity with a biologically characterized sequence, e.g., protein sequence, cDNA or expressed sequence tag (EST)

© Springer International Publishing AG 2016
Z. You et al. (Eds.): CCBR 2016, LNCS 9967, pp. 747–755, 2016.
DOI: 10.1007/978-3-319-46654-5_82

sequence, and intrinsic statistical properties such as codon usage(a triplet of DNA bases), hexamer frequency, nucleotide composition, GC content and base occurrence periodicity.

Many early approaches only focused on those signal sensors to roughly locate the position of gene in genomic DNA sequences. Subsequently, in order to predict entire gene structures precisely, the approaches have been developed by integrating multiple types of information which include splice signal sensors, compositional properties of coding and non-coding DNA, and database homology searching in some cases. Some typical programs show: GENEID [4], Genie [5], GENSCAN [2] and AUGUSTUS [6]. However, early available programs have two important limitations [7]: one is that their algorithms assume that the input sequence contains exactly one complete gene. If the sequence contains a partial or multiple genes, the results they provide do not make sense. The other is that due to evaluating by independent control sets, the accuracy is usually worse than originally thought. Fortunately, some methods emerging afterwards supply these gaps, such as GENSCAN and AUGUSTUS. They use an explicitly double-stranded genomic sequence model to simultaneously analyze potential genes occurring on both DNA strands. Additionally, the model treats the general case in which the sequence can contain a partial gene, a complete gene, multiple complete genes, or no gene at all. The combination of double-stranded nature of model and the capacity to deal with variable numbers of genes may prove useful for long human genomic segments, e.g. those of a hundred kilobases or more, which usually contain more than a gene on one or both strands. We follow the model design, integrate some other different innovations of submodels and implement a prediction system of Human Genes in DNA. The system has functional advantages mentioned above and a high performance in accuracy.

Finally, regardless of benefits of function and performance in our model, the difficulties of handling overlapping transcription units and explicitly addressing alternative splicing are still presence. As both of them are still challenging problems and short board of all gene prediction programs, we will try to further exploit it individually in future work.

2   Method

2.1   Algorithmic Issues of the GHMM

Hidden Markov Models (HMM) has been used in pattern recognition for decades and its applicability to computational biology has also been widely recognized. But as we know, a standard Hidden Markov model is just a state-based generative model which transitions stochastically from state to state and emits a single symbol from each state [8]. Although it can produce a certain effect in gene prediction, the recognition accuracy is still far from satisfactory. The GHMM have a better performance by allowing an individual state to emit a string of symbols rather than only one symbol at a time. The model is generally parameterized by its transition probabilities, state duration (i.e., feature length) probabilities, and state emission probabilities. These probabilities influence the output of the model by determining which sequences are more likely to be emitted and which series of states are more likely to be visited by it.

Eukaryotic gene prediction with a GHMM means to decode an input sequence into a most probable set of putative functional segments having a specific biological significance [9]. Suppose that X denotes an input DNA sequence with a length n, $x_i (1 \leq i \ll k)$ denotes a subsequence of X,and its length is $d_i (1 \leq d_i \leq n)$, we can get that $X = x_1 x_2 \cdots x_k$ (the concatenation of subsequences), and define $\emptyset$ is a correct parse corresponding to the input sequence, having that $\emptyset = \{(q_1, x_1), \cdots, (q_i, x_i), \cdots (q_k, x_k)\} (1 \leq i \leq k)$, and q_i denotes a hidden state which signifies a specific functional segment mentioned above. But in general, we still need to supplement two additional states producing no output, as start and end flags of decoding operation of a program. And then, how to set the optimal value of $\emptyset$ is what we concern and difficult to gain. In the case of standard Hidden Markov Models, the well-known Viterbi algorithm [10], a dynamic programming algorithm with running time linear to the sequence length for a fixed number of states, is the most classic means to solve with this problem, similarly, it is also applicable to the case of GHMM. However, since each state can emit more than one symbol at a time, the algorithm needs to be modified to result in the following optimization problem [11]:

$$
\begin{aligned}
\Phi_{optimal} &= \arg \max p(\Phi|X) \\
&= \arg \max \frac{p(\Phi, X)}{p(X)} \\
&\simeq \arg \max p(\Phi, X) \\
&= \arg \max p(X|\Phi) p(\Phi) \\
&= \arg \max \prod_{i=1}^{k} P_e(x_i|q_i, d_i) p_t(q_i|q_{i-1}) p_d(d_i|q_i)
\end{aligned}
\tag{1}
$$

where $P_e(x_i|q_i, d_i)$ means the probability that state q_i emits the subsequence x_i, given duration $d_i, P_t(q_i|q_{i-1})$ denotes the probability that the GHMM translates from q_{i-1} state to state q_i; and $P_d(d_i|q_i)$ is the probability that state q_i has the duration d_i, the arg max is to select the best one from all parses of the DNA sequence into well-formed exon-intron structures.

We introduce a common approach, named the Prefix Sum Arrays (PSA), to evaluate Eq. 1. According to a dynamic programming algorithm, the method needs to allocate several arrays for one per variable-length feature state and assess them left-to-right along the length of the input sequence. It can also conclude that the values in the aforementioned arrays represent cumulative scores for prefixes of the sequence only in term of the surface meaning of its name. Here, we show its recursive expressions of the GHMM in log space as follows:

$$
R_I(q_j, r_j) = \arg \max_{q_i} (R_I(q_i, r_i) + R_T(q_i, q_j) + R_D(q_i, q_j) + R_C(q_i, q_j, r_j))
\tag{2}
$$

$$
q_i, q_j \in Q
$$

In Eq. 2, Q denotes the set of states in GHMM, $R_I(q_i, r_i)$ denotes the logarithmic inductive score for signal q_i in phase r_i, and the next three expressions respectively mean the logarithmic scores of state translation from q_i to q_j, state duration of content region delimited by signals q_i and q_j, and sequence emission between current signal q_j and predecessor q_i in phase r_j, additionally, it is still necessary to emphasize that $r_j = r_i$ or $r_j = (r_i \pm \Delta) \bmod 3$ (Δ denotes the sequence length of special putative state), depending on the different situations.

2.2   Modeling Gene Structure

To expound completely the process of gene prediction based on a GHMM, Fig. 1 shows the states of the Hidden Markov Models in the system and some certain probabilities of possible transitions between them (as to others that cannot be depicted explicitly at the arrows, their values are always 1). In Fig. 1, Esng denotes a single exon gene; EI, E and EF respectively denote the first, internal and last exon of a multi exon gene (the exon only referred to the coding part of exons); I is the intron, IR is the intergenic region between genes, DSS and ASS separately are the donor and acceptor splice sites including branch point, as for the states S and T, they are the start codon emitting the string ATG with probability 1 and stop codon generally only including TAG, TGA and TAA whose emission probabilities are respectively 24 %, 48 % and 28 %. Furthermore, the states with names beginning with r mean to be on the reverse strand, and the exponents (0, 1, 2) stand for the phase of the reading frame, and for an exon it denotes the position of the last coding nucleotide of the exon in its codon.

In the GHMM, each state emits a random DNA string with random length, and their emission probabilities mainly depends on the annotated sequences which correspond to the respective biometrics in training set. In order to seize the feature information of this distribution for each state, we mainly made use of five established models, a Markov chain, a higher order windowed weight array model (WWAM), a weight array model (WAM) [12], simple interpolated Markov Models (IMM) [13] and the method based on similarity weighting of sequence patterns [6], whose good results have been verified by other gene finders.

In term of the details of the Markov Chain, WAM and WWAM, there is no need to elaborate too much again, since that they have been widely used in bioinformatics for many years, and here, we briefly illustrate our usage on them. We adopt a Markov model of order 5 to the model of non-coding region such as I, rI and IR as mentioned above meanwhile using a WAM of order 2 and a WWAM of order 2 and of window size 5 in other related states. As for the IMM, it's a special case in our coding models, in which only the transition probabilities of order 5 and 4 are considered and the respective inter-polation weights are either 0 or 1 with the frequency threshold of occurrence of the given string in training set 400. Finally, we focus on the method of similarity-based weighting of sequence patterns, which is solely applied in the DSS model. Given a fixed sequence pattern size, training patterns $q_1, q_2 \cdots, q_m$ and a similarity scoring function s, weighting pairs of patterns, we estimate the probability that a random pattern equals a given pattern q as

$$p(q) = c \sum_{i=1}^{m} s(q, q_i) \tag{3}$$

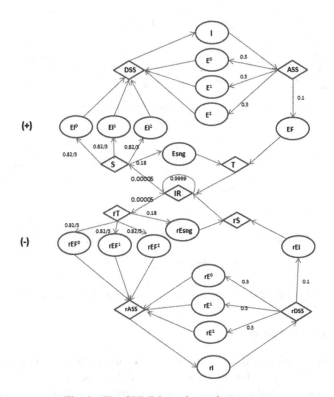

Fig. 1. The GHMM topology of our system

where c is a modulus keeping that the sum of all p(q) is 1. Regarding the similarity scoring function s, we follow the definition in AUGUSTUS as

$$s(r,q) = \begin{cases} 1 & \text{if } r=q \\ 0.001 & \text{if } r \text{ and } q \text{ differ at exactly one pos}, \\ 0 & \text{otherwise} \end{cases} \tag{4}$$

and the resulting distribution obtained by this way is the discretely smoothed empirical distribution which respects the complicated statistical dependencies that exist between the nucleotide positions.

Figure 2 shows detailed model distribution of human gene structure with single and multiple exons in our system. According to it, we once more simply describe the emission distribution for those states which are not mentioned above. The models of fixed length, translation initiation motif and ASS model respectively emitting 20 and 23 nucleotides per time, are trained by the WWAM of order 2 and window size 5, while the model of translation end motif emitting 30 nucleotides per time introduces the WAM of order 2 to evaluate.

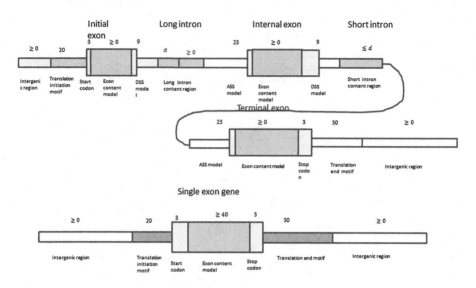

Fig. 2. My model distribution of gene structure with single and multiple exons

2.3   Intron Length Model

In the GHMM, length distribution of states with variable length, such as intron and exon, is also significant information which can determine the prediction accuracy. We adopt a typical smoothing technique using a kernel estimator with discrete Gaussian kernel function and variable bandwidth to evaluate them. And because of compact length density of coding exons (only 0.3 % of the human exons were longer than 3000 nucleotides), the evaluation effect is fairly satisfactory. However, to a long biological intron, for example, the human neurexin-3 gene on chromosome 14 has an intron of length 479 Kb, results in a large range of length span, and it is practically infeasible to explicitly model the whole length distribution in a HMM. In order to deal with this problem, we have combined the method mentioned above with a simple geometric distribution to model it. Define a length threshold d, a probability parameter p for determining to choose a short intron, and parameter q which is only used by the geometric distribution function, the concrete formula expression as follows:

$$P(M = l) = \begin{cases} pP(L = l)/P(L \leq d) & l \leq d \\ (1 - p)(1 - q)^{l-d-1}q & l > d \end{cases} \tag{5}$$

where M denotes a model variable to be evaluated and L denotes the variable based on the discrete Gaussian kernel function and variable bandwidth. Firstly, to keep the continuity of functions, we can get an equation that $P_-(M = d + 1) = P_+(M = d)$, stating that there is no jump in the distribution of M between positions d and $d + 1$. Secondly, we need to set q so that the expectations of M and L are equivalent, when $M > d, L > d$, for instance, $d + 1/q = E[L|L > d]$. Thirdly, to better take into account both of accuracy (large d) and speed (small d), we choose the smallest d so that parameter p approximately equal to $P(L \leq d)$. Finally, combining all of the three points, we have obtained a group of evaluation values using my training set that $q \approx 1/1764, p \approx 0.47, d = 592$.

2.4 Training Data Set

The training set was retrieved from 22 autosomal sequences of human genome, which is in the light of the corresponding version of the gene annotation files issued in Genbank. After getting rid of the case in which sequences are overlapping with another sequence by our self-made checking procedure, we luckily extract most of gene sequences with single transcription as the master training sets, about 941 sequences, and randomly select a certain number of genes with multiple transcriptions, e.g. approximately 400, as the addition of our training set (naturally, the genes of test sets provided by AUGUSTUS, h178 and sag178, have been removed from it). Then, making most use of the two data sets, we train the each relevant state model in our GHMM.

3   Results and Discussion

We tested our program on two data sets, called h178 and sag178, which can be downloaded from the official website of AUGUSTUS. The h178 is a set of 178 human genomic sequences which are from EMBL and have been used by the author of GENSCAN for evaluation; each sequence only contains one complete gene and their mean sequence length is 7169 bases, shortest 622 and longest 86640 bases. The sag178 has the same 178 human genes in which 40 genes are single exon genes, but all of them are included in a set of 43 sequences on both strands. These sequences are taken from Guigo et al. (2000) as like the h178 and have been done some necessary special process, their mean length is 177 kilo bases (shortest 70, longest 282) and the average number of genes is 4.1.

Table 1. Accuracy results on human data sets h178

		base	exon	gene
GENEID	sn	89	66	14
	sp	91	75	13
GENSCAN	sn	97	83	40
	sp	86	75	36
AUGUSTUS	sn	93	80	46
	sp	90	80	45
OUR SYSTEM	sn	92	74	31
	sp	89	72	27

In order to evaluate the gene prediction performance, we also adopted the usual measures, sensitivity and specificity, for a feature such as base, exon and gene. The sensitivity is defined as the number of correctly predicted features divided by the number of annotated features. The specificity is the ratio of the number of correctly predicted features to the number of predicted features. A predicted exon is considered to be correct if both splice sites are at the annotated position of an exon. A gene is considered to be predicted correctly if all the exons are correctly predicted and no additional exons are not in the annotation. Predicted partial genes were counted as predicted genes. The testing results on both of test sets are depicted in the following tables (Tables 1 and 2).

Table 2. Accuracy results on human data set sag178

		base	exon	gene
GENEID	sn	89	67	17
	sp	78	60	17
GENSCAN	sn	94	68	18
	sp	64	45	14
AUGUSTUS	sn	93	78	40
	sp	81	71	35
OUR SYSTEM	sn	90	73	23
	sp	76	61	19

Comparing the above two tables carefully, we can analyze that my system can have similar prediction accuracy with AUGUSTUS and GENSCAN in term of the mean of sensitivity and specificity on the base and exon level. GENSCAN is more sensitive, AUGUSTUS is more specific, and our program is indeed worse a little in both aspects but superior than GENEID. Whether on long or short gene set, our model predicted exactly more genes than GENEID and GENESCAN, stating that the design combining main model structures of the AUGUSTUS and GENSCAN with the more precise evaluation of length distribution in intron is effective. However, the number of genes predicted correctly is only slightly higher than GENSCAN's while far lower than AUGUSUTS', we guess, which is likely due to ignoring the influence of the GC-content in genes. Besides, comparatively speaking, our model tends to produce many more genes in which only partly exons are evaluated correctly and is therefore less specific than others. To solve with this problem, it is necessary to introduce some further follow-up design and optimization.

4   Conclusion

In our paper, with the integration and modification of some mainly related submodels, we personally implemented a GHMM-based gene prediction system. Despite a certain degree of performance promotion, there is still a lot of space to further improve by considering the influence of the GC-content in genes and training a better classification model of spite sites with other superior machine learning methods like SVM. In the future, we will continue to deepen our research from two above-mentioned aspects.

Acknowledgement. This article is partly supported by the Shenzhen Municipal Science and Technology Innovation Council (Nos. JCYJ20140904154645958).

References

1. Cairui, L., Changsong, Z., Guoli, S.: Recent progress in gene mapping through high-throughput sequencing technology and forward genetic approaches. Yi chuan = Hereditas/Zhongguo yi chuan xue hui bian ji **37**(8), 765–776 (2015)
2. Burge, C., Karlin, S.: Prediction of complete gene structures in human genomic DNA. J. Mol. Biol. **268**(1), 78–94 (1997)
3. Burset, M., Seledtsov, I.A., Solovyev, V.V.: Analysis of canonical and non-canonical splice sites in mammalian genomes. Nucleic Acids Res. **28**(21), 4364–4375 (2000)
4. Guigó, R., et al.: Prediction of gene structure ☆. J. Mol. Biol. **226**(1), 141–157 (1992)
5. Haussler, D., David, K., Reese, M.G., Eeckman, F.H.: A generalized hidden Markov model for the recognition of human genes in DNA. In: Proceedings of the International Conference on Intelligent Systems for Molecular Biology, St. Louis (1996)
6. Stanke, M., Waack, S.: Gene prediction with a hidden Markov model and a new intron submodel. Bioinformatics **19**(suppl 2), 215–225 (2003)
7. Fickett, J.W.: Finding genes by computer: the state of the art. Trends Genet. **12**(8), 316–320 (1996)
8. Krogh, A., Mian, I.S., Haussler, D.: A hidden Markov model that finds genes in E. coli DNA. Nucleic Acids Res. **22**(22), 4768–4778 (1994)
9. Salzberg, Steven L., D. B. Searls, and S. Kasif. "Computational methods in molecular biology." Computational Methods in Molecular Biology49.2(1999):191-192
10. Ryan, M.S., Nudd, G.R.: The viterbi algorithm. Warwick Res. Rep. Rr **37**(2), 160–163 (1993)
11. Majoros, W.H., et al.: Efficient decoding algorithms for generalized hidden Markov model gene finders. BMC Bioinform. **6**(2), 8–16 (2005)
12. Zhang, M.Q., Marr, T.G.: A weight array method for splicing signal analysis. Comput. Appl. Biosci. Cabios **9**(5), 499–509 (1993)
13. Salzberg, S.L., et al.: Microbial gene identification using interpolated Markov models. Nucleic Acids Res. **26**(2), 544–548 (1998)

User Authentication Using Motion Sensor Data from Both Wearables and Smartphones

Jianmin Dong and Zhongmin Cai[✉]

MOE KLINNS Lab, Xi'an Jiaotong University, Xi'an 710049, Shaanxi, China
shujmdong@163.com, zmcai@mail.xjtu.edu.cn

Abstract. With the increasing popularity of wearable devices, it is common to use several smart devices simultaneously including smartphones. With embedded accelerometers and gyroscopes, the smart devices naturally constitute a multiple sensor system to measure the activities of the user more comprehensively and accurately. This paper proposed a new approach to perform authentication by using motion data collected from both wearables and smartphones. We propose a set of simple timedomain features to characterize the motion data collected from daily activities such as walking and train a one-class classifier to differentiate legitimate and illegitimate users. The experiments on data collected from 20 subjects demonstrate the proposed multiple sensor approach does lead to obvious performance improvements compared with traditional single sensor approaches.

Keywords: User authentication · Smartphones · Wearables · Motion sensor

1 Introduction

With the increasing popularity of wearable devices such as smart wristbands, watches and shoes, it is more and more common for an ordinary user to use multiple smart devices simultaneously including smartphones. As a basic component, most smart devices are equipped with motion sensors such as accelerometer and gyroscope. Although the motion sensors are designed for different purposes for different devices, such as posture awareness for smartphones and step counting for wristbands, the basic function of motion sensing makes all the smart devices carried by a user constitute a multiple sensor system for measuring the physical activities of the user. For analysis of human activities, this multiple sensor system usually exhibits advantages over single sensor approaches. The motion of human body is complex and different parts of human body usually conduct different movements when a person performs certain tasks such as walking. The multiple sensor system constituted of multiple smart devices can measure the activities of the user more comprehensively and be more resilient to noise in analysis of the sensed motion data.

Motion data collected from either smartphones or wearables have been used to perform authentication in previous research. [6, 8, 9] investigated the approaches of using motion data from a smartphone to perform authentication. [7, 10] investigated the approaches of using motion data collected from a smartwatch to perform user authentication. These efforts demonstrated the feasibility of using motion data collected by

© Springer International Publishing AG 2016
Z. You et al. (Eds.): CCBR 2016, LNCS 9967, pp. 756–764, 2016.
DOI: 10.1007/978-3-319-46654-5_83

smart devices as a useful source of biometric information. But all the previous work only utilized motion data from one device, either a smartphone or a smartwatch. This single sensor approach only characterizes human activities partially and may be more subjective to noise.

In this paper, we explore the mulitple sensor approach to perform authentication by using motion data collected from not only smartphones, but wearables as well. We demonstrate the combined data approach does lead to obvious performance improvements compared with traditional single sensor approaches. We extract simple timedomain features from motion data collected from both a smartphone and a smartwatch. We train a one-class SVM classifier to differentiate legitimate and illegitimate users. We perform experiments on data collected from 20 subjects and achieve a best equalerror rate of 0.09 % for the combined data approach. The major contributions of this paper are summarized as following:

- We proposed a new method of user authentication by using daily physical activity data collected from smartphone and wearables simultaneously.
- We established a public motion sensor dataset, not only for this study but also for further research. This dataset contains motion sensor data for 20 subjects collected by smartphone and wearables simultaneously.

The rest of this paper is organized as follows: Sect. 2 describes the related works. Section 3 introduces the data collection. Section 4 defines and extracts the motion data features. Section 5 explains evaluation methodology. Section 6 shows the experiments and analysis. Finally, in Sect. 7 we discuss conclusions and future work.

2　Related Work

User authentication on smart devices such as smartphones is a hot topic in recent years. It is believed PIN and passcode based authentication are not secure, which are exposed shoulder-surfing attacks and some PINs and passcodes are guessable [1]. Fingerprint is becoming more and more popular but there are still a large number of smart devices without the fingerprint reader to perform fingerprint authentication [2]. Thus to improve the security of smart devices without a fingerprint reader, behavior-based authentication attracted a lot of efforts in recent research of biometrics. We can generally divide behavior based authentication methods for smart devices into two categories: operation behavior based and daily physical activity based.

Operation behavior based approaches utilize behavior data of a user when he is operating the smart devices to authenticate the user. Cai et al. [3] utilized user interaction data on touchscreen of mobile phones to authenticate users in 2013. Napa et al. [4] proposed to use touch traces of five-finger gestures on touchscreen for authentication on multi-touch tablets in 2014. Shen et al. [5] utilized behavior data collected by accelerometer and gyroscope when a user inputs the PIN code on a smartphone to perform second layer authentication besides the checking of PIN input.

For wearables, operational behavior are simple and less frequent, which may not provide enough information for authentication. However, these wearables are able to record people's data activities which may provide another source of personal information for authentication. Some recent papers use daily physical activity for smartphone authentication [6–10]. Jani et al. [6] identified users via a small accelerometer-based device placed on a belt when users walked at fast, normal, and slow walking speeds in 2005. Davrondzhon et al. [7] analyzed data collected from accelerometer-based sensors placed on the foot, hip, pocket, and arm to authenticate user's identities in 2009. Kwapisz et al. [8] compared the authentication performances of using daily activities such as walking, jogging, and climbing stairs. The motion data are collected by a smartphone put in the front pants leg pocket. And Kunnathu [9] in 2015 attempted to build an authentication model using tri-axial accelerometer based on how the user picked up the phone and how he/she held the phone to the ear. Johnston et al. [10] analyzed the feasibility of using motion data of walking collected from a smartwatch for authentication in 2015.

The efforts in [6–10] all used the single sensor approach and showed the daily physical behavior sensed by accelerometer and gyroscope has a rich potential for user authentication. However, human activity is complicated and the human body is consisted of limbs, body and head. The movements of different parts of the body in an activity such as walking are different. Therefore, using two or more smart devices placed in different positions of the human body may provide more comprehensive information about human activities. Multiple sensors are also more robust to noises and irregular fluctuations in human activities.

In this paper, we propose a multiple sensor approach of using motion data collected by wearable and smartphone simultaneously for authentication. The experimental results indicate that this approach leads to better performance compared with traditional single sensor approaches.

3   Data Collection

This section explains how we set up a data-collection system and the protocol for recording activity data from recruited subjects for authentication, using smartwatches and smartphones.

3.1   Motion Data Collection

We use walking as the activity to be performed when we collect motion data from a subject. This is because walking is the most common activity people perform every day. We use a smartwatch as the wearable device in our study and developed a data collection system to control a smartwatch and a smartphone via Bluetooth to simultaneously collect motion sensor data from a moving subject. The motion sensor data are the data recorded by accelerometers and gyroscopes on the smartwatch and smartphone.

The smartwatch used in our data collection is Samsung Galaxy Gear 1 and the smartphone is Samsung Galaxy S4. The sampling rates of accelerometer and gyroscope in the smartwatch are 50 Hz, while the sampling rate of smartphone is 90 Hz. The formats of the collected motion data in the smartwatch and smartphone are the same and shown in Table 1. x_{nm}, y_{nm}, z_{nm} in Table 1 refer to the reading of the corresponding sensor at a particular instant of $Time_{mn}$ for the 3 axes of the device coordinate system respectively.

Table 1. Formats of motion data.

Acceleration sequence	Angular velocity sequence
$Time_{11}$: x_{11}, y_{11}, z_{11},	$Time_{21}$: x_{12}, y_{12}, z_{12},
$Time_{12}$: x_{21}, y_{21}, z_{21},	$Time_{22}$: x_{22}, y_{22}, z_{22},
......	......
$Time_{1n}$: x_{n1}, y_{n1}, z_{n1},	$Time_{2n}$: x_{n2}, y_{n2}, z_{n2},
......	......

Each time, a subject is asked to walk for some time and we record the motion sensor data by both the smartwatch worn on his right wrist and the smartphone in his right pocket of trousers. The data collected constitute one sample of walking activity of the subject. To eliminate confounding factors, all the data collections are performed at the same corridor in the same building. And the route of walking is fixed. All the subjects are asked to wear flat-bottom shoes and not to carry a bag or backpack.

Table 2. Motion features.

Feature name	Description	Number of features
Mean	Means of x, y, z acceleration or angular velocity	3
Mode	Modes of x, y, z acceleration or angular velocity	3
Min	Minimums of x, y, z acceleration or angular velocity	3
Max	Maximums of x, y, z acceleration or angular velocity	3
Std	Standard deviations of x, y, z acceleration or angular velocity	3
Peak	Peaks of x, y, z acceleration or angular velocity	3
Kurtosis	Kurtoses of x, y, z acceleration or angular velocity	3
Energy	Summed energy of acceleration or angular velocity	3
RMS	Root mean square of x, y, z acceleration or angular velocity	3
Median	Medians of x, y, z acceleration or angular velocity	3

3.2 Subjects

We recruited 20 subjects from our campus. Many of them are within our lab, but some from the university at large. For each subject, he is required to walk for 50 times and we collected 50 samples of walking data sensed by the wearing smartwatch and the carrying smartphone. The dataset will be published with the publishing of this paper.

4 Features

We extracted a set of motion features for walking behavior. All of them are in the time domain. These features are easy to be calculated and will not pose a serious sanction on the performance of mobile devices. The proposed features are shown in the Table 2. We define 10 features for every dimension of the accelerometer and gyroscope signal for each sample of walking data. Thus for each device of either the smartwatch or the smartphone, we extracted 30 features from the acceleration signal and 30 features from the angular velocity signal of one sample. And if data from both devices are used together, we totally have 120 features for one sample.

5 Classifiers

In this study, the problem of user authentication is investigated as a one-class classification problem. We use a feature vector consisting of motion features to represent a sample of user's walking activity. Since usually we only have samples from legitimate users, the classifier should be trained solely from the legitimate samples. Then the trained classifier classifies a testing feature vector to be legitimate or illegitimate.

6 Experimental Evaluations

We employ a one-class SVM using the RBF kernel as the classifier in our experiment. To evaluate the performance of our approach, we calculate the false-acceptance rate (FAR) and false-rejection rate (FRR) based on the collected dataset in Sect. 3. FAR is the fraction of samples of imposters that are recognized as the samples of the legitimate user. FRR is the fraction of samples of the legitimate user that are rejected by the classifier. By varying the threshold of the classification, we generate sequences of FARs and FRRs to obtain the ROC curves. We also compute equal-error rate (EER) where FAR equals FRR.

We will evaluate our approach in three experiments: 1. Comparing different data sources; 2. Impacts of different observation time, i.e., how long the subject walks in an sample; 3. Impacts of different sizes of training dataset.

6.1   User Authentication Using Smartphone and Wearables

In this experiment, we compare the authentication performances under three scenarios: only using data collected by the smartwatch, only using data collected by the smartphone and using data collected by smartwatch and smartphone simultaneously. We have 20 subjects totally, each subject contributes 50 samples and we set each sample contains 10 s of walking data. We select randomly 40 samples out of 50 samples of one subject as training data, and the rest 10 samples of this subject are as legal testing data. The 950 samples from the rest 19 subjects are used as illegal testing data. The resulted ROC curves are shown in Fig. 1.

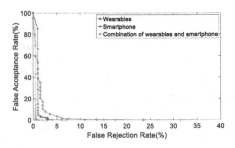

Fig. 1. ROC curves of user authentication under three scenarios.

As shown in Fig. 1, the EERs of activity authentication for only using smartwatch, only using smartphone and using smartwatch and smartphone simultaneously are 4.36 %, 2.40 % and 0.65 % respectively. The ROC curves also show using smartwatch and smartphone simultaneously achieves the best performance in general since the corresponding curve (in green) is the closest to the x and y axes. This results demonstrate the combined data approach exhibits obvious performance improvements over original single sensor approaches.

6.2   User Authentication on Different Observation Time

Observation time means how long a subject should perform a particular task for the authentication. In this experiment, we will investigate the impact of observation time on the performance of daily physical activity based authentication. We compare the authentication results using three observation time: 10 s, 5 s and 3 s under three scenarios: only using smartwatch, only using smartphone and using smartwatch and smartphone simultaneously. As in Sect. 6.1, we select randomly 40 samples from 50 samples of one subject as training data, and the rest 10 samples are used as legal testing data. The 950 samples from the rest 19 subjects are used as illegal testing data. The results are shown in Table 3.

Table 3 shows the average EERs for three different observation time under three scenarios. In general, the longer the observation time, the better the authentication accuracy. This is consistent with our expectation that the longer we observe a user, the more information we can get from the observation which lead to a higher accuracy of authentication. Specifically, the best performance is achieved for the combined scenario which has an EER of 0.65 % for the observation time of 10 s. We also notice that the data collected by smartwatch are noisier so that longer observation time are required to obtain enough identity information. This may explain why for the 3 s observation time, the combined approach performs slightly better than the approach using only smartphone.

Table 3. Average EERs for user authentication on different observation time.

Scenarios	Time (s)	Average EER (%)
Smartwatch	10	4.36
	5	6.82
	3	8.69
Smartphone	10	2.40
	5	2.77
	3	3.50
Combination of smartwatch and smartphone	10	0.65
	5	2.00
	3	3.49

6.3   User Authentication for Different Sizes of Training Data

To investigate the effect of size of training dataset on authentication performance, we set the training data sizes to be 45(90 %), 35(70 %), 25(50 %), 15(30 %), and 5(10 %) under the scenario that data from both smartwatch and smartphone are used for authentication. The results are shown in Fig. 2 and Table 4.

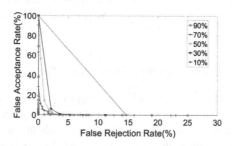

Fig. 2. ROC curves for five different training data sizes.

It shows that the authentication accuracies for small training data sizes are worse than large sizes of training data. Specifically, with only 10 % of legitimate samples for training, the average EER is 12.80 %; while with 30 % of samples for training, the average EER decreases dramatically to 2.98 %; and with 90 % legitimate samples for training, the average EER reaches 0.09 %. In practice, daily physical activity based authentication is usually used as a continuous authentication scheme, where behavior samples are continuously collected and fed to the classifier for analysis. Collecting many training data may not pose a difficult problem if an online learning approach is adopted.

Table 4. Average EERs on different training sample size.

Training data	Average EER (%)
90%	0.09
70%	1.67
50%	2.25
30%	2.98
10%	12.80

7 Conclusions and Future Work

This work explores a mulitple sensor approach to perform authentication by using motion data collected from not only smartphones, but wearables as well. We propose a set of simple motion features to characterize the acceleration signal and the angular velocity signal recorded by the smart devices in user daily activities. We train a one-class SVM classifier to perform authentication. Experiments on a dataset collected from 20 subjects showed that the proposed multiple sensor approach leads to better performance compared with traditional single sensor approaches and achieves an EER of 0.09 % with 10 s walking data. The collected dataset will be published to facilitate future research.

Acknowledgments. The research is supported by NFSC (61175039, 61221063, 61403301), 863 High Tech Development Plan (2012AA011003), Research Fund for Doctoral Program of Higher Education of China (20090201120032), International Research Collaboration Project of Shaanxi Province (2013KW11) and Fundamental Research Funds for Central Universities (2012jdhz08).

References

1. Mazurek, M.L., Komanduri, S., Vidas, T., et al.: Measuring password guessability for an entire university. In: Proceedings of the 2013 ACM SIGSAC Conference on Computer & Communications Security (2013)
2. Moorthy, M.S., Jayaraj, R., Jagadeesan, J.: Fingerprint Authentication System Using Minutiae Matching and Application. IJCSMC, **3** (2014)
3. Cai, Z., Shen, C., Wang, M., Song, Y., Wang, J.: Mobile authentication through touch-behavior features. In: Sun, Z., Shan, S., Yang, G., Zhou, J., Wang, Y., Yin, Y. (eds.) CCBR 2013. LNCS, vol. 8232, pp. 386–393. Springer, Heidelberg (2013)
4. Napa, S.B., Nasir, M., Katherine, I., et al.: Multitouch gesture-based authentication. IEEE Trans. Inf. Forensics Secur. **9**, 933–947 (2014)
5. Shen, C., Yu, T.W., Yuan, S., et al.: Performance analysis of motion-sensor behavior for user authentication on smartphones. Sensors **16**, 345 (2016)
6. Jani, M., Mikko, L., Elena, V., et al.: Identifying users of portable devices from gait pattern with accelerometers. In: Proceedings of Acoustics, Speech, and Signal Processing, (ICASSP 2005), vol. 2 (2005)

7. Davrondzhon, G., Einar, S.: Gait recognition using wearable motion recording sensors. J. Adv. Sig. Process. **1**, 1–6 (2009)
8. Kwapisz, J.R., Weiss, G.M., Moore, S.A.: Cell phone-based biometric identification. In: Fourth IEEE International Conference on Biometrics: Theory Applications and Systems (2010)
9. Kunnathu, N.: Biometric user authentication on smartphone accelerometer sensor data. In: Proceedings of Student-Faculty Research Day, CSIS, Pace University (2015)
10. Johnston, A.H., Weiss, G.M.: Smartwatch-based biometric gait recognition. In: IEEE, International Conference on Biometrics Theory, Applications and Systems (2015)

Person Authentication Using Finger Snapping — A New Biometric Trait

Yanni Yang[1], Feng Hong[1($\boxtimes$)], Yongtuo Zhang[2], and Zhongwen Guo[1]

[1] Department of Computer Science and Technology, Ocean University of China, Qingdao, China
hongfeng@ouc.edu.cn

[2] School of Computer Science and Engineering, University of New South Wales, Sydney, Australia

Abstract. This paper presents a new biometric trait, finger snapping, which can be applied for person authentication. We extract a set of features from finger snapping traces according to time and frequency domain analysis. A prototype is developed on Android smartphones to realize authentication for users. We collect 6160 snapping traces from 22 subjects for continuous 7 days and 324 traces from 54 volunteers across three weeks. Extensive experiments confirm the measurability, permanence, uniqueness, circumvention, universality and acceptability of the finger snapping to realize biometrics based authentication. It shows that the system achieves 6.1% average False Rejection Rate (FRR) and 5.9% average False Acceptance Rate (FAR).

Keywords: Finger snapping · Biometric trait · DTW · Smart device

1 Introduction

The security of smart devices has been a major concern for people nowadays. For example, a range of methods have been applied for user authentication on smartphones and smart watches, such as password, PIN and fingerprint [1]. They can be either easily stolen by attackers or need extra sensors for input. In this paper, a new biometric trait, finger snapping, is applied for person authentication. The sound of finger snapping is easy to capture with the microphone embedded in the smart devices. Besides, it is easy to perform and do not require explicit remembrance for the reason that finger snapping only depends on muscle memory.

Finger snapping is an act of making an impulsive sound with one's fingers and palm [2]. It is often done by connecting the thumb with another (middle, index or ring) finger, and then moving the other finger immediately downward to hit the palm. Such act of finger snapping involves physiological characteristics which refer to inherited traits that are related to human body, as the sound of finger snapping is differentiated by the size of palm and skin texture. In addition, it also involves behavioral characteristics which refer to learned pattern of a person, as it is the movement of the finger creates the sound.

© Springer International Publishing AG 2016
Z. You et al. (Eds.): CCBR 2016, LNCS 9967, pp. 765–774, 2016.
DOI: 10.1007/978-3-319-46654-5_84

Intuitively, the original time series of finger snapping sound is applied to authenticate users. However, through experiments in Sect. 2, the average FAR of this method is 45 %, which is relatively high for person authentication purpose. So we concentrate our research to the direction of *finding the unique features contained in the finger snapping sound for user authentication*. This problem is solved by investigating features which represent the physiological and behavioral characteristics of finger snapping from the original snapping sounds. On the one hand, time domain features of finger snapping sound are explored, since it is a motion during which fingers hit the palm. On the other hand, we regard the person's palm as a musical instrument and try to locate features in frequency domain. Overall, we extract zero-crossing rate, and root mean square as time domain features, and the Mel-Frequency Cepstral Coefficiets (MFCC), spectrum power and spectral centroid as frequency domain features. Finally, Dynamic Time Warping (DTW) [3] is applied to realize authentication. Through the evaluation phase, we verify that the finger snapping, as a biometric trait, can meet the requirements of a combination of several factors including measurability, permanence, uniqueness, circumvention, universality and acceptability [4].

2 Related Work

Biometric traits have been widely used in user authentication on smart devices, like fingerprint which requires an extra scanner to input the trait. In terms of the biometric trait, it generally falls into two categories: physiological and behavioral characteristics. Physiological characteristics are related to the shape of the body, such as face [5], fingerprint [1], iris [6], etc. Physiological characteristics rely on biological features that users uniquely have, but often require special sensors like extra sensors or user engagement. For iris and retina based identification, bespoke special sensors and making eyes close to certain scanner are both required, which increase the cost and inconvenience for users.

Behavioral characteristics take the implicit patterns of user behavior for authentication, including but not limited to typing rhythm, gait [7], voice [8] and motion [9]. For example, motion based authentication utilize the way of user waving smartphones [9] which calls for the user to remember the fixed gesture and try to perform the same gestures all the time, restricting accuracy and convenience. Another type of behavioral characteristics is voice, which is also an authentication method using sound traces like finger snapping. Many acoustic features and recognition algorithms have been put forward, giving us clues on finger snapping sound processing.

Compared with the above biometrics, finger snapping contains both physiological and behavioral characteristics, and it requires no special sensors and explicit remembrance as the finger snapping depends only on muscle memory.

3 Constitution and Detection of Finger Snapping

This section first introduces the constitution of finger snapping sound and explains the motivation why it can be taken as a biometric trait. Then we describe our data collection process and bring forward the method to detect and extract the raw snapping traces from the whole snapping sound files. At last, we give the authentication results on raw time series comparison to illustrate the importance of feature extraction.

3.1   Constitution of Finger Snapping

The finger snapping sound is made of three parts [2]: (1) The friction sound between the middle finger and the thumb which is weak and unnoticeable. (2) The impact sound made by the middle finger colliding with the cavity formed by contacting the ring finger with the palm. (3) The pop sound created by the fast compression and the pursuant decompression of air. The pop sound is the clearest sound among the three parts as it is caused by a compression of air between the fast moving middle finger and the cavity formed by the palm and middle finger.

The snapping sound is differentiated by the skin texture and the cavity created by palm and finger which can be categorized as physiological characteristics. In addition, the finger movement also has an impact on the snapping sound, with different strength and speed, which can be related to behavioral characteristics. So finger snapping is a combination of both physiological and behavioral characteristics.

3.2   Collection of Finger Snapping

We collect the finger snapping traces on a commercial Android based smartphone, HUAWEI Honor 7. An application is developed on the smartphone to collect snapping sounds and interact with the user to tell whether he is the owner or not. Two datasets are collected: Training Set and Testing Set. Training Set consists of 22 subjects' 6160 snapping sounds across continuous 7 days. These subjects' ages are from 19 to 39, including 14 males and 8 females. Testing Set consists of 54 volunteers' 324 snapping traces, which are collected when they are doing the attacking experiment on the smartphone. We collect each volunteer's finger snapping traces every Tuesday and Thursday for three weeks. Collection is carried out in two common laboratories.

3.3   Finger Snapping Detection

Finger snapping detection is to locate the exact proportion of snapping sound in the whole file. Through our empirical observation, it is found that the time span of the exact finger snapping is generally below 3 ms. Hence, with the sampling rate of 44.1 kHz, the exact snapping sound is within 1350 sample points. Therefore, a sliding window is applied to detect the largest power difference of the whole sound samples and cut out 1350 sample points as the exact finger snapping sound, called snapping trace in the following. Figure 1 shows examples of finger snapping detection for two subjects, and the part between the two vertical solid lines is the detected snapping sound.

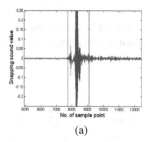 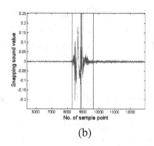

(a)   (b)

Fig. 1. Finger snapping detection of (a) subject1 (b) subject2

3.4 Raw Data Analysis

Intuitively, the whole raw time series of snapping trace (i.e., the whole 1350 samples) is applied to authenticate users. Here, Hidden Markov Model (HMM) [10] is applied to the raw time series of the snapping traces, as the process of finger snapping can be considered as a Markov process with hidden states. The HMM model is trained with 40 traces of each subject to get an authentication threshold. All the other subjects' traces are used to test the model for each subject. However, the average FAR among all the subjects of the direct comparison is 45 %, which is not acceptable for person authentication purpose. So we concentrate our research to the direction of *finding the unique features underlying in the finger snapping sound for user authentication*.

4 Feature Extraction

We extract features from the finger snapping traces for person authentication based on Training Set. Here several features referring to acoustic analysis on time and frequency domain are investigated step by step.

4.1 Time Domain Feature

We explore time domain features because they reflect the behavioral characteristics. Two widely used time domain features are selected for finger snapping authentication, including zero-crossing rate (ZCR) and root mean square (RMS). Figure 2(a) shows the ZCR and RMS values of 40 snapping traces from each of the 4 subjects. It can be seen that the point sets are distributed without too much intersection. We only show 4 subjects' values for clear visualization, and all the traces of other 18 subjects also receive the similar results.

4.2 Frequency Domain Feature

We regard the hand as a musical instrument for snapping fingers. Considering that musical instruments may have their own particular frequency, we study frequency domain features of the snapping sounds. We select the MFCC, spectrum power and spectral centroid features because they can reflect the uniqueness of different individuals' finger snapping.

Spectrum Power and Spectral Centroid: After taking the FFT of the snapping trace, we calculate the total spectrum power and spectral centroid of the snapping trace. Spectral centroid is the gravity center of the power spectrum [11]. The values of spectrum power and spectral centroid are normalized between 0 and 10. Figure 2(b) shows the spectrum power and spectral centroid of 40 snapping traces from each of the 4 subject. The point set boundaries are clear among different individuals, so spectrum power and spectral centroid will be useful for user authentication. We only show 4 subjects' values for clear visualization in Fig. 2(b), and the traces of other 18 subjects also receive the similar results.

MFCC: Mel-Frequency Cepstral Coefficients (MFCC) are proposed to realize speech and speaker recognition [5]. It is an approximation of the human auditory system's response. Figure 2(c) shows two subjects MFCC value distributions of 15 snapping traces respectively. There are obvious differences between these two subjects which indicate the uniqueness for different individuals and the MFCC sets of the same individual remain a similar trend. In order to facilitate observation, we only give 2 subjects MFCC sets in Fig. 2(c), and the other 20 subjects present the observable distinctiveness as well.

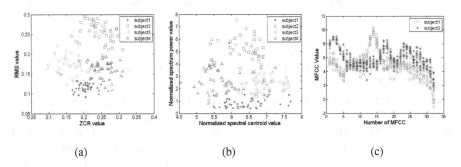

(a)   (b)   (c)

Fig. 2. Visualization of (a) ZCR and RMS (b) Spectrum power and spectral centroid (c) MFCC

5   System Design

The design of our user authentication system based on finger snapping is shown in Fig. 3. The system leverages snapping sound sensed by the microphones in smart devices and does not rely on the priori that knowing any ambient environment information. The result of the system is a decision: owner or attacker. The system contains five steps:

Sensing: To record the finger snapping sound using the embedded microphone in smart devices. Then the exact sound of the finger snapping is detected.

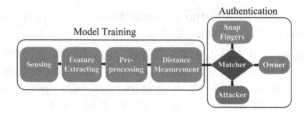

Fig. 3. System Design

Feature Extracting: A set of acoustic features from both the time and frequency domain are extracted from the snapping sound traces.

Preprocessing: Since noises can overwhelm the snapping sound, there may be a few low quality snapping inputs. Enrollment threshold is defined to remove low quality traces for model training. First, we calculate the feature vector's Manhattan distance between one trace and all the other traces from the owner. Each trace gets its own average Manhattan distance d_i, which represents the relevance with the owner's normal snapping state. The enrollment threshold δ is represented in Eq. (1), where m and var are the mean and standard variance of all d_i. Those traces with d_i values exceeding δ are the invalid enrollments. It is emphasized that preprocessing is only applied on traces used to train the model.

$$\delta = m + 2 \times var \tag{1}$$

Distance Measurement: DTW distance measurement is applied for authentication. DTW finds a non-linear warping path between two feature vectors to obtain an optimized similarity distance. Here, DTW is not applied to cope with length diversity, as the feature vector of finger snapping is length-fixed. It is the special property of MFCC that makes us use DTW algorithm. In the process of calculating MFCC, the spectrum power is mapped to mel-scale using overlapping windows which share some common areas with each other. This indicates that adjacent MFCC values can be similar, so number 1 MFCC in one feature set can be aligned with number 2 MFCC in another set.

Matcher: It decides whether the snapping sound is made by the owner or the attacker with the DTW output. As only owner's traces are available for authentication situation, DTW needs a template and a threshold to get the result. The template is selected to be the trace from the owner which achieves the highest pairwise similarity with all the other training traces. All the training traces will be compared with the template and the outputs are sorted to get a certain value as the authentication threshold. The procedure of determining the template and threshold can be regarded as the training process. A test trace will be compared with the template to get the distance output. If the output is smaller than the threshold, the test trace will be accepted as the owner's.

6   Evaluation

In this section, the performance of finger snapping authentication is evaluated. Based on Training Set of 6160 snapping traces from 22 subjects across 7 days, we evaluate the FER, select the training parameters and analyze the permanence of finger snapping. Combining Training Set with Testing Set, we verify the uniqueness of finger snapping. Circumvention results are evaluated by recording owner's snapping sound with attacker's smartphone. We further do a survey of 74 people on universality and acceptance issue of finger snapping authentication. Finally, the cost of finger snapping authentication is analyzed, including the computational time and power consumption on smartphones.

6.1   Failure to Enroll Rate

FER is the rate at which low quality inputs occur and they are regarded as invalid enrollment. The preprocessing phase eliminates the low quality inputs before training models. In order to give a comprehensive result, all the collected traces of 22 subjects are used to obtain FER. The average FER among all subjects is 4.4 %, which shows that finger snapping can be effectively collected.

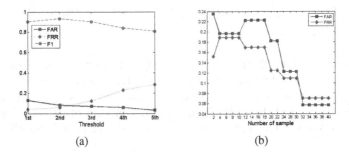

(a)   (b)

Fig. 4. Performance of different (a) threshold (b) trace capacity

6.2   Threshold and Trace Capacity

We investigate the effect of the choice of authentication threshold and the number of training traces on authentication performance with all the snapping traces in Training Set. The template is selected from the Day0' traces for each subject. Then all the training traces are compared with the template by DTW and the outputs are sorted to get the $1st$, $2nd$, $3rd$, $4th$ and $5th$ highest values. They are respectively taken as the authentication threshold. Figure 4(a) depicts the average FRR, FAR and F1 score of different thresholds for all subjects. It shows that the $2nd$ highest value is proper to be set as the authentication threshold as it achieves the highest F1 score with low FRR and FAR.

For the capacity of training traces, we vary the number from 1 to 40 to obtain the template and threshold. The performance on average FRR and FAR for all subjects with different trace capacity is shown in Fig. 4(b). When the number is higher than 32, the FRR and FAR will stay at the lowest level, so we choose 32 as the capacity length.

6.3 Permanence and Uniqueness

The snapping traces in Training Set and Testing traces are used to evaluate the permanence and uniqueness of finger snapping.

FRR: To obtain FRR, we use each subject Day0's traces for training and use Day1-Day6's traces for testing. The average FRRs among all 22 subjects from Day1 to Day6 are shown in Table 1. The average FRR (6.1%) across 7 days and the standard variance (0.9%) show that the FRRs stay low and relatively stable across days. Besides, the testing traces are not preprocessed. Among the FRR traces, some owner's traces are rejected because of low quality inputs (FER traces).

Table 1. Average FRR of all subjects on Day0

Day	1	2	3	4	5	6	Mean	std
FRR	6.4%	4.8%	5.9%	7.2%	5.4%	6.7%	6.1%	0.9%

FAR: To obtain FAR, 22 subjects in Training Set are regarded as owners. All the snapping traces in Testing Set which is collected from 54 volunteers and the other 21 subjects' traces are used to attack the owner's finger snapping. The FAR is illustrated in Table 2. It shows the FAR is kind of subject dependent. The average FAR is 5.9%, and all the FARs are lower than 10% for all subjects.

Table 2. FAR of all subjects on Day0

Subject	1	2	3	4	5	6	7	8	9	10	11
FAR	3.8%	6.5%	4.5%	6.2%	4.7%	5.8%	7.6%	3.5%	7.9%	8.5%	5.5%
Subject	12	13	14	15	16	17	18	19	20	21	22
FAR	6.4%	5.6%	7.4%	6.8%	5.2%	4.8%	7.5%	4.4%	5.7%	5.8%	4.9%

6.4 Circumvention

In terms of circumvention, one question might be brought up: What if the attacker records the owner's snapping sound to attack the owner's device? We imitate this situation by recording the owner's snapping with the attacker's smartphone side by side to the owner's phone. Then the attacker replays the recorded file to attack owner's model. The owner's phone type is HUAWEI Honor

7, and the attacker's phone types are HUAWEI Honor 7, Samsung Galaxy 3 and 4, Google Nexus 5, iPhone 5 and 6. All the 22 subjects play the role of the owner in turn, and attack attempts all failed. This is because the frequency response of the microphone and speaker of the off-the-shelf devices, like smartphones, does not match with each other. So the snapping sounds recorded by the microphone are thereby badly distorted through the speaker when being replayed.

6.5   Universality and Acceptability

A survey is carried out on 74 people about whether they can snap their fingers and accept the finger snapping authentication. Results show that 86.5 % of the respondents can snap fingers, of which 89.2 % would like to authenticate themselves using a simple finger snap. Besides, through our finger snapping collecting phase, we come to find out that people who could not snap their fingers can learn to do it after understanding the method of finger snapping.

6.6   Computational Time and Power Consumption

For each of the 22 subjects, we further measure the time and energy cost with 32 snapping traces. The average time on calculating DTW distances and deciding the template and threshold is $7.144s$ on the smartphone of HUAWEI Honor 7. The average time to decide whether a test snapping trace is the owner's or not is only $0.118s$ on the smartphone. In terms of the power consumption on the smartphone, it costs totally $4.36J$ for the training process, and $0.12J$ for authenticating a test snapping trace.

7   Conclusion

This paper proposes a new biometric trait, finger snapping, to realize person authentication. Finger snapping is recorded and detected with the microphone embedded in the off-the-shelf smart devices. The acoustic features are extracted from both time and frequency domain, including zero-crossing rate, root mean square, time average energy, MFCC, spectrum power and spectral centroid. We apply DTW to evaluate the similarity between the feature vectors of the snapping traces. Experiments have confirmed the measurability, uniqueness, permanence, circumvention, universality and acceptability of the finger snapping authentication.

Acknowledgments. We show thanks to the volunteers who participated in the process of finger snapping collection. This research is partially supported by the National Science Foundation of China (NSFC) under Grant Number 61379128 and 61379127.

References

1. Maltoni, D., Maio, D., Jain, A.K., Prabhakar, S.: Handbook of Fingerprint Recognition, 2nd edn. Springer, Heidelberg (2009)
2. "Wikipedia" "Finger snapping". https://en.wikipedia.org/w/index.php?title=Finger_snapping&oldid=691142888
3. Müller, M.: Dynamic time warping. In: Müller, M. (ed.) Information Retrieval for Music and Motion, pp. 69–84. Springer, Heidelberg (2007)
4. Jain, A.K., Ross, A., Nandakumar, K.: Introduction to Biometrics. Springer, Heidelberg (2011). ISBN 978-0-387-77325-4
5. Li, S.Z., Jain, A.K. (eds.): Handbook of Face Recognition, 2nd edn. Springer, Heidelberg (2011). ISBN 978-0-85729-931-4
6. Kevin, W.B., Karen, H., Patrick, J.F.: Image understanding for iris biometrics: a survey. Comput. Vis. Image Underst. 110(2), 281–307 (2008)
7. Yu, G., Li, C.-T.: A robust speed-invariant gait recognition system for walker and runner identification. In: 2013 International Conference on Biometrics (ICB) (2013)
8. Shannon, R.V., and Zeng, F.-G., Kamath, V., Wygonski, J., Ekelid, M.: Speech recognition with primarily temporal cues. In: American Association for the Advancement of Science (1995)
9. Hong, F., Wei, M., You, S., Feng, Y., Guo, Z.: Waving authentication: your smartphone authenticate you on motion gesture. In: Proceedings of the 33rd Annual ACM Conference Extended Abstracts on Human Factors in Computing Systems (2015)
10. Nadeu, C., Macho, D., Hernando, J.: Time and frequency filtering of filter-bank energies for robust HMM speech recognition. In: Speech Communication. Elsevier (2001)
11. Wang, J., Lee, H., Wang, J., Lin, C.: Robust environmental sound recognition for home automation. IEEE Trans. Autom. Sci. Eng. 5(1), 25–31 (2008)

Author Index

Printed in the United States
By Bookmasters